integrated marketing communication (IMC) 509
internal customers 262
Internet 528
intrapreneur 182
ISO 9000 48
just-in-time inventory control (JIT) 283
line and staff organization 254
logistics 473
marketing concept 409
marketing mix 413
MFN 107
middle management 217
mixed economy 64
monetary policy 76
multiculturalism 43
multinational corporation 107
NAFTA 105
network marketing 484
niche market 425
nonprofit organization 32
organizational culture 263
outsourcing 262
patent 132
preferred stock 616
product development 434
product differentiation (competitive) 437
product life cycle 448
product mix 436
productivity 74
promotion mix 492
quality 48

quality control 291
reengineering 260
relationship marketing 411
restructuring 245
Securities and Exchange Commission (SEC) 621
segmentation 422
self-managed teams 228
Sherman Act 137
shopping goods 437
Small Business Administration 183
social audit 124
social responsibility 116
specialty goods 438
stakeholders 40
strategic alliances 46
strategic planning 215
supply chain management 472
tactical planning 215
target market 422
teamwork 41
telecommuting 538
total quality management (TQM) 259
trade deficit 92
trade protectionism 102
utility 415
value package 435
value pricing 453
virtualization 525
welfare capitalism 64
wholesaler 464
word of mouth 503

UNDERSTANDING BUSINESS

Fourth Edition

William G. Nickels
University of Maryland

James M. McHugh
St. Louis Community College at Forest Park

Susan M. McHugh

IRWIN
Chicago • Bogotá • Boston • Buenos Aires • Caracas
London • Madrid • Mexico City • Sydney • Toronto

Irwin Book Team

Executive editor: *Craig Beytien*
Senior marketing manager: *Jim Lewis*
Developmental editor: *Burrston House*
Project editor: *Jane Lightell*
Production supervisor: *Laurie Kersch*
Interior designer: *Mercedes Santos*
Cover designer: *Mercedes Santos*
Cover Illustrator: *Jack Harris/Visual Logic*
Art Studio: *PC&F, Inc.*
Manager, graphics and desktop services: *Kim Meriwether*
Assistant manager, graphics: *Charlene R. Breeden*
Compositor: *PC&F, Inc.*
Typeface: *10/12 New Astor*
Printer: *Von Hoffman Press, Inc.*

Times Mirror
Higher Education Group

Library of Congress Cataloging-in-Publication Data

Nickels, William G.
    Understanding business / William G. Nickels, James M. McHugh,
Susan M. McHugh. — 4th ed.
        p. cm.
    Includes index.
    ISBN 0-256-14054-5. — ISBN 0-256-19074-7 (annotated instructor's
ed.)
    1. Industrial management.   2. Business.   3. Business—Vocational
guidance.
I. McHugh, James M.   II. McHugh, Susan M.   III. Title.
HD31.N4897   1996
650—dc20   95–22442

Printed in the United States of America
3 4 5 6 7 8 9 0 VH 2 1 0 9 8 7 6

DEDICATION

To Marsha and Joel, who make all the effort worthwhile, and to all the students and faculty who have praised, criticized, and guided us to this market-leading Fourth Edition.

Bill Nickels

To our children: Casey, who used the third edition in class last year and gave us an abundance of frank feedback, and Molly and Michael, future users of the eighth and ninth editions, thanks for being patient and supportive.

Jim and Susan McHugh

BRIEF CONTENTS

PART 1
Business Trends: Cultivating a Business in Diverse, Global Environments   1

Prologue: Using Career and Course Resources   2
Appendix: Getting the Job You Want   15
1   Exploring Trends in Dynamic Business Environments   26
2   Understanding Global and Domestic Economics   58
3   Competing in Global Markets   86
4   Demonstrating Ethical Behavior and Social Responsibility   114
Appendix: Working within the Legal Environment of Business   130

PART 2
Business Ownership: Starting a Small Business   145

5   Owning a Business   146
6   Entrepreneurship and the Challenge of Starting a Small Business   176
Appendix: Entrepreneur Readiness Questionnaire   204
Career Portfolio: Business Formation   206

PART 3
Business Management: Empowering Employees to Satisfy Customers   209

7   Leadership, Management, and Employee Empowerment   210
8   Organizing a Customer-Driven Business   242
9   Producing World-Class Products and Services   274
Career Portfolio: Management   301

PART 4
Management of Human Resources: Motivating Employees to Produce Quality Goods and Services   305

10   Motivating Employees and Building Self-Managed Teams   306
11   Human Resource Management: Finding and Keeping the Best Employees   336
12   Dealing with Employment–Management Issues and Relationships   370
Career Portfolio: Management of Human Resources   400

PART 5
Marketing: Developing and Implementing Customer-Oriented Marketing Plans   403

13   Marketing: Building Customer Relationships   404
14   Developing and Pricing Quality Products and Services   432
15   Distributing Products Efficiently and Competitively   462
16   Promoting Products Using Integrated Marketing Communication   490
Career Portfolio: Fundamentals of Marketing   517

PART 6
Decision-Making: Managing Information   521

17   Using Technology to Manage Information   522
18   Understanding Financial Information and Accounting   548
Career Portfolio: Managing Information (Information Systems)   577

PART 7
Managing Financial Resources   581

19   Using Financial Resources   582
20   Financing and Investing Through Securities Markets   608
21   Understanding Money and Financial Institutions   640
22   Developing and Managing Your Personal Finances   666
Appendix: Managing Risk   685
Career Portfolio: Financial Management (Finance and Accounting)   692

Chapter Notes   CN1
Glossary   G1
Credits   CR1
Name Index   I1
Company and Product Index   I5
General Index   I7

CONTENTS

Technology, especially in communications, continues to accelerate change and to shrink our planet.

PART 1

BUSINESS TRENDS: CULTIVATING A BUSINESS IN DIVERSE, GLOBAL ENVIRONMENTS

Prologue
Using Career and Course Resources 2

Profile: Kelly Stratico-Smith, Laura Biondi-Williams, and Other Entrepreneurs 3

Business Skills Can Be Applied Anywhere 4
The Value of a College Education 4

Learning about Careers 4
Getting Started 5   Assessing Your Skills and Personality 5   Which College Is Best for Me? 6
Establishing Resource Files 7   Career Preparation 7

Resources for the Course 8
The Professor as a Resource 9   This Text as a Resource 9   Outside Readings as a Resource 10
Your Classmates as a Resource 11   The Returning Student 11   Outside Contacts as a Resource 11
The Learning Resource Center or Library as a Resource 12   Pretest Your Business I.Q. 14

Appendix: Getting the Job You Want 15

Chapter 1
Exploring Trends in Dynamic Business Environments 26

Profile: La-Van Hawkins and Raymond O'Neal: Urban Entrepreneurs 27

Opportunities for Entrepreneurs 28
What Is a Business? 29   Matching Risk with Profit 29
Entrepreneur Magazine: Quoting Mary Rogers of Computer Tots 30   How Much Profit Do Businesses Make? 30

Businesses Can Provide Wealth for Almost Everyone 30
The Importance of Entrepreneurship to Wealth 32
Nonprofit Organizations Work with Businesses 32
The Factors of Production 33

The Business Environment 34
Spotlight on Small Business: Teams Lead to Responsiveness 35
The Economic Environment 35   *Legal Briefcase: Creating a Climate for Growth 37*

The Technological Environment 37
The Importance of Information Technology 37
Responding to the Consumer 38   Electronic Data Interchange 38

The Competitive Environment 39
Competing by Delighting the Customer 39
Competing by Meeting the Needs of the Community 40
Competing by Restructuring to Meet the Needs of Employees 41   Competing by Concern for the Natural Environment 41   *Making Ethical Decisions: Competing with a Strong Ethical Base 42*

The Multicultural Environment 42
Multiculturalism and Its Advantages for Business 43
The Increase in the Number of Older Americans 44
Two-Income Families 44   Single-Parent Households 45

The Global Environment 45
Global Opportunities and Free Trade Agreements 46
Reaching Beyond Our Borders: From NAFTA to AFTA 47
How Global Changes Affect You 47

The Quality Imperative 48
The New Quality Standard: The Baldrige Award 48
Quality and ISO 9000 48

The Evolution of American Business 49
Progress in the Agricultural and Manufacturing Industries 49   Progress in Service Industries 50
The Pain of Transition 50   Your Future in the Global Economy 51

Case: Women Entrepreneurs in Small Business 55
Video Case: Opportunity Unlimited 56

Chapter 2
Understanding Global and Domestic Economics 58

Profile: Pablo Tesak, Entrepreneur from El Salvador 59

The Importance of the Study of Economics 60
What Is Economics? 60   The Economic Theory of Wealth Creation: Adam Smith 61   The "Invisible Hand" 61   *Entrepreneur Magazine: For Goodness' Sake 62*

The History of Business and Economics 62
The Search for Equality 62   The Consequences of Socialism 63   The Trend toward Mixed Economies 63
Reaching Beyond Our Borders: Free Market Friendliness 64
The Emergence of Welfare Capitalism 64

The Foundations of Capitalism 66
How Free Markets Work 67   How Prices Are Determined 67   Supply 68   Demand 69
Equilibrium Point 69   World Markets: Supply and Demand 70   Limitations of the Free-Market System 71

Understanding the Economic System of the United States 71
Key Economic Indicators 72   *Spotlight on Small Business: Creating Jobs 73*   Distribution of GNP 74
Productivity in the United States 74   Productivity in the Service Sector 74

Inflation and the Consumer Price Index 75
Inflation and the Rule of 72 75   The Issue of Recession versus Inflation 76

The Issue of Monetary Policy 76
Tight versus Loose Monetary Policy 77

The Issue of Fiscal Policy 77
How Taxes and Spending Affect Businesspeople 77
Regulation: The Hidden Tax 78   *Making Ethical Decisions: Tax Fairness 79*   The Federal Deficit 79
The National Debt 79

Case: Let's Just Tax the Rich and Pay Off the Debt 84
Video Case: Ogre Faces a Market Economy 85

Chapter 3
Competing in Global Markets 86

Profile: Virginia Kamsky, China Trader 87

The Dynamic Global Market 88

Why Trade with Other Nations? 89
The Theories of Comparative and Absolute Advantage 89

Getting Involved in Global Trade 90
Importing Goods and Services 90   Exporting Goods and Services 91   *Reaching Beyond Our Borders: Where's the Beef? Not in India 92*   Measuring Global Trade 92

Trading in Global Markets: The U.S. Experience 93

Strategies for Reaching Global Markets 95
Exporting 95   Licensing 95   Creating Subsidiaries 96   Contract Manufacturing 96   Franchising 97
International Joint Ventures 97   Countertrading 98

Hurdles of Trading in Global Markets 98
Cultural Differences 98   *Entrepreneur Magazine: Funding Global Ventures 100*   Societal and Economic Differences 100   Legal and Regulatory Differences 101   Problems with Currency Shifts 101
Making Ethical Decisions: Global Hand-Me-Downs 102

Trade Protectionism 102
General Agreement on Tariffs and Trade (GATT) 104
Common Markets 104   *Legal Briefcase: Two Sides of the Tariff Issue 105*   The North American Free Trade Agreement (NAFTA) 105

Multinational Corporations 107

The Future of Global Trade 107
Spotlight on Small Business: A Place to Call Home: The Top 10 Export States 108   Globalization and You 109

Case: The Ghosts of Smoot–Hawley 112
Video Case: Learning to Do Business Globally 113

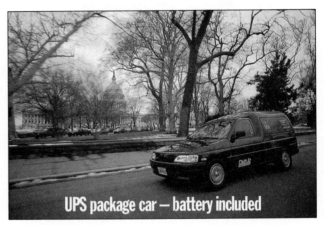

Businesses are becoming more socially responsible. Ford and UPS have joined forces to develop and test an electric car.

Chapter 4
Demonstrating Ethical Behavior and Social Responsibility 114

Profile: Jaynell Grayson, Co-owner of Food from the 'Hood 115

Managing Business Ethically and Responsibly 116

Legality Is Only the First Ethical Standard 116
Making Ethical Decisions: Competing for Young Customers 117   Ethics Is More than an Individual Concern 117   Organizational Ethics Begins at the Top 118   Personal Ethics Begins at Home 118

Setting Corporate Ethical Standards 119

Corporate Social Responsibility 120
Legal Briefcase: The 1991 Federal Sentencing Guidelines 122
Entrepreneur Magazine: Ethics in Global Trade 123
Social Auditing 124

International Ethics and Social Responsibility 124
Reaching Beyond Our Borders: A Global View of Business Ethics 125

Case: Ethics in Hollywood and the Entertainment Industry 127

Video Case: Doing Things Right versus Doing the Right Thing 128

Appendix: Working within the Legal Environment of Business 130

Entrepreneur Cynthia Jones and her graphic design company, Jones Worley Design, Inc., of Atlanta, is participating in more Olympic projects than any other minority-owned company.

PART 2

BUSINESS OWNERSHIP: STARTING A SMALL BUSINESSCHAPTER 5

Chapter 5
Owning a Business 146

Profile: Tony Conza of Blimpie International Sandwich Shops 147

Basic Forms of Business Ownership 148

Sole Proprietorships 149
　Advantages of Sole Proprietorships 149
　Disadvantages of Sole Proprietorships 150

Partnerships 151
　Advantages of Partnerships 152　　Disadvantages of Partnerships 152　　*How to Form a Partnership 153*
　Spotlight on Small Business: Choose Your Partner 154

Corporations 155
　Advantages of Corporations 155　　*Making Ethical Decisions: Outsourcing or Outsmarting 156*　　Disadvantages of Corporations 156　　*How to Incorporate 158*
　Corporate Types 159　　Individuals Can Incorporate 159
　S Corporations 159　　Limited Liability Companies 160

Corporate Expansion: Mergers and Acquisitions 161

Special Forms of Business Ownership 163
　Franchises 163　　*Buying a Franchise 166*
　Cooperatives 168　　*Reaching Beyond Our Borders: Joining Hands across the Waters: Strategic Alliances 169*
　Entrepreneur Magazine: Co-ops Allow Small Businesses to Compete against Big Odds 170

Which Form of Ownership Is for You? 170

Case: Should Cooperatives Go Corporate? 173

Video Case: Ben and Jerry's Choose among Forms of Business 174

Chapter 6
Entrepreneurship and the Challenge of Starting a Small Business 176

Profile: Tomima Edmark of Topsytail Co. 177

The Job-Creating Power of Entrepreneurs in the United States 178

Why People Take the Entrepreneurial Challenge 179
　What Does It Take to Be an Entrepreneur? 179
　Entrepreneurial Teams 181　　Encouraging Entrepreneurship 181　　*Making Ethical Decisions: Competing with Your Old Boss 182*　　Entrepreneurship within Firms 182

Getting Started in Small Business 183
　Small versus Big Business 183　　Importance of Small Business 184　　Small-Business Success and Failure 184
　Spotlight on Small Business: Situations for Success 185
　Spotlight on Small Business: Causes for Failures 186

Learning about Small-Business Operations 186
　Learn from Others 187　　Get Some Experience 187
　Take Over a Successful Firm 187

Managing a Small Business 188
　Beginning with Planning 188　　Getting Money to Fund a Small Business 189　　*Outline of a Comprehensive Business Plan 190*　　*Entrepreneur Magazine: Seed Money for Rural Entrepreneurs 191*　　Knowing Your Customers 193　　Managing Employees 194　　Keeping Records 194　　*Legal Briefcase: How Laws Affect Home-Based Businesses 195*　　Looking for Help 195

Going International: Small-Business Prospects 197
　Reaching Beyond Our Borders: Exporters' Tips 198

Case: BMOC: Starting a Small Business at School 200

Video Case: Taking the Entrepreneurial Challenge 202

Appendix: Entrepreneur Readiness Questionnaire 204

Career Portfolio: Business Formation 206

More and more companies are making the goals of product quality and pleasing customers the focus of their business strategy.

PART 3

BUSINESS MANAGEMENT: EMPOWERING EMPLOYEES TO SATISFY CUSTOMERS

Chapter 7
Leadership, Management, and Employee Empowerment 210

Profile: Mary Parker Follett: Mother of Modern Management 211

The Management Challenge of the Future 212
  The Changing Role of Managers 212   The Definition and Functions of Management 213

Planning: Creating a Vision for the Organization 214

Organizing: Creating a Unified System Out of Multiple Organizations 217
  The Customer-Oriented Organization 218
  Organization Is Becoming Interfirm 219   *Making Ethical Decisions: Ethics on the Front Line 220*

Directing and Empowering 220
  From Direction to Empowerment of Teams 220

Controlling 222
  Spotlight on Small Business: Leadership in Small Business 223   New Criteria for Measurement: Customer Satisfaction 223

Leadership: Vision and Values 224
  Leadership Styles 225   The Trend toward Self-Managed Teams 228   *Entrepreneur Magazine: Testing Your Leadership Ability 229*

Tasks and Skills at Different Levels of Management 229
  Delegating: Becoming a Team Leader 230   Decision Making: Finding the Best Ethical Alternative 231

Learning Managerial Skills 232
  Verbal Skills 232   Writing Skills 233   Computer Skills 233   Human Relations Skills 233   *Reaching Beyond Our Borders: Learning about Managing Businesses in Global Markets 234*   Time Management Skills 234   Technical Skills 234

Managers and Leaders Are Needed Everywhere 235

Case: Changing the Paradigm 238

Video Case: Waking Up to Starbucks 239

Chapter 8
Organizing a Customer-Driven Business 242

Profile: Betty Wagner of Cavalier Gage and Electronic 243

The Development of Organizational Hierarchy 244
  The Fundamentals of Bureaucracy 244

How Organizations Have Evolved 245
  The Background of Organizational Theory 246
  Fayol's Principles of Organization 246   Max Weber and Organization Theory 247

Designing More Responsive Organizations 248
  Tall versus Flat Organization Structures 249   Span of Control 249   *Entrepreneur Magazine: Give Bureaucracy the Boot 250*   Departmentalization 250   Centralization versus Decentralization of Authority 251

Organization Models 253
  Line Organizations 253   Line and Staff Organizations 254   Matrix Organizations 254   Cross-Functional, Self-Managed Teams 256   *Reaching Beyond Our Borders: Self-Managed Teams Overseas 258*

The Restructuring Process and Total Quality 259
  Spotlight on Small Business: Networking to Win 260   Turning the Organization Upside Down to Empower Employees 261   Turning the Organization Inside Out (Outsourcing) 262   *Making Ethical Decisions: Restructuring Responsibility 263*

Organizational Service-Oriented Culture 263
  The Informal Organization Helps Create Teamwork 266

Case: Creating Cross-Functional Teams in Service Organizations 270

Video Case: Big Apple Bagels and the Saint Louis Bread Company 271

Chapter 9
Producing World-Class Products and Services 274

Profile: Thomas L. Kassouf of Carrier 275

America's Manufacturing Base 276
    Production Management 276   Fundamentals of Production and Productivity 277

Keeping Costs Low: Site Selection 278
    Locating Close to Markets to Serve Customers Better 279   Site Selection in the Future 279   *Making Ethical Decisions: Stay or Leave? 280*

Production Processes 281
    Materials Requirement Planning: The Right Place at the Right Time 282

Modern Production Techniques 283
    Just-in-Time Inventory Control 283   *Entrepreneur Magazine: Lean Manufacturing Means Fat City for Small Producers 284*   Flexible Manufacturing 284   Lean Manufacturing 285   Mass Customization 285   Competing in Time 286

Computer-Aided Design and Manufacturing 286
    The Computerized Factory 288   People Problems on the Plant Floor 288   *Spotlight on Small Business: Computer-Integrated Manufacturing for Small Businesses 289*

Control Procedures: PERT and Gantt Charts 290
    Total Quality in Production Management 291   *Reaching Beyond Our Borders: Benchmark on the Best 292*

Improving Productivity 292
    Productivity in the Service Sector 293   Productivity and Quality in Nonprofit Organizations 294   Preparing for the Future 294   *Legal Briefcase 295*

Case: Competing in Time at Digital Equipment Corporation 298

Video Case: The Production Process at Washburn Guitars 299

Career Portfolio: Mangement 301

Major corporations such as Dial now recognize that constant change within the competitive environment must be viewed and managed as an opportunity.

PART 4

MANAGEMENT OF HUMAN RESOURCES: MOTIVATING EMPLOYEES TO PRODUCE QUALITY GOODS AND SERVICES

Chapter 10
Motivating Employees and Building Self-Managed Teams 306

Profile: Herb Kelleher of Southwest Airlines 307

The Importance of Motivation 308
    Legal Briefcase: Productivity versus Job Stress 309   Early Management Studies (Taylor) 309   The Hawthorne Studies (Mayo) 310

Maslow's Hierarchy of Needs 312
    Applying Maslow's Theory 313

McGregor's Theory X and Theory Y 313
    Theory X 314   Theory Y 314   Applying Theory X and Theory Y 315

Ouchi's Theory Z 316

Herzberg's Motivating Factors 317
    Applying Herzberg's Theories 319

Job Enrichment 319
    Entrepreneur Magazine: Motivation in Small Business 320

Goal-Setting Theory and Managment by Objectives 321
> *Spotlight on Small Business: Building the Team Small-Business Style 323*

Building Teamwork through Communication 324
Motivation through Self-Managed Teams 325 *Teamwork Calls for Team Compensation 326* Rethinking the Corporation 326 *Making Ethical Decisions: Motivating Temporary Employees 327* Changing Organizations Is Not Easy 327 A Team-Building Model for the Future: Mary Kay Cosmetics 328 *Reaching Beyond Our Borders: Exporting Motivation to Aspiring Capitalists 329* Motivation in the Future 329

Case: Theories X and Y: That's How the Cookie Crumbles 333

Video Case: Motivate and Innovate or Die 334

Chapter 11
Human Resource Management: Finding and Keeping the Best Employees 336

Profile: Jillian Perlberger, Temporary Employee 337

Working with People Is Just the Beginning 338
Developing the Ultimate Resource 338 The Human Resource Challenge 339 *Entrepreneur Magaizine: Diversity and the Human Resource Department 340*

Determining Your Human Resource Needs 341

Recruiting Employees from a Diverse Population 343

Selecting Employees Who Will Be Productive 344
> *Making Ethical Decisions: Recruiting Employees from the Competition 347*

Training and Developing Employees for Optimum Performance 347
Making New Employees Feel at Home 348 On-the-Job Training: Working with Others 348 Apprentice Programs: Learning Advanced Skills 348 Off-the-Job Training: Learning from the Best 349 Vestibule Training: Getting Used to the Equipment 349 Job Simulation: Try before You Fly 349 Management Development: Learning to Be Customer-Responsive 350 *Reaching Beyond Our Borders: Wanted: International Executives 352*

Appraising Employee Performance to Get Optimum Results 352

Compensating Employees: Attracting and Keeping the Best 353
Pay Systems 354 Fringe Benefits 355

Scheduling Programs That Meet Organizational and Employee Needs 356
Job-Sharing Plans 357 Flextime Plans 357 Home-Based Work 358

Moving Employees Up, Over, and Out to Maintain Morale 359
Promoting and Reassigning Employees 359 Terminating Employment and Downsizing 360 Retiring Employees 360

Laws Affecting Human Resource Management 361
Laws Protecting the Disabled and Older Employees 362 Proposed Wages and Benefits Legislation 362 *Legal Briefcase: Government Legislation 363* Effects of Legislation 364

Case: Dual-Career Planning 366

Video Case: Modern Training Methods 367

Chapter 12
Dealing with Employee–Management Issues and Relationships 370

Profile: David Stern, Commissioner of the National Basketball Association 371

Employee–Management Issues 372

Labor Unions from Different Perspectives 372
The Early History of Organized Labor 373 *Spotlight on Small Business: No More Homework, Please! 375*

Labor Legislation and Collective Bargaining 375
Goals of Organized Labor 377 Resolving Labor–Management Disagreements 378

Tactics Used in Labor–Management Conflicts 379
Entrepreneur Magazine: Unions in Small Business 380 Union Tactics 380 Management Tactics 382 The Future of Labor–Management Relations 383 *Reaching Beyond Our Borders: The Armor Cracks in German Labor Unions 384*

Controversial Employee–Management Issues 386
The Issue of Executive Compensation 386 The Issue of Pay Equity: Equal Pay for Comparable Jobs 388 The Issue of Sexual Harassment 389 The Issue of Child Care 390 The Issue of Elder Care 391 The Issues of AIDS, Drug Testing, and Violence in the Workplace 391 The Issue of Employee Stock Ownership Plans (ESOPs) 392 *Making Ethical Decisions: Coping with AIDS in the Workplace 393*

Case: Replacing Striking Workers 397

Video Case: Managing Diversity 398

Career Portfolio: Management of Human Resources 400

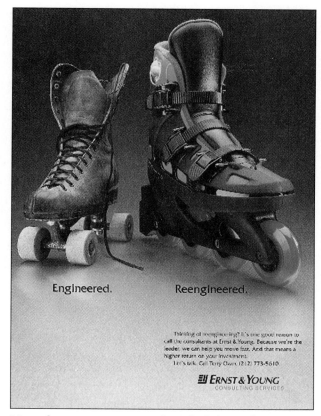

More than ever, success and profitability in business depend on adaptability.

PART 5

MARKETING: DEVELOPING AND IMPLEMENTING CUSTOMER-ORIENTED MARKETING PLANS

Chapter 13
Marketing: Building Customer Relationships 404
Profile: Bob and Candy Kocher and Gail Sundling, Customer-Oriented Marketers 405

What Is Marketing? 406
   Buying Is Marketing Too 406

Understanding the Marketing Process 406
   Designing a Product to Meet Needs 407   Getting the Product to Customers 407   Establishing a Relationship with Customers 407   *Reaching Beyond Our Borders: Yak Paks 408*

Total Qualtiy and the Marketing Concept 408
   A Brief History of the Marketing Concept 408
   Legal Briefcase: Don't Say, "Xerox That Article about Rollerblades." 409   From a Customer Orientation to Delighting Customers and Other Stakeholders 409
   From Training All Employees to Uniting Organizations 410   Maintaining a Profit Orientation 410

Relationship Marketing 411
   The Movement Away from Mass Marketing 411
   Entrepreneur Magazine: Niche Marketing 412

Marketing Management and the Marketing Mix 412
   The Eight Functions of Marketing 414   The Utilities Created by Marketing 415

Determining What Customers Want 416
   The Marketing Research Process 417   Using Research to Understand Consumers 419   *Making Ethical Decisions: No Kidding 421*

Recognizing Different Markets: Consumer and Business-to-Business 421
   The Consumer Market 422   Segmenting the Consumer Market 422   *Spotlight on Small Business: Bull's Eye Marketing 423*   Selecting a Target Market 424   Business-to-Business Marketing 426

Career Prospects in Marketing 427

Case: Applying Total Quality Marketing Concepts at Thermos 430

Video Case: Selling Coca-Cola in Japan 431

Chapter 14
Developing and Pricing Quality Products and Services 432

Profile: Wolfgang Schmitt of Rubbermaid 433

Product Development and the Value Package 434
   Developing a Value Package 435   Product Lines and the Product Mix 436

Product Differentiation 437
   Marketing Different Classes of Consumer Goods and Services 437   *Spotlight on Small Business: Product Design for Entrepreneurs and Small Businesses 438*   Marketing Industrial Goods and Services 438

Packaging Changes the Product 439
   The Growing Importance of Packaging 440
   Making Ethical Decisions: It's Not Easy Being Green 441

Building a Brand Equity 441
   Brand Categories 442   Building Brand Equity and Loyalty 443   Building Brand Associations 443

Product Management 444
   New-Product Success 444   *Top Ten Reasons Products Fail 444*   The New-Product Development Process 444   Generating New-Product Ideas 445   Product Screening and Analysis 445   Product Development and Testing 446   Commercialization 447   The International Challenge 448

The Product Life Cycle 448
   Reaching Beyond Our Borders: A Global View of Product Design 449   Example of the Product Life Cycle 450   The Importance of the Product Life Cycle 450   Extending the Life Cycle 451

Competitive Pricing 452
   Pricing Objectives 452   Cost-Based Pricing 453   Value Pricing 453   Break-Even Analysis 454

Monica A. Thomas
18 Nautical Lane
Gloucester, Mass.

Age: 21
Height: 5' 6"
Weight: 123 lbs.
Hair: Red
Eyes: Hazel
Marital status: Single
Health: Good

OBJECTIVE

To apply management experience and French language skills in an international firm.

EDUCATION

B.A. Management, Georgia State University, Atlanta, Ga.

Also completed a semester of study abroad in London, England (Georgia State University)

Additional Areas of Academic Competence:
8 credit hours in Computers, Small Business Counseling

College courses included Marketing, French, English Literature, Computer Programming, Data Processing, Statistics, Sociology, Economics.

High School Diploma: St. Agatha's High School, Gloucester, Mass.: College preparatory, National Honor Society, graduated in top 25% of class.

WORK EXPERIENCE

1995–Present

Flowers by Joann, Rockport, Mass. Responsibilities included bookkeeping, inventory, floral design, and selling merchandise both person-to-person and by use of computer.

Summer 1994

Waitress, Citronella's Taverna, London, England. Learned to work effectively with an international clientele.

Summer 1993

Hostess, The Clam Shell, Salem, Mass.

ACTIVITIES

American Marketing Association, Student Marketing Association, Fencing Club.

Source: Special Advertising Section in *Business Week's Guide to Careers* ("The Chrysler–Plymouth Guide to Building a Résumé").

FIGURE A.4

STAMP OUT BAD RÉSUMÉS

A good résumé should

1. Invite you to read it, have a clear layout and top-quality printing, and eliminate extraneous information.

2. Start sentences with action verbs (such as organized, managed, and designed) rather than with lead-ins ("I was the person responsible for . . .").

3. Highlight those accomplishments related to future work.

4. Be free of spelling, punctuation, and grammatical errors.

5. Speak the reader's language by using the vocabulary of the industry you're targeting.

6. Make a strong statement; this means using only the most relevant information—nothing less, nothing more.

Your résumé is an advertisement for yourself. If your ad is better than the other person's ad, you're more likely to get the interview. In this case, "better" means that your ad highlights your attributes in an attractive way.

In discussing your education, for example, be sure to highlight your extracurricular activities such as part-time jobs, sports, clubs, and other such activities. If you did well in school, put down your grades. The idea is to make yourself look as good on paper as you are in reality.

The same is true for your job experience. Be sure to describe what you did, any special projects in which you participated, and any responsibilities you had.

For the Other Interests section, if you include one, don't just list your interests, but describe how deeply you were involved. If you organized the club, volunteered your time, or participated more often than usual in an organization, make sure to say so in the résumé. Figure A.4 shows an unedited version of a résumé. It was a part of a guide to building a résumé prepared by

Additional Pricing Tactics 455 *Pricing Strategies 455*
Nonprice Competition 456 *Entrepreneur Magazine:*
Hello Dolly 457

Case: Everyday Low Pricing (EDLP) 460

Video Case: Product Development and the Pricing
Factor 461

Chapter 15
Distributing Products Efficiently and Competitively 462

Profile: Robert May of Business Logistics Services at FedEx 463

The Role of Distribution in Business 464
Why We Need Middlemen 464 Middlemen and
Exchange Efficiency 465 *Entrepreneur Magazine:*
The Growing Importance of the Fourth P 466 The
Value Created by Middlemen 466

How Middlemen Add Utility to Goods 468
Form Utility 469 Time Utility 469 Place
Utility 469 Possession Utility 469 Information
Utility 470

Building Cooperation in Channel Systems 470
Corporate Distribution Systems 470 Contractual
Distribution Systems 470 *Top 10 Fast-Food*
Chains 471 Administered Distribution Systems 471
The Channel Captain 471 Supply Chain
Management and Quick Response 471 Electronic
Data Interchange (EDI) 472 Efficient Consumer
Response (ECR) 472

Physical Distribution (Logistics) Management 473
Methods Used to Move Raw Materials and Finished
Goods 473 Criteria Used to Select Physical
Distribution Systems 475 *Reaching Beyond Our*
Borders: Distribution in International Markets 476
Containerization 476 The Storage Function 477
Materials Handling 477

Wholesale Middlemen 478
Merchant Wholesalers 478

Retail Middlemen 479
Spotlight on Small Business: Small Retailers and Computer
Technology 480 Top 10 Retailers (Sales) 480 How
Retailers Compete: Benchmarking Against the
Best 480 *Making Ethical Decisions: Bribery or*
Business? 482 Retail Distribution Strategy 482
The Wheel of Retailing 483

Nonstore Retailing 483
Telemarketing 483 Vending Machines, Kiosks, and
Carts 484 *Top Vending Machine Products 484*
Direct Selling 484 Network Marketing 484
Direct Marketing Goes On-Line 485

Case: Network Marketing 488

Video Case: Wholesaling, Logistics, and UPS 489

Chapter 16
Promoting Products Using Integrated Marketing Communication 490

Profile: Jerry Winter of Pepsico 491

The Importance of Marketing Communications 492
The Promotion Mix 492

Advertising 493
The Importance of Advertising 493 *Major Categories*
of Advertising 494 Advertising Using Infomercials
495 Using Technology in Advertising 495
Spotlight on Small Business: Shopping from Home 498
Customized Advertising versus Global Advertising 498
Reaching Beyond Our Borders: Culture Shock 499

Personal Selling 500
Steps in the Selling Process 500 Business-to-
Business Selling 502

Word-of-Mouth and Sales Promotion 503
Sales Promotion 504 *Entrepreneur Magazine:*
Word-of-Mouth Promotions 505

Public Relations and Publicity 505
Making Ethical Decisions: Guilt by Association 506
Global Public Relations 506 Publicity 506

Preparing the Promotion Mix 507
Promotion Strategies 507 Opening
Communications with All Stakeholders 508

Integrated Marketing Communication (IMC)
Systems 509
Implementing an Integrated Marketing
Communication System 509 The Effect on
Traditional Marketing Organizations 510

From Integrated Marketing Communication to
Integrated Marketing 510
Implementing an Integrated Marketing Strategy 510

Case: Waking Up the Coffee Industry 514

Video Case: Integrated Marketing Communication at
Sprint 515

Career Portfolio: Fundamentals of Marketing 517

As this 3D video-projection system demonstrates, advances in technology will continue to transform the way products are designed and sold.

PART 6

DECISION-MAKING: MANAGING
INFORMATION

Chapter 17
Using Technology to Manage Information 522

Profile: Harriet Donnelly of AT&T 523

The Role of Information Technology 524
How Information Technology Changes Business 524
Moving from Information Technology Toward
Knowledge Technology 525   *Spotlight on Small
Business: Field of Dreams 526*

Cruising the Information Highway 526
Drivers Ed for the Information Highway 528   How
to Drive in the Fast Lane: The Internet 529
*Reaching Beyond Our Borders: The Internet Helps Small
Businesses Reach Beyond Their Borders 531*

Managing Information 531

The Enabling Technology: Hardware 532
Computer Networks 534

Software 534
*Legal Briefcase: Needed: A Balance of Free Trade and Public
Policy 535*   Word Processing Programs 535
Spreadsheet Programs 536   Database Programs 536
Graphics Programs 537   Communications
Programs 537   Integrated Programs 537
Groupware 537   *Making Ethical Decisions:
Superhighway Robbery 538*

Effects of Information Technology on
Management 538
Entrepreneur Magazine: Home-Based Business 539

Technology and You 540
Case: Electronic Shopping—What Next? 544
Video Case: Cruising the Internet 545

Chapter 18
Understanding Financial Information and Accounting 548

**Profile: Connie Connors of CVC
Communications 549**

The Importance of Financial Information 550

What Is Accounting? 550

Areas of Accounting 551
Managerial Accounting 551   Financial Accounting
552   *Entrepreneur Magazine: Details, Details 553*
Auditing 553   Tax Accounting 554

Accounting versus Bookkeeping 554
Double-Entry Bookkeeping 555   The Six-Step
Accounting Cycle 555

Key Financial Statements 557
The Balance Sheet 557   The Accounts of the
Balance Sheet 558   Liabilities and Owners' Equity
Accounts 558   The Fundamental Accounting
Equation 560   The Income Statement 560
Revenue 561   Cost of Goods Sold (Cost of Goods
Manufactured) 562   Operating Expenses 562
Legal Briefcase: Who's Accountable? 563   The
Importance of Cash Flow Analysis 563   *Reaching
Beyond Our Borders: The Oil's Flowing but the Cash Isn't
564*   The Statement of Cash Flows 565   *Making
Ethical Decisions: Oh, My Aching Bank! 566*

Applying Accounting Knowledge 566

Using Financial Ratios 567
Liquidity Ratios 567   Leverage (Debt) Ratios 568
Profitability (Performance) Ratios 568 Activity
Ratios 569 *Spotlight on Small Business: Keeping a Smile on
Your Banker's Face 570*

The Impact of Computer Technology in
Accounting 570

Case: Applying Financial Information 574

Video Case: Learning the Language of Business 575

Career Portfolio: Managing Information
(Information Systems) 577

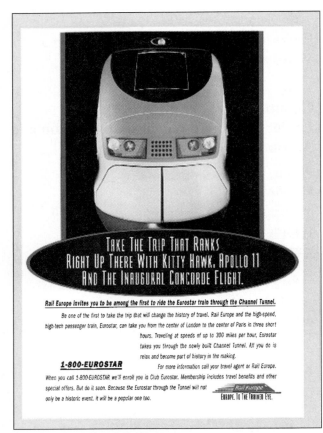

Financing construction of the Channel Tunnel between France and Great Britain required the cooperation of a large group of the world's foremost financial institutions.

PART 7

MANAGING FINANCIAL RESOURCES

Chapter 19
Using Financial Resources 582

Profile: Judy Lewent, CFO of Merck & Company 583

The Role of Finance 584
   The Importance of Understanding Finance 584

What Is Finance? 585

Financial Planning 586
   Forecasting Financial Needs 587   *Reaching Beyond Our Borders: Dear Walt and Mickey, Welcome to Realityland 588*
   Developing Budgets 588   Establishing Financial Controls 589   *Making Ethical Decisions: How Much Is Enough? 590*

The Need for Operating Funds 590
   Managing Daily Business Operations 590   *Entrepreneur Magazine: Advice from the Ice Man 591*   Managing Accounts Receivable 591   Obtaining Needed Inventory 592   Major Capital Expenditures 592

Alternative Sources of Funds 592

Obtaining Short-Term Financing 593
   Trade Credit 593   Promissory Notes 594   Family and Friends 594   Commercial Banks 594   Factoring 596   Commercial Paper 596   *Spotlight on Small Business: Financing a Small Business 597*

Obtaining Long-Term Financing 598
   Debt Financing 598   Equity Financing 599   Retained Earnings 600   Venture Capital 600   *Legal Briefcase: Derivatives Are Risky Business 601*   Using Leverage 601

Case: Financing Nonprofit Organizations 605

Video Case: The Role of the Financial Manager 605

Chapter 20
Financing and Investing through Securities Markets 608

Profile: Jerome Dodson, Mutual Fund Manager 609

The Function of Securities Markets 610

Debt Financing through Selling Bonds 610
   The Language of Bonds 611   Advantages and Disadvantages of Selling Bonds 611   Different Classes of Bonds 612   Special Features of Bonds 612

Equity Financing through Selling Stock 614
   The Language of Stock 614   Advantages and Disadvantages of Issuing Stock 615   Issuing Shares of Preferred Stock 616   Special Features of Preferred Stock 616   Issuing Common Stock 617   *Entrepreneur Magazine: Initial Public Offerings (IPOs) 618*

Stock Exchanges 618
   U.S. Exchanges 619   The Over-the-Counter (OTC) Market 619   *Reaching Beyond Our Borders: Calling All Brokers: How to Build New Exchanges 620*   Securities Regulations 620

How to Invest in Securities Markets 621
   Choosing the Right Investment Strategy 621

Investing in Bonds 622
   Investing in High-Risk Bonds 623

Investing in Stocks and Other Investments 623
   Buying Stock: Market and Limit Orders 624   Buying Stock on Margin 624   *Spotlight on Small Business: How to Make Money in Hot Growth Companies 625*   Stock Splits 625   Investing in Mutual Funds 626   Diversifying Investments 626   Investing in Commodities 627

Understanding Securities Market Information 628
   Bond Quotations 628   Stock Quotations 629   Mutual Fund Quotations 630   The Dow Jones Averages 631   Investment Bankers and Institutional Investors 631   *Legal Briefcase: Institutional Investors Have Unfair Advantages in IPO Markets 632*   The Stock Market Crash of 1987 632   *Making Ethical Decisions: Inside Scoop 633*

Case: Bonds or Stocks? That Is the Question. 636

Video Case: Why Stock, Why Bonds? 637

Chapter 21
Understanding Money and Financial Institutions 640

Profile: Alan Greenspan, Chairman of the Federal Reserve 641

The Importance of Money 642
  What Is Money? 642   What Is the Money Supply? 643
  Why Does the Money Supply Need to Be
  Controlled? 643   The Global Exchange of Money 644

Control of the Money Supply 645
  The Reserve Requirement 645   Open-Market
  Operations 645   The Discount Rate 646

The Development of the Federal Reserve System 646
  The Great Depression 647   The Federal Reserve
  and the Banking Industry 647

The American Banking System 648
  Commercial Banks 648   Savings and Loan
  Associations (S&Ls) 651   *Entrepreneur Magazine:
  Checking Out Credit Unions 652*   Credit Unions 652
  Other Financial Institutions 652

Protecting Your Funds 654
  The Federal Deposit Insurance Corporation
  (FDIC) 654   The Savings Association Insurance
  Fund (SAIF) 654   *Making Ethical Decisions: How
  High Can You Go? 655*

The Future of Banking 655
  Interstate Banking 655   *Spotlight on Small Business:
  The Success of 1st Business Bank 656*   Expanding What
  Banks Do 656   The Electronic Funds Transfer
  System (EFTS) 656

International Banking and Banking Services 657
  Leaders in International Banking 658   *Reaching
  Beyond Our Borders: BCCI, the Bank of Crooks and
  Criminals, International 659*

Case: Learning about the Federal Reserve System 662

Video Case: The Federal Reserve System 663

Chapter 22
Developing and Managing Your Personal Finances 666

Profile: Eillen Dorsey and Walter Hill, Jr., of ECS Technologies 667

The Need for Personal Financial Planning 668
  Six Steps in Learning to Control Your Assets 668
  *Entrepreneur Magazine: From Paper Boy to Entrepreneur
  669*   Education—The Best Investment 671

Building Your Capital Account 671
  Applying the Strategy 672   Real Estate: A Secure
  Investment 672   Tax Deduction and Home
  Ownership 673

Learning to Manage Credit and Insurance 673
  College Students Need Credit Education 674   Buying
  Life Insurance 675   Buying Health Insurance 676
  Buying Other Insurance 676

Planning Your Retirement 677
  Social Security 677   Individual Retirement Accounts
  (IRAs) 678   401(k) Plans 679   Keogh Plans 679
  Financial Planners 680

Case: Becoming Financially Secure 682

Video Case: Employee Savings Plans—Working with Brokers 683

Appendix: Managing Risk 685

Career Portfolio: Financial Management (Finance and Accounting) 692

Chapter Notes CN1

Glossary G1

Credits CR1

Name Index I1

Company and Product Index I5

General Index I7

ABOUT THE AUTHORS

Dr. William G. Nickels is an associate professor of business at the University of Maryland, College Park, Maryland. With over 25 years of teaching experience, Bill teaches introduction to business and marketing principles to large sections (250 students) each semester. Bill won the Outstanding Teacher on Campus Award in 1985 and teaching excellence awards in the Division of Behavioral Science and in the College of Business and Management. He was again nominated for the Outstanding Teacher on Campus three out of the last five years. Bill received his M.B.A. degree from Case Western Reserve University and his Ph.D. from the Ohio State University. He has written a principles of marketing text and a marketing communications text in addition to many articles in business publications. Bill is a marketing consultant and a lecturer on many business topics.

Jim McHugh is an associate professor of business at St. Louis Community College/Forest Park. Jim holds an M.B.A. degree and has broad experience in both education and business. In addition to teaching several sections of introduction to business each semester for 16 years, Jim maintains an adjunct professorship at Lindenwood College, teaching in the marketing and management areas at both the undergraduate and graduate levels. Jim has conducted numerous seminars in business and maintains several consulting positions with small and large business enterprises in the St. Louis area. He is also involved in a consulting capacity in the public sector.

Susan McHugh is an educational learning specialist with extensive training and experience in adult learning and curriculum development. She holds an M.Ed. degree and has completed her course work for a Ph.D. in education administration with a specialty in adult learning theory. As a professional curriculum developer she has directed numerous curriculum projects and educator training programs. She has worked in the public and private sector as a consultant in training and employee development. In addition to her role as co-author of the text, Susan designed the instructor's manual, test bank, and computer simulation program.

PREFACE

In the early days of television, there was a program called "You Asked For It." Even then good businesspeople knew that the way to win customers was to give them what they wanted. And now that businesses are in the midst of a customer-driven revolution, what better way for business textbook authors to win customers than by asking them what they want and then giving it to them. That's what we did as we developed the fourth edition of *Understanding Business*. We asked and you answered.

This new edition of *Understanding Business* is the most customer-driven text on the market. In the process of developing this edition, we met with dozens of Introduction to Business instructors from around the country in intensive focus group sessions. These instructors told us what they liked and didn't like about their current texts and what they wanted to see in our new edition. We also sent detailed surveys to many of the nation's Intro instructors. Remarkably, almost two hundred were returned with specific recommendations concerning what you expect in an Intro text.

We didn't stop at instructors as we gathered information. We met with several focus groups of end customers—students. We visited classrooms and talked to students about the strengths and weaknesses of their current texts. We found that students are not shy when you ask them what they think of the value of their texts!

The recommendations from instructors and the input from students in over 500 schools have all been compiled, reviewed, integrated, and in effect, have guided the development of the Fourth Edition. The results of this research not only determined which concepts and topics we covered, but the amount of space that we allocated to each, which concepts were integrated throughout the text, and which were segregated into separate chapters. Here are a few of the major changes.

YOU ASKED FOR IT: CURRENT ISSUES THAT REFLECT THE CHANGING BUSINESS ENVIRONMENT

One of our major efforts was to keep the text the most current on the market. To do that, we added new material right up until publication time! Current issues in this edition include:

- Focus on the customer.
- Diversity and multiculturalism in the workplace.
- Technology.
- Self-managed teams.
- Integrated marketing.
- Cross-functional cooperation among departments.
- Strategic alliances.
- Empowerment of employees.
- Outsourcing.

- Narrowcasting.
- Limited liability companies.
- Competitive benchmarking.
- Internet.
- Integrated marketing communication.
- Mass communications.
- Infomercials.
- Interactive television.
- Virtual banking.
- Efficient consumer response.
- Reengineering.
- Downsizing.
- Relationship marketing.
- Online computer services.
- Globalization.
- Trade alliances: GATT, NAFTA, EU, etc.
- Small business networking.
- Inverted organizations.
- Lean manufacturing.
- Home-based work and businesses.

Some of these topics, such as teams, quality, small business, and pleasing customers, are so important that you advised us and we agreed that coverage should not be segregated into separate, distinct chapters. Instead, we continuously integrated their discussion throughout the text. Let's use a story to illustrate the importance and advantages of concept integration. Picture a piece of cake. When you eat the cake you can't see or taste the egg that is in it, but you know that it holds everything together, makes it moist, more palatable. As important as the egg is to the success of the cake's recipe, the integration of key concepts is to the success of a business course. Think about it. Would you serve your students a piece of dry, falling-apart cake with some egg *on the side?* Chances are they'll pass on the cake, and they won't ask for the recipe! Well, we've thoroughly blended the following concepts throughout the Fourth Edition, and it makes for a winning recipe:

- **Pleasing customers.**
- **Teams.**
- **Quality.**
- **Small business.**
- **Technology.**
- **Cultural diversity.**
- **Change as a constant force.**

••• YOU ASKED FOR IT: A SHORTER TEXT •••

Everyone wants to cover the entire text, but who has the time? Of course, each of us has chapters we drop to give us time to cover our pet topics in more detail. Since these chapters vary from instructor to instructor, it was difficult to cut complete chapters. However, there were some topics that the great majority of you said should be saved for later courses, moved to appendixes, or condensed. As a result of this feedback the following major changes were made:

- The two economics chapters in the third edition were condensed into a single chapter: Chapter 2—Understanding Global and Domestic Economics.
- The three chapters on business formation were condensed into two: Chapter 5—Owning a Business and Chapter 6—Entrepreneurship and the Challenge of Starting a Small Business.
- The chapter on management tools (computers) was replaced with a discussion of managing information and driving on the information superhighway in Chapter 17—Using Technology to Manage Information.
- The material on financial ratios was moved into Chapter 18—Understanding Financial Information and Accounting.
- Part of the material from the chapter on risk management was integrated within the text and other topics were moved to an end-of-book appendix.
- Coverage of business law was moved out of the chapter on ethics and into an Appendix: Working within the Legal Environment of Business. In addition and **new** to this edition, Legal Briefcase boxes, each covering a single issue, have been added to most chapters.
- The appendix on personal financial planning became Chapter 22—Developing and Managing Your Personal Finances.

These and other changes resulted in a more efficient text with 15 percent fewer pages than the previous edition without losing the personal, interactive tone. Detailed explanations of these changes can be found in the Instructor's Manual.

YOU ASKED FOR IT: GLOBAL EMPHASIS EARLIER IN THE TEXT

We all know the importance of understanding the global economy. In previous editions, we chose to introduce global concepts early, integrate them throughout the book, and summarize specific global issues in the last chapter. Most of you applauded the integration of global topics, but indicated you would like to cover the global chapter sooner. We heard you and moved the material up to Chapter 3—Competing in Global Markets.

YOU ASKED FOR IT: EARLIER ETHICS DISCUSSION

Again, you were pleased with the ethics coverage, but wanted to see it earlier in the text. Chapter 4, now titled Demonstrating Ethical Behavior and Social Responsibility, satisfies this recommendation, while we continue to integrate the topic throughout the text with chapter boxes entitled "Making Ethical Decisions."

YOU ASKED FOR IT: MANAGEMENT BEFORE MARKETING

As businesses in the 1990s focus on the customer more and more, we continue to hold that marketing is at the center of all business activities. It was this philosophy that led to presenting the marketing chapters before management in our previous editions. Then why switch the management chapters before marketing in this edition? The easy explanation is that the vast majority of you told us to. The complex explanation deals with what is happening in business today.

As the lines between functions blur, focusing on customers has become the responsibility of *all* employees, not just those in the marketing department. Businesses are changing the way they are organized in order to beat the competition in satisfying the needs of their customers. This is evident in the cross-functional teams that are replacing line and staff in many organizations. Understanding these changes and concepts in the marketing chapters requires an understanding of the new relationships and principles presented in the management chapters.

YOU ASKED FOR IT: EMPHASIS ON CRITICAL THINKING

Education is a social process . . . Education is growth . . . Education is not a preparation for life; education is life itself.

John Dewey

I have never let my schooling interfere with my education.

Mark Twain

"Education is life itself." This is even more true today than it was in Dewey's day. The volume and speed of changes in today's world require that continuous education be an integral part of each of our lives. We cannot tell our students as we hand them their degrees, "Here, now you know all you need to know." Even if we were successful in teaching them what we thought they needed to know, much of it will be obsolete before their diplomas are framed. The best way that we can make sure that our students' schooling doesn't interfere with their education is to teach them how to learn, how to think, how to analyze and question.

Helping students learn how to think is what *Understanding Business,* Fourth Edition, strives to do. The design of the text and the accompanying instructional materials are based on learning principles that put the responsibility for learning where it belongs—on the students' shoulders.

SECRETARY'S COMMISSION ON ACHIEVING NECESSARY SKILLS (SCANS)

The Secretary of Labor appointed a commission, the Secretary's Commission on Achieving Necessary Skills (SCANS), to identify the skills people need to succeed in the workplace. SCANS' fundamental purpose is to encourage a high-performance economy characterized by high-skill, high-wage employment. The commission's message to educators is this: Help your students connect what they learn in class to the world outside.

To help educators prepare their students for the workplace, SCANS identified five workplace competencies that should be taught: (1) Resources—ability to allocate time, money, materials, space, and staff; (2) Interpersonal skills—ability to work on teams, teach others, serve customers, lead, negotiate, and work well with people from culturally diverse backgrounds; (3) Information—ability to acquire and evaluate data, organize and maintain files, interpret and communicate, and use computers to process information; (4) Systems—understanding of social, organizational, and technological systems; ability to monitor and correct performance and to design or improve systems; and (5) Technology—ability to select equipment and tools, apply technology to specific tasks, and maintain and troubleshoot equipment. The pedagogical tools in the text and package are designed to facilitate these SCANS competencies.

Here are the major pedagogical devices used in the text.

- **Learning Goals.**   Tied directly to the summaries at the end of the chapter and to the test questions, these learning goals help students preview what they are supposed to know after reading the chapter, and then test that knowledge by answering the questions in the summary. The study guide is also closely linked to the learning goals as part of the total integrated teaching, learning, and testing system.

- **Opening Profiles.**   Each chapter begins with a profile of a person whose career illustrates an important point covered in the chapter. Not all the personalities are famous since many of them work in small businesses and nonprofit organizations. These profiles provide a transition between chapters and a good introduction to the text material.

- **Progress Checks.**   Throughout the chapters there are Progress Checks that ask students to remember what they have just read. If students are not understanding and retaining the material, the Progress Checks will stop them and show them that they need to review before proceeding. We have all experienced times when we were studying and our minds wandered. Progress Checks are a great tool to prevent that from happening for more than a few pages.

- **Critical Thinking Questions.**   These **new** and unique inserts, found throughout each chapter, ask students to pause and think about how the material they are reading applies to their own lives. This device is an excellent tool for linking the text material to the student's past experience to enhance retention. It greatly increases student involvement in the text and course as recommended by SCANS.

- **Boxes.**   Each chapter includes boxed inserts that apply the chapter concepts to particular themes, including **small business, entrepreneurship, business law, making ethical decisions,** and **global business.** Although examples of such topics are integrated throughout the text, these boxes highlight the application in a particular area. The entrepreneurship boxes, **new** to this edition, were developed in cooperation with *Entrepreneur* magazine. The ethics boxes, entitled "Making Ethical Decisions," pose questions that require students to evaluate their own ethical behavior as recommended by SCANS.

- **Key Terms.**   Key terms are developed and reinforced through a three-tiered system. They are introduced in boldface, repeated and defined in the margin, listed at the end of each chapter with page references, and defined in a glossary at the end of the text.

- **Cross-Reference System.**   This system, unique to our text and **new** to this edition, refers students back to the primary discussion and examples of key concepts. An icon and specific page reference appear each time a key concept occurs in a chapter subsequent to its original discussion. This allows students to quickly review that concept (if necessary) and improve their comprehension of the material. It eliminates the need to continuously revisit and restate key concepts, reducing overall text length. Students participating in our focus groups ranked this learning/study tool first in utility from more than 20 different aids.

- **Photo and Illustration Essays.** Each photo and illustration in the text is accompanied by a short paragraph that shows the relevance of the visual to the material in the text. The accompanying descriptions help the student understand what is being shown in the graphic and how it applies to the text. In order to enhance their pedagogical value, many of these photos were commissioned specifically for use in this edition.

- **Interactive Summaries.** The end-of-chapter summaries are directly tied with the learning goals and are written in a unique question and answer format. Answering the questions and getting immediate feedback helps prepare students for quizzes and exams. The students in our focus groups were extremely positive about this format.

- **Developing Workplace Skills.** **New** to this edition are Developing Workplace Skills activities designed to increase student involvement in the learning process. Some of these miniprojects require library work, but many of them involve talking with people to obtain their reactions and advice on certain subjects. Students then come to class better prepared to discuss the topics at hand. These assignments can be divided among groups of students so they can learn a great deal from outside sources and about teamwork without any one student having to do too much work. These are the type of learning experiences that facilitate the SCANS competencies.

- **Practice Cases.** Each chapter concludes with a short case to allow students to practice managerial decision making. They are intentionally brief and meant to be discussion starters rather than take up the entire class period. The answers to the cases are in the instructor's manual. Again these examples of real-world problem solving will help students achieve the SCANS competencies.

- **Video Cases.** New to this edition are video *cases* for each chapter. These are placed at the end of the chapter and are optional as assignments. They feature companies, processes, practices, and managers that highlight and bring to life the key concepts, and especially the themes of the Fourth Edition. Highlighted companies, managers, and topics include accessing and using the Internet, Checkers and La-Van Hawkins, St. Louis Bread Company, Big Apple Bagels, Tellabs, Nike, and Coca-Cola. In their report, SCANS stated that video and multimedia materials are essential to creating the realistic contexts in which the competencies are used. Most segments are 8 to 15 minutes in length and are suitable for classroom, home, or lab viewing. Detailed notes regarding content, running time, suggestions for use, and questions are included in the instructor's material.

YOU ASKED FOR IT: MORE EMPHASIS ON CAREERS

Our student focus group recommended that we give more emphasis to information about potential careers. In response to this request, and **new** to the Fourth Edition, are unique career portfolios at the end of each part.

Each portfolio includes a vignette which profiles the career development of a *recent* college student. They also include charts of specific careers including titles, job descriptions, requirements, potential earnings, responsibilities, and future growth possibilities.

YOU ASKED FOR IT: INSTRUCTIONAL MATERIALS THAT ARE ACCURATE AND EASY TO USE

Perhaps it is because we use these materials in our own classrooms that we were so meticulous with their preparation. Jim teaches traditional-size classes of 30–50 students in an urban community college, and Bill teaches large classes of 250 in lecture halls in a four-year institution. As a result, everything in the Fourth Edition is designed to help instructors be more effective and make this course more practical and interesting for students. No introductory business text package is as market responsive, easy to use, and fully integrated as this one. To accomplish this integration, the authors designed and contributed to the instructor's manual, test bank, and computer software. They also prepared the new acetates and the accompanying annotations and notes. The other supplements were prepared by outstanding practitioners who used the materials in their own classes.

In addition to the text, the integrated teaching and testing system includes: Instructor's Manual, Electronic Instructor's Manual, Annotated Instructor's Edition, Test Bank, Computest 4, Teletest, Study Guide, Interactive Computerized Tutorial, Color Overhead Transparency Acetates, Transparency Masters, Videos, Videodisc, and other useful instructional tools.

KEY SUPPLEMENTS

Instructor's Manual   All material in the Instructor's Manual is easy to use and has been widely praised by new instructors, part-timers, and experienced educators alike. Many instructors tell us that the IM is a valuable time-saver that makes them look good in class. **The Instructor's Manual is unique in its thorough integration with both the text and package**. Each chapter opens with a description of the differences between the third and fourth editions in order to facilitate the conversion of your own teaching notes to the new edition.

After a short topic outline of the chapter and listing of the chapter objectives and key terms, you will find a resource checklist with all of the supplements that correspond to each chapter. Consequently, there is no need to flip through half a dozen sources to find which supplementary materials are available for each chapter.

To make the system even easier to use, the detailed lecture outline contains marginal notes recommending where to use acetates, supplementary cases, lecture enhancers, and critical thinking exercises. Space is also available to add personal notes of your own so that they too may be integrated into the system.

Each chapter contains lecture enhancers—short article summaries that provide additional examples—allowing you to implement the latest business and social issues. Supplementary cases, similar to those in the text, are provided for each chapter for use as outside assignments and/or classroom discussions. The critical thinking exercises require students to analyze and apply chapter concepts, a tremendous aid in getting students more involved in the learning process as recommended by SCANS. The Instructor's Manual has been revised and reformatted by Gayle Ross, based on feedback from three separate focus groups.

Electronic Instructor's Manual   The lecture outline in the Instructor's Manual is available in WordPerfect or ASCII files so you can modify it to fit your own teaching style. Using this disk and your word processor, you can customize the instructor's manual by integrating your own unique notes to the lecture outline.

Annotated Instructor's Edition   **New** to this edition, the AIE is a reproduction of the student edition of the text with the addition of marginal notes that suggest where to use various instructional tools such as the overhead transparencies, supplementary cases, and lecture enhancers. It also identifies the activities that facilitate the SCANS competencies.

Test Bank   This part of our Integrated Teaching and Testing System always receives more attention than the rest. We're keenly aware that the success of your course depends on tests that are comprehensive and fair, and we have provided questions that measure recall and require students to apply the material to real-world situations.

The Nickels/McHugh/McHugh Test Bank is like no other on the market. It is designed to test three levels of learning.

1. **Knowledge** of key terms.
2. **Understanding** of concepts and principles.
3. **Application** of principles.

A rationale for the correct answer and the corresponding text page add to the uniqueness of our 4,000-question Test Bank.

Another helpful tool is our unique "Test Table." This chart helps you develop balanced tests by quickly identifying items according to objective and level of learning.

For the ultimate in ease, each chapter concludes with a Quick Quiz. These 10-item tests are ready for reproduction and distribution for testing or for outside assignments. The Test Bank was revised by the very capable team of Dennis Shannon and Jim McGowen of Belleville Area College. To assure clarity and accuracy, the Test Bank was reviewed by the text authors and Donald White of Prince George's Community College.

Computest 4   The Test Bank also comes in a computerized version. This enhanced test-generation software allows users to add and edit questions; save and reload multiple test versions; select questions based on type, difficulty, or key word; and utilize password protection. It supports over 250 printers; links graphics, tables, and text to a series of questions; supports numerous graphics including special characters, complex equations, subscripts, superscripts, bolds, underlines, and italics; and can run on a network.

Teletest   For those who prefer not to use the computerized test-generator, Irwin provides the Teletest Service. Using a toll-free phone number, the instructor can order an exam prepared from the *Understanding Business* Test Bank. A master copy of the exam, with answer key, is sent first class mail the same day it is requested. Fax is also available within 30 minutes of the request.

Study Guide   The *Study Guide to Understanding Business*, written by Barbara Barrett of St. Louis Community College/Meramec, is not merely a synopsis of the text or a collection of multiple choice questions. The exercises contain various forms of open-ended questions that require the student to write out his or her personal grasp of the material. It is not an easy study guide; it is an effective one that demands active participation. If your students use this guide, they will be fully prepared for class discussions and exams. It has been reviewed by several instructors for accuracy and utility.

Videotapes   See previous description under Videocases.

Overhead Transparency Acetates   Two hundred color acetates, none of which reproduce textual exhibits, augment the concepts and examples presented in the text. These acetates enable you to illustrate your lectures with colorful visual aids. Detailed annotations regarding content and suggested uses for each acetate are found on the acetate divider sheets and in the Instructor's Manual.

Transparency Masters   In addition to the acetates, all important charts, graphs, and tables in the text are reproduced as transparency masters for your easy use in the classroom.

NEW Technologies   Several new elements are being introduced to our cadre of market-driven supplements. These include:

Classroom Presentation Software Using Microsoft PowerPoint with Electronic Lecture Notes. Over 200 electronic "slides" keyed to the text. These slides can be modified with PowerPoint. Accompanying lecture notes are available for Windows and DOS word processors.

McNick Plus for Windows. A self-contained interactive tutorial based on setting up a small business venture. Introductory scenarios are followed by guided questions (feedback is provided for all answers).

Business Plan Templates. Word processing templates designed for popular Windows-based word processors carefully guide students through the necessary steps to develop a business plan.

CD-ROM Case Analysis Software. An interactive CD-ROM product containing video cases and self-directed study questions.

Business Simulation (Union Pacific). An interactive CD-ROM from Allen Communications, which guides the students through the decision-making process in running a business (the Union Pacific Railroad).

Instructor's Orientation Video. Preparing for a course with a new text can be time-consuming for even the most experienced instructor and often overwhelming for part-time instructors scheduled on short notice. In response to your feedback and in an effort to ease the transition and to introduce the features of the text and package as quickly as possible, we have prepared for this edition an orientation video that walks you through each of the various elements, with our suggestions as to when and how instructors can use them.

We are proud of the text and the integrated teaching and testing system that you have helped us develop over the years. The many accolades from loyal text and supplements users are gratifying and rewarding. We continue to strive to provide the strongest instructional package to help you support the text in the classroom. Our goal is to join you in ensuring that, indeed, your students' schooling does not interfere with their education. After all, you asked for it!

Bill Nickels
Jim McHugh
Susan McHugh

ACKNOWLEDGMENTS

Our names may appear on the cover of this book, but we are only three of the people responsible for its evolution. We were blessed to work with a great team of professionals in making this book and package a reality. Craig Beytien gallantly served as our executive editor. As manager of the project, it was Craig's job to recruit the best team members and he did an outstanding job. Craig saw to it that somehow all of the pieces came together—on time and within budget!

Glenn Turner and Meg Turner of Burrston House were tireless in their roles as developmental editors. Their persistence in gathering market research and their diligence in keeping us focused on priorities were indispensable in assuring that the product responds to market needs. Glenn's thoroughness and Meg's graciousness produced an appealing blend of skill in drawing the best from their other teammates.

Victoria Gregor and Nancy Shanahan, also from Burrston House, skillfully searched for photos that effectively reflect the concepts presented in the text. Their choice of photos beautifully complement the new text design created under the direction of Michael Warrell. Michael successfully blended divergent ideas into a shared vision, an achievement that reveals his diplomatic as well as aesthetic intuitions.

Many thanks to our industry sources for their suggestions and advice on current technologies and "real-world" business concepts. Special thanks to Edward Tennent of IBM and Devar Burbage of Manugistics for their ideas and help.

Many dedicated educators contributed to the text and package. Lowell Lamberton of Central Oregon Community College developed the unique career portfolios that appear at the end of each part. Dennis Shannon and Jim McGowen of Belleville Area College revised the Test Bank. Gayle Ross of Ross Publishing gave the Instructors' Manual a face lift. Billie Petersen of the University of Central Oklahoma updated McNick. Barbara Barrett of St. Louis Community College/Meramec wrote the Study Guide.

Jane Lightell, the world's most patient senior project editor, never once admonished us for our continuous changes to "completed" manuscript—at least not to our faces! The complexity of this project was a difficult task under ideal circumstances, but with so many cooks in the kitchen Jane outdid herself in keeping us all in line and on schedule.

We want to thank Bruce Sylvester for his excellent copyediting, Charlene Breeden for photo coordination, Kim Meriwether and Laurie Kersch and the Irwin production team, and Betty Hadala for overseeing the new technology supplements. Special thanks to Irwin's in-house composition team and their fearless leader, Jim Cronin. Many more people than we can ever acknowledge worked behind the scenes to translate our manuscript into the text you see; we thank them all.

Having a great text and package doesn't mean a thing if we don't find a way to get it to you. The excitement and energy of our exceptional marketing manager, Jim Lewis, was contagious as he spread the word of the project's progress to the sales reps. We appreciate the renowned service and commitment of these dedicated sales reps as much as you do.

We have many instructors, more than ever before, to thank for contributing to the development of *Understanding Business*. An exceptional group of reviewers dedicated many long hours to critiquing the previous edition and subsequent drafts of this edition. Their recommendations and contributions were invaluable in making this edition a stronger instructional tool. Our sincere thanks to the following reviewers:

Kenneth Anderson, *Charles S. Mott Community College*

Alec Beaudoin, *Triton College*

Harvey Bronstein, *Oakland Community College*

William Chittenden, *Texas Tech University*

Bobbie Corbett, *Northern Virginia Community College*

Vincent Deni, *Oakland Community College*

Janice Feldbauer, *Austin Community College*

Michael Fritz, *Portland Community College*

Stephen Griffin, *Tarrant County Junior College*

John Gubbay, *Moraine Valley Community College*

Daniel Hallock, *St. Edward's University*

Gene Hastings, *Portland Community College*

Frederic Hawkins, *Westchester Business Institute*

Jim Lentz, *Moraine Valley Community College*

Bob Mathews, *Oakton Communitiy College*

William Motz, *Lansing Community College*

Edward O'Brien, *Scotsdale Community College*

Donald Radtke, *Richard J. Daley College*

Anne Ranczuch, *Monroe Community College*

Richard Randall, *Nassau Community College*

Jill Russell, *Camden County College*

Nicholas Sarantakes, *Austin Community College*

Leon Singleton, *Santa Monica College*

Carl Stem, *Texas Tech University*

Susan Thompson, *Palm Beach Community College*

Robert Ulbrich, *Parkland College*

Michael Vijuk, *Harper College*

Donald White, *Prince Georges Community College*

Gayla Jo Wilson, *Mesa State College*

Judy Eng Woo, *Bellevue Community College*

Ron Young, *Kalamazoo Valley Community College*

Four separate groups of reviewers agreed to give us intensive recommendations by meeting with us in focus groups. Two of these groups even braved bitter Chicago snowstorms to help us. We hope this text, the reflection of their suggestions, in some way repays them for their efforts. Members of the Fourth Edition focus groups include:

Harold Babson, *Columbus State Community College*

Xenia Balabkins, *Middlesex Community College*

John Balek, *Morton College*

Carol Bibly, *Triton College*

Jim Boeger, *Rock Valley College*

Willie Caldwell, *Houston Community College*

Sandra Cece, *Triton College*

Allen Coon, *Robert Morris College*

Al Fabian, *IVY Tech*

John Foster, *Montgomery College*

Bernette Glover, *Olive Harvey College*

Mike Graves, *Portland Community College*

John Gubbay, *Moraine Valley Community College*

Clark Hallpike, *Elgin Community College*

Tim Helton, *Joliet Junior College*

Gloria Jackson, *San Antonio College*

Bill Jedlicka, *Harper College*

John Kalaras, *DeVry Institute of Technology*

Jim Lentz, *Moraine Valley Community College*

Willy Morris, *Northwestern Business College*

Elaine Novak, *San Jacinto College*

George Otto, *Truman College*

Robert Pollero, *Ann Arundel Community College*

James Reinemann, *College of Lake County*

Ellen Reynolds Ligons, *Pasadena City College*

Doug Richardson, *Eastfield College*

Karen Richardson, *Tarrant County Junior College*

Cathy Sanders, *San Antonio College*

Wallace Satchell, *St. Phillip's College*

Kurt Schindler, *Wilbur Wright College*

Jim Seeck, *Harper College*

Dennis Shannon, *Belleville Area Community College*

Nora Jo Sherman, *Houston Community College*

Scott Steinkamp, *Northwestern Business College*

Paul Sunko, *Olive Harvey College*

Darrell Thompson, *Mountain View College*

Robert Ulbrich, *Parkland College*

Wallace Wirth, *South Suburban Community College*

It was our honor to receive direct input from a very special group of users—students. These introduction to business students gave up their time to visit with us in a day-long session in order to help us better meet the needs of students that will follow them. We thank the following for sharing their ideas and course experiences:

Carol Griesbach, *Rock Valley Community College*

Leslie Hanson, *Moraine Valley Community College*

Ken Kuh, *Moraine Valley Community College*

Tom Martin, *Harper College*

Kathy Sarich, *DeVry Institute of Technology*

Kevis Smith, *Olive Harvey College*

Donna Wendling, *Elgin Community College*

Approximately 200 instructors, both adopters and nonadopters alike, from around the country agreed to complete a comprehensive questionnaire as a way of telling us what they would like to see in an Intro text and supplements package. Their collective advice was critical to our decision-making for this edition. Respondents include:

Dennis G. Allen, *Grand Rapids Community College*, Larry Arp, *University of Southern Indiana*, Doug Ashby, *Lewis & Clark Community College*, Hal Babson, *Columbus State Community College*, Xenia Balabkins, *Middlesex Community College*, Michael Baldigo, *Sonoma State University*, John Balek, *Morton College*, Barbara Barrett, *St. Louis Community College*, Richard Bartlett, *Muskigan Area Technical College*, Lorraine Bassette, *Prince George's Community College*, Jade Beavers, *Jeferson State Community College*, Dean Bittick, *East Central College*, Mary Jo Boehms, *Jackson State Community College*, John Bowdidge, *Southwest Missouri State University*, Debbie Brown, *Santa Fe Community College*, Joseph Brum, *Fayetteville Technical Community College*, xxx

ACKNOWLEDGMENTS

Albert Bundons, *Johnson County Community College*, J. Callahan, *Florida Institute of Technology*, Professor Carman, *Bucks County Community College*, Mary Margaret Cavera, *Davenport College*, Bonnie Chavez, *Santa Barbara City College*, Larry Chonko, *Baylor University*, Michael Cicero, *Highline Community College*, J. Cicheberger, *Hillsborough Community College*, Professor Connell, *Montgomery County Community College*, Jeffrey Conte, *Westchester Community College*, Doug Copeland, *Johnson County Community College*, John Coppage, *Saginaw Valley State University*, James Cox, *Jefferson Community College*, Bruce Cudney, *Middlesex Community College*, C. Culbreth, *Brevard Community College*, Clifford Davis, *SUNY–Cobleskill*, Kathleen Denisco, *SUNY–Buffalo*, S. Desai, *Cedar Valley College*, Katherine Dillon, *Ocean County College*, Samuel DiRoberto, *Penn State University–Ogontz*, Ronald Eggers, *Barton College*, Pat Ellsberg, *Lower Columbia College*, John Evans, *New Hampshire College*, Karen Fager, *Umpqua Community College*, S. Fante, *Central Florida Community College*, Edward Fay, *Canton College of Technology*, David Felt, *Northern Virginia Community College–Manassas*, Bob Ferrentino, *Lansing Community College*, Steve Floyd, *Manatee Community College*, Leatrice Freer, *Pitt Community College*, Thomas Frizzel, *Masasoit Community College*, Alan Gbur, *Richard J. Daley College*, Eileen Baker Glassman, *Montgomery College*, Joe Gray, *Nassau Community College*, Gary Green, *Manatee Community College*, Steve Griffin, *Tarrant Co. Jr. College*, Johnathan Gueverra, *Newbury College*, James J. Hagel, *Davenport College*, Dan Hall, *East Central College*, Ron Halsac, *Community College Allegheny North*, E. Hamm, *Tidewater Community College*, Bob Harmel, *Midwestern State University*, Gene Hastings, *Portland Community College*, Joseph Hecht, *Montclair State College*,

Douglas Heeter, *Ferris State University*, Michael Heim, *Lakewood Community College*, Edward Henn, *Broward Community College*, Dave Hickman, *Frederick Community College*, George Hicks, *Muskigan Area Technical College*, Nathan Himmelstein, *Essex County College*, Eric Hoogstra, *Davenport College*, B. Hoover, *Brevard Community College*, Vince Howe, *University of North Carolina–Wilmington*, Joseph Hrebenak, *Community College Allegheny County*, Tom Humphrey, *Palomar College*, Howard Hunnius, *John Tyler Community College*, Robert Ironside, *North Lake College*, James Isherwood, *Community College of Rhode Island*, Paloma Jalife, *SUNY–Oswego*, Michael Johnson, *Delaware County Community College*, Wallace Johnston, *Virginia Commonwealth University*, Norman Karl, *Johnson County Community College*, Jim Kennedy, *Angelina College*, Daniel Kent, *Northern Kentucky University*, Professor Kern, *Reading Area Community College*, Betty Ann Kirk, *Tallahassee Community College*, Barbara G. Kreichbaum, *Hagerstown Business College*, Patrick C. Kumpf, *University of Cincinnati*, Jay LaGregs, *Tyler Junior College*, Professor Lander, *Montgomery County Community College*, Donna Lees, *Butte College*, Joseph Liebreich, *Reading Area Community College*, Donald Linner, *Essex County College*, Thomas Lloyd, *Westmoreland County Community College*, Anthony Lucas, *Allegheny Community College*, Joyce Luckman, *Jackson Community College*, Rippy Madan, *Frostburg State University*, Richard Maringer, *University of Akron–Wayne College*, Alan Marks, *DeVry Institute of Technology*, Christine McCallum, *University of Akron–Wayne College*, Mark M. McCarthy, *Davenport College*, Yet Mee Lim, *Alabama State University*, Carl Meskimen, *Sinclair Community College*, Duane Miller, *SUNY–Cobleskill*, Herbert Miller, *Indiana University– Kokomo*,

Bill Motz, *Lansing Community College*, Micah Mukabi, *Essex County College*, Herschel Nelson, *Polk Community College*, Sharon Nickels, *St. Petersburg Junior College*, Phil Nufrio, *Essex County College*, Susan Oleson, *Central Piedmont Community College*, J. Ashton Oravetz, *Tyler Junior College*, Nikki Paahana, *DeVry Institute of Technology*, Dennis Pappas, *Columbus State Community College*, Knowles Parker, *Wake Technical Community College*, Patricia Parker, *Maryville University*, Darlene Raney Perry, *Columbus State*, Stephen Peters, *Walla Walla Community College*, A. Pittman, *Brevard Community College*, Wayne Podgorski, *University of Memphis*, Raymond Pokhon, *M A T C*, Geraldine Powers, *Northern Essex Community College*, Mary E. Ray, *Indiana Business College*, Carla Rich, *Pensacola Junior College*, Bob Roswell, *Jackson Community College*, Tom Rutkowski, *SUNY–Cobleskill*, Cathy Sanders, *San Antonio College*, Billie Sargent, *National College*, Gordon Saul, *National Business College*, Patricia A. Serraro, *Clark College*, Donald Shifter, *Fontbonne College*, Noel Smith, *Palm Beach Community College*, Bill Snider, *Cuesta College*, Rieann Spence-Gale, *Northern Virginia Community College*, Emanual Stein, *Queensborough Community College*, David Stringer, *DeAnza College*, Jacinto Suarez, *Bronx Community College*, Carl Swartz, *Three Rivers Community College*, James Taggart, *University of Akron*, Vern Timmer, *SUNY–Alfred*, Amy Toth, *Northampton County Area Community College*, Robert Ulbrich, *Parkland College*, Richard Van Ness, *Schenectady County Community College*, William Vincent, *Santa Barbara City College*, Philip Weatherford, *Embry-Riddle Aeronautical University*, Pete Weiksner, *Lehigh County Community College*, Henry Weiman, *Bronx Community College*, Bill Weisgerber, *Saddleback College*, Sally Wells, *Columbia College*, Walter Wilfong, *Florida Technical College*, Dick Williams, *Laramie County Community College*, Wallace Wirth, *South Suburban College*, Bennie Woods, *Burlington County College*, Greg Worosz, *Schoolcraft College*, William F. Wright, *Mt. Hood Community College*, Merv Yeagle, *Hagerstown Junior College*, C. Yin, *DeVry Institute of Technology*, Ned Young, *Sinclair Community College*, C. Zarycki, *Hillsborough Community College*, Richard Zollinger, *Central Piedmont College*.

Of course, we continue to thank the reviewers of previous editions. Their contributions remain the backbone of this text.

Milton Alderfer, *Miami-Dade Community College*, Dan Anderson, *Sullivan Jr. College*, John Anstey, *University of Nebraska—Omaha*, Ed Aronson, *Golden West College*, Alec Beaudoin, *Triton College*, John Beem, *College of DuPage*, John Blackburn *The Ohio State University*, John Bowdidge, *Southwest Missouri State University*, Stephen Branz, *Triton College*, Robert Brechner, *Miami-Dade Community College*, Harvey Bronstein, *Oakland Community College*, Joseph Brum, *Fayetteville Technical Institute*, Thomas Buchl, *Northern Michigan University*, Dennis Butler, *Orange Coast Community College*, Ron Bytnar, *South Suburban College*, B.J. Campsey, *San Jose State University*, Bruce Charnov, *Hofstra University*, Jill Chown, *Mankato State University*, Monico Cisneros, *Austin Community College*, James Cocke, *Pima County Community College*, Ron Cooley, *South Suburban College*, R.K. Davis, *University of Akron*, Ted Erickson, *Normandale Community College*, Alton Evans, *Tarrant County Community College*, C.S. Everett, *Des Moines Area Community College*, Frank Falcetta, *Middlesex Community College*, Robert Fishco, *Middlesex County Community College*, Charles FitzPatrick, *Central Michigan University*,

Jane Flagello, *DeVry Institute of Technology–Lombard*, John Foster, *Montgomery College*, Donald Gordon, *Illinois Central College*, Patricia Graber, *Middlesex County College*, Roberta Greene, *Central Piedmont Community College*, Sanford B. Helman, *Middlesex County College*, Paul Jenner, *Southwest Missouri State University*, Gene Johnson, *Clark College*, Alan Kardoff, *Northern Illinois University*, Allen Kartchner, *Utah State University*, Bob Kegel, *Cypress College*, Warren Keller, *Grossmont College*, Robert Kersten, *St. Louis Community College–Florissant Valley*, John A. Knarr, *University of Maryland–European Division*, Kenneth Lacho, *University of New Orleans*, Roger Lattanza, *University of New Mexico*, George Leonard, *St. Petersburg Junior College*, John Lloyd, *Monroe Community College*, Paul Londrigan, *C.S. Mott Community College*, Patricia Long, *Tarrant Junior College*, Jerry Lynch, *Purdue University*, Judith Lyles, *Illinois State University*, Diana McCann, *Kentucky College of Business*, Terrance Mitchell, *South Suburban College*, Joyce Mooneyhan, *Pasadena City College*, William Motz, *Lansing Community College*, Gary R. Murray, *Rose State College*, Sharon J. Nickels, *Saint Petersburg Junior College*, Cletus O'Drobinak, *South Suburban College*, Katherine Olson, *Northern Virginia Community College*, Eugene O'Connor, *California Polytechnical University–San Luis Obispo*, Mike Padbury, *Arapahoe Community College*, Dennis Pappas, *Columbus Technical Institute*, Joseph Platts, *Miami-Dade Community College*, Roderick Powers, *Iowa State University*, Renee Prim, *Central Piedmont Community College*, Richard Randall, *Nassau Community College*, Richard J. Randolph, *Johnson County Community College*, Betsy Ray, *Indiana Business College*, Robert Redick, *Lincoln Land Community College*, Scott Reedy, *Brookes College*, John Rich, *Illinois State University*, Jeri Rubin, *University of Alaska*, Karl Rutkowski, *Peirce Jr. College*, Nicholas Sarantakes, *Austin Community College*, Larry Saville, *Des Moines Area Community College*, Dennis Schmitt, *Emporia State University*, Daniel C. Segebath, *South Suburban College*, Guy Sessions, *Spokane Falls Community College*, Richard Shapiro, *Cuyahoga Community College*, Jerry Sitek, *Southern Illinois University*, Michelle Slagle, *The George Washington University*, Paul Solomon, *San Jose State University*, Carl Sonntag, *Pikes Peak Community College*, Richard Stanish, *Tulsa Junior College*, Robert Stivender, *Wake Technical Community College*, David Stringer, *DeAnza College*, George Sutcliffe, *Central Piedmont Community College*, Lorraine Suzuki, *University of Maryland—Asian Division*, Merle E. Taylor, *Santa Barbara City College*, Verna Teasdale, *Prince George's Community College*, Ray Tewell, *American River College*, Robert Ulbrich, *Parkland College*, Pablo Ulloa, *El Paso Community College*, Heidi Vernon-Wortzel, *Northeastern University*, Janna P. Vice, *Eastern Kentucky University*, Michael Vijuk, *Harper College*, Bernard Weinrich, *St. Louis Community College–Forest Park*, Paul Williams, *Mott Community College*, Wallace Wirth, *South Suburban College*, William Wright, *Mt. Hood Community College*, Ron Young, *Kalamazoo Valley Community College*

The fourth edition is all the stronger due to involvement of these committed instructors and students. We thank them all.

Bill Nickels
Jim McHugh
Susan McHugh

P A R T 1

BUSINESS TRENDS: CULTIVATING A BUSINESS IN DIVERSE, GLOBAL ENVIRONMENTS

PROLOGUE
USING CAREER AND
COURSE RESOURCES

APPENDIX
GETTING THE JOB
YOU WANT

CHAPTER 1
EXPLORING TRENDS IN
DYNAMIC BUSINESS
ENVIRONMENTS

CHAPTER 2
UNDERSTANDING
GLOBAL AND
DOMESTIC ECONOMICS

CHAPTER 3
COMPETING IN
GLOBAL MARKETS

CHAPTER 4
DEMONSTRATING
ETHICAL BEHAVIOR
AND SOCIAL
RESPONSIBILITY

APPENDIX
WORKING WITHIN THE
LEGAL ENVIRONMENT
OF BUSINESS

Using Career and Course Resources

KELLY STRATICO-SMITH, LAURA BIONDI-WILLIAMS, AND OTHER ENTREPRENEURS

Kelly Stratico-Smith and Laura Biondi-Williams each has two children. Like many mothers today, they were both busy carting their children to school, music lessons, dentist appointments, and more. Unable to obtain help or relief from these transportation duties, Kelly and Laura decided to assist other mothers in the area with similar needs. They started a part-time service in Santa Cruz, California, that for a fee would pick up children at their homes and take them to various activities. They bought a couple of white vans and put signs on them saying, "KART! Kids Area Rapid Transit."

Smith and Williams didn't do any special marketing research before starting their business. They simply saw a need and filled it. It turned out that there was no competition in the area and their service increased to 400 rides a week (at $6 a ride) and seven employees. Now these entrepreneurs are planning to expand into all of California's major cities. These two women represent a major trend in the country today. People of all ages are discovering the rewards, and the challenges, of owning and building their own businesses.

Linda Grabill is another entrepreneur who as an 18-year-old student decided to start her own summer lawn-care company. Her motivation to do so came from the realization that if successful she could make $30 an hour rather than the $6 she could earn as a store cashier. Linda's Lawn Care is a success, has two additional employees, and pays for many of her college expenses.

For various reasons beyond their control, many students and young married people are finding it harder to find attractive jobs in local businesses. The result has been positive for many, however, because the scarcity of jobs has opened their eyes to the opportunities of owning their own businesses.

Colleges and universities throughout the country are responding to the desire for students to own their own businesses. Community demand led Montgomery College in Rockville, Maryland, to offer a summer course that teaches students how to develop business plans and to learn other business skills. Howard University in Washington, D.C., has a Small Business Development Center that teaches teenagers how to start and manage businesses. Students line up early in the morning to register for the University of Southern California's Entrepreneurship Program.

A survey by the Higher Education Research Institute at the University of California at Los Angeles found that 42 percent of college freshmen said that eventually owning their own business was very important to them. Many of today's students are individualistic and idealistic. To them, starting a business is more than a way to make money. It is also a way to be on your own and to make a difference in the world.

There are many risks involved in starting your own business and much that you must learn. For those who don't want to assume that much risk, there are many excellent career opportunities working for others in business firms, nonprofit organizations, and government. This text provides a firm foundation for anyone eager to learn about business and business functions.

> ***Tell me, I'll forget. Show me, I may remember. But involve me and I'll understand.***
>
> *Chinese proverb*

BUSINESS SKILLS CAN BE APPLIED ANYWHERE

Smith, Williams, and Grabill represent thousands of small-business operators who begin their own businesses each year. Some, like Smith and Williams, are women with children who are starting businesses in their own homes. Others, like Grabill, are young people eager to earn more than the minimum wage. Some of these entrepreneurs are new immigrants who are finding tremendous opportunity in this country. We shall explore many such stories throughout the text. The purpose of these stories is to show you that the American dream is still alive and well. Business opportunities have never been greater.

This book and this course together may be one of the most important learning experiences of your life. They're meant to help you understand business so that you can use business principles in your own life. But you don't have to be in business to use business principles. You can use *marketing* principles to get a job and to sell your ideas to others. You can use your knowledge of *investments* to make money in the stock market. Similarly, you'll be able to use the *management skills* and general business knowledge wherever you go and in whatever career you pursue.

THE VALUE OF A COLLEGE EDUCATION

The earnings gap between high school and college graduates was about 33 percent in 1979. Today, *The Washington Post* reports that community college graduates make over 22 percent more than high school graduates and people with a bachelor's degree make 57 percent more.[1] Research has shown that 40 percent of the increase in these gaps is due to computer skills. The benefit of computer knowledge for women is even greater. Some 56 percent of the increased wage difference for women is computer-based.[2]

To get the most out of your college education, you must become familiar with computers. Your instructor can provide you with exercises to help you develop computer skills while mastering the material in this text. We encourage you to take any opportunity that arises to use the computer and to learn the latest computer capabilities, including word processing, desktop publishing, E-mail, and using the Internet.

Clearly, the investment in college and computer skills is worthwhile. It will be even more valuable if you study your text carefully and put in extra effort.

LEARNING ABOUT CAREERS

Almost all of us want to find a rewarding career and to be successful and happy. We just find it hard to decide what that career should be. Even many of those who have relatively successful careers tend to look for something more fulfilling, more challenging, and more interesting. One purpose of this text is to introduce you to the wide variety of careers available in business and management. You'll learn about production, marketing, finance, accounting, management, economics, and more.

When you're finished, you should have a much better idea about what kind of business career would be best for you. Not only that, you'll be prepared to use basic business terms and concepts that are necessary to be a success in any organization—including government agencies, charities, and social causes—or in your own small business.

This book is written in a different style from most textbooks. It's written to you and for you, the student. It's not just a text full of facts and figures; it's a guidebook for understanding business. Special attention is given to career opportunities, techniques for starting and managing your own business, managing businesses for others, and strategies for finding and getting the rewarding career you want.

••• GETTING STARTED •••

A great place to start in your career search is with a course like this one. Each chapter in this book will begin with a profile of someone in the business world. The stories of Linda Grabill and Kelly Smith are two examples. Many of the people you'll meet in the profiles learned the hard way that it's easy to fail in business if you don't know what you're doing. These stories are a good way to learn from the experiences of others.

••• ASSESSING YOUR SKILLS AND PERSONALITY •••

The earlier you can do a personal assessment of your interests, skills, and values, the better it will be for finding some career direction. In recognition of this need, many colleges have assessment programs you can take. About 300 schools use a software exercise called SIGI (System for Interactive Guidance and Information). A different version called DISCOVER is used at 400 other schools. Both feature self-assessment exercises, create personalized lists of occupations based on your interests and skills, and provide information about careers and the preparation required. The Strong–Campbell Interest Inventory and the Meyers–Briggs personality indicator can be used to supplement DISCOVER and SIGI, and reinforce the results.

It would be helpful to take such programs early in this course so you can determine, while you're learning about the different business fields, which ones most closely fit your interests and skills. These self-assessment programs will help you assess the kind of work environment you'd prefer (for example, technical, social service, or business), what values you seek to fulfill in a career (for example, security, variety, or independence), what abilities you have (for example, creative/artistic, numerical, or sales), and what important job characteristics you stress most (for example, income, travel, or amount of job pressure).

If you're one of the 42 percent of college students who are over 25 years old, you may be interested in the kind of aptitude test given by the Johnson O'Connor Research Foundation's Human Engineering Laboratory in Los Angeles. The lab has tested some 300,000 people since it began. Most are in their 30s and 40s, and come to the lab because they're not satisfied with what they're doing. Many such people are now back in college. To ensure that they choose the right career this time, such aptitude testing can be valuable. Armed with such information, you too are more likely to make a career choice that will be personally fulfilling. Such assessment tests are available in college placement centers, career labs, and libraries.

Visit the career center on your campus to learn about self-assessment, career opportunities today, and other information relative to your career. Shown here is the Career Exchange Center at Triton College in River Grove, Illinois. The Lyphomed booth is one example of the employers who visit Triton College on Career Exchange Day.

In doing career research, you will discover that the tourism industry is the number one employer in the majority of states. There are many interesting jobs related to tourism such as developing the "It's Like A Whole Other Country" campaign for the state of Texas. How many different careers and companies can you think of that depend on tourism?

EVERY COUNTRY OWNS A COLOR. *England has dibs on gray sky. Italy owns cities of gold. And in Texas, we've got blue all to ourselves. Each spring, bluebonnets dot our hillsides from rugged Big Bend to lush East Texas. We've also got cowboys in silver spurs, hikers in red canyons and shoppers in big-city neon. Come to Texas. It's a colorful place.*

For the new 272-page Texas Travel Guide, call 1-800-8888-TEX, Ext. 311.

TEXAS

It's Like A Whole Other Country.

••• WHICH COLLEGE IS BEST FOR ME? •••

The trend in higher education is for students to start out in community colleges. In the early 1990s, an estimated 45 percent of all postsecondary students taking courses for college credit were enrolled in community, technical, and junior colleges. This compares to just 37.4 percent in 1980. Over half of all first-time students taking credit classes are enrolled in two-year colleges. Accessibility is cited as one of the big advantages of community colleges. Accessibility includes location, time, and money.

When students complete their associate degrees at community colleges, they usually perform well at other colleges. Community colleges have a teaching focus that helps students get a firm foundation. Community colleges are particularly attractive to adult students who want to upgrade their skills, especially in technical areas such as computers. Community colleges are often uniquely able to handle such students because they usually offer evening courses and weekend programs geared to the part-time student. Community colleges typically develop close working relationships with local businesses so that graduates can be educated to fit the needs of the local community. Community colleges are also very effective at preparing students for jobs that don't require a bachelor's degree, such as nursing and police work.

About 39 percent of community college students plan to transfer to other colleges. There are advantages to studying at a university as well. Some careers require a bachelor's degree or more. One benefit of education in the United States is the diversity available in colleges. Some students prefer to attend a religious institution or to pursue a particular field of study, while others want the opportunity to play for or support nationally ranked athletic teams, and still others seek the camaraderie of fraternities and sororities.

This text is used in both community colleges and universities throughout the United States and around the world. The Canadian version is called *Understanding Canadian Business*.

••• ESTABLISHING RESOURCE FILES •••

One thing that links all students in all colleges is the need to retain what they learn in business courses. While it's important to learn about various careers and businesses, one tends to forget such data. You need a strategy to remember what you've learned. It's also extremely important to keep the names of contact people at various organizations. In addition, you may want to keep facts and figures of all kinds about the economy and business-related subjects. That's why you should develop resource files.

There are many programs on TV about business. "Wall $treet Week" is an interesting program about stocks and bonds. By watching such shows, you will learn what is happening in the business world and will pick up some new business terms. If there are terms you hear, but don't understand, ask your instructor to explain them.

An effective way to become an expert on almost any business subject is to set up your own information system. Eventually you may want to store data on computer disks for retrieval on your personal computer and to access professional data bases. Meanwhile, it's effective to establish a comprehensive paper filing system.

Each time you read a story about a firm that interests you, either cut it out of the magazine or photocopy it and then place it in an appropriate file. You might begin with files labeled Careers, Small Business, Economics, Management, and Resource People. You definitely want to have a personal data file titled Credentials for My Résumé or something similar. In that file, you'll place all reference letters and other job-related information. Soon you'll have a tremendous amount of information available to you. Later you can add to these initial files until you have your own comprehensive information system.

If you start now, you'll soon have at your fingertips information that will prove invaluable for use in term papers and throughout your career. Few college students do this filing, and, as a consequence, they lose most of the information they read in college or thereafter. Developing this habit is one of the most effective ways of educating yourself and having the information available when you need it. The only space you'll need to start is a 12-inch by 12-inch corner of your room to hold a portable file box. In these files you might put your course notes, with the names of your professors and the books you used, and so on. You may need this information later for employment references. Also, be sure to keep all the notes you make when talking with people about careers, including salary information, courses needed, and contacts.

Television shows such as "Wall $treet Week" are another good way to learn about business and investments. Have you ever watched Adam Smith's "Money World," the "Nightly Business Report," or other business shows? Try watching some or listening to similar shows on the radio, and see which ones you like best. Take notes and put them in your files.

••• CAREER PREPARATION •••

If you're typical of many college students, you may not have any idea what career you'd like to pursue. That isn't necessarily a big disadvantage in today's fast-changing job market. There are no perfect or certain ways to prepare for the most interesting and challenging jobs of tomorrow, many of which have yet to be created. Rather, you should continue your college education; develop strong computer skills and applications; improve your verbal and written communication; and remain flexible while you explore the job market.

RESOURCES  THE COURSE

College courses are best at teaching you concepts and ways of thinking about business. However, to learn first hand about real-world applications, you will need to explore and interact with actual businesses. Textbooks are like comprehensive tour guides in that they tell you what to look for and where to look, but they can never replace experience.

This text, then, isn't meant to be the only resource for this class. In fact, it's not even the primary resource. Your professor is much better at responding to your specific questions and needs. This book is just one of the resources he or she can use with you to satisfy your desire to understand what the business world is all about. There are six basic resources for the class in addition to the text:

1. *The professor.* Your instructor is more than a teacher of facts and concepts. He or she is a resource who's there to answer questions and guide you to the answers for others. One of the most valuable facets of college is the chance to study with experienced professors.

2. *The text*, Understanding Business, *and the* Study Guide *that comes with it*. The *Study Guide* will help you review and interpret key material and give you practice answering test questions.

3. *Outside readings.* Not only should you read magazines such as *Business Week* and *Nation's Business*, you should briefly review some of the latest business trade books. Three that will give you some indication of what business will be like in the 21st century are Don Peppers and Martha Rogers' *The One-to-One Future* (New York: Doubleday, 1993), Jessica Lipnack and Jeffrey Stamps' *The TeamNet Factor* (Essex Junction, VT: Oliver Wight Publications, 1993); and Earl Naumann's *Creating Customer Value* (Cincinnati, OH: Thompson Executive Press, 1995).

4. *Your own experience and that of your classmates.* Many college students have had experience working in a retail store, a factory, warehouse, or some other business or nonprofit organization. Talking together about those experiences exposes you to many real-life examples that are invaluable for understanding business. Students from other countries can also teach you about their culture and business opportunities around the world.

5. *Outside contacts.* One of the best ways to learn about business is to personally visit them. Who can tell you more about what it's like to start a career in accounting than someone who's doing it now? The same is true of other jobs. The world can be your classroom if you let it.

6. *The library or learning resource center.* Here you'll find newspapers, magazines, and various online data sources to find additional information about business. Take a day to review what's available. The library and the librarian are excellent resources.

••• THE PROFESSOR AS A RESOURCE •••

It's important for you to develop a friendly relationship with your professors. One reason for doing so is that many professors get job leads that they can pass on to you. They're also excellent references for future jobs. But most of all, your professor is one more experienced person who can help you find and access resource materials, and answer questions about business.

••• THIS TEXT AS A RESOURCE •••

Many learning aids appear throughout this text to help you understand the material. The first learning aid is a list of Learning Goals at the beginning of each chapter. Reading through these goals will help you set the framework and focus for the chapter material. Since every student at one time or other has found it difficult to get into studying, the Learning Goals are there to provide an introduction and to get your mind into a learning mode. Periodically, within each chapter, you'll encounter a set-off list of questions called a Progress Check. These questions give you a chance to pause, think carefully about, and recall what you've just read. We've all experienced having our minds wander while we read. These Progress Checks help you realize whether you're really absorbing the material. They're also an excellent review device.

Developing a strong business vocabulary is one of the most important and useful aspects of this course. To assist you, all key terms in the book are highlighted in boldface type. Key terms are also defined in the margins, and page references to these terms are given at the end of each chapter. A full glossary is located in the back of the book. You should rely heavily on these learning aids in adding these terms to your vocabulary.

The Critical Thinking sections are designed to help you relate the material to your own experiences. They should cause you to think about the meaning of what you have read and studied beyond the course. Research has shown that it is much easier to retain information and concepts that you can relate to your own life.

Each chapter contains a box titled Making Ethical Decisions. These examples emphasize the need for businesspeople to make moral and ethical decisions in business. As mentioned earlier, one purpose of this text is to teach you how to be successful in business. But another, very important objective is to teach you the *proper* as well as the profitable way to conduct business. Because

There are several learning devices in the text to help you master business. They include the Critical Thinking exercises and Developing Workplace Skills questions. These essay questions will help you think through business situations for yourself, encourage you to talk with businesspeople about their experiences, and recommend business publications that will provide valuable background. Such research will indeed prepare you for "real life" in business.

FRANK & ERNEST® by Bob Thaves

SCHOOL IS MOSTLY TRUE-FALSE, KID, BUT REAL LIFE IS ALL ESSAY QUESTIONS.

THAVES 10-7

© 1992 by NEA, Inc.

we believe business ethics are so important, in addition to the boxed examples we have an entire chapter devoted to the issue of ethical decision making. We encourage you to study this material thoroughly and to think over the moral and ethical implications of the various incidents we present.

Each chapter also has a separate box which considers small-business issues related to the topic of that chapter. These examples are taken from *Entrepreneur*, a popular magazine which calls itself "The Small Business Authority." Most jobs in the future will be created by small and medium-sized businesses, and small-business owners must deal with many challenges that are uncommon in larger firms. If you want to start and manage your own small business, you will need to be aware of and knowledgeable about the issues we present in these boxes.

As we approach the next century, nothing is more important to the future growth of U.S. businesses, in many instances regardless of size, than understanding global markets. Therefore, and similar to the emphasis we place on ethics, we include a discussion of global issues within boxes in each chapter. Additionally, Chapter 3 provides a comprehensive overview of the international business environment and its implications for our future.

The photographs, boxes, figures, and other highlighted material are designed to reinforce and highlight key concepts and to make the book a more effective learning tool as well as a pleasure to read. Great care has been used in selecting them to make sure these objectives are achieved.

The summaries are not mere reviews of what has been said. Rather, they're written in question-and-answer form, much like a classroom dialogue. This format makes the material more lively and should help you remember it better. Furthermore, the summaries are directly tied to the learning goals so you can see whether you've accomplished the chapter's objectives.

Regardless of how hard we try to make learning easier, the truth is that students tend to forget most of what they read and hear. To really remember something, it's best to do it. That's why there are Developing Workplace Skills sections at the end of each chapter. The purpose of Developing Workplace Skills questions is to have you do small projects that reinforce what you've read. You may find it easiest to divide these projects among the class and come back and share what you've learned.

The end-of-the-chapter cases (Practicing Management Decisions) give you another chance to think about the material and apply it in real-life situations. Don't skip the cases even if they're not reviewed in class. They're an integral part of the learning process because they enable you to think about and apply what you've studied.

If you use all of these learning aids plus the *Study Guide,* you will not simply "take a course in business." Instead, you'll have actively participated in a learning experience that will help you greatly in your chosen career.

Learning business is a lifetime occupation. Now is a good time to become familiar with business newspapers and magazines such as those pictured here. If you are interested in small business, you may want to read *Inc., Entrepreneur,* and *Nation's Business*. If you are more interested in big business, try reading *Fortune, Forbes,* and *Business Week*. Glance through the other business publications as well. You may find something of interest in each.

... OUTSIDE READINGS ...
AS A RESOURCE

We've noted that business periodicals are one of the major resources of the course. It's recommended that you review the following magazines and newspapers as well as other resources during the course and throughout your career: *The Wall Street Journal, Forbes, Inc., Business Week, Fortune,* the *Harvard Business Review, Nation's Business, Black Enterprise,* and *Entrepreneur.* You may also want to read your local paper's business section to keep up with current issues.

If you're not familiar with these sources, it's time to get to know them. You don't necessarily have to become a regular subscriber, but you should learn what information is available in these sources over time, especially information that will help you get a job. All of these sources are probably available free of charge in your school learning resource center or local public library.

••• YOUR CLASSMATES AS A RESOURCE •••

It's often quite productive to interact with your classmates both in and out of class. They know people and have had experiences that would be very beneficial for you. Don't rely totally on the professor for answers to the cases and other exercises in this book. Often there is no single "right" answer, and your classmates may open up new ways of looking at things for you.

Part of being a successful businessperson is knowing how to work with others. College classrooms are excellent places to practice this skill. Some professors encourage their students to work together in small groups by providing them opportunities to do so. Such exercises build teamwork as well as presentation and analytical skills. Some of the students in your class may be quite experienced in their use of these skills. Next, we'll discuss such students.

THE RETURNING STUDENT   Of the 10.6 million undergraduates enrolled in U.S. colleges, it's estimated that 45 percent are older than 25. *Modern Maturity* magazine reported that 1 in 10 college students is actually over 50. Furthermore, a much larger percentage of older students are women, the number of female students over 22 years of age having more than doubled in the past decade. In urban institutions, the average age of students is 28 years. More students in such colleges now go to class after 4 P.M. than earlier in the day.

Returning students often are more serious about college than younger students because they've experienced the need for certain skills in the real world. They may work harder and longer than the average students. However, returning students often are as uncertain as younger students about career choices and strategies for finding the right job in the right firm. This book is designed for all students who want to further their career by understanding business better.

If you are interested in global business, and everyone should at least check it out, examine magazines such as *International Business* to learn the latest trends. Check your libraries to see what other international business periodicals are available. The variety has never been greater.

••• OUTSIDE CONTACTS AS A RESOURCE •••

After you've completed a personal assessment, it's a good idea to begin exploring potential career possibilities in the areas that seem to fit you best. The time to begin studying career opportunities is now, not when you're closer to graduation. As you read about the various business functions (marketing, finance, etc.), try to imagine what it would be like doing such jobs. Do they sound interesting? Do you have the needed skills? This book will give you some guidance, but the best way to learn about careers is to visit various organizations and talk with people in the different occupations.

When you go shopping, for example, think

about whether you would enjoy working in and managing a store. Talk with the clerks and the manager to see how they feel about the job. Think about the possibilities of owning or managing a restaurant, an auto body shop, a health club, a print shop, or any other establishment you visit. If something looks interesting, talk to the employees and learn more about the job and industry. Soon you may discover fascinating careers in places or industries such as the zoo, travel, computer sales, and health clubs. Do these careers look interesting? How much do they pay? Is there a chance to advance? The best way to find out is to ask.

What's it like to be a salesperson for a sporting goods company? Call a salesperson and ask. What's it like to be an accountant in a major firm? What do stockbrokers do? Is it interesting? How do people feel about selling real estate, life insurance, or financial services?

What courses should a college student take to prepare for such jobs? You'll never know unless you ask people doing them. It's not enough to read about careers; articles can make jobs look more exciting and glamorous than they really are. Visit an accounting office and observe for yourself. Go to an advertising agency if that's what interests you. Don't make up your mind until you've investigated. In short, be constantly on the alert to find career possibilities, and don't hesitate to talk with people about their careers. Typically, they'll be pleased to give you their time because they're talking about their favorite subject—themselves.

It's as important to learn which jobs you would not as well as those you would enjoy. Eliminating some jobs from your list takes you that much closer to the best job for you.

In the Appendix to this Prologue, we'll discuss a step-by-step procedure for getting a job, including writing a résumé, writing a cover letter, and managing job interviews. Before you get involved in such details, you need to become familiar with some other resources.

··· THE LEARNING RESOURCE CENTER ···
OR LIBRARY AS A RESOURCE

Few exercises you do in this class will be more important to you than this one. Your assignment is to research the resources you might use to begin a successful career search. While you're in college, you may want to work as an intern in various firms to get a better feel for what people do. Some schools offer a cooperative education program where you go to school for a while and then work for a while in a local firm. If your school doesn't offer such a program, you can create one on your own. Here's a source you can use for finding such jobs:

Internships 1995 (Princeton, N.J.: Peterson's Guides, 1995).

What other sources are available in your library for finding internships? Write this information down and put it in your career file. If you'd like a head start in finding businesses that are looking for students, there are many sources. See if you can find

Peterson's Hidden Job Market 1995 (Princeton, N.J.: Peterson's Guides, 1994).
The Adams Job Almanac 1995 (Holbrook, Mass.: Adams Publishing, 1995).
Kathryn Petras and Ross Petras, *Jobs '95* (N.Y.: Simon and Schuster, 1995).

When you find the section where such books are kept, look at the other titles and list them along with their call letters. See if you can find books on specific careers or careers for minorities such as

Tom Fischgrund, *Top 20 Careers in Business and Management* (N.Y.: McGraw-Hill, 1994).

Barbara A. Ganim, *How to Approach an Advertising Agency & Walk Away with the Job You Want* (Lincolnwood, Ill.: NTC Publishing Group, 1993).

Business and Management Jobs (Princeton, N.J.: Peterson's Guides). This book is written especially for business, humanities, and social science majors. Look for the newest edition.

Mary Elizabeth Pitz, *Careers in Government* (Lincolnwood, Ill.: NTC Publishing Group, 1994).

Michael F. Kastre, Nydia Rodriguez Kastre, and Alfred G. Edwards, *The Minority Career Guide* (Princeton, N.J.: Peterson's Guides, 1993).

Daniel Lauber, *Non-Profits' Job Finder* (River Forest, Ill.: Planning/ Communications, 1994–1995).

What books are available on the careers you prefer now? Add them to your resource file. Finally, look for books that will help you set up a successful strategy for winning the job you want. A good one for starters is *What Color Is Your Parachute 1995* (Berkeley, Calif.: Ten Speed Press, 1995).

Look for books on how to write cover letters and résumés, on how to conduct job interviews, and on special job-getting strategies for women. Examples include

Peter D. Weddle, *Electronic Resumes for the New Job Market* (Manassas Park, Va.: Impact Publications, 1995).

Laura Morin, *Every Woman's Essential Job Hunting and Resume Book* (Holbrook, Mass.: Bob Adams, Inc., 1994).

The Adams Resume Almanac (Holbrook, Mass.: Bob Adams, Inc., 1994).

J. I. Biegeleisen, *Make Your Job Interview a Success* (N.Y.: Prentice-Hall General Reference, 1994).

You also need skills to find summer employment. You may find some help in

America's Top 100 Internships, 1995 edition (N.Y.: Villard Books, 1995).

Summer Jobs USA 1995 (Princeton, N.J.: Peterson's Guides, 1995).

To make this assignment and all the other assignments in the book work the best for you, you should (1) do careful research, (2) keep good notes, (3) share your notes with the class, (4) discuss your findings, and (5) put your notes into your Career file.

Before you go further into the text, take a few minutes to see how many of the questions on the next page you can already answer. This short test will give you some indication of your current business I.Q. and will introduce you to the types of material you'll be studying. (The answers are found at the bottom of the page.)

Good luck in the course; we hope you enjoy it.

Bill Nickels
Jim McHugh
Susan McHugh

••• PRETEST YOUR BUSINESS I.Q. •••

1. About how many new businesses are started in the United States every year?
   A. 10,000   B. 50,000   C. 160,000   D. 700,000

2. In the United States, what signal tells farmers and other producers what to produce?
   A. Supply   B. Demand   C. Price   D. News reports

3. Which of the following refers to taxes and spending by the government?
   A. Fiscal policy   B. Monetary policy   C. National policy   D. Deficit policy

4. What are people who take the risk of starting and managing a business called?
   A. Bureaucrats   B. Entrepreneurs   C. Speculators   D. Designers

5. What is the term used to describe working four 10-hour days instead of five 8-hour days every week?
   A. Job sharing   B. Compressed workweek   C. Flextime   D. Weekending

6. Which of the following utilities provided by marketers brings strawberries to the market in winter?
   A. Time   B. Place   C. Possession   D. Information

7. Which of the following marketing terms describes a product that's better for the environment than competing products?
   A. Green products   B. Pure products   C. Eco-friendly products   D. Crystal-clear products

8. Which kind of goods are consumers more likely to go out of town to find?
   A. Convenience goods   B. Shopping goods   C. Specialty goods   D. Dry goods

9. Which kind of marketing intermediary is most likely to sell to consumers like you and me?
   A. Wholesalers   B. Retailers   C. Sales agents   D. Manufacturer's agents

10. What are TV programs devoted exclusively to selling goods and services called?
   A. Infomercials   B. Advertorials   C. Promotional videos   D. Sales pitches

11. Which of the following leadership styles involves making decisions without consulting others?
   A. Democratic   B. Laissez-faire   C. Autocratic   D. Participative

12. Making goods using less input is called:
   A. Skimping   B. Lean manufacturing   C. Downsizing   D. Short-changing

13. Which of the following is the biggest motivator of workers?
   A. Money   B. Recognition   C. Achievement   D. The work itself

14. Which form of business provides limited liability to the owners?
   A. Sole proprietorship   B. Partnership   C. Cooperative   D. Corporation

15. Who controls the money supply of the United States?
   A. Congress   B. The president   C. The Federal Reserve   D. Local banks

16. Which of the following provides a tax deduction?
   A. Your car   B. Your home   C. Your education   D. Interest you receive from the bank

17. What do accountants call items such as trucks and machinery?
   A. Liabilities   B. Assets   C. Revenues   D. Goods

18. Which function in business is responsible for obtaining money and deciding how it should be spent?
   A. Finance   B. Accounting   C. Credit   D. Logistics

19. What is equal pay for comparable work called?
   A. Equality   B. Pay equity   C. Civil rights   D. The fairness doctrine

20. The connection of tens of thousands of interconnected computer networks that includes 1.7 million host computers is called
   A. The Internet   B. Shareware   C. Interconnectedness   D. Database management

Answers: 1. D, 2. C, 3. A, 4. B, 5. B, 6. A, 7. A, 8. C, 9. B, 10. A, 11. C, 12. B, 13. D, 14. D, 15. C, 16. B, 17. B, 18. A, 19. B, 20. A

A PPENDIX

GETTING THE JOB YOU WANT

One of the more important objectives of this text is to help you get *the* job that you want. First of all, you have to decide what job you want. We'll help you decide that issue by explaining what people do in the various business functions: accounting, marketing, human resource management, and so on.

If you follow the advice in the Prologue, you've done a self-assessment to determine what kind of career would be best for you. You've also gone to the library and done some background research into organizations that need people with your skills and knowledge.

If you're older and looking for a new career, your self-assessment has probably revealed that you have handicaps and blessings that younger students do not have. First of all, you may already have a full-time job. Working while going to school is exhausting. Many older students must juggle family responsibilities in addition to the responsibilities of school and work. But take heart. You have also acquired many skills from these experiences. Even if they were acquired in unrelated fields, these skills will be invaluable as you enter your new career.

Whether you're beginning your first career or your latest career, it's time to develop a strategy for finding and obtaining a personally satisfying job.

Life is a constant process of deciding what we are going to do.
José Ortega y Gasset

A FIVE-STEP JOB SEARCH STRATEGY

There are several good books available that provide guidance for finding the right job. This appendix summarizes the important steps:

1. *Complete a self-analysis inventory.* A couple of such programs were discussed earlier. If you want to do an assessment on your own, see Richard Nelson Bolles, *What Color Is Your Parachute* (Berkeley, Calif.: Ten Speed Press, 1995 edition). See Figure A.1 for a sample assessment. Career Navigator is a software program that will walk you through five modules of job-seeking strategies from "Know Yourself" to "Land That Job." Call Drake Beam Morin Inc. at 1–800–345–JOBS. This program will also help you establish an interview strategy.

2. *Search for jobs you would enjoy.* Begin at your college placement office if your school has one. Keep interviewing people in various careers, even after you've found a job. Career progress demands continuous research.

Interests
1. How do I like to spend my time?
2. Do I enjoy being with people?
3. Do I like working with mechanical things?
4. Do I enjoy working with numbers?
5. Am I a member of many organizations?
6. Do I enjoy physical activities?
7. Do I like to read?

Abilities
1. Am I adept at working with numbers?
2. Am I adept at working with mechanical things?
3. Do I have good verbal and written communication skills?
4. What special talents do I have?
5. In which abilities do I wish I were more adept?

Education
1. Have I taken certain courses that have prepared me for a particular job?
2. In which subjects did I perform the best? The worst?
3. Which subjects did I enjoy the most? The least?
4. How have my extracurricular activities prepared me for a particular job?
5. Is my GPA an accurate picture of my academic ability? Why?
6. Do I want a graduate degree? Do I want to earn it before beginning my job?
7. Why did I choose my major?

Experience
1. What previous jobs have I held? What were my responsibilities in each?
2. Were any of my jobs applicable to positions I may be seeking? How?
3. What did I like the most about my previous jobs? Like the least?
4. Why did I work in the jobs I did?
5. If I had it to do over again, would I work in these jobs? Why?

Personality
1. What are my good and bad traits?
2. Am I competitive?
3. Do I work well with others?
4. Am I outspoken?
5. Am I a leader or a follower?
6. Do I work well under pressure?
7. Do I work quickly, or am I methodical?
8. Do I get along well with others?
9. Am I ambitious?
10. Do I work well independently of others?

Desired Job Environment
1. Am I willing to relocate? Why?
2. Do I have a geographic preference? Why?
3. Would I mind traveling in my job?
4. Do I have to work for a large, nationally known firm to be satisfied?
5. Must I have a job that initially offers a high salary?
6. Must the job I assume offer rapid promotion opportunities?
7. In what kind of job environment would I feel most comfortable?
8. If I could design my own job, what characteristics would it have?

Personal Goals
1. What are my short- and long-term goals? Why?
2. Am I career-oriented, or do I have broader interests?
3. What are my career goals?
4. What jobs are likely to help me achieve my goals?
5. What do I hope to be doing in 5 years? In 10 years?
6. What do I want out of life?

Source: Eric N. Berkowitz, Roger A. Kerin, Steven Hartley, and William Rudelius, *Marketing*, 3rd ed. (Homewood, Ill.: Richard D. Irwin, 1992), p. 663.

FIGURE A.1

A PERSONAL ASSESSMENT SCALE

3. *Begin the networking process as discussed in this chapter.* You can start with your family, relatives, neighbors, friends, professors, and local businesspeople. Be sure to keep a file with the names, addresses, and phone numbers of contacts, where they work, the person who recommended them to you, and the relationship between the source person and the contact.

4. *Prepare a good cover letter and résumé.* Samples are provided in this appendix.

5. *Develop interviewing skills.* We'll give you some clues as to how to do this.

••• THE JOB SEARCH •••

The placement bureau at your school is a good place to begin reading about potential employers. On-campus interviewing is by far the number one source of jobs. (See Figure A.2)

The second most important source of jobs involves writing to companies and sending a good cover letter and résumé. You can identify companies to contact in your library. Check such sources as the *Million Dollar Directory* or the *Standard*

SOURCE OF JOB	PERCENTAGE OF NEW EMPLOYEES
On-campus interviewing	49.3%
Write-ins	9.8
Current employee referrals	7.2
Job listings with placement office	6.5
Responses from want ads	5.6
Walk-ins	5.5
Cooperative education programs	4.8
Summer employment	4.7
College faculty/staff referrals	4.5
Internship programs	4.5
High-demand major programs	4.4
Minority career programs	2.9
Part-time employment	2.4
Unsolicited referrals from placement	2.1
Women's career programs	2.1
Job listings with employment agencies	1.9
Referrals from campus organizations	1.8

Source: J. Singleton and P. Scheetz, *Recruiting Trends*, Michigan State University.

FIGURE A.2

WHERE COLLEGE STUDENTS FIND JOBS
When looking for a job, be sure to check the sources listed in the figure. Use those sources that will guarantee your success as you begin your job search. Total is over 100% because students use multiple sources.

Directory of Advertisers. Your library may also have annual reports that will give you even more information about your selected companies.

The third best source of jobs is networking; that is, finding someone in a firm to recommend you. You find those people by asking friends, neighbors, family, and others if they know anyone who knows someone, and then you track those people down, interview them, and seek their recommendation.

Other good sources of jobs include the placement center, want ads, summer and internship programs, and walking into firms that appeal to you and asking for an interview.

The *Occupational Outlook Quarterly,* produced by the U.S. Department of Labor, says this about job hunting:

> *The skills that make a person employable are not so much the ones needed on the job as the ones needed to get the job, skills like the ability to find a job opening, complete an application, prepare the résumé, and survive an interview.*

Before you read on, check the Interview Rating Sheet in Figure A.3. Note what recruiters want. Interviewers will be checking your appearance (clothes, haircut, fingernails, shoes), your attitude (friendliness is desired), your verbal ability (speak loud enough to be heard clearly), and your motivation (be enthusiastic). Note also that interviewers want you to have been active in clubs and activities and to have set goals. Have someone evaluate you on these scales now to see if you have any weak points. You can then work on those points before you have any actual job interviews.

It's never too early in your career to begin designing a résumé and thinking of cover letters. Preparing such documents reveals your strengths and weaknesses more clearly than most other techniques. Your résumé lists all your education, work experience, and activities. By preparing a résumé now, you may discover that you haven't been active enough in outside activities to impress an employer. That information may prompt you to join some student groups, to become a volunteer, or to otherwise enhance your social skills.

Some employers use an interview rating sheet like the one in this figure. When you go for a job interview, put your best foot forward.

Candidate: "For each characteristic listed below there is a rating scale of 1 through 7, where '1' is generally the most unfavorable rating of the characteristic and '7' the most favorable. Rate each characteristic by *circling* just *one* number to represent the impression you gave the interview that you have just completed."

Name of Candidate _____

1. **Appearance**
   Sloppy   1   2   3   4   5   6   7   Neat

2. **Attitude**
   Unfriendly   1   2   3   4   5   6   7   Friendly

3. **Assertiveness/Verbal Ability**
   a. Responded completely to questions asked
      Poor   1   2   3   4   5   6   7   Excellent
   b. Clarified personal background and related to job opening and description
      Poor   1   2   3   4   5   6   7   Excellent
   c. Able to explain and sell job abilities
      Poor   1   2   3   4   5   6   7   Excellent
   d. Initiated questions regarding position and firm
      Poor   1   2   3   4   5   6   7   Excellent
   e. Expressed thorough knowledge of personal goals and abilities
      Poor   1   2   3   4   5   6   7   Excellent

4. **Motivation**
   Poor   1   2   3   4   5   6   7   High

5. **Subject/Academic Knowledge**
   Poor   1   2   3   4   5   6   7   Good

6. **Stability**
   Poor   1   2   3   4   5   6   7   Good

7. **Composure**
   Ill at ease   1   2   3   4   5   6   7   Relaxed

8. **Personal Involvement/Activities, Clubs, Etc.**
   Low   1   2   3   4   5   6   7   Very High

9. **Mental Impression**
   Dull   1   2   3   4   5   6   7   Alert

10. **Adaptability**
    Poor   1   2   3   4   5   6   7   Good

11. **Speech Pronunciation**
    Poor   1   2   3   4   5   6   7   Good

12. **Overall Impression**
    Unsatisfactory   1   2   3   4   5   6   7   Highly satisfactory

13. Would you hire this individual if you were permitted to make a decision right now?
              Yes   No

You may also discover that you're weak on experience, and seek an internship or part-time job to fill in that gap. In any event, it's not too soon to prepare a résumé. It will certainly be helpful in deciding what you'd like to see in the area marked Education and help you to choose a major and other coursework. Given that background, let's discuss how to prepare these materials.

••• WRITING A RÉSUMÉ •••

A *résumé* is a document that lists information an employer would need to evaluate you and your background. It explains your immediate goals and career objectives. This information is followed by an explanation of your educational background, experience, interests, and other relevant data.

If you have exceptional abilities but don't communicate them to the employer on the résumé, those abilities aren't part of the person he or she will evaluate. You must be comprehensive and clear in your résumé if you are to communicate all your attributes.

FIGURE A.5

BUILDING A RÉSUMÉ

Check out the new and upgraded version of Monica's résumé, and compare its impact with the former version. Things to notice:

1. You would be surprised how many people forget to include their home (permanent) phone number. You can use a second—school—number as well.

2. It's permissible to eliminate high school data if it doesn't add to the total picture. Employers will get this information on the application form anyway.

3. Use action words (see Figure A.9) at beginnings of sentences and paragraphs where you can.

4. Use numbers and quantities where possible.

5. It simplifies matters to eliminate month designations.

6. Rewards and citations help.

7. Note more detail on real results, and the communication of value stressed over simple "duties."

8. It's permissible to claim a piece of the overall successes.

Monica A. Thomas
18 Nautical Lane
Gloucester, Mass. 01930
(508) 281-0568

EDUCATION

1997	B.A. in Management, GEORGIA STATE UNIVERSITY
1995	Semester, GSU-London, England
1993–1994	8 credit hours, Small Business Training–Computer Science

OBJECTIVE

To apply management experience and French language skills in a corporation overseas.

CAPABILITIES

- Perceive motivations in others, allowing them to produce results based on their goals and commitments.
- Listen to subtle communications and convert them into active resolutions.
- Provide spirit of trust and enthusiasm so that business transactions can occur harmoniously.
- Handle administrative details under pressure so as to allow boss to pursue higher levels of thinking and decision making.

EXPERIENCE

- Sold floral arrangements at $800–$1,200/month in person and by telephone and computer.
- Managed all administrative details of medium-size floral shop for five seasons.
- Recognized by British restaurant manager for outstanding courtesy and efficiency.
- Served as restaurant hostess/junior manager where patronage increased over 33% in a three-month period.

1995–Present	FLOWERS BY JOANN, Rockport, Mass. Sales Assistant
1994 (Summer)	CITRONELLA'S TAVERNA London, England. Waitress
1993 (Summer)	THE CLAM SHELL, Salem, Mass. Hostess/Junior Manager

ACTIVITIES

Member: American Marketing Association, Student Marketing Association

Source: Special Advertising Section in *Business Week's Guide to Careers* ("The Chrysler–Plymouth Guide to Building a Résumé").

the Chrysler–Plymouth Corporation. Look over the résumé and see what you think. Then turn to Figure A.5 for an improved version. Can you see how important planning and writing a résumé can be?

••• WRITING A COVER LETTER •••

A cover letter is used to announce your availability and to introduce the résumé. The cover letter is probably one of the most important advertisements anyone will write in a lifetime—so it should be done right.

First, the cover letter should indicate that you've researched the organization in question and are interested in a job there. Let the organization know what sources you used and what you know about it in the first paragraph to get the attention of the reader and show your interest.

Dear Mr. Franklin:

A recent article in *Business Week* mentioned that Donahue Corporation is expanding its operations into the Southwest. I have always had an interest in your firm, and so I read more about you in *Forbes* and *Standard & Poor's*. It seems as though you wil be needing good salespeople to handle your expanding business. Harold Jones, your Detroit sales representative, is a neighbor of mine. He told me about your training program, compensation system, and career opportunities. He convinced me that Donahue is the place for an ambitious college graduate.

I will be graduating from State College in June with a degree in marketing. My courses in marketing management, sales management, consumer behavior, and marketing research have given me some insight into marketing for a growing organization like yours. My three years' experience as a salesman for Korvalis Shoes has given me valuable skills that I could apply at Donahue. You will notice when you read the attached résumé that I have always been active in the organizations I have joined. Could I do as well at Donahue?

I will be in the New York area the week of November 17–25. Please let me know which time and date would be convenient for you to discuss a future at Donahue. I am looking forward to hearing from you.

Sincerely,

Thomas Smith

Thomas J. Smith

FIGURE A.6

A MODEL COVER LETTER
Things to notice:

1. The first paragraph of the letter mentions someone in the firm (a networking strategy).

2. The second paragraph mentions specific courses and experience applicable to the job.

3. The third paragraph asks for a specific time and date for the interview.

You may have heard people say, "It's not what you know, but whom you know that counts." This is only partly true, but it's important nonetheless. If you don't know someone, you can get to know someone. You do this by calling the organization (or better yet, visiting its offices) and talking to people who already have the kind of job you're hoping to get. Ask about training, salary, and other relevant issues. Then, in your cover letter, mention that you've talked with some of the firm's employees and that this discussion increased your interest. You thereby show the letter reader that you "know someone," if only casually, and that you're interested enough to actively pursue the organization. This is all part of networking.

Second, in the description of yourself, be sure to say how your attributes will benefit the organization. For example, don't just say, "I will be graduating with a degree in marketing." Say, "You will find that my college training in marketing and marketing research has prepared me to learn your marketing system quickly and begin making a contribution right away." The sample cover letter in Figure A.6 will give you a better feel for how this looks.

Third, be sure to "ask for the order." That is, say in your final paragraph that you're available for an interview at a time and place convenient for the interviewer. Again, see the sample cover letter in Figure A.6 for guidance. Notice in this letter how Tom subtly showed that he read business publications and drew attention to his résumé.

Principles to follow in writing a cover letter and preparing your résumé include

- Be self-confident. List all your good qualities and attributes.

- Don't be apologetic or negative. Write as one professional to another, not as a humble student begging for a job.

- Research every prospective employer thoroughly before writing anything. Use a rifle approach rather than a shotgun approach. That is, write effective marketing-oriented letters to a few select companies rather than to a general list.

- Have your materials prepared on a word processor by an experienced typist. For best results, have your résumé printed. (If you have access to a word processing system with a letter-quality laser printer, you could produce individualized letters efficiently.)

- Have someone edit your materials for spelling, grammar, and style. Don't be like the student who sent out a second résumé to correct "some mixtakes." Or another who said, "I am acurite with numbers."

- Don't send the names of references until asked. Put "References furnished on request" at the bottom of the last page of your résumé.

PREPARING FOR JOB INTERVIEWS

Companies usually don't conduct job interviews unless they're somewhat certain that the candidate has the requirements for the job. The interview, therefore, is pretty much a make-or-break situation. If it goes well, you have a greater chance of being hired. Therefore, you must be prepared for your interviews. There are five stages of interview preparation:

1. *Do research about the prospective employers.* Learn what industry the firm is in, its competitors, the products or services it produces and their acceptance in the market, and the title of your desired position. You can find such information in the firm's annual reports, in *Standard & Poor's*, Moody's manuals, and various business publications such as *Fortune, Business Week,* and *Forbes.* Ask your librarian for help. Together you can look in the *Reader's Guide to Business Literature* to locate the company name and to look for articles about it. This important first step shows you have initiative and interest in the firm.

2. *Practice the interview.* Figure A.7 lists some of the more frequently asked questions in an interview. Practice answering these questions and more at the placement office and with your roommate, parents, or friends. Don't memorize your answers, but be prepared—know what you're going to say. Also, develop a series of questions to ask the interviewer. Figure A.8 shows sample questions you might ask. Be sure you know whom to contact, and write down the names of everyone you meet. Review the action words in Figure A.9 and try to fit them into your answers.

3. *Be professional during the interview.* "You don't have a second chance to make a good first impression," the saying goes. That means that you should look and sound professional throughout the interview. Do your homework and find out how managers dress at the firm. Then buy an appropriate outfit.

〈〈 FIGURE A.7 〉〉

BE PREPARED FOR THESE FREQUENTLY ASKED QUESTIONS

- How would you describe yourself?
- What are your greatest strengths and weaknesses?
- How did you choose this company?
- What do you know about the company?
- What are your long-range career goals?
- What courses did you like best? Least?
- What are your hobbies?

- Do you prefer a specific geographic location?
- Are you willing to travel (or move)?
- Which accomplishments have given you the most satisfaction?
- What things are most important to you in a job?
- Why should I hire you?
- What experience have you had in this type of work?
- How much do you expect to earn?

- Who are your major competitors and how would you rate their products and marketing relative to yours?
- How long does the training program last and what is included?
- How soon after school would I be expected to start?
- What are the advantages of working for this firm?
- How much travel is normally expected?
- What managerial style should I expect in my area?
- How would you describe the working environment in my area?
- How would I be evaluated?
- What is the company's promotion policy?
- What is the corporate culture?
- What is the next step in the selection procedures?
- How soon should I expect to hear from you?
- What other information would you like about my background, experience, or education?
- What is your highest priority in the next six months and how could someone like me help?

When you meet the interviewers, greet them by name, smile, and maintain good eye contact. Sit up straight in your chair and be alert and enthusiastic. If you have practiced, you should be able to relax and be confident. Other than that, be yourself, answer questions, and be friendly and responsive.

When you leave, thank the interviewers and, if you're still interested in the job, tell them so. If they don't tell you, ask them what the next step is. Maintain a positive attitude. Figure A.10 outlines what the interviewers will be evaluating.

4. *Follow up on the interview.* First, write down what you can remember from the interview: names of the interviewers and their titles, any salary figures mentioned, dates for training, and so on. Put the information in your career file. You can send a follow-up letter thanking each interviewer for his or her time. You can also send a letter of recommendation or some other piece of added information to keep their interest. "The squeaky wheel gets the grease" is the operating slogan. Your enthusiasm for working for the company could be a major factor in hiring you.

Managed	Wrote	Budgeted	Improved
Planned	Produced	Designed	Increased
Organized	Scheduled	Directed	Investigated
Coordinated	Operated	Developed	Sold
Supervised	Conducted	Established	Served
Trained	Administered	Implemented	Handled

FIGURE A.10

SIXTEEN TRAITS RECRUITERS SEEK IN JOB PROSPECTS

1. **Ability to communicate.** Do you have the ability to organize your thoughts and ideas effectively? Can you express them clearly when speaking or writing? Can you present your ideas to others in a persuasive way?
2. **Intelligence.** Do you have the ability to understand the job assignment? Learn the details of operation? Contribute original ideas to your work?
3. **Self-confidence.** Do you demonstrate a sense of maturity that enables you to deal positively and effectively with situations and people?
4. **Willingness to accept responsibility.** Are you someone who recognizes what needs to be done and is willing to do it?
5. **Initiative.** Do you have the ability to identify the purpose for work and to take action?
6. **Leadership.** Can you guide and direct others to obtain the recognized objectives?
7. **Energy level.** Do you demonstrate a forcefulness and capacity to make things move ahead? Can you maintain your work effort at an above-average rate?
8. **Imagination.** Can you confront and deal with problems that may not have standard solutions?
9. **Flexibility.** Are you capable of changing and being receptive to new situations and ideas?
10. **Interpersonal skills.** Can you bring out the best efforts of individuals so they become effective, enthusiastic members of a team?
11. **Self-knowledge.** Can you realistically assess your own capabilities? See yourself as others see you? Clearly recognize your strengths and weaknesses?
12. **Ability to handle conflict.** Can you successfully contend with stress situations and antagonism?
13. **Competitiveness.** Do you have the capacity to compete with others and the willingness to be measured by your performance in relation to that of others?
14. **Goal achievement.** Do you have the ability to identify and work toward specific goals? Do such goals challenge your abilities?
15. **Vocational skills.** Do you possess the positive combination of education and skills required for the position you are seeking?
16. **Direction.** Have you defined your basic personal needs? Have you determined what type of position will satisfy your knowledge, skills, and goals?

Source: "So You're Looking for a Job?" The College Placement Council.

5. *Be prepared to act.* Know what you want to say if you do get a job offer. You may not want the job once you know all the information. Don't expect to receive a job offer from everyone you meet, but do expect to learn something from every interview. With some practice and persistence, you should find a rewarding and challenging job.

BE PREPARED  TO CHANGE JOBS

If you're like most people, you'll find that you'll follow several different career paths over your lifetime. This is a good thing in that it enables you to try different jobs and stay fresh and enthusiastic. The key to moving forward in your career is a willingness to change jobs, always searching for the career that will bring the most personal satisfaction and growth. This means that you'll have to write many cover letters and résumés and go through many interviews. Each time you change jobs, go through the steps in this appendix to be sure you're fully prepared. Good luck.

CHAPTER 1

EXPLORING TRENDS IN DYNAMIC BUSINESS ENVIRONMENTS

LEARNING GOALS

After you have read and studied this chapter, you should be able to

1. Define profit and show the relationship of profit with risk assumption.

2. Describe how businesses add to the standard of living and quality of life.

3. Explain how the economic environment and taxes affect businesses.

4. Give examples to show how the technological environment has affected businesses.

5. Describe various ways that businesses can meet and beat competition.

6. Show how the social environment has changed and what the reaction of business has been.

7. Tell businesses what they must do to meet the global challenge.

8. Explain the new quality standards and what businesses are doing to meet those standards.

9. Show how trends from the past are being repeated in the present and what that will mean for the service sector.

LA-VAN HAWKINS AND RAYMOND O'NEAL: URBAN ENTREPRENEURS

Pickles, ketchup, and mustard may come to mind when you think of hamburgers, but the words "economic empowerment" probably don't. It may sound odd at first—burgers helping to build neighborhoods—but that's what one man is determined to accomplish.

La-Van Hawkins, President and Chief Executive Officer of Inner City Foods Incorporated, is one of America's most extraordinary and successful entrepreneurs. His story demonstrates both the potential and the importance of entrepreneurship to the continued success of American business.

La-Van Hawkins grew up in the Cabrini Green housing project, one of Chicago's poorest and most dangerous areas. His first job was sweeping floors at McDonald's. Early in his career he observed that many businesses would not locate in mostly African-American, urban neighborhoods. Unlike others, he saw this circumstance as an opportunity, not only for personal benefit, but as a way to provide employment and income for these communities.

What sets Hawkins and his Inner City Foods Incorporated apart is that while other businesses go to great lengths to avoid poor, mostly black urban neighborhoods, Hawkins seeks them out. He now owns over 30 Checkers restaurant franchises in the inner city areas of Atlanta, Baltimore, and Philadelphia, all providing jobs and income to communities that are usually passed over by national chains and fast-food outlets as too great a risk. In 1994 his restaurants generated sales of $50 million, and he's just been given a seat on the board of directors of the Checkers Corporation. Perhaps more important, his growing fast-food empire is providing a fast track into the business world for hundreds of young African-American men and women.

With the financial backing of the Checkers Corporation, Hawkins expects to open 100 more inner-city restaurants in the next three years, including New York, in places like Harlem and Bedford-Stuyvesant.

Material signs of success—designer suits and a luxury sports car—might get attention. But it's La-Van Hawkins's unique and successful business strategies that are drawing the attention of urban business and political leaders around the country.

On a smaller scale, Raymond O'Neal, another Chicago entrepreneur, saw his business opportunity with the growth of the Midwest's hip-hop community, especially in his Wicker Park neighborhood. O'Neal started *FlyPaper*, a tabloid filled with underground urban news, commentary, and music advertisements. Atlantic Records often turns to *FlyPaper* when it wants to reach the Chicago market. "We employ a staff of three, we give fledgling writers a forum, and we pay taxes," O'Neal says. He and two business partners also manage six local rap groups.

La-Van Hawkins and Raymond O'Neal are just two of thousands of entrepreneurs who are creating jobs and contributing to the economic growth and vitality of the United States and countries throughout the world. This text will help future entrepreneurs understand business terms and concepts so that they can start businesses and create more jobs and opportunities for others. It will also help students find rewarding jobs in *established* businesses and contribute to society in other ways. The new global economy is creating business opportunities throughout the world.

"Americans are more open-minded than any other people in the world. This is a good country. There's opportunity for everyone."

Ezzat Reda, an entrepreneur from Lebanon

OPPORTUNITIES FOR ENTREPRENEURS

entrepreneur
A person who takes the risk of starting and managing a business.

An **entrepreneur** is a person who takes the risk of starting and managing a business. La-Van Hawkins and Raymond O'Neal are just two of the millions of business owners who've taken that risk and succeeded. Although we begin this text by profiling two male entrepreneurs, women are starting small businesses at twice the pace of men. Case 1 at the end of the chapter has more details about women entrepreneurs.

One woman entrepreneur, Lois Jackman, contracted polio as a teenager and is now in a wheelchair. When she was shopping for her chair, she found that medical supply stores selling such chairs were depressing places. Because of this, she decided to open her own shop, Yes I Can, in Cathedral City near Palm Springs, California. Her store is bright and attractive. Jackman has hired others with disabilities to work in the store, and sales are climbing dramatically every year.[1] Sales volume doubled in the second year and was expected to increase by 50 percent the third year. People with disabilities are more likely to start their own businesses than to seek employment, according to Urban Miyares, president of the San Diego–based Disabled Businesspersons Association (DBA).[2]

downsizing
Making organizations more efficient by laying off workers.

Entrepreneurs have come from all over the world to prosper in America. Ezzat Reda is from Lebanon. He and his younger brother Hussein now own one of the "liveliest, best-stocked magazine stores of its kind in Manhattan." [3] Some 30 percent of Koreans who have immigrated to the United States own their own businesses.[4] Entrepreneurs like Chinese-Americans Yee-Ping Wu and her husband Philip Lui have been very successful in the United States. They make multimedia software in their loft in New York City.[5] Clearly, the United States remains a land of opportunity—and most of that opportunity is in small business.

Entrepreneurs not only create wealth for themselves and their families; they also create jobs for the community. La-Van Hawkins has provided many jobs for others in his Checkers restaurants. This grand opening ceremony, featuring various public officials in Atlanta, is just one of many that he conducts each year.

Many of our major corporations are downsizing. **Downsizing** means laying off workers. Some of these cutbacks are due to a slow economy; others result from new strategies to assign (outsource) nonessential work to other firms. During the first part of 1994, for example, businesses were laying off workers at a pace of 3,000 per day! Government began a similar downsizing in 1995.[6] *Entrepreneur* magazine points out, however, that such layoffs are creating new opportunities for entrepreneurs who provide business services such as advertising, building maintenance, computer-related services, and security services.[7] In short, there are many business opportunities available today, largely in smaller businesses. In the following sections, we'll define "business" and explain some of the major concepts of business.

••• WHAT IS A BUSINESS? •••

A **business** is any activity that seeks profit by providing goods and services to others. Businesses provide us with food, clothing, housing, medical care, transportation, and almost everything else that makes life easier and better. Businesses also provide people with the opportunity to become wealthy, as La-Van Hawkins' story clearly shows. Sam Walton of Wal-Mart began by opening one store in Arkansas and, over time, became the richest person in America. (His heirs now have billions of dollars.)[8]

This is an exciting time to study business because the opportunities and challenges have never been greater. Over 700,000 new businesses are started in the United States every year.[9] People open new businesses because they see the opportunity to become independent (not work for others). They also see the opportunity through profits to make more money than they might earn working for someone else.

Profit is money a business earns above and beyond what it spends for salaries, expenses, and other costs. For example, if you were to rent a vending cart and sell hot dogs this summer, you would have to pay for the cart, for the hot dogs and other materials, and for someone to run the business while you were away. After you'd paid your employee and yourself, paid for the food and materials you used, paid the rent on the cart, and paid your taxes, any money left over would be profit. It's over and above the money you pay yourself in salary. You could use that profit to rent a second cart and hire another employee. After a few summers, you might have a dozen carts employing dozens of employees.

Not all businesses make a profit. A **loss** occurs when a business's costs and expenses are more than its revenues. Revenue is the money a business earns by selling goods and services. If a business loses money over time, it will likely have to close, putting its employees out of work. Starting a business, therefore, involves risk. **Risk** is the chance you take of losing time and money on a business that may not prove profitable.

••• MATCHING RISK WITH PROFIT •••

There are different things that people can do with their money. One thing is to spend that money to buy goods and services that they want and need. Another thing that people can do with their money is invest. You *invest* when you use your money to earn more money. You can, for example, put your money into a bank or savings and loan and then make money in the form of interest. You can also use that money to start your own business.

Why would you start a business rather than put your money in the bank? If you find a company that has a product that many people would want, there's a good chance that the company will make a lot of profit. La-Van Hawkins, for example, saw the opportunity for profits with Checkers, an established fast-food restaurant. However, not all companies make the same amount of profit. Those companies that take the most risk may make the most profit. For example, it would be a tremendous risk to start a new company that designs and manufactures computer games. However, if you succeed, you may become very wealthy.

It's also risky opening a fast-food franchise in the inner city because costs of insurance and land are usually high. On the other hand, your chance for making substantial profits is also good because there's less competition. As a potential business owner, you want to invest your money in a company that's likely to make a lot of profit, but isn't too risky. If it's too risky, you're more likely to lose your investment.

---

business
Any activity that seeks profit by providing needed goods and services to others.

profit
Earnings above and beyond what a business spends for salaries, expenses, and other costs.

loss
When a business's costs and expenses are more than its revenues.

risk
The chance you take of losing time and money on a business that may not prove profitable.

FROM THE PAGES OF...
Entrepreneur
MAGAZINE

Quoting Mary Rogers of Computer Tots

Franchising is a growing industry. This is especially true for service providers like us. Today's (and tomorrow's) baby boomers are our prime customers, and they will be more likely to part with their dollars than previous generations.

Also, the fear of buying a franchise has lessened. People now get more information and are more educated when it comes time to make a decision. Another major step forward is that franchise documents are written in plain English. The "mystique" about what you're really getting is disappearing. When presented with such earnings claims, the buyer knows more about the profit potential.

Source: *Entrepreneur's 1995 Buyer's Guide to Franchise and Business Opportunities*, a special issue of *Entrepreneur* magazine, 1994, p. 46.

You need to do research (e.g., talking to other businesspeople) to find the right balance between risk and profit. In the box from *Entrepreneur* magazine, you'll read about franchisors' attempts to give potential investors more information about earnings and risks.

••• HOW MUCH PROFIT DO BUSINESSES MAKE? •••

There's almost no risk involved in putting your money into a bank. On the other hand, you only get a small return on your investment. How much money do business owners earn on investment? Well, Wal-Mart stores returned over 20 percent on investment after taxes in 1993. So did Nike, Safeway, and many other companies.[10] Before you even think about starting

FIGURE 1.1

Where Your Money Goes When You Buy a Coke

Ingredients	$.04
Can	.07
Advertising/promotion	.03
Delivery	.06
Vending machine	.03
Sales tax	.04
Other*	.12
Coca-Cola Co./ bottler profit	.05
Location owner commission	.16
RETAIL PRICE	**$.60**

*Includes executive and sales salaries, administrative expenses, interest, and taxes.

Source: "Why It Costs 60¢ for a Can of Coke from a Vending Machine," *Washington Post*, May 14, 1994, p. C1.

your own business, you'll want to learn what the return on investment has been for others in the same field. If the return is worth the risk, go for it! Most businesses strive for a profit of about 10 to 15 percent.

But you must understand that profits go to owners of a company, not to managers or employees. Of course, managers and employees can buy stock in companies themselves and make money if the company is profitable.

One company that makes a good return (profit) on investment is Coca-Cola. Let's see what happens to the money you pay for a can of Coke in a vending machine. (See Figure 1.1.) If you pay 60 cents for a can of Coke, the Coca-Cola Company and the bottler together make 5 cents in profit (8.3 percent) and the location owner makes 16 cents (26.6 percent). Note that the government collects 4 cents. Part of the money reported as "other" goes to taxes as well. Thus, you can see how a business earns money for its owners and provides money to the government at the same time. An issue in America today is how much money from businesses should go to government and how much should go to owners to keep the economy growing and to provide jobs. We'll explore that issue in the following chapter.

It's not many luxury-performance sedans that can scare traffic into the slow lane on looks alone. But that's how the new Aurora is. Aggressive.

Bold. With a 32-valve, 250hp, DOHC V8, ABS, leather,* walnut and CD stereo sound. All of which make the left-hand lane a much more enjoyable

place to be. Aurora by Oldsmobile. See what happens when you Demand Better. 1-800-718-7778.   *AURORA — An American Dream*

BUSINESSES CAN PROVIDE WEALTH FOR ALMOST EVERYONE
• • • • • • •

Entrepreneurs like La-Van Hawkins and Sam Walton not only become wealthy themselves, but provide employment for other people. Wal-Mart is the nation's second largest private employer after GM. In the 32 months prior to April 1994, Wal-Mart created about 153,000 jobs.[11] It then had about 520,000 employees.[12] Those workers pay taxes that the federal government and local communities use to build hospitals, schools, roads, playgrounds, and other facilities. Taxes are also used to keep the environment clean and to support people in need. Businesses too pay taxes to the federal government and local community. By starting a business, therefore, you're *generating wealth* that helps everyone in the community. You become part of an economic system that helps to create a higher standard of living and quality of life for everyone.

Businesses, first of all, add to the standard of living. The **standard of living** of a country refers to the amount of goods and services people can buy with the money they have. For example, the United States has the second highest standard of living (to Luxembourg) in the world even though people in some other countries, such as Germany and Japan, make more money per hour.[13] How can that be? Prices for goods and services in Germany and Japan are higher, so what a person can buy with the same amount of money is less than people in the United States can buy. The United States has such a high standard of living largely because of the wealth created by businesses. Figure 1.2 shows purchasing power in various countries.

The **quality of life** of a country refers to the general well-being of a society in terms of freedom, clean environment, schools, health care, safety, free time, and everything else that leads to satisfaction and joy. Such results

The standard of living in a country refers to the goods and services people can buy with the money they earn. The success of the new Oldsmobile Aurora is just one indication of the high standard of living businesses have created. Businesses also contribute to the quality of life by providing the funds used to clean up the air and water and to fund other social projects.

standard of living
The level of ability to buy goods and services.

quality of life
The general well-being of a society.

FIGURE 1.2

PER CAPITA INCOME
ADJUSTED FOR
PURCHASING-POWER
PARITY, IN DOLLARS

Source: World Bank

require the combined efforts of businesses, government agencies, and non-profit organizations. The more money that business creates, the more is available for such causes.

CRITICAL THINKING

Since businesses provide the wealth that society needs to clean up the environment, to provide for the needy, and to build schools and roads, why are some people in the United States and around the world so hostile toward businesspeople? Wouldn't society be better off if businesspeople were given more support and encouragement?

··· THE IMPORTANCE OF ENTREPRENEURSHIP ··· TO WEALTH

Look what entrepreneurs of the past have done to create wealth. The state of Delaware doesn't need to charge a sales tax on retail purchases because of the great wealth created by E. I. du Pont, a chemicals entrepreneur. The DuPont Company has over 114,000 employees. DuPont and Hercules, another chemical company, are the two largest employers in Delaware.

Texas is a relatively rich state because of the entrepreneurs who took the risk of finding oil in that state. Now the leading companies in the state are Exxon, Shell, Tenneco, and Coastal. To find the largest companies in your state, see the April 1994 issue of *Fortune* magazine.

··· NONPROFIT ORGANIZATIONS WORK WITH BUSINESSES ···

Not everything that makes life easier and better is provided by businesses. Nonprofit organizations such as government agencies, public schools, associations, charities, and social causes help make a country and the world more responsive to all the needs of citizens. **A nonprofit organization** is an organization whose goals don't include making a personal profit for its

nonprofit organization
An organization whose goals do not include making a personal profit for its owners.

They built more than a ballpark in Portland, Maine

They transformed the way government works

The Portland Sea Dogs wouldn't have a new home today had the city relied on business-as-usual.

Instead of giving up when they couldn't afford a private contractor to build the stadium, city officials tried something new. They asked city workers to do the job. It was a home run of an idea.

The winter was long and cold, but the city workers completed the stadium in just 7 months. And in the process they saved taxpayers $1 million. The Sea Dogs had a home in time for spring.

This wasn't just a stroke of good luck. In 1990 Portland made a commitment to better government. There was a recession and the city needed cash. But instead of layoffs and angry words, the city and the public employees union, AFSCME Local 481, established a labor-management partnership to streamline public services.

That changed everything. Workers were given equal say. They were urged to submit cost-saving ideas. Responsibility was theirs to take.

And taxpayers saw results. A sidewalk project was done for thousands less than a contractor would have charged -- despite a large increase in the project's scale. A new in-house supply store gave city workers everything from lumber to lugnuts when they needed them -- and cut purchase orders from 40,000 to 1,000 in one year.

There's no magic to Portland's enterprise. It's what successful corporations are doing. Treat workers as resources. Trust them to make decisions. Train them for more responsibility. Cut out unnecessary management layers. Redesign the government workplace.

Taxpayers benefit. Services improve. Everyone wins. Sometimes all it takes to build a stadium is a little bit of teamwork.

PUBLIC EMPLOYEES
PARTNERS FOR CHANGE

For more information on how to redesign government and improve public services, call 1-800-634-0409.    AFSCME
in the public service

Sometimes all that's required for government to be more effective is a little teamwork. When the city of Portland, Maine, could not afford to hire a private contractor, the city government and the public employees union worked together as entrepreneurs to build a new baseball stadium. Due in part to the cost-saving ideas submitted by city workers, the ballpark was built in under 7 months with a $1 million savings for taxpayers.

owners. Nonprofit organizations often do strive for gains; such gains are used to meet the stated social or educational goals of the organization, not to enrich the owners.

If you want to work in a nonprofit organization, you'll need to learn business skills such as information management, leadership, marketing, and financial management. Therefore, the knowledge and skills you can acquire in this course and other business courses will be useful for careers in any organization, including nonprofit organizations. Because such cross-over is possible, many businesspeople volunteer their expertise in nonprofit organizations.

Businesses, nonprofit organizations, and volunteer groups often help to accomplish the same objectives. All such groups can help feed people, provide them with clothing and housing, clean up the environment and keep it clean, and improve the standard of living and quality of life for all. To accomplish those objectives, though, this nation's businesses must remain competitive with the best businesses in the world.

- What is profit and who gets the profits businesses make?
- What is risk and how is it related to profit?
- What is the difference between standard of living and quality of life?

PROGRESS CHECK

••• THE FACTORS OF PRODUCTION •••

U.S. businesses can remain competitive with the best businesses in the world only if they manage carefully the factors of production. **Factors of production** refer to the resources businesses use to create wealth. Today, there are five

factors of production
The resources used to create wealth: land, labor, capital, entrepreneurship, and information.

FIGURE 1.3

THE FIVE FACTORS OF
PRODUCTION

Land: Land and other natural resources are used to make homes, cars, and other products.

Labor: People have always been an important resource in producing goods and services, but many people are now being replaced by machinery.

Capital: Capital includes machines, tools, buildings, and other means of manufacturing.

Entrepreneurship: All the resources in the world have little value unless entrepreneurs are willing to take the risk of starting businesses to *use* those resources.

Information: Information technology has revolutionized business, making it possible to quickly determine wants and needs and to respond with desired goods and services.

factors of production that businesses use: (1) land (and other natural resources), (2) labor (workers), (3) capital (e.g., machines, tools, and buildings), (4) entrepreneurship, and (5) information. (Information has become so important that this is called the "Information Era" in business.) (See Figure 1.3.)

Management expert and business consultant Peter Drucker is one of the most respected business advisors in the world. In his book *Post-Capitalist Society*, he says that the most important factor of production in our economy isn't capital, natural resources, or labor. "It is and will be knowledge," he says. Knowledge comes from information; information management will be a major issue in the 21st century.

If you were to analyze rich countries versus poor countries to see what caused the difference, you'd have to look at the factors of production in the various countries. Such an analysis reveals that poor countries usually have plenty of land. Russia, for example, has vast areas of land with many resources, but it's not a rich country. Therefore, land isn't the critical element for wealth creation. Japan is a rich country, but is poor in land and other natural resources.

Most poor countries have many unemployed laborers, so it's not labor that's the primary source of wealth today. Furthermore, capital is widely available in world markets. In 1993, for example, investors purchased almost $160 billion of stocks in other countries, including the fast-growing Asian countries.[14] Thus, money for machinery and tools is available, and capital isn't the missing ingredient.

What makes rich countries rich today is entrepreneurship and the effective use of information. Lack of entrepreneurship and the absence of good information keeps poor countries poor. Similarly, entrepreneurship makes some states and cities in the United States rich while others remain poor. The business environment either encourages or discourages entrepreneurship. In the following section, we'll explore the business environment and how to create an environment that encourages growth and job creation throughout the world.

THE BUSINESS ENVIRONMENT

The business environment has a tremendous effect on the success of entrepreneurs. Figure 1.4 identifies five key environmental factors that are critical to the success of business:

1. The economic environment, including taxes and regulation.
2. The technological environment.

SPOTLIGHT ON SMALL BUSINESS

Teams Lead to Responsiveness

When we read about Sam Walton and the thousands of people he employs, we tend to forget that Sam Walton started out as a small business owner. His entrepreneurial skills are what led his company to its extraordinary growth. But big companies like Wal-Mart aren't the major job creators in the United States. Small and medium-sized companies were responsible for generating 5.8 million new jobs from 1987 to 1992. Larger companies with more than 500 employees had a net loss of 2.3 million jobs. In 1993, small companies added 1.7 million jobs while big companies were losing 300,000. In short, small companies represent the fastest-growing and major job-creating sector of the U.S. economy.

Small businesses are growing partly because they're faster at responding to customers' needs. A recent survey showed that small companies produce 2.4 times as many innovations as large companies. So small companies not only produce jobs, but they produce the technological change that keeps America strong.

Competition from small businesses is forcing larger businesses to become more responsive and entrepreneurial. That is, they're firing middle managers who historically have slowed the decision-making process. One trend in business is toward more intrapreneuring and intraprise. This means that firms are encouraging employees to take more risks inside larger firms. Management gives these innovators the resources and support they need to make large firms more creative, responsive, and competitive.

Intraprise is the creation of small businesses within larger firms to service other workers within the firms. For example, the accounting department may become an intraprise that competes with accounting firms from the outside. If the intraprise fails to please its customers (employees), the company will give the accounting function to an outside firm. Small teams of employees make it possible for large firms to get close to internal and external customers and respond to their needs quickly. Such teams, if successful, will make it possible for these larger businesses to be flexible and responsive, similar to small businesses, and to begin expanding and generating more jobs.

Source: "Enterprise: How Entrepreneurs Are Reshaping the Economy and What Big Companies Can Learn," *Business Week* Special Bonus Issue, 1993; and Gifford Pinchot and Elizabeth Pinchot, *The End of Bureaucracy and the Rise of the Intelligent Organization* (San Francisco: Berrett-Koehler, 1993).

---

3. The competitive environment.
4. The social environment.
5. The global business environment.

Business grows and prospers in a healthy environment. The result is job growth and the wealth that makes it possible to have both a high standard of living and a high quality of life. The wrong environmental conditions, on the other hand, lead to business failure, loss of jobs, and a low standard of living and quality of life. In short, creating the right business environment is the foundation for social progress of all kinds, including good schools, clean air and water, good hospitals, and low crime.

••• THE ECONOMIC ENVIRONMENT •••

People are willing to take the risk of starting businesses if they feel that the risk isn't too great. Part of that risk involves the economic system and how government treats businesses. Government can do a lot to lessen the risk of starting businesses and thus increase entrepreneurship and wealth. One key

FIGURE 1.4

THE BUSINESS
ENVIRONMENT

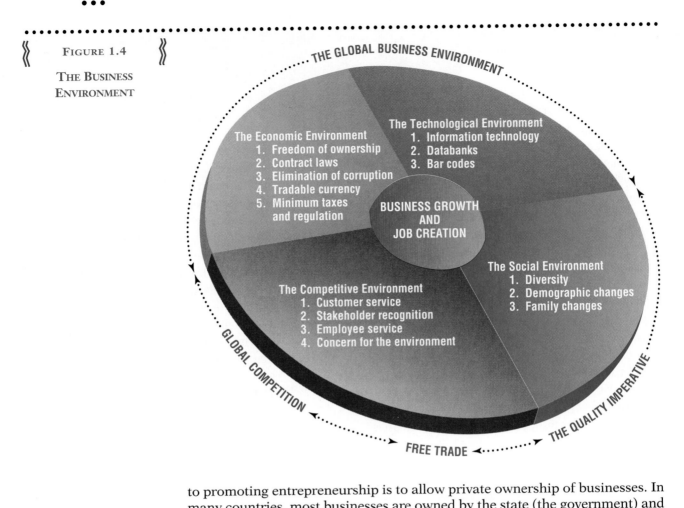

to promoting entrepreneurship is to allow private ownership of businesses. In many countries, most businesses are owned by the state (the government) and there's little incentive to work hard or create profit. All around the world today, various countries are selling government-owned businesses to private individuals to create more wealth.[15] Let's explore what else the government can do to foster entrepreneurial growth:

- The government can lessen the risks of entrepreneurship by passing laws that enable businesspeople to write contracts that are enforceable in court. Many countries don't yet have such laws, making the risks of starting a business that much greater.

- The government can establish a currency that's tradable in world markets. One element preventing Russia from joining world markets and gaining economic strength is its lack of a tradable currency.

- The government can focus on eliminating corruption in business and government. It's hard to do business in many poor countries because the governments are so corrupt. It's nearly impossible to get permission to build a factory or open a store without a government permit, which is obtained largely through bribery of public officials. Corrupt business leaders can threaten competitors and minimize competition. There are many laws in the United States to minimize corruption, and businesses can flourish as a result.

- The government can keep taxes and regulations to a minimum. Entrepreneurs are looking for a high return on investment, including the investment of their time. If the government takes away much of

Legal Briefcase

Creating a Climate for Growth

Critics of government regulations argue that the government has created an environment for businesses that's slowing growth. For example, U.S. export regulations comprise more than 1,500 pages as compared to 145 pages in the United Kingdom. Small business owners believe that the government is passing new laws and regulations at a pace that's simply too fast for them to absorb.

A strong society demands business–government cooperation in creating a climate of growth where more wealth will be available for all social goals. A major challenge of the 21st century will be for business and government leaders to work together to solve the social problems of the United States and the world while continuing economic growth. Government laws and regulation of businesses are even more strict in many other countries. As a consequence, there's higher unemployment and slower growth throughout much of the world. Thus, business–government cooperation is a global issue as well as a national issue.

Source: "Silly Summit," *Forbes*, April 25, 1994, p. 24, Sally Jacobsen, "Europe in Uphill Battle against Joblessness," *The Washington Times*, March 11, 1994, p. A7; and Dan Moore, "Exporting and the Law," *International Business*, October 1994, p. 12.

what a business earns through high taxes, the returns may no longer be worth the risk. This is true even within rich countries. States and cities that have high taxes and regulations are likely to drive entrepreneurs out; states and cities with low taxes attract them. This is happening all across the United States and the world.[16]

The economic environment is so important to businesses that we'll devote all of Chapter 2 to that subject. There you'll learn more about the influence of government on business success and failure.

THE TECHNOLOGICAL ENVIRONMENT

The most successful college graduates of tomorrow will be those who can find their way on the information superhighway. The **information superhighway (I-way)** is the network of computer and telecommunications equipment that links people throughout the world into one unified communications system. Information on almost any topic will be available. To access that information, you must be able to use computers and other telecommunications equipment. It would be a mistake to think you can escape learning such information because you plan to work as a mechanic or farmer, or in some other job that hasn't required computer literacy in the past. Mechanics now order parts by computer and read repair manuals on computer screens. Farmers often have cellular phones and even computers on their combines. These tools now link them to suppliers and enable them to schedule everything on the farm.

information superhighway (I-way)
The network of computer and telecommunications equipment that links people throughout the world into one unified communications system.

••• THE IMPORTANCE OF INFORMATION TECHNOLOGY •••

Many companies now have a chief information officer. A chief information officer (CIO) is responsible for getting workers and managers the information they need to become world-class competitors. That information includes information about customers, competitors, and the changing business environment.

Information technology has revolutionized businesses of all kinds. Agricultural workers now use computers for all kinds of tasks that were once done manually. Keeping current with the latest in computer and telecommunications technology has become critical for workers in almost all industries.

Charles Wang is the entrepreneur who started the second largest computer software company. Only Microsoft is larger. The name of his company is Computer Associates International. Wang says that information management is the most important part of a business. The problem today, however, is that few businesses are now managing information well. The information manager's most important role is to establish information flows between businesses and their customers. Because information technology (IT) has become such a central part of an organization's success, we'll devote Chapter 17 to that issue. Information technology (linked computers, cellular phones, modems, and the like) will be used in the future to monitor the business environment so that firms can quickly adapt to changing conditions.

••• RESPONDING TO THE CONSUMER •••

Technology has also made it possible for businesses to become much more responsive to consumers. For example, businesses are now marking goods with bar codes, those series of lines that you see on most grocery goods. Those bar codes tell retailers what size product you bought, what color, and at what price. A scanner at the checkout counter reads that information and puts it into a databank. A **databank** is an electronic storage file where information is kept. One use of databanks is to store vast amounts of information about consumers. For example, a retailer may ask for your name, address, and other information such as how many children are in your family, how old they are, and whether you have pets. That information is added to the databank. Soon retailers know what you buy and for whom you buy it.

Using this information, retailers can send you catalogs and other direct mail advertising which offers the kind of products you might want, as indicated by your past purchases. Databases enable stores to carry only the merchandise that the local population wants. They also enable stores to carry fewer items, and less inventory, saving them money.

databank
Electronic storage file for information.

••• ELECTRONIC DATA INTERCHANGE •••

Electronic data interchange (EDI) means that the sales data from bar codes are sent directly to manufacturers, which then replace the items quickly. The flow of information from retailers to manufacturers is seamless. That is, there are no barriers to communication. Likewise, the flow of goods from manufacturers to retailers is much smoother. The growing use of this technology is making it possible for businesses to save time and money, resulting in less expensive products. Thus, technology now makes it possible for you to receive the right ads about the right products at the right time for you to purchase. Moreover, the price is usually more attractive because the new distribution process is so efficient. We'll discuss distribution systems in detail in Chapter 15.

THE COMPETITIVE ENVIRONMENT

Competition among businesses has never been greater. Some companies found a competitive edge in the 1980s by focusing on making *quality* products. The goal was zero defects—no mistakes in making the product. Some companies, such as Motorola in the United States and Toyota in Japan, came close to meeting that standard. And soon, in order to remain competitive, other companies from all over the world were striving to make quality products.

By the early 1990s, making a quality product wasn't enough to stay competitive in world markets. Companies now have to offer quality products *and* outstanding service at competitive prices. GM, for example, is catching up rapidly. Its Saturn division, for example, made quality automobiles that were competitively priced. Saturn dealers pleased customers by offering a one-price policy that ended the haggling that once went on between customers and car dealers. Furthermore, Saturn dealers invited customers to barbecue dinners and treated them as valued long-term customers with outstanding service. Saturn thus became one of GM's best-selling cars. Despite their success, Saturn will now have to develop a more sophisticated car to satisfy the needs of affluent customers with large families. What Saturn has learned is that the market is constantly changing and you have to change with it.

••• COMPETING BY DELIGHTING THE CUSTOMER •••

Manufacturers and service organizations throughout the world have learned that today's customers are very demanding. They not only want good quality at low prices, but they want great service as well. In fact, products in the 21st

FIGURE 1.5

HOW COMPETITION HAS
CHANGED BUSINESSES

TRADITIONAL BUSINESSES	WORLD-CLASS BUSINESSES
Customer satisfaction	Delighting the customer[1]
Customer orientation	Customer and stakeholder orientation[2]
Profit orientation	Profit and social orientation[3]
Reactive ethics	Proactive ethics[4]
Product orientation	Quality and service orientation
Managerial focus	Customer focus

1. *Delight* is a term from total quality management. *Bewitch* and *fascinate* are alternative terms.
2. Stakeholders include employees, stockholders, suppliers, dealers, and the community; the goal is to please *all* stakeholders.
3. A social orientation goes beyond profit to do what is right and good for others.
4. *Proactive* means doing the right thing before anyone tells you to do it. *Reactive* means reacting to criticism after it happens.

century will be designed to "fascinate, bewitch, and delight." Every manufacturing and service organization in the world should have a sign over its door telling its workers that the customer is king.

Business is becoming customer-driven, not management-driven as in the past. (See Figure 1.5.) This means that customers' wants and needs come first. Successful oganizations must now listen to customers to determine their wants and needs, then adjust the firm's products, policies, and practices to meet these demands.

... COMPETING BY MEETING THE NEEDS ...
OF THE COMMUNITY

It is possible for businesses today to please their customers and still not meet some needs of the community in which they operate. For example, in their efforts to please employees and customers, firms may take actions that pollute the environment. Such an outcome or by-product is highly undesirable in today's business environment. World-class organizations in the future must attempt to meet the needs of all their stakeholders. **Stakeholders** are all the people affected by the policies and activities of an organization. Stakeholders include customers, employees, stockholders, suppliers, dealers, people in the local community, environmentalists, and government officials. (See Figure 1.6.)

The challenge of the 21st century will be for organizations to work together to ensure that all stakeholders' needs are considered and satisfied as much as possible. Such an ambitious goal calls for both world-class employees and world-class organizational leaders.

stakeholders
Those people who can affect or are affected by the achievement of an organization's objectives.

CRITICAL THINKING

The newest business books talk about having teams of employees work together to satisfy the needs of all stakeholders, including the community. Some recommend having environmentalists and community leaders sit in on team discussions so that businesses can respond more quickly to community needs. What community needs aren't being met by businesses in your area? Can you see the benefit of having community leaders sit in on planning sessions to see that those needs are met? What, if any, drawbacks to such a policy can you see from the company's perspective?

STAKEHOLDERS

FIGURE 1.6

A BUSINESS AND ITS
STAKEHOLDERS

... COMPETING BY RESTRUCTURING TO ...
MEET THE NEEDS OF EMPLOYEES

To meet the needs of customers, firms must give their front-line workers (clerks, front-desk people at motels, salespeople, and so forth) more freedom to respond quickly to customer requests. This is called *empowerment,* and we'll be talking about that process throughout the book. In this chapter, we simply want to acknowledge the fact that businesses must reorganize to make their front-line people more effective. In many firms, that has meant the formation of cross-functional teams (people from various departments working together). These teams have learned to work without close supervision; thus they are often called *self-managed cross-functional teams.* One cause of the downsizing we mentioned earlier is the firing of managers as lower-level workers learn to work in self-managed teams.

Because of self-managed teams, employers in the future will expect a lot more from their lower-level workers than they have in the past. Because they will have less management oversight, such workers will need more education. Furthermore, lower-level employees will need to receive higher pay and be treated more as partners in the firm. Increasingly, managers' jobs will be to train, support, coach, and motivate lower-level employees. As companies such as Motorola have discovered, it sometimes takes years to restructure an organization so that managers are willing to give up some of their authority and employees are willing to assume more responsibility.

More employees will demand increased compensation based on performance. Often, in larger firms, that will mean giving employees partial ownership of the firm. It will also mean developing entirely new organizational structures to meet the changing needs of customers and employees. We'll discuss such organizational changes and models in Chapter 8.

... COMPETING BY CONCERN FOR ...
THE NATURAL ENVIRONMENT

In their rush to give consumers what they want and need, managers must be careful that they cause minimal damage to the environment. Business and government leaders throughout the coming years will be discussing issues

Making Ethical Decisions

Competing with a Strong Ethical Base

Television, movies, and the print media all paint a dismal picture of ethics among businesspeople, government officials, and citizens in general. Often the reality seems to match the image. In the past several years, we've seen the largest world banking scandal ever (the BCCI case). Illegal and unethical practices among business leaders throughout the world are in the news regularly.

Immoral and unethical behavior among government officials is also global in scope. One positive element in all this sordid behavior is that much of it is being reported, and the public seems genuinely upset at the findings. The first step toward improving a negative social condition is to admit that it exists. The next step is to do something about it. The second step is now being implemented. Business schools across the country have made ethics an integral part of the curriculum. Many businesses are working hard to alter their behavior in a positive way. There's a growing trend toward greater commitment to ethics policies—written codes that clearly communicate management expectations—programs to implement these guidelines, and surveys to monitor compliance.

Ethical business behavior is much more than not doing what society (customers) concludes is improper. It means getting involved in society to help improve conditions. A national poll by the Gallup organization found that half the people who were surveyed were involved in charitable or social service activities such as helping the poor, the sick, or the elderly. This healthy sign indicates that businesspeople aren't just talking about moral and ethical behavior; they're starting to do something about it.

We feel this trend toward improving ethical behavior is so important that we've made it a major theme of this text. Throughout the text you'll see boxes called *Making Ethical Decisions*. The boxes contain short descriptions of situations that pose ethical dilemmas and ask what you would do in these situations. The idea is for you to think about the moral and ethical dimensions of every decision you make. If all of us were more concerned about and responsive to others, were honest, and were more reliable, the business and social environment would greatly improve.

---

such as the potential benefits and hazards of nuclear power, recycling, the management of forests, the ethical treatment of animals, and the protection of the air we breathe and the water we drink.

Environmentalism must not be a social cause of a few; it must be a major focus of everyone, and it's becoming increasingly so. Today, over $200 billion is spent annually to keep North America clean. By the year 2000, spending is predicted to reach $400 billion.

THE MULTICULTURAL ENVIRONMENT

demography
The statistical study of human population to learn its size, density, and other characteristics.

Demography is the statistical study of the human population to learn its size, density, and characteristics. In this book, we're particularly interested in the demographic trends that most affect businesses and career choices. We're going through a kind of social revolution in the United States that's dramatically impacting how we live, where we live, what we buy, and how we spend our time. Furthermore, tremendous population shifts lead to new opportunities for some firms and declining opportunities for others.

FIGURE 1.7

NUMBERS FOR THE 90s

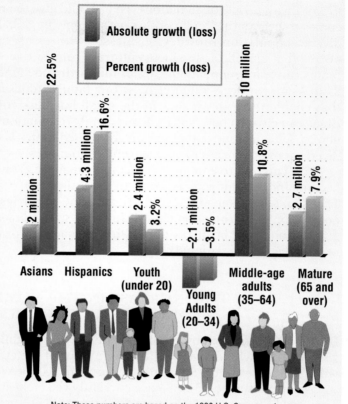

Demographic groups such as Asians, Hispanics, and middle-age adults will increase significantly as the U.S. approaches the turn of the century, according to 1994–99 demographic estimates and projections by Strategic Mapping Inc., Santa Clara, Calif. SMI estimates the U.S. population will reach 273.8 million by 1999. The most rapidly growing regions are expected to be the West (8.5%) and South (6.2%), which combined would account for more than three-fourths of the nation's growth.
These projections represent population growth and percentage growth of specific demographic groups by 1999.

Absolute growth (loss)

Percent growth (loss)

Asians — 2 million, 22.5%
Hispanics — 4.3 million, 16.6%
Youth (under 20) — 2.4 million, 3.2%
Young Adults (20–34) — −2.1 million, −3.5%
Middle-age adults (35–64) — 10 million, 10.8%
Mature (65 and over) — 2.7 million, 7.9%

Note: These numbers are based on the 1990 U.S. Census and use current estimates and 5-year projections of key demographic variables.

Source: *Advertising Age*, September 19, 1994, p. 3.

MULTICULTURALISM AND ITS ADVANTAGES FOR BUSINESS

The Bureau of the Census predicts that the U.S. population in 2050 will be very different from what it is today. First, our population will increase by approximately 50 percent: 383 million versus 260 million today. As the population grows, the more need there will be for the goods and services today's students will be providing.

The population's makeup in the year 2050 will also be very different from today. The Hispanic and Latino population will increase from 9 percent of the total to 21 percent and the Asian population will rise from 3 percent to 11 percent. Think of the business opportunities and challenges such shifts will create. Figure 1.7 shows the short-term changes in these groups.

In a business context, **multiculturalism** is the process of optimizing (in the workplace) the contributions of people from different cultures. A

multiculturalism
Process of optimizing the contribution of people from different cultures.

A diverse work group like this one keeps the United States competitive in world markets. Working together, people from different cultural backgrounds have unique ways of approaching problems that cannot be matched in a work environment where everyone comes from a similar background. Managing such a diverse work force will be a major challenge in the future as businesses try to optimize the benefits of diversity.

multicultural population provides an opportunity for all U.S. citizens to learn to work with people of all nations. That should give them an advantage when it comes to negotiating and working with people in global markets. Moreover, a diverse population provides businesses with ideas, concepts, and cultural norms that enrich the business culture. From Native Americans, the United States can learn more about care of the earth and community living. Citizens from Asian countries often bring strong family values and financial planning that enable them to prosper in the small-business community. Many Latin American citizens have spiritual and family orientations that strengthen businesses. All in all, one of the reasons the United States is strong is because of its diversity and openness to people from all countries.

You can't go to Japan and become Japanese. You can't go to India and become Indian. But you can come to the United States and become American. That's an advantage and a strength that few countries can match. A diverse population is a strong population. Just as a strong lawn is made up of diverse grasses, a strong business population is made up of people of all different races, creeds, and national origins.

··· THE INCREASE IN THE NUMBER ···
OF OLDER AMERICANS

By 2030, the entire baby-boom generation (the 76 million people born from 1946 to 1964 who make up almost one third of the current U.S. population) will be senior citizens. Soon more Americans will be working into their 70s.

Americans aged 45 to 54 are currently the richest group in U.S. society. They spend more than others on everything except health care and thus represent a lucrative market for restaurants, transportation, entertainment, education, and so on. What do such demographic changes mean for you and for businesses in the future? Think of the products the middle-aged and elderly will need—medicine, nursing homes, assisted-living facilities, adult day care, home health care, recreation, and the like—and you'll see opportunities for successful businesses of the 21st century. Older citizens with money will demand more and better health care, more recreation and travel, and new and different products and services of all kinds. Businesses that cater to them will have the opportunity for exceptional growth in the near future.

··· TWO-INCOME FAMILIES ···

Several factors have led to a dramatic growth in two-income families. The high costs of housing and of maintaining a comfortable lifestyle have made it difficult if not impossible for many households to live on just one income. Furthermore, many women today simply want a career outside the home.

One result of this trend is a host of programs that companies are implementing to assist two-income families. IBM and Procter & Gamble, for example, have pregnancy benefits, parental leave, flexible work schedules, and elder care programs. Some companies offer referral services that provide counseling to parents in search of child care or elder care. Such trends are creating many new opportunities for graduates in human resource management.

Many employers provide child care benefits of some type; some of these programs, such as the one at Johnson Wax, are on-site. Such centers are expensive to operate and often cause resentment from employees who don't use the benefits. The resentment has led companies to offer *cafeteria benefits* packages, which enable families to choose from a "menu" of benefits. A couple may choose day care instead of a dental plan, for instance.

Many companies are increasing the number of part-time workers to enable mothers and fathers to stay home with children and still earn income. Others allow workers to stay home and send in their work by telecommunications. That is called **telecommuting**. The net result of these trends is increased opportunity for men and women to enhance their standard of living and raise a family. They also create many job opportunities in day care, counseling, and other related fields. You'll learn more about what's happening in human resource management in Chapters 11 and 12.

telecommuting
Working at home and keeping in touch with others in the work force using telecommunications.

••• SINGLE-PARENT HOUSEHOLDS •••

One trend in the United States is the growing number of single-parent families. Today 30 percent of all births and 70 percent of African-American births are to single parents. It's projected that the figures will soon be 40 percent of all births and 80 percent of African-American births.[17] One problem with single parenthood is that it can lead to poverty. The median or average annual income for a two-parent family is over $40,000. For divorced mothers, it's just over $16,000; for never-married mothers it's just under $9,000.

Single parents have an especially hard time finishing high school and college—a near necessity for tomorrow's well-paying jobs. Single parents also have problems maintaining a job and a home at the same time. Extended families and government assistance help, but such assistance isn't the path to wealth and prosperity. The more that businesses and people in general can do to halt the single-parenthood rate or to support single parents with part-time jobs and other flexible employment opportunities, the stronger the economy and the country will be.[18]

- What are the five factors of production?
- How can government encourage entrepreneurial growth?
- How does information technology help businesses to be more customer-oriented?
- What are stakeholders? Discuss how a business can compete by being more responsive to all its stakeholders.

PROGRESS CHECK

THE GLOBAL ENVIRONMENT

The global environment of business is so important that we show it as surrounding all other environmental influences. It affects all of them. (See Figure 1.4). Perhaps the number one global environmental change is the growth of international competition and the opening of free trade among nations. In the recent past, Japanese manufacturers like Honda and Sony won much of the market for automobiles, videocassette recorders, TV sets, and other products by offering global consumers better-quality products than U.S. manufacturers. This competition hurt many U.S. industries and many jobs were lost.

Today, manufacturers in countries such as China, India, South Korea, and Mexico can produce high-quality goods at low prices because their workers are paid less money than U.S. workers and they've learned quality concepts from Japanese, German, and U.S. producers.

U.S. manufacturers have been analyzing and many have implemented the more advanced quality methods and skills the Japanese have developed. In fact, U.S. workers in many industries are now more productive than workers

productivity
The total output of goods and services in a given period of time divided by work hours (output per work hour).

in Japan and other countries. **Productivity** is the volume of goods and services that one worker can produce. Better technology, machinery, and tools enable each worker to be more productive.

U.S. businesses are rapidly changing their ways of operating to become world-class competitors. The Ford Taurus, the Chrysler Minivan, and the Oldsmobile Aurora are now competitive with the best automobiles in the world. Companies such as Motorola, Wal-Mart, Disney, Federal Express, Intel, and Microsoft are as good or better than competing organizations anywhere in the world. But businesses have gone beyond simply *competing* with organizations in other countries. They have learned to *cooperate* with international firms. That cooperation has the potential to create rapidly growing world markets that can generate prosperity beyond most people's expectations. That is the hope. That is the goal. The challenge is tremendous, but so is the will to achieve.

As these two photographs demonstrate, the signing of NAFTA was very controversial. Business owners and many politicians claim that the free trade agreement with Canada and Mexico has the potential for creating jobs in all three countries. However, many U.S. workers believed jobs would be lost to lower-paid Mexican workers. Despite the collapse of the peso in the early part of 1995, most economists remain confident that NAFTA will result in job growth in the U.S. as the Mexican economy recovers. Overall, the best way for the U.S. to compete against low-wage workers is to continue to increase productivity and quality.

... GLOBAL OPPORTUNITIES AND ... FREE TRADE AGREEMENTS

Recently the United States signed the North American Free Trade Agreement (NAFTA) opening trade between the United States, Canada, and Mexico. Previously, there were trade restrictions among the countries that made it hard to sell goods and services across the borders. Now it's easier for U.S. auto manufacturers to sell cars in Mexico and it's easier for Mexican companies to export their goods, such as cement, to the United States. The intended goal is for consumers and businesses in all three countries to benefit from unrestricted trade. Some U.S. companies will lose business to Mexican and Canadian companies, but other companies such as Wal-Mart will gain markets. It will take years for the results to be clear, but there's evidence that free trade is better than restricted trade.

Note, for example, how prosperous people are in the United States as a result of free trade between the states. Many jobs were lost when companies shifted production from the Northeast to states like North Carolina, but overall the country continued to prosper. Trying to protect manufacturers from international competition often leads to stagnation and the inability to compete globally.

Most European leaders recognize the benefits of free trade as well. As a consequence, free trade agreements have been negotiated among the various European countries (the European Union or EU). As the agreements are successfully

Reaching Beyond Our Borders

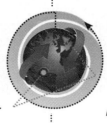

From NAFTA to AFTA

Now that NAFTA has passed, the United States is looking at the potential for negotiating a similar free trade agreement with other countries in the Western Hemisphere. Chile is a free-market economy that would be a major trading partner. Argentina is rapidly changing to a free-market economy. Soon all of Latin America may enter into a trade agreement (AFTA—American Free Trade Agreement) with the United States, Mexico, and Canada. If this occurs it would constitute one of the largest and most prosperous free-trade regions in the world. Similar agreements are likely to be made among European nations and among East Asian Rim nations. Possible members of an East Asian trading bloc are Japan, China, South Korea, Taiwan, Indonesia, Thailand, Hong Kong, the Philippines, Malaysia, Singapore, Vietnam, Brunei, Cambodia, and Laos. If these trading blocs result in benefits for such large geographical areas, then the obvious question is, Why not free trade among all nations?

Source: "After NAFTA May Come AFTA," *U.S. News & World Report*, December 27, 1993, p. 14.

completed, European trade is likely to grow much faster than it grew in recent years. More countries may join the European Union because they too see the benefit of free trade. (See Figure 1.8.)

Trade agreements have also been established in Asia, South America, and other parts of the world. World trade agreements and the global environment in general are so important to businesses today that Chapter 3 is devoted entirely to that subject.

••• HOW GLOBAL CHANGES AFFECT YOU •••

The fair trade agreements concluded in 1994 will lead to many career opportunities for American college students. As businesses expand to serve global markets, new jobs will be created in both manufacturing and service industries. As exports grow, new jobs are created. Exports are expected to increase under the new trade agreements. New jobs will be created both in the United States and overseas.

Global trade also means global competition. The students who will prosper are those who are prepared for the markets of tomorrow. That means that you must prepare yourself now to compete in a rapidly changing environment. This will require you to recognize the need for continuous learning. In other words, be prepared to continue your education *throughout* your career. Colleges will

Austria	Germany	Luxembourg
Belgium	Great Britain	Netherlands
Denmark	Greece	Portugal
Finland	Ireland	Spain
France	Italy	Sweden

FIGURE 1.8

MEMBERS OF THE EUROPEAN UNION

offer updated courses in computer, telecommunications, and language skills, and other subjects you'll need to stay competitive. Students have every reason to be optimistic about job opportunities in the future if they have prepared well. There will be plenty of jobs, but you'll need the required education.

THE QUALITY IMPERATIVE

One consequence of global competition is that no country dares fall behind other countries in providing high-quality products. Quality production techniques have been in place for over a decade in countries such as Japan, the United States, and Germany. That means that top-quality manufacturers, such as Motorola, are able to make products with almost no defects and to make them quickly. Global consumers will fast become accustomed to such quality.

quality
Providing customers with high quality goods and services that go beyond the expected.

Quality in today's firms is defined as providing customers with high-quality goods and services that go beyond the expected. At IBM, for example, quality is defined as "meeting the requirements of our customers, both inside and outside the organization, for defect-free products, services, and business processes." *Fortune* magazine devoted its Autumn/Winter 1993 edition to "The Tough New Consumer/Changing Demands." It said that consumer and industrial buyers (buyers who buy goods from other businesses) are getting used to high standards of quality but, being squeezed by merciless budgetary constraints, they aren't willing to pay top dollar for it. In other words, consumers are increasingly demanding the best quality at the lowest prices. Much of Wal-Mart's success is that it provides such value. Companies that can't provide this combination will be less able to compete in the 21st century.

••• THE NEW QUALITY STANDARD: THE BALDRIGE AWARD •••

In the United States, a new standard was set for quality with the introduction of the *Baldrige Awards* in 1987. To qualify for this award, a company has to show quality as measured three ways: (1) by customer satisfaction, (2) by product and service quality, and (3) by quality of internal operations. Among other things, the Baldrige award requires companies to increase employee involvement, measure themselves against industry leaders, and shorten the time it takes to introduce products. A major criterion for the award is that customer wants and needs are being met, and customer satisfaction ratings are better than those of competitors. As you can see, focus is shifting away from just making quality goods and services to providing top-quality customer service in all respects.

••• QUALITY AND ISO 9000 •••

ISO 9000
Quality management and assurance standards published by the International Organization for Standardization (ISO).

The new global measures for quality are called *ISO 9000 standards*. **ISO 9000** refers to quality management and assurance standards published by the International Organization for Standardization (ISO). Prior to the establishment of such standards in 1987, there were no international standards of quality with which to measure companies. Now ISO standards, established in Europe, provide a "common denominator" of business quality accepted around the world.

What makes ISO 9000 so important is that the European Union—the group of European countries that are establishing free-trade agreements—is demanding that companies that want to do business with the EU be certified by ISO standards. There are several accreditation agencies in Europe and in the United States. They certify that a company meets standards for all phases of its operations, from product development through production and testing to installation. Many European companies have already been certified, but only a few in the United States.

Those companies that qualify for the Baldrige Award will have little trouble passing the certification process for ISO 9000, but most U.S. companies have a long way to go to qualify. It's no longer enough to have a total quality program to compete in certain areas of the world. Now in order to do so that program must be certified by international standards.

THE EVOLUTION OF AMERICAN BUSINESS

Many managers and workers are losing their jobs in major manufacturing firms. Businesses in the United States have become so productive that fewer workers are needed in the industrial sector (that is, industries that produce goods). **Goods** are tangible products such as computers, food, clothing, cars, and appliances.

goods
Tangible products such as houses, food, and clothing.

You may think such layoffs are a sign of U.S. businesses becoming less competitive. In fact, in most instances just the opposite is true. Many U.S. manufacturers have become so efficient that they need fewer employees. Some jobs that have been eliminated were those that were the most physically difficult. Most of the newer plants and factories are cleaner, air conditioned, and more attractive places to work. In many industries the United States is now a world-class producer of goods. The leaders of these companies can take pride in the fact that the technological innovations and methodologies they introduced are now being adopted throughout the world, enabling people in less developed countries to achieve a higher standard of living and quality of life.

Due to the increasing impact of technology and global competition, shouldn't we be concerned about the future and the prospect of higher unemployment and lower incomes? Where will the jobs be when today's students graduate? These important questions force us to look carefully at the U.S. economy and its future. Let's begin by examing history to give you a better understanding of where the economy is now and where it's going.

PROGRESS IN THE AGRICULTURAL AND MANUFACTURING INDUSTRIES

The United States has been a leader in economic development since the beginning of the 1900s. The agricultural industry led the way, providing food for the United States and much of the world. That industry became so efficient through the use of technology that the number of farmers has dropped from about a third of the population to less than 2 percent. The number of farms in the United States has declined from some 5.7 million at the turn of the century to about 2 million today. However, average farm size is now about 455 acres versus 160 acres. Owners of the most profitable 1 percent of these farms now control 30 percent of the farmland.[19] In other words, agriculture is still a major industry in the United States. What has changed is that millions of smaller farms were replaced by some that are huge, some that are large, and some that are small, but highly specialized. The loss of farm workers was not a negative sign. It was instead an indication that U.S. agricultural workers were the most productive in the world, and they still are despite the fact that there are fewer of them.

Many farmers who lost their jobs went to work in factories. Some of those factories were hot, dirty, unpleasant places to work. Most of them are now closed. The manufacturing industry, much like agriculture, used technology to become world class. The natural consequence, as in farming, was the elimination of many jobs. Again, the loss to society is minimal if the wealth created by increased productivity and efficiency creates new jobs elsewhere, and that's exactly what has happened over the past 50 years. Nonetheless, some individuals suffer greatly as they're displaced, forced to retrain and find new employment.

••• PROGRESS IN SERVICE INDUSTRIES •••

services
Intangible products such as education, health care, and insurance.

Many workers who could no longer find employment in manufacturing were able to find jobs in the service industry. **Services** are intangible products (e.g. products that can't be held in your hand) such as education, health care, insurance, recreation, and travel and transportation. In the past, the dominant industries in the United States produced goods (steel, railroads, machine tools, and the like). Today, the leading firms are in services (legal, telecommunications, entertainment, financial, and so on). Travel and tourism is now the nation's number two employer and its leading export.[20]

Since the mid-1980s, the service industry has generated almost all of our economy's increases in employment. Although service sector growth has slowed, it remains the largest. Chances are very high that you'll work in it at some point in your career. Figure 1.9 lists many service sector jobs. Look it over to see where the careers of the future are likely to be. Retailers like Wal-Mart are part of the service sector. Each new store creates many managerial jobs for college graduates. Another bit of good news is that there are more high-paying jobs in the service sector than in the goods-producing sector. High-paying service sector jobs can be found in health care, accounting, finance, telecommunications, architecture, law, and software engineering.

SLOWER GROWTH PROJECTED FOR THE FUTURE   Projections are that the service sector will grow slowly in the coming decades. (See Figure 1.10.) Nonetheless, it's predicted that about 88 percent of the labor force will be in the service sector by the year 2000. Some sectors, such as telecommunications, will grow rapidly while others, such as advertising agencies, may have much slower growth. The strategy for college graduates is to remain flexible, find where the jobs are being created, and move when appropriate.

Most people thought that the service era in the United States would last a lot longer, but it seems to be losing out to a new era in the 21st century. The new era could be described as a global revolution that will affect all sectors of the economy: agricultural, industrial, and service. The global "information revolution" is breaking down barriers between nations. As a result global competition will intensify, but so will the opportunity for international cooperation.

••• THE PAIN OF TRANSITION •••

The transition from an agricultural economy to an industrial economy was a painful one. In fact, the United States went through a major depression in the 1930s as workers were forced off the farm, while industry wasn't creating new jobs fast enough to absorb them. The demands of a wartime economy during World War II accelerated industry's growth and resulted in putting most of the labor force of the United States back to work.

There's much talk about the service sector, but few discussions actually list what it includes. Here's a representative list of services as classified by the government:

Lodging Services
Hotels, rooming houses, and other lodging places
Sporting and recreation camps
Trailering parks and camp sites for transients

Personal Services

Laundries	Child care
Linen supply	Shoe repair
Diaper service	Funeral homes
Carpet cleaning	Tax preparation
Photographic studios	Beauty shops
Health clubs	

Business services

Accounting	Exterminating
Ad agencies	Employment agencies
Collection agencies	Computer programming
Commercial photography	Research and development labs
Commercial art	Management services
Stenographic services	Public relations
Window cleaning	Detective agencies
Consulting	Interior design
Equipment rental	

Automotive Repair Services and Garages

Auto rental	Tire retreading
Truck rental	Exhaust system shops
Parking lots	Car washes
Paint shops	Transmission repair

Miscellaneous Repair Services

Radio and television	Welding
Watch	Sharpening
Reupholstery	Septic tank cleaning

Motion Picture Industry

Production	Theaters
Distribution	Drive-ins

Amusement and Recreation Services

Dance halls	Racetracks
Symphony orchestras	Golf courses
Pool halls	Amusement parks
Bowling alleys	Carnivals
Fairs	Ice skating rinks
Botanical gardens	Circuses
Video rentals	

Health Services

Physicians	Nursery care
Dentists	Medical labs
Chiropractors	Dental labs

Legal Services

Educational Services

Libraries	Correspondence schools
Schools	Data processing schools

Social Services

Child care	Family services
Job training	

Noncommercial Museums, Art Galleries, and Botanical and Zoological Gardens

Selected Membership Organizations
Business associations
Civic associations

Financial Services

Banking	Investment firms (brokers)
Insurance	
Real estate agencies	

Miscellaneous Services

Architectural	Surveying
Engineering	Utilities

FIGURE 1.9

WHAT IS THE SERVICE SECTOR?

Many people are now experiencing similar pain as the United States transitions from a national to a world economy. There has already been a slowdown in economic growth resulting in continued unemployment, although the unemployment rate is relatively low. More unemployment may occur when growth in the service sector slows even further. The future of the U.S. economy and the economies of the rest of the world depends largely on how quickly businesses adapt to these changes.

You now live in a global economy and to compete in the 21st century, businesses will have to provide world-class goods and services. The competition will be great, as we have experienced in the past from countries such as Japan and Germany, but the potential for success is great as well. In the following sections, we'll explore the business challenges you'll face in the 21st century.

••• YOUR FUTURE IN THE GLOBAL ECONOMY •••

We're now in a new, information-based global revolution that will alter the way business is done in the future. It's exciting to think about the role you'll play in that revolution. You may be a leader. You may be one of the people who will implement the changes and accept the challenges of world competition based on world quality standards. This book will introduce you to some of the concepts that will make such a revolution possible.

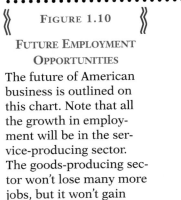

FIGURE 1.10

FUTURE EMPLOYMENT OPPORTUNITIES
The future of American business is outlined on this chart. Note that all the growth in employment will be in the service-producing sector. The goods-producing sector won't lose many more jobs, but it won't gain many either.

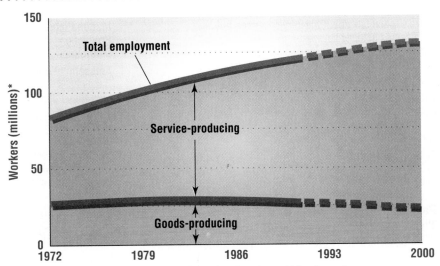

*Includes wage and salary workers, the self-employed, and unpaid family workers.

Source: *Occupational Outlook Handbook*, U.S. Department of Labor.

Remember that most of the concepts and principles that make businesses more effective and efficient are applicable in government agencies and non-profit organizations as well. This is an introductory business text, so we'll tend to focus on business. Nonetheless, we'll remind you periodically that you can apply these concepts in other areas. Business can't prosper in the future without the cooperation of government and social leaders throughout the world.

PROGRESS CHECK

What is AFTA and how does it relate to NAFTA?
What is the Baldrige Award?
How do ISO 9000 standards affect U.S. businesses?
If the service sector is in decline, where will future job opportunities be?

SUMMARY

1. Define profit and show the relationship of profit with risk assumption.

1. A business is any activity that seeks profit by providing goods and services to others.
   ● ***What are the importances of profit, loss, and risk to a business?***
   Profit is money a business earns above and beyond the money that it spends for salaries, expenses, and other costs. Businesspeople make profits by taking risks. Risk is the chance you take of losing time and money on a business that may not prove profitable. A loss occurs when a business's costs and expenses are more than its revenues. If a business loses money over an extended period of time, it will likely have to close, putting its employees out of work. A nonprofit organization is an organization whose goals don't include making a personal profit for its owners.

2. Describe how businesses add to the standard of living and quality of life.

2. The standard of living of a country refers to the amount of goods and services people can buy with the money they have.
   ● ***Where does the money come from that people use to buy goods and services?***
   Businesses and their employees create the wealth that people use to buy goods and services. Businesses also are the source of funds for government agencies and nonprofit organizations that improve the quality of life of society. The quality of life of a country refers to the general well-being

of its people because of freedom, a clean environment, safety, schools, health care, free time, and other things that lead to satisfaction and joy. Thus, business adds to both the quality of life and standard of living by creating the wealth needed to fund progress in these areas.

• *What factors of production do businesses use to create wealth?*
Businesses use five factors of production: land, labor (workers), capital, entrepreneurship, and information. Of these, the most important are entrepreneurship and information.

3. People are willing to take the risk of starting businesses if they feel that the risk isn't too great.

   • *What are some economic factors that increase the risks of starting and managing a business?*
   Part of that risk involves the way that government treats businesses. There's much a government can do to lessen the risk of starting businesses: allow private ownership of businesses, pass laws that enable businesspeople to write contracts that are enforceable in court, establish a currency that's tradable in world markets, focus on the elimination of corruption in business and government, and keep taxes and regulations to a minimum. From a business perspective, low taxes mean lower risks, more growth, and more money for workers and the government.

3. Explain how the economic environment and taxes affect businesses.

4. The most successful college graduates of tomorrow will be those who can find their way on the information superhighway, the I-way.

   • *How has technology benefited businesses and consumers?*
   Information technology (linked computers, cellular phones, modems, and the like) are used by business to monitor the business environment so that firms can quickly adapt to changing conditions. Technology has also made it possible for businesses to become much more responsive to consumers. Bar codes tell retailers what size product you bought, what color, and at what price. Using that information, the retailers can send you catalogs and direct mail pieces offering you exactly what you want, as indicated by your past purchases.

4. Give examples to show how the technological environment has affected businesses.

5. Competition among businesses has never been greater.

   • *What are some ways that businesses meet and beat competition?*
   Some companies found a competitive edge in the 1980s by focusing on making *quality* products. By the early 1990s, meeting the challenge of making a quality product was not enough to stay competitive in world markets. Companies had to offer quality products *and* outstanding service at competitive prices. World-class organizations meet the needs of all their stakeholders. Modern businesses have *teams* of employees who work together to satisfy the needs of all stakeholders, including employees, the community, and people concerned about the natural environment.

5. Describe various ways that businesses can meet and beat competition.

6. The United States is going through a social revolution that's having a dramatic impact on how we live, where we live, what we buy, and how we spend our time.

   • *How have such social changes affected businesses?*
   Social changes are resulting in new opportunities for some firms and declining opportunities for others. As the world population grows, there will be many new opportunities for businesses to sell more products and services. Moreover, a diverse population provides businesses with ideas, concepts, and cultural norms that enrich the business culture. Because many more women have entered the labor force, companies have implemented

6. Show how the social environment has changed and what the reaction of business has been.

a variety of programs to assist two-income and single-parent families. Many employers provide child-care benefits of some type to keep their valued employees.

7. Tell businesses what they must do to meet the global challenge.

7. The number one global environmental change is growth of international competition and the opening of free trade among nations.
   - *How can businesses meet the global challenge?*
   Many businesses in the United States have met the challenge of quality. Now they're moving to form alliances with businesses all over the globe to take advantage of the best business practices in the world. Free trade agreements are expected to create even more opportunities and challenges. The North American Free Trade Agreement (NAFTA) opened trade between the United States, Canada, and Mexico and other such agreements are opening the world to free trade and the potential for achieving greater prosperity.

8. Explain the new quality standards and what businesses are doing to meet those standards.

8. ISO 9000 refers to quality management and assurance standards published by the International Organization for Standardization.
   - *How important is quality to the future of businesses?*
   Quality in today's firms is defined as providing customers with high-quality goods and services that go beyond the expected. Quality and service will be the two major competitive factors in the 21st century. If you include service in quality, then quality is the competitive advantage for the future.

9. Show how trends from the past are being repeated in the present and what that will mean for the service sector.

9. The United States has been a leader in economic development since the beginning of the 1900s.
   - *What is the history of our economic development and what does it tell us about the future?*
   What has sustained America as the world's economic leader is the development and use of technology to improve productivity. Productivity is the volume of goods and services one worker can produce. Due to productivity gains, the agricultural sector was able to produce more food with fewer workers. Those displaced agricultural workers eventually went to work in factories producing more industrial goods. Improved productivity resulting from technology and increased competition from foreign firms combined to reduce the need for factory workers and contributed to the development in the United States of a service economy where more than 75 percent of workers are now employed.

KEY TERMS

business 29
databank 38
demography 42
downsizing 28
entrepreneur 28
factors of
  production 33
goods 49

information super-
  highway (I-way) 37
ISO 9000 48
loss 29
multiculturalism 43
nonprofit
  organization 32
productivity 46

profit 29
quality 48
quality of life 31
risk 29
services 50
stakeholders 40
standard of living 31
telecommuting 45

DEVELOPING WORKPLACE SKILLS

1. Interview both business and government leaders in your community about their major concerns. Then ask them how much they rely on each other to jointly solve mutual problems. Compare your findings with those of your classmates.

2. The text describes the growth trend in the numbers of businesses in the service sector. Look through your local phone book and list five businesses that provide services in your area. The text also describes how certain demographic and social changes affect businesses. Look at your list of local service businesses and consider how these trends affect them. Create a chart that distinguishes the businesses that are negatively affected and those that are positively affected. Be prepared to explain your answers.

3. Use a computer word processing program to write a report on how technology will change society in the next 10 years. Use a computer graphics program to create a chart that illustrates the increase of personal computers used in American homes since 1980.

4. Research current business publications to identify which countries have the fastest growing economies. Read about those countries to see if you would like working there, at least some of the time. What languages should you take in order to prepare for working in these countries? Compose a list of the other skills you'll need. Remember, no area of business has more promise for growth than international trade.

5. Plan for educational advancement throughout your business career by creating a time-line showing key steps you need to take in order to meet your goals.

• •

PRACTICING MANAGEMENT DECISIONS

⟩⟩ C A S E   WOMEN ENTREPRENEURS IN SMALL BUSINESS ⟨⟨

Business Week reported in 1994 that approximately 6.5 million women-owned businesses were operating in the United States. Together these businesses employed more people than all the Fortune 500 companies combined. There are more than 49 metropolitan areas where women-owned businesses had sales of over $1 billion. In 1994, women were forming small businesses at twice the rate of men. In other words, much of the future growth of small businesses in the United States will be among women, and small businesses are the ones creating most of the new jobs.

One reason for women starting their own businesses is that they feel that corporations have established a "glass ceiling" that prevents women (and minorities) from reaching top levels of management. A 1990 study, for example, found that among 4,000 executives in a variety of U.S. companies, only 19 were women. Many firms are working to correct this problem, but progress has been slow. The U.S. Department of Labor is working to establish rules for government contractors that would eliminate any glass ceilings that they perceive.

Women entrepreneurs are frequently the business leaders in developing countries. Women tend to be the ones to take the risk of starting small businesses. To encourage their growth, the Women's World Bank encourages banks to make loans to women by backing 75 percent of each loan. The focus has been on ownership of very small businesses (microenterprises) but is now shifting to larger firms.

Women in America are expected to own 50 percent of small businesses by the year 2000. Women now make up 55 percent of the enrollment in higher education, so they may be better trained than men for tomorrow's executive positions if they major in business and related subjects.

Decision Questions

1. The number of women in developing countries who are becoming entrepreneurs is increasing. What can the governments of these developing countries do to promote and encourage such risk taking among their entrepreneurs?

2. What progress, if any, can you cite in breaking the glass ceiling for women in U.S. businesses, government agencies, and nonprofit organizations?

3. What advantages and/or disadvantages do you see from women taking over top positions in business, nonprofit organizations, and government?

Source: "The Status of Women-Owned Start-Ups," *Inc.*, November 1993, p. 34; and Wendy Zellner, Resa W. King, Veronica N. Byrd, Gail DeGeorge, and Jane Birbaum, "Women Entrepreneurs," *Business Week*, April 18, 1994, pp. 104–10.

⟨ VIDEO CASE　Opportunity Unlimited ⟩

Many teenagers in the inner city drop out of high school because they believe that good job opportunities are not and will not be available. Furthermore, they don't believe that an education is the path to success. And, most of all, they often shun the opportunity to work at a fast-food restaurant for minimum wage because "there is no future in a minimum wage job." La-Van Hawkins is one role model to show that these beliefs are not only untrue but they are keeping young people from experiencing the real opportunities that are available in today's economy.

First, a minimum wage job enables teenagers to prove they are reliable workers. On the job, they can pick up skills and work habits that will transfer to almost any company. La-Van Hawkins began by sweeping floors, but that was only a start. By observing what was going on around him, he saw *opportunity* where others saw only despair.

Hawkins worked his way up the employment ladder until he was offered a job as assistant restaurant manager at Kentucky Fried Chicken. He continued to succeed and ultimately became the director of operations and regional manager, supervising 80 KFC stores in the Philadelphia/Baltimore markets. All along the way Hawkins was learning and observing. He was so successful that the Checkers operation lured him away to supervise their stores.

What was most apparent to Hawkins was the need for fast-food stores in the inner city. He began opening such stores. In just three years he started more than 30 Checkers franchises in three states: 20 in Atlanta, 8 in Philadelphia, and 6 in the Baltimore–D.C. area. In the fourth year he opened 40 more. More will be opening soon in these and other cities, including New York.

What is exciting about such entrepreneurship is that it creates wealth for Hawkins *and* for the community. New stores create new jobs and the community collects taxes to use for all kinds of projects, including schools, playgrounds, and more. By encouraging such entrepreneurship, communities can grow and prosper and students can find rewarding career opportunities. But it all begins at a basic level: working at a low wage to develop the discipline and knowledge needed to become an assistant manager, then a manager, then an owner who shares his or her wealth and knowledge with the community. The world certainly needs more entrepreneurs (wealth creators) like La-Van Hawkins. Will you be one of them?

Discussion Questions

1. Talk with successful businesspeople in your area and ask them how they got started. Did they have to begin by working for a low wage? What did they learn on those jobs that led to the success they now enjoy?

2. What opportunities do you see in your community to become an entrepreneur and employ people from your area?

3. What are some of the conditions in the inner city that make entrepreneurship more difficult there? What can business and city officials do to improve such conditions?

CHAPTER 2

UNDERSTANDING GLOBAL AND DOMESTIC ECONOMICS

LEARNING GOALS

After you have read and studied this chapter, you should be able to

1. Explain how wealth is created in an economy by the "invisible hand."

2. Discuss the major differences between capitalism, socialism, and a mixed economy.

3. Describe how the free-market system works.

4. Use key terms (e.g., *GDP* and *productivity*) to explain the U.S. economic condition.

5. Explain how inflation is measured and the rule of 72.

6. Describe monetary policy and its importance to the economy.

7. Discuss fiscal policy and its importance to the economy.

PABLO TESAK, ENTREPRENEUR FROM EL SALVADOR

When Pablo Tesak came to El Salvador in 1951, most of the wealth of the country was owned by a few families. The majority of consumer products were imported from the United States and Europe. Tesak decided to develop a line of snack products for the poor people of El Salvador. He knew these snacks would have to be simple and cheap, and they would have to be tailored to the tastes of the local population. Tesak began making such snacks and prospered. Later, a civil war in the country caused dissent among his workers. In order to stabilize his work force Tesak raised salaries, but discovered that his employees needed more.

To keep his workers and increase their productivity, Tesak opened a "price club" for his workers. He arranged to buy local products from nearby factories and make them available to employees at cost, with interest-free monthly payments. The club now sells beds, refrigerators, and other household goods to employees and provides them with services such as medical care, English courses, and a summer camp for children. Tesak then set up a $500,000 home credit line so that his employees could borrow money to buy homes. As a result of these new benefits, employee morale and productivity increased substantially. Tesak learned that entrepreneurship can flourish even in the most trying of conditions—with hunger, war, poverty, and disease as constant threats.

Over the past few years, the collapse of communism in Eastern Europe, economic reforms in Latin America, and peace in places like Vietnam have opened such countries to the idea of a market economy. Investors in America and Japan have poured money into funds that invest in emerging economies around the world. But some countries are cautious about adopting free-market principles. Many are uncertain about how such economies are built. One purpose of this chapter is to discuss economic concepts so that you'll understand how free markets work and how businesses and the government can work together to encourage entrepreneurship and growth.

The nation's elected leaders face a critical policy choice—either impose meaningful limits on the growth of government or an ever-increasing government will set de facto limits on America's future economic prosperity.

James Buchanan
Nobel Laureate economist

THE IMPORTANCE OF THE STUDY OF ECONOMICS

The success of the *American* business system is based on an economic and political climate that allows businesses to operate freely. Any change in the economic or political system has a major influence on the success of the business system. The *world* economic situation and world politics also have a major influence on businesses in the United States. Therefore, to understand business, you must also understand basic economics and politics.

Pablo Tesak is just one of millions of men and women who are willing and able to create jobs and wealth if given the chance. That chance comes when a market system is introduced. As you can see from the El Salvador experience, one person can make a huge difference to an economy, providing not only jobs, but also housing, medical care, and more. A million such people could dramatically change the world.

The three basic objectives of this chapter are to teach you (1) how the free enterprise system works to create wealth and prosperity, (2) how free markets differ from government-controlled markets, and (3) some basic terms and concepts from economics so that when you read business periodicals you'll understand what they mean when you encounter them.

••• WHAT IS ECONOMICS? •••

economics
The study of how society chooses to employ resources to produce various goods and services and distribute them for consumption among various competing groups and individuals.

Economics is the study of how society chooses to employ resources to produce various goods and services and distribute them for consumption among various competing groups and individuals. One of businesses' contributions to an economic system is that they have the potential to invent products that greatly increase available resources. Resources are continually expanding as businesses discover new energy sources, new ways of growing food, and new ways of creating needed goods and services. Just recently, for example, a new kind of rice plant was developed that will greatly increase production. As you can see from the example of Pablo Tesak, businesses also can help in the distribution of goods and the provision of services.

Adam Smith developed a theory of wealth creation more than 200 years ago. His theory relied on entrepreneurs working to improve their lives. To make money, they would provide goods and services, as well as jobs, for others.

There's no way to create peace and prosperity in the world by merely dividing known resources among all the various nations. There aren't enough known resources available to do that. *Resource development* is the study of how to use technology to *increase* the known resources of the world and to create the conditions that will make better use of those resources.

THE ECONOMIC THEORY OF WEALTH CREATION: ADAM SMITH

Adam Smith was one of the first economists to imagine a system for creating wealth through the promotion of entrepreneurship. ⟨ **P.28** ⟩ Rather than divide fixed resources among competing groups and individuals, Smith envisioned creating *more* resources so that everyone could become wealthier. The year was 1776. Adam Smith named his book *An Inquiry into the Nature and Causes of the Wealth of Nations*; it's often simply called *The Wealth of Nations*.

Adam Smith was the father of capitalism. **Capitalism** is an economic system in which all or most of the means of production and distribution (for example, land, factories, railroads, and stores) are privately owned (not owned by the government) and operated for profit. In other words, Adam Smith believed that businesspeople would create wealth if given the opportunity. Remember, this was before any country had tried such a system.

Smith believed that *freedom* was vital to the survival of any economy. He believed that people would work hard (have incentives) if they knew they would be rewarded for doing so. He made the desire for improving one's condition in life the foundation of his theory. According to Smith, as long as farmers, laborers, and businesspeople (entrepreneurs) could see economic reward for their efforts (i.e., receive more money in the form of profits), they would work long hours. As a result of those efforts, the economy would prosper with plenty of food and products available of all kinds.

capitalism
An economic system in which all or most of the means of production and distribution are privately owned and operated for profit.

••• THE "INVISIBLE HAND" •••

How is it that people working in their own self-interest can produce wealth for others? It became clear to Adam Smith that the only way farmers could become wealthy would be to sell some of their crops to others. To become even wealthier, the farmer would have to hire others to produce more food. As a consequence, people in the town would have plenty of food and some would have jobs on the farm.

A shoemaker might see that farmers had become wealthy by producing as much food as possible. That meant working long hours and hiring others. So shoemakers would do the same thing as farmers. They would work longer hours and hire others to make shoes. As a consequence, people in the town would have plenty of shoes and even more would have jobs.

Soon there would be hat makers and furniture makers and house builders who would follow the same pattern. They would work hard and hire others in order to become wealthy. As a consequence, nearly everyone in the town would have homes, furniture, and so on—and everyone who was willing and able to work would have a job. Who or what was enabling everyone to have a job and to buy what they wanted? Adam Smith called the mechanism for creating wealth and jobs an *invisible hand*. Under his system of capitalism, businesspeople don't deliberately set out to help others. In fact, they work only for their own prosperity and growth. Yet, like an invisible hand, through people trying to improve their own situation in life, an economy grows and prospers through the production of needed goods, services, and ideas.

The **invisible hand** turns self-directed gain into social and economic benefits for all. One way it does this is by creating jobs. As people became more wealthy, it was assumed that they would naturally reach out to help the less fortunate in the community, as Pablo Tesak did. Adam Smith didn't anticipate the government creating a welfare society where individuals turned much of the care for others over to the government. Many U.S. businesspeople are concerned about social issues and their obligation to return to society some of what they've earned. The box from *Entrepreneur* magazine cites such efforts.

invisible hand
The term coined by Adam Smith to describe the mechanism for creating wealth and jobs.

FROM THE PAGES OF...

Entrepreneur

MAGAZINE

For Goodness' Sake

Helen Mills believes that entrepreneurs can merge profits and principles without sacrificing either. Mills hopes to improve the image of businesspeople by promoting a unified commitment to social responsibility in the workplace and in the community. To do that, she formed an organization called Business for Social Responsibility (BSR) in Washington, D.C. The organization has over 800 members, including companies such as Levi Strauss, Stride Rite, Ben & Jerry's Homemade, and Reebok. The organization's agenda includes increasing environmental accountability, creating a more employee-friendly workplace, and directly helping the community.

Source: "For Goodness' Sake," *Entrepreneur*, August 1994, p. 14.

THE HISTORY OF BUSINESS AND ECONOMICS

Following the ideas of Adam Smith, businesspeople in the United States, Europe, Japan, Canada, and other countries began to create wealth. They hired people to work on their farms and in their factories, and these countries began to prosper as a result. Businesspeople soon became the wealthiest people in town.

Great disparities in wealth began to appear. Businesspeople owned large homes and fancy carriages while workers lived in more humble surroundings. Nonetheless, there was always the promise of better times. If you wanted to be wealthy like the businesspeople in town, all you had to do was start a business of your own. Of course, it wasn't that easy. It never has been. You have to accumulate some money to buy or start a business and you have to work long hours to make it grow. But the opportunities have always been there, especially where there are free markets.

> While business owners rode in fancy carriages with teams of horses, workers could not afford such a lifestyle. Nonetheless, the incentive to become wealthy encouraged many workers to become entrepreneurs themselves. They learned that running a business was hard work, but the rewards were great as well.

••• THE SEARCH FOR EQUALITY •••

Free-market capitalism (capitalism without any government regulation) naturally leads to inequality of wealth. Business owners and managers will make more money and have more wealth than workers. Similarly, people who are disabled or sick may not be able to start and manage a business. Others may not have the talent or the drive to start and manage a business or farm. What does society do about such inequality? Not all people are as generous as Pablo Tesak. In fact, the search to produce as much as possible and to create as much wealth as possible led some businesspeople to such practices as slavery and child labor. Living conditions for workers throughout the world were modest at best.

One person living in such poor conditions was Karl Marx. Marx saw the wealth created by capitalism, but he also noted the poor working

and living conditions of laborers. He decided that workers should take over ownership of businesses and share in the wealth. He wrote *The Communist Manifesto* in 1848.

Marx thus became the father of socialism. **Socialism** is an economic system based on the premise that businesses should be owned by the state. Marx acknowledged the benefits of capitalism—wealth creation—but he believed that wealth should be more evenly distributed.

Socialism became the guiding economic platform for countries such as Russia, China, France, and much of the rest of the world, including Western Europe. In some countries, such as Sweden, businesses were expected to prosper, but business owners and workers were forced to pay extremely high taxes. In other countries, such as China, key businesses were taken over by the state. Socialist nations rely heavily on the government to provide education, health care, retirement benefits, unemployment benefits, and care for everyone not able to work.

••• THE CONSEQUENCES OF SOCIALISM •••

Socialism creates more equality, but it takes away some of businesspeople's incentives to start work early and leave work late. The motto of socialism is, From each according to his ability, to each according to his need. Thus, those who work hard must share with those who don't work so hard or those who don't have such well-paying jobs. Marginal tax rates in Sweden once reached 85 percent. (The marginal tax rate is the rate you pay over a certain income level.) Thus, professional tennis players, doctors, lawyers, business owners, and others who made a lot of money were taxed very highly. As a consequence, many of them left Sweden for other countries with lower taxes, such as the United States.

It turned out that socialism didn't create the jobs or the wealth that capitalism did. Over the past decade or so, socialist countries have simply not kept up with the United States in job creation or wealth creation. *Forbes* magazine reported that "Western Europe suffers almost twice as much unemployment as the U.S. because of its extraordinary burdensome tax codes, onerous regulations and suffocating social policies."[1]

••• THE TREND TOWARD MIXED ECONOMIES •••

The nations of the world have largely been divided between those that followed the concepts of Adam Smith and those that adopted the concepts of Karl Marx. Thus, there are two major economic systems vying for dominance in the world:

1. **Free market economies** exist when the marketplace largely determines what goods and services get produced, who gets them, and how the economy grows. *Capitalism* is the popular term used to describe this economic system. It's based on principles from Adam Smith.

2. **Command economies** exist when the government largely decides what goods and services will be produced, who'll get them, and how the economy will grow. *Socialism* is the popular term used to describe this economic system. It's based on principles from Karl Marx.

socialism
An economic system based on the premise that businesses should be owned by the state.

free market economies
Economic systems in which decisions about what to produce and in what quantities are decided by the market; that is, by buyers and sellers negotiating prices for goods and services.

command economies
Economic systems in which the government largely decides what goods and services will be produced, who will get them, and how the economy will grow.

Poor treatment of workers in the 19th century led many countries to adopt socialism as their economic system. The goal was to create more equality and to help those with special needs. Eventually, almost all countries introduced some socialism into their systems, creating a mixed economy of both capitalism and socialism.

Free Market Friendliness

When Poland was a command economy, people had money, but there were few goods to buy. Under a new, freer-market economy, there are more goods available, but prices are so high that many people can't afford what's available. Most people prefer to have goods available, even at high prices, because they hope (have incentive) to earn more money under the free-market system.

Problems remain, however. For example, under the old system, workers in Polish retail shops were never taught customer service. They treated customers badly and forced them to wait in line. Now that the lines are gone, the clerks still don't act in the friendly, helpful style that free markets and competition bring. It may take years for old habits to die and for free-market values and behaviors to take hold. One desperate need in socialist countries is for Western-style managers who can train workers in a customer orientation and who understand competition and the need for quality.

The experience of the world has been that neither free markets nor socialism has resulted in optimum economic conditions. Free-market mechanisms weren't believed to be responsive enough to the needs of the disabled, the elderly, and the environment. Voters in relatively free market countries, such as the United States, elected officials who adopted many social programs such as social security, welfare, and unemployment compensation.

Socialism, on the other hand, didn't create enough jobs or wealth to keep economies growing fast enough. As a consequence, socialist governments have been cutting back on social programs and lowering taxes on businesses and workers. The idea is to generate more business growth and thus more revenue.

The trend, then, is for so-called capitalist countries, such as the United States, to move toward more socialism and for so-called socialist countries, such as Sweden, to move toward more capitalism. We say "so-called" because there are no countries that are purely capitalist or purely socialist. All countries have some mix of the two systems.

mixed economies
Economic systems in which some allocation of resources is made by the market and some is made by the government.

The net effect of capitalist systems moving toward socialism and socialist systems moving toward free markets is the emergence throughout the world of mixed economies. **Mixed economies** exist where some allocation of resources is made by the market and some by government. Most countries don't have a name for such a system. If the dominant way of allocating resources is by free-market mechanisms, then the leaders of such countries still call their system capitalism. If the dominant way of allocating resources is by the government, then the leaders call their system socialism. Figure 2.1 compares the various economic systems.

••• THE EMERGENCE OF WELFARE CAPITALISM •••

welfare capitalism
A mixed economy in which most of the wealth is generated by businesses, but the government plays a major part in allocating resources.

The economic system that seems to be developing worldwide could well be called *welfare capitalism.* **Welfare capitalism** is a mixed economy where most wealth is generated by businesses, but the government plays a major part in allocating resources. Those resources are obtained from businesses and workers in the form of taxes.

Russia, China, most of Eastern Europe and South America, and other countries throughout the world are moving away from command economies toward welfare capitalism. Entrepreneurship is now being encouraged in

	Capitalism	Mixed Economy	Socialism
Social and economic goals	Private ownership of land and business. Liberty and the pursuit of happiness. Free trade. Emphasis on freedom and the profit motive for economic growth.	Private ownership of land and business with government regulation. Government control of some institutions (e.g., mail). High taxation for defense and the common welfare. Emphasis on a balance between freedom and equality.	Public ownership of major businesses. Some private ownership of smaller businesses and shops. Government control of education, health care, utilities, mining, transportation, and media. Very high taxation. Emphasis on equality.
Motivation of workers	Much incentive to work efficiently and hard because profits are retained by owners. Workers are rewarded for high productivity.	Incentives are similar to capitalism except in government-owned enterprises, which have few incentives. High marginal taxes can discourage overtime work.	Capitalist incentives exist in private businesses. Government control of wages in public institutions limits incentives.
Control over markets	Complete freedom of trade within and among nations. No government control of markets.	Some government control of trade within and among nations (trade protectionism). Government regulation to ensure fair trade within the country.	Some markets are controlled by the government and some are free. Trade restrictions among nations vary and include some free-trade agreements.
Choices in the market	A wide variety of goods and services is available. Almost no scarcity or oversupply exists for long because supply and demand control the market.	Similar to capitalism, but scarcity and oversupply may be caused by government involvement in the market (e.g., subsidies for farms).	Variety in the marketplace varies considerably from country to country. Choice is directly related to government involvement in markets.
Social freedoms	Freedom of speech, press, assembly, religion, job choice, movement, and elections.	Similar to capitalism. Some restrictions on freedoms of assembly and speech. Separation of church and state may limit religious practices in schools.	Similar to mixed economy. Governments may restrict job choice, movement among countries, and who may attend upper-level schools (i.e., college).

FIGURE 2.1

COMPARISONS OF KEY ECONOMIC SYSTEMS

most countries, but the foundations for business growth haven't always been set. For example, Russia doesn't yet have a currency that is tradable on world markets. China is experimenting with capitalism only in certain areas. A major story of the early 21st century will be the movement of formerly command economies toward welfare capitalism (a mixed economic system). If free-market principles are allowed to grow, Russia, China, and other formerly command economies are likely to become much wealthier—and more powerful too.

The United States isn't a purely capitalist nation. Rather, it has a mixed economy like most of the other nations of the world. The degree of government involvement in the economy is a matter of some debate in the United States today. The government has now become the largest employer in the United States. The number of workers in the public sector—18.6 million—is more than the number in the entire manufacturing sector. The Institute for Policy Innovation says, "If this keeps up, pretty soon we'll have more people redistributing wealth than creating it."[2] There's much debate about the role of government in health care. There was so much uncertainty about proposed health care programs in 1994 that no one could anticipate just how expensive a program would be or how involved the government would be. Additionally, the federal government continues to mandate other programs without providing

Many government agencies have been created to monitor business practices and to optimize competition and fair practices. The United States government is now in the process of reviewing such agencies to determine whether they should be restructured or eliminated entirely. Both government and business sectors must remain effective and efficient for the United States to stay competitive in world markets.

funds to the states to implement them.[3] The 1994 election was said to change the direction of the United States toward less government and less regulation. The next few years will reveal whether this is true.[4]

The government has a great effect on the success of businesses in the United States and throughout the world. Later in the chapter, we'll explore many issues having to do with the U.S. government and the economy. Keep in mind as you read this material that the foundation of the U.S. economy is capitalism. The government serves as a means to *supplement* that basic system and tries to promote both growth and greater equality. Changes in the tax codes may have a significant effect on the economy over the next few years. Lower taxes may give the economy a needed boost. Watch for yourself to see what happens. This is an interesting time to monitor the relationship between business and government in the United States.

Many students don't understand how the free-market system works or what the benefits and drawbacks are. Without that knowledge, citizens can't determine what the best economic system is. You should understand how the U.S. economy works and what mechanisms exist to promote further growth. Let's begin the process by exploring how the free market works.

PROGRESS CHECK

- What's the most important resource for wealth creation?
- What did Adam Smith mean by the "invisible hand," and how does it create wealth for a country?
- What led to the emergence of socialism?
- What are some negative consequences of socialism?
- Why have both socialist and capitalist countries moved toward welfare capitalism?

THE FOUNDATIONS OF CAPITALISM

Individuals living in a capitalist (free-market) system have four basic rights:

- *The right to private property.* This is the most fundamental of all rights under capitalism. It means that people can buy, sell, and use land, buildings, machinery, inventions, and other forms of property. They can also pass the property on to their children.
- *The right to keep all of a business's profits after taxes.*
- *The right to freedom of competition.* Within certain guidelines established by the government, a company is free to compete with new products and promotions. To survive and grow, businesses need laws

and regulations such as the laws of contracts, which ensure that people will do what they say they'll do.

- *The right to freedom of choice.* People are free to choose where they want to work and what career they want to follow. Other freedoms of choice include where to live and what to buy or sell.

Given these rights and freedoms, how do businesspeople know what goods to produce and in what quantity? What role do we, as consumers, play in the process? How do businesses learn about changes in consumer desires? These questions and more are answered next.

When the demand for paper goes up, as it did in 1995, the price goes up as well. This encourages manufacturers to increase production. As the supply increases, the price will fall until the quantity demanded and supplied reach an equilibrium point.

••• HOW FREE MARKETS WORK •••

The free-market system is one in which decisions about what to produce and in what quantities are made by the market; that is, by buyers and sellers negotiating prices for goods and services. You and I and other consumers in the United States and in other relatively free markets (e.g., Germany and Hong Kong) send signals to tell producers what to make, how many, in what color, and so on. We do that by going to the store and buying products and services. For example, if all of us decided we wanted more fish, we would signal the fishing industry to provide more fish. The message is sent by the price.

As demand for fish goes up, the price goes up as well because people are willing to pay more than before. People in the fishing industry notice this price increase and know they can make more money by catching more fish. Thus, they have incentive to get up earlier and fish later. Furthermore, more people go fishing and start fish farms. These are people who previously couldn't make enough profit fishing or raising fish, but now can because of the higher price. The kind of fish they raise and catch depends on the kind of fish we request in the store.

The same process occurs with all products. The *price* tells producers how much to produce. As a consequence, there's rarely a long-term shortage of goods in the United States. If something is wanted but isn't available, the price tends to go up until someone begins making that product, sells the ones they already have, or makes a substitute.

••• HOW PRICES ARE DETERMINED •••

The previous discussion about supply, demand, and pricing is an important part of economics. It illustrates the fact that in a free market, prices aren't determined by sellers alone. They're determined by buyers and sellers negotiating in the marketplace. A seller may want to receive $10 a pound for fish, but the quantity demanded at that price may be quite low. The lower the price, the higher the quantity demanded is likely to be. How is a price determined that's acceptable to both buyers and sellers? The answer is found in the economic concepts of supply and demand.

FIGURE 2.2

THE SUPPLY CURVE AT
VARIOUS PRICES

The supply line rises
from left to right. Think
it through. The higher the
price of fish goes (the left
margin), the greater the
quantity that the fish
industry will be willing to
supply.

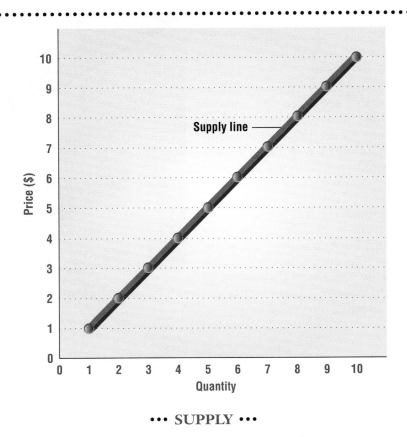

••• SUPPLY •••

supply
The quantity of products that
manufacturers or owners are
willing to sell at different prices
at a specific time.

Supply refers to the quantity of a product that manufacturers or owners are willing to sell at different prices at a specific time. Generally speaking, the amount supplied will increase as the price increases because sellers can make more money with a higher price.

Economists show this relationship between quantity supplied and price on a graph. Figure 2.2 shows a simple supply line. (Actually, the line is curved, but it is easier to picture the relationship between supply and demand using straight lines.) The price of an item in dollars is shown vertically on the left of the graph. Quantity is given horizontally at the bottom of the graph. The various points on the graph indicate how many fish people would provide at different

The line outside a
Reeboks store in Russia,
illustrates how eager
Russians are to buy this
brand of athletic shoe.
Such demand raises
prices and potentially
attracts other shoe com-
panies to open stores in
Russia. In the past, the
Russian government has
hindered free trade, causing great shortages in
consumer goods.

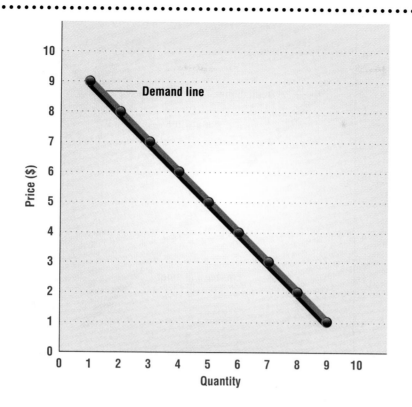

FIGURE 2.3

THE CURVE AT VARIOUS PRICES

A simple demand curve showing the quantity of fish demanded at different prices. The demand curve falls from left to right. It is easy to understand why. The higher the price of fish, the lower the quantity demanded. As the price falls, the quantity demanded goes up. We drew the line straight so you could see the relationships more clearly.

prices. For example, at a price of $2, people in the fish industry would provide only two fish, but at $8, they would supply eight fish. The line connecting the dots is called a *supply line*. The supply line indicates the relationship between the price and the quantity supplied. All things being equal, the higher the price, the more the fishing industry will be willing to supply.

··· DEMAND ···

Demand refers to the quantity of a product that people are willing to buy at different prices at a specific time. Generally speaking, the quantity demanded will decrease as the price increases. Again, the relationship between price and quantity demanded can be shown in a graph. Figure 2.3 shows a simple demand line. The various points on the graph indicate the quantity demanded at various prices. For example, at a price of $8, the quantity demanded is just two fish. But if the price were $2, the quantity demanded would increase to eight. The line connecting the dots is a *demand line*. It shows the relationship between quantity demanded and price.

demand
The quantity of products that people are willing to buy at different prices at a specific time.

··· EQUILIBRIUM POINT ···

After reviewing the graphs, it should be clear to you that the key factor in determining the quantity supplied and the quantity demanded is *price*. Sellers prefer a high price and buyers prefer a low price. If you were to lay one of the two graphs on top of the other, the supply line and the demand line would cross. At that crossing point, the quantity demanded and the quantity supplied would be equal, as Figure 2.4 shows. At a price of $5, the quantity demanded and the quantity supplied are equal. That crossing point is known as the *equilibrium point*. In the long run, that price would become the market price. Market price, then, is determined by supply and demand.

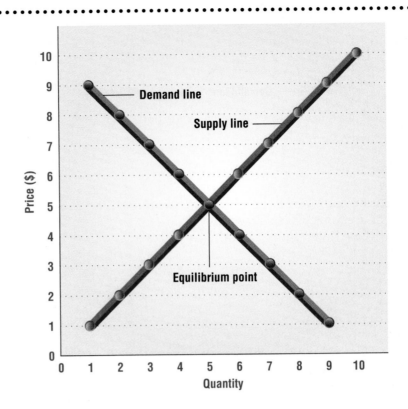

FIGURE 2.4

THE EQUILIBRIUM POINT
The interaction of quantity demanded and supplied is the equilibrium point. When we put supply and demand lines on one graph, we find that they interact at a price where the quantity supplied and the quantity demanded are equal. This is therefore called the equilibrium point. In the long run, the market price will tend toward the equilibrium point.

What would happen if the seller moved his or her price up to $6? At that price, the buyer would be willing to buy only four fish, but the seller would be willing to sell six fish. Similarly, if the price were cut to $4, then buyers would be willing to buy six fish, but sellers would be willing to sell only four. In a free market, prices will always tend toward the equilibrium price.

It's this interaction between supply and demand that determines the market price in the long run. Proponents of a free market would argue that there's no need for government involvement or government planning. If surpluses develop (i.e., if quantity supplied exceeds quantity demanded), a signal is sent to sellers to lower the price. If shortages develop (i.e., if quantity supplied is less than quantity demanded), a signal is sent to sellers to increase the price. Eventually, supply will again equal demand if nothing interferes with market forces.

••• WORLD MARKETS: SUPPLY AND DEMAND •••

Every day billions of consumers throughout the world are sending signals to millions of producers throughout the world telling them what they (the consumers) want. The signals are sent by the *prices* of various goods and services. The signals are sent very quickly, so that there should be little delay in ending surpluses and shortages.

In the real world, however, there are many interferences to the free exchange of goods and services among countries. Consequently, some countries have surpluses (for example, the United States has a surplus of many crops) and others suffer from scarcity (many countries lack sufficient food). A global free-market system would seem to be a good system for improving the world's economic condition. Given the advantages of such a system, there must be offsetting disadvantages or else the world would move more quickly toward one unified free market.

••• LIMITATIONS OF THE FREE-MARKET SYSTEM •••

The free-market system, with its freedom and incentives, was a major factor in creating the wealth that developed countries now enjoy. Some people even talk of the free-market system as an economic miracle. Capitalism, more than any other system, provides opportunities for the poor to work their way out of poverty. Capitalism, through competition, also encourages businesses to be more efficient so that they can successfully compete on price and quality. Thus, capitalism brought prosperity to the United States, but it brought inequality as well.

As soon as Poland, China, and other countries introduced capitalist principles, inequality increased dramatically. The new entrepreneurs (mostly manufacturers and store owners) became wealthy while the average worker didn't. That inequality has caused much national and world tension. In the search to create more equality in the United States and around the world, governments have intervened in the free-market system to create more social fairness and a more even distribution of wealth. That's how mixed economies got started.

Government entities at the state, local, and federal levels (or the equivalent in other countries) take a large share of total national output and reallocate it to create more equality. Some money goes to schools, some goes to help those who are unemployed, and so on. The economic question becomes, How much money should be available to the government for national defense and social welfare, and how much should be left to free-market forces to provide incentives for more output? If more is left to business, then the economic pie may grow faster and there will be more money to distribute. But if all money is allocated by free markets, then some people who can't participate in the capitalist system may suffer.

A major question is, what's the proper blend of government and free markets? We'll discuss that issue in the second half of this chapter.

Adam Smith anticipated that businesspeople would be like Pablo Tesak and would voluntarily support those in need. In the past, churches, temples, and other nonprofit organizations took a leadership position in supporting those in need. If the government were to stop supporting the needy, would those organizations provide the extra needed support? What are the advantages and disadvantages of the government being the major source of welfare?

CRITICAL THINKING

UNDERSTANDING THE ECONOMIC SYSTEM OF THE UNITED STATES

Over the past few years, while most of the world was moving toward freer markets, the United States was moving toward more social programs. As a consequence, there was much conflict between business leaders and government leaders. Many business leaders believed that there were too many taxes and regulations. Government leaders were divided as to the direction the economy should take. Some believed that the government should be more involved in health care, education, day care, and environmental issues. Others believed that the government spent too much on social programs already. The midterm elections in 1994 seemed to slow the movement toward more social programs. Some may even be cut.[5]

The need for soup kitchens in the nation's capital indicates that much inequality persists in the United States. The government has raised taxes to lessen that inequality, but the problem persists. The question today is, "How much tax money should the government acquire in order to help the poor when those dollars retained in businesses can create more wealth with jobs?"

gross domestic product (GDP)
The total value of goods and services produced in a country in a given year.

unemployment rate
The number of civilians who are unemployed and tried to find a job within the prior four weeks.

Because of such uncertain economic policies, the U.S. economic system is in a state of flux. The following sections will introduce the terms and concepts you'll need to understand the issues facing government and business leaders today. As an informed citizen, you can then become a leader in helping to create a world economy that is best for all.

••• KEY ECONOMIC INDICATORS •••

Three major indicators of economic conditions are (1) the gross domestic product (GDP), (2) the unemployment rate, and (3) the price indexes. When you read business literature, you'll see these terms used again and again. It will greatly increase your understanding if your learn the terms now.

GROSS DOMESTIC PRODUCT (GDP) **Gross domestic product (GDP)** is the total value of a country's output of goods and services in a given year. If GDP growth slows or declines, there are often many negative effects on businesses. A major influence on the growth of GDP is how productive the work force is; that is, how much output workers create with a given amount of inputs such as machinery.

Almost every discussion about a nation's economy is based on GDP. The total U.S. GDP in 1995 was about $6 trillion. The level of U.S. economic activity is actually larger than the GDP figures show because they don't take into account illegal activities (e.g., illegal drug sales). The high GDP in the United States is what enables people to enjoy such a high standard of living.

THE UNEMPLOYMENT RATE The **unemployment rate** refers to the number of civilians, 16 years old or older, who are unemployed and tried to find a job within the prior four weeks. The unemployment rate at the beginning of 1995 was the lowest in years—5.4 percent. There are four types of unemployment: frictional, structural, cyclical, and seasonal.

Frictional unemployment refers to those people who have quit work because they didn't like the job, the boss, or working conditions and who haven't yet found a new job. It also refers to those people who are entering the labor force for the first time (for example, new graduates) or are returning to the labor force. There will always be some frictional unemployment because it takes some time to find a new job or a first job. Frictional unemployment has little negative effect on the economy.

Structural unemployment refers to unemployment caused by the restructuring of firms or by a mismatch between the skills (or location) of job seekers and the requirements (or location) of available jobs (for example, coal miners in an area where mines have been closed). Structural unemployment calls for industry retraining programs to move workers into growth industries. One problem has been that many high-paying jobs in firms such as steel mills have been lost and the people have been retrained for much lower-paying jobs in the service sector.

Cyclical unemployment occurs because of a recession or a similar downturn in the business cycle. This type of unemployment lasts until the economy recovers and businesses begin rehiring. The 1990s unemployment figures reflect degrees of both structural and cyclical layoffs. *Seasonal employment* occurs where demand for labor varies over the year, as with the harvesting of crops.

SPOTLIGHT ON SMALL BUSINESS

Creating Jobs

Small businesses have the potential to create the jobs needed to substantially reduce the U.S. unemployment rate. There are about 15 million small enterprises that don't have any workers other than the owner. If the country's economic, tax, and budget policies encouraged each of those businesses to hire just one employee, that would be 15 million new jobs.

There are 6.3 million businesses in the United States with under 100 employees. If each of those businesses added just one employee, there would be another 6 million workers. Add that number to the 15 million and you'd have about 21 million new jobs. That's more than the number of workers added throughout the 1980s, a period of rapid expansion in the United States. Much of the growth in business employment over the next couple of years will be from midsize companies.

In other words, unemployment in the United States could be improved by giving small and midsized businesses some incentive to hire new workers. The problem in the past has been that some government programs did just the opposite. Businesses have frequently been faced with new taxes and regulations. For example, an increase in the minimum wage was proposed in 1995. If passed, some business leaders and economists predicted it would result in additional unemployment.

In short, government policies, laws, and regulations have frequently created obstacles to job growth in the economy. Business leaders are now working to persuade government leaders to work closely with them to devise job growth legislation.

Source: Steven Pearlstein, "Small Isn't All When It Comes to Creating Jobs," *Washington Post*, July 28, 1993, pp. D1 and D4; and Rick Tetzelli, "Midsize Firms: The New Job Engine?" *Fortune*, June 14, 1993, p. 10.

The United States tries to protect those people who are unemployed because of factors such as recessions and industry shifts. Nonetheless, for a variety of factors, many of these individuals do not receive these unemployment benefits.

CRITICAL THINKING

Would the United States be better off today if we hadn't introduced modern farm machinery? There would be more people employed on the farm if we hadn't. Would the world be better off in the future if we didn't introduce new computers, robots, and machinery? They do take away jobs in the short run. What happened to the farmers who were displaced by machines? What will happen to today's workers who are being replaced by machines?

THE PRICE INDEXES   The **consumer price index (CPI)** consists of monthly statistics that measure the pace of inflation (consumer prices going up) or deflation (consumer prices going down). The producer price index (PPI) measures prices at the wholesale level.

Other indicators of the economy's condition include housing starts, retail sales, and changes in personal income. You can learn more about such indicators by reading business periodicals and listening to business broadcasts on radio and television.

The government plays a major role in trying to maintain growth in the economy without causing prices to increase too much. How the government does that and how much of GDP the government should have to work with are two critical issues.

consumer price index (CPI)
Monthly statistics that measure changes in the prices of about 400 goods and services that consumers buy.

••• DISTRIBUTION OF GDP •••

The income earned from producing goods and services goes to the people who own businesses (stockholders) in the form of dividends and to the government in the form of taxes. Some countries take a much larger percentage of GDP for the government than other countries. The question in the United States each year is, How much of GDP should go to the government and how much should go to businesses and the owners of businesses?

In the United States, the percentage of GDP given to the government at all levels (federal, state, and local) was about 20 percent in the early 1950s. By 1994, that figure had risen to about 33.3 percent.[6] When you count all fees, sales taxes, and more, the government share can exceed 50 percent.

••• PRODUCTIVITY IN THE UNITED STATES •••

productivity
The total output of goods and services in a given period of time divided by work hours (output per work hour).

Productivity is the total output of goods and services in a given period of time divided by work hours (output per work hour). An increase in productivity means that the same amount of labor input is now able to produce more goods and services than before. The higher productivity is, the lower costs are in producing goods and services, and the lower prices can be. Therefore, businesspeople are eager to increase productivity.

At the beginning of the 20th century in the United States, one out of three workers was needed to produce enough food to feed everyone and create some surplus for world use. Today it takes fewer than 2 out of 100 workers to produce far greater quantities of food that contribute a much larger share of world production. What made the difference?[7] The answer is that the use of tractors, chemical fertilizers, combines, silos, and other machines and resources (capital) raised farmers' productivity.

Now that we're in a service economy, productivity is an issue because service firms are so labor intensive. Machinery helps labor increase productivity. Spurred by foreign competition, productivity in the manufacturing sector is rising rapidly. But manufacturing provides just over 20 percent of our economy's output. It's the nonmanufacturing sector (the service sector) that's holding back productivity gains.

Robots increase productivity. They also do many of the repetitive and dangerous jobs workers once did by hand. As productivity increases, businesses are able to pay employees more, but fewer workers may be needed. However, the low unemployment rate in the United States indicates that high productivity and high rates of employment are attainable.

••• PRODUCTIVITY IN THE SERVICE SECTOR •••

In the service sector, computers, word processors, and other machines are making service workers more productive. The United States is ahead of much of the world in service productivity. However, one problem with the service industry is that an influx of machinery may add to the *quality* of the service provided but not to the output per worker (productivity).

For example, you've probably noticed how many computers are being installed on college campuses. They add to the quality of education but don't necessarily boost professors' productivity. The same is true of some new equipment in hospitals, such as CAT scans. They improve patient care but don't necessarily increase the number of patients that can be seen. In other words, today's productivity measures fail to capture the increase in quality caused by today's new technology.

The United States and the world need to develop new measures of productivity for the service economy, measures that include quality as well as quantity of output. Otherwise, it will appear that the United States isn't making much progress toward improving the quality of life when, in fact, it's likely that the quality of life is continuing to improve. New measures would prove the case, one way or the other.

INFLATION AND THE CONSUMER PRICE INDEX

One measure of an economy is its ability to control inflation. **Inflation** basically refers to a general rise in the price level of goods and services over time. Two of the more popular measures of price changes over time (inflation indicators) are the consumer price index and the producer price index. The consumer price index measures changes in the prices of about 400 goods and services that consumers buy. The CPI measures the price of an average market basket of goods for an average family over time. Among the items included in the basket of goods are food, automobiles, clothing, homes, furniture, drugs, and medical and legal fees. The consumer price index is closely followed because so many companies and government programs base their salary and payment increases on it.

inflation
A general rise in the prices of goods and services over time.

••• INFLATION AND THE RULE OF 72 •••

No formula is more useful for understanding inflation than the rule of 72. Basically, the idea is to quickly compute how long it takes the cost of goods and services to double at various compounded rates of growth. For example, if houses were increasing in cost at 9 percent a year, how long would it take for the price of a home to double? The answer is easy to calculate. Simply divide the annual increase (9 percent) into 72 and you get the number of years it takes to double the price (eight years). If houses go up in price by 12 percent, it only takes six years to double in price (72 ÷ 12 = 6) and so on. Of course, the same calculation can be used to predict how high food prices or car prices will be 10 years from now.

Here's an example of how you can use this formula. Let's say you wanted to buy a house for $100,000 but found interest rates were so high that you'd end up paying almost $500,000 for the house after 30 years (assuming no money down). It sounds as if you'd be paying way too much for the house, given the information so far. But if you calculate how much the house may be worth after 30 years, you may change your mind. If housing prices increase 10 percent per year, prices will double every seven years or so (72 ÷ 10 = 7.2).

Farm equipment such as this has helped U.S. farmers become the most productive in the world. Agriculture has become one of our most successful and important export commodities. Similar productivity gains in manufacturing will provide the world with cars, clothes, and other consumer goods.

In 30 years, then, the price will double about four times (30 ÷ 7 = 4.3). Your $100,000 house would then sell for about $1.6 million in 30 years. Since you would have paid less than $500,000, the home would be a good deal (assuming a 10 percent increase). What if the price only went up 6 percent a year? Then what would the price be after 30 years? It would double in 12 years, so it would double about 2.5 times in 30 years. In other words, it would be worth about $600,000, still more than you paid for it.

CRITICAL THINKING

If one year in college costs $9,000 today, how much will it cost when a six-year-old goes to school 12 years from now, if college costs go up 6 percent a year?

••• THE ISSUE OF RECESSION VERSUS INFLATION •••

recession
Two consecutive quarters of decline in the GDP.

A **recession** is two consecutive quarters of decline in the GDP. When recession occurs, prices fall, people purchase fewer products, and businesses begin to fail. A recession has severe consequences for an economy: high unemployment, business failures, and an overall drop in living standards. For years (since the Great Depression of the 1930s) the government has put much of its effort into preventing another recession or depression. (A **depression** is a severe recession.) Whenever business has slowed or unemployment has increased, the Federal Reserve has pumped money into the economy to revive it. We'll explain that process next.

depression
A severe recession.

monetary policy
The management of the amount of money placed into the economy by the government and the management of interest rates.

There's much debate about the future of the U.S. economy as the government tries to keep employment high, inflation low, and business growing. To fight inflation and recession, the government and the Federal Reserve System try to manage the economy. To understand the economic situation in the United States and the world today with regard to inflation, recession, unemployment, and other economic matters, you must understand the government's and the Federal Reserve System's roles. Two terms that are crucial to your understanding are *monetary policy* and *fiscal policy*.

Headlines such as these from the *Chicago Tribune* show the importance of the Federal Reserve to the economy. As the economy grows, the Fed increases interest rates in an attempt to reduce inflation. If the economy slows down too much, the Fed will lower interest rates to stimulate it.

THE ISSUE OF MONETARY POLICY

Monetary policy is the management of the money supply and interest rates. In learning about monetary policy, the first thing one must understand is the role of the Federal Reserve System (the Fed). The Fed is one of the sources of money in

More growth probably means more rate hikes

Fed pushes interest rates to 3-year high

Experts already look to next hike

the economy; it can add or subtract money from the economy as it sees fit. For example, the Fed can increase the interest rate on money it lends to banks if it thinks such action is warranted. Banks would pass this increase on to businesses, thus slowing the economy as businesses borrow less. The Federal Reserve System operates independently of the president and Congress and has the goal of keeping the economy growing without causing inflation. It does that by trying to manage the money supply and interest rates. (Chapter 21 discusses it in detail.)

••• TIGHT VERSUS LOOSE MONETARY POLICY •••

Inflation is sometimes caused by having too much money in the economy. When that happens, the Fed cuts the money supply and increases interest rates. That makes less money available for spending and discourages businesses and consumers from borrowing money (because of high interest rates). When businesses find it hard to borrow money, they often cut back on production and lay off workers or cut workers' hours instead. In either case, this slows the economy and lowers inflation.

When unemployment gets too high, the Federal Reserve may put more money into the economy and lower interest rates. This stimulates spending and encourages business growth, which leads to the hiring of more people.

When you read that the Fed is "loosening up on the money supply" or "lowering interest rates," it means that the Fed is trying to stimulate the economy (that is, increase consumer spending and increase business investment). A tight monetary policy is one in which the Fed is restricting the supply of money and increasing credit costs to lower inflation. The Federal Reserve raised interest rates throughout 1994 and early 1995. The effect should be slower growth in the economy.

THE ISSUE OF FISCAL POLICY

Fiscal policy refers to the federal government's efforts to keep the economy stable by increasing or decreasing taxes and/or government spending. For many years, the government has tended to raise taxes to fund more and more social and defense programs. More recently, the government has tried to cut spending to balance the budget (that is, make income equal spending). But such attempts were rather unsuccessful; they merely cut the *growth* in spending rather than spending itself. Figure 2.5 shows how federal expenses have been exceeding federal revenues for years. The result is an increasing federal debt. The debate is whether to lower the debt through more taxes or through less spending or both.

Remember, the total amount that the government takes at all levels can now exceed 50 percent of all that we earn.[8] U.S. citizens are so accustomed to thinking about the federal tax bite that we tend to ignore state and local taxes, various fees, and sales taxes. Fiscal issues will dominate the political scene throughout the coming decades. It's important for you to follow the debate. After all, half of your money may be involved.

fiscal policy
Government efforts to keep the economy stable by increasing or decreasing taxes or government spending.

••• HOW TAXES AND SPENDING AFFECT BUSINESSPEOPLE •••

A major issue in most political campaigns concerns fiscal policy—taxes and spending. Tax rates for the richest people in the United States, mostly businesspeople, were recently raised. Many of those people are owners of small

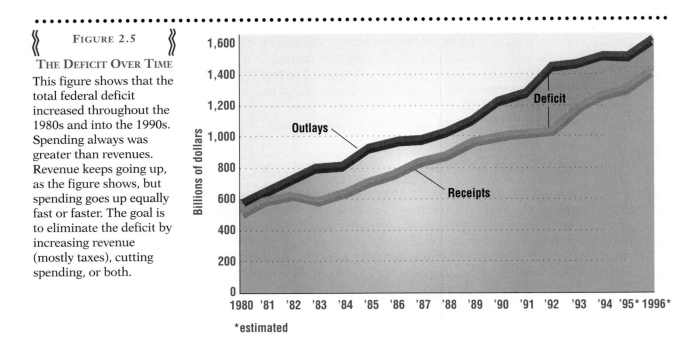

⟨⟨ FIGURE 2.5 ⟩⟩

THE DEFICIT OVER TIME

This figure shows that the total federal deficit increased throughout the 1980s and into the 1990s. Spending always was greater than revenues. Revenue keeps going up, as the figure shows, but spending goes up equally fast or faster. The goal is to eliminate the deficit by increasing revenue (mostly taxes), cutting spending, or both.

and intermediate-sized businesses who were creating jobs and wealth for the rest of the economy. The tendency of some small business owners is to cut back on hiring when taxes go up. Increased tax rates may result in less revenue for the government. That's exactly what has happened in Canada. The government keeps raising tax rates, but revenues don't increase.

Time will tell what the effect of the new U.S. tax rates will be. What's important for you to understand at this point is that fiscal policy has a major influence on businesses and businesspeople. These effects are eventually felt by employees and the entire economy as businesspeople decide whether to hire more people and invest more money.

Government spending is also an issue today. The government is spending more each year, even though the rate of growth in spending is slowing. Almost everyone agrees that government spending should be lowered; what people don't agree on is which programs should be cut. You can learn more about this issue and fiscal policy in general by reading the business section of your daily paper or *The Wall Street Journal*.

••• REGULATION: THE HIDDEN TAX •••

The government is running out of money, but not out of defense or social programs that it wishes to implement. For example, the government recently proposed a new health care program to be paid for by businesses. Thus, the government would be able to increase health care coverage in the United States without raising taxes. Nonetheless, a cost is imposed on businesses that has the same effect as a tax.

The health care proposal was part of a trend by the government to increase its regulatory efforts rather than raise taxes. Thus, in 1993 the federal government passed a law requiring businesses with more than 50 employees to provide parental leave (requiring employers to give workers unpaid time off to cope with childbirth and family illnesses and to guarantee their job when they return) and other benefits that, in the past, have been optional.

Tax Fairness

Imagine that you've been out of school for a while and you and your spouse are now earning $50,000 a year. To get to that point, you both paid your way through college. You look forward to buying a home, cars, and other goods and services that you've been postponing all these years to get your education.

You decide to buy a nice home. The government allows you to deduct all the mortgage interest charges on that home and the property taxes from your taxable income. That makes the payments much easier at first. In fact, almost all the money you're paying into the home the first few years goes for taxes and mortgage interest, and all of that is tax deductible. That means that you won't have to give the government as much money in taxes.

You also feel that you should give some money to your religious group and other charities. The money you give these nonprofit organizations is also deductible from your taxes if you itemize such deductions. You read in the paper that you and other people who buy homes and give money to charity are receiving unfair tax breaks. After all, poor people can't get deductions for the rent they pay and they can't afford to give to charity. Some people feel that you shouldn't receive a "government subsidy" to buy your home. You, on the other hand, feel that you're paying enough in taxes, but you want to give your fair share.

Is it ethical for the government to give tax breaks to people? Some people can buy tax-free bonds, get deductions for interest payments on their homes, receive deductions for money given to charity, and get tax breaks to rent out a second home. Businesses can write off some entertainment and travel expenses, and more. What percentage of a person's income should go to the government? Should everyone pay equally or should the rich pay more? What are the moral and ethical reasons for your position?

We'll discuss such concepts in more detail later. At this point, it's important to note that there are ways for the government to affect the nation's social system without raising taxes. Whether or not taxes are raised, the effects of such government actions are additional costs to businesses and higher prices to consumers.

••• THE FEDERAL DEFICIT •••

The **federal deficit** is the difference between federal revenue and federal spending in any given year. There was much concern about deficit spending throughout the 1980s and into the 1990s. The estimated deficit was only 2.1 percent of GDP in 1995. That is lower than Germany (2.4 percent), Canada (4.7 percent), Britain (4.7 percent), or Italy (9 percent).[9] Nonetheless, government spending is exceeding revenue by hundreds of billions of dollars every year. Therefore, a major topic of conversation in the 1990s was: How can we cut the budget deficit? Each year there's a federal deficit, the amount not paid is added to the national debt. The **national debt**, then, is the sum of all the federal deficits over time.

federal deficit
The difference between federal revenue and federal spending in any given year.

national debt
The sum of all the federal deficits over time.

••• THE NATIONAL DEBT •••

Government spending has exceeded government income for so long that the national debt is now nearing $5 trillion.[10] That's about $19,000 for every man, woman, and child in the United States, or $76,000 for a family of four.[11] What does a trillion dollars look like? If you had a stack of $1,000 bills in your hand only four inches high, you'd be a millionaire. A trillion dollars would be a

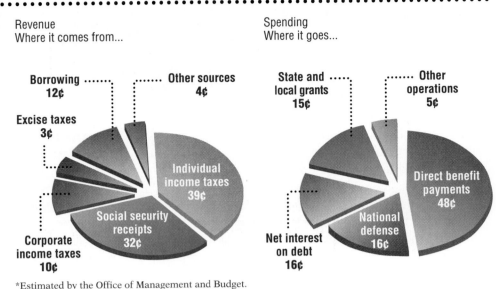

FIGURE 2.6

1996 GOVERNMENT REVENUE AND EXPENSES*

Most of the government's revenue comes from you and me and other taxpayers in the form of taxes and social security payments. Corporate tax provides a much smaller revenue source. The bulk of spending goes to individuals in the form of welfare, social security, and related programs. Defense takes 16 percent. The national debt gobbles up 16 percent of every dollar in interest payments.

Revenue
Where it comes from...

Spending
Where it goes...

Borrowing 12¢

Other sources 4¢

Excise taxes 3¢

Individual income taxes 39¢

Social security receipts 32¢

Corporate income taxes 10¢

State and local grants 15¢

Other operations 5¢

Direct benefit payments 48¢

National defense 16¢

Net interest on debt 16¢

*Estimated by the Office of Management and Budget.

stack of $1,000 bills 67 miles high. If we were able to pay off the national debt in one payment, we would need a stack of $1,000 bills over 300 miles high.

Most people believe that something must be done about the national debt, and soon. The questions are, How did the national debt get so enormous? What can be done about it? First, let's look at how the national debt got so large. Figure 2.6 gives some details about the sources of government funds and the way that money is spent. Government expenditures are growing faster than the economy's ability to support its programs. Most government programs have automatic increases built into them, so spending goes up automatically every year. Since World War II, every dollar of legislated higher taxes has been matched by $1.28 to $1.58 in higher spending. The way to have smaller deficits, therefore, isn't higher taxes. Spending must be cut as well. (Figure 2.7 shows how the national debt is growing.)

One question that economists, government officials, and ultimately you and other taxpayers must answer is: What are our national priorities? That is, do we want a strong military capability, including nuclear weapons and a strategic defense system, and how much are we willing to pay for such a capability? Can we shift some defense money to domestic programs and international aid? These are the kinds of questions being posed in the media.

A huge chunk of federal income goes for social security payments. Social security wasn't originally meant to be a retirement program, but a supplement to savings. Many people now ignore that fact and rely on social security for survival. Given this, do you think it's reasonable for government to reduce these benefits, or should people retire later and lessen the burden on social security? These will be major issues throughout the coming years.

Millions of people receive medicare treatment, school lunches, medicaid, food stamps, housing subsidies, low-cost student loans, and other government-paid (taxpayer-paid) assistance. Certain industries, for example, dairy farmers and gas and oil companies, receive subsidies or tax deductions to support their production. What is the national priority regarding such payments? Should the government continue such payments and expand the programs when hard times come, or should such payments be limited somehow? Are such payments more or less important than defense or social security? What should the policy be if such payments threaten the

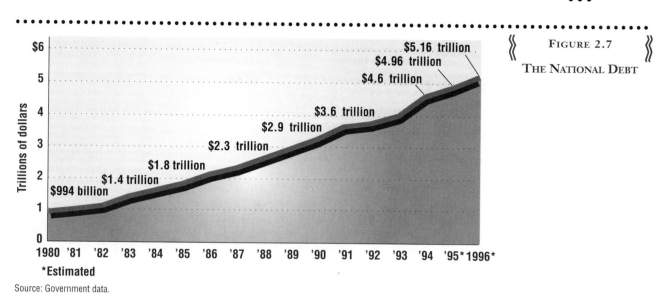

FIGURE 2.7

THE NATIONAL DEBT

*Estimated

Source: Government data.

economy by siphoning too much money from business? These are the issues you'll be seeing in the various media. They have a direct effect on you (in taxes) and on business.

PROGRESS CHECK

- What's the difference between a recession and a depression?
- How does the government manage the economy using monetary policy?
- How does the government manage the economy using fiscal policy?
- How big is the U.S. national debt?
- What's the difference between the federal deficit and the federal debt?

SUMMARY

1. **Economics** is the study of how society chooses to employ resources to produce various goods and services and to distribute them for consumption among various competing groups and individuals.
   - ***How can wealth be created in a society so that more is available for distribution?***
   Adam Smith called the mechanism for creating wealth and jobs an *invisible hand*. Under his system of capitalism, nobody deliberately sets out to help others. In fact, they work only for their own prosperity and growth. Yet, like an invisible hand, through people trying to improve their own situation in life, an economy grows and prospers through the production of needed goods, services, and ideas.

1. Explain how wealth is created in an economy by the "invisible hand."

2. **Capitalism** is an economic system in which all or most of the means of production and distribution (for example, land, factories, railroads, and stores) are privately owned and operated for profit. **Socialism** is an economic system based on the premise that businesses should be owned by the people (workers).
   - ***Discuss the major differences between capitalism and socialism.***
   The major difference between capitalism and socialism is the involvement of the government. Under capitalism, the government isn't very involved

2. Discuss the major differences between capitalism, socialism, and a mixed economy.

in the distribution of wealth and much freedom is given to businesspeople. Under socialism, the government owns and controls many key businesses; private businesses and individuals are taxed relatively steeply to pay for social programs such as health, education, unemployment insurance, and social security. The trend today is toward **mixed economies** or welfare capitalism where the government taxes businesses and individuals heavily, but owns few businesses.

3. Describe how the free-market system works.

3. The free-market system is one in which decisions about what to produce and in what quantities are made by the market; that is, by buyers and sellers negotiating prices for goods and services.

- ● **Describe how the free-market system works.**
Buyers tell sellers what to produce and in what quantity by the buying decisions they make in the marketplace. When buyers demand more goods, the price goes up, signaling sellers to produce more. The higher the price, the more gets produced. Price, then, is the mechanism that allows free markets to work.

4. Use key terms (e.g, *GDP* and *productivity*) to explain the U.S. economic condition.

4. Three major indicators of economic conditions are (1) the gross domestic product (GDP), (2) the unemployment rate, and (3) the price indexes.

- ● **What are the key terms used to describe the U.S. economic system?**
Gross domestic product (GDP) is the total value of a country's output of goods and services in a given year. The **unemployment rate** refers to the number of civilians, 16 years old or older, who are unemployed and who tried to find a job within the most recent four weeks.

  The **consumer price index (CPI)** consists of monthly statistics that measure the pace of inflation (consumer prices going up) or deflation (consumer prices going down). **Productivity** is the total output of goods and services in a given period of time divided by work hours (output per work hour).

5. Explain how inflation is measured and the rule of 72.

5. Inflation refers to a general rise in the price level of goods and services over time.

- ● **How does the United States measure inflation?**
Two of the more popular measures of price changes over time (inflation indicators) are the consumer price index (CPI) and the producer price index (PPI). The **consumer price index (CPI)** measures changes in the prices of about 400 goods and services that consumers buy. The PPI measures price increases at the wholesale level.
- ● **What is the "rule of 72"?**
Basically, the idea is to quickly compute how long it takes the cost of goods and services to double at various compounded rates of growth. For example, if houses were increasing in cost at 9 percent a year, how long would it take for the price of a home to double? The answer is easy to calculate. Simply divide the annual increase (9 percent) into 72 and you get the number of years it takes to double the price (eight years).

6. Describe monetary policy and its importance to the economy.

6. **Monetary policy** is the management of the money supply and interest rates.

- ● **What is the importance of monetary policy to the economy?**
When unemployment gets too high, the Federal Reserve may put more money into the economy and lower interest rates. This stimulates spending and encourages business growth, which leads to the hiring of more people. On the other hand, when unemployment is low and prices are rising, the Fed may take money out of the economy and raise interest rates. This slows spending, and businesses hire fewer workers.

7. **Fiscal policy** refers to government efforts to keep the economy stable by increasing or decreasing taxes and/or government spending.

• *Why is fiscal policy important to the economy?*

The government in recent years has tended to raise taxes to fund more and more social and defense programs. The government is trying to cut spending to balance the budget (that is, make income equal spending). But such attempts have been rather unsuccessful; Congress merely cut the growth in spending rather than spending itself. The result is an increasing federal debt. The debate is whether to lower the debt through more taxes, through less spending, or through both.

7. Discuss fiscal policy and its importance to the economy.

capitalism 61
command
  economies 63
consumer price index
  (CPI) 73
demand 69
depression 76
economics 60
federal deficit 79

fiscal policy 77
free market
  economies 63
gross domestic
  product (GDP) 72
inflation 75
invisible hand 61
mixed economies 64
monetary policy 76

national debt 79
productivity 74
recession 76
socialism 63
supply 68
unemployment
  rate 72
welfare capitalism 64

KEY TERMS

1. What are some of the disadvantages of living in a free society? How could such disadvantages be minimized? What are the advantages? Write a short essay describing why a poor person in India might reject capitalism and prefer a socialist state. How could the United States overcome this situation to broaden the base of the free-market system? Two students could debate capitalist versus socialist societies to further reveal the issues.

2. Identify one of the most widely debated economic issues and discuss the various viewpoints with your classmates and instructor. Choose a position and be ready to defend it by researching facts and figures to support it. Have you set up a filing system yet to maintain such information?

3. The text discusses three major indicators of an economy's health: gross domestic product (GDP), unemployment rate, and consumer price index (CPI). The text also describes the close relationship of productivity to GDP. Each of these indicators rises and falls during periods of recession and periods of growth. Devise a chart that illustrates whether each economic indicator goes up, down, or remains the same during a condition of economic recession or growth.

4. Most of the world's nations are moving toward some variation of a mixed economy that could be labeled welfare capitalism. What do you see as the primary differences between the emergence of welfare capitalism and pure capitalism? Which would you favor and recommend? Why?

5. Demonstrate your understanding of the rule of 72 by using it to calculate the impact of inflation. For example, calculate how much a new car will cost a child now 5 years old when he or she reaches age 17 if the car prices increase by 6 percent a year. Assume the cost of a new car is now $15,000. How much will a textbook cost if prices go up by 12 percent a year, and the book now costs $40?

DEVELOPING WORKPLACE SKILLS

PRACTICING MANAGEMENT DECISIONS

⟨⟨ C A S E   LET'S JUST TAX THE RICH AND PAY OFF THE DEBT ⟩⟩

For years, economics has been defined as the allocation of *scarce* resources among competing groups and individuals. No two groups would seem more in competition in the United States than the rich versus the poor. The feeling among many people is that the rich got rich by exploiting the poor (labor). In their search for more equality, such people suggest increasing taxes on the rich and giving the additional money to the poor. Such was the thinking behind most socialist governments until the 1980s and 1990s, when socialism lost its glow, even in Sweden, the model socialist country for many people.

The problem with such thinking is that there simply aren't enough wealthy people making enough money so that by increasing their taxes the government would be able to pay for all its programs. A few years back, *Forbes* magazine reported that if the federal government took 100 percent of the income of the 35,875 millionaires in the United States, the increase in revenue would run the government for just 12 days. If the total wealth of the 400 richest were confiscated, it would pay for just three months.

Wealthy people make most of their money from investing in businesses. If the government were to increase their taxes, that investment money would no longer be there, and the economy would slow. Therefore, it's clear that "taxing the rich" isn't a solution to the government's problems. The tax burden always falls on the middle class, those people who are struggling to pay their mortgages, send their kids to school, and so forth. Increasing their taxes makes them poorer, and nobody feels better off.

The only long-term solution to meeting government needs is for the economy to grow. That increases the size of the pie and makes it possible for everyone to have more without taking it from someone else. The problem is that growth strategies are directly in conflict with goals of more equality. Growth often comes from cutting taxes on the rich. That encourages them to invest more and to make the economy grow. The rich get richer and the poor get richer too, but at a slower rate. The net result is a bigger gap between rich and poor. It's interesting to note, however, that half of the families in the bottom 20 percent of income aren't there seven years later. In other words, there's a good chance that people on the bottom will become middle-income earners sometime in their lives. The persistently poor make up only about 3 percent of the population in the United States.

Many businesses in the 1980s and early 1990s cut workers from their payroll because competition and a failing economy forced them to do so. At the same time, the number of government workers increased in some areas. There's some room, therefore, for government spending cuts. There's also the potential for less spending on the military as tensions relax in the world. In short, there's an opportunity to cut taxes, spur growth, and still provide necessary social programs.

Decision Questions

1. Recently, Sweden joined many of the other nations in the world in cutting taxes. The Swedish people also voted against a socialist government. Taxing the rich is no longer the preferred way to balance government budgets. What are the alternatives?

2. There are thousands of millionaires and some billionaires in the United States. What are the advantages and disadvantages of taxing such people at much higher rates than now prevail?

3. The notion that "a rising tide lifts all ships" is true in the United States for all but 3 percent of the population. What can be done to help raise those people as well?

4. Every year, there seems to be a call for a cut in government waste and corruption. Years pass, and no such cuts appear to be made. What steps would you recommend for making local, state, and federal government agencies more efficient and effective?

•••

〉〉 VIDEO CASE OGRE FACES A MARKET ECONOMY 〈〈

Ogre Mills in Latvia is a typical factory in a command economy. As the world opens to free competition, these factories will have to compete with world-class factories in countries such as the United States, Germany, and Japan. Are they ready for such competition?

Under a command economy, the factory submitted a budget to the government. The government then set quotas for the factory, decided who would supply the factory with raw materials, distributed final goods, and set the price. The government even decided how much workers would be paid. Management pay was based on whether or not quotas were met and whether the budget was followed.

Now that the mill faces a market economy, things will be very different. The firm must acquire materials in global markets, pay for those goods in hard currency, find final markets willing to pay for the goods in hard currency, and price the goods competitively.

In most advanced countries, businesses rely on information systems to provide the information needed to set global prices, track inventory and shipping, and track profits. The Russian information systems are not world class and the firms will thus have trouble competing.

The firm has been able to find enough hard currency to buy raw materials overseas. It has also joined the International Wool Society to make sure that its products meet the world's quality standards. Nonetheless, the company still has obsolete production equipment and information systems.

Discussion Questions

1. Explain how prices are determined in free markets. How does such a system result in few surpluses or shortages? Contrast that system with the command economy to which Ogre once belonged.

2. What are some of the advantages and disadvantages that people in Latvia will experience as the country moves toward free markets. Explain how a mixed economy would alleviate some of the problems.

3. What advantages do Latvian firms have over firms in the United States and Germany, if any?

4. If you were a counselor to the Latvian people, what kind of economic system would you recommend: socialism, capitalism, or a mixed economy? Explain your reasons.

CHAPTER 3

COMPETING IN GLOBAL MARKETS

LEARNING GOALS

After you have read and studied this chapter, you should be able to

1. Discuss the increasing importance of the global market and the roles of comparative advantage and absolute advantage in international trade.

2. Explain how the marketing motto "Find a need and fill it" applies to global markets and understand key terms used in international business.

3. Describe the current status of the United States in global business.

4. Illustrate the strategies used in reaching global markets.

5. Identify the hurdles of trading in world markets.

6. Debate the advantages and disadvantages of trade protectionism.

7. Evaluate the role of multinational corporations in global markets.

VIRGINIA KAMSKY, CHINA TRADER

The road to international trade isn't always obvious, even to the most successful. Take Virginia Kamsky, for example. When Virginia was 10, she read *The Good Earth,* a book about China by Pearl Buck. She decided to learn Chinese, so at 11 she signed up for an introductory course in the language. By 17 she was fluent in it.

Kamsky went on to Princeton to study Japanese and classical Chinese. After taking an elective macroeconomics course, she became fascinated by economics.

After graduation, she was an economic analyst for the U.S. embassy in Singapore when Chase Manhattan Bank lured her away to join their global credit training program. She made it to the top of her class and went to Tokyo to be assistant treasurer of Chase. Kamsky became the first and only woman bank officer in Japan at age 23. Handling credit transactions at the bank, Ms. Kamsky became interested in world trade. She went back to New York and learned more about trade as a lending officer.

One day, Chase's president had to go to China. He took Kamsky along because of her language skills and knowledge. She loved it, and has been part of Chinese trade ever since. She became vice president in charge of the bank's corporate division in China. She spent much of her time helping the bank's clients get through the bureaucracy, paperwork, and cultural details involved in negotiating real estate projects and trading contracts of all kinds. Eventually, Kamsky left Chase to start her own firm, Kamsky Associates. Kamsky Associates has been responsible for helping U.S. and foreign firms sign between $3 and $4 billion in joint ventures, developments, and trade agreements with the People's Republic of China. Kamsky Associates now employs 35 consultants and has satellite offices in Hong Kong and New York. She was still very positive about China's potential in 1995.

Ms. Kamsky represents the successful international businessperson of the future: that is, one who knows several languages, who goes into countries where trade is minimal, and who creates huge trade agreements. The future of world economic growth is in international trade. The future of U.S. growth is directly tied to this growth in world trade. That's what this chapter is all about.

> *We have to accept the fact that we are going to be increasingly dependent on the international economy, while the international economy is likely to be less dependent on us. . . . Indeed, both economic growth and full employment will increasingly depend on success in competing in the international economy.*
>
> *Peter Drucker*
> *Management Consultant and Author*

THE DYNAMIC GLOBAL MARKET

Do you dream of traveling to exotic cities like Paris, Hong Kong, Rio de Janiero, or Cairo? Years ago, the closest most Americans would get to these cities was in their dreams. However, the situation has changed. A career in international business could very well take you to these cities.

Have you thought about the possibilities of a career in international business? Maybe a few statistics will make the possibility more interesting:

There are about 250 million people in the United States, but there are about 5.5 billion potential customers in the global market. Of the 5.5 billion people in the world, approximately 75 percent live in developing areas.[1]

Today we buy $107 billion worth of goods annually from one country, Japan.[2] In Germany, 80 percent of all American Express card usage is by Germans. Sales of pagers made by Motorola in the People's Republic of China increased from 100,000 in 1991 to over 4 million in 1993. The company notes this is the fastest growing foreign market for its pagers and cellular phones in the world.[3]

Thanks to a new service on the Internet called Tradepoint small-business owners will be able to market their products in 50 countries. The service provides a multimedia catalog to assist them.

The United States is the largest importer in the world. It's the largest exporter as well. **Importing** is buying products from another country. **Exporting** is selling products to another country. Competition in exporting is

importing
Buying products from another country.

exporting
Sellling products to another country.

As the world's largest importer, the United States offers enormous opportunities for imported products from aggressive export nations like Japan. Here we see imported Sanyo televisions from Japan on sale at Best Buy. By producing first-class electronics products, exporters like Japan have gained a significant share of the U.S. electronics market.

intense. The United States must compete against aggressive exporters such as Germany and Japan.

These facts show that international trade is big business today and will be even more important in the coming decades. Will you be ready? Are you studying a foreign language in school? Have you talked with anyone about the excitement and rewards of traveling to and trading with other countries? Do you recognize the many challenges the United States will face in the 1990s and beyond? Many colleges offer study-abroad programs. Check with your counselor or faculty advisor to see what international study programs your school offers.

The purpose of this chapter is to expose you to global business, including its potential and problems. There aren't yet many students preparing for such a career. That means that demand for students with such training is likely to exceed the supply as international trade grows. Maybe you'll be one of the lucky ones to find a challenging, rewarding career in international business.

WHY TRADE WITH OTHER NATIONS?

There are several reasons why one country would trade with others. First, no nation, even a technologically advanced one, can produce all of the products that its people want and need. Second, even if a country became self-sufficient, other nations would demand trade with that country to meet their people's needs. Third, some nations have an abundance of natural resources and a lack of technological know-how. Other countries (for example, Japan) have sophisticated technology, but few natural resources. Trade relations enable each nation to produce what it's most capable of producing and to buy what it needs in a mutually beneficial exchange relationship. This happens through the process of free trade. **Free trade** is the movement of goods and services among nations without political or economic obstruction.

free trade
The movement of goods and services among nations without political or economic obstruction.

... THE THEORIES OF COMPARATIVE ...
AND ABSOLUTE ADVANTAGE

International trade is the exchange of goods and services across national borders. Exchanges between and among countries involve more than goods and services, however. Countries also exchange art, athletes, cultural events, medical advances, space exploration, and labor. The guiding principle behind international economic exchanges is the economic **comparative advantage theory**. This theory states that a country should produce and sell to other countries those products that it produces most effectively and efficiently, and it should buy from other countries those products that it can't produce as effectively or efficiently.

comparative advantage theory
Theory which asserts that a country should produce and sell to other countries those products that it produces most efficiently.

The United States has a comparative advantage in producing many goods and services, such as those in high-tech products and engineering services. Figure 3.1 lists successful U.S. exporters. On the other hand, the United States doesn't have a comparative advantage in producing some shoes, coffee, videotape recorders, and other products that it imports.

A country has an **absolute advantage** if it has a monopoly on the production of a specific product or can produce it more cheaply than all other nations. For instance, South Africa dominates diamond production. There are very few instances of absolute advantage in today's competitive global economy.

absolute advantage
When a country has a monopoly on producing a product or is able to produce it at a cost below that of all other countries.

FIGURE 3.1

SUCCESSFUL U.S.
EXPORTERS

COMPANY	EXPORTS AS A PERCENTAGE OF TOTAL SALES
Boeing	57.5%
Sun Microsystems	49.2
Intel	39.1
Caterpillar	32.8
McDonnell Douglas	28.5
Hewlett-Packard	22.6
Chrysler	19.1
General Electric	13.2

Source: "The Top U.S. Exporters," *Fortune*, June 14, 1993, p. 131.

GETTING INVOLVED IN GLOBAL TRADE

Students often wonder which U.S. firms are best for finding a job in international business. Naturally, the discussion focuses on large multinational firms (for example, Boeing, GM, Ford, GE, IBM, and DuPont), which have large global accounts. But the real secret to success in international business may be with small businesses. Getting started is often a matter of observation, determination, and risk. What does that mean? First of all, it's important to research and study those global markets that interest you. The college library is often a good first stop. If possible, travel internationally to get some feel for the culture and lifestyles of various countries to see if you really want to work and trade outside the United States.

For example, a traveler in one part of Africa noticed that there was no ice available for drinks, for keeping foods fresh, and so on. Further research showed that, in fact, there was no ice factory for hundreds of miles, yet the market seemed huge. The man returned to the United States, found some willing investors, and went back to Africa to build an ice-making plant. Much negotiation was necessary with the authorities (negotiation best done by locals who know the system), and the plant was built. Now the man is indeed wealthy and the country has a needed resource available.

••• IMPORTING GOODS AND SERVICES •••

Students frequently find that importing goods into the United States can be quite profitable. International students attending U.S. colleges and universities often notice that some products widely available in their countries aren't available in the United States or are more costly here. By working with native producers and finding some working capital, these students have become major importers.

Several years ago, executives from Minnetonka, Inc., of Chaska, Minnesota, were browsing in a German supermarket when they noticed a fascinating new product—toothpaste in a pump dispenser. The company contacted Henkel,

One way to participate in global exchanges is to import products from other countries. The picture shows the Tullycross Fine Irish Imports store in Philadelphia, which sells quality goods from Ireland. No doubt you have seen similar stores selling shoes from Italy, and so on. If not, shop around and see if managing or owning such stores might be an interesting career possibility.

the German manufacturer, and together they introduced the product into the United States as Check-Up toothpaste. It became so popular that Colgate, Crest, and other major brands soon followed with their own versions of the pump. Maybe you too could find such products to bring back to the United States.

••• EXPORTING GOODS AND SERVICES •••

Once you decide to get into international trade, you'll be surprised at what you can sell globally. Who would think, for example, that a U.S. firm could sell beer in Germany, where there are so many good beers? Yet right around the corner from a famous beer hall in Munich you can buy Samuel Adams Boston Lager. Some 16,000 cases have been sold, and a local licensing agreement will ensure more sales to come. American brewing giant Anheuser-Busch took the hint. It has leveled its firepower at the global market and expects sales globally to expand to $30 million in 1994.[4] But you haven't heard anything yet. Can you imagine selling sand to the Middle East? Meridan Group sells a special kind of sand used in swimming pool filters. A Rhode Island fishery sells sushi to Japan.

So what can you sell to other countries? You can sell them just about anything of quality you can sell in the United States. You can sell snowplows to the Saudi Arabians. Why? They use them to plow sand off their driveways. Just about any good or service that's used in the United States is needed in other countries, and the competition is often not nearly as stiff for most of them.

But don't be mistaken—that isn't to say that selling internationally is easy. We'll discuss many of the hurdles later in the chapter. Adapting products to specific global markets is often essential. A good example of this is in the box Reaching beyond Our Borders.

To get started in exporting, write for *The Basic Guide to Exporting* (Government Printing Office, Superintendent of Documents, Washington, D.C., 20402). More advice can be found in *Business America*, a trade magazine published by the U.S. Department of Commerce's International Trade Administration. You can order it from the Government Printing Office as well. Also, call the Small Business Administration and ask for a copy of *Exportise*. A visit to your campus library is also a big help.

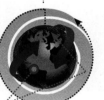

Reaching Beyond Our Borders

Where's the Beef? Not in India!

"**W**ould you like fries with that?" is a question asked daily around the globe. That's because McDonald's is one of the world's most successful multinational corporations and global franchisors. With 4,400 of its over 13,000 restaurants located outside the United States, the golden arches stand tall in world markets. Now India, one of the last holdouts, is about to add the arches to its landscape. However, Big Mac faces a problem. In India, four out of five Indians are Hindu, and the cow is sacred! How do you serve a beefless burger?

No problem, says McDonald's. The company plans to serve a nonbeef meat substitute between its famous buns. With a market of over 844 million people and the government's new economic reform drive, India presents an opportunity too good to pass up. McDonald's

hasn't decided yet whether to serve up grilled lamb or a chickenburger. The only thing the company has promised is the same quality and good taste that can be found in all its restaurants around the globe. However, Surendra Pratap Singh, an Indian columnist, warns that the product will be somewhat of a luxury in India, much different from the fast-food notion in the United States. McDonald's spokesperson Brad Trask seems unconcerned. "With an educated middle class larger than the population of the United States, that's an impressive market." The company planned to open its first Indian restaurant in 1995.

Source: Valerie Reitman, "India Anticipates the Arrival of the Beefless Big Mac," *The Wall Street Journal*, January 4, 1994, p. B1; and "American Firms Chasing Golden Calf in India," *St. Louis Post-Dispatch*, January 2, 1994, p. 2A.

••• MEASURING GLOBAL TRADE •••

balance of trade
The relationship of exports to imports.

trade deficit
Buying more goods from other nations than are sold to them.

balance of payments
The difference between money coming into a country (from exports) and money leaving the country (for imports) plus money flows from other factors such as tourism, foreign aid, military expenditures, and foreign investment.

dumping
Selling products for less in a foreign country than is charged in the producing country.

In measuring the effectiveness of global trade, nations carefully follow two key indicators: balance of trade and balance of payments. The **balance of trade** is the relationship of exports to imports. A *favorable balance of trade,* or trade surplus, occurs when the value of exports exceeds imports. An *unfavorable balance of trade,* or **trade deficit**, occurs when the value of imports exceeds exports. It's easy to understand why countries prefer to export more than they import. If I sell you $200 worth of goods and buy only $100 worth, I have an extra $100 available to buy other things. However, I'm in an unfavorable position if I buy $200 worth of goods and sell only $100.

The **balance of payments** is the difference between money coming into a country (from exports) and money leaving the country (for imports) plus money flows from other factors such as tourism, foreign aid, military expenditures, and foreign investment. The amount of money flowing into or out of a country for tourism and other reasons may offset a trade imbalance. The goal is always to have more money flowing into the country than flowing out of the country. This is called a *favorable balance of payments*.

To make certain trade is being conducted globally on a fair basis, laws have been enforced to prohibit dumping. **Dumping** is the practice of selling products in foreign countries for less than you charge for the same products in your own country. This tactic is sometimes applied to unload surplus products in foreign markets or to gain a foothold in a new market by offering products cheaper than domestic competitors. South Korea and Japan, for example, have been accused of such dumping practices. The United States has laws against dumping, specifying that foreign firms must price their products to include 10 percent overhead costs plus 8 percent profit margin. Dumping is hard to prove, however. Also, some governments will subsidize certain industries to sell goods in international markets for less. Charges of dumping have been made against manufacturers of several products, including steel, motorcycles, and computer flat-panel screens.[5]

Now that you understand some terms, we can discuss global business in depth. The first question to address is how and what the United States is doing in world trade. Before doing so, however, let's check your progress.

PROGRESS CHECK

- Explain why statistics show that international trade is the real key to the future for U.S. business. (The statistics include world population, size of market, and growth of market).

- Examine the difference between comparative advantage and absolute advantage. State some examples in actual global markets.

- What's the difference between balance of trade and balance of payments?

TRADING IN GLOBAL MARKETS: THE U.S. EXPERIENCE

Fully 95 percent of the world's population lies outside the United States; this group is growing 70 percent faster than the American population. However, the United States in general has never been very active at exporting. How can this be true when the United States is the world's largest exporter? Even though the United States exports the largest *volume* of goods, we export a much lower *percentage* of our products than other countries. In the early 1980s, no more than 10 percent of U.S. businesses exported products. However, slow economic growth in the United States and the lower value of the dollar lured more businesses to overseas markets in the late 1980s and early 1990s. Now some 55 percent of large businesses are involved in global trade, and growing numbers of small businesses are going global.

Although the United States is the world's largest exporter, it doesn't export a significant percentage of its gross domestic product (GDP) ◀-- P.72 --▶. In other words, the United States doesn't depend on exporting as much as other industrialized economies such as Japan and Germany. For many years it exported more goods and services than it imported. In 1985, however, the United States bought more goods from other nations than it sold to other nations. Remember, this is called a *trade deficit* or *unfavorable balance of trade*. The highest trade deficit is with Japan. For that reason, the U.S. and Japanese governments are trying to devise strategies acceptable to both countries. However, in 1994 the merchandise trade deficit with Japan stood at $59.3 billion. This caused President Clinton to threaten to retaliate against the Japanese if their market wasn't opened to more U.S. products.[6] As you'll note in Figure 3.2, foreign companies do very little business in Japan.

France	28%
United Kingdom	24
United States	16
Germany	14
Japan	1

Source: *1994 Economic Report of the President.*

FIGURE 3.2

MARKET SHARE OF FOREIGN COMPANIES IN FIVE MAJOR COUNTRIES

In 1994, the U.S. trade deficit for goods (merchandise) was approximately $170 billion. However, the United States has a surplus trading in the service sector.[7] This trade surplus in the service sector may help pull the American goods and services balance of trade up to surplus levels in the future.

Another way that economists measure a nation's economic activity is to compare the amount of money a country owes to foreign creditors and the value of assets it owns in foreign countries with the money foreigners owe to it and the value of assets that foreigners own in the country. During the 1980s, it was widely reported that the United States had become a **debtor nation** (a country that owes more money to other nations than they owe it). At first, it was reported that we were the "greatest debtor nation in the world," which created quite a stir. Eventually, the Bureau of Economic Analysis revised the figures for the 1980s and concluded that the "debt" wasn't as high as some people imagined. In reality, the United States in 1990 took in some $7 billion more in investment income from its foreign holdings than it paid out to foreign creditors. Such figures indicate that the federal government's data are often questionable if not incorrect. Nonetheless, there's a trend toward foreign direct investment in the United States.

Foreign direct investment is the buying of permanent property and businesses in foreign nations. Visible examples of this in the United States are the purchase of Firestone by Bridgestone (a Japanese tire producer) and Honda's opening an auto plant in Marysville, Ohio.[8] Many viewed these events as well as the sale of Rockefeller Center and Columbia Records as a wholesale selling out of America to the Japanese. However, those who view foreign investment in the United States as a sign of strength contend that foreign firms are investing in the United States because the American economy over the past several years has been very strong. Property, buildings, and stock in U.S. firms have simply been more attractive than their counterparts in other countries. The time to worry is when investors find other countries more attractive. Figure 3.3 shows the nations with the largest direct foreign investment in the United States.

Contrary to what some people imply, it isn't necessarily a good sign when U.S. businesses invest more internationally than foreign businesses invest here. It may mean that the United States is no longer perceived as a strong economic leader, and foreign investors are no longer investing in our businesses' stock or building new plants here.

debtor nation
Country that owes more money to other nations than they owe it.

foreign direct investment
Buying of permanent property and businesses in foreign nations.

The size of the U.S. market and the competitiveness of American workers make foreign direct investment in the United States attractive. Here, former South Carolina Governor Carroll Campbell and BMW Chief Executive Eberhard Kuenheim break ground for the auto maker's new plant in South Carolina. The state provided incentives to the auto maker for its long-term investment.

United Kingdom	$110 billion
Japan	$80 billion
Netherlands	$68 billion
Canada	$38 billion

Source: U.S. Commerce Department.

FIGURE 3.3

COUNTRIES WITH THE HIGHEST FOREIGN DIRECT INVESTMENT IN THE UNITED STATES

If you're getting the idea that the national income accounting (which determines a nation's debt status) is confusing, you're right. You may need to take a course in international economics or international accounting if you plan to get involved in international trade. This will help you understand what's behind the sometimes misleading statistics.

CRITICAL THINKING

You've read that some 95 percent of the world's population lives outside the United States, but a relatively small percentage of U.S. companies engage in world trade. In 1992, exports were only 10.6 percent of GDP.[9] Why is that? What do such figures indicate about the future potential for increasing U.S. exports? What do they say about future careers in international business?

STRATEGIES FOR REACHING GLOBAL MARKETS

An organization may participate in international trade in many ways, including exporting and importing, joint venturing, licensing, creating subsidiaries, contract manufacturing, franchising, and countertrading. Pay close attention to these topics because they represent future careers that will be both challenging and rewarding for the savvy college graduate.

••• EXPORTING •••

Because so many U.S. firms are reluctant to go through the trouble of establishing international trading relationships, it makes sense that some organization would step in to negotiate such exchanges for them. In fact, Congress authorized such organizations in 1982. They're called **export trading companies**. An export trading company serves the role of matching buyers and sellers from different countries. A good place to get experience in international trade is at such an export house. Some companies handle exporting functions internally in the form of an export department or an export section in marketing. GE's trading department has 60 bilingual workers with M.B.A. (master of business administration) degrees, 70 percent of whom are foreign-born. Students who learn foreign languages in school and enter international trade have an opportunity to improve the success of export trading firms and make good money besides.

export trading companies
Companies that attempt to match buyers and sellers from different countries.

••• LICENSING •••

A firm may decide to service a growing global market by **licensing** to a foreign company the right to manufacture its product or use its trademark on a royalty basis. The company generally sends representatives to the foreign producer to help set up the production process. It may also assist in such areas as distribution and promotion.

licensing
Agreement in which a producer allows a foreign company to produce its product in exchange for royalties.

Coke has licensing agreements in several countries. This is a Coke can as sold in China. It is sometimes amusing to see American products overseas with pictures of Mickey Mouse or other well-known U.S. characters. Foreign companies buy the rights to use such images on their products.

foreign subsidiary
A company owned by another company (parent company) in a foreign country.

contract manufacturing
Production of private-label goods by a company to which another company then attaches its brand name or trademark.

A licensing agreement can be beneficial to a firm in several different ways. Through licensing, an organization can gain additional revenues from a product that it wouldn't have normally generated domestically. In addition, foreign licensees often must purchase start-up supplies, component materials, and consulting services from the licensing firm. Coke and Pepsi often enter foreign markets through licensing agreements that typically extend into long-term service contracts. One final advantage of licensing worth noting is that licensors spend little or no money to produce and market their products. These costs come from the licensee's pocket. Therefore, licensees generally work very hard to see that the product succeeds in their market. The more sales, the more royalties.

Unfortunately, licensing agreements may provide some disadvantages to a company. One major problem is that often a firm must grant licensing rights to its product for an extended period, maybe as long as 20 years. If a product experiences remarkable growth in the foreign market, the bulk of the revenues go to the licensee. Perhaps even more threatening is that a licensing firm is actually selling its expertise in a product area. If a foreign licensee learns the technology, it may break the agreement and begin to produce a similar product on its own. If legal remedies aren't available, the licensing firm loses its trade secrets, not to mention the agreed-upon royalties.

••• CREATING SUBSIDIARIES •••

As the size of a foreign market expands, a firm may want to establish a foreign subsidiary. A **foreign subsidiary** is a company that's owned by another company (called a parent company) in a foreign country. Such a subsidiary would operate much like a domestic firm, with production, distribution, promotion, pricing, and other business functions under the control of the foreign subsidiary's management. Of course, the legal requirements of both home and host countries would have to be observed. The primary advantage of a subsidiary is that the company maintains complete control over any technology or expertise it may possess. Nestlé is one example of a major firm with many foreign subsidiaries. The Swiss company has spent over $10 billion to acquire foreign subsidiaries such as Carnation in the United States and Perrier in France.[10]

The major shortcoming associated with creating a foreign subsidiary is that the company is committing a large amount of funds and technology within foreign boundaries. Should relations with the host country falter, the firm's assets could be taken over by that nation's government.

••• CONTRACT MANUFACTURING •••

Contract manufacturing involves the production of private-label goods by a company to which another company then attaches its brand name or trademark. This is also called *outsourcing*. Many well-known firms such as Levi Strauss and Nike practice contract manufacturing. In such a situation, factors such as distribution or promotion can be handled by the firm or its foreign producer. Through contract manufacturing a company can often experiment in a new market without heavy start-up costs. If the brand name becomes a success, the company has penetrated a new market with reduced risk.

• • • FRANCHISING • • •

Franchising is popular both domestically and in global markets. We'll discuss franchising in depth in Chapter 5. Firms such as McDonald's, 7-Eleven, Ramada Inn, Avis, and Dunkin' Donuts have many overseas units operated by franchisees. McDonald's alone has over 1,000 outlets in Japan, 275 in Latin America, and 3 in China.[11] Franchisors have to be careful to adapt in the countries they serve. For example, Kentucky Fried Chicken's first 11 Hong Kong outlets failed within two years. Apparently, the chicken was too greasy and messy to be eaten with fingers by the fastidious people of Hong Kong. McDonald's also made a mistake when entering the Amsterdam market. It originally set up operations in the suburbs, as it does in the United States, but soon learned that Europeans mostly live in the cities. Therefore, McDonald's began to open outlets downtown. Pizza Hut serves spinach and sauerkraut pizza in Germany; corned beef, corn, and pea pizza in Hong Kong; and sardine, tuna, and mackerel pizza in Russia.

Nike Town in Chicago offers footware fanciers the ultimate stroll through sneakerland. Nike is one of many U.S. companies that make use of contract manufacturing. With contract manufacturing (or outsourcing) a company contracts with another firm to produce its products and then attach its brand name to them. Nike does most of its outsourcing with firms in the Far East.

• • • INTERNATIONAL JOINT VENTURES • • •

A **joint venture** is a partnership in which companies (often from two different countries) join to undertake a major project. Such alliances increased 47 percent annually from 1984 to 1994. A survey of affiliations by U.S.–based companies reported about 12,000 in which the American company owned a 10 to 50 percent equity position in a foreign firm. As noted in the profile about Virginia Kamsky, it's often hard to gain entry into a country like China whose economy is centrally planned. Joint ventures often help. For example, Campbell Soup formed a joint venture with Nakano Vinegar Company, a Japanese food concern. The alliance gives Campbell a chance to expand its rather skimpy 3 percent market share in Japan's "Western" soup market.

America's largest retailer, Wal-Mart, formed a joint venture with Mexico's top retailer, CIFRA SA, in 1991. Mexico's small retail industry makes it fertile territory for U.S. retailers like Wal-Mart. Even law firms are entering into joint ventures with foreign firms. For instance, a Washington, D.C., firm that specializes in transportation law has negotiated a joint venture law practice with a Belgian firm. The company offers American businesses European expertise and experience, and helps European businesses in the United States.

Joint ventures are nothing new in international trade. Perhaps the most visible example is the cooperation between major department stores and foreign producers of TV sets, videotape recorders, and other such goods. The foreign company produces the goods, and U.S. corporations provide the distribution and promotion expertise. In the United States, names such as Panasonic, Samsung, and Sony are as familiar as GE and Westinghouse because of joint ventures.

The benefits of international joint ventures are clear: shared technology, shared marketing expertise, entry into markets where foreign goods aren't allowed unless produced locally, and shared risk. The drawbacks aren't so

joint venture
A partnership in which companies (often from two or more different countries) join to undertake a major project.

obvious. An important one is that the partner can learn your technology and practices and go off on its own as a competitor—a rather common practice. Also, over time, the technology may become obsolete, or the partnership may be too large to be as flexible as needed.[12]

••• COUNTERTRADING •••

bartering
The exchange of goods or services for goods or services.

countertrading
Bartering among several countries.

One of the oldest forms of trade is called **bartering**, the exchange of merchandise for merchandise, service for service, or service for merchandise with no money involved. **Countertrading** is more complex than bartering in that several countries may be involved, each trading goods for goods or services for services. It has been estimated that countertrading accounts for 25 percent of all international exchanges.

Examples of countertrade and bartering agreements are many. Chrysler traded its vehicles in Jamaica for bauxite. McDonnell Douglas traded jets in the former Yugoslavia for canned hams. General Motors has traded vehicles with China for industrial gloves and cutting tools.

Barter is especially important to poor countries that have little cash available for trade. Such countries may barter with all kinds of raw materials, food, or whatever resources they have.[13] Colombia has traded coffee for buses. Romania traded cement for steam engines. The Sudan pays for Pepsi concentrate with sesame seeds. Tanzania uses sisal, and Nicaragua uses sesame seeds and molasses for barter.

With many emerging economies still in a state of flux, countertrading surely will grow in importance throughout the 1990s. Trading products for products helps avoid some problems and hurdles experienced in global markets.

HURDLES OF TRADING IN GLOBAL MARKETS

Succeeding in any business takes work and effort, due to the many hurdles you encounter. Unfortunately, the hurdles get higher and more complex in world markets. This is particularly true in dealing with differences in cultural perspectives, societies and economies, laws and regulations, and fluctuations in currencies. Let's look at each of these hurdles next.

••• CULTURAL DIFFERENCES •••

ethnocentricity
The feeling that one's culture is superior to all others.

If you hope to get involved in international trade, one thing you must learn is the cultural differences among nations. Different nations have very different ways of conducting business, and American businesspeople are notoriously bad at adapting. In fact, American businesspeople have consistently been accused of **ethnocentricity.** This means they feel that our culture is superior to all others and that our job is to teach others the American way of doing things. On the other hand, most foreign businesspeople are very good at adapting to the American culture. Let's give you a couple of examples to show how American businesses have difficulty in adapting to important cultural differences.

Religion—an important part of any society's culture—can have a significant impact on business operations. Consider the tragedy in Bosnia. Think how this clash between the Islamic and Christian communities there has crippled the economy. In Islamic countries, dawn-to-dusk fasting during the month of Ramadan causes workers' output to drop considerably. Also, the requirement to pray five times daily can affect output. For example, an American manager in Islamic Pakistan toured a new plant under his control in full operation. He went to his office to make some pre liminary forecasts of production. As he was working, suddenly all the machinery in the plant stopped. He rushed out expecting a possible power failure and instead found his production workers on their prayer rugs. He returned to his office and lowered his production estimates.

Cultural differences also impact such important business factors as human resource management. In Latin American countries, workers see managers as authoritarian figures responsible for their well-being. Consider what happened to one American manager who believed workers should participate in managerial functions. This person neglected one important cultural characteristic. This manager was convinced he could motivate his workers in Peru to higher levels of productivity by instituting a more democratic decision-making style. He even brought in trainers from the United States to teach his supervisors to solicit suggestions and feedback from workers. Shortly after his new style was put in place, workers began quitting their jobs in droves. When asked why, Peruvian workers said the new production manager and supervisors didn't know their jobs and were asking the workers what to do. All stated they wanted to quit and find new jobs since obviously this company was doomed because of incompetent managers.

Without question, culture presents a significant hurdle for global managers. The reality of growing cultural diversity in the U.S. workplace highlights differences and distinctions even in our domestic market. Therefore, learning about important cultural perspectives about time, change, competition, natural resources, achievement, and even work itself in global markets can be of great assistance. Today, firms often provide classes and training for managers and their families on how to adapt to different cultures and avoid culture shock. Involvement in courses in cultural variations and anthropology can assist you in understanding foreign cultures.

Cultural differences affect not only management behaviors but global marketing strategies as well. **Global marketing** is the term used to describe selling the same product in essentially the same way everywhere in the world. The growth of satellite systems makes it possible to have worldwide promotions. The question is whether international promotions will be successful given the problems we just discussed. Some companies have developed universal appeals. Brand names such as Coca-Cola, Disney, IBM, Ford, and Toyota have widespread global appeal and recognition. Apple Computer shifted its focus from "global sales" to global marketing. The company intends to have the same brand identity every place and have the same promotional campaigns running worldwide to the extent that the campaign makes sense.[14] Others, unfortunately, have hit the hurdles and failed. Some past experiences reveal the problems of global marketing. For example, translating a theme into a different language can be disastrous. Look at the trouble General Motors had with two products:

"Body by Fisher" was translated as "Corpse by Fisher."

The Chevrolet Nova had little appeal in Spanish-speaking countries because *no va* in Spanish means, It doesn't go.

Thousands of similar stories could be told. The truth is that many U.S. manufacturers often fail to think globally. For example, most auto producers still don't adapt cars to drive on the left side of the road, as is done in many countries. They often print instructions only in English. We're one of only five nations

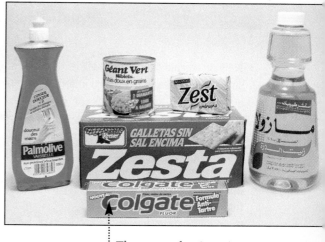

These popular American products are packaged for international markets. U.S. producers must learn the cultures of other nations so that the design of products and packages and the selection of distribution channels match the needs of different countries. Each country poses a different challenge calling for a different marketing strategy.

global marketing
Selling the same product in essentially the same way everywhere in the world.

FROM THE PAGES OF... Entrepreneur MAGAZINE

Funding Global Ventures

Nothing has inhibited the growth of small businesses trying to sell internationally more than the lack of reliable sources of working capital. A small business may get an order and its banker may be somewhat interested, but the money may take so long in coming that the small business loses the order. Businesses whose assets are already pledged for long-term loans are not likely to get any more money from banks.

Recognizing this problem, the Small Business Administration (SBA) recently started an Export Working Capital Program (EWCP) which replaces the SBA's Export Revolving Line of Credit. Under this program, the SBA guarantees up to 90 percent of loans up to $750,000. Guarantees can be extended for pre-shipment working capital (used to finance the production or acquisition of goods and services for export) or post-shipment working capital (used to finance receivables from export sales).

The loans are for a 12-month period, but may be renewed twice, up to a total of 36 months. When reviewing such loans, the SBA looks at each transaction's viability, the reliability of the repayment sources, and the exporter's ability to perform. Small businesses can apply directly to the SBA for such loans.

The SBA offers other services for exporters. A free publication called *Bankable Deals: A Question and Answer Guide to Trade Finance for Small Businesses* answers questions about export financing. Counseling and training programs are also available to small business exporters. For more on what the SBA offers the small business exporter, you can call the Office of International Trade at 1-800-U-ASK-SBA.

Source: Erskine Bowles, "Export Help," *Entrepreneur*, November 1994, p. 202.

---

that refuse to conform to the metric system. The problems go on and on. Since global marketing works only in limited cases, it's critical that U.S. exporters thoroughly research foreign markets before attempting to penetrate global markets.

••• SOCIETAL AND ECONOMIC DIFFERENCES •••

Certain social and economic realities are often overlooked by American businesses. Kids 'R' Us, the clothing subsidiary of Toys 'R' Us, missed the mark in Puerto Rico. The company banked heavily on back-to-school sales, but failed to understand that Puerto Rican kids all wear uniforms to school. Also, a good deal of the clothing line was too heavy for the climate. Jeff Handler, the company marketing director, admitted it missed on the market's tastes.[15] You'd think the close association of Puerto Rico to the United States would make the market almost identical to ours. Unfortunately, as Kids 'R' Us found out, that's not always so.

Surely it's hard for us to imagine buying chewing gum by the stick instead of by the package. However, in economically depressed nations like the Philippines this buying behavior is commonplace because consumers have only enough money to buy small quantities. What might seem like an opportunity of a lifetime may in fact be unreachable due to economic conditions.

Technological constraints may also make it difficult or impossible to carry on effective trade. For example, some less developed countries have such primitive transportation and storage systems that international food exchanges are ineffective, because the food is spoiled by the time it reaches consumers. Americans are astonished at conditions in nations such as Somalia. These constraints are often further complicated by the tremendous geographic distances between and within some countries.

American exporters must also be aware that certain technological differences affect the nature of exportable products. For example, how would the differences in electricity available (110 versus 220 volts) affect an American appliance manufacturer wishing to export?

• • • LEGAL AND REGULATORY DIFFERENCES • • •

In any economy, the conduct and direction of business is firmly tied to the legal and regulatory environment. In the United States, business operations are heavily impacted by various federal, state, and local laws and regulations. In global markets, several groups of laws and regulations may apply. This makes conducting world business even tougher.

What businesspeople find in global markets is a myriad of laws and regulations that are often inconsistent. Important legal questions related to antitrust rules, labor relations, patents, copyrights, trade practices, taxes, product liability, child labor, prison labor, and other issues are written and interpreted differently country by country. To compound problems, American businesspeople are required to follow U.S. laws and regulations in conducting business affairs. For example, legislation such as the **Foreign Corrupt Practices Act of 1978** can create hardships for American businesspeople in competing with other foreign competitors. This law specifically prohibits "questionable" or "dubious" payments to foreign officials to secure business contracts. In many countries, corporate bribery is acceptable and perhaps the only way to secure a lucrative contract.

To be a successful trader in foreign countries, you might choose to begin by contacting local businesspeople and gaining their cooperation and sponsorship. The problem is that foreign bureaucracies are often stumbling blocks to successful international trade. To penetrate those barriers, often you must find a local sponsor who can pay the necessary fees to gain government permission. As we saw in the Profile at the start of this chapter, Ms. Kamsky's job in China is to smooth the way toward trade with China, one of the more difficult international jobs because of the Chinese bureaucracy.

Foreign Corrupt Practices Act of 1978
Law that prohibits "questionable" or "dubious" payments to foreign officials to secure business contracts.

• • • PROBLEMS WITH CURRENCY SHIFTS • • •

The global market doesn't have a universal currency. Mexicans shop with pesos, Germans with deutsche marks, South Koreans with won, the British with pounds, and Americans with dollars. These currencies' widely fluctuating values make world trade difficult. For example, today one dollar may be exchanged for 2 deutsche marks, but tomorrow you may only get 1.5 marks for your dollar. The **exchange rate** is the value of one currency relative to the currencies of other countries. Global markets operate under a system of **floating exchange rates** in which currencies "float" according to the supply and demand in the market for the currency. For example, a *high value of the dollar* means that a dollar would buy more foreign goods (or would be traded for more foreign currency) than normal. *Lowering the value of the dollar* means that a dollar can buy less internationally than it once did (or is traded for less foreign currency). That makes foreign goods more expensive because it takes more dollars to buy them. It also makes American goods cheaper to foreign buyers because it takes less foreign currency to buy American goods. At certain times, countries will intervene and adjust the value of their currencies. **Devaluation** is lowering the value of a nation's currency relative to other currencies.

Changes in currencies cause many problems. Consider the H. B. Fuller Company, which has 43 plants in 27 foreign countries making paints, adhesives, and coatings. Mr. Fuller feels that his most dramatic problem is in the

exchange rate
The value of one currency relative to the currencies of other countries.

floating exchange rate
Value of currencies fluctuate according to the supply and demand in the market for the currency.

devaluation
Lowering the value of a nation's currency relative to other currencies.

Making Ethical Decisions

Global Hand-Me-Downs

As a top manager of Nightie Nite, a maker of children's sleepwear, you're aware of all the U.S. government regulations that affect your industry. A recent safety regulation prohibits the use of the fabric that you've been using for girls' nightgowns for the past 15 years. Apparently, the fabric lacks sufficient flame-retardant capabilities to meet U.S. government standards. In fact, last week Nightie Nite lost a lawsuit brought against it by the parents of a severely burned young child whose nightgown burst into flames when she got too close to a gas stove. Not only did you lose the lawsuit, but you may also lose your nightshirt if you don't find another market for your warehouse full of nightgowns in inventory. You realize that some countries don't have such restrictive laws concerning products sold within their borders. You're considering exporting your products to these countries. What are your alternatives? What are the consequences of each alternative? What will you do?

currency area. He has an adhesive plant in Japan, where the yen's value went from 260 yen to an American dollar to below 90. Since you can't control currency, you must learn to control your business. Mr. Fuller uses currency fluctuations to his advantage now by buying raw materials from sources with relatively weak currencies.

Never before have so many economies used U.S. dollars. The Federal Reserve Board estimates that nearly two thirds of the $300 billion of U.S. currency in circulation has gone abroad.[16] This may sound like a rather worrisome statement. However, cash accounts for less than 9 percent of the U.S. money supply.

Understanding currency fluctuations and financing opportunities is vital to success in the global market. It isn't surprising that Virginia Kamsky started out in banking. Banks traditionally have led the way in financing export operations in the United States. However, American banks aren't always willing to provide export financing, and U.S. exporters have to turn to foreign banks and other sources for financing. This is often especially true for small and medium-sized businesses. They have to use their wits and scour the globe for financing. Fortunately, a growing number of U.S. government, multilateral, and interregional agencies are available for financing.[17] Figure 3.4 lists some of them.

What this means for you is that there will be a tremendous opportunity in banking for people who are knowledgeable about the global market and willing to make loans for international trade.

CRITICAL THINKING

Many countries in the world are called less developed countries. Why are they less developed? Is it because they lack natural resources? Then how do you explain the success of Japan, which has few natural resources?

trade protectionism
The use of government regulations to limit the import of goods and services; based on the theory that domestic producers can survive and grow, producing more jobs.

TRADE PROTECTIONISM

Trade protectionism is the use of government regulations to limit the import of goods and services. Countries often use trade protectionism measures to protect their industries against dumping and foreign competition that hurts

FIGURE 3.4

U. S. GOVERNMENT,
MULTILATERAL, AND
INTRAREGIONAL SOURCES
OF GLOBAL FINANCING

Export-Import Bank It makes loans to exporters that can't secure financing through private sources and to foreign countries that use the funds to buy American goods.

International Finance Corporation (IFC) This organization makes loans to private businesses when they can't obtain loans from more conventional sources. It's affiliated with the World Bank.

International Development Association (IDA) This organization makes loans to private businesses and to member countries of the World Bank.

Inter-American Investment Corporation (IIC) It operates as an autonomous merchant banking corporation that will give preference to small and midsized companies that wish to expand.

European Bank for Reconstruction and Development Based in London, it has a mandate to devote 60 percent of its investment activity to private sector loans.

Overseas Private Investment Corporation This organization sells insurance to U.S. firms that operate overseas. It covers damages caused by war, revolution, or insurrection; inability to convert local currencies to U.S. dollars; and expropriation (takeover by foreign governments).

domestic industry. Protectionism is based on the theory that such practices will help domestic producers survive and grow, producing more jobs. Generally, it's not a good idea. As we said in the previous section, cultural differences, societal and economic factors, legal and regulatory requirements, and currency shifts are all hurdles to those wishing to trade globally. Often a much greater barrier to international trade is the overall political atmosphere between nations. This barrier is best understood through a review of some economic history of world trade.

Business, economics, and politics have always been closely linked. In fact, economics was once referred to as *political economy*, indicating the close ties between politics (government) and economics. For centuries, businesspeople have tried to influence economists and government officials. Back in the 16th, 17th, and 18th centuries, nations were trading goods (mostly farm products) with one another. Businesspeople at that time advocated an economic principle called *mercantilism*. Basically, the idea of **mercantilism** was to sell more goods to other nations than you bought from them, that is, to have a favorable balance of trade. This results in a flow of money to the country that sells the most. Governments assisted in this process by charging a tariff (basically a tax) on imports, making them more expensive.

There are two different kinds of tariffs: protective and revenue. **Protective tariffs** are designed to raise the retail price of imported products so that domestic products will be more competitive. These tariffs are meant to save jobs for domestic workers and to keep industries from closing down entirely because of foreign competition. **Revenue tariffs**, on the other hand, are designed to raise money for the government. Revenue tariffs are commonly used by developing countries. There's still much debate about the degree of protectionism a government should practice.

The term that describes limiting the number of products in certain categories that can be imported is **import quota**. The United States has had import quotas on a number of products such as beef and steel. Again, the goal was to protect industry to preserve jobs. An **embargo** is a complete ban on the import or export of certain products. The ban on the sale of Cuban cigars in the United States is one example. The United States also prohibits the export of some products. The Export Administration Act prohibits exporting goods that would endanger national security. Political considerations have caused many countries to establish embargoes.

mercantilism
The economic principle advocating the selling of more goods to other nations than a country buys.

protective tariff
Import tax designed to raise the price of imported products so that domestic products are more competitive.

revenue tariff
Import tax designed to raise money for the government.

import quota
Limiting the number of products in certain categories that can be imported.

embargo
A complete ban on the import or export of certain products.

James Thwaits, president of international operations of the 3M Company, says that as much as half of all world trade is limited by *nontariff barriers*. Japan has some of the lowest tariffs in the world, yet American businesses find it hard to establish trade relationships with the Japanese. The most important reason that even foreign companies offering high-quality products and services have difficulty penetrating Japanese markets is the Japanese tradition of forging semipermanent ties with suppliers, customers, and distributors. The Japanese believe that stable alliances provide economic payoffs by nurturing long-term strategic thinking and mutually beneficial cooperation.[18] Southwire Company (a small-town, Georgia-based company) found this out when it tried to penetrate the Japanese market. Southwire knew it could provide high-quality wire for Japanese utilities at prices 20 to 30 percent lower than its competitors in Japan. The company found no specific tariffs, quotas, or government obstacles apparent. Yet, it couldn't get a foothold in the market. Company officials complained that cozy relationships among buyers and sellers in Japan dictated keeping foreign suppliers out.[19] The U.S. government is investigating such practices and has threatened a possible trade war with Japan.

Such constraints on world trade could be viewed as good reasons to avoid world trade. But such constraints could also be viewed as a tremendous opportunity. The General Agreement on Tariffs and Trade (GATT) was established to deal with such trade questions. Let's look at the issues involved in the GATT agreement.

••• GENERAL AGREEMENT ON TARIFFS AND TRADE (GATT) •••

General Agreement on Tariffs and Trade (GATT)
Agreement among 124 countries which provided a forum for negotiating mutual reductions in trade restrictions.

In 1948, the **General Agreement on Tariffs and Trade (GATT)** was established. This agreement among 23 countries provided a forum for negotiating mutual reductions in trade restrictions. In short, government leaders from nations throughout the world have cooperated to create monetary and trade agreements that facilitate the exchange of goods, services, ideas, and cultural programs. In 1986, the Uruguay Round of GATT talks were convened to renegotiate trade agreements. After eight years of meetings, 124 nations agreed to a new GATT agreement. The U.S. House of Representatives and Senate approved the pact in 1994. The new GATT agreement lowered tariffs on average by 38 percent worldwide, extended GATT rules to new areas such as agriculture, services, and the protection of copyrights and patents, and created a new World Trade Organization (WTO) to mediate trade disputes.[20] It's estimated that the GATT agreement will slash tariffs on 8,000 categories of manufactured goods. The Clinton administration predicted the boost in trade could add $150 billion to the U.S. economy when the pact is fully in effect in 2004.[21] Trade Representative Mickey Kantor estimates an additional 2 million jobs could be added to the U.S. economy.[22]

Before you get too excited though, it's important to note the GATT agreement didn't resolve many of the internal national laws that impede trade expansion. For example, France was able to limit the import of popular U.S. films and TV programs under cultural customs claims. Also, questions arise about foreign countries' ability to challenge U.S. laws protecting consumers, workers, and the environment as unfair barriers to trade. The GATT's achievements were impressive, but many problems remain.[23]

••• COMMON MARKETS •••

One of the issues not resolved by the GATT talks is the concern that regional agreements such as NAFTA, and common markets such as the European Union (EU), will create regional alliances at the expense of global expansion.

Legal Briefcase

Two Sides of the Tariff Issue

Some people feel that tariffs are necessary to protect national markets from foreign competition. Their arguments include:

Tariffs save jobs. Tariffs should be used to keep cheap foreign labor from taking over American jobs.

Tariffs are imposed on the United States by its competitors. To make competition fair, we have to take mutual measures.

Tariffs protect industries vital to American security. The U.S. government has been protecting certain industries that are sensitive for our defense, such as the auto, aerospace, and shipbuilding industries.

Tariffs are needed to protect new domestic industries from established foreign competition. The so-called *infant industry argument* supports tariffs for new industries until they can compete with foreign competitors.

Opponents of tariffs respond by presenting the following negative effects tariffs can have:

Tariffs reduce competition. Any tool used to restrain international trade in effect reduces competition, with all the negative implications this has on the economy.

Tariffs tend to increase inflationary pressure. Tariffs raise consumer prices and, as such, stimulate inflation.

Tariffs tend to support special-interest groups. Tariffs usually benefit special-interest groups, such as local manufacturers.

Tariffs can lead to foreign retaliation and subsequent trade wars. If the United States imposes tariffs, so will its major trading partners.

Debate over trade restrictions will be a major part of international politics for the next decade. You may want to stay current with such discussions, because the future of global trade may very well depend on them.

A **common market** is a regional group of countries that have no internal tariffs, a common external tariff, and the coordination of laws to facilitate exchange among countries.

The EU is a group of nations in Western Europe that dissolved their economic borders in the early 1990s. Europe hopes to become a vast market of some 320 million people who trade freely and live and work where they please. Europe sees such integration as the only way to compete with Japan and the United States for world markets. There are signs that the United States may join Europe to form a Trans-Atlantic Free Trade Union (TRAFTA).[24]

The path to such unification is more difficult than we might imagine. The idea of free movement of labor, shared social programs, new and strange tax systems, and shared professional standards is rather scary to countries that are more used to fighting with one another than working as an economic unit. Imagine the struggles that emerge over a community language, just for starters! One advantage for Americans is that English has become Europe's common business language. Some American observers, however, fear that a European protectionist superstate may emerge. But early signs haven't justified those fears.

common market
A regional group of countries that have no internal tariffs, a common external tariff, and a coordination of laws to facilitate exchange; an example is the European Union.

••• THE NORTH AMERICAN FREE ••• TRADE AGREEMENT (NAFTA)

One of the most debated issues of the early 1990s was the **North American Free Trade Agreement (NAFTA)**. Opponents led primarily by organized labor and billionaire Ross Perot promised nothing short of economic disaster if the

North American Free Trade Agreement (NAFTA)
An agreement through which the United States, Canada, and Mexico formed a free trade area.

After years of intense negotiating and sometimes bitter debate, the U.S. Congress passed and President Bill Clinton signed the North American Free Trade Agreement (NAFTA) in 1994. In this photo, the president formally signs the bill in the presence of the vice president and former Democratic and Republican House leaders.

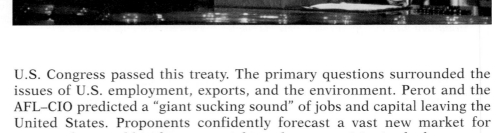

U.S. Congress passed this treaty. The primary questions surrounded the issues of U.S. employment, exports, and the environment. Perot and the AFL–CIO predicted a "giant sucking sound" of jobs and capital leaving the United States. Proponents confidently forecast a vast new market for exports that would in fact create jobs and opportunities in the long term. After a bitter debate, the U.S. House of Representatives narrowly passed the legislation. The Senate was more supportive and President Clinton signed the treaty into law. The combination of the United States, Canada, and Mexico creates a market of over 369 million people with a gross domestic product of $6.9 trillion.

free trade area

Market in which nations can trade freely without tariffs or other trade barriers.

NAFTA creates a **free trade area** where nations can trade freely with each other without tariffs or other trade barriers. The unification under NAFTA creates a market larger than the EU. However, as the EU discovered, the mechanics of making the system work are often more difficult than originally anticipated. NAFTA has already faced the difficulties caused by the devaluation of the peso in 1995.[25] The only certainty is that the emergence of economic blocs in North America, Europe, and the Far East will change the landscape of global trade in the 1990s and beyond. Some economists are concerned that as the world divides itself into three major trading blocs, poorer countries that don't fit into one of the blocs will suffer.

PROGRESS CHECK

- What are the major hurdles to successful international trade?
- American businesspeople are often said to suffer from ethnocentricity. What is ethnocentricity?
- Identify at least two cultural and societal differences that can affect global trade efforts.
- How could the Foreign Corrupt Practices Act affect U.S. foreign trade?
- What are the advantages and disadvantages of trade protectionism? Of tariffs?

MULTINATIONAL CORPORATIONS

There has been much discussion about the power of multinational corporations. It's helpful to first understand what they are and what they mean for international business. A **multinational corporation (MNC) is** an organization that does manufacturing and marketing in many different countries; it has multinational stock ownership and multinational management. The more multinational a company is, the more it attempts to operate without being influenced by restrictions from various governments.

Multinational corporations are typically extremely large corporations. Barnett and Muller's best-selling book *Global Reach* points out,

> *If we compare the annual sales of multinational corporations with the gross national product of countries . . . we discover that GM is bigger than Switzerland, Pakistan and South Africa, that Royal Dutch Shell is bigger than Iran, Venezuela and Turkey and that Goodyear Tire is bigger than Saudi Arabia.*

The size and scope of multinational businesses are evident. The multinational corporation is constantly checking opportunities for expansion all over the globe. It aggressively markets its products, capitalizing on its technological and managerial expertise. Caution should be exercised, however, before calling a company *multinational*. Not all firms involved in global business are multinationals. A company may be exporting its entire product, thus deriving 100 percent of its sales and profits internationally, but that alone wouldn't make it a multinational. Only firms that have manufacturing capacity or other physical presence in various nations can be called multinational.

THE FUTURE OF GLOBAL TRADE

The future of global trade gets brighter every day. New and growing markets present new opportunities. It's hoped that free trade will continue to lessen international tensions so that capital is freed up to invest in *business* rather than in military equipment. This is particularly true for nations such as the People's Republic of China and Russia. Just think about it: If consumers in China drank an average of just one extra can of Coca-Cola a year, the company would sell over a billion more Cokes.[26] This is obviously why Coca-Cola recently invested over $150 million in China. Foreign direct investment in China has grown from under $5 billion in 1987 to over $25 billion in 1993.[27] This is a major turnaround for the world's most populous country. Just a few years ago, investment in China was considered to be too risky and not worth the effort. Today, companies are flocking to China. Motorola has even established a training center for Chinese engineers, Motorola University, in Beijing.[28] The United States is obviously eager to trade with the Chinese. However, its most favored nation (MFN) status (an agreement that provides

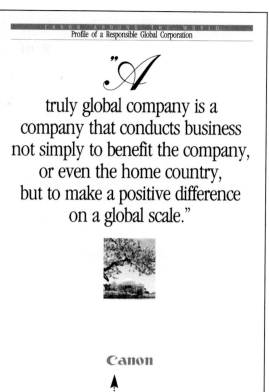

This ad captures the essence of effective global competition. International business is more than an economic game among competing nations. It is a way to bring prosperity to all, or at least make a good start.

multinational corporation
An organization that does manufacturing and marketing in many different countries; it has multinational stock ownership and multinational management.

SPOTLIGHT ON SMALL BUSINESS

A Place to Call Home: The Top 10 Export States

An old adage in retailing says three things are important for success: location, location, and location. The same holds true for success in global markets. Small and medium-sized businesses must closely look for the "right" location to base operations. Robert North of Tredegar Industries advises that the place with the best price isn't necessarily the best place. Factors such as great transportation, access to qualified labor and R&D, and international infrastructure are critical to compete in global markets.

With these criteria in mind, let's look at the top 10 U.S. locations in terms of exporting. Who knows, someday you may call one of these states home for your global venture:

1. *California.* Access to the Pacific Rim, Mexico, science and engineering talent, and high-tech vendors.

2. *Texas.* Strong international infrastructure without high cost. Business-friendly government, excellent transportation, good R&D, well-educated work force.

3. *Washington.* One out of five jobs is tied to international trade. Easy access to the Pacific Rim and European markets.

4. *New York.* Expensive but worth it. All the services you need for global success.

5. *Michigan.* Exports more than 27 percent of its factory output to Canada, Mexico, Germany, and Japan. State has 12-office export assistance network.

6. *Louisiana.* Ports of New Orleans and Baton Rouge send goods and services all around the world.

7. *Ohio.* Cutting edge customs system, export tax credit, financial incentives, and support services.

8. *Illinois.* Heart of the country and a direct link to diverse markets. Chicago offers traders the full spectrum of trade support services.

9. *Florida.* Natural export state has strong international banking system. Gateway to South and Central America.

10. *North Carolina.* Today's most favorite site has a host of benefits. Plans to be a global hub for air cargo. Raleigh/Durham cited as best area for knowledge workers.

Source: Kenneth Labich, "The Best Cities for Knowledge Workers," *Fortune*, November 15, 1993, pp. 50–58; and Robin Tierney, "The Top Ten Export States," *World Trade*, March 1993, pp. 66–73.

favorable trade benefits with the U.S.) has been threatened by China's policies on human rights and violations of intellectual property rights.[29] Let's hope both sides come to an accommodation.[30]

Since the fall of communism, Russia has been a prize coveted by many global traders. Like China, Russia presents enormous opportunities. Philip Morris, RJR Nabisco, Coca-Cola, Bristol-Myers, Squibb, and Gillette have established manufacturing facilities in Russia. Despite many political and social problems, firms are clearly attracted by Russia's 150 million potential customers craving consumer goods.[31] Music television (MTV) has found a home in Russia,[32] and Snickers virtually owns the chocolate market.[33] Free trade could be the ticket to the prosperity Russian citizens so desperately seek.

Many economists and business experts feel that Asia will be the primary growth market of the late 1990s. The U.S. decision to resume trade with Vietnam presents another opportunity for global expansion. The Big Three U.S. automakers feel direct investment in assembly plants in Vietnam is very likely. Add Vietnam to the growing list of emerging markets (such as India, Indonesia, Thailand, Singapore, Hong Kong, and Malaysia) and it's easy to see the great potential the Asian market holds for U.S. business.

••• GLOBALIZATION AND YOU •••

North American International Business magazine says we urgently need to improve U.S. managers' global skills. The same is true of students. As future entrepreneurs, managers, and business leaders, it's important now to *think globally* as you plan your future career. As the chapter points out, global markets are huge and basically untapped. By studying foreign languages and taking courses in foreign cultures, you'll develop a global perspective as you study business and think about a future career. The potential of global markets doesn't belong only to the multinational corporations. Small businesses are often better prepared to take the leap into global markets than large, cumbersome corporations saddled with bureaucracies. Read the Spotlight on Small Business box to see the best global locations. Also, don't forget the potential of franchising (which we examine in Chapter 5).

- What is a multinational corporation (MNC)? Can you name at least three multinational corporations?
- What are the major risks of doing business in countries like the People's Republic of China and Russia?
- How does the future for international trade appear?
- What factors might have an important impact on global trading?

PROGRESS CHECK

1. The world market for trade is huge. Some 95 percent of the people in the world live outside the United States.
   - **Why should nations trade with other nations?**
   (1) No country is self-sufficient. (2) Other countries need products that prosperous countries produce. (3) There's a world imbalance of natural resources and technological skills.
   - **What is the theory of comparative advantage?**
   The theory of comparative advantage contends that a country should produce and then sell those products it produces most efficiently but buy those it can't produce as efficiently.
   - **What is absolute advantage?**
   Absolute advantage means that a country has a monopoly on a certain product or can produce the product more efficiently than any other country can. For example, the U.S. has an absolute advantage in space satellite technology.

2. Students can get involved in world trade through importing and exporting. They don't have to work for big multinational corporations.
   - **What kinds of products can be imported and exported?**
   Just about any kind of product can be imported and exported. A potential importer or exporter has to find a need and fill it.
   - **What terms are important in understanding world trade?**
   Exporting is selling products to other countries. *Importing* is buying products from other countries. The *balance of trade* is the relationship of exports to imports. The *balance of payments* is the balance of trade plus other money flows such as tourism and foreign aid. *Dumping* is selling products for less in a foreign country than in your own country. *Trade protectionism* is the use of government regulations to limit the importation of products. Other important terms appear on the Key Terms list at the end of the chapter.

SUMMARY

1. Discuss the increasing importance of the global market and the roles of comparative advantage and absolute advantage in international trade.

2. Explain how the marketing motto "Find a need and fill it" applies to global markets and understand key terms used in international business.

3. Describe the current status of the United States in global business.

3. It was widely reported during the late 1980s and early 1990s that the United States was a "debtor nation." In fact, it was called the largest debtor nation in the world. However, the United States was earning more on its investments overseas than foreign investors were earning on their investments in the United States. That indicates that the United States was never in a debtor position, and the government data were faulty.

- ***How did the government make such a mistake?***

The government reported U.S. holdings at cost when the actual value of such holdings had increased dramatically. The best way to determine whether a nation is a net debtor is to look at income flows among nations. When income from foreign investments exceeds outgo, a nation isn't likely to be a debtor.

4. Illustrate the strategies used in reaching global markets.

4. A company can participate in world trade in a number of ways.

- ***What are some ways that a company can get involved in international business?***

Ways of entering world trade include exporting and importing, joint venturing, licensing, creating subsidiaries, franchising, and countertrading.

5. Identify the hurdles of trading in world markets.

5. There are many restrictions on foreign trade.

- ***What are some hurdles that can discourage participation in international business?***

Potential stumbling blocks to world trade include cultural differences, societal and economic differences, legal and regulatory differences, and fluctuations in different currencies.

6. Debate the advantages and disadvantages of trade protectionism.

6. Political differences are often the most difficult hurdles to international trade.

- ***What is trade protectionism?***

Trade protectionism is the use of government regulations to limit the import of goods and services, based on the theory that domestic producers can survive and grow, producing more jobs. The tools of protectionism are tariffs and embargoes.

- ***What are tariffs?***

Tariffs are taxes on foreign products. There are two kinds of tariffs: protective tariffs (which are used to raise the price of foreign products) and revenue tariffs (which are used to raise money for the government).

- ***What is an embargo?***

An embargo prohibits the importing or exporting of certain products.

- ***Is trade protectionism good for domestic producers?***

That's debatable. Trade protectionism hurt the United States badly during the Great Depression because other countries responded to U.S. tariffs with tariffs of their own.

- ***Why do governments continue such practices?***

The theory of mercantilism started the practice of trade protectionism and it has persisted, in a lesser form, ever since.

7. Evaluate the role of multinational corporations in the global markets.

7. Multinational corporations have a huge impact on world trade.

- ***How do multinational corporations differ from other companies that participate in international business?***

Unlike other companies involved in exporting or importing, multinational corporations also have manufacturing facilities or other types of physical presence in various nations.

absolute advantage 89
balance of payments 92
balance of trade 92
bartering 98
common market 105
comparative
  advantage theory 89
contract
  manufacturing 96
countertrading 98
debtor nation 94
devaluation 101
dumping 92
embargo 103
ethnocentricity 98
exchange rate 101

export trading
  companies 95
exporting 88
floating exchange
  rate 101
Foreign Corrupt
  Practices Act of
  1978 101
foreign direct
  investment 94
foreign subsidiary 96
free trade 89
free trade area 106
General Agreement
  on Tariffs and Trade
  (GATT) 104

global marketing 99
import quota 103
importing 88
joint venture 97
licensing 95
mercantilism 103
multinational
  corporation 107
North American Free
  Trade Agreement
  (NAFTA) 105
protective tariff 103
revenue tariff 103
trade deficit 92
trade
  protectionism 102

DEVELOPING WORKPLACE SKILLS

1. One of the difficulties of engaging in international trade is the constant shift in exchange rates. How much do exchange rates change over a 30-day period? Research this by choosing five countries and recording the exchange rate for their currency (Austria's schilling, Italy's lira, Japan's yen, Mexico's peso, etc.) for 30 days. The rates are available daily in the *The Wall Street Journal* (in the "Currency Markets" chart in the "Money and Investing" section.) Chart the amount of foreign currency per dollar. What effect would these currency shifts have on your company's trade with each of these countries?

2. Visit an Oriental rug dealer or some other importer of foreign goods. Interview the owner/manager about the problems and rewards of being involved in international trade. Compile a list of advantages and disadvantages. Then compare your list with others in the class.

3. Write a short essay describing the benefits and disadvantages of trade protectionism. Have your class divide into two sides and debate this issue: "Should the United States increase trade protection to save American jobs and American companies?"

4. Many U.S. firms have made embarrassing mistakes when trying to sell products internationally. Sometimes the product is not adapted to the needs of the country, sometimes the advertising makes no sense, sometimes the product color is wrong, and so forth. Discuss the steps U.S. businesses should follow to be more responsive to the needs of foreign markets. Discuss your list with others, and together form a plan for improving U.S. international trade.

5. I.M. Windy is a candidate for the U.S. House of Representatives from your district. He just delivered an excellent speech at your college. He spoke at great length on the topic of tariffs. His major arguments were that we need tariffs to:
   a. Provide revenues.
   b. Protect our young industries.
   c. Encourage Americans to buy U.S. made products because it is patriotic.
   d. Keep us militarily strong.
   e. Protect American workers and wages.
   f. Help us maintain a favorable balance of trade.
   g. Create a favorable balance of payments.

   Do you agree or disagree with Mr. Windy? Evaluate each of the candidate's major points by indicating whether you consider it valid or invalid. Justify your position.

PRACTICING MANAGEMENT DECISIONS
⟨⟨ C A S E   THE GHOSTS OF SMOOT–HAWLEY ⟩⟩

No subject of this chapter has received more interest in the early 1990s than trade protectionism. Ever so often newspaper headlines or TV commentators refer to "Smoot–Hawley." What is Smoot–Hawley? Some history may help clarify the issue.

The date: June 13, 1930 (Friday the 13th). The time: 2:13 P.M. The place: the U.S. Senate. The Great Depression had started, and the air was full of talk about trade protection. Over 1,000 economists warned the government that protectionism was dangerous and petitioned it not to pass the Smoot–Hawley Act. (Hawley was a professor of economics at Willamette University. Smoot was a banker and wool manufacturer.) But, by a vote of 44 to 42, the bill passed. It was an act conceived by Republican congressmen, passed by a Republican Congress, and signed into law by conservative President Herbert Hoover.

The bill imposed duties of up to 60 percent on almost everything imported into the United States. The concept was to protect the Western beet sugar farmer by raising the duty for sugar; protect the Northwestern wheat farmer by raising the duty on wheat; and protect the Imperial Valley cotton farmer by raising the duty on cotton from Egypt. The list went on: cattle and dairy products, hides, shoes, velvet, silk, china, pocket knives, watch parts, and so on.

World trade fell by one third, and a global trade war started. Exports dropped from $4.8 billion to $1.7 billion from 1929 to 1932. Imports dropped from $5.4 billion to $2.4 billion. Other countries were plunged into depression also as world trade fell. In 1934, Congress passed the Reciprocal Trade Agreement Act to reduce tariffs, but it was too little too late.

The issue of world trade regulation continued. From 1987 until 1993, the GATT discussions often reached impasse points or stalemates. A collapse of the negotiations would have actually pleased protectionists. In response to protectionist legislation throughout the world, three trading blocs have emerged: the United States of North America (led by the United States), the United States of Europe, and the United States of Asia (led by Japan). Such trading blocs allow for free trade among nations in the same trading bloc, but may lead to even greater protectionist legislation and less free trade between nations in competing trading blocs.

Decision Questions

1. Why might some politicians push for trade protection? What economic conditions would call for protectionism?

2. Has Congress learned the lessons of the early 1930s such that we'll not repeat the mistake of passing overly restrictive legislation on world trade? What could cause Congress to reverse itself on this issue?

3. What should be the U.S. government's role with regard to world trade? How much effort should be made to protect American workers from foreign competition? What can the United States do to open trade among the three major trading blocs?

Source: Ashby Bladen, "1991: 1931 with a Difference," *Forbes*, January 21, 1991; and Louis S. Richman, "What's Next after GATT's Victory?" *Fortune*, January 10, 1994, pp. 66–71.

⟨⟨ VIDEO CASE   LEARNING TO DO BUSINESS GLOBALLY ⟨⟨

The Profile to this chapter featured Virginia Kamsky, a woman who teaches businesses how to trade with China. China does not have an "open door" policy to world traders; rather, it views trade as a bridge. That is, goods should flow both ways so that both countries benefit. It is important, when attempting to do business with another country, to understand the social and economic conditions of that country. In China, for example, Nike found that only 15 percent of the population could afford its athletic shoes. Thus it had to focus its advertising and promotional efforts toward those people. Nike was able to penetrate the Chinese market by subsidizing the Chinese track and field team.

McDonald's has had similar experiences around the world. It has learned that most of the world enjoys the Big Mac. On the other hand, the company has learned to adapt to local tastes as well. For example, it sells beer in its restaurants in Germany. Some sell pasta. In Japan, it sells rice instead of potatoes.

Benetton, an Italian clothing company, discovered that it could experience tremendous growth in a relatively static market by going global. It now has some 7,000 shops in 80 countries. Benetton uses information systems to tie together its worldwide organization. When you manufacture in 25 different countries and work with 15 import companies, it is important to have a sophisticated information system to tie the entire network together.

Whether you are selling Caterpillar generators and equipment to Arab countries or infrastructure-developing materials to Russia, it is best to partner with local businesses and to adapt to local customs. Similarly, companies that want to do business in the United States have to adapt to our business practices and our culture. Honda, for example, has been successful in building plants in the United States and making automobiles that meet the wants and needs of U.S. consumers. By locating their plants in the United States, such firms create jobs and additional tax revenues. Thus multinational firms create mutually beneficial exchange relationships around the world. They do that by bridging gaps and removing wedges that have separated nations in the past.

Decision Questions
1. Recently the United States has had to impose sanctions on China for not recognizing patent rights on intellectual property: books, music tapes, and the like. How important is the U.S. government in creating bridges between U.S. and foreign firms?

2. If McDonald's sells beer in German outlets, what beverage might it sell in France? England? Can you see why it might have cabbage instead of lettuce on its Big Mac in Russia? How might McDonald's adjust its menu in countries that don't eat beef?

3. What are some of the other adjustments U.S. firms may have to make to conform to the cultural, economic, business, and social practices of other countries?

CHAPTER 4

DEMONSTRATING ETHICAL BEHAVIOR AND SOCIAL RESPONSIBILITY

LEARNING GOALS

After you have read and studied this chapter, you should be able to

1. Explain why legality is only the first step in behaving ethically.

2. Describe management's role in setting ethical standards.

3. Ask the three questions one should answer when faced with a potentially unethical action.

4. Distinguish between compliance-based and integrity-based ethics codes and list the six steps in setting up a corporate ethics code.

5. Define social responsibility and compare the three views of corporate responsibility to stakeholders.

6. Discuss the role of American businesses in influencing ethical and social responsibility in global markets.

JAYNELL GRAYSON, CO-OWNER OF FOOD FROM THE 'HOOD

Jaynell Grayson, a junior at Crenshaw High School in Los Angeles, takes three buses from her grandfather's house in Watts to her new company housed in the high school. The company, founded by Grayson and 38 other inner-city teenagers, launched its first product, a bottled salad dressing, in 1993.

The company got its seed (start-up) money from a grant provided by Rebuild LA, the city's riot recovery agency. More importantly, the company later received help from marketing consultant Norris Bernstein. Bernstein read in the newspaper about how the kids were unsure how to market their product. Grayson's group first attempted to distribute it by appealing to the Lucky supermarket where Grayson works after school. He then volunteered to teach them the basics of distribution. He also introduced them to key contacts in the packaged goods and supermarket industries.

Nearly every supermarket in Southern California has agreed to stock the salad dressing thanks to the philanthropic nature of the store managers. Obtaining shelf space for the product cleared one major hurdle any new food item must overcome, but now the product will have to stand on its own to win sales and vital market share. So far, it looks like it stands a good chance of succeeding. An executive at California's largest grocer who plans to carry the dressing chainwide says, "We see lots of companies trying to develop new products that don't do half the research that these high school kids did. They've done all the work necessary to introduce a product to the marketplace and develop it into a good business."

What will Food from the 'Hood do with its profits? The students will follow the examples of those who helped them by donating a quarter of the profits to the needy and putting the rest into a college scholarship fund for the student owners.

In this chapter we'll explore the moral and ethical responsibilities of businesspeople like Norris Bernstein and Jaynell Grayson. This is a new era in business, an era when social responsibility is receiving top attention. Many companies like Food from the 'Hood are giving back to the communities in which they do business.

> *The performance of the corporation must be not only legal but ethical, fair, open, and considerate; it must accord with the total well-being requirements set by society.*
>
> Coy G. Eckland
> CEO of Equitable Life Assurance

MANAGING BUSINESS ETHICALLY AND RESPONSIBLY

social responsibility
A business's concern for the welfare of society as a whole.

Knowing what's right and wrong and behaving accordingly is what ethical behavior is all about. **Social responsibility** means that a business shows concern for the welfare of society as a whole. In this chapter we'll look at ethics from both an organizational and an individual perspective, and then we'll look at how organizations show social responsibility.

LEGALITY IS ONLY THE FIRST ETHICAL STANDARD

Some people wonder if being ethical these days means no more than having escaped conviction. The "ethical" question seems to have become, Was it legal? We get ourselves in trouble when a society considers ethics and legality to be the same. Ethical behavior requires more than following the law, but following the law is an important first step. Ethics and law are two very different things. Ethics reflects people's proper relations with one another: How should they treat each other? What responsibility should they feel for others? Legality

A picture says a thousand words—but not always the truth! In 1993, NBC used photographs of a rigged GM truck bursting into flames upon impact from another car to illustrate the truck's fuel tank's defects. The use of setup pictures undermined the story the network wanted to promote. Upon pressure from GM, NBC acknowledged the bogus footage. GM is satisfied that NBC was adequately humbled, but how's your confidence level in NBC's news reporting?

3a

Making Ethical Decisions

Competing for Young Customers

Joe Camel has been taking a lot of heat lately from people who say his ads appeal to adolescents and could encourage them to smoke. Converse is on the run from people who say the name of its new basketball shoe, Run 'N Gun, might encourage adolescent violence, especially in inner cities where handguns are as common as basketballs. Liquor producers are swallowing the criticism of folks that say their new drinks with sweet taste, brightly colored labels, and cutesy names like Tahitian Tangerine and Dixie Jazzberry could encourage adolescents to start drinking.

All of the offending companies respond that they aren't encouraging adolescent misbehavior. What do you think? Do you think the companies are trying to attract adolescents as new customers? If so, is such luring ethical? What are the companies' responsibilities to the well-being of the young members of society?

Source: Ellen Neuborne, "Uproar Adds to Joe Camel's Image," *USA Today*, February 24, 1994, p. 2B; Lawrence Ingrassia, "Run 'N Gun, a New Converse Sneaker, Kicks Up Fears It May Promote Violence," *The Wall Street Journal*, February 8, 1993, p. B7; and Eben Shapiro, "Low-Alcohol, Brightly Labeled Cocktails Stir Fears They Will Tempt Teenagers," *The Wall Street Journal*, August 4, 1993, p. B1.

is more limiting. It refers to laws we've written to protect ourselves from fraud, theft, and violence. Many immoral and unethical acts fall well within our laws.

Before we go further in this discussion, we need to clarify some terms:

Ethics is the study of standards of conduct and moral judgment.

Morality refers to the attempt to live by certain values and standards of conduct accepted by society as right and wrong.

Integrity refers to the honesty, sincerity, and morality of a person.

ethics
The study of standards of conduct and moral judgment.

morality
The attempt to live by certain values and standards of conduct accepted by society as right and wrong.

integrity
The honesty, sincerity, and morality of a person.

• • • ETHICS IS MORE THAN AN INDIVIDUAL CONCERN • • •

Some managers think ethics is a personal matter. They believe that either individuals have ethical principles or they don't. They feel management isn't responsible for an individual's misdeeds and that ethics has nothing to do with management. But a growing number of people think that ethics has *everything* to do with management. Individuals don't usually act alone. They need the implied cooperation—if not the direct cooperation—of others to behave unethically in a corporation.

For example, in 1992, Sears, Roebuck & Company was besieged with complaints about its automotive services. Sears management had tried earlier to improve its auto centers' performance by introducing new goals and incentives for its employees. Increased pressure on Sears employees to meet these quotas caused them to become careless and to exaggerate the need for repairs. Did the managers say directly, "Deceive the customers"? No, but the message was clear anyway. The goals and incentives created an environment in which mistakes did occur and managers didn't make efforts to correct the mistakes. Sears settled pending lawsuits by offering coupons to customers who paid for certain services between 1990 and 1992. The estimated cost was $60 million. Such misbehavior doesn't reflect a management philosophy that intends to deceive. It does, however, show an insensitivity or indifference to ethical considerations.[1]

••• ORGANIZATIONAL ETHICS BEGINS AT THE TOP •••

Ethics is caught more than it's taught. That is, people learn their standards and values from observing what others do, not what they say. This is as true in business as it is at home. Corporate values are instilled by the leadership and example of strong top managers.

Companies such as IBM, Xerox, McDonald's, Ben & Jerry's Homemade, Levi Strauss & Co., and Marriott are known to have strong, effective, ethical leadership.[2] Within these firms, a high value system has become pervasive, and employees feel part of a corporate mission that's socially beneficial. On the other hand, corporate standards can work the other way too, as you learned from the Sears example. Managers with strong personal values may compromise those values if they feel that the corporation's profits are compromised.

••• PERSONAL ETHICS BEGINS AT HOME •••

It's easy to criticize business for its moral and ethical shortcomings, but we must be careful in our criticism to note that society as a whole isn't too socially minded either. A recent book, *The Day America Told the Truth*, revealed that most Americans have few moral absolutes. Many decide situationally whether it's all right to steal, lie, or drink and drive. Two thirds of the population reported never giving any time to the community. Nearly one third said they never contributed to a charity. Both managers and workers cited low managerial ethics as a major cause of our competitive woes. Employees report that they often violate safety standards and goof off as much as seven hours a week. Robert Wallach, CEO of auto insurer Robert Plan Corp., says that 70 percent of the applications his company receives are "misstated," with fibs about whether the applicant drives to work, whether the driver is under age 21, and other details that could increase premiums.[3]

It's always healthy when discussing moral and ethical issues to remind ourselves that ethical behavior begins with you and me. We can't expect "society" to become more moral and ethical unless we as individuals commit to becoming more moral and ethical ourselves.

The purpose of the Making Ethical Decisions boxes you see throughout the text is to demonstrate to you that it's important to keep ethics in mind whenever you're making a business decision. It's helpful to ask yourself the following questions when faced with a potentially unethical action:[4]

1. **Is it legal?** Am I violating any law or company policy? Whether you're gathering marketing intelligence, designing a product, hiring or firing employees, planning on how to get rid of waste, or using a nickname for a secretary, it's necessary to think of the legal implications of what you do. This is the most basic step in an ethics-based management system, but ethics goes way beyond legality.

2. **Is it balanced?** Am I acting fairly? Would I want to be treated this way? Will I win everything at the expense of another party? Win–lose situations often end up lose–lose situations. There's nothing like a major loss to generate retaliation from the loser. This can eventually lead to using your limited resources to combat the competition in the "backroom" rather than using them to compete in the marketplace. Not every situation can be completely balanced, but it's important to the health of our relationships that we avoid major imbalances over time. An ethics-based manager has a win–win attitude.

3. **How will it make me feel about myself?** Will I feel proud if my family learns of my decision? Could I discuss the proposed situation or action with my immediate supervisor or the company's clients? How

would I feel if my decision were announced on the evening news? Will I have to hide or keep my actions secret? Has someone warned me not to disclose my actions? Am I feeling unusually nervous? Decisions that go against our sense of right and wrong make us feel bad—they corrode our self-esteem. That's why an ethics-based manager does what's proper as well as what's profitable.

If there's to be trust and cooperation between workers and managers, that trust must be based on a foundation of fairness, honesty, openness, kindness, and moral integrity. The same can be said about relationships among businesses and among nations. In many dealings, the Golden Rule ("Do unto others as you would have them do unto you") is as good a guideline as any.

There are no easy solutions to ethical problems. Companies and individuals that develop a strong ethics code and use the three preceding ethics-check questions have a better chance than most of behaving ethically.

- Think of a situation you were involved in recently that tested your ethical behavior. Would it have been easier to make a choice if you had asked yourself the three questions listed above? Try answering them now and see if you would have made a different choice.

CRITICAL THINKING

SETTING CORPORATE ETHICAL STANDARDS

Formal corporate ethics codes are popular these days. Companies without them are scrambling to commit corporate values to paper. Companies that already have codes are rushing to update, distribute, and interpret them.

Although ethics codes vary greatly, they can be classified into two major categories: compliance-based and integrity-based. **Compliance-based ethics codes** emphasize preventing unlawful behavior by increasing control and by penalizing wrongdoers. Whereas compliance-based ethics codes are based on avoiding legal punishment, **integrity-based ethics codes** define the organization's guiding values, create an environment that supports ethically sound behavior, and stress a shared accountability among employees. Figure 4.1 compares compliance-based and integrity-based ethics codes.

To be effective, all ethics codes must be enforced and employees must be held responsible for their behavior. A long-term improvement of America's business ethics calls for a six-step approach:[5]

- First, top management must adopt and unconditionally support an explicit corporate code of conduct.
- Second, employees must understand that expectations for ethical behavior begin at the top and that senior management expects all employees to act accordingly.
- Third, managers and others must be trained to consider the ethical implications of all business decisions.
- Fourth, an ethics office must be set up. Phone lines to the office should be established so that employees who don't necessarily want to be seen with an ethics officer can inquire about ethical matters anonymously.

compliance-based ethics codes
Ethical standards that emphasize preventing unlawful behavior by increasing control and by penalizing wrongdoers.

integrity-based ethics codes
Ethical standards that define the organization's guiding values, create an environment that supports ethically sound behavior, and stress a shared accountability among employees.

FIGURE 4.1

STRATEGIES FOR ETHICS MANAGEMENT

As you can see from this chart, integrity-based ethics codes are similar to compliance-based ethics codes in that both have a concern for the law and use penalties as enforcement. Integrity-based ethics codes move beyond legal compliance to create a "do-it-right" climate that emphasizes core values such as honesty, fair play, good service to customers, a commitment to diversity, and involvement in the community. These values are ethically desirable, but not necessarily legally mandatory.

Features of Compliance-Based Ethics Codes

Ideal:	Conform to outside standards (laws and regulations)
Objective:	Avoid criminal misconduct
Leaders:	Lawyers
Methods:	Education, reduced employee discretion, controls, penalties

Features of Integrity-Based Ethics Codes

Ideal:	Conform to outside standards (laws and regulations) and chosen internal standards
Objective:	Enable responsible employee conduct
Leaders:	Managers with aid of lawyers and others
Methods:	Education, leadership, accountability, decision processes, controls, and penalties

- Fifth, outsiders such as suppliers, subcontractors, distributors, and customers must be told about the ethics program. Often pressure to put aside ethical considerations comes from the outside, and it helps employees resist such pressure when everyone knows what the ethical standards are.

- Sixth, the ethics code must be enforced. It's important to back any ethics program with timely action if any rules are broken. That's the best way to communicate to all employees that the code is serious and cannot be broken.

PROGRESS CHECK

- What's the difference between ethics, integrity, and morality?
- What are the six steps to follow in establishing an effective ethics program in a business?

CORPORATE SOCIAL RESPONSIBILITY

As we said at the start of the chapter, corporate social responsibility is the concern businesses have for the welfare of society. Business needs to accept social responsibility in a structured way. A company's social performance has several dimensions:

corporate philanthropy
Dimension of social responsibility that includes charitable donations.

- **Corporate philanthropy** includes charitable donations to nonprofit groups of all kinds.

corporate responsibility
Dimension of social responsibility that includes everything from minority hiring practices to the making of safe products.

- **Corporate responsibility** includes everything from minority hiring practices to the making of safe products, minimization of pollution, wise energy use, provision of a safe work environment, and more.

corporate policy
Dimension of social responsibility that refers to the position a firm takes on social and political issues.

- **Corporate policy** refers to the position a firm takes on issues that affect the firm and society, including political issues.

Corporations are less likely to give money to other organizations (charities) than they are to start their own programs of social responsibility. It would be instructive for you to read about the thousands of programs sponsored by leading U.S. firms. So much news coverage is devoted to the social *problems* caused by corporations that people tend to get a one-sided view of the social impact of companies. Few people know, for example, that Xerox has a program called Social Leave whereby employees can leave for up to a year and work for a nonprofit organization. The employee gets his or her full salary and benefits while away and has job security. IBM and Wells-Fargo Bank have similar programs. In fact, over 900 companies have some kind of program to allow employees to volunteer their help part-time to social agencies of all kinds.

What should be the guiding philosophy for business in the 21st century? For most of the 20th century, there has been uncertainty regarding the position top managers should take. The question revolves around the treatment of stakeholders « P.40 ». Remember, stakeholders are those people who can affect or are affected by the achievement of an organization's objectives; they include stockholders, employees, customers, suppliers, distributors, competitors, and the general public. Three different views of corporate responsibility to these stakeholders have been presented:[6]

1. *The strategic approach*. The strategic approach requires that management's primary orientation be toward the economic interests of stockholders. The rationale is this: As owners, the stockholders have the right to expect management to work in their best interests (to optimize profits). Furthermore, Adam Smith's invisible hand says that the maximum social gain is realized when managers attend only to their shareholder's interests. For example, IBM's John Akers said that if IBM would decide whether to cease operations in a country, it would be a business decision. He said, "We are not in business to conduct moral

"I work in finance.

But money can't buy the feeling I get working with these kids."

Carmen Rolón

CARMEN ROLÓN
REGIONAL MANAGER, ITT ISLAND FINANCE
SAN JUAN

Carmen Rolón knows the importance of teamwork. She stresses it every day to her staff at ITT Island Finance. Then on weekends she teaches it to a very special group of boys, the basketball team she coaches. She wants to see them succeed on the court, and in life, like she has at ITT Island Finance.

ITT Island Finance is part of the ITT Corporation, a global, $23 billion enterprise that employs 100,000 people around the world.

And whether it's ITT Sheraton, ITT Automotive, or ITT World Directories, these companies and all of our businesses share a common goal: To improve the quality of life. Because helping people is more than our job. It's our responsibility. Just ask Carmen Rolón. For more information about ITT, write to: ITT Corporation, 1330 Avenue of the Americas, New York, NY 10019.

ITT

Some corporate employees extend their commitment to teamwork to stakeholders outside of the company. Like Carmen Rolon shown here, these people believe that social responsibility means working to improve the quality of life both in and out of the office.

Mining ranks as one of the most dangerous professions in the United States. As you can see from this photo showing the effects of coal mining in the Cumberland Plateau region of Tennessee, mining is dangerous for the environment as well as miners. What do you think is the most ethical way of dealing with this problem?

Legal Briefcase

The 1991 Federal Sentencing Guidelines

How much does a company have to pay for bending the law? It all depends. Does the company have a record of similar misconduct? Does it have a program to prevent and detect unlawful behavior? Does it accept responsibility for the misconduct and agree to cooperate with authorities? Did the company report the crime in the first place? The answers to these questions can mean a big difference in the fine the offending company must pay.

The 1991 Federal Sentencing Guidelines have had an effect on how managers' actions influence organizational fines. Let's take the case of Acme Corporation, a company convicted of mail fraud. The chart at the bottom of the box shows the minimum and maximum that the company can be fined. As you see, the company could be fined from a maximum of approximately 55 million dollars to a minimum of two thirds of a million dollars depending on how active management was in crime prevention or crime promotion. Who says crime doesn't pay! Just ask the courts; looks like it pays big time!

Source: Based on Case No. 88-266, United States Sentencing Commission, *Supplementary Report on Sentencing Guidlines for Organization;* and Lynn Sharp Paine, "Managing for Organizational Integrity," *Harvard Business Review*, March–April 1994, pp. 106–17.

	MAXIMUM	MINIMUM
Ethics program, reporting, cooperation, responsibility	$ 2,740,000	$ 685,000
Program only	10,960,000	5,480,000
No program, no reporting, no cooperation, no responsibility	27,400,000	13,700,000
No program, no reporting, no cooperation, no responsibility, involvement of high-level personnel	54,800,000	27,400,000

activity; we are not in business to conduct socially responsible action. We are in business to conduct business." The strategic approach encourages managers to consider actions' effects on stakeholders other than owners, but others' interests are secondary. Often those interests are considered only when they would adversely affect profits if ignored.

2. *The socialist approach.* Using the socialist approach, management gives equal attention to all stakeholders: owners, employees, the local community, and so forth. A recent law in Pennsylvania is based on this approach. The law seeks to protect companies from hostile takeovers. The idea is to protect customers, employees, and the public at large from decisions that may benefit owners, but harm the others. The argument against such an approach is that it turns private organizations into public institutions with no special responsibility to their owners. Special-interest groups could lobby managers to take all kinds of actions that may cut into profits and damage the success or life of the firm.

3. *The pluralist approach.* This approach recognizes the special responsibility of management to optimize profits, but not at the expense of

FROM THE PAGES OF...
Entrepreneur®
MAGAZINE

Ethics in Global Trade

Jonathan Rosenthal is co-founder and executive director of Equal Exchange Inc. in Stoughton, Massachusetts. His company buys coffee in places such as Nicaragua and El Salvador. It also serves as an international trade advisor to other companies. Equal Exchange buys directly from farmers rather than relying on brokers and agents. The idea is to empower farmers to succeed. To do that Rosenthal pays farmers more than they would normally receive for their coffee. In turn, Rosenthal expects the farmers to assure that their workers are paid a decent wage. They should get rest breaks and work a reasonable number of hours each day.

Furthermore, the farmer should get rid of waste properly and try to renew resources such as trees, topsoil, and animal life.

Rosenthal feels that suppliers are partners and that their social responsibility is linked with your own social responsibilities. By offering incentives in the form of additional money for coffee, Rosenthal is able to create positive benefits for workers and the environment. His is a proactive ethical stance that works in a global setting.

Source: Erika Kotite, "Keeping Tabs," *Entrepreneur*, December 1994, p. 43.

employees, suppliers, and members of the community. This approach recognizes the moral responsibilities of management that apply to all human beings. Managers don't have moral immunity when making managerial decisions. This view says that corporations can maintain their economic viability only when they fulfill their moral responsibilities to society as a whole. When stockholders' interests compete with the interests of the community, as they often do, managers must decide using ethical and moral principles.

The guiding philosophy for the 21st century will be some version of the pluralist approach. Managerial decision making won't be easy, and new ethical guidelines may have to be drawn. But the process toward such guidelines has been started, and a new era of more responsible and responsive management is beginning.

Many corporations are publishing reports that document their net social contribution. To do that, a company must measure its social contributions and subtract its negative social impacts. We'll discuss that process next.

Businesses may be "shot down" if they ignore their social responsibilities to all stakeholders. For example, Disney surrendered to historians and writers who criticized a proposed theme park in the midst of Civil War battlefields in Virginia. A group called Protect Historic America pointed out that the site was important to all Americans—not just Virginians—and should be preserved.

••• SOCIAL AUDITING •••

It's nice to talk about having organizations become more socially responsible. It's also hopeful to see some efforts made toward creating safer products, cleaning up the environment, designing more honest advertising, treating women and minorities fairly, and so forth. But is there any indication that organizations are making social responsiveness an integral part of top management's decision making? The answer is yes, and the term that represents that effort is *social auditing*.

social audit

A systematic evaluation of an organization's progress toward implementing programs that are socially responsible and responsive.

A **social audit** is a systematic evaluation of an organization's progress toward implementing programs that are socially responsible and responsive.[7] One of the more difficult problems with social auditing is how to define *socially responsible and responsive*. Is it being socially responsible to delay putting in the latest technology (for example, robots and computers) to save jobs, even if that makes the firm less competitive? Hundreds of such questions make the design of social audits difficult.

Another major problem is establishing procedures for measuring a firm's activities and their effects on society. What should be measured? Figure 4.2 outlines business activities that could be considered socially responsible.

There's some question as to whether positive actions should be added and then negative effects (for example, pollution, layoffs) subtracted to get a net social contribution. Or should just positive actions be recorded?

In general, social auditing has become a concern of business. It's becoming one of the aspects of corporate success that business evaluates, measures, and develops.

INTERNATIONAL ETHICS AND SOCIAL RESPONSIBILITY

Ethical problems and issues of social responsibility aren't unique to the United States. Top business and government leaders in Japan were caught in a major "influence peddling" (read *bribery*) scheme in Japan. Similar charges have been brought against top officials in South Korea and the People's Republic of China.

What's new about these changes in moral and ethical standards by which government leaders are being judged? They're much more strict than in

---

FIGURE 4.2

SOCIALLY RESPONSIBLE BUSINESS ACTIVITIES

- Community-related activities such as participating in local fund-raising campaigns, donating executive time to various nonprofit organizations (including local government), and participating in urban planning and development.

- Employee-related activities such as equal opportunity programs, flextime, improved benefits, job enrichment, job safety, and employee development programs. (You'll learn more about these activities in Chapters 11 and 12.)

- Political activities such as taking a position on issues such as nuclear safety, gun control, pollution control, and consumer protection; and working more closely with local, state, and federal government officials.

- Support for higher education, the arts, and other nonprofit social agencies.

- Consumer activities such as product safety, honest advertising, prompt complaint handling, honest pricing policies, and extensive consumer education programs.

Reaching Beyond Our Borders

A Global View of Business Ethics

How can a producer control the ethical behavior of the factories of their suppliers? Perhaps the model of determined policy enforcement is Levi Strauss & Co. Levi didn't just send its 600 suppliers a list of tough standards of conduct. It inspected each supplier, dropping 30 of them and requiring reforms in 120 others. In addition, Levi left Myanmar because the government violated the company's vision of human rights. The company compromised in Bangladesh, where it's commonplace for factories to hire children under 14. Levi protected 40 of the children who would have been fired, avoiding sending their families deeper into poverty. The company will educate the children while the suppliers continue to pay them their regular salaries until their 14th birthdays.

Source: John McCormick and Marc Levinson, "The Supply Police," *Newsweek*, February 15, 1993, pp. 48–49; and "Levi's Values: One Size Does Not Fit All," *Business Week*, August 22, 1994.

---

previous years. Top leaders are being held to a new, higher standard. The late 1990s or early 21st century may be the era when a new morality is recognized.

We all look forward to the day when American businesses and consumers will not only be the *economic* leaders of the world, but will be the *moral* and *ethical* leaders as well. Many American businesses are already demanding socially responsible behavior from their international suppliers.

Many American companies are working to make sure their suppliers don't violate U.S. human rights and environmental standards. For example, Sears won't import products made by Chinese prison labor. Phillips Van Heusen said it would cancel orders from suppliers that violate its ethical, environmental, and human rights code. Dow Chemical expects its suppliers to conform to tough American pollution and safety laws rather than just to local laws. McDonald's denied rumors that one of its suppliers grazes cattle on cleared rain forest land, but wrote a ban on the practice anyway.

Three types of tactics are used to see that companies enforce their ethical policies: (1) Socially conscious investors insist that companies extend their own high standards to all their suppliers. (2) Environmentalists apply pressure by naming names of companies that don't abide by their standards. (3) Union officials hunt down violations and force companies to comply to avoid negative publicity.[8] In the 1960s, one of the first to pressure the enforcement of corporate ethics was a young lawyer named Ralph Nader. Nader almost single-handedly took on mighty General Motors. Nader began challenging GM because of its defective Corvair, which had been responsible for many fatal accidents caused by sudden, erratic, and uncontrollable behavior. At first, Nader annoyed GM like a pesky mosquito might annoy an elephant. Gradually, however, Nader's efforts got more and more support. Despite GM's strenuous opposition, including hiring private detectives to look for dirt on Nader's personal life, GM was forced for the first time in the history of auto manufacturing to recall cars to correct the problems. This was the

Paul Newman donates all profits from the sale of his Newman's Own products to charity. Newman uses his entrepreneurial talents as well as his famous name to help the less fortunate.

first important signal of a move toward recognizing that corporations must take into account the ethical standards of society.

The important thing to remember is that it isn't enough for a company to be right when it comes to ethics and social responsibility. It also has to convince its customers that it's right.

PROGRESS CHECK

- What are three different views of corporate responsibility to stakeholders?
- What is a social audit, and what kinds of activities are monitored in such a program?

SUMMARY

1. Explain why legality is only the first step in behaving ethically.

2. Describe management's role in setting ethical standards.

1. Ethics goes beyond obeying laws. It also involves abiding by the moral standards accepted by society.
   - ***How is legality different from ethics?***
   Ethics reflects people's proper relation with one another. Legality is more limiting. It refers to laws written to protect us from fraud, theft, and violence.

2. Some managers think ethics is an individual issue that has nothing to do with management, while others believe ethics has everything to do with management.
   - ***What is management's role in setting ethical standards?***
   Managers often set formal ethical standards, but more important are the messages they send through their actions. Tolerance or intolerance of ethical misconduct influences employees more than any written ethics codes.

3. Ask the three questions one should answer when faced with a potentially unethical action.

3. It's often difficult to know when a decision is ethical.
   - ***How can we tell if our business decisions are ethical?***
   Our business decisions can be put through an ethics check by asking three questions: (1) Is it legal? (2) Is it balanced? (3) How will it make me feel?

4. Distinguish between compliance-based and integrity-based ethics codes and list the six steps in setting up a corporate ethics code.

4. Ethics codes can be classified as complianced-based or integrity-based.
   - ***What's the difference between compliance-based and integrity-based ethics codes?***
   Whereas compliance-based ethics codes are based on avoiding legal punishment, integrity-based ethics codes define the organization's guiding values, create an environment that supports ethically sound behavior, and stress a shared accountability among employees.

5. Define social responsibility and compare the three views of corporate responsibility to stakeholders.

5. Social responsibility is the concern businesses have for society.
   - ***What are the three different views of corporate responsibility toward stakeholders?***
   (1) The *strategic* approach contends that businesses should abide by the laws and let ethics be regulated by the invisible hand of the free-market system. (2) The socialist approach recognizes all the stakeholders of a firm and holds that the law and the political process should regulate ethical objectives. (3) The *pluralist* approach recognizes management's special responsibility to optimize profits, but not at the expense of employees, suppliers, and members of the community.
   - ***How are a company's social responsibility efforts measured?***
   A corporate social audit measures the effects of positive social programs and subtracts the negative effects of business (for example, pollution) to get a net social benefit.

6. Many customers are demanding that companies deal only with other companies that share a commitment to environmental and human rights issues.
   - ***How can companies influence the ethical behavior of its international suppliers?***
   Companies like Sears, Phillips Van Heusen, and Dow Chemical won't import products from companies that don't meet their ethical and social responsibility standards. Levi Strauss enforces its standards to the point of educating underage laborers in Bangladesh.

6. Discuss the role of American businesses in influencing ethical and social responsibility in global markets.

compliance-based ethics codes 119
corporate philanthropy 120
corporate policy 120

corporate responsibility 120
ethics 117
integrity 117
integrity-based ethics codes 119

morality 117
social audit 124
social responsibility 116

KEY TERMS

1. Poll your class to see how many students have had to make recent ethical decisions. How many used the three questions outlined in this chapter to help them make their decisions?

2. Newspapers and magazines are full of stories about individuals and businesses that are *not* socially responsible. What about those individuals and organizations that *do* take social responsibility seriously? We don't normally read or hear about them as often. Do a little investigative reporting of your own. List two of the public interest power groups in your community and identify their officers, their objectives, their sources and amount of financial support, the size and characteristics of their membership, and examples of their recent actions and/or accomplishments. Call the local Chamber of Commerce or Better Business Bureau for help. Call local government agencies and see what private interest groups are operating in your area that have the public interest in mind. For example, there are likely to be environmental groups, animal protection groups, and political action committees.

3. You are manager of a coffee house called the Morning Cup. One of your best employees desires to be promoted to a managerial position; however, the owner is grooming his slow-thinking son for the promotion your employee seeks. This nepotism may hurt a valuable employee's chances for advancement, but complaining may hurt your own chances for promotion. What do you do?

4. Contact a local corporation and ask for a copy of its written ethics code. Would you classify its code as compliance-based or integrity based? Explain.

5. Where do you see leadership emerging to improve the moral standards of the United States? What could you do as an employee to encourage your company to support such leadership?

DEVELOPING WORKPLACE SKILLS

PRACTICING MANAGEMENT DECISIONS

》 C A S E   ETHICS IN HOLLYWOOD AND THE ENTERTAINMENT INDUSTRY 》

Many people say that the foundation for ethical behavior begins with the family and what the family says and does. Family values seem to persist into adulthood. Part of what influences a child is the kind of movies and TV shows the family watches. Nobody has to tell you how low the moral and ethical standards for some TV shows and movies have become.

A Hollywood film producer sends 10 copies of a script to 10 different directors, saying "You're my first choice" to all 10. A major studio agrees to the pay demands of a big star but insists on paying some of the money "on the side" so that agents and other stars won't insist on a similar amount. A scene in a script calls for a tennis court, so the producer volunteers his yard, has a court built there, and charges the cost of the court to the film's budget. Creative accounting in the costing of movies means that most movies make no money. That way, some investors in films get no money even though the film brought in huge revenues. The industry thinks such accounting practices are ethical because they're legal.

The corruption of youth doesn't stop in Hollywood, though. The singing group 2 Live Crew says things in their songs that professors may be fired for saying in front of their classes. The "proof" that such songs aren't too bad is that the courts haven't forbidden them. Madonna's videos are shown repeatedly on cable TV in the middle of the day. They aren't illegal. Neither are shows like "Beavis and Butthead" even though they show dangerous behavior (like saying that playing with fire is fun) that can be and has been copied by young children.

Children watch such shows—sometimes with their parents in the room. Often the parents are busy doing something else and don't carefully monitor what their children watch. Many shows feature businesspeople who are greedy, mean, and dangerous. Often, businesspeople on TV and in the movies lie, cheat, and kill to get what they want. This happens on TV every night of the year. That's the ethical foundation being established in some of the children of America in the 1990s. Value-free education is widespread in U.S. public schools. This creates a greater need for parents to instill values in the home, but TV and other influences make that task difficult.

Decision Questions

1. In recent survey of college students by the Josephson Institute of Ethics in Los Angeles, 75 percent of the undergraduates said they cheated at least once last year. A similar survey by the Higher Education Research Institute at UCLA found that 37 percent of students admitted to cheating on exams, while 57 percent said they copied homework. Such figures are higher than they were in the past. How much of such cheating do you feel is influenced by the amount of cheating students see on TV and in the movies?

2. Hollywood movie studios and other businesses are careful not to break the law. That's their standard of morality these days. If Hollywood suffers few social sanctions for its behavior, why should other businesses maintain a higher standard of ethics and morality? After all, they often can make more money, as Hollywood can, by pushing the ethical boundary as far out as possible.

3. What influences have helped shape your personal code of ethics and morality? What influences, if any, have pressured you to compromise those standards in recent years?

4. At one time, there were many words that performers weren't allowed to say on TV and in movies, and they were restricted as to what they could do as well. What benefits and disadvantages would occur if America were to return to those standards?

VIDEO CASE   DOING THINGS RIGHT VERSUS DOING THE RIGHT THING

You can take college courses that will teach you all the correct accounting principles (doing things right). But no course can teach you how to do the right thing each time you are challenged by the many ethical choices that you will be faced with each day (doing the right thing). For example, what would you do if you worked at an accounting firm and your boss told you to not report some income on a customer's account. "After all," the boss says, "This income is not being reported by the customer because it is gambling income. The IRS won't know; why not leave it out?"

Decisions aren't much easier in the marketing department. What happens if your boss tells you to sell outdated games to your customers so that you can get rid of excess inventory? You know that customers would prefer to wait for the newer, updated version. Would you do what your boss tells you to do or what you believe is right? What are the consequences of such decisions?

The same is true in the purchasing department. Here your boss tells you to buy a part from an old fraternity buddy. The cost is not much more and the supplier is actually closer. You can justify buying from someone you know and trust, but is it the right thing to do? What if it goes against company policy?

And how far should you go in trying to promote a product? If you are asked to design a sexist campaign, should you go along because such promotional efforts are effective or should you do what you believe is the right thing in your heart? How do you know when to trust and follow your own beliefs and when to follow orders?

What if you see someone else violating what you believe are ethical standards. Should you tell others in the firm? What are the consequences of doing so?

Decision Questions

1. Maintaining ethical standards is one of the most difficult parts of work today. There are so many situations where doing the right thing seems to have negative consequences. What are some of the most difficult ethical decisions you have had to make on the job?

2. What do you think happens to people who follow their ethical standards completely, even when it goes against the wishes of their supervisors? What would you advise such people to do?

3. In this case, the boss recommends an unethical practice, but often the choice is up to you, with no one watching. For example, you have the opportunity to take home pencils, paper, paper clips, and other materials from work. Is it harder or easier to do what is right when faced with such ethical decisions?

WORKING WITHIN THE LEGAL ENVIRONMENT OF BUSINESS

THE NEED FOR LAWS

Imagine a society without laws. Just think—no speed limits to control how fast we drive, no age restrictions on the consumption of alcoholic beverages, no limitations on who can practice medicine. A society free to do whatever it chooses with no interference. Obviously, the more we consider this possibility, the more unrealistic we realize it is. Laws are an essential part of a civilized nation. Over time, the depth and scope of the body of laws must change to reflect the needs and changes in society. The judiciary is the branch of government chosen to oversee the legal system.

The world of business is also governed by laws. In the 1990s, the government seems to be stepping in more and more to govern the behavior of businesspeople. Thus, you see more laws and regulations regarding sexual harassment on the job as well as the hiring and firing of employees, plus increased enforcement of environmental and safety laws. Even business responsibilities for health care coverage are being debated as a matter of law. As you may suspect, businesspeople prefer to set their own standards of behavior. However, business hasn't been perceived as implementing acceptable practices fast enough. To hasten the process, the government has expanded its control and enforcement procedures. In this appendix we'll look at some of the laws and regulations now in place. You can't obey or understand the law unless you know what the law is.

BUSINESS LAW

business law
Rules, statutes, codes, and regulations established to provide a legal framework within which business may be conducted and that are enforceable in court.

Business law refers to rules, statutes, codes, and regulations established to provide a legal framework within which business may be conducted and that are enforceable by court action. A businessperson should be familiar with the laws regarding product liability, sales, contracts, fair competition, protection of consumers, taxes, and bankruptcy. Let's begin at the beginning and discuss the foundations of the law.

••• STATUTORY AND COMMON LAW •••

There are two major kinds of law: statutory law and common law. Both are important for businesspeople.

Statutory law (written law) includes state and federal constitutions, legislative enactments, treaties of the federal government, and ordinances (written laws). You can read these laws, but many are written in such a form that their meaning must be determined in court. That's one reason why there are so many lawyers.

Common law is the body of law that comes from decisions handed down by judges. Common law is often referred to as unwritten law, because it doesn't appear in any legislative enactments, treaties, and so forth. What judges have decided in previous cases is important to today's cases. Such decisions are called *precedent*, and they guide judges in the handling of new cases. Common law evolves through decisions made in trial courts, appellate courts, and special courts. Lower courts must abide by the precedents set by the U.S. Supreme Court. In law classes, therefore, students study case after case to learn about common law as well as statutory law.

statutory law
State and federal constitutions, legislative enactments, treaties, and ordinances (written laws).

common law
The body of law that comes from judges' decisions; also known as "unwritten law."

••• ADMINISTRATIVE AGENCIES •••

Many rules, regulations, and orders are issued by branches of government referred to as **administrative agencies**. These are institutions created by Congress with delegated power to pass rules and regulations within their mandated area of authority. Since Congress creates administrative agencies, it can also terminate them. Administrative agencies hold both *quasi-legislative* and *quasi-judicial powers*. This means the agency is allowed to pass rules and regulations within its area of authority and hold hearings when it feels the rules and regulations have been violated. Administrative agencies issue more rulings and settle more disputes than courts. Figure A2.1 describes the powers and functions of several leading federal administrative agencies within the executive branch of government.

administrative agencies
Institutions created by Congress with delegated power to pass rules and regulations within their mandated area of authority.

TORT LAW

The tort system is an example of common law at work. **Tort law** relates to wrongful conduct that causes injury to another person's body, property, or reputation. Although torts are noncriminal acts, victims can be awarded compensation, especially if the harmful conduct is considered intentional. An intentional tort is a willful act purposely inflicted that results in injury. Negligence deals with questionable but unintentional behavior that causes harm or injury. One of the more controversial areas of tort law deals with the question of product liability. Let's look briefly at this issue.

tort
Wrongful conduct that causes injury to another person's body, property, or reputation.

••• PRODUCT LIABILITY •••

Few issues in business law have caused as much debate as product liability. **Product liability** is covered under tort law and holds businesses liable for negligence in the production, design, sale, or use of products it markets. At one

product liability
Laws that hold businesses liable for negligence in the production, design, sale, or use of products it markets.

Agency	Function
Federal Trade Commission (FTC)	Enforces laws and guidelines regarding unfair business practices and acts to stop false and deceptive advertising and labeling.
Food and Drug Administration (FDA)	Enforces laws and regulations to prevent distribution of adulterated or misbranded foods, drugs, medical devices, cosmetics, veterinary products, and hazardous consumer products.
Consumer Products Safety Commission	Ensures compliance with the Consumer Product Safety Act and seeks to protect the public from unreasonable risk of injury from any consumer product not covered by other regulatory agencies.
Interstate Commerce Commission (ICC)	Regulates rates, finances, and franchises of interstate rail, bus, truck, and water carriers.
Federal Communications Commission (FCC)	Regulates wire, radio, and TV communication in interstate and foreign commerce.
Environmental Protection Agency (EPA)	Develops and enforces environmental protection standards and researches the effects of pollution.
Federal Power Commission (FPC)	Regulates rates and sales of natural gas producers, wholesale rates for electricity and gas, pipeline construction, and imports and exports of natural gas and electricity to and from the United States.

FIGURE A2.1

FEDERAL REGULATORY AGENCIES

time the legal standard for measuring product liability was if a producer *knowingly* placed a hazardous product on the market. Today, many states have extended business liability for its products to the level of strict liability. Legally, this means *without regard to fault*. Therefore, a company could be liable for damages (financial compensation) caused by placing a product on the market with a defect, even if the defect wasn't known by the company at the time of sale. The rule of strict liability has caused serious problems, particularly for chemical and drug manufacturers. A producer may place a drug or chemical on the market that everyone thinks is safe. Years later, a side effect or other health problem could emerge. Under the doctrine of strict liability, the manufacturer can be held liable. Insurance companies and businesses are calling for relief from huge losses from such damage suits by lobbying Congress to set limits on the amount of damages they are liable for should harm to consumers occur.

LAWS PROTECTING IDEAS: PATENTS, COPYRIGHTS, AND TRADEMARKS

patent
Exclusive rights for inventors to their inventions for 17 years.

Many people, including students, invent products that they feel are of commercial value, and then they wonder what to do next. One step may be to apply for a patent. A **patent** gives inventors exclusive rights to their inventions for 17 years. Patent owners may sell or license the use of the patent to others. Filing a patent with the U.S. Patent Office requires a search to make sure the patent is truly unique, followed by the filing of forms. A lawyer's advice is usually recommended. Figure A2.2 reviews patent laws. Penalties for violating a patent can be severe. Polaroid forced Kodak to recall all of its instant cameras because Polaroid had several patents that Kodak violated. Kodak lost millions of dollars, and Polaroid maintained market leadership in instant cameras.

- A U.S. patent is enforceable for 17 years from its issue date. An issued patent excludes others from making, using, or selling a patented product or using a patented process.

- A patent defines its protected product or process in claims that set forth the required elements and features of that product or process. An unauthorized product or process that incorporates *all* of the claimed elements and features typically infringes the patent—even if the product or process utilizes additional elements or features not set forth in the claims.

- A patent must be issued before it can be infringed, which means that a patent pending has no legal effect—it serves only as an advance warning.

- A patent application generally takes from six months to about four years to issue as a patent, and is kept secret by the Patent & Trademark Office up until the time the patent is issued.

- If the Patent & Trademark Office or a court determines that a claimed invention has been marketed for more than a year before a patent application is filed, the patent will be rejected or declared invalid.

Source: *Inc.* magazine (July 1988). Copyright ©1988 by *Inc.* Publishing Company, 38 Commercial Wharf, Boston, MA 02110.

FIGURE A2.2

PATENT LAW

How good are your chances of receiving a patent if you file for one? Some 65 percent are approved, costing the inventor a minimum of $6,600 in fees over the life of the patent. The time it takes to process a patent is just over 18 months. Less than 2 percent of inventors file on their own. The rest hire a lawyer. However, there are only 10,000 patent lawyers to handle 165,000 applications. If you file successfully, you can make a lot of money if someone violates your patent. For example, Robert Kearns recently won a $10.2 million award from Ford Motor Company and $21 million from Chrysler for a patent on intermittent windshield wipers!

A **copyright** protects an individual's rights to materials such as books, articles, photos, and cartoons. Copyrights are filed with the Library of Congress and involve a minimum of paperwork. They last for the lifetime of the author or artist plus 50 years. You may charge a fee to allow someone to use copyrighted material.

copyright
Exclusive rights to materials such as books, articles, photos, and cartoons.

Coca-Cola is one of the best known products in the world. The brand name, Coca-Cola, is a registered trademark of the Coca-Cola Company. The small circle at the end of the word Cola with the "R" inside signifies this company has exclusive legal protection to use this name and symbol.

A trademark gives exclusive legal protection to a name, symbol, or design (or combination of them) that identifies one seller's goods or services from those of competitors. Trademarks generally belong to the owner forever, so long as they're properly registered and renewed every 20 years. We'll discuss trademarks in detail in Chapter 14.

SALES LAW: THE UNIFORM COMMERCIAL CODE

Uniform Commercial Code (UCC)
A comprehensive commercial law adopted by every state in the United States; it covers sales laws and other commercial law.

At one time, laws involving businesses varied from state to state, making interstate trade extremely complicated. Today, all states have adopted the same commercial law. The **Uniform Commercial Code (UCC)** is a comprehensive commercial law that covers sales laws and other commercial laws. Since all states have adopted the law, the UCC simplifies trading across state lines. The UCC's 11 articles contain laws covering sales; commercial paper; bank deposits and collections; letters of credit; bulk transfers; warehouse receipts, bills of lading, and other documents of title; investment securities; and secured transactions. We don't have space to discuss all of these articles, but we'd like to tell you about two of them: Article 2 (which regards warranties) and Article 3 (which covers negotiable instruments).

••• WARRANTIES •••

express warranties
Specific representations by the seller regarding the goods.

implied warranties
Guarantees legally imposed on the seller.

Express warranties are specific representations made by the seller and relied upon by the buyer regarding the goods and services. The warranty you receive in the box with a clock or toaster is the express warranty. It spells out the seller's warranty agreement. **Implied warranties** are legally imposed on the seller. It's implied, for example, that the product will conform to the customary standards of the trade in which it passes. Many of the buyers' rights, including the acceptance and rejection of goods, are spelled out in Article 2 of the UCC. Both buyers and sellers should become familiar with the UCC. You can read more about it in business law books in the library.

••• NEGOTIABLE INSTRUMENTS •••

negotiable instruments
Forms of commercial paper (such as checks) that are transferable among businesses and individuals.

Negotiable instruments are forms of commercial paper (such as checks) that are transferable among businesses and individuals. Article 3 of the UCC states that a negotiable instrument must be written and (1) signed by the maker, (2) made payable on demand at a certain time, (3) made payable to the bearer or to order, and (4) contain an unconditional promise to pay a specified amount of money.

CONTRACT LAW

If I offer to sell you my bike for $35 and later change my mind, can you force me to sell the bike, saying we had a contract? If I lose $120 to you in a poker game, can you sue in court to get your money? If I agree to sing at your wedding for free and back out at the last minute, can you claim we had a contract? These are the kinds of questions that contract law answers.

A **contract** is a legally enforceable agreement between two or more parties. **Contract law** specifies what a legally enforceable agreement is. Basically, a contract is legally binding if the following conditions are met:

1. *An offer is made.* An offer to do something or sell something can be oral or written. If I agree to sell you my bike for $35, I have made an offer. That offer isn't legally binding, however, until other conditions are met.

2. *There must be voluntary acceptance of the offer.* If I use "duress or undue influence" to get you to agree to buy my bike, the contract isn't legal. The principle of mutual acceptance means that both parties to a contract must agree on the terms. You couldn't use duress to get me to sell, either. Even if we both agree, though, the contract is still not legally binding without the following.

3. **Both parties must give consideration.** **Consideration** means something of value. If I agree to sell you my bike for $35, the bike and the $35 are consideration, and we have a legally binding contract. If I agree to sing at your wedding and you don't give me anything in return, we have no contract.

4. *Both parties must be competent.* A drunk, drug addict, or an insane person (one who has been legally declared incompetent), for example, can't be held to a contract. In many cases, a minor may not be held to a contract, either. For example, if a 15-year-old agrees to pay $10,000 for a car, the seller may not be able to enforce the contract.

5. *The contract must be legal.* Gambling losses aren't legally collectible. If I lose money to you in poker, you can't legally collect. The sale of illegal drugs is another example of an unenforceable contract.

6. *The contract must be in proper form.* An agreement for the sale of goods worth $500 or more must be in writing. Contracts that can't be fulfilled within one year also must be put in writing. Contracts regarding real property (land and everything attached to it) must be in writing.

• • • BREACH OF CONTRACT • • •

Breach of contract means that one party fails to follow the terms of the contract. Both parties may agree to end a contract, but if just one person violates the contract, the following may occur:

1. *Specific performance.* The person who violated the contract may be required to live up to the agreement if no money damages would be adequate. For example, if I offered to sell you a rare painting, I would have to sell you that painting.

2. *Payment of damages.* The term **damages** refers to the monetary settlement awarded to a person who's injured by a breach of contract. If I fail to live up to a contract, you can sue me for damages, usually the amount you would lose from my nonperformance. If we had a legally binding contract for me to sing at your wedding, for example, and I failed to come, you could sue me for the cost of hiring a new singer.

3. *Discharge of obligation.* If I fail to live up to my end of a contract, you could agree to drop the matter, and then you wouldn't have to live up to your agreement, either. This is often referred to contractually as *restitution*.

contract
A legally enforceable agreement between two or more parties.

contract law
Laws which specify what constitutes a legally enforceable agreement.

consideration
Something of value; it's one of the requirements of a legal contract.

breach of contract
Violation when one party fails to follow the terms of a contract.

damages
The monetary settlement awarded to a person who is injured by a breach of contract.

Lawyers wouldn't make so much money if the law were as simple as implied in these rules of contract. In fact, it's always best to have a contract in writing even if it's not required under law. The offer and consideration should be clearly specified, and the contract should be signed and dated. A contract doesn't have to be long and complicated as long as it has these elements: (1) It's in writing. (2) Mutual consideration is specified. (3) There's a clear offer and agreement.

LAWS TO PROMOTE FAIR AND COMPETITIVE PRACTICES

One objective of legislators and judges is to pass laws that will maintain a competitive atmosphere among businesses and promote fair business practices. Competition is a cornerstone of the free-market system. In the United States, the U.S. Department of Justice's antitrust division and other government agencies serve as watchdogs to ensure that trade among sellers flows freely and that new competitors have open access to the market. However, competition exists in different degrees, ranging from perfect to nonexistent. Economists generally agree that four different degrees of competition exist: (1) perfect competition, (2) monopolistic competition, (3) oligopoly, and (4) monopoly.

perfect competition
The market situation where there are many sellers of nearly identical products and no seller is large enough to dictate the price of the product.

Perfect competition exists when there are many sellers in a market and no seller is large enough to dictate the price of a product. Under perfect competition, sellers produce products that appear to be identical. Agricultural products are often considered to be the closest examples of perfect competition at work. However, you should know that there are no true examples of perfect competition. Today, government price supports and drastic reductions in the number of farms make it hard to argue that even farming is an example of perfect competition.

monopolistic competition
The market situation where there are a large number of sellers that produce similar products, but the products are perceived by buyers as different.

Monopolistic competition exists when a large number of sellers produce products that are very similar but are perceived by buyers as different. Under monopolistic competition, product differentiation (the attempt to make buyers think similar products are different in some way) is a key to success. Think about what that means for just a moment. Through tactics such as advertising, branding, and packaging, sellers try to convince buyers that their product is different from those of competitors. Actually, the competing products may be similar or even interchangeable. Under monopolistic competition, prices are set by individual sellers. Retail stores are a familiar example of monopolistic competition.

oligopoly
A form of competition where the market is dominated by just a few sellers.

An **oligopoly** is a form of competition in which a market is dominated by just a few sellers. Generally, oligopolies exist in industries that produce products such as steel, cereal, automobiles, aluminum, and aircraft. One reason some industries remain in the hands of a few sellers is that the initial investment to enter an oligopolistic industry is usually tremendous. In an oligopoly, prices tend to be close to the same. The reason for this is simple. Intense price competition would lower profits for all the competitors, since a price cut by one producer would most likely be matched by the others. Product differentiation, rather than price differences, is usually the major factor in market success in a situation of oligopoly.

monopoly
A market in which there is only one seller.

A **monopoly** occurs when there's only one seller for a product or service. Since one seller controls the supply of a product, the price may rise dramatically. In the United States, laws prohibit the creation of monopolies except in a few sectors. The legal system does permit approved monopolies such as public utilities that sell gas, water, and electric power. These utilities' prices and profits are usually monitored carefully by public service commissions that are supposed to protect the interest of buyers.

There was a time when businesses operated under relatively free market ≪ P.63 ≫ conditions. Big businesses were able to drive smaller competitors out of business with little recourse. The following discussion shows the government's response to these troubling situations and how business must deal with them today.

••• THE INTERSTATE COMMERCE ACT OF 1887 •••

When the railroads started to grow after the Civil War, their managers thought little about what was good for the country and a great deal about what was good for the railroads. The public complained enough about such practices (e.g., the railroads agreeing among themselves to fix prices) that Congress passed the Interstate Commerce Act in 1887. The act stipulated that railroad rates must be "reasonable"; it prohibited discriminatory rates, rebates, and other forms of favoritism; and it outlawed price fixing agreements between railroads. The act established the Interstate Commerce Commission to enforce these provisions.

••• THE SHERMAN ANTITRUST ACT OF ••• 1890 AND LATER RELATED ACTS

In the late 19th century, big oil companies, big railroads, big steel companies, and other large firms dominated the U.S. economy. People were afraid that such large, powerful companies would crush any competitors and then be able to charge high prices. It was in that atmosphere that Congress passed the Sherman Act in 1890. The Sherman Antitrust Act was designed to prevent large organizations from stifling the competition of smaller or newer firms. The Sherman Act forbids (1) contracts, combinations, or conspiracies in restraint of trade and (2) actual monopolies or attempts to monopolize any part of trade or commerce. Because of the act's vague language, there was some doubt about just what practices were prohibited under the Sherman Act of 1890. The following laws were passed later to clarify some of the legal concepts in the Sherman Act.

The Clayton Act of 1914 prohibits exclusive dealing, tying contracts, interlocking directorates, and buying large amounts of stock in competing corporations. *Exclusive dealing* is selling goods with the condition that the buyer won't buy goods from a competitor (when the effect lessens competition). A *tying contract* requires a buyer to purchase unwanted items in order to purchase the desired items. An *interlocking directorate* occurs when a board of directors includes members of the board of competing corporations.

The Federal Trade Commission Act of 1914 prohibits unfair methods of competition in commerce. The act set up a five-member Federal Trade Commission (FTC) to enforce compliance with this act. The involvement of the FTC depends on the members on the board at the time. The FTC conducted three times as many investigations and brought twice as many cases in the 1990s than it did in a typical year in the 1980s.

The Robinson–Patman Act of 1936 prohibits price discrimination. One interesting aspect of the act is that it applies to both sellers and buyers who "knowingly" induce or receive an unlawful discrimination in price. It also stipulates that certain types of price cutting shall be criminal offenses punishable by fine and imprisonment.

The Wheeler–Lea Amendment of 1938 gave the FTC additional jurisdiction over false or misleading advertising. It also gave the FTC power to increase fines if its requirements aren't met within 60 days.

Government often passes excise taxes on the manufacturer, retailer, or both on selected items such as tobacco and alcoholic beverages. Revenue raised from such *sin taxes* will often go toward a specific objective. Suggestions have been made to levy excise taxes on alcohol in order to help pay for national health insurance.

The laws have grown more precise and the punishments more definite as the years have passed. Congress is continuing to monitor business practices and to pass laws regulating those practices when necessary.

LAWS TO PROTECT CONSUMERS

consumerism

A social movement that tries to increase the rights and powers of buyers in relation to sellers.

Consumerism is a social movement that seeks to increase and strengthen buyers' rights and powers in relation to sellers. President John F. Kennedy proposed four basic rights of consumers: (1) the right to safety, (2) the right to be informed, (3) the right to choose, and (4) the right to be heard. Unfortunately, these rights won't be realized if consumers passively wait for all businesses to recognize them; they will come partially from consumer action in the marketplace. **Consumerism** is the people's way of getting their fair share in marketing exchanges. Although consumerism isn't a new movement, it has taken on new vigor and direction in the past decade or so. Figure A2.3 lists the major consumer protection laws.

TAX LAWS

taxes

Federal, state, and local governments' way of raising money.

Mention the word *taxes* and most people frown. That's because taxes affect almost every individual and business in the United States. **Taxes** are federal, state, and local governments' way of raising money. Traditionally, taxes have been used primarily as a source of funding for government operations and programs. They've also been used as a method of encouraging or discouraging taxpayers from doing something. For example, if the government wishes to reduce the use of certain classes of products (cigarettes, beer, etc.), it passes what are referred to as *sin taxes*. The additional cost of the product from increased taxes *perhaps* discourages additional consumption. In other situations, government may encourage businesses to hire new employees or purchase new equipment by offering a tax credit. A tax credit is an amount that can be deducted from a tax bill.

Legislation	Purpose
Pure Food and Drug Act (1906)	Protects against the adulteration and misbranding of foods and drugs sold in interstate commerce.
Food, Drug, and Cosmetic Act (1938)	Protects against the adulteration and sale of foods, drugs, cosmetics, or therapeutic devices and allows the Food and Drug Administration to set minimum standards and guidelines for food products.
Wool Products Labeling Act (1940)	Protects manufacturers, distributors, and consumers from undisclosed substitutes and mixtures in manufactured wool products.
Fur Products Labeling Act (1951)	Protects consumers from misbranding, false advertising, and false invoicing of furs and fur products.
Flammable Fabrics Act (1953)	Prohibits the interstate transportation of dangerously flammable wearing apparel and fabrics.
Automobile Information Disclosure Act (1958)	Requires auto manufacturers to put suggested retail prices on all new passenger vehicles.
Textile Fiber Products Identification Act (1958)	Protects producers and consumers against misbranding and false advertising of fiber content of textile fiber products.
Cigarette Labeling Act (1965)	Requires cigarette manufacturers to label cigarettes as hazardous to health.
Fair Packaging and Labeling Act (1966)	Makes unfair or deceptive packaging or labeling of certain consumer commodities illegal.
Child Protection Act (1966)	Removes from sale potentially harmful toys and allows the FDA to pull dangerous products from the market.
Truth-in-Lending Act (1968)	Requires full disclosure of all finance charges on consumer credit agreements and in advertisements of credit plans.
Child Protection and Toy Safety Act (1969)	Protects children from toys and other products that contain thermal, electrical, or mechanical hazards.
Fair Credit Reporting Act (1970)	Requires that consumer credit reports contain only accurate, relevant, and recent information and are confidential unless a proper party requests them for an appropriate reason.
Consumer Product Safety Act (1972)	Created an independent agency to protect consumers from unreasonable risk of injury arising from consumer products and to set safety standards.
Magnuson–Moss Warranty–Federal Trade Commission Improvement Act (1975)	Provides for minimum disclosure standards for written consumer product warranties and allows the FTC to prescribe interpretive rules and policy statements regarding unfair or deceptive practices.
Alcohol Labeling Legislation (1988)	Provides for warning labels on liquor saying that women shouldn't drink when pregnant and that alcohol impairs your abilities.
Nutrition Labeling and Education Act (1990)	Requires truthful and uniform nutritional labeling on every food the FDA regulates.

FIGURE A2.3

CONSUMER PROTECTION LAWS

Taxes are levied from a variety of sources. Income (personal and business), sales, and property are the major bases of tax revenue. The federal government receives its largest share of revenue from income taxes. States and local communities often make extensive use of sales taxes. The tax policies of states and cities are taken into consideration when businesses seek to locate operations. Tax policies also affect personal decisions such as retirement. Figure A2.4 highlights the primary types of taxes levied on individuals and businesses.

Type	Purpose
Income taxes	Taxes paid on the income received by businesses and individuals. Income taxes are the largest source of tax income received by the government.
Property taxes	Taxes paid on real and personal property. *Real property* is real estate owned by individuals and businesses. *Personal property* is a broader category that includes any movable property such as tangible goods (wedding rings, equipment, etc.) or intangible items (stocks, checks, mortgages, etc.) Taxes are based on their assessed value.
Sales taxes	Taxes paid on merchandise when it's sold at the retail level.
Excise taxes	Taxes paid on selected items such as tobacco, alcoholic beverages, airline travel, gasoline, and firearms. These are often referred to as *sin taxes*. Income generated from the tax goes toward a specifically designated purpose. For example, gasoline taxes often help the federal government and state governments pay for highway construction or improvements.

BANKRUPTCY LAWS

bankruptcy
The legal process by which a person or business, unable to meet financial obligations, is relieved of those debts by having the court divide any assets among creditors, freeing the debtor to begin anew.

Bankruptcy is the legal process by which a person, business, or government entity that can't meet its financial obligations is relieved of those debts by a court. The court divides any assets among creditors, allowing creditors to get at least part of their money and freeing the debtor to begin anew. The U.S. Constitution gives Congress the power to establish bankruptcy laws. There has been bankruptcy legislation since the 1890s, but the Bankruptcy Code was amended by the Bankruptcy Amendments and Federal Judgeships Act of 1984. This act allows a bankrupt person to keep part of the equity (ownership) in a house, $1,200 in a car, and some other personal property. Exemptions vary by state.

There have been about 1 million bankruptcies a year in the 1990s. The United States averaged only 250,000 bankruptcies in the 1960s and 1970s. The number of bankruptcies picked up in the late 1980s and grew tremendously in the 1990s. Bankruptcy attorneys say the increase in filings is due to a lessening of the stigma of bankruptcy, the changing economy, an increase in understanding of bankruptcy law and the protection it offers, and the ease with which some consumers can get credit.

voluntary bankruptcy
Legal procedures initiated by a debtor.

involuntary bankruptcy
Bankruptcy procedures filed by a debtor's creditors.

Bankruptcy can be either voluntary or involuntary. In **voluntary bankruptcy** cases, the debtor applies for bankruptcy, whereas in **involuntary bankruptcy** cases, the creditors start legal procedures against the debtor. Most bankruptcies today are voluntary because creditors usually want to wait in hopes that they'll be paid *all* of the money due them rather than settle for only part of it.

Bankruptcy procedures begin when a petition is filed with the court under one of the following sections of the Bankruptcy Code:

Chapter 7—"straight bankruptcy" or liquidation (used by businesses and individuals).

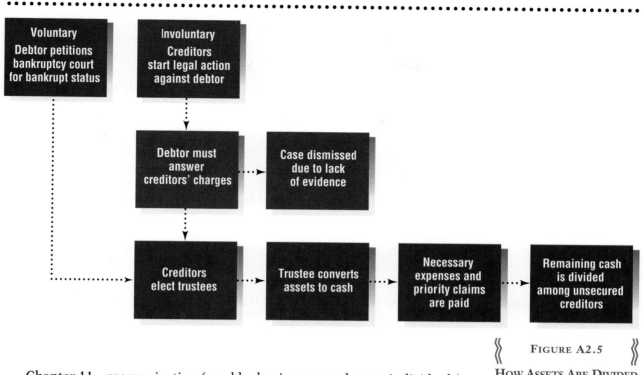

HOW ASSETS ARE DIVIDED IN BANKRUPTCY
This figure shows that the creditor (the person owed money) selects the trustee (the person or organization that handles the sale of assets). Note that the process may be started by the debtor or the creditors.

Chapter 11—reorganization (used by businesses and some individuals).

Chapter 13—repayment (used by individuals).

Chapter 7 calls for "straight bankruptcy," which requires the sale of nonexempt assets of debtors. A debtor may be able to retain up to $7,500 of equity in a home ($15,000 in a joint case); up to $1,200 of equity in an automobile; up to $4,000 in household furnishings, apparel, and musical instruments; and up to $500 in jewelry. When the sale of assets is over, the resulting cash is divided among creditors, including the government. Almost 70 percent of bankruptcies follow these procedures. Chapter 7 stipulates the order in which the assets are to be distributed among the creditors. First, creditors with *secured claims* receive the collateral for their claims or repossess the claimed asset. Then *unsecured claims* are paid in this order:

1. Costs involved in the bankruptcy case.
2. Any business costs incurred after bankruptcy was filed.
3. Wages, salaries, or commissions (limited to $2,000 per person).
4. Employee benefit plan contributions.
5. Refunds to consumers who paid for products that weren't delivered (limited to $900 per claimant).
6. Federal and state taxes.
7. The remainder (if any) is divided among unsecured creditors in proportion to their claims. Figure A2.5 shows the steps used in liquidating assets under Chapter 7.

In actuality, nearly 90 percent of the growing number of Chapter 7 filers escape any attachments of property. Creditors simply lose their investment. It's estimated that the total amount written off in personal bankruptcies in 1990 was $6 billion. Such a large amount affects the cost of credit for the rest of us since creditors face such huge potential losses.

Chapter 11 allows a company to reorganize and continue operations while paying only a limited proportion of its debts. Five percent of all bankruptcies are handled this way. Under some conditions, the company can sell assets, borrow money, and change officers to strengthen its position. All such matters usually are supervised by a trustee appointed by the court to protect the interests of creditors. Chapter 11 is designed to help both debtors and creditors find the best solution.

Under Chapter 11, a company continues to operate, but has court protection against creditors' lawsuits while it tries to work out a plan for paying off its debts. In theory, Chapter 11 is a way for sick companies to recover. In reality, less than 12 percent of Chapter 11 companies emerge healthy—usually only the big ones with lots of cash available to start with. In 1991, the U.S. Supreme Court gave individuals the right to file bankruptcy under Chapter 11, so we can expect to see many more Chapter 11 filings in the future.

Chapter 13 permits individuals, including small-business owners, to pay back creditors over a three-to-five-year period. Chapter 13 proceedings are less complicated and less expensive than Chapter 7 proceedings. The debtor files a proposed plan for paying off debts to the court. If the plan is approved, the debtor pays a court-appointed trustee in monthly installments as agreed upon in the repayment plan. The trustee then pays each creditor. About 25 percent of all bankruptcies take this form.

⧘ **FIGURE A2.6** ⧘

HAMBURGER REGULATIONS
Does this amount of regulation seem just right, too little, or too much for you?

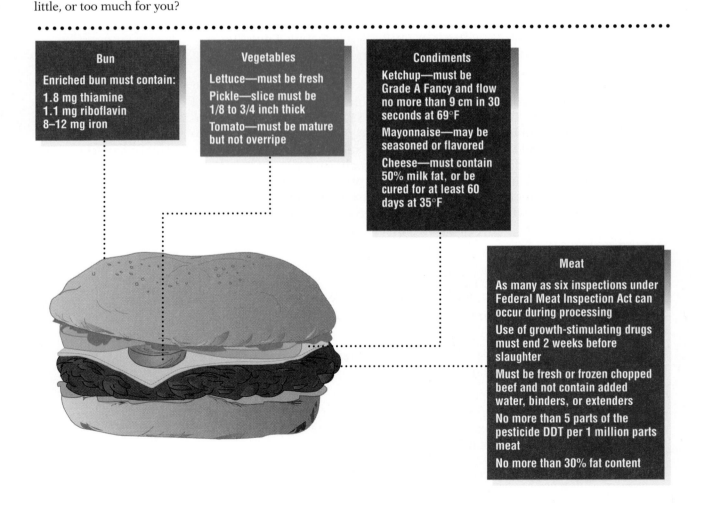

Bun

Enriched bun must contain:
1.8 mg thiamine
1.1 mg riboflavin
8–12 mg iron

Vegetables

Lettuce—must be fresh

Pickle—slice must be 1/8 to 3/4 inch thick

Tomato—must be mature but not overripe

Condiments

Ketchup—must be Grade A Fancy and flow no more than 9 cm in 30 seconds at 69°F

Mayonnaise—may be seasoned or flavored

Cheese—must contain 50% milk fat, or be cured for at least 60 days at 35°F

Meat

As many as six inspections under Federal Meat Inspection Act can occur during processing

Use of growth-stimulating drugs must end 2 weeks before slaughter

Must be fresh or frozen chopped beef and not contain added water, binders, or extenders

No more than 5 parts of the pesticide DDT per 1 million parts meat

No more than 30% fat content

DEREGULATION

By 1980, there were laws and regulations covering almost every aspect of business. There was concern that there were too many laws and regulations, and that these laws and regulations were costing the public money. (See Figure A2.6.) Thus began the movement toward deregulation. **Deregulation** means that the government withdraws certain laws and regulations that seem to hinder competition. Perhaps the most publicized example is the deregulation of the airlines. At one time, airlines were restricted by the government as to where they could fly and land. When such restrictions were lifted, airlines began competing for different routes and charging lower prices. This was a clear benefit to consumers, but it put tremendous pressure on the airlines to be more competitive. New airlines were born to take advantage of the opportunities. Similar deregulation of the trucking industry has made it more competitive as well. Today there's some call for reregulation of the airlines because they aren't serving smaller cities as well as some would like.

There's also a call for new regulations for the banking industry as a result of the savings and loan crisis of the 1980s and early 1990s. Some banks and S&Ls seem to have taken too much liberty in their unregulated state. Some regulation of business seems necessary to ensure fair and honest dealings with the public. Of course, that would be less important if businesses took on more social responsibility themselves.

There now appears to be more dialogue and more cooperation between business and government than in the past. Businesses have adapted to the laws and regulations, and have done much toward producing safer, more effective products. Competition is increasingly fierce, as many small and innovative firms have been started to capture selected markets. Global competition is also increasing. Business and government need to continue to work together to create a competitive environment that's fair and open. If businesses don't want additional regulation, they must accept their responsibilities to society.

deregulation
Government withdrawal of certain laws and regulations that seem to hinder competition (for example, airline regulations).

administrative
  agencies 131
bankruptcy 138
breach of
  contract 135
business law 130
common law 131
consideration 135
consumerism 138
contract 135
contract law 135
copyright 133

damages 135
deregulation 142
express
  warranties 134
implied
  warranties 134
involuntary
  bankruptcy 140
monopolistic
  competition 136
monopoly 136
negotiable
  instruments 134

oligopoly 136
patent 132
perfect
  competition 136
product liability 131
statutory law 131
taxes 138
tort 131
Uniform Commercial
  Code (UCC) 134
voluntary
  bankruptcy 140

KEY TERMS
•••

PART 2

BUSINESS OWNERSHIP: STARTING A SMALL BUSINESS

CHAPTER 5
OWNING A BUSINESS

CHAPTER 6
ENTREPRENEURSHIP AND THE CHALLENGE OF STARTING A SMALL BUSINESS

APPENDIX
ENTREPRENEURSHIP READINESS QUESTIONNAIRE

CHAPTER 5

OWNING A BUSINESS

LEARNING GOALS

After you have read and studied this chapter, you should be able to

1. Compare the advantages and disadvantages of sole proprietorships.

2. Describe the differences between general and limited partnerships and compare the advantages and disadvantages of partnerships.

3. Compare the advantages and disadvantages of corporations and summarize the differences between C corporations, S corporations, and limited liability companies.

4. Define and give examples of three types of corporate mergers and explain the role of leveraged buyouts and taking a firm private.

5. Outline the advantages and disadvantages of franchises and discuss the opportunities for diversity in franchising and the challenges of international franchising.

6. Explain the role of cooperatives.

TONY CONZA OF BLIMPIE
INTERNATIONAL
SANDWICH SHOPS

Tony Conza borrowed $2,000 to open his first sandwich shop with two of his old schoolmates in Hoboken, New Jersey, in 1964. Three years later, they had 10 stores. What they didn't have was enough experience to manage the business. The growing losses pushed the partners out, but Conza's self-confidence told him to stick with it. He hired an operations expert to help him learn management skills. As the business grew stronger, he hired a lawyer to prepare franchise arrangements. By 1983, there were 150 franchises and company revenues were approaching $1 million a year. Conza went public that year, putting Blimpie stock on the open market.

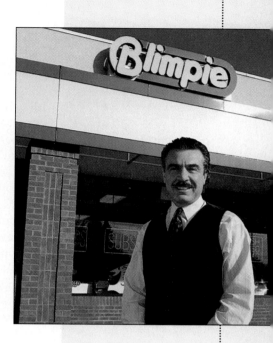

Blimpie added only 50 new franchises in the next five years. Conza grew restless. He felt that he let the details of managing deflate his entrepreneurial passion. He vowed to change from being a manager drowning in day-to-day details into a leader who could create a vision and inspire his employees and franchisees to maximize their talents. Conza chose a team of his senior managers to set goals for the company; he then delegated the new responsibilities to meet those goals to his managers. Since then, Blimpie has more than tripled in size to more than 700 stores. Now there are Blimpie outlets in such diverse places as the University of Texas at Austin campus, a bowling alley in Collinsville, Illinois, some Delta airline flights, and a hospital in Atlanta, Georgia.

Conza's business started as a partnership, changed to a sole proprietorship, changed again to a franchise operation, and finally changed to a franchise corporation. Each form of ownership has its advantages and disadvantages. You'll learn about them in this chapter.

sole proprietorship
A business that is owned, and usually managed, by one person.

partnership
A legal form of business with two or more owners.

corporation
A legal entity with authority to act and have liability separate from its owners.

Due in part to the services provided by firms such as Bell South, minority and woman-owned businesses have many opportunities for success in today's markets *if* they can provide quality goods and services at competitive prices.

BASIC FORMS OF BUSINESS OWNERSHIP

Like Tony Conza, hundreds of thousands of Americans start new businesses every year. Chances are you've thought of owning your own business or know someone who has. One key to success in a new business is knowing how to get the resources you need to start. You may need to take on partners or find other ways of obtaining money. To stay in business, you may need help from someone with more expertise than you have in certain areas, or you may need to raise more money to expand. How you form your business can make a tremendous difference in your long-term success. You can form a business in several ways. The three major forms of business ownership are (1) sole proprietorships, (2) partnerships, and (3) corporations.

It's easy to get started in your own business. You can begin a word processing service out of your home, open a car repair center, start a restaurant, or go about meeting other wants and needs of the community on your own. An organization that is owned, and usually managed, by one person is called a **sole proprietorship**. That's the most common form of business ownership (over 12 million firms).

Many people lack the money, time, or desire to run a business on their own. They prefer to have someone else or some group of people get together to form the business. When two or more people legally agree to become co-owners of a business, the organization is called a **partnership** (about 1.4 million firms).

There are advantages to creating a business that's separate and distinct from the owners. A legal entity with authority to act and have liability separate from its owners is called a **corporation**. There are only 2.8 million corporations in the United States (17 percent of all businesses), but they do 87 percent of the business. (See Figure 5.1.)

As you'll learn in this chapter, each form of business ownership has its advantages and disadvantages. You must understand these advantages and disadvantages before starting a business. Keep in mind that just because a business starts in one form of ownership, it doesn't always stay in that form. Many companies start out in one form (like Blimpie International sandwich shops in the Profile), then add or drop a partner or two, and eventually become corporations and/or franchisors. Let's begin our research by looking at the most basic form of ownership, the sole proprietorship.

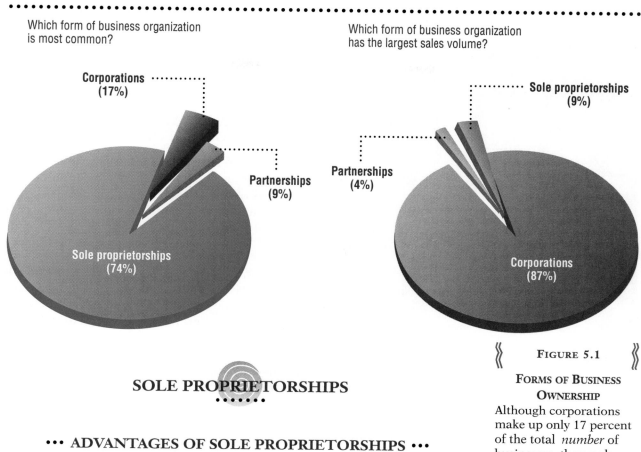

Which form of business organization is most common?

Corporations (17%)

Partnerships (9%)

Sole proprietorships (74%)

Which form of business organization has the largest sales volume?

Sole proprietorships (9%)

Partnerships (4%)

Corporations (87%)

FIGURE 5.1

FORMS OF BUSINESS OWNERSHIP
Although corporations make up only 17 percent of the total *number* of businesses, they make 87 percent of the sales volume. Sole proprietorships are the most common form of ownership (74 percent), but they represent only 9 percent of sales volume.

SOLE PROPRIETORSHIPS

••• ADVANTAGES OF SOLE PROPRIETORSHIPS •••

Sole proprietorships are the easiest kind of business for you to explore in your quest for an interesting career. Every town has some sole proprietorships that you can visit. There's the local produce stand, the beauty shop, and the auto repair garage. You'll find sole proprietors who do income taxes, repair household appliances, and provide all kinds of local services. Talk with them about the joys and frustrations of being on their own. Most people will mention the benefits of being their own boss and setting their own hours. Other advantages they may mention include

1. *Ease of starting and ending the business.* All you have to do to start a sole proprietorship is buy or lease the needed equipment (for example, a saw, word processor, tractor, or lawn mower) and generate some form of an announcement that you're in business. It's just as easy to get out of business; you simply stop. There's no one to consult or to disagree with about such decisions. You may have to get a permit or license from the local government, but that's often no problem.

2. *Being your own boss.* "Working for others simply doesn't have the same excitement as working for yourself," many sole proprietors say. You may make mistakes, but they're your mistakes—and so are the many small victories each day.

3. *Pride of ownership.* People who own and manage their own businesses are rightfully proud of their work. They deserve all the credit for taking the risks and providing needed goods or services.

4. *Retention of profit.* Other than the joy of being your own boss, there's nothing like the pleasure of knowing that you can make as much as you can and don't have to share that money with anyone else (except the government, in taxes).

Natalie Towles owns her own catering business. She has the freedom to make all her own business decisions that she would not necessarily have if she had a partner. But this increased freedom also includes increased risks. Just as Natalie gets to keep all the profits her business makes, she must also pay for any mistakes she makes.

unlimited liability
The responsibility of business owners for all of the debts of the business; making the personal assets of the owners vulnerable to claims against the business. Sole proprietors and general partners have unlimited liability.

5. *No special taxes.* All the profits of a sole proprietorship are taxed as the personal income of the owner, and he or she pays the normal income tax on that money. Owners do have to file an estimated tax return and make quarterly payments.

··· DISADVANTAGES OF ···
SOLE PROPRIETORSHIPS

Not everyone is cut out to own and manage a business. Often it's hard to save enough money to start a business and keep it going. Often the costs of inventory, supplies, insurance, advertising, rent, utilities, and other factors are simply too much to cover alone. There are other disadvantages of owning your own business:

1. *Unlimited liability—the risk of losses.* When you work for others, it's their problem if the business isn't profitable. When you own your own business, you and the business are considered one. You have **unlimited liability**; that is, any debts or damages incurred by the business are your debts and you must pay them, even if it means selling your home, your car, and so forth. This is a serious risk—one that requires thought and discussion with a lawyer, insurance agent, and others.

2. *Limited financial resources.* Funds available to the business are limited to the funds that the one (sole) owner can gather. Since there are serious limits to how much money one person can raise, partnerships and corporations have a greater probability of recruiting the needed financial backing to start a business and keep it going.

3. *Difficulty in management.* Most businesses need some management; that is, someone must keep inventory records, accounting records, tax records, and so on. Many people who are skilled at selling things or providing a service aren't so skilled in keeping records. Sole proprietors may have no one to help them. It's often hard to find good, qualified people to help run the business.

4. *Overwhelming time commitment.* It's hard to own a business, manage it, train people, and have time for anything else in life. The owner must spend long hours working. The owner of a store, for example, may put in 12 hours a day at least six days a week—almost twice the hours worked by a salaried laborer. Imagine how this time commitment affects the sole proprietor's family life. Tim DeMello, founder of successful Wall Street Games Inc., echoes countless sole proprietors when he says, "It's not a job, it's not a career, it's a way of life."[1]

5. *Few fringe benefits.* If you're your own boss, you lose the fringe benefits that come from working for others. You have no health insurance, no disability insurance, no sick leave, no vacation pay, and so on. These benefits may add up to 30 percent or more of a worker's income.

6. *Limited growth.* If the owner becomes incapacitated, the business often comes to a standstill. Expansion is often slow since a sole proprietorship relies on its owner for most of its creativity, business know-how, and funding.

7. *Limited life span.* If the sole proprietor dies or retires, the business no longer exists unless it's sold or taken over by the sole proprietor's heirs.

Many of the disadvantages of owning your own business are taken care of when you find a business partner. When one partner is not there, the other can take over operations. Although the funding for partnerships is easier than for sole proprietorships, it is harder than for corporations. David Tran and his son Robert, shown here standing in front of the Little Saigon Supermarket, have formed a family partnership.

Talk with a few local entrepreneurs about the problems they've faced in being on their own. They're likely to have many interesting stories to tell, such as problems getting loans from the bank, problems with theft, and problems simply keeping up with the business. These problems are also reasons why many sole proprietors choose to find partners to share the load.

Have you ever dreamed of opening your own business? If you did, what would it be? What talents or skills do you have that you could use? Could you start a business in your own home? How much would it cost to start? Could you begin part time while you worked elsewhere? What satisfaction and profit could you get from owning your own business? What would you lose?

PARTNERSHIPS

A partnership is a legal form of business with two or more owners. All states except Louisiana have adopted the Uniform Partnership Act (UPA) to replace laws relating to partnerships. The UPA defines the three key elements of any general partnership as (1) common ownership, (2) shared profits and losses, and (3) the right to participate in managing the operations of the business.[2]

There are several types of partnerships: (1) general partnerships, (2) limited partnerships, and (3) master limited partnerships. A **general partnership** is a partnership in which all owners share in operating the business and in assuming liability for the business's debts. A **limited partnership** is a partnership with one or more general partners and one or more limited partners. A **general partner** is an owner (partner) who has unlimited liability and is active in managing the firm. A **limited partner** risks an investment in the firm, but enjoys limited liability and cannot legally help manage the company. **Limited liability** means that limited partners aren't responsible for the business's debts beyond the amount of their investment—their liability (debts they must pay) is limited to the amount they put into the company; their personal assets aren't at risk.

CRITICAL THINKING

general partnership
A partnership in which all owners share in operating the business and in assuming liability for the business's debts.

limited partnership
A partnership with one or more general partners and one or more limited partners.

general partner
An owner (partner) who has unlimited liability and is active in managing the firm.

limited partner
Owner who invests money in the business but does not have any management responsibility or liability for losses beyond the investment.

limited liability
The responsibility of a business's owners for losses only up to the amount they invest; limited partners and shareholders have limited liability.

**master limited
partnership (MLP)**
A partnership that looks much like
a corporation in that it acts like a
corporation, but is taxed like a
partnership and thus avoids the
corporate income tax.

A new form of partnership, the **master limited partnership (MLP)**, looks much like a corporation in that it acts like a corporation and is traded on the stock exchanges like a corporation, but is taxed like a partnership and thus avoids the corporate income tax. Some well-known MLPs include Burger King and Perkins Family Restaurants.[3]

••• ADVANTAGES OF PARTNERSHIPS •••

There are many advantages of having one or more partners in a business. Often, it's much easier to own and manage a business with one or more partners. Your partner can cover for you when you're sick or go on vacation. Your partner may be skilled at inventory keeping and accounting, while you do the selling or servicing. A partner can also provide additional money, support, and expertise. People enjoying the advantages of partnerships today include doctors, lawyers, dentists, and other professionals. Partnerships usually have these advantages:

1. *More financial resources*. Naturally, when two or more people pool their money and credit, it's easier to pay the business's rent, utilities, and other bills. A limited partnership is specially designed to help raise capital (money). As mentioned earlier, a limited partner invests money in the business, but can't legally have any management responsibility and has limited liability.

2. *Shared management and pooled knowledge*. It's simply much easier to manage the day-to-day activities of a business with carefully chosen partners than to do it alone. Partners give each other free time from the business and provide different skills and perspectives. Many people find that the best partner is a spouse. That's why you see so many husband–wife teams managing restaurants, service shops, and other businesses.

3. *Longer survival*. Partnerships may be more likely to succeed than sole proprietorships. Having a partner helps a businessperson to become more disciplined because someone is watching over him or her.

••• DISADVANTAGES OF PARTNERSHIPS •••

Any time two people must agree on anything, there's the possibility of conflict and tension. Partnerships have caused splits among families, friends, and marriages. Let's explore four disadvantages of partnerships:

1. *Unlimited liability*. Each general partner is liable for the debts of the firm, no matter who was responsible for causing those debts. You're liable for your partners' mistakes as well as your own. Like a sole proprietor, general partners can lose their homes, cars, and everything else they own if the business is sued by someone. Many states are allowing partners to form limited liability partnerships (LLPs) to end this disadvantage.[4]

2. *Division of profits*. Sharing the risk means sharing the profit, and that can cause conflicts. For example, two people form a partnership; one puts in more money and the other puts in more hours. Each may feel justified in asking for a bigger share of the profits. Imagine the resulting conflicts.

• •

How to Form a Partnership

It's not hard to form a partnership, but it's wise for each prospective partner to get the counsel of a lawyer experienced with such agreements. Lawyers' services are usually expensive, so would-be partners should read all about partnerships and reach some basic agreements before calling a lawyer. One good book that covers the basics of forming a partnership is *The New Jacoby & Meyers Practical Guide to Everyday Law* (Fireside Press/Simon & Schuster, 1994).

For your protection, be sure to put your partnership agreement in writing. The Model Business Corporation Act recommends including the following in a written partnership agreement:

1. The name of the business. Many states require the firm's name to be registered with state and/or county officials if the firm's name is different from the name of any of the partners.

2. The names and addresses of all partners.

3. The purpose and nature of the business, the location of the principal offices, and any other locations where the business will be conducted.

4. The date the partnership will start and how long it will last. Will it exist for a specific length of time or will it stop when one of the partners dies or when the partners agree to discontinue?

5. The contributions made by each partner. Will some partners contribute money, while others provide real estate, personal property, expertise, or labor? When are the contributions due?

6. The management responsibilities. Will all partners have equal voices in management or will there be senior and junior partners?

7. The duties of each partner.

8. The salaries and drawing accounts of each partner.

9. Provision for sharing of profits or losses.

10. Provision for accounting procedures. Who'll keep the accounts? What bookkeeping and accounting methods will be used? Where will the books be kept?

11. The requirements for taking in new partners.

12. Any special restrictions, rights, or duties of any partner.

13. Provision for a retiring partner.

14. Provision for the purchase of a deceased or retiring partner's share of the business.

15. Provision for how grievances will be handled.

16. Provision for how to dissolve the partnership and distribute the assets to the partners.

• •

3. *Disagreements among partners.* Disagreements over money are just one example of potential conflict in a partnership. Who has final authority over employees? Who hires and fires employees? Who works what hours? What if one partner wants to buy expensive equipment for the firm and the other partner disagrees? Potential conflicts are many. Because of such problems, all terms of partnership should be spelled out in writing to protect all parties and to minimize misunderstanding in the future (see the list above).

4. *Difficult to terminate.* Once you've committed yourself to a partnership, it's not easy to get out of it. Sure, you can end a partnership by just saying, "I quit." However, questions about who gets what and what happens next are often difficult to solve when the business is closed. Surprisingly, law firms often have faulty partnership agreements and find that breaking up is hard to do. How do you get rid of a partner you don't like? It's best to decide that up front—in the partnership agreement.

SPOTLIGHT ON SMALL BUSINESS

Choose Your Partner

Suppose you need money and want help running your business, and you decide to take on a partner. You know that partnerships are like marriages and that you won't really know the other person until after you live together. How do you choose the right partner? C. D. Peterson, a business broker who wrote *How to Leave Your Job and Buy a Business of Your Own* and *How to Sell Your Business,* suggests you do three things before you plunge into a partnership:

1. Talk to people who've been in successful—and unsuccessful—partnerships. Find out what worked and what didn't. Ask them how conflicts were resolved and decisions were made.

2. Interview your prospective partner carefully. What skills does the person have? Are they the same as yours or do they complement your skills? What contacts, resources, or special attributes will the person bring to the business? Do the two of you feel the same about family members working for the business? Do you share the same vision for the company's future?

3. Evaluate your prospective partner as a decision maker. Ask yourself, "Is this someone with whom I could happily share authority for all major business decisions?"

Corey Sandler used this process when he searched for his partner for his editorial services business. He made a list of the characteristics he wanted in a business mate. At the top of his list were flexible work habits, varied experience in writing, and honesty. He then made another list of the people he knew and respected; next he applied his criteria to the list. He tossed out every name but one—Tom Badgett. The new partners divide their work according to their particular strengths, and then pass portions of their works in progress back and forth. Somehow it all comes together—just like most other good marriages! On the other hand, a 1992 *Inc.* magazine survey found that 60 percent of respondents felt that "Personal conflicts outweigh the benefits of partnerships." The best way to avoid major conflicts is to begin with an honest communication of what each partner expects to give and get from the partnership.

Source: Don Wallace, "Power in Numbers," *Home Office Computing,* February 1994, pp. 56–61; C. D. Peterson, "Build Your Power Base: How to Choose the Right Partner," *Success,* April 1991, p. 12; Corey Sandler, "Taking On a Partner," *Home Office Computing,* May 1990, pp. 49–50; and "Are Partners Bad for Business?" *Inc.,* February 1992, p. 24.

Again, the best way to learn about the advantages and disadvantages of partnerships is to interview people with experience doing such agreements. They'll give you insights and hints on how to avoid problems.

One fear of owning your own business or having a partner is the fear of losing everything you own if the business loses a lot of money or someone sues the business. Many businesspeople try to avoid this and the other disadvantages of sole proprietorships and partnerships by forming corporations. We'll discuss this basic form of business ownership next.

PROGRESS CHECK

- Most Americans who start a business are sole proprietors. What are the advantages and disadvantages of this form of business?
- What are some advantages of partnerships over sole proprietorships?
- Why would unlimited liability be considered one of the biggest drawbacks to sole proprietorships and general partnerships?
- What's the difference between a limited partner and a general partner?

Size and money are just two substantial advantages enjoyed by corporations such as Nike. Clearly, corporations have many advantages over other forms of business, but there are disadvantages as well. How many can you identify?

CORPORATIONS

Although the word *corporation* makes people think of big businesses like General Motors, IBM, FedEx, Exxon, GE, Westinghouse, and USX (formerly U.S. Steel), it's not necessary to be big in order to incorporate (start a corporation). Obviously, many corporations are big. However, incorporating may be beneficial for small businesses also.

A conventional (C) corporation is a state-chartered legal entity with authority to act and have liability separate from its owners. What this means for the corporation's owners (stockholders) is that they aren't liable for the debts or any other problems of the corporation beyond the money they invest. Owners no longer have to worry about losing their house, car, and other property because of some business problem—a significant benefit. A corporation not only limits owners' liability, it enables many people to share in the ownership (and profits) of a business without working there or having other commitments to it.

••• ADVANTAGES OF CORPORATIONS •••

Most people aren't willing to risk everything to go into business. Yet, for businesses to grow and prosper and create abundance, many people would have to be willing to invest their money in businesses. The way to solve this problem was to create an artificial entity, one that exists only in the eyes of the law—a corporation. Let's explore some of the advantages:

1. *More money for investment.* To raise money, a corporation sells ownership (stock) to anyone who's interested. This means that millions of people can own part of major companies like IBM, Xerox, and General Motors and smaller companies as well. If a company sold 10 million shares for $50 each, it would have $500 million available to build plants, buy materials, hire people, build products, and so on. Such a large amount of money would be difficult to raise any other way. Corporations may also find it easier to obtain loans since lenders find it easier to place a value on the company when it can review how the stock is trading.

2. *Limited liability.* A major advantage of corporations is the limited liability of owners. Corporations in England and Canada often have the letters *Ltd.* after their name, as in British Motors, Ltd. *Ltd.*

stands for *limited liability*, which is probably the most significant advantage of corporations. Remember, limited liability means that the owners of a business are responsible for losses only up to the amount they invest.

3. *Size.* That one word summarizes many advantages of corporations. Because they have large amounts of money to work with, corporations can build large, modern factories with the latest equipment. They can also hire experts or specialists in all areas of operation. Furthermore, they can buy other corporations in other fields to diversify their risk. (This means that a corporation can be involved in many businesses at once so that if one fails, the effect on the total corporation is lessened.) In short, a major advantage of corporations is that they have the size and resources to take advantage of opportunities anywhere in the world. Corporations don't have to be large to enjoy the benefits of incorporating. Many doctors, lawyers, and individuals and partners in a variety of businesses have incorporated. There are many small corporations in the United States.

4. *Perpetual life.* Because corporations are separate from the people who own them, the death of one or more owners doesn't terminate the corporation.

5. *Ease of ownership change.* It's easy to change the owners of a corporation. Simply sell the stock to someone else.

6. *Ease of drawing talented employees.* Corporations can attract skilled employees by offering such benefits as stock options (the right to purchase shares of the corporation for a fixed price).

7. *Separation of ownership from management.* Corporations can raise money from many different investors without getting them involved in management. Figure 5.2 shows the corporate hierarchy.

The pyramid in Figure 5.2 shows that the owners/shareholders are separate from the managers and employers. The owners elect a board of directors. The directors select the officers. They, in turn, hire managers and employees. The owners thus have some say in who runs the corporation, but no control.

••• DISADVANTAGES OF CORPORATIONS •••

There are so many sole proprietorships and partnerships in the United States that there clearly must be some disadvantages to incorporating. Otherwise, more people would incorporate their businesses. Here are a few disadvantages:

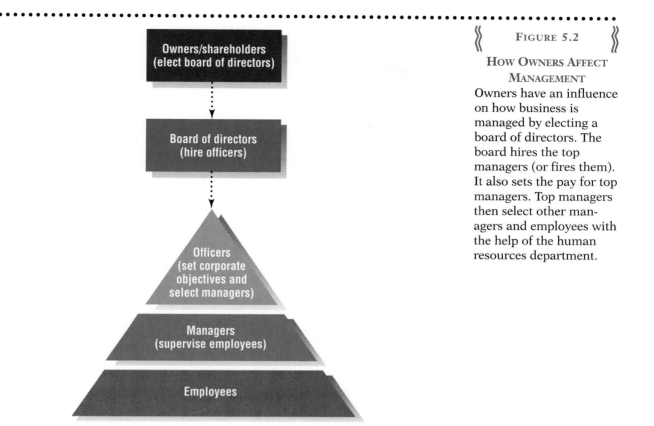

FIGURE 5.2

HOW OWNERS AFFECT
MANAGEMENT
Owners have an influence
on how business is
managed by electing a
board of directors. The
board hires the top
managers (or fires them).
It also sets the pay for top
managers. Top managers
then select other man-
agers and employees with
the help of the human
resources department.

1. *Initial cost.* Incorporation may cost thousands of dollars and involve expensive lawyers and accountants. There are less expensive ways of incorporating in certain states. (See the subsection "Individuals Can Incorporate" later in this chapter.) But few people have the time or confidence to go through this procedure without a lawyer's help.

2. *Paperwork.* The papers to be filed to start a corporation are just the beginning. Tax laws demand that a corporation prove all its expenses and deductions are legitimate.[5] A corporation, therefore, must process many forms. A sole proprietor or partnership may keep rather broad accounting records; a corporation, on the other hand, must keep detailed records, the minutes of meetings, and more.

3. *Two tax returns.* If an individual incorporates, he or she must file both a corporate tax return and an individual tax return. The corporate return can be quite complex.

4. *Size.* Size may be one advantage of corporations, but it can be a dis- advantage as well. Large corporations sometimes become too inflexi- ble and too tied down in red tape to respond quickly to market changes. One analyst, for example, said that IBM lost market share because is was "big and bloated."[6]

5. *Difficulty of termination.* Once a corporation is started, it's relatively hard to end.

6. *Double taxation.* Corporate income is taxed twice. First, the corpora- tion pays tax on income before it can distribute any to stockholders. Then the stockholders pay tax on the income (dividends) they receive from the corporation. States often tax corporations more harshly than other enterprises. Sometimes they levy special taxes that apply to cor- porations, but not to other forms of business.

How to Incorporate

The process of forming a corporation varies somewhat from state to state. The articles of incorporation are usually filed with the secretary of state's office in the state in which the company incorporates. The articles contain

- The corporation's name.
- The names of the people who incorporated it.
- Its purposes.
- Its duration (usually perpetual).
- The number of shares that can be issued, their voting rights, and any other rights the shareholders have.
- The corporation's minimum capital.
- The address of the corporation's office.
- The name and address of the person responsible for the corporation's legal service.
- The names and addresses of the first directors.
- Any other public information the incorporators wish to include.

Before a business can so much as open a bank account or hire employees, it needs a federal tax identification number. To apply for one, get an SS-4 form from the IRS.

In addition to the articles of incorporation listed, a corporation also has bylaws. These describe how the firm is to be operated from both legal and managerial points of view. The bylaws include

- How, when, and where shareholders' and directors' meetings are held, and how long directors are to serve.
- Directors' authority.
- Duties and responsibilities of officers, and the length of their service.
- How stock is issued.
- Other matters, including employment contracts.

Source: Stephen L. Nelson, "How Not to Incorporate," *Home Office Computing,* February 1994, pp. 28–30.

7. *Possible conflict with the board of directors.* Some conflict may brew if the stockholders elect a board of directors that disagrees with the present management. Since the board of directors chooses the company's officers, an entrepreneur could find himself forced out of the very company he founded—which happened to Steve Jobs at Apple Computer.

Many people are discouraged by the costs, paperwork, and special taxes corporations must pay. Partners may feel that the hassles of incorporation outweigh the advantages.

Here we see a nonprofit corporation in action during Hurricane Andrew. The Red Cross is there when disaster strikes. Nonprofit corporations ≪ P.32 ≫ get tax breaks from the government because of the good work they do.

Corporate Types

You may find some confusing types of corporations when reading about them. Here are a few of the more widely used terms:

An *alien corporation* does business in the United States, but is chartered (incorporated) in another country.

A *domestic corporation* does business in the state in which it's chartered (incorporated).

A *foreign corporation* does business in one state, but is chartered in another. About one third of all corporations are chartered in Delaware because of its relatively attractive rules for incorporation. A foreign corporation must register in states where it operates.

A *closed (private) corporation* is one whose stock is held by a few people and isn't available to the general public.

An *open (public) corporation* sells stock to the general public. General Motors and Exxon are examples of public corporations.

A *quasi-public corporation* is a corporation chartered by government as an approved monopoly to perform services to the general public. Public utilities are examples of quasi-public corporations.

A *professional corporation* is one whose owners offer professional services (doctors, lawyers, etc.). Shares in professional corporations aren't publicly traded.

A *nonprofit corporation* is one that doesn't seek personal profit for its owners.

A *multinational corporation* is a firm that operates in several countries.

••• INDIVIDUALS CAN INCORPORATE •••

A corporation doesn't need to have hundreds of employees or thousands of stockholders. Individuals (for example, doctors, lawyers, and rock stars) can also incorporate. By doing so, they may save on taxes and receive other benefits of incorporation. Many firms incorporate in Delaware because it's relatively easy to do so there. Ted S. Nicholas's book *How to Form Your Own Corporation without a Lawyer for Under $500* (Enterprise Publications) tells you the steps to take.

••• S CORPORATIONS •••

A form of ownership receiving growing attention in the past few years is the S corporation. An **S corporation** is a unique government creation that looks like a corporation but is taxed like sole proprietorships and partnerships. S corporations have the benefit of limited liability. The paperwork and details of S corporations are similar to those of regular corporations. S corporations have shareholders, directors, and employees, but the profits are taxed as the personal income of the shareholders—thus avoiding the double taxation of conventional corporations. However, S corporations must pay self-employment taxes.[7]

Avoiding the double corporate tax rate was enough reason for 1.6 million small U.S. companies to operate as S corporations. The benefits of S corporations change every time the tax rules change. The best way to learn all the benefits for a specific business is to go over the tax advantages and liability differences with a lawyer or accountant or both.

Not all businesses can become S corporations. To qualify, a company must

1. Have shareholders who are individuals or estates and are citizens or permanent residents of the United States.

2. Have only one class of outstanding stock.

3. Not own 80 percent or more of the stock of another corporation.

4. Not have more than 25 percent of income derived from passive sources (rents, royalties, interest, etc.).

S corporation
A unique government creation that looks like a corporation but is taxed like sole proprietorships and partnerships.

Recently (1995) the IRS increased the number of shareholders who could participate in an S corporation. There is now no real limit to the number of shareholders. The rules regarding S corporations change often, however, so check with an attorney before choosing *any* form of business.[8]

S corporations lost much of their attraction in the early 1990s for two reasons: (1) Tax law changes increased the top rate on the owners of S corporations to 39.6 percent—nearly six percentage points higher than the top rate on a C corporation's earnings. (2) States were passing new legislation creating limited liability companies that had much the same appeal.

Fast-growing small businesses are switching to C corporation status to avoid the higher taxes. They don't intend to pay dividends to owners because they need the money for new investment. Thus, they aren't subject to double taxation. Slower-growing businesses, on the other hand, have been keeping the S corporation form of ownership.[9] Next we'll discuss limited liability companies—the newest form of business ownership.

••• LIMITED LIABILITY COMPANIES •••

limited-liability company
A company similar to an S corporation but without the special eligibility requirements.

Billed as the "business entity of the future," a **limited-liability company** is similar to an S corporation without the special eligibility requirements. The concept of limited liability companies is so new that the various states haven't adopted uniform legislation regarding them. However, a draft law called the Uniform Limited Liability Company Act was prepared for the National Conference of Commissioners on Uniform State Laws. Therefore, most states will soon have some type of legislation about this form of ownership.

Two features of the draft are important to small-business owners. The first feature is the adoption of a sole-member limited liability company, which would provide liability protection for sole proprietorships. When this law passes, it's expected that the majority of sole proprietors will adopt this form of ownership. The second feature is the adoption of at-will limited liability companies, which would enable every member of the company to withdraw at any time and receive fair market value for his or her interest.[10] Limited liability companies are likely to become one of the most popular forms of business ownership. Watch the business press to see the latest developments.

Limited liability companies have all the flexibility of partnerships with the same kind of liability protection provided for corporations. It's relatively easy to switch from a limited liability company to a C corporation status if you so desire. You would do that to raise more money. Limited liability companies are so new that you may want to do some research on your own before making any final decision. You can get such information by contacting the Association of Limited Liability Companies in Washington, D.C. (telephone (202) 965–6565). The Commerce Clearing House also has a user-friendly introduction called *A Guide to Limited Liability Companies*. Call 1–800–835–5224 for information. Figure 5.3 on page 162 lists advantages and disadvantages of the major forms of business ownership.

PROGRESS CHECK

- What are the major advantages and disadvantages of incorporating a business?
- What is the role of owners (stockholders) in the corporate hierarchy?
- If you buy stock in a corporation and someone gets injured by one of the corporation's products, can you be sued? Why or why not?
- Could you be sued if you were a general partner in a partnership?

	Sole Proprietorship	Partnerships		Corporations		
		General Partnership	Limited Partnership	Conventional Corporation	S Corporations	Limited Liability Company
Documents needed to start business	None, may need permit or license	Partnership agreement (oral or written)	Written agreement. Must file certificate of limited partnership	Articles of incorporation, bylaws	Articles of incorporation, bylaws, must meet criteria	Articles of organization and operating agreement. No eligibility requirements
Ease of termination	Easy to terminate: just pay debts and quit	May be hard to terminate, depending on the partnership agreement	Same as general partnership	Hard and expensive to terminate	Same as conventional corporation	May be difficult, depending upon operating agreement
Length of life	Terminates on the death of owner	Terminates on the death or withdrawal of partner	Same as general partnership	Perpetual life	Same as conventional corporation	Same as partnership
Transfer of ownership	Business can be sold to qualified buyer	Must have other partner(s)' agreement	Same as general partnership	Easy to change owners; just sell stock	Can sell stock, but with restrictions	Can't sell stock
Financial resources	Limited to owner's capital and loans	Limited to partners' capital and loans	Same as general partnership	More money to start and operate; may sell stocks and bonds	Same as conventional corporation	Same as partnership
Risk of losses	Unlimited liability	Unlimited liability	Limited liability	Limited liability	Limited liability	Limited liability
Taxes	Taxed as personal income	Taxed as personal income	Same as general partnership	Corporate, double taxation	Taxed as personal income	Taxed as personal income
Management responsibilities	Owner manages *all* areas of the business	Partners share management	Can't participate in management	Separate management from ownership	Same as conventional corporation	Varies
Employee benefits	Usually fewer benefits and lower wages	Often fewer benefits and lower wages; promising employee could become a partner	Same as general partnership	Usually better benefits and wages, advancement opportunities	Same as conventional corporation	Varies

{{ FIGURE 5.3 }}

COMPARISON OF FORMS OF
BUSINESS OWNERSHIP

In the past, forming a corporation was the only way to achieve limited liability. Why would most sole proprietors and partners be expected to form limited liability companies in the future rather than corporations if they have the chance?

CRITICAL THINKING

CORPORATE EXPANSION: MERGERS AND ACQUISITIONS

Merger mania continued in corporate America through the mid 1990s as the number of mergers surged to near the record level of the 1980s.[11] The trend is a result of major changes in the entertainment, drug, and telecommunications industries. We saw such megadeals as the $10 billion battle for Paramount between QVC and Viacom, AT&T's $17.6 billion purchase of McCaw Cellular, and Merck's $6 billion acquisition of Medco. Most of the new deals involve companies trying to expand within their own fields to save costs, enter new markets, or adapt to changing technologies or regulations.[12]

What's the difference between mergers and acquisitions? A **merger** is the result of two firms forming one company. Sounds like a marriage, doesn't it? An **acquisition** is one company buying the property and obligations of another company. It is more like buying a house than entering a marriage.

There are three major types of corporate mergers: vertical, horizontal, and conglomerate. A **vertical merger** is the joining of two firms involved in different stages of related businesses. Think of a merger between a bicycle company and a company that produces wheels. Such a merger would ensure a constant supply of wheels needed by the bicycle company. It could also help ensure quality control of the bicycle company's product. A **horizontal merger** joins two firms in the same industry and allows them to diversify or expand their products. An example of a horizontal merger is the merger of a bicycle company and a tricycle company. The business can now supply a variety of cycling products. A **conglomerate merger** unites firms in completely unrelated industries. The primary purpose of a conglomerate merger is to diversify business operations and investments. The acquisition of a restaurant chain by a bicycle company would be an example of a conglomerate merger. Figure 5.4 distinguishes between the three types of mergers.

Rather than merge or sell to another company, some corporations decide to maintain control of the firm internally. For example, Cox Communications, a large firm in the cable TV industry, decided to take the firm private. What does this mean? Taking a firm private involves the efforts of a group of stockholders or management to obtain all the firm's stock for themselves. In the Cox situation, the Cox family successfully gained total control of the company. The stock can no longer be purchased by investors in the open market.

Suppose the employees in an organization believe that there's a good possibility they may lose their jobs. Or what if management believes that corporate performance could be enhanced if it owned the company? Do either of these groups have an opportunity to take ownership of the company? Yes— they might attempt a leveraged buyout. A **leveraged buyout (LBO)** is an attempt by employees, management, or a group of investors to purchase an organization primarily through borrowing. The funds borrowed are used to buy out the company's stockholders. The employees, managers, or group of investors now become the owners of the firm.

Merger mania isn't restricted to American companies. For example, foreign companies are gobbling up U.S. food companies. British candy and soft drink producer Cadbury Schweppes bought the largest American root beer producer, A&W, for $334 million in 1993. Unilever, a Dutch company, bought Kraft General Foods' ice cream division (makers of Breyers and Sealtest). Why the buying binge? Some analysts suggest the spree was brought on by a slumping dollar, depressed stock prices, sluggish U.S. spending, and increasing globalization. Foreign companies have found that the quickest way to grow is to buy an established U.S. operation and bring the brands and technology to Europe.[13]

merger
The result of two firms forming one company.

acquisition
A company's purchase of the property and obligations of another company.

vertical merger
The joining of two companies involved in different stages of related businesses.

horizontal merger
The joining of two firms in the same industry.

conglomerate merger
The joining of firms in completely unrelated industries.

leveraged buyout (LBO)
An attempt by employees, management, or a group of investors to purchase an organization primarily through borrowing.

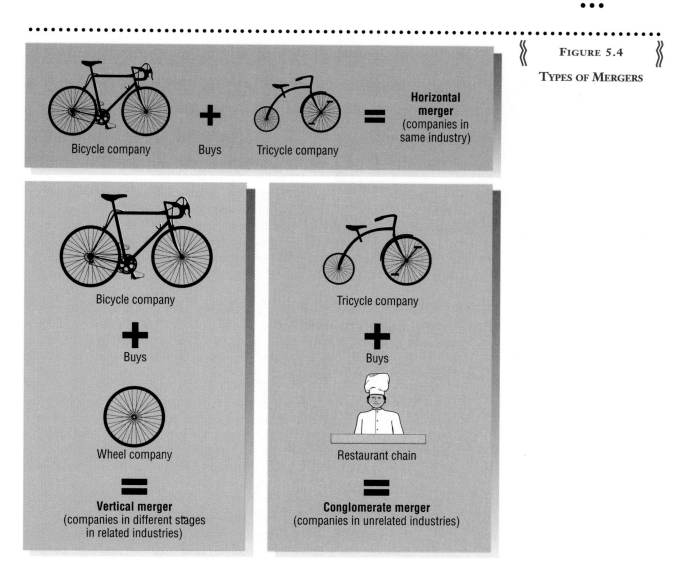

FIGURE 5.4

TYPES OF MERGERS

Bicycle company   Buys   Tricycle company   =   **Horizontal merger** (companies in same industry)

Bicycle company
+
Buys
Wheel company
=
Vertical merger (companies in different stages in related industries)

Tricycle company
+
Buys
Restaurant chain
=
Conglomerate merger (companies in unrelated industries)

SPECIAL FORMS OF BUSINESS OWNERSHIP

In addition to the three basic forms of business ownership, we'll discuss two special forms of ownership: franchises and cooperatives.

Basically, a **franchise agreement** is an arrangement whereby someone with a good idea for a business (the **franchisor**) sells the rights to use the business name and to sell a product or service (the **franchise**) to others (the **franchisee**) in a given territory. A **cooperative** is an organization owned by members/customers who pay an annual membership fee and share in any profits (if it's a profit-making organization). Let's look at franchises first.

••• FRANCHISES •••

Some people are more comfortable not starting their own business from scratch. They'd rather join a business with a proven track record through a franchise agreement. A franchise can be formed as a sole proprietorship, partnership, or corporation. Some of the best known franchises include McDonald's, Domino's, 7-Eleven, and Holiday Inn.

franchise agreement
An arrangement whereby someone with a good idea for a business sells the rights to use the business name and sell its products or services to others in a given territory.

franchisor
A company that develops a product concept and sells others the rights to make and sell the products.

franchise
The right to use a specific business's name and sell its products or services in a given territory.

franchisee
A person who buys a franchise.

cooperative
An organization owned by members/customers who pay an annual membership fee and share in any profits (if it is a profit-making organization).

Who would have thought what the world needed was another steakhouse? But now Outback Steakhouse, started in 1988 in Tampa, Florida, is one of the hottest and most successful new franchises. Original plans called for only five restaurants, all within the Tampa Bay area. Six years later there were 210 stores and growth remains in full swing. Founders Robert Basham, Chris Sullivan, and Tim Gannon, who previously worked for the Steak & Ale restaurant chain, were named Entrepreneurs of the Year by *Inc.* magazine in 1994.

The potential in franchising is impressive. In 1993, there were over 540,000 franchised outlets in the United States.[14] Government projections show that franchising sales could account for nearly 50 percent of all retail sales in the United States during the 1990s.[15] With about one out of every three retailers now operating as a franchise, you shouldn't have much difficulty finding places to visit where you can get more information from franchise owners/managers.

When you think of franchising, however, don't confine your thoughts to the United States. Some enterprising entrepreneurs have had great success taking American franchises overseas. For example, McDonald's has nearly 4,500 restaurants outside the United States.[16]

ADVANTAGES OF FRANCHISES   Franchising has penetrated every aspect of American and global business life by offering products and services that are reliable, convenient, and cost effective. The growth experienced in franchising throughout the world couldn't have been accomplished by accident. Franchising clearly has some advantages:

1. *Management assistance.* A franchisee (the person who buys a franchise) may have a greater chance of succeeding in business because he or she has (1) an established product (for example, McDonald's hamburgers), (2) help with choosing a location and with promotion, and (3) assistance in all phases of operation. It's like having your own store with full-time consultants available when you need them. Furthermore, you have a whole network of peers who are facing similar problems and can share their experiences with you.

2. *Personal ownership.* A franchise operation is still your store, and you enjoy much of the freedom, incentives, and profit of any sole proprietor. You're still your own boss, although you must follow more rules, regulations, and procedures than you would with your own privately owned store.

3. *Nationally recognized name.* It's one thing to open a new hamburger outlet or ice cream store. It is quite another to open a new McDonald's or a Baskin-Robbins ice cream shop. In most cases, with an established franchise, you get instant recognition and support from a product group with established customers.

4. *Financial advice and assistance.* A major problem with small businesses is arranging financing and learning to keep good records. Franchisees get valuable assistance in these areas and periodic advice from people with expertise in these areas. In fact, some franchisors will even provide financing to potential franchisees they feel will be valuable parts of the franchise system.

5. *Lower failure rate.* Historically, the failure rate for franchises has been lower than that of other business ventures. More recently, however, franchising has grown so rapidly that there are many weaker franchises that have entered the field. Even strong franchises may not do well. Some research now indicates that survival rates for franchises are even *lower* than other start-ups.[17] This shows that you should carefully research any franchise before buying. Mountain Mike's Pizza

franchise offers a radical way to reduce risk of failure. Mountain Mike's will buy back the franchise after 33 months of ownership for the full initial franchise fee if the franchisee chooses. Thought to be making the first offer of this kind, Mountain Mike's hopes to attract 60 additional franchisees with its low-risk option.

DISADVANTAGES OF FRANCHISES   It almost sounds like the potential of owning a franchise is too good to be true. However, you should carefully investigate and check out any such arrangement with present franchisees and discuss the idea with an attorney.[18] Disadvantages of franchises include

1. *Large start-up costs.* Most franchises demand a fee just to obtain the rights to the franchise. Fees for franchises can vary considerably. Start-up costs for a Jazzercise outlet ranges from as little as $2,000 to $3,000. Compare that to the $610,000 needed to start a McDonald's restaurant.

2. *Shared profit.* The franchisor often demands a large share of the profits or a percentage commission based on sales, not profit. This share is generally referred to as a *royalty*.

3. *Management regulation.* Management assistance has a way of becoming managerial orders, directives, and limitations. Franchisees may feel burdened by the company's rules and regulations and lose the spirit and incentive of being their own boss with their own business. For example, because of Pearle Vision's management's price slashing programs, many Pearle franchisees are in financial distress. Franchisees filed a complaint with the FTC accusing Pearle of violating federal rules governing disclosures to prospective franchisees. To avoid litigation in issues such as this, 28 franchisors have recently joined a dispute-resolution program called the National Franchise Mediation Program.[19]

4. *Coattail effects.* What happens to your franchise if fellow franchisees fail? Quite possibly you could be forced out of business even if your particular franchise was profitable. This is often referred to as a *coattail effect.* Other franchisees' actions clearly have an impact on your future growth and level of profitability. Franchisees must also look out for competition from fellow franchisees. For example, TCBY franchisees' love for frozen yogurt has thawed as the market has become more competitive and flooded with new TCBY stores. The same thing happened to some Subway franchises.

5. *Restrictions on selling.* Unlike owners of private businesses who can sell their companies to whomever they choose on their own terms, many franchisees face restrictions in the reselling of their franchises. To control the quality of their franchisees, franchisors often insist on approving the new owner, who must meet their standards.

6. *Fraudulent franchisors.* Contrary to common belief, most franchisors aren't large systems like McDonald's. Many are small, rather obscure franchises that prospective franchisees may know little about. Most franchisors are honest, but there has been an increase in complaints to the FTC about franchisors that delivered little or nothing that they promised.

Figure 5.5 summarizes benefits and drawbacks in franchising.

Buying a Franchise

Since buying a franchise is a major investment, be sure to check out a company's financial strength before you get involved. Watch out for scams, too. Scams called *bust-outs* usually involve people coming to town, renting nice offices, taking out ads, and persuading people to invest. Then they disappear with the investors' money. For example, in San Francisco a company called T.B.S. Inc. sold distributorships for in-home AIDS tests. It promised an enormous market and potential profits of $3,000 for an investment of less than $200. The test turned out to be nothing more than a mail order questionnaire about lifestyle.

A good source of information about franchise possibilities is available from Franchise Watchdog in Burlington, Vermont. It compares what franchisors have to offer, including fees and support services, and also rates franchisors by sampling franchisees. Another good resource for evaluating a franchise deal is the handbook *Investigate before Investing* available from International Franchise Association Publications.

Checklist for Evaluating a Franchise

The Franchise

Did your lawyer approve the franchise contract you're considering after he or she studied it paragraph by paragraph?

Does the franchise give you an exclusive territory for the length of the franchise?

Under what circumstances can you terminate the franchise contract and at what cost to you?

If you sell your franchise, will you be compensated for your goodwill (the value of your business's reputation and other intangibles)?

If the franchisor sells the company, will your investment be protected?

The Franchisor

How many years has the firm offering you a franchise been in operation?

Does it have a reputation for honesty and fair dealing among the local firms holding its franchise?

Has the franchisor shown you any certified figures indicating exact net profits of one or more going firms that you personally checked yourself with the franchisee? Ask for the company's disclosure statement.

Will the firm assist you with

> A management training program?
> An employee training program?
> A public relations program?
> Capital?
> Credit?
> Merchandising ideas?

Will the firm help you find a good location for your new business?

Has the franchisor investigated you carefully enough to assure itself that you can successfully operate one of its franchises at a profit both to itself and to you?

You, the Franchisee

How much equity capital will you need to purchase the franchise and operate it until your income equals your expenses?

Does the franchisor offer financing for a portion of the franchising fees? On what terms?

Are you prepared to give up some independence of action to secure the advantages offered by the franchise? Do you have your family's support?

Does the industry appeal to you? Are you ready to spend much or all of the remainder of your business life with this franchisor, offering its product or service to the public?

Your Market

Have you made any study to determine whether the product or service that you propose to sell under the franchise has a market in your territory at the prices you'll have to charge?

Will the population in the territory given to you increase, remain static, or decrease over the next five years?

Will demand for the product or service you're considering be greater, about the same, or less five years from now than it is today?

What competition already exists in your territory for the product or service you contemplate selling?

Source: *Franchise Opportunities Handbook* (U.S. Department of Commerce); and Derek Dingle, "Franchising's Fast Track to Freedom," *Money Extra*, 1990, pp. 35–44.

DIVERSITY IN FRANCHISING   There's a strong likelihood that women and minorities will assume a much larger role in franchising than they have in the past. A 1990 survey by Women in Franchising indicates that women currently own 30 percent of the country's franchised businesses. Women aren't just franchisees anymore either; they're becoming franchisors as well. Top-rated franchise companies Decorating Den and Jazzercise are owned by women.

BENEFITS	DRAWBACKS
• Nationally recognized name and established reputation	• High initial franchise fee
• Help with finding a good location	• Additional fees may be charged for marketing
• A proven management system	• A monthly percentage of gross sales may go to the franchisor
• Tested methods for inventory and operations management	• Possible competition from other nearby franchisees
• Financial advice and assistance	• No freedom to select decor or other design features
• Training in all phases of operation	• Little freedom to determine management procedures
• Promotional assistance	• Many rules and regulations to follow
• Periodic management counseling	
• Proven record of success	
• It's your business!	

FIGURE 5.5

ADDITIONAL BENEFITS AND DRAWBACKS OF FRANCHISING
The start-up fees and monthly fees can be killers. Ask around. Don't be shy. This is the time to learn about opportunities.

When women found it difficult to find financing for expanding their businesses, they often turned to finding franchisees to sidestep expansion costs. For example, Marilyn Ounijan, founder and CEO of Careers USA, claims that having franchisees pay for inventory and other costs of growing a business allowed her company to grow from her office in her home to 22 locations throughout the country. Franchising provided Careers USA with a cost-effective way to enter new markets.

The U.S. Department of Commerce's Federal Minority Business Development Agency provides minorities with training in how to run franchises. It reports that 46 percent of these minority companies are in California, Texas, and Florida.[20] Franchising opportunities seem perfectly attuned to the needs of aspiring minority businesspersons. (See Chapter 1's Profile about La-Van Hawkins.)

HOME-BASED FRANCHISES   Home-based businesses offer many obvious advantages including relief from the time and stress of commuting, extra time for family activities, and low overhead expense. But one of the disadvantages of owning a business based at home is the feeling of isolation.

Unlike home-based entrepreneurs, home-based franchisees feel less isolated. Experienced franchisors share their knowledge of building a profitable enterprise with franchisees. For example, when Henry and Paula Feldman decided to quit sales jobs that kept them on the road for weeks, they wanted to find a business to run at home together. The Feldmans started their Money Mailer, Inc., home-based franchise with nothing more than a table and a telephone. Five years later, they own 15 territories that they run from an office full of state-of-the-art equipment and have reached gross revenues of more than $600,000. Henry says that the real value of being in a franchise is that the systems are in place. "You don't have to develop them yourself. Just be willing to work hard, listen, and learn. There's no greater magic than that."[21] Figure 5.6 describes some interesting home-based franchises.

FRANCHISING IN INTERNATIONAL MARKETS   The attraction of global markets has carried over into franchising. Today, American franchisors are counting their profits in pesos, lira, francs, won, deutsche marks, krona, bahts, yen, and many other global currencies. More than 450 of the 3,000 U.S.-based franchisors have international outlets. Canada is by far the most popular target

BUSINESS	DESCRIPTION	FRANCHISE FEE	TOTAL INITIAL INVESTMENT
Comprehensive Business Services	All-round financial consultants relieving small businesses of record-keeping, business analysis, tax preparation and payroll	$25,000	$30,000-$50,000
Computertots	Innovative approach to teaching small children in day care and nursery schools about computers	$15,900-$23,900	$28,000-$45,000
Money Mailer	Franchises sell advertising space in Money Mailer. They send the cooperative mailings to a minimum of 30,000 homes up to eight times a year	$20,000 for the first 40,000 homes and $5,000 for each additional 10,000	$30,000 and up, depending on size of territory
Ident-A-Kid	Market laminated photo IDs for kids through schools	$12,500	$12,500
The Bride's Day Magazine	Sell ad space in magazine that's offered free to brides through retail stores	$14,900	$14,900

Source: Gregory Matusky, "The Best Home-Based Franchises," *Home Office Computing,* December, 1993, pp. 70–83.

FIGURE 5.6

EXAMPLES OF HOME-BASED FRANCHISES

because of proximity and language. Many franchisors are finding it surprisingly easy to move into South Africa and the Philippines. Even though franchisors feel costs of franchising are high in these markets, the costs are counterbalanced by less competition and a rapidly expanding consumer base.

Newer, smaller franchises are going international as well. Smaller franchises such as SpeeDee Oil Change & Tune-Up, Rug Doctor Pro, and Merry Maids have all ventured into the international market. What makes franchising successful in international markets is what makes it successful in the United States: convenience and a predictable level of service and quality.

Many U.S. firms such as Astro Pizza have moved rapidly to establish a strong presence in Russia and other countries in Eastern Europe.

Franchisors must be careful to adapt to the region. For example, in France, some people thought a furniture stripping place called Dip 'N' Strip was a bar that featured strippers. In general, however, U.S. franchises are doing well all over the world and are adapting to the local customs and desires of consumers.

COOPERATIVES

Some people dislike the notion of having owners, managers, workers, and buyers as separate individuals with separate goals. They envision a world where people cooperate with one another more fully and share the wealth more evenly. These people have formed a different kind of organization that reflects their social orientation. Such an organization is called a cooperative.

Reaching Beyond Our Borders

Joining Hands across the Waters: Strategic Alliances

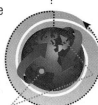

With Europe, Asia, and the Third World buying a wide range of products and services, American companies find the opportunities almost unlimited. Joint ventures and mergers with companies native to these global markets provide businesses a chance to enter those markets less warily. Joint venturing involves both participants in sales, distribution, or manufacturing.

For example, an American company with a design for a high-efficiency boiler decided to sell the technology internationally. Rather than take on a foreign market single-handedly, the company entered a joint venture with a German business that produced a similarly designed high-efficiency burner that could be fitted to the boiler.

Since the products fit together, both companies decided to produce each other's design in their own markets. This gave the German company an immediate outlet in the United States and gave the American company an entry into the vigorous German economy.

Joint ventures and mergers aren't always easy to pull off. Even a large company such as McDonald's had its problems when it opened its first restaurant in Moscow. After ensuring a steady supply of quality meat and potatoes from its partner (the Moscow municipal authorities), McDonald's officials were told the price for beef would increase from 2.4 rubles per kilogram to 14 rubles and that rent would increase by 10 times. The increases forced McDonald's to double its prices soon after opening.

Joint ventures and mergers with foreign firms will continue to dominate the headlines throughout the 1990s.

Source: Don Clark, "Fujitsu and Hyundai Electronics Form Unusual Joint Venture in Memory Chips," *The Wall Street Journal*, October 7, 1993, p. B6; Mark Stevens, "Expand Overseas in Joint Ventures," *The Washington Times*, January 17, 1991, p. C10; and Marshall Goldman, "An Answer to Perestroika: Joint Ventures," *Harvard Business Review*, March-April 1991, pp. 191–94.

Often the members/customers work in the organization so many hours a month as part of their duties. Owners, managers, workers, and customers are all the same people. You may have one of the country's 4,000 food cooperatives near you. If so, stop by and chat with the people and learn more about this growing aspect of American trade. If you're interested in starting your own food co-op, contact the National Cooperative Business Association (telephone (202) 638–6222).[22]

There's another kind of cooperative in the United States, set up for different reasons. These cooperatives are formed to give members more economic power as a group than they would have as individuals. The best example of such cooperatives is a farm cooperative. The idea at first was for farmers to join together to get better prices for their food products. Eventually, however, the organization expanded so that farm cooperatives now buy and sell fertilizer, farm equipment, seed, and other products needed on the farm. This has become a multibillion dollar industry. The cooperatives now own many manufacturing facilities. Farm cooperatives don't pay the same kind of taxes that corporations do, so they have an advantage in the marketplace. Farm cooperatives have thus been called one of the next boom industries.[23]

To give you some idea of farm cooperatives' size, let's look at Farmland Industries, Inc. As the country's largest farm cooperative, the company reports an annual revenue of $4.5 billion. Its 1,800 member cooperatives include 250,000 farmers in 19 states. Farmland Industries owns manufacturing facilities, oil wells and refineries, fertilizer plants, feed mills, and plants that produce everything from grease and paint to steel buildings. Besides offering insurance plus financial and technical services, it owns a network of warehouses.

As word spreads, the idea of business cooperatives (member-owned organizations established by a large group of small business owners) is spreading. According to the National Cooperative Bank, 2 million businesses belong to 20,000 co-ops nationwide. Franchisees, for example, are starting their own co-ops to lower costs. The Employers' Health Purchasing Co-op in Seattle negotiates for favorable health plans for small businesses.

Co-ops Allow Small Businesses to Compete against Big Odds

Contract Sheet is a cooperative public relations firm. Aldus, the manufacturer of Pagemaker, has invited more than 140 independent software writers to develop complementary software for its company. In short, "Cooperation allows the entrepreneur to tap much larger resources for purchasing, marketing, or accessing technology."

Source: Janean Huber, "All Together Now," *Entrepreneur*, April 1994, p. 14.

In spite of debt and mergers, cooperatives are still a major force in agriculture today. Some top farm co-ops have familiar names such as Land O'Lakes, Sunkist, Ocean Spray, Blue Diamond, and Welch's.

WHICH FORM OF OWNERSHIP IS FOR YOU?

As you can see, you may participate in the business world in a variety of ways. You can start your own sole proprietorship, partnership, corporation, or cooperative, or you can buy a franchise. There are advantages and disadvantages to each. Before you choose the form for you, you should carefully evaluate each alternative and its risks.

The miracle of free enterprise is that the freedom and incentives of capitalism make risks acceptable to many people, who go on to create the great corporations of America. You know many of their names: J. C. Penney, Malcolm Forbes, Sears and Roebuck, Levi Strauss, Ford, Edison. They started small, accumulated capital, grew, and became industrial leaders. Could you do the same?

PROGRESS CHECK

- What are some factors to consider before buying a franchise?
- What opportunities are available for starting an international franchise?
- What is a cooperative?

SUMMARY

1. Compare the advantages and disadvantages of sole proprietorships.

1. The major forms of business ownership are sole proprietorships, partnerships, and corporations.
   - ***What are the advantages and disadvantages of sole proprietorships?*** Advantages of a sole proprietorship include the ease of starting and ending, being your own boss, pride of ownership, retention of profit, and no special taxes. Disadvantages include unlimited liability, limited financial resources, difficulty in management, overwhelming time commitment, few fringe benefits, limited growth, and limited life span.

2. The three key elements of a general partnership are common ownership, shared profits and losses, and the right to participate in managing the operations of the business.
- **What are the main differences between general and limited partners?**
General partners are owners (partners) who have unlimited liability and are active in managing the company. Limited partners are owners (partners) who have limited liability and aren't active in the company.
- **What does unlimited liability mean?**
Unlimited liability means that sole proprietors and general partners must pay all debts and damages caused by their business. They may have to sell their houses, cars, or other personal possessions to pay business debts.
- **What does limited liability mean?**
Limited liability means that corporate owners (stockholders) and limited partners are responsible for losses only up to the amount they invest. Their other personal property isn't at risk.
- **What is a master limited partnership?**
A master limited partnership is a partnership that acts like a corporation but is taxed like a partnership. Burger King is a well-known master limited partnership.
- **What are the advantages and disadvantages of partnerships?**
Advantages include more financial resources, shared management and pooled knowledge, and longer survival. Disadvantages include unlimited liability, division of profits, disagreements among partners, and difficulty in termination.

2. Describe the differences between general and limited partnerships and compare the advantages and disadvantages of partnerships.

3. A corporation is a state-chartered legal entity with authority to act and have liability separate from its owners.
- **What are the advantages and disadvantages of corporations?**
Advantages include more money for investment, limited liability, size, perpetual life, ease of ownership change, ease of drawing talented employees, and separation of ownership from management. Disadvantages include initial cost, paperwork, need to file two tax returns (double taxation), size, difficulty of termination, and possible conflict with board of directors.
- **Why do people incorporate?**
Two important reasons for incorporating are special tax advantages and limited liability.
- **What are the advantages of S corporations?**
S corporations have the advantages of limited liability (like a corporation) and simpler taxes (like a partnership). To qualify for S corporation status, stockholders must be individuals or estates and U.S. citizens or permanent residents; the company can't own more than 80 percent of another corporation; and the company can't have more than 25 percent of its income derived from passive sources.
- **What are the advantages of limited liability companies?**
Limited liability companies have the advantage of limited liability without the hassles of forming a corporation or the limitations imposed by S corporations. They also may have tax advantages over corporations.

3. Compare the advantages and disadvantages of corporations and summarize the differences between C corporations, S corporations, and limited liability companies.

4. The number of mergers increased during the mid-1990s.
- **What is a merger?**
A merger is the result of two firms forming one company. The three major types of mergers are vertical mergers, horizontal mergers, and conglomerate mergers.

4. Define and give examples of three types of corporate mergers and explain the role of leveraged buyouts and taking a firm private.

> • *What are leveraged buyouts and what does it mean to "take a company private"?*
> Leveraged buyouts are attempts by managers and employees to borrow money and purchase the company. Individuals who, together or alone, buy all of the stock for themselves are said to take the company private.

5. Outline the advantages and disadvantages of franchises and discuss the opportunities for diversity in franchising and the challenges of international franchising.

5. A person can participate in the entrepreneurial age by buying the rights to market a new product innovation in his or her area.
> • *What is this arrangement called?*
> A franchise is an arrangement to buy the rights to use the business name and sell its products or services in a given territory.
> • *What is a franchisee?*
> A franchisee is a person who buys a franchise.
> • *What are the benefits and drawbacks of being a franchisee?*
> Benefits include a nationally recognized name and reputation, a proven management system, promotional assistance, and the pride of ownership. Drawbacks include high franchise fees, managerial regulation, shared profits, and transfer of adverse effects if other franchisees fail.
> • *What are the opportunities for women and minorities in franchising?*
> Women are buying franchises at a faster rate than men are. In fact, women now own 30 percent of the nation's franchises. Minority franchise ownership isn't growing as quickly, largely due to trouble getting the large start-up capital needed to purchase a franchise.
> • *What is the major challenge to international franchises?*
> It's often hard to transfer an idea or product that worked well in the United States to another culture. It's essential to adapt to the region.

6. Explain the role of cooperatives.

6. People who dislike organizations in which owners, managers, workers, and buyers have separate goals often form cooperatives.
> • *What's the role of a cooperative?*
> Cooperatives are organizations owned by members/customers. Some people form cooperatives (Farmland, for example) to give members more economic power than they would have as individuals. Small businesses often form cooperatives to give them more purchasing, marketing, or product development strength.

KEY TERMS

acquisition 162	general partner 151	limited partnership 151
conglomerate merger 162	general partnership 151	master limited partnership (MLP) 152
cooperative 163	horizontal merger 162	merger 162
corporation 148	leveraged buyout (LBO) 162	partnership 148
franchise 163	limited liability 151	S corporation 159
franchise agreement 163	limited liability company 160	sole proprietorship 148
franchisee 163	limited partner 151	unlimited liability 150
franchisor 163		vertical merger 162

DEVELOPING WORKPLACE SKILLS

1. Research businesses in your area and identify companies using each of the following forms of ownership: sole proprietorships, partnerships, and corporations. Arrange and conduct interviews with managers from each form of ownership and get their impressions, hints, and warnings. How much does it cost to start? How many hours do they work? What are the specific benefits? Share the results with your class.

2. Contact a publicly owned company (e.g., water company, electric company, or local transportation company). Ask the manager how he or she sees the company as being different from privately owned businesses. Find out how government regulations affect the company.

3. Have you thought about starting your own business? What opportunities seem attractive? Think of a friend (s) whom you might want for a partner in the business. List all the financial resources and personal skills you will need to launch the business. Then make separate lists of the capital and personal skills that you and your friend (s) might bring to your new venture. What capital and personal skills do you need, but neither of you have? Develop an action plan to obtain them.

4. Review the Yellow Pages for your area and find a business cooperative in your community. Arrange a visit to find out how it was formed, who may belong to it, and how it operates.

5. Obtain an annual report of a large corporation from your library or by writing the company. What are the firm's annual sales? Net income (profit)? Number of common shareholders? Profit shareholders receive in dividends?

• •

PRACTICING MANAGEMENT DECISIONS

〳 C A S E   SHOULD COOPERATIVES GO CORPORATE? 〳

The idea of starting a cooperative to meet a social need is not new in the United States. The first formal American co-op was organized by Ben Franklin in 1752 and is still operating today. Today, cooperatives usually evolve because some need hasn't been met by the other three forms of business: proprietorships, partnerships, and corporations. For example, many homes in rural areas are serviced by telephone and electric co-ops because no one else would provide those services back in the 1930s when they were needed for farmers to enjoy the benefits of new technology.

Today, the need is for child care and care of the aged. Because such needs aren't being met by traditional organizations or are being offered at too great a cost, new cooperatives are emerging. A group of agricultural leaders in Texas, for example, has started a co-op to meet special needs of retired people who want small houses with less upkeep; greater security; easy access to health care, shops, and recreational facilities; and so forth.

Similarly, child care cooperatives are emerging in various places to assist parents in finding a good, reliable place to leave their children as they work. In a child care cooperative, the parents select a board of directors, help determine what kind of services will be provided, and volunteer in various ways to keep costs down.

Smaller, independent druggists and other small businesses rely on cooperatives to allow them to compete with mass merchandisers. They usually form some kind of co-op wholesale facility where they can get goods for less.

As we discussed in the chapter, some of the larger cooperatives are in farming. Ocean Spray is a farmer-owned cooperative that's now the number three juice marketer in the United States. Because of the growth in sales revenues of co-ops such as Ocean Spray, many of the top cooperatives are thinking of selling shares to the public. They would thus become corporations much like the big companies they compete with, such as Coca-Cola.

Decision Questions

1. What are some advantages and disadvantages of a cooperative's changing to a corporation? What would be the major reason for them to do so?

2. What's the future of cooperatives that provide housing and other services to the elderly? What are some of the differences you'd expect to see between a cooperative housing development and one owned and operated by a real estate corporation?

3. What advantages do you see in the fact that members of a cooperative often volunteer their time to help run the organization?

4. Might farmers lose some control over the production and marketing of their goods if farm cooperatives were to begin going corporate?

VIDEO CASE BEN AND JERRY'S CHOOSE AMONG FORMS OF BUSINESS

When Ben and Jerry decided to go into the ice cream business, they thought that they would be operating a small ice cream parlor for a few years. They chose to become a partnership rather than a sole proprietorship because they had complementary skills to bring to the venture. Ben was the creative one who was never satisfied with things the way they were. He wanted to continuously improve operations. Jerry, on the other hand, was comfortable doing routine things. In short, they worked well together.

When outside consultants recommended that they form a corporation, they decided to do that. They had to choose between an S corporation and a regular C corporation, and decided to go with the regular form (that allowed for more stockholders). There are many differences between a corporation and a partnership. These include:

Partnership	Corporation
Voluntary association	Separate legal entity
Unlimited liability	Limited liability
Mutual agency	Limited stockholder powers
Limited life	Unlimited life
Limited access to capital	Ease of capital formation
Partners maintain control	Owners may lose control
Relatively unregulated	Government regulation
Single taxation	Double taxation

Of these differences, two stand out as extremely important. One is limited liability. By forming a corporation, Ben and Jerry were not liable for losses beyond what they invested in the company. Furthermore, Ben and Jerry needed more money, and a corporation enabled them to sell stock to others to raise money.

Ben and Jerry had a community orientation from the start. Therefore, they sold stock to their neighbors, the residents of Vermont for as little as $126 a share. Many took advantage of that opportunity. The company had a strong sense of ethical and social responsibility ◀·· P.116 ··▶ from the start. As a result, Ben & Jerry's has earned a tremendous amount of publicity, and the company has prospered. However, business growth slowed in the 1990s which led Ben and Jerry to conclude that they needed some new thinking and the experience provided by an outsider with experience in running a large organization. In 1995 they hired a new president with the hope that he would lead the company to bigger and better things.

Discussion Questions

1. What other alternatives did Ben and Jerry have when deciding what form of business to take? Why was incorporating the best choice?

2. Few companies in the world have generated more publicity from their social responsibility stance than Ben & Jerry's. What lessons could other companies learn from their experience?

3. What are the major disadvantages of incorporating a company?

CHAPTER 6

ENTREPRENEURSHIP AND THE CHALLENGE OF STARTING A SMALL BUSINESS

LEARNING GOALS

After you have read and studied this chapter, you should be able to

1. Explain why people are willing to take the risks of entrepreneurship; list the attributes of successful entrepreneurs; and describe the benefits of entrepreneurial teams and intrapreneurs.

2. Discuss the importance of small business to the American economy and summarize the major causes of small-business failure.

3. Summarize ways to learn about how small businesses operate.

4. Analyze what it takes to start and run a small business, including the writing of a business plan.

5. Outline the advantages and disadvantages of small businesses entering global markets.

TOMIMA EDMARK OF TOPSYTAIL CO.

Tomima Edmark considers her dyslexia (a condition where letters and words are seen backwards or upside down) a gift rather than a handicap. "Would a normal person ever think to turn a ponytail inside out? Think about it, that's a really dyslexic concept."

Edmark's concept resulted in a red plastic hoop that looks like a butterfly net without the net. This little plastic hoop has turned thousands of pony tails inside out since Edmark started using direct marketing in 1991. TopsyTail Company's gross retail sales for 1993 topped $80 million. Not bad for a three-employee operation that has just moved from the kitchen table to an office above Edmark's garage.

Edmark's invention is so simple that the most common comment she hears from hairdressers is, "I could have done that." But they didn't. And that's what makes Tomima Edmark an entrepreneur. She took a risk and it paid off. Stories about people taking risks by starting their own businesses are commonplace in this age of the entrepreneur. We'll discuss such risk takers in this chapter. Maybe you'll be inspired to become an entrepreneur yourself.

> *If there is one coefficient of entrepreneurial success, it is energy. You may have all the ambition in the world, gobs of capital, a gambling man's soul, and business degrees covering an entire wall, but if you are not a human dynamo, forget it.*
>
> Joseph R. Mancuso
> *in* Have You Got What It Takes?

THE JOB-CREATING POWER OF ENTREPRENEURS IN THE UNITED STATES

A major issue in the United States today is the need to create more jobs. To get some idea about the job-creating power of entrepreneurs « P.28 », look at some of the great American entrepreneurs from the past and the present. The history of the United States is the history of its entrepreneurs. **Entrepreneurship** is accepting the risk of starting and running a business. Consider just a few of the many entrepreneurs who have helped shape the American economy:

entrepreneurship
The acceptance of the risk of starting and managing a new business.

- DuPont was started in 1802 by Eleuthere Irenee du Pont. Some 18 shareholders provided $36,000 in start-up money.
- Avon started in 1886 on $500 David McConnell borrowed from a friend.
- Kodak was launched by George Eastman in 1880 with a $3,000 investment.
- Procter & Gamble was formed in 1837 by William Procter and James Gamble with a total of $7,000 in capital.
- Ford Motor Company began with an investment of $28,000 by Henry Ford and 11 associates.

The stories are all about the same. One entrepreneur or a couple of entrepreneurs had a good idea, borrowed a few dollars from friends and family, and started a business. That business now employs thousands of people and

T. J. Walker and Carl Jones saw that multiculturalism could pay when they started designing and advertising their inner-city-looking clothes for the mass market. Their fashion company, Threads 4 Life, had sales of over $70 million in 1993. Now they are trying to predict the next trend to come from the black urban experience. Entrepreneurs like Walker and Jones look for opportunities overlooked by others.

helps the country prosper. Today, the United States still has plenty of entrepreneurial talent. Names such as Steve Jobs (Apple Computer), Anita Roddick (Body Shop), Michael Dell (Dell Computer), William Gates (Microsoft), Howard Schultz (Starbucks), Craig McCaw (McCaw Cellular Communications), and Scott Cook (Intuit) have become as familiar as those of the great entrepreneurs of the past.[1]

WHY PEOPLE TAKE THE ENTREPRENEURIAL CHALLENGE

There are many reasons why people are willing to take the risks of starting a business:

- *Opportunity.* Many immigrants lack the necessary skills for working in today's complex organizations. They do have the initiative and drive to work the long hours demanded by entrepreneurship. To them, the opportunity to share in the American dream is a tremendous lure. The same is true of many corporate managers who left the security of the corporate life—either by choice or as a result of corporate downsizing « P.28 » to run businesses of their own.[2]
- *Profit.* Profit is another important reason to become an entrepreneur. At one time, the richest person in America was Sam Walton, the entrepreneur who started Wal-Mart. Now, one of the richest people in America is William Henry Gates III, the entrepreneur who founded Microsoft Corporation. Recently, *The Wall Street Journal* reported that "Entrepreneurial gambles have been the fastest road to riches since the days of Marco Polo, and today remain a major creator of jobs in the American economy."[3]
- *Independence.* Many entrepreneurs simply don't enjoy working for someone else. Many lawyers, for example, don't like the stress and demands of big law firms. Some have found more enjoyment and self-satisfaction in starting their own businesses.[4]
- *Challenge.* Entrepreneurs are excitement junkies who flourish on taking risks. However, they contend that entrepreneurs take moderate, calculated risks; they aren't just gambling. In general, though, entrepreneurs seek achievement more than power.

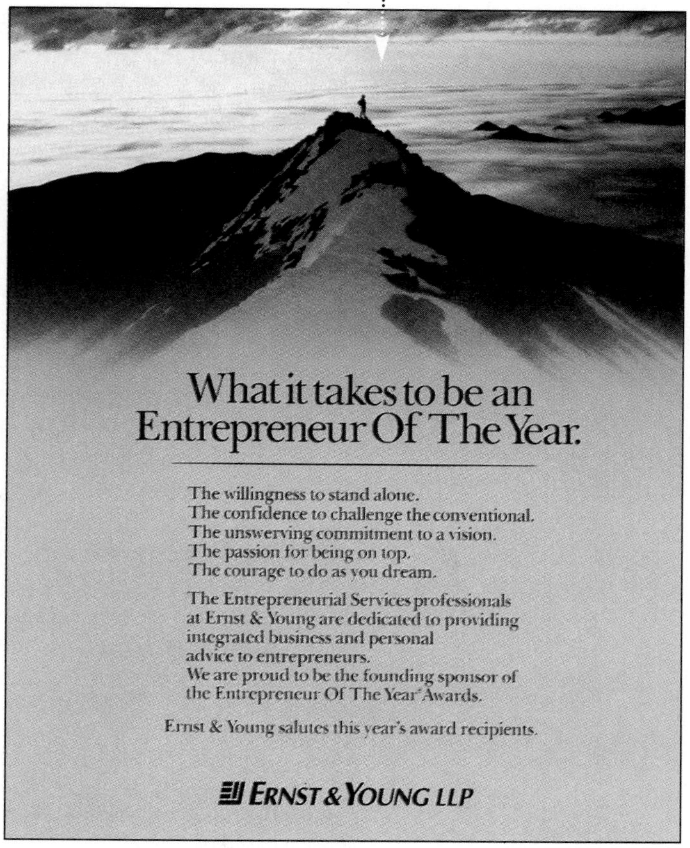
What it takes to be an Entrepreneur Of The Year.
The willingness to stand alone.
The confidence to challenge the conventional.
The unswerving commitment to a vision.
The passion for being on top.
The courage to do as you dream.
The Entrepreneurial Services professionals at Ernst & Young are dedicated to providing integrated business and personal advice to entrepreneurs.
We are proud to be the founding sponsor of the Entrepreneur Of The Year® Awards.
Ernst & Young salutes this year's award recipients.
ERNST & YOUNG LLP

Many existing companies offer support to entrepreneurs as they start their new businesses. As you see here, for example, Ernst & Young, a large public accounting firm, offers business and personal advice to entrepreneurs and also sponsors the Entrepreneur of the Year Awards. How many of the traits listed in this ad do you have?

WHAT DOES IT TAKE TO BE AN ENTREPRENEUR?

Would you succeed as an entrepreneur? You can learn the managerial and leadership skills needed to run a firm. However, you may not have the personality to assume the risks, take the initiative, create the vision, and rally others to follow your lead. Those traits are harder to learn or acquire. A list of entrepreneurial traits you would look for in yourself includes[5]

1. *Self-directed.* You should be thoroughly comfortable and thoroughly self-disciplined even though you're your own boss. You'll be responsible for your success or possible failure.

2. *Self-nurturing.* You must believe in your idea even if no one else does, and be able to replenish your own enthusiasm. When Walt Disney suggested the possibility of a full-length animated feature film, *Snow White*, the industry laughed. His personal commitment and enthusiasm caused the Bank of America to back his venture. The rest is history.

3. *Action-oriented.* Great business ideas aren't enough. The most important thing is a burning desire to build your dream into reality.

4. *Highly energetic.* It's your business, and you must be emotionally, mentally, and physically able to work long and hard.

5. *Tolerant of uncertainty.* Successful entrepreneurs take only calculated risks (if they can help it). Still, they must be able to take some risks. Remember, entrepreneurship isn't for the squeamish or the person bent on security.

If you're interested in seeing if you may have the entrepreneurial spirit in your blood, there's an entrepreneurial test you can take on page 205. There's more advice for would-be entrepreneurs in Figure 6.1.

CRITICAL THINKING

Do you know anyone who seems to have the entrepreneurial spirit? What about him or her makes you say that? Are there any similarities between the characteristics demanded of an entrepreneur and those of a professional athlete? Would an athlete be a good prospect for entrepreneurship? Why? Could teamwork be important in an entrepreneurial effort?

FIGURE 6.1

ADVICE FOR POTENTIAL ENTREPRENEURS

- Research your market, but don't take too long to act.
- Work for other people first and learn on their money.
- Start out slowly. Start your business when you have a customer. Maybe try your venture as a sideline at first.
- Set specific objectives, but don't set your goals too high. Remember, there's no easy money.
- Plan your objectives within specific time frames.
- Surround yourself with people who are smarter than you—including an accountant and an outside board of directors who are interested in your well-being and who'll give you straight answers.
- Don't be afraid to fail. Former football coach Vince Lombardi summarized the entrepreneurial philosophy when he said, "We didn't lose any games this season, we just ran out of time twice." New entrepreneurs must be ready to run out of time a few times before they succeed.

Source: Joseph Mancuso, "The Right Stuff: Do You Have What It Takes to Start Your Own Business?" *THe Wall Street Journal's Managing Your Career*, Spring 1991, pp. 15–19.

••• ENTREPRENEURIAL TEAMS •••

An **entrepreneurial team** is a group of experienced people from different areas of business who join together to form a managerial team with the skills needed to develop, make, and market a new product or service. A team may be better than an individual entrepreneur because it can combine creative skills with production and marketing skills right from the start. The team ensures more cooperation and coordination among functions.

One exciting new company that developed in the 1980s was Compaq Computer. It was started by three senior managers at Texas Instruments: Bill Murto, Jim Harris, and Rod Canion. All three were bitten by the entrepreneurial bug and decided to go out on their own. They debated what industry to enter but finally decided to build a portable personal computer that was compatible with the IBM PC.

The key to Compaq's early success was that it was built around this "smart team" of experienced managers. The team wanted to combine the discipline of a big company with an environment where people could feel they were participating in a successful venture. This trio of entrepreneurs recruited seasoned managers with similar desires. All the managers worked as a cross-functional team. That is, the company's treasurer and top engineer contributed to production and marketing decisions. Everyone worked together to conceive, develop, and market products.

Today, Compaq sells more PCs in the United States than any of its competitors and is ranked 1, 2, or 3 in all other markets it competes in worldwide. The person who made Compaq global is Eckhard Pfeiffer. He was recruited from Texas Instruments to take this entrepreneurial company international. That has become a pattern in the past few decades. Entrepreneurs such as Steve Jobs (Apple Computer) and the three from Compaq frequently turn their companies over to professional managers once they reach a certain size.[6] Often such a change is good for the firm because new ideas are introduced and new entrepreneurial spirit is instilled.

entrepreneurial team
A group of experienced people from different areas of business who join together to form a managerial team with the skills needed to develop, make, and market new products or services.

••• ENCOURAGING ENTREPRENEURSHIP •••

To encourage more entrepreneurs to come to the United States, the government passed the Immigration Act of 1990. It created a category of "investor visas" that allows as many as 10,000 people to come to the United States each year if they are willing to invest $1 million in an enterprise that creates or preserves 10 jobs. Some people are promoting the idea of increasing the number of such immigrants. They believe that the more entrepreneurs that can be lured to the United States, the more jobs will be created and the more the economy will grow.

One way to encourage entrepreneurship is through enterprise zones that feature low taxes and government support. The government could have a significant effect on entrepreneurship by offering investment tax credits that would give tax breaks to businesses that make the kind of investments that would create jobs. The government could also institute a plan of public investment to rebuild the nation's infrastructure (bridges, roads, and so forth). Such money would go to businesses that would then hire people whose spending would stimulate economic growth.

- Name some famous entrepreneurs from the past and present.
- Why are people willing to take the risks of entrepreneurship?
- What are the advantages of entrepreneurial teams?

PROGRESS CHECK

Making Ethical Decisions

Competing with Your Old Boss

Suppose you've worked for two years in a company and you see signs that the business is beginning to falter. You and a co-worker have ideas about how to make a company like your boss's succeed. You're considering quitting your jobs and starting your own company together. Should you approach other co-workers about working for your new venture? Will you try to lure your old boss's customers to your own business? What are your alternatives? What are the consequences of each alternative? What's the most ethical choice?

••• ENTREPRENEURSHIP WITHIN FIRMS •••

intrapreneur

A person with entrepreneurial skills who is employed in a corporation to launch new products; such people take hands-on responsibility for creating innovation of any kind in an organization.

Entrepreneurship in a large organization is often reflected in the efforts and achievements of intrapreneurs. **Intrapreneurs** are creative people, usually working together as teams, who function as entrepreneurs within corporations. The idea is to use a company's existing resources—human, financial, and physical—to launch new products and generate new profits. At 3M Company, for example, managers are expected to come up with at least 30 percent new products for 3M every four years.[7]

Have you seen those yellow Post-it™ note pads people use to stick messages everywhere? That product was developed by Art Fry, a 3M employee. He needed to mark the pages of a hymnal in a way that wouldn't damage the book or fall out. He came up with the idea of the sticky paper. The 3M labs soon produced a sample, but distributors thought the product was silly, and market surveys were negative. Nonetheless, 3M kept sending samples to secretaries of top executives. Eventually, after 12 years, the orders began pouring in, and Post-its became a major revenue producer. The company continues to update the product and now offers Post-it notes in a variety of colors and sizes, some for different uses, and all of which are made from recycled paper. Post-it notes have gone global as well. The pads sent to Japan are long and narrow to accommodate vertical writing.

Livio "Desi" DeSimone, chairman of 3M, says he doesn't want his employees to get too comfortable with past successes. 3M has a reputation for encouraging intrapreneurship by setting the goal of deriving 30 percent of its sales from products introduced in the last four years. The company had the highest rate of new product introductions in its history in 1993 and was issued 418 new patents.

Hewlett-Packard calls its entrepreneurial approach the Triad Development Process. The idea is to link the design engineer, the manufacturer, and the marketer (the three thus forming the Triad) in a cross-functional team from the design phase forward. Everything, even the assembly line, shuts own if the Triad team wants to test an innovation.

The classic intrapreneurial venture is the Skunkworks of Lockheed Corp. The Skunkworks is a top secret research and development center that turned out such monumental products as the first fighter jet in 1943 and the Stealth fighter.[8]

GETTING STARTED IN SMALL BUSINESS

Let's suppose you decide you have a great idea for a new business, you have the attributes of an entrepreneur, and you're ready to take the leap into business for yourself. How do you start a business? How much paperwork is involved? That's what the rest of this chapter concerns. We'll explore small businesses, their role in the economy, and small-business management. It's easier to identify with a small neighborhood business than a giant global firm, yet the principles of management are very similar. The management of charities, government agencies, churches, schools, and unions is much the same as the management of small and large businesses. So, as you learn about small-business management, you'll make a giant step toward understanding management in general. All organizations demand capital, good ideas, planning, information management, budgets (and financial management in general), accounting, marketing, good employee relations, and good overall managerial know-how. We'll explore these areas as they relate to small businesses; later in the book, we'll apply the concepts to large firms, even global organizations.

••• SMALL VERSUS BIG BUSINESS •••

The Small Business Administration (SBA) defines a **small business** as one that's independently owned and operated, not dominant in its field of operation, and meets certain standards of size in terms of employees or annual receipts (for example, less than $2 million a year for service businesses). Figure 6.2 gives guidelines on sizes of various kinds of small businesses.

A small business is considered "small" only in relation to other businesses in its industry. A wholesaler may sell up to $22 million and still be considered a small business by the SBA. In manufacturing, a plant can have 1,500 employees and still be considered small. For example, before its merger with Chrysler, American Motors was considered small because it was tiny compared to Ford, General Motors, and Chrysler. Let's look at some interesting statistics about small businesses:

small business
A business that is independently operated, is not dominant in its field, and meets certain size standards in terms of number of employees and annual receipts.

- There are about 25.4 million full- and part-time home-based businesses in the United States.[9]
- Of all nonfarm businesses in the United States, almost 97 percent are considered small by SBA standards.
- Small businesses account for over 40 percent of gross domestic product (GDP) ⇐ **P.72** ⇒ .
- The total number of employees who work in small business is greater than the populations of Australia and Canada combined.
- The first jobs of about 80 percent of all Americans are in small business.
- The number of women owning small businesses has increased 11-fold since 1960. Studies predict that women will own half of the small businesses by 2000.
- The number of minority-owned businesses increased more than 64 percent between 1962 and 1987 (the latest date for government figures).[10]
- Small companies produced 90 percent of the new jobs in 1994.[11]

As you can see, small business is really a big part of the U.S. economy. How big a part? We'll explore that question next.

••• IMPORTANCE OF SMALL BUSINESSES •••

In the 1980s, large companies lost 4.1 million jobs; small businesses created 1.5 million jobs in 1992 and 1993 alone. Ninety percent of the nation's new jobs in the private sector are in small businesses. Two-thirds of the new jobs are in companies with fewer than 25 employees.[12] That means there's a very good chance that you'll either work in a small business someday or start one.

Dun & Bradstreet reports that the biggest employment increases in 1994 were in services (979,000), manufacturing (776,000), retail (468,000), and construction (349,000). The smallest job increases were in transportation, public utilities, mining, and government. More than half of all businesses complain of shortages of qualified workers.[13]

Did you notice in the preceding statistics that manufacturing firms are producing almost as many jobs as service firms? Why is this? Many analysts believe that the declining value of the dollar has spurred a revival in American exports as they become less expensive in global markets. As a result, small manufacturers that supply exporting industries are among the winners in the 1990s.

In addition to providing employment opportunities, small firms believe that they offer other advantages that larger companies lack. Owners of small companies report that their greatest advantages over big companies are their more personal customer service ◀·· **P.39** ··▶ and their ability to respond quickly to opportunities. As big businesses cut employees, they often find that they don't always have the staff they need and are increasingly contracting with small companies to temporarily fill their needs. Management guru Tom Peters calls this subcontracting "contract employment."[14] Figure 6.3 and the Small Business box show other areas in which small businesses believe they have advantages over big businesses.

As you can see, bigger isn't always better. Picture a hole in the ground. If you fill it with sand, there's no space between the grains. However, if you fill it with big boulders, there are many empty spaces between them. That's how it is in business. Big businesses don't serve all the needs of the market. There's plenty of room for small companies to make a profit filling those niches.

••• SMALL-BUSINESS SUCCESS AND FAILURE •••

You can't be naive about business practices, or you'll go broke. There's some debate about how many new small businesses fail each year. Conventional wisdom says that four out of five businesses (80 percent) fail in their first five

)) **FIGURE 6.2** ((

CLASSIFICATION OF SMALL BUSINESSES
There's no one definition of *small business*, but the U.S. Small Business Administration uses these guidelines for classification.

SMALL BUSINESS	EMPLOYMENT SIZE	ASSET SIZE	SALES SIZE
Independent contractor	0	0	Under 100,000
Family size	1–4	Under $100,000	$100,000–500,000
Small	5–19	$100,000–500,000	$500,000–1 million
Medium	20–99	$500,000–5 million	$1–10 million
Large	100–499	$5–25 million	$10 million–50 million
Total small business	0–500	$0–25 million	$0–50 million
Medium business	500–999	$25–100 million	$50–250 million
Large business	1,000 +	$100 million +	$250 million +
Government-size business	10,000 +	$2 billion	$2 billion +

Source: Office of Economic Research, U.S. Small Business Administration.

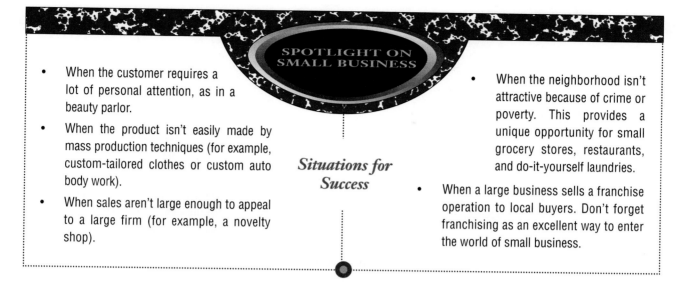

SPOTLIGHT ON SMALL BUSINESS

Situations for Success

- When the customer requires a lot of personal attention, as in a beauty parlor.

- When the product isn't easily made by mass production techniques (for example, custom-tailored clothes or custom auto body work).

- When sales aren't large enough to appeal to a large firm (for example, a novelty shop).

- When the neighborhood isn't attractive because of crime or poverty. This provides a unique opportunity for small grocery stores, restaurants, and do-it-yourself laundries.

- When a large business sells a franchise operation to local buyers. Don't forget franchising as an excellent way to enter the world of small business.

years; yet the SBA reports a 62 percent death rate within six years. However, a recent study by economist Bruce Kirchhoff shows that the failure rate is only 18 percent over the first eight years. Kirchhoff contends that the other failure rates resulted from a misinterpretation of Dun and Bradstreet statistics. When small business owners went out of business to start new and different businesses, they were included in the "business failure" category when obviously that wasn't the case. Similarly, when a business changed its form of ownership from partnership to corporation, it was considered as a failure. Retirements of sole owners were also included in the "business death" category.[15] All in all, the good news for entrepreneurs is that business failures are much lower than has traditionally been reported.

Although chances of business survival may be greater than some used to think, keep in mind that even the most optimistic interpretation of the statistics shows that nearly one out of five businesses that fails is left owing money to creditors. As you can see in the box listing causes of small-business failure, many small businesses fail because of managerial incompetence and inadequate financial planning.

Choosing the right type of business is critical to success. Many of the businesses with the lowest failure rates—such as veterinary services, dentists' offices, and physicians' offices—require advanced training to start. While

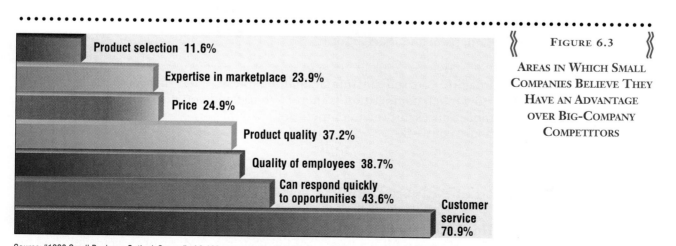

Product selection 11.6%
Expertise in marketplace 23.9%
Price 24.9%
Product quality 37.2%
Quality of employees 38.7%
Can respond quickly to opportunities 43.6%
Customer service 70.9%

FIGURE 6.3

AREAS IN WHICH SMALL COMPANIES BELIEVE THEY HAVE AN ADVANTAGE OVER BIG-COMPANY COMPETITORS

Source: "1990 Small Business Outlook Survey" of 3,100 companies by Reliable Corp., Chicago, as reported in "A Manager's Notebook," *Inc.*, July 1990, p. 94.

SPOTLIGHT ON SMALL BUSINESS

Causes for Failure

- Plunging in without first testing the waters on a small scale.
- Underpricing or overpricing goods or services.
- Underestimating how much time it will take to build a market.
- Starting with too little capital.
- Starting with too much capital and being careless in its use.
- Going into business with little or no experience and without first learning something about it.
- Borrowing money without planning just how and when to pay it back.
- Attempting to do too much business with too little capital.
- Not allowing for setbacks and unexpected expenses.

- Buying too much on credit.
- Extending credit too freely.
- Expanding credit too rapidly.
- Failing to keep complete, accurate records, so that the owners drift into trouble without realizing it.
- Carrying habits of personal extravagance into the business.
- Not understanding business cycles.
- Forgetting about taxes, insurance, and other costs of doing business.
- Mistaking the freedom of being in business for oneself, for liberty to work or not according to whim.

Source: The Service Corps of Retired Executives (SCORE), a part of the Small Business Administration; and Judith Gross, "Autopsy of a Business," *Home Office Computing*, October 1993, pp. 52–60.

training and degrees may buy security, they don't tend to produce much growth. If you want to be both independent and rich, you need to go after growth. The businesses with the highest odds of significant growth are in manufacturing. But these aren't easy businesses to start and are even more difficult to keep going.

In general, it seems that the easiest businesses to start are the ones that tend to have the least growth and the greatest failure rate. The easiest businesses to keep alive are difficult ones to get started. And the ones that can make you rich are the ones that are both hard to start and hard to keep going.

When you decide to start your own business, you must think carefully about what kind of business you want. You aren't likely to find everything you want in one business—easy entry, security, and reward. Choose those characteristics that matter the most to you; accept the absence of the others; plan, plan, plan; and then go for it!

CRITICAL THINKING

Imagine yourself starting a small business. What markets look attractive? How much competition is there? What could you do to make your business more successful than competitors'? Would you be willing to work 60 to 70 hours per week?

LEARNING ABOUT SMALL-BUSINESS OPERATIONS

Hundreds of would-be entrepreneurs of all ages have asked the same question, How can I learn to run my own business? Many of these people had no idea what kind of business they wanted to start; they simply wanted to be in business for themselves. That seems to be a major trend among students today. So here are some hints for learning about small business.

••• LEARN FROM OTHERS •••

Your search for small-business knowledge might begin by investigating your local college for such classes. One good thing about such courses is that they usually bring together entrepreneurs. One of the best ways to learn to run a small business is to talk to others who've already done it.[16] They'll tell you that location is critical. They'll caution you not to be undercapitalized (not have enough money to start). They'll warn you about problems of finding and retaining good workers. And, most of all, they'll tell you to keep good records and hire a good accountant and lawyer before you start. This free advice is invaluable.

••• GET SOME EXPERIENCE •••

There's no better way to learn small-business management than by becoming an apprentice or working for a successful entrepreneur. In fact, 42 percent of small-business owners got the idea for their businesses from their prior jobs. The rule of thumb is, have three years' experience in a comparable business.

The new entrepreneurs of the 1990s often come from corporate management. Many corporate managers are tired of the big-business life and/or are being laid off because of downsizing. One of every four middle managers who lost their positions in corporations in 1990 started his or her own business.[17] Such managers bring their managerial expertise and enthusiasm with them.

Getting experience before you start your own business isn't a new concept. In fact, way back in 1818, Cornelius Vanderbilt sold his own sailing vessels and went to work for a steamboat company so he could learn the rules of the new game of steam. After learning what he needed to know, he quit, started his own steam shipping company, and became the first American to accumulate $100 million.[18]

By starting a business part time, during your off hours or on weekends, you can experience the rewards of working for yourself while still enjoying a regular paycheck. Some 12.7 million people in the United States are self-employed part time.[19]

Tom Simonds, Hoyt Hudson, and Steve Norton are "20-something" partners in one of Chicago's most promising new entrepreneurial ventures—InterAccess. Simonds started the comany in 1993 (with $31,000 in cash) to provide access for customers to the Internet through use of their user-friendly software. InterAccess emphasizes exceptional customer service and technical support at reasonable prices. Revenues in 1995 are expected to exceed $1 million.

••• TAKE OVER A SUCCESSFUL FIRM •••

Small-business management takes long hours, dedication, and determination. Owners work long hours and rarely take vacations. After many years, they may feel stuck in their business. They may think that they can't get out because they have too much time and effort invested. Consequently, there are millions of small business owners out there eager to get away, at least for a long vacation.

This is where you come in. Find a mature businessperson (50 to 60 or more years old) who owns a small business. Tell him or her that you're eager to learn the business and would like to serve an apprenticeship, a training period. At the end of that period (one year or so), you would like to help the owner/manager by becoming assistant manager. As assistant manager, you would free the owner to take off weekends and holidays, and to take a long vacation—a good deal for him or her. For another year or so, work very hard to learn all about the business—suppliers, inventory, bookkeeping, customers, promotion, and so on. At the end of two years, make the owner this offer: He

• • •

or she can retire or work only part-time, and you'll take over the business. You can establish a profit-sharing plan for yourself plus a salary. Be generous with yourself; you'll earn it if you manage the business. You can even ask for 40 percent or more of the profits.

The owner benefits by keeping ownership in the business and making 60 percent of what he or she earned before—without having to work. You benefit by making 40 percent of the profits of a successful firm. This is an excellent deal for an owner about to retire who can keep his or her firm and a healthy profit flow. It's also a clever and successful way to share in the profits of a successful small business without any personal money investment. Andrew and Abigail Ashley are starting their own organic vegetable business by taking over the heavy farm chores from Al and Caroline Mueller. The Muellers are tired from working 15-hour days for the past 40 years, but they don't want to sell their farm. The Ashleys are young and eager to start their business, but can't afford to buy a farm. Their deal allows Ashley to make most of the management decisions and contribute most of the labor. Mueller contributes his wealth of knowledge, some well-used equipment, and most important, the land. When the Muellers are ready to sell the farm, the Ashleys should be able to buy it and manage it alone.[20]

If profit sharing doesn't appeal to the owner, you may want to buy the business outright. How do you determine a fair price for a business? Value is based on (1) what the business owns, (2) what it earns, and (3) what makes it unique. Naturally, your accountant will need to help you determine the business's value.

If your efforts to take over the business through either profit sharing or buying fail, you can quit and start your own business fully trained.

MANAGING A SMALL BUSINESS

The Small Business Administration has reported that 90 percent of all failures are a result of "poor management." The problem is that "poor management" covers a number of faults. It could mean poor planning, poor record keeping, poor inventory control, poor promotion, or poor employee relations. Most likely it would include poor capitalization. This chapter gives us a chance to explore the functions of business in a small-business setting so you can become one of the successful owners. The functions we'll explore are

- Planning your business.
- Financing your business.
- Knowing your customers (marketing).
- Managing your employees (human resource development).
- Keeping records (accounting).

Although all of the functions are important in both the start-up phase and the management phase of the business, the first two functions, planning and financing, are the primary concerns when you start your business. The remaining functions are the heart of the actual running of the business once it's started.

• • • BEGINNING WITH PLANNING • • •

It's amazing how many people are eager to start a small business but have only a vague notion of what they want to do. Eventually, they come up with an idea for a business and begin discussing the idea with professors, friends, and other businesspeople. It's at this stage that the entrepreneur needs a business plan. A **business plan** is a detailed written statement that describes the nature of the business, the target market, the advantages the business will have in relation to competition, and the resources and qualifications of the owner(s). Stop here and review the nearby box about business plans on p. 190 for details. A business plan forces potential owners of small businesses to be quite specific about the products or services they intend to offer. They must analyze the competition, the money needed to start, and other details of operation. It is also essential to plan for ending the business when the time comes. You owe it to your partners and family to plan for succession early.[21] A business plan is also mandatory for talking with bankers or other investors.

A good business plan is the foundation for business success. It spells out the intended market, how much capital will be needed, and how the business will meet and beat the competition. Business plan software packages, such as those pictured here, are available to assist entrepreneurs in organzing and developing their business plans.

Michael Celello, president of the People's Commercial Bank, says that fewer than 10 percent of prospective borrowers come to a bank adequately prepared. He offers several tips to small-business owners, including picking a bank that serves businesses the size of yours, having a good accountant prepare a complete set of financial statements and personal balance sheet, going to the bank with an accountant and all the necessary financial information, making an appointment before going to the bank, and demonstrating to the banker that you're a person of good character, civic-minded and respected in business and community circles. Finally, he says to ask for all the money you need and be specific and be prepared to personally guarantee the loan.

business plan
A detailed written statement that describes the nature of the business, the target market, the advantages the business will have over competitors, and the resources and qualifications of the owners.

WRITING A BUSINESS PLAN   According to Joseph Mancuso, author of a book on how to prepare business plans and director of the Center for Entrepreneurial Management in New York, a good business plan takes a minimum of five months to write, but you've got to convince your readers in five minutes not to throw the plan away.

Mr. Mancuso says there's no such thing as a "perfect business plan" and suggests that prospective entrepreneurs think out the smallest details. Getting the completed business plan in the right hands is almost as important as getting the right information in the plan. Finding the right hands requires research.

Next we'll discuss some of the many sources of money available to new business ventures. All of them call for a comprehensive business plan. The time and effort invested before a business is started will pay off many times later. With small businesses, the big payoff is survival.

••• GETTING MONEY TO FUND A SMALL BUSINESS •••

Entrepreneurs, like most people, often aren't highly skilled at obtaining, managing, and using money. Inadequate capitalization or poor financial management can destroy a business, even when the basic idea behind the business is good and the products are accepted in the marketplace. One secret of finding the money to start your business is knowing where to look for it.

An entrepreneur has several sources of capital: personal savings, relatives, former employers, banks, finance companies, venture capital organizations, government agencies such as the Small Business Administration, the Farmers Home Administration, the Economic Development Authority, and more.

You may even want to consider borrowing from a potential supplier to your future business. Helping you get started may be in the supplier's interest if there's a chance you'll be a big customer later.

Outline of a Comprehensive Business Plan

Cover letter

Only one thing is for certain when you go hunting for money to start a business: You won't be the only hunter out there. You need to make potential funders want to read your business plan instead of the hundreds of others on their desks. Your cover letter should summarize the most attractive points of your project in as few words as possible. Be sure to address the letter to the potential investor by name. "To whom it may concern" or "Dear Sir" isn't the best way to win an investor's support.

Section 1

Introduction. Begin with a two-page or three-page management overview of the proposed venture. Include a short description of the business, and discuss major goals and objectives.

Section 2

Company background. Describe company operations to date (if any), potential legal considerations, and areas of risk and opportunity. Summarize the firm's financial condition, and include past and current balance sheets, income and cash flow statements, and other relevant financial records (you'll read about these financial statements in Chapter 18.) It's also wise to describe your insurance coverage. Investors want to be assured that death or other mishaps don't pose major threats to the company.

Section 3

Management team. Include an organization chart, job descriptions of listed positions, and detailed résumés of the current and proposed executives. A mediocre idea with a proven management team is funded more often than a great idea with an inexperienced team. Managers should have expertise in all disciplines necessary to start and run a business. If they don't, mention outside consultants who'll serve in these roles and describe their qualifications.

Section 4

Financial plan. Provide five-year projections for income, expenses, and funding sources. Don't assume the business will grow in a straight line. Adjust your planning to allow for funding at various stages of the company's growth. Explain the rationale and assumptions used to determine the estimates. Assumptions should be reasonable and based on industry/historical trends. Make sure all totals add up and are consistent throughout the plan. If necessary, hire a professional accountant or financial analyst to prepare these statements.

Stay clear of excessively ambitious sales projections; rather, offer best-case, expected, and worst-case scenarios. These not only reveal how sensitive the bottom line is to sales fluctuations but also serve as good management guides.

Section 5

Capital required. Indicate the amount of capital needed to begin or continue operations and describe how these funds are to be used. Make sure the totals are the same as the ones on the cash flow statement. This area will receive a great deal of review from potential investors, so it must be clear and concise.

Section 6

Marketing plan. Don't underestimate the competition. Review industry size, trends, and the target market segment. Discuss strengths and weaknesses of the product or service. The most important things investors want to know are what makes the product more desirable than what's already available and whether the product can be patented. Compare pricing to the competition's. Forecast sales in dollars and units. Outline sales, advertising, promotion, and PR programs. Make sure the costs agree with those projected in the financial statements.

Section 7

Location analysis. In retailing and certain other industries, the location of the business is one of the most important factors. Provide a comprehensive demographic analysis of consumers in the area of the proposed store as well as a traffic-pattern analysis and vehicular and pedestrian counts.

Section 8

Manufacturing plan. Describe minimum plant size, machinery required, production capacity, inventory and inventory-control methods, quality control, plant personnel requirements, and so on. Estimates of product costs should be based on primary research.

Section 9

Appendix. Include all marketing research on the product or service (off-the-shelf reports, article reprints, etc.) and other information about the product concept or market size. Provide a bibliography of all the reference materials you consulted. This section should demonstrate that the proposed company won't be entering a declining industry or market segment.

Source: Eric Adams, "Growing Your Business Plan," *Home Office Computing*, May 1991, pp. 44–48; R. Richard Bruno, "How to Write a Business Plan for a New Venture," *Marketing News*, March 15, 1985, p. 10; and Ellyn Spragins, "Venture Capital Express," *Inc.*, November 1990, pp. 159–60.

> **FROM THE PAGES OF... Entrepreneur MAGAZINE**
>
> ## Seed Money for Rural Entrepreneurs
>
> The Farmer's Home Administration (FmHA) in Washington, D.C., is lending young people aged 10 to 20 up to $5,000 to start their own businesses. Youth Project Loan applicants must live in a small town (population less than 10,000) or in the open country. Crop production, catering services, and farm equipment repair are just a few of the business possibilities open to these young rural entrepreneurs. Many of the applicants are members of 4-H Clubs or Future Farmers of America. You can get more information from your local FmHA office.
>
> Source: "Seed Money," *Entrepreneur*, June 1994, p. 14.

States are becoming stronger supporters of entrepreneurs as they create programs that invest directly in new businesses. Often, state commerce departments serve as clearinghouses for such investment programs. States are also creating incubators and technology centers to reduce start-up capital needs.[22] **Incubators** provide low-cost offices with basic business services such as accounting, legal advice, and secretarial help. The number of incubators now exceeds 500.

incubators
Centers which provide "newborn" businesses (usually in technological industries) with low-cost offices and basic business services.

Technology-minded entrepreneurs often have the best shot at attracting start-up capital. Not only are such potential businesses more attractive to venture capitalists and state governments, but also the federal government has several grant programs that provide funds for computer-related ventures.

Other than personal savings, individual investors are the primary source of capital for most entrepreneurs. Such investors provide 6 of every 10 dollars for firms with fewer than four employees and sales of under $150,000 a year. About $56 billion in risk capital comes from these "business angels" each year. Computer networks are now available that link entrepreneurs with such potential investors.

Investors known as *venture capitalists* may finance your project—for a price. **Venture capitalists** may ask for a hefty stake (as much as 60 percent) in your company in exchange for the cash to start your business. Experts recommend that you talk with at least five investment firms and their clients to find the right venture capitalist. You can get a list of venture capitalists from the Small Business Administration. Ask for the "Directory of Operating Small Business Investment Companies." You can also follow the ups and downs of venture capital availability in *Inc.* magazine.

venture capitalist
Individuals or organizations which invest in new businesses in exchange for partial ownership pf the company.

Two good books about finding venture capital are Robert J. Gaston's, *Finding Private Venture Capital for Your Firm* (John Wiley & Sons) and G. Steven Barrill and Craig T. Norback's *The Arthur Young Guide to Raising Venture Capital* (Liberty House).

THE SMALL BUSINESS ADMINISTRATION (SBA)   The Small Business Administration is a valuable source of expertise on starting a new business. The SBA has produced many publications to assist small-business owners in all areas of management. You can get many of its booklets at your local library. The SBA provides the following types of financial assistance:

- Direct loans—loans made directly to selected small-business owners who have difficulty securing conventional loans (for example, disabled owners, veterans, and other special cases).

Budding entrepreneurs can find start-up capital in a variety of places, including corporations. For example, AT&T sponsors the Working Woman Startup grant for women who want to start their own businesses.

- Guaranteed loans—loans made by a financial institution that the government will repay if the borrower stops making payments.

- Participation loans—combination direct and guaranteed loans. The SBA will guarantee part of the loan and will loan the balance directly.

- Loans from Minority Enterprise Small Business Investment Companies (MESBICs). MESBICs are finance companies that make loans to minority-owned businesses.

- Loans from the Women's Financing Section—guaranteed loans to qualified women for less than $50,000, created by the Women's Business Ownership Act of 1988.[23]

- Microloans—amounts ranging from $250 to $50,000 (average $7,000) to people such as single mothers and public housing tenants.

The SBA started the five-year microloan demonstration program in 1992. The program now provides $75 million a year to 47 existing nonprofit microloan programs. Plans are to expand to 1,000 microloan programs across the country. Rather than base the awarding of loans on collateral, credit history, or previous business success, these programs decide worthiness on the basis of belief in the borrowers' integrity and the soundness of their business ideas.[24]

The SBA microloan program is modeled after similar programs like the Women's Economic Development Corp. (Wedco) in St. Paul, Minnesota. Such programs have seen many good results. For example, Leslie Johnson received a $500 Wedco loan to buy roses to sell on Valentine's Day. According to the program's rules, she had to repay the loan in five days, which she could easily do with the $2,500 she made selling the flowers. After a series of such loans, Johnson now has three locations and grosses about $740,000 annually.[25]

If you want to know what loan officers look for when reviewing SBA-guaranteed loan applications, invest $69 in *SBA Lending Made Easy*, a book put out by the American Bankers Association (telephone 1–800–338–0626) to help out loan officers.[26] The SBA has recently revised its loan-guarantee forms for loans under $50,000 to a single-page application. That's a far cry from its 150-page predecessor.[27]

You may also want to consider requesting funds from **Small Business Investment Companies (SBICs)**, private investment companies that the Small Business Administration licenses to lend money to small businesses. An SBIC must have a minimum of $1 million in capital and can borrow up to four dollars from the SBA for each dollar of capital it has. It loans to or invests in small businesses that meet its criteria. Often the SBICs are able to keep defaults to a minimum by identifying a business's trouble spots early; giving entrepreneurs advice; and, in some cases, rescheduling payments.

You may want to write or call the SBA in Washington, D.C., for the latest information about SBA programs and report to the class. The SBA's address is 1441 L Street NW, Washington, D.C. 20005; its public communication line is : (202) 205–6740. The SBA is also on the Internet. Its e-mail address is http://www.sbaonline.sba.gov.[28]

Obtaining money from banks, venture capitalists, and government sources is difficult for most small businesses. (You'll learn more about financing in Chapter 19.) Those who do survive the planning and financing of their new ventures are eager to get their businesses up and running. Your success in running a business depends on many factors. Four important factors for success are knowing your customers, managing employees, keeping efficient records, and looking for help.

Small Business Investment Companies (SBICs)
Private investment companies which the Small Business Administration licenses to lend money to small businesses.

- There were nine sections in the business plan on page 190. This is probably the most important document a small-business owner will ever make. Can you describe at least five of those sections now?
- The U.S. Small Business Administration gives reasons why small businesses fail financially. Can you name three?

PROGRESS CHECK

••• KNOWING YOUR CUSTOMERS •••

One of the most important elements of small-business success is knowing the market. In business, a **market** consists of people with unsatisfied wants and needs who have both the resources and willingness to buy. For example, we can confidently state that most of our students have the willingness to take a Caribbean cruise during their spring break. However, few of them have the resources necessary to satisfy this want. Would they be considered a good market for the local travel agency to pursue?

Once you have identified your market and its needs, you must set out to fill those needs. The way to meet your customers' needs in the 1990s is to offer top quality at a fair price with great service. Remember, it isn't enough just to get customers; you also have to keep them. As Victoria Jackson, founder of the $50 million Victoria Jackson Cosmetics Company, says of the stars that push her products on TV infomercials, "All the glamorous faces in the world wouldn't mean a thing if my customers weren't happy with the product and didn't come back for more." Everything must be geared to bring the customers the satisfaction they deserve.[29]

You'll gain more insights about markets in Chapters 13 and 14. Now let's consider the importance of effectively managing the employees who help you serve your market.

market
People with unsatisfied wants and needs who have both the resources and willingness to buy.

R. Terren Dunlap had a good idea for a dual-deck videocassette recorder. His initial financing came from using 10 personal credit cards. Once developed, he ran into problems getting the machine manufactured. Dunlap learned that even the best ideas call for advice from finance, production, and marketing experts.

••• MANAGING EMPLOYEES •••

As a business grows, it becomes impossible for an entrepreneur to oversee every detail, even if he or she is putting in 60 hours per week. This means that hiring, training, and motivating employees is critical.

It's not easy to find good, qualified help when you offer less money, skimpier benefits, and less room for advancement than larger firms. That's one reason why employee relations is such an important part of small-business management. Employees of small companies are often more satisfied with their jobs than are their counterparts in big business. Why? Quite often they find their jobs more challenging, their ideas more accepted, and their bosses more respectful. Over 90 percent of the small, top growth companies listed by *Inc.* magazine share ownership and profits with their employees.

Often entrepreneurs reluctantly face the reality that to keep growing, delegating authority to others is essential. Nagging questions such as "Who should be delegated authority?" and "How much control should they have?" create perplexing problems.

This can be a particularly touchy issue in small businesses with long-term employees as well as in family businesses. As you might expect, entrepreneurs who've built their companies from scratch often feel compelled to promote employees who've been with them from the start—even when those employees aren't qualified to serve as managers. Common sense probably tells you this could harm the business.

The same can be true of family-run businesses that are expanding. Attitudes such as "You can't fire family" or you must promote someone because "they're family" can hinder growth. Entrepreneurs can best serve themselves and the business if they gradually recruit and groom employees for management positions. By doing this, trust and support of the manager are enhanced among other employees and the entrepreneur.

When Heida Thurlow of Chantal Cookware suffered an extended illness, she let her employees handle the work she once had insisted on doing herself. The experience transformed her company from an entrepreneurial company into a managerial one. "Over the long run that makes us stronger than we were."[30] You'll learn more about managing employees in Chapters 7 through 12.

••• KEEPING RECORDS •••

Small-business owners often say that the most important assistance they needed in starting and managing the business involved accounting. A businessperson who sets up an effective accounting system early will save much grief later. Computers make record keeping much easier and enable a small business owner to follow the firm's progress (in terms of sales, expenses, and profits) on a daily basis. An inexpensive computer system can also help with other record keeping chores, such as inventory control, customer records, and payroll.

A good accountant is invaluable in setting up such systems and showing you how to keep the system operating smoothly. Many business failures are caused by poor accounting practices. A good accountant can help make decisions such as whether to buy or lease equipment and whether to own or rent the building. Help may also be provided for tax planning, financial forecasting, choosing sources of financing, and writing up requests for funds.

Legal Briefcase

How Laws Affect Home-Based Businesses

Laws and regulations can sometimes be a headache for the budding entrepreneur. Local zoning laws prohibiting businesses in residential areas can limit home-based businesses. Expenses such as social security taxes, unemployment insurance, pension contributions, and workers' compensation insurance can be crippling. Adherence to the Family Leave and Americans with Disabilities Acts (ADA) can also be expensive.

The impact of what seems at times to be a government crusade against small businesses can, in some instances, actually spur entrepreneurial activity. For example, the expenses of hiring an employee may force both small and large businesses into using small independent contractors rather than keeping employees on the payroll to perform certain tasks. This creates a significant opportunity for the self-employed. For example, home-office consultant Bonnie Feingold used to beg companies to work with her. Now she shows them that she can save them 35 percent over a salaried employee who requires health insurance and workers' compensation insurance—and she's having an easy time landing clients.

Source: Mary McAleer Vizard, "Home-Business Outlaws," *Home Office Computing*, February 1993, pp. 32–34; and Wesley J. Smith, "The Face-Off: Clinton and Small Business," *Home Office Computing*, August 1993, pp. 42–48.

Other small businesses may give you an idea of where to find an accountant experienced in small business. It pays to shop around for advice.[31] You will learn more about accounting in Chapter 18.

••• LOOKING FOR HELP •••

Small-business owners have learned, sometimes the hard way, that they need outside consulting advice early in the process. This is especially true of legal, tax, and accounting advice, but may also be true of marketing, finance, and information systems advice. About 60 percent of leading entrepreneurs believe that getting help with information technology is important.[32] Most small and medium-size firms can't afford to hire such experts as employees, so they must turn to outside assistance. (See Figure 6.4.)

SOURCE	PERCENTAGE USING SOURCE	IMPORTANCE RANK OF SOURCE
Accountant	78%	1
Other business owners	77	3
Friends/relatives	76	5
Bankers	72	2
Lawyers	63	6
Books/manuals	62	7
Suppliers	59	4
Trade organizations	47	9
Seminars	41	8
Government sources	33	10

FIGURE 6.4

INFORMATION SOURCES FOR SMALL BUSINESSES
Small-business managers turn to accountants and bankers for important advice. They also question other business owners and friends for ideas.

A necessary and invaluable aide is a competent, experienced lawyer—one who knows and understands small businesses. Partners have a way of forgetting agreements unless the contract is written by a lawyer and signed. Lawyers can help with a variety of matters including leases, contracts, and protection against liabilities. Lawyers don't have to be expensive. In fact, there are several prepaid legal plans that offer legal services such as drafting legal documents for an annual rate of $150 to $350. Attorneys that offer plans for small businesses include Lawphone (telephone 1–800–255–3352), Prodigy (1–800–284–5933), and Caldwell Legal (1–800–222–3035).[33]

Marketing decisions should be made long before a product is produced or a store is opened. An inexpensive marketing research study may help you determine where to locate, whom to select as your target market, and what would be an effective strategy for reaching those people. Thus, a marketing consultant with small-business experience can be of great help to you.

Two other invaluable experts are a commercial loan officer and an insurance agent. The commercial loan officer can help you design an acceptable business plan and give you financial advice as well as loan you money when you need it. An insurance agent will explain all the risks associated with a small business and how to cover them most efficiently with insurance and other means (for example, safety devices and sprinkler systems).

An important source of information for small businesses is the **Service Corps of Retired Executives (SCORE)**. This SBA office has 13,000 volunteers who provide consulting services for small businesses free (except for expenses). You can find a SCORE counselor by calling your local SBA office or SCORE's Washington, D.C., number, (202) 205–6762. The SBA also sponsors volunteers from industry, trade associations, and education who counsel small businesses. They are called the **Active Corps of Executives (ACE)**.

Often a local college has business professors who'll advise small-business owners for free or a small fee. Some universities have clubs or programs that provide consulting services by MBA candidates for a nominal fee. For example, Columbia University's Small Business Consulting Group charges only $15 an hour for the consulting services of a team of three MBA students with complementary skills (for example, marketing, finance, and management).[34]

It also is wise to seek the counsel of other small-business owners. Other sources of counsel include chambers of commerce, the Better Business Bureau, national and local trade associations, and the business reference section of your library. Many entrepreneurs are using computer bulletin boards on the Internet for advice and support as well as for a way to find clients.[35]

Service Corps of Retired Executives (SCORE)
Part of SBA made up of experienced businesspeople who provide consulting services to small businesses for free (minus expenses).

Active Corps of Executives (ACE)
Volunteers from industry, trade associations, and education who counsel small businesses.

FIGURE 6.5

U.S. INDUSTRIES WITH THE HIGHEST POTENTIAL IN INTERNATIONAL MARKETS

1. Computers and peripherals (hardware)
2. Telecommunications equipment and systems
3. Computer software and services
4. Medical instruments, equipment, and supplies
5. Electronic parts
6. Analytical and scientific laboratory instruments
7. Industrial process control instruments
8. Aircraft and parts and avionics and ground support equipment
9. Automotive parts and service equipment and accessories
10. Electronic production and test equipment
11. Electronic power generation and distribution systems and transmission equipment
12. Food processing and packaging equipment and machinery
13. Safety and security equipment
14. Printing and graphic arts equipment
15. Water resources equipment

GOING INTERNATIONAL: SMALL-BUSINESS PROSPECTS
• • • • • • •

There are only about 250 million people in the United States, but there are over 5 billion people in the world. Obviously, the world market is potentially a much larger and more lucrative market for small businesses than the United States alone. In spite of that potential, most small businesses still don't think internationally. Only 20 percent of small-business executives say they export.[36] By U.S. Department of Commerce estimates, there are 18,000 manufacturers (most of them small) that could export their products but don't. Only 2,000 U.S. firms are responsible for 80 percent of our exports. Figure 6.5 lists the industries with the highest potential in global markets.

Why are so many companies missing the boat to huge global markets? Primarily because the voyage involves a few major hurdles: (1) Financing is often difficult to find. (2) Many would-be exporters don't know how to get started. (3) Potential global businesspeople don't understand the cultural differences of prospective markets. (4) The bureaucratic paperwork can bury a small business.

Beside the fact that most of the world's market lies outside the United States, there are other good reasons for going international. For instance, exporting products can absorb excess inventory, soften downturns in the domestic market, and extend product lives. It can also spice up dull routines.

Small businesses have several advantages over large businesses in international trade:

- Overseas buyers enjoy dealing with individuals rather than with large corporate bureaucracies.
- Small companies can usually begin shipping much faster than large ones.
- Small companies provide a wide variety of suppliers.
- Small companies can give more personal service and more undivided attention, because each overseas account is a major source of business to them.

There are many opportunities to start small businesses elsewhere in the world. Often the competition is not as stiff. This 7-Eleven store in Norway, for example, will not have many similar stores nearby. With over 5 billion people in the world market, there are many, many opportunities to take a successful concept from the United States to another country.

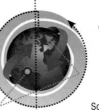

Reaching Beyond Our Borders

Exporters' Tips

1. Examine your product or service to see if it has export potential.

2. Learn as much as you can about the foreign markets you're considering entering.

3. Study local customs carefully so you don't insult potential customers.

4. Explore state and federal programs for funds available for small-business exporting.

5. Be patient. If you're willing to wait for results, long-term relationships pay off. Take on the world one market at a time.

6. Invest your own time in meetings and travel rather than delegating such activities to subordi-

nates. Many foreign businesspeople prefer dealing with the top person.

7. Set up an appropriate financing and payment plan, and buy commercial and political risk insurance for protection.

8. Go to workshops and seminars that teach export skills.

9. Get qualified export counseling and work with a written business plan.

Source: Jane Applegate, "Exporting Doesn't Need to Be So Foreign," *Washington Post*, January 4, 1991, pp. D3–D12; and Mary Beth Sammons, "Preparing for the Plunge," *Chicago Tribune*, October 27, 1993, section 7, p. 5.

The growth potential for small businesses in global markets is phenomenal. The pioneers among U.S. firms in international expansion were franchised organizations such as McDonald's, Avis, Hertz, Kentucky Fried Chicken, and Hanna car washes. They were soon followed by other entrepreneurs who saw the opportunity to start small businesses in foreign countries. For example, John Stollenwerk found customers for his Wisconsin-made shoes in Italy, and Ohio's Andrew Bohnengel opened an entire world for his tape company by adopting the metric standard.

There's an abundance of inexpensive information about exporting. A good place to start is with the Department of Commerce. Other sources of information include the SBA, banks, local freight forwarders, export management companies, and export trading companies. "Exportise," a step-by-step guide to exporting, is available from the Small Business Foundation. You can call the SBA Office of International Trade at (202) 634–1500.

PROGRESS CHECK

- Why do many small businesses avoid doing business internationally?
- What are some advantages small businesses have over large businesses in selling in global markets?

SUMMARY

1. Explain why people are willing to take the risks of entrepreneurship; list the attributes of successful entrepreneurs; and describe the benefits of entrepreneurial teams and intrapreneurs.

1. There are many reasons why people are willing to take the risks of entrepreneurship.
- ***What are a few of the reasons people start their own businesses?***
Reasons include profit, independence, opportunity, and challenge.
- ***What have modern entrepreneurs done to ensure longer terms of management?***
They've formed entrepreneurial teams that have expertise in the many different skills needed to start and manage a business.
- ***What is intrapreneuring?***
It's the establishment of entrepreneurial centers within a larger firm where people can innovate and develop new product ideas internally.

2. Of all the nonfarm businesses in the United States, almost 97 percent are considered small by the Small Business Administration.
   - ***Why are small businesses important to the U.S. economy?***
   Small business accounts for over 40 percent of GDP. Perhaps more important to tomorrow's graduates, 80 percent of American workers' first jobs are in small businesses.
   - ***What does the*** small ***in small business mean?***
   The Small Business Administration defines a small business as one that's independently owned and operated, that's not dominant in its field of operation, and that meets certain standards of size in terms of employees or sales. (These standards depend on the size of other firms in the industry.)
   - ***Why do many small businesses fail?***
   Many small businesses fail because of managerial incompetence and inadequate financial planning. See the box on page 186 for a list of causes of business failure.

   2. Discuss the importance of small business to the American economy and summarize the major causes of small-business failure.

3. Most people have no idea how to go about starting a small business.
   - ***What advice would you give someone who wants to learn about starting a small business?***
   First, learn from others. Take related courses and talk with some small-business owners. Second, get some experience working for others. Third, take over a successful firm. Finally, study the latest in small-business management techniques, including the use of computers for things like payroll, inventory control, and mailing lists.

   3. Summarize ways to learn about how small businesses operate.

4. Writing a business plan is the first step in organizing a business.
   - ***What goes into a business plan?***
   See the box on page 190.
   - ***Someone you know wants to start a new business. What sources of funds would you suggest that she investigate?***
   A new entrepreneur has several sources of capital: personal savings, relatives, former employers, banks, finance companies, venture capital organizations, government agencies, and more.
   - ***Name some special problems that small-business owners have in dealing with employees.***
   Small-business owners often have difficulty finding competent employees and grooming employees for management responsibilities.
   - ***Where can budding entrepreneurs find help in starting their businesses?***
   Help can be found in many places: accountants, lawyers, marketing researchers, loan officers, insurance agents, the SBA, SBICs, and college professors. (See Figure 6.4.)

   4. Analyze what it takes to start and run a small business, including the writing of a business plan.

5. The future growth of some small businesses is in foreign markets.
   - ***What are some advantages small businesses have over large businesses in global markets?***
   Foreign buyers enjoy dealing with individuals rather than large corporations because (1) small companies typically provide a wider variety of suppliers and can ship more quickly and (2) small companies give more personal service.
   - ***Why don't more small businesses start trading internationally?***
   There are several reasons: (1) Financing is often difficult to find. (2) Many people don't know how to get started. (3) Many don't understand the cultural differences of foreign markets. (4) The bureaucratic red tape is often overwhelming.

   5. Outline the advantages and disadvantages of small businesses entering global markets.

KEY TERMS

Active Corps of
Executives
(ACE) 196
business plan 189
entrepreneurial
team 181
entrepreneurship 178

incubators 191
intrapreneur 182
market 193
Service Corps of
Retired Executives
(SCORE) 196
small business 183

Small Business
Investment
Companies
(SBICs) 193
venture capitalist 191

DEVELOPING WORKPLACE SKILLS

1. Review past issues of *Entrepreneur, Today's Business,* and *Inc.* magazines. Read about the entrepreneurs who are heading today's dynamic new businesses. Write profiles about two or more of these entrepreneurs focusing on their similarities. Report your findings to the class.

2. Obtain the 80-page 1993 federal government publication "Small Business Handbook" (item number 574A) by sending $1 to S. James, Consumer Information Center-4A, P.O. Box 100, Pueblo, Colorado, 81002. The booklet will come in handy in later chapters since it covers such management issues as minimum and overtime pay, child labor laws, employment of alien workers, veterans, family leave, and much more. Discuss the contents of this handbook in class.

3. Select two small businesses in your area that look attractive as career possibilities for you. Interview at least two people who manage such businesses. Ask them how they started, about financing, personnel problems (hiring, firing, training, scheduling), accounting problems, and other managerial matters. Pick their brains. Let them be your instructors. Share your findings with the class, including whether or not these individuals find their jobs rewarding, interesting, and challenging, and why.

4. Contact your local Small Business Administration office and arrange to visit it if you can. Learn as much as possible about the programs and brochures offered there.

5. Choose a partner from among your classmates and put together a list of factors that might mean the difference between success and failure for a new company entering the business software industry. Can small startups realistically hope to compete with companies such as Microsoft and Lotus? Discuss the list and your conclusions in class.

PRACTICING MANAGEMENT DECISIONS

〈〈 C A S E   BMOC: STARTING A SMALL BUSINESS AT SCHOOL 〉〉

Many students don't wait until they complete school before they try to get their feet wet in small-business management. Many students go beyond the planning stage and actually run their businesses while still in school. For example, college freshman Jason Bernard runs his drawing firm, Architectural Rendering, from his bedroom. Other young people look around, see thousands of students, and try to develop small businesses that would appeal to students. For example, some students assemble and sell "Home Emergency Kits" for students returning in the fall. The kits contain items like pens and pencils, chocolate chip cookies, aspirin, and other college "necessities." The kits are sold to the parents and distributed to students the first week of class as a start-the-year-right gift from home.

Some students produce and sell calendars with pictures of beautiful women on campus or male hunks. Others sell desk mats with advertising messages printed on the sides. Some students become salespeople for cosmetic companies and other more traditional firms. They too feel as if they're in their own business on campus, because they have exclusive sales rights but unlike independent entrepreneurs they don't have to assume as many risks.

One student makes more than his professors by selling ice cream from a truck. Others try to learn the retail business by delivering pizza or other fast foods. Some students have started moving services, moving students' goods from home to school and back.

Dick Gilbertson considered such options as a student at Indiana University. He felt students might enjoy having food other than pizza and subs delivered to the dorms. His research showed that students preferred McDonald's hamburgers and Taco Bell burritos. Students said they were willing to pay $1.00 more for a Big Mac, fries, and a Coke rather than ride the mile or so to the fast-food stores. Mr. Gilbertson's company, Fast Breaks, now serves the 13,000 on-campus students at his school. Guess who his partner is? A professor of entrepreneurship at Indiana University.

Jimmy Enriquez was busy getting a degree in accounting at the University of Texas when he started two companies. One, a construction-site cleaning business run by his sister, has 15 employees, grosses about $4,000 a week, and has expanded to Dallas and Houston. The other business is a vending company that leases foosball games. Foosball was dead when Jimmy and his brother Rocky started. But they started foosball leagues, let beginners play for free, and built a prosperous business. Jimmy's advice to potential entrepreneurs:

If you wait until you're out of school and working for somebody else, you're going to get used to that big car—and you're not going to want to gamble with that stuff. It's better to start a company when you're a student, while you're still used to driving a junker and living like a dog.

Jimmy started an entrepreneurs club at the University of Texas that has 260 members. There are now more than 350 entrepreneurship clubs on college campuses. The Association of Collegiate Entrepreneurs published a list of the top 100 businesses started by people under 30. All are worth over $1 million.

College campuses aren't the only places to find guidance in entrepreneurship. The National Foundation for Teaching Entrepreneurship to Handicapped and Disadvantaged Youth in Newark, New Jersey, trains former drug dealers, street toughs, and special-education students to sell goods and services. Their businesses range from sneakers and lingerie to manicures and car repair. Maybe you should consider getting started now, too.

Decision Questions

1. What are the advantages and potential problems of starting a business while in school?

2. What kinds of entrepreneurs are operating around your school? Talk to them and learn from their experiences.

3. What opportunities exist for satisfying student needs at your school? Pick one idea, write a brief business plan, and discuss it in class (unless it's so good you don't want to share it; in that case, good luck).

VIDEO CASE　Taking the Entrepreneurial Challenge

Of all the factors of production, none is more important than entrepreneurship, the willingness to accept the risk of starting and managing a new business. Fortunately, the other side of assuming risk is making profits. One of the fastest paths to wealth creation—for yourself and others—is through successful entrepreneurship. Two relatively new businesses are good examples: Big Apple Bagels and the Saint Louis Bread Company.

Paul Stoler saw independence, opportunity, challenge and profit potential in starting his own business. Stoler is from New York where he had a successful career going in risk management. He knew that opening your own business involved risk, so choosing the right business was critical. There is much less risk, of course, if you can find a successful business and take it over. Big Apple Bagels was such a business. It launched its first franchise in1993 and soon had 75 franchises in addition to 22 company stores. Stoler, as president, finds that Big Apple Bagels gives him freedom to innovate and he's having fun running this fast growing business.

Ken Rosenthal's plans were even more ambitious than Paul Stoler's. He knew from the beginning that he wanted to own a chain of stores. He also knew there was great risk involved; his friends were constanly telling him so. Furthermore, owning your own business can be exhausting, especially a bakery. You have to get up very early to begin baking and you work late. Again, the key was to find the right product or idea. Rosenthal found his in San Francisco. He had an idea that the sourdough bread that is common there would appeal to St. Louisans, did some research, (found a great model in California), served an apprenticeship, and then sought capital to get started. A sound business plan was critical to getting capital needed to start the business and keep it going. The Saint Louis Bread Company, started in 1988, is now one of the most impressive American success stories with 565 employees in its headquarters, central baking plant, and 17 bakery/cafes.

Both Big Apple Bagels and the Saint Louis Bread Company have created jobs in their communities and have created wealth for their owners. They have also contributed to the well-being of the surrounding community. Both companies give away excess food to local food pantries and soup kitchens.

The long-term success and continued growth of these firms will heavily depend upon good marketing; that is, keeping close to customers and constantly adjusting to satisfy and meet customer wants and needs. However, it will also depend on good management in all areas such as accounting, finance, and information systems. Typically, that means finding others to help. These individuals may become partners or remain as outside consultants. Rosenthal took on partners, but also sought the counsel of a team of facilitators.

The failure rate of small businesses is very high. Since there are typically few people to manage all of the necessary business functions, the whole process frequently becomes overwhelming, and many entrepreneurs quit from shear exhaustion. Is the risk worth it? Some 700,000 people think so, for every year that's how many new businesses are started. The success of Big Apple Bagels, the Saint Louis Bread Company, and other entrepreneurial ventures show it can be done. In 1994, Rosenthal and his partners hit the entrepreneurial jackpot by selling their company to Au Bon Pain for more than $90 million.

Discussion Questions

1. What enables one bakery or bagel place to succeed when others fail?

2. What are some of the best sources that a small business can tap for capital?

3. What other entrepreneurial success stories have you recently observed in your area? What have those businesses done to succeed with customers and rise above competition?

4. How important is a business plan to the *long-term* success of a small business?

ENTREPRENEUR READINESS QUESTIONNAIRE

Not everyone is cut out to be an entrepreneur. The fact is, though, that all kinds of people with all kinds of personalities have succeeded in starting small and large businesses. There are certain traits, however, that seem to separate those who'll be successful as entrepreneurs from those who may not be. The following questionnaire will help you determine in which category you fit. Take a couple of minutes to answer the questions and then score yourself at the end. Making a low score doesn't mean you won't succeed as an entrepreneur. It does indicate, however, that you may be happier working for someone else.

Each of the following items describes something that you may or may not feel represents your personality or other characteristics about you. Read each item and then circle the response (1, 2, 3, 4, or 5) that most nearly reflects the extent to which you agree or disagree that the item seems to fit you.

Scoring: Give yourself one point for each 1 or 2 responses you circled for questions 1, 2, 6, 8, 10, 11, 16, 17, 21, 22, 23.
Give yourself one point for each 4 or 5 response you circled for questions 3, 4, 5, 7, 9, 12, 13, 14, 15, 18, 19, 20, 24, 25.

Add your points and see how you rate in the following categories:

21–25   Your entrepreneurial potential looks great if you have a suitable opportunity to use it. What are you waiting for?

16–20   This is close to the high entrepreneurial range. You could be quite successful if your other talents and resources are right.

11–15   Your score is in the transitional range. With some serious work you can probably develop the outlook you need for running your own business.

6–10   Things look pretty doubtful for you as an entrepreneur. It would take considerable rearranging of your life philosophy and behavior to make it.

0–5   Let's face it. Entrepreneurship isn't really for you. Still, learning what it's all about won't hurt anything.

Looking at my overall philosophy of life and typical behavior, I would say that . . .	Agree Completely (1)	Mostly Agree (2)	Partially Agree (3)	Mostly Disagree (4)	Disagree Completely (5)
1. I am generally optimistic.	1	2	3	4	5
2. I enjoy competing and doing things better than someone else.	1	2	3	4	5
3. When solving a problem, I try to arrive at the best solution first without worrying about other possibilities.	1	2	3	4	5
4. I enjoy associating with co-workers after working hours.	1	2	3	4	5
5. If betting on a horse race I would prefer to take a chance on a high-payoff "long shot."	1	2	3	4	5
6. I like setting my own goals and working hard to achieve them.	1	2	3	4	5
7. I am generally casual and easy-going with others.	1	2	3	4	5
8. I like to know what is going on and take action to find out.	1	2	3	4	5
9. I work best when someone else is guiding me along the way.	1	2	3	4	5
10. When I am right I can convince others.	1	2	3	4	5
11. I find that other people frequently waste my valuable time.	1	2	3	4	5
12. I enjoy watching football, baseball, and similar sports events.	1	2	3	4	5
13. I tend to communicate about myself very openly with other people.	1	2	3	4	5
14. I don't mind following orders from superiors who have legitimate authority.	1	2	3	4	5
15. I enjoy planning things more than actually carrying out the plans.	1	2	3	4	5
16. I don't think it's much fun to bet on a "sure thing."	1	2	3	4	5
17. If faced with failure, I would shift quickly to something else rather than sticking to my guns.	1	2	3	4	5
18. Part of being successful in business is reserving adequate time for family.	1	2	3	4	5
19. Once I have earned something, I feel that keeping it secure is important.	1	2	3	4	5
20. Making a lot of money is largely a matter of getting the right breaks.	1	2	3	4	5
21. Problem solving is usually more effective when a number of alternatives are considered.	1	2	3	4	5
22. I enjoy impressing others with the things I can do.	1	2	3	4	5
23. I enjoy playing games like tennis and handball with someone who is slightly better than I am.	1	2	3	4	5
24. Sometimes moral ethics must be bent a little in business dealings.	1	2	3	4	5
25. I think that good friends would make the best subordinates in an organization.	1	2	3	4	5

Source: Kenneth R. Van Voorhis, *Entrepreneurship and Small Business Management* (New York: Allyn & Bacon, 1980).

Part 2
BUSINESS FORMATION

When you drive through any town or city, you see dozens, often hundreds and thousands, of small businesses. The kinds of businesses are as varied as the people who own and operate them. If you were to interview the owners, you would also find a great variety of reasons for choosing a specific business, for settling in a certain location, and for choosing business ownership as a way of life.

Many people become entrepreneurs today because they see the risks as similar to working for someone else—but the rewards much greater. The workplace as a whole is becoming increasingly risk-intensive. Many jobs are riskier propositions than they would have been 10 years ago. Downsizing « P.28 » and restructuring are just two reasons that job security assumptions are changing. The incentive for some risk-taking with a payoff of independence, high job satisfaction, and possible high profits just might be more enticing to you in the future than it already is now.

One of the first objections people often have when encouraged to start their own business is that "Everything has already been tried." That simply isn't true. You have probably seen ideas of your own that were put into practice by someone else—someone else who made all the profits. Although the number of possibilities seem smaller than, say, 50 years ago, the opportunities for new, creative business ideas are still lurking in a veiled reality somewhere, awaiting discovery by an innovative entrepreneur—maybe you.

SKILLS

You will need certain qualities to succeed, no matter what type of business you choose to start.

1. You must be willing to take risks. This doesn't mean being reckless; it means being comfortable with trying things that could possibly fail. It means feeling that you control your own fate—that you affect circumstances at least as much as they affect you.

2. You must be able to see the possibilities in new ways of doing things. You need to be able to "see the big picture" with both creativity and practicality. An entrepreneur cannot be too set in the old ways of doing things—or of perceiving reality.

3. You need to be a self-starter—someone who doesn't need to have others tell you what to do and when. An entrepreneur should be motivated. Getting up in the morning should be exciting and challenging rather than threatening or depressing.

4. You need to be ambitious and competitive. Entrepreneurs often have to work hard and long hours, especially in the first few years in busi-

ness. A successful entrepreneur sees himself or herself as a winner and *expects* to win. You also need the health and physical stamina to work long hours day after day.

5. You need to be someone who is not easily discouraged. Many successful businesspeople have experienced setback after setback, but they refuse to see setbacks as "failures." An entrepreneur should see setbacks as lessons that won't have to be learned again.

CAREER PATHS

Entrepreneurs get started in many ways. One way is to purchase an existing business. Another is to get involved with a franchise operation. Still another is to create an original idea and develop it on your own. Whatever starting point you choose, remember that entrepreneurship usually offers rewards that are commensurate with the energy you are willing to put into the enterprise. Beyond that, the career path is up to you, the entrepreneur.

SOME POSSIBLE POSITIONS FOR WOULD-BE ENTREPRENEURS

Opportunity	Earnings	Investment	Tasks and responsibilities/Career path	Growth possibilities
Home-based, owner-run businesses	Low at first; will grow faster than overhead, because overhead will remain low.	Will vary; usually very low compared with other entrepreneurial slots.	Bookkeeping, marketing, customer relations, organization of business. Must be self-motivated and able to see opportunities.	Home-based businesses promise to be a growing trend through the year 2005.
Franchising	Considerably higher than nonfranchise operations from the first month of operation.	Varies roughly from $28,000–several million, depending on size and scope of franchise.	Most franchisees provide considerable training and support for the beginning of operations. Owner must accept less freedom, but trades that for a greater chance of success. Opportunities in fast foods, office backup, auto repair, and many others.	Franchising will continue to be popular well into the next century.
Small business consultant	Earnings vary greatly, based on number of contacts and ability to market the service.	Can work for large consulting firms and thus not actually be in business. Operating on one's own, very little investment necessary.	Act as adviser to businesses in various stages of success or failure. A degree in business will help your credibility greatly. Should have a background of both experience and education.	The demands for consultants will continue to grow, especially in the areas of international business and high technology.
Franchise director	Usually depends on the number of franchises in the territory and the size and scope of the overall operation.	Once on its feet, your business can grow using mostly the investment of others (franchisees).	Provide direction for the franchisee, provide training, and help the franchisee become successful. Many franchisors start by working first for another franchise to learn the strategies necessary for success.	Franchising will continue to be popular well past the year 2005.

Norma Rufkahr, Entrepreneur

Norma Rufkahr is a graduate of Belleville Area College in Belleville, Illinois. Twelve years ago, she and her husband owned two video stores. Norma noticed that her next-door business neighbor, a tanning salon, was doing a great amount of volume. But when she thought of changing businesses, the seasonal nature of tanning salons stopped her. "At least the video store is steady and dependable," she told herself. But Norma is not one to stick to conventional thinking—a trait she shares with most other successful entrepreneurs. "Why not combine the two businesses?" she asked herself one day, "and have the best of both worlds?" When the couple parted, each emerged as owner of one store. Being alone presented both challenges and opportunities to the young entrepreneur. Immediately, Norma started back to college. She felt that she needed new skills to become the kind of business success she wanted to be.

Norma had started her first video/tanning store in Troy, Illinois. The idea caught on right away. Customers found the combined services a unique convenience. A few months after parting from her husband, Norma opened another combination store in nearby Fairview Heights. This time, though, the tanning succeeded considerably better than video rental business. Deciding that location and adequate space were the problems, she found another location and moved across the street. Now, with more tanning rooms for customers, the second store is solely a tanning salon.

There was only one problem: What to do with all of the video cassettes from the Fairview Heights store? "Simple," thought Norma, "I opened a third store in Lebanon, Illinois." This store, like the first in Troy, Illinois, offered customers tanning as well as video rentals. With hard work and clever marketing, the idea is working again.

"Succeeding as an entrepreneur takes a while," Norma explains. "It doesn't happen overnight. Even a great idea will often take a couple of years to work out—sometimes even longer." She explains that creativity, energy, and drive are important traits for an entrepreneur, but another one is patience, the ability to wait for growth to develop.

Norma credits her success in part to her educational growth in college and her current learning, which involves attending as many classes and management seminars as she can crowd into her busy schedule. "Getting ideas from the classroom and applying them is really exciting," she reflects. "For example, I've experimented with price and volume. Sure enough, volume increases as prices decrease—just as I learned in economics."

Norma is realistic about changes coming to the video rental industry. As video-on-demand and other innovations grow in popularity, Norma Rufkahr will have to use her talent for innovation. The future doesn't frighten her. On the contrary, she's excited about applying her entrepreneurial skills to a changing environment. Will the tanning salon–video store idea continue to work? If it doesn't, she will be ready with other new ideas to meet the challenge.

Special thanks to Dennis Shannon and James McGowen, faculty at Belleville Area College, for recommending Norma Rufkahr for this Career Portfolio.

BUSINESS MANAGEMENT: EMPOWERING EMPLOYEES TO SATISFY CUSTOMERS

CHAPTER 7
LEADERSHIP, MANAGEMENT, AND EMPLOYEE EMPOWERMENT

CHAPTER 8
ORGANIZING A CUSTOMER-DRIVEN BUSINESS

CHAPTER 9
PRODUCING WORLD-CLASS PRODUCTS AND SERVICES

LEADERSHIP, MANAGEMENT, AND EMPLOYEE EMPOWERMENT

LEARNING GOALS

After you have read and studied this chapter, you should be able to

1. Explain the four functions of management and why the role of managers is changing.

2. Distinguish between goals and objectives; distinguish between strategic, tactical, and contingency planning; and explain the relationships of goals and objectives to various types of planning.

3. Describe the significance of an organization chart and explain how organizations are changing to meet the needs of customers.

4. Describe the directing function of management and illustrate how the function differs at various management levels.

5. Summarize the five steps of the control function of management.

6. Explain the differences between managers and leaders, and compare the characteristics and uses of the various leadership styles.

7. Describe the three general categories of skills needed by top, middle, and first-line managers.

8. Illustrate the skills you will need to develop your managerial potential and outline activities you could use to develop these skills.

MARY PARKER FOLLETT: MOTHER OF MODERN MANAGEMENT

Mary Parker Follett graduated from Thayer College and Radcliffe. While she was in college, Follett taught political science at a nearby secondary school. She was a part of Boston high society and participated on committees that set minimum wages for women and children. The management theorist of that time (the early 1900s) was Frederick Taylor, the "father of scientific management." His writings favored command-style, hierarchical organizations. Employees were treated much like robots or computers; things to be manipulated and directed. Taylor did not believe in participative management. Managers acted more like dictators.

Mary Parker Follett, on the other hand, believed very strongly that the person doing the job was the person most likely to know how to do the job better. She felt that it was human nature to want to be self-managed. Furthermore, Follett believed in the concept of cross-functional rather than vertical authority. Her idea was for people in various departments to share information with one another to the benefit of all.

Follett believed that managers should be leaders rather than dictators. They were to provide a "vision" and help focus all the resources of the firm on meeting that vision. Follett also felt that knowledge and experience, not titles and seniority, should decide who should lead.

Follett's concepts, written in the 1920s and 1930s, were way ahead of her time. She was relatively ignored while Frederick Taylor grew in importance. But times change and innovative ideas from the past suddenly take on new meaning. That is exactly what has happened to Follett's writings. A new book titled *Mary Parker Follett—Prophet of Management: A Celebration of Writings from the 1920s* was recently released by the Harvard Business School Press (1995).

London School of Economics Chairman Sir Peter Parker says that he is not sure who the father of management is, but he is sure who the mother is: Mary Parker Follett. Her ideas about empowerment, self-management, cross-functional cooperation, and conflict resolution are now being implemented in leading firms throughout the world. In this chapter, we shall explore both traditional and new management concepts. Much of it is based on the fundamentals that Mary Parker Follett established 70 years ago.

If you really believe in quality, when you cut through everything, it's empowering your people, and it's empowering your people that leads to teams.

Jaime Houghton

THE MANAGEMENT CHALLENGE OF THE FUTURE

Jack Welch of GE (General Electric) is just one example of many managers who are radically changing the whole approach to corporate management. Changes are necessary because of global competition, technological change, and the growing importance of pleasing customers. Many top managers have delegated more authority and responsibility to lower-level managers and employees who can respond more quickly to consumer requests. Foreign competitors have the reputation for being more responsive to the market and for bringing out innovations earlier. American firms are restructuring (for example, downsizing « P.28 ») and changing their management styles to become more responsive and better able to produce new products quickly.

Accelerating technological change also increases the need for a new breed of worker, one who is more educated and has higher skill levels. Such workers demand more freedom of operation and a different managerial style. The increasing diversity of the work force is creating additional challenges.

In short, the decade of the 1990s is an era for corporate housecleaning—a time to get rid of the old divisions and managerial styles that have been accumulating in the attic and to introduce a new way of operating. In short, the ideas of Mary Parker Follett have superceded those of Frederick Taylor, and this is causing much disruption in business. Many managers have been fired and are seeking new jobs. The same is true of blue-collar workers. GE is only one of hundreds of firms that have gone through sweeping organizational and managerial changes. As a result, U.S. firms are becoming leaner and meaner and ready to take on world competition. As they become more competitive, they'll begin rehiring managers and workers, but the new hires will have different skills, especially skills in communication, teamwork, and information technology.

In the following sections, we'll describe the foundations of management, but it takes an entire book to learn how to implement the concepts of leadership in today's competitive environment. One book that outlines where organizations are heading in the 21st century is Gifford and Elizabeth Pinchot's *The End of Bureaucracy and the Rise of the Intelligent Organization*. The organizations that it describes are even more flexible and responsive to market changes. To understand where we are going, however, it is important to understand where we are. Let's begin by exploring some basic managerial principles.

••• THE CHANGING ROLE OF MANAGERS •••

Mary Parker Follett defined management as "the art of getting things done through people." At one time, that meant that managers were called *bosses*, and their job was to tell people what to do and watch over them to be sure they did it. Bosses tended to reprimand those who didn't do things correctly and generally acted stern and "bossy." Many managers still behave that way. Perhaps you've witnessed such managers yelling at employees at fast-food restaurants or on shop floors.

Management is the art of getting things done through people. Today that means that managers work with employees rather than simply directing them. The new managerial style is more casual (including dress) and people are more likely to work in teams, as this photo shows.

Today, management is changing from that kind of behavior. Managers are being educated to guide, train, support, motivate, and coach employees rather than to boss them around.[1] Modern managers in progressive companies emphasize teamwork and cooperation rather than discipline and order giving. Managers in some high-tech and progressive firms of all kinds dress more casually, are more friendly, and generally treat employees as partners rather than unruly workers.

In general, therefore, management is experiencing a revolution. Managers in the future are much more likely to be working in teams, they'll be appraised by those below them as well as those above, and they'll be assuming completely new roles in the firm. We'll discuss these roles in detail later.

What this means for tomorrow's graduates like you is that managerial careers will demand a new kind of person. That person is a skilled communicator and team player as well as a planner, coordinator, organizer, and supervisor. These trends will be addressed in the next few chapters to help you decide whether management is the kind of field you'd like.

••• THE DEFINITION AND FUNCTIONS OF MANAGEMENT •••

One reason people go to college is that college prepares them to become managers. Students have told us, "I don't know what I want to do, really. I guess I'd like to be in management." Management is attractive to students because it represents authority, money, prestige, and so on. But few students can describe just what managers do. That's what this chapter is for. It describes what managers are, what they do, and how they do it.

Management could be called the art of getting things done through people and other resources. Well-known management consultant Peter Drucker says managers give direction to their organizations, provide leadership, and decide how to use organizational resources to accomplish goals. Both descriptions give you some feel for what managers do. The definition that provides the outline of this chapter is: **management** is the process used to accomplish organizational goals through planning, organizing, directing, and controlling people and other organizational resources. This definition spells out the four key functions of management: (1) planning, (2) organizing, (3) directing, and (4) controlling. (See Figure 7.1.)

management
The process used to accomplish organizational goals through planning, organizing, directing, and controlling people and other organizational resources.

FIGURE 7.1

WHAT MANAGERS DO

Some modern managers perform all of these tasks with the full cooperation and participation of workers. Empowering employees means allowing them to participate more fully in decision making.

Planning
- Setting organizational goals.
- Developing strategies to reach those goals.
- Determining resources needed.
- Setting standards.

Organizing
- Allocating resources, assigning tasks, and establishing procedures for accomplishing goals.
- Preparing a structure (organization chart) showing lines of authority and responsibility.
- Recruiting, selecting, training, and developing employees.
- Placing employees where they'll be most effective.

Directing
- Leading, guiding, and motivating employees to work effectively to accomplish organizational goals and objectives.
- Giving assignments.
- Explaining routines.
- Clarifying policies.
- Providing feedback on performance.

Controlling
- Measuring results against corporate objectives.
- Monitoring performance relative to standards.
- Taking corrective action.

planning

Management function that involves anticipating future trends and determining the best strategies and tactics to achieve organizational objectives.

organizing

Management function that involves designing the organizational structure, attracting people to the organization (staffing), and creating conditions and systems that ensure that everyone and everything work together to achieve the objectives of the organization.

directing

Management function that involves guiding and motivating others to achieve the goals and objectives of the organization.

controlling

Management function that involves checking to determine whether or not an organization is progressing toward its goals and objectives, and taking corrective action if it is not.

Planning includes anticipating future trends and determining the best strategies and tactics to achieve organizational goals and objectives. The trend today is to have planning *teams* to help monitor the environment, to find business opportunities, and to watch for challenges.

Organizing includes designing the organization structure, attracting people to the organization (staffing), and creating conditions and systems that ensure that everyone and everything works together to achieve the organization's goals and objectives. Today's organizations are being designed around the customer. The idea is to design the firm so that everyone is working to please the customer at a profit.

Directing is guiding and motivating others to work effectively to achieve the organization's goals and objectives. The trend is to give employees as much freedom as possible to become self-directed and self-motivated. Often that means working in teams.

Controlling is checking to determine whether an organization is progressing toward its goals and objectives, and then taking corrective action if it's not. In the past, the greatest attention was given to corporate goals such as profit. The trend today is toward measuring customer satisfaction as well as profit.

The four functions just listed are the heart of management, so let's explore them in more detail. The process begins with planning. We'll look at planning right after the Progress Check.

PROGRESS CHECK

- What were some of the factors that have forced executives to change their organizations and managerial styles?
- What's the definition of *management* used in this chapter, and what are the four functions in that definition?

PLANNING: CREATING A VISION FOR THE ORGANIZATION

vision

A sense of why the organization exists and where it's heading.

Planning is the first managerial function. Planning involves the setting of the organizational vision, goals, and objectives. Top managers are expected to create a vision for the firm. A **vision** is more than a goal; it's the larger explanation of why the organization exists and where it's trying to head. A vision gives the organization a sense of purpose and values to unite workers in a common destiny.[2] Managing an organization without a common vision can be counterproductive. It's like motivating everyone in a row boat to get really excited about getting somewhere, but not giving them any direction. As a result, the boat just keeps heading off in different directions rather than speeding toward an agreed-upon goal.

Goals are the broad, long-term accomplishments an organization wishes to attain. These goals need to be mutually agreed upon by workers and management. Thus, goal setting is often a team process. At GE, the goal is to be number one or two in every business it undertakes.

Objectives are specific, short-term statements detailing how to achieve the goals. One of your goals for reading this chapter, for example, may be to learn basic concepts of management. An objective you could use to achieve this goal is to plan to answer correctly the chapter's Critical Thinking exercise and Progress Checks.

Planning is a continuous process. It's unlikely that a plan that worked yesterday would be successful in today's market. Most planning follows a pattern. The procedure you would follow in planning your life and career is basically the same as those used by businesses for their plans. Planning answers three fundamental questions for businesses:

1. What is the situation now? What is the state of the economy? What opportunities exist for meeting people's needs? What products and customers are most profitable? Why do people buy (or not buy) our products? Who are our major competitors?

2. Where do we want to go? How much growth do we want? What is our profit goal? What are our social objectives? What are our personal development objectives?

3. How can we get there from here? This is the most important part of planning. It takes three forms (Figure 7.2):
   a. **Strategic (long-range) planning** determines the major goals of the organization as well as the policies and strategies for obtaining and using resources to achieve those goals. In this definition, *policies* are broad guides to action, and *strategies* determine the best way to use resources. At the strategic planning stage, the company decides which customers to serve, what products or services to sell, and the geographic areas in which the firm will compete.

      In today's rapidly changing environment, long-range planning is rapidly being replaced by quick response to customer needs and requests. The long-range goal is to be flexible and responsive to the market.

   b. **Tactical (short-range) planning** is the process of developing detailed, short-term strategies about what's to be done, who's to do it, and how it's to be done. Just as objectives are specific plans to meet broad goals, tactical

goals
Broad, long-term accomplishments an organization wishes to attain.

objectives
Specific, short-term statements detailing how to achieve an organization's goals.

strategic (long-range) planning
Process of determining the major goals of the organization and the policies and strategies for obtaining and using resources to achieve those goals.

tactical (short-range) planning
Process of developing detailed, short-term strategies about what is to be done, who is to do it, and how it is to be done.

The first managerial function is to create a shared vision for the organization. A vision gives a sense of purpose and direction for the organization, including its ethical base. Goals and objectives are based on the vision and are developed with as much participation as possible.

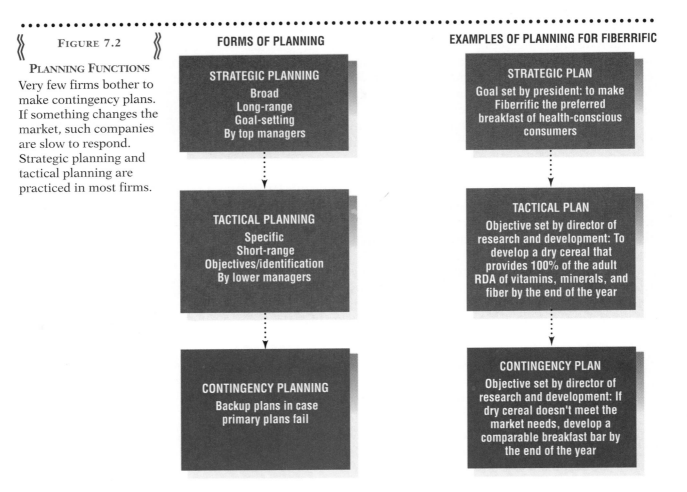

FIGURE 7.2

PLANNING FUNCTIONS
Very few firms bother to make contingency plans. If something changes the market, such companies are slow to respond. Strategic planning and tactical planning are practiced in most firms.

planning involves defining specific plans to achieve broad strategic plans. Tactical planning is normally done by managers or teams of managers at lower levels of the organization, whereas strategic planning is done by the top managers of the firm (for example, the president and vice presidents of the organization). Tactical planning, for example, involves setting annual budgets and deciding on other details of how to meet the strategic objectives.

contingency planning
Process of preparing alternative courses of action that may be used if the primary plans do not achieve the objectives of the organization.

c. **Contingency planning** is the preparation of alternative courses of action that may be used if the primary plans don't achieve the organization's objectives. The economic and competitive environments change so rapidly that it's wise to have alternative plans of action ready in anticipation of such changes.

The leaders of market-based companies set direction, not detailed strategy. The idea is to stay flexible, listen for opportunities, and seize opportunities when they come, whether they were planned or not.

PROGRESS CHECK

- What's the difference between strategic, tactical, and contingency planning?
- Why would organizations today be less concerned about strategic planning than they once were? What has become of even greater concern? Could strategic planning get in the way of an organization being flexible enough to respond to market changes?

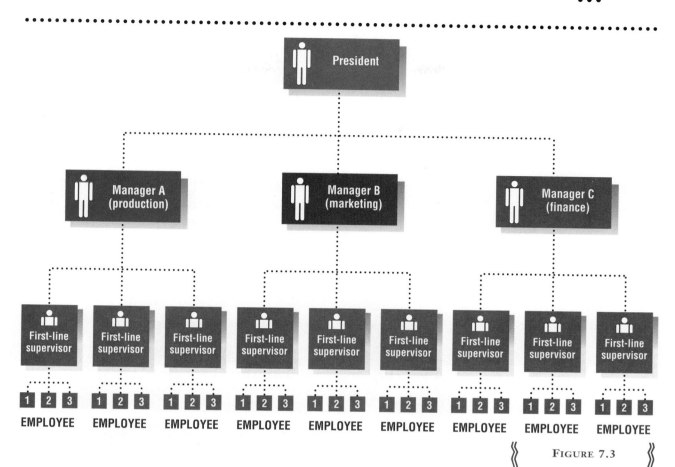

FIGURE 7.3

TYPICAL ORGANIZATION CHART

This is a rather standard chart with managers for major functions and supervisors reporting to the managers. Each supervisor manages three employees.

ORGANIZING: CREATING A UNIFIED SYSTEM OUT OF MULTIPLE ORGANIZATIONS

After managers have planned a course of action, they must organize the firm to accomplish their goals. Basically, organizing means allocating resources, assigning tasks, and establishing procedures for accomplishing the organizational objectives. When organizing, a manager develops a structure or framework that relates all workers, tasks, and resources to each other. That framework is called the *organization structure*. Most organizations draw a chart showing these relationships. This is called an *organization chart*. Figure 7.3 shows a simple one. The organization chart pictures who reports to whom and who's responsible for each task. The problem of developing organization structure will be discussed in more detail in the next chapter. For now, it's important to know that the corporate hierarchy illustrated on the organization chart above includes top, middle, and first-line managers.

Top management (the highest level of management) consists of the president and other key company executives who develop strategic plans. Two terms you're likely to see often are *chief executive officer (CEO)* and *chief operating officer (COO)*. The CEO is often the president of the firm and is responsible for all top-level decisions in the firm. CEOs are responsible for introducing changes into an organization. The COO is responsible for putting those changes into effect. His or her tasks include structuring, controlling, and rewarding to ensure that people carry out the leader's vision.

Middle management includes branch and plant managers, deans, and department heads who are responsible for tactical planning and controlling. **Supervisory (first-line) management** includes people directly responsible

top management
Highest level of management, consisting of the president and other key company executives who develop strategic plans.

middle management
Level of management that includes plant managers and department heads who are responsible for tactical plans.

supervisory (first-line) management
First level of management above workers; includes people directly responsible for assigning specific jobs to employees and evaluating their daily performance.

LEVELS OF MANAGEMENT
This figure shows the three levels of management. In many firms, there are several levels of middle management. Recently, however, firms have been eliminating middle-level managers in a cost-cutting attempt.

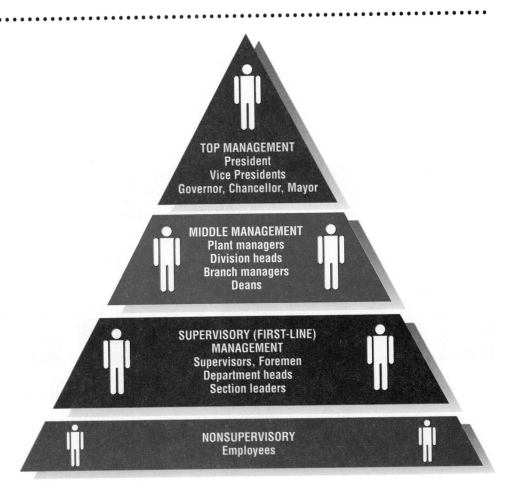

TOP MANAGEMENT
President
Vice Presidents
Governor, Chancellor, Mayor

MIDDLE MANAGEMENT
Plant managers
Division heads
Branch managers
Deans

SUPERVISORY (FIRST-LINE) MANAGEMENT
Supervisors, Foremen
Department heads
Section leaders

NONSUPERVISORY
Employees

for assigning specific jobs to workers and evaluating their daily performance; they're often known as *first-line managers* because they're the first level above workers (see Figure 7.4).

All of this work of gathering materials and people together and assigning tasks is called *organizing*. An important part of organizing is staffing, getting the right people on the organizational team. You're probably most familiar with the term *personnel* to describe that function. Today it's called *human resource management* because it's as important to develop employees' potential as it is to recruit good people in the first place. We'll discuss human resource management in Chapter 11.

••• THE CUSTOMER-ORIENTED ORGANIZATION •••

A dominating question of the past 20 years or so has been how to best organize the firm to respond to the needs of customers and other stakeholders. *Stakeholders* **‹‹–** P.40 **–»** include anyone who's affected by the organization and its policies and products. That includes employees, customers, suppliers, dealers, environmental groups, and the surrounding communities. The consensus seems to be that smaller organizations are more responsive than large organizations. Therefore, most large firms are being redesigned into smaller, more customer-focused units.

Domino's Pizza, for example, is a chain of 4,500 highly decentralized outlets that encourage managers to regard themselves as individual entrepreneurs. Meanwhile, headquarters takes responsibility for all paperwork.

Thus, managers can focus on customers, the most important part of management.

Small businesses, such as independent tire dealer Direct Tire Sales, realize the importance of pleasing customers too. The dealership provides services such as loaning customers cars while theirs are in the shop, fixing flats for free on all tires purchased, and guaranteeing linings and brake pads for the life of the car. They'll even pick up the tab for the cab ride home when you have your brakes changed. But what really excites customers is the customer lounge. The spotless, tastefully decorated room sports an aquarium, hot coffee, fresh donuts, and current magazines. Customers ignore the 10 to 15 percent premium for this exceptional service. The dealership was awarded the *Modern Tire Dealer*'s dealer of the year award.[3]

Domino's Pizza is an example of a firm that has highly independent (decentralized) outlets that are responsive to the needs of the surrounding communities. Headquarters is responsible for paperwork, freeing the local managers to focus on customer service. For example, Domino's no longer emphasizes a 30-minute delivery because local communities were afraid that hurried delivery people may not pay as much attention to safety as required.

Other industries, both large and small, are equally customer-oriented. They include investment banking, health care, construction, engineering, and more. The point is that companies are no longer organizing to make it easy for *managers* to have control. Instead, they're organizing so that *customers* have control.

••• ORGANIZATION IS BECOMING INTERFIRM •••

In the past, the goal of organization in the firm was to clearly specify who does what *within the firm*. Today, the organization task is much more complex because firms are forming partnerships, joint ventures, and other arrangements that make it necessary to organize the *whole system*.[4]

There's no way an organization can provide quality goods and services to customers unless suppliers provide world-class parts and materials with which to work. Thus, managers have to establish close relationships with suppliers. To make the entire system work, similar relationships have to be established with those organizations that sell directly to consumers—retailers.

Each firm is striving to have every process (e.g., order processing and delivery) as good as the best companies in the world. Often that means finding other firms to do various processes. Top management must contact those firms and work closely with them to coordinate processes. None of this was possible 20 years ago because the information technology simply wasn't available. Today, however, firms throughout the world are linked by computers and communications technology so that they operate as one.

According to management guru Tom Peters, small businesses are key forces in shaping American business in this time of interfirm relationships. In fact, Peters claims that big businesses depend on small companies for success.[5] Consider the example of Fields & Associates, a company that helps large companies reduce overhead. Fields found that the bureaucracy of one of its big-company clients sometimes made duplicate payments. The company had paid the same $40,000 bill twice —with one $80,000 check. Intel Corp, the big computer chip maker, says that Fields can find errors for them much more efficiently than it could. Fields recovered $1 million for Intel in exchange for part of the savings.[6]

Making Ethical Decisions

Ethics on the Front Line

First-line managers assist in the decisions made by their department heads. The department heads retain full responsibility for the decisions—if a plan succeeds, it's their success; if a plan fails, it's their failure. Now picture this: As a first-line manager, you have new information that your department head hasn't seen. The findings in this report indicate that your manager's recent plans are sure to fail. If the plans do fail, the manager will probably be demoted and you're the most likely candidate to fill the vacancy. Will you give your department head the report? What will be the consequences of your decision?

It makes no sense to introduce the latest management concepts and try to make them work in an organization that's not designed correctly. And one organization is often not as effective as many organizations working together.[7] Many small businesses are pooling their efforts in such fields as marketing and distribution. Many are forming purchasing cooperatives so they can buy in bulk and get better prices from suppliers.

Creating a unified *system* out of multiple organizations will be one of the greatest management challenges of the 21st century. We'll discuss this issue in more depth in Chapter 8.

DIRECTING AND EMPOWERING

After the plans are made and the interfirm connections are made, traditional managers direct the workers in activities to meet the goals and objectives of the organization. In traditional organizations, directing involves giving assignments, explaining routines, clarifying policies, and providing feedback on performance.

In traditional organizations, all managers, from top managers to first-line supervisors, direct employees. The process of directing is quite different, however, at the various levels of the organization. The top managers are concerned with the broad overview of where the company is headed. Their immediate subordinates are middle managers, who are responsible, in turn, for directing employees to meet company objectives. Top managers' directions to subordinates, therefore, are characteristically broad and open-ended. The further down the corporate ladder, the more specific the manager's directions become. First-line managers traditionally allocate much of their time to giving specific, detailed instructions to employees.

••• FROM DIRECTION TO EMPOWERMENT OF TEAMS •••

empowerment
Giving employees the authority and responsibility to respond quickly to customer requests.

Progressive managers in the future are less likely to be giving specific instructions to employees. Rather, they're more likely to empower them to make decisions on their own. **Empowerment** is a total quality term that means giving employees the authority and responsibility to respond quickly to customer requests. In cooperation with employees, managers will set up teams that will work together to accomplish objectives and goals. The manager's role will be less that of a "boss" and more that of a coach, assistant, counselor, and team member. This shift in managerial direction gives employees more participation in decision making and more flexibility in how to get the job done. That usually results in better work and more employee motivation.

A leading company in the United States, Boeing makes most of the airplanes you see flying around the United States. In 1988, Boeing tried to upgrade its 747 airplane. Redesigned parts didn't fit together well and Boeing had to use thousands of workers to correct the problems. Today, however, Boeing has adopted the team approach, grouping together experts in design, manufacturing, and tooling. The 777 was the first plane designed by a team. Airline customers sat in on the planning sessions. When the plane was finally assembled, the parts fit together within thousandths of an inch. Everything went much smoother than before. Now managers are evaluated by employees as well as the managers above them, and employee morale is up.[8]

Business Week noted how Boeing, Motorola, GE, AT&T, DuPont, and other top U.S. firms were moving toward self-managed teams. Self-managed, cross-functional teams are groups of employees from various departments such as purchasing, marketing, and engineering. You'll learn more about such teams in Chapter 8. For now it's important to know that self-managed teams function as independent elements of the firm with an inherent group intelligence of their own. Because they think and act on their own and seek out any information they need, such teams are known as *smart teams*. One purpose of cross-functional teams is to respond quickly to customer needs and market changes. Another purpose is to empower those who know the most about products and what makes them good (the employees themselves) to do what needs to be done to make world-class products. To ensure such responsiveness and responsibility, these teams are self-organizing as well as self-managing.[9]

Training must also be upgraded so that employees become more flexible and ready to take on more responsibility. Customers should be brought into regular contact with the teams, as should suppliers. If they're willing, customers and suppliers can join the teams. Such teams function most effectively when management provides them with all the information the company has (including accounting data) and lets the teams make decisions on their own.

This self-managed team at Boeing is just one example of a trend that is sweeping industry. Employees are empowered to make more decisions on their own and management backs them with training, coaching, and needed materials. Often customers and suppliers are brought into these team meetings to ensure that their input and needs are considered when designing products.

CONTROLLING

Often managers get so involved with the firm's planning process and day-to-day crisis management that they tend to shortchange the control function. The control function involves measuring performance relative to objectives and standards and then taking corrective action when necessary. Thus, the control function (Figure 7.5) is the heart of the management system because it provides the feedback that enables managers and workers to adjust to any deviations from plans and to changes in the environment that have affected performance.

Controlling consists of five steps:

1. Setting clear performance standards.
2. Monitoring and recording actual performance (results).
3. Comparing results against plans and standards.
4. Communicating results and deviations to the employees involved.
5. Taking corrective action when needed.

FIGURE 7.5

THE CONTROL PROCESS
The whole control process is based on clear standards. Without such standards, the other steps are difficult, if not impossible. With clear standards, performance measurement is relatively easy and the proper action can be taken.

The control system's weakest link tends to be the setting of standards. To measure results against standards, the standards must be specific, attainable, and measurable.[10] Vague goals and standards such as "better quality," "more efficiency," and "improved performance" aren't sufficient because they don't describe what you're trying to achieve. For example, let's say you're a runner and you say you want to "improve" your distance. When you started your improvement plan last year, you ran two miles a day. Now you run 2.1 miles a day. Did you meet your goal? Well, you did increase your distance, but certainly not by very much. A more appropriate goal statement would be, To increase running distance from two miles a day to four miles a day by January 1. It's important to have a time period established when goals are to be met. Here are examples of goals and standards that meet these criteria:

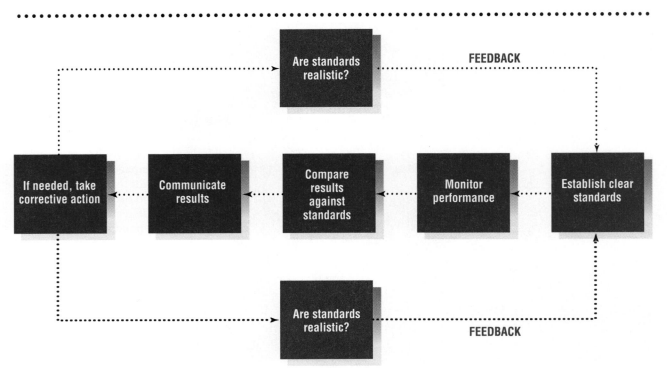

SPOTLIGHT ON SMALL BUSINESS

Leadership in Small Business

Successful leaders build their teams in different ways. Ralph Stayer of Johnsonville Foods does more than inform his workers—he empowers them. He doesn't think that managers have communication problems—he thinks that they have responsi-bility-is-in-the-wrong-spot problems. The real problem is to have people understand that they're responsible for their own workplace. Believing that the people who are responsible should make the decisions, Stayer gives his employees the power and authority to solve their own problems.

For example, when a group of employees complained about the loud noise from other employees' boom boxes, they first asked him to solve the problem. Stayer told them, "That's your workplace; you guys decide. You solve this any way you want." After the employees solved that problem, they started looking at other things that bothered them and fixed them as well.

Stayer sees the role of the manager as getting people to want to do whatever it takes to make the company prof-

itable. "You don't have time to baby them. They just have to do it. So your role is to make sure people see it's in their own best interest to do that." All Stayer's employees are paid for performance, and a regular pool of profits is divided among them. Productivity increased between 200 and 300 percent between 1982 and 1990.

Richard Difede has a small business that makes power catamarans and multihull sail-boats. His firm is in St. Croix, so he knows about living the good life. Over time, the firm learned that its power came not from manage-ment, but from its employees. Difede says, "Management has to learn to delegate, learn to empower, and allow the decision-making process to per-colate through the organization from top to bottom and bottom to top."

Source: "Managing the Journey," *Inc.*, November 1990, pp. 45–54; and Sharon Nelton, "Yachts at the Cutting Edge," *Nation's Business*, November 1993, pp. 13-14.

- Cutting the number of finished product rejects from 10 per 1,000 to 5 per 1,000 by March 31.
- Increasing the times managers praise employees from 3 times per week to 12 per week.
- Increasing sales of product X from 10,000 in the month of July to 12,000 in that same period.

One key to making control systems work is the establishment of clear pro-cedures for monitoring performance. Naturally, management shouldn't be burdened with such control procedures unless the goals are important enough to justify such reporting. Most managers have seen, for example, elaborate accident reports that took hours of management time and that reported, "All is well." To minimize paperwork, such reports could be limited to exceptions.

• • • NEW CRITERIA FOR MEASUREMENT: • • •
CUSTOMER SATISFACTION

The criteria for measuring success in a customer-oriented firm is customer satisfaction of both internal and external customers. **Internal customers** are units within the firm that receive services from other units.

Other criteria of organizational effectiveness may include the firm's con-tribution to society or improvements in the quality of air and water surround-ing the plant. The traditional measures of success are usually financial, defined in terms of profits or return on investment. Certainly these measures

internal customers
Units within the firm that receive services from other units.

One of the measures of success used today by many firms is whether the organization delights its customers with its products and services. Saturn tries to accomplish this with a high-quality product, no-hassle buying, and great service. Relationship building is an important goal as a way of building a strong bond with its customers. Saturn recently sponsored a three-day celebration for more than 20,000 of them at their plant in Spring Hill, Tennessee.

are still important, but they're not the whole purpose of the firm. The purpose of the firm today is to please employees, customers, and other stakeholders. Thus, measurements of success must take all these groups into account. Firms have to ask questions such as

Do we have good relations with our employees, our suppliers, our dealers, our community leaders, the local media, our stockholders, and our bankers?

What more could we do to please these groups?

Are the corporate needs (such as making a profit) being met as well?

LEADERSHIP: VISION AND VALUES

In the literature of business there's a trend toward separating the notion of manager from that of leader. One person could be a good manager and not a good leader. Another could be a good leader without being a good manager. One difference between managers and leaders is that managers produce order and stability while leaders embrace and manage change. **Leadership** is creating a vision for others to follow, establishing corporate values and ethics, and transforming the way the organization does business so that it's more effective and efficient. Management is the carrying out of the vision.

leadership
Creating a vision for others to follow, establishing corporate values and ethics, and transforming the way the organization does business so it is more effective and efficient.

Like managers, leaders plan, organize, direct, and control. But when leaders plan, they plan more globally than managers in terms of setting the agenda for the firm. Leaders organize, but their focus is on structuring or restructuring the organization to be competitive in world markets. Leaders direct and control, but their direction involves creating a vision and their control consists of empowering people and holding them responsible for finding their own means to those ends. Let's look at other ways that leaders differ from managers.

In the future, all organizations will need leaders who can supply the vision as well as the moral and ethical foundation for growth. All organizations will

MANAGERS	LEADERS
Do things right	Do the right thing
Command and control	Inspire and empower
Seek stability and predictability	Seek flexibility and change
Are internally focused	Are externally oriented
Work within the firm	Coordinate the whole system
Are locally oriented	Are globally oriented
Think mostly of workers	Think mostly of customers and other stakeholders

also need managers who share in the vision and know how to get things done with the cooperation of all employees. The workplace is changing from a place where a few dictate what to do to others to a place where all employees work together to accomplish common goals.

To summarize, leaders are supposed to

1. Have a vision and rally others around that vision. Rather than manage, the leader is supposed to be openly sensitive to the concerns of followers, give them responsibility, and win their trust.

2. Establish corporate values. These values include a concern for employees, for customers, and for the quality of the company's products. When companies set their goals today, they're going beyond just business goals and are defining the values of the company as well. Levi Strauss, for example, uses words such as *empowerment*, *honesty*, and *teamwork* in its goals statement.

3. Emphasize corporate ethics. This means an unfailing demand for honesty and an insistence that everyone in the company gets a fair shake. That's why we've stressed ethical decision making throughout this text.

4. Not fear change, but embrace change and create it. The most important job may be to transform the way the company does business so that it's more effective and efficient.

Managers work within organizational boundaries. Leaders set those boundaries and constantly change the organization to meet new challenges. Today's excellent corporations, more often than not, are reflections of their leaders. The leaders of successful corporations have had a vision of excellence and have led others to share that vision. For example, Walt Disney's leadership can still be seen in Disney amusement parks and movies.

••• LEADERSHIP STYLES •••

Nothing has challenged researchers in the area of management more than the search for the "best" leadership traits, behaviors, or styles. Thousands of studies have been made just to find leadership traits; that is, characteristics that make

Bobby Knight is a good example of the effectiveness of autocratic leadership in selected situations. Such a leadership style is not appropriate for all groups or all managers. Managers must learn to be flexible and use the appropriate leadership style.

leaders different from others. Intuitively, you would conclude about the same thing that researchers found: that the research findings were neither statistically valid nor reliable.[11] You and I know that some leaders seem to have traits such as good appearance and tact while others appear unkempt and abrasive.

Just as there's no one set of traits that can describe a leader, there's also no one style of leadership that works best in all situations. Let's look briefly at a few of the most commonly recognized leadership styles and see how they may be effective

1. **Autocratic leadership** involves making managerial decisions without consulting others; it implies power over others. Many businesspeople who were sports leaders seem to use an autocratic style that consists of issuing orders and telling employees what to do. Motivation comes from threats, punishment, and intimidation of all kinds. Such a style is effective in emergencies and when absolute followership is needed (for example, on army maneuvers). Some football, basketball, and soccer coaches have successfully used this style. Bobby Knight, basketball coach of Indiana University, is one.

2. **Democratic or participative leadership** consists of managers and employees working together to make decisions. Research has found that employee participation in decisions may not always increase effectiveness, but it usually increases job satisfaction. Many new, progressive organizations are highly successful at using a democratic style of leadership where traits such as flexibility, good listening skills, and empathy are dominant. Organizations that have successfully used this style include Wal-Mart, Federal Express, IBM, Xerox, and AT&T.

3. **Laissez-faire or free rein leadership** involves managers setting objectives and employees being relatively free to do whatever it takes to accomplish those objectives. In certain professional organizations, where managers deal with doctors, engineers, and other professionals, the most successful leadership style is often one of laissez-faire

autocratic leadership
Leadership style that involves making decisions without consulting others and implies power over others.

democratic (participative) leadership
Leadership style that consists of managers and employees working together to make decisions.

laissez-faire (free-reign) leadership
Leadership style that involves managers setting objectives and employees being relatively free to do whatever it takes to accomplish those objectives.

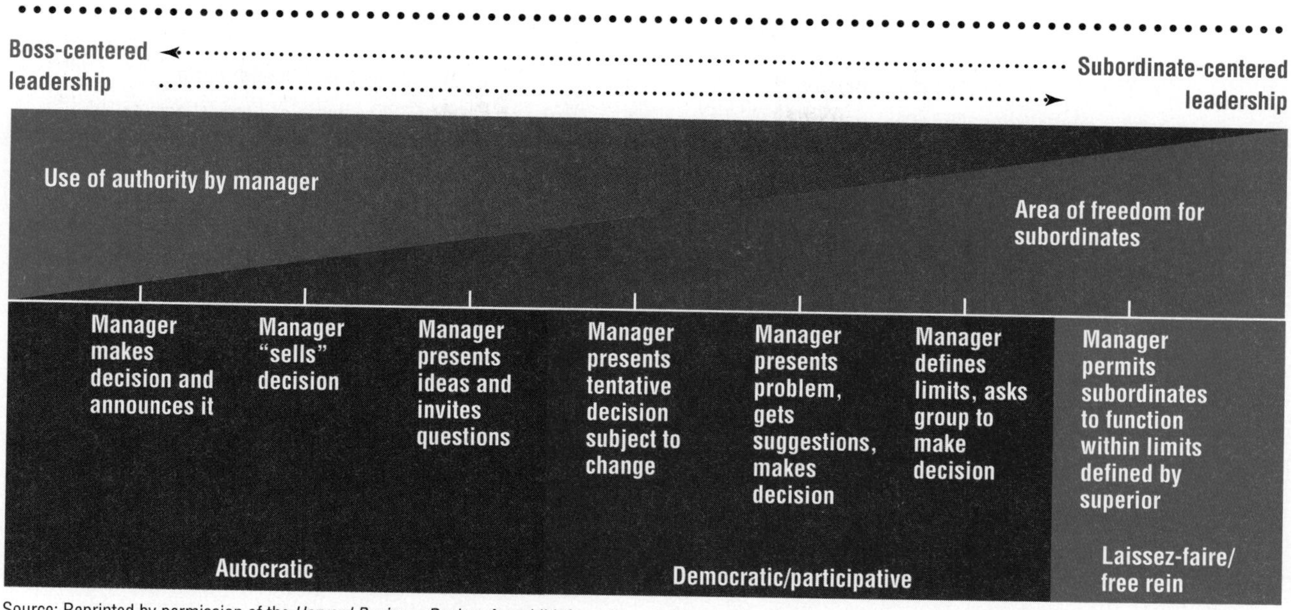
Boss-centered leadership
Subordinate-centered leadership
Use of authority by manager
Area of freedom for subordinates
Manager makes decision and announces it
Manager "sells" decision
Manager presents ideas and invites questions
Manager presents tentative decision subject to change
Manager presents problem, gets suggestions, makes decision
Manager defines limits, asks group to make decision
Manager permits subordinates to function within limits defined by superior
Autocratic
Democratic/participative
Laissez-faire/ free rein

Source: Reprinted by permission of the *Harvard Business Review*. An exhibit from "How to Choose a Leadership Pattern" by Robert Tannenbaum and Warren Schmidt (May/June 1973). Copyright © 1973 by the President and Fellows of Harvard College, all rights reserved.

FIGURE 7.6

VARIOUS LEADERSHIP STYLES

leadership. The traits needed by managers in such organizations include warmth, friendliness, and understanding. More and more firms are adopting this style of leadership.

Individual leaders rarely fit neatly into just one of these categories. Researchers Tannenbaum and Schmidt illustrate leadership as a continuum with varying amounts of employee participation ranging from purely boss-centered leadership to subordinate-centered leadership. (See Figure 7.6).

Which leadership style is best? Research tells us that successful leadership depends largely on who's being led and in what situations. It also supports the notion that different leadership styles ranging from autocratic to laissez-faire may be successful depending on the people and the situation.

In fact, any one manager may use a variety of leadership styles depending on whom he or she is dealing with and the situation. A manager may be autocratic but friendly with a new trainee; democratic with an experienced employee who has many good ideas that can only be fostered by a manager who's a good listener and flexible; and laissez-faire with a trusted, long-term supervisor who probably knows more about operations than the manager does.

Let's summarize what we've just said.

- There's no such thing as leadership traits that are effective in all situations, nor are there leadership styles that always work best.
- Different styles of leadership can be used effectively. They range from autocratic to laissez-faire. Which style is most effective depends on the people and the situation.
- A truly successful leader has the ability to use the leadership style most appropriate to the situation and the employee involved.
- Leadership depends on followership, and followership depends on the traits and circumstances of the follower. In general, though, one could say that good leaders tend to be visionary, value driven, flexible, able to identify with the goals and values of followers, good communicators, sensitive to the needs of others, and decisive when the situation demands it. (See Figure 7.7.)

The 12 Golden Rules of Leadership

1. *Set a good example.* Your subordinates will take their cue from you. If your work habits are good, theirs are likely to be too.

2. *Give your people a set of objectives and a sense of direction.* Good people seldom like to work aimlessly from day to day. They want to know not only what they're doing but why.

3. *Keep your people informed* of new developments at the company and how they'll affect them. Let people know where they stand with you. Let your close assistants in on your plans at an early stage. Let people know as early as possible of any changes that will affect them. Let them know of changes that won't affect them but about which they may be worrying.

4. *Ask your people for advice.* Let them know that they have a say in your decisions whenever possible. Make them feel a problem is their problem too. Encourage individual thinking.

5. *Let your people know that you support them.* There's no greater morale killer than a boss who resents a subordinate's ambition.

6. *Don't give orders.* Suggest, direct, and request.

7. *Emphasize skills, not rules.* Judge results, not methods. Give a person a job to do and let him or her do it. Let an employee improve his or her own job methods.

8. *Give credit where credit is due.* Appreciation for a job well done is the most appreciated of "fringe benefits."

9. *Praise in public.* This is where it will do the most good.

10. *Criticize in private.*

11. *Criticize constructively.* Concentrate on correction, not blame. Allow a person to retain his or her dignity. Suggest specific steps to prevent recurrence of the mistake. Forgive and encourage desired results.

12. *Make it known that you welcome new ideas.* No idea is too small for a hearing or too wild for consideration. Make it easy for them to communicate their ideas to you. Follow through on their ideas.

The Seven Sins of Leadership

On the other hand, these items can cancel any constructive image you might try to establish.

1. *Trying to be liked rather than respected.* Don't accept favors from your subordinates. Don't do special favors in trying to be liked. Don't try for popular decisions. Don't be soft about discipline. Have a sense of humor. Don't give up.

2. *Failing to ask subordinates for their advice and help.*

3. *Failing to develop a sense of responsibility in subordinates.* Allow freedom of expression. Give each person a chance to learn his or her superior's job. When you give responsibility, give authority too. Hold subordinates accountable for results.

4. *Emphasizing rules rather than skill.*

5. *Failing to keep criticism constructive.* When something goes wrong, do you tend to assume who's at fault? Do you do your best to get all the facts first? Do you control your temper? Do you praise before you criticize? Do you listen to the other side of the story?

6. *Not paying attention to employee gripes and complaints.* Make it easy for them to come to you. Get rid of red tape. Explain the grievance machinery. Help a person voice his or her complaint. Always grant a hearing. Practice patience. Ask a complainant what he or she wants to do. Don't render a hasty or biased judgment. Get all the facts. Let the complainant know what your decision is. Double-check your results. Be concerned.

7. *Failing to keep people informed.*

Source: "To Become an 'Effective Executive,' Develop Leadership and Other Skills," *Marketing News*, April 1984, p.1.

FIGURE 7.7

RULES OF LEADERSHIP

••• THE TREND TOWARD SELF-MANAGED TEAMS •••

The trend in the United States is toward self-managed teams and away from management, with its emphasis on planning, organizing, directing, and controlling. The trend is toward leadership, with its emphasis on vision and empowerment. What will these trends mean for managers and leaders in the 1990s? It means, for one thing, that the trend is away from autocratic leadership toward laissez-faire leadership. This is a real challenge for traditional managers because it means giving up their traditional command-and-control style of management.

Managers in the future will be empowering teams rather than individual employees. This is an entirely different role for managers, one that will take some time to develop. In the end, however, the concept of self-managed teams will enable U.S. manufacturers to compete with anyone in the world.

FROM THE PAGES OF...
Entrepreneur
MAGAZINE

Testing Your Leadership Ability

Danny Cox, author of *Leadership: When the Heat's On,* developed the following questionnaire to test your leadership potential. Score yourself from 1 to 10 (10 being the highest) for each item.

1. High ethics
2. High energy
3. Hard worker
4. Enthusiastic
5. Goal-oriented
6. Courageous
7. Priority-driven
8. Nonconformist
9. Levelheaded
10. Committed to developing employees

Cox believes that leaders are made, not born. Therefore, you can learn to become a leader by developing the preceding traits. You can learn, for example, to be a hard worker and to commit yourself to developing your employees. It may be harder to develop traits such as courage and enthusiasm, but it can be done. Note that the most important trait is a high level of ethics, a commitment to doing the right thing.

Most wannabe leaders give themselves a grade of 90 or above on this test, but when their employees grade them, they get a much lower score. To develop your leadership skills, Cox says, you need to have a dream, to study diligently, to plan, and to take action.

Source: Robert McGarvey, "Learn to Lead," *Entrepreneur,* October 1994, pp. 139–43.

PROGRESS CHECK

- What are some characteristics of leadership today that make leaders different from traditional managers?
- Explain the differences between autocratic and democratic leadership styles.
- What's a smart team and how is it managed?

CRITICAL THINKING

Do you see any problems with a participative managerial style? Do you think it could be adopted by football teams? It's already practiced by some baseball teams. What's the difference between football and baseball players, what they do, and how they're managed? How does that relate to the business world?

Can you see a manager getting frustrated when he or she can't be bossy? Can someone who's trained to give orders (for example, a military sergeant) be retrained to be a participative manager? What problems may emerge? What kind of boss would you be? Do you have evidence to show that?

TASKS AND SKILLS AT DIFFERENT LEVELS OF MANAGEMENT

Anyone who has ever played a sport such as basketball, football, or soccer knows there's a tremendous difference between being an excellent player and an excellent coach (manager). Often a good player will volunteer to coach the neighborhood team and be a disaster as a manager. The same thing happens in business. Few people are trained to be managers. Rather, the process of becoming

	Technical skills	Human relations skills	Conceptual skills
Top managers	Technical skills	Human relations skills	Conceptual skills
Middle managers	Technical skills	Human relations skills	Conceptual skills
First-line managers	Technical skills	Human relations skills	Conceptual skills

a manager is similar to the sports example. A person learns how to be a skilled accountant or salesperson or production line worker, and then—because of his or her skill—is selected to be a manager. The tendency is for such managers to become deeply involved in showing others how to do things, helping them, supervising them, and generally being very active in the operating task.

The further up the managerial ladder a person moves, the less such skills are required. Instead, the need is for people who are visionaries, good planners, organizers, coordinators, communicators, morale builders, and motivators. Figure 7.8 shows that a manager must have three categories of skills:

1. Technical skills.
2. Human relations skills.
3. Conceptual skills.

Let's pause here to clarify the terms:

technical skills
Ability to perform tasks of a specific department (such as selling or bookkeeping).

Technical skills involve the ability to perform tasks of a specific department such as selling (marketing) or bookkeeping (accounting).

human relations skills
Ability to lead, communicate, motivate, coach, build morale, train, support, and delegate.

Human relations skills include leadership, motivation, coaching, communication, morale building, training and development, help and supportiveness, and delegating.

conceptual skills
Ability to picture the organization as a whole and the relationship between the various parts.

Conceptual skills refer to a manager's ability to picture the organization as a whole and the relationship of various parts to perform tasks such as planning, organizing, controlling, systems development, problem analysis, decision making, coordinating, and delegating.

Looking at Figure 7.8, you'll notice that first-line managers need to be skilled in all three areas. Most of their time is spent on technical and human relations tasks (assisting operating personnel, giving direction, and so forth). First-line managers spend little time on conceptual tasks. Top managers, on the other hand, need to use few technical skills. Instead, almost all of their time is devoted to human relations and conceptual tasks. One who's competent at one level of management may not be competent at higher levels and vice versa. The skills needed are different at different levels.

Spend some time reviewing the definitions of conceptual and human relations skills, which are so important to top management. Note that the word *delegate* is in our definition of human relations skills. Another one of the key managerial tasks is decision making. Because of their importance, we'll explore both delegating and decision making in more detail.

••• DELEGATING: BECOMING A TEAM LEADER •••

delegating
Assigning authority and accountability to others while retaining responsibility for results.

The most difficult task for most managers to learn is **delegating** (assigning authority and accountability to others while retaining responsibility for results). Remember, managers are usually selected from those who are most

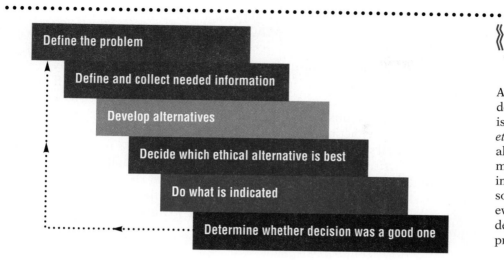

FIGURE 7.9

THE DECISION-MAKING PROCESS
An important step in the decision-making process is to choose the best *ethical* alternative. Other alternatives may generate more money but be immoral or improper in some way. After an evaluation is made of the decision, the whole process begins again.

skilled at doing what the people they manage are doing. The inclination is for managers to pitch in and help or do it themselves. Of course, this keeps workers from learning and having the satisfaction of doing it themselves. A great leader is one whose workers say, "We did it ourselves."

As we noted earlier, most progressive managers of the 21st century will be team leaders. They will set specific goals in cooperation with a team of workers, set up feedback and communication procedures (control procedures), and minimize the tendency to continually look over the team's shoulder to make sure it's doing things the manager's way. Employees will be given the freedom (empowered) to decide the hows and whens of completion of specific tasks as long as the goals are accomplished on time.

... DECISION MAKING: FINDING THE ... BEST ETHICAL ALTERNATIVE

Decision making is choosing among two or more alternatives. It sounds easier than it is in practice. In fact, decision making is the heart of all the management functions: planning, organizing, directing, and controlling. As Figure 7.9 shows, the rational decision-making model is a series of steps managers should follow to make logical, intelligent, and well-founded decisions. These six Ds of decision making are

1 Define the problem.
2. Describe and collect needed information.
3. Develop alternatives.
4. Decide which ethical alternative is best.
5. Do what's indicated (implement solution).
6. Determine whether the decision was a good one and follow up.

The best decisions are based on sound information. That's why this is known as the Information Age. Managers often have computer terminals at their desks so they can get internal records and external data of all kinds. But all the data in the world can't replace a manager who's creative and makes brilliant decisions. Decision making is more an art than a science. It's the one skill most needed by managers and leaders in that all the other functions depend on it.

decision making
Choosing among two or more alternatives.

LEARNING MANAGERIAL SKILLS

Now that you know some of the broad categories of skills needed by various levels of management, we can look at the more specific skills you'll need to learn to be a good manager. As you build your skills, it helps to think of yourself as a one-person business. Like any business, you must strive for quality and customer satisfaction.[12]

In general, it's a good idea to take as many courses as you can in oral communication, writing, computers, and human relations. In all managerial jobs, these are the skills in greatest demand. Naturally, you'll also have to develop technical skills in your chosen area. Figure 7.10 lists the six skills you'll need to develop your managerial potential: verbal skills, writing skills, computer skills, human relations skills, time management skills, and other technical skills.

••• VERBAL SKILLS •••

The bulk of your duties as a manager will involve communicating with others. You'll have to give talks, conduct meetings, make presentations, and generally communicate your ideas to others. To prepare for such tasks, you should take oral communication courses and become active in various student groups. Become an officer so that you're responsible for conducting meetings and giving speeches. You may want to join a choir or other group to become comfortable performing in front of others.

At least half of communication is skilled listening. A good manager mixes with other managers, workers, clients, stockholders, and others outside the firm. He or she listens to recommendations and complaints and acts on them. Active listening requires the asking of questions and feeding back what you've heard to let others know you're truly interested in what they say.

FIGURE 7.10

EVALUATING YOUR MANAGEMENT POTENTIAL
If you find yourself needing improvement in any of these areas, it's a good idea to take courses or read books to improve yourself. The best time to do this is *before* you seek work so you're fully prepared when you go job hunting.

Evaluating your management potential

Skill needed	Personal evaluation			
	Excellent	Good	Fair	Need work
Verbal skills				
Writing skills				
Computer skills				
Human relations skills				
Time management skills				
Other technical skills				

••• WRITING SKILLS •••

Managers must also be able to write clearly and precisely. Much of what you want others to do must be communicated through memos, reports, policies, and letters. Organizations everywhere are complaining about many college graduates' inability to write clearly. If you develop good writing skills, you'll be miles ahead of your competition. That means you should take courses in grammar and composition. To learn to write, you must practice writing! It helps to write anything: a diary, letters, notes, and so on. With practice, you'll develop the ability to write easily—just as you speak. With this skill, you'll be more ready for a career in management.

••• COMPUTER SKILLS •••

The office of the future will be an office full of computers and related technology. Memos, charts, letters, and most of your other communication efforts will involve the computer. When you're practicing writing, practice on a word processor. The truly efficient manager of the future will be able to effectively use and take advantage of the continuing developments in technology.

••• HUMAN RELATIONS SKILLS •••

A manager works with people, and that means that good managers know how to get along with people, motivate them, and inspire them.[13] People skills are learned by working with people. That means you should join student groups, volunteer to help at your church or temple and local charities, and get involved in political organizations. Try to assume leadership positions where you're responsible for contacting others, assigning them work, and motivating them. Good leaders begin early by assuming leadership positions in sports, community groups, and so on.

Be aware of how others react to you. If you cause negative feelings or reactions, learn why. Don't be afraid to make mistakes and upset others. That's how you learn. But do learn how to work with others. Ask your friends what you could do to be a more effective and attractive leader.

MANAGING DIVERSITY   **Managing diversity** means building systems and a culture that unite different people in a common pursuit without undermining their diversity. The problem of diversity is more than dealing with questions about race, gender, ethnicity, sexual orientation, and disabilities. If people are to work on teams, they have to learn to deal with people who have different personalities, different priorities, and different lifestyles. In the past, firms tended to look for people much like the people already working at the firm. Today such recruiting would probably be illegal, and it certainly would be less than optimal.

Research has shown that heterogeneous (mixed) groups are more productive than homogeneous (similar) groups in the workplace.[14] Men and women, young and old, gay and straight, and all other mixes of people can learn not only to work together, but to work together with more success. In the future, managers must learn how to deal effectively with people from many differ-

managing diversity
Building systems and a culture that unite different people in a common pursuit without undermining their diversity.

Managing diversity means building a culture within the company that unites different people in a common pursuit without ignoring their cultural heritage. Each person has something unique to contribute, and that uniqueness should not be lost in the team or organizational culture. Successfully managing diversity will be more critical in the 21st century for U.S. firms as more and more employees come from diverse cultural backgrounds.

Reaching Beyond Our Borders

Learning about Managing Businesses in Global Markets

Business schools are seeing a mood change these days. As students read about countries that make up the former Soviet Union going to a market economy and Eastern Europeans opening their doors to Western businesses, they're demanding to know more about global business management. Many young people know they'll be involved in international business even if they never leave the United States. They also know that American companies are looking to business schools for managers who know how to work in the new global context.

How are business schools responding to this student demand? Many are revamping their existing curriculum by integrating international examples into basic courses. This reduces the need for specifically international courses. The idea is to bring international dimensions into the mainstream.

Still, some students demand more. They feel that global enterprise is too important to be mixed in with other courses, and they want courses that are entirely international. Many business schools now offer semester exchange programs with business schools in other countries. Professors are encouraged to participate in international research and to gain teaching experience overseas. Students are encouraged—and in some cases required—to study foreign languages. Students have caught the international fever and have passed the sense of urgency on to colleges.

Businesses too are changing the way they educate employees. Rather than send them for a traditional MBA, firms are teaching their managers how to work on teams, how to use the latest technology, and how to operate in a global economy. It's possible, if not likely, that the entire nature of business education will change over the next decade. Much more information will be available and accessible via computers and computer networks. More courses will be customized to fit the needs of individual firms. In any case, the future of management promises to be exciting, and so does the future of management education.

Source: Brian O'Reilly, "How Execs Learn Now," *Business Week*, April 5, 1993, pp. 52–58; and Brian O'Reilly, "Reengineering the MBA," *Fortune*, January 24, 1994, pp. 38–47.

ent cultures. Managers will also be asked to work in foreign countries. The more skilled you can become now in other languages and in working with diverse cultural groups, the better off you'll be when you become a manager.

••• TIME MANAGEMENT SKILLS •••

One of the most important skills for new managers to learn is how to budget their time effectively. There are many demands on managers' time that they need to learn to control: telephone interruptions, visits from colleagues, questions from subordinates, meetings scheduled by higher management, and such. See if your school offers courses in time management. Time management courses or workshops will help you develop such skills as setting priorities, delegating work, choosing activities that produce the most results, doing your work when you're at your best, and dealing with interruptions. Learning these skills now will help you increase your productivity at school and home.

••• TECHNICAL SKILLS •••

To rise through the ranks of accounting, marketing, finance, production, or any other functional area, you'll have to be proficient in that area. Therefore, you should begin now to choose some area of specialization. To rise to top management, you might supplement your undergraduate studies with an

M.B.A. (master of business administration) or some similar degree in government, economics, or hospital administration. More and more students are going on to take advanced degrees. About 60 percent of top managers have taken courses beyond the bachelor's degree. The most common areas of technical expertise among top managers are accounting and finance together. Marketing came in second. Slightly more than half of the top 1,000 chief executive officers in the country have a graduate degree.[15]

MANAGERS AND LEADERS ARE NEEDED EVERYWHERE

One exciting thing about studying management and leadership is that it prepares you for a career in any organization. Managers and leaders are needed in schools, churches, charities, government organizations, unions, associations, clubs, and all other organizations. Naturally, an important need for managers and leaders is in business.

When selecting a career in management, a student has several decisions to make:

What kind of organization is most attractive? That is, would you like to work for government, business, or some nonprofit organization?

What type of managerial position seems most interesting? A person may become a production manager, a sales manager, a human resource manager, an accounting manager, a traffic (distribution) manager, a credit manager, and so on. There are dozens of managerial positions from which to choose. In the future, you're likely to move among several different functions, so it pays to have a broad education in business.

What type of industry appeals to you: sporting goods, computers, auto, tourism, aircraft, or what? Would you prefer to work for a relatively new firm or an established one?

What courses and training are needed to prepare for various managerial careers? Only careful research will answer this question.

Management will be discussed in more detail in the next few chapters. Let's pause now, review, and do some exercises. Management is doing, not just reading.

What kind of management are you best suited for: human resource, marketing, finance, accounting, production, credit, or what? Why do you feel this area is most appropriate?

Would you like to work for a large firm or a small business? Private or government? In an office or out in the field? Would you like being a manager? If you aren't sure, read on and see what's involved.

CRITICAL THINKING

• Which managerial skills are used more by supervisors than by top managers and vice versa?

• What are the six Ds of decision making?

• What are the six skills you should be working on now to become a good manager later?

PROGRESS CHECK

SUMMARY

1. Explain the four functions of management and why the role of managers is changing.

1. Many managers are changing their approach to corporate management.
   - *What reasons can you give to account for these changes in management?*
   The three major reasons given in this text for management changes are (1) global competition, (2) technological change, and (3) the growing importance of pleasing customers. Managers are now being trained to guide and coach employees rather than boss them. The trend is toward working with employees as a team to meet organizational goals.
   - *What are the four functions of management?*
   Management is the process used to pursue organizational goals through (1) planning, (2) organizing, (3) directing, and (4) controlling.

2. Distinguish between goals and objectives; distinguish between strategic, tactical, and contingency planning; and explain the relationships of goals and objectives to the various types of planning.

2. The planning function involves the process of setting objectives to meet the organizational goals.
   - *What's the difference between goals and objectives?*
   Goals are broad, long-term achievements that organizations aim to accomplish, whereas objectives are specific, short-term plans made to help reach the goals.
   - *What are the three types of planning and how are they related to the organization's goals and objectives?*
   Strategic planning is broad, long-range planning that outlines the goals of the organization. Tactical planning, on the other hand, is specific, short-term planning that lists organizational objectives. Contingency planning involves developing an alternative set of plans in case the first set doesn't work out.

3. Describe the significance of an organization chart and explain how organizations are changing to meet the needs of customers.

3. Managers develop a framework that illustrates the relationship of workers, tasks, and resources.
   - *What is this framework or chart called, and what are the three major levels of management illustrated on the chart?*
   The organization chart pictures who reports to whom and who is responsible for what task. It illustrates the top, middle, and first-line management levels.
   - *How are organizations changing to become more customer-oriented?*
   Organizations are becoming smaller so that they can respond more quickly to customers. Furthermore, each firm is striving to have every process as good as the best companies in the world. Often that means finding other firms to do various processes. Top management must make contact with those firms and work very closely with them to coordinate processes so that customers get the highest-quality goods and services possible.

4. Describe the directing function of management and illustrate how the function differs at the various management levels.

4. The directing function of management involves giving assignments, explaining routines, clarifying policies, and providing feedback on performance.
   - *How does the directing function vary at different levels of management?*
   The further down the corporate ladder, the more specific the manager's directions become. First-line managers once spent a great deal of their time giving very specific, detailed instructions to their subordinates. Now they're more likely to work with employees to set goals and to allow more freedom to employees to decide how to reach those goals. Top managers direct middle managers, who require only broad, general directions.

5. Summarize the five steps of the control function of management.

5. The control function of management involves measuring employee performance against objectives and standards and taking corrective action if necessary.
   - *What are the five steps of the control function?*
   Controlling incorporates (1) setting clear standards, (2) monitoring and recording performance, (3) comparing performance with plans and

standards, (4) communicating results and deviations to employees, and (5) taking corrective action if necessary.

• **What qualities must standards possess to be used to measure performance results?**

Standards must be specific, attainable, and measurable.

6. Executives today must be more than just managers; they must be leaders as well.

• **What's the difference between a manager and a leader?**

A manager sees that the organization runs smoothly and that order is maintained. A leader does this and more. A leader has vision and inspires others to grasp that vision, establishes corporate values, emphasizes corporate ethics, and doesn't fear change.

• **Describe the various leadership styles.**

Figure 7.7 shows a continuum of leadership styles ranging from boss-centered to subordinate-centered leadership.

• **Which leadership style is best?**

The best (most effective) leadership style depends on the people being led and the situation. The challenge of the future will be to empower self-managed teams to manage themselves. This is a move away from command-and-control management.

7. Managers must be good planners, organizers, coordinators, communicators, morale builders, and motivators.

• **What skills must a manager have to be all these things?**

Managers must have three categories of skills: (1) technical skills (ability to perform tasks such as bookkeeping or selling), (2) human relations skills (ability to communicate and motivate), and (3) conceptual skills (ability to see organizations as a whole and how all the parts fit together).

• **Are these skills equally important at all management levels?**

The skills needed are different at different levels. Top managers rely heavily on human relations and conceptual skills and rarely use technical skills, while first-line supervisors need strong technical and human relations skills but use conceptual skills less often. (See Figure 7.8.)

8. Now that you've examined what managers do, you may be considering a career in management.

• **What skills should you be developing now to help you become a better manager in the future?**

You'll need to develop six skills to sharpen your managerial potential: (1) verbal skills, (2) writing skills, (3) computer skills, (4) human relations skills, (5) time management skills, and (6) technical skills.

6. Explain the differences between managers and leaders, and compare the characteristics and uses of the various leadership styles.

7. Describe the three general categories of skills needed by top, middle, and first-line managers.

8. Illustrate the skills you will need to develop your managerial potential and outline activities you could use to develop these skills.

---

autocratic
   leadership 226
conceptual skills 230
contingency
   planning 216
controlling 214
decision making 231
delegating 230
democratic
   (participative)
   leadership 226
directing 214
empowerment 220

goals 215
human relations
   skills 230
internal customers 223
laissez-faire (free rein)
   leadership 226
leadership 224
management 213
managing diversity 233
middle
   management 217
objectives 215

organizing 214
planning 214
strategic (long-range)
   planning 215
supervisory (first-line)
   management 217
tactical (short-range)
   planning 215
technical skills 230
top management 217
vision 214

KEY TERMS

DEVELOPING WORKPLACE SKILLS

1. Discuss the merits of working as a manager in the following types of organizations: government, business, and nonprofit. To learn the advantages of each, talk to managers from each area and share what you learn with the class.

2. Interview two or more managers of local businesses (preferably of different sizes) and find out what they spend the majority of their time doing. Is it planning, organizing, controlling, or directing? Use a computer graphics program to create a pie chart illustrating the average amount of time spent on each type of activity. If you have a chance to talk with different levels of managers, it would be interesting to create a chart comparing their allocation of time. Discuss the results with the class.

3. Discuss the disadvantages of becoming a manager. Does the size of the business make a difference? Do managers or workers seem to enjoy better lifestyles? Discuss.

4. Review *Business Week, Forbes, Inc.*, and other business journals and read about key executives and managers. How much do they make? (See *Business Week*'s annual survey.) How many hours do they work? Do you believe they earn their pay? Discuss.

5. Review Figure 7.7 and discuss managers you have known, worked for, or read about who have practiced each style. Which did you like best? Why? Which were most effective? Why?

· ·

PRACTICING MANAGEMENT DECISIONS

⟨⟨ C a s e   CHANGING THE PARADIGM ⟩⟩

Noel Tichy, a business professor at the University of Michigan, advises you not to try this at home. Consider the two ways to boil a live frog. The first way is to drop little Kermit into boiling water. He'll hop right out according to those acquainted with the classic physiological phenomenon. But try placing Kermit in a pot of cold water and gradually raising the temperature. He'll sit there and boil to death. This is meant to be a parable for business leadership in the 1990s, not a lesson in animal torture. Kermit failed to adjust to a shifting paradigm. He ignored a critical, though gradual, change in his environment. Before coming to a full boil, he should have remembered the words of American patriot Thomas Paine, "A long habit of not thinking a thing wrong gives it the superficial appearance of being right."

Used in business, the word *paradigm* (pronounced as in "Brother, can you paradigm?") simply refers to the accepted view of how things have always been done and should continue to be done. A paradigm shifter is someone who throws out the rules of the game and starts radical change. Tichy, who worked with General Electric's ultimate paradigm shifter, Jack Welch, adds, "It's not just quantum ideas, but the guts to stick with them. In industry after industry, a lot of frogs are waking up and finding it's too late to jump. Banking is there. Auto has had two chances and may not get a third. And now the computer industry is feeling the heat."

Jack Welch's restructuring of GE meant far fewer middle managers and more power to those who remained. John Trani (the Welch lieutenant who overhauled and runs GE Medical Systems) says, "People come to me and ask, 'Why was I good enough yesterday, but not today?' It's simple. In 1954, Roger Bannister won world acclaim for breaking the four-minute mile. Today high schoolers can do that. The standard is always changing, but there's always a top 10 and a bottom 10." As a matter of policy, Welch demands that all GE businesses be number one or number two in their industry.

Decision Questions

1. How is the business environment changing from what it was 10 or 20 years ago? What can managers do to adapt to these changes?

2. Noel Tichy suggests that companies that don't adjust to shifting paradigms face death. As an example, he points to buggy makers who turned up their noses at Henry Ford's smelly exhaust. Can you think of other victims of shifting paradigms?

3. Experts say that for a real paradigm shift to occur within a corporation, top management has to have a strong commitment to change. Says Ram Charan, a consultant to many Fortune 500 companies, "There has to be divine discontent with the status quo at the very top, and courage to do something about it." Explain why top management's commitment to change is crucial to change within a corporation.

Source: John Huey, "Nothing Is Impossible," *Fortune*, September 23, 1991, pp. 134–40.

• •

⟨⟨ VIDEO CASE   THE CHANGING ROLE OF MANAGEMENT ⟨⟨

The traditional role of managers has been to plan, organize, direct, and control the work of others to achieve the objectives of the organization. In the past, emphasis was placed on strategic (long-range) planning, on telling employees what to do and how to do it, and on closely supervising employees and discouraging errors and defects. All of that is changing in today's fast-paced industries. One of those rapidly changing industries is telecommunications. The deregulation of phone companies, the introduction of fiber optics, the growth of cellular phone systems, and more are making competition and the need for innovation more important than ever.

Tellabs is one company that has successfully implemented all of the newest management concepts: just-in-time inventory control, total quality management, continuous improvement, and cross-functional teams. The company realizes that customer expectations are what determine quality standards. To get close to customers, the company sends out cross-functional teams to determine customer wants and needs and expectations. *Planning* takes on a much shorter horizon as the company continually innovates to stay ahead of competition.

An entirely new kind of *organization*, the cross-functional team, is used to facilitate innovation and motivation. The company designed and constructed its plant so that there literally are no walls between functional units.

Directing is minimized at Tellabs. Instead, members of cross-functional teams are encouraged to be self managed, to make mistakes (if you don't make mistakes, you're being too cautious and not sufficiently innovative), and to respond quickly to customers.

Control is less a matter of looking over the shoulder of workers and more a matter of measuring customer satisfaction and making adjustments when needed. In short, management at Tellabs is largely a matter of leadership. What is the difference? Leadership is more involved with creating a vision. At Tellabs, that vision is one of a global leader. The leadership style is more democratic than most firms; some might say it resembles laissez faire.

A decision by management to give more authority and responsibility to employees doesn't come easy. It means that managers give up some of their own authority in order to become coaches, supporters, and motivators instead. On the other hand, every employee becomes his or her own manager in that they assume more and more responsibility. That is what self management is all about. It helps to have people working in teams because shared responsibility and authority also help to optimize the diverse experiences of group members. At Tellabs, that teamwork has led to new innovations and a more motivated workforce.

Discussion Questions

1. In the future, more and more college graduates will be working on cross-functional teams. What kind of training in college would help students be more productive on such teams?

2. What kinds of problems might managers experience in the future as a result of the growth of cross-functional teams? Will it be more difficult to evaluate, compensate, and promote people?

3. Is information management more or less important now that the planning horizon for managers is much shorter? Why?

4. Would you rather work at a firm with a traditional organizational structure or one with cross-functional teams? Why?

CHAPTER 8

ORGANIZING A CUSTOMER-DRIVEN BUSINESS

LEARNING GOALS

After you have read and studied this chapter, you should be able to

1. Describe the traditional hierarchical, bureaucratic organization structure and how it is being restructured.

2. Explain the organizational theories of Fayol and Weber.

3. Discuss the various issues connected with organizational design.

4. Describe the differences between line, line and staff, matrix, and cross-functional organizations.

5. Explain the benefits of turning organizations upside down and inside out.

6. Give examples to show how organizational culture and the informal organization can hinder or assist organizational change.

BETTY WAGNER OF CAVALIER GAGE AND ELECTRONIC

Betty Wagner graduated from a community college and went to work for a small metal fabricator called Cavalier Gage & Electronic. She began as a secretary, but moved up through the ranks, eventually buying the company from its owner. When Betty had her third child (the second still being a toddler), she found that managing the company by herself was too much. Therefore, she turned her company from a boss-driven firm into a team operation. She began by opening her books and sharing the information with her managers. Together they developed the company's first business plan. They decided to target small medical equipment manufacturers.

Working together, a cross-functional team was able to cut bidding time on new contracts from two days to less than an hour. Using total quality concepts such as continuous improvement, the company eventually became one of only 2,500 U.S. companies to be certified for ISO 9000 international standards «·· P.48 ··» . It's quite possibly the smallest company to be so certified. The company was in trouble when Betty decided to go to cross-functional teams. Now it's thriving and she's rehiring many of the workers she had to let go when times were tough.

Betty Wagner is just one of thousands of managers throughout the world who've restructured their organizations to stay competitive in global markets. Many leading U.S. firms—including Motorola, American Express, Bell Atlantic, General Motors, AT&T, IBM, Kodak, Taco Bell, and Mack Trucks—have gone through drastic organizational changes in the past few years. Ms. Wagner shows, however, that such changes are equally important in smaller firms.

In this chapter, we'll explore traditional organizational design and theory and then discuss the newest trends. Few developments in business have more far-reaching implications for today's students than the organizational changes now taking place.

}} *America's business problem is that it is entering the twenty-first century with companies designed during the nineteenth century to work well in the twentieth.* {{

Michael Hammer and James Champy
Reengineering the Corporation

THE CHANGING ORGANIZATIONAL HIERARCHY

Moving from a boss-driven to an employee-driven company isn't easy. Managers often resist giving up their authority over workers, while workers often resist the responsibility that comes with self management. Nonetheless, many leading organizations in the world are moving in that direction. They're trying to develop an organizational design that best serves the needs of customers, stockholders, employees, and the community.

Organizational design is the structuring of workers so that they can best accomplish all of the firm's goals. In the past, many organizations were designed so that managers could *control* workers. Everything was set up in a hierarchy. A **hierarchy** means that there's one person at the top of the organization and there are many levels of managers who are responsible to that person. Since one person can't keep track of thousands of workers, the top manager needs many lower-level managers to help. Figure 8.1 shows a typical hierarchical organization structure.

Some organizations had as many as 10 to 14 layers of management between the chief executive officer (CEO) and the lowest-level employees. If employees wanted to introduce work changes, they would ask their supervisors who would ask their managers who would ask the manager above them and so on. Eventually a decision would be made and passed down from manager to manager until it reached the employee. Such decisions could take days, weeks, or months. **Bureaucracy** is the term used in organizations to describe having many layers of management who set rules and regulations and participate in all decisions.

organizational design
The establishment of manageable groups of people who have clear responsibilities and who know how to accomplish the objectives of the organization and the group.

hierarchy
Organization with several levels of managers.

bureaucracy
Organization with three layers of authority: (1) top managers who make decisions, (2) middle managers who develop procedures for implementing decisions, and (3) workers and supervisors who do the work.

••• THE FUNDAMENTALS OF BUREAUCRACY •••

In a bureaucratic organization, a chain of command goes from the top down. There are many rules and regulations that everyone is expected to follow. To make the process easier, organizations are set up by function. That is, there are separate departments for design, engineering, production, marketing, finance, human resource management, accounting, legal, and so on. People tend to specialize in one function in school and then on the job. Communication among departments is minimal. The typical career is to move up within a function. For example, one might move up from salesperson to sales trainer to sales manager to regional manager to marketing manager to marketing vice president. Such a career progression doesn't regularly expose people to other functions in the firm and therefore doesn't create much interfunctional cooperation.

In the past, such an organization structure worked well because employees could specialize in one area and learn to do it well. The problem today is that such organizations aren't very responsive to customers. Employees tend to follow the rules and aren't very flexible in responding to customer wants and needs. Such slow response to consumer demands cuts dramatically into

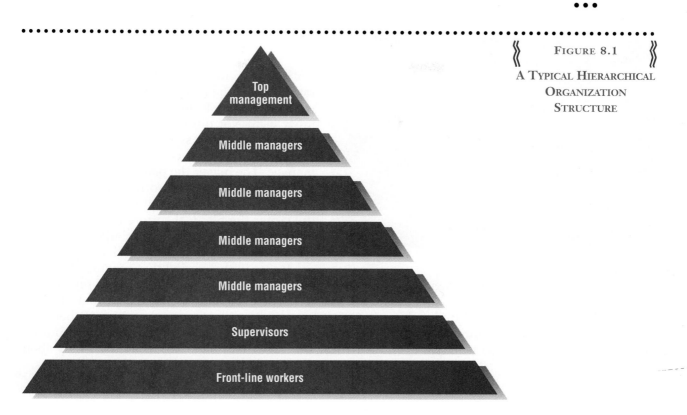

FIGURE 8.1

A TYPICAL HIERARCHICAL
ORGANIZATION
STRUCTURE

sales by leading firms such as IBM, GM, and Kodak. They responded by restructuring their firms. **Restructuring** means redesigning an organization so that it can more effectively and efficiently service customers. Often that means breaking down barriers between functions. It may also mean giving more authority to lower-level employees and ending top-down management. Those organizations that have made such changes—like Cavalier Gage—have regained market leadership. Many others are quickly following their lead.

There are still many remnants of bureaucracy among today's organizations. Most universities are still slow to adapt to customer (student) wants and needs. So are most government agencies. Often you can see the consequences of bureaucracy in agencies such as the Department of Motor Vehicles or the Postal Service. Such agencies are starting to explore new ways of organizing. Otherwise, they may lose their function to more efficient organizations. For example, the postal service in England has been taken over by private firms.

restructuring
Redesigning organizations to make them more productive.

Start noticing how many clerks and other customer-contact people say things like, "That's not our policy" or "We don't do things that way" when you request some unusual service. Such answers are the result of bureaucratic rules and regulations that employees are forced to follow. Imagine a day when employees are free to adjust to the wants and needs of customers. What organizational changes would have to be made? Would the results be worth the effort?

CRITICAL THINKING

HOW ORGANIZATIONS HAVE EVOLVED

To understand traditional managers and their approach to business, you have to understand traditional organization theory. In the next few sections, we'll review those theories. Then we'll outline the new approaches that will guide organizations in the 21st century.

Bureaucracy frequently means delay in meeting the needs of customers. Often lines such as these at the Department of Motor Vehicles occur because the employees are not empowered to respond quickly to requests by customers. Instead, they tend to follow rules and procedures that are slow and inefficient. What is different about government organizations that typically makes them slower to respond to consumer needs than businesses?

··· THE BACKGROUND OF ··· ORGANIZATION THEORY

Until this century, most organizations were rather small, the processes for producing goods were rather simple, and organizing workers was fairly easy. Not until the 20th century and the introduction of mass production did business organizations grow complex and difficult to manage. The bigger the plant, the more efficient production became, or so it seemed. The concept was called economy of scale. It meant that the larger the plant, the more efficient it could be because all the employees could specialize in a function that they could do efficiently.

It was in this period that organization theorists emerged. In France, Henri Fayol published his book *Administration Industrielle et Generale* in 1919. It was popularized in the United States in 1949 under the title *General and Industrial Management*. Max Weber (pronounced *Vay-ber*) was writing organization theories in Germany about the same time Fayol was writing his books in France. Note that it was only about 50 years ago that organization theory became popular in the United States.

··· FAYOL'S PRINCIPLES OF ORGANIZATION ···

Fayol introduced such "principles" as

Unity of command. Each worker is to report to one, and only one, boss. The benefits of this principle are obvious. What happens if two different bosses give you two different assignments? Which one should you follow? To prevent such confusion, each person is to report to only one manager.

Hierarchy of authority. Each person should know to whom they should report. Managers should have the right to give orders and expect others to follow.

Division of labor. Functions are to be divided into areas of specialization such as production, marketing, and finance.

Subordination of individual interests to the general interest. Workers are to think of themselves as a coordinated team. Goals of the team are more important than the goals of individual workers.

Authority. Managers have the right to give orders and the power to exact obedience. Authority and responsibility are related: Whenever authority is exercised, responsibility arises.

Degree of centralization. The amount of decision-making power vested in top management should vary by circumstances. In a small organization, it's possible to centralize all decision-making power in the top manager. In a larger organization, however, some decision-making power should be delegated to lower-level managers and employees on both major and minor issues.

Clear communication channels.

Order. Materials and people should be placed and maintained in the proper location.

Equity. A manager should treat employees and peers with respect and justice.

Esprit de corps. A spirit of pride and loyalty should be created among people in the firm.

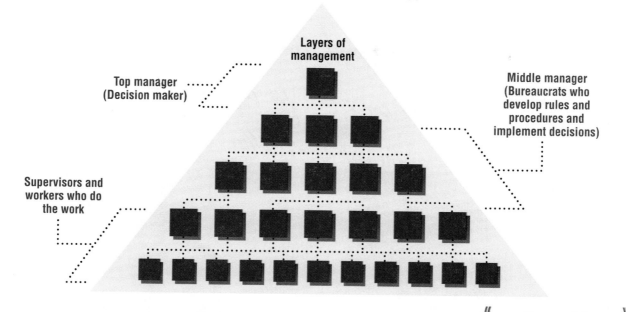

FIGURE 8.2

BUREAUCRATIC
ORGANIZATION
STRUCTURE
This chart shows Weber's
concept of a bureacratic
organization—one with
clear lines of authority
and several layers of
management.

Management courses in colleges throughout the world taught these principles for years, and they became synonymous with the concept of management. Organizations were designed so that no person had more than one boss, lines of authority were clear, and everyone knew to whom they were to report. Naturally, these principles tended to become rules and policies as organizations grew larger. That led to rather rigid organizations and a feeling among workers that they belonged to an inflexible system rather than to a group of friendly, cooperative workers joined together in a common effort.

••• MAX WEBER AND ORGANIZATION THEORY •••

Max Weber used the term *bureaucrats* to describe middle managers whose function was to implement top management's orders. His book *The Theory of Social and Economic Organizations* was introduced to the United States in the late 1940s. Weber's concept of a bureaucratic organization basically consisted of three layers of authority: (1) top managers, who were the decision makers, (2) middle managers (the bureaucracy), who developed rules and procedures for implementing the decisions, and (3) workers and supervisors who did the work. (See Figure 8.2.)

It was Weber who promoted the pyramid-shaped organization structure that became so popular in large firms. Weber put great trust in managers and felt that the firm would do well if employees simply did what they were told. The less decision making employees had to do, the better. Clearly, this is a reasonable way to operate if you're dealing with relatively uneducated and untrained workers. Often, such workers were the only ones available at that time. Today, however, many firms believe that workers are the best source of ideas, and that managers are there to support workers rather than boss them around.

Weber's principles of organization were similar to Fayol's. In addition, Weber emphasized

Job descriptions.

Written rules, decision guidelines, and detailed records.

Consistent procedures, regulations, and policies.

Staffing and promotions based on qualifications.

General Motors.

"If the people who make the car don't fit together, the car won't either."

Welcome to the Excel training course. Before it's over, Saturn's Dennis Bowman will take these General Motors employees on a real adventure. They'll scale walls. Walk across high wires. Plunge backwards into the waiting arms of their coworkers. And take away some valuable lessons about trust, cooperation and seeing things from the other person's point of view. Developed by Saturn, Excel is now used throughout General Motors. It's turning out graduates who know the power of teamwork. Who go a little further to build quality automobiles. And who believe that the right way to treat a customer is the way you'd want to be treated yourself.

One of the most important goals of organizations today is teamwork. This concept was a key part of Fayol's principles. Teamwork builds trust, cooperation and joint commitments to achieve the firm's objectives. What have you observed coaches or managers doing that has fostered a feeling of teamwork?

Weber believed that large organizations demanded clearly established rules and guidelines that were to be followed precisely. Although the word *bureaucrat* didn't have any negative connotations as used by Weber, the practice of establishing rules and procedures sometimes becomes so rigid that *bureaucracy* has become almost a nasty name for an organization with many managers who seem to do nothing but make and enforce rules.

Together, Fayol and Weber introduced organizational concepts such as (1) unity of command (one employee, one boss), (2) division of labor (specialized jobs), (3) job descriptions, (4) rules, guidelines, procedures, and policies, (5) clear lines of authority and communication, (6) placement of materials and people in some established order, (7) the establishment of departments, (8) detailed record keeping, (9) the establishment of an esprit de corps (a feeling of enthusiasm and devotion to the firm), and (10) the assignment of a limited number of people to each manager. You can see the benefits of such concepts. What's needed today is a way to implement those concepts while still maintaining employees' freedom and incentives to work productively on their own.

DESIGNING MORE RESPONSIVE ORGANIZATIONS

It wasn't until the late 1970s that management began the process of reorganizing firms, making them smaller, less complex, and more efficient. That process continues today. New technologies and international competition forced these changes. Organizational issues that have led to design changes include (1) tall versus flat organization structures, (2) span of control, (3) departmentalization, and (4) centralization versus decentralization.

••• TALL VERSUS FLAT ORGANIZATION STRUCTURES •••

Over time, organizations have grown bigger and bigger, adding layer after layer of management. Such organizations have what are called *tall* organization structures. This means, simply, that the organization chart would be quite tall because of the various levels of management. The organization structure of the U.S. Army is an example of how tall an organization can get. There are many layers of management between a private and a general (e.g., sergeant, lieutenant, captain, major, colonel). You can imagine how a message may be distorted as it moves up through so many layers of management.

Business organizations took on the same style of organization as the military. Organizations were divided into regions, divisions, centers, and plants. Each plant might have several layers of management. The net effect was a huge complex of managers, management assistants, secretaries, assistant secretaries, supervisors, trainers, and so on. The cost of keeping all these managers and support people was quite high. The paperwork they generated was enormous, and the inefficiencies in communication and decision making became intolerable.

The development of computers helped to bring more efficiency to large operations. But the more important trend was to eliminate several layers of management. Throughout the 1990s, companies fired managers and tried to become more efficient. This trend toward trimming management positions is likely to continue into the next century.[1] Those organizations that do cut management are tending to create teams. Business majors, therefore, need to practice working and thinking in teams. You're likely to get a job because of functional expertise (e.g., as a finance major), but your career is likely to take you into many different areas of the firm and demand more general skills. You may thus have to be a jack of all trades *and* a master of at least one.

••• SPAN OF CONTROL •••

Span of control refers to the optimum number of subordinates a manager supervises or should supervise. There are many factors to consider when determining span of control. At lower levels, where work is standardized, it's possible to implement a wide span of control (15 to 40 workers). However, the number gradually narrows at higher levels of the organization because work is less standardized and there's more need for face-to-face communication. Variables in span of control include

span of control
The optimum number of subordinates a manager should supervise.

1. *Capabilities of the manager.* The more experienced and capable a manager is, the broader the span of control can be. (More workers can report to one supervisor.)

2. *Capabilities of the subordinates.* The more subordinates who need supervision, the narrower the span of control should be. (Fewer workers report to one supervisor.)

3. *Complexity of the job.*

   a. *Geographical closeness.* The more concentrated the work area is, the broader the span of control can be.

   b. *Functional similarity.* The more similar the functions are, the broader the span of control can be.

FROM THE PAGES OF...
Entrepreneur.
MAGAZINE

*Give
Bureaucracy
the Boot*

Carstar Automotive Inc. in Overland Park, Kansas, is a 36-employee franchisor of auto body shops in 34 states. The head of the firm, Lirel Holt, tries to maintain an organizational environment that favors informal teams and open doors. His employees are cross-trained and instructed to ignore traditional communication barriers. Holt based his organizational design on the boundaryless organizational principles developed at larger firms such as GE.

The common element among such firms is the horizontal versus vertical organizational design. The organizational form is very flat. Communication among departments is free flowing; management tends to go across depart-

ments, not down through the organization. The goal is to respond faster to customer wants and needs. Anyone who answers the phone should be able to help the customer. That's one purpose of cross-training—everyone knows how to deal with customers. The span of control for top management in such organizations is very wide.

Therefore, top management must learn to delegate authority and let teams decide what needs to be done and when. Where such horizontal management has been tried, the results have been very positive.

Source: Mark Hendricks, "New Horizons," *Entrepreneur*, June 1994, pp. 42–45.

c. Need for coordination. The greater the need for coordination, the narrower the span of control might be.

d. Planning demands. The more involved the plan, the narrower the span of control might be.

e. Functional complexity. The more complex the functions are, the narrower the span of control might be.

Other factors to consider include the professionalism of superiors and subordinates and the number of new problems that occur in a day. In business, the span of control varies widely. The number of people reporting to the president may range from 1 to 80 or more. The trend is to expand the span of control as organizations get rid of middle managers. It's possible to increase the span of control as employees become more professional, as information technology makes it possible for managers to handle more information, and as employees take on more responsibility for self-management.

••• DEPARTMENTALIZATION •••

departmentalization
Dividing tasks into homogeneous departments such as manufacturing and marketing.

Departmentalization is the dividing of organizational functions into separate units. The traditional technique for departmentalizing organizations is by function. Functional structure is the grouping of workers into departments based on similar skills, expertise, or resource use. There might be, for example, a production department, a transportation department, a finance department, an accounting department, a marketing department, a data processing department, and so on. Such units enable employees to specialize and work together more efficiently. Advantages of such a structure include

1. Skills can be developed in depth, and employees can progress within a department as their skills develop.

2. It allows for economies of scale in that all the resources needed can be centralized and various experts can be located in that area.

3. There's good coordination within the function, and top management can easily direct and control various departments' activities.

As for disadvantages,

1. There's a lack of communication among the different departments. For example, production may be isolated from marketing so that the people making the product do not get the proper feedback from customers.

2. Individual employees begin to identify with their department and its goals rather than with the goals of the organization as a whole.

3. Response to external changes is slow.

4. People aren't trained to take different managerial responsibilities; rather, they tend to become narrow specialists.

Given the limitations of departmentalization, businesses are now trying to redesign their structures to optimize skill development while increasing communication among employees in different departments. The goal, remember, is to better serve customers and to win their loyalty. When Mack Truck found itself near bankruptcy because its quality was deteriorating and market penetration was plummeting, it turned to some 400 employee teams to break down barriers between departments. Those teams were so successful that warranty claims are down 53 percent and sales increased over 38 percent in 1993 alone.[2]

DIFFERENT WAYS TO DEPARTMENTALIZE   In the past, companies have tried various ways to departmentalize to better serve customers. Figure 8.3 shows five ways a firm can departmentalize. Companies may use a variety of methods of departmentalization in structuring the same company. One form of departmentalization is by product. A book publisher might have a trade book department, textbook department, and technical book department. Customers for each type of book are very different, so separate development and marketing processes are developed to better serve each type of customer.

The most basic way to departmentalize, as we discussed above, is by function. This text is divided by business function because such groupings are most common. Production, marketing, finance, human resource management, and accounting are all distinct functions calling for separate skills. Companies are now discovering, however, that functional separation isn't always the most responsive form of organization.

It makes more sense in some organizations to departmentalize by customer group. A pharmaceutical company, for example, might have one department that focuses on the consumer market, another that calls on hospitals (institutional market), and another that targets doctors.

Some firms group their units by geographic location because customers vary so greatly by region. The United States is usually considered one market area. Japan, Europe, and Korea may involve separate departments.

The decision about which way to departmentalize depends greatly on the nature of the product and the customers served. A few firms departmentalize by process because it's more efficient to separate activities that way. For example, a firm that makes leather coats may have one department cut the leather, another dye it, and a third sew the coat together.

••• **CENTRALIZATION VERSUS DECENTRALIZATION** •••
OF AUTHORITY

Imagine for a minute that you're a top manager for a retail company such as J.C. Penney. Your temptation may be to preserve control over all your stores in order to maintain a uniform image and merchandise. You've noticed such

FIGURE 8.3

WAYS TO
DEPARTMENTALIZE
A publisher may want to
departmentalize by prod-
uct, a manufacturer by
function, a pharmaceuti-
cal company by customer
group, and a computer
company by geographic
location (countries). A
leather manufacturer
may prefer departmental-
ization by process. In
each case, the structure
must fit the firm's goals.

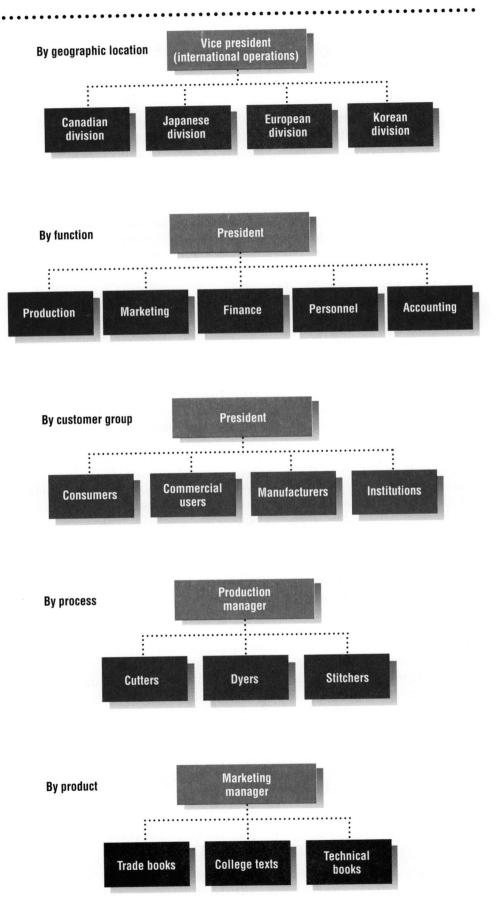

control works well for McDonald's; why not J.C. Penney? The degree to which an organization allows managers at the lower levels of the managerial hierarchy to make decisions determines the degree of decentralization that an organization practices.

Centralized authority means that decision-making authority is maintained at the top level of management at headquarters or central management. **Decentralized authority** means that decision-making authority is delegated to lower-level managers and employees who are more familiar with local conditions than headquarters management could be.

At J.C. Penney, for example, customers in California are likely to demand clothing styles different from those demanded in Minnesota or Maine. It makes sense, therefore, to give store managers in various cities the authority to buy, price, and promote merchandise appropriate for each area. Such a delegation of authority is an example of decentralized management.

On the other hand, McDonald's feels that purchasing, promotion, and other such decisions are best handled centrally. There's little need for each McDonald's store to carry different food products. McDonald's, therefore, would lean toward centralized authority. Today's rapidly changing markets, added to global differences in consumer tastes, tend to favor more decentralization and thus more delegation of authority. McDonald's, for example, has learned that stores in England should provide tea, stores in Germany should provide beer, stores in Japan should provide rice, and so on.

centralized authority
Maintaining decision-making authority with the top level of management at headquarters.

decentralized authority
Delegating decision-making authority to lower-level managers who are more familiar with local conditions.

- What is bureaucracy and why has it led to the need for restructuring organizations?
- How many of Fayol's 10 principles can you name?
- What principles did Weber add?
- What are the trends in tall versus flat organizations, a narrow versus wide span of control, departmentalization, and the centralization versus decentralization of authority?

PROGRESS CHECK

ORGANIZATION MODELS

Now that we've explored the basic principles of organizational design, we can explore in depth the various ways to structure an organization to accomplish our goals. The four forms of organization we'll look at are (1) line organizations, (2) line and staff organizations, (3) matrix-style organizations, and (4) cross-functional, self-managed teams. Figure 8.4 compares their advantages and disadvantages.

••• LINE ORGANIZATIONS •••

A line organization has direct two-way lines of responsibility, authority, and communication running from the top to the bottom of the organization, with all people reporting to only one supervisor. The most obvious example is the army, which has a clear line of authority going from general to colonel to major to lieutenant to sergeant to corporal to private. A private reports to a corporal, the corporal to a sergeant, and so on back up to the generals. A line organization has the advantages of having clearly defined responsibility and authority, of being easy to understand, and of providing one supervisor for each person. The principles of good organizational design are met. Most very small companies are organized this way.

	Advantages	Disadvantages
Line	Clearly defined responsibility and authority Easy to understand One supervisor for each group of employees	Too inflexible Few specialists to advise Long lines of communication Unable to handle complex questions quickly Tons of paperwork
Line and staff	Expert advice from staff to line personnel Establishes lines of authority Encourages cooperation and better communication at all levels	Potential overstaffing Potential overanalyzing Lines of communication can be blurred Staff frustrations because of lack of authority
Matrix	Flexible Encourages cooperation among departments Can produce creative solutions to problems Allows organization to take on new projects without adding to the organization structure	Costly and complex Can confuse employees Requires good interpersonal skills and cooperative managers and employees Difficult to evaluate employees and to set up reward systems
Cross-functional, self-managed teams	Greatly increases interdepartmental coordination and cooperation Quicker response to customers and market conditions Increased employee motivation and morale	Some confusion over responsibility and authority Perceived loss of control by management Difficult to evaluate employees and set up reward systems Requires self-motivated, highly trained workers

FIGURE 8.4

ORGANIZATION TYPES
Each form of organization has its own advantages and disadvantages.

However, a line organization may have the disadvantages of being too inflexible, of having few specialists or experts to advise people along the line, of having lines of communication that are too long, and of being unable to handle the complex decisions involved in an organization with thousands of sometimes unrelated products and literally tons of paperwork.

LINE AND STAFF ORGANIZATIONS

To minimize the disadvantages of simple line organizations, many organizations today have both line and staff personnel. A couple of definitions will help:

line personnel
Employees who perform functions that contribute directly to the primary goals of the organization.

staff personnel
Employees who perform functions that assist line personnel in achieving their goals.

Line personnel perform functions that contribute directly to the primary goals of the organization (e.g., making the product, distributing it, and selling it). **Staff personnel** perform functions that advise and assist line personnel in performing their goals (e.g., marketing research, legal advising, and personnel).

Many organizations have benefited from the expert advice of staff assistants in areas such as safety, quality control, computer technology, human resource management, and investing. Such positions strengthen the line positions and are by no means inferior or lower-paid positions. It's like having well-paid consultants on the organization's payroll.

MATRIX ORGANIZATIONS

Both line, and line and staff organization structures suffer from a certain inflexibility. Both have established lines of authority and communication, and both work well in organizations with a relatively stable environment and evo-

Everyone in this small print shop is a line employee. The tasks performed by each one will have an impact on satisfying the company's customers. Due to its size there are no staff employees or departments dedicated to legal, accounting, or similar specialized functions. However, if the business should grow, enabling it to begin hiring staff positions, which function do you think they would address first? Why?

lutionary development (such as firms selling consumer products like toasters and refrigerators). In such firms, clear lines of authority and relatively fixed organization structures are assets that ensure efficient operations.

Today's economic scene is dominated by new kinds of organizations in high-growth industries (e.g., robotics, biotechnology, and aerospace) unlike anything seen in the past. In such industries, new projects are developed, competition with similar projects elsewhere is stiff, and the life cycle of new ideas is very short. The economic, technological, and competitive environments are rapidly changing. In such organizations, emphasis is on new product development, creativity, special projects, rapid communication, and interdepartmental teamwork.

From that environment grew the popularity of the matrix organization. In **matrix organizations**, specialists from different parts of the organization are brought together to work on specific projects, but they still remain part of a line and staff structure. (See Figure 8.5.) In other words, a project manager can borrow people from different departments to help design and market new product ideas.

Matrix organization structures were developed in the aerospace industry at firms such as Boeing, Lockheed, and McDonnell Douglas. The structure is now used in banking, management consulting firms, accounting firms, ad agencies, and school systems. Although it works well in some organizations, it doesn't work in others. Advantages of a matrix organization structure include

- It gives flexibility to managers in assigning people to projects.
- It encourages interorganizational cooperation and teamwork.
- It's flexible and can result in creative solutions to problems such as new product development.

As for disadvantages,

- It's costly to implement, and it's complex.
- It can cause confusion among employees as to where their loyalty belongs—to the project manager or to their functional unit.
- It requires good interpersonal skills and cooperative employees and managers.

matrix organization
Organization in which specialists from different parts of the organization are brought together to work on specific projects but still remain part of a traditional line and staff structure.

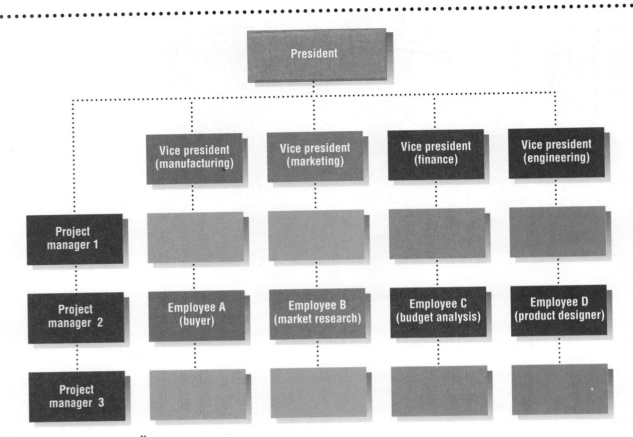

FIGURE 8.5

A MATRIX-STYLE ORGANIZATION
In a matrix organization, project managers are in charge of teams made up of members of several departments. In this case, project manager 2 supervises employees A, B, C, and D. These employees are accountable not only to project manager 2, but also to the head of their individual departments. For example, employee B, a market researcher, reports to project manager 2 *and* to the vice president of marketing.

cross-functional teams
Groups of employees from different departments who work together on a semipermanent basis (as opposed to the temporary teams established in matrix-style organizations).

If it seems to you that matrix organizations violate some traditional managerial principles, you're right. Normally a person can't work effectively for two bosses. (Who has the real authority? Which directive has the first priority: the one from the project manager or the one from one's immediate supervisor?) In reality, the system functions more effectively than we might imagine. To develop a new product idea, a project manager may be given temporary authority to "borrow" line personnel from engineering, production, marketing, and other line functions. Together, they work to complete the project and then return to their regular positions. In fact, then, they really don't report to more than one manager at a time.

The effectiveness of matrix-style organizations in high-tech firms eventually led to the adoption of similar concepts in many firms, including such low-tech firms as Rubbermaid. Rubbermaid now turns out an average of one new product every day using the team concept from matrix management.

••• CROSS-FUNCTIONAL, SELF-MANAGED TEAMS •••

The matrix-style of organization eventually led to cross-functional teams. **Cross-functional teams** are groups of employees from different departments who work together on a semipermanent basis (as opposed to the temporary teams established in matrix-style organizations). Often the teams are empowered «⋯ P.220 ⋯» to make decisions on their own without seeking the approval of management. That's why the teams are called *self-managed*. The barriers between design, engineering, marketing, distribution, and other functions fall as members of each department work on teams.

Honeywell's Building Controls Division used cross-functional teams to reduce product development time by 50 percent, reduce product costs by 5 to 10 percent, and make products 97.6 percent defect free. AT&T cut development

Working together in teams is much different from working in your own functional specialty. You have to be a jack of all trades and a master of one. That is, you have to be skilled at one function and still be able to understand and work with people in other activities. What kind of interdisciplinary courses could you take in school to prepare you for such teamwork?

time for its cordless phone from two years to 12 months using cross-functional teams.[3] Procter & Gamble reports from 30 to 40 percent higher productivity in plants that are team based. Self-directed teams at General Mills' plant in Georgia produce cereal with quality far exceeding that in other plants. In General Electric's Canadian operations, self-managed teams of 4 to 12 people have improved the productivity of accounts payable, payroll, and other financial functions. Roanoke, Virginia's Shenandoah Life processed 50 percent more paperwork with 10 percent fewer people after it began self-managed teams. Tektronix in Beaverton, Oregon, turns out as many products in three days with one self-managed team as a whole assembly line used to produce in 14 days. In 1994, about half of America's corporations were experimenting with self-managed teams, which were expected to be *the* productivity breakthrough of the 1990s.[4] Even small companies like Cavalier Gage & Electronics have had great success with such teams. (See the Profile at the start of this chapter.) Although more and more companies are adopting the team concepts, the total number of workers involved is only 10 percent of the workers.[5] It's estimated that teams will be the foundation for organizations for the next 50 years.[6] The box Reaching Beyond Our Borders illustrates how one such firm in Denmark has applied the concepts.

LIMITATIONS OF CROSS-FUNCTIONAL TEAMS   Setting up cross-functional teams isn't easy. Often managers of functional areas will resist the move toward teams. Furthermore, team members are often unsure of what their duties are, how they'll be compensated, and who's responsible if mistakes are made. Working on a team takes different skills from working alone. Therefore, additional training is needed to prepare workers for teamwork.[7] The change to such teams is often so disruptive that a company may falter for years while the changes are being made. That has been the case at IBM, for example.

The most common problem with teams is that companies rush out and form the wrong kind of team for the wrong kind of job. Figure 8.6 illustrates five different types of teams. Sometimes teams can be overused. Cross-functional teams aren't the answer to every management problem. Some problems can be solved faster by a single person. For example, making creative types sit in a team meeting waiting to reach a consensus can stifle creativity.

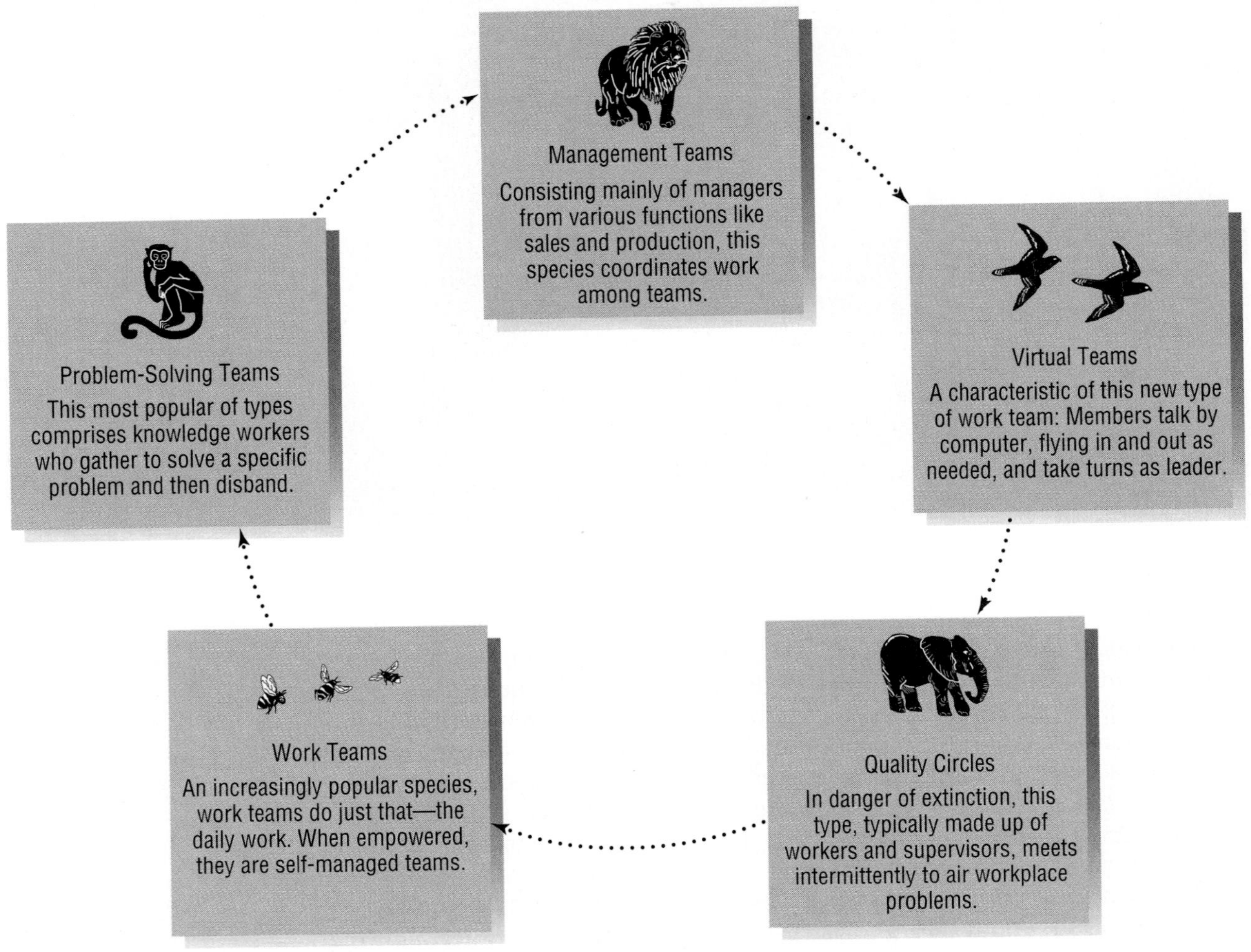

Management Teams
Consisting mainly of managers from various functions like sales and production, this species coordinates work among teams.

Problem-Solving Teams
This most popular of types comprises knowledge workers who gather to solve a specific problem and then disband.

Virtual Teams
A characteristic of this new type of work team: Members talk by computer, flying in and out as needed, and take turns as leader.

Work Teams
An increasingly popular species, work teams do just that—the daily work. When empowered, they are self-managed teams.

Quality Circles
In danger of extinction, this type, typically made up of workers and supervisors, meets intermittently to air workplace problems.

Source: Brian Dumaine, "The Trouble With Teams," *Fortune*, September 5, 1994, pp. 86–92.

〈〈 **FIGURE 8.6** 〉〉

CROSS-FUNCTIONAL TEAMS LEAD TO NETWORKING Cross-functional teams work best when the "voice of the customer" is brought into organizations. That's why it's a good idea to include customers on cross-functional product development teams. To ensure that suppliers and distributors are part of the process, they should be included on the team as well. Now you have cross-functional teams that cross organizational boundaries.

Some of those suppliers and distributors may be in other countries. Thus, cross-functional teams may cross national boundaries. Such teams may share market information with teams from other countries. The government may encourage this networking of teams, and government coordinators may assist such projects. In that case, cross-functional teams break the barriers between government and business. **Networking**, in this context, means the linking of organizations with communications technology and other means to work together on common objectives. The Japanese term for networking major enterprises is *keiretsu*.[8]

The net result of cross-functional teams, therefore, is that organizational design has now expanded way beyond the design of a single firm. It has become the design of an integrated system of firms that all work together to satisfy the wants and needs of customers and other stakeholders of the *system*.[9] Imagine, for example, a piece of hockey equipment designed in Scandinavia, engineered in the United States to meet the needs of the Canadian market,

networking
Linking organizations with communications technology in order for them to work together on common objectives.

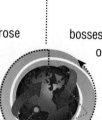

Reaching Beyond Our Borders

Self-Managed Teams Overseas

Oticon A/S is an 80-year-old Danish hearing aid manufacturer. Few companies in the world were more conservative and bureaucratic than Oticon. The organization structure wasn't working well, however, and in 1987 the company lost half of its equity. Something had to be done. The company decided to completely overhaul its organization structure. As a consequence, profits rose sixfold and are still growing. Employee satisfaction is at an all-time high even though 15 percent of the staff had to be let go. Oticon's reorganization will give you some feel for the radical changes now occurring in organizations.

Workers at Oticon no longer have a job; instead they have a portfolio of jobs that they choose for themselves. For example, a woman in accounting serves as the company's contact for all Spanish-language calls. Between calls, she does her accounting work. An engineer may sign up to write the company's newsletter or help with the marketing plan. The idea is to fit the work to the people rather than fit the people to the work. Employees set their own hours and vacations. Everyone knows how the company's projects are doing and what the financial results are. If something needs to be done, anyone can volunteer to do it. There's no hierarchy.

All titles have been eliminated so there are no bosses or managers, but there are leaders. Employees are organized into highly flexible project teams. Chaos is prevented by a high level of communication. Everyone knows the strategies and policies of the firm. Project leaders keep the self-managed teams coordinated and a leadership group decides which projects to follow. Project leaders also set salaries.

As a result of cross-functional, self-managed work teams and open communication, time to market for new products has been cut in half. Oticon, in other words, has taken a lead in designing a nonbureaucratic office.

Source: Gifford Pinchot and Elizabeth Pinchot, *The End of Bureaucracy & the Rise of the Intelligent Organization* (San Francisco: Berrett-Koehler, 1993).

---

manufactured in Korea, and distributed in a global market with initial distribution from Japan. Such linked organizations are what's happening today.[10] As such systems become global «·· P.99 ·», the orientation of managers becomes global as well, and barriers between cooperating countries become weaker.

- Can you cite the advantages and disadvantages of line, line and staff, matrix, and cross-functional organizational forms?
- Why do cross-functional teams often lead to networking?

PROGRESS CHECK

THE RESTRUCTURING PROCESS AND TOTAL QUALITY

It's not easy to move from an organization dominated by managers to one that relies heavily on self-managed teams. How you restructure an organization depends on the status of the present system. If the system already has a customer focus, but isn't working well, a total quality management approach may work.

Total quality management (TQM) is the practice of striving for maximum internal and external customer satisfaction by developing and providing them with high-quality, high-value, want-satisfying goods, services, and ideas. Total quality management calls for *continuous improvement* of *present processes. Processes* are sets of activities strung together for a reason, such as the process for handling a customer's order. **Continuous improvement** means constantly improving the way the organization does things so that customer needs can be better satisfied.

total quality management (TQM)
Satisfying customers by building in and ensuring quality from all departments in an organization.

continuous improvement
Procedures designed to insure and inspire constant creative interaction and problem solving.

SPOTLIGHT ON SMALL BUSINESS

Networking to Win

Networking helps organizations, large and small, to compete in global markets. Beginning in 1989, for example, 3,500 small Danish firms organized into networks, small groups of businesses that work together. In less than two years, they made a substantial contribution to completely reversing a three-decade–long deficit in the country's trade exports. Networking thus creates jobs. CD (Corporate Design) Line is one of the Danish success stories. A network of 14 textile firms produces part of a complete collection: shirts, suits, skirts, women's knitwear, ties, scarves, and more. Marketing the entire collection together benefits all the firms. Together they hire a quality manager and set up salespeople in their best foreign markets: Sweden and Germany. They jointly contract with famous designers. They even share an electronic data interchange network on a cost-sharing basis.

Together, this network can now compete with large companies. Smaller organizations use networking to purchase cooperatively, to market jointly, to combine research and development, to establish quality programs, to share in distribution research and costs, and more.

Source: Jessica Lipnack and Jeffrey Stamps, The TeamNet Factor (Essex Junction, Vt.: Oliver Wight Publications, 1993).

It's possible, in an organization with few layers of management and a customer focus, that new computer software and employee training could lead to a team-oriented approach with few problems. In old, bureaucratic organizations with many layers of management, however, the total quality approach to change will simply not work. Continuous improvement doesn't work when the whole process is being done incorrectly. When an organization needs dramatic changes, only reengineering will do. **Reengineering** is the fundamental rethinking and radical redesign of organizational processes to achieve dramatic improvements in critical measures of performance. Note the words *radical redesign* and *dramatic improvements*.[11]

At IBM credit corporation, for example, the process for handling a customer's request for credit went through a five-step process that took an average of six days. By completely reengineering the customer-request *process*, IBM credit cut its processing time from six *days* to four *hours*! When you reengineer a process, jobs evolve from narrow and task-oriented to multidimensional. Employees who once did as they were told now make decisions on their own.[12] Functional departments lose their reason for being. Managers stop acting like supervisors and instead behave like coaches. Workers focus more on the customers' needs and less on their bosses'. Attitudes and values change in response to new incentives. Practically every aspect of the organization is transformed, often beyond recognition. Because of the complexity of the process, many reengineering efforts fail.[13]

reengineering
The rethinking and radical redesign of organizational processes to achieve dramatic improvements in critical measures of performance.

CRITICAL THINKING

Given the dramatic changes that occur when companies adopt cross-functional, self-managed teams, what would prevent the majority of companies from adopting such an organization structure? Given the flexibility and high education requirements of empowered employees, what changes must occur in U.S. schools to prepare students for such jobs?

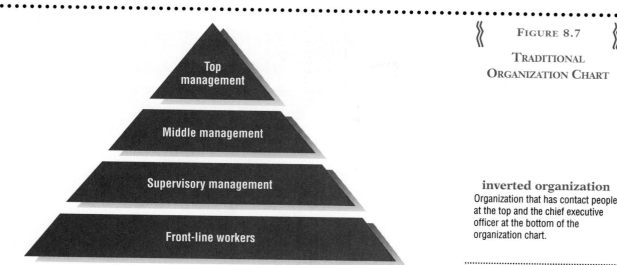

FIGURE 8.7

TRADITIONAL
ORGANIZATION CHART

inverted organization
Organization that has contact people at the top and the chief executive officer at the bottom of the organization chart.

... TURNING THE ORGANIZATION UPSIDE ... DOWN TO EMPOWER EMPLOYEES

Many firms are discovering that the key to long-term success in a competitive market is to empower front-line people (often in teams) to respond quickly to customer wants and needs. That means major restructuring of the firm to make front-line workers the most important people in the firm. For example, doctors have long been treated as the most important people in hospitals, pilots are the focus of airlines, and professors are the central focus of universities. However, front-desk people in hotels, clerks in department stores, and tellers in banks haven't been considered key personnel in the past. Instead, managers were considered the key people, and they were responsible for "managing" the front-line people. The organization chart in a typical firm, therefore, looked something like Figure 8.7's pyramid.

The most advanced service organizations have turned the traditional organization structure upside down. These **inverted organizations** have contact people at the top and the chief executive officer at the bottom. There are few layers of management, and their job is to assist and support front-line people, not boss them around. Figure 8.8 shows the new inverted organization structure.

A good example of an inverted organization is NovaCare, a provider of rehabilitation care. At its top are some 3,500 physical, occupational, and speech therapists. The rest of the organization is structured to serve those therapists. Managers consider the therapists as their bosses, and the manager's job is to support them by arranging contacts with nursing homes, handling accounting and credit activities, and providing training for the therapists.

Companies based on this organization structure support front-line personnel with internal and external databanks, advanced communication systems, and professional assistance. Naturally, this means that front-line people have to be better educated, better trained, and better paid than in the past. It takes a lot of trust for top managers to implement such a system—but when they do, the payoff for

Working in an inverted organization such as Avis is much different from working in a firm with a more traditional structure. As a front-line person, you are treated with the utmost respect and typically receive or have the potential for more pay. You are also given more training and responsibility and are expected to do more. These factors make the job more exciting and motivating. On the other hand, managers have less authority. From your perspective, which would be the better postion, manager or front-line worker?

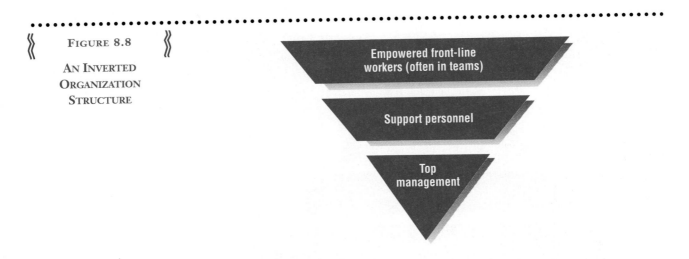

FIGURE 8.8

AN INVERTED ORGANIZATION STRUCTURE

customers and profits is often well worth the effort.[14] In the past, managers controlled information, and that gave them power. In more progressive organizations, everyone shares information and that gives everyone power.

... TURNING THE ORGANIZATION ... INSIDE OUT (OUTSOURCING)

In the past, organizations have tried to do everything themselves. That is, each organization had a separate department for accounting, finance, marketing, production, and so on. Today's organizations are turning inside out. Total quality demands that organizations benchmark each function against the best in the world. **Competitive benchmarking** is rating an organization's practices, processes, and products against the world's best.

    If the organization can't do as well as the best, the idea is to outsource the function to an organization that *is* the best. **Outsourcing** is assigning various functions, such as accounting and legal work, to outside organizations. Some functions, such as information management and marketing, may be too important to assign to outside firms. In that case, the organization should benchmark on the best firms and reengineer their departments to try to be equally good.

    When a firm has completed its outsourcing process, the remaining functions are the firm's core competency. **Core competencies** are those functions that the organization can do as well as or better than anyone else in the world. Gallo Winery, for example, doesn't grow most of its own grapes. Instead, it sticks to what it does best: producing and marketing (including distributing) wine products. Gallo spends more money on market research than its primary competitors and thus knows more about the market for wines. It also has the most up-to-date information and distribution system. Gallo isn't as skilled in retailing and promotion, so it outsources those functions.

CREATING INTERNAL CUSTOMERS   Some departments in organizations are reluctant to join the total quality revolution. They would rather function "the old way" where each department had its own agenda and method of operating. Executives who believe in total quality have a way of transforming such departments. They create internal customers within the firm. To improve such internal services, management sets up buy–sell relationships among teams and business units in the organization. If the team isn't happy with the products and services provided by an *internal* unit, the team can purchase those services from *outside vendors*.[15] This creates a competitive situation

competitive benchmarking
Rating an organization's practices, processes, and products against the world's best.

outsourcing
Assigning various functions, such as accounting and legal work, to outside organizations.

core competencies
Functions that the organization can do as well as or better than anyone else in the world.

BUREAUCRATIC	CUSTOMER-FOCUSED
Coordination from the top	Self-management
Top-down chain of command	Bottom-up power relationships
Many rules and regulations	Employees free to make decisions
Departmentalization by function	Cross-functional teams
Specialization	Integration and cooperation
One firm does it all	Outsourcing
Management controls information	Information goes to all
Largely domestic orientation	Global orientation
Focus on external customers	Focus on both internal and external customers

FIGURE 8.9

BUREAUCRATIC VERSUS CUSTOMER-FOCUSED ORGANIZATIONAL STRUCTURES

between, for example, the internal accounting department and outside public accounting firms. This competition forces internal units to become more internally customer oriented or lose their business to outsiders.

Clark Equipment (the South Bend, Indiana, construction equipment maker) began such a program in 1982 when it learned that the quality of its internal components (transmissions, axles, and the like) was uncompetitive. Clark's management subjected every unit to outside competition—make world-class products or else. To keep their jobs, the production department cut workers, invested in state-of-the-art equipment, and instituted new quality controls. Clark's revenues, profits, and stock price soared as a result. Figure 8.9 summarizes the changes that occur as an organization moves from being bureaucratic to being customer-oriented.

ORGANIZATIONAL SERVICE-ORIENTED CULTURE

Any organizational change is bound to cause some stress and resistance among members of the firm. Therefore, any change should be accompanied by the establishment of an organizational culture that facilitates such change.[16] **Organizational culture** may be defined as widely shared values within an organization that provide coherence and cooperation to achieve common goals. Usually the culture of an organization is reflected in stories, traditions, and myths.

Anyone who has been to Disneyland or Disney World can't fail to be impressed by the obvious values instilled by Walt Disney that permeate the organization. One may have heard about or read about the focus on cleanliness, helpfulness, and friendliness, but such stories can't prepare you for the near-perfect implementation of those values at the parks.

It's also obvious from visiting any McDonald's restaurant that every effort has been made to maintain a culture that emphasizes "quality, service, cleanliness, and value." Each restaurant has the same "feel," the same "look," and the same "atmosphere." In short, each has a similar organizational culture.

Disney and McDonald's are two examples of favorable organizational cultures that lead to successful operations. But an organizational culture can also be negative. Have you ever been in an organization where you feel that no one cares about service or quality? The clerks may seem uniformly glum, indifferent, and testy. The mood often seems to pervade the atmosphere so

organizational culture
Widely shared values within an organization that provide coherence and cooperation to achieve common goals.

Making Ethical Decisions

Restructuring Responsibility

One consequence of restructuring organizations in the United States is that many people are being fired. GE alone laid off 100,000 workers, and GM laid off 74,000 workers over a space of a few years. Other large firms are making similar cuts in both workers and managers.

Some firms are restructuring and outsourcing, but top management has a commitment to make such changes as nonthreatening to employees as possible. Such companies minimize layoffs by reassignment, normal attrition through retirement, early retirement, and retraining.

Many American firms must restructure to be more competitive with foreign producers, but it isn't necessary to fire workers and managers whenever they don't live up to your expectations and then bring in new ones. That can lower morale and create stress and fear in the organization.

What's the moral and ethical thing for a top executive to do when faced with the prospect of firing workers? Do top managers have a greater responsibility to stockholders or to employees? What if the two interests conflict? Should a firm not restructure if it results in massive layoffs? What would be the long-run benefits and drawbacks if all firms restrustured?

that patrons become moody and upset. You know the feeling. It gets so that one can hardly believe that an organization can be run so badly and survive, especially a profit-making organization. Are there examples in your area?

Managers who move to another corporation sometimes find that their old management styles don't fit the corporate culture of the new company. For example, when Richard Snyder, the extravagant head of the Simon & Schuster publishing firm, joined the Viacom team, he found that his free-spending ways represented a fundamental clash of values with Viacom owner Sumner Redstone. Snyder's limo bills riled Redstone, who still lives in a modest home and buys suits off the rack. Viacom is proud of its freewheeling culture that produces MTV and "Beavis and Butt-head." Snyder, on the other hand, demanded so much control that people in his company were often afraid to express their opinions and be creative. He was forced to leave the company in 1994.[17]

The organizational culture at Disney is a model for other firms. Talk with a Disney worker sometime and you are likely to see someone who is excited about their work and finds it enjoyable. That same atmosphere can be created in other companies. However, creating such an atmosphere takes time and requires a strong, long-term commitment from management.

But the productivity increases and satisfaction that result are worth the effort. What are some things managers can do to make work more pleasurable and exciting?

The very best organizations have cultures that emphasize service to others, especially customers. The atmosphere is one of friendly, concerned, caring people who enjoy working together to provide a good product at a reasonable price. Those companies that have such cultures have less need for close supervision of employees, not to mention policy manuals, organization charts, and formal rules, procedures, and controls.

Good organizational leaders create a culture that emphasizes cooperation and joy in serving customers, and that culture results in self-motivated employees who need minimal supervision. Within that atmosphere, self-managed teams can develop and flourish. The key to productive culture is mutual trust. You get it by giving it. The very best companies stress high moral and ethical values such as honesty, reliability, fairness, environmental protection, and social involvement.

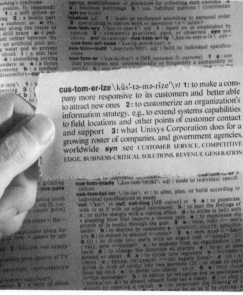
This ad for Unisys says it all. To "customerize" means a shift in a company's goals to become more responsive to its customers and, therefore, better able to attract and retain them. Getting close to customers calls for gathering more information about them. Unisys is an example of a company that designs programs and systems to assist in gathering and using customer information to gain competitive advantage.

Thus far, we've been talking as if organizational matters were mostly controllable by management. The fact is that the formal organization structure is just one element of the total organizational system. To create organizational culture, the informal organization is of equal or greater importance. Let's explore this notion next.

··· THE INFORMAL ORGANIZATION HELPS ···
CREATE TEAMWORK

All organizations have two organizational systems. One is the formal organization. It's the official system that details each person's responsibility, authority, and position. Formal organization is used for baseball teams and for companies. But there's also an informal organization. It consists of the various cliques, relationships, and lines of authority that develop outside the formal organization. The basic ideas, therefore, are these:

The **formal organization** is the structure that details lines of responsibility, authority, and position. It's the structure shown on organization charts. The **informal organization** is the system of relationships that develop spontaneously as employees meet and form power centers. It's the human side of the organization that doesn't show on any organization chart.

No organization can operate effectively without both types of organization. The formal system is often too slow and bureaucratic to enable the organization to adapt quickly. However, the formal organization does provide helpful guidelines and lines of authority to follow in routine situations.

The informal organization is often too unstructured and emotional to allow careful, reasoned decision making on critical matters. It's extremely effective, however, in generating creative solutions to short-term problems and providing a feeling of camaraderie and teamwork among employees.

In any organization, it's wise to learn quickly who the important people are in the informal organization. Typically, there are rules and procedures to follow for getting certain supplies or equipment, but those procedures may take days. Who in the organization knows how to obtain these items immediately without following the normal procedures? Which secretaries should you see if you want your work given first priority? These are the questions you need to answer in order to work effectively in many organizations.

The informal organization's nerve center is the grapevine (the system through which unofficial information flows between and among managers and employees). It consists of rumors, facts, suspicions, accusations, and all kinds of accurate and inaccurate information. The key people in the information system usually have the most influence in the organization.

In the old "us-versus-them" system of organizations, where managers and employees were often at odds, the informal system often hindered effective management. In the new, more open organizations, where managers and employees work together to set objectives and design procedures, the informal organization can be an invaluable managerial asset that often promotes harmony among workers and establishes the corporate culture. That's a major advantage, for example, of self-managed teams. Two of the more important aspects of the informal organization are group norms and group cohesiveness.

1. *Group norms.* Group norms are the informal rules and procedures that guide group members' behavior. They include often unspoken but very clear guidelines regarding things like proper dress, language, work habits (e.g., how fast one works, how many breaks one takes,

---

formal organization
The structure that details lines of responsibility, authority, and position. It is the structure that is shown on organizational charts.

informal organization
The system of relationships and lines of authority that develops spontaneously as employees meet and form power centers. It is the human side of the organization and does not show on any formal charts.

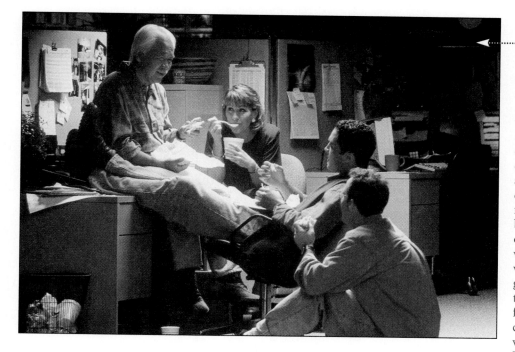

An organization can either work together like a successful sports team or fight each other like unruly children. The secret to creating a powerful team is to celebrate diversity « P.42 » and bring out the best in different people. That means successfully blending younger and older workers, men and women, and people from various ethnic backgrounds. You see such teamwork on the football field and the basketball court. In the future, you will see equal dedication, hard work, and teamwork in businesses of all sizes. What is it that successfully converts a group of individuals into a winning team? Could these same factors be used in all organizations? Government agencies?

who one turns to for assistance), and social behavior (where one goes for recreation, with whom, how often, and more). Deviants from the norm are often verbally abused, isolated, or harassed.

2. *Group cohesiveness*. Often a work group will develop alliances and commitments over time that tie them together strongly. The term used to describe such feelings of group loyalty is *cohesiveness*. Historically, unions have been a strong cohesive force as workers united to fight management. The goal today is to generate such cohesiveness among all corporate employees to create excellence in all phases of operation. For such cohesiveness to develop, employees must feel that they're part of a total corporate team. Often, the informal network created by corporate athletic teams, unions, and other such affiliations can help to create teamwork and cooperation. In summary, the informal organization of a firm can strongly reinforce a feeling of teamwork and cooperation or can effectively prevent any such unity; managers who maintain open, honest communication with employees can create an informal atmosphere that promotes willing commitment and group cohesiveness.

As effective as the informal organization may be in creating group cooperation, it can be equally powerful in resisting management directives. Employees may form unions, go on strike together, and generally disrupt operations. Learning to create the right corporate culture and to work within the informal organization is a key to managerial success.

- What's the difference between continuous improvement and reengineering?
- What does it mean to turn an organization chart upside down? Inside out?
- What's an internal customer?
- How important is the informal organization to the success of organizational change?

PROGRESS CHECK

SUMMARY

1. Describe the traditional hierarchical, bureaucratic organization structure and how it is being restructured.

1. Organizational design is the coordinating of workers so that they can best accomplish all the firm's goals.

● *What's the traditional organization structure and how is it being restructured?*
The typical organization is hierarchical and bureaucratic. Restructuring means redesigning an organization so that it can more effectively and efficiently service customers. Often that means breaking down the barriers between functions. It may also mean giving more authority to lower-level employees and ending top-down management.

2. Explain the organizational theories of Fayol and Weber.

2. Economy of scale means that the larger the plant, the more efficient it can be because all the employees can specialize in a function that they can do efficiently.

● *What concepts did Fayol and Weber contribute?*
Fayol introduced "principles" such as unity of command, hierarchy of authority, division of labor, subordination of individual interests to the general interest, authority, clear communication channels, order, and equity. Weber added principles of bureaucracy such as job descriptions, written rules and decision guidelines, consistent procedures, and staffing and promotions based on qualifications.

3. Discuss the various issues connected with organizational design.

3. Organizational issues that have led to design changes include (1) tall versus flat organization structures, (2) span of control, (3) departmentalization, and (4) centralization versus decentralization.

● *What are the major issues of each?*
The issue of tall organizations is that they slow communications. The trend is to eliminate managers and flatten organizations. The span of control is getting larger as employees are becoming self-directed. Departments are often being replaced or supplemented by matrix organizations and cross-functional teams. In matrix organizations, people can be borrowed from departments to be put on project teams. Cross-functional teams have been very effective in making organizations faster and more responsive to the market. They've also led to decentralization of authority.

4. Describe the differences between line, line and staff, matrix, and cross-functional organizations.

4. The four forms of organization explored in the text are (1) line organizations, (2) line and staff organizations, (3) matrix–style organizations, and (4) cross-functional, self-managed teams.

● *What are the advantages of each?*
A line organization has the advantages of having clearly defined responsibility and authority, of being easy to understand, and of providing one supervisor for each person. Most organizations have benefited from the expert advice of staff assistants in areas such as safety, quality control, computer technology, human resource management, and investing. Matrix organizations give flexibility to managers in assigning people to projects and encourage interorganizational cooperation and teamwork. Cross-functional, self-managed teams are more permanent and have all the benefits of the matrix style.

5. Explain the benefits of turning organizations upside down and inside out.

5. Reengineering is the fundamental rethinking and radical redesign of organizational processes to improve critical measures of performance.

● *What are the benefits of turning organizations upside down and inside out?*
By turning organizations upside down, more authority and responsibility are given front-line workers so they can better serve customers. Managers serve workers instead of the other way around. Outsourcing is assigning various functions, such as accounting and legal work, to outside organi-

zations. By setting up competition between internal and external functions, a corporation can become world class.

6. Organizational culture may be defined as widely shared values within an organization that provide coherence and cooperation to achieve common goals.

   • *How can organizational culture and the informal organization hinder or assist organizational change?*

   The very best organizations have cultures that emphasize service to others, especially customers. The atmosphere is one of friendly, concerned, caring people who enjoy working together to provide a good product at a reasonable price. Companies with such cultures have less need for close supervision of employees; policy manuals; organization charts; and formal rules, procedures, and controls. This opens the way for self-managed teams.

6. Give examples to show how organizational culture and the informal organization can hinder or assist organizational change.

KEY TERMS
••••••

bureaucracy 244
centralized authority 253
competitive benchmarking 262
continuous improvement 259
core competencies 262
cross-functional teams 256
decentralized authority 253

departmentalization 250
formal organization 266
hierarchy 244
informal organization 266
inverted organization 261
line personnel 254
matrix organization 255
networking 258

organizational culture 263
organizational design 244
outsourcing 262
reengineering 260
restructuring 245
span of control 249
staff personnel 254
total quality management (TQM) 259

DEVELOPING WORKPLACE SKILLS
•••••••

1. There is no way to better understand the effects of having 10 layers of management on communication accuracy than to play the game of Message Relay. Take 10 members of the class and have them line up from 1 to 10. Have the first person read the following story and whisper it to number 2, who whispers it to number 3, and so on. Have number 10 tell the story out loud and compare it to the original. The distortions and mistakes in the story are often quite humorous, but they are not so funny in organizations such as Ford, which had 22 layers of management.

   Here's the story:

   Dealers in the Midwest region have received over 130 complaints about steering on the new Commander and Roadhandler models of our minivans. Apparently, the front suspension system is weak and the ball joints are wearing too fast. This causes slippage in the linkage and results in oversteering. Mr. Berenstein has been notified, but so far only 213 out of 4,300 dealers have received repair kits.

2. You are probably familiar with the informal network of communication in schools, communities, and various organizations. Assume you work in a large company with several such networks. Draft a memo to the manager of your division making suggestions as to how management could use the power of these groups to increase productivity and meet the needs of workers at the same time.

3. Imagine you are working for Kitchen Magic, an appliance manufacturer that produces, among other things, dishwashers for the home. Imagine

further that a competitor introduces a new dishwasher that uses sound waves to clean dishes. The result is a dishwasher that cleans even the worst burnt-on food and sterilizes the dishes and silverware as well. You need to develop a similar offering fast or lose the market. Write a memo to management outlining the problem and explaining your rationale for recommending use of a cross-functional team to respond quickly.

4. If you were free to start over, how would you organize your college or university? Would you have the same departments? What kind of staff people would you hire? Compose two lists, one explaining why the school should reorganize and the other why they might oppose restructuring. Discuss this issue with the class.

5. As discussed in this chapter, many of the work groups of the future, including management, will be cross-functional and self-managed. To practice working in such a group, break your class up into groups of five or so students (try to find students with different backgrounds and interests) and work together to prepare a report on the advantages and disadvantages of working in teams. Many of the problems and advantages should emerge in your group as you try to complete this assignment.

· ·

PRACTICING MANAGEMENT DECISIONS

CASE   CREATING CROSS-FUNCTIONAL TEAMS IN SERVICE ORGANIZATIONS

The Direct Response Group (DRG) at Capital Holding is a direct marketer of life, health, property, and casualty insurance. In the past, it sold a mass-produced product to a mass market. Over time, however, sales slowed, profits eroded, and the company decided it had to refocus its efforts. That meant, for one thing, selling to particular, identifiable customers and giving those customers a customized product/service package that was world class, enabling the company to compete globally.

Organizational change began with a vision statement that emphasized caring, listening to, and satisfying customers—one on one. To accomplish that goal, the company formed a cross-functional team to study the sales, service, and marketing *processes* and completely redesign those functional areas. The idea was to have a world-class customer-driven company. That meant gathering as much information as possible about customers.

Front-line customer-contact people were empowered with user-friendly information systems that made it possible for one contact person, working with a support team, to handle any question that customers had. Management used external databases to get detailed information on some 15 million consumers. The combined internal and external databases were used to develop custom-made products for specific customer groups.

The whole company was focused on satisfying customer wants and needs. That meant changing *processes* within the firm so that they were geared toward the customer. For example, one case worker is now attached to each customer, and that case worker is responsible for following an application through the entire approval and product design process. Previously, many people handled the application and no one person was responsible for it.

An analysis of the corporate culture showed that people were more concerned with pleasing their bosses than pleasing the customer. People hoarded information instead of sharing information because the people with information had power. The information *system* had to be changed to encourage sharing.

A pilot program was started whereby a customer–management team was formed to serve 40,000 customers. The team consisted of 10 customer service representatives and their support team (a marketer, an expert in company operations, and an information systems person). Employees are now rewarded for performance, and merit raises are based on *team* performance to encourage team participation.

Decision Questions

1. Are traditional bureaucracies set up to provide custom-made products to individual consumers? Could they be, or is it always better to have customer-oriented teams design such products?

2. Anyone who has worked in team situations has discovered that some members of the team work harder than others; nonetheless, the whole team is often rewarded based on the overall results, not individual effort. How could team evaluations be made so that individual efforts could be recognized and rewarded?

3. What service organizations, private or public, would you like to see become more customer-oriented? How could this case be used as a model for that organization?

4. What are some major impediments to implementing customer-oriented teams in service organizations?

Source: Michael Hammer and James Champy, *Reengineering the Corporation* (New York: HarperCollins, 1993).

• •

VIDEO CASE   BIG APPLE BAGELS AND THE SAINT LOUIS BREAD COMPANY

In the past many businesses were organized according to concepts and structures learned from the military and the church. There were clear lines of authority and responsibility and people at the top made virtually all decisions. To maintain control over employees, certain bureaucratic rules and regulations were passed which didn't allow employees much flexibility in decision making or in responding to customer wants and needs.

Today's organizations, in order to remain competitive, are being restructured to be more responsive to customers. This means that many layers of management, especially those in the middle, are being eliminated (middle managers are now equated with bureaucracy). It also means that front-line workers are being empowered and challenged to respond to customer wants and needs quickly. The literature is full of stories about GM, Motorola, and other big companies and their reengineering processes. However, stories about smaller firms are less common.

Big Apple Bagels and the Saint Louis Bread Company are two examples of smaller organizations that have been restructured to meet the needs of today's marketplace. As Big Apple Bagels grew, it tried to maintain its open-door policy so that everyone could have access to top management. But the larger a firm becomes, the more difficult this is. As the firm grew larger, it decentralized authority allowing its stores to innovate by creating their own variety of bagels.

The Saint Louis Bread Company has had a similar experience. The process of radically changing organizational structure is called reengineering. At the Saint Louis Bread Company, that process called for the introduction of high technology for production processes and for gathering information on the latest advances and product features in cash registers.

The Saint Louis Bread Company is now striving to become boundaryless. This means that the divisions or boundaries between jobs and functions are being eliminated through the implementation of cross-functional self-managed teams. The focus is on the customer, and front-line workers are now empowered to be responsive to customers and give them what they want without resorting to the slow process of involving management.

Discussion Questions

1. Which of Fayol's principles of organization are still being maintained at Big Apple Bagels and the Saint Louis Bread Company and which are not being followed? Why?

2. Weber was the founder of concepts such as written rules, job descriptions, and consistent procedures. Why are these principles no longer as effective in meeting the needs of customers?

3. To what extent has information technology changed the way organizations can be and are structured?

CHAPTER 9

PRODUCING WORLD-CLASS PRODUCTS AND SERVICES

LEARNING GOALS

After you have read and studied this chapter, you should be able to

1. Describe the production process and explain the importance of productivity.

2. Explain the importance of site selection in keeping down costs and identify the criteria used to evaluate different sites.

3. Classify the various production processes and how materials requirement planning links organizations in performing those processes.

4. Describe manufacturing techniques such as just-in-time inventory control, flexible manufacturing, lean manufacturing, and competing in time.

5. Show how CAD/CAM improves the production process, but can lead to people problems on the plant floor.

6. Illustrate the use of PERT and Gantt charts in production planning.

7. Explain the importance of productivity in all sectors: manufacturing, service, and nonprofit.

THOMAS L. KASSOUF OF CARLYLE

America's manufacturing base was once anchored by large manufacturers like General Motors and Ford. But General Motors and almost all other large manufacturers are cutting back dramatically on the number of people they employ. On the surface, it looks like America is losing its manufacturing base.

Below the surface, however, you'll find a new manufacturing base being established by thousands of small and medium-sized manufacturing plants. For example, Eaton Corporation (a Cleveland-based auto parts maker) built a 120-employee plant in Hamilton, Indiana. Intel Corporation built a computer chip plant in Santa Clara, California, that created some 250 jobs. Thousands of other examples could be given of small, flexible plants that are changing the nature of manufacturing in the United States.

Thomas Kassouf is president of one of those flexible plants—the Carlyle Compressor Company (a division of the Carrier Corporation) in Arkadelphia, Arkansas. If you visited his plant, you'd see the new face of American manufacturing. The plant makes compressors for air conditioners. The first thing you'd notice is how clean and quiet the factory is. But many of the innovations aren't so apparent. The plant now has 450 workers, and they're very different from their counterparts in the past. For example, potential employees must take a state test. Only those scoring in the top third may advance. Their references are checked carefully to make sure that the candidates can work well with others and they're interviewed by fellow workers. Only 1 in 16 applicants is hired.

Those who get past the interviews must take a six-week course at night to learn blueprint reading, math (e.g., metric calculations), statistical process control methods, computer skills, and human relations skills. All this occurs before the person is hired. Kassouf is careful to hire top people because he then empowers those workers to make decisions on their own. For example, workers can install the machines and may determine their layout. Working in teams, employees are virtually self-managed. Men and women work side by side because the plant was designed so that no heavy lifting is involved.

Recognizing the benefits of such plants, the county underwrote the costs to build a sewer line to the industrial park where Carlyle is located. The state gave the company tax breaks. The plant is competitive with the best in the world because it practices the latest in total quality concepts «·· P.259 ··». In this chapter you'll learn more about these concepts plus the other strategies U.S. businesses must adopt if they wish to remain competitive in world markets.

> *If you're not better than the best on a worldwide basis, you're not going to make a living.*
>
> *Jack Welch of GE*

AMERICA'S MANUFACTURING BASE

The heart of the free enterprise system in the United States has always been its manufacturers. Names such as General Electric, USX (formerly U.S. Steel), Westinghouse, and Navistar (formerly International Harvester) have represented the finest in production technology since the turn of the century. But, as you read in the Profile, we're in a new era in the industrial evolution. Today, manufacturing produces less than one fourth of the U.S. gross domestic product (the total output of goods and services) ◀┈ P.72 ┈▶.

Bethlehem Steel and other traditional manufacturing leaders declined through much of the past 20 years. Foreign manufacturers captured huge chunks of the market for basic products such as steel, cement, machinery, and farm equipment. That competition forced U.S. companies to greatly alter their production techniques and managerial styles. You read about the managerial changes in Chapter 7. In this chapter, we'll explore the changes that have occurred in production. Many U.S. firms are now as good or better than competitors anywhere in the world. What have American manufacturers done to regain a competitive edge? They've implemented all of the following:

1. A customer focus.
2. Cost savings through site selection.
3. A faster response to the market through flexible manufacturing.
4. More savings on the plant floor through lean manufacturing.
5. Computer-aided manufacturing and other modern practices.
6. Total quality management.
7. Better control procedures.

We'll discuss these developments in detail in this chapter. You'll see that production and operations management have become challenging and vital elements of American business. The rebuilding of America's manufacturing base will likely remain a major business issue in the near future. There will be debates about the merits of moving production facilities to foreign countries. Serious questions will be raised about replacing workers with robots and other machinery. Major political decisions will be made regarding protection of American manufacturers through quotas and other restrictions of free trade. Regardless of how these issues are decided, however, tomorrow's college graduates will face tremendous challenges (and career opportunities) in redesigning and rebuilding America's manufacturing base.

••• PRODUCTION MANAGEMENT •••

production and operations management
Activities managers do to create goods and services.

One purpose of this chapter is to introduce the basic concepts and issues in production management. **Production and operations management** is all the activities managers do to create goods and services. In today's firms, most of what gets done actually falls into the service category. For example, a very small percentage of the people working for manufacturers are actually on the assembly line. The rest do service work such as accounting, finance, legal

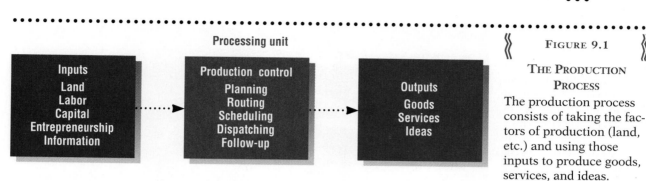

FIGURE 9.1

THE PRODUCTION
PROCESS
The production process
consists of taking the factors of production (land,
etc.) and using those
inputs to produce goods,
services, and ideas.
Planning, routing, sched-
uling, and the other activities are the means to
accomplish the objec-
tive—output.

advice, and so on.[1] Therefore, the concepts that apply to service organizations apply almost entirely to manufacturing organizations.

New production techniques make it possible to virtually custom-make products for individual industrial buyers. The job then becomes one of getting closer to customers to find out what their product needs are. What the future is coming down to, in other words, is effective marketing combined with effective production and management to make U.S. producers number one in the world again.

The United States remains a major industrial country and is likely to become even stronger. This means tremendous opportunities for careers in production and operations management. Today there are relatively few college students majoring in production and operations management, inventory management, and other careers involving manufacturing and mining. That means more opportunities for those student entrepreneurs who can see the future trends and have the skills (such as computer literacy) to own or work in tomorrow's highly automated, efficient factories and mines. The profile at the start of this chapter dramatically illustrated the fact that unskilled workers will have fewer employment opportunities as new firms become automated. To prepare for a career in production and operations management, you must learn the basics of production. That's the subject of an entire course or courses, but in this chapter we'll simply review some of the fundamentals you should know.

••• FUNDAMENTALS OF PRODUCTION AND PRODUCTIVITY •••

Common sense and some experience have already taught you much of what you need to know about production and operations management. You know what it takes to build a model of an airplane or make a dress. You need a place to work, you need money to buy the materials, and you need to be organized to get the task done. The same is true of production. It uses basic inputs to produce outputs. (See Figure 9.1.) **Production**, then, is the creation of finished goods and services using the factors of production (inputs): land, labor, capital, entrepreneurship, and information. Production creates what is known as *form utility* (*utility* means value added). **Form utility** is the value added by the creation of finished goods and services using raw materials, components, and other inputs.

Production is a broad term that describes the creative process in all industries that produce goods and services, including mining, lumbering, manufacturing, education, and health care. Manufacturing is one part of production. It means making goods by hand or with machinery as opposed to extracting things from the earth (mining and fishing) or producing services.

To be competitive, manufacturers must keep the costs of *inputs* down. That is, the costs of workers, machinery, and so on must be kept as low as possible. Similarly, the amount of *output* must be relatively high. *Productivity* is the term used to describe output per worker. *Output* could mean goods like cars and

production
The creation of finished goods and services using the factors of production: land, labor, capital, entrepreneurship, and information.

form utility
The value added by the creation of finished goods and services using raw materials, components, and other inputs.

New machinery makes mass customization possible. Mass customization means tailoring products to meet the specifications of many different customers. The task involves using technology to gather necessary information and to design and customize each product. Today, with the use of machinery flexible enough to adjust to the unique needs of each order, customization is being achieved in many industries.

furniture, or services such as education and health care. In either case, the question is the same: How does a producer keep costs low and still produce more (that is, increase productivity)? This question will dominate thinking in the manufacturing and service sectors for years to come.

KEEPING COSTS LOW: SITE SELECTION

A major issue of the 1990s has been the shift of manufacturing and service organizations from one city or state to another in the United States or to foreign sites. Such shifts sometimes result in pockets of unemployment in some parts of the country and the world and lead to tremendous economic growth in others.

Why would entrepreneurs spend millions of dollars to move their facilities from one location to another? One major reason some businesses move is the availability of cheap labor or the right kind of skilled labor. Even though labor cost is becoming a smaller percentage of total cost in some highly automated industries, cheap labor remains a key reason many less technologically advanced producers move their plants. For example, cheap labor is one reason why some firms are moving to Malaysia, Mexico, and other countries with low wage rates.

The southern part of the United States has also attracted many manufacturers because the region has mostly nonunion labor. In general, such workers demand lower wages and fringe benefits. By moving south, U.S. businesses can compete more effectively with those foreign producers that have much lower labor costs.

Businesses are often called greedy and uncaring when they move production facilities. But the very survival of the U.S. manufacturing industry depends on its ability to remain competitive, and that means either cheaper inputs or increased outputs from present inputs (increased productivity).

Cheaper resources are another major reason for moving production facilities. Companies usually need water, electricity, wood, coal, and other basic resources. By moving to areas where such resources are cheap and plentiful,

The United States represents a large and stable market for many international firms. Foreign owned companies such as Mercedes-Benz are continuing to build production plants in the United States in order to be closer to U.S. customers. Also, by locating manufacturing facilities in this country they benefit from workers who can better understand the culture and the wants and needs of U.S. customers. Shipment is also easier and less expensive. Furthermore, the United States has some of the finest workers in the world. Do you think it equally wise or necessary for U.S. firms to have factories in other countries in order to get closer to those markets and to better understand international customers?

firms can significantly lower costs—not only the cost of buying such resources, but the cost of shipping as well. Water shortages in the West, for example, often discourage manufacturing plants from locating there.

Reducing time to market is a new hot concept. As manufacturers attempt to compete globally, they need sites that allow products to move through the system quickly, at the lowest costs, so that they can be delivered rapidly to customers. Information technology (IT) is such a key to quick response that many firms are seeking countries with the most advanced information systems.[2]

••• LOCATING CLOSE TO MARKETS TO SERVE CUSTOMERS BETTER •••

One reason businesses choose to remain in an area such as Chicago, New York, New Jersey, or California is because that's where their customers are. Much of the buying power of the United States is still centered in the Midwest, Northeast, and Far West (California). By locating close to their customers, businesses lower transportation costs and can be more responsive to customer needs for service. It's especially important for service organizations to be located in urban areas where they can serve their customers best.

Many businesses are building factories in foreign countries to get closer to their international customers. That's a major reason why Honda builds cars in Ohio. It's also the reason why Mercedes is building automobiles in Alabama. When U.S. firms select foreign sites, they consider whether they are near airports, waterways, and highways so that raw materials and finished goods can be moved quickly and easily. Businesses also study the quality of life for workers and managers.[3] Quality of life questions include: Are there good schools nearby? Is the weather nice? And, Is the crime rate low? Robert Wilkins, for example, moved his mail order computer company, Mac's Place, from Redmond, Washington, to northwest Montana to save money and to live within a 35-minute drive of skiing, fly fishing, river rafting, and the like.[4]

The bottom line is that site location has become a critical issue in production and operations management. Companies want to be close to their markets around the world, but also need a skilled or trainable labor supply.[5]

••• SITE SELECTION IN THE FUTURE •••

The cost of land is becoming a more critical factor in choosing a plant location. Some businesses are forced to leave cities such as New York, where land is expensive, and move to rural areas where land is much, much cheaper. Some employers also enjoy living away from the noise, pollution, and traffic

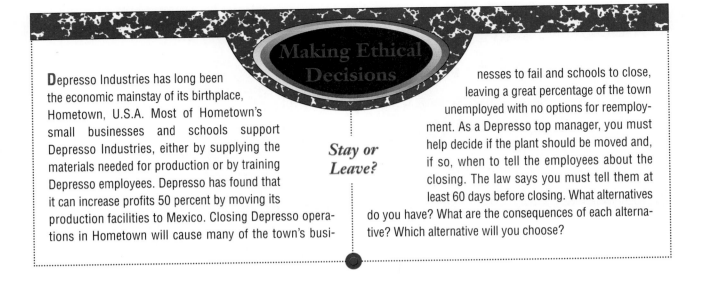

Making Ethical Decisions

Stay or Leave?

Depresso Industries has long been the economic mainstay of its birthplace, Hometown, U.S.A. Most of Hometown's small businesses and schools support Depresso Industries, either by supplying the materials needed for production or by training Depresso employees. Depresso has found that it can increase profits 50 percent by moving its production facilities to Mexico. Closing Depresso operations in Hometown will cause many of the town's busi- nesses to fail and schools to close, leaving a great percentage of the town unemployed with no options for reemploy- ment. As a Depresso top manager, you must help decide if the plant should be moved and, if so, when to tell the employees about the closing. The law says you must tell them at least 60 days before closing. What alternatives do you have? What are the consequences of each alterna- tive? Which alternative will you choose?

of big cities. New developments in information technology (computers, modems, e-mail, voice mail, teleconferencing, etc.) are enabling firms and employees even more flexibility in choosing locations while staying in the competitive mainstream.

Today, another big incentive to locate or relocate in a particular city or state is the tax situation and degree of government support. Some states and local governments have higher taxes than others yet many engage in fierce competition by giving tax reductions and other support, such as zoning changes and financial aid, so that businesses will locate there. In the bidding war to get the Mercedes plant, for example, North Carolina proposed building a $35 million training center at the company's plant to train auto workers. Alabama not only matched the offer, but paid employee salaries while they studied. Alabama also gave the company huge tax cuts and offered to buy more than 2,500 Mercedes for state use. In total, Alabama offered Mercedes $300 million in incentives. South Carolina won a BMW plant by offering the company some $130 million in incentives.

Some cities attract business by designing industrial parks.[6] An industrial park is a planned area where businesses can find land, shipping facilities, and waste disposal outlets so they can build a manufacturing plant or storage facility. In summary, then, businesses today are trying to cut production costs and improve lifestyles by locating their plants where

Resources are plentiful and inexpensive.

Skilled workers are available or are trainable.

Labor is relatively inexpensive.

Taxes are low and the local government offers support.

Energy and water are available.

Land is available, inexpensive, and close to markets.

Transportation costs are low.

Quality of life is high.

Quality of education is high.

Once a location is selected, production can begin. We'll go through the entire production process to see how it can be improved to become more competitive.

PRODUCTION PROCESSES

After a site is selected and a factory has been built, manufacturers begin the process of actually making products. There are several different processes manufacturers use. This material is probably new to you, so we'll use familiar examples to help you visualize these processes. Andrew S. Grove, chief executive officer of Intel, uses a great analogy to explain the production process:[7]

> *To understand the principles of production, imagine that you're a chef . . . and that your task is to serve a breakfast consisting of a three-minute soft-boiled egg, buttered toast, and coffee. Your job is to prepare and deliver the three items simultaneously, each of them fresh and hot.*

Grove goes on to say that the task here encompasses the three basic requirements of production: (1) to build and deliver products in response to the demands of the customer at a scheduled delivery time, (2) to provide an acceptable quality level, and (3) to provide everything at the lowest possible cost.

From the breakfast example, it's easy to understand two manufacturing processes: process and assembly. **Process manufacturing** physically or chemically changes materials. For example, boiling physically changes the egg. **Assembly processes** put together components (such as eggs, toast, and coffee—to make a breakfast). These two processes are called *synthetic systems*. **Synthetic systems** either change raw materials into other products (process manufacturing) or combine raw materials or parts into a finished product (assembly process).

The reverse of a synthetic system is called an *analytic system*. **Analytic systems** break down raw materials into components to extract other products. For example, crude oil can be reduced to gasoline, wax, and jet fuel. So, the production process will be either synthetic or analytic. In addition, production processes are either continuous or intermittent.

A *continuous process* is one in which long production runs turn out finished goods over time. In our diner, for example, you could have eggs on a conveyor belt that lowered them into boiling water for three minutes and then lifted them out on a continuous basis. A three-minute egg would be available whenever you wanted one. An automobile factory is run on a continuous process.

It usually makes more sense when responding to specific customer orders (job-order production) to use an *intermittent process*. This is an operation where the production run is short (one or two eggs) and the machines are changed frequently to produce different products (like the oven in a bakery or the toaster in the diner). Manufacturers of custom-designed furniture would use an intermittent process.

Today, most new manufacturers use intermittent processes. They use computers, robots, and flexible manufacturing processes that make it possible to make custom-made goods almost as fast as mass-produced goods were once made. We'll discuss how they do that in detail later in the chapter.

Managers use five indicators of whether they can meet their production goals on any given day:

1. *Sales forecast.* How many breakfasts should you plan to deliver?
2. *Raw material inventory.* Do you have enough eggs, bread, butter, and coffee on hand?
3. *Equipment.* Is everything ready to produce the breakfast?

process manufacturing
Production process which physically or chemically changes materials.

assembly process
Production process that puts together components.

synthetic systems
Production processes which either change raw materials into other products or combine raw materials or parts into finished products.

analytic systems
Manufacturing systems that break down raw materials into components to extract other products.

4. *Manpower*. Are there enough people available to make the forecasted number of breakfasts?

5. *Quality*. Are customers satisfied?

The production of breakfasts begins with the purchase of the needed food and equipment. The food and supplies must be stored in refrigerators and other storage equipment. One place we can look for production efficiency and savings, therefore, is in purchasing and storage.

... MATERIALS REQUIREMENT PLANNING: ... THE RIGHT PLACE AT THE RIGHT TIME

One thing for certain about the technological changes now taking place in manufacturing is that they've resulted in an entirely new terminology for production and operations management. Today's students need to be familiar with this terminology before they can discuss such advances in any depth.

One important term from the past is *materials requirement planning (MRP)*, a computer-based production and operations management system that uses sales forecasts to make sure that needed parts and materials are available at the right place and the right time. In our diner, for example, we could feed the sales forecast into the computer, which would specify how many of each ingredient to order and then print out the proper scheduling and routing sequence.

MRP was most popular with companies that made products with a lot of different parts. For example, Holly Carburetor used MRP to solve an inventory problem. Using MRP, the company cut inventory costs (e.g., storage, spoilage) from $30 million to $20 million, making it well worthwhile to invest $250,000 for the computer program.

MRP quickly led to MRP II. *MRP II* was an advanced version of MRP that allowed plants to include all the resources involved in the efficient making of a product, including projected sales, personnel, plant capacity, and distribution limitations. It was called *manufacturing resource planning* because the planning involved more than just materials.

The newest version of such systems is called *enterprise resource planning*. **Enterprise resource planning (ERP)** is a computer-based production and operations system that links multiple firms into one integrated production unit. The software enables the monitoring of quality and customer satisfaction as it's happening. ERP is much more sophisticated than MRP II because it monitors processes in multiple firms at the same time. For example, it monitors inventory at the supplier as well as at the manufacturing plant.

Eventually, such programs will link suppliers, manufacturers, and retailers in a completely integrated manufacturing and distribution system that will be constantly monitored for the smooth flow of goods from the time they're ordered to the time they reach the ultimate consumer. Companies now using such systems include Coors Ceramics (structural products), Phoenix Designs (office systems and furniture), and Red Devil (sealants, caulks, and hand tools).[8]

enterprise resource planning (ERP)
Computer-based production and operations system that links multiple firms into one, integrated production unit.

PROGRESS CHECK

- What is production?
- What are the major factors that determine where a plant locates?
- Can you explain the differences among the following production processes: process, assembly, analytic, continuous, and intermittent?
- What is enterprise resource planning?

MODERN PRODUCTION TECHNIQUES

The ultimate goal of manufacturing and process management is to provide high-quality goods and services instantaneously in response to customer demand. Traditional organizations were simply not designed to be so responsive to the customer. Rather, they were designed to make goods efficiently. The whole idea of mass production was to make a limited variety of products at very low cost. Low cost came at the expense of quality and flexibility. Furthermore, suppliers didn't always deliver when they said they would, so manufacturers had to carry large inventories of raw materials and components.

As a result of global competition, largely from Japan and Germany, companies today must make a wide variety of high-quality custom-designed products at very low cost. Clearly, something had to change on the production floor to make that possible. Also, something had to change in supplier–producer relationships. Five major developments have radically changed the production process in the United States: (1) just-in-time inventory control, (2) flexible manufacturing, (3) lean manufacturing, (4) mass customization, and (5) competing in time.

••• JUST-IN-TIME INVENTORY CONTROL •••

One major cost of production is holding parts, motors, and other items in warehouses. To cut such costs, the Japanese implemented a concept called *just-in-time (JIT) inventory control.* They learned the concept from U.S. quality consultants. The idea is to have suppliers deliver their products "just in time" to go on the assembly line. A minimum of inventory is kept on the premises. Some U.S. manufacturers have adopted the practice and are quite happy with the results.

Here's how it works: A manufacturer sets a production schedule using enterprise requirement planning (ERP) or one of the other systems just described, and determines what parts and supplies will be needed. It then informs its suppliers of what will be needed. The supplier must deliver the goods just in time to go on the assembly line. Naturally, this calls for more effort on the supplier's part (and more costs). Efficiency is maintained by having the supplier linked by computer to the producer so that the supplier becomes more like another department in the firm than a separate business. The supplier delivers its materials just in time to be used in the production process, so a bare minimum must be kept in storage just in case the delivery is held up for some reason.

The latest version of JIT is called JIT II. This system is designed to create more harmony and trust than was the case with JIT. There is much more sharing of information. In fact, an employee from the supplier may work full time at the buyer's plant handling the smooth flow of materials.[9]

You can imagine how the system would work in Andrew Grove's breakfast example. Rather than ordering enough eggs, butter, bread, and coffee for the week and storing it, the chef would have his suppliers deliver every morning. That way the food would be fresh and deliveries could be varied depending on customer demand. An employee from the supplier would be on hand at all times to ensure freshness.

At the Unisys plant in Flemington, New Jersey, about 200 deliveries arrive daily. The combination of just-in-time inventory management and a faster process time has allowed Unisys to pare inventories to a 1.3-month supply from a seven-month supply.

ERP and JIT systems make sure the right materials are at the right place at the right time at the cheapest cost to meet customer needs and production needs. That's the first step in modern production innovation. The next step in innovation is to change the production process itself. We'll discuss those changes next.

••• FLEXIBLE MANUFACTURING •••

When researchers from America visited the Toyota-Takaoka auto plant in Japan, they were stunned by the contrast they saw with the GM plant in Framingham, Massachusetts. The GM plant had wide aisles full of indirect workers; that is, workers on their way to relieve a fellow employee, workers en route to troubleshoot a problem, and so forth. These workers were adding no immediate value to the product whereas in Japan almost all workers were engaged in adding value to the auto. Furthermore, the Framingham plant had several weeks' worth of inventory piled around the plant. The Toyota plant had no more than an hour's worth of materials near the workstation and there was no warehouse to store surplus inventory.[10]

In addition to just-in-time inventory control, the Toyota plant practiced flexible manufacturing. **Flexible manufacturing** is the design of machines to do multiple tasks so that they can produce a variety of products. In other words, a few machines were used to produce a variety of cars.

Today, U.S. auto plants do flexible manufacturing as well.[11] Ford Motor Company, for example, uses flexible manufacturing at its Romeo, Michigan, plant. It designed V-8 and V-6 engines around a basic building block (a combustion chamber designed for maximum fuel economy). As many as six new V-8s and V-6s can be built from the same machinery.

Allen-Bradley uses flexible manufacturing to build motor starters. Orders come in daily and within 24 hours, 26 machines are used to manufacture, test, and package them—untouched by human hands. The machines are so flexible that a special order, even a single item, can be included in the assembly without slowing down the process. The system was one of the first to use *simultaneous engineering*—designing the product and the process to make the product at the same time.[12]

flexible manufacturing
Totally automated production centers that can perform a variety of functions to produce different products.

CRITICAL THINKING

Earlier we talked about continuous processes versus intermittent processes. Can you see how flexible manufacturing makes it possible for intermittent processes to become as fast as continuous processes? What are the implications for saving time on the assembly line, saving money, and cutting back on labor?

••• LEAN MANUFACTURING •••

Lean manufacturing is the production of goods using less of everything compared to mass production: half the human effort, half the manufacturing space, half the investment in tools, half the engineering time to develop a new product in half the time.[13] A company becomes lean by continuously increasing the capacity to produce more, higher quality results with fewer resources.[14]

Investing eight years and $3.5 billion, GM redesigned its production process, abandoning the assembly line. The name given the changeover was Project Saturn. The fundamental purpose of restructuring was to dramatically cut the number of worker-hours needed to build a car.

The changes GM made were many, but the most dramatic was to switch to modular construction. This means that most parts are preassembled into a few large components called *modules*. Workers are no longer strung out along miles of assembly line. Instead, they're grouped at various workstations where they put the modules together. Rather than do a few tasks, workers perform a whole cluster of tasks. Trolleys carry the partly completed car from station to station. Such a process takes up less space and calls for fewer workers—both money-saving steps. Suppliers were asked to provide a wider variety of parts and to subassemble certain parts before shipping them.

In addition to these changes, GM designed a casting process for building the engine block that uses 40 percent less machinery. This, too, saves money and time. And finally, GM greatly expanded its use of robots in the manufacturing process. A **robot** is a computer-controlled machine capable of performing many tasks requiring the use of materials and tools. Robots, for example, spray paint cars and do welding. Robots usually are fast, efficient, and accurate.[15]

Robots and machinery can never completely replace a creative worker. Such workers can make the most of the new technology. Therefore, GM devotes 70,000 square feet to its training and development center.

GM is just one example of how innovations are occurring in U.S. manufacturing. In general, firms are using more robots, more computers, and less labor. Nabisco makes Oreos in a Garner, North Carolina, plant. The cookies are "untouched by human hands" until you take them apart to eat them. You do take them apart, don't you? Manufacturing plants tend to be smaller and more fuel-efficient. Again, the goal is to cut costs and increase productivity to keep American business competitive.

Lean manufacturing enables U.S. firms to compete with firms anywhere in the world. Other countries may have cheaper labor, but U.S. firms can get by with less labor by using robots and other automated equipment. By staying competitive, U.S. firms keep high-tech jobs in the United States. Are you surprised by the fact that the United States has such low unemployment when it has replaced so many workers with machines?

lean manufacturing
The production of goods using less of everything compared to mass production: half the human effort, half the manufacturing space, half the investment in tools, half the engineering time to develop a new product in half the time.

robot
A computer-controlled machine capable of performing many tasks.

mass customization
Tailoring products to meet the needs of individual customers.

••• MASS CUSTOMIZATION •••

Mass customization means tailoring products to meet the needs of individual customers. The National Bicycle Industrial Company in Japan, for example, makes 18 bicycle models in more than 11 million combinations, with each combination designed to fit the needs of a specific customer. The customer chooses the model, size, color, and design. The retailer measures the buyer and faxes the data to the factory, where robots handle the bulk of the assembly.[16]

GiftMaker is a software program that lets you sit at your computer and custom-design T-shirts, baseball caps, and other gift items for your friends. Once you're finished with the design, you enter the addresses where you want the items sent, enter a credit card number, and send it by modem to the manufacturer. The manufacturer will then custom-make your products and send them to your friends.[17]

Flexible manufacturing systems enable manufacturers to custom-make goods as quickly as mass-produced items were once made. This enables producers to more closely meet the wants and needs of customers. As manufacturing learns to work more closely with design, distribution, and marketing throughout the system (which is what enterprise resource planning is all about), U.S. firms will be able to continue to provide quality goods and services that are as good as the best in the world.

• • • COMPETING IN TIME • • •

Competing in time is essential to competing at all in a global marketplace. McKinsey & Co., a major consulting firm, estimates that going over budget by 50 percent to get the product out on time reduces profit 4 percent. However, staying on budget and getting the product out six months late reduces profit 33 percent. Speed is of the essence. Ford estimates that it must be 25 percent faster than it is now in creating new products to match the best.

In their book, *Competing Against Time*, Tom Hout and George Stalk, Jr., describe *the 0.05 to 5 rule*: "Most products and many services are actually receiving value [something is actually happening to them] for only 0.05 to 5 percent of the time they are in the systems of their companies."[18] For example, a manufacturer may take 45 days to get a special-order car to a buyer, but it only takes 16 hours to assemble the car. Hout and Stalk say we routinely waste 95 percent of our time. That gives us lots of opportunity for improvement!

Next we'll explore dramatic changes that are restoring American competitive strength in manufacturing: computer-aided design and computer-aided manufacturing (CAD/CAM). They enable firms to compete in time and efficiency.

COMPUTER-AIDED DESIGN AND MANUFACTURING

If one development in the recent past changed production techniques and strategies more than any other, it was the integration of computers into the design and manufacturing of products. The first thing computers did was help

This picture shows gym shoes being designed on a computer-aided design (CAD) system. Some day you will be able to buy custom-made shoes for the same price (or nearly so) as mass-produced shoes because of computer-aided design and manufacturing and flexible manufacturing systems.

in the design of products; this is called **computer-aided design (CAD)**. The next step was to involve computers directly in the production process; this is called **computer-aided manufacturing (CAM)**.

CAD/CAM has made it possible to custom-design products to meet the needs of small markets with very little increase in cost. A producer programs the computer to make a simple design change, and that change can be incorporated directly into the production line. For example, some consumers in the Midwest like hamburger on their pizza rather than pepperoni or sausage. The Pillsbury Company added a hamburger pizza to its Midwest line by making a few simple changes in the CAD computer program for pizzas.

Computer-aided design and manufacturing are also invading the clothing industry. A computer program establishes a pattern and cuts the cloth automatically. Soon, a person's dimensions will be programmed into the machines to create custom-cut clothing at little additional cost. Computer-aided manufacturing is used to make cookies in those new fresh-baked cookie shops. On-site, small-scale, semiautomated, sensor-controlled baking makes consistent quality easy.

Computer-aided design has increased productivity by 2 to 1. The problem in the past was that computer-aided design machines couldn't talk to computer-aided manufacturing machines. It's one thing to design a product; it's quite another to set the specifications to make a machine do the work. Recently, however, new software programs have been designed to unite CAD with CAM: *computer-integrated manufacturing* (CIM). The new software is expensive, but it cuts 80 percent of the time needed to program machines to cut parts and eliminates many errors.[19]

In summary, computer-aided design and computer-aided manufacturing (CAD/CAM) have revolutionized the production process. Now, everything from cookies to cars can be designed and manufactured much more cheaply. Furthermore, customized changes can be made with very little increase in cost. Think what that will mean for the clothing industry, the shoe industry, and other fashion-conscious industries. The age of custom-designed consumer and industrial goods has arrived.

More important for you is the effect such changes will have on jobs in manufacturing. Employees of manufacturing facilities in the future will be working with sophisticated computers and other equipment rather than performing dull, repetitive work. That means more education and constant updating of skills to stay current. (See the box Spotlight on Small Business.)

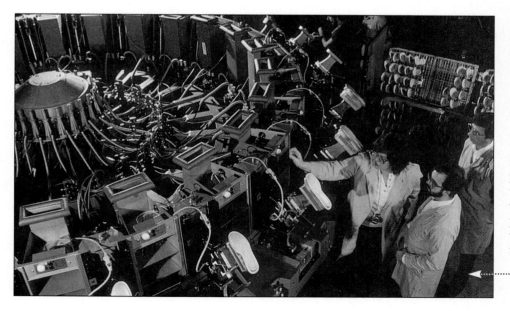

computer-aided design (CAD)
The use of computers in the design of products.

computer-aided manufacturing (CAM)
The use of computers in the manufacturing of products.

All the talk about robots and machinery today may lead you to think that people are not as important in today's production facilities. Just the opposite is true. The difference is that workers are much better educated and highly skilled. Human integrated manufacturing makes sure that the voice of the customer gets into the firm. It also makes sure that workers are not treated like robots, but as important inputs into the process. Are U.S. schools turning out the kind of workers that production plants using advanced technology will need in the future?

The Computerized Factory

Because of new ideas such as CAD/CAM, the United States is now on the brink of a new era in production and operations management. The force behind the change is new technology, especially computers and robots. Some terms you'll be seeing over the next decade include:

1. *Computer-aided engineering (CAE)*. CAE includes the designing and analysis of products, the programming of robots and machine tools, the designing of molds and tools, and the planning of the production process and quality control. In the past, engineering involved a lot of paperwork—blueprints, drawings, and so forth. Many inefficiencies resulted from the shuffling of such papers from desk to desk to shop floor and so on. Today, the whole engineering process from conception to production can be and is being done by computer in some firms.

2. *Flexible manufacturing systems (FMS)*. These are totally automated production centers that include robots, automatic materials handling equipment, and computer-controlled machine tools that can perform a variety of functions to produce different products. GM's new plants use flexible manufacturing systems.

3. *Design for manufacturability and assembly (DFMA)*. This innovation is based on the premise that the best-engineered part may be no part at all. Reducing the number of parts needed to build a product reduces the product's cost. Savings come from less time to assemble, ease in installation and maintenance, and less field service. NCR's newest electronic cash register has only 15 parts (85 percent fewer parts from 65 percent fewer vendors than its previous model). The terminal takes only one quarter of the time previously required to assemble it.

4. *Computer-Aided Acquisition and Logistics Support (CALS)*. This communications system allows manufacturers to send design specifications to suppliers over a phone line directly to the machine that will do the work. This system makes it possible to reduce inventories even further because new parts can be ordered and processed at once, and sent almost immediately.

What you should learn from all this is that factories are being fully automated. That is, most of the jobs that traditionally have been involved in the manufacturing process are being eliminated. Everything from customer order processing, to inventory control planning, to forecasting through production, quality control, and shipping is being made more productive through the use of computers and robots. The remaining workers are and will be highly skilled technical workers who have the training needed to use and develop such equipment.

••• PEOPLE PROBLEMS ON THE PLANT FLOOR •••

With all of this talk of automation and computers, it's easy to get the idea that using machine-centered production like CAD/CAM is the only remedy for improving ailing productivity levels. Recent studies by another consulting firm, Ernst & Young, indicate that the manufacturing companies that did the best job were those that had a heavy people orientation as well. They call it *human-integrated manufacturing (HIM)*.

Tracy O'Rourke introduced HIM at Varian Corporation with a communications campaign. He communicated the importance of a customer focus, quality, fast response, flexible factories, time-to-market, and organizational excellence. Before instituting HIM, customer focus was almost nonexistent at Varian. The firm took technology, converted it to products, and then took it to the market. Now it begins with finding out what the customer wants first. How's it working? O'Rourke lets the numbers do the talking. The cost of goods sold dropped from 70 cents per sales dollar to 65 cents in his first 12 months, and O'Rourke expects it to drop another 5 cents in the next two years.

It's important to remember that production is still dependent upon people, and it will be people who determine future systems' success or failure. Several steps must occur before people and machines will be combined to revolutionize manufacturing:

SPOTLIGHT ON SMALL BUSINESS

Computer-Integrated Manufacturing for Small Businesses

The bulk of manufacturing automation is in large companies. For instance, 80 percent of the robots used in the United States are in companies like Ford and IBM. Although experts have been saying for over a decade that factory automation will soon be common in small companies, it just hasn't happened yet.

As the gap widens between the skills workers need and the skills they have, small companies' need for sophisticated equipment increases. To attract quality workers, small companies must have the right equipment.

Why are small companies slower to automate? There are lots of reasons. At the top of the list are the high initial equipment costs and the high cost of training. Many small firms simply don't have the money to do it. Whereas large companies have greater resources and can spread the cost of technology over several products, small-business owners spend their own money and can lose the business if the technology doesn't pay for itself. One way to overcome these disadvantages is for several smaller manufacturers to pool their resources and buy or lease equipment.

The software for implementing CAD/CAM often costs $30,000 or more. Small businesses must think of creative ways to finance such an expense or to share the expense with others. Often larger firms will help finance such a purchase for their suppliers. They do this because they want their suppliers to have the most modern equipment so they can supply them with the best parts and materials. They also want their suppliers to become compatible with their own automated systems. Vendors of automated equipment now recognize the problems caused by their customers' skill deficiencies. Their sales pitches now emphasize training and technical support. Small businesses can also work closely with local educational institutions to help train their employees. Community colleges across the country have increased their attention to "manufacturing education." Their aim is to teach current workers basic literacy, critical thinking, and technical skills.

Another problem is that firms are introducing computer manufacturing piecemeal, one step at a time. This sounds like a good idea because of the high cost, but it often results in a system that's not as efficient as it could be. The most successful automation users implement the new technology as a whole, from order entry to moving the product out the door.

As computer integration becomes more popular, the price of CAD/CAM systems should go down. Then even the smallest firms should be able to take advantage of the technology.

- There's an obvious need to train future production workers in the use and repair of computers, robots, and automatic machinery.
- Today's production workers must be retrained or relocated to adapt to the new high-tech systems.
- Major adjustments must be made in the relationships between suppliers and producers to implement concepts such as just-in-time inventory programs and enterprise networking.
- Production managers must be retrained to deal with more highly skilled workers who demand a much more participative managerial style.
- Employees must be trained to work in teams and to understand the concepts of competing in time, empowerment, total quality, and continuous improvement.

- What is just-in-time inventory control?
- How does flexible manufacturing differ from lean manufacturing?
- What is meant by competing in time?
- What is human-integrated manufacturing?

PROGRESS CHECK

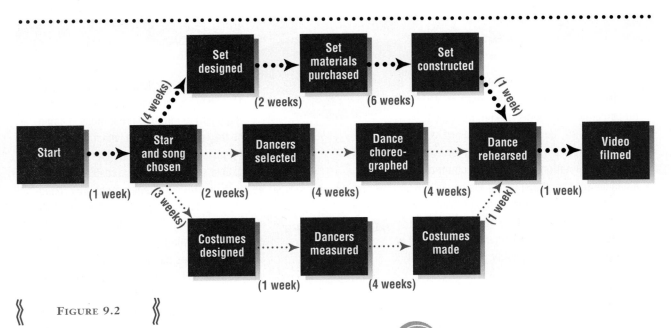

FIGURE 9.2

PERT CHART FOR A VIDEO

The minimum amount of time it will take to produce this video is 15 weeks. To get that number, you add the week it takes to pick a star and a song to the four weeks to design a set, the two weeks to purchase set materials, the six weeks to construct the set, the week before rehearsals, and the final week when the video is made. That's the critical path. Any delay in that process will delay the final video. Delays in other processes (selecting and choreographing dancers and costume design) wouldn't necessarily delay the video because there are more weeks in the critical path.

program evaluation and review technique (PERT)

A method for analyzing the tasks involved in completing a given project, estimating the time needed to complete each task, and identifying the minimum time needed to complete the total project.

critical path

The sequence of tasks that takes the longest time to complete.

CONTROL PROCEDURES: PERT AND GANTT CHARTS

Obviously, an important function of a production manager is to be sure that products are manufactured and delivered on time. The question is, How can one be sure that all of the assembly processes will go smoothly and end up completed by the required time? A popular strategy for maintaining some feel for the progress of the production process is called the *program evaluation and review technique*, a process developed in the 1950s for constructing nuclear submarines. The **program evaluation and review technique (PERT)** is a method for analyzing the tasks involved in completing a given project, estimating the time needed to complete each task, and identifying the minimum time needed to complete the total project.

The steps involved in using PERT are (1) analyzing and sequencing tasks that need to be done, (2) estimating the time needed to complete each task, (3) drawing a PERT network illustrating the information from steps 1 and 2, and (4) identifying the critical path. The critical path is the sequence of tasks that takes the longest time to complete. This path is referred to as the **critical path** because a delay in the time needed to complete this path would cause the project or production run to be late.

Figure 9.2 illustrates a PERT chart for producing a music video. Note that the squares on the chart indicate completed tasks and the arrows leading to the squares indicate the time needed to complete each task. The path from one completed task to the other illustrates the relationships among tasks. For example, the arrow from "set designed" to "set materials purchased" shows that designing the set must be completed before the materials can be purchased. The critical path (indicated by the bold black arrows) reflects that producing the set takes more time than auditioning dancers and choreographing dances as well as designing and making costumes. The project manager now knows that it's critical that set construction remain on schedule if the project is to be completed on time, but short delays in the dance and costume preparation shouldn't affect the total project.

A PERT network can be made up of thousands of events over many months. Today, this complex procedure is done by computer. Another, more basic, strategy used by manufacturers for measuring production progress is a Gantt chart. The **Gantt chart** (named after its developer, Henry L. Gantt) is a bar graph that

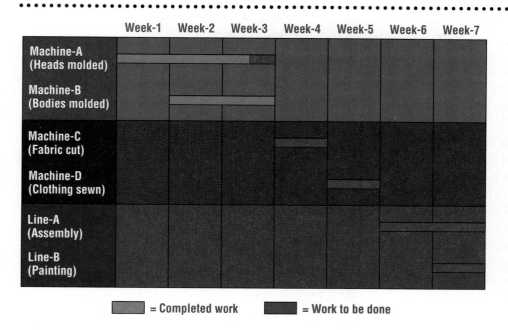

	Week-1	Week-2	Week-3	Week-4	Week-5	Week-6	Week-7
Machine-A (Heads molded)							
Machine-B (Bodies molded)							
Machine-C (Fabric cut)							
Machine-D (Clothing sewn)							
Line-A (Assembly)							
Line-B (Painting)							

= Completed work   = Work to be done

FIGURE 9.3

A GANTT CHART FOR A DOLL MANUFACTURER
A Gantt chart enables a production manager to see at a glance when projects are scheduled to be completed and what the status now is. For example, the dolls' heads and bodies should be completed before the clothing is sewn, but could be a little late, as long as everything is ready for assembly in week 6. This chart shows that at the end of week 3, the dolls' bodies are ready, but the heads are about half a week behind.

Gantt chart
Bar graph showing production managers what projects are being worked on and what stage they are in on a daily basis.

clearly shows what projects are being worked on and how much has been completed (on a daily basis). Figure 9.3 shows a Gantt chart for a doll manufacturer. The chart shows that the dolls' heads and bodies should be completed before the clothing is sewn. It also shows that at the end of week 3, the dolls' bodies are ready, but the heads are about half a week behind. All of this calculation was once done by hand. Now the computer has taken over.

••• TOTAL QUALITY IN PRODUCTION MANAGEMENT •••

Quality control is the measurement of products and services against set standards. Earlier in America, quality control was often done at the end of the production line. It was done by a quality control department. Today, things have changed. As Ford says in its ads, "Quality Is Job One."

Total quality means satisfying customers by building in and ensuring quality from product planning to production, purchasing, sales, and service. Emphasis is placed on customer satisfaction and the fact that quality is everyone's concern, not just the quality control people at the end of the assembly line. In TQM ◀-- P.259 --▶, everybody is permitted—and expected—to contribute to change.

Remember that the purpose of quality goods and services is to make the consumer happy. Therefore, a TQM program begins by analyzing the consumer to see what quality standards need to be established. Quality is then designed into products, and every product must meet those standards every step of the way in the production process.

Here are examples of how quality is being introduced into the production process:

- Motorola set a goal of attaining "six sigma" quality—just 3.4 defects per million products. It has already exceeded such a standard for its calculators and is planning to reach that level of quality for its other product lines soon.

- In 1980, Xerox found 97 defects for every 100 copiers coming off the assembly line. Now it finds only 12. As a consequence, it raised its market share for small-business copiers from 1 percent to 20 percent.

quality control
The measurement of products and services against set standards.

Reaching Beyond Our Borders

Benchmark on the Best

The term *globalization* means that the world's best manufacturers can enter almost any market almost any time. In other words, if you aren't one of the world's best manufacturers, you're likely to go out of business. In fact, you can be one of the world's best producers and still lose the bulk of your business if you aren't also one of the most innovative and cost-efficient producers. Mercedes and BMW, for example, were known as two of the best manufacturers in the world. Along came Lexus and Infiniti not only to challenge their technological lead, but to offer similar quality at a much lower price. Consequently, you now see models of Mercedes that are less expensive. If Mercedes hadn't responded, it would have continued to lose its market.

Even being an industry leader doesn't ensure world dominance for long. Japan, for example, introduced high-definition TV (HDTV) in 1988 at the Olympics in Seoul. U.S. manufacturers considered this a challenge much like the challenge to get to the moon. Working together, U.S. manufacturers developed a better technol-

ogy that leapfrogged Japanese products. European companies are doing the same. Similarly, IBM once led the world in computer technology, but it's now just one of many competitors, not the dominant industry leader.

Staying on top means meeting the world's standard (that is, benchmarking on the best companies in the world). Compare each process in your company to that same process as practiced by the best. Then bring your processes up to the world-class standard or outsource the process to someone who can. Empower workers to become the best in the world. And never be content. Continuously improve processes and products to maintain a leadership position. Often that means developing products that will make your own products obsolete. So be it. If you don't, someone else will.

Source: Stratford Sherman, "Are You as Good as the Best in the World?" *Fortune*, December 13, 1993, pp. 95–96; and Bill Powell, "Losing Their Lead," *Newsweek*, December 13, 1993, pp. 51–53.

- Holiday Inn authorized its hotel staff to do almost anything to satisfy an unhappy customer from handing out gift certificates to eliminating the charge for a service. Managers were given the authority to waive charges for the night's stay if the customer was still unhappy. Note that the customer is ultimately the one who determines what the standard for quality should be.

Dozens of other manufacturers and service organizations could be discussed here, but you get the idea. American businesses are getting serious about providing top customer service, and many are already doing it.

IMPROVING PRODUCTIVITY

You may have had the impression that in the battle of producing goods the United States is losing to other countries, but in truth it's merely losing its huge lead. Actually, manufacturing productivity ◀--- P.74 --▶ in the United States grew at an average rate of 3.5 percent from 1981 to 1990. This compares with an average growth rate of 2.3 percent in the 1970s. Losing part of our lead is to be expected as other countries learn from U.S. experiences and adopt the latest technologies while some of our older plants become obsolete. There's no doubt that the United States might lose out to competitors if manufacturers and service organizations fail to adopt the concepts from this chapter—but as you've seen, many of them have already done so and others are quickly following their lead. Thus, the United States should continue to be a manufacturing leader for the foreseeable future.

••• PRODUCTIVITY IN THE ••• SERVICE SECTOR

The greatest productivity problem in the United States is reported to be in the service economy. While productivity growth was relatively good for manufacturers during the 1980s, it was reported to be next to nothing (0.2 percent) for service organizations. We've already learned that over 7 of 10 U.S. jobs are now in the service sector, with more to come. A truly strong America, therefore, has to be progressive in introducing the latest technology to services as well as to manufacturing.

There's strong evidence that productivity in the service sector *is* rising, but the government simply doesn't have the means to measure it.[20] The quality of service is greatly improving, but quality is difficult to measure. The traditional way to measure productivity involves tracking inputs (worker-hours) compared to outputs (dollars). New information systems must be developed to measure the *speed* of delivery of goods and services, the quality, and customer satisfaction. In fact, researchers recently discovered that companies, including service firms, earned an amazing 67 percent return on investment in information technology.[21]

Operations management has added greatly to the productivity of the service sector. This automatic ticketing machine from Southwest Airlines is just one example. The problem is that measures for service productivity have not kept up with the advances. As a consequence, productivity increases in the service sector do not yet accurately appear in national figures.

Computers are only the beginning of improving service sector productivity. Think about labor-intensive businesses like McDonald's and Burger King. Automation plays a big role in controlling costs and improving service. Today, you go in Burger King, order your meal, get your food, and fill your own drink cup. Because the people working at the drive-up window now wear headsets instead of using stationary mikes, they aren't glued to one spot anymore and can do four or five tasks while taking an order.

Most of us have been exposed to similar productivity gains in banking. For example, people in many towns no longer have to wait in long lines for harassed tellers to help them deposit and withdraw money. Instead, they use automatic tellers that take a few seconds and are available 24 hours a day.

Another service that was once annoyingly slow was the checkout counter at the grocery store. The new system of marking goods with universal product codes enables computerized checkout and allows cashiers to be much more productive when providing this service.[22]

Airlines are another service industry experiencing tremendous productivity increases through the use of computers for everything from processing reservations, to the heavy use of prepackaged meals on board, to more standardization of all movements of luggage, passengers, and so on.

In short, operations management has led to tremendous productivity increases in the service sector. Those gains haven't been reflected in national productivity figures because the government doesn't yet know how to accurately measure them. Nonetheless, service workers are losing jobs to machines just as manufacturing workers are. Again, the secret to obtaining and holding a good job is education and training. That message can't be repeated too frequently.

... PRODUCTIVITY AND QUALITY IN ...
NONPROFIT ORGANIZATIONS

The United States can't remain competitive with the rest of the world if inefficient government agencies keep draining funds away from businesses. In the early 1990s, state and local government agencies found themselves with reduced revenues because of a national recession. Some responded with programs as dramatic as those instituted at the most progressive manufacturing firms. A case in point is the city of Madison, Wisconsin.

Mayor Joseph Sensenbrenner went to a seminar given by quality expert W. Edwards Deming. He listened to case histories of how organizations like American Express can mail out a new credit card in less than a week. It was taking six weeks to get a driver's license renewed in Madison.

The idea, Deming said, is to institute proven quality techniques. You've learned that quality includes continuous improvement in pleasing customers and reducing the variation in whatever product or service is offered. Mayor Sensenbrenner decided to try the quality process in the city garage, which serviced some 765 vehicles. It took an average of nine days to service a vehicle, so police cars and other important vehicles were off the road for too long.

The problem turned out to be that the city was ordering the cheapest vehicles every year. That meant that there were different models purchased every year and thousands of parts were needed to service all those different vehicles (leading to waste in inventory). A team of people analyzed the problem and came up with a new purchasing plan that saved an impressive $700,000 a year. Furthermore, turnaround time for repairs fell from nine days to just three.

What's most interesting about the Madison case is that the city adopted many of the most advanced production and operations management concepts. A formal quality and productivity program was established, and a full-time quality and productivity administrator was hired. The city's mission statement includes continuous improvement, customer input, employee involvement, innovation, and trust.

Most government departments aren't designed to work with each other cooperatively. Bureaucracy prevails. That is, it's hard to get anything done because the thousands of rules and procedures normally prohibit a government worker from being flexible in response to citizen complaints and needs. That's all being changed in Madison through the efforts of one educated leader. Market forces are exerting great pressure on businesspeople to make fundamental changes for efficiency and survival. Deep federal deficits, state and local government budget-balancing requirements, and the slowdown in government revenues are forcing government agencies to make similar changes. In fact, the next decade could well become known as the era of productivity improvement in *all* organizations.

··· PREPARING FOR THE FUTURE ···

What does all this mean to you? It means that college graduates of the future will have marvelous new technological advances available to them. It means new opportunities and a higher standard of living and quality of life. But it also means preparing for such changes. Clearly, the workplace will be dominated by computers, robots, and other advanced machinery. Even the service sector will require the widespread use of hand-held computers.

If all this sounds terribly cold and impersonal, then you recognize one of the needs of the future. People will need much more contact with people outside the work environment. There will be new demands for recreation, social clubs, travel, and other diversions. The America of the next century will be

Legal Briefcase

All businesses must adhere to certain workplace safety standards as prescribed by the Occupational Safety and Health Act (OSHA). This law was enacted in 1970 to ensure that workers in all organizations have healthy, safe working conditions. It provides specific safety regulations as well as inspectors to see that the regulations are enforced. Inspections are carried out both randomly and specifically to investigate complaints of unsafe conditions. OSHA officials are empowered to issue warnings, to impose fines, and even to invoke court-ordered shutdowns for unsafe conditions.

Early experience with OSHA was mixed. Although OSHA caused a general improvement in working conditions and safety records, sometimes overzealous inspectors demanded strict compliance with certain regulations that many employers felt were too detailed and unrealistic in terms of cost and benefits. Congress subsequently ordered OSHA to eliminate nuisance regulations and try to be more realistic in administering federal regulations.

Source: William J. Stevenson, *Production/Operations Management*, 4th ed. (Homewood, Ill.: Richard D. Irwin, 1993, p. 375).

radically different from the America of the 1990s. It will take both technically trained people and people skilled in human relationships to guide us through the transition.

Carnegie-Mellon University now requires a course in manufacturing management for its M.B.A. degree. Other courses are offered in robotics and manufacturing strategy. Some students act as consultants to manufacturers in the Pittsburgh area. Stanford University has the Institute for Manufacturing and Automation. Georgia Tech has a program in computer-integrated manufacturing. Such programs will become commonplace as other schools follow the leadership of these schools in introducing such courses at both the undergraduate and graduate levels.

Other schools are training students to manage the new high-tech work force. Emphasis is on participative management and the design of attractive work environments. All this will come together in the next decade to bring a new era in both the manufacturing and service sectors. You have every reason to be optimistic about the future for both U.S. and world economic growth because of these changes. You can also expect to find many exciting new careers in America's new industrial boom.

- Could you draw a PERT chart for making a breakfast of three-minute eggs, buttered toast, and coffee? Which process would be the critical path, the longest process? How could you use a Gantt chart to keep track of production?

- Why does service productivity seem to lag behind industrial productivity, and what can be done about it?

PROGRESS CHECK

1. Production and operations management consists of those activities managers do to create goods and services.
   - ***Describe the production process and explain the importance of productivity.***
   Production is the creation of finished goods and services using inputs—land, labor, capital, entrepreneurship, and information. *Productivity* is the

SUMMARY
• • • • • •

1. Describe the production process and explain the importance of productivity.

term used to describe output per worker. Output could mean goods like cars and furniture, or services such as education and health care.

2. Explain the importance of site selection in keeping down costs and identify the criteria used to evaluate different sites.

2. A major issue of the 1990s has been the shift of manufacturing and service organizations from one city or state to another in the United States or to foreign countries.
   - *Why is site selection so important and what criteria are used to evaluate different sites?*
   The very survival of the U.S. manufacturing industry depends on its ability to remain competitive, and that means either cheaper inputs, such as cheaper costs of labor and land, or increased outputs from present inputs (increased productivity). Cheaper labor and land are two major criteria for selecting the right sites. Other criteria include whether (1) resources are plentiful and inexpensive, (2) skilled workers are available or are trainable, (3) taxes are low and the local government offers support, (4) energy and water are available, (5) transportation costs are low, and (6) the quality of life and quality of education are high.

3. Classify the various production processes and how materials requirement planning links organizations in performing those processes.

3. Process manufacturing physically or chemically changes materials. Assembly processes put together components. These two processes are called *synthetic systems.*
   - *Are there other production processes?*
   Yes, the reverse of a synthetic system is called an *analytic system.* Analytic systems break down raw materials into components to extract other products. In addition, production processes are either continuous or intermittent. A continuous process is one in which long production runs turn out finished goods over time. An intermittent process is an operation where the production run is short (e.g., one or two eggs) and the machines are changed frequently to produce different products.
   - *What relationship does MRP have with the production process?*
   A manufacturer sets a production schedule. It then informs its suppliers of what will be needed. The supplier must deliver the goods just in time to go on the assembly line, making the supplier part of the process.

4. Describe manufacturing techniques such as just-in-time inventory control, flexible manufacturing, lean manufacturing, and competing in time.

4. Flexible manufacturing is the design of machines to do multiple tasks so that they can produce a variety of products.
   - *What's the relationship between flexible manufacturing and lean manufacturing?*
   Lean manufacturing is the production of goods using less of everything compared to mass production: half the human effort, half the manufacturing space, half the investment in tools, half the engineering time to develop a new product in half the time. Flexible manufacturing enables the firm to use less equipment to make more goods; thus, it could be considered part of lean manufacturing.
   - *What is mass customization?*
   Mass customization means making custom-designed goods for all customers. Flexible manufacturing makes mass customization possible. Given the exact needs of a customer, flexible manufacturing machines can produce a customized good as fast as mass-produced goods were once made.
   - *How do competing in time and JIT fit into the process?*
   Getting your product to market before your competitors is essential today, particularly in the electronic sector. Thus, competing in time is critical. JIT inventory control allows for less inventory and fewer machines to move goods. This allows for more flexibility and faster response times.

5. CAD/CAM has made it possible to custom-design products to meet the tastes of small markets with very little increase in cost.
   • **How might CAD/CAM lead to people problems?**
   Workers must be trained to deal with the new technology. Better relationships must be established between the firm and suppliers, customers, and other stakeholders.

5. Show how CAD/CAM improves the production process, but can lead to people problems on the plant floor.

6. The program evaluation and review technique (PERT) is a method for analyzing the tasks involved in completing a given project, estimating the time needed to complete each task, and identifying the minimum time needed to complete the total project.
   • **How can I learn to draw such a chart? Is there any relationship between it and a Gantt chart?**
   Figure 9.3 shows a PERT chart. A Gantt chart is a bar graph that clearly shows what projects are being worked on and how much has been completed (on a daily basis). Whereas PERT is a planning tool, Gantt is a tool used to measure progress.

6. Illustrate the use of PERT and Gantt charts in production planning.

7. Because the United States is a service society now, automation of the service sector is extremely important.
   • **Why is service productivity not increasing as rapidly as manufacturing productivity?**
   One important reason is that the service sector is labor-intensive. Keep in mind however that productivity and quality are rising in the service sector, but they're harder to measure than outputs of the industrial sector.

7. Explain the importance of productivity in all sectors: manufacturing, service, and nonprofit.

analytic system 281	form utility 277	program evaluation and review technique (PERT) 290
assembly process 281	Gantt chart 291	
computer-aided design (CAD) 287	lean manufacturing 285	
computer-aided manufacturing (CAM) 287	mass customization 285	quality control 291
critical path 290	process manufacturing 281	robot 285
enterprise resource planning (ERP) 282	production 277	synthetic systems 281
flexible manufacturing 284	production and operations management 276	

KEY TERMS

1. Review the terms in this chapter: CAD, CAM, CIM, MRP, JIT, and so on. These are among the most important business terms of the 1990s. Try to use them in class so that they become familiar. Soon you will be thinking of new ways to advance business yourself, based on your understanding of these terms.

2. Compose a list of as many of the applications of advanced technology in the service sector that have already occurred as you can. Using this information, brainstorm further uses of technology in areas such as recreation, travel, retailing, wholesaling, insurance, banking, finance, and government.

3. Choose one of your classmates to debate the following proposition: Should the federal government become more involved in the future of U.S. industry through implementation of a national industrial policy? Take

DEVELOPING WORKPLACE SKILLS

whichever side of the issue you did not previously agree with to broaden your thinking on this issue.

4. Debate the following proposition: Should or can U.S. manufacturers limit in some fashion the growth and spread of computers and robots used in manufacturing in order to save jobs for U.S. workers? Again, take the other side of this issue from your normal position.

5. Think about some of the experiences you have had with service organizations recently, including your school, and select one incident where you had to wait for an unreasonable time to get what you wanted. Prepare a letter to the management of that organization explaining how they could make their operation more efficient and customer-oriented.

PRACTICING MANAGEMENT DECISIONS

《 CASE COMPETING IN TIME AT DIGITAL EQUIPMENT CORPORATION 《

Marketing strategists at Digital Equipment Corporation (DEC) spotted a window of opportunity in the late 1980s for a new minicomputer. The problem was that there were less than two years to design, manufacture, test, market, deliver, and service a highly complex computer. However, 15 months later the company was producing computers in plants in New England, the Caribbean, and Europe. How did DEC do it? It used cross-functional teams ◀-- P.256 --▶ from various parts of the world that worked together to create the product. The project, named Calypso, eventually generated huge profits for Digital.

The project began with a vision for the product. A small group took the idea to various parts of the company to find people who'd be interested in working on the project. Some 50 core people from 14 separate company locations joined the team. They were located in New England, California, the Caribbean, and Ireland. They communicated with each other by phone, telephone conferences, electronic mail, and computer conferencing. A common database was created to hold all the information about the project and from time to time certain team members flew to various sites to work with others.

The core team then went to other companies to find key components. Digital was surprised to find that one of its customers, Raytheon, shared its vision so it proposed an alliance. Raytheon would do a parallel product for its military market. Thus, teams of workers from Digital and teams from Raytheon worked together and came up with solutions and products at the same time.

The secrets to the success of this project were a shared vision, common purpose, clear goals, and well-articulated tasks. But the methods used didn't look anything like a traditional production process. There was a project manager—Pauline Nist—but not all the engineers reported to her. Some members of the teams reported to their own functional areas in the firm, while others reported to the production teams. It's hard to believe that such a loosely aligned group of people could produce a product so quickly. But that's the benefit of production teams. They follow no set rules. They do not answer to a bureaucracy. They're free to do what's necessary to get done. Empowerment ◀-- P.220 --▶ is critical to the project's success. So is "partnering" with another company. In short, businesses today are forming cross-functional multifirm teams to create products quickly. This is true in the aircraft, software, computer, and other high-tech industries where fast product development is important.

Decision Questions

1. What skills will tomorrow's college graduates need to participate in cross-functional multifirm teams?

2. Note that some team members lived in other countries. How might multinational teams working together affect global politics and cooperation?

3. What technological advances have made such multinational teams possible?

4. Once every company learns to network with other companies to produce and market products quickly, what can such networks do to make their products more attractive to potential customers?

Source: Jessica Lipnack and Jeffrey Stamps, *The TeamNet Factor* (Essex Junction, Vt.: Oliver Wight Publications, 1993).

VIDEO CASE   THE PRODUCTION PROCESS AT WASHBURN GUITARS

When you think of manufacturing firms, names like GM and IBM come to mind. But there are thousands of smaller manufacturers in the marketplace providing us with many of the products that make life more enjoyable. Certainly guitars are one of those products. Washburn guitars in Chicago, Illinois, is a manufacturing company that uses the *intermittent process* of production. That is, they make a few of one model of guitar and then shift production to a different one. They call it *small batch production*.

Even though Washburn makes only a few products each day (about fifteen guitars), they still need to use the latest in production techniques to stay competitive. For example, they use *flexible manufacturing*. They have a machine that is capable of doing many different tasks: building guitar necks, drilling holes for the fretboard, and so on.

Washburn also follows the total quality concepts that other, larger firms follow. When planning the production process, the company also keeps in mind the need for profits. Therefore, popular, more-expensive guitars take precedence over less-expensive items. Today, all of Washburn's acoustic guitars are made overseas, but they have plans to make them in a new facility in Nashville, Tennessee. Total quality management and modern production techniques now make it possible to manufacture them in the United States and still stay competitive on price.

When making career plans, it is important to include smaller firms like Washburn Guitars in your thoughts. It is often more exciting to work in a smaller, more intimate work environment, especially if the firm practices participative management and other modern techniques.

Discussion Questions

1. What small manufacturing facilities are located in or near your city or town? Visit them and see for yourself what it's like working for a small manufacturer.

2. Do you think that guitars are the kind of item that lends itself well to continuous process manufacturing? Why?

3. One of the more important aspects of small-batch manufacturing is scheduling. What kinds of scheduling techniques have you learned in this chapter that you could use in a business similar to Washburn?

4. Does a career in production management seem attractive to you? Why or why not?

Part 3
MANAGEMENT

Management is the people part of business. Although managers are also responsible for managing finance, information, and various processes, their main responsibility is to the people who work for them. The managers are the people who run the organization. Without managers, there would be no business.

As everything else in the human realm is constantly changing, so is management and our attitudes toward it. Management careers have always been among the most challenging and fulfilling in the field of business. They still are. And the role of managers is changing rapidly as we approach the end of the century.

SKILLS

Managers today need different skills from those they needed a generation ago. Today's managers must know how to be both team players and team leaders. They cannot get away with the "jump when I say jump" mentality of the past. More than ever, managers need to be effective communicators. They especially need to know how to listen, to hear, and to understand the needs of both their subordinates and their own managers. They also need the ability to organize and to keep others organized and to possess the know-how to motivate workers.

CAREER PATHS

Today's management opportunities often start out as management training positions that later develop into full-blown management opportunities. Both government and larger companies have management training programs. Some of these organizations will hire workers through campus recruiters. Others look for skills that can be acquired outside the classroom. Another common way to become a manager is to start as an employee and work your way up the management ladder. College courses and other forms of management training are often available tuition-free to the ambitious employee.

Once a manager is hired, the progress into middle and top management is far from automatic. As one gets closer to the top, there are fewer and fewer opportunities. Getting to the top, then, means learning to be competitive and good at what you do. Understanding office politics is also certainly a plus, though some companies are more political than others.

As a manager moves up in an organization, his or her responsibilities and authority increase. Becoming an integral part of planning and running an organization brings excitement as well as rewards.

Some Possible Positions in Management

Job title	Salary	Job duties	Career path	Prospects
General manager; CEO; executive vice president	Amount varies widely. Top companies: $3.2 million average; mid-level managers average $59,400.	Establish the organization's general goals and policies. Act as liaison with other companies; direct the individual department or division; direct supervisor in motivation and control of workers.	Most general managers and top CEOs have college degrees, but some do not. Qualifications vary widely. Most vacancies are filled by promoting lower-level managers up through the ranks.	Slow growth in opportunities through year 2005.
Management trainee	$19,500–$23,000 (to start).	Learn basic responsibilities of a manager, training for the specific industry. Work in closely supervised situations in departments such as production, sales, research and development, finance. Training period usually specified and is treated as probationary.	Usually, a two-year associate degree is the minimum. Four-year degrees are preferred. Previous management experience can be helpful, though some companies want applicants to have none, so they can be trained the company way.	Outlook through 2005 is very good to excellent.
Supervisor, blue collar	$21,000 (often based on 140–155% of subordinate's wages).	Manage and train employees; keep track of time and scheduling, oversee use of equipment and materials. Work with union when union is present.	Knowledge of the technical part of the workers' task is the most important knowledge area. A two- or four-year degree is usually an aid in obtaining promotion.	Outlook through 2005 is fair to average. No dramatic growth expected.
Management consultant	Varies greatly, based on reputation of consulting firm.	Act as an adviser and analyst of management concerns in host organizations.	Degree and work experience help market credibility of the consultant. However, knowledge of the industry and self-confidence are most important qualities.	Demand will increase through 2005, especially in firms doing business internationally.

Kris Savignac, Manager and Entrepreneur

As a freshman at Palm Beach Community College, Kris Savignac was half-hearted. He didn't have enough direction to know where he was going. Soon he decided that he would need a four-year degree to succeed in business and changed his program to a two-year transfer. That was about the same time he discovered Delta Epsilon Chi, the collegiate division of Distributive Education Clubs of America (DECA). Kris asked his club advisor, Susan Thompson, what he could do to succeed in the club—and in business. Her answer helped him succeed at both. "Ask a successful person," she replied.

Kris went to Max Davis Associates, a local company that sold copiers and computer products. The sales manager suggested Kris spend time with one of his sales representatives who liked working as a mentor. This sales rep helped Kris prepare for national competition in Sales Representative, one of the business skills contest areas conducted at the National Delta Epsilon Chi convention which that year was held in Salt Lake City. Kris won first place in the nation that year and was told by the company that groomed him to come to them for a job as soon as he graduated.

Thus, unlike many of his classmates, Kris had a job waiting for him. He transferred to Flagler College in St. Augustine. Upon his graduation, he went to work for Max Davis, as promised. There he worked for several years, with great success. This is where he learned to take pride in his work. He won "Top Producer of the Quarter" several times. The prize for his last success was a trip to sunny Jamaica. It was there that he decided that his job as a sales representative wasn't fulfilling him as much as he had hoped.

When he returned to Florida, he gave his notice. The same day he quit his sales job, he drove across town to visit a friend who owned and developed golf courses. By coincidence—or providence—they were in the market for someone just like Kris. They were trying to decide whether to hire someone with knowledge of golf, to whom they would teach sales, or a salesperson, who they would teach about golf courses. Because Kris had worked at a golf course while he was in college, he fit in both directions. He was hired immediately. The golf course business has proven to be Kris's first love. As this book goes to press, Kris is dealing with Donald Trump about the possibility of developing a custom-built country club in northern Florida. In the golf course business, Kris has succeeded above even his own expectations.

Kris has some advice for anyone in any business career. He says "Get into something you really love; don't just go for the greatest monetary reward." If you're really happy at what you do and if what you do makes sense, the money will likely take care of itself. Also, learn to communicate. Especially, learn to be a good listener. "All of business is about communicating," he concludes. "And don't be afraid to ask for advice. There are successful people everywhere who can give you the direction you need; help from others has been priceless."

Kris's future includes managing his own golf course construction company, Global Golf Corporation. The challenge of managing people, rather than simply selling to them, presents a change in thought processes. When asked how he will deal with those problems, his answer is simple: "I'll just ask another successful person."

Special thanks to Susan Thompson, faculty member at Palm Beach Community College, for recommending Kris Savignac for this career portfolio.

PART 4

MANAGEMENT OF HUMAN RESOURCES: MOTIVATING EMPLOYEES TO PRODUCE QUALITY GOODS AND SERVICES

CHAPTER 10
MOTIVATING
EMPLOYEES AND
BUILDING SELF-
MANAGED TEAMS

CHAPTER 11
HUMAN RESOURCE
MANAGEMENT:
FINDING AND KEEPING
THE BEST EMPLOYEES

CHAPTER 12
DEALING WITH
EMPLOYEE–
MANAGEMENT ISSUES
AND RELATIONSHIPS

MOTIVATING EMPLOYEES AND BUILDING SELF-MANAGED TEAMS

LEARNING GOALS

After you have read and studied this chapter, you should be able to

1. Explain Taylor's scientific management.

2. Describe the Hawthorne studies and relate their significance to human-based management.

3. Identify the levels of Maslow's hierarchy of needs and relate their importance to employee motivation.

4. Differentiate among Theory X, Theory Y, and Theory Z.

5. Distinguish between motivators and hygiene factors identified by Herzberg.

6. Explain how job enrichment affects employee motivation and performance.

7. Identify the steps involved in implementing a management by objectives (MBO) program.

8. Describe the implementation of motivation theory in the 1990s.

HERB KELLEHER OF SOUTHWEST AIRLINES

The sky is anything but friendly for all but one airline. As the other airlines struggle to stay aloft, Southwest Airlines is flying high as the only airline to remain profitable every year since 1973. Analysts credit this achievement to the engaging management style of the company's chairman, Herb Kelleher. Known to show up dressed as Elvis or the Easter Bunny, Kelleher is the jokemeister of the airline industry. He's usually at the center of Southwest's frequent employee activities. Asked to speak to a group about his accomplishments he's most proud of, he took the podium and said, "Well, I'm here to tell you that I *am* proud of a couple of things. First, I'm very good at projectile vomiting." Such unorthodox statements rarely fail to capture his audience's attention.

Kelleher has his employees' attention most of the time. For the past several years, under his leadership, Southwest has captured the U.S. Department of Transportation's Service Triple Crown for highest customer satisfaction, most on-time flights, and best baggage handling. Kelleher's employees are far more productive than those of other airlines, so Kelleher can fly more planes and serve more passengers with fewer workers than his competitors. Southwest employees pitch in wherever needed. Pilots might work the boarding gate if things back up; ticket agents might haul luggage to get the plane out on time. And, get this, Kelleher pays his employees *less* than many other carriers.

How does he do it? His employees say Kelleher motivates them because he doesn't just say that people are his most important resource, he acts on it. Kelleher states, "I feel that you have to be with your employees through all their difficulties, that you have to be interested in them personally. They may be disappointed in their country. Even their family might not be working out the way they wish it would. But I want them to know that Southwest will always be there for them."

⟨⟨ *The test of leadership is not to put greatness into humanity, but to elicit it, for the greatness is already there.* ⟩⟩

James Buchanan

THE IMPORTANCE OF MOTIVATION

No matter where you end up being a leader—in school, in business, in sports, in the military, wherever—the key to your success will be whether you can motivate others to do their best. That's no easy task today when so many people feel bored and disinterested in their work. Yet people are willing to work, and work hard, if they feel that their work is appreciated and makes a difference. People are motivated by a variety of things, such as recognition, accomplishment, and status. **Intrinsic reward** is the good feeling you have when you've done a job well. An **extrinsic reward** is given to you by someone else as recognition for good work. Such things as pay increases, praise, bonuses, and promotions are examples of extrinsic rewards. Ultimately, motivation—the drive to satisfy a need—comes from within. There are ways to stimulate people that bring out the natural drive to do a good job.

This chapter teaches you the concepts, theories, and practice of motivation. The most important person to motivate, of course, is yourself. One way to do that is to find the right job in the right organization, one that enables you to reach your goals in life. The whole purpose of this book is to help you in that search and to teach you how to succeed once you get there. One secret of success is to recognize that everyone else is on a similar search. Naturally, some are more committed than others. The job of a manager is to find that commitment, encourage it, and focus it on some common goal.

This chapter will begin with a look at some traditional theories of motivation. You'll learn about the Hawthorne studies because they created an entirely new interest in worker satisfaction and motivation. Then you'll look at some assumptions about employees: Are they basically lazy, or willing to work if given the proper incentives? You'll explore the traditional theorists.

intrinsic reward
The good feeling you have when you have done a job well.

extrinsic reward
Reinforcement from someone else as recognition for good work, including pay increases, praise, and promotions.

Southwest Airlines has proven itself to be a high flier. In an industry plagued with massive financial losses and increasing costs, Southwest has enjoyed continuous profitability. The company's secret is low cost yet high productivity from its work force. As this photograph shows, Southwest employees work as a team and pitch in wherever and whenever needed. Here a pilot unloads luggage in order to get the plane back in the air on time. What should other airlines do to compete with Southwest?

Legal Briefcase

Productivity versus Job Stress

United Parcel Service is the largest transportation company in the United States. In fact, UPS is twice the size of its closest competitor, Federal Express. The company's 128,000 trucks and 458 aircraft deliver three fourths of the ground packages and one fourth of the air packages in the United States. UPS grew from a small bicycle messenger service in 1907 to today's mammoth delivery service by dictating every task for its employees. Drivers are required to step out of their trucks with their right foot, fold their money face-up, and carry packages under their left arm. If they're considered slow, their supervisor rides with them, prodding them with stopwatches and clipboards. Until recently, drivers accepted such direction, taking comfort in their $40,000 to $50,000 salaries, generous benefits, and an attractive profit-sharing plan.

The need to increase productivity to meet increased competition from other delivery services prompted UPS to add 20 new services that require more skill. Drivers must learn an assortment of new codes and billing systems and handle an increasing number of packages that have special handling and time-sensitive requirements. All this pressure has taken its toll. A study showed that UPS employees scored in the 91st per- centile of U.S. workers for job stress. Many suffer from anxiety, phobias, or back strain. In April 1994, UPS settled a $3 million OSHA complaint that it didn't provide adequate safety for workers handling hazardous wastes. UPS paid $12 million to more than 2,000 drivers in 1993 when a judge ruled that UPS forced them to work through lunch. Labor problems cost the company more than $100 million from added expenses and customer defections when workers walked off their jobs on February 7, 1994.

UPS CEO Kent Nelson says UPS is using new technologies and better planning to achieve greater productivity without overloading employees. He says that what's different is that the variety of new services require the drivers to remember more things. Because the jobs now require more thinking, the company is hiring a new breed of more skilled and college-educated workers. In exchange for generous compensation, do you think the new breed of UPS workers will be more or less tolerant of the company's rules and demands?

Source: Robert Frank, "Driving Harder: As UPS Tries to Deliver More to Its Customers, Labor Problems Grow," *The Wall Street Journal*, May 25, 1994, pp. A1 and A5.

You'll see their names over and over in the business literature: Mayo, Maslow, McGregor, Herzberg. Finally, you'll look at modern applications of these theories and the managerial procedures for implementing them.

• • • EARLY MANAGEMENT STUDIES (TAYLOR) • • •

Several books in the 19th century presented management principles. For example, Charles Babbage (1792–1871) designed a mechanical computer and wrote a book on how to manage a manufacturing firm. However, Frederick Taylor earned the title Father of Scientific Management. His book, *The Principles of Scientific Management*, was published in 1911. Taylor's goal was to increase worker productivity so that both the firm and the worker could benefit from higher earnings. The way to improve productivity, Taylor thought, was to scientifically study the most efficient way to do things and then teach people those methods **(scientific management)**. Three elements were basic to his approach: time, methods, and rules of work. His most important tools were observation and the stopwatch.

A classic Taylor story involves his study of men shoveling rice, coal, and iron ore with the same shovel. Taylor felt that different materials called for different shovels. He proceeded to invent a wide variety of sizes and shapes of

scientific management
The study of workers to find the most efficient way of doing things and then teaching people those techniques.

time–motion studies

Studies of the tasks performed to complete a job and the time needed to do each task.

motion economy

Theory that every job can be broken down into a series of elementary motions.

shovels. Then, with stopwatch in hand, he measured output over time in what were called **time–motion studies**—studies of the tasks performed to complete a job and the time needed to do each task. Sure enough, an average person could shovel more (from 25 tons to 35 tons per day) with the proper shovel using the most efficient motions. This led to time–motion studies of virtually every factory job. The most efficient way of doing things was determined and became the standard for setting goals.

Taylor's scientific management became the dominant strategy for improving productivity in the early 1900s. There were hundreds of time–motion specialists in plants throughout the country. One follower of Taylor was H. L. Gantt. He developed charts by which managers plotted the employees' work a day in advance down to the smallest detail. (See Chapter 9 for a discussion of Gantt charts.) Frank and Lillian Gilbreth used Taylor's ideas in a three-year study of bricklaying. They developed the principle of **motion economy**, which showed that every job could be broken down into a series of elementary motions called a *therblig* (*Gilbreth* spelled backward). They then analyzed each motion to make it more efficient.

You can imagine how workers felt having time–motion people studying their every move. Scientific management viewed people largely as machines that needed to be properly programmed. There was little concern for the psychological or human aspects of work. Taylor felt that workers would perform at a high level of effectiveness (that is, be motivated) if they received high enough pay because money would allow them to meet their basic needs.

There's much evidence today that some of Taylor's ideas are still being implemented. The difference is that machinery is being used to standardize how work is done. Much emphasis in some companies is still placed on conformity to work rules rather than on creativity, flexibility, and responsiveness. For example, United Parcel Service (UPS), a highly successful global company, tells drivers how fast to walk (three feet per second), how many packages to pick up and deliver a day (average of 400), and even how to hold their keys (teeth up, third finger).[1] Nonetheless, the benefits of relying on workers to come up with creative solutions to productivity problems have long been recognized, as we'll discover next.

••• THE HAWTHORNE STUDIES (MAYO) •••

One of the studies that grew out of Taylor's research was conducted at the Western Electric Company's Hawthorne plant in Cicero, Illinois. The study began in 1927 and ended six years later. Let's see why it was one of the major studies in management literature.

The studies were conducted by Elton Mayo and his colleagues from Harvard University. The idea was to test the degree of lighting associated with optimum productivity. In this respect, it was a traditional scientific management study: The method was to keep records of productivity under different levels of illumination.

The problem with the initial experiments was that the productivity of the experimental group compared to other workers doing the same job went up regardless of whether the lighting was bright or dim. This was true even when the lighting was reduced to about the level of moonlight. These results confused and frustrated the researchers.

A second series of experiments was conducted. A separate test room was set up where temperature, humidity, and other environmental factors could be manipulated. A series of 13 experimental periods was recorded, and productivity went up each time. Productivity went up by 50 percent. When the

MAGNET WIRE INSULATING DEPARTMENT

This picture inside the Hawthorne plant is a classic in the study of motivation. It was at the Hawthorne plant that Elton Mayo and his team from Harvard University gave birth to human-based motivational theory. Before the studies at Hawthorne, workers were often programmed to work like human robots.

experimenters repeated the original condition (expecting productivity to fall to original levels), productivity kept increasing. The experiments were considered a total failure at this point. No matter what the experimenters did, productivity went up. What was causing the increase?

Mayo guessed that some human or psychological factor was involved. Thus, workers were interviewed about their feelings and attitudes toward the experiment. What the researchers found was to have a profound change in management thinking that continues today. Here's what they concluded:

- The women in the test room thought of themselves as a social group. The atmosphere was informal, they could talk freely, and they interacted regularly with their supervisors and the experimenters. They felt special and worked hard to stay in the group. This motivated them.

- The women were involved in planning the experiments. For example, they rejected one kind of pay schedule and recommended another, which was used. The women felt that their ideas were respected and that they were involved in managerial decision making. This, too, motivated them.

- The women enjoyed the atmosphere of their special room and the additional pay they got for more productivity. Job satisfaction increased dramatically.

Researchers now use the term **Hawthorne effect** to refer to people's tendency to behave differently when they know they're being studied. The Hawthorne studies' results encouraged researchers to begin to study human motivation and the managerial styles that lead to more productivity. The emphasis of research shifted away from Taylor's *scientific* management to Mayo's new *human-based* management.

Hawthorne effect
The tendency for people to behave differently when they know they are being studied.

Mayo's findings led to completely new assumptions about employees. One of those assumptions, of course, was that pay wasn't the only motivator. In fact, money was found to be a relatively low motivator. That change in assumptions led to many theories about the human side of motivation. One of the best-known motivation theorists was Abraham Maslow.

MASLOW'S HIERARCHY OF NEEDS

Abraham Maslow believed that to understand motivation at work, we must understand human motivation in general. It seemed to him that motivation arises from need. That is, people are motivated to satisfy *unmet needs*; needs that have been satisfied no longer provide motivation. He thought that needs could be placed on a hierarchy of importance.

Figure 10.1 shows Maslow's hierarchy of needs. The basic needs are

physiological needs
The needs for basic, life-giving elements such as food, water, and shelter.

safety needs
The needs for peace and security.

social needs
The needs to feel loved, accepted, and part of the group.

esteem needs
The needs for self-confidence and status.

self-actualization needs
The needs to achieve and to be all you can be.

1. **Physiological needs:** Basic survival needs including the need to drink, eat, and be sheltered from heat and cold.
2. **Safety needs:** The need to feel secure at work and at home.
3. **Social needs:** The need to feel loved, accepted, and part of the group.
4. **Esteem needs:** The need for recognition and acknowledgment from others, as well as self-respect and a sense of status or importance.
5. **Self-actualization needs:** The need to accomplish established goals and develop to your fullest potential.

When one need is satisfied, a higher-level need emerges and motivates the person to do something to satisfy it. The satisfied need is no longer a motivator.[2] For example, if you just ate a full dinner, food would no longer be a

FIGURE 10.1

MASLOW'S HIERARCHY OF NEEDS

Maslow's hierarchy of needs is based on the idea that motivation comes from need. If a need is met, it's no longer a motivator so a higher-level need becomes the motivator. This chart shows the various levels of need.

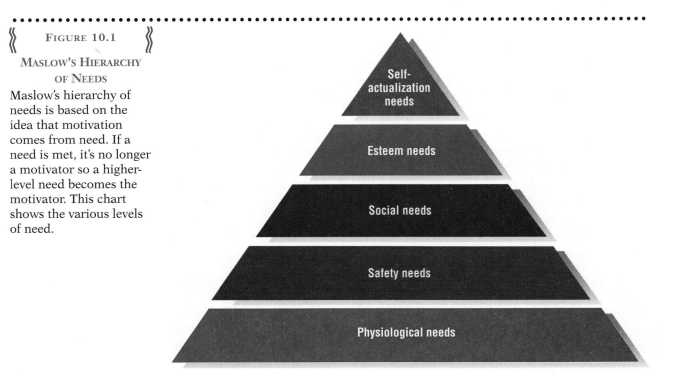

motivator. Also, lower-level needs (for example, food and drink) may emerge at any time they aren't met, and take our attention away from higher-level needs such as recognition or status.

Most of the world's workers struggle all day simply to meet the basic needs for food, shelter, and safety. In developed countries, such needs no longer dominate, and workers seek to satisfy growth needs (social, esteem, and self-actualization needs).

To compete successfully, U.S. firms must create a corporate environment that motivates the best and brightest workers. That means establishing a corporate culture that includes goals such as social contribution, honesty, reliability, service, quality, dependability, and unity.

Your job right now is to finish reading this chapter. How strongly would you be motivated to do that if you were sweating in a 105-degree room? Imagine now that your roommate turns on the air conditioning. Now that you're more comfortable, are you more likely to read? Look at Maslow's hierarchy of needs to see what need would be motivating you at both times. Can you see how helpful Maslow's theory is in understanding motivation by applying it to your own life?

CRITICAL THINKING

••• APPLYING MASLOW'S THEORY •••

Andrew Grove, president of Intel, observed Maslow's concepts in action in his firm. One woman, for example, took a low-paying job, which did little for her family's standard of living. Why? Because she needed the companionship her work offered (social/affiliation need). One of Grove's friends had a midlife crisis when he was made a vice president. This position had been a lifelong goal, and when the man reached it he had to find another way to motivate himself. People at a research and development lab were knowledge-centered. They were self-actualized by the desire to know more, but they had little desire to produce results, so little was achieved. Grove had to find new people who were results-oriented.

Once we understand employees' need level, it's easier to design programs that will trigger self-motivation. Grove believes that all motivation comes from within. He believes that self-actualized persons are achievement-oriented. Personally, Grove was motivated to earn a doctorate degree from the University of California at Berkeley. He proceeded at Intel to design a managerial program that emphasized achievement. Now Intel's managers are highly motivated to achieve their objectives because they feel rewarded for doing so.[3]

- What are the similarities and differences between Taylor's scientific management and Mayo's Hawthorne studies? How did Mayo's findings influence scientific management?
- Can you draw Maslow's hierarchy of needs and label the parts?
- According to Andrew Grove, what's the ultimate source of all motivation?

PROGRESS CHECK

MCGREGOR'S THEORY X AND THEORY Y
• • • • • • •

The way managers go about motivating people at work depends greatly on their attitudes toward workers. Douglas McGregor observed that managers had two different attitudes that led to entirely different managerial styles. He called the two systems *Theory X* and *Theory Y*.

••• THEORY X •••

Theory X management assumes:

- The average person dislikes work and will avoid it if possible.
- Because of this dislike, the average person must be forced, controlled, directed, or threatened with punishment to make him or her put forth the effort to achieve the organization's goals.
- The average worker prefers to be directed, wishes to avoid responsibility, has relatively little ambition, and wants security.
- Primary motivators are fear and money.

The natural consequence of such attitudes, beliefs, and assumptions is a manager who is very "busy" and who hangs over people telling them what to do and how to do it. Motivation is more likely to take the form of punishment for bad work rather than reward for good work. Workers are given little responsibility, authority, or flexibility. Those were the assumptions behind Taylor's scientific management and all the theorists who preceded Taylor. No doubt you've seen such managers in action. How did this make you feel? Is that how you prefer to be managed? Are these assumptions accurate regarding your work attitudes?

For years, the typical manager operated from such assumptions. That's why management literature focused on time–motion studies that calculated the "one best" way to perform a task and the "optimum" time to be devoted to a task. It was assumed that workers needed to be trained and carefully watched to see that they conformed to the standards. Would you like to be told exactly how to do something in a given amount of time with no room for creativity, flexibility, or time to relax and take a breather?

••• THEORY Y •••

Theory Y makes entirely different assumptions about people:

- The average person likes work; it's as natural as play or rest.
- The average person naturally works toward goals to which he or she is committed.

When football coaches or drill sergeants sound the order for their players or recruits to "jump," the only response they expect to hear is "How high?" Football coaches and drill sergeants generally serve in job situations where Theory X principles are appropriate. Can you think of other situations in which Theory X managers thrive?

- The depth of a person's commitment to goals depends on the perceived rewards for achieving them.

- Under certain conditions, the average person not only accepts but also seeks responsibility.

- People are capable of using a relatively high degree of imagination, creativity, and cleverness to solve problems.

- In industry, the average person's intellectual potential is only partially realized.

- People are motivated by a variety of rewards. Each worker is stimulated by a reward unique to that worker (time off, money, recognition, etc.).

Rather than emphasize authority, direction, and close supervision, Theory Y emphasizes a relatively free managerial atmosphere in which workers are free to set objectives, be creative, be flexible, and go beyond the goals set by management.[4] A key technique in meeting these objectives is empowerment ◀-- P.220 --▶. Empowerment gives employees both the right to make decisions and the tools to implement those decisions. For empowerment to be a real motivator, management should follow three steps: (1) Find out what people think the problems in the organization are. (2) Let them design the solutions. (3) Get out of the way and let them put those solutions into action.

Often employees complain that they're asked to become involved in company decision making, but their managers fail to actually empower them to make decisions. Have you ever worked in such an atmosphere? How did that make you feel?

Traditional managerial styles were based on one of two major assumptions:

- Workers are basically lazy and must be given direction, threatened, and negatively motivated (Theory X); or

- Workers are basically goal-oriented and self-motivated. The best managerial style is to offer them incentives and freedom (Theory Y).

The trend in most U.S. businesses is toward Theory Y management. One reason is that many service industries are finding Theory Y helpful in dealing with on-the-spot problems. Dan Kaplan of Hertz Rental Corporation would attest to this. He empowers his employees in the field to think and work as entrepreneurs ◀-- P.28 --▶. Another reason for a more flexible, permissive managerial style is to meet competition from foreign firms such as those in Japan. William Ouchi, a business professor at UCLA, wrote a best-selling management book called *Theory Z: How American Business Can Meet the Japanese Challenge.* We'll explore this theory after we summarize Theories X and Y.

••• APPLYING THEORY X AND THEORY Y •••

The trouble with these neat theories is that no organization that we know of is run strictly according to either Theory X or Theory Y—not even the army. You've probably known managers who are self-starters and perform best when they share in decision making. They may even resent taking orders. You've probably also known managers who don't want responsibility for making crucial decisions and prefer to be told what to do. After they're told what to do, they do their jobs with care and determination. Both types of managers could work for the same company. It's wise for managers to be flexible in applying Theory X or Y to those they supervise. Some people do better with direction; others do better with more freedom. Your natural inclination may be to choose a Theory Y–type manager as your supervisor, while your friend may prefer a Theory X–type supervisor. At the end of this chapter, a case discusses how two companies in the same industry use different approaches to management. One, Mrs. Fields Cookies, uses Theory Y techniques. The other, David's Cookies, uses Theory X. If you were the chief executive, how would you run that company—by Theory X or Theory Y? Or would you use your common sense and act according to the circumstances at hand?

OUCHI'S THEORY Z

Many organizations in Japan are run quite differently from those in the United States. Out of the Japanese system has come a concept called *Theory Z.* Its major elements include[5]

- Virtually guaranteed long-term employment for all employees.
- Emphasis on collective decision making.
- Relatively slow evaluation and promotion.
- Creation of a sense of involvement, closeness, and cooperation in the organization (family atmosphere).
- Expectation of individual responsibility (like Theory Y).
- Trust among all managers and workers.
- Few levels of management.

Several U.S. firms have attempted to adopt aspects of this managerial style. Citing Hewlett-Packard as an example, Ouchi quotes from a preamble to corporate objectives written by David Packard and William Hewlett: "The achievements of an organization are the results of the combined efforts of each individual in the organization working toward common objectives." The preamble goes on to list several requirements, including (1) the most capable people should be selected for each assignment, (2) enthusiasm should exist at all levels, and (3) all levels should work in unison toward common objectives.

The corporate philosophy at Hewlett-Packard is to have overall objectives that are clearly stated and agreed to, and to give people the freedom to work toward those goals in ways they determine best for their own areas of responsibility. When Harold Geneen was chief executive officer of ITT, he reviewed Theory Z. He noted that the basics of U.S. corporate life are just the opposite from those of Theory Z: relatively short-term employment, rapid promotions and dismissals, individual decision making and responsibilities, and a sense of personal rather than corporate loyalty.

Geneen questioned whether Americans would want to trade their heritage of personal freedoms and individual opportunity for the ingrown paternalism, humility, and selflessness of the Japanese. He doubted whether we could instill such feelings, even if we wanted to, even though Japanese-style

Organizations in the 1990s are learning to rely on the efforts of teams to enhance motivation and productivity. Teamwork is an integral part of the "HP WAY," Hewlett-Packard Company's philosophy and style of doing business. While recognition is based on individual contribution, the company emphasizes working together and sharing rewards.

management has been effective in some firms in England. A job for life in a firm may sound good until you think of the implications: no chance to change jobs and no opportunity to move up quickly through the ranks. There are fewer layers of management in Japan and, thus, fewer management positions. Geneen concluded that Theory Z wouldn't work as well in the United States as in Japan because of cultural differences. This emphasizes the fact that the appropriate managerial style is one that matches the culture, the situation, and the specific needs of individual employees. Ouchi recognized that fact in his book and didn't expect Theory Z to catch on in many U.S. firms. Figure 10.2 summarizes Theories X, Y, and Z.

What *are* the factors that motivate workers in the United States? That's the question we address next.

HERZBERG'S MOTIVATING FACTORS

Theories X, Y, and Z are concerned with *styles* of management. Another direction in managerial theory is to explore what managers can do with the job itself to motivate employees (a modern-day look at Taylor's research). Of all the factors controllable by managers, which are most effective in generating an enthusiastic work effort? In other words, this section is more concerned with the content of work than with style of management.

The most discussed study in this area was conducted by Frederick Herzberg in the mid-1960s.[6] He asked workers to rank various job-related factors in the order of importance relative to motivation. That is, what creates enthusiasm for workers and makes them work to full potential? The results, in order of importance, were

1. Sense of achievement.
2. Earned recognition.
3. Interest in the work itself.
4. Opportunity for growth.
5. Opportunity for advancement.
6. Importance of responsibility.

FIGURE 10.2

A COMPARISON OF THEORIES X, Y, AND Z

Theory X	Theory Y	Theory Z
1. Employees dislike work and will try to avoid it.	1. Employees view work as a natural part of life.	1. Employee involvement is the key to increased productivity.
2. Employees prefer to be controlled and directed.	2. Employees prefer limited control and direction.	2. Employee control is implied and informal.
3. Employees seek security, not responsibility.	3. Employees will seek responsibility under proper work conditions.	3. Employees prefer to share responsibility and decision making.
4. Employees must be intimidated by managers to perform.	4. Employees perform better in work environments that are nonintimidating.	4. Employees perform better in environments that foster trust and cooperation.
5. Employees are motivated by financial rewards.	5. Employees are motivated by many different needs.	5. Employees need guaranteed employment and will accept slow evaluations and promotions.

7. Peer and group relationships.

8. Pay.

9. Supervisor's fairness.

10. Company policies and rules.

11. Status.

12. Job security.

13. Supervisor's friendliness.

14. Working conditions.

Herzberg noted that the factors receiving the most votes were all clustered around job content. Workers like to feel that they contribute. (Sense of achievement was number 1.) They want to earn recognition (number 2) and feel their jobs are important (number 6). They want responsibility (which is why learning is so important) and want recognition for that responsibility by having a chance for growth and advancement. Of course, workers also want the job to be interesting.

Herzberg noted further that factors having to do with the job environment weren't considered motivators by workers. It was interesting to find that one of those factors was pay. Workers felt that the absence of good pay, job security, friendly supervisors, and the like could cause dissatisfaction, but the presence of those factors didn't motivate them; they just provided satisfaction and contentment in the work situation.

The conclusions of Herzberg's study were that certain factors, called **motivators**, did motivate employees and gave them a great deal of satisfaction. (See Figure 10.3.) These factors mostly had to do with job content and were grouped as follows:

motivators
Factors that provide satisfaction and motivate people to work.

- The work itself.
- Achievement.
- Recognition.
- Responsibility.
- Growth and advancement.

hygiene factors
Factors that cause dissatisfaction if they are missing, but do not motivate if they are increased.

Other elements of the job were what Herzberg called **hygiene factors**. These had to do mostly with job environment and could cause dissatisfaction if they were missing, but they wouldn't necessarily motivate if they were increased. They were

- Company policy and administration.
- Supervision.
- Working conditions.
- Interpersonal relations.
- Salary.

Combining McGregor's Theory Y with Herzberg's motivating factors, we can conclude

- Employees work best when management assumes that they're competent and self-motivated (Theory Y). Theory Y calls for a participative style of management.
- The best way to motivate employees is to make the job interesting, help them to achieve their objectives, and recognize that achievement through advancement and added responsibility.

MOTIVATORS	HYGIENE FACTORS
(These factors can be used to motivate workers.)	(These factors can cause dissatisfaction, but changing them will have little motivational effect.)
Work itself	Company policy and administration
Achievement	Supervision
Recognition	Working conditions
Responsibility	Interpersonal relations (co-workers)
Growth and advancement	Salary, status, and job security

FIGURE 10.3

HERZBERG'S MOTIVATORS AND HYGIENE FACTORS
There's some controversy over Herzberg's results. For example, sales managers often use money as a motivator. Recent studies have shown that money can be a motivator if used as part of a recognition program.

••• APPLYING HERZBERG'S THEORIES •••

Pat Blake, a Sunnen Products Co. employee, says that what makes her happy to work extra hours or to learn new skills is less tangible than money or bonuses—it's a kind word from her boss. "When something good happens, like we have a shipping day with so many thousands of dollars going out the door, they let us know about that," Blake said. "It kind of makes you want to go for the gold."[7] Improved working conditions (such as better wages or tighter security) are taken for granted after workers get used to them. This is what Herzberg meant by *hygiene factors*; their absence causes dissatisfaction, but their presence doesn't motivate. The best motivator may be a simple and sincere "I really appreciate what you're doing."

Many surveys have been conducted to test Herzberg's theories. They support Herzberg's finding that the number one motivator isn't money, but a sense of achievement and recognition for a job well done. In fact, a 1994 survey by *Industry Week* showed that 80 percent of the employees asked to pick the most important factor in fostering company loyalty chose recognition of good work.[8]

When asked what makes them content with their current jobs, more than half of those surveyed listed open communication with higher-ups, the nature of the work, the quality of management, control over work content, the opportunity to gain new skills, the quality of co-workers, and the opportunity for intellectually stimulating work. Only a third mentioned salary as important.[9]

JOB ENRICHMENT

Both Maslow's and Herzberg's theories were extended by job enrichment theory. **Job enrichment** is a motivational strategy that emphasizes motivating the worker through the job itself. Work is assigned to individuals so that they have the opportunity to complete an identifiable task from beginning to end. They're held responsible for successful completion of the task. The motivational effect of job enrichment can come from the opportunities for personal achievement, challenge, and recognition. Go back and review Maslow's and Herzberg's work to see how job enrichment grew out of those theories. Five characteristics of work are believed to be important in affecting individual motivation and performance:

job enrichment
Efforts to make jobs more interesting, challenging, and rewarding.

FROM THE PAGES OF...

Entrepreneur
MAGAZINE

Motivation in Small Business

This chapter teaches you how to motivate employees, but what motivates the management of smaller firms? They face all kinds of adversity every day. What makes them willing to work six days a week, 15 hours a day? *Entrepreneur* magazine talked to a few managers to learn the answer. Anita Roddick, founder of The Body Shop, Inc., says, "Every time I walk by one of my shops and see what an educational role my company plays in a community, it sends chills down my spine. . . . In America, we have a shop in Harlem where 50 percent of the profits go into community development, and the other 50 percent go toward the funding of a similar shop elsewhere in the United States. The pride that shop brings to the staff and local residents motivates me." Anita Roddick is clearly at the top of Maslow's hierarchy.

Sheri Poe of Ryka Inc. says, "I think it's really important that people you're working with are as committed to the same vision as you are, so you can support each other and keep each other motivated." Management by objectives is one strategy for maintaining a common vision in the firm.

Richard Melman the visionary behind Chicago's highly successful restaurant development group, Lettuce Entertain You Enterprises Inc., states, "I think it all adds up to having fun. When it stops being fun, I'll stop doing it." It's helpful to remember that all motivation ultimately comes from within and nothing motivates a person like having fun on the job.

Source: Liza Leung, "Turn It On," *Entrepreneur*, May 1994, pp. 92–96.

1. *Skill variety.* The extent to which a job demands different skills of the person.
2. *Task identity.* The degree to which the job requires doing a job with a visible outcome from beginning to end.
3. *Task significance.* The degree to which the job has a substantial impact on the lives or work of others in the company.
4. *Autonomy.* The degree of freedom, independence, and discretion in scheduling work and determining procedures.
5. *Feedback.* The amount of direct and clear information received about job performance.

Variety, identity, and significance contribute to a job's meaningfulness. Autonomy gives employees a feeling of responsibility, and feedback contributes to a feeling of achievement and recognition.

Sherwin-Williams began a job enrichment program in its Richmond, Kentucky, plant in 1975. Employees were grouped into self-managed teams « P.228 », and members were trained to do all of the jobs assigned to their team. Teams have autonomy to decide where members work, what they do, and how they train other team members. The team is responsible for its own results. Compensation is based on a pay-for-knowledge system, and team members' performance is evaluated by their team leaders and peers. Employees are made to feel responsible for the entire production process.

The program was extremely successful. Overall, absenteeism is lower than at other Sherwin-Williams plants and runs less than 2 percent. Turnover is very low, and productivity is 30 percent higher than at similar plants. Cost per gallon of paint is 45 percent lower than at traditional paint plants. The firm has expanded the program to other plants and distribution centers.

Enriching jobs motivates workers by appealing to personal values such as achievement, challenge, and recognition. Harley-Davidson is a company committed to the principles of job enrichment. At Harley-Davidson, self-managed teams of workers are trained to perform different tasks and have clear autonomy over how their job is organized. The team is also responsible for its own results.

Job enrichment is based on Herzberg's higher motivators such as responsibility, achievement, and recognition. This is in contrast to **job simplification**, which produces task efficiency by breaking down the job into simple steps and assigning people to each of those steps. There isn't much motivation in doing boring, repetitive work, but some managers still operate on the Taylor level of motivation and use job simplification. One way to increase motivation is to use **job enlargement**, which combines a series of tasks into one assignment that's more challenging, interesting, and motivating. For example, Maytag redesigned its work so that employees could work on an entire water pump instead of separate parts. **Job rotation** also makes work more interesting and motivating by moving employees from one job to another. You can see the problem of having to train employees to do several different operations, but usually the resulting increase in morale and motivation offsets the additional costs.

Job design is clearly a way to rethink jobs so that people feel responsibility and a sense of accomplishment. Another way is to get everyone to agree on specific corporate objectives.

job simplification
Process of producing task efficiency by breaking down the job into simple steps and assigning people to each of those steps.

job enlargement
Job enrichment strategy involving combining a series of tasks into one assignment that is more challenging and interesting.

job rotation
Job enrichment strategy involving moving employees from one job to another.

GOAL-SETTING THEORY AND MANAGEMENT BY OBJECTIVES

Goal-setting theory is based on the notion that the setting of specific ambitious but attainable goals is related to high levels of motivation and performance if the goals are accepted, are accompanied by feedback, and are facilitated by organizational conditions. Nothing makes more sense intuitively than the idea that all members of an organization should have some basic agreement about the organization's overall goals and the specific objectives to be met by each department and individual in the organization. It follows, then, that someone would develop a system to involve everyone in the organization in goal setting and implementation. Such a system is called *management by objectives (MBO)*. MBO was developed by Peter Drucker and was very popular in the 1960s. Big corporations such as Ford Motor Company used it. Ford executives taught the method to the U.S. Department of Defense, and from there it spread to other government agencies.

goal-setting theory
Theory that setting specific, attainable goals can motivate workers and improve performance if the goals are accepted, are accompanied by feedback, and are facilitated by organizational conditions.

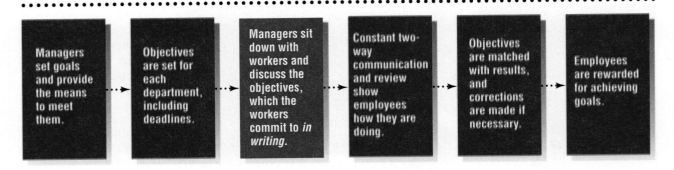

Managers set goals and provide the means to meet them.

Objectives are set for each department, including deadlines.

Managers sit down with workers and discuss the objectives, which the workers commit to *in writing*.

Constant two-way communication and review show employees how they are doing.

Objectives are matched with results, and corrections are made if necessary.

Employees are rewarded for achieving goals.

〈〈 **FIGURE 10.4** 〉〉

MANAGEMENT BY OBJECTIVES

The critical step in the MBO process is the one where managers sit down with workers, discuss the objectives, and get the workers to commit to those objectives in writing. Commitment is the key!

management by objectives (MBO)

A system of goal setting and implementation that involves a cycle of discussion, review, and evaluation of objectives among top and middle-level managers, supervisors, and employees.

Management by objectives (MBO) is a system of goal setting and implementation that involves a cycle of discussion, review, and evaluation of objectives among top and middle-level managers, supervisors, and employees. It meets the criteria of goal-setting theory when implemented properly and can be quite effective. Figure 10.4 shows six steps in the motivational MBO process:

1. Top management consults with managers throughout the organization to set long-range goals and the means to determine whether those goals are being met over time.

2. Overall corporate goals are clearly formulated, and subgoals are determined for each department. These subgoals are further divided into objectives for each unit and each individual within the unit. All this is done with the full participation and cooperation of the people involved, including deciding the means for reaching the overall goals and the deadlines.

3. The key to success of the MBO system is a third step where managers and workers sit down with their superiors, review the objectives, adjust them if necessary, and then commit themselves to those objectives in a written contract or agreement that states clearly the objectives, the means for reaching the objectives, and the time periods involved. The idea is that participation in goal setting involves everyone in the goals and motivates them by making them feel part of a team. This is consistent with the Hawthorne effect, discussed earlier.

4. Implementation of the plan calls for periodic reviews of progress, constant two-way communication among all participants, and the application of good management so that the spirit of mutual cooperation toward agreed-upon goals is maintained.

5. The next step is to monitor progress by matching objectives to accomplishments, noting deviations, making needed corrections, communicating the results to all participants, and adjusting to any unanticipated situations.

6. The final step is to reward employees for achieving the desired goals or to assist employees in reaching the goals in the future.

Management by objectives is most effective in relatively stable situations where long-range plans can be made and implemented with little need for major changes. Even in rapidly changing high-tech industries, such as computers and biotechnology, MBO may be effective. That is, managers should formulate plans in cooperation with everyone, commit people to those plans, monitor results, and reward accomplishment. To summarize, management by

SPOTLIGHT ON SMALL BUSINESS

Building the Team Small-Business Style

Both large and small companies would agree that attracting and keeping skilled employees is essential for growing a successful business. But small-business owners would probably be the first to admit that often it's the little things they do that keep employees motivated.

As a small business with limited resources, Big Wheel/Rossi Auto Stores in Mendota Heights, Minnesota, can't always sweeten the economic pie for its employees. Does this bother Vice President Jerry Johnson? No! He feels recognition and incentive programs work better than high hourly wages in motivating the firm's employees. Big Wheel recognizes performance excellence through specially marked parking spots and tickets for sporting events and concerts. Also, the monthly President's Award and a bimonthly merchandise award offer prizes ranging from dinners and department store gift certificates to trophies for outstanding employ-

ees in multiple categories. All winners are acknowledged in the company newsletter and are singled out at the company awards banquet. Motivation at Big Wheel extends beyond the workplace. The company newsletter recognizes employees who make their mark in community activities and service. "Winners in any aspect of life are usually winners in the workplace," according to Johnson.

Developing an environment in which workers can feel motivated is an important challenge to small businesses. Perhaps David Young of the Friendly Ice Cream Corporation of Wilbraham, Massachusetts, said it best: "We don't motivate employees. They motivate themselves."

Source: Gail Krueger-Nicholson, "Use Incentive Programs to Keep Employees Motivated," *Automotive Marketing*, September 1, 1990; and Alan Liddle, "Personnel Execs: Motivation Is the Key to Quality Work," *Nation's Restaurant News*, October 29, 1990.

---

objectives is a strategy for involving all members of an organization in goal setting and implementation. Properly conducted, it generates a feeling of involvement and cooperation (motivation). MBO is also an excellent way to determine who deserves a promotion and increased pay and who doesn't, based on results.

Problems arise when management uses MBO as a strategy for *forcing* managers and workers to commit to goals that aren't really mutually agreed upon, but are set by top management. Also, care must be taken to maintain open two-way communication and an organizational culture that values the stated objectives. For example, all universities talk about the importance of teaching, but few give full recognition to good teachers in promotion decisions. The objectives are clear, but the reward system contradicts the objectives. The same kind of conflict may occur in other organizations.

It's also important for managers to understand the difference between helping and coaching subordinates. *Helping* means to work with the subordinate, doing part of the work if necessary. *Coaching* means acting as a resource—teaching, guiding, recommending—but not helping (that is, not participating actively in the task).

Helping subordinates tends to make them weak, dependent, and irresponsible. Coaching subordinates tends to make them feel like they're part of a team and capable of doing their work on their own once they learn the system, and this is highly motivating. Bill Eaton of Levi Strauss's executive management committee says that "on a day-to-day basis, his passion and satisfaction come from backing the efforts of his employees, getting them what they need for the job, educating them and working with them as members of the team."[10]

PROGRESS CHECK

- Briefly describe the managerial attitudes behind Theories X, Y, and Z.
- Relate job enrichment to Herzberg's motivating factors.
- What are the six steps in management by objectives?
- What's the difference between helping and coaching? Which motivates workers more?

BUILDING TEAMWORK THROUGH COMMUNICATION

Management by objectives teaches us that in any organization, one key to successful management and motivation is the establishment and maintenance of open two-way communication between and among managers and workers so that everyone understands the objectives and works together effectively and efficiently to achieve them. Communication must flow two ways among all members of an organization. The problem today is that most communication flows only one way: from top management down. This communication takes the form of directives, policies, announcements, memos, rules, procedures, and the like.

The flow upward, from workers to managers, is usually severely clogged. Rarely do organizations have any formal means of upward communication (from employees to management) equivalent to directives and announcements. Instead, the burden falls on workers to initiate contact with supervisors and present their ideas and suggestions. As you know, few people in any organization tell the boss when things aren't going well. Children don't tell parents when they've broken something, students don't tell teachers when someone has goofed, and employees don't tell bosses. Such a system creates an "us against them" attitude, where workers feel united in their distrust and avoidance of managers. To create an atmosphere of "us working together," managers have to become active listeners and valued assistants to workers. Such a change demands a long-term commitment, radical retraining of managers, and careful creation of new attitudes and beliefs among workers.

Teamwork between and among managers and employees doesn't just happen. The whole organization must be structured to facilitate dialogue. Here are three procedures for encouraging open communication:

- Top management must first create an organizational culture that rewards listening by being listeners themselves; by creating facilities (for example, conference rooms) for having dialogues; and by showing others that talking with superiors counts—by providing feedback, adopting employee suggestions, and rewarding upward communication—even if the discussion is negative. Employees must feel free to say anything.
- Supervisors and managers must be trained in listening skills. Most people receive no such training in school or anywhere else, so organizations must do the training themselves or hire someone to do it.
- Barriers to open communication must be removed; facilitating mechanisms must be installed. Barriers include separate offices, parking spaces, bathrooms, dining rooms, and other such facilities for various levels of management and workers. Such facilities foster an "us versus them" attitude. Other barriers are different dress codes, different ways of addressing one another (for example, calling workers by their first

names and managers by their last), and so on. Removing such barriers takes imagination and a willingness to give up the special privileges of management. Facilitating efforts include large lunch tables where all organization members eat, conference rooms, organizational picnics, organizational athletic teams, and other such outings where managers mix with and socialize with each other and with workers. George Fisher, Kodak's CEO, feels it is important for managers to be visible and accessible. Fisher frequently drops in on researchers for updates on projects and chats with employees each morning as he eats his breakfast in the company cafeteria. He invites employees to send him e-mail messages. He personally responds to the approximately 30 messages a day with handwritten notes.[11]

Let's see how some organizations are addressing the challenge of open communication.

••• MOTIVATION THROUGH SELF-MANAGED TEAMS •••

Companies that have developed highly motivated work forces usually have several things in common. Among the most important are open communication systems and self-managed teams. This is a feature at the Canadian plant of Phillips Cables Ltd., which produces hair-thin fiber-optic cable in a state-of-the-art factory. The company is in a joint venture with Furukawa Electric of Japan called Phillips-Fitel.

Despite the fact that the Furukawa managers speak no French and the plant employees speak almost no English, there's an open communication system that has helped to create a strongly motivated work force. According to union president Marcel Rouleau, "The only boss we have is the plant manager. We don't have incompetents telling us what to do when we know better. Now they consult us. . . . We feel a lot more creative and it's rewarding."[12]

Kenneth Kohrs, vice president of car product development at Ford Motor Co., says that an inside group known as Team Mustang set the guidelines for how production teams should be formed. Given the challenge to create a car that will make people dust off their old "Mustang Sally" records and dance into the showrooms, the 400-member team was also given the freedom to make decisions without waiting for approval from headquarters or other departments. The team moved everyone from various departments into cramped offices under one roof of an old warehouse. Draftsmen sat next to "bean counters," engineers next to stylists. Budgetary walls that divided departments were knocked down as department managers were persuaded to surrender some control over their subordinates.

When the Mustang convertible displayed shaking problems, suppliers were called in and the team worked around the clock to solve the problem. The engineers were so motivated to complete the program on schedule and under budget that they slept on the floors of the warehouse. Senior

Highly motivated work teams depend on open communications and self-management. Ford Motor Company provided such an atmosphere for its 400-member Team Mustang work group. What did the company get for its trust and commitment in this self-managed team? A showroom winner that came in under budget and was finished a couple of months early.

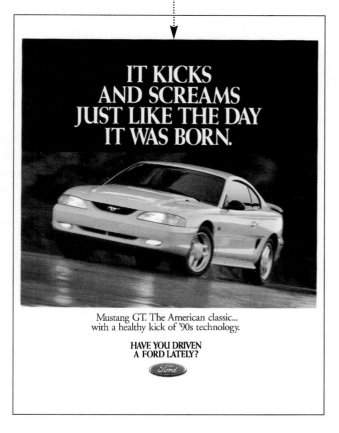

IT KICKS AND SCREAMS JUST LIKE THE DAY IT WAS BORN.

Mustang GT. The American classic... with a healthy kick of '90s technology.

HAVE YOU DRIVEN A FORD LATELY?

Teamwork Calls for Team Compensation

In many companies the movement toward cross-functional teams has proceeded much faster than the systems needed to support the change. Technological and training systems are keeping up, but the performance appraisal and compensation systems in many cases are lagging. A recent study of 4,500 teams in more than 500 organizations found that 80 percent of the firms still based compensation solely on *individual* performance. The ultimate goal, however, is to reward individuals based on *group* performance. A separate study of Fortune 1000 firms found that the number of such plans was quite small, but since most teams had only been in operation for a short time (three years or less) most believe this circumstance will change. Guidelines currently being used to design team incentive systems include:

1. Formulate team awards that reinforce the cross-functional team concept. The belief among team members should be that none of them can win unless they all win. In a major New York bank, for example, measurable goals were established for product sales, customer service, and profitability. All personnel are included on cross-functional teams to reach those goals. No one wins in terms of bonuses unless all three objectives are achieved. Initial results have exceeded management's highest expectations.

2. Any individual rewards must reinforce the cross-functional team concept. The compensation system must be designed from scratch to reward team efforts, not reconfigured from a functional base due to the likelihood that team members will tend to be more loyal to their function than the team if the function controls the funds.

3. Bring the rewards down to the team level. Gainsharing and profit-sharing plans are too far removed from the team to offer true incentives for teamwork. There should always be a clear, direct connection between team success and team rewards.

4. Reward individual team players also. Outstanding team players—those that go beyond what is required and make an outstanding individual contribution to the firm—should be separately recognized for their additional contribution. Some firms use knowledge-based pay to reward individuals. At Johnsonville Foods in Sheboygan Falls, Wisconsin, for example, employees are paid the market value of their jobs. When they master a series of skills, they receive a raise. Bonuses are also given those who exceed quality and efficiency standards or teach teammates something new.

5. Use noncash as well as cash rewards. Team members are often incentivized by such things as free vacation trips, briefcases, home computers, or some other noncash reward.

6. Use informal methods of reward until the team compensation plan is in place. Teams can be mentioned in company newsletters or bulletin boards. Verbal recognition can be given at staff meetings. Teams can be sent to baseball games or similar events, or given team-building symbols such as shirts, coffee mugs, and other gifts with the team name and goals on them.

Measuring and rewarding individual performance on teams while at the same time rewarding team performance can be tricky. Nonetheless, it can be done. Football players are rewarded as a team when the team goes to the play-offs and Super Bowl, but they are paid individually as well. Companies are now experimenting with and developing similar incentive systems.[13]

Ford executives were tempted to overrule the program, but they stuck with their promise not to meddle. The team solved the shaking problem and still came in under budget and a couple of months early.[14]

For companies to implement such groups or teams, managers must reinvent work groups. We'll discuss that next.

••• RETHINKING THE CORPORATION •••

In their book *Re-inventing the Corporation* (New York: Warner Books, 1985), John Naisbitt and Patricia Aburdene say the goal of management is to adopt "new humanistic values." Such new values enable employees to *motivate themselves* because they feel more a part of a unified corporate team.

Naisbitt and Aburdene suggest certain steps for creating a new, better corporate atmosphere; these include some suggestions we referred to earlier: calling everyone by his or her first name, eliminating executive parking spots and bathrooms, having everyone answer his or her own phone, and throwing out the organization chart.

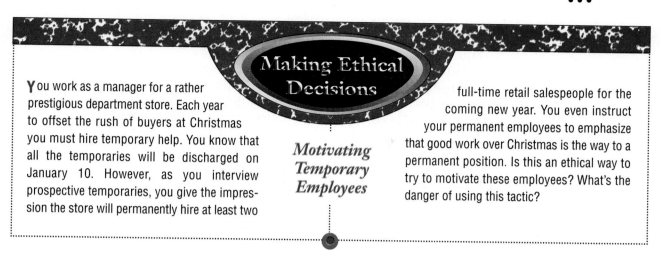

Making Ethical Decisions

Motivating Temporary Employees

You work as a manager for a rather prestigious department store. Each year to offset the rush of buyers at Christmas you must hire temporary help. You know that all the temporaries will be discharged on January 10. However, as you interview prospective temporaries, you give the impression the store will permanently hire at least two full-time retail salespeople for the coming new year. You even instruct your permanent employees to emphasize that good work over Christmas is the way to a permanent position. Is this an ethical way to try to motivate these employees? What's the danger of using this tactic?

The authors also suggested that managers "reinvent work." This means respecting workers, providing interesting work, rewarding good work, developing workers' skills, allowing some autonomy, and decentralizing authority.

Other points include the following: (1) The manager's role is that of teacher, mentor, and coach; (2) the best people want ownership in the firm; (3) the best managerial style isn't a top-down style, but a networking, people style; (4) quality is the new key to success; (5) successful large corporations copy the entrepreneurial flavor of small businesses; and (6) the Information Age enables firms to locate where there's a high quality of life since they don't have to be concerned with such industrial considerations as raw materials.

All these ideas are consistent with management thought in the 1990s. Clearly, there's a trend toward different management styles, as we described earlier. What's important to learn from this chapter is that the new management styles are largely motivational tools to bring out the best in more educated, better trained workers.[15] Those are the workers of the future, and they include you and me. Look through the points just outlined and see if you don't agree that it would be fun and productive to work in such an organization and that would help motivate you to do a better job.

••• CHANGING ORGANIZATIONS ISN'T EASY •••

We've come a long way from the time–motion studies of Frederick Taylor. Maslow, Mayo, Herzberg, and others have taught us to treat employees as associates and to get them more involved in decision making. This increases motivation and leads to greater productivity.

The problem is that many managers were brought up under a different system. Some were in the military and are used to telling people what to do rather than consulting with them. Others come from the football coach school of management. They tend to yell and direct rather than consult and discuss.

Furthermore, employees are often not used to participative management. The transition from Theory X to Theory Y management, from Taylor to Herzberg, is still going on. It's important, then, to have examples to follow when trying to implement the new approaches.

Mary Kay Ash of Mary Kay Cosmetics is certainly a manager who succeeded at taking a lead in employee motivation, customer service « P.39 », and establishment of a general partnership with employees. Let's review her story to see what lessons she can teach us.

... A TEAM-BUILDING MODEL FOR THE FUTURE: ...
MARY KAY COSMETICS

More than 36,000 Mary Kay beauty consultants invade Dallas every summer to participate in a three-day sales rally called Seminar. Seminar is part convention, part *Hello Dolly*. Caught up in the Mary Kay enthusiasm, the women laugh, cry, and sing as Mary Kay doles out diamonds and pink Cadillacs under enough spotlights and sequins to rival any Broadway musical.

Mary Kay started the $613 million company in 1963 when the promotion she'd been working toward was given to her male assistant, whom she'd just spent nine months training. She vowed to run a company that would treat women right and "not ruin their self-esteem" or limit how much money they can make. Developing women's leadership potential gives national sales director Shirley Hutton a lot of pride. "Give me a hard-working waitress and in a year I'll turn her into a director making $35,000." Today, the new Mary Kay consultant is more likely to be a refugee from corporate America. There are lawyers, a Harvard MBA, and even a pediatrician in the Mary Kay ranks.

But everyone starts off on the same foot. Say you were a rocket scientist in your last job. Great. Buy a beauty case and start calling your friends. Earnings increase as sales rise and as the consultant recruits more consultants. More important, especially for those who have healthy earnings, is the emotional compensation. At Seminar, there's plenty of it.

Color-coded suits, badges, sashes, crowns, and other emblems show how far each person has come. Like generals inspecting ribbons, they immediately see who's done what. Despite the glitter of the diamonds and cars, the most treasured rewards are the vacations. On one trip to London, Mary Kay had Harrods closed for an hour so that only Mary Kay consultants could shop. Mary Kay herself goes on many of these trips. Her consultants consider her uniquely approachable. "Mary Kay calls you her daughter and looks you dead in the eye. She is so sincerely concerned about your welfare that you feel you can do anything," reports one consultant. The consultants treat their customers with the same interest by remembering their birthdays, sending them notes, and showing that they're interested.

Gloria Hilliard Mayfield, a Harvard MBA, left her marketing manager position to sell Mary Kay full-time. Did her former classmates give her a hard time? You bet. "When you're from Harvard and you say you're starting an entrepreneurial venture, people are all ears. Then you tell them it's Mary Kay; they say *what*?! I try to explain it's no different from my having a Ford dealership. The Ford dealer's an independent entrepreneur. So am I." In fact, Mary Kay consultants consider themselves less cosmetic salespeople than sellers of the premier business opportunity for women.[16]

LEARNING FROM THE MARY KAY EXPERIENCE Mary Kay developed not just a business but a true American success story. She believes that success in business depends on several key factors such as believing in yourself and showing interest in your employees and your customers. You can prepare for a business career by getting involved in campus activities and learning to (1) get along with people by practicing listening skills, (2) be a concise, clear writer so that you can write short, readable memos and reports, and (3) be a public speaker by becoming an officer in a campus club and giving talks. Today, corporate recruiters complain that business graduates lack creativity, people skills, aptitude for teamwork, and the ability to speak and write clearly and concisely. Remember, the best way to lead is by example, and Mary Kay is a model for employees and for managers in all types of firms as well. Lessons we can learn from the Mary Kay example include

Reaching Beyond Our Borders

Exporting Motivation to Aspiring Capitalists

The fall of the Berlin Wall, the opening of Eastern Europe, and the spread of free enterprise in the former Soviet Union presented many opportunities for ambitious businesspeople. Dollar signs danced in the minds of would-be capitalist adventurers as they dreamed of building a niche in these budding free-market frontiers. However, a major stumbling block also plagued the flood of entrepreneurs pouring into Eastern Europe and the former Soviet Union. How do you motivate workers who had little reason to be motivated in the state-controlled systems in which they were employed?

The former Soviet Union is a good case to explore. Russians have worked under the communist/socialist system since 1917. Few are old enough to remember anything different. Empowering and motivating these workers to perform is no small feat. This challenge seems especially difficult and acute in staffing the emerging service industry in the new Commonwealth of Independent States. The obvious question is, How do you change the mind-set of workers who've worked and survived in non–service-oriented state-owned enterprises?

Radisson Hotels International thinks it has a solution. The company exported its successful "Yes I Can" program to the 430-room Radisson Slavjanskaya Hotel, which opened in Moscow in 1991. Juergen Bartels, president of the Carlson Hospitality Group (Radisson's parent company), recognizes that the firm's biggest challenge is to find, train, and motivate the hotel's employees. Bartels decided to recruit workers with service experience, such as teachers and hospital workers. He believes these workers are more likely to have developed some service attitudes. To motivate the workers, the hotel offers incentives such as Western goods like VCRs, TVs, jeans, and other items in short supply in Russia. Employees are able to redeem incentive points for goods in the hotel store.

The Radisson experiment is being closely followed, as are other attempts to motivate workers in Poland, Hungary, Bulgaria, and other Eastern European nations where worker motivation has never been a high priority.

Source: "'Yes I Can' Gives Hotels a Boost," *Lodging Hospitality*, October 1, 1990.

- The future growth of industry and business in general depends on a motivated, productive work force.
- Motivation is for the most part internally generated by workers themselves. The process that releases that energy includes giving employees more freedom to be creative and rewarding achievement when it occurs.
- The first step in any motivational program is to establish open communication among workers and managers so that the feeling generated is one of cooperation and teamwork, a family-type atmosphere.

• • • MOTIVATION IN THE FUTURE • • •

What can you learn from all the theories and experiences discussed in this chapter? You should have learned that people can be motivated to improve productivity and quality of work if managers know which technique to use and when.

Today's customers expect high-quality, customized goods and services. That means employees must provide extensive personal service and pay close attention to details. Employees will have to work smart as well as hard. No

Yes I Can! Customer Service Training

A Powerful Marketing Strategy

▲ **Focuses on Building Repeat Business**
▲ **Communicates a Service Level**
▲ **Distinguishes Radisson**
▲ **Has Worldwide Understanding**

amount of supervision can force an employee to smile or go the extra mile to help a customer. In fact, no theory of motivation will work with all workers.

The point is that employees aren't alike; different employees respond to different managerial and motivational styles. Tomorrow's managers won't be able to use any one formula for all employees. Rather, they'll have to get to know each worker as an individual and taylor (pun intended) the motivational effort to the individual.

In general, motivation will come from the job itself rather than from external punishments or rewards. Managers need to give workers what they need to do a good job: the right tools, the right information, and the right amount of cooperation.

You see, motivation isn't so difficult. It begins with acknowledging a job well done and telling those who do such a job that you appreciate them, especially in front of others. After all is said and done, the best and cheapest motivator is frequently the words, "Thanks, I appreciate what you've done for me."[17]

PROGRESS CHECK

- What are several steps firms can use to increase internal communications and, thus, motivation?
- What are the six steps in "reinventing work," and how are they related to motivation?
- What problems may emerge when trying to implement participative management?
- Why is it important today to adjust motivational styles to individual employees? Are there any general principles of motivation that today's managers should follow?

SUMMARY
••••••

1. Explain Taylor's scientific management.

1. Frederick Taylor was one of the first people to study management.
   - ***Who is Frederick Taylor?***
   Frederick Taylor is the father of scientific management. He did time–motion studies to learn the most efficient way of doing a job and then trained workers in those procedures. He published his book on scientific management in 1911. The Gilbreths and H. L. Gantt were followers of Taylor.

2. Describe the Hawthorne studies and relate their significance to human-based management.

2. Management theory moved away from Taylor's scientific management and toward theories that stress human factors of motivation.
   - ***What led to the more humane managerial styles to increase motivation?***

The greatest impact on motivation theory was generated by the Hawthorne studies in the late 1920s and early 1930s. Elton Mayo found that human factors such as feelings of involvement and participation led to greater productivity gains than did physical changes in the workplace.

3. Maslow studied basic human motivation and found that motivation was based on need—an unfilled need motivated people to satisfy it, while a satisfied need no longer motivated.
   • ***What were the various levels of need identified by Maslow?***
   Moving up from the bottom of Maslow's hierarchy of needs, the needs are physiological, safety, social, esteem, and self-actualization.
   • ***Can managers use this theory?***
   Yes, they can recognize a person's unmet needs and have work provide the satisfaction.

   3. Identify the levels of Maslow's hierarchy of needs and relate their importance to employee motivation.

4. McGregor held that managers can have two attitudes toward employees. They are called Theory X and Theory Y. Ouchi introduced Theory Z in response to McGregor.
   • ***What are Theory X and Theory Y and when were they developed?***
   Theory X assumes that the average person dislikes work and will avoid it if possible. Therefore, people must be forced, controlled, and threatened with punishment to accomplish organizational goals. Theory Y assumes that people like working and will accept responsibility for achieving goals if rewarded for doing so. Douglas McGregor published these theories in 1970.
   • ***What is Theory Z?***
   Theory Z comes out of Japanese management. Among other factors it stresses long-term employment.

   4. Differentiate among Theory X, Theory Y, and Theory Z.

5. Herzberg found that some factors are motivators and others are hygiene factors; that is, they cause job dissatisfaction if they're missing, but they aren't motivators if they're present.
   • ***What are the factors called* motivators?**
   The work itself, achievement, recognition, responsibility, growth, and advancement.
   • ***What are hygiene factors?***
   Factors that don't motivate but must be present for employee satisfaction, such as company policies, supervision, working conditions, interpersonal relations, and salary.

   5. Distinguish between motivators and hygiene factors identified by Herzberg.

6. Job enrichment describes efforts to make jobs more interesting.
   • ***What characteristics of work affect motivation and performance?***
   The job characteristics that influence motivation are (1) skill variety, (2) task identity, (3) task significance, (4) autonomy, and (5) feedback.
   • ***Name two forms of job enrichment that increase motivation.***
   Job enrichment strategies include job enlargement and job rotation.

   6. Explain how job enrichment affects employee motivation and performance.

7. One procedure for establishing objectives and gaining employee commitment to those objectives is management by objectives (MBO).
   • ***What are the steps in an MBO program?***
   (1) Managers set goals. (2) Objectives are established for each department. (3) Workers discuss the objectives and commit themselves in writing to meeting them. (4) Progress is reviewed. (5) Feedback is provided and adjustments are made. (6) Employees are rewarded for achieving goals or are assisted in reaching goals in the future.

   7. Identify the steps involved in implementing a management by objectives (MBO) program.

8. Describe the implementation of motivation theory in the 1990s.

8. The transition from scientific management to human-based management is still going on.

● *What's the key to successful human-based management?*

In a word, the key to successful management is communication. That means training managers to listen and facilitating listening by removing barriers (for example, executive dining rooms) and providing necessary facilities (for example, conference rooms).

KEY TERMS

esteem needs 312
extrinsic reward 308
goal-setting theory 321
Hawthorne effect 311
hygiene factors 318
intrinsic reward 308
job enlargement 321
job enrichment 319
job rotation 321

job simplification 321
management by objectives (MBO) 322
motion economy 310
motivators 318
physiological needs 312
safety needs 312

scientific management 309
self-actualization needs 312
social needs 312
time–motion studies 310

DEVELOPING WORKPLACE SKILLS

1. Conduct some informal research with several of your friends on the subject of motivation. What motivates them to work or not to work hard in school and on the job? How important is self-motivation to them? Assume you are an entrepreneur running your own bookstore. Based on the results of your survey prepare a questionnaire asking your employees to rate the importance of each motivational factor (e.g., salary, benefits, flexible work hours, etc.)

2. Assume you are a branch manager for a large car rental company that continues to lose market share to smaller companies offering superior customer service. Draft a memo to your company's training director describing the steps and policies you recommend the company adopt and implement in order to motivate your front-line employees to become customer-oriented.

3. One of the newest managerial ideas is to let employees work in self-managed teams. Is there a reason why such teams could not be formed in colleges as well as businesses? Discuss the benefits and drawbacks of dividing your class into self-managed teams for the purpose of studying, doing cases, and so forth.

4. Think of all of the groups with whom you have been associated over the years—sports teams, clubs, friendship groups, and so on—and try to recall how the leaders of those groups motivated the group to action. Did the leaders assume a Theory X or Theory Y attitude? What motivational tools were used and to what effect?

5. Herzberg concluded that pay was not a motivator. If you were paid to get better grades, would you be able to get them? In your employment experiences have you ever worked harder to obtain or as a result of receiving a large raise? Do you agree with Herzberg? Assume you are a sales manager in a large department store. Word process a memo to your sales representatives explaining and advocating the company's recent decision to reduce salaries and increase bonus potential for sales personnel.

• •

PRACTICING MANAGEMENT DECISIONS

⟨⟨ C A S E   THEORIES X AND Y: THAT'S HOW THE COOKIE CRUMBLES ⟩⟩

No two firms better illustrate Theory X and Theory Y than David's Cookies and Mrs. Fields Cookies stores. You'll see what we mean.

First, let's look at David's Cookies. When owner David Liederman first opened his stores, food reviewers criticized his cookies. However, when the *New York Times* had a cookie-tasting contest, David's won. Today, even though the market for cookies has softened, David's Cookies operates specialty stores and compact self-contained modular stores (called *kiosks*), and sells frozen cookie dough and ice cream to 2,000 New York–area supermarkets. David has also entered the restaurant business in New York. His latest venture, Emmi's, is a casual dining restaurant that serves American-style dishes. David's a big success thanks to his cookies.

How much confidence does David have in his employees in the cookie business? Apparently not much. David feels it necessary to minimize employee involvement in cookie making so employees can't mess things up. He does that by making all the dough in a factory and shipping it to the stores. All the employee has to do is put the dough on a tray, put it in an automatic oven, and take it out seven and a half minutes later. David has even admitted he was hesitant to sell brownies because he feels workers can't handle the job of adding eggs. He says, "One of the reasons we do well . . . is that a chimpanzee could take cookies out of that bag and more often than not put them on the tray properly." David has also minimized his own risk by franchising his stores.

In contrast, let's look at one of David's main competitors, Mrs. Fields Cookies. Debbi Fields has about 650 company-owned cookie stores. She also has agreements with companies such as Host International, which plans to open 57 more stores by 1996, and National Convenience Stores Inc., which plans to sell her cookies throughout its convenience stores. Mrs. Fields has even entered into head-to-head competition in the consumer packaged chip market with her Mrs. Fields semisweet chocolate chips. Not bad either.

Does Mrs. Fields have the same attitude about her employees as David Liederman? No way! She feels that people "will do their very best provided that they are getting proper support." Mrs. Fields adds, "It's a people company. That's what it's all about. . . . What we really do is . . . we take care of people." This philosophy is reflected in how Mrs. Fields makes cookies. Store employees combine ingredients right in the store (some in proportioned containers). The ovens aren't automatic. Employees put in the raw dough to bake and take out the finished cookies when it feels right. "We tell them that we want them to have fun," Mrs. Fields says. "People come to work because they need to be productive. They need to feel successful in whatever they do." Mrs. Fields's idea is to have her managers out where they can be most useful—with employees and customers. Here's how Debbi sums up her job: "To make people feel important and to create an opportunity for them. That's really my role as cookie president, the cookie person."

To keep this momentum going, Mrs. Fields has expanded into a line of Mrs. Fields Bakery Cafes and has scheduled in a low-calorie dessert line. The firm will offer products such as chocolate mousse cake and lemon meringue pie made with Nutrasweet brand sweetener. As Debbi Fields puts it, "When there's a cookie opportunity, we want to be there. Cookies will always be in our future."

Decision Questions

1. What motivational philosophies are in use at David's and Mrs. Fields Cookies? How do you support your conclusions?
2. Which store is more likely to build employee honesty and loyalty?
3. In which company would you rather be a manager? Employee? Investor? Why?

Source: Tom Richman, "A Tale of Two Companies," *Inc.*, July 1984, pp. 37–43; Brian Quinton, "Mrs. Fields Bakery Cafes Seek New Fortune Beyond Cookies," *Restaurants and Institutions*, February 20, 1991; Paul Frumkin, "Liederman Shutters Chez Louis, Plans to Open More Casual Spot," *Nation's Restaurant News*, April 8, 1991; and "National Convenience to Expand Pizza Hut, Mrs. Fields Products Sales," Dow Jones News Service, June 4, 1991.

VIDEO CASE MOTIVATE AND INNOVATE OR DIE

In the fast-paced telecommunication industry, a company must have fewer defects, shorter time to the market, and newer innovations than competitors or lose out. One of the companies that has thrived in this atmosphere is Tellabs. It is one of the faster-growing firms in a rapidly growing industry. How does Tellabs do it? It doesn't; its employees are what make the company great. Just how then does Tellabs motivate its employees?

First, Tellabs' employees are trained to understand the competitive environment within which they function. The opportunities are fantastic, but so are the challenges. To win in this market requires Tellabs to be more customer-oriented than its competition. It also means being a leader in technology using total quality management «-- P.259 --» techniques. None of this is possible without motivated workers like Grace Pastiak. She started out as a clerk in the purchasing department. When she learned of Tellab's move into just-in-time inventory control, she began reading about the system and became the resident authority. Her contribution was quickly recognized and she was put in charge of a cross-functional team to focus on new uses for their primary product.

Ms. Pastiak and her team members spent months talking to customers, company engineers, and production people. She created a situation whereby everyone on her team made a contribution to the process and could feel part of the action. Workers aren't just employees at Tellabs; they are stakeholders «-- P.40 --». That is, they have an intimate interest in the success of the firm. To encourage teamwork, most of the walls in the manufacturing area have been eliminated. As a result, laboratories, engineering offices, and manufacturing cells are blended into one, unified system. And, in order to maintain and stimulate employee interest, they are encouraged to rotate among jobs.

In motivational terms, Tellabs is a Theory Y company. It assumes that its workers are self-motivated and capable. The company optimizes that potential with continuous training. Cross-functional teams «-- P.256 --» are a form of job enlargement in that each team member has a fundamental understanding of what his or her colleagues in engineering, marketing, production, and so on are doing. Achievement is recognized, just as Herzberg would recommend. Ms. Pastiak went from a clerk to a team leader because of her achievements. Everyone understands the objectives of the firm and works together to achieve them. Employees are encouraged to take risks and are supported if their efforts aren't always successful. In short, Tellabs is poised to be a major competitor not only in the United States but worldwide. It is truly a world-class company with a world-class system of motivation.

Discussion Questions

1. Why is a stock ownership plan a good way to motivate Tellab employees?

2. How do cross-functional teams work to keep employees motivated and involved?

3. At what level of Maslow's need hierarchy would you expect to find most of Tellab's employees?

4. What are some of the benefits and drawbacks of job rotation, as you see them?

CHAPTER 11

HUMAN RESOURCE MANAGEMENT: FINDING AND KEEPING THE BEST EMPLOYEES

LEARNING GOALS

After you have read and studied this chapter, you should be able to

1. Explain the importance of human resource management and describe current issues in managing human resources.

2. Summarize the six steps in planning human resources.

3. Describe methods companies use to recruit new employees and explain some of the problems that make recruitment difficult.

4. Outline the six steps in selecting employees.

5. Illustrate the use of various types of employee training and development methods.

6. Trace the six steps in appraising employee performance.

7. Summarize the objectives of employee compensation programs and describe various pay systems and fringe benefits.

8. Explain the scheduling plans managers use to adjust to workers' needs.

9. Describe the ways employees can move through a company: promotion, reassignment, termination, and retirement.

10. Illustrate the effects of legislation on human resource management.

JILLIAN PERLBERGER, TEMPORARY EMPLOYEE

Since Jillian Perlberger graduated from Williams College in 1992, she has been circulating among the law firms and ad agencies of New York City. Temping in secretarial pools, Perlberger earns $16 an hour while she thinks about what to do next. Law school is one option. Until she decides, Perlberger is one of America's 1.6 million temporary or part-time job holders.

One out of four American workers is what economists call a contingent worker—a person hired to meet an unexpected or temporary challenge. These workers include part-timers, freelancers, subcontractors, and independent professionals. Some analysts have gone as far as to predict that half of all working Americans will be freelance providers by the year 2000. Even top executives are joining the temp ranks. In 1990 there were only 40 companies that supplied temporary managers, but by 1994 there were 140 such services across the country.

Supporters of temporary employees say that contingent workers are less expensive since they rarely receive fringe benefits that add over $13,000 to the annual cost of the average permanent worker. They also argue that contingent workers increase companies' flexibility and therefore their competitiveness. However, detractors contend that the drive for cost cutting and flexibility crashes head-on into another important aspect: the belief that competitive success is based on retaining a motivated, creative, empowered «·· P.220 ··» work force. They believe this goal will never be met by a largely disposable work force.

Both permanent employees and contingent workers need to be trained and managed. That's what this chapter is all about. It discusses present and future challenges of human resource management.

{{ *Our time on earth is finite. The majority of everyone's waking hours are spent at work. A company has an obligation to the people it employs to make that part of life pleasant and happy.* }}

Hal Rosenbluth
CEO of Rosenbluth Travel Inc.

WORKING WITH PEOPLE IS JUST THE BEGINNING

In your career search, you may be in and out of many human resource management offices (formerly called *personnel offices*). While you're there, take a few minutes to observe. Talk to some of the employees and managers. Perhaps human resource management is the field in which you'd like to work.

There's an old story about the student who wanted to go into human resource management "because I want to work with people." It's true that human resource managers work with people, but they're also deeply involved in planning, policy formulation, record keeping, and other administrative duties. To begin a career in human resource management, you need to develop a better reason than "I want to work with people." This chapter will discuss all the aspects of human resource management, which involves recruiting, hiring, training, evaluating, and compensating people. **Human resource management** is the process of evaluating human resource needs, finding people to fill those needs, and getting the best work from each employee by providing the right incentives and job environment, all with the goal of meeting the objectives of the organization. (See Figure 11.1.) Let's explore some trends in human resource management.

human resource management

The process of evaluating human resource needs, finding people to fill those needs, and getting the best work from each employee by providing the right incentives and job enrichment, all with the goal of meeting the objectives of the organization.

... DEVELOPING THE ULTIMATE RESOURCE ...

One reason that human resource management is receiving increased attention is the major shift from traditional manufacturing industries to service and high-tech manufacturing industries that require more technical job skills. A major problem today is retraining workers for new, more challenging jobs. For example, when Crown Zellerbach modernized a Louisiana pulp mill, it set up a training facility nearby and paid workers full wages to learn new skills. There are also other examples:

- Hewlett-Packard spent $1 million to move 350 workers to new jobs, and Boeing enrolled laid-off electronics technicians in college to learn new microprocessor skills. The idea was to retrain their own people before going outside for skilled employees.[1]

- At Motorola, continuous learning is built into the culture. The company's training programs are run from Motorola University in Schaumburg, Illinois, and regional campuses in Phoenix and Austin. The school—staffed by engineers, scientists, and former managers—trains employees, suppliers, and customers. That the employees have learned to learn is evidenced by the fact that so many employees volunteered to participate in the company's "Total Customer Satisfaction" competition that the plant had to close during presentation week.[2]

- Stelco, Inc., has been contracted to conduct management retraining for Bohumin Steel & Wire Co. in Czechoslovakia. The company is converting its management and sales methods from those suitable for a communist-controlled economy to techniques designed for a free-market system.[3]

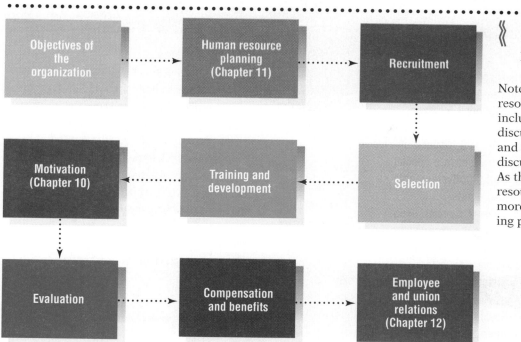

FIGURE 11.1

HUMAN RESOURCE MANAGEMENT Note that human resource management includes motivation as discussed in Chapter 10 and union relations as discussed in Chapter 12. As this shows, human resource management is more than hiring and firing personnel.

- Not all retraining programs are complex. Parker Jewish Geriatric Institute, a full-service geriatric and rehabilitation facility in New York, uses retraining to cut employee turnover. It began by training night-shift security guards to handle the switchboard so an operator wouldn't be needed on that shift.[4]

Some people have called employees the ultimate resource. Indeed, when you think about it, nothing could be more true. People develop the ideas that eventually become the products that satisfy our wants and needs. Take away their creative minds, and leading firms such as IBM, GE, Hewlett-Packard, and Intel would be nothing. The problem is that this resource has always been relatively plentiful, so there was little need to nurture and develop it. If you needed qualified people, you simply went out and hired them. If they didn't work out, you fired them and found others. *Qualified* labor is growing more scarce today; that makes recruiting more difficult.

Historically, most firms assigned the job of recruiting, selecting, training, evaluating, compensating, motivating, and, yes, firing people to the various functional departments. For years, the personnel department was viewed more or less as a clerical function responsible for screening applications, keeping records, processing payroll, and finding people when necessary.

Today, the job of human resource management has taken on an entirely new role in the firm. In the future, it may become the most critical function in that it's responsible for the most critical resource—people. In fact, the human resource function has become so important that it's no longer the function of just one department; it's a function of all managers. Most human resource functions are shared between the professional human resource manager and other managers.

••• THE HUMAN RESOURCE CHALLENGE •••

No changes in the American business system have been more dramatic and had more impact on the future success of the free-enterprise system than changes in the labor force. The U.S. business system's ability to compete in international markets depends on an increase in new ideas, new products,

FROM THE PAGES OF...
Entrepreneur
MAGAZINE

Diversity and the Human Resource Department

The 1990 U.S. census counted more than 30 million African-Americans, 22 million Hispanics, and about 7.5 million Asian/Pacific Islanders. Together, these people make up one fourth of the U.S. population. Human resource people thus have a special challenge to hire, train, and motivate people from diverse cultural backgrounds.

Small businesses have a special need because they don't often have the expertise or the resources to adapt to the new multiculturalism «··· P.43 ···». However, to help compensate for these circumstances, managers of smaller businesses can rent films such as Griggs Productions' *Valuing Diversity*. The film has vignettes showing cultural misunderstandings and how to deal with them. Local community colleges,

chambers of commerce, and Small Business Administration offices often have diversity training seminars. It's wise to go to such seminars and to have as many employees as possible attend as well.

A diverse work force is a strong work force if the strengths of every culture are promoted. Similarly, a diverse work force can better meet the needs of a culturally diverse marketplace if every attempt is made to do so. The human resource department must take a leadership position in promoting diversity in the organization.

Source: Jane Easter Bahls, "Culture Shock," *Entrepreneur*, February 1994, pp. 66–72.

and a higher level of productivity from its workers. All these critical factors depend on the ultimate resource—people with good ideas. Here are some problems in the human resource area:

- Shortages in people trained to work in the growth areas of the future, such as computers, biotechnology, robotics, and the sciences.
- A huge population of skilled and unskilled workers from declining industries, such as steel and automobiles, who are unemployed or underemployed and who need retraining. Underemployed workers are those who have higher-level skills than their current job requires.
- A growing population of African-Americans, Hispanics, Asians, and other minorities, many of whom are undereducated and poor and who lack adequate preparation for jobs in the contemporary business environment. (A study by the Institute of Educational Leadership indicated that 20 million new workers will be in the labor force by the year 2000, 83 percent of whom will be women, minorities, and immigrants.)
- A shift in the age composition in the work force, including many older workers.
- A complex set of laws and regulations involving hiring, safety, unionization, and equal pay that limits organizations' freedom to create an optimum labor force. For example, it's becoming more difficult to fire an inefficient or ineffective worker.
- A tremendous influx of women into the labor force and the resulting demand for day care, job sharing, maternity leave, and special career advancement programs for women.
- A shift in employee attitudes toward work. Leisure time has become a much higher priority, as have concepts such as flextime and a shorter workweek.
- Relentless downsizing «··· P.28 ···» is taking its toll on employee morale as well as increasing the demand for contingent workers. (See the profile at the start of this chapter.)

Human resource managers must forecast human resource needs and conduct formal and informal inventories to evaluate how prepared they are to meet these anticipated changes. At Rockwell International, advanced technology has compounded this challenge and caused human resource managers to devote increased efforts to training and developing its work force in high-tech jobs.

- A challenge from foreign labor pools available to U.S. firms at lower wages and subject to far fewer laws and regulations. This results in many jobs being shifted to foreign countries.

- An increased demand for benefits tailored to the individual. We'll discuss these cafeteria-style fringe benefit plans later in the chapter.

- A growing concern over such issues as health care and day care (discussed in Chapter 12), equal opportunities for people with disabilities, and special attention given to affirmative action programs.

- The bedrock of workers' beliefs crumbling as they see their clergy accused of child abuse and stockbrokers being thrown in jail. Remarkably, many workers turn to corporations to find values such as integrity, taking responsibility, and respecting diversity  « P.42 » [5]

Given all these issues plus others that are sure to develop, you can see why human resource management has taken a more central position in management thinking. Let's see what's involved.

Based on the complex problems you'd be addressing, does human resource management seem like a challenging career? Do you see any other issues, such as the compensation of cross-functional teams, that are likely to affect this function? What have been your experiences in dealing with people who work in human resource management? Would you enjoy working in such an environment?

CRITICAL THINKING

DETERMINING YOUR  HUMAN RESOURCE NEEDS

All management, including human resource management, begins with planning. Six steps are involved in the human resource planning process:

1. Preparing forecasts of future human resource needs.

2. Preparing a human resource inventory that includes ages, names, education, capabilities, training, specialized skills, and other information

FIGURE 11.2

JOB ANALYSIS

A job analysis yields two important statements: job descriptions and job specifications. Here you have a job description and job specifications for a Fiberrific cereal sales representative.

Job Analysis

Observe current sales representatives doing the job.
Discuss job with sales managers.
Have current sales reps keep a diary of their activities.

Job Description	Job Specifications
Primary responsibility is to sell Fiberrific to food stores in Territory Z. Other duties include servicing accounts and maintaining positive relationships with clients. Duties required include	Characteristics of the person qualifying for this job include

Job Description

Primary responsibility is to sell Fiberrific to food stores in Territory Z. Other duties include servicing accounts and maintaining positive relationships with clients. Duties required include

- Introducing the new cereal to store managers in the area.
- Helping the store managers estimate the volume to order.
- Negotiating prime shelf space.
- Explaining sales promotion activities to store managers.
- Stocking and maintaining shelves in stores that wish such service.

Job Specifications

Characteristics of the person qualifying for this job include

- Two years' sales experience.
- Positive attitude.
- Well-groomed appearance.
- Good communication skills.
- High school diploma and two years of college credit.

job analysis

A study of what is done by employees who fill various job titles.

job description

A summary of the objectives of a job, the type of work, the responsibilities of the job, the necessary skills, the working conditions, and the relationship of the job to other functions.

job specifications

Written summary of the qualifications required of workers to do a particular job.

pertinent to the specific organization (for example, languages spoken). Such information reveals whether the labor force is technically up-to-date, thoroughly trained, and so forth.

3. Preparing a job analysis. A **job analysis** is a study of what's done by employees who fill various job titles. It answers the question, What do employees who fill various job titles do? Such analyses are necessary to recruit and train employees with the necessary skills to do the job. The results of job analysis are two written statements: job descriptions and job specifications. A **job description** specifies the objectives of the job, the type of work to be done, the responsibilities and duties, the working conditions, and the relationship of the job to other functions. **Job specifications** specify the *minimum* qualifications (education, skills, etc.) required of a worker to fill specific jobs. In short, job descriptions are statements about the job, whereas job specifications are statements about the person who does the job. (Figure 11.2 shows a job description and job specifications.)

4. Assessing future demand. Changing technology often means that training programs must be started long before the need is apparent. Human resource managers who are proactive (that is, who anticipate the future of their organization) have the trained human resources available when needed.

5. Assessing future supply. The labor force is constantly shifting: getting older, becoming more technically oriented, attracting more women, and so forth. There are likely to be increased shortages of some skills in the future (for example, computer and robotic repair) and oversupply of others (for example, assembly line workers).

6. Establishing a strategic plan for recruiting, selecting, training and developing, appraising, compensating, and scheduling the labor force, given the previous analysis.

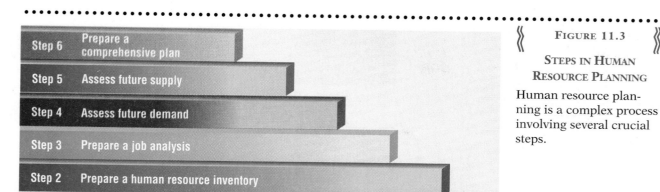

FIGURE 11.3

STEPS IN HUMAN RESOURCE PLANNING

Human resource planning is a complex process involving several crucial steps.

Step 6	Prepare a comprehensive plan
Step 5	Assess future supply
Step 4	Assess future demand
Step 3	Prepare a job analysis
Step 2	Prepare a human resource inventory
Step 1	Prepare a future needs forecast

We'll look at each of these elements of the strategic human resource plan in the next sections. Figure 11.3 gives an overview of the planning process.

RECRUITING EMPLOYEES FROM A DIVERSE POPULATION

Recruitment is the set of lawful activities used to obtain a sufficient number of the right people at the right time to select those who best meet the needs of the organization. You'd think that, with a continuous flow of new people into the work force, recruiting would be easy. On the contrary, recruiting has become very difficult for several reasons.

recruitment

The set of legal activities used to obtain a sufficient number of the right people at the right time to select those who best meet the needs of the organization.

- Legal restrictions such as the Civil Rights Act of 1991 make it necessary legally to recruit the proper mix of women, minorities, and other individuals. Often people with the necessary skills aren't available, but must be hired and then trained internally.
- The emphasis on corporate culture 《· P.263 ·》, teamwork, and participative management makes it important to hire skilled people who also fit in with the organization's culture and leadership style.

Your college placement office is one of the best places to start when searching for a career. It's important to visit your placement office early to find out what resources they have available and what services they provide. Here at the College of Lake County Placement Office, students are provided many career services to help them get a jump on the competition in the market.

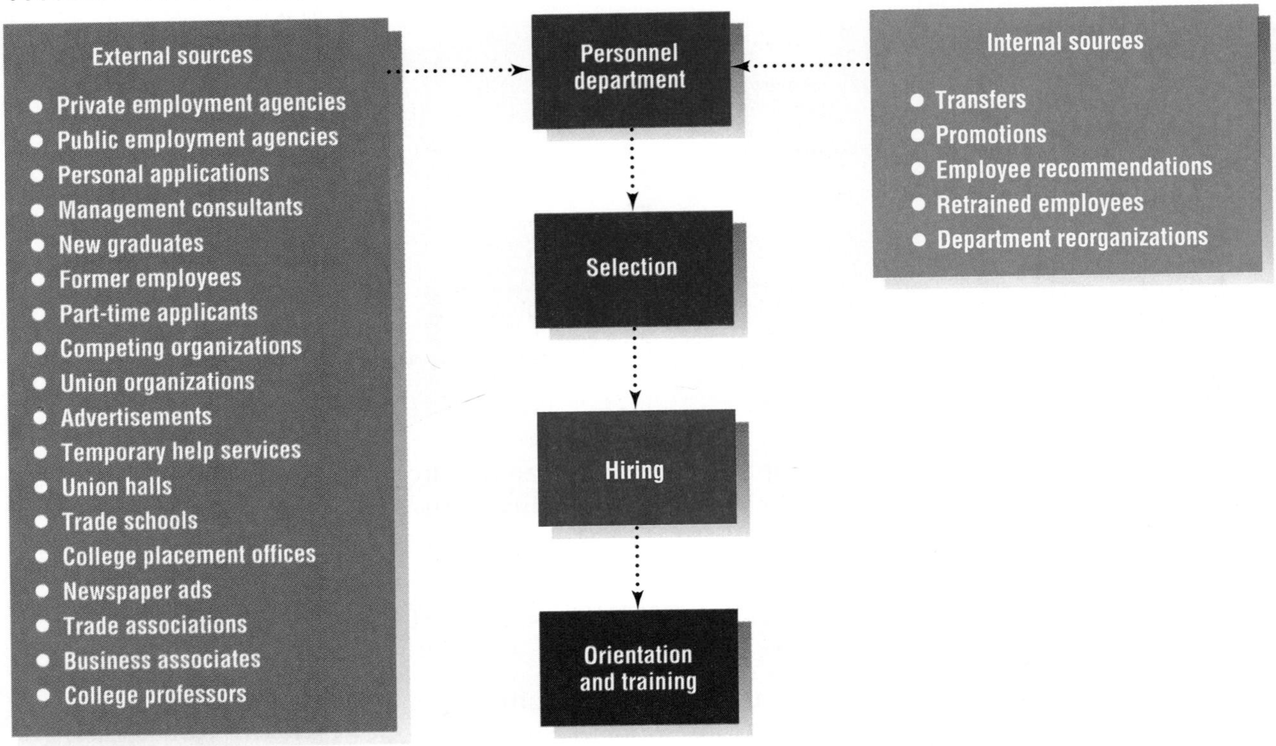
External sources
Private employment agencies
Public employment agencies
Personal applications
Management consultants
New graduates
Former employees
Part-time applicants
Competing organizations
Union organizations
Advertisements
Temporary help services
Union halls
Trade schools
College placement offices
Newspaper ads
Trade associations
Business associates
College professors
Personnel department
Selection
Hiring
Orientation and training
Internal sources
Transfers
Promotions
Employee recommendations
Retrained employees
Department reorganizations

FIGURE 11.4

EMPLOYEE SOURCES

Internal sources are often given first consideration. Therefore, it's useful for you to get a recommendation from a current employee of the firm for which you want to work. College placement offices are also an important source. Be sure to learn about such facilities early so you can plan a strategy throughout your college career.

- As we've noted, firing unsatisfactory employees is getting harder to justify legally. This is especially true of discharges involving possible discrimination by factors such as age, sex, or race. Therefore, it's necessary to screen and evaluate employees carefully to be sure they'll be effective long-term members of the organization.
- Some organizations have unattractive workplaces, have policies that demand promotions from within, operate under union regulations, or offer low wages, which makes recruiting and keeping employees difficult or subject to outside influence and restrictions.

Because recruiting is a difficult chore that involves finding, hiring, and training people who are an appropriate technical and social fit, human resource managers turn to many sources for assistance. (See Figure 11.4.) These sources are classified as either internal or external. Internal sources include hiring from within the firm (transfers, promotions, etc.) and employee recommendations. Internal sources are less expensive than recruiting outside the company. The greatest advantage of hiring from within is that it helps maintain employee morale. However, it isn't always possible to find qualified workers within the company, so human resource managers must use external recruitment sources such as ads, public and private employment agencies, college placement bureaus, management consultants, professional organizations, referrals, and applicants who simply show up at the office.

SELECTING EMPLOYEES WHO WILL BE PRODUCTIVE

selection
The process of gathering information to decide who should be hired, under legal guidelines, for the best interests of the individual and the organization.

Selection is the process of gathering information to decide who should be hired, under legal guidelines, for the best interests of the individual and the organization. Because of high turnover, the cost of selecting and training

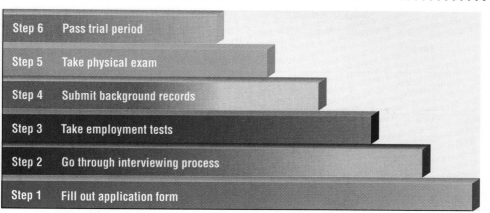

FIGURE 11.5

STEPS IN THE SELECTION PROCESS
You must take serveral steps to obtain a job. First, you fill out an application blank. (See Figure 11.6.) Then you must go through an interviewing process and the steps illustrated here. The goal is to find a job that's satisfying to you and to your employer.

employees has become prohibitively high in some firms. Think of the costs involved: interview time, medical exams, training costs, unproductive time spent learning the job, moving expenses, and so on. It's easy to see how such expenses can run over $50,000 for a manager. Even entry-level workers can cost thousands of dollars to recruit, process, and train. Thus, the selection process is an important element in any human resource program. Figure 11.5 shows the six steps in a typical selection process:

1. *Completion of an application form.* Once this was a simple procedure with few complications. Today, legal guidelines limit the kind of questions one can ask. Still, such forms help the employer discover the applicant's educational background, past work experience, career objectives, and other information directly related to the job's requirements. (See Figure 11.6.)

2. *Initial and follow-up interviews.* Applicants are often screened in a first interview by a member of the human resource department staff. If the interviewer considers the applicant a potential employee, the manager who'll supervise the new employee interviews the applicant as well. It's important that managers prepare adequately for the interview process to avoid selection errors they may regret. Asking the wrong question such as asking a female about her family, no matter how innocent the intention, could be used as evidence if the applicant files discrimination charges.[6]

3. *Employment tests.* Employment tests have been severely criticized because of charges of discrimination. Nonetheless, organizations continue to use them to measure basic competencies in specific job skills (for example, welding, typing) and to help evaluate applicants' personalities and interests. An employment test must be directly related to the job. This will make the selection process more efficient and often satisfy legal requirements.

4. *Background investigations.* Most organizations are investigating a candidate's work record, school record, credit history, and recommendations more carefully than they have in the past. It's simply too costly to hire, train, motivate, and lose people and then have to start the process over. Background checks help weed out candidates least likely to succeed and identify those most likely to succeed.

5. *Physical exams.* A complete medical background and checkup helps screen candidates. There are obvious benefits in hiring physically and mentally healthy people. However, medical tests can't be given just to

FIGURE 11.6

APPLICATION FORM
Look over the application form. Note that it asks whether you can use personal computers. It also asks about scholastic honors and scholarships. For maximum effect, you should attach a cover letter and a résumé, like the ones we suggest in the appendix to the Prologue at the beginning of the text.

GENERAL DYNAMICS

| Date |
| Mo. | Day | Year |

GENERAL DYNAMICS IS AN EQUAL OPPORTUNITY EMPLOYER

APPLICATION FOR EMPLOYMENT

INSTRUCTIONS: Fill in all iInformation. Incomplete applications will not be considered for employment. Print or write with black ink or type if preferred. Upcoming college graduates attach a coursework transcript. Overflow information may be put in remarks section.

PERSONAL

Last name	First name	Middle name	Social security number
Current address		City	State	Zip code	(A/C)	Telephone
Permanent address		City	State	Zip code	(A/C)	Telephone

In case of emergency notify: (A/C) Telephone
Address of person listed for emergency City State Zip code

Are you at least 18 years of age? ☐ Yes ☐ No
How were you referred? ☐ Newspaper—which one? _____

If employed, can you provide proof of United States citizenship? ☐ No ☐ Yes
If not a U.S. citizen, specify alien registration number:
Have you ever been known by any other names? (Include nicknames.) If so, what?
Do you have any physical or mental limitations which could affect your ability to perform the job or jobs for which you are applying? If yes, give details.
☐ No ☐ Yes Accommodations required: _____

☐ Agency
☐ Governmental employment service
☐ Friend/employee
☐ College placement office
☐ Other—please specify _____

Geographical preference _____ Relocations restrictions _____ Travel restrictions _____

EDUCATION

Circle highest education completed

Grade school 1 2 3 4 5 6 7 8 | High school 9 10 11 12 | College* 1 2 3 4 5 | Graduate school 1 2 3 4 5

	Name & Location	Dates attended		Graduated	Degree** Certificate Diploma	Majored in	Minored in	GPA/ Possible
		Mo./Yr.	Mo./Yr.	Mo./Yr.				
High school								
College(s)								
Graduate school(s)								
Military/other								

Scholastic honors, scholarships, etc. _____

List publications, thesis, etc. _____

Professional licenses _____

*If co-op graduate, specify total work periods .... Semester _____ Quarter _____

**Specify number of college hours earned if no degree obtained .... Semester _____ Quarter _____

JOB INTEREST

Type of work preferred: ☐ Fulltime ☐ Parttime ☐ Co-op ☐ Summer ☐ Other _____

Have you ever worked for General Dynamics? ☐ No ☐ Yes
Division: Dates:
Have you ever been granted a U.S. Government security clearance? ☐ No ☐ Yes
Type/Level: Employer: Dates:
Have you ever had a security clearance suspended, denied or revoked? ☐ No ☐ Yes Employer: Date:
Do you have relatives employed at G.D.? ☐ No ☐ Yes Name: _____
Relationship: G.D. division:

Will you work:
	Yes	No
Any shift	☐	☐
Overtime	☐	☐
Saturdays	☐	☐
Sundays	☐	☐

Date available for employment:
May we contact your present employer? ☐ No ☐ Yes

Can you operate word processing equipment? ☐ No ☐ Yes Make/Model:
Can you utilize personal computers? ☐ No ☐ Yes Make/Model:
Typing speed _____ WPM Shorthand speed _____ WPM

MILITARY STATUS

| Branch of U.S. armed forces | Date entered | Date and type of discharge/retirement | Rank/rate at discharge |
| Other military service (including Reserves) | Date entered | Date and type of discharge/retirement | Rank/rate at discharge |

screen out individuals. If such tests are given, they must be given to everyone applying for the same position. There has been some controversy about preemployment testing to detect drug or alcohol abuse as well as AIDS screening to detect carriers of the virus. Eighty-seven percent of major companies now test their employees and job applicants for drug use.[7]

6. *Trial periods*. Often an organization will hire an employee conditionally. This enables the person to prove his or her worth on the job. During a period of perhaps six months or a year, the firm has the right

Making Ethical Decisions

Recruiting Employees from the Competition

As human resource manager for Technocrat, Inc., you must recruit the best employees. You completed a human resource inventory that indicated that Technocrat currently has an abundance of qualified designers and that several lower-level workers will soon be eligible for promotions to designer positions as well. In spite of the surplus of qualified designers, you're considering offering a similar position to a designer who's now with a major competitor. Your thinking is that the new employee will be a source of information about the competition's new products. What are your ethical considerations in this case? Will you lure the employee away from the competition even though you have no need for a designer? What will be the consequences of your decision?

to discharge that employee based on evaluations from supervisors. Such systems make it easier to fire inefficient or problem employees, but don't eliminate the high cost of turnover.

The selection process is often long and difficult, but it's worth the effort because of the high costs of replacing workers. The process helps ensure that people hired are competent in all relevant areas, including communication skills, education, technical skills, experience, social fit, and health.[8]

Most firms recruit people who have the potential to be productive employees. They realize that potential involves effective training programs and proper managerial incentives. Carefully orienting an individual to the new environment can be an important step for the human resource manager.

- What is human resource management?
- What are the six steps in human resource planning?
- What factors make it hard to recruit qualified employees?
- What are the six steps in the selection process?

PROGRESS CHECK

TRAINING AND DEVELOPING EMPLOYEES FOR OPTIMUM PERFORMANCE

Technologies involving computers and robots have made it necessary to do more and more training, much of which is quite sophisticated. Today's forward-thinking organizations are recognizing that people are their most vital resource and an integral part in achieving increased productivity. Therefore, many firms are getting much more involved in continuing education and development programs for their employees. Career development is no longer just a haphazard system of promotions, moves, and occasional training programs. Rather, it's a long-term organizational strategy for assisting employees in optimizing their skills and advancing their education. In fact, the growing use of cross-functional teams ← P.256 → has led to cross-training programs that enable workers to handle more than just their own jobs and to help them understand the relationship of their jobs to others.[9]

training and development
All attempts to improve employee performance by increasing an employee's ability to perform through learning.

Training and development include all attempts to improve performance by increasing an employee's ability to perform through learning. The process of creating training and development programs includes (1) assessing the organization's needs and employees' skills to determine training needs, (2) designing training activities to meet the identified needs, and (3) evaluating the training's effectiveness. In the next sections, we'll look at various training and development activities: employee orientation, on-the-job training, apprenticeship, off-the-job training, vestibule training, job simulation, and management training.

••• MAKING NEW EMPLOYEES FEEL AT HOME •••

employee orientation
The activity that introduces new employees to the organization, to fellow employees, to their immediate supervisors, and to the policies, practices, and objectives of the firm.

Employee orientation is the activity that initiates new employees to the organization, to fellow employees, to their immediate supervisors, and to the firm's policies, practices, and objectives. Orientation programs vary from quite informal, primarily verbal efforts to formal schedules that feature employee visits to various departments for a day or more, and include lengthy handouts. Formal orientation programs may cover

- History and general policies of the organization.
- Descriptions of products or services offered by the organization to the public.
- The organization's chain of command (organization chart).
- Company safety measures and regulations.
- Human resources policies and practices.
- Compensation, benefits, and employee services.
- Daily routines and regulations.
- Introduction to the corporate culture—the values and orientation of the organization.
- Organizational objectives and the new recruit's role in accomplishing those objectives.

••• ON-THE-JOB TRAINING: WORKING WITH OTHERS •••

on-the-job training
Training program in which the employee immediately begins his or her tasks and learns by doing, or watches others for a while and then imitates them, all right at the workplace.

The most fundamental training programs involve on-the-job training. **On-the-job training** means that the employee immediately begins his or her tasks and learns by doing, or watches others for a while and then imitates them, right at the workplace. Salespeople, for example, are often trained by watching experienced salespeople perform. Naturally, this can be either quite effective or disastrous, depending on the skills and habits of the person being observed. On-the-job training is obviously the easiest kind of training to implement and can be effective where the job is easily learned (such as clerking in a store), or performing repetitive physical tasks (such as collecting refuse, cleaning carpets, and mowing lawns). More tedious or intricate jobs require a more intense training effort.

••• APPRENTICE PROGRAMS: LEARNING ADVANCED SKILLS •••

apprenticeship
Training involving a new worker working alongside a master technician to learn the skills and procedures of a job.

Many skilled crafts, such as bricklaying or plumbing, require a new worker to serve several years as an apprentice. An **apprenticeship** is a period of time when a learner works alongside a skilled worker to learn the skills and procedures of a craft. Trade unions often require such periods to ensure excellence among their members as well as to limit entry to the union. Workers who successfully complete an apprenticeship earn the classification of journeyman.

In the future, there are likely to be more but shorter apprenticeship programs to prepare people for skilled jobs in changing industries. For example, auto repair will require more intense training as new car models include the use of more computers and other electronic advances.

••• OFF-THE-JOB TRAINING: ••• LEARNING FROM THE BEST

Training is becoming more sophisticated as jobs become more complex. Furthermore, training is expanding to include education (through the Ph.D.) and personal development (for example, time management, stress management, health education, wellness training, physical education, nutrition, and even art and languages).

Some firms do such training internally and have elaborate training facilities, whereas other firms must assign it to outside sources. **Off-the-job training** occurs away from the workplace. It consists of internal and external programs to develop a variety of skills and to foster personal development. This includes classroom lectures, conferences, and films as well as workshops, tapes, reading programs, and the like. Struggling Euro Disney is considering starting a special 6- to 12-month training program that would include how to please customers. The school will include a dorm in the hope that it will attract students from all over Europe.[10]

Vestibule training is an effective way to teach computer skills. Such training is conducted away from the job site and involves use of equipment similar to that used on the job.

••• VESTIBULE TRAINING: GETTING ••• USED TO THE EQUIPMENT

Vestibule training is done in schools where employees are taught on equipment similar to that used on the job. Such schools enable employees to learn proper methods and safety procedures before assuming a specific job assignment in an organization. Training in the use of computers and robots is often completed in a vestibule school.

••• JOB SIMULATION: TRY BEFORE YOU FLY •••

One of the faster-growing areas of training is simulation exercises. **Job simulation** is the use of equipment that duplicates job conditions and tasks so that trainees can learn skills before attempting them on the job. Job simulation differs from vestibule training in that the simulation attempts to duplicate the *exact* combination of conditions that occur on the job. This is the kind of training given astronauts, airline pilots, army tank operators, ship captains, and others who must learn highly skilled jobs off the job. Astronauts, for example, must learn to work, eat, sleep, wash, and live in an environment of weightlessness. Simulation training sometimes takes place underwater (to simulate weightlessness) and in a variety of laboratories that can artificially create real-life experiences before attempting them.

Imagine the benefits of simulating the landing of an airplane in a major storm for the first time or docking a huge ocean liner in a small port facility. Such tasks are better learned in a simulator where many variables can be programmed to give people practical experience in a lab setting.

off-the-job training
Internal and external programs to develop a variety of skills and foster personal development away from the workplace.

vestibule training
Training conducted out of the workplace where employees are given instructions on equipment similar to that used on the job.

job simulation
A training method that uses equipment that duplicates job conditions and tasks so that trainees can learn skills before attempting them on the job.

Should an intricate task like flying an airplane be taught by trial and error? Hardly. Therefore, flight simulators such as the one pictured here simulate the actual sights, sounds, and feel of flying a plane. Naturally, it's also much safer for the trainee and less costly for a company to employ this type of training. Some virtual reality simulators can actually create storms and other hazards that give flight experience in all sorts of situations.

Computers can simulate the sounds, sights, smells, and feel of the most trying circumstances (for example, fighting another jet plane in aerial combat). Given this capability, it's possible to simulate other skills, such as managing a power plant's operating room or handling new equipment of any kind.

... MANAGEMENT DEVELOPMENT: LEARNING TO ... BE CUSTOMER-RESPONSIVE

Managers need special training. They need to be good communicators and especially need to learn listening skills and empathy. They also need time management, planning, coaching, training, and other human relations skills.

management development
The process of training and educating employees to become good managers and then developing managerial skills over time.

Management development, then, is the process of (1) training and educating employees to become good managers and (2) then developing managerial skills over time. Management development programs have sprung up everywhere, especially at colleges, universities, and private management development firms. Managers participate in various role-playing exercises, solve various management cases, and are exposed to films, lectures, and all kinds of management development processes. In some organizations, managers are paid to take college courses through the graduate level.

Increasingly, executive education is being used as a tool to accomplish business objectives. For example, Ford Motor Co. is using education to teach executives how to be more customer-responsive «--- **P.40** --».[11] Most management training programs also include several of the following:

- *On-the-job coaching.* This means that a senior manager will assist a lower-level manager by teaching him or her needed skills and generally providing direction, advice, and helpful criticism. Such programs are effective only when the senior managers are skilled themselves and have the ability to educate others. This isn't always the case.
- *Understudy positions.* Job titles such as *undersecretary* and *assistant* reveal a relatively successful way of developing managers. They work as assistants to higher-level managers and participate in planning and

other managerial functions until they can assume such positions themselves. Such assistants may take over when higher-level managers are on vacation or on business trips.

- *Job rotation.* To expose managers to different functions of the organization, they're often given assignments in a variety of departments. Top managers, of course, must have a broad picture of the organization. Rotation gives them that exposure.

- *Off-the-job courses and training.* Managers periodically go to schools or seminars for a week or more to hone their technical and human relations skills. Such courses expose them to the latest concepts and create a sense of camaraderie as the managers live, eat, and work together in a college-type atmosphere. This is often where case studies and simulation exercises of all kinds are employed.

THE IMPORTANCE OF NETWORKING Over time, male managers have developed what has been called an *old-boy network*, through which certain senior managers become mentors to certain junior managers. They introduce them to the important managers, enroll them in the "right" clubs, and guide them into the "right" social groups. Young male managers are thus socialized regarding proper dress, behavior, and procedures to follow to rise up the corporate hierarchy.

Networking, then, is the process of establishing and maintaining contacts with key managers in one's own organization and in other organizations and using those contacts to weave strong relationships that serve as informal development systems. Of equal or greater importance to potential managers is the need for **mentors**, corporate managers who supervise, coach, and guide selected lower-level employees by introducing them to the right people and groups and generally being their organizational sponsors. In reality, an informal type of mentoring goes on in most organizations on a regular basis as older employees assist younger workers. However, many organizations, such as Merrill Lynch and Federal Express, use a formal system of assigning mentors to employees considered to have strong potential.

As women moved into management they also learned the importance and value of such networking and of having mentors. But since most older managers are male, women often have difficulty finding mentors and entering the network. Women managers won a major victory when the U.S. Supreme Court ruled that it was illegal to bar females from men-only clubs where business activity and contact-making flowed. More and more, women are now entering this system or, in some instances, creating their own networking systems.

Similarly, African-American managers are learning the value of networking. Working together, African-Americans are forming pools of capital and new opportunities that are helping to overcome traditional barriers to success.[12] *Black Enterprise* magazine sponsors several networking forums each year for African-American professionals; call 1–800–54–FORUM for information.

It's also important to remember that networking can go beyond the business environment. For example, your college experience is a perfect environment in which to begin your networking. Associations you nurture with professors, with local businesspeople, and especially with your classmates might provide you with a valuable network through which you can work for the rest of your career.

networking
The process of establishing and maintaining contacts with key managers in one's own organization and in other organizations and using those contacts to weave strong relationships that serve as informal development systems.

mentor
An experienced employee who supervises, coaches, and guides lower-level employees by introducing them to the right people and groups and generally being their organizational sponsors.

*Wanted:
International
Executives*

You'd think that with the reality of a global economy, the United States would be bursting at the seams with international executives. On the contrary, the number is actually decreasing. Part of this has to do with the costs of moving to and living in a foreign country: relocation costs, sky-high monthly rents, international school tuition for dependents, and cost of living differences in food and clothing.

But even with the high costs, demand for international executives is far greater than the supply. The most common reason, more so than costs, is that American businesses don't train their employees for international careers. Only 33 percent of the American firms surveyed provide language training, whereas all Japanese companies provide language and cultural training. For example, each year Samsung hands 400 employees a fistful of money and sends them out of

the country for 12 months to do whatever they want. They're expected to return with a solid understanding of their host country's customs and language.

Lack of training isn't the only reason American executives haven't chosen the international track. Many perceive an international assignment as being taken out of their company's "power loop." They fear losing touch with the political structure of the home office. To persuade more managers to choose the international route, companies must be sure that an international assignment is encouraged, supported with proper training, and viewed as something good for a person's career path.

Source: Ronald E. Yates, "Demand Great, Supply Short for Overseas Execs," *Chicago Tribune*, March 6, 1994, Section 7, p. 4; and Laxmi Nakarmi and Robert Neff, "Samsung's Radical Shakeup," *Business Week*, February 28, 1994, pp. 74–76.

APPRAISING EMPLOYEE PERFORMANCE TO GET OPTIMUM RESULTS

All managers must supervise employees. Therefore, they must be able to determine whether their workers are doing an effective, efficient job with a minimum of errors and disruptions. Such a determination is called a *performance appraisal*. A **performance appraisal** is an evaluation of the employees' performance level against established standards to make decisions about promotions, compensation, additional training, or firing. Performance appraisals consist of six steps:

performance appraisal
An evaluation of the performance level of employees against standards to make decisions about promotions, compensation, additional training, or firing.

1. *Establishing performance standards*. This is a crucial step. Standards must be understandable, subject to measurement, and reasonable.

2. *Communicating those standards*. Often managers assume that employees know what's expected of them, but such assumptions are dangerous at best. Employees must be told clearly and precisely what the standards and expectations are and how they're to be met.

3. *Evaluating performance*. If the first two steps are done correctly, performance evaluation is relatively easy. It's a matter of evaluating the employee's behavior to see if it matches standards.

4. *Discussing results with employees*. Most people will make mistakes and fail to meet expectations at first. It takes time to learn a new job and do it well. Discussing an employee's successes and areas that need improvement is an opportunity to be understanding and helpful and to guide the employee to better performance. Additionally, the performance appraisal can be a good source of employee suggestions on how a particular task could perhaps be better performed.

1. **DON'T** attack the employee personally. Critically evaluate his or her work.
2. **DO** allow sufficient time, without distractions, for appraisal. (Take the phone off the hook or close the office door.)
3. **DON'T** make the employee feel uncomfortable or uneasy. *Never* conduct an appraisal where other employees are present (such as on the shop floor).
4. **DO** include the employee in the process as much as possible. (Let the employee prepare a self-improvement program.)
5. **DON'T** wait until the appraisal to raise problems about the employee's work that have been developing for some time.
6. **DO** end the appraisal with positive suggestions for employee improvement.

FIGURE 11.7

MAKING APPRAISALS AND REVIEWS MORE EFFECTIVE

5. *Taking corrective action.* The performance appraisal is an appropriate time for a manager to take corrective action or provide corrective feedback to help the employee perform his or her job better. Remember, the key word is *performance*. The primary purpose of conducting a performance appraisal is to increase employee performance if possible.

6. *Using the results to make decisions.* Decisions about promotions, compensation, additional training, and firing are all based on performance evaluations. An effective performance appraisal system is a way of satisfying certain legal conditions concerning promotions, compensation, and firing policies.

Management means getting results through top performance by employees. That's what performance appraisals are for—at all levels of the organization. Figure 11.7 illustrates how managers can make performance appraisals more meaningful.

- Can you name and describe four training techniques?
- Why is employee orientation important? Did your college do a good job of orienting you to college life?
- What's the primary purpose of a performance appraisal?
- What are the six steps in a performance appraisal?

PROGRESS CHECK

COMPENSATING EMPLOYEES: ATTRACTING AND KEEPING THE BEST

Employee compensation is one of the largest operating costs for many organizations. The long-term success of a firm—perhaps even its survival—may depend on how well it can control employee costs and optimize employee efficiency. For example, service organizations such as hospitals, airlines, and banks have recently struggled with managing high employee costs. This isn't unusual since these firms are considered labor intensive. That is, their primary cost of operations is the cost of labor. Manufacturing firms in the auto and steel industries have asked employees to take reductions in wages to make the firm more competitive or risk going out of business and losing their jobs forever. Many employees have agreed, even union employees who traditionally resisted such cuts. In other words, the competitive environment of the 1990s is such that compensation and benefit packages are being given special attention. In fact, some experts believe that figuring out how to best pay people has replaced downsizing as the human resources challenge of the 1990s.

One of the least popular tasks that managers perform is performance appraisal. However, such appraisals are effective for both managers and employees if clear standards are established and communicated. With such standards, appraisals are easier to perform and more relevant to the employee in improving productivity.

A carefully managed compensation and benefit program can accomplish several objectives:

- Attracting the kind of people needed by the organization, and in sufficient numbers.
- Providing employees with incentive to work efficiently and productively.
- Keeping valued employees from leaving and going to competitors or starting competing firms.
- Maintaining a competitive position in the marketplace by keeping costs low through high productivity.
- Protecting employees from unexpected problems such as layoffs, sickness, and disability.
- Ensuring employees of funds to carry them through retirement.

••• PAY SYSTEMS •••

One of the heroes in China during the 1980s was a man named Bu Xinsheng.[13] He ran a highly successful shirt factory. From the mid-1970s to the mid-1980s, Mr. Bu raised the factory's assets from $10,000 to $600,000 and increased its number of workers from 73 to 630. So how did he do it? He switched his factory from straight wages to piecework. That increased the maximum possible wage from $18 a month to the equivalent of $41 a month, but workers had to work much harder to earn more. The government was thrilled with Mr. Bu's success and supported Mr. Bu in implementing capitalist ideas such as performing market research, developing private brands, implementing graduated benefits for his workers, and buying equipment to expand production for export sales.

It's evident from this story that the type of pay system in an organization can have a dramatic effect on efficiency and productivity. Let's look at six different pay systems.

- *Salary systems* are systems of fixed compensation computed on weekly, biweekly, or monthly pay periods (for example, $1,500 per month or $400 per week). It's probable that many of you who graduate from college will be paid a salary.

- *Hourly wage or daywork* is the system used for most blue-collar and clerical workers. Often, employees must punch a time clock when they arrive at work and when they leave. Hourly wages vary greatly. The federal minimum wage is $4.25 as of early 1995. Top wages go as high as $20 to $40 for skilled craftspeople. This doesn't include benefits such as retirement systems that add 25 percent to 30 percent more to the value of the total package.

- *Piecework* means that employees are paid according to the number of items they produce rather than by the hour or day. This system creates powerful incentives to work efficiently and productively. It was so effective for Mr. Bu that he has become a model manager in China.

- *Commission plans* are often used to compensate salespeople. They actually resemble a piecework system; the commission is based on some percentage of sales.

- *Bonus plans* are used for executives, salespeople, and many other employees. They earn bonuses for accomplishing or surpassing certain objectives. Called "gain-sharing" at Rogan Corp., employees receive a bonus each month when productivity targets are met or surpassed.[14] The number of companies that use bonus plans of some type has increased to 68 percent.[15]

- *Profit-sharing plans* give employees some share of profits over and above their normal pay. In 1994, Chrysler paid average profit-sharing bonuses of $4,300 a person to 81,000 workers.[16]

Managers want to find a system that compensates employees fairly. Most companies still use the pay system devised by Edward Hay for General Foods. Known as the Hay system, it's based on job tiers, each of which has a strict pay range. In some firms, you're guaranteed a raise after 13 weeks if you're still breathing. Conflict arises when an employee who's performing well earns less than a lower-achieving worker simply because the other person has worked for the company longer.

Perhaps the most offensive pay system is the two-tier wage scheme devised by some airlines. Under the system, new hires work under a different pay scale than veteran workers. For example, a newly hired ticket agent could hit a permanent ceiling of $18,000 while another agent doing the same job but hired six months earlier could earn up to $34,000 after 10 years.[17] Imagine the tension such situations create.

John Whitney, author of *The Trust Factor*, believes that the market should use a base pay and give all employees the same percentage merit raise because it sends out the message that everyone in the company is important.[18] Fairness remains the issue. What do you think is the fairest pay system?

••• FRINGE BENEFITS •••

Fringe benefits include sick leave pay, vacation pay, pension plans, and health plans that provide additional compensation to employees. Fringe benefits in the 1980s grew faster than wages. In fact, since employee benefits can't really be considered "fringe" anymore many managers now call such benefits "indirect compensation." While these benefits only accounted for 1.7 percent of payroll in 1929, recently they were 39.2 percent of payroll. According to a study by the U.S. Chamber of Commerce, U.S. companies now spend an

fringe benefits
Benefits such as sick leave pay, vacation pay, pension plans, and health plans that represent additional compensation to employees.

One fringe benefit being offered at more and more firms is a health and fitness room such as this one. Managers and employees can use their lunch hour or after-work hours to stay fit and alert on the job. Such programs are also good for stress management.

cafeteria-style fringe benefits
Fringe benefits plan which allows employees to choose the benefits they want up to a certain dollar amount.

average of $14,807 a year per employee for benefits.[19] Many employees request more fringe benefits instead of more salary to avoid higher taxes. This has resulted in much debate and much government investigation.

The range of fringe benefits companies provide runs from paid vacations, health care programs, recreation facilities, company cars, country club memberships, and day care services to executive dining rooms. Managing the benefit package will continue to be a major human resource issue in the future. Employees want packages to include dental care, mental health care, elder care, legal counseling, eye care, and shorter workweeks.

To address these growing demands, many firms are offering **cafeteria-style fringe benefits** from which employees can choose the benefits they want up to a certain dollar amount. Choice is the key to flexible, cafeteria-style benefits plans. At one time, most employees' needs were similar. Today, employees are more varied and more demanding. Some employees may need child care benefits whereas others may need more pension benefits. Rather than giving all employees identical benefits, managers can equitably and cost-effectively meet employees' individual needs by providing benefits choices.[20]

The cost of administering benefits programs has become so great that a number of companies are contracting with outside companies (outsourcing «--- P.262 ---») to run their employee benefits plans. IBM, for example, decided to spin off its human resources and benefits operation into a separate company called Workforce Solutions. Workforce Solutions provides customized services to each of IBM's independent units. The company saves IBM $45 million each year.[21] Workforce Solutions now handles benefits for other organizations such as the National Geographic Society. In addition to the cost savings, companies outsource their benefits plan administration because of the growing complexity and technical requirements involved in administering such plans.[22]

To put it simply, benefits are as important to wage negotiations now as salary. In the future, they may be even more important.

SCHEDULING PROGRAMS THAT MEET ORGANIZATIONAL AND EMPLOYEE NEEDS

By now, you're quite familiar with trends in the work force. You know, for example, that many more women are working now. You also know that managers and workers are demanding more from jobs in the way of flexibility and responsiveness. From these trends have emerged several new or renewed ideas such as job sharing, flextime, and in-home employment. Sixty percent of national companies surveyed offer flexible schedules as part of their employee benefits packages.[23] Computer software programs are available that help managers schedule workers' hours. Let's see how these innovations affect managing human resources.

••• JOB-SHARING PLANS •••

Job sharing is an arrangement whereby two part-time employees share one full-time job. The concept has received great attention in the 1990s as more and more women with small children have entered the labor force. Job sharing enables mothers and fathers to work part-time while their children are in school and then return to the home when the children come home. Job sharing has also proved beneficial to students, older people who want to work part-time before fully retiring, and others who can only work part-time. The benefits are impressive:

job sharing
An arrangement whereby two or more part-time employees share one full-time job.

- It offers employment opportunities to those who can't or prefer not to work full-time.

- An employee is more likely to maintain a high level of enthusiasm and productivity for four hours than eight hours; therefore, two part-time employees are often much more productive than one full-time employee.

- Problems such as absenteeism and tardiness are greatly reduced by using part-time employees. These people are able to handle other duties or problems in their off hours.

- Employers are better able to schedule people into peak demand periods (for example, banks on payday) when part-time people are available.

However, as you might suspect, disadvantages include having to hire, train, motivate, and supervise twice as many people and to prorate some fringe benefits. Nonetheless, most firms that were at first reluctant to try job sharing are finding the benefits outweigh the disadvantages.

••• FLEXTIME PLANS •••

Flextime plans give employees some freedom to adjust when they work, as long as they work the required number of hours. The most popular plans allow employees to come to work at 7, 8, or 9 A.M. and leave between 4 and 6 P.M. Usually flextime plans incorporate what is called *core time*. **Core time** refers to particular hours of the day when all employees are expected to be at their job stations. For example, an organization may designate core time hours as 10 A.M. to noon and 2 to 4 P.M. During these hours all employees are required to be at work. (See Figure 11.8.) Flextime plans, like job-sharing plans, are designed to allow employees to adjust to the new demands of the times, especially the trend toward two-income families. The federal government has experimented extensively with flextime and found it to be a boost to employee productivity and morale. Specific advantages of flextime include

flextime plans
Work schedule that gives employees some freedom to adjust when they work as long as they work the required number of hours.

core time
The period when all employees are present in a flextime system.

- Working mothers and fathers can schedule their days so that one partner can be home to see the children off to school and the other partner can be home soon after school.

- Employees can schedule doctor's appointments and other personal tasks during working hours by coming in early and leaving at 3 or 4 P.M. (or by coming in late and working late).

- Traffic congestion is greatly reduced as employees arrive and leave over several hours instead of all at once.

- Employees can work when they're most productive. Some people are most alert early in the morning, while others can't get going until 9 A.M.

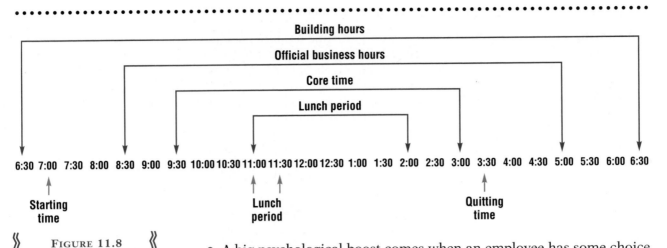

{{ **FIGURE 11.8** }}

A FLEXTIME CHART
Employees can start any time between 6:30 and 9:30. They later take a half hour for lunch and can quit from 3 to 6:30. Everyone works an eight-hour day. The red arrows show a typical flextime day.

- A big psychological boost comes when an employee has some choice about sleeping late once in a while or taking off early on Friday afternoon in the spring.
- It has obvious advantages for creative people who are most productive at certain times of the day. But it's also helpful for anyone who must work long hours when a proposal is due.
- It helps companies keep employees who might leave otherwise.

There are some real disadvantages to flextime as well. Flextime is certainly not for all organizations. For example, it doesn't work in assembly line processes where everyone must be at work at the same time. It also isn't effective for shift work.

Another disadvantage to flextime is that managers often have to work longer days to be there to assist and supervise employees. Some organizations operate from 6 A.M. to 6 P.M. under flextime, a long day for supervisors. Flextime also makes communication more difficult; certain employees may not be there when others need to talk to them. Furthermore, some employees could abuse the system if they weren't carefully supervised, and that could cause resentment among others. Imagine how you'd feel if half the work force left at 3 P.M. on Friday and you had to work until 6 P.M.

compressed workweek
Work schedule that involves same number of hours per week in fewer days.

Another popular option used in 24 percent of the companies surveyed is a **compressed workweek**. That means that an employee works a full number of hours in fewer days. For example, an employee may work four 10-hour days and then enjoy a long weekend instead of working five 8-hour days with a traditional two-day weekend. There are the obvious advantages of working only four days and having three days off, but some employees get tired working such long hours, and productivity could decline. Many employees find such a system of great benefit, however, and are quite enthusiastic about it.

In spite of the fact that flexible schedules are offered by so many companies, only 2 percent of the workers use the programs.[24] Most workers report that they resist using the programs because they fear it would hurt their careers. Some managers send a signal that if they change their hours, they aren't serious about their careers.[25]

••• HOME-BASED WORK •••

In nations such as Japan, in-home employment has traditionally been very common. These *cottage industries*, as they're called, are often key suppliers to large multinational firms in Japan. In the United States over 6 million workers work at home. Many of these homebound workers are women who want to pursue career goals and family goals at the same time. Many say they work at home to have more control over their lives, but others had no choice in the matter. Some were fired or laid off from good-paying jobs and decided to work for themselves.

The old term for working at home is *tele-commuting*.[26] The new term is *virtual office* to reflect the practice of carrying office technology in your briefcase or car so you're ready to work anywhere.[27] Peter Firestone, a senior manager in Ernst & Young's information technology consulting division, has no permanent office. His clients provide him with a desk for the duration of each project and he stays linked to his employer by computer and voice mail. The flexibility is a plus, but the downside is not having the camaraderie of fellow workers.[28]

Advances in technology and telecommunications are causing more and more companies, employees, and entrepreneurs to reconsider the traditional workplace environment. Today, home-based businesses are growing at record levels and more workers are telecommuting. Some employees do not require any type of permanent office, working instead out of their home, briefcase, or car.

What effects have dual-career families had on the personnel function? Have you noticed any changes in nepotism rules with so many marriages involving two professionals? (*Nepotism* means hiring relatives.) What problems can arise when family members work together in the same firm? What's your reaction to employees who date one another?

CRITICAL THINKING

• Name and describe five alternative compensation techniques.
• What advantages do compensation plans such as profit sharing offer an organization?

PROGRESS CHECK

MOVING EMPLOYEES UP, OVER, AND OUT TO MAINTAIN MORALE

Employees don't always stay in the position they were initially hired to fill. They may excel and move up the corporate ladder or fail and move out the front door. Besides promotions and terminations, other ways of moving employees is by reassignment and retirement.

••• PROMOTING AND REASSIGNING EMPLOYEES •••

Many companies find it improves employee morale to promote from within the company. Promotions are also cost-effective in that the employees are already familiar with the corporate culture and procedures.

Due to the growth in the number of firms who are flattening their corporate structures, there are fewer positions for employees to reach. Therefore, it's becoming more common today for workers to move over to a new position than to move up to one. Such transfers allow employees to develop and display new skills in more challenging jobs. This is one way of motivating experienced employees to remain in a company where few advancement opportunities are available.

••• TERMINATING EMPLOYMENT AND DOWNSIZING •••

Downsizing ◄- P.28 -► and restructuring ◄- P.245 -►, increasing customer demands for greater value, and the relentless pressure of global competition and shifts in technology have human resource managers struggling to manage layoffs and firings. Companies like Gillette, Eli Lilly, GTE, and Arco made mammoth employee cuts in 1994.[29]

However, as companies regain financial strength, they're hesitant to rehire permanent employees. Why? One reason is that the cost of terminating employees is so high that managers are increasingly choosing to avoid the costs of firing employees by not hiring them in the first place. Instead, companies are using temporary employees or outsourcing certain functions. The cost of firing comes from severance compensation, lost training costs, and damages and legal fees paid in wrongful discharge suits.

At one time the prevailing employment doctrine was "employment at will." This meant that managers had as much freedom to fire workers as workers had to leave voluntarily. Most states now have written employment laws that limit the "at will" doctrine to protect employees from wrongful firing because of discrimination or because the employee exposed the employer's illegal actions or refused to violate a law. This well-meaning legislation eroded management's firing rights as it increased workers' rights to their jobs. Now workers fired for drug use can sue on the ground that they're protected by laws barring discrimination against the disabled.

Consultants offer this advice to minimize the chance of a lawsuit for wrongful discharge:[30]

- Prepare before hiring by requiring recruits to sign a statement that retains management's freedom to terminate at will.
- Don't make unintentional promises by using terms such as *permanent employment*.
- Document reasons before firing and make sure you have an unquestionable business reason for the firing.
- Fire the worst first and be consistent in discipline.
- Buy out bad risks by offering severance pay in exchange for a signed release from any claims.

••• RETIRING EMPLOYEES •••

In addition to laying off employees, another tool used to downsize companies is to offer early retirement benefits to entice older (and more expensive) workers to resign. These benefits usually involve such financial incentives as one-time cash payments. Studies have shown that if you're offered early retirement, you're better off taking the first offer when employers are more likely to feel guilty and, therefore, generous.[31] The advantage of offering early retirement benefits rather than the less expensive downsizing strategy of laying off employees is that early retirement offers boost the morale of remaining employees. Retiring senior workers also increases promotion opportunities for younger employees.

LAWS AFFECTING HUMAN RESOURCE MANAGEMENT

Legislation has made hiring, promoting, firing, and managing employee relations in general very complex and subject to many legal complications and challenges. Let's see how these changes in law have expanded the role and the challenge of human resource management.

The government had little to do with human resource decisions until the 1930s. Since then, though, legislation and legal decisions have greatly affected all areas of human resource management, from hiring to training and working conditions. (See Legal Briefcase box on page 363.)

One of the most important pieces of social legislation ever passed by Congress was the Civil Rights Act of 1964. This act was passed with much debate and was actually amended 97 times before final passage. Title VII of that act brought the government directly into the operations of human resource management. Title VII prohibits discrimination in hiring, firing, compensation, apprenticeships, training, terms, conditions, or privileges of employment based on race, religion, creed, sex, or national origin. Age was later added to the conditions of the act. The Civil Rights Act of 1964 was expected to stamp out the vestiges of discrimination in the workplace. However, specific language in the legislation often made its enforcement difficult. With this in mind, Congress took on the task of amending the law.

In 1972, the Equal Employment Opportunity Act (EEOA) was added as an amendment to Title VII. It strengthened the Equal Employment Opportunity Commission (EEOC), which was created by the Civil Rights Act of 1964. Congress gave rather broad powers to the EEOC. For example, the commission was permitted to issue guidelines for acceptable employer conduct in administering equal employment opportunity. Also, specific record-keeping procedures as set forth by the EEOC became mandatory. In addition, the commission was vested with the power of enforcement to ensure that these mandates were carried out. The EEOC became a formidable regulatory force in the administration of human resource management.

The most controversial program enforced by the EEOC is probably **affirmative action;** that is, activities designed to increase opportunities for minorities and women. The purpose of affirmative action was to "right past wrongs" endured by females and minorities in the administration of human resource management. Interpretation of the law eventually led employers to actively recruit and give preference to females and minority group members. As you might expect, interpretation and enforcement of the program are often difficult. Legal questions persist about the program's legality and whether it creates reverse discrimination in the workplace. **Reverse discrimination** refers to the sense of unfairness unprotected groups may have when protected groups are given preference in hiring and promoting. Laws are now being proposed at both the state and federal levels to end *all* discrimination, reverse discrimination included.

The Civil Rights Act of 1991 expands the remedies available to victims of discrimination by amending Title VII of the Civil Rights Act of 1964. Now victims of discrimination have the right to a jury trial and punitive damages. There was much debate about whether this act would lead to reverse discrimination or quotas in hiring during the 1990s.[32] Human resource managers should follow court cases closely to see how the law is enforced.

The Civil Rights Act of 1991 created the Glass Ceiling Commission to investigate the invisible barriers that women and minorities bump into when they rise close to the top of the organization hierarchy. The commission's report, released in early 1995, revealed that 95 to 97 percent of the senior

affirmative action
Employment activities designed to "right past wrongs" endured by females and minorities.

reverse discrimination
The feeling of unfairness unprotected groups may have when protected groups are given preference in hiring and promoting.

managers in the country's biggest companies are men and that women or minorities do not hold the jobs that lead to top management promotions. One of the commission's conclusions was that govvernment was not doing enough to enforce existing policies that encourage hiring and promoting women and minorities. It planned to meet later to outline recommendations for solving these problems. These issues are likely to persist for years to come.[33]

••• LAWS PROTECTING THE DISABLED •••
AND OLDER EMPLOYEES

The courts have continued their activity in issues involving human resource management. As you just read, the courts look carefully into any improprieties concerning possible discrimination in hiring, firing, training, and so forth specifically related to race or sex. The Vocational Rehabilitation Act (1973) extended the same protection given to minorities and women to people with disabilities. Today, businesses can't discriminate against people with disabilities on the basis of their physical or mental handicap.

The Americans with Disabilities Act of 1990 (ADA) requires that disabled applicants be given the same consideration for employment as people without disabilities. It also requires that businesses make "reasonable accommodations" to people with disabilities. This means doing such things as modifying equipment or widening doorways. Not all reasonable accommodations are expensive. For about $6 a month, a company can rent a headset phone allowing someone with cerebral palsy to talk on the phone and write at the same time. ADA also protects disabled individuals from discrimination in public accommodations, transportation, and telecommunications. Equal opportunity for people with disabilities promises to be a continuing issue in the 1990s. Most companies aren't having trouble making structural changes to be accommodating. What they're finding difficult are the cultural changes. Employers used to think being fair meant treating everyone the same. Now they believe accommodation means that they must treat people differently.[34]

Older employees (between 40 and 69) are also guaranteed protection against discrimination in the workplace. Courts have ruled against firms in unlawful discharge suits where age appeared to be the major factor in the dismissal. Additionally, protection through the Age Discrimination in Employment Act outlawed mandatory retirement in most organizations before age 70. Mandatory retirement after age 70 is voluntarily being phased out by many companies as well.

••• PROPOSED WAGES AND BENEFITS LEGISLATION •••

Some controversy has been raised about legislation regarding wages and employee benefits. Of major concern is the minimum wage law and mandatory health insurance protection. In 1991, the minimum wage was increased from $3.35 to $4.25 per hour. In 1994 President Clinton failed to convince enough business leaders and politicians of the merits of mandatory health care. There's much controversy over the effect of such legislation on business. Good arguments abound for raising the minimum wage and providing health insurance, but the question remains, Does legislation raising the minimum wage and requiring health care coverage prevent employers from hiring entry-level workers and thus cause a loss of jobs among people least able to find jobs? Some European countries took this path and their average unemployment rate ballooned from 2.6 percent in 1970 to 11 percent in 1993.[35]

Legal Briefcase

Government Legislation

National Labor Relations Act of 1935. Established collective bargaining in labor–management relations and limited management interference in the right of employees to have a collective bargaining agent.

Fair Labor Standards Act of 1938. Established a minimum wage and overtime pay for employees working more than 40 hours a week.

Manpower Development and Training Act of 1962. Provided for the training and retraining of unemployed workers.

Equal Pay Act of 1963. Specified that men and women doing equal jobs must be paid the same wage.

The Civil Rights Act of 1964. Outlawed discrimination in employment based on sex, race, color, religion, or national origin.

Age Discrimination in Employment Act of 1967. Outlawed personnel practices that discriminate against people aged 40 to 69. An amendment outlaws company policies that require employees to retire before age 70.

Occupational Safety and Health Act of 1970 (OSHA). Regulated the degree to which employees can be exposed to hazardous substances and specified the safety equipment to be provided by the employer.

Equal Employment Opportunity Act of 1972. Created the Equal Employment Opportunity Commission (EEOC) and authorized the EEOC to set guidelines for human resource management.

The Comprehensive Employment and Training Act of 1973. Provided funds for training unemployed workers (was known as the *CETA program*).

Employee Retirement Income Security Act of 1974. Regulated company retirement programs and provided a federal insurance program for bankrupt retirement plans.

Immigration Reform and Control Act of 1986. Required employers to verify the eligibility for employment of *all* their new hires (including U.S. citizens).

Supreme Court ruling against set aside programs (affirmative action), 1989. Declared that setting aside 30 percent of contracting jobs for minority businesses was reverse discrimination and unconstitutional.

Older Workers Benefit Protection Act, 1990. Protects older people from signing away their rights to things like pensions or to fight against illegal age discrimination.

Civil Rights Act of 1991. Applies to firms with over 15 employees. It extends the right to a jury trial and punitive damages to victims of intentional job discrimination.

Americans with Disabilities Act (1992 implementation). Employers must not discriminate against qualified disabled individuals in hiring, advancement, or compensation and must adapt the workplace if necessary.

Family and Medical Leave Act of 1993. Businesses with 50 or more employees must provide up to 12 weeks of unpaid leave per year upon birth or adoption of employee's child or upon serious illness of parent, spouse, or child.

As small and large businesses complain of not being able to find qualified workers, the government has proposed several training programs. The School-to-Work Opportunities Act of 1993 was proposed by the Clinton administration to address training needs of entry-level workers. The law would establish national standards and provide grants to states planning school-to-work systems. Another legislative measure to prepare students for the job market is the Workforce Readiness Act of 1993. This law would establish a national board on work force skills and a comprehensive school-to-work transition program. Three appointees to the board would be required to be winners of the Baldrige Award ◄-- P.49 --► [36]

••• EFFECTS OF LEGISLATION •••

Clearly, legislation affects all areas of human resource management. Such legislation ranges from the Social Security Act of 1935, to the Occupational Safety and Health Act (OSHA) of 1970, to the Employment Retirement Income Security Act (ERISA) of 1974. Read *The Wall Street Journal, Business Week,* and other periodicals to keep up with human resource legislation and rulings.

Legislation clearly has enormous impact on human resource programs. In summary,

- Employers must be sensitive to the legal rights of women, minorities, the disabled, and older employees or else risk costly court cases.

- Legislation affects all areas of human resource management, from hiring and training to wages and benefits.

- Court cases have made it clear that it's legal in certain instances to go beyond providing equal rights for minorities and women in order to provide special employment (affirmative action) and training to correct discrimination in the past.

- New court cases and legislation change human resource management almost daily. The only way to keep current is to read the business literature and become familiar with the issues.

PROGRESS CHECK

- Explain what was covered by the following laws:
  The Civil Rights Act of 1964.
  The Equal Employment Opportunity Act of 1972.
  The Americans with Disabilities Act of 1990.

SUMMARY
•••••••

1. Explain the importance of human resource management and describe current issues in managing human resources.

1. Human resource management is the process of evaluating human resource needs, finding people to fill those needs, and getting the best work from each employee by providing the right incentives and job environment, all with the goal of meeting organizational objectives.
   - ***What are some current problems in the human resource area?***
   Many of the current problems revolve around the changing demographics of workers: more women, minorities, immigrants, and older workers. Other problems concern a shortage of trained workers and an abundance of unskilled workers; skilled workers in declining industries requiring retraining; changing employee work attitudes; and complex laws and regulations.

2. Summarize the six steps in planning human resources.

2. Like all other types of management, human resource management begins with planning.
   - ***What are the steps in human resource planning?***
   The six steps are (1) preparing forecasts of future human resource needs, (2) preparing a human resource inventory, (3) preparing job analyses, (4) assessing future demands, (5) assessing future supply, and (6) establishing a plan for recruiting, hiring, educating, and developing employees.

3. Describe methods companies use to recruit new employees and explain some of the problems that make recruitment difficult.

3. Recruitment is the set of lawful activities used to obtain a sufficient number of the right people at the right time and to select those who will best meet the organization's needs.
   - ***Why has recruitment become more difficult?***
   Legal restrictions complicate hiring and firing practices. Finding suitable employees can also be hard if companies are considered unattractive workplaces.

4. Selection is the process of gathering and interpreting information to decide which applicants should be hired.
   - **What are the six steps in the selection process?**
   (1) Obtain complete application forms. (2) Give initial interviews and follow-up interviews. (3) Give employment tests. (4) Conduct background investigations. (5) Give physical exams. (6) Conduct a trial period of employment.

   4. Outline the six steps in selecting employees.

5. Employee training and development include all attempts to improve employee performance by increasing an employee's ability to perform through learning.
   - **What are some of the procedures used for training?**
   They include employee orientation, on- and off-the-job training, apprentice programs, vestibule training, and job simulation.
   - **What methods are used to develop managerial skills?**
   Management development methods include on-the-job coaching, understudy positions, job rotation, and off-the-job courses and training.
   - **How does networking fit in this process?**
   Networking is the process of establishing contacts with key managers within and outside the organization to get additional development assistance.

   5. Illustrate the use of various types of employee training and development methods.

6. A performance appraisal is an evaluation of employees' performance level against established standards to make decisions about promotions, compensation, additional training, or firing.
   - **How is performance evaluated?**
   The steps are (1) establish performance standards, (2) communicate those standards, (3) evaluate performance, (4) discuss results, (5) take corrective action when needed, and (6) use the results for decisions about promotions, compensation, additional training, or firing.

   6. Trace the six steps in appraising employee performance.

7. Employee compensation is one of the largest operating costs for many organizations.
   - **What kind of compensation systems are used?**
   They include salary systems, hourly wages, piecework, commission plans, bonus plans, and profit-sharing plans.
   - **What are fringe benefits?**
   Fringe benefits include such items as sick leave, vacation pay, pension plans, and health plans that provide additional compensation to employees.

   7. Summarize the objectives of employee compensation programs and describe various pay systems and fringe benefits.

8. Workers' increasing need for flexibility has generated new innovations in scheduling.
   - **What scheduling plans can be used to adjust to employees' need for flexibility?**
   Such plans include job sharing, flextime, compressed workweeks, and working at home.

   8. Explain the scheduling plans managers use to adjust to workers' needs.

9. Employees often move from their original positions in a company.
   - **How can employees move within a company?**
   Employees can move up (promotion), over (reassignment), or out (termination or retirement) of a company.

   9. Describe the ways employees can move through a company: promotion, reassignment, termination, and retirement.

10. Many laws affect human resource management.
    - **What are those laws?**
    See the Legal Briefcase box and review the section on laws. This is an important subject for future managers to study.

    10. Illustrate the effects of legislation on human resource management.

KEY TERMS

affirmative action 361
apprenticeship 348
cafeteria-style fringe benefits 356
compressed workweek 358
core time 357
employee orientation 348
flextime plans 357
fringe benefits 355
human resource management 338
job analysis 342
job description 342
job sharing 357
job simulation 349
job specifications 342
management development 350
mentor 351
networking 351
off-the-job training 349
on-the-job training 348
performance appraisal 352
recruitment 343
reverse discrimination 361
selection 344
training and development 348
vestibule training 349

DEVELOPING WORKPLACE SKILLS

1. If you experience a typical career you are likely to have about eight different jobs in your lifetime. Therefore, you will have to prepare several résumés and cover letters. Write a cover letter and résumé seeking employment for an entry level position in your local area. Ask your instructor to critique them.
2. Read the current business periodicals to find the latest court rulings on issues such as fringe benefits, affirmative action, and other human resource–related issues. Compose a summary of your findings. What are the major trends? What will these mean for tomorrow's college graduates?
3. Recall the various training programs you have experienced. Think of both on-the-job and off-the-job training sessions. What is your evaluation of such programs? Write a brief critique of each. How would you improve them? Share your ideas with the class.
4. Use the library to look up the current unemployment figures for individual states. Notice there are pockets of very high unemployment. Analyze the causes of such uneven figures? What can be done to retrain workers whose skills are obsolete because of a restructured economy? Is that the role of government or business? Discuss. Could government and business cooperate in this function?
5. Find several people who work under flextime or part-time systems and interview them regarding their experiences and preferences. Using this information, draft a proposal to your company's management advocating an option for a four-day work week. Debate this proposal with your class.

PRACTICING MANAGEMENT DECISIONS

CASE DUAL-CAREER PLANNING

Carey Moler is a 32-year-old account executive for a communications company. She's married to Mitchell Moler, a lawyer. They have one child. Carey and Mitchell hadn't made any definite plans about how to juggle their careers and family life until Carey reached age 30. Then she decided to have a baby, and career planning took on entirely new dimensions. A company named Catalyst talked to 815 dual-career couples and found most of them, like the Molers, hadn't made any long-range career decisions regarding family lifestyle.

From the business perspective, such dual-career families create real concerns. Problems with relocations, child care, and so on affect recruiting, productivity, morale, and promotion policies.

For a couple such as the Molers, having both career and family responsibilities is exhausting. But that's just one problem. If Carey is moving up in the firm, what happens if Mitchell gets a terrific job offer 1,500 miles away? What if Carey gets such an offer? Who's going to care for the baby? What happens if the baby becomes ill? How do they plan their vacations when there are three schedules to balance? Who'll do the housework?

Dual careers require careful planning and discussion, and those plans need to be reviewed over time. A couple who decide at age 22 to do certain things may change their minds at 30. Whether to have children, where to locate, and how to manage the household can become major problems if not carefully planned.

The same is true for corporations. They too must plan for dual-career families. They must give more attention to job sharing, flextime, paternity leave policies for men, transfer policies, nepotism rules, and more.

Decision Questions

1. What are some issues you can see developing because of dual-career families? How is this affecting children in such families?

2. What kind of corporate policies need changing to adapt to these new realities?

3. How can newlywed couples minimize the problems of dual careers? What are the advantages of dual careers? Disadvantages? How can a couple achieve the advantages with a minimum number of problems?

••

〉〉 VIDEO CASE MODERN TRAINING METHODS 〉〉

An important part of the human resource manager's function is to keep employees of the firm up to date with regard to use of the latest equipment and processes. In the past, such training has taken place in the classroom, through one-on-one instruction, and through the use of videotapes, audiotapes, workbooks, and the like. Today, information systems technology is making it possible to provide such training for less cost and with better results. Two companies that are using the latest technology are Allstate Insurance and United Air Lines.

Allstate is one of the larger insurance companies selling personal, business, and life insurance. It needs to do a lot of advanced underwriting and claims training. To do that, it uses computer-based training (CBT). Interactive workstations—using a combination of tools such as CD-ROM, video discs, and printers—enable employees at Allstate to sit down at a workstation and take any one of 200 lessons.

There are some 12,000 employees to be trained at Allstate, making the use of such systems extremely important to the firm. The company estimates that it costs $375 to train off-site in the traditional way (classroom training) compared to only $75 for computer-based training. Furthermore, the computer-based training is more flexible. It allows employees to log on when they want, take the training program most appropriate to their individual needs, and come back to it at any time. There is a bookmark command that takes them back to where they left off.

United Airlines flies a greater variety of planes than other airlines. Accordingly, its 19,000 flight attendants need to be brought up to date on the newest planes and their operating systems (e.g., galley equipment, saftey features, emergency equipment, and so forth). The company has 133 multimedia computers located strategically around the country where employees travel: San Francisco, Washington, D.C., New York, Miami, and so on. Flight attendants therefore find it easy to log on at one of the airports, take training, log off, and come back whenever they have additional time.

Information technology gives both companies the advantage of:

- Automatic scoring and tracking
- Consistency of training
- User control
- Mixed media applications: animation, graphics, text, audio, visual, and databases.

The companies can immedialtely implement new training, monitor employee progress, check which programs are most popular, and custom-design programs for each employee. In short, with computer-based training human resource managers now have a flexible new tool to assist them in their training function.

Discussion Questions

1. What are the advantages and disadvantages of such training as you see it? Can computerized instruction ever replace face-to-face instruction?

2. What are some other industries that could benefit from computer-based training? Would you include college education?

3. Can you see the value of such training in companies that use cross-functional teams?

CHAPTER 12

DEALING WITH EMPLOYEE–MANAGEMENT ISSUES AND RELATIONSHIPS

LEARNING GOALS

After you have read and studied this chapter, you should be able to

1. Trace the history of organized labor in the United States and discuss the major legislation affecting labor unions.

2. Outline the objectives of labor unions.

3. Describe the tactics used by labor and management during conflicts and discuss the role of unions in the future.

4. Explain some of the controversial employee–management issues such as executive compensation, comparable worth, child care and elder care, AIDS, drug testing, violence in the workplace, and employee stock ownership plans (ESOPs).

DAVID STERN, COMMISSIONER OF THE NATIONAL BASKETBALL ASSOCIATION

As a boy, David Stern learned about business from working at his parents' delicatessen in New York City. From these humble beginnings, he worked his way through school and earned a law degree. Stern became a respected corporate attorney with a thriving law practice in New York. He seemed bound for an illustrious legal career. However, in 1984 Stern was attracted to a more challenging offer. He was asked to accept the job as commissioner of the National Basketball Association (NBA) and help rejuvenate this American sports institution.

What David Stern found was a league beset with problems. Players were dissatisfied, owners were grumbling about inadequate revenue sharing, and fan support was stagnant. He addressed these issues by applying solid management techniques. For example, the NBA was the first sports association to tie players' salaries directly to revenues. The players' union agreed to a revenue-sharing plan that capped salaries at 53 percent of the league's sales. Therefore, the league avoided the cost escalations that hurt other professional sports but still provided an incentive for players.

Stern was able to triple the NBA's television contract and greatly expand its sales of merchandise such as jackets, hats, and warm-up suits to $1 billion. He launched a draft lottery that generated a tremendous amount of free publicity and stimulated new interest from both fans and the press. Marquee players such as Larry Bird, Magic Johnson, and Michael Jordan were marketed as league ambassadors. The once disgruntled owners started beaming with pride when talking about the commissioner's performance. It seems he accomplished the impossible: He satisfied both management and labor. Stern's next objective is expansion in the global market, which he says is perfect for basketball. In 1994, the NBA granted its first Canadian franchise.

David Stern is credited with molding the NBA into an outstanding example of modern sports management. Professional sports isn't the only industry that has problems dealing with labor–management relations, employee compensation, and other work-related issues. Managers of business and nonprofit organizations address these issues every day. This chapter will discuss unions, executive pay, comparable worth, ESOPs, and many other issues that will dominate the headlines and the thoughts of business managers throughout the coming years.

By working faithfully 8 hours a day, you may eventually get to be boss and work 12 hours a day.

Robert Frost

EMPLOYEE–MANAGEMENT ISSUES

The relationship between owners/managers and employees has rarely been smooth. Management has the responsibility to produce a profit through maximum productivity. Labor is interested in fair and competent management, human dignity, and a reasonable share in the wealth its work generates. Many issues affect the relationship between managers and employees: executive compensation, comparable worth, child care and elder care, AIDS, drug testing, violence in the workplace, and employee stock ownership plans (ESOPs).

This chapter discusses such issues. Like all other managerial problems, these issues must be worked out through open discussion, goodwill, and compromise. It's important to know both sides of the issues, however, to make reasoned decisions.

Any discussion of employee–management relations in the United States probably should begin with a discussion of unions. Workers formed unions to protect themselves from unfair managers and to have some say in the operations of their jobs. This gave workers more negotiating power with managers and more political power as well. **Unions** are employee organizations whose main goal is to represent members in employee–management bargaining over job-related issues.

union
Employee organizations that have the main goal of representing members in employee–management bargaining about job-related issues.

Employees have historically turned to unions to assist them in gaining specific rights and benefits. However, in the 1980s and 1990s, unions lost much of the power they'd previously achieved and continued to decrease in membership. Nonetheless, some labor analysts forecast that unions may still regain strength among workers in the later 1990s. There's no question that unions' future role and position will arouse emotions and opinions that contrast considerably. Let's briefly look at some contrasting viewpoints concerning labor unions. Then we'll look at the other issues affecting employee–management relations.

LABOR UNIONS FROM DIFFERENT PERSPECTIVES

Are labor unions essential in the American economy today? This question is certain to evoke emotional responses from various participants in the workplace. The textile worker carrying a picket sign in New York will elaborate on the dangers to our free society if employers continue to try to bust authorized unions.

A different perspective is often embraced by small manufacturers who are forced to operate under union wage and benefit obligations and work rules. Such manufacturers argue that competition in an expanding global market is very difficult under strict union conditions.

Fundamentally, most people would agree that the union movement of today is an outgrowth of the economic transition caused by the Industrial Revolution of the 19th and early 20th centuries. The workers who once toiled in the fields, dependent on the mercies of nature for survival, instead became dependent on the continuous roll of the factory presses and assembly lines for their living. The steps in breaking away from an agrarian (agricultural)

Striking members of the United Auto Workers (UAW) attempt to block the entry of temporary replacement workers at the Caterpillar plant in Aurora, Illinois. The use of replacement workers intensified hostilities in this labor dispute. Which position do you defend? Why?

economy to an industrial economy were quite difficult. Nonetheless, over time workers learned that strength through unity could lead to improved job conditions, better wages, and job security.

Today, critics of organized labor maintain that few of the inhuman conditions that once dominated U.S. industry can be found in the workplace. They charge that organized labor has in fact become a large industrial entity in itself, and the real issue of protecting workers has become secondary because the legal system and current management attitudes prohibit the reappearance of the sweatshops of the late 19th and early 20th centuries. Are these assumptions correct? A short discussion of the history of labor unions may cast a better light on these differing positions.

••• THE EARLY HISTORY OF ORGANIZED LABOR •••

Formal labor organizations in the United States date back to near the time of the American Revolution. As early as 1792, cordwainers (shoemakers) in Philadelphia met to discuss the fundamental work issues of pay, hours, conditions, and job security. (Many of the same issues dominate labor negotiations today.) The shoemakers were a **craft union** (an organization of skilled specialists in a particular craft or trade). They were typical of the early labor organizations formed before the Civil War in that they were local or regional in membership. Also, most were established to achieve some short-range goal such as curtailing the use of convict labor as an alternative to available local labor. Often after a specific objective was attained, the labor group disbanded. This situation changed dramatically in the late 19th century with the expansion of the Industrial Revolution.

The Industrial Revolution changed the economic structure of the United States. Productivity rose enormously due to mass production and job specialization, making the United States a true world power. However, this rapid shift in economic focus brought problems for workers in terms of productivity, hours of work, wages, and unemployment.

Workers were faced with the reality that production was vital. If you failed to produce, you lost your job. Often, this caused workers to go to work even if they were ill or had family problems. Over time, the increased emphasis on production led firms to expand the hours of work. The average workweek in 1900 was 60 hours, but 80 hours wasn't uncommon for some industries.

craft union
Labor organization of skilled specialists in a particular craft or trade.

No More Homework, Please!

No, this is not the voice of thousands of college students around the country offering an impassioned plea for relief. This is the latest cause being pressed by labor unions. It seems unions are extremely concerned with "industrial homeworkers" and feel they present the newest challenge to labor's growth and stability. Industrial homeworkers are workers like Carol Roberts of Gorham, Maine. Carol works at home knitting various items for a distributor who then sells her goods to retailers. The distributor supplies Carol with yarn and designs that she produces on a piece-rate basis. With consistent work, Carol can earn up to $10 per hour of income she and her husband (who's employed full-time) desperately need. The AFL–CIO estimates there are more than 600,000 industrial homeworkers around the country.

Unions complain that workers like Carol compete against union labor. In 1938, Congress and the U.S. Department of Labor agreed, and barred industrial homework in seven industries: ladies' garments, jewelry, gloves

BUSINESS

and mittens, buttons and buckles, handkerchiefs, embroideries, and knitted outerwear. But in the 1980s, exceptions were made permitting industrial homework in all but ladies' garments and some jewelry. In many service industries, employees now work at computers at home rather than go to an office. Also, the majority of homeworkers are female, and argue that working at home lets them spend more time with their children. Unions such as the International Ladies Garment Workers' Union are unmoved and plan to ask Congress to strictly adhere to the law and prohibit such work practices. Labor unions feel the potential for abuse is also rampant in industrial homework. They charge that children are often brought into the work process by industrial homeworkers in violation of child labor laws. It looks like it will be up to Congress to decide if this is an example of free enterprise at its best or a violation of fair labor practices.

Source: Jody Brennan, "New Outlaws?" *Forbes*, February 15, 1993, p. 70.

Wages were low and child labor was common. Furthermore, periods of unemployment were hard on families who lived on subsistence wages. As you can sense, these weren't short-term issues that would easily go away. The workplace was ripe for the emergence of national labor organizations.

Knights of Labor
The first national labor union (1869).

The first truly national labor organization was the Noble Order of the **Knights of Labor** formed by Uriah Smith Stephens in 1869. By 1886, the Knights of Labor claimed 700,000 members. The Knights of Labor offered membership to all working people (including employers), and promoted social causes as well as labor and economic issues. However, their stewardship was short lived because of the rather revolutionary attitudes of their leadership. In essence, the Knights of Labor's goal was to gain significant *political* power and eventually restructure the entire U.S. economy. They fell from prominence after receiving the blame for a bomb that exploded during a labor rally at Haymarket Square in Chicago which killed eight policemen.

American Federation of Labor (AFL)
An organization of craft unions that championed bread-and-butter labor issues.

A rival group to the Knights of Labor, the **American Federation of Labor (AFL)**, was formed in 1886. By 1890, the AFL, under the dynamic leadership of Samuel Gompers, had moved to the forefront of the labor movement. The AFL was an organization of craft unions that championed bread-and-butter labor issues. They intentionally limited membership to skilled workers (craftspeople), assuming they would have bargaining power in attaining concessions from some employers. It's important to note that the AFL was never one big union. Rather, it functioned as a federation of many separate unions that could become members, yet keep separate union status. Over time, an unauthorized committee in the AFL began to organize workers in **industrial unions**, which were organizations of unskilled and semiskilled workers in

industrial unions
Labor organizations of unskilled workers in mass production-related industries such as automobiles and mining.

Norris–La Guardia Act, 1932	Prohibited courts from issuing injunctions against nonviolent union activities; outlawed contracts forbidding union activities; outlawed the use of yellow-dog contracts by employers. (Yellow-dog contracts were contractual agreements forced on workers by employers whereby the employee agreed not to join a union as a condition of employment.)
National Labor Relations Act (Wagner Act), 1935	Gave employees the right to form or join labor organizations (or to refuse to form or join); the right to collectively bargain with employers through elected union representatives; and the right to engage in labor activities such as strikes, picketing, and boycotts. Prohibited certain unfair labor practices by the employer and the union, and established the National Labor Relations Board to oversee union election campaigns and investigate labor practices. This act gave great impetus to the union movement.
Fair Labor Standards Act, 1938	Set a minimum wage and maximum basic hours for workers in interstate commerce industries. The first minimum wage set was 25 cents an hour, except for farm and retail workers.
Labor–Management Relations Act (Taft-Hartley Act), 1947	Amended the Wagner Act; permitted states to pass laws prohibiting compulsory union membership (right-to-work laws); set up methods to deal with strikes that affect national health and safety; prohibited secondary boycotts, closed-shop agreements, and featherbedding (the requiring of wage payments for work not performed) by unions. This act gave more power to management.
Labor–Management Reporting and Disclosure Act (Landrum-Griffin Act), 1959	Amended the Taft-Hartley Act and the Wagner Act; guaranteed individual rights of union members in dealing with their union, such as the right to nominate candidates for union office, vote in union elections, attend and participate in union meetings, vote on union business, and examine union records and accounts; required annual financial reports to be filed with the U.S. Department of Labor. One goal of this act was to clean up union corruption, but some corruption continues today.

mass production–related industries such as automobiles and mining. This committee, called the Committee of Industrial Organization, was led by John L. Lewis, president of the United Mine Workers Union.

Lewis's goal was to organize both craftspeople (craft unions) and unskilled workers (industrial unions). When his proposal was rejected, Lewis broke with the AFL and formed a rival organization called the **Congress of Industrial Organizations (CIO)** in 1935. The CIO soon rivaled the AFL in membership, partly because of passage of the Wagner Act the same year. (Figure 12.1 describes major labor–management legislation.) For 20 years, the two organizations contested for leadership of the labor movement. It wasn't until the passage of legislation unfavorable to unions (such as the Taft-Hartley Act) that the two organizations saw the benefits of a merger. In 1955, under the leadership of George Meany, 16 million labor members united to form the AFL–CIO. Today, the AFL–CIO includes affiliations with over 100 labor unions, including the Teamsters, the second largest labor organization in the United States. The nation's largest labor group, the National Education Association, isn't formally affiliated with the AFL–CIO.

⟨⟨ **FIGURE 12.1** ⟩⟩

MAJOR LEGISLATION AFFECTING LABOR–MANAGEMENT RELATIONS

Congress of Industrial Organizations (CIO)

Union organization of unskilled workers which broke away from the AFL in 1935 and rejoined it in 1955.

LABOR LEGISLATION AND COLLECTIVE BARGAINING

Organized labor's growth and strength have always depended on two major factors: the law and public opinion. Figure 12.1 outlines five major federal laws that have had a significant impact on labor unions' rights and operations.

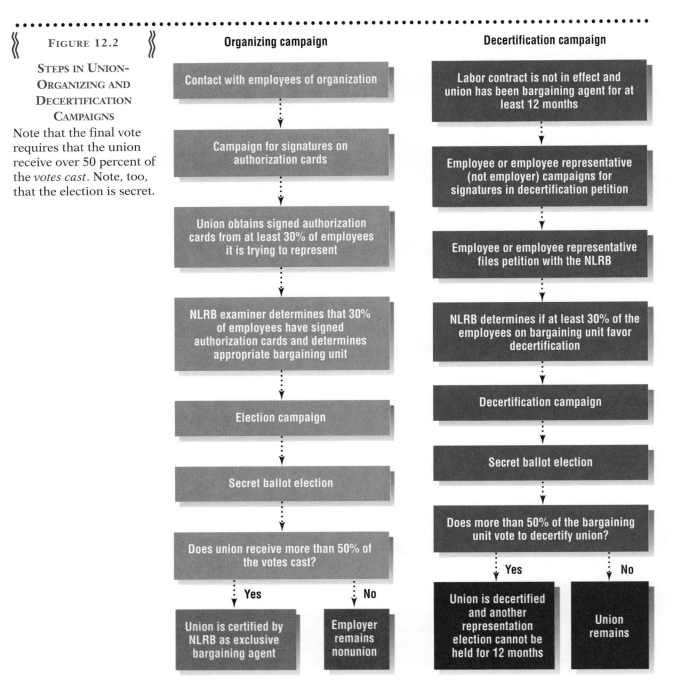

FIGURE 12.2

STEPS IN UNION-ORGANIZING AND DECERTIFICATION CAMPAIGNS

Note that the final vote requires that the union receive over 50 percent of the *votes cast*. Note, too, that the election is secret.

Organizing campaign

Contact with employees of organization

Campaign for signatures on authorization cards

Union obtains signed authorization cards from at least 30% of employees it is trying to represent

NLRB examiner determines that 30% of employees have signed authorization cards and determines appropriate bargaining unit

Election campaign

Secret ballot election

Does union receive more than 50% of the votes cast?

Yes — Union is certified by NLRB as exclusive bargaining agent

No — Employer remains nonunion

Decertification campaign

Labor contract is not in effect and union has been bargaining agent for at least 12 months

Employee or employee representative (not employer) campaigns for signatures in decertification petition

Employee or employee representative files petition with the NLRB

NLRB determines if at least 30% of the employees on bargaining unit favor decertification

Decertification campaign

Secret ballot election

Does more than 50% of the bargaining unit vote to decertify union?

Yes — Union is decertified and another representation election cannot be held for 12 months

No — Union remains

certification
Process of a union's becoming recognized by the NLRB as the bargaining agent for a group of employees.

decertification
Process by which workers take away a union's right to represent them.

collective bargaining
The process whereby union and management representatives reach a negotiated labor-management agreement.

The Wagner Act provided labor with legal justification to pursue the issues supported by Samuel Gompers and the AFL. This act of Congress established an administrative agency, the National Labor Relations Board (NLRB), to oversee labor–management relations. It also provided guidelines and offers legal protection to workers seeking to vote on "organizing" a union to represent them in the workplace. This process of a union's being recognized by the NLRB as the authorized bargaining agent for a group of employees is called **certification**. The act also provided workers and management with a clear process to decertify a union. **Decertification** is the process by which workers take away a union's right to represent them. (Figure 12.2 describes the steps in union-organizing and decertification campaigns.)

The equalization of unequals through collective bargaining was a vital issue, according to Gompers. **Collective bargaining** is the process whereby union representatives sit down with management and work out a mutually

1. Management rights
2. Union recognition
3. Union security clause
4. Strikes and lockouts
5. Union activities and responsibilities
   a. Dues checkoff
   b. Union bulletin boards
   c. Work slowdowns
6. Wages
   a. Wage structure
   b. Shift differentials
   c. Wage incentives
   d. Bonuses
   e. Piecework conditions
   f. Tiered wage structures
7. Hours of work and time-off policies
   a. Regular hours of work
   b. Holidays
   c. Vacation policies

d. Overtime regulations
e. Leaves of absence
f. Break periods
g. Flextime
h. Meal time allotments
8. Job rights and seniority principles
   a. Seniority regulations
   b. Transfer policies and bumping
   c. Promotions
   d. Layoffs and recall procedures
   e. Job bidding and posting
9. Discharge and discipline
   a. Suspension
   b. Conditions for discharge
10. Grievance procedures
    a. Arbitration agreement
    b. Mediation procedures
11. Employee benefits, health, and welfare

FIGURE 12.3

ISSUES IN A LABOR–MANAGEMENT AGREEMENT

Labor and management often meet to discuss and clarify the terms that specify employees' functions within the company. The topics listed in this figure are typically discussed during these meetings. Notice that the union is concerned about the employees' benefits and rights.

agreed upon contract for the workers. The Wagner Act expanded the right to collectively bargain and obligated employers to meet at reasonable times and bargain in *good faith* with respect to wages, hours, and other terms and conditions of employment. Gompers and his followers were true believers in the capitalist system. They believed collective bargaining was the means to attain a fairer share of the economic pie and attain specific objectives important to members' well-being.

••• GOALS OF ORGANIZED LABOR •••

As you might suspect, organized labor's objectives frequently change according to shifts in social and economic trends. For example, in the 1970s most labor unions' primary objective was additional pay and benefits for their members. Throughout the 1980s, there was a significant shift toward issues related to job security and union recognition. The 1990s have certainly focused on these objectives, but the issue of global competition and its effects has also taken center stage. For example, the AFL–CIO split with the Clinton administration concerning NAFTA ◄·· P.105 ··►.

The **negotiated labor–management agreement** sets the tone and clarifies the terms and conditions under which management and labor agree to function over a specific period of time. Figure 12.3 lists topics commonly negotiated in labor–management agreements.

Union security clauses stipulate that employees who reap benefits from a union must either join or pay dues to the union. After passage of the Wagner Act, organized labor sought security in the form of the closed shop. The **closed-shop agreement** specified that workers had to be members of a union before being hired. The Taft-Hartley Act outlawed this practice in 1947. (Figure 12.4 covers types of union contracts.) Under an **agency shop agreement**, employers may hire nonunion workers who aren't required to join the union but must pay a union fee.

Labor today favors the union shop as the primary means for ensuring security. Under the **union shop agreement**, workers don't have to be members of a union to be hired for a job, but must agree to join the union within a prescribed period (usually 30, 60, or 90 days). The Taft-Hartley Act recognizes the legality of the union shop but grants individual states the power to outlaw

negotiated labor-management agreement
Settlement which sets the tone and clarifies the terms under which management and labor agree to function over a period of time.

union security clause
Provision in a negotiated labor-management agreement which stipulates that employees who benefit from a union must either join or pay dues to the union.

closed-shop agreement
Clause in labor–management agreement specified that workers had to be members of a union before being hired.

agency shop agreement
Clause in labor–management agreement that says employers may hire nonunion workers who are not required to join the union but must pay a union fee.

union shop agreement
Clause in labor–management agreement which says workers do not have to be members of a union to be hired, but must agree to join the union within a prescribed period.

FIGURE 12.4

DIFFERENT FORMS OF UNION CONTRACTS
Passed in 1947, the Taft-Hartley Act stated that employees don't have to be members of a union before being hired. Prior to this act, union membership could be a condition for employment. Now most union contracts are union shop agreeements.

TYPE OF CONTRACT	DESCRIPTION
Union shop	The majority of union contracts are of this type. The employer can hire anyone, but employees must join the union to keep their jobs.
Agency shop	Employers may hire anyone. Employees need not join the union, but are required to pay a union fee. Less than 10 percent of union contracts are of this nature.
Closed shop (no longer used)	The Taft-Hartley Act made this form illegal. Only union members could be hired under this system.
Open shop	Union membership is voluntary for new and existing employees. Those who don't join the union don't have to pay union dues. Few union contracts are of this type.

right-to-work laws
Legislation which gives workers the right, under an open shop, to join or not join a union if it is present.

open-shop agreement
Agreement in right-to-work states which gives workers the option to join or not join a union, if one exists in their workplace.

the union shop through passage of **right-to-work laws**. To date, 21 states have passed such legislation. (See Figure 12.5.) In a right-to-work state, workers under the **open-shop agreement** have the option to join a union, if one is present in the workplace, or to not join.

In the future, union negotiations' focus will no doubt shift as issues such as child and elder care, worker retraining, two-tiered wage plans, employee empowerment, and even integrity and honesty testing further challenge union members. Unions also intend to carefully monitor global agreements such as NAFTA and GATT «··· P.104 ···» to see that U.S. jobs aren't lost.

••• RESOLVING LABOR–MANAGEMENT DISAGREEMENTS •••

The rights of labor and management are outlined in the negotiated labor–management agreement. Upon acceptance by both sides, the agreement becomes a guide to work relations between the firm's employees and managers. However, the signed agreement doesn't necessarily mean the end to employee–management negotiations. As you might suspect, there are sometimes differences concerning interpretations of the labor–management agreement. For example, managers may interpret the agreement to mean that they decide who works overtime, while employees may interpret it to mean that managers must select employees for overtime based on employee seniority. If such controversies can't be resolved between the two parties, a grievance may be filed.

grievance
A charge by employees that management is not abiding by the terms of the negotiated labor agreement.

A **grievance** is a charge by employees that management isn't abiding by terms of the negotiated labor agreement. Issues such as overtime rules, promotions, layoffs, transfers, and job assignments are generally sources of employee grievances. A grievance can be filed by an individual or the entire labor organization. Handling employee grievances demands a good deal of contact between labor officials and managers.

shop steward
A labor official who works permanently in an organization and represents employee interests on a daily basis.

The majority of grievances are negotiated by **shop stewards** (labor officials who work permanently in an organization and represent employee interests on a daily basis) and supervisory managers. However, if a grievance isn't resolved at this level, formal grievance procedures will begin. Figure 12.6 on page 380 illustrates steps in the formal grievance procedure.

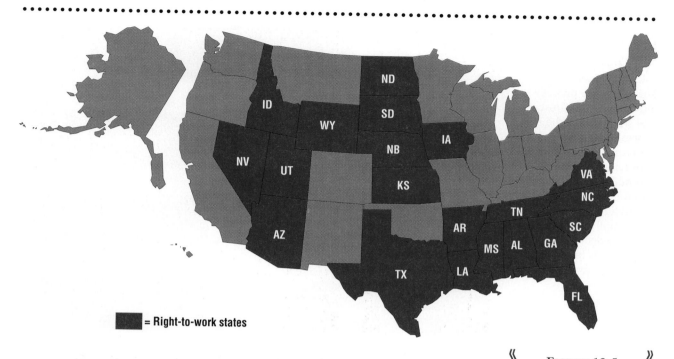

= Right-to-work states

FIGURE 12.5

STATES WITH RIGHT-TO-WORK LAWS

MEDIATION AND ARBITRATION   During the negotiation process, there's a **bargaining zone** or range of options between the initial and final offer that each party will consider before a union will strike or before management will close a plant. If labor–management negotiators can't agree on alternatives within this bargaining zone, mediation may be necessary. **Mediation** is the use of a third party, called a *mediator*, to encourage both sides to continue negotiating. Mediators often make suggestions for resolving a work dispute. But remember that mediators make suggestions, not decisions, as to how a dispute should be settled. Elected officials, attorneys, and college professors are often called on to serve as mediators in labor disputes. For example, W. J. Usery, former U.S. Secretary of Labor, served as a mediator in the baseball player's strike in 1994–95.

Another tool used to resolve labor–management conflicts is arbitration. **Arbitration** is the agreement to bring in an impartial third party (an arbitrator) to render a binding decision in a labor dispute. Many negotiated labor–management agreements in the United States call for the use of an arbitrator to end labor disputes. The arbitrator must be acceptable to both labor and management. The nonprofit American Arbitration Association is the dominant force in dispute resolution.[1] You may have heard of baseball players filing for arbitration to resolve a salary dispute.

bargaining zone
Range of options between the initial and final offer that each party will consider before a union will strike or before management will close a plant.

mediation
The use of a third party, called a mediator, to encourage both parties to continue negotiating.

arbitration
The agreement to bring in an impartial third party (an arbitrator) to render a binding decision in a labor dispute.

TACTICS USED IN LABOR–MANAGEMENT CONFLICTS

When labor and management reach an impasse in their collective bargaining and negotiations break down, either side or both sides will use specific tactics to further their objectives and perhaps sway public opinion. The primary tactics of labor are the strike and boycott. Unions might also use pickets and work slowdowns as tactics. Management tactics include lockouts, injunctions, strikebreakers, and perhaps even bankruptcy. Before they were outlawed by the Norris–La Guardia Act, management used yellow-dog contracts. In the following sections, we'll look at each of these labor and management strategies.

FIGURE 12.6

THE GRIEVANCE
RESOLUTION PROCESS
The grievance process
may move through sev-
eral steps before the issue
is resolved. At each step,
the issue is negotiated
between union officials
and managers. If no reso-
lution comes internally,
an outside arbitrator may
be mutually agreed upon.
If so, the decision by the
arbitrator is binding
(legally enforceable).

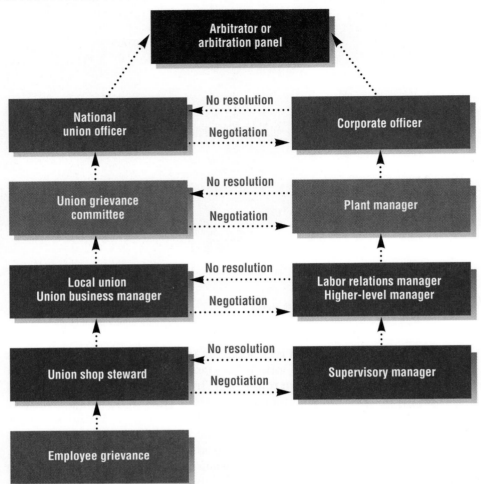

••• UNION TACTICS •••

strike
Union strategy of workers refusing
to go to work in order to further
their objectives after an impasse in
collective bargaining.

The strike has historically been the most potent union tactic. A **strike** means
that workers refuse to go to work. The strike provides public focus on the situation and at times causes operations to shut down totally. Often strikers
also *picket* the firm. This means that they walk around outside the organization carrying signs and talking with the public and the media about the
issues. You may recall the United Auto Workers (UAW) picketing against
Caterpillar, Inc., in 1992 and 1994. Unfortunately, strikes have often generated violence and extended bitterness since emotions on both sides frequently reach a boiling point. Strikes against Greyhound and the *New York
Daily News* brought out the dark side of strikes as a union tactic. There were
more than 500 incidents of threats or violence during the *New York Daily
News* strike. Delivery trucks were firebombed, bundles of newspapers were
stolen or scattered, and drivers were beaten. During the 1994 Teamsters
strike, a union picketer was struck and injured trying to block a truck driven
by a strikebreaker from leaving the terminal. Such violence often happens
when unions go on strike.

The public often realizes how important a worker is when he or she goes
on strike. Can you imagine what an economic and social disaster it would be
if doctors and nurses went on strike or if all police officers in a town left work
at once? Several cities have already experienced the smell and disruption

FROM THE PAGES OF... Entrepreneur MAGAZINE

Unions in Small Businesses

No matter how small your business is, it's important to understand how unions operate and what you can and can't do if your employees start talking about unionizing. If you build a strong working relationship with your employees and give them a stake in the business, they may not have any interest in forming a union. As the government passes legislation mandating some things unions have fought for in the past (such as family and medical leave), there's less need for union activity. Nonetheless, unions give employees a collective voice and are still an important part of the business environment.

If employees vote to have a union, a simple majority wins. There are certain things that employers aren't allowed to do to prevent unionizing. They can be summarized with the acronym *TIPS;* it's illegal to **t**hreaten, **i**nterrogate, **p**romise, or **s**py. For example, you aren't allowed to promise employees wage or benefit increases if they promise not to unionize. If you follow the principles of management and motivation outlined in this book, and keep open the lines of communication with employees, you'll minimize the chances of them forming a union. If you're already working with unionized employees, open communication will make them allies and can be a positive force for change.

Source: Jane Easter Bahls, "Strike!" *Entrepreneur*, March 1994, pp. 64–67.

---

caused when garbage collectors strike. How would college students react if the faculty struck? Today the strike is used less often as a labor tactic. There were 470 strikes in 1952, but only 45 in 1994.[2] Figure 12.7 on page 382 identifies the major reasons why both labor and management seek to avoid strikes if at all possible. Nonetheless, as strikes in transportation, publishing, airlines, and professional sports have shown, the strike isn't dead as a labor tactic.

Unions also use boycotts in an attempt to obtain their objectives. Boycotts can be classified as primary or secondary. A **primary boycott** occurs when organized labor encourages its membership, as well as the general public, not to buy product(s) of a firm involved in a labor dispute. A **secondary boycott** is an attempt by labor to convince others to stop doing business with a firm that's the subject of a primary boycott. For example, if a union initiated a boycott against a supermarket chain because it carried products of a target of a primary boycott, this would be considered a secondary boycott. The law permits labor to conduct authorized primary boycotts.

The Taft-Hartley Act seemed to prohibit the use of secondary boycotts by labor unions. However, a 1988 Supreme Court decision opened the door for unions to use secondary boycotts. In this case, a firm hired a contractor (H. J. High Construction Company) to build a store in a new mall. The construction union thought that High was paying substandard wages and passed out handbills asking customers not to shop at the mall's 85 stores. That case opened the door for unions to initiate boycotts against virtually any company that has a connection with a unionized employer. For example, one union instituted secondary boycotts against banks that financed International Paper because the union was on strike against International Paper, and this put more pressure on the company. The United Food & Commercial Workers Union began a secondary boycott against a newly opened Price Chopper supermarket because the supermarket's low wages might cause a trend. You can see the power of such tactics. As a consumer, you can also see the costs such tactics add to food shopping. You may also sympathize with the union workers who want to maintain their income levels.

primary boycott
Union encouragement of members not to buy products of a firm involved in a labor dispute.

secondary boycott
An attempt by labor to convince others to stop doing business with a firm that is the subject of a primary boycott.

PRESTRIKE COSTS	STRIKE COSTS	POSTSTRIKE COSTS
Legal expenses	Legal expenditures	Needed overtime to catch up on past orders
Potential loss of orders from customers	Loss of profits from production stoppage or slowdown	Loss of customers who switched allegiance
Expense of executive negotiations	Cost of executive negotiations	Productivity slump
Potential slowdowns in productivity	Added public relations costs	Possible training of replacement workers
Downturn in worker morale	Inventory-carrying costs	Chance of boycotts
Alterations in strategic planning scheme	Possible extra security costs	Loss of consumer goodwill and loyalties
	Overtime in other plants	
	Continuing salary expense for nonunion workers	
	Cost of executive strike negotiations	
	Continuing fringe benefits for strikers	
	Management cost in performing operative tasks	
	Potential loss of goodwill	
	Cost of hiring strikebreakers	

〈〈 **FIGURE 12.7** 〉〉

THE GROWING COSTS OF STRIKES

Note that there are legal expenses and costs in morale as well as lost profits. After the strike, there are overtime costs and the cost of lost customers.

yellow-dog contract
A contract agreement whereby employees agreed not to join a union as a condition of employment (outlawed by the Norris–La Guardia Act).

lockout
A management tool for putting pressure on unions by closing the business.

injunction
A court order directing someone to do something or refrain from doing something.

strikebreaker
Workers hired to do the jobs of striking workers until the labor dispute is resolved.

••• MANAGEMENT TACTICS •••

Management also uses specific tactics to attain its goals. Historically, management thwarted labor demands by **yellow-dog contracts** (in which employees had to agree as a condition of employment not to join a union) and **lockouts** (which put pressure on unions by temporarily closing the business and denying workers employment). Yellow-dog contracts are now outlawed by the Norris-La Guardia Act and lockouts are rarely used (though many of us remember the sight of major league baseball players locked out of spring training in 1990 and the National Hockey League players locked off the ice in 1994). Today, management most often calls on injunctions and the use of strikebreakers to stymie labor demands it sees as unreasonable.

An **injunction** is a court order directing someone to do something or to refrain from doing something. Management has sought injunctions to order striking workers back to work, limit the number of pickets that can be used during a strike, or otherwise deal with actions that could harm public welfare. For a court to issue an injunction, management must show a "just cause." During the Greyhound bus strike, management obtained an injunction limiting the number of pickets at bus terminals. Fear of violence was considered a "just cause" to limit picketing.

The use of strikebreakers has been a source of hostility and violence in labor relations. **Strikebreakers** (called *scabs* by unions) are workers hired to do the jobs of striking employees until the labor dispute is resolved. Employers have had the right to replace strikers since a 1938 Supreme Court ruling. However, it wasn't until the 1980s that we saw this tactic frequently used.[3] Labor analysts suggest that President Reagan's use of this tactic in the 1981 air traffic controllers' strike provided the momentum. Strikebreakers were used in the the Greyhound, *New York Daily News*, and Caterpillar strikes in the early 1990s and the Teamsters strike in 1994. Even Major League Baseball fielded replacement players in spring training in 1995.

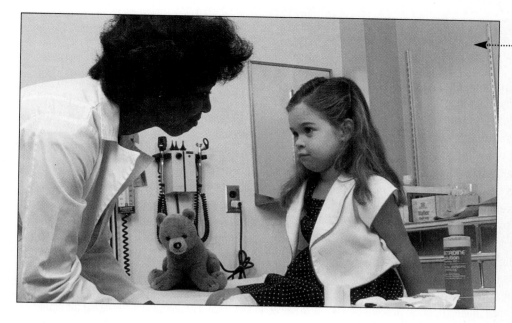

Doctors are one example of service workers who are now evaluating the benefits of unionization. Doctors are feeling the pressure from cost-cutting measures that limit what they can charge and inhibit freedoms they once had. The Florida-based Federation of Physicians & Dentists has already signed up 500 private practice physicians in that state.

Certain workers have such important positions that they're not allowed to strike. For example, it would be chaotic if we allowed the army or police officers to strike. Employees of the federal government can organize unions but are denied the right to strike. In fact, under the Taft-Hartley Act, the president can ask for a cooling-off period to prevent a strike in a critical industry. During a **cooling-off period**, workers return to their jobs while the union and management continue negotiations.

Some labor analysts suggest that management has used bankruptcy laws as a tactic to void union contracts. (Bankruptcy laws were discussed in the business law appendix following Chapter 4.) The U.S. Supreme Court has upheld this tactic against the labor movement. In such cases, companies wishing to escape a negotiated labor–management agreement declare bankruptcy, thereby releasing them from agreements with labor unions. For example, Continental Airlines once employed this tactic to escape from its union contracts. This tactic's effectiveness for management is still unclear.

cooling-off period
Period during which workers return to their jobs while the union and management continue negotiations.

••• THE FUTURE OF LABOR–MANAGEMENT RELATIONS •••

Many emerging labor–management issues may encourage certain employees to join unions. Increased global competition and advanced technology have certainly threatened many workers' jobs. Also, some employees feel that their pay is way below standards in other industries. This is especially true of female employees in service industries (e.g., dental technicians, secretaries, and social workers). It has been predicted that trained women, especially those in the service and information sectors, could be the catalyst and the leadership of the labor movement in the 1990s. In fact, the number of female union members in the United States doubled to 6.2 million from 3.1 million between 1960 and 1990. Today, women comprise 37percent of the unionized work force.[4] With membership in heavy industries declining, labor organizations are rushing to shore up their clout in the service sector, where most of the growth has been for the past decade.[5] Labor has mustered less than half of all ballots cast for unionization in service industries even though unions called for elections only in companies where they felt they had a chance of winning.[6] It's obvious that for unions to grow, they must adapt to a work force

*The Armor
Cracks in
German Labor
Unions*

German workers and unions have had things going their way for a long time. Since the passage of the Codetermination Act of 1976, German workers have enjoyed lucrative labor pacts and boast the shortest workweek in the industrialized world. Wages paid to industrial workers are the highest of any developed country, averaging $28.67 per hour in 1993. According to the codetermination law, corporations and limited partnerships with more than 2,000 employees were to be run by supervisory boards composed of representatives of management and labor. The law granted German unions considerable influence since about 30 percent of company board seats were designated for labor unions. But the tide seems to be shifting, and German labor unions' clout is waning.

I.G. Metall, Germany's largest labor union with 3.3 million members, is even expected to make concessions rather than risk a collapse of the model labor agreement enjoyed by German workers. Recession, global competition, and the cost of reunification have stalled the $2 trillion German economy and caused employers to seek relief. Wage agreements and the appreciation of the deutsche mark have caused labor costs in Germany to run 25 percent higher than in the United States, and 33 percent higher than in

Japan. Employers are asking for concessions—especially on limited shift work and the ban on weekend work. It's also apparent that more companies are interested in negotiating more local labor pacts rather than the traditional industrywide contracts insisted on by the unions. Wolfgang Schroeder, a strategic advisor to I.G. Metall, warns that Germany can't be the exception in global markets P.99 where competition has intensified. I.G. Metall appears willing to cooperate to boost productivity and innovation, but it isn't certain that cutting wages and benefits is the best alternative. In fact, recent agreements have called for higher wages and shorter workweeks. Time will tell if the German unions go the way of their counterparts in the United States and England, where unions' power and ranks have dwindled over the past 10 years.

Source: Peter Engardio, "Time to Leave the Cocoon," *Business Week*, October 18, 1993, pp. 46–47; John Templeman, "Crunch Time for Germany's Unions," *Business Week*, June 7, 1993, p. 47; Robert Neff and Douglas Harbrecht, "Germany's Mighty Unions Are Being Forced to Bend," *Business Week*, March 1, 1993, pp. 52–56; and Ray Marshall and Marc Tucker, *Thinking for a Living: Education and the Wealth of Nations* (New York: Basic Books, division of HarperCollins 1992), pp. 47–48; John Templeman, "A Serious Blow to German Competitiveness," *Business Week*, March 13, 1995, p. 60.

that's increasingly culturally diverse, white-collar, female, foreign-born, and professional. Note that the nation's largest labor union is the National Education Association with over 2 million members.[7]

Organized labor is evidently at a crossroads. The unionized share of the nonfarm work force has declined from a peak of 35.5 percent in 1945 to 12.8 percent today.[8] (See Figure 12.8.) AFL–CIO membership fell by 700,000 between 1991 and 1993.[9] The United Steelworkers Union reports a 60 percent drop in membership that was more than a million strong in 1975; the United Mine Workers has all but disappeared as a major force in the labor movement.[10] Labor's approval rating among the working public has dropped noticeably and foreign competition has forced union workers and management to sit down and work out reasonable agreements that enable U.S. firms to stay competitive. To save jobs, many unions are granting concessions or **givebacks** to management. For example, United Press International workers took a temporary 35 percent pay cut so the company could be sold to new owners. Princeton University researchers Henry Farber and Alan Krueger don't expect the union's position to improve as long as nonunion workers remain satisfied with their paychecks and job security. However, if job cutbacks continue, workers may again look to unions.[11]

givebacks
Concessions made by unions to help employers remain competitive and save jobs.

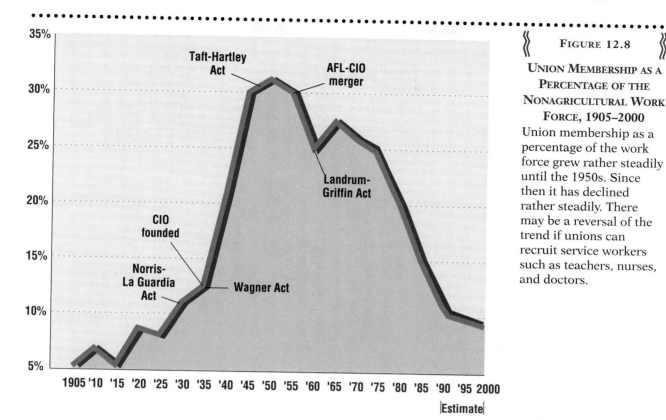

FIGURE 12.8

UNION MEMBERSHIP AS A PERCENTAGE OF THE NONAGRICULTURAL WORK FORCE, 1905–2000
Union membership as a percentage of the work force grew rather steadily until the 1950s. Since then it has declined rather steadily. There may be a reversal of the trend if unions can recruit service workers such as teachers, nurses, and doctors.

FROM NEGOTIATION TO COOPERATION   For the rest of the century, organized labors' role is likely to be much different than in the past. Union members know as well as anyone the necessity for U.S. firms to remain competitive with foreign firms. One way to do that is through team production. Concepts such as continuous improvement ⟨⟨ P.259 ⟩⟩, constant creative innovation, and employee involvement programs can't be implemented without employees' cooperation. Unions have taken a leadership role in making that happen. In exchange for cooperating with management, unions are getting improved job security, gain sharing (profit sharing), and, sometimes higher wages. Lynn Williams, president of the Steelworkers Union, summed it up well: "When it comes to dividing up the pie, we'll be adversaries. But now we have to grow the pie, and that means working together."[12]

Corning Glass is one company that has benefited from union cooperation. Management decided to shift to self-managing work teams ⟨⟨ P.228 ⟩⟩ . When the American Flint Glass Workers union became involved, the company was easily able to implement the changes. It was said that the union "bought ownership" in the plan, which led to "partnership in the workplace."

Unions in the future will assist management in training, work redesign, and assimilating the new work force; that is, recruiting and training foreign workers, unskilled workers, minority workers, and others who may need special help in adapting to job requirements of the workplace. Such competition among workers may result in further union–management agreements and cooperation or may result in further union–management conflicts. Employee stock ownership plans (ESOPs)—which we'll discuss later in this chapter—could help motivate unions to be partners with management since they'll be partial owners of the firm and interested in profits as well as job security. However, two nagging problems—global competition and a negative public image—promise to plague organized labor into the next century. How it handles these major challenges may well define labor unions' future.

PROGRESS CHECK

- What kinds of workers are joining unions today and why are they joining?
- What major pieces of legislation affected union growth? What's covered in each?
- How have unions' objectives changed over time and why?
- What major tactics do unions and management use to assert their power?

CONTROVERSIAL EMPLOYEE–MANAGEMENT ISSUES

This is an interesting time in the history of employee–management relations because the government is taking a much more active role in mandating what benefits businesses must provide. In many instances, the government can't afford to provide social benefits given the huge national debt, so the idea is to force businesses to provide the benefits. In other instances, the question of fairness applies. Let's look at a few of the growing controversies, starting with the issue of executive compensation.

How does $3.9 million a week plus all the free rides at Disneyland you can handle strike you? That's what CEO Michael Eisner earned with Mickey & Company in 1993. His $203 million in compensation included cashing in of stock options that he accumulated from previous years. Disney shareholders, pleased with Mr. Eisner's performance at the company, had few complaints regarding his compensation. Many companies today tie the top manager's compensation to the company's performance.

••• THE ISSUE OF EXECUTIVE COMPENSATION •••

How much should a top executive earn? Larry Johnson of the Charlotte Hornets dribbles his way to $6 million per year. Arnold Schwartzenegger flexes his way to over $25 million per year. Oprah Winfrey talks her way to over $80 million per year. For years, top performers in sports, movies, and entertainment have walked away with hefty paychecks with few complaints from the public that supports them.

Is it out of line, therefore, that the chief executive of IBM should make over $4.5 million and that Robert Allen of AT&T should make over $5 million?[13] In Chapter 2 you learned that the U.S. free enterprise system is built on the incentives that allow executives to make that much. However, in the 1990s, government, boards of directors, and stockholders challenged this fundamental principle and argued that executive compensation is way too high. The Securities and Exchange Commission (SEC) obtained new disclosure rules that removed a companies' opportunities to hide extravagant incentive pay for executives. A new restriction was made on executive pay with the adoption of a $1 million pay cap on the tax deductibility of executive salaries.[14] Directors exerted more effort in determining compensation by hiring consultants and by demanding more information and analysis concerning pay plans. What was the result of these efforts? Companies such as Eastman Kodak, Gillette, Kellogg, and Motorola ignored the government pay cap and passed up the tax deduction.[15] New York executive pay consultant Arnold S. Ross argued that President Clinton in fact created a "minimum wage for CEO's."[16] Furthermore, the average CEO of a major company rose to $3,841,273 in salary and bonuses in 1993—a far cry from the $160,000 average in 1960.[17]

In the past, executive compensation and bonuses were generally determined by the firm's profitability or increase in stock price. Today, many

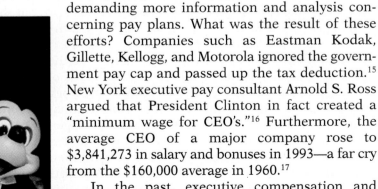

executives receive stock options (the ability to buy the company's stock at a set price at a later date) as part of their compensation. However, executive pay can soar even when the company does poorly. For example, CEO Anthony J. O'Reilly of H.J. Heinz earned approximately $115 million over a three-year period even though the firm's financial performance had been spotty and the stock price had lagged. How can corporate boards justify such a questionable increase? Graef Crystal, a pay consultant and business professor at the University of California at Berkeley, suggests a link between executive pay and board director's pay and benefits: "Wherever you find highly paid CEOs, you'll find highly paid directors," says Crystal.[18] He also decries the use of so-called *quickie options* for executives. With a quickie option, an executive stands to gain handsomely from increasing a firm's stock price after just 12 months. Crystal argues this type of incentive can affect executive decisions that may not benefit the firm over the long term. Crystal suggests longer-term incentives and bonuses.[19]

Management consultant Peter Drucker has been critical of executive pay levels since the mid-1980s, when he suggested that CEOs shouldn't earn much more than 20 times as much as the company's lowest-paid employee. Some companies have followed his advice, such as Herman Miller Inc., a Michigan producer of office furniture. Its chief executive is limited to 20 times the average worker's pay. At Ben & Jerry's Homemade of Vermont, the CEO's pay was restricted to eight times that of the lowest-paid worker, but that made it hard to find a good top executive.[20] Today the average chief executive of a major corporation makes 149 times the pay of a typical American factory worker.[21]

Lavishly compensating executives who order cutbacks, layoffs, and general corporate austerity for everyone else rankles employees, small investors, and unions. Nonetheless, the belief persists among many experts that the law of supply and demand holds and that executives are worth what they get or else the market wouldn't pay them that much. It's also interesting to note that Disney stockholders had few questions or complaints about CEO Michael Eisner earning over $203 million in 1993.

Since firms compete globally, checking what executives in other countries make is revealing. In the United States, a chief executive of one of the 200 largest firms makes over $3 million on average, including salary, bonuses, and stock options. In Japan, the CEO of a large corporation makes approximately 32 times what the average factory worker makes (compared to 149 times in the United States). Also, in Japan stock options for chief executives are unheard of. American CEOs typically earn two to three times as much as executives in Europe and Canada. However, European companies often have workers on the board of directors. Since boards set executive pay, this could be a reason why the imbalance between starting pay and top pay is less for European executives. What do these figures say about the level of executive pay in the United States, if anything? Does it affect the issue of leadership?

It's important to recognize that most U.S. executives are responsible for billion-dollar corporations and work 70–plus hours a week. Many can show their stockholders that their decisions turned potential problems into success (Michael Eisner at Disney, for example). There's no "answer" to fair compensation for executives. What's your opinion? This subject could be debated in class. After all, you may be one of those executives some day.

GOLDEN PARACHUTES A **golden parachute** is a hefty severance package for corporate managers whose jobs may be threatened by a takeover by another firm. To attract an executive to a firm, the board may offer that executive a golden parachute to assure him or her that the job is a secure one—or else the

golden parachute
A sizable severance package for corporate managers whose jobs may be threatened by a takeover by another firm.

golden parachute will protect against a crash. Why is this an issue? Because golden parachutes are often huge. In fact, the average golden parachute gives executives three times their salaries plus their bonuses. Golden parachutes sometimes provide such a cushion that some executives are tempted to jump and pull the cord.[22] They were, however, designed to have the opposite effect.

To receive a golden parachute, executives must be terminated, demoted, relocated, or given a pay cut by the acquiring company. However, many companies are now putting "windows" into the parachute deals. The parachute opens if the executive quits during a 30-day window after the first six months or first year of the new ownership. Do executives deserve millions of dollars for losing their jobs? Are golden parachutes fair? These are questions that call for serious analysis and debate.

CRITICAL THINKING

Top executives' high pay creates tremendous incentives for lower-level executives to work hard to get those jobs. Their high pay also creates resentment among workers, some stockholders, and some members of the general public. What's your position on the proper level of top-executive compensation? Is there a way to make the pay more equitable?

How do you justify the fact that many sports and TV stars make millions of dollars? Should top executives take a cut in pay when these people don't? What's the difference between the two groups?

... THE ISSUE OF PAY EQUITY: EQUAL PAY ... FOR COMPARABLE JOBS

The challenge of pay equity for women takes on growing importance as more women continue to enter the labor force. In 1890, only 15 percent of the labor force was female. By 1950, that figure had risen, but to only 25 percent. By 1980, women made up 40 percent of the labor force; in 1992 the rate was 47 percent.[23] According to the U.S. Department of Labor, almost 60 percent of women with children under age six were in the labor force in 1992.[24] More women joining the labor force means more issues: day care centers, flextime, job sharing, and so forth. Another hot issue is that of pay equity (comparable worth). **Comparable worth** is the demand for equal pay for jobs requiring similar levels of education, training, and skills.

> **comparable worth**
> The demand for equal pay for jobs requiring similar levels of education, training, and skills.

Part of the problem has been understanding just what comparable worth means. It doesn't mean that equal wages should be paid to men and women who do the same job. The Equal Pay Act of 1963 already requires equal pay for equal work. It's against the law, for example, to pay a female nurse less than a male nurse. Rather, the issue of comparable worth centers on comparing the value of jobs such as nurse or librarian (traditionally women's jobs) with jobs such as truck driver or plumber (traditionally men's jobs). Such a comparison shows that women's jobs pay less—sometimes much less.

Today, women earn on average approximately 71 percent of what men earn, though the disparity varies considerably by profession and level of education.[25] In the past, the primary explanation for this disparity was that women were only in the workplace 50 percent to 60 percent of their available years once they left school, whereas men, on the whole, worked all of those years. This changed in the 1990s as fewer women left the work force for an extended period of time. Another explanation is that many women try to work as well as care for their families and fall off the career track. This is especially true in professions such as medicine and law. Others opt for more flexible jobs that pay less such as bookkeeping, nursing, or secretarial work. But the main argument is that women make less because they are women and are discriminated against. The idea of *pay equity* is to correct past discrimination by raising the pay in so-called women's jobs.

Many firms have started comparable-worth–type analyses. AT&T, for example, evaluated 20 categories of employment using 14 measurements. The results of the study are now being implemented. Other firms have also implemented changes. An *Industry Week* survey showed that employees feel that pay scales should be standardized and open to employee review. Unfortunately, this usually occurs only with union and nonsalaried jobs. Comparable worth will be an ongoing issue as women make up an even larger percentage of the labor force.

••• THE ISSUE OF SEXUAL HARASSMENT •••

In the 1990s, sexual harassment became a critical employment issue. The furor grew in 1991 with the nationally televised confirmation hearings of Supreme Court Justice Clarence Thomas. Claims against Thomas by his former co-worker Anita Hill sparked demands that the issue be dealt with more aggressively. That issue rose again in 1994 with the publication of a new book about the case. Disclosures of U.S. Navy personnel's behavior at its Tailhook convention and charges of sexual harassment against U.S. Senator Robert Packwood further accelerated the debate. Even the president of the United States was accused of sexual harassment.

Sexual harassment refers to unwelcome sexual advances, requests for sexual favors, and other conduct of a sexual nature (verbal or physical). Such conduct becomes illegal when (1) an employee's submission to such conduct is made either explicitly or implicitly a term or condition of employment, (2) an employee's submission to or rejection of such conduct is used as the basis for employment decisions affecting the worker's status, or (3) the conduct unreasonably interferes with a worker's job performance or creates an intimidating, hostile, or offensive working environment. Both men and women are covered under the Civil Rights Act of 1991 ❮··· P.361 ··❯ , but 9 out of 10 sexual harassment cases are filed against men.[26]

> **sexual harassment**
> Unwelcome sexual advances, requests for sexual favors, and other conduct of sexual nature (verbal or physical).

There's no question that many managers and workers have become more sensitive to comments and behavior of a sexual nature. The Thomas hearings introduced managers to the concept of a *hostile workplace* that implies a work atmosphere or behavior that would offend a reasonable male or female.[27] One major problem is that workers and managers often know a sexual harassment policy exists, but they have no idea what it says. Towers Perrin, a major consulting firm, notes that executives at 600 major U.S. companies plan to increase sexual harassment training for managers and employees. Such efforts may save businesses millions of dollars in lawsuits and make the workplace more productive and harmonious. Nonetheless, it's safe to bet this will be an important issue throughout the 1990s.

- How does top executive pay in the United States compare with that in other countries?
- What's a golden parachute, and why are they so important today?
- What's the difference between comparable worth and equal pay for equal work?
- How is sexual harassment defined and when does it become illegal?

PROGRESS CHECK

This day care center in Bethesda, Maryland, is for the children of Marriott Corporation employees. Marriott is one of many companies that recognizes the need to adjust to the changing needs of its work force. Child care and elder care are two issues gaining attention of employers due to the large number of workers affected by these demands.

CRITICAL THINKING

Should college football coaches be paid the same as college volleyball coaches using the comparable worth argument? How would that affect the supply and demand for football coaches? What role should the market play in determining wages? What about working conditions? How do they factor in the argument?

••• THE ISSUE OF CHILD CARE •••

Another controversial issue today involves child care. Responsibilities for child care subsidies, child care programs, and even child care leave are being addressed in both the private and public sectors of the economy. In February 1993, Congress passed and President Clinton signed the Family and Medical Leave Act that permits up to 12 weeks of unpaid leave per year to qualified workers upon the birth of a child. Federal child care assistance has risen significantly. Some taxpayers question whether single workers or families that have one member stay home to take care of children should subsidize families that don't have anyone stay home. However, the need for child care is obvious. According to the Bureau of Labor Statistics, 55 percent of the women in the labor force with children at home have children under three years old.[28] Also, 25 percent of the single-parent households in the United States have children under age 18. The U.S. Bureau of the Census forecasts that nearly 90 percent of the over 50 million working women are likely to become pregnant during their working years. American businesses could lose billions annually due to child care–related employee absences. It's obvious that child care issues are critical in the workplace and won't go away. The question is, Who should provide child care services and who should pay for them?

The number of companies providing such services is growing. However, only 29 percent of U.S. companies provide child care of any sort.[29] Some of the more extensive child care programs are offered at large firms such as AT&T, Marriott, Johnson & Johnson, Stride Rite, and Campbell Soup. However, many small companies are competing for available talent with creative programs that meet specific employee needs. For example, Haemonetics Corporation in Braintree, Massachusetts, set up Camp Haemonetics, a summer camp for its employees' children who often become bored on summer vacation. The kids come to work with their parents and then get bused off for swimming, hiking, and so forth at a nearby state park. At noon, they come back for lunch with Mom or Dad, and then finish their activities at about 5 P.M.[30] Working parents have made it clear that safe, affordable child care is an issue on which they won't compromise. Companies have responded by providing

- Discount arrangements with national child care chains.
- Vouchers that offer payments toward whatever child care the employee chooses.
- Referral services that help identify quality child care facilities they recommend to employees.
- On-site child care centers where parents can visit children at lunch or lag times during the workday.
- Sick-child centers to care for moderately ill children.

As single-parent and two-income households continue to grow, it will be interesting to follow this controversial issue.[31] However, a new storm is brewing over the workplace that hasn't been clearly addressed—the issue of elder care. Let's look at this next.

••• THE ISSUE OF ELDER CARE •••

The U.S. work force is aging. By 2005, 37 percent of U.S. workers will be aged 40 to 54.[32] Many of these workers won't have to concern themselves with finding care for children, but they'll confront another problem—the responsibility of caring for older parents and other relatives. Sally Coberly, a specialist in aging at the Washington Business Group, predicts that in coming years elder care will have a greater impact on the workplace than child care. Some firms are already experiencing this situation. In 1994 at U.S. West's work/family referral service, employee calls for elder care exceeded calls for child care for the first time in the firm's history. The situation isn't expected to get any better, yet businesses aren't responding as quickly as they might.

A 1992 survey by the Society for Human Resource Management disclosed that of 1,004 employers surveyed, only one third were involved in any elder care services whatsoever.[33] Andrew Scharlach, a professor of aging at the University of California at Berkeley, estimates that elder care givers cost employers approximately $17 billion in lost output and replacement costs. These costs are expected to rise even higher as more employees become involved in caring for older parents. Businesses find the problem is also compounded because the elder care provider is generally an older, more experienced employee. They're often more critical to the company than the younger worker affected by child care problems. Some companies even note that transfer decisions and promotions are becoming impacted more and more by decisions involving elderly parents needing care. With an aging work force, this issue will intensify in the future.

••• THE ISSUES OF AIDS, DRUG TESTING, •••
AND VIOLENCE IN THE WORKPLACE

The spread of AIDS is certainly a top national concern. The Centers for Disease Control and Prevention estimate that as of 1994, almost 1 million Americans were infected with the HIV virus but didn't yet have AIDS.[34] The numbers include such notables as former basketball superstar Earvin "Magic"

While extensive research to discover the causes and potential cure for AIDS continues, more and more Americans are falling prey to the deadly disease. Olympic diving gold medalist Greg Louganis disclosed in early 1995 that he was HIV positive. AIDS testing and management of HIV positive workers is likely to remain a key employee issue throughout the remainder of this century. Would you favor mandatory testing for new employees? Why?

Johnson of the Los Angeles Lakers and Olympic diving champion Greg Louganis. Since no one predicts an easy solution to or quick victory over AIDS, the development of clear-cut business policies is needed to confront this critical issue.

One of the more controversial employee–management policies concerns mandatory testing for the AIDS antibody. If administered, the tests must be given to everyone across the board. More and more firms are insisting on mandatory AIDS testing for potential employees. A major reason is the cost to an employer that an AIDS-afflicted employee can incur in terms of insurance, losses in productivity, absenteeism, and employee turnover. However, many firms have gone beyond pre-employment testing and have suggested that all employees be tested for the antibody. Managers argue that the information gained allows for the development of a uniform and humanitarian AIDS policy at the workplace.

The grim reality of AIDS hits at the heart of a company's legal and ethical standards. Managers are faced with the challenge of how to best protect the firm without infringing on an employee's legal rights or personal privacy. Employees question the propriety and safety of such testing. Most experts agree that AIDS education in the workplace is the best answer. Nevertheless, this issue has no easy answer and certainly bears watching.

Some companies feel that alcohol and drug abuse is an even more serious issue because so many more workers are involved. According to the American Management Association, drug testing in the workplace has grown at a rapid pace, with 85 percent of major companies now testing workers and job applicants.[35]

Employers are also struggling with a growing trend of violence in the workplace. The U.S. Postal Service holds focus groups for employee input and has begun hiring managers with strong interpersonal skills to deal with growing employee violence on the job. Between 1986 and July 1993, 38 postal employees died violently while at work.[36]

While issues such as AIDS, drug testing, and violence present a somewhat negative and grim picture of the workplace in the 1990s, many employees are assuming new roles within their companies. In fact, some are becoming owners. Let's look next at how this is happening.

··· THE ISSUE OF EMPLOYEE STOCK ··· OWNERSHIP PLANS (ESOPS)

employee stock ownership plan (ESOP)
A plan whereby employees can buy part or total ownership of the firm where they work.

No matter how long and hard workers fight for better pay, they'll never become as wealthy as people who actually own companies. At least that's the theory behind employee stock ownership plans (ESOPs). An **ESOP** is a program that enables employees to buy part or even all of the firm. The notion for ESOPs was started by Louis O. Kelso about 50 years ago.[37] His idea was to turn workers into owners by selling them stock. Using this concept, he helped

Making Ethical Decisions

Coping with AIDS in the Workplace

You own a small regional brewery that serves a specialized market in three Midwest states. In the past you've considered automating one of the brewery's operations, the racking room, because it could easily be robotized. But employees in the racking room have been loyal and hardworking. In the past they even voted down union representation, feeling it could cause your plant difficulties. Also, you're aware that these workers' chance of finding alternative employment is slim. However, the other day you heard that an employee in the racking room was diagnosed as having the AIDS antibody. You realize that this person's medical bills could escalate to over $150,000 over the course of the illness, not to mention missed workdays, production slowdowns, and so forth. Without a doubt, insurance premiums for your firm will increase. You know that legally this employee can't be dismissed because of this medical misfortune, but you could close the racking room, pleading the necessity to automate. What would you do? Is your decision good for the business? Is your decision ethical?

employees of a newspaper buy their company. Since then, the idea of employees taking over all or some of the ownership of their companies has gained much favor. Many people consider ESOPs to be examples of capitalism at its best. The facts are, however, that ESOPs have had mixed results.

BENEFITS OF ESOPS   ESOPs have enjoyed considerable growth. Just under 10,000 businesses have ESOPs covering over 10 million workers. Approximately 1,500 of these companies are majority-owned by employees, and only a handful are publicly traded.[38] Much of this growth can be tied to congressional action making ESOPs attractive for corporations as well as workers.

During the past few years, employee participation in ownership has emerged as an important issue in just about every industry and every type of company: steel foundries, airlines, bakeries, agencies, industrial equipment suppliers, publishing companies, mutual fund organizations, radio stations, and on and on. Organizations with ESOPs include Polaroid, Procter & Gamble, Pepsico, J.C. Penney, and General Mills.

The basic purpose of employee ownership is to give employees a share in the firm's profits and thus increase their involvement and commitment to the firm. Advantages include

- Higher morale as a result of being part owner of the firm.
- Incentives to produce more efficiently. Any increased profits are shared by the workers.
- Tax benefits. ESOPs are considered as a special type of pension plan by the government; thus, there are tax breaks.
- More employee participation in managerial decision making.
- More commitment by all workers to the firm and its success.
- A lure to attract highly skilled people at lower salaries with the promise that they'll earn more in the long run as the company prospers. Some employees at Microsoft, for example, have become millionaires because of stock ownership.[39]

Well, getting your own airline feels even better.

Come meet the 54,000 new owners of United. Come fly *our* friendly skies.

UNITED AIRLINES

Louis Kelso believed that making employees owners of a company would heighten their performance. His idea of establishing ESOPs (employee stock ownership plans) started approximately 50 years ago. United Airlines initiated this cooperative spirit by selling 54 percent of the airline to its employees. Here, the new owners invite us to "fly our friendly skies."

- Feelings of cooperation and participation that can't be matched in any other way.
- An ability to discourage an unwanted purchase of the firm since employee-owners would most likely vote with management against a takeover attempt.

Results at firms such as Avis support the concept of ESOPs. Avis Chairperson Joseph Vittoria actually postponed his retirement because of the success of the company's ESOP. His company enjoyed record profits in 1992 and paid off most of its $785 million acquisition debt ahead of schedule.[40] Avis credits its success to having employees think like owners and make managers listen to them. The company's EPGs (employee participation groups) meet frequently around the country to discuss how to make the company more successful. Equity participation created a bond that joins people and makes them think and work harder together. It's this cooperative spirit that encouraged the 76,000 employees of United Airlines to work together in finalizing the sale of 54 percent of the airline to its employees. It would be misleading, however, to say that ESOPs are easy to implement and an unqualified success. Let's look at the other side.

PROBLEMS WITH ESOPS   Not all ESOPs work as planned. They can be used to refinance a firm with employees' money without giving employees added participation or more job security. Weirton Steel was once praised as the ideal model of an ESOP. Unfortunately, between 1983 and 1993, its employees' mood has changed from cooperation to confrontation. Workers' primary frustration is that even though they control 77 percent of the firm's voting stock and 3 of its 13 board seats, they have little power in the company.[41] Workers complain that they've accepted pay cuts and layoffs, and watched management spend $550 million to revamp operations, yet the company is still losing money. Unfortunately, it's only management or financial institutions that benefit from an ESOP in some cases. In 85 percent of the companies with ESOPs, employees don't have voting rights and rarely have a strong voice on the company's board of directors. North American Rayon employees lost their jobs when they went on strike. They didn't think that could happen because they were the owners.[42]

In summary, ESOPs' goals—employee ownership and pride, better customer relations, improved profits, and so on—are good, but the implementation of such programs is often less than satisfactory. ESOPs aren't for every company. They certainly imply a degree of risk. When used correctly, ESOPs can be a powerful strategy for improving corporate profitability as well as employee satisfaction, participation, and income.

There's some concern about U.S. business's future competitiveness. Firms with healthy employee–management relations have a better chance to prosper. As managers, a *proactive approach* is the best strategy to ensure workable employee–management environments. The proactive manager anticipates potential problems and works toward resolving those problems before they get out of hand. Do you foresee any major issues in employee–management relations in the latter half of the 1990s? Do you have possible solutions to those issues?

- What are the issues related to child care and elder care?
- How are some companies addressing those issues?
- What are ESOPs, and what are their benefits and drawbacks?

PROGRESS CHECK

SUMMARY

1. There were organized labor unions in the United States before the American Revolution.
   - ***What was the first union?***
   The cordwainers (shoemakers) organized a craft union of skilled specialists in 1792. The Knights of Labor (formed in 1869), was the first national labor organization.
   - ***How did the AFL–CIO evolve?***
   The American Federation of Labor (AFL), formed in 1886, was an organization of craft unions. The Congress of Industrial Organization (CIO), a group of unskilled and semiskilled workers, broke off from the AFL in 1935. Over time, the two groups saw the benefits of joining together and thus became the AFL–CIO in 1955.

1. Trace the history of organized labor in the United States and discuss the major legislation affecting labor unions.

2. Much legislation has been passed to balance the power of labor and management.
   - ***What are the provisions of the major legislation affecting labor unions?***
   See Figure 12.1.

2. Outline the objectives of labor unions.

3. Labor unions' objectives shift in response to changes in social and economic trends.
   - ***What topics typically appear in labor–management agreements?***
   See Figure 12.3.
   - ***What weapons do unions and management use in conflicts?***
   Unions can use strikes and boycotts. Management can use injunctions and lockouts.

3. Describe the tactics used by labor and management during conflicts and discuss the role of unions in the future.

4. Explain some of the controversial employee–management issues such as executive compensation, comparable worth, child care and elder care, AIDS, drug testing, violence in the workplace, and employee stock ownership plans (ESOPs).

• **What must unions do to cope with declining membership?**

In order to grow, unions must adapt to a work force that's becoming more white-collar, female, foreign-born, and professional. To help keep American business competitive in international markets, unions must soften their historic "us versus them" attitude and build a new "we" attitude with management.

4. Top executives' median salary in the top 100 industrial companies exceeds $3 million a year.

• **What's a fair wage for managers?**

Managers' salaries are set by the market and organizations. What's fair is open to debate.

• **What's comparable worth?**

Comparable worth is the demand for equal pay for jobs requiring similar levels of education, training, and skills.

• **Why is this an issue?**

Comparable worth is an issue because supply and demand has been the major factor in deciding who gets paid what, and overriding market forces is difficult.

• **Isn't pay inequity caused by sexism?**

There's evidence on both sides of that question. Government and corporate actions indicate that some remedial action will be taken regardless of causes.

• **How are some companies addressing the child care issue?**

Responsive companies are providing day care on the premises, emergency care when scheduled care is interrupted, discounts with child care chains, vouchers to be used with employee's chosen care center, and/or referral services.

• **What's elder care and what problems do companies face with this growing problem?**

Elder care involves workers in caring for older parents or other relatives. This problem may outpace the need for child care. Workers who must care for dependent parents are generally more experienced and vital to the organization. Cost to business in time lost is currently measured at over $17 billion per year.

• **What are some concerns surrounding AIDS and mandatory AIDS testing?**

Employers want to cut the costs that an employee with AIDS can incur in terms of insurance increases, losses in productivity, absenteeism, and employee turnover. Employees question the tests' accuracy and their infringement on their personal right to privacy.

• **How well are employee stock ownership plans (ESOPs) working?**

ESOPs have had mixed results, but the overall trend is favorable. Some 10,000 businesses now have ESOPs. Properly implemented, such plans can increase morale, motivation, commitment, profits, and job satisfaction. The problem is that many firms have used ESOPs as a capital-raising scheme, but haven't given employees more participation in management. ESOP administration will be a major issue in the next decade.

KEY TERMS

agency shop agreement 377
American Federation of Labor (AFL) 374
arbitration 379
bargaining zone 379

certification 376
closed-shop agreement 377
collective bargaining 376
comparable worth 388

Congress of Industrial Organizations (CIO) 375
cooling-off period 383
craft union 373
decertification 376

employee stock
  ownership plan
  (ESOP) 392
givebacks 384
golden parachute 387
grievance 378
industrial unions 374
injunction 382
Knights of Labor 374
lockout 382

mediation 379
negotiated labor–
  management
  agreement 377
open-shop
  agreement 378
primary boycott 381
right-to-work laws 378
secondary boycott 381
sexual harassment 389

shop steward 378
strike 380
strikebreaker 382
union 372
union security
  clause 377
union shop
  agreement 377
yellow-dog
  contract 382

**DEVELOPING
WORKPLACE
SKILLS**
• • • • • •

1. Many college faculty members do not belong to a union. Faculty pay in many disciplines has fallen significantly behind pay in industry. Talk with several faculty members about their feelings toward unions. Assuming faculty salaries aren't increased to match those in industry, do you think unions will eventually be able to recruit more faculty members?

2. Debate the following in class: "Business executives receive a total compensation package that is far beyond their value." Take the opposite side of the issue from your normal stance to get a better feel for the other point of view.

3. Use the library to research the latest information on legislation relating to child care, parental leave, and elder care benefits for employees. What are the trends? What will the cost to businesses be of these new programs? On balance, do you support or reject such legislation? Why?

4. Develop a list of three worker issues not covered in this chapter. Contact and interview a labor official and the human resource director of a large company in your area. Solicit their opinions and positions with respect to these three issues. Report your findings to the class.

5. Should businesses and government agencies be required to provide child care for employees? What about health care? What if some employees would prefer not to have the company provide child care because they have no children? Devise a fringe benefits system that you consider fair for both employers and for employees with a variety of needs.

• •

PRACTICING MANAGEMENT DECISIONS

〉〉 C A S E REPLACING STRIKING WORKERS 〈〈

As you learned in this chapter, the strike is a major weapon used by unions to attain their objectives in a contract dispute. During a strike, workers generally set up picket lines to inform the general public about the contract impasse. In fact, organized labor's fundamental purpose often is to win public support for its position.

In years past, companies would rarely try to replace striking workers with strikebreakers (called *scabs* by the union). Many unionists felt this trend shifted when President Ronald Reagan replaced striking air traffic controllers with nonunion controllers in the 1980s. Businesses felt that Reagan legitimatized the process of replacing striking workers. Furthermore, a loophole in the National Labor Relations Act made the process legal. In the 1990s, it's not uncommon for firms to advertise for replacement workers if they believe a strike may be forthcoming. That happened during the Caterpillar, Inc., strike in 1992, Teamsters strike in 1994, and the baseball strike in 1995.

Needless to say, unions are much opposed to firms hiring replacement workers during a strike. At Ravenswood Aluminum Company, replacement workers became full-time replacements, taking jobs of former union workers. Unions have taken their displeasure to the door of the U.S. Congress, but the legislation has been stalled. President Clinton signed an executive order in 1995 to discourage replacement workers and has promised to sign a law prohibiting the use of permanent replacement workers if it reaches his desk. Organized labor is pushing the legislation hard to restrict the hiring of replacement workers during a strike, but the results of congressional elections in 1994 make chances for passage slim.

Decision Questions

1. Should companies have the legal right to replace striking workers with replacement workers? If so, should replacement workers be permitted to keep their jobs after the labor dispute has ended?

2. What are some potentially negative effects of replacing striking workers?

3. Does either the company or the union really ever win during a strike? Can you cite examples of each case? What are some negative effects for both the company and the union?

4. Would you cross a picket line and fill the job of a striking worker? Why?

Source: Dana Milbank, "Row Escalates over Striker Replacements," *The Wall Street Journal*, July 3, 1991, pp. B1 and B4; Aaron Bernstein, "Busting Unions Can Backfire on the Bottom Line," *Business Week*, March 18, 1991, p. 108; Michael Abramowitz, "The Agony of Crossing the Line," *Washington Post*, April 8, 1992, pp. C1 and C3; David Warner, "A Bill to Outlaw Replacing Strikers," *Nation's Business*, June 1993, p. 56; and Stan Crock, "Clinton May Be Playing a Risky Game of Solitare," *Business Week*, March 27, 1995, pp. 41–42.

⟨⟨ VIDEO CASE   MANAGING DIVERSITY ⟨⟨

No issue is likely to have more relevance for human resource managers in the coming years than management of diversity. Only 46 percent of the total work force is now comprised of white males. In the future, some 75 percent of all new employees will be minorities and women. In short, diversity is a fact of life. Diversity means working with employees who are young and old, male and female, gay and straight, and from several different ethnic, religious, and cultural backgrounds. It also means making provisions for optimizing the contributions of disabled individuals. The demographics of the future only show a greater need to successfully manage such a diverse work force.

What does management of diversity mean? For one thing, it means avoiding stereotyping. Assumptions about groups of people and individuals within groups are often wrong. Today, in order to become an effective manager or team leader you have to learn to accept all people as they are and learn to optimize their performance. Productivity, getting the most out of people, is the goal of diversity management.

In the past, the contributions of women were often ignored. We can all identify with the woman in the video whose suggestions were ignored by her boss until brought up by a man. We can also identify with the stereotypes about various groups. Thankfully, such incidents are becoming less common in business and other organizations, but they are far from being eliminated.

Today's organizations are learning to value differences because multicultural work forces add to the nation's productivity. Young people have new ideas and older workers have maturity and experience. Women and men often approach problems differently, and by using each of their experiences businesses can better adapt to a diverse marketplace. Different ethnic groups have different cultural norms and different ways of approaching problems. Often such new ways of doing things are improvements over traditional ways. But only by valuing differences, by seeking multicultural inputs, can government agencies, businesses, schools, and other organizations reach their maximum potential. That is what the management of diversity is all about.

Discussion Questions

1. What kinds of stereotyping do you still see in business, government, and other organizations? What is behind such stereotypes and how can organizations teach people to end such behavior?

2. Think of the outstanding leaders of this country in politics, sports, and entertainment. Think also of the diversity of indivduals in those groups. Discuss how much stronger those groups are as a result of that diversity.

3. There is much debate today about the merits and drawbacks of opening up U.S. borders to more immigrants. What are the advantages and disadvantages of bringing in more people from diverse backgrounds to work in business and government?

Part 4

MANAGEMENT OF HUMAN RESOURCES

Human resources are the people in an organization. How those people are hired, managed, and treated is the responsibility of human resource managers. These key people used to be called personnel managers or directors—and still are in some companies. They are personnel specialists who help to make management more effective in hiring and in overall job satisfaction. Many organizations are too large to allow close contact between top management and most subordinates. In such firms, human resource people provide this link.

Human resource specialists select, interview, and recommend prospective employees for job openings. They are involved in training for both employees and managers. Human resource personnel will often be directly involved in writing training guides, and they keep everyone in the organization informed about training opportunities. A director of human resources may manage several departments in larger companies, including equal employment opportunity specialists and recruitment specialists.

SKILLS

A human resource manager must have a thorough knowledge of current laws. Since the early 1960s, many new laws affecting employment have been passed, especially in the area of equal employment opportunity. Not knowing the law can damage a company and even cause it to lose credibility with the public.

Like other managers, human resource mangers need the ability to organize themselves and to keep others organized. They also need good communications skills, both oral and written. Since human resource planning is an integral part of the job, they must also be good planners, able to project both long- and short-term needs. Good human resource managers should also like to persuade and influence the actions of others. Often they have to sell their ideas on such issues as creative training programs, changing company traditions, and staffing changes.

Other skills are more specific to the careers in the area. For example, training specialists need skills in teaching and developing training programs. Directors of labor relations need to have extensive training in labor union operations and law. Human resource planning specialists must be adept at forecasting future trends and planning for them.

CAREER PATHS

In today's workplace, most companies want to hire college graduates, even for entry-level human resource positions. An increasing number of colleges offer programs that lead to a human resources management degree. Graduate programs leading to master's and doctoral degrees are also numerous. Human resource management is also one field that remains open to women and minorities.

Entry-level jobs include administrative assistant, human resource assistant, or office assistant. Even with the academic training that is required, experience in a human resource department is important for success as a human resource manager. Just as in other management positions, promotion to the top in a large organization is likely to be competitive—and even political.

SOME POSSIBLE POSITIONS IN HUMAN RESOURCE MANAGEMENT

Job Title	Salary	Job Duties	Career Path	Prospects
Training specialist	$17,000–$64,000 Median: $37,200	Assess needs for training, plan and implement training programs. Conduct orientation and on-the-job training programs.	A background in teaching or psychology is helpful. Degree in human resource management can also help. Often will be promoted into management within human resource department.	Above average growth through 2005.
Employment interviewer/ counselor	$18,000–$27,000+ (limited data available)	Act as broker, bringing job and applicant together.	College degree desirable, but not always necessary. Jobs are available in state employment agencies and in private career placement companies.	Average growth through 2005.
Employee benefits specialist	$19,200–$55,000 Median: $47,500	Administer programs in health insurance, retirement plans, profit sharing, etc. Apply ever-changing federal laws to the process.	Begin by following orders of human resource manager; Given more responsibility with experience. Degree not essential in most companies.	Above average growth through 2005.
Labor relations specialist	$50,000 (average)	Assist management in conducting negotiations with the union and help in labor–management disputes.	Entry-level specialists deal with minor grievances and other minor labor–management issues. After experience, they become involved in higher-level negotiations.	Average or below average growth due to declining union membership.

KATHLEEN MCGRATH, HUMAN RESOURCE MANAGER

Kathleen McGrath finds the job of the human resource manager both challenging and fulfilling. However, she didn't know that in the beginning. At first, she set out to be a physical therapist. "I was just average," she says of her physical therapy studies at Illinois State University. After three years of college, Kathy got a job in the retail sector, thinking that maybe this is where she would find her niche.

The Hart, Schaffner, and Marx company put her through management training, and she maintained a good track record as a troubleshooter with them until they went out of business in 1989. Her next stop on the career ladder was with Kohl's Department Store, where she became an assistant store manager. In that capacity, Kathy found herself involved in recruiting and staffing for the first time. Although those tasks were fulfilling, retail was still leaving something to be desired. Soon she became a store manager, controlling a $13 million operation. After two and a half years, though, she burned out. One of the ingredients that was missing was the "people" ingredient in her daily activities. She simply hadn't realized how important that element is to her work life.

"It was time for some soul-searching," she remembers. After a few months off, she returned to college. While attending William Rainey Harper College, she became involved in a work-study program. "I thought maybe I was too old for work-study, but I sent out my résumé, and Coldwell Banker Relocation hired me." At Coldwell Banker, Kathy worked with the human resource manager. "That manager brought me up to high gear," Kathy recalls. For the first time she became acquainted with EEO laws, affirmative action debates, and other issues she had never dealt with directly before.

After receiving her associate degree, Kathleen McGrath was finally ready for the field that really suited her: human resource management. After an energetic job search, she was hired by DFT Lighting as a human resource assistant. DFT is a division of the Genlyte Group, Inc., a leading manufacturer of lighting fixtures.

Kathy says that to succeed at human resource management, you have to be flexible. "This is not accounting," she says. "It's not an exact science. An HRM person is there for the people, and working with people requires creativity and social skills." You try to make sure that employees are safe, happy, and well-paid. While thinking about the human element, you need also to emphasize efficiency—and computer skills are mandatory.

As for the future, Kathy plans to stay in human resource management and to grow with that field. While working, she will continue taking courses in psychology, management—whatever she can learn to help her grow and develop as a human resource manager. She has finally found her niche in this exciting and dynamic career.

Special thanks to Mike Vijuk, William Rainey Harper College, for recommending Kathleen McGrath for this career portfolio.

PART

5

MARKETING:
DEVELOPING
AND
IMPLEMENTING
CUSTOMER-
ORIENTED
MARKETING
PLANS

CHAPTER 13
MARKETING:
BUILDING CUSTOMER
RELATIONSHIPS

CHAPTER 14
DEVELOPING AND
PRICING QUALITY
PRODUCTS AND
SERVICES

CHAPTER 15
DISTRIBUTING
PRODUCTS
EFFICIENTLY AND
COMPETITIVELY

CHAPTER 16
PROMOTING PRODUCTS
USING INTEGRATED
MARKETING
COMMUNICATION

MARKETING: BUILDING CUSTOMER RELATIONSHIPS

LEARNING GOALS

After you have read and studied this chapter, you should be able to

1. Define marketing and summarize the steps involved in the marketing process.

2. Describe marketing's changing role in society and the merging of the marketing concept with total quality management.

3. Illustrate how marketing is evolving from mass marketing to custom marketing.

4. List the eight functions of marketing and the utilities created by marketing, and give examples of each.

5. Apply the four parts of the marketing research process to a business problem.

6. Differentiate between consumer and industrial markets and compare the various forms of market segmentation.

7. Discuss present and future prospects for careers in marketing.

BOB AND CANDY KOCHER AND GAIL SUNDLING, CUSTOMER-ORIENTED MARKETERS

Bob and Candy Kocher own Price's Market, a convenience store in Richmond, Virginia. When business slowed, Bob and Candy could have done what most businesses do: launch an expensive campaign or cut prices. But Bob and Candy had a better idea. They asked their neighborhood customers, "What are you always looking for, but can't get?" The overwhelming answer, much to their surprise, was "Imported beer." The Kochers went out and bought every imported beer they could find and stocked their store with them. Soon Price's Market was the hottest store in town. People came from miles around to buy their exotic beers. Profits flowed.

The secret to marketing, the Kochers learned, is rather simple: Find out what people want and give it to them. Once you've established a customer base, it's important to keep them coming back because keeping a customer costs about one fifth of what it takes to get a new one.

Delmar Bootery in Albany, New York, creates loyal customers by giving them quality goods and services that go far beyond the expected. The Bootery did research and found the finest shoes there are. To keep those shoes looking good, the Bootery provides free shoe shines for the life of the shoes.

Gail Sundling, owner of Delmar Bootery, realizes that establishing *and maintaining* friendly relations with customers depends largely on having friendly, helpful store personnel. Those employees must be able to quickly respond to customer requests. Therefore, Sundling gives her employees authority to keep customers happy. That means that employees have to be thoroughly trained to assume such responsibility. Given that training, employees can be trusted to please customers within some reasonable cost to the store.

Price's Market and the Delmar Bootery meet the three criteria for a successful marketing program: (1) Please customers and make them loyal to the firm. (2) Make sure that employees are trained to do that. (3) Make a profit as a result. To accomplish these three goals, many firms are combining marketing with total quality management ◄--- P.259 ---►. We'll explore that process in this chapter.

Customer loyalty is earned by consistently delivering superior value.

Frederick F. Reichheld of Bain & Company

WHAT IS MARKETING?

marketing

The process of determining customer wants and needs and then providing customers with goods and services that meet or exceed their expectations.

From an organizational perspective, **marketing** is the process of determining customer wants and needs and then profitably providing customers with goods and services that meet or exceed their expectations. More simply, the marketing process has been described as:

FIND A NEED AND FILL IT

In the past, it was believed that businesses made products first and marketing was then responsible for selling and distributing those products. In other words, production came first. That approach is obsolete in an era when the customer is king. In such an environment, marketing comes first. Its role is to determine exactly what consumers want and then to provide goods and services that fill those needs.

••• BUYING IS MARKETING TOO •••

There's no getting away from using marketing in your life. As a consumer, you can use marketing to get what you want. You no doubt have noticed the want ads in the paper. These represent buyers advertising for what they want. Buyers can use their persuasive skills in negotiating with sellers just as salespeople do. Thus, both buying and selling are part of marketing.

GTE Sprint has the right idea when it comes to marketing: "Find a Need and Fill It." They know that listening to customers is as important as talking. "We hear you loud and clear" is an effective slogan if implemented properly.

UNDERSTANDING THE MARKETING PROCESS

The best way for you to understand marketing is to take one product and follow the marketing process that led to the development and sale of that product. (See Figure 13.1). You may start the process by remembering that the basis of marketing is finding a need and filling it. So your first step is to find a need. Imagine that you and your friends don't eat big breakfasts. You want something for breakfast that's fast, nutritious, and good tasting. Some of your friends eat Quaker's 100% Natural cereal but may not be happy with its sugar content.

You ask around among your acquaintances and find a huge demand for a good-tasting breakfast cereal that's nutritious, high in fiber, and low in sugar. That leads you to conduct a more extensive marketing research study to determine whether there's a large market for such a cereal. Your research supports your hypothesis: there's a large market for a high-fiber cereal. "Aha," you say to yourself. "I've found a need."

You've now completed one of the first steps in marketing. You've researched consumer wants and needs and found a need for a product that's not yet available.

••• DESIGNING A PRODUCT TO MEET NEEDS •••

The next step is to develop a product to fill that need. A **product** is any physical good, service, or idea that satisfies a want or need. In this case, your proposed product is a multigrain cereal made with an artificial sweetener.

It's a good idea at this point to do *concept testing*. That is, you develop an accurate description of your product and ask people whether the concept (the idea of the cereal) appeals to them. If it does, you might go to a manufacturer that has the equipment and skills to design such a cereal, and begin making prototypes. *Prototypes* are samples of the product that you take to consumers to test their reactions. The process of testing products among potential users is called *test marketing*.

If consumers like the product, you may turn the production process over to an existing manufacturer or you may produce the cereal yourself. *Outsourcing*, remember, is the term used to describe the allocation of production and other functions to outside firms. The idea is to retain only those functions that you can do best and outsource the rest.

Once the product is made, you have to design a package, think up a brand name for the product, and set a price. A **brand name** is a word, letter, or group of words or letters that differentiates one seller's goods and services from those of competitors. Cereal brand names, for example, include Cheerios, Team Flakes, and Raisin Bran. You name your cereal Fiberrific to emphasize the high fiber content and terrific taste. We'll discuss the product development process, including packaging, branding, and pricing, in the next chapter. Now we're simply picturing the whole process to get an overall picture of what marketing is all about.

••• GETTING THE PRODUCT TO CONSUMERS •••

Once the product is manufactured, you have to choose how to get it to the consumer. You may want to sell it directly to supermarkets or health food stores, or you may want to sell it through organizations that specialize in distributing food products. Such organizations are called *marketing middlemen* because they're in the middle of a series of organizations that distribute goods from producers to consumers. We'll discuss middlemen and distribution in detail in Chapter 15.

••• ESTABLISHING A RELATIONSHIP WITH CUSTOMERS •••

One of the last steps in the marketing process is to promote the product to consumers. Promotion consists of all the techniques sellers use to capture markets. They include advertising, personal selling, publicity, word of mouth, and various sales promotion efforts such as coupons, rebates, samples, and cents-off deals. Promotion is discussed in Chapter 16.

The last step in the marketing process consists of relationship building with customers. That includes responding to any suggestions they may make to improve the product or its marketing. Postpurchase service may include exchanging goods that weren't satisfactory and making other adjustments to ensure consumer satisfaction, including recycling. Marketing is an ongoing process. A company must continually adapt to changes in the market and to changes in consumer wants and needs. The box Reaching Beyond Our Borders shows how this process works in international markets.

FIGURE 13.1

THE MARKETING PROCESS

- Find a need
- Conduct research
- Design a product to meet the need based on research
- Do product testing
- Determine a brand name, design a package, and set a price
- Select a distribution system
- Design a promotional program
- Build a relationship with customers

product
Any physical good, service, or idea that satisfies a want or need.

brand name
A word, letter, or group of words or letters that differentiates the goods and services of a seller from those of competitors.

Reaching Beyond Our Borders

Yak Paks

Can a young person get involved in international marketing while still in college? It's not only possible, it can be quite profitable as well. Stephen Holt, for example, was an exchange student in China. He noticed how inexpensive labor was in China and thought about possible products he could sell back home. He decided he could sell suede backpacks if the price were right—and it would be by using inexpensive labor.

Stephen noticed that dealing in China was different from the United States. For one thing, the older you are the more Chinese businesspeople respect you. Since he was so young, Stephen did all he could to look professional. He prepared business cards in English and Chinese and hired an experienced translator to help him negotiate with a contractor. Soon Stephen and his roommate were in the backpack business. They now run their company out of a former Brillo pad factory in Brooklyn, New York. Sales are expected to top $1 million annually now that they've added suede hats, high-end leather bags, and other items from China.

Source: Mary Talbott, "Ventures Abroad," *Success*, November 1993, p. 16.

TOTAL QUALITY AND THE MARKETING CONCEPT

Marketing has changed over time as the wants and needs of consumers have changed. A brief review of marketing's history will show its adaptability and give you a glimpse of what's likely to come next.

The marketing concept calls for a customer orientation. To measure customer satisfaction, companies often stop consumers when they are shopping to ask them how satisfied they were with the experience and to find ways to improve service. Listening and responding to customer wants and needs is the heart of marketing.

••• A BRIEF HISTORY OF THE MARKETING CONCEPT •••

From the time the first settlers began their struggle to survive in America until after the Civil War, one philosophy of business was, "Produce as much as you can because there's a limitless market." Given the limited production capability and the vast demand for products in those days, such a philosophy was both logical and profitable for most firms. Business owners were mostly farmers, carpenters, and trade workers who were catering to the public's basic needs for housing, food, and clothing. There was a need for greater productive capacity, and most businesses naturally had a production orientation. A *production orientation* means that the goals of business center on production rather than marketing. This was satisfactory in the early 1900s because most goods were bought as soon as they became available. The most important marketing functions at that time were distribution and storage.

From 1890 to 1920, businesses developed mass production techniques. Production capacity often exceeded the immediate market demand. Therefore, in the 1920s the business philosophy turned from a production orientation to a sales orientation. A *sales orientation* means that businesses focus on promoting their products and mobilize much of their resources toward selling, advertising, publicity, and other promotional efforts.

After World War II ended in 1945, there was tremendous demand for goods and services among the returning soldiers who were starting a new life with new families. These postwar years launched the baby boom (reflecting the sudden jump in the

Legal Briefcase

Businesses often spend a lot of money developing a brand name, only to find later that the brand name cannot be used or is overused and becomes generic. Furthermore, someone could copy your brand name and take some of its effectiveness away. In short, the legal issues surrounding the branding of a product are quite significant.

To minimize legal problems, it is best to register a brand name with the appropriate state agency and the U.S. Patent and Trademark Office. You first do a records search to ensure that your chosen brand name isn't already in use. The U.S. patent office has libraries throughout the country where you can conduct such a search.

After you have chosen a name, it is important to protect it. One danger a business faces is having its

Don't say, "Xerox that article about Rollerblades."

brand name become a generic name; that is, the name of the product category rather than one brand. Aspirin, for example, was once a brand name. So were corn flakes, escalator, cellophane, thermos, yo-yo, and raisin bran. In potential danger today are Xerox and Rollerblades. Those companies wish you would say, "Copy that article about in-line skates," not "Xerox that article about Rollerblades." Otherwise, their brand names may go generic.

A company's brand name (Pepsi-Cola or Avis) is often an asset worth millions of dollars. It pays to protect that name legally so that others cannot destroy that valuable asset.

Source: Maxine S. Lans, "On Your Mark: Get Set or It May Go," *Marketing News*, September 26, 1994, p. 12.

birthrate after the war) and a boom in consumer spending. Competition for consumers' dollars was fierce. Business owners recognized the need to be more responsive to consumers, and a new orientation emerged called the *marketing concept*. The **marketing concept** had three parts:

1. A customer orientation; that is, find out what consumers want and provide it for them.

2. The training of employees from all departments in customer service so that everyone in the organization has the same objective—consumer satisfaction. This is a total and integrated organizational effort.

3. A profit orientation; that is, market those goods and services that will earn the firm a profit and enable it to survive and expand to serve more customer wants and needs.

marketing concept
Refers to a three-part business philosophy: (1) a customer orientation, (2) training of all employees in customer service, and (3) a profit orientation.

During the 1980s, businesses began to more aggressively implement the marketing concept. In the 1990s, they extended the marketing concept by adopting the concepts of total quality management (TQM) that focus on delighting the customer «⋯ P.39 ⋯». In the following sections, we'll explore how the marketing concept and total quality management have merged.

••• FROM A CUSTOMER ORIENTATION TO DELIGHTING •••
CUSTOMERS AND OTHER STAKEHOLDERS

The phrase *delighting the customer* comes out of the literature of TQM. Marketing's goal in the past was to provide customer satisfaction. Today, the goal of total quality firms is to please, dazzle, or delight customers by providing goods and services that exactly meet their requirements. AT&T Universal Card Services, for example, sets customer delight at the foundation of everything it does.[1] One objective of its marketing effort, therefore, is to make sure that the response to customer wants and needs is so fast and courteous that customers are truly surprised and pleased by the experience. One author says the goal is to create "raving" customers. You can see how TQM is just an extension of the marketing concept.

You don't have to look far to see that most organizations haven't yet reached the goal of dazzling customers. Most retail stores, government agencies, and other organizations still irritate customers as often as they please them. Nonetheless, global competition is forcing organizations to adopt total quality concepts, which means, above all, adapting organizations to customers.

Businesses have learned that employees won't provide first-class goods and services to customers unless they receive first-class treatment themselves. Marketers, therefore, must work with others in the firm, such as human resource personnel, to help make sure that employees are pleased. In some firms, such as IBM, employees are called *internal customers* ◀-- P.262 --▶.

... FROM TRAINING ALL EMPLOYEES TO UNITING ... ORGANIZATIONS

Once it became clear that everyone in the firm had to work together to please internal and external customers and all other stakeholders ◀-- P.40 --▶, many changes started to happen in firms' organization. First of all, barriers between departments began to fall. Marketers formed cross-functional teams with designers, engineers, production personnel, and others in the firm to develop quality products. See the case at the end of the chapter for more on cross-functional teams ◀-- P.256 --▶. Such a team at Chrysler developed the Neon. Texas Instruments, Westinghouse, GM, Ford, and many other leading companies—large and small alike—have moved to such teams.[2]

In Boston, Eric Gershman organized his *small* newsletter-publishing concern, Published Image, into four self-managed teams ◀-- P.228 --▶. His employees set their own work schedules, prepare their own budgets, and receive group bonuses based on their team's performance. Gershman renamed his managers *coaches* to reflect their largely advisory roles. As a consequence, turnover has virtually halted, revenues have doubled, and profit margins increased to 20 percent from 3 percent.[3]

In quality-oriented firms, cross-functional teams practice continuous improvement. ◀-- P.259 --▶ Organizations today are uniting in a *joint effort* to produce goods and services that will please customers and ensure a profit for everyone involved in producing and distributing those products. Baxter Healthcare Corporation, for example, produces medical and health care products. They have cross-functional teams that practice continuous improvement. They found that services that dazzle customers today may be expected services tomorrow. Therefore, the firm must constantly improve products and services.

Determining whether the various organizations are providing first-class service and quality is done through competitive benchmarking. ◀-- P.262 --▶ Xerox Corporation, for example, has benchmarked its functions against corporate leaders such as American Express (for billing), Ford (for manufacturing floor layout), Westinghouse (for bar coding), Mary Kay Cosmetics (for warehousing and distribution), and Florida Power & Light (for quality processes).

••• MAINTAINING A PROFIT ORIENTATION •••

Marketing must make sure that everyone in the organization understands that the purpose behind pleasing customers is to ensure a profit for the firm. Using that profit, the organization can then satisfy other stakeholders of the firm such as stockholders, environmentalists, and the local community.

It has been estimated that reducing the number of customers who defect by 5 percent can increase profit by as much as 85 percent. (It varies by industry.) Some of that profit comes from increased purchases and some from referrals.[4] In the next section, we'll explore the marketing process in more detail so you can see how relationships are established. But first, stop and do the Critical Thinking exercise.

The government is now starting to implement total quality concepts, just as business is doing. What barriers will make the process more difficult? For example, why can't the Post Office delight customers like UPS and Federal Express do?

CRITICAL THINKING

- What are the three parts of the marketing concept?
- Can you define the following terms from total quality management: *continuous improvement* and *competitive benchmarking*?

PROGRESS CHECK

RELATIONSHIP MARKETING

The traditional marketing concept called for giving *customers* what they want. Relationship marketing goes further by recognizing the need to please other stakeholders as well. For example, you could go so far to give customers what they want that the organization would lose money. That would hurt stockholders. You could please customers and harm the environment, thus harming the relationship with the community. Balancing the wants and needs of all the firm's stakeholders is a much bigger challenge than marketing has attempted in the past.

Relationship marketing, then, is establishing and maintaining mutually beneficial exchange relationships with internal and external customers and all the other stakeholders of the organization. Organizations that adopt relationship marketing take the community's needs into mind when designing and marketing products. For example, more products are now designed to be biodegradable so that they cause less pollution than earlier products.

Many companies have responded to the environmental movement by introducing "green products" into the marketplace. A **green product** is one whose production, use, and disposal don't damage the environment.

relationship marketing
Establishing and maintaining mutually beneficial exchange relationships with internal and external customers and all the other stakeholders of the organization.

green product
A product whose production, use, and disposal don't damage the environment.

••• THE MOVEMENT AWAY FROM MASS MARKETING •••

In the world of mass production, marketers responded with mass marketing. **Mass marketing** means developing products and promotions to please large groups of people. The mass marketer tries to sell products to as many people as possible. That means using mass media such as TV, radio, and newspapers. Many marketing managers got so caught up with their products and competition that they became insensitive to the market. They began "selling to everybody and listening to nobody."[5]

Mass marketing tends to lead to adversarial marketing. **Adversarial marketing** means that buyers and sellers have different, often conflicting goals, so that what's good for one may not be good for the other. The jargon of adversarial marketing sounds more like war than relationship building. For example, traditional marketers *aim* their promotional messages at the *target market*, and hope to *make a killing* in the market. Each marketer *fights* for a share of the market.

mass marketing
Developing products and promotions that are designed to please large groups of people.

adversarial marketing
Buyers and sellers have different, often conflicting goals, so that what is good for one may not be good for the other.

FROM THE PAGES OF...
Entrepreneur®
MAGAZINE

Niche Marketing

With all the greeting card companies, you'd think that there would be an appropriate greeting card for almost everyone. But you'd be wrong. There are lots of niche markets out there from which small companies can profit. If you're looking for a card to celebrate Kwanzaa, Bodhi Day, or some other ethnic holiday, good luck.

Enter EthnoGraphics, a Santa Barbara, California–based multicultural card company. Its revenues are expected to triple this year for the third year in a row. Why? Because EthnoGraphics' current multicultural mix includes about 800 different cards. Its target markets are African-Americans, Native Americans, Chinese-Americans, Latino-Americans, and Jewish-Americans. The artists are as diverse as the customer base.

Jodee Weinstock similarly has had success developing cards for the gay market. Her Chicago company, Cardthartic LLC, has three lifestyle card lines geared toward gay friends and family. These niche marketers represent the wave of the future in marketing: specialized products for small market segments.

Source: Gayle Sato Stodder, "The Greeting of America," *Entrepreneur,* September 1994, pp. 210–14.

Relationship marketing moves away from mass production toward custom-made goods. The latest in technology enables sellers to *work with* buyers to determine their *individual* wants and needs and to develop goods and services specifically designed for those individuals. One-way messages in mass media give way to a personal dialogue among participants. Examples of relationship marketing include

- MCI's Friends and Family Program custom-designs services that enable customers to reach up to 20 friends or family members at a discount. This program is a good deal for customers and a good deal for MCI because all 20 people have to subscribe. That makes the deal mutually beneficial. Over 10 million people have signed up for the program.[6]
- Rental car companies, airlines, and hotels have frequent user programs where loyal customers can earn special services. For example, a traveler can earn free flights on an airline, special treatment at a car rental agency (e.g., no stopping at the rental desk—just pick up a car and go), and all kinds of special services at a hotel (e.g., faster check-in and check-out procedures, flowers in the room, free breakfasts, free exercise rooms).

Robert Reichheld of Bain & Company estimated that retaining 2 percent more customers has the same effect on profit as cutting costs by 10 percent. At regional banks, for example, a 20-year customer is worth 85 percent more profits than a 10-year customer.[7] Relationship marketing means establishing *and maintaining* long-term relationships with customers.

MARKETING MANAGEMENT AND THE MARKETING MIX

It's marketing managers who are responsible for getting everyone in the firm to establish and maintain mutually beneficial relationships with all the stakeholders. Traditionally, however, the main focus of marketing managers is to

The benefits offered by frequent flyer programs are just one example of the trend toward relationship marketing. The idea is to develop a long-term relationship with customers so that they feel committed to and will continue to purchase a company's products or services. Such relationships are built on mutual trust, communication, and going beyond the expected.

please customers. Given that goal, managing the marketing process involves four factors: (1) designing a want-satisfying product, (2) setting a price for the product, (3) getting the product to a place where people will buy it, and (4) promoting the product. These four factors (product, price, place, and promotion) have become known as the *four Ps of marketing* or the **marketing mix** because they're the ingredients that go into a marketing program. Each factor of the marketing mix will be discussed in detail in the following three chapters. Note that the marketing mix is surrounded by the marketing environment. (See Figure 13.2.) Changes in the social, economic, technological, and global environment force marketers to constantly adapt.

A marketing manager designs a marketing program that effectively combines these ingredients of the marketing mix. (See Figure 13.3.) **Marketing management**, therefore, is the process of planning and executing the conception, pricing, promotion, and distribution (place) of ideas, goods, and services (products) to create mutually beneficial exchanges.

marketing mix
The ingredients that go into a marketing program: product, price, place, and promotion.

marketing management
The process of planning and executing the conception, pricing, promotion, and distribution [place] of ideas, goods, and services [products] to create mutually beneficial exchanges.

FIGURE 13.2

THE MARKETING ENVIRONMENT

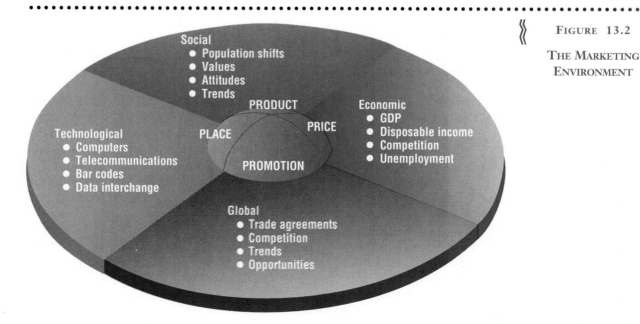

· ·

 FIGURE 13.3

THE FOUR PS AND THE MARKETING MANAGER'S ROLE

The marketing manager chooses the proper price, promotion, and place to develop a comprehensive marketing program. This figure shows the mix for Fiberrific cereal. Included would be decisions about packaging, couponing, and more.

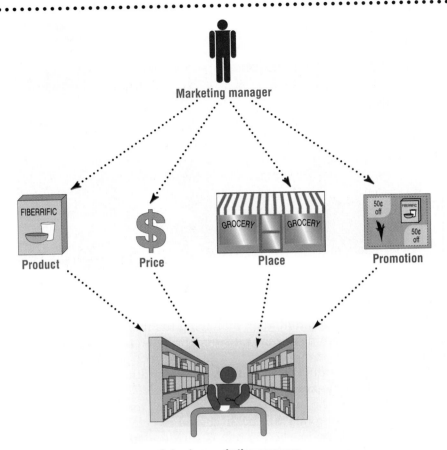

Marketing manager

Product   Price   Place   Promotion

Cohesive marketing program aimed at satisfying customers

· · · THE EIGHT FUNCTIONS OF MARKETING · · ·

In their efforts to give consumers what they want, marketing managers perform eight functions (see Figure 13.4):

Research	Storage
Buying	Finance (credit)
Selling	Risk bearing
Transportation	Standardization

Let's see how these eight functions apply to Fiberrific. First of all, marketing research was needed to (1) find an unmet need, (2) test the product in the market, and (3) determine the most effective way to price, promote, and distribute the cereal. Marketing research is thus important throughout the design of the marketing mix.

To produce the cereal, we have to buy raw materials such as wheat, oats, and corn from farmers. Retail stores will buy the cereal from us, and consumers will buy from the retail store. Thus, buying and selling are important marketing functions.

Financing (credit) was once an important marketing function because expensive items couldn't be bought without credit, and marketers provided the credit. Today, credit is often a separate department with separate managers, but it's still an important function to marketing managers. Many supermarkets, for example, buy cereal and other foods on credit from their suppliers.

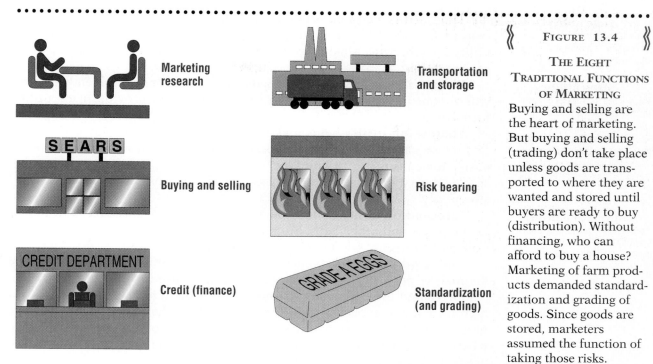

FIGURE 13.4

THE EIGHT
TRADITIONAL FUNCTIONS
OF MARKETING
Buying and selling are
the heart of marketing.
But buying and selling
(trading) don't take place
unless goods are trans-
ported to where they are
wanted and stored until
buyers are ready to buy
(distribution). Without
financing, who can
afford to buy a house?
Marketing of farm prod-
ucts demanded standard-
ization and grading of
goods. Since goods are
stored, marketers
assumed the function of
taking those risks.
Finally, the whole
process begins and ends
with research (knowing
what the market wants).

Transportation involves moving grain from the farm to the producer and then moving boxes of cereal from the producer to the retailer and other middlemen on the way to consumers. Consumers also perform the transportation function by bringing the cereal home from the store.

The word *store* comes from the fact that retailers store items on their shelves so that consumers can buy goods whenever they want. Producers and middlemen also have storage facilities. Consumers may also perform the storage function by buying several boxes of cereal on sale and storing them in their homes.

Whenever you buy products for resale and store them, you bear the risk of their being stolen or damaged or becoming obsolete. Assuming the risks of storage and distribution has traditionally been considered a marketing function. Risk management has now become a separate function (not part of marketing).

The last marketing function is standardization or grading. No doubt you've seen "grade A eggs" and various classifications of beef (e.g., prime). These are forms of grading. Standardization is important for products such as lumber and plumbing materials. The computer industry got into trouble in the past decade because it ignored the importance of standardization. As a result, computer software programs from Apple and IBM couldn't communicate with each other. Apple and IBM are now working together to develop software that's compatible with both computers.

A major function of marketing is to deliver products to customers when they want and need them. This photo shows fresh produce being delivered to a restaurant. Such daily deliveries ensure fresh-tasting salads for the restaurant and a strong relationship with suppliers that results in profits for both.

... THE UTILITIES CREATED ...
BY MARKETING

All of marketing's functions are performed to move goods from producers to consumers. During this process, marketing adds four types of utility (value) to goods and services: (1) time, (2) place, (3) possession, and (4) information.

time utility
Value added to products by making them available when they are needed.

place utility
Value added to products by having them where people want them.

possession utility
Value added to products by doing whatever is necessary to transfer ownership from one party to another.

information utility
Value added to products by opening two-way flows of information between marketing participants.

Time utility helps consumers by making products available when the consumer wishes. Supermarkets that are open 24 hours a day provide time utility for Fiberrific. Making fresh fruit available in the winter is also a form of time utility.

Place utility makes sure that goods and services are conveniently located where consumers want them. 7–Eleven stores help provide place utility for Fiberrific.

Possession utility helps make the exchange of goods between buyers and sellers easier. For example, supermarket check-cashing services make it easier for consumers to buy Fiberrific. Anything that helps complete the sale—delivery, installation, warranties, credit—is considered part of possession utility.

Information utility informs buyers of the product's existence, how to use it, the price, and other facts. Such information is provided through means such as advertising, salespeople, and packaging.

The word marketing comes from the root word market. A *market* is defined as people with unsatisfied wants and needs who have both the resources and the willingness to buy. Thus, if there are people who want a high-fiber, low-sugar cereal like Fiberrific and have the resources and willingness to buy it, then we say that there's a market for Fiberrific. We learn whether there's a market for our cereal by studying consumer wants and needs. We'll look at how marketers determine customer wants and needs after the Progress Check.

PROGRESS CHECK

- What is relationship marketing? How does it differ from mass marketing?
- What are the four Ps of the marketing mix?
- What are the eight functions of marketing?
- What are the four types of utility (value) added to goods and services by marketing?

DETERMINING WHAT CUSTOMERS WANT

marketing research
The process used both to determine what consumer and industrial clients want and need and to select the most effective way to satisfy those wants and needs.

Marketing research is the analysis of markets to determine opportunities and challenges. One goal of research is to determine exactly what consumers want and need. That isn't easy because consumer wants and needs are constantly changing. Therefore, marketing must establish close relationships with customers. Marketing research helps determine what customers have purchased in the past, what situational changes have occurred to change what consumers want, and what they're likely to want in the future. In addition, marketers research business trends, the ecological impact of their decisions, international trends, and more. (See Figure 13.5.) Businesses need information to compete effectively, and marketing research is the activity that gathers that information.

Finding out what people want means more than sending out questionnaires regularly. It means getting out of the office and sitting down with people and listening to them. It also means paying attention to what shareholders, dealers, consumer advocates, employees, and other stakeholders have to say.

Advertising Research

1. Motivation research
2. Copy research
3. Media research
4. Studies of ad effectiveness
5. Studies of competitive advertising

Business Economics and Corporate Research

1. Short-range forecasting (up to 1 year)
2. Long-range forecasting (over 1 year)
3. Studies of business trends
4. Pricing studies
5. Plant and warehouse location studies
6. Acquisition studies
7. Export and international studies
8. MIS (management information system)
9. Operations research
10. Internal company employees

Corporate Responsibility Research

1. Consumers' "right-to-know" studies
2. Ecological impact studies
3. Studies of legal constraints on advertising and promotion
4. Social values and policies studies

Product Research

1. New product acceptance and potential
2. Competitive product studies
3. Testing of existing products
4. Packaging research

Sales and Market Research

1. Measurement of market potentials
2. Market share analysis
3. Determination of market characteristics
4. Sales analysis
5. Establishment of sales quotas and territories
6. Distribution channel studies
7. Test markets and store audits
8. Consumer panel operations
9. Sales compensation studies
10. Promotional studies

⸨ **FIGURE 13.5** ⸩

MARKETING RESEARCH TOPICS

Many organizations do research to determine market potential, to evaluate market share, and to learn more about the people in various markets. Most also do short- and long-range sales forecasting and competitor analysis.

••• THE MARKETING RESEARCH PROCESS •••

The key steps in the marketing research process are

1. Define the problem and determine the present situation.
2. Collect data.
3. Analyze the research data.
4. Choose the best ethical solutions.

The following sections look at each of these steps.

DEFINE THE GOAL AND DETERMINE THE PRESENT SITUATION
It's as important to know what an organization does well as what it doesn't do well. Marketing research should report both sides. Marketing researchers should be given the freedom to help discover what the problems are, what the alternatives are, what information is needed, and how to go about gathering and analyzing data.

COLLECT DATA   Obtaining usable information is vital to the marketing research process. Nevertheless, you must first determine the scope and estimated costs of doing research. Research can become quite expensive, so some trade-off must be made between information needs and cost.

To minimize costs, it's best to explore first all already-published research reports from journals, trade associations, the government, information services, libraries, and so forth. There's no sense in reinventing the wheel, so find out what other research has been done first. Figure 13.6 lists some popular sources of marketing information (secondary data).

The authors of this text relied heavily on focus groups to tell them what information and features students and faculty wanted and in what form. In composing this edition, focus groups were used both before and after changes were made to get as much advice as possible from potential users. This one occurred in 1994 with a group of students from the Chicago area.

focus group
A small group of people who meet under the direction of a discussion leader to communicate their feelings concerning an organization, its products, or other important issues.

sample
A representative group of a market population.

Usually, previously published research doesn't provide all the information necessary for important business decisions. When additional, more in-depth information is needed, marketers must do their own studies. Such studies include the observation method, the survey method, and focus groups.

In the observation method, data are collected by observing the actions of potential buyers. Can you think of a way we could use the observation method to gather the information we need to promote Fiberrific?

The survey method involves direct questioning of people to gather facts, opinions, or other information. The survey method is the most widely used technique for collecting primary data. *Primary data* are facts and figures not previously published that you gather on your own. Telephone surveys, mail surveys, and personal interviews are the most common methods of gathering survey information. Focus groups have become a popular method of surveying individuals. **A focus group** consists of a small group of people (8 to 14 individuals) who meet under the direction of a discussion leader to communicate their opinions about an organization, its products, or other important issues. Figure 13.6 lists the principle sources of primary data.

Realistically, it's impossible for an organization to survey all the potential buyers of a product. Therefore, marketers select a sample of the target market. A **sample** is the selection of a representative group of a market population. A *random sample* means that all people have an equal chance of being selected to be part of the representative group.

ANALYZE THE RESEARCH DATA   Careful, honest interpretation of data collected can help you find useful alternatives to specific marketing problems. The same data can mean different things to different people. Sometimes people become so intent on a project that they're tempted to ignore or misinterpret data. For example, if our data indicate the market won't support another brand of cereal, we'd do well to accept the information and drop Fiberrific rather than to slant the results as we'd like to see them and go ahead with the project.

CHOOSE THE BEST ETHICAL SOLUTIONS   Researchers are supposed to present alternative strategies and make recommendations as to which strategy may be best and why. It's important to include ethical and moral considerations at this point. That is, we must consider what's the *right* thing to do as well as the *profitable* thing to do. This step could add greatly to the social benefits of marketing decisions. The last steps in a research effort involve

SECONDARY SOURCES

Government Publications

Statistical Abstract of the United States
Survey of Current Business
Census of Retail Trade
Census of Transportation
Annual Survey of Manufacturers

Commercial Publications

A.C. Nielsen Company studies on retailing and media
Marketing Research Corporation of America studies on consumer purchases
Selling Areas–Marketing, Inc., reports on food sales

Magazines

Entrepreneur	*Journal of Marketing*	Trade Magazines
Business Week	*Journal of Retailing*	appropriate to your industry
Fortune	*Journal of Consumer Research*	such as *Progressive Grocer*
Inc.	*Journal of Advertising*	Reports from various
Advertising Age	*Journal of Marketing Research*	Chambers of Commerce
Forbes	*Marketing News*	
Harvard Business Review	*Journal of Advertising Research*	

Newspapers

The Wall Street Journal
Barron's

Computer searches
  Check your library for various software programs that
  will research articles in various business and trade publications for you

Internal Sources

Company records
Balance sheets
Income statements
Prior research reports

PRINCIPAL SOURCES OF PRIMARY DATA

Observation
Surveys
Experiments
Focus groups
Questionnaires

following up on the actions taken to see if the results were as expected. If not, corrective action can be taken and new research studies done in the ongoing attempt to provide consumer satisfaction at the lowest cost.

In the past, marketing research data were given to top managers in the firm who were then expected to make decisions based on those data. Quality-oriented organizations no longer operate that way. Instead, data are made available to customer contact people and everyone else in the organization who may benefit from the information. The most important competitive tool in the future will be an educated, trained, and informed work team. Marketing research information is critical to the success of such teams.

⟨ FIGURE 13.6 ⟩

SELECTED SOURCES OF SECONDARY AND PRIMARY INFORMATION
You should spend a day or two at the library becoming familiar with these sources. You can read about primary research in any marketing research text from the library.

••• USING RESEARCH TO UNDERSTAND CONSUMERS •••

The secret to understanding consumers is simply to listen to them. There are many techniques for doing that, such as focus groups. At this point, it's important to note that effective marketing research calls for getting out of the office

FIGURE 13.7

THE CONSUMER
DECISION-MAKING
PROCESS AND OUTSIDE
INFLUENCES

There are many influences on consumers as they decide which goods and services to buy. Marketers have some influence, but it's not usually as strong as sociocultural influences. Helping consumers in their information search and their evaluation of alternatives is a major function of marketing.

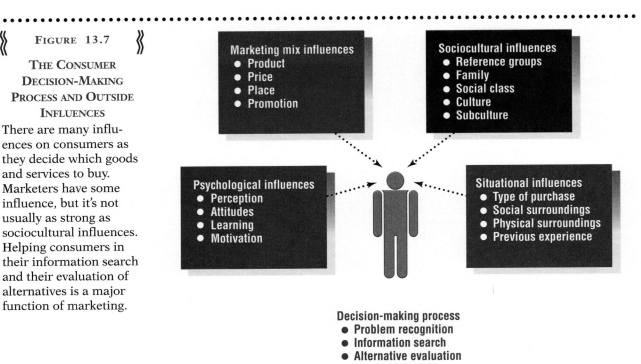

and getting close to customers to find out what they want and need. Laboratory research and consumer panels can never replace going into people's homes, watching them use products, and asking them what improvements they seek. Many U.S. producers now do that, but many don't.

In international markets, the need for marketing research is even greater. One must learn the culture of the people and talk with them directly. What's attractive in one country may be insulting to another country's value system. Marketing often is easier than some people make it. The goal, remember, is to find a need and fill it. That means listening to people constantly and adapting to what they say. It doesn't mean trying to sell them what they don't want.

THE CONSUMER DECISION-MAKING PROCESS   Figure 13.7 shows the kinds of subjects studied in a consumer behavior course. The core involves studying the consumer purchase decision process. "Problem recognition" may be the fact that your washing machine broke down. This leads to an information search—you look for ads about washing machines and read brochures about them. You may even consult *Consumer Reports* and other information sources. Then you evaluate alternatives and make a purchase decision. After the purchase, you may ask others how much they paid for their machines and do other comparisons, such as how other machines perform. Marketing researchers investigate consumer thought processes and behavior at each stage to determine the best way to facilitate marketing exchanges.

Consumer behavior researchers also study the various influences on consumer behavior. Figure 13.7 shows that such influences include the marketing mix variables, psychological influences such as perception and attitudes, situational influences such as the type of purchase and the physical surroundings, and sociocultural influences such as reference groups and culture. Here are some terms that may be unfamiliar to you:

Making Ethical Decisions

No Kidding

Marketers have long recognized that children can be an important influence on their parents' buying decisions. In fact, many direct appeals for products are focused directly at children. At Fiberrific, we've experienced a great response to our new high-fiber, high-protein cereal among health-conscious consumers. The one important group we haven't been able to attract is children. Therefore, the product management team is considering introducing Fiberrific Jr to help solve this problem.

Fiberrific Jr may have strong market potential if we follow two recommendations of our research department. First, we coat the flakes generously with sugar (significantly changing the cereal's nutritional benefits). Second, we promote the product exclusively on children's TV programs. Such a promotional strategy should create a strong demand for the product, especially if we offer a premium in each box. The consensus among the research department is that "Kids will love the new taste," plus parents will agree to buy Fiberrific Jr because of their positive impression of our best-selling brand. The research director commented, "The chance of a parent actually reading our label and noting the addition of sugar is nil!"

Would you introduce Fiberrific Jr according to the recommendations of research? What are the benefits of doing this? What are the risks involved in using the recommendations? What would you do if you were the marketing manager?

- *Culture* is the set of values, attitudes, and ways of doing things that are transmitted from one generation to another in a given society. The American culture, for example, emphasizes education, freedom, and diversity.

- *Learning* involves changes in an individual's behavior resulting from previous experiences and information.

- *Reference group* is the group that an individual uses as a reference point in the formation of his or her beliefs, attitudes, values, or behavior. For example, a college student may carry a briefcase instead of a backpack because his or her reference group is businesspeople.

- *Subculture* is the set of values, attitudes, and ways of doing things that result from belonging to a certain ethnic group, religious group, racial group, or other group with which one closely identifies (e.g., teenagers). Your subculture may prefer rap and hip-hop music, while your parents' subculture may prefer opera.

- **Cognitive dissonance** means that after the purchase, consumers may have doubts about whether they got the best product at the best price. That means marketers must reassure consumers after the sale if they want to establish a long-term relationship.[8]

cognitive dissonance
Consumer doubts after the purchase about whether or not the purchase was the best product at the best price.

RECOGNIZING DIFFERENT MARKETS: CONSUMER AND BUSINESS-TO-BUSINESS

There are two major markets in marketing: the consumer market and the industrial or business-to-business market. The **consumer market** consists of all the individuals or households who want goods and services for personal consumption or use. McDonald's Happy Meals, Toro lawn mowers, and Prudential health insurance policies are examples of items commonly considered consumer products.

consumer market
All individuals or households who want goods and services for personal consumption or use.

industrial market
All individuals and organizations that want goods and services to produce other goods and services or to sell, rent, or supply the goods to others.

The **industrial market** consists of all the individuals and organizations that want goods and services to produce other goods and services or to sell, rent, or supply the goods to others. Oil drilling bits, cash registers, display cases, office desks, public accounting audits, and corporate legal advice are examples of such goods and services (products).

The important thing to remember is that the buyer's reason for buying and the end use of the product are what determine whether a product is considered a consumer product or an industrial product. For example, a box of Fiberrific bought for a family's breakfast is considered a consumer product. However, if the same box of Fiberrific were purchased by Dinnie's Diner to sell to its breakfast customers, it would be considered an industrial product.

••• THE CONSUMER MARKET •••

The consumer market consists of the approximately 260 million people in the United States and the over 5½ billion people in world markets. Obviously, consumers vary greatly in age, education level, income, and taste. Because consumers differ so greatly, marketers must learn to select different consumer groups to develop products and services specially tailored to their needs. If a consumer group is large enough, a company may design a marketing program to serve that market.

market segmentation
The process of dividing the total market into several groups that have similar characteristics.

target marketing
The process by which an organization decides which market segments to serve.

Take Campbell soups, for example. You know Campbell for its line of traditional soups such as chicken noodle and tomato soup. But Campbell noticed the growth in the South and the increase in the Latino population so it's experimenting with a Creole soup for the southern market and a red bean soup for the Latino market. In Texas and California, where people like their food with a bit of kick, Campbell makes its nacho cheese soup spicier than in other parts of the country. Campbell is just one company that has had success studying the consumer market, breaking it down into categories, and then developing products for those separate groups.

The process of dividing the total market into several groups (segments) that have similar characteristics is called **market segmentation**. Usually a business can't serve all of these markets. A business must decide which markets to serve. **Target marketing** is the process by which an organization decides which market segments to serve.

The industrial market includes companies that buy goods to sell to other organizations. Therefore, this process is often referred to as business-to-business marketing. This photo shows a food distributor that buys goods from farmers and sells them to supermarkets and restaurants for resale to consumers.

••• SEGMENTING THE CONSUMER MARKET •••

There are several ways in which a firm can segment (divide) the consumer market. Let's say, for example, in trying to sell Fiberrific we begin our marketing campaign by focusing on a certain region, such as the Far West, where fitness is a major issue. Dividing the market by geographic area is called *geographic segmentation.* (See Figure 13.8.)

Alternatively, we could aim our promotions toward people aged 25 to 45 who have some college training and have high incomes—young urban professionals (yuppies)—like Campbell soup did with its Le Menu line. Segmentation by age, income, and education level is part of *demographic segmentation.* (See Figure 13.9 on page 424.)

We may want our ads to portray a group's lifestyle. To do that, we could study the group's values, attitudes, and interests. This segmentation strategy is called *psychographic segmentation.* (See Figure 13.10 on page 424.)

SPOTLIGHT ON SMALL BUSINESS

Bull's Eye Marketing

One of the most valuable lessons a new small-business owner can learn is that you can't take a shotgun approach to marketing and be all things to all people. If you do, you end up shooting a lot of shells and missing the target. A helter-skelter method of marketing can quickly drain your limited resources.

Entrepreneurs selecting target markets ask themselves, "Who are my best prospects—the people most likely to buy my goods and services and continue to buy them regularly?" Businesspeople not using target marketing normally give answers such as "Anyone who wants his or her windows washed," "Anyone who has a computer," or "Anyone who wants to remodel his or her house."

Entrepreneurs who use target marketing, however, know that it's hard to sell to "anyone" you happen to meet. There are specific people who have a specific need that you can fill—you'll find it easy to sell to them. The shortest way to marketing success, therefore, is to select target markets.

Gerry Foster, president of Foster Marketing Resources, uses a computer software program to track characteristics of his key clients—the 20 percent who account for 80 percent of his revenue. He calls this group his A clients. Examining their characteristics gives him a good idea of the type of prospects to seek in the future for new business. He avoids prospects who don't have characteristics of his A clients because they are less likely to be profitable.

Donna Barson of Barson Marketing, Inc., feels you need to do "primary research"—in other words, go directly to your target market. If you can't afford to hire professional researchers, Ms. Barson recommends contacting the local Small Business Development Center, Small Business Administration office, or business school for assistance.

Source: Gerry Foster, "Bull's-Eye Marketing—The Key to Profitability," *Home-Office Computing*, April 1991, pp. 24–25; and "Know Thy Market," *Entrepreneur*, March 1994, p. 91.

What benefits should we talk about? Should we emphasize high fiber, low sugar, price, health in general, or what? Determining which benefits are preferred is called *benefit segmentation*. (See Figure 13.11 on page 425.)

Who are the big eaters of cereal? Children eat cereal, but so do adults. Separating the market by usage (volume of use) is called *volume segmentation*. Most cereal companies seem to aim at children. Why not go for adults, a less competitive market? (See Figure 13.12 on page 425.)

VARIABLE	TYPICAL SEGMENTS
Region	New England, Mideast, Great Lakes, Plains, Southeast, Southwest, Rocky Mountain, Far West
City or county size	Under 5,000; 5,000–19,999; 20,000–49,999; 50,000–99,999; and so on
Population density	Urban, suburban, rural
Zip codes	Furs and stationwagons, blue blood estates, shotguns and pickups

FIGURE 13.8

GEOGRAPHIC SEGMENTATION VARIABLES
This table shows one method marketers use to divide the market. The aim of segmentation is to break the market into smaller units.

FIGURE 13.9

DEMOGRAPHIC SEGMENTATION VARIABLES

These variables divide the market into groups having similar ages and occupations. When would you use demographic information?

VARIABLE	TYPICAL SEGMENTS
Age	Under 5; 5–10; 11–18; 19–34; 35–49; 50–64; 65 and over
Education	Grade school or less; some high school; high school graduate; some college; college graduate; advanced college degree
Family size	1; 2–3; 4–5; over 6
Family life cycle	Young, single; young, married, no children; young, married, oldest child less than 6 years old; young, married, youngest child 6 or over; older, married, with children; older, married, no children; older, single; other
Income	Under $9,999; $10,000–$14,999; $15,000–$19,999; $20,000–$40,000; over $40,000
Nationality	American, Asian, British, Eastern European, French, German, Italian, Japanese, Latin American, Middle Eastern, Scandinavian, and so forth
Occupation	Professional, managerial; technical, officials, and proprietors; clerical, sales; supervisors; operatives; farmers; students; home managers; retired; unemployed
Race	White, African-American, Indian, Asian, and so forth
Religion	Catholic, Protestant, Jewish, and so forth
Sex	Male, female
Social class	Lower lower, upper lower, lower middle, upper middle, lower upper, upper upper

••• SELECTING A TARGET MARKET •••

The best segmentation strategy is to use all the variables to come up with a consumer profile (a target market) that's sizable, reachable, and profitable. Let's look more closely at procedures for selecting a target market. Variables include

FIGURE 13.10

PSYCHOGRAPHIC SEGMENTATION VARIABLES

Using the variables in this figure would identify the lifestyles of a group of people. Can you think of an ad related to attitudes?

VARIABLE	TYPICAL SEGMENTS
Attitudes	LOV (list of values)
Behavior problems	Self-respect
Interests	Security
Lifestyles	Warm relationship with others
Opinions	Sense of accomplishment
Personality	Self-fulfillment
Self-image	Being well respected
Values	Sense of belonging
	Fun and enjoyment in life

VARIABLE	TYPICAL SEGMENTS
Comfort	Benefit segmentation divides an already established market into smaller, more homogeneous segments. Those people who desire economy in a car would be an example. The benefit desired varies by product.
Convenience	
Durability	
Economy	
Health	
Luxury	
Safety	
Status	

FIGURE 13.11

BENEFIT SEGMENTATION VARIABLES
Which of these benefits are most important to you? Marketing managers need to know which variables people value.

1. *Size and growth potential of the segment*. The proper size for a market segment depends on the size of the seller and the objectives of the firm. A small business might select a small market segment that has been ignored by larger firms but is large enough to be profitable for the small firm.

2. *How reachable the segment is*. The marketer must be able to reach the target group and still make a profit. One may see the potential of selling a product in China because there are over a billion consumers there, but the cost of trying to reach those consumers may be too high.

3. *The nature of the market*. A marketer must look at how many competitors are already going after that market, potential new competitors, and customers' buying power. If there are too many existing competitors or potential competitors, one may hesitate to enter certain markets. The same is true if the target market's buying power is too low.

4. *The nature of the company*. The fact that a market need exists and could be profitable doesn't mean a company should enter that market. Management must consider its present product mix, company strengths, and competence.

During the 1990s, marketers became more focused on smaller market segments that provide profit potential in spite of their small size. For example, new manufacturing techniques make it possible to develop specialized products for small market segments. **Niche marketing** is the process of finding small, but profitable market segments and designing custom-made products for those groups. For example, Evergreen makes upgraded central processing units (CPUs) for computers, a market not pursued by giants such as Intel.[9]

niche marketing
The process of finding very small but profitable market segments and designing custom-made products for those people.

VARIABLE	TYPICAL SEGMENTS
Usage	Heavy users, light users, nonusers
Loyalty status	None, medium, strong

FIGURE 13.12

VOLUME MARKET SEGMENTATION
Knowing who uses a product most is an important consideration in marketing.

••• BUSINESS-TO-BUSINESS MARKETING •••

The marketing of goods and services to manufacturers, institutions (for example, hospitals or schools), commercial operations (retail stores), and the government is called **industrial marketing**. It's also known as *business-to-business marketing*.

industrial marketing
The marketing of goods and services to manufacturers, institutions, commercial operations, and the government.

The basic principle of this kind of marketing is still "Find a need and fill it," but the strategies are different from consumer marketing because the buyers are different. Seven factors make industrial marketing different:

1. The market for industrial goods is a derived demand; that is, demand for consumer products such as cars creates demand for industrial goods and services including tires, batteries, glass, metal, plastics, and engines.

2. Demand for industrial goods is relatively inelastic; that is, the quantity demanded doesn't always change significantly with minor changes in price. The reason for this is that industrial products are made up of so many parts that a price increase for one part isn't usually a significant problem.

3. The number of customers in the industrial market is relatively few; that is, there are just a few construction firms or mining operations compared to the consumer market of 70 million or so households.

4. The size of industrial customers is relatively large; that is, a few large organizations account for most of the employment and production of various goods and services. Nonetheless, there are many small to medium-size firms in the United States that together make an attractive market.

5. Industrial markets tend to be concentrated. For example, oil fields tend to be concentrated in the Southwest and Alaska. Consequently, marketing efforts often may be concentrated on a particular geographic area, and distribution problems are often minimized by locating warehouses near industrial centers.

6. Industrial buyers generally are more rational than consumers in their selection of goods and services; they use specifications and carefully weigh the "total product offer," including quality, price, and service.

7. Industrial sales tend to be direct. Manufacturers sell products such as tires directly to auto manufacturers, but tend to use wholesalers and retailers to sell to consumers.

Industrial markets are often more complex than consumer markets because the products are sold many times before they reach the ultimate consumer. Many universities now have courses in industrial (business-to-business) marketing. In such courses, you learn (1) how to segment industrial markets using government data and (2) how the various kinds of industrial goods are marketed. In general, industrial firms rely more on personal selling, whereas consumer goods rely more heavily on advertising. That's because business customers tend to be large and concentrated, and it's more efficient and effective to call on them with a salesperson.

CRITICAL THINKING

When businesses buy goods and services from other businesses, they usually buy in very large volume. Salespeople in the industrial field usually are paid on a commission basis; that is, they make a certain percentage of every sale. Can you see, therefore, why industrial sales may be a more rewarding career (monetarily) than consumer sales? Industrial salespeople sell goods such as steel, lumber, computers, engines, parts, and supplies. Where would you find the names of such companies?

Because many industrial customers buy certain products in large volume, there has been a tendency for suppliers to locate their factories nearby. In this case, the supplier is Grainger and the buyer is the M&M*Mars plant that manufactures Dove ice cream bars. The Grainger plant is actually located right across the street from Mars so that deliveries can be made quickly and efficiently.

CAREER PROSPECTS IN MARKETING

If you were to major in marketing, a wide variety of careers would be available to you. You could work in a retail store or for a wholesaler. You could do marketing research or get involved in product management. You could go into selling, advertising, sales promotion, or public relations. You could get involved in transportation, storage, or international distribution. As you read through the following marketing chapters, consider whether a marketing career would interest you.

PROGRESS CHECK

- What are the four parts of the marketing research process?
- Can you give examples of how a company would use the following segmentation strategies: geographic, demographic, psychographic, benefit, and volume?
- What criteria do marketers use to select a market segment to service?
- What are five factors that make industrial markets different from consumer markets?

SUMMARY

1. Marketing is the process of determining customer wants and needs and then providing customers with goods and services that meet or exceed their expectations.
   ● ***What is a simple description of marketing?***
   Find a need and fill it.
   ● ***What are the basic steps in the marketing process?***
   After finding a need, the next step in the marketing process is finding a product or the proposed product and testing it in the marketplace. The product development process includes packaging, branding, and pricing. Marketing middlemen distribute the product to consumers. The final steps in the marketing process are promoting the product to consumers and building a relationship with customers.

1. Define marketing and summarize the steps involved in the marketing process.

2. The role of marketing has changed as the wants and needs of consumers have changed.
   ● ***How is the role of marketing changing?***
   Marketing is becoming much more customer-oriented. Whereas the goal once was to satisfy customers, the goal now is to please, dazzle, or delight customers. Furthermore, more consideration is being given to the buyer's role in creating marketing exchanges.

2. Describe marketing's changing role in society and the merging of the marketing concept with total quality management.

- *What are the three parts of the marketing concept?*

The three parts of the marketing concepts are (1) a customer orientation, (2) training employees from all departments in customer service so that everyone in the organization has the same objective—consumer satisfaction (this is a total and integrated organizational effort), and (3) a profit orientation; that is, market those goods and services that will earn the firm a profit and enable it to survive and expand to serve more customer wants and needs.

- *How has the total quality movement affected the marketing concept?*

Total quality has led firms to have a wider orientation than just customers. Marketing now is concerned with employees, customers, and other stakeholders of the firm (e.g., suppliers, dealers, and the local communities). Furthermore, marketing is establishing close relationships among firms so that the whole marketing *system* is customer-oriented. Finally, everyone in the system must keep the profit orientation in mind.

3. Illustrate how marketing is evolving from mass marketing to custom marketing.

3. The marketing process involves research, developing product ideas, branding and pricing products, distributing products to customers, and establishing long-term relationships with customers.

- *What is relationship marketing?*

Relationship marketing is establishing and maintaining mutually beneficial exchange relationships with internal and external customers and all the other stakeholders of the organization. Organizations that adopt relationship marketing take the community's needs into mind when designing and marketing products.

- *What's the difference between relationship marketing and mass marketing?*

Mass marketing means developing products and promotions that are designed to please large groups of people. That means using mass media such as TV, radio, and newspapers. Mass marketing tended to lead to adversarial marketing. Relationship marketing moves away from mass production toward custom-made goods.

4. List the eight functions of marketing and the utilities created by marketing, and give examples of each.

4. Marketers perform various functions that create value for consumers. Marketers call those values *utility*.

- *What is the marketing mix?*

The marketing mix consists of the four Ps of marketing: product, price, place, and promotion.

- *What functions do marketers perform?*

Marketers perform eight functions: research, buying, selling, transportation, storage, credit, risk bearing, and standardization (or grading).

- *What utilities to marketers create?*

Marketers create *time* utility by having goods available when you want them. *Place* utility gets goods where you want them. *Possession* utility makes it possible for you to obtain the goods by providing credit, delivery, installation, and whatever else you need to enjoy the product. *Information* utility tells you when and where the product is available, the price, and other information you need to make an intelligent marketing decision.

5. Apply the four parts of the marketing research process to a business problem.

5. Marketing research is the first step in the "Find a need and fill it" process.

- *What are the four steps in the marketing research process?*

The four steps are (1) define the problem and determine the present situation, (2) collect data, (3) analyze the research data, and (4) choose the best ethical solutions.

6. There are two major markets: the consumer market and the industrial or business-to-business market.
   - ***What are the differences between the two markets?***
   The consumer market is people who buy products for their own use—people like you and me. The industrial market consists of all the individuals and organizations that want goods and services to produce other goods and services or to sell, rent, or supply the goods to others. Industrial buyers buy products to use in other products or for resale.
   - ***How do businesses segment the consumer market?***
   Segmentation techniques include geographic, demographic, psychographic, benefit, and volume. Using these techniques, marketers choose a target market that's sizable, reachable, and profitable.

6. Differentiate between consumer and industrial markets and compare the various forms of market segmentation.

7. Job prospects for marketing graduates have never been better.
   - ***What kinds of jobs can a marketing major find?***
   Marketing majors can find jobs in retailing, wholesaling, advertising, selling, public relations, sales promotion, transportation, and international trade.

7. Discuss present and future prospects for careers in marketing.

adversarial marketing 411	information utility 416	niche marketing 425
brand name 407	market segmentation 422	place utility 416
cognitive dissonance 421	marketing 406	possession utility 416
consumer market 421	marketing concept 409	product 407
focus group 418	marketing management 413	relationship marketing 411
green product 411	marketing mix 413	sample 418
industrial market 422	marketing research 416	target marketing 422
industrial marketing 426	mass marketing 411	time utility 416

KEY TERMS

1. Imagine that you are the president of a small liberal arts college. Enrollment has declined dramatically. The college is in danger of closing. Show how you might revive the college by applying the marketing concept. Develop an action plan outlining how you would implement the three phases: (1) a consumer orientation, (2) the training of employees in all departments in customer service, and (3) a profit orientation.

2. Think of a product other than cereal that your friends want but cannot get near campus. Invent a product to fill that need. Do a concept test, evaluate the total market, think of a brand name and a package, develop a promotional scheme, and design a system to distribute it to students.

3. Research companies in your area, identifying one involved in business-to-business marketing. Interview a manager of this firm regarding the ways business-to-business differs from consumer marketing. Report your findings to the class.

4. How many segmentation strategies could you use to segment the market for a new, nutritious soft drink that contains no sugar but does have all the vitamins required for a day? Use all the strategies together to describe a target market that you feel would be the most profitable.

5. Divide into groups of four or five students. Conduct a marketing research study by identifying a problem on your campus that your group agrees needs attention. Collect information about that problem, analyze the data, and make written recommendations to the proper authority.

DEVELOPING WORKPLACE SKILLS

PRACTICING MANAGEMENT DECISIONS

CASE   APPLYING TOTAL QUALITY MARKETING CONCEPTS AT THERMOS

Thermos is the company made famous by its Thermos bottles and lunch boxes. Thermos also manufacturers cookout grills. Its competitors include Sunbeam and Weber. To become a world-class competitor, Thermos completely reinvented the way it conducted its marketing operations. By reviewing what Thermos did, you can see how new marketing concepts affect organizations.

First of all, Thermos replaced its corporate culture ◀·· P.263 ··▶. It had become a bureaucratic firm organized by function: design, engineering, manufacturing, marketing, and so on. That organizational structure was replaced by flexible, cross-functional ◀·· P.256 ··▶, self-managed teams ◀·· P.228 ··▶. The idea was to focus on a customer group—for example, buyers of outdoor grills—and build a product development team to create a product for that market.

The product development team for grills consisted of six middle managers from various disciplines, including engineering, manufacturing, finance, and marketing. They called themselves the Lifestyle team because their job was to study grill users to see how they lived and what they were looking for in an outdoor grill. To get an outside perspective, the company hired Fitch, Inc., an outside consulting firm, to help with design and marketing research. Leadership of the team rotated based on needs of the moment. For example, the marketing person took the lead in doing field research, but the R&D person took over when technical developments became the issue.

The team's first step was to analyze the market. The team spent about a month on the road talking with people, videotaping barbecues, conducting focus groups, and learning what people wanted in an outdoor grill. The company found that people wanted nice-looking grills that didn't pollute the air and that were easy to use. It also had to be safe enough for apartment dwellers, which meant it had to be electric.

As the research results came in, engineering began playing with ways of improving electric grills. Manufacturing kept in touch to make sure that any new ideas could be produced economically. Design people were already building models of the new product. R&D people relied heavily on Thermos's strengths. Thermos's core strength was its vacuum technology. It was used to keep in hot and cold in Thermos bottles. Using that knowledge, the engineers developed a domed lid that contained the heat inside the grill.

Once a prototype was developed, the company showed the model to potential customers who made several suggestions for changes. Employees took sample grills home and tried to find weaknesses. Using the input from potential customers and employees, the company used continuous improvement ◀·· P.259 ··▶ to manufacture what became a world-class product.

No product can become a success without communicating with the market. The team took the grill on the road, showing it at trade shows and in retail stores. The product was such a success that Thermos is now using self-managed customer-oriented teams to develop all its product lines.

Decision Questions

1. How could the growth of self-managed cross-functional teams affect you and your future career in business?

2. Can you see the advantage of having teams of people from auto repair shops researching consumers in the same way that Thermos did?

3. Which people in an organization do you anticipate being most resistant to forming self-managed, cross-functional teams? Why?

4. What do you think the Thermos team would have found if they had asked customers what they thought about having consumers put the grills together rather than buying them assembled?

Source: Brian Dumaine, "Payoff from the New Management," *Fortune*, December 13, 1993, pp. 103–10.

〉〉 VIDEO CASE   SELLING COCA-COLA IN JAPAN 〈〈

Coca-Cola and Pepsi are major competitors throughout the world as well as in the United States. When it comes to Japan, however, Coke is the clear winner. Why? The sale of soft drinks in Japan began on military bases after WWII. However, the rapid growth stage didn't begin until 1957 when a Japanese businessperson bought a license to manufacture Coke in Japan.

What made Coke a success in Japan over time was its willingness to partner with local businesspeople. Rather than simply being a multinational firm, Coke was successful in becoming a multilocal firm. That is, it found partners in various cities and worked closely with them to develop sales in those areas.

As many U.S. firms have found, it wasn't easy to break into the Japanese market. For one thing, Coke wanted to sell directly to retailers. That simply was not—and *is* not—the tradition in Japan. The tradition is to sell through a whole series of middlemen that control the distribution.

It is fundamentally important when trying to sell in a different country to adapt as much as possible to the local culture. Coca-Cola did that by setting up social clubs in its facilities like those in other Japanese firms. It also helped employees buy homes with low interest loans. Every effort was made to adjust to the tastes of the local people, including the creation of a new 50 percent juice drink.

Relationship marketing is especially important in Japan where negotiations take time, and patience is truly a virtue. Consensus building is the norm, and that requires more time than U.S. firms are used to investing. Nonetheless, the payoff can be extraordinary. For example, Coke has some 1,000,000 dealers and 700,000 vending machines in Japan as a result of its patience and care in establishing local relationships.

Pepsi, on the other hand, remains a minor competitor due to its failure to invest the time necessary to establish local partners and relationships. As a consequence Pepsi's market penetration continues to be hindered and shallow.

Discussion Questions

1. What evidence can you cite showing that foreign firms have been very careful to adapt to U.S. culture when marketing their products here?

2. Many U.S. firms have had difficulty establishing relationships in Japan. Do you think that they could learn from Coke's experience and try again? Would a similar approach work for U.S. automakers?

3. Talk with a local store owner or manager who sells products from various parts of the world. Ask him or her what foreign manufacturers do to establish and maintain good relationships with that store and its suppliers.

CHAPTER 14

DEVELOPING AND PRICING QUALITY PRODUCTS AND SERVICES

LEARNING GOALS

After you have read and studied this chapter, you should be able to

1. Explain the difference between a product and a value package and between a product line and a product mix.

2. Describe how businesses create product differentiation for their goods and services in both consumer and industrial markets.

3. List the six functions of packaging.

4. Give examples of a brand, a brand name, and a trademark, and explain how to prevent a brand name from becoming generic.

5. Explain the role of product managers and the five steps of the new-product development process.

6. Identify and describe the stages of the product life cycle and describe marketing strategies at each stage.

7. Give examples of various pricing objectives and show how break-even analysis helps in pricing decisions.

WOLFGANG SCHMITT OF RUBBERMAID

Fortune magazine takes a survey of leading businesspeople each year to determine which companies are most admired. It wasn't surprising that IBM led the list in the early 1980s. Then Merck dominated the list from 1986 to 1992. But guess who was second for five of those six years? Rubbermaid. Finally in 1993 and 1994 Rubbermaid earned the most-admired award. Why do top executives rate Rubbermaid so highly?

Rubbermaid has sales of $1.8 billion and profits of $182.4 million. But, more important is how Rubbermaid earns those profits: by continuously bringing out new products and by constantly improving old products. Most Rubbermaid products are common household goods such as mops, toys, spatulas, storage boxes, and dish drainers. Rubbermaid sells some 5,000 different items.

Rubbermaid's chief executive officer is Wolfgang Schmitt. Not satisfied with the 5,000 products Rubbermaid was selling, Schmitt set a goal of entering a new *product category* every 12 to 18 months. Recent categories include hardware cabinets and garden sheds. As a result of such aggressive new-product development, 33 percent of sales are from products developed in the past five years. Rubbermaid is known as a "new-product machine." In 1993, it turned out new products at the rate of one a day! Yes, one a day.

How does the company come up with so many new products? It uses cross-functional teams ◀·· **P.256** ··▶. Some 21 teams of five to seven people from manufacturing, marketing, research and development, finance, and other departments focus on specific product lines, such as birdhouses. The company now offers 25 different birdhouse models.

But Schmitt knows that *making* products isn't the key to success. *Selling* products is! So Rubbermaid has a Customer Center where buyers like Wal-Mart come to hear presentations about its new products. Rubbermaid shows customers competing products and demonstrates why Rubbermaid's are better. It then shows customers how they can increase their profits by selling the right combination of Rubbermaid products in their stores. Using such tactics, Schmitt expects to double sales by the year 2000 and raise foreign sales from 18 percent to 30 percent of revenues. The story of Rubbermaid sets the stage for this important chapter on product development and pricing.

> *If a man can make a better mousetrap than his neighbor, though he builds his house in the woods the world will make a beaten path to his door.*
>
> *Ralph Waldo Emerson*

PRODUCT DEVELOPMENT AND THE VALUE PACKAGE

International competition today is so strong that American businesses are losing some markets to foreign producers. The only way to regain those markets is to design and promote better products—meaning products that are perceived to have high quality at a fair price. As we'll see in this chapter, whether a consumer perceives a product as better depends on many factors. To satisfy consumers, marketers must learn to listen better and to adapt constantly to changing market demands. Managers must also constantly adapt to price challenges from competitors. This further stirs up the waters of product management.

Constant white water

The unremitting turmoil in today's corporate life.

Constant white water is the unremitting turmoil in today's corporate life, demanding quick response to market changes, constant innovation, great flexibility, and crisis management skills. The comparision to white-water rafting is accurate in that some white water on a rafting trip is fun, but constant turbulence takes a lot out of you. Learning to manage change, especially new-product changes, is critical for tomorrow's managers.[1] A critical part of the impression consumers get about products is the price. This chapter, therefore, will explore two critical parts of the marketing mix: product development and price.

Wolfgang Schmitt and other marketers have learned that the problem of adapting products to markets is a continuous one. An organization can't do a one-time survey of consumer wants and needs, design a line of products to meet those needs, put them in the stores, and relax. There must be a constant monitoring of customer wants and needs because consumer and business needs change over time.

Fast-food organizations must constantly monitor all sources of information for new-product ideas. Chicken McNuggets were developed at McDonald's when the head chef was experimenting with Onion McNuggets. Fast-food

Most fast-food restaurants are constantly developing new offerings to appeal to different markets. About 300 KFC stores, for example, cater specifically to African-Americans. They offer hot and spicy chicken along with Mean Greens, red beans and rice, and, in some locations, peach cobbler and sweet potato pie. In Latino neighborhoods, stores have experimented with side dishes such as fried plantains and black beans and rice.

researchers also monitor grocery store shelves and cookbooks for new ideas. CEO Robert Autry of Hardee's Food System claims to bring out more new products than anyone. Each Hardee's offers 12 to 15 different sandwiches. Offerings differ in various locations, based on the wants of the local community. In Iowa, pork tenderloin is big, but in Oklahoma City, it's tortilla scramblers.

Product development, then, is a key activity in any modern business. There's a lot more to new-product development than merely introducing new products, however. What marketers do to create excitement and demand for those products (product strategy) is as important as the products themselves.

••• DEVELOPING A VALUE PACKAGE •••

From a strategic marketing viewpoint, a value package is more than just the physical good or service. A **value package** consists of everything that consumers evaluate when deciding whether to buy something. Thus, the basic product or service may be a washing machine, an insurance policy, or a bottle of beer, but the value package also consists of

value package
Everything that consumers evaluate when deciding whether or not to buy something.

Price

Package

Store surroundings (atmospherics)

Image created by advertising

Guarantee

Reputation of the producer

Brand name

Service

Buyers' past experience

Speed of delivery

When people buy a product, they evaluate and compare value packages on all these dimensions. Therefore, a successful marketer must begin to think like a consumer and evaluate the product offer as a total collection of impressions created by all the factors listed above.

Let's go back and look at our highly nutritious, high-fiber, low-sugar breakfast cereal, Fiberrific, for example. The value package as perceived by the consumer is much more than the cereal itself. Anything that affects consumer perceptions about the cereal's benefits and value may determine whether the cereal is purchased. The price certainly is an important part of the perception of product value.

Often a high price indicates exceptional quality. The store surroundings also are important. If the cereal is being sold in an exclusive health food store, it takes on many characteristics of the store (e.g., healthy and upscale). A guarantee of satisfaction can increase the product's value in the mind of consumers, as can a well-known brand name. Advertising can create an attractive image, and word of mouth can enhance the reputation. Thus, Fiberrific is more than a cereal as a value package; it's a an entire bundle of impressions.

Sometimes an organization can use low price to create an attractive value package. For example, Hull Industries, a small company in Twinsburg, Ohio, developed a steering-wheel–locking device (Lockjaw) to compete with The Club. Its wholesale price is $5 less than The Club's, and Lockjaw fits all cars whereas The Club comes in multiple sizes. Furthermore, the lock is said to be stronger and thieves would have to cut the Lockjaw in two places (versus just one for The Club). However, a better product still needs great promotion to capture the market from a leader.[2]

CRITICAL THINKING

What's the product of a library? One branch of the Chicago Public Library actually lends expensive power tools and such accessories as fiberglass extension ladders. At the Carnegie library in Pittsburgh, volunteer psychologists go to the library, listen to people's troubles, and refer them to appropriate help. The Broome High School Media Center in Spartanburg, South Carolina, lends prom, wedding, and mother-of-the-bride dresses donated by members of the community. What do you think prompted libraries to be so creative in their product offers? What's the product of a college or university?

PRODUCT LINES AND THE PRODUCT MIX

product line
A group of products that are physically similar or are intended for a similar market.

product mix
The combination of product lines offered by a manufacturer.

Companies usually don't have just one product that they sell. Rather, they sell several different but complementary products. The profile about Rubbermaid showed that new-product lines can be added continually with the right amount of research. Figure 14.1 shows Procter & Gamble's product lines. A **product line**, as the figure shows, is a group of products that are physically similar or are intended for a similar market. Procter & Gamble's product lines include bar soaps, detergents, and dishwashing detergents. In one product line, there may be several competing brands. Thus, Procter & Gamble has many brands of detergent in its product line, including Bold, Cheer, Tide, and Ivory Snow. All of P&G's product lines make up its product mix.

Product mix is the term used to describe the combination of product lines offered by a manufacturer. As we see in Figure 14.1, P&G's product mix consists of product lines of soap, detergents, toothpastes, shampoos, and so forth.

Small companies may find it best to keep the product mix short and simple. Sashco Sealants Inc., for example, cut its product line from 11 to 3 to focus on the most profitable lines: Lexel and Big Stretch (sealants) and Glue Buddy (an adhesive). Revenues and profits increased the first year the line was cut.

The company also decided not to sell through discounters like Kmart because it believed that such exposure would ruin the firm's top-quality image. Instead, the company sold only through independent dealers. Les

FIGURE 14.1

PROCTER & GAMBLE'S PRODUCT MIX INCLUDING ALL ITS PRODUCT LINES
Most large companies make more than one product. Here we see the various products and brands Procter & Gamble makes. Note how physically similar the products are.

PRODUCT MIX

PRODUCT LINES	BRANDS
Bar soaps	Camay, Coast, Ivory, Kirk's, Lava, Monchel, Safeguard, Zest
Detergents	Bold, Cheer, Dash, Dreft, Era, Gain, Ivory Snow, Liquid Bold-3, Liquid Cheer, Liquid Tide, Oxydol, Solo, Tide
Dishwashing detergents	Cascade, Dawn, Ivory Liquid, Joy, Liquid Cascade
Cleaners and cleansers	Comet, Comet Liquid, Mr. Clean, Spic & Span, Spic & Span Pine Liquid, Top Job
Shampoos	Head & Shoulders, Ivory, Lilt, Pert Plus, Prell
Toothpastes	Crest, Denquel, Gleem
Paper tissue products	Banner, Charmin, Puffs, White Cloud
Disposable diapers	Luvs, Pampers
Shortening and cooking oils	Crisco, Crisco Oil, Crisco Corn Oil, Puritan

Burch, the president, says, "By reducing our product line and clarifying our distribution policy, we became more important to our customers, and I learned that there is more growth potential in focusing yourself than in answering every call."[3]

Service providers have product lines and product mixes as well. For example, a bank may offer a variety of ways to deposit money, from savings accounts to money market funds. A bank's product mix may include safety deposit boxes, loans (home, car, etc.), traveler's checks, and more. AT&T combines services (telephone) with goods (computers, phones) in its product mix. Companies must decide what product mix is best. The mix may include both goods and services to spread the risk among several industries.

PRODUCT DIFFERENTIATION

Product differentiation is the creation of real product differences or perceptions that make one product seem superior to others. Actual product differences are sometimes quite small, so marketers must use a clever mix of pricing, advertising, and packaging to create a unique, attractive image. Evian, for example, successfully attempted product differentiation. Evian made its water so attractive through pricing and promotion that often people order it by brand name instead of a Coke or Pepsi. There's no reason why you couldn't create an attractive image for Fiberrific. With a high price and creative advertising, it could become the Evian of cereals. Different products call for different marketing strategies, as we'll see next.

Small businesses can often win market share with creative product differentiation. For example, photographer Charlie Clark competes with other yearbook photographers by offering multiple clothing changes, backgrounds, and poses along with special allowances, discounts, and guarantees. He has been so successful that companies use him as a speaker at photography conventions. Small businesses usually have the advantage of being more flexible in adapting to customer wants and needs and giving them product differences that make a difference. See the Spotlight on Small Business box for more ideas.

product differentiation
The attempt to create product perceptions in the minds of consumers so that one product seems superior to others.

... MARKETING DIFFERENT CLASSES OF ... CONSUMER GOODS AND SERVICES

Several attempts have been made to classify consumer goods and services. One of the more traditional classifications has three general categories—convenience, shopping, and specialty—based on consumer shopping habits and preferences.

1. **Convenience goods and services** are products that the consumer wants to purchase frequently and with a minimum of effort (for example, candy, snacks, banking). Location, brand awareness, and image are important for marketers of convenience goods and services.

2. **Shopping goods and services** are those products that the consumer buys only after comparing value, quality, and price from a variety of sellers. Shopping goods and services are sold largely through shopping centers where consumers can "shop around." Because many consumers carefully compare such products, marketers can emphasize price differences, quality differences, or some combination of the two. Examples include clothes, shoes, appliances, and auto repair services.

convenience goods and services
Products that the consumer wants to purchase frequently and with a minimum of effort.

shopping goods and services
Products that the consumer buys only after comparing quality and price from a variety of sellers.

specialty goods and services
Products that have a special attraction to consumers who are willing to go out of their way to obtain them.

3. **Specialty goods and services** are products that have a special attraction to consumers who are willing to go out of their way to obtain them. Examples are fur coats, jewelry, and exotic candy and cigars as well as services provided by medical specialists or business consultants. These products are often marketed through specialty magazines. For example, specialty skis may be sold through ski magazines and specialty foods through gourmet magazines.

The marketing task varies depending on the kind of product; that is, convenience goods are marketed differently from specialty goods, and so forth. The best way to promote convenience goods is to make them readily available and to create the proper image. Price and quality are the best appeals for shopping goods. Specialty goods rely on reaching special market segments through advertising.

Whether a good or service falls into a particular class depends on the individual consumer. What's a shopping good for one consumer (for example, coffee) could be a specialty good for another consumer (for example, imported coffee). Some people shop around to compare different dry cleaners, so dry cleaning is a shopping service for them. Others go to the closest store, making it a convenience service. Therefore, marketers must carefully monitor their customer base to determine how consumers perceive their products.

••• MARKETING INDUSTRIAL GOODS AND SERVICES •••

industrial goods
Products used in the production of other products.

Industrial goods are products used in the production of other products. Some products can be classified as both consumer goods and industrial goods. For example, personal computers could be sold to consumer markets

Environmentally concerned marketing (green marketing ◀ P.411 ▶) has become an important part of packaging. Jerry Smith developed a biodegradable cleaner/degreaser. He then needed a package that matched the environmental benefits of the product. He chose a standup pouch that requires less plastic than a bottle with the same capacity. The pouch is also cheaper to ship and takes up less room in landfills. Have you noticed other companies that are using packaging that is more environmentally sound?

or industrial markets. As a consumer good, the computer might be sold through computer stores like CompUSA or through computer magazines. Most of the promotional task would go to advertising. As an industrial good, personal computers are more likely to be sold by salespeople. Advertising would be less of a factor in the promotion strategy. You can see that classifying goods by user category helps determine the proper marketing mix strategy. Figure 14.2 shows some categories of both consumer and industrial goods and services.

- • What's the difference between a product and a value package?
- • What's the difference between a product line and a product mix?
- • Name the three classes of consumer goods and services, and give examples of each.

PROGRESS CHECK

PACKAGING CHANGES THE PRODUCT

We've said that consumers evaluate many aspects of the value package, including the brand. It's surprising how important packaging can be in such evaluations. Many years ago people had problems with table salt because it would stick together and form lumps during humid or damp weather. The Morton Salt Company solved that problem by designing a package that kept salt dry in all kinds of weather. Thus, the slogan "When it rains, it pours." Packaging made Morton's salt more desirable than competing products—it's still the best-known salt in the United States.

The Morton Salt Company knew how to use packaging to change and improve its basic product—salt. Other companies have used similar techniques. Thus, we've had squeezable catsup bottles, plastic bottles for motor oil that eliminate the need for funnels, stackable potato chips in a can, toothpaste pumps, plastic cans for tennis balls, microwavable popcorn packages, dinners that can be boiled in a pouch and served immediately, whipped cream in dispenser cans, and so forth. In each case, the package changed the product in the minds of consumers and opened large markets. Packaging can also help make

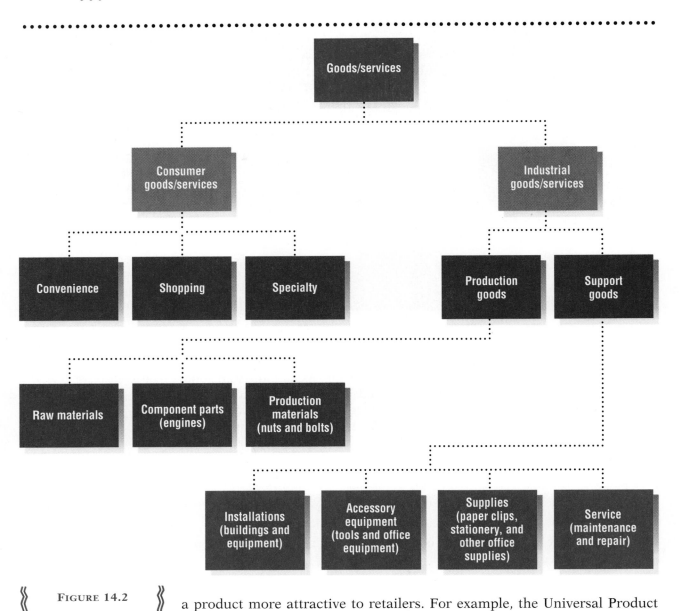

FIGURE 14.2

VARIOUS CLASSES OF CONSUMER AND INDUSTRIAL GOODS AND SERVICES

a product more attractive to retailers. For example, the Universal Product Codes on many packages make it easier to control inventory. In short, packaging changes the product by changing its visibility, usefulness, or attractiveness.

The latest in packaging is jumbo-sized portions. Pillsbury Company's Grands—biscuits that are 40 percent larger than the traditional biscuit—is Pillsbury's most successful new product in 126 years.[4] Other big-sized package successes include Healthy Choice's extra portion dinners, Oscar Mayer's Big & Juicy hot dogs, and Pizza Hut's Big Foot pizza.

••• THE GROWING IMPORTANCE OF PACKAGING •••

Packaging has always been an important aspect of the product offer, but today it's carrying more of the promotional burden than in the past. Many goods that were once sold by salespersons are now being sold in self-service outlets, and the package has been given more sales responsibility. As such the package must perform the following functions: (1) attract the buyer's attention, (2) describe the contents and give information about the contents, (3) explain the benefits of the good inside, (4) provide information on warranties, warnings, and other consumer matters, (5) give some indication of price, value,

Making Ethical Decisions

It's Not Easy Being Green

Manufacturers are increasingly torn between using packages that are good for the environment versus those that are good for marketing. Compact discs, for example, were packaged in 6-inch by 12-inch cardboard or plastic boxes a half-inch thick to hold a wafer-thin disc. This excess packaging created an environmental problem and the record industry responded by using a new, smaller package.

In Canada and Europe two record producers have voluntarily agreed to eliminate the "long box" for CDs. U.S. producers saw the large box as an excellent marketing tool. They used large, eye-catching graphics on them, which can't be placed on the current, smaller boxes. Also, large boxes discouraged shoplifting. Nonetheless, in a movement spearheaded by the Rykodisc record company, manufacturers responded to environmental concerns and changed the CD package. The cost to retailers was high because they had to put in new display units.

Environmentalists have put great pressure on all U.S. firms to be more environmentally concerned in their packaging. McDonald's, for example, trashed its foam sandwich containers made of polystyrene. Both Coke and Pepsi have announced that they plan to use recycled bottles.

Many people are now separating their rubbish into different categories to aid the recycling process. But it turns out that not all such efforts can be justified at this time on a cost basis alone. In fact, until technology improves, in certain instances it can still be more costly to recycle. However, with the goals of cleaning up the environment and saving natural resources recycling is a process businesses must continue to pursue.

When forced to choose between a package that makes a product more marketable and one that's recyclable or less damaging to the environment (e.g., that leads to less litter), which package should a marketer choose? What if you knew that another form of packaging was better for the environment than coated paper, but you could get a lot of publicity by shifting to paper? Would you shift to paper to get the publicity? What would be the consequences of your actions?

Would you have supported new laws to require U.S. producers to make smaller packages for CDs even if that resulted in fewer sales? What are the ethical issues?

Source: Faye Rice, "Who Scores Best on the Environment," *Fortune*, July 26, 1993, pp. 114–22; and Jeff Bailey, "Recycling Mania Crashes and Burns in California," *The Wall Street Journal*, April 26, 1994, pp. B1 and B5.

and uses, and (6) protect the goods inside, stand up under handling and storage, be tamperproof, and yet be easy to open and use. Clearly, packaging has become a critical part of product design. Even Perrier has added artwork to its signature green bottle to make it stand out from the crowd.

BUILDING A BRAND EQUITY

Closely related to packaging is branding. A **brand** is a name, symbol, or design (or combination of them) that identifies the goods or services of one seller or group of sellers and distinguishes them from those of competitors. The term *brand* is sufficiently comprehensive to include practically all means of identification of a product except perhaps the package and its shape. A *brand name*, remember, is that part of the brand consisting of a word, letter, or group of words or letters comprising a name that differentiates a seller's goods or services from those of competitors. Brand names you may be familiar with include QVC, Sony, Del Monte, Campbell, Levi, Snackwell's, Borden, Michelob, and Macintosh. Such brand names give products a distinction that tends to make them attractive to consumers.

brand
A name, symbol, or design (or combination of these) that identifies the goods or services of one seller or group of sellers and distinguishes them from those of competitors.

trademark
Brand that has been given exclusive legal protection for both the brand name and the pictorial design.

A **trademark** is a brand that has been given exclusive legal protection for both the brand name and the pictorial design. The trademarks shown below are widely recognized. So are trademarks such as McDonald's golden arches.

People are often impressed by certain brand names, even though they say they know there's no difference between brands in a given product category. For example, when people say that all aspirin is alike, put two bottles in front of them—one with the Anacin label and one labeled with an unknown brand. See which they choose. Most people choose the brand name even when they say there's no difference.

••• BRAND CATEGORIES •••

Several categories of brands are familiar to you. *National brand names* are the brand names of manufacturers that distribute the product nationally—Xerox, Polaroid, Kodak, Sony, and Chevrolet, for example.

Knockoff brands are illegal copies of national brand name goods such as Izod shirts or Rolex watches. If you see an expensive brand name item for sale at a ridiculously low price, you can be pretty sure it's a knockoff. Counterfeiters who copy U.S. brand names steal some $20 billion in business a year.

private brands
Products that do not carry the manufacturer's name, and carry the name of a distributor or retailer instead.

Private brands are products that don't carry the manufacturer's name, but carry a distributor or retailer's name instead. Kenmore and Diehard (Sears) are examples. These brands are also known as *house brands* or *distributor brands*.

generic name
The name of a product category.

Many manufacturers fear having their brand names become generic names. A **generic name** is the name for a product category. Did you know that aspirin and linoleum, which are now generic names for products, were once brand names? So were nylon, escalator, kerosene, and zipper. All those names became so popular, so identified with the product, that they lost their brand status and became generic (the name of the product category). Their producers then had to come up with new names. The original Aspirin, for example, became Bayer aspirin. Companies that are working hard to protect

Do you recognize these trademarks? What other trademarks stand out in your mind? McDonald's golden arches are known throughout the world. Is there any symbol more readily recognized?

their brand names today include Xerox (one ad reads, "Don't say 'Xerox it'; say 'Copy it' "), Styrofoam, and Rollerblade (in-line skating).

Generic goods are nonbranded products that usually sell at a sizable discount compared to national or private brands. They feature very basic packaging and are backed with little or no advertising. Some are copies of national brand names and may be close to the same quality, but others may be of minimum quality. There are generic tissues, generic cigarettes, generic peaches, and so forth. Consumers today are buying more generic products because their quality has improved so greatly that they approximate that of more expensive brand names.

••• BUILDING BRAND EQUITY AND LOYALTY •••

A major goal of advertisers in the future will be to reestablish the notion of brand equity. **Brand equity** is a combination of factors including awareness, loyalty, perceived quality, the feeling and images, and any other emotion people associate with a brand name. What has happened in the past is that companies have tried to boost their short-term performance by offering coupons and price discounts to move goods quickly. This eroded consumers' commitment to brand names. Now, companies realize the value of brand equity and are trying to measure the earning power of strong brand names.[5]

The core of brand equity is brand loyalty. **Brand loyalty** is the degree to which customers are satisfied, like the brand, and are committed to further purchases. A loyal group of customers represents substantial value to a firm, and that value can be calculated. Relationship marketing is designed to create brand loyalty.

Brand awareness means that your product is the first that comes to mind when a product category is mentioned. Advertising helps build strong brand awareness. Older brands, such as Coca-Cola and Pepsi, are usually the highest in brand awareness. *Event sponsorship* (the Winston-Salem auto races and Virginia Slims tennis tournament, for example) help improve awareness.

Perceived quality is an important part of brand equity. A product that's perceived as better quality than its competitors can be priced higher and thus improve profits. The key to creating a quality image is to identify what the consumer looks for in a quality product and then communicate a quality message in everything the company does. Quality cues include a high price, appearance, and reputation.

Today, it's so easy to copy a product's benefits that off-brand products are being developed to capture the market from brand name goods. Brand X diapers, for example, has increased its market share from 7 to 20 percent. Paragon Trade Brands gives retailers higher than normal margins and quickly matches the product innovations of the major companies. Brand name manufacturers have to develop new products even faster and promote their names better to hold off the challenge of lower-priced competitors.[6]

••• BUILDING BRAND ASSOCIATIONS •••

The name, symbol, and slogan a company uses can be great assets as they assist brand recognition and association. **Brand association** is the linking of a brand to other favorable images. For example, you can link a brand to other product users, to a popular celebrity, to a particular geographic area, or to competitors. Note, for example, how ads for Mercedes-Benz and

generic goods
Nonbranded products that usually sell at a sizable discount from national or private brands, have very basic packaging, and are backed with little or no advertising.

brand equity
Combination of factors such as awareness, loyalty, perceived quality, the feeling and images, and any other emotion people associate with a brand name.

brand loyalty
The degree to which customers are satisfied, like the brand, and are committed to further purchases.

brand awareness
The first product recalled when a product category is mentioned.

Associating brand names with famous athletic stars gives those brands more recognition and acceptance among young players and wannabe players. Shaquille O'Neal, who promotes Reebok, is just one such celebrity. Michael Jordan, Nike's most famous promoter, is such an influential athlete that the price of the stock of each of the major companies he endorses increased with his announcement in 1995, "I'm back!"

brand association
The linking of a brand to other, favorable images.

Cadillac associate those cars with rich people such as polo players. Note too the success of associating basketball shoes to stars such as Shaquille O'Neal and Michael Jordan (especially after his comeback). The person responsible for building brands is known as a *brand manager* or *product manager*. We'll explore that position right after the Progress Check.

PROGRESS CHECK

- What five functions does packaging now perform?
- What's the difference between a brand name and a trademark?
- Can you explain the difference between a national brand, a private brand, and a generic brand?
- What are the key components of brand equity?

PRODUCT MANAGEMENT

product manager
Coordinates all the marketing efforts for a particular product (or product line) or brand.

A **product manager** has direct responsibility for one brand or one product line, including all the elements of the marketing mix: product, place, promotion, and price. Imagine being the product manager for Fiberrific. You'd be responsible for everything having to do with that one brand. One reason many large consumer product producers have created this position is to have greater control over new-product development and product promotion. Many companies are now challenging the value of product managers. As some national brand names become less important to retailers, customers' brand loyalty declines. This gives product managers less power. The product management concept seems to be fading, and cross-functional teams and similar consumer-oriented forms of marketing are taking their place.

••• NEW-PRODUCT SUCCESS •••

Top Ten Reasons Products Fail

1. Strategic direction.
2. Product didn't deliver promise.
3. Positioning.
4. Little competitive difference.
5. Price/value relationship.
6. Management commitment.
7. Packaging.
8. Misleading research.
9. Development process.
10. Creative execution.

Source: *Marketing Tools*, November–December 1994, p. 20.

Chances that a new product will fail are overwhelmingly high, according to *The Wall Street Journal*, which reported that 86 percent of products introduced in one year failed to reach their business objectives. There were some 20,000 new products introduced in 1993. Products that don't deliver what they promise is a leading cause of new-product failure.[7] Other reasons for failure include poor positioning, not enough differences from competitors, and poor packaging. (See the chart in the margin.) Smaller firms may experience a lower success rate, but shouldn't if they do proper product planning. We'll discuss such planning next.

••• THE NEW-PRODUCT DEVELOPMENT PROCESS •••

As Figure 14.3 shows, product development for producers consists of several stages:

1. Idea generation.
2. Screening and analysis.
3. Development.
4. Testing.
5. Commercialization (bringing the product to the market).

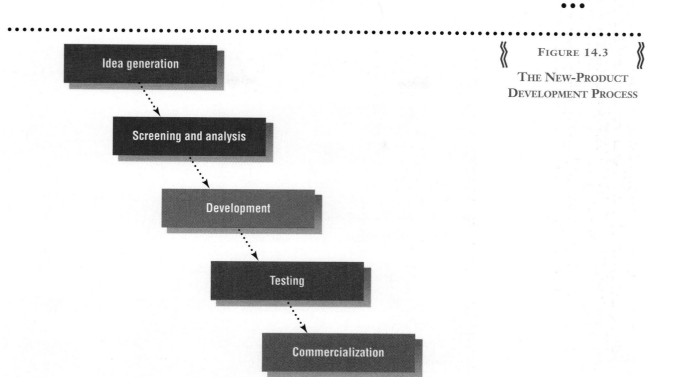

FIGURE 14.3

THE NEW-PRODUCT
DEVELOPMENT PROCESS

New products continue to pour into the market every year, and the profit potential looks tremendous. Think, for example, of the potential of interactive TV, large-screen HDTV sets, virtual reality games and products, hand-held computers, and other innovations. Where do these ideas come from? How are they tested? What's the life span for an innovation? The following material looks at these issues.

••• GENERATING NEW-PRODUCT IDEAS •••

Figure 14.4 gives you a good idea of where new-product ideas come from. Note that 38 percent of the new-product ideas for consumer goods come from analyzing competitors (the source of 27 percent of ideas for new industrial products). Such copying of competitors (as opposed to discovering new products) slows the introduction of new ideas.

A strong point can be made for listening to employee suggestions for new-product ideas.[8] The number one source of ideas for new industrial products has been company sources other than research and development. It was also a major source for new consumer goods. Part of that is due to successful marketing communication systems that monitor suggestions from all sources.

Look through Figure 14.4 carefully and think about the implications. Notice that more than a third of all new-product ideas for industrial products came from users, user research, or supplier suggestions. This finding emphasizes the principle that a firm should listen to its suppliers and customers and give them what they want.

••• PRODUCT SCREENING AND ANALYSIS •••

Product screening is designed to reduce the number of ideas being worked on at any one time. Criteria needed for screening include whether the product fits in well with present products, profit potential, marketability, and personnel requirements. (See Figure 14.5.) Each of these factors may be assigned a weight, and total scores are then computed.

FIGURE 14.4

SOURCES OF
NEW-PRODUCT IDEAS

This survey shows where ideas for new products originate. As you know, research plays an important role in the development of new products.

CONSUMER PRODUCTS (based on a survey of 79 new products)	
Analysis of the competition	38.0%
Company sources other than research and development	31.6
Consumer research	17.7
Research and development	13.9
Consumer suggestions	12.7
Published information	11.4
Supplier suggestions	3.8

INDUSTRIAL PRODUCTS (based on a survey of 152 new products)	
Company sources other than research and development	36.2%
Analysis of the competition	27.0
Research and development	24.3
Product users	15.8
Supplier suggestions	12.5
Product user research	10.5
Published information	7.9

When products reach the mature stage of the product life cycle, it is usually necessary to introduce new products or ideas in order to generate growth. This Hearth Express restaurant in Darien, Illinois, developed by McDonalds, is an experimental restaurant testing out the idea of family-style meals to compete with Boston Market and other similar restaurants.

Product analysis is done after product screening. It's largely a matter of making cost estimates and sales forecasts to get a feeling for profitability. Products that don't meet the established criteria are withdrawn from further consideration.

••• PRODUCT DEVELOPMENT AND TESTING •••

If a product passes the screening and analysis phase, the firm begins to develop it further. A product idea can be developed into many different product concepts (alternative product offerings based on the same product idea that have different meanings and values to consumers). For example, a firm might want to test the concept of a chicken dog—a hot dog made of chicken that tastes like an all-beef hot dog.

Concept testing involves taking a product idea to consumers to test their reactions. (See Figure 14.6.) Do they see the benefits of this new product? How frequently would they buy it? At what price? What features do they like and dislike? What changes would they make? Different samples are tested using different packaging, branding, ingredients, and so forth until a product emerges that's desirable from both production and marketing perspectives. Can you see the importance of concept testing for Fiberrific?

Areas of company strengths and weaknesses	Consumer promotional considerations
Tie-ins with, or potential impact on, other company brands	Nature of competition
	Market segments
Production capabilities	Distribution channels
Consumer attitudes toward category	Trade perceptions of category
Awareness	Turnover rates/optimum inventory
Satisfaction with existing brands	allocations
Regional consumer differences	Seasonal characteristics
Advertising and merchandising norms, timing, and directions	Price margins

FIGURE 14.5

CRITERIA FOR SCREENING NEW-PRODUCT IDEAS
Ideas for new products are carefully screened. This screening helps the company identify the areas where new products are needed and reduces the chance of a company working on too many ideas at a time.

••• COMMERCIALIZATION •••

Even if a product tests well, it may take quite a while before the product achieves success in the market. Take the introduction of the zipper, for example. It was one of the longest development efforts on record for a consumer product. Whitcomb Judson received his first patents in the early 1890s. It took more than 15 years to perfect the product, but even then consumers weren't interested. The company suffered numerous financial setbacks, name changes, and relocations before settling in Meadville, Pennsylvania. Finally, the U.S. Navy started using Judson's zippers during World War I. Today, Talon Inc. is the leading U.S. maker of zippers, producing some 500 million of them a year.

This example shows that the marketing effort must include commercialization. This includes (1) promoting the product to distributors and retailers to get wide distribution and (2) developing strong advertising and sales campaigns to generate and maintain interest in the product among distributors and consumers.

FIGURE 14.6

STEPS TO TAKE BEFORE TEST MARKETING A PRODUCT
Product development, communication development, and strategy development all are used as a company develops a new product. Extensive testing is used to guarantee the new product's success.

PRODUCT DEVELOPMENT	COMMUNICATION DEVELOPMENT	STRATEGY DEVELOPMENT
Identify unfilled need	Select a name	Set marketing goals
Preliminary profit/payout plan for each concept	Design a package and test	Establish marketing strategy
Concept test	Create a copy theme and test	Develop marketing mix (after communication developed)
Determine whether the product can be made	Develop complete ads and test	Estimate cost of marketing plan and payout (after product development)
Test the concept and product (and revise as indicated)		
Develop the product		
Run extended product use tests		

••• THE INTERNATIONAL CHALLENGE •••

> "Product development time is going to be a great competitive battleground in the 1990s—as intense, I would say, as the revolutionary push for quality in the Eighties."
>
> Allan Gilmour, executive vice president of Ford Motor Company

Wolfgang Schmitt of Rubbermaid learned through experience that the secret to success in today's rapidly changing environment is to bring out new products, high in quality, and to bring them out quickly. This is especially true in light of the rapid development process occurring in other countries.

Xerox executives were surprised by Japanese competitors who were developing new copier models twice as fast as Xerox and at half the cost. Xerox had to slash its traditional four-to-five-year product development cycle. After millions of dollars of investment, Xerox can now produce a new model in two years—which still isn't as fast as the Japanese.

The big three automakers all recently formed task forces to cut product development cycles that had swollen to nearly five years. The Japanese were taking about three-and-a-half-year cycles. To stay competitive in world markets, U.S. businesses must develop an entirely new product development process. To keep products competitive requires continuous, incremental improvements in function, cost, and quality. Cost-sensitive design and new process technologies are critical. Remember, constant white water is always threatening to wash you overboard.

More attention in the United States must be given the product development process; that is, developing products in cooperation with their users. To implement the new-product development process, managers must go out into the market and interact closely with their dealers and their ultimate customers. Successful new-product development is an interactive process whereby customers present their needs, and new-product designs are prepared to meet those needs. Changes are made over time to make sure that the total product offer exactly meets the customer's needs. The focus shifts from internal product development processes to external customer responsiveness.

Global marketers today use cross-functional teams to develop new products. Teams from production, marketing, engineering, and other departments go to customers in other countries and learn what they want. The team then works together to quickly meet those customers' needs.

product life cycle
The four-stage theoretical depiction of the process from birth to death of a product class: introduction, growth, maturity, and decline.

Product modification is one way companies seek to extend the product life cycle. For example, the VW beetle, introduced commercially in 1946, was extremely popular in the United States until the 1980s, but then lost some appeal. The new version of the product is clearly more modern, yet recognizes its ancestry. Do you think VW has a winner this time?

THE PRODUCT LIFE CYCLE

Once a product has been developed, tested, and placed on the market, it goes through a life cycle consisting of four stages: introduction, growth, maturity, and decline. This is called the *product life cycle*. (See Figure 14.7.) The **product life cycle** is a theoretical model of what happens to sales and profits for a product class (for example, all dishwasher soaps) over time. However, not all

Reaching Beyond Our Borders

A Global View of Product Design

American product development specialists can learn much from studying how the Japanese have so successfully introduced products into the U.S. market. The secret is rather simple. They carefully observe what Americans do and buy; then they design products specifically for observed wants and needs. For example, a Japanese shoe manufacturer flew to New York with a high-powered camera and lens to film people's feet as they walked by. The purpose? The manufacturer wanted to see the kinds of shoes worn by people in a hurry to get someplace. This type of observational research has helped the Japanese penetrate many U.S. markets.

To compete with such dedication to customer satisfaction, U.S. manufacturers must become equally devoted to finding out what people want in other countries. "Find a need and fill it" will still be a viable slogan throughout the 21st century. That includes studying the culture, history, and values of people in various countries.

Product design specialists must do as the Japanese do: visit and research consumers in various countries. Learn how they shop and use products. Study their reactions to price promotions, advertising, and other marketing efforts. Learn the culture and the language. Only then can the United States produce products that will be as well accepted in international markets as foreign products that were designed in this way are accepted in the United States.

Source: Kerry Pechter, "Sound Strategy?" *International Business*, April 1994, p. 84; Stephen J. Simurda, "Trade Secrets," *Entrepreneur*, May 1994, pp. 99–103; and Cyndee Miller, "Going Overseas Requires Marketers to Learn More than a New Language," *Marketing News*, March 28, 1994, p. 8.

products follow the life cycle, and particular brands may act differently. For example, while frozen foods as a generic class may go through the entire cycle, one brand may never get beyond the introduction stage. Nonetheless, the product life cycle provides a basis for anticipating future market developments and for planning marketing strategies. Some products, such as microwave ovens, stay in the introductory stage for years. Other products, such as fad clothing, may go through the entire cycle in a few months.

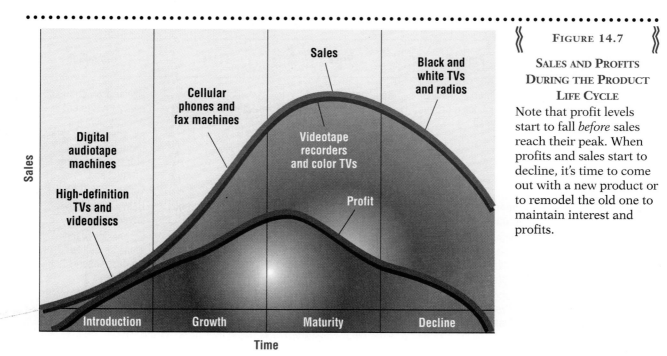

FIGURE 14.7

SALES AND PROFITS DURING THE PRODUCT LIFE CYCLE
Note that profit levels start to fall *before* sales reach their peak. When profits and sales start to decline, it's time to come out with a new product or to remodel the old one to maintain interest and profits.

••• EXAMPLE OF THE PRODUCT LIFE CYCLE •••

You can see how the product life cycle works by looking at the introduction of instant coffee. When it was introduced, most people didn't like it as well as "regular" coffee, and it took several years to gain general acceptance (introduction stage). At one point, though, instant coffee grew rapidly in popularity, and many brands were introduced (rapid-growth stage). After a while, people became attached to one brand and sales leveled off (maturity stage). Sales then went into a slight decline when freeze-dried coffees were introduced (decline stage). At present, freeze-dried coffee is at the maturity stage. It's extremely important to recognize what stage a product is in because such an analysis leads to more intelligent and efficient marketing decisions.

••• THE IMPORTANCE OF THE PRODUCT LIFE CYCLE •••

The importance of the product life cycle to marketers is this: Different stages in the product life cycle call for different strategies. Figure 14.8 outlines the marketing mix decisions that might be made. As you go through the table, you'll see that each stage calls for multiple marketing mix changes. Next, we'll walk through the product life cycle together and discuss what happens at each stage.

Figure 14.9 shows what happens to sales volume, competition, and profit/loss during the product life cycle. Such figures are revealing. For instance, they show that a product at the mature stage may reach the top in sales growth while profit is decreasing. At that stage, a marketing manager may decide to create a new image for the product to start a new growth cycle. Note, for example, how Arm & Hammer baking soda gets a new image every few years to generate new sales. One year it's positioned as a deodorant for refrigerators and the next as a substitute for harsh chemicals in swimming pools. Knowing what stage in the cycle a product is in helps marketing managers decide when such strategic changes are needed. Figure 14.8 summarizes the decision making that occurs at each level of the product life cycle.

FIGURE 14.8

SAMPLE STRATEGIES FOLLOWED DURING THE PRODUCT LIFE CYCLE

	Marketing Mix Elements			
Life Cycle Stage	**Product**	**Price**	**Place**	**Promotion**
Introduction	Offer market-tested product; keep product mix small	Go after innovators with high introductory price (skimming strategy) or use penetration pricing	Use wholesalers, selective distribution	Dealer promotion and heavy investment in primary demand advertising and sales promotion to get stores to carry the product and consumers to try it.
Growth	Improve product; keep product mix limited	Adjust price to meet competition	Increase distribution	Heavy competitive advertising
Maturity	Differentiate your product to satisfy different market segments	Further reduce price	Take over wholesaling function and intensify distribution	Emphasize brand name as well as product benefits and differences
Decline	Cut product mix; develop new-product ideas	Consider price increase	Consolidate distribution; drop some outlets	Reduce advertising to only loyal customers

In what stage of the product life cycle are laptop computers? What does Figure 14.8 indicate firms should do at that stage? What will the next stage be? What might you do at that stage to optimize profits?

Peanut butter is in the maturity or decline stage of the product life cycle. Does that explain why Skippy introduced a reduced fat version of its peanut butter? What other variations on older products have been introduced in the last few years?

••• EXTENDING THE LIFE CYCLE •••

Most products are in the maturity stage of the product life cycle; therefore, marketing managers deal often with mature products. The goal is to extend product life so that sales and profits don't decline. One strategy is called *market modification*. **Market modification** means that marketing managers look for new users and market segments. Did you know, for example, that the backpacks that so many college students carry were originally designed for the military? The search for new users led to the present-day backpack.

Market modification also means searching for increased usage among present customers. That's what Arm & Hammer does by finding new uses for its baking soda. Finally, a marketer may reposition the product to appeal to new market segments. Once 7-Up was considered a mix for drinks using whiskey or bourbon. It was repositioned as an alternative to colas (the UnCola) and penetrated new markets. What could we do to extend Fiberrific's product life cycle when it reaches the decline stage? Alternatives include going for a different market, such as senior citizens, or positioning the product as a snack as well as a cereal.

Another product extension strategy, **product modification**, involves changing product quality, features, or style to attract new users or more usage from present users. American auto manufacturers are using quality improvement to recapture world markets. Similarly, new features are keeping the sales of videotape recorders going. Customers can now edit tapes, receive stereo broadcasts, watch one show, have another show in the corner of the screen, and more. Style changes can also extend a product's life. Note, for example, how auto manufacturers once changed styles dramatically from year to year to keep demand from falling. That strategy was called *planned obsolescence* because it made autos obsolete in style long before they were obsolete in engineering.

Different stages in the product life cycle call for different pricing strategies. Next we'll discuss pricing—a key management decision in product design.

market modification
Technique used to extend the life cycle of mature products by finding new users and market segments.

product modification
Technique used to extend the life cycle of mature products by changing the product quality, features, or style to attract new users or more usage from present users.

〉〉 **FIGURE 14.9** 〈〈

HOW SALES, PROFITS, AND COMPETITION VARY OVER THE PRODUCT LIFE CYCLE
All products go through these stages at various times in their life cycle. What happens to sales as a product matures?

LIFE CYCLE STAGE	SALES	PROFITS	COMPETITORS
Introduction	Low sales	Losses may occur	Few
Growth	Rapidly rising sales	Very high profits	Growing number
Maturity	Peak sales	Declining profits	Stable number, then declining
Decline	Falling sales	Profits may fall to become losses	Declining number

- What are the five steps in the new-product development process?
- Can you draw a product life cycle and label its parts?
- Can you give one marketing strategy in product, price, place, or advertising for each stage? (See Figure 14.8.)
- Can you explain the difference between market modification and product modification, and give examples of each?

COMPETITIVE PRICING

Pricing is so important to marketing that it has been singled out as one of the four Ps in the marketing mix, along with product, place, and promotion. Price is also a critical ingredient in consumer evaluations of the product. In this section, we'll explore price both as an ingredient of the product and as a strategic marketing tool.

••• PRICING OBJECTIVES •••

A firm may have several objectives in mind when setting a pricing strategy. When pricing Fiberrific, we may want to promote the product's image. If we price it high and use the right promotion, maybe we can make it the Evian of cereals, which we discussed earlier. We also might price it high to achieve a certain profit objective. We could also price Fiberrific lower than its competitors because we want poor people and older people to be able to afford this nutritional cereal. That is, we could have some social or ethical goal in mind. Low pricing may also discourage competition because the profit potential is less in this case. A low price may also help us capture a larger share of the market. The point is that a firm may have several pricing strategies, and it must formulate these objectives clearly before developing an overall pricing objective. Popular strategies include

1. *Achieving a target profit*. Ultimately, the goal of marketing is to make a profit by providing goods and services to others. Naturally, one long-run pricing objective of almost all firms is to optimize profit.

2. *Building traffic*. Supermarkets often advertise certain products at or below cost to attract people to the store. These products are called *loss leaders*. The long-run objective is to make profits by following the short-run objective of building a customer base.

3. *Achieving greater market share*. The auto industry is in a fierce international battle to capture and hold market share. U.S. producers lost market share to foreign producers and have used price incentives (and quality) to win it back.

4. *Increasing sales*. Sometimes a firm will lower prices to increase sales even though such low prices may harm short-run profit margins. For example, RJR Reynolds lowered its cigarette prices in 1993 to pay off debts. Such a move could hurt profit margins in the short run, but will enable the company to become more financially secure for the long run. Then prices could again be raised.[9]

5. *Creating an image*. Certain watches, perfumes, and other socially visible products are priced high to give them an image of exclusivity and status.

6. *Furthering social objectives.* A firm may want to price a product low so that people with less money can afford the product. Often, governments get involved in pricing farm products so that everyone can get basic needs such as milk and bread at a low price.

Another objective may be to avoid government investigation and control. Large, powerful firms can't price their products so low that they drive out competitors for fear of government involvement. Wal-Mart gained much of its market share with a simple motto: "Always the low price. Always." But recently an Arkansas judge ruled that Wal-Mart's prices were too low and that the chain had illegally engaged in predatory pricing tactics (tactics designed to drive competitors out of business). Although the ruling applied only to Arkansas, Wal-Mart may be more careful in setting such low prices in the future.[10]

Note that a firm may have short-run objectives that differ greatly from its long-run objectives. Both should be understood at the beginning and put into the strategic marketing plan. Pricing objectives should be influenced by other marketing decisions regarding product design, packaging, branding, distribution, and promotion. All of these marketing decisions are interrelated.

People believe rather intuitively that the price charged for a product must bear some relation to the cost of producing the product. In fact, we'd generally agree that prices are usually set somewhere above cost. But as we'll see, prices and cost aren't always related.

• • • COST-BASED PRICING • • •

Producers often use cost as a primary basis for setting price. They develop elaborate cost accounting systems to measure production costs (including materials, labor, and overhead), add in some margin of profit, and come up with a price. The question is whether the price will be satisfactory to the market as well. In the long run, the market—not the producer—determines what the price will be.

Cost-driven pricing has been cited as the reason that the United States lost much of the consumer electronics industry. The United States had the technology and the products, but it used cost-based pricing. The price ended up being too high. The Japanese, on the other hand, used price-led costing. That is, the Japanese determined what the market was willing to pay (price) and then designed products to fit those prices. Eventually, the Japanese won most of the market.[11] Today, many U.S. producers are as good as the best in the world and are begining to recapture lost market share, such as automobiles, from international competitors.

• • • VALUE PRICING • • •

Value pricing means that marketers are providing consumers with brand name goods and services at fair prices. Apple Computer, for example, offered an Apple Macintosh Classic for half the price of the equivalent Macintosh SE computers that it had sold in the past. It was a great computer for a lot less money than earlier models. In short, it was a strong value.

value pricing
Offering consumers brand name goods and services at fair prices.

Taco Bell had great success with a "value" menu offering 59-cent tacos and 14 other items for 79 cents or 99 cents. General Motors joined the "value" pricers by offering a special two-door Pontiac Grand Prix for $17,000 that had sold for $26,000 the previous year.

Manufacturers and service organizations, as you might expect, are finding it hard to maintain profits while offering value pricing to consumers. The only way to offer value prices and not go broke is to redesign products from the

Value pricing has been a big success for Taco Bell. Its value meals at 59 cents, 79 cents, and 99 cents are major competitors for the hamburger chains. Taco Bell did some additional product modification recently to broaden its appeal to health conscious consumers by introducing a line of low-fat meals. What other strategies could Taco Bell develop to generate growth?

bottom up and to cut costs wherever possible. Taco Bell, for example, cut its kitchen space to provide more seating and specifically designed its menu to make more items that took little kitchen space to prepare. Now 70 percent of the restaurant is seating compared with 30 percent in the past.

McDonald's had to respond to Taco Bell's value pricing with its own value package. It began, for example, offering "value meals" such as a Big Mac, a large order of fries, and a medium drink for $3.59. Some companies are refurbishing old equipment and selling it at attractive prices. Again, the idea is to sell brand name items at low prices.

••• VALUE PRICING IN THE SERVICE SECTOR •••

Value pricing isn't just for fast-food restaurants and grocery stores. It's rapidly becoming part of the service sector as well. Airlines, for example, are struggling to meet the pricing challenge of low-cost carriers such as Southwest Airlines.[12] The chairman of Seabrook Marketing calls Southwest's pricing strategy "Sam's Club with wings."

Continental Airlines and USAir Group are actively trying to meet the price competition. Continental, for example, introduced no-frills Peanuts Fares on more than half of its daily flights. Its ads said, "Big airline service. Small airline prices." USAir responded with ads saying, "USAir's low fares. No strings attached."

Service industries are adopting many of the same pricing tactics as goods-producing firms. They begin by cutting costs as much as possible. Then they determine what services are most important to customers. Those services that aren't important are cut. For example, some airlines have eliminated meals on their flights. Southwest doesn't incur the administrative costs of assigned seats. In return, customers get good value.

The bigger airlines are trying to cut costs, but are stuck with high fixed costs. American Airlines often won't even try to match other airlines' prices. It must offer exceptional service to compete. United Airlines is creating an airline within the airline, called U2, that will offer low fares on shorter routes. New airlines like Kiwi International Airlines out of New Jersey, Midway Airlines out of Raleigh-Durham, and Valu-Jet Airlines out of Atlanta all offer low fares for short-haul flights.[13]

With both goods and services, the idea is to give the consumer value. But trying to give the consumer value while maintaining profits is a challenge. Break-even analysis helps an organization relate sales, profit, and price. We'll explore that concept next.

••• BREAK-EVEN ANALYSIS •••

break-even analysis
The process used to determine profitability at various levels of sales.

Before we go into the business of producing Fiberrific cereal, it may be wise to determine how many boxes of cereal we'd have to sell before making a profit. We'd then determine whether we could reach such a sales goal. **Break-even analysis** is the process used to determine profitability at various levels

Additional Pricing Tactics

It's impossible to cover all pricing tactics in detail in this book, but you should at least be familiar with the following terms:

1. *Adaptive pricing* allows an organization to vary its prices based on factors such as competition, market conditions, and resource costs. Rather than relying on one set price, the firm adjusts the price to fit different situations.

2. *Cost-oriented pricing* is the "strategy of setting prices primarily on the basis of cost." For example, retailers often use cost plus a certain markup, while producers use a system of cost-plus pricing.

3. *Customary pricing* means that most sellers will adapt the product to some established, universally accepted price such as the price for gum or candy bars. Notice that when the price goes up, almost all producers adjust their price upward.

4. *Product-line pricing* is the procedure used to set prices for a group of products that are similar but aimed at different market segments. For example, a beer producer might have a low-priced beer, a popular-priced beer, and a premium-priced beer.

5. *Target pricing* means that an organization will set some goal such as a certain share of the market or a certain return on investment as a basis for setting a price. Usually, market conditions prevent a firm from establishing prices this way, but such goals do give some direction to pricing policies.

6. *Uniform pricing*, also known as a *single-price policy*, means that all customers buying the product (given similar circumstances) pay the same price. Although it's the most common policy in the United States, uniform pricing is unusual in many foreign markets, especially among private sellers.

7. *Odd pricing* or *psychological pricing* means pricing an item a few cents under a round price ($9.98 instead of $10) to make the product appear less expensive.

8. *Price lining* is the practice of offering goods at a few set prices such as $30, $40, and $50. Such a tactic makes both pricing and checkout easier, and it appeals to a market segment interested in that level of pricing.

of sales. The break-even point is the point where revenues from sales equal all costs. Let's say it costs you $1,000 to build and stock a vending cart that sells ice cream products and your average revenue is $5 per sale. You have to sell 200 products to cover the fixed costs of the cart and the cost of all the products you bought to go into the cart. Anything sold in excess of 200 products results in a profit; fewer than 200 items sold results in a loss.

What would the break-even point be if the cost of the cart and products sold was only $500? How would increasing the price affect the break-even point?

CRITICAL THINKING

••• PRICING STRATEGIES •••

Let's say a firm has just developed a new line of products, such as high-definition television (HDTV) sets. The firm has to decide how to price these sets at the introductory stage of the product life cycle. One strategy would be to price them high to recover the costs of developing the sets and to take advantage of the fact that there are few competitors. A **skimming price strategy** is one in which a new product is priced high to make optimum profit while there's little competition. Of course, those large profits will attract competitors. That happened with the high-priced HDTVs introduced in the 1990s.

A second strategy is to price them low. This would attract more buyers and discourage others companies from making sets because the profit is so low. This strategy enables the firm to penetrate or capture a large share of the market quickly. A **penetration strategy**, therefore, is one in which a product is priced low to attract more customers and discourage competitors.[14] The Japanese successfully used a penetration strategy with videotape recorders. No U.S. firm could compete with the low prices the Japanese offered.

skimming price strategy
Method of pricing by which the product is priced high to make optimum profit while there is little competition.

penetration strategy
Method of pricing by which a product is priced low to attract more customers and discourage competitors.

We think we've figured out why people hate shopping for a car.

Oldsmobile Simplified Pricing

It's very simple, really. Shopping for a car has become too complicated. All those confusing option packages and rebates. Hours of haggling. Ugh. That's why we're making it simpler. By equipping every new Oldsmobile with the most popular options, standard. By taking out confusing rebates – but leaving in the savings. So our retailers can give you their best price right upfront. Without a lot of haggling. Funny, but people really seem to like our new way of doing business. Go figure. Demand Better. Oldsmobile

Oldsmobile recognized and responded to the discontent among consumers with regard to pricing. It introduced its new no-haggle pricing with this ad. What do you think of no-haggle pricing by auto dealers? Do you think that there are some consumers out there who actually prefer negotiating the price because they think they can get a better deal? How should dealers handle such people?

Ultimately, price is determined by supply and demand in the marketplace, as described in Chapter 2. For example, if we charge $2 for our cereal and nobody buys it at that price, we'll have to lower the price until we reach a price that's acceptable to customers and to us. The price that results from the interaction of buyers and sellers in the marketplace is called the *market price*.

Recognizing the fact that different consumers may be willing to pay different prices, marketers sometimes price on the basis of consumer demand rather than cost or some other calculation. That's called *demand-oriented pricing* and is reflected by movie theaters with low rates for children and by drugstores with discounts for senior citizens.

Besides supply and demand forces, another factor in the marketplace is competition. *Price leadership* is the procedure by which all competitors in an industry follow the pricing practices of one or more dominant firms. You may have noticed that practice among oil and cigarette companies. *Competition-oriented pricing* is a strategy based on what all the other competitors are doing. The price can be at, above, or below competitors' prices. Pricing depends on customer loyalty, perceived differences, and the competitive climate.

••• NONPRICE COMPETITION •••

In spite of the emphasis placed on price in microeconomic theory, marketers often compete on product attributes other than price. You may have noted that price differences between products such as gasoline, men's haircuts, candy bars, and even major products such as compact cars and private colleges are often small, if there's any difference at all. Typically, you will not see price used as a major promotional appeal on television. Instead, marketers tend to stress product images and consumer benefits such as comfort, style, convenience, and durability.

Many organizations promote the services that accompany basic products rather than price. The idea is to make a relatively homogeneous product "better" by offering more service. For example, some airlines stress friendliness, promptness, more flights, better meals, and other such services. Higher priced hotels stress "no surprises," cable TV, business services, health clubs, and other extras.

Often marketers emphasize nonprice differences because prices are so easy to match. On the other hand, few competitors can match the image of a friendly, responsive, consumer-oriented company. Other strategies for avoiding price wars include[15]

1. *Add value.* Some drugstores with elderly customers add value by offering home delivery. Training videos add value to any product that's difficult to use. Toro gives lawn parties during which it teaches customers lawn care strategies.

2. *Educate consumers.* Home Depot teaches its customers how to use the equipment it sells and how to build decks and other do-it-yourself

••

FROM THE PAGES OF...
Entrepreneur®
MAGAZINE

Deborah Hellman runs the Northbrook, Illinois, doll art gallery, Dolls Etcetera Ltd. Hellman began by collecting dolls herself. When she found that there were few places to buy doll art, she opened her own gallery. She says that her dolls aren't really collectibles or toys. "They are a new art form."

You can see that the dolls aren't toys when you examine the prices—the average is $4,000. Some run as high as $22,000. The more realistic the doll, the more

Hello Dolly

popular it tends to be. Despite their high prices, customers have continued to buy them even when the economy has been in a slump.

Do you think that Hellman could earn more money by pricing her dolls lower? Higher? How does one go about pricing such rare art objects? As a consumer, how do you know if the price is too high or too low?

Source: Karen Sulkis, "Hello Dolly," *Entrepreneur*, September 1994, p. 192.

---

projects. The Iowa Beef Processors educate their customers about the value of buying better-grade beef with less waste.

3. *Establish relationships.* Customers will pay a little more for products and services when they have a friendly relationship with the seller. Today some auto dealers, for example, Saturn, may send out cards reminding people when service is needed. They may also have picnics and other special events for customers. Airlines, supermarkets, hotels, and car rental agencies have frequent buyer clubs that offer all kinds of fringe benefits to frequent users. The services aren't less expensive, but they offer more value.

As you can see, this chapter begins and ends with one theme: Give customers value and they'll give you their loyalty.

- Can you list two short-term and two long-term pricing objectives? Are the two compatible?
- What's wrong with using a cost-based pricing strategy?
- What's the purpose of break-even analysis?
- Can you calculate a product's break-even point if producing it costs $10,000 and revenue from the sale of one unit is $20?

PROGRESS CHECK

---

1. Product development means developing a value package for each product and developing a product mix that will appeal to a variety of consumers.

- ***What's the difference between a product and a value package?***

A product is any physical good, service, or idea that satisfies a want or need. A value package is much more than a physical object. A value package consists of all the tangibles and intangibles (things you can't touch) that consumers evaluate when deciding whether to buy something. A value package includes price, brand name, satisfaction in use, and more.

- ***What's the difference between a product line and a product mix?***

A product line is a group of physically similar products. (A product line of gum may include chewing gum, sugarless gum, bubble gum, etc.) A product mix is a company's combination of product lines. (A manufacturer may offer lines of gum, candy bars, chewing tobacco, etc.)

SUMMARY
••••••

1. Explain the difference between a product and a value package and between a product line and a product mix.

2. Describe how businesses create product differentiation for their goods and services in both consumer and industrial markets.

2. Product differentiation is what makes one product appear better than the competition in both consumer and industrial markets.
   - *How do marketers create product differentiation for their goods and services?*
   Marketers use a mix of pricing, advertising, and packaging to make their products seem unique and attractive.
   - *What are the three classifications of consumer goods and services and how are they marketed?*
   There are convenience goods and services (requiring minimum shopping effort), shopping goods and services (for which people compare price and quality), and specialty goods and services (which consumers go out of their way to get). Convenience goods and services are best promoted by location, shopping goods and services by some price/quality appeal, and specialty goods and services by word of mouth.
   - *What are industrial goods and how are they marketed differently from consumer goods?*
   Industrial goods are products used in the production of other products. They're sold largely through salespeople and rely less on advertising.

3. List the six functions of packaging.

3. Packaging changes the product and is becoming increasingly important, taking over much of the sales function for consumer goods.
   - *What are the six functions of packaging?*
   The six functions are (1) to attract the buyer's attention, (2) to describe the contents, (3) to explain the benefits of the product inside, (4) to provide information on warranties, warnings, and other consumer matters, (5) to indicate price, value, and uses, and (6) to protect the goods inside, stand up under handling and storage, be tamperproof, and yet be easy to open and use.

4. Give examples of a brand, a brand name, and a trademark, and explain how to prevent a brand name from becoming generic.

4. Branding also changes a product.
   - *Can you give examples of a brand, a brand name, and a trademark?*
   There are endless examples. One example of a brand name of crackers is Waverly by Nabisco. The brand consists of the name Waverly as well as the symbol (a red triangle in the corner with Nabisco circled in white). The brand name and the symbol are also trademarks, since Nabisco has been given legal protection for this brand.

5. Explain the role of product managers and the five steps of the new-product development process.

5. Product managers are like presidents of one-product firms.
   - *What are the functions of a product manager?*
   Product managers coordinate product, place, promotion, and price decisions for a particular product. In many companies the product manager's role is gradually losing its importance as consumer brand loyalty decreases.
   - *What are the five steps of the product development process?*
   The steps are: (1) generation of new-product ideas, (2) screening and analysis, (3) development, (4) testing, and (5) commercialization.

6. Identify and describe the stages of the product life cycle and describe marketing strategies at each stage.

6. Once a product is placed on the market, marketing strategy varies as the product goes through various stages of acceptance called the product life cycle.
   - *What are the stages of the product life cycle?*
   They are introduction, growth, maturity, and decline.
   - *How do marketing strategies change at the various stages?*
   See Figure 14.7.

7. Pricing is one of the four Ps of marketing. It can also be viewed as part of the product concept.

- ***What are pricing objectives?***

  Objectives include achieving a target profit, building traffic, increasing market share, increasing sales, creating an image, and meeting social goals.

- ***What's the break-even point?***

  At the break-even point, total cost equals total revenue. Sales beyond that point are profitable.

- ***What strategies can marketers use to determine a product's price?***

  A skimming price strategy is one in which the product is priced high to make optimum profit while there's little competition, whereas a penetration strategy is one in which a product is priced low to attract more customers and discourage competitors. Demand-oriented pricing is based on consumer demand rather than cost. Competition-oriented pricing is based on all competitors' prices. Price leadership occurs when all competitors follow the pricing practice of one or more dominant companies. Please review p. 445 to be sure you understand all the terms used for other pricing tactics.

7. Give examples of various pricing objectives and show how break-even analysis helps in pricing decisions.

KEY TERMS

brand 441
brand association 444
brand awareness 443
brand equity 443
brand loyalty 443
break-even
 analysis 454
constant white-
 water 434
convenience goods
 and services 437
generic goods 443
generic name 442

industrial goods 438
market
 modification 451
penetration
 strategy 455
private brands 442
product
 differentiation 437
product life cycle 448
product line 436
product manager 444
product mix 436

product
 modification 451
shopping goods and
 services 437
skimming price
 strategy 455
specialty goods and
 services 438
trademark 442
value package 435
value pricing 453

DEVELOPING WORKPLACE SKILLS

1. Notice the different types of shoes that students are wearing. What product qualities were they looking for when they chose those shoes? What was the importance of price, style, brand name, and color? Describe the product offerings you would feature in a new shoe store designed to appeal to college students.

2. A product offer consists of all the tangibles and intangibles that consumers evaluate when choosing among products including price, package, service, reputation, and so on. Compose a list of as many tangibles and intangibles that consumers might consider when evaluating the following products: a vacation resort, tennis shoes, a college, and a new car.

3. Discuss how the faculty at your college could increase student satisfaction by working more closely with students in developing new products (courses) and changing existing products (courses). Would it be a good idea for all marketers to work with their customers that way? Discuss.

4. Go to your medicine cabinet and inventory all the branded and non-branded items. Then discuss with the class the brand names they buy for the same goods. Do most students buy brand name goods or generic goods? Why?

5. Determine where in the product life cycle you would place each of the following products and then prepare a marketing strategy for each product based on the recommendations in this chapter:

a. Alka Seltzer

b. Cellular phones

c. Electric automobiles

d. Campbell's chicken noodle soup

. . . .

PRACTICING MANAGEMENT DECISIONS

⧚ CASE   EVERYDAY LOW PRICING (EDLP) ⧚

Wal-Mart, Kmart, and wholesale clubs such as Price Club have had great success with a concept they call *everyday low pricing (EDLP)*. Rather than have relatively high prices and then barrage consumers with coupons and price discounts, such stores promote the fact that they offer lower prices every day. Similarly, some manufacturers are offering everyday low purchasing prices. Instead of having a relatively high price for products sold **to** retailers, manufacturers such as Procter & Gamble have everyday low purchase prices. It's the same concept as EDLP applied to retailers instead of consumers.

Many retailers have decided to follow the lead of Wal-Mart and others by cutting prices on all their goods. But recent research shows that this isn't always wise. Dominick's Finer Foods, with 28 percent of the Chicago-area food business, tried an EDLP policy and boosted sales by 3 percent. On the other hand, profits declined by 18 percent. It has been calculated, in fact, that supermarket volume would have to increase by 39 percent for supermarkets to avoid losing money after a 7 percent price drop. Consumers say location is usually their most important factor in choosing a supermarket. Thus, supermarkets shouldn't have to have the lowest prices to keep market share.

In spite of the potential drawbacks of everyday low pricing, 7-Eleven implemented it in 250 stores in the Dallas–Fort Worth area. This pricing policy was just one part of an overall revamping of 7-Eleven's image, including updated interiors, fresh produce, and gourmet items. In fact, 7-Eleven no longer wants the image of a high-priced convenience store, but seeks to appear more as a smaller, yet viable alternative to supermarkets.

Decision Questions

1. As a consumer, would you prefer that your local supermarket offer everyday low prices, offer some products at major discounts (half off) periodically, or offer some combination of the two?

2. What could your local supermarket do other than offer low prices or price discounts to win your business (delight you) and still maintain a high profit margin?

3. What advantages and disadvantages do you see for manufacturers to offer everyday low purchase prices to retailers?

4. Are manufacturers and retailers pushing price so much that they're in danger of lowering profits? Why is price competition so common?

Source: "Everyday Low Profits," *Harvard Business Review*, March-April 1994, p. 13; and "The Concept of EDLP Is Changing," *Advertising Age*, August 16, 1993, pp. 33–34.

VIDEO CASE PRODUCT DEVELOPMENT AND THE PRICING FACTOR

Sometimes the idea for a new product can come from your everyday experiences. That's what happened to Mary Anne Jackson. When she was faced with making lunches for her kids every day, she noted the lack of nutritious easy-to-make meals. From that discovery came her company: My Own Meals, Inc. At first Jackson had the market to herself and was doing well, but soon the big guns—Hormel, Banquet, and Tyson—came out with similar products. Jackson then found that she wasn't making money with her quick-to-serve meals, but she still expected to return to profitability as her advertising costs subsided.

Jackson had set a high price for her meals to reflect the quality ingredients she used. Nonetheless, she tested the market to see how they would react to different prices. It turned out that sales (and profits) were optimum at the median price range tested. It was also important to show stores that carrying her products would be profitable for them (direct product profitability). Demand factors for her meals include consumer incomes, the price and availability of competitive products and substitutes (such as fast-food restaurants), and consumer tastes.

As it turned out, Jackson did have trouble competing with the giants, which points out that the best strategy is to develop a product that doesn't face such tough competition. Ultimately, Jackson discovered that the military didn't provide kosher meals for Jewish soldiers and by specializing in such meals, she's been able to capture a market and make a better profit.

Outboard Marine Corporation found that it could charge premium prices by bringing out a technologically superior boat engine. Their lone competitor could try to match that product, but would then face stiff price competition because OMC could use the profits from the new innovation to reduce prices. Those profits could also be used for more innovations, keeping competitors at bay. As this example shows, product innovation and pricing are two factors that can be used together to create a value package that is hard to beat.

In another industry, the design and manufacture of large trucks, the value package depends more on the long-run cost of buying *and* running the truck. Therefore, it is important to build one that gets good mileage, is durable, *and* is priced competitively.

Each product category, therefore, calls for a different value package based on the operating demand factors. In all cases, price is an important ingredient.

Discussion Questions

1. If the economy were to go into a slump, Outboard Marine would suffer more than My Own Meals because people need food more than boat engines. What could the company do to maintain sales and profitability when the economy slows?

2. Is there anything that Mary Anne Jackson could have done to meet the competition of major competitors other than take them on head to head?

3. Mary Anne Jackson expanded her product mix by going into kosher meals. What else could she do to extend that product line?

4. Since My Own Meals are shelf stable, they could be sold through vending machines. Are there any new markets that Jackson might attempt to reach using vending?

CHAPTER 15

DISTRIBUTING PRODUCTS EFFICIENTLY AND COMPETITIVELY

LEARNING GOALS

After you have read and studied this chapter, you should be able to

1. Explain why we need marketing middlemen.

2. Give examples of how middlemen perform the five utilities.

3. Discuss how a manufacturer can get wholesalers and retailers in a channel system to cooperate by the formation of systems.

4. Describe in detail what's involved in physical distribution management.

5. Describe the various wholesale organizations that help move goods from manufacturers to consumers.

6. List and explain the ways that retailers compete.

7. Explain the various kinds of nonstore retailing.

ROBERT MAY OF BUSINESS LOGISTICS SERVICES AT FEDEX

FedEx is one of the leaders in the field of distribution. Its Business Logistics Services (BLS) division has 3,000 employees. Their goal is to provide full logistics support to manufacturers. That includes generating orders, handling purchase orders, monitoring receipt of goods, warehousing, shipping, collecting accounts receivable, and more. FedEx uses electronic technology to unite all these functions into one efficient logistics system, and management is confident that few companies in the world can match its competence. Only Wal-Mart's internal system is comparable.

National Semiconductor gave Business Logistics Services its finished goods delivery business from Southeast Asia to customers worldwide. Robert May, as president of this division, guaranteed 2-day delivery as opposed to the manufacturer's previous 5-to-18–day deliveries. Eventually FedEx will also handle Semiconductor's internal logistics (that is, warehousing of goods and moving those goods onto the assembly line).

National Semiconductor (NSC) tried to design its own logistics system, but couldn't design a global system as fast and cost-effective as BLS provided. BLS now stores finished goods from NSC's plants in a Singapore warehouse. It then flies the goods around the world, clears them through customs, and delivers them to customers. NSC can track the goods by tapping into the BLS database. Based on this new arrangement, NSC projects that it will be able to reduce its inventory and transportation costs by half.

May also captured global distribution for Laura Ashley with its two-day delivery guarantee. BLS even agreed to hire interior designers to handle telephone-order inquiries related to Ashley's home furnishings products.

In a highly competitive industry, FedEx is just one of about 50 companies offering some degree of logistics service. One of its major competitors, for example, is United Parcel Service (UPS), also highly successful. Resourceful companies such as these will provide leadership in dramatically cutting marketing costs in the coming decades. Information technology has made most of this possible with its ability to track shipments and schedule deliveries.

> *Companies facing the inevitability of global competition are learning a critical component of their marketing strategy is smart distribution; satisfying customers and improving services by fitting products to specific markets at the lowest cost and quickest speed.*
>
> *Douglas Fisher of Yellow Freight Systems*

THE ROLE OF DISTRIBUTION IN BUSINESS

Thus far, we've looked at two of the four Ps of the marketing mix: product and price. In this chapter, we'll look at the third of the four Ps: place. Products have to be physically moved from where they're produced to a convenient place where consumer and industrial buyers can see and purchase them. **Physical distribution (logistics)** is the movement of goods from producers to industrial and consumer users; it involves functions such as transportation and storage. It includes activities involved in purchasing goods, receiving them, moving them through the plant, inventorying them, storing them, and shipping finished goods to final users (including all the warehousing, reshipping, and physical movements involved).

How efficiently those tasks are performed often makes the difference between success and failure of the whole system. For example, the ultimate success or failure of the transition from a communist to a capitalist system in the former Soviet Union will depend to a considerable degree on its ability to build an effective logistics system. Such a system is made up of a series of marketing organizations called *middlemen*.

Marketing middlemen are organizations that assist in moving goods and services from producer to industrial and consumer users. They're called *middlemen* because they're organizations in the middle of a whole series of organizations that join together to help distribute goods from producers to consumers. You can see, therefore, why these organizations as a group are known as a *channel of distribution*. A **channel of distribution** consists of marketing middlemen such as wholesalers and retailers who join together to transport and store goods in their path (channel, if you will) from producers to consumers. A **wholesaler** is a marketing middleman that sells to organizations and individuals, but not final consumers. A **retailer** is an organization that sells to ultimate consumers. Figure 15.1 pictures channels of distribution for both consumer and industrial goods.

Channels of distribution enhance communication flows and the flow of money and title to goods. They also help ensure that the right quantity and assortment of goods will be available when and where needed.

Not too many people are aware of all the different wholesale and retail institutions and the careers available in them. Therefore, competition for jobs in the lesser-known institutions isn't as stiff. There are many career opportunities in logistics, and the number of students majoring in that area is lower than the growing demand as more and more firms move into international distribution. It has been estimated that the total U.S. logistics bill is nearly $600 billion.[1] Imagine the bill for companies throughout the world!

••• WHY WE NEED MIDDLEMEN •••

Manufacturers don't need marketing middlemen to sell their goods to consumer and industrial markets. Figure 15.1 shows manufacturers that sell directly to buyers. So why have marketing middlemen at all? The answer is

physical distribution (logistics)
The movement of goods and services from producer to industrial and consumer users.

marketing middlemen
Organizations that assist in the movement of goods and services from producer to industrial and consumer users.

channel of distribution
Marketing middlemen such as wholesalers and retailers who join together to transport and store goods in their path (channel) from producers to consumers.

wholesaler
A marketing middleman that sells to organizations and individuals, but not final consumers.

retailer
A marketing middleman that sells to consumers.

that middlemen perform certain marketing tasks such as transportation, storage, selling, and advertising more effectively and efficiently than most manufacturers could. A simple analogy is this: You could deliver your own packages to people anywhere in the world, but usually you don't. Why not? Because it's usually cheaper and faster to have them delivered by the post office or some private agency such as UPS or Emery.

Similarly, you could sell your own home or buy stock directly from other people, but most people don't. Why? Again, because there are specialists (brokers) who make the process more efficient and easier. Brokers are marketing middlemen who bring buyers and sellers together and assist in negotiating an exchange, but don't take title to (own) the goods. Usually, they don't carry inventory, provide credit, or assume risk. Examples include insurance brokers, real estate brokers, and stock brokers.

••• HOW MIDDLEMEN CREATE EXCHANGE EFFICIENCY •••

The benefits of marketing middlemen can be illustrated rather easily. Suppose that five manufacturers of various food products each tried to sell directly to five retailers. The number of exchange relationships that would have to be established is 5 times 5, or 25. But picture what happens when a wholesaler enters the system. The five manufacturers would contact one wholesaler to establish five exchange relationships. The wholesaler would have to establish

FIGURE 15.1

CHANNELS OF DISTRIBUTION FOR INDUSTRIAL AND CONSUMER GOODS AND SERVICES

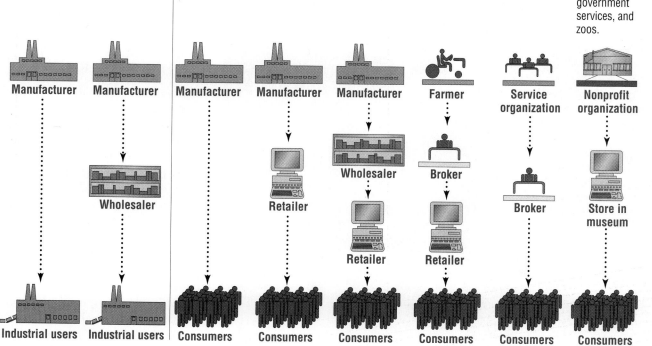

Channels for industrial goods

This is the common channel for industrial products such as glass, tires, and paint for automobiles.

This is the way that lower-cost items such as supplies are distributed. The wholesaler is called an industrial distributor.

This channel is used by craftspeople and small farmers.

This channel is used for cars, furniture, and clothing.

Channels for consumer goods

This channel is the most common channel for consumer goods such as groceries, drugs, and cosmetics. This is the path soup takes.

This is a common channel for food items such as produce.

This is a common channel for consumer services such as real estate, stocks and bonds, insurance, and nonprofit theater groups.

This is a common channel for nonprofit organizations that want to raise funds. Included are museums, government services, and zoos.

FROM THE PAGES OF...
Entrepreneur.
MAGAZINE

The Growing Importance of the Fourth P

The fourth P of the marketing mix, place, is growing in importance as the other three lose some of their power. The first P, product, is losing its clout because new production techniques allow competitors to match your product innovations very quickly. They can also match your price, while promotional techniques are losing some of their punch because they're so pervasive and because consumers are bored with most commercials.

On the other hand, Americans feel more and more that there just aren't enough hours in the day. Anything that marketers can do to make it easier to find and purchase products contributes to a winning strategy. For example, Domino's Pizza captured a huge share of the market with fast delivery. Virginia-based Takeout Taxi Inc. now delivers a wide variety of meals from local restaurants. Kindercare has made it easy for parents to use their day care center in Lombard, Illinois, by placing it next to the parking lot of the commuter train. Dean College in Franklin, Massachusetts, is offering classes on commuter trains.

No matter what business you're in, you may be able to capture more market share by making it more convenient for the buyer to find and use your products. That may mean home delivery; placing vending machines in convenient locations; offering products in catalogs or on the Internet; or simply locating your business in a more convenient place. In any case, the fourth P of marketing will become more and more important in coming years.

Source: Bob Jones, "Know Your Place," *Entrepreneur*, June 1994, pp. 52–55.

---

contact with the five retailers. That would mean another five exchange relationships. Note that the number of exchanges is reduced from 25 to only 10 by the addition of a wholesaler. Figure 15.2 shows this process. Not only are middlemen an efficient way to conduct exchanges, but they're often more effective as well. This means that middlemen are often better at performing their functions than a manufacturer or consumer could be.

Businesses could deliver their own packages to customers and others, but distribution middlemen such as UPS can typically do the job much faster and better. For example, UPS can immediately show you that your package was delivered and who signed for it. With the availability of services such as these offered by UPS, why would some companies continue to ask customers to, "Allow six weeks for delivery"?

... THE VALUE CREATED ... BY MIDDLEMEN

Marketing middlemen have always been viewed by the public with some suspicion. Some surveys have shown that about half the cost of the things we buy are marketing costs that are largely to pay for the work of middlemen. People reason that if we could only get rid of middlemen, we could greatly reduce the cost of everything we buy. Sounds good, but is the solution really that simple?

Let's take as an example a box of Fiberrific cereal. How could we, as consumers, get the cereal

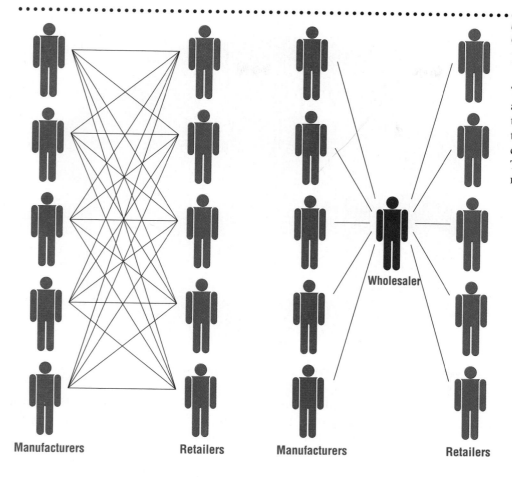

Manufacturers   Retailers   Manufacturers   Retailers

FIGURE 15.2

HOW MIDDLEMEN CREATE EXCHANGE EFFICIENCY
This figure shows that adding a wholesaler to the channel of distribution cuts the number of contacts from 25 to 10. This makes distribution more efficient.

for less? Well, we could all drive to Michigan where some of the cereal is produced and save some shipping costs. But would that be practical? Can you imagine millions of people getting in their cars and driving to Michigan just to buy some cereal? No, it doesn't make sense. It's much cheaper to have middlemen bring the cereal to major cities. That might involve transportation and warehousing by wholesalers. But these steps add cost, don't they? Yes, but they add value as well, the value of not having to drive to Michigan.

The cereal is now in a warehouse somewhere on the outskirts of the city. We could all drive down to the wholesaler and pick it up. But that isn't really the most economical way to buy cereal. If we figure in the cost of gas and time, the cereal would be rather expensive. Instead, we prefer to have someone move the cereal from the warehouse to a truck, drive it to the corner supermarket, unload it, unpack it, stamp it with a price, put it on the shelf, and wait for us to come in to buy it. To make it even more convenient, the supermarket may stay open for 24 hours a day, seven days a week. Think of the costs. Think also of the value! For about $4, we can get a box of cereal when we want, where we want, and with little effort on our part.

If we were to get rid of the retailer, we could buy a box of cereal for a little less, but we'd have to drive miles more and spend time in the warehouse looking through rows of cereals. If we got rid of the wholesaler, we could save a little more, but then we'd have to drive to Michigan. But a few cents here and a few cents there add up—to the point where marketing may add up to 75 cents for every 25 cents in manufacturing costs. Figure 15.3 shows where your money goes in the distribution process. Notice that the largest percentage goes to people who drive trucks and work in wholesale and retail organizations.

⟨⟨ **FIGURE 15.3** ⟩⟩

DISTRIBUTION'S EFFECT ON YOUR FOOD DOLLAR
Note that the farmer gets only 25 cents of your food dollar. The bulk of your money goes to middlemen to pay distribution costs. Their biggest cost is labor (truck drivers, clerks), followed by the costs for warehouses and storage.

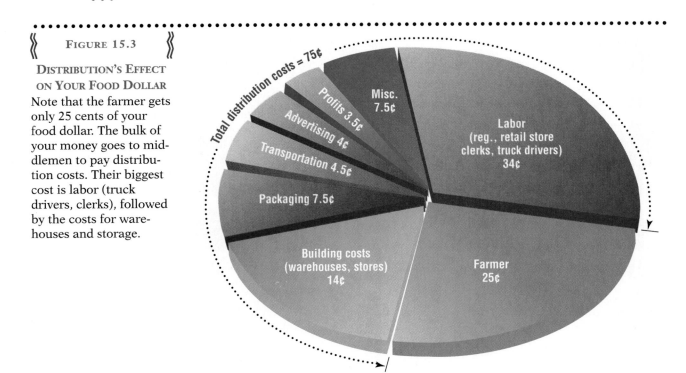

Source: U.S. Department of Agriculture reporting on food dollars spent in stores and restaurants.

Only 3.5 cents goes to profit. Figure 15.4 shows the share of distribution costs that go to various middlemen. Note that the percentages vary greatly among products. Here are three basic points about middlemen:

- Marketing middlemen can be eliminated, but their activities can't; that is, you could get rid of retailers, but then consumers or someone else would have to perform the retailer's tasks, including transportation, storage, finding suppliers, and establishing communication with suppliers.

- Middleman organizations survive because they perform marketing functions more effectively and efficiently than others can.

- Middlemen add costs to products, but these costs are usually more than offset by the values they create.

CRITICAL THINKING

Imagine that we eliminate middlemen and you had to go shopping for groceries and shoes. How would you find out where the shoes and groceries were? How far would you have to travel to get them? How much money do you think you'd save for your time and effort? Which middleman do you think is most important and why?

HOW MIDDLEMEN ADD UTILITY TO GOODS

Utility ⟨⟨--- P.415 ---⟩⟩ is an economic term that refers to the value or want-satisfying ability that's added to goods or services by organizations because the products are made more useful or accessible to consumers. Five utilities are mentioned in the economics literature: form, time, place, possession, and information.

ITEM	FARMER	PROCESSOR	WHOLESALER	RETAILER
1 pound choice beef	66.3%	5.4%	7.4%	20.9%
1 dozen grade A large eggs	69.7	11.5	5.1	13.7
1 half-gallon milk	50.8	21.6	19.8	7.8

FIGURE 15.4

HOW MIDDLEMEN SHARE YOUR FOOD DOLLAR

••• FORM UTILITY •••

The first of the five, form utility, is performed mostly by producers. It consists of taking raw materials and changing their form so that they become useful products. Thus, a farmer who separates the wheat from the chaff and the processor who turns that wheat into flour are creating form utility. Marketers sometimes perform form utility as well. For example, a retail butcher may cut pork chops off of a larger roast and trim off the fat. Normally, however, marketers perform the other four utilities: time, place, possession, and information. The following are some examples of how they do that.

••• TIME UTILITY •••

Middlemen, such as retailers, add time utility to products by making them available *when* they're needed. For example, Devar Tennent lives in Montana. One winter evening while watching TV with his brother, he suddenly got the urge for a hot dog and Coke. The problem was that there were no hot dogs or Cokes in the house. Devar ran down to the corner delicatessen and bought some hot dogs, buns, Cokes, and potato chips. He also bought some fresh strawberries. Devar was able to get these groceries at 10 P.M. because the store was open from 7 A.M. to 11 P.M. That's time utility.

••• PLACE UTILITY •••

Middlemen add place utility to products by having them *where* people want them. For example, while traveling through the badlands of South Dakota, Juanita Ruiz grew hungry and thirsty. She saw a sign saying that Wall Drug with fountain service was up ahead. She stopped at the store for refreshments. She also bought sunglasses and souvenir items there.

••• POSSESSION UTILITY •••

Middlemen add possession utility by doing whatever is necessary to *transfer ownership* from one party to another, including providing credit. Activities associated with possession utility include delivery, installation, guarantees, and follow-up service. For those consumers who don't want to own goods, possession utility makes it possible for them to use goods through renting or leasing.

Doc Martens boots and shoes are produced in England. Initially, they were popular among the rock and roll set but have now gained more interest among all consumers. In fact, their success is so widespread that they have decided to open their own stores. Do you see any advantage for Dr. Martens to own its own stores rather than selling through department stores?

For example, Larry Rosenberg wanted to buy a nice home in the suburbs. He found just what he wanted, but he didn't have the money he needed. So he went with the real estate broker to a local savings and loan and borrowed the money to buy the home. Both the real estate broker and the savings and loan were marketing middlemen.

••• INFORMATION UTILITY •••

Middlemen add information utility by opening two-way flows of information between marketing participants. For example, Jerome Washington couldn't decide what kind of TV set to buy. He looked at various ads in the newspaper, talked to salespeople at several stores, and read material at the library. He also got some booklets from the government about radiation hazards and consumer buying tips. The newspaper, salespeople, library, and government publications were all information sources made available by middlemen.

For consumers to receive the maximum benefit from marketing middlemen, the various organizations must work together to ensure a smooth flow of goods and services to the consumer. Historically, there hasn't always been total harmony in the channel of distribution. As a result, channel members have created channel systems that make the flows more efficient. We'll discuss those systems next.

BUILDING COOPERATION IN CHANNEL SYSTEMS

How can manufacturers get wholesalers and retailers to cooperate to form an efficient distribution system? One way is to link the firms together somehow in a formal relationship. Three systems have emerged to tie firms together: corporate systems, contractual systems, and administered systems.

••• CORPORATE DISTRIBUTION SYSTEMS •••

corporate distribution system
Distribution system in which all the organizations in the channel are owned by one firm.

A **corporate distribution system** is one in which all the organizations in the channel are owned by one firm. If the manufacturer owns the retail firm, clearly it can influence much greater control over its operations. Sherwin-Williams, for example, owns its own retail stores and thus coordinates everything: display, pricing, promotion, inventory control, and so on. Other companies that have tried corporate systems include GE, Firestone, and Xerox.

••• CONTRACTUAL DISTRIBUTION SYSTEMS •••

contractual distribution system
Distribution system in which members are bound to cooperate through contractual agreements.

If a manufacturer can't buy retail stores, it can try to get retailers to sign a contract to cooperate. A **contractual distribution system** is one in which members are bound to cooperate through contractual agreements. There are three forms of contractual systems:

1. *Franchise systems* such as McDonald's, Kentucky Fried Chicken, Baskin-Robbins, and AAMCO. The franchisee agrees to all of the rules, regulations, and procedures established by the franchisor. This results in the consistent quality and level of service you find in most franchised organizations.

2. *Wholesaler-sponsored chains* such as Western Auto and IGA food stores. Each store signs an agreement to use the same name, participate in chain promotions, and cooperate as a unified system of stores even though each store is independently owned and managed.

3. *Retail cooperatives* such as Associated Grocers. This arrangement is much like a wholesaler-sponsored chain except it's initiated by the retailers. The same cooperation is agreed to, however, and the stores remain independent. The normal way such a system is formed is for retailers to agree to focus their purchases on one wholesaler, but cooperative retailers could also purchase a wholesale organization to ensure better service.

••• ADMINISTERED DISTRIBUTION SYSTEMS •••

If you were a producer, what would you do if you couldn't get retailers to sign an agreement to cooperate? One thing you could do is to manage all the marketing functions yourself, including display, inventory control, pricing, and promotion. The management by producers of all the marketing functions at the retail level is called an **administered distribution system**. Kraft does that for its cheeses; Scott does it for its seed and other lawn care products. Retailers cooperate with producers in such systems because they get so much free help. All the retailer has to do is ring up the sale.

administered distribution system
Distribution system in which all the marketing functions at the retail level are managed by producers.

••• THE CHANNEL CAPTAIN •••

The greatest problems in traditional independent systems are human problems. People just don't want to give up some of their freedom to benefit the system. Thus, retailers don't like to do what wholesalers want, wholesalers don't want to do what manufacturers want, and manufacturers don't always respond to the needs of their suppliers, distributors, and dealers. The channel becomes a source of conflict, antagonism, and inefficiency.

The channel captain's role is to somehow gain control over the channel members and get them to work together. The channel captain may be the manufacturer, the wholesaler, or the retailer. For example, in the automobile distribution system, the manufacturer has much control over what the dealers do and when and how they do it. Retailers such as Sears have the power to control manufacturers that supply them. In other cases, it's the wholesaler who takes charge.

In each case, however, a channel captain has the power to get the other channel members to cooperate. A **channel captain**, therefore, is one organization in the channel of distribution that gets all the channel members to work together in a cooperative effort so that the whole channel is more efficient and more competitive with other channels in the same industry. The captain may have more financial resources, better marketing intelligence, or more managerial know-how. Regardless of the source of power, this organization maintains control. You can see how channel captains benefit all the members of the channel by motivating them to cooperate.

channel captain
The organization in the marketing channel that gets the other members to work together in a cooperative effort.

••• SUPPLY CHAIN MANAGEMENT AND QUICK RESPONSE •••

Most firms in a channel of distribution are forced to carry higher levels of inventory than absolutely necessary to ensure that goods will be available when needed. Much lower levels of inventory could be carried if those firms had

New electronic equipment connects retailers directly with manufacturers. The system is called supply chain management. In the supermarket industry, it is called efficient consumer response. Regardless of the name, electronic data interchange makes it possible for manufacturers to know immediately what is being sold at the retail level and replace those items immediately.

What advantages are apparent to you of taking inventory using electronic equipment?

supply chain management (SCM)

The overall process of minimizing inventory and moving goods through the channel faster by using computers to improve communications among the channel members.

electronic data interchange (EDI)

Software that enables the computers of producers, wholesalers, and retailers to talk with each other.

efficient consumer response (ECR)

The electronic linking of firms to provide more efficient response to consumer needs.

better communication links with and faster response times from their suppliers. That's exactly what's happening today. **Supply chain management (SCM)** is the overall process of minimizing inventory and moving goods through the channel faster by using computers to improve communication among the channel members.[2]

In 1993, U.S. companies spent $670 billion (15 percent of GDP) to wrap, bundle, load, unload, sort, reload, and transport goods. The distribution channel is so inefficient that the grocery industry believes it can cut costs by $30 billion. The industry notes, for example, that it takes 104 days for a box of cereal to get from the factory to the supermarket floor.[3] Every effort is now being made to reduce delivery time.

Quick response is the term used to describe the efforts by producers and suppliers to send goods to retailers and to each other as quickly as possible. One way to minimize response time is to link retailers with suppliers and producers by computer so that suppliers and producers can send replacement stock quickly when something is needed. Computerized checkout machines read the bar codes on goods that are sold and send that information to suppliers instantly so that a replacement good can be on the way immediately.

••• ELECTRONIC DATA INTERCHANGE (EDI) •••

Electronic data interchange (EDI) enables producers', wholesalers', and retailers' computers to "talk" with each other. EDI makes it possible for a retailer to be directly linked with a supplier electronically. As a result, the supplier knows that new goods must be shipped as soon as the retail sale is made. EDI thus becomes a critical part of an effective supply chain management system. Target and Ace Hardware were two of the first retailers to use EDI on a global basis. Many retailers are now following suit and are tracking shipments from Asia and other countries minute by minute so that the transportation time is minimized. The next step is to integrate transportation information directly into order entry and credit and collections. Thus, shippers are moving into the *information* business as well as the shipping business.[4]

••• EFFICIENT CONSUMER RESPONSE (ECR) •••

Efficient consumer response (ECR) is the term used in the grocery industry to describe the linking of firms to provide more efficient response to consumer needs.[5] Total cost reductions using supply chain management have been 30 percent or more. Similar reductions in inventory have also been achieved. Bergin Brunswig, a major distributor of pharmaceuticals and health care products, has cut the time between order placement and its delivery to just 12 hours. A retailer can carry much less inventory and still never be out of a product with such quick response time.

Companies such as Procter & Gamble, Xerox, 3M, Nabisco, and Black & Decker have cut inventory and improved service using supply chain management. Such companies implement the system by working together on functions such as forecasting, distribution, and marketing. Data are shared among firms so the whole system can be operated as a unit and so world-class products can be sent through the system in world-class time. New EDI computer software makes all this possible. Such high-quality service and management are demanded in the highly competitive global economy. Such service is part of a total logistics system. We'll discuss management of such systems next.

PROGRESS
CHECK

- What's the relationship among middlemen, channels of distribution, and physical distribution?
- Why do we need middlemen? Can you illustrate how middlemen create exchange efficiency? How would you defend middlemen to someone who said that getting rid of them would save millions of dollars?
- Can you give examples of the five utilities and how middlemen perform them?
- Could you tell a firm how to implement a corporate, a contractual, and an administered system? What are EDI and ECR?

PHYSICAL DISTRIBUTION (LOGISTICS) MANAGEMENT

Historically, middlemen helped to perform the distribution function; that is, they helped to move goods from the farm to consumer markets, move raw materials to factories, and so forth. It involved moving goods by truck, train, and other modes, and storing goods in warehouses along the way. (A *mode*, in the language of distribution, refers to the various means used to transport goods such as trucks, trains, planes, ships, and pipelines.) Today, *logistics systems* involve more than simply moving products from place to place. They involve all kinds of activities such as processing orders and inventorying products. In other words, logistics systems involve whatever it takes to see that the right products are sent to the right place quickly and efficiently.

Logistics systems, like all marketing activities, are becoming more customer-oriented. AT&T network systems were once driven primarily by productivity considerations. (How can we do it cheaply?) Today, however, the company's logistics planning director says, "Now there's a customer focus that demands we design flexibility into how we shift stuff out the door. We are actually becoming part of a customer team that meets with customers to satisfy specific logistics requirements."[6]

Many firms have introduced customer-oriented logistical strategies such as just-in-time (JIT) inventory controls ◀·· P.283 ··▶ . JIT means that manufacturers (1) can cut back substantially on their inventory in warehouses and (2) count on suppliers to deliver needed parts and materials *just in time* to go onto production lines. None of this would be possible without an efficient, reliable logistics system supported by trucking. Thanks to improved logistics systems (1) businesses now carry less in inventory and (2) total national logistics costs have decreased dramatically.[7]

··· METHODS USED TO MOVE RAW ···
MATERIALS AND FINISHED GOODS

A primary concern of distribution managers is selecting a transportation mode that will minimize costs and ensure a certain level of service. The largest percentage of goods is shipped by rail. Railroad shipment is best for

MODE	COST	PERCENTAGE OF DOMESTIC VOLUME	SPEED	ON-TIME DEPENDABILITY	FLEXIBILITY HANDLING PRODUCTS	FREQUENCY OF SHIPMENTS	REACH
Railroad	Medium	38%	Slow	Medium	High	Low	High
Trucks	High	25	Fast	High	Medium	High	Most
Pipeline	Low	21	Medium	Highest	Lowest	Highest	Lowest
Ships (water)	Lowest	15	Slowest	Lowest	Highest	Lowest	Low
Airplane	Highest	1	Fastest	Low	Low	Medium	Medium

《 **FIGURE 15.5** 》

COMPARING TRANSPORTATION MODES
Combining trucks with railroads lowers cost and increases the number of locations reached. The same is true when combining trucks with ships. Combining trucks with airlines speeds goods over long distances and gets them to almost any location.

bulky items such as coal, wheat, automobiles, and heavy equipment. Figure 15.5 compares the various modes on several dimensions.

For the past 20 years or so, railroads have handled about 35 to 40 percent of the total volume of goods in the United States. As you're no doubt aware, railroad lines are in a state of transition. As a result of practices such as piggyback shipments, railroads should continue to hold better than a 38 percent share of the market. (*Piggyback* means that a truck trailer is loaded onto a flatcar and taken to a destination from which it will be driven to plants by a truck driver.) Railroad shipment is a relatively energy-efficient way to move goods and could therefore experience significant gains if energy prices climb.

The second-largest surface transportation mode is motor vehicles (trucks, vans, and so forth). Such vehicles handle a little over 25 percent of the volume. As Figure 15.5 shows, trucks reach more locations than trains. Trucks can deliver almost any commodity door-to-door.

Railroads have joined with trucking firms to further the process of piggybacking. The difference lately is that the new railroad cars are 20 feet high and are called *double-stacks* because they carry two truck trailers over one another. As a consequence, the Norfolk Southern Railroad is in the process of lowering the floors of some tunnels and blasting off the top of others to allow these taller train cars to go through. It's worth the cost and effort, however, because it makes transportation costs much lower.

Water transportation moves a greater volume of goods than you might expect. Over the past 20 years, water transportation has carried 15 to 17 percent of the total. If you live near the Mississippi River, you've likely seen towboats hauling as many as 30 barges at a time with a cargo of up to 35,000 tons. On smaller rivers, about eight barges can be hauled carrying up to 20,000 tons—that's the equivalent of four 100-car railroad trains. Thus, you can see the importance of river traffic. Add to that Great Lakes shipping, shipping from coast to coast and along the coasts, and international shipments, and water transportation takes on a new dimension as a key transportation mode. When truck trailers are placed on ships to travel long distances at lower rates, the process is called *fishyback*.

One transportation mode that's not visible to the average consumer is movement by pipeline. About 21 percent of the total volume moves this way. Pipelines are used primarily for transporting petroleum and petroleum products. The Cleveland Electric Illuminating Company has experimented with a coal pipeline, and several more are either planned or in operation now. Here's how it works. The coal is broken down into small pieces, mixed with water to

This picture shows the piggyback process in action. A truck chassis is positioned to receive a container from a double-stack train in Chicago. The truck can move the cargo directly to a retail store or other user.

form what's called *slurry*, and piped to its destination, where it often must be dried before use. Such coal may not burn as cleanly as dry coal, and there's some resistance to such pipelines from environmentalists. There have been experiments with sending other solids in pipelines, which could be a major mode of distribution in the future.

Today, only a small part of shipping is done by air. Nonetheless, air transportation is a critical factor in many industries. Airlines carry everything from small packages to luxury cars and elephants, and could expand to be a very competitive mode for other goods. The primary benefit of air transportation is speed. No firm knows this better than Federal Express. Its theme is "When it absolutely, positively has to be there overnight." Federal Express is just one of several competitors vying for the fast-delivery market. As you read in the profile, FedEx is using air transport to expand into global markets.

The air freight industry is starting to focus on global distribution. Emery Worldwide, for example, anticipates that 50 percent of its business will come from global distribution in the next few years, up from 35 percent today.[8] Emery has been an industry pioneer in establishing specialized sales and operations teams aimed at serving the logistics needs of specific industries. KLM Royal Dutch Airlines has cargo/passenger planes that handle high-profit items such as diplomatic pouches and medical supplies. Specializing in such cargo has enabled KLM to compete with Federal Express, TNT, and DHL, which carry bulk items.[9]

INTERMODAL SHIPPING   *Intermodal shipping* uses multiple modes of transportation—highway, air, water, rail—to complete a single long-distance movement of freight. It now accounts for nearly 25 percent of trailerload shipments moving 500 miles or more.[10] Services that specialize in intermodal shipping are known as *intermodal marketing companies*.

... CRITERIA USED TO SELECT PHYSICAL ... DISTRIBUTION SYSTEMS

Two criteria dominate thinking in physical distribution planning. One criterion is customer service « P.39 ». Customer wants and needs come first. A goal would be to serve all a firm's customers' needs with 100 percent reliability.

Distribution in International Markets

It's one thing to decide to sell a product internationally; it's something else again to try to implement such a program. How are you going to reach the consumer? You could, of course, send sales representatives to contact people directly, but that would be costly and risky. How can you get your product into foreign markets at a minimum cost and still have wide distribution?

• *Use brokers.* A broker is a middleman who keeps no inventory and takes no risk. A broker can find distributors for you. Brokers sell for you and make a commission on the sale. This is the least expensive way to enter foreign markets, but you still assume the risks of transportation.

• *Use importers and exporters.* Importers and exporters take all the risks of business and sell your products to international markets. Their commission is much higher than brokers', but they do much more for you. They may find you distributors or do the selling to ultimate consumers themselves.

• *Call on distributors directly.* You can bypass exporters and brokers and call on distributors yourself. In that case, you actually become your own exporter and deliver directly to distributors, but again you assume the risks of transportation.

• *Sell direct.* The most costly and risky way to sell internationally is to set up your own distribution system of wholesalers and retailers. On the other hand, this maximizes potential profits in the long run. Many firms start out selling through importers and exporters and end up setting up their own distribution system as sales increase.

International distribution will be a major growth area in marketing with many challenges and opportunities for tomorrow's college graduates. Does such a career sound interesting to you?

Such a goal would be prohibitively expensive. But distribution managers strive for an 85 to 95 percent level of customer satisfaction.

The other criterion is cost. Distribution's aim is to provide a certain standard of customer service at the lowest cost that will still result in a profit for the seller.

Transportation modes vary from relatively slow carriers, such as barges, to high-speed jet airplanes. Generally speaking, the faster the mode, the higher the cost. Marketers must select those transportation modes that deliver goods at a reasonable price and maintain an acceptable level of customer service.

••• CONTAINERIZATION •••

You can imagine the problem of moving many small items from place to place in large trucks, railroad cars, or other forms of transportation. There's the danger of theft and loss, especially of small items. An effective answer is to pack and seal groups of items in one large package that can be easily moved and stored. The process of packing and sealing a number of items into one unit that's easily moved and shipped is called *containerization*. Some items are wrapped in plastic and then heated so that the plastic shrinks and holds all the items securely in place. This is called *shrink wrapping.*

As more companies use containerization techniques, shipping will become more efficient and goods will move more smoothly. The most efficient container is an entire truck trailer filled with goods. The trailer can be placed on a train, on a ship, or behind a truck cab. As noted earlier, the newest train cars can load two trailers on top of one another.

If you do not live near a body of water, you may not appreciate the volume of freight that is moved by barge. This picture shows how busy some waterways are. This is the Mississippi River near St. Louis, Missouri.

• • • THE STORAGE FUNCTION • • •

About 25 to 30 percent of the total cost of physical distribution is for storage. This includes the cost of the warehouse and its operation plus movement of goods within the warehouse. There are two kinds of warehouses: storage and distribution. A *storage warehouse* stores products for a relatively long time. Seasonal goods such as lawn mowers would be stored in such a warehouse.

Distribution warehouses are facilities used to gather and redistribute products. You can picture a distribution warehouse for Federal Express or United Parcel Service handling thousands of packages for a very short time. GE's combination storage and distribution facility in San Gabriel Valley, California, gives you a feel for how large such buildings can be. At only 475 feet short of a half-mile in length and 465 feet wide, it's big enough to hold three Statues of Liberty, two *Queen Marys*, and one Empire State Building.

• • • MATERIALS HANDLING • • •

Materials handling is the movement of goods within a warehouse, factory, or store. Go to a warehouse and watch the operations for a while. You may see forklift trucks picking up stacks of merchandise and moving them around. In more modern warehouses, computerized vehicles and robots move the materials. Warehouse management could be an interesting career possibility for business students.

materials handling
The movement of goods within a warehouse, factory, or store.

- What are some activities involved in physical distribution?
- Which transportation mode is fastest, cheapest, and most flexible?
- Which transportation modes can be combined to improve the distribution process?
- What percentage of the distribution cost comes from storage?

PROGRESS CHECK

WHOLESALE MIDDLEMEN

Now that we've talked about channels of distribution and physical distribution management, we can talk about the organizations that make up the channel. Let's begin with wholesalers. Remember that one goal of this discussion is to introduce you to the variety of careers in this area. Most college students know little or nothing about wholesaling, yet the rapid growth of warehouse clubs offers many career possibilities.

There's much confusion as to the difference between wholesalers and retailers. For example, many retail outlets have signs that say WHOLESALE DISTRIBUTORS or something similar. What difference does it make whether an organization is called a wholesaler or a retailer? One difference is that many states impose a sales tax on retail sales. To collect such a tax, the state must know which sales are retail sales and which aren't. Retailers are sometimes subject to other rules and regulations that don't apply to wholesalers.

For practical marketing purposes, it's helpful to distinguish wholesaling from retailing and to clearly define the functions performed so that more effective systems of distribution can be designed. Some producers won't sell directly to retailers but will deal only with wholesalers. Some producers give wholesalers a bigger discount than retailers. What confuses the issue is that some organizations sell much of their merchandise to other middlemen (a wholesale sale) but also sell to ultimate consumers (a retail sale). Warehouse clubs are a good example.

The issue is really rather simple: A *retail sale* is the sale of goods and services to consumers for their own use. A *wholesale sale* is the sale of goods and services to businesses and institutions (e.g., hospitals) for use in the business or to wholesalers, retailers, and individuals for resale. Wholesalers can't legally sell goods to consumers for their own use. If a wholesaler sells something to you for your use, that's called a retail sale, and the wholesaler must pay a retail tax on that sale (where such taxes are collected). One organization can be both a retailer and a wholesaler, but that gets confusing when it comes time to collect or not collect the retail sales tax.

••• MERCHANT WHOLESALERS •••

full-service wholesaler
A merchant wholesaler that performs all distribution functions.

limited-function wholesaler
A merchant wholesaler that performs only selected distribution functions.

rack jobber
A full-service wholesaler that furnishes racks or shelves full of merchandise to retailers, displays products, and sells on consignment.

cash-and-carry wholesaler
A limited-function wholesaler that serves mostly smaller retailers with a limited assortment of products.

Merchant wholesalers are independently owned firms that take title to (own) goods that they handle. About 80 percent of wholesalers fall in this category. There are two types of merchant wholesalers: **full-service wholesalers** and **limited-function wholesalers.** Full-service wholesalers perform all distribution functions: transportation, storage, risk bearing, credit, market information, grading, buying, and selling (see Figure 15.6). Limited-function wholesalers perform only selected functions, but try to do them especially well.

Rack jobbers furnish racks or shelves full of merchandise to retailers, display products, and sell on consignment. This means that they keep title to the goods until they're sold, and then they share the profits with the retailer. Merchandise such as toys, hosiery, and health and beauty aids are sold by rack jobbers. (A rack jobber who doesn't supply credit to customers is classified as a limited-function wholesaler.)

Cash-and-carry wholesalers serve mostly smaller retailers with a limited assortment of products. Retailers go to them, pay cash, and carry the goods home—thus, the term *cash-and-carry wholesaler*. Cash-and-carry wholesalers have begun selling to the general public in what are called *warehouse clubs*. Warehouse clubs are open to members only and sell merchandise at 20 to 40

A Full-Function Wholesaler

1. Provide a sales force to sell the goods to retailers and other buyers.

2. Communicate manufacturers' advertising deals and plans.

3. Maintain inventory, thus reducing the level of the inventory suppliers have to carry.

4. Arrange or undertake transportation.

5. Provide capital by paying cash or quick payments for goods.

6. Provide suppliers with market information they can't afford or can't obtain themselves.

7. Undertake credit risk by granting credit to customers and absorbing any bad debts, thus relieving the supplier of this burden.

8. Assume the risk for the product by taking title.

The wholesaler may perform the following services for customers:

1. Buy goods the end market will desire and make them available to customers.

2. Maintain inventory, thus reducing customers' costs.

3. Transport goods to customers quickly.

4. Provide market information and business consulting services.

5. Provide financing through granting credit, which is critical to small retailers especially.

6. Order goods in the types and quantities customers desire.

Source: Thomas C. Kinnear and Kenneth L. Bernhardt, *Principles of Marketing*, 2d ed. (Glenview, Ill.: Scott, Foresman, 1986), p. 369.

> **FIGURE 15.6**
>
> **A FULL-FUNCTION WHOLESALER**

percent below supermarkets and discount stores. One function of such clubs is to provide small businesses (those too small to have wholesalers service them) with merchandise and supplies at low prices.

What makes these new stores different is that you and I can join these clubs for an annual fee (usually $25) and buy goods at a 5 percent markup if we belong to a credit union, are government employees, or otherwise meet the qualifications. One example is Sam's Clubs, which were started by Sam Walton of Wal-Mart Stores.

Drop shippers solicit orders from retailers and other wholesalers and have the merchandise shipped directly from a producer to a buyer. They own the merchandise but don't handle, stock, or deliver it. That's done by the producer. Drop shippers tend to handle bulky products such as coal, lumber, and chemicals.

Truck jobbers are small wholesalers who deliver goods by truck to retailers. They're like a cash-and-carry wholesaler on wheels. They provide no credit. They handle items like bakery goods, dairy products, and tobacco products.

Perhaps the most useful marketing middlemen as far as you're concerned are *retailers*. They're the ones who bring goods and services to your neighborhood and make them available day and night. Let's look at retailers in more detail.

drop shipper
A limited-function wholesaler that solicits orders from retailers and other wholesalers and has the merchandise shipped directly from a producer to a buyer.

truck jobber
A small limited-function wholesaler that delivers goods by truck to retailers.

RETAIL  MIDDLEMEN

Next time you go to the supermarket to buy groceries, stop for a minute and look at the tremendous variety of products in the store. Think of how many marketing exchanges were involved to bring you the 18,000 or so items that you see. Some products (spices, for example) may have been imported from halfway around the world. Other products have been processed and frozen so that you can eat them out of season (for example, strawberries).

A supermarket is a retail store. A retailer, remember, is a marketing middleman who sells to consumers. The United States boasts approximately 2.3 million retail stores selling everything from apples to zoo souvenirs. Retail

TOP 10 RETAILERS (SALES)

Wal-Mart

Kmart

Sears

Dayton Hudson

J.C. Penney

May

Walgreens

The Limited

Federated

Macy

organizations employ more than 11 million people and are one of the major employers of marketing graduates. There are many careers available in retailing in all kinds of firms.

HOW RETAILERS COMPETE: BENCHMARKING AGAINST THE BEST

There are four different ways for retailers to compete for the consumer's dollar: price, service, selection, and total quality.

PRICE COMPETITION   Discount stores such as Wal-Mart, Target, Kmart, Marshalls, and Caldor succeed with low prices. It's hard to compete with these price discounters over time, especially when they offer good service as well. Warehouse stores are now trying to win the grocery store market by offering lower prices than neighborhood supermarkets. Price competition from warehouse stores has hurt many retailers. For example, there are few independent retailers left to service the office supply market since the advent of Staples, Office Depot, and other office-supply giants.[11] Those stores that have survived have suffered huge sales and profit declines unless they offer truly outstanding service and selection.

Service organizations also compete on price. Note, for example, Southwest Airlines' success with its low-price strategy. The same is true of H & R Block in income tax preparation services, Hyatt for legal services, and Motel 6 or Red Roof Inns for motel rentals.

SERVICE COMPETITION   A second competitive strategy for retailers is service. Retail service involves putting the customer first. This requires all frontline people being courteous and accommodating to customers. Retail service also means follow-up service such as on-time delivery, guarantees, and fast installation. Consumers are frequently willing to pay a little more for goods and services if the retailer offers *outstanding service*.

The benchmark companies in this regard are Dayton's, Lord & Taylor, Dillard's, and Nordstrom.[12] These retailers show that if you hire good people, train them well, and pay them fairly, you will be able to provide world-class service.

Service organizations that have successfully competed using service include Scandinavian Airlines, Tokyo's Imperial Hotel, Metropolitan Life Insurance Company, and Florida Power & Light.

Some retailers compete by offering such a large selection that people prefer to shop there rather than go from store to store to find exactly what they want. PetsMart, one of the new pet supply superstores, has everything for your pet including veterinary services. Which would you rather do: shop at a store with everything you need or where you have less selection but can get a small discount? Does your answer depend on the cost of the item?

SELECTION COMPETITION A third competitive strategy for retailers is selection. Selection is the offering of a wide variety of items in the same product category. Toys "R" Us carries some 18,000 toys and has over 500 stores all around the world. Small, independent toy stores are closing their doors because they simply can't compete with the low prices and selection found at Toys "R" Us. *Category killer stores* offer wide selection at competitive prices. Tower Records, for example, carries over 75,000 titles. Borders Books carries some 150,000 different titles. Sportmart carries over 100,000 sporting goods items. Petstuff and other pet food superstores have some 10,000 items.[13]

Smaller retailers compete with category killers by offering more selection within a smaller category of items. Thus, you have successful smaller stores selling nothing but coffee or party products. Smaller retailers also compete with more personalized service.

Service organizations that compete successfully on selection include Blockbuster Video (wide selection of rental videos), most community colleges (wide selection of courses), and Schwab Mutual Funds (hundreds of funds).

TOTAL QUALITY COMPETITION A fourth competitive strategy is total quality ◀─ P.259 ─▶. A total quality retailer offers low price, good service, wide selection, and total quality management. The benchmark retailer for total quality

CATEGORY	HIGHEST-RATED STORE	〈〈 HOW SHOPPERS 〉〉 RATE RETAILERS
Overall customer satisfaction	Dayton's	
Friendly, professional, and helpful employees	Nordstrom	
Newest fashions	Bloomingdale's	
Women's clothing	Lord & Taylor	
Cosmetics	Hudson's	
Competitive prices	Wal-Mart	

Source: *Marketing News*, June 6, 1994, p. 8.

marketing is Wal-Mart, which treats its "associates" well, gives them ownership incentives, and backs them up with information and the latest in technology and tools to do their job.

Wal-Mart can offer low prices because its marketing process is world-class. It uses electronic data interchange and supply chain management to keep its inventories low and its turnover high. Wal-Mart has a societal orientation that recognizes the wants and needs of all its stakeholders, including stockholders, employees, suppliers, and the local community.

Wal-Mart tries to please its customers with better service than its competitors'.[14] It believes in continuous improvement and benchmarks on the best in the world for logistics, pricing, and other retail practices. Kmart, Sears, and other competitors are getting stronger by competing with Wal-Mart. Service organizations competing on total quality include the Ritz-Carlton Hotel Company, Federal Express, and AT&T Universal Card.

••• RETAIL DISTRIBUTION STRATEGY •••

A major decision marketers must make is selecting retailers to sell their products. Different products call for different retail distribution strategies. There are three categories of retail distribution: intensive distribution, selective distribution, and exclusive distribution.

intensive distribution
The distribution strategy that puts products into as many retail outlets as possible, including vending machines.

Intensive distribution puts products into as many retail outlets as possible, including vending machines. Products that need intensive distribution include candy, cigarettes, gum, and popular magazines (convenience goods).

selective distribution
Distribution strategy that uses only a preferred group of the available retailers in an area.

Selective distribution is the use of only a preferred group of the available retailers in an area. Such selection helps to assure producers of quality sales and service. Manufacturers of appliances, furniture, and clothing (shopping goods) usually use selective distribution.

exclusive distribution
The distribution strategy that uses only one retail outlet in a given geographic area.

Exclusive distribution is the use of only one retail outlet in a given geographic area. Because the retailer has exclusive rights to sell the product, he or she's more likely to carry more inventory, give better service, and pay more attention to this brand than others. Auto manufacturers usually use exclusive distribution, as do producers of specialty goods.

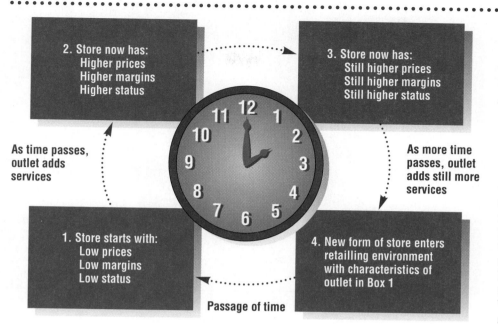

2. Store now has:
Higher prices
Higher margins
Higher status

As time passes, outlet adds services

1. Store starts with:
Low prices
Low margins
Low status

3. Store now has:
Still higher prices
Still higher margins
Still higher status

As more time passes, outlet adds still more services

4. New form of store enters retailing environment with characteristics of outlet in Box 1

Passage of time

FIGURE 15.7

WHEEL OF RETAILING
Discount department stores provide an example of the wheel of retailing. They began by offering low prices and few services. They added services such as credit and delivery to meet competition. The new services forced them to raise prices, making their products less competitive. New stores such as catalog stores and warehouse clubs entered the market with low prices. Watch for them to add services and get more expensive too.

••• THE WHEEL OF RETAILING •••

The *wheel of retailing* describes a process that has occurred in retailing over the years. What happens is that new retailers tend to enter a market by emphasizing low price, limited service, and out-of-the-way locations. The new warehouse clubs are a good example. As business improves, they add services such as credit and get better locations. Soon, prices must be raised to cover the added services and the store must now compete with traditional department stores and specialty stores. Once a store has added services, it's hard to go back. Because the store is now competing more directly with department stores that are more attractive, it often fails. (Korvette's and Robert Hall are examples.) New stores then enter the market using low prices and repeat the cycle. Figure 15.7 shows the wheel of retailing.

NONSTORE RETAILING

For every dollar consumers spend in stores like Safeway and Nordstrom, they spend 37.5 cents at home ordering goods and services by mail and by phone from sources such as Lands' End. The store figures don't include supermarkets, service stations, restaurants, and car dealerships. Still, the out-of-store shopping trend is growing. Categories include telemarketing; vending machines, kiosks, and carts; direct selling; network marketing; and direct marketing.

••• TELEMARKETING •••

Telemarketing is the sale of goods and services by telephone. Some 80,000 companies use telemarketing today to supplement or replace in-store selling. Many send a catalog to consumers and let them order by calling a toll-free 800 number. The organization Occupational Forecasting has predicted that telemarketing will continue to be one of the fastest-growing areas in marketing.

telemarketing
The sale of goods and services by telephone.

Shopping by computer is becoming more convenient as company after company goes on-line offering an increasing variety of goods and services over the Internet. You can wander through virtual stores looking at various products and services, you can ask for more information, and you can place your order, all without leaving home. What will be the effect on department stores if large numbers of consumers turn to computers for purchasing what they want? Will computerized kiosks such as this one add efficiency to in-store shopping?

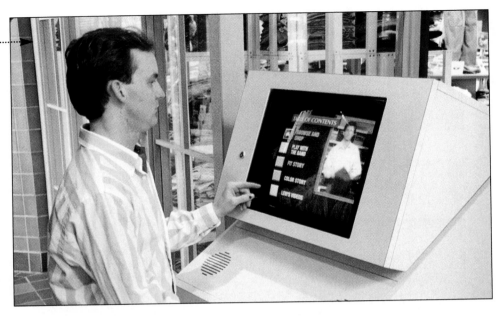

TOP VENDING MACHINE PRODUCTS

Cold beverages

Confections

Food products

Hot beverages

Cigarettes

Dairy products

••• VENDING MACHINES, KIOSKS, AND CARTS •••

A vending machine dispenses convenience goods when consumers deposit sufficient money in the machine. The benefit of vending machines is their convenient location in airports, office buildings, schools, service stations, and other areas where people want convenience items. Vending machines in Japan sell everything from bandages and face cloths to salads and spiced seafood. Such vending will be an interesting area to watch as such innovations are introduced around the United States.

Carts and kiosks have lower costs than stores; therefore, they can offer lower prices on items such as T-shirts and umbrellas. You often see vending carts outside stores on the sidewalk or along walkways in malls. Mall owners love them because they're colorful and create a marketplace atmosphere. Retailers, however, see them as parasites and would like to see them banned.[15]

••• DIRECT SELLING •••

Direct selling involves selling to consumers in their homes or where they work. Major users of this category include encyclopedia publishers (Britannica), cosmetics producers (Avon), and vacuum cleaner manufacturers (Electrolux). The newest trend is to sell lingerie, artwork, plants, and other goods at house "parties" sponsored by sellers. No doubt you've heard of Tupperware parties.

Because so many women work now and aren't at home during the day, such companies are sponsoring parties at workplaces and on weekends and evenings.

••• NETWORK MARKETING •••

Some 2,000 companies have had great success using network marketing (also known as *multilevel marketing*). This means that people are recruited to recruit other people until a huge network of salespeople and users is created. Examples of this marketing strategy include Amway and Mary Kay Cosmetics. Network marketing has been successful around the world in selling a wide variety of products.

A new salesperson's job is to sell the products provided by the company and to recruit several people who will use the product and will recruit others to sell and use the product. If you recruit 10 people and they each recruit 10 people and they recruit 10 people and so on, you'll soon have thousands of people under you. You receive a commission for all those sales. On the other hand, many people who've tried multilevel marketing have been disappointed with their success. The secret is to do your homework and talk to several people before getting involved in such ventures. Like any venture, multilevel marketing calls for hard work and dedication, but its rewards can be high.

••• DIRECT MARKETING GOES ON-LINE •••

One of the fastest-growing aspects of retailing is direct marketing. Direct marketing includes any activity that directly links manufacturers or intermediaries with the ultimate consumer. Thus, direct retail marketing includes direct mail, catalog sales, telemarketing, and on-line shopping (e.g., Prodigy Information Service shopping). Two popular direct marketing names are L.L. Bean (there's also an L.L. Bean store) and Lands' End. Direct marketing has created tremendous competition in some high-tech areas as well. For example, direct mail sales of computers by Dell Computers, Gateway 2000, and others led to the price cutting tactics by IBM and Compaq to meet the competition.

Direct marketing has become popular because it's more convenient for consumers than going to stores. Instead of driving to a mall they can "shop" in catalogs and free-standing advertising supplements in the newspaper and then buy by phone, by mail, or by computer. On-line computer sales will be a major competitor for retailers in the near future. Stanley Marcus of Neiman Marcus says, "You lose everything if you don't think like the customer. If customers don't want to get off their butts and go to your stores, you've got to go to them."

Direct marketing will take on a new dimension when consumers become more involved with interactive video. Producers will provide all kinds of information on CD-ROM discs that consumers access with their computers. Such systems' potential seems almost limitless. You'll be able to ask questions, seek the best price, and order goods and services—all by computer. Such systems will become major competitors for those who market by catalog today.

How important are middlemen such as wholesalers, retailers, trucking firms, and warehouse operators to the progress of less developed countries? Is there a lack of middlemen in less developed countries? How do middlemen contribute to the development of a less developed country?

CRITICAL THINKING

- What are the four major ways retailers compete with each other?
- What advantages and disadvantages do you see to having an intensive distribution strategy versus an exclusive one?
- Can you explain the wheel of retailing?

PROGRESS CHECK

---

1. Marketing middlemen are organizations that assist in moving goods and services from producer to industrial and consumer users.
   - ***Why do we need marketing middlemen?***
   We need middlemen because they perform marketing functions more effectively and efficiently than others can. Marketing middlemen can be eliminated, but their activities can't. Middlemen add costs to products, but these costs are usually more than offset by the values they create.

SUMMARY
•••••••

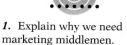

1. Explain why we need marketing middlemen.

2. Give examples of how middlemen perform the five utilities.

2. *Utility* is an economic term that refers to the value or want-satisfying ability that's added to goods or services by organizations because the products are made more useful or accessible to consumers.

- ● ***What different types of utilities do middlemen add?***
  Normally, marketing middlemen perform the following utilities: form, time, place, possession, and information.
- ● ***How do middlemen perform the five utilities?***
  A retail grocer may cut the fat off of meat, providing some form utility. But marketers are more responsible for the four other utilities. Time utility is provided by having goods available *when* people want them. Place utility is provided by having goods *where* people want them. Possession utility is provided by making it possible for people to own things by providing them with credit, delivery, installation, guarantees, and anything else that will help complete the sale. Finally, marketers inform consumers of the availability of goods and services with advertising, publicity, and other means. That provides information utility.

3. Discuss how a manufacturer can get wholesalers and retailers in a channel system to cooperate by the formation of systems.

3. One way of getting manufacturers, wholesalers, and retailers to cooperate in distributing products is to form efficient distribution (logistics) systems.

- ● ***What are the three types of distribution systems?***
  The three distribution systems that tie firms together are (1) corporate systems, in which all organizations in the channel are owned by one firm, (2) contractual systems, in which members are bound to cooperate through contractual agreements, and (3) administered systems, in which all marketing functions at the retail level are managed by manufacturers. The latest trends in system cooperation are called *supply chain management* and *quick response*. Retailers send sales data directly to manufacturers (electronic data interchange), who quickly replenish inventories so that retailers can carry fewer items, thus saving on inventory carrying costs. In the grocery industry, this is known as *efficient consumer response*.

4. Describe in detail what's involved in physical distribution management.

4. Physical distribution can be a complex process because it involves all the activities needed to get products from producers to consumers as quickly and efficiently as possible.

- ● ***What's involved in physical distribution management?***
  A primary concern of distribution managers is the selection of a transportation mode that will minimize costs and ensure a certain level of service. Logistics managers must also keep down storage costs. That's why supply chain management has become so popular. Furthermore, logistics managers are responsible for materials handling, moving goods within the warehouse and from the warehouse to the production or selling floor. Less inventory means less materials handling.

5. Describe the various wholesale organizations that help move goods from manufacturers to consumers.

5. A wholesaler is a marketing middleman that sells to organizations and individuals, but not to final consumers.

- ● ***What are some wholesale organizations that assist in the movement of goods from manufacturers to consumers?***
  Merchant wholesalers are independently owned firms that take title to (own) goods that they handle. Rack jobbers furnish racks or shelves full of merchandise to retailers, display products, and sell on consignment. Cash-and-carry wholesalers serve mostly smaller retailers with a limited assortment of products. Drop shippers solicit orders from retailers and other wholesalers and have the merchandise shipped directly from a producer to a buyer. Truck jobbers are small wholesalers who deliver goods by truck to retailers.

6. A retailer is an organization that sells to ultimate consumers.
   • ***How do retailers compete in today's market?***
   There are four different ways of competing for the consumer's dollar today: price, service, selection, and total quality.

6. List and explain the ways that retailers compete.

7. For every dollar consumers spend in stores like Safeway and Nordstrom, they spend 37.5 cents at home ordering goods and services by mail and by phone.
   • ***What are the various kinds of nonstore retailing?***
   Nonstore retailing includes telemarketing; selling goods in vending machines, kiosks, and carts; network marketing or multilevel marketing; and direct marketing.

7. Explain the various kinds of nonstore retailing.

KEY TERMS

administered distribution system 471
cash-and-carry wholesaler 478
channel captain 471
channel of distribution 464
contractual distribution system 470
corporate distribution system 470
drop shipper 479
efficient consumer response (ECR) 472

electronic data interchange (EDI) 472
exclusive distribution 482
full-service wholesaler 478
general merchandise wholesaler
intensive distribution 482
limited-function wholesaler 478
marketing middlemen 464
materials handling 477

physical distribution (logistics) 464
rack jobber 478
retailer 464
selective distribution 482
supply chain management (SCM) 472
telemarketing 483
truck jobber 479
wholesaler 464

DEVELOPING WORKPLACE SKILLS
• • • • • • •

1. The four utilities of marketing are time, place, possession, and information. Give examples of organizations specifically designed to perform each of these functions.

2. Research businesses in your community to identify the different kinds of wholesalers. Arrange visits to two or more of them in order to observe their operations. Draft a report for presentation to your class on the various ways they use technology.

3. Visit several retailers in a shopping mall in your area making notes about their merchandise, product displays, pricing strategies, location, and store design. Draw a map showing both the customer and auto traffic patterns in and out of the mall. Which stores enjoy an advantage due to location? Explain why.

4. Visit the newest stores in your community such as warehouse clubs, hypermarkets, or giant supermarkets. Compare their prices with the older stores. What are the trends in retailing that seem most significant to you? How do the products and prices offered by these newer, warehouse type stores compare to those sold by the Home Shopping Network?

5. Arrange to visit a telemarketer or firm in your area that uses telemarketing. Ask questions and learn all you can. Imagine then that you are employed as a sales representative for a telemarketing services company. Use a computer to develop a sales proposal outlining the advantages and reasons why a new sporting goods manufacturer should engage your firm's services.

PRACTICING MANAGEMENT DECISIONS

〉〉 C A S E   NETWORK MARKETING 〉〉

Network marketing (also called *multilevel marketing*) often doesn't get the respect it deserves in the marketing literature. When network marketing companies succeed, their growth is often unbelievable. Over six multilevel marketing companies have reached the $500 million level in sales.

Multilevel marketing companies work like this: The founders begin by recruiting a few good people to go out and find managers to sell their products and to recruit other supervisors. These supervisors then recruit additional salespeople. That is, 20 people recruit 6 people each. That means 120 salespeople. Those people then recruit 6 people each, and you have 720 salespeople. If in turn those people all recruit 6 people, you then have almost 5,000 salespeople. All supervisors earn commissions on what they sell as well as on what everyone under them sells. When you get thousands of salespeople selling for you, commissions can be quite large. One company promotes the fact that 1 percent from 100 salespeople is as good as 100 percent from one successful salesperson. Companies often add new products or expand to other countries to keep a continuous growth pattern.

Nu Skin will soon have $1 billion in sales. Looking for more growth, the company started a new division, Interior Design Nutrition, to make and sell vitamins and weight control products. Sales in this division are projected to reach $500 million by 1996 and Nu Skin is now expanding to Japan.

Amway has chosen the international route for growth. Thirteen years ago, it launched Amway, Japan. That company had $135 million in profits on $1 billion in sales in 1991. Japanese sales now make up one fourth of Amway's revenues. The sales force in Japan grew from 10 in 1979 to 870,000 in 1992. Full-time salespeople can earn as much as $300,000 annually. Other multilevel marketers have had success in Japan. For example, Shaklee has some 250,000 salespeople selling nutrition, personal care, and household products.

Decision Questions:

1. Amway and others have been successful in Japan. What other countries could you lead such companies to so that you could become a top earner?

2. Would it be possible to set up multilevel marketers who sold by catalog or by telemarketing from home?

3. Why do you suppose multilevel marketing hasn't received the same acceptance as other retail innovations such as catalog sales? What could the companies do to improve their image?

4. If multilevel marketing works so well for beauty products and health care products, why not use the same concept to sell other products?

〉〉 V I D E O   C A S E   WHOLESALING, LOGISTICS AND UPS 〉〉

Wholesalers are called middlemen or intermediaries because they are in the middle of the channel of distribution from manufacturers to consumers. You can get rid of wholesalers, but you can't rid your company of the necessity of performing their functions. That is, you can transport goods yourself, store them yourself, and obtain needed market information, on your own, but it is usually cheaper and more effective to have an expert do it—a wholesaler.

There are several kinds of wholesalers performing a wide variety of services for manufacturers. The movement of goods and information from manufacturers to consumers, including transportation, storage, and materials handling, and everything connected to those functions, is called logistics. Logistics planning is becoming more and more critical as a marketing function as global markets open, necessitating the rapid movement of goods throughout the world. UPS is a world-class provider of logistics support. Their services include ease of order entry, reliable and timely delivery, error-free paperwork, and ease of claim handling.

Technology has dramatically changed the logistics function in the last few years. UPS shows those changes in everything it does. First, every address is electronically mapped so that UPS can find senders and receivers quickly. When you want to send a package, UPS can be there within the hour. Its new image recognition equipment makes it possible to record delivery time, the account number, and who signed for the delivery. Intelligent packages are created by encoding them with UPS codes that are similar to bar codes. These codes track and trace packages and are used to bill clients. They also allow for automated sorting.

UPS is truly global, serving some 4 billion people, more than are served even by telephones and it is technology that makes this rapid worldwide movement of goods possible. The company is also electronically linked with customs agencies so that goods can be cleared before they reach the appropriate customs station, and when they do arrive, they move quickly and efficiently through the system.

UPS succeeds by providing efficient customized service for each of its customers.

Discussion Questions

1. Periodically you will hear ads that say, "Allow four to six weeks for delivery." Is there any reason you should wait that long, given the capability of delivering within two days by UPS and others?

2. There are many careers available in logistics, including careers at various wholesale organizations. What are some of those organizations and what services do they provide?

3. What all is involved in logistics management? Why is this function more important than ever?

CHAPTER 16

PROMOTING PRODUCTS USING INTEGRATED MARKETING COMMUNICATION

LEARNING GOALS

After you have read and studied this chapter, you should be able to

1. List and describe the various elements of the promotion mix.

2. Describe advantages and disadvantages of various advertising media and explain the latest advertising techniques.

3. Illustrate the seven steps of the selling process.

4. Explain the importance of word of mouth and sales promotion as promotional tools.

5. Describe the functions of the public relations department and the role of publicity in those functions.

6. Compare and contrast various promotional strategies such as push and pull strategies.

7. Describe the three parts of an integrated marketing communication system and how such systems affect ad agencies.

8. Discuss how integrated marketing evolves from integrated marketing communication.

JERRY WINTER OF PEPSICO

Few companies face stronger global competition than the Pepsi-Cola Company, especially from the Coca-Cola Company. Pepsico decided that the best way to compete with Coke was to get closer to the customer. Pepsico then concluded that the best means to do that was by gathering more information about customers, its own as well as those of Coke, and then targeting those people with an integrated promotional effort.

Jerry Winter, as the manager of database marketing at Pepsico, had the job of managing information about customers and competitors. But Winter needed help in creating a unified promotional campaign based on that information. He suggested hiring Rapp Collins Worldwide as Pepsico's first direct marketing agency.

Over the years, Winter's area had gathered extensive information about Pepsi's frequent customers as well as those of its biggest rival, Coke. During this period, he also noted that customers for Pepsico's other products—Frito Lay snack foods, Pizza Hut, Kentucky Fried Chicken, and Taco Bell—are mostly the same people: teens and families. He determined that it would be possible to develop similar campaigns to reach these targets. Rapp Collins was also commissioned by Pizza Hut to create a program rewarding frequent customers. When people buy Pizza Hut pizza, they're likely to buy Pepsi also, so the campaign would help two parts of the company.

Using Rapp Collins's input and Pepsico's database, the company intends to use direct mail and other promotional techniques to win Coke customers over to Pepsi. For example, a Diet Pepsi campaign called "Convert a Million" aimed to get Diet Coke users to switch to Diet Pepsi. Sample cases of Diet Pepsi were mailed to 1 million Diet Coke–drinking households. The idea was to send each Diet Coke drinker enough Diet Pepsi to last a while until the users got used to the taste, and hopefully were attracted to it.

Pepsico is just one of many companies seeking new ways of reaching the consumer with database marketing and integrated promotional messages. This chapter will outline the newest promotional strategies. Using such strategies, organizations will become more efficient marketers and get much closer to their customers.

The idea of coordinating advertising, sales, marketing and promotion to produce something greater than just mass media ad tonnage is marketing's boldest Big Idea.

Advertising Age *editorial, May 3, 1993*

THE IMPORTANCE OF MARKETING COMMUNICATIONS

Promotion is the last, but not the least, of the four Ps of marketing. Marketers now spend over $138 billion yearly on advertising alone trying to convince industrial and consumer buyers to choose their products. They spend even more on sales promotion efforts such as conventions and trade shows where producers and customers meet to discuss marketing exchanges.

direct marketing
Marketing that allows consumers to buy products by interacting with various advertising media without meeting a salesperson face-to-face.

Marketers spend the most money sending salespeople into the field to talk personally with customers. Direct marketing is often much cheaper and more effective than personal selling, as Pepsico is learning. **Direct marketing** allows consumers to buy products by interacting with various advertising media without meeting a salesperson face-to-face. Direct marketing includes direct mail selling, catalog sales, telemarketing (marketing by phone), televised home shopping, and selling through interactive computer systems on the Internet.

··· THE PROMOTION MIX ···

promotion
An attempt by marketers to inform people about products to persuade them to participate in an exchange.

Promotion is an attempt by marketers to inform people about products and to persuade them to participate in an exchange. Marketers use many different tools to promote their products and services. These tools include advertising, personal selling, word of mouth, sales promotion, public relations, and publicity. The combination of promotion tools an organization uses is called its

FIGURE 16.1

THE PROMOTION MIX

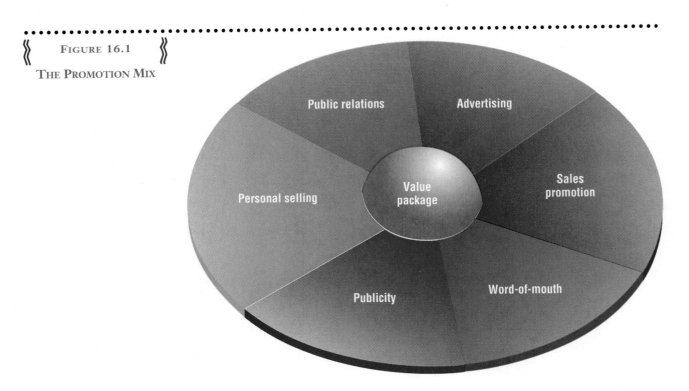

promotion mix. (See Figure 16.1.) The value package is shown in the middle of the figure to illustrate the fact that the product itself can be a promotional tool (e.g., through sampling), and that all promotional efforts are designed to sell products. We'll discuss each of these promotional tools in this chapter. Let's begin by looking at advertising.

promotion mix
The combination of tools marketers use to promote their products or services.

advertising
Paid, nonpersonal communication through various media by organizations and individuals who are in some way identified in the advertising message.

ADVERTISING

Many people equate promotion with advertising because they are not aware of the differences among promotional tools such as advertising, personal selling, publicity, and word of mouth. **Advertising** is limited to paid, nonpersonal communication through various media by organizations and individuals who are in some way identified in the advertising message. Word of mouth is *not* a form of advertising because it doesn't go through a medium (newspaper, TV, etc.), it's not paid for, and it's personal. Publicity is different from advertising in that media space for publicity isn't paid for. Personal selling is face-to-face communication and doesn't go through a medium; therefore, it's not advertising.

••• THE IMPORTANCE OF ADVERTISING •••

The importance of advertising in the United States is easy to document; just look at the figures. The total ad volume exceeds $138 billion yearly. The number one advertising medium in terms of total dollars spent is newspapers (see Figure 16.2) with over 23 percent of the total. Many people erroneously think that the number one medium is TV, so take some time to look at the real figures.

The public benefits greatly from advertising expenditures. First, ads are informative. The number one medium, newspaper advertising, is full of information about products, prices, features, and more. Are you surprised that businesses spend more on direct mail than on radio or magazine advertising? Direct mail (the use of mailing lists to reach an organization's most likely customers) is an informative shopping aid for consumers. Each day, consumers receive minicatalogs in their newspapers or in the mail that tell them what's on sale, where, at what price, for how long, and more.

Advertising not only informs us about products; it also provides us with free TV and radio programs because advertisers pay for the production costs. Advertising also covers the major costs of producing newspapers and magazines. When we buy a magazine, we pay mostly for mailing or promotional costs. Figure 16.3 discusses advantages and disadvantages of various advertising media to the advertiser. Newspaper, radio, and Yellow Page ads are especially attractive to local advertisers.

TV has many advantages to national advertisers, but it's expensive. Figure 16.4 shows how the cost of one minute of advertising during the Super Bowl telecast has leaped to $2 million. How many

This single ad demonstrates the power of promotion to achieve several things at once. First, the ad introduces eight new products. It also ties those products to eight community activists, helping to maintain Ben & Jerry's image as a socially conscious firm. Finally, the ad offers posters of these activists and the proceeds from the sale go to the Children's Defense Fund.

MEDIUM	SALES ($ MILLIONS)	PERCENTAGE OF TOTAL
Newspapers	$ 32,025	23.2%
Television	30,584	22.1
Direct mail	27,266	19.7
Yellow Pages	9,517	6.9
Radio	9,457	6.8
Magazines	7,600	5.5
Business papers	3,260	2.7
Outdoor	1,090	.8
Miscellaneous	17,281	12.3
Total	$138,080	100 %

FIGURE 16.2

ADVERTISING VOLUME IN THE VARIOUS MEDIA

bottles of beer or bags of dog food must a company sell to pay for such a commercial? Is it any wonder that companies are now buying 15-second commercials to save money and that they're thinking of alternative ways to reach the public? The box titled Major Categories of Advertising lists some of the various forms of advertising.

Major Categories of Advertising

Different kinds of advertising are used by various organizations to reach different market targets. Major categories include

● *Retail advertising*—advertising to consumers by various retail stores such as supermarkets and shoe stores.

● *Trade advertising*—advertising to wholesalers and retailers by manufacturers to encourage them to carry their products.

● *Industrial advertising*—advertising from manufacturers to other manufacturers. A firm selling motors to auto companies would use industrial advertising.

● *Institutional advertising*—advertising designed to create an attractive image for an organization rather than for a product. "We Care about You" at Giant Food is an example. "Virginia Is for Lovers" and "I ♥ New York" are two institutional campaigns by government agencies.

● *Product advertising*—advertising for a good or service to create interest among consumer, commercial, and industrial buyers.

● *Advocacy advertising*—advertising that supports a particular view of an issue (for example, an ad in support of gun control or against nuclear power plants). Such advertising is also known as *cause advertising*.

● *Comparison advertising*—advertising that compares competitive products. For example, an ad that compares cold care products' speed and benefits is a comparative ad.

● *Interactive advertising*—customer-oriented communication that enables customers to choose the information they receive, such as interactive video catalogs that let customers select which items to view.

● *On-line advertising*—advertising messages that are available by computer when customers want to receive them.

Medium	Advantages	Disadvantages
Newspapers	Good coverage of local markets; ads can be placed quickly; high consumer acceptance; ads can be clipped and saved.	Ads compete with other features in paper; poor color; ads get thrown away with paper (short life span).
Television	Uses sight, sound, and motion; reaches all audiences; high attention with no competition from other material.	High cost; short exposure time; takes time to prepare ads.
Radio	Low cost; can target specific audiences; very flexible; good for local marketing.	People may not listen to ad; depends on one sense (listening); short exposure time; audience can't keep ad.
Magazines	Can target specific audiences; good use of color; long life of ad; ads can be clipped and saved.	Inflexible; ads often must be placed weeks before publication; cost is relatively high.
Outdoor	High visibility and repeat exposures; low cost; local market focus.	Limited message; low selectivity of audience.
Direct mail	Best for targeting specific markets; very flexible; ad can be saved.	High cost; consumers may reject ad as "junk mail"; must conform to Post Office regulations.
Yellow Pages advertising	Great coverage of local markets; widely used by consumers; available at point of purchase.	Competition with other ads; cost may be too high for very small businesses.

FIGURE 16.3

ADVANTAGES AND DISADVANTAGES OF VARIOUS ADVERTISING MEDIA
The most effective media are often very expensive. The inexpensive media may not reach your market. The goal is to use the most efficient medium that can reach your desired market.

infomercials
TV programs that are devoted exclusively to promoting goods and services.

• • • ADVERTISING USING INFOMERCIALS • • •

One of the faster-growing forms of advertising is the use of infomercials. **Infomercials** are TV programs devoted exclusively to promoting goods and services. They're so successful because they show the product in great detail. A great product can sell itself if there's some means to show the public how it works. Infomercials provide that opportunity. People have said that a half-hour infomercial is the equivalent of sending your very best salespeople to a person's home where they can use everything in their power to make the sale: drama, demonstration, testimonials, graphics, and more.

Some products, such as personal development seminars or work-out tapes, are hard to sell without showing people testimonials and a sample of how they work. Infomercials have sold such services so well that major companies are now trying to buy time for their own infomercials.[1]

• • • USING TECHNOLOGY IN ADVERTISING • • •

The technology revolution is having a major impact on advertising. For example, promoters are using interactive TV to carry on a dialogue with customers instead of merely sending them messages, and they're using CD-ROM technology to provide more information.

Salespeople are using hand-held computers to place orders and to help consumers design custom-made products. Customers can now request information via e-mail and can reach service people from almost any location using cellular phone technology and pagers. In short, the information revolution has greatly affected advertising in a positive way for both seller and buyer. Here's what Terence Westmacott of InForm Incorporated has to say about empowering customers with information technology:[2]

FIGURE 16.4

THE COST OF SUPER BOWL ADS

The growth of America's premier sporting event is reflected in the rising cost of a 60-second TV commercial over the years. One minute of advertising during the 1995 Super Bowl cost $2 million.*

SUPER BOWL	YEAR	COST OF "60 SPOT"
I	1967	$ 80,000
IV	1970	200,000
VIII	1974	214,000
XIII	1979	444,000
XVII	1983	800,000
XXII	1988	1,300,000
XXVI	1992	1,700,000
XXIX	1995	2,000,000

*Now commercials are sold in 30-second spots; the first six Super Bowls had only 60-second spots.

Changes in technology and society have given all consumers the power and the desire to screen and discard most of the traditional means used to reach them. Even when product information is narrowcast, pushing information out to potential customers is a less and less effective way to reach them. Customers want to be able to understand a product easily and quickly. And they want to control access to that product information.

In the dialogue between producers and consumers, consumers are increasingly in charge. Companies must actively assist their customers in controlling this communication process. By structuring product information to support customers as they do their jobs, companies can become an indispensable strategic partner and not just a supplier of goods or services.

Next, let's look at some specific ways marketers are using technology in advertising.

USING ON-LINE COMPUTER SERVICES IN ADVERTISING   On-line services, such as Prodigy, America Online, and CompuServe, are computer services that provide information on a variety of subjects such as business, entertainment, financial, and sports news. (See Chapter 17.) On-line services are expected to have some 20 million users by 1998. Recently, marketers have been devising ways to provide marketing information to users via such services. The first attempts at such advertising were rejected by users, but the future is promising. What on-line services on the Internet can do is provide massive product information when customers want it.[3]

Once potential customers see what information is available, they can go on-line with sellers (directly contact them by computer) and get additional information immediately. The potential for such communication between buyers and sellers is almost endless. Any data that can be put into a computer can be accessed by others. The challenge is to make such searches easy and profitable.

ProductView Interactive is developing an on-line service that will offer advertising—and nothing but advertising—on demand. This will be a database

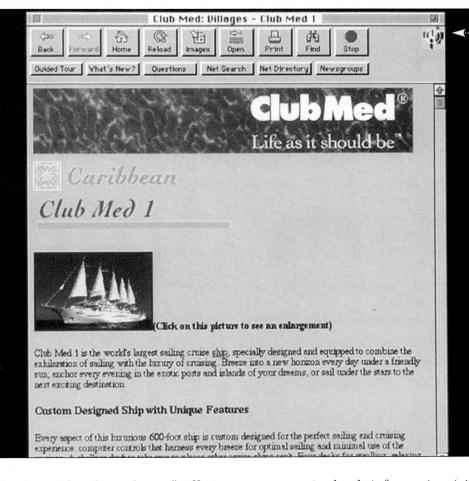

Advertising in cyber-space? This on-line ad for ClubMed illustrates many of its advantages. An advertiser can use sight, sound, and interactivity to show information and respond to individual consumer inquiries. This gives consumers more control and makes it possible for advertisers to provide consumers with much more infor-mation. What will hap-pen to the mass media when the bulk of con-sumers get their product information on-line?

for "considered purchases," offering consumers in-depth information (via text, pictures, and sound) about cars, travel, consumer electronics, and other high-priced items.[4]

To see what on-line services can do, let's look at Larry Chase's business. Chase started an on-line advertising agency. More than 50 people are available at the agency to help in areas such as creative, media planning, and produc-tion. Copy, design, and media plans can be sent by modem to customers. Pastel Development Company is using the on-line agency for package design and communications.[5]

USING INTERACTIVE TELEVISION IN ADVERTISING   Interactive television is a technology that enables TV viewers to respond or get involved with TV programs and commercials electronically. Rather than passively *receive* programming—news, entertainment, and commercials—consumers using interactive TV can actively *control* what they receive and can conduct a dialogue with advertisers. They can eliminate commercials from shows or watch the commercials and respond electronically (including placing orders).

In such an environment, advertisers must be more creative and efficient when communicating with consumers. *Broadcasting*—sending generic mes-sages to mass markets—will give way to *narrowcasting*—preparing targeted messages for selected audiences. There will be whole channels dedicated to relatively narrow market segments—for example, a 24-hour golf channel, a health and fitness channel, a military channel, and a sports channel aimed at people who like sports other than just football, basketball, and baseball.

interactive television
Technology that enables TV viewers to respond or get involved with TV programs and commercials electronically.

In the past small businesses have felt that it was their responsibility to advertise to buyers in order to persuade them to buy. However, as a buyer you know that there are products you're interested in buying, but what often prevents you from making a decision to purchase is information. The question then becomes, How can small businesses make more information available so that buyers can obtain it whenever they want? One answer is to use a system like MarketFax. Here's how it works: You set up a data system at your company that contains all the information you want your potential customers to have. For example, the Boston Computer Exchange took all the documents it normally mailed to clients and put them in a MarketFax system.

Then you give customers and potential customers a special phone number. When they call that number, the system asks them what information they desire and requests a fax number. Clients key in their fax numbers and then hang up. A few moments later, the system sends the information desired by fax machine. All the information needed is sent instantly in printed form. Through this system the Boston Computer Exchange makes available price sheets, news items, popular products, policy statements, order forms, and more. This is just one more example of how small companies can use the latest in technology to establish the kinds of communication with its customers that create long-term marketing relationships.

Source: "FutureFax," an ad in *Nation's Business*, April 1995, p. 59.

... CUSTOMIZED ADVERTISING VERSUS ... GLOBAL ADVERTISING

Harvard professor Theodore Levitt is a big proponent of global marketing «‑ P.99 ‑» and advertising. His idea is to develop a product and promotional strategy that can be implemented worldwide. Certainly that would save money in research costs and advertising design. However, other experts think that promotion targeted at specific countries may be much more successful since each country has its own culture, language, and buying habits.

The evidence supports the theory that promotional efforts specifically designed for individual countries work best.[6] For example, commercials for Camay soap that showed men complimenting women on their appearance were jarring in cultures where men don't express themselves that way. A different campaign is needed in such countries.

People in Brazil rarely eat breakfast and treat Kellogg's Corn Flakes as a dry snack like potato chips. Kellogg is trying a promotional strategy of showing people in Brazil how to eat cereal—with cold milk in the morning. The box Reaching Beyond Our Borders gives further examples. Many more situations could be cited to show that international advertising calls for researching the wants, needs, and culture of each specific country and then designing appropriate ads and testing them.

Even in the United States, selected groups are large enough and different enough to call for specially designed promotions. For example, Maybelline is targeting special promotions to African-American women. In short, advertising today is moving from the trend toward *globalism* (one ad for everyone in the world) to *regionalism* (specific ads for each country and for specific groups within a country). In the future, marketers will prepare more custom-designed promotions to reach smaller audiences—audiences as small as one person.

mass customization
The design of custom-made products and promotions, including advertising.

Mass customization is the term used to describe the design of custom-made products and promotions, including advertising.[7] For example, Coke Classic made over two dozen commercials for 20 different TV networks. For

Reaching Beyond Our Borders

Culture Shock

"*Ich bin ein Berliner.*" John F. Kennedy used these famous words to tell the people of Berlin that he was a "Berliner" too. The local people had trouble getting the message. You see, to them Berliner was a jelly donut, so they thought he said, "I'm a donut."

Communicating in global advertising is more than a little tricky. For example, using white roses for a joyous occasion in a commercial to be shown in China would backfire because white is a symbol of mourning in the Chinese culture. Using a bull's horn as a symbol of a men's product would work against you in Spain. For many Spaniards, the horns symbolize a man whose wife has committed adultery. As you can see, insensitivity to cultural considerations can be embarrassing—and costly.

How do some companies avoid such embarrassment? Richard Becker, president of the soft drink company Blue Sky, addressed the cultural question by contracting with a Japanese distributor to direct his company's marketing campaign in Japan. The American version of a Blue Sky commercial features lots of condensation-covered cans of Blue Sky against a view of the New Mexico desert. Every once in a while a cowgirl in a halter top and string tie stares longingly at the can. Everything is in pastels to stress the all-natural, no-preservative features of the drink. The closing line is "Blue Sky: the new taste of the old West."

The Japanese ad is more than a little different. It has a blood-red background with just two cans of Blue Sky. The written message is shoved into the lower-left corner: "We are drinking it again in Japan. Direct from Santa Fe's clear blue sky to the Japanese throat. Natural soda, Blue Sky, new introduction. No additives, no artificial color, no caffeine that your mom recommends (against)."

Not every company finds it necessary to make such drastic changes to appeal to global markets. Gillette introduced its Sensor razor to American men in commercials during the Super Bowl. The same spots were also introduced in 19 other countries with little modification. Gillette did change a few things. For example, *perfection* is a feminine word in French. The French Gillette theme, "*La perfection au masculin,*" translates into something like "perfection, male-style." Also, U.S. football scenes were replaced with soccer shots in the non-American commercials. Other than that, the models in Gillette's commercials speak 26 different languages, all with the same pitch: not macho but not too soft. They're regular guys. Regular is what you look for when you're building a worldwide mass-market brand.

Other successful global campaigns include L'Oreal's "It's expensive, but I'm worth it" campaign, Clinique's product-as-hero campaign, and Snuggles fabric softener's campaign. The Snuggles brand name changes to fit the country, however. In Germany, it's Kuschelweich. In Italy it's Coccolino. It's Mimosin in France.

Source: J. Roy Parcels, "Making Your Mark," *R&D Strategist*, Fall 1990, pp. 32–34; Paul B. Brown, "Over There," *Inc.*, April 1990, p. 105; and Ashish Banerjee, "Global Campaigns Don't Work; Multinationals Do," *Advertising Age*, April 18, 1994, p. 23.

MTV, the ads are kind of strange (to traditional viewers) and cut from one shot to another quickly, whereas the ads are more wholesome and heart-tugging on adult shows like "Murder She Wrote." MCI developed some 50 different ads to target various narrow market segments.[8] Other marketers may soon follow Coke and MCI's lead in developing separate ads for separate groups.

PROGRESS CHECK

- What are the various forms of direct marketing?
- What are the six elements of the promotion mix?
- Can you explain the differences between industrial advertising, trade advertising, and institutional advertising?
- What are the advantages and disadvantages of TV, magazine, and radio advertising?

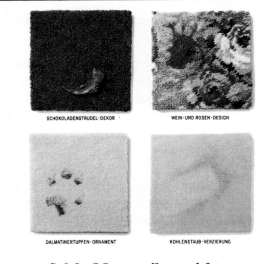

SCHOKOLADENSTRUDEL·DEKOR ·   WEIN· UND ROSEN· DESIGN

DALMATINERTUPFEN· ORNAMENT   KOHLENSTAUB· VERZIERUNG

Solche Muster gibt es nicht – mit Scotchgard™ Imprägnierung.

Die Wahl eines Teppichbodenmusters ist eine persönliche Sache. Von eigenen Kreationen wie kunstvollen Pfotenabdrücken Ihres Vierbeiners und Ketchupstreifen in gewagtem Schwung ist jedoch abzuraten.

Die Scotchgard™ Imprägnierung bewahrt Sie vor solchen 'plötzlichen Inspirationen.' Sie bildet einen unsichtbaren Schutzschild um jede einzelne Faser und schützt vor Schmutz und verschütteten Flüssigkeiten. Wenn Flüssigkeit auf den Teppichboden gelangt, dringt sie nicht in die Faser ein, sondern perlt auf der Faseroberfläche ab und kann leichter abgetupft werden.

Wenn Schmutz in den Teppichboden eingetreten wird, bleibt er nicht an den Fasern haften und ist leichter abzusaugen. Und weil Ihr Teppichboden einfacher gepflegt

werden kann, sieht er bis zu dreimal so lange aus wie neu.

Natürlich werden immer neue Teppichbodenarten entwickelt – deshalb wird auch die Scotchgard™ Imprägnierung fortlaufend verbessert.

Dies sichert die ungewöhnlich hohe Leistungsfähigkeit so vieler Teppichboden-Faserarten. Von Polyamid und Reine Schurwolle bis hin zu Polypropylen – die Scotchgard™ Imprägnierung ist bei vielen Materialien wirkungsvoll.

Deshalb sollten Sie Teppichböden wählen, die mit Scotchgard™ Imprägnierung veredelt sind. Damit das Muster Ihrer Wahl auch auf Dauer das Muster Ihrer Wahl bleibt.

Scotchgard

3M™ und Scotchgard™ sind eingetragene Warenzeichen der 3M Company. 3M Deutschland GmbH, Carl-Schurz-Str. 1, Postfach 100422, 41453 Neuss.

3M *Innovation*

Does global advertising mean using the same message in every country? Certainly such advertising is easier to make, but does it respond to the specific needs of each country? You can imagine similar ads for Coke and Pepsi. Even this ad for Scotchgard has almost universal appeal. What kind of products do you suppose need to change their messages in different countries or even among different people in the same country?

personal selling
Face-to-face presentation and promotion of products and services plus searching out prospects and providing follow-up service.

prospecting
Researching potential buyers and choosing those most likely to buy.

PERSONAL SELLING
• • • • • •

Personal selling is the face-to-face presentation and promotion of products and services. It also involves the search for new prospects and follow-up service after the sale. Effective selling isn't simply a matter of persuading others to buy. (See Figure 16.5.) In fact, it's more accurately described today as helping others to satisfy their wants and needs.

To illustrate personal selling's importance in our economy and the career opportunities it provides, let's look at a few figures. First, U.S. census data show that nearly 10 percent of the total labor force is employed in personal selling. When we add those who sell for nonprofit organizations, we find that over 7 million people are employed in sales.

The average cost of a single sales call to a potential industrial buyer is over $250. Surely no firm would pay that much to send out anyone but a highly skilled, professional marketer and consultant. But how does one get to be that kind of sales representative? What are the steps along the way? Let's take a closer look at the process of selling.

• • • STEPS IN THE SELLING PROCESS • • •

The best way to get a feel for personal selling is to go through the selling process with a product and see what's involved. One product that you're probably familiar with is life insurance. An insurance salesperson has the job of showing people the advantages of life insurance and persuading people to buy one company's policy versus another. Let's go through the selling process with a salesperson to see what can be done to make the sale.

1. *Prospect and qualify*. The first step in the selling process is prospecting. **Prospecting** involves researching potential buyers and choosing those most likely to buy. That selection process is called *qualifying*. To qualify people means to make sure they have a need for the product, the authority to buy, the ability to pay, and the willingness to listen to a sales message. People who meet these criteria are called *prospects*. You may find prospects by asking present customers for names, by calling on people randomly (this is called a *cold call*), and by looking through public records. One source of prospects for life insurance, for example, is public records of people who were recently married or had children.

2. *Preapproach*. Before making a sales call, the sales representative must do further research. As much as possible should be learned about customers and their wants and needs. Before you try to sell people insurance, for example, you would want to know their names, know whether they have children, and have some idea of their family

Prospect and qualify	This first step involves researching potential buyers and choosing those most likely to buy. These people are called ***prospects.*** You may learn the names of prospects from present customers, from surveys, from public records, and so forth.
Preapproach	Before making a sales call, the sales representative must do further research. As much as possible should be learned about the customer and his or her wants and needs. What products are they using now? Are they satisfied? Why or why not? Before a call, a salesperson should know the customer well and have a specific objective for the call. This is probably ***the* most important step in selling.**
Approach	"You don't have a second chance to make a good first impression." That's why the approach is so important. The idea is to give an impression of friendly professionalism, to create rapport, and to build credibility. This is the time to listen carefully to determine customer wants and needs.
Make presentation	This is the actual demonstration or presentation of the product and its benefits to the prospect. This may involve audiovisual aids. Showing advantages versus competition is often included.
Answer objections	Sometimes a prospect may question facts or figures and ask for more information. Often a sales representative must come back several times. The goal is to make sure that the customer is informed and committed to the purchase.
Close sale	You have to "ask for the sale" to finalize the sales process. "Would you like the red one or the green one?" "And when would you want delivery?" are examples of questions used to close the sale.
Follow up	The selling process isn't over until the product is delivered, installed, and working satisfactorily. The selling relationship often continues for years as the salesperson responds to customer requests and introduces new products over time. Selling is a matter of establishing relationships, not just selling goods and services.

The steps in the selling process (shown as a staircase from bottom to top): Prospect, Preapproach, Approach, Make presentation, Answer objections, Close sale, Follow up.

FIGURE 16.5

STEPS IN THE SELLING PROCESS

income. Such information can be obtained when a customer refers you to another client. You can also observe the neighborhood to get an idea of family income.

3. *Approach.* "You don't have a second chance to make a good first impression." That's why the approach is so important. When you call on a customer for the first time, your appearance and your opening comments are important. The idea is to give an impression of friendly professionalism, to create rapport, and to build credibility. The objective of the initial sales call probably won't be to make a sale that day. Rather, the goal may be to set the client at ease. That is, listen to the client, learn what the insurance needs are, get some idea for the amount desired, determine what kind of insurance would be appropriate, and create some interest in the product. Of course, if the client seems ready to buy, an order could be taken that day.

Sales presentations are becoming more and more sophisticated as technology enables sales people to become more creative in presenting their products and services. For example, salespeople can now use laptop computers to show videos, call up database information, and access and tailor all kinds of product information for the customer. Salespeople have become point-of-purchase information sources with almost unlimited flexibility as a result of this new technology.

4. *Make presentation.* This is the actual presentation of the policy and its benefits to the prospect. The idea is to match the benefits of your product to the client's needs. The presentation may involve audiovisual aids and flip charts. Showing the advantages of your product versus competition is often included. Since you've done your homework and know the prospect's wants and needs, the policy will be tailored to the family's needs and be relatively easy to present. Many insurance salespeople today carry laptop computers that enable them to custom-design a policy for each person or family. Once the policy is designed, the computer will tell the family what the payments will be.

5. *Answer objections.* A salesperson should anticipate potential objections clients may raise and determine proper responses. Questions should be viewed as opportunities for creating better relationships, not as a challenge to what you're saying. Customers have legitimate doubts, and salespeople are there to resolve those doubts. If such a dialogue weren't necessary, salespeople could easily be replaced by advertising. Salespeople are taught several strategies for overcoming objections.

6. *Close sale.* You have to "ask for the sale" to finalize the sales process. A salesperson has limited time and can't spend forever with one client answering questions and objections. Closing techniques include getting a series of small commitments and then asking for the order and showing the client where to sign. Salespeople are taught to remember their "ABCs"—Always Be Closing.

7. *Follow up.* The selling process isn't over until the policy is written and signed, and the customer is happy. The selling relationship often continues for years as the salesperson responds to new customer requests for information. Each time a new child is born, a client may want a new insurance policy or may want to increase the insurance coverage on the existing policy. Selling is a matter of establishing relationships, not just selling goods or services. Thus, follow-up includes handling customer complaints and making sure that the customer's questions are answered. Often customer service is as important to the sale as the product itself.

The selling process varies somewhat among different goods and services, but the general idea is the same. Your goals as a salesperson are to help the buyer buy and to make sure that the buyer is satisfied after the sale.

••• BUSINESS-TO-BUSINESS SELLING •••

Salespeople who sell to commercial accounts (wholesalers and retailers), institutional accounts (hospitals and schools), and industrial accounts (manufacturers and service providers) often make more money and have a more challenging experience than those selling to consumers. The customers tend to buy in larger quantities, and as a result the salesperson often makes a larger commission.

Customers are often easier to find because the government classifies business customers using Standard Industrial Classification Codes. Using those codes, once a salesperson has found one customer in an industry, he or she can easily find other customers with the same SIC code. Industrial salespeople are often called *marketing consultants* because they help their business customers become more effective at marketing. Ice cream salespeople can sell more ice cream to dairy stores if they teach the store personnel how to sell more ice cream to final customers.

Xerox believes that selling is based largely on understanding buyers' thought processes. That's true whether you're selling copiers or banking services. Therefore, Xerox is training salespeople from all kinds of companies in customer-oriented selling.[9]

What kind of products do you think you would enjoy selling? Think of the customers for that product. Can you imagine yourself going through the seven-step selling process with them? Which steps would be hardest? Which would be easiest? Which step could you avoid by selling in a retail store? Can you picture yourself going through the sales process on the phone (telemarketing)?

CRITICAL THINKING

WORD-OF-MOUTH  SALES PROMOTION

Word-of-mouth promotion encourages people to tell other people about products they've enjoyed. Word of mouth is one of the most effective promotional tools, but most marketers don't use it to full effectiveness. Ivan R. Misner's book *The World's Best Known Marketing Secret: Building Your Business with Word-of-Mouth Marketing* is a hands-on, how-to book on managing word-of-mouth promotions. Such books teach marketers the effectiveness of word-of-mouth communication.

word-of-mouth promotion
Consumers talking about products they have liked or disliked.

Anything that encourages people to talk favorably about an organization is effective word of mouth. Notice, for example, how stores use clowns, banners, music, fairs, and other attention-getting devices to create word of mouth. Clever commercials can generate much word of mouth. You can ask people to tell others about your product or even pay them to do so. Samples are another way to generate word of mouth. But the best way to generate word of mouth is to have a good product, provide good services, and keep customers happy. Word-of-mouth promotion thus includes (1) focusing on customer satisfaction and quality, (2) delivering on promises, and (3) targeting opinion leaders.

We consumers are happy to tell others where to get good services and reliable products. Lynn Gordon of French Meadow Bakery in Minneapolis learned about the power of word of mouth when she developed a recipe for old-fashioned bread. Word of mouth enlarged her business from selling 40 loaves a week at local co-ops to running her own 13,500-square-foot bakery employing 15 people. But we consumers are also quick to tell others when we're unhappy with products and services. Negative word of mouth hurts a firm badly. Taking care of consumer complaints quickly and effectively is one of the best ways to reduce the negative effects of word of mouth.

To promote positive word-of-mouth, advertise to people who already use your product. Yes, we said, "to people who already use your product." They have a commitment to that product and are more likely to read the ad. They

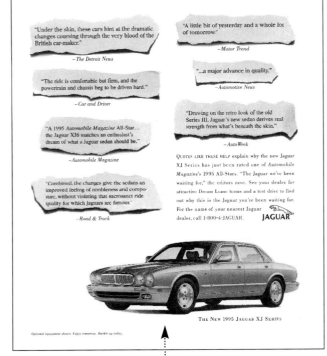

The greatest form of advertising is still word of mouth.

"Under the skin, these cars hint at the dramatic changes coursing through the very blood of the British car-maker."
– *The Detroit News*

"A little bit of yesterday and a whole lot of tomorrow."
– *Motor Trend*

"The ride is comfortable but firm, and the powertrain and chassis beg to be driven hard."
– *Car and Driver*

"...a major advance in quality."
– *Automotive News*

"A 1995 *Automobile Magazine* All-Star... the Jaguar XJ6 matches an enthusiast's dream of what a Jaguar sedan should be."
–*Automobile Magazine*

"Drawing on the retro look of the old Series III, Jaguar's new sedan derives real strength from what's beneath the skin."
– *AutoWeek*

"Combined, the changes give the sedans an improved feeling of nimbleness and composure, without violating that sacrosanct ride quality for which Jaguars are famous."
– *Road & Track*

QUOTES LIKE THESE HELP explain why the new Jaguar XJ Series has just been rated one of *Automobile Magazine*'s 1995 All-Stars. "The Jaguar we've been waiting for," the editors rave. See your dealer for attractive Dream Lease terms and a test drive to find out why this is the Jaguar you've been waiting for. For the name of your nearest Jaguar dealer, call 1-800-4-JAGUAR. **JAGUAR**

THE NEW 1995 JAGUAR XJ SERIES

Optional equipment shown. Enjoy tomorrow. Buckle up today.

Word of mouth is really not a form of advertising because advertising, by definition, goes through a medium such as newspapers or magazines. Nonetheless, word of mouth *is* one of the most potent forms of promotion. What customers and professionals say about a product is often more powerful than what marketers say in their ads. By putting word-of-mouth messages into their ads, Jaguar has the best of both worlds.

sales promotion
The promotional tool that stimulates consumer purchasing and dealer interest by means of short-term activities (displays, shows and exhibitions, contests, etc.).

may then go out and tell others how smart they were in buying the product. This results in positive word of mouth for you. For example, sending brochures about a beautiful vacation resort to people who've already been there gives them something to use to show and tell others how exciting the place was. Such word-of-mouth promotion is very effective in getting others to visit.

One strategy for spreading word of mouth is to send testimonials to current customers. Most companies use testimonials only in promoting to new customers. But testimonials are effective in confirming customers' belief that they chose the right company. Positive word of mouth from other users further confirms their choice.[10]

••• SALES PROMOTION •••

Sales promotion is the promotional tool that stimulates consumer purchasing and dealer interest by means of short-term activities (such things as displays, shows and exhibitions, and contests). Figure 16.6 lists some sales promotion techniques.

Those free samples of products that people get in the mail, the cents-off coupons that they clip from newspapers, the contests that various retail stores sponsor, and those premiums you find in Cracker Jack boxes are examples of sales promotion activities. Sales promotion programs are designed to supplement personal selling, advertising, and public relations efforts by creating enthusiasm for the overall promotional program. Coupons were especially popular in the early part of this decade, but manufacturers decided that coupons were costing them too much money and began cutting back on coupon use in the mid-1990s.[11] Leaders in this cutback include such large firms as Procter & Gamble, Philip Morris, and Ralston Purina.

Sales promotion can be both internal (within the company) and external (outside the company). It's just as important to get employees enthusiastic about a sale as it is to attract potential customers. The most important internal sales promotion efforts are directed at salespeople and other customer-contact people such as complaint handlers and clerks. Sales promotion is an attempt to keep salespeople enthusiastic about the company through (1) sales training, (2) the development of sales aids such as flip charts, portable audio-visual displays, and videotapes, and (3) participation in trade shows where salespeople can get leads. Other employees who deal with the public may also be given special training to make them more aware of company programs and a more integral part of the total promotional effort.

After enthusiasm is generated internally, it's important to get distributors and dealers involved so that they too are enthusiastic and will cooperate by putting up signs and helping to promote the product.

After the company's employees and salespeople have been motivated with sales promotion efforts and middlemen have become involved, the next step is to promote to final consumers using samples, coupons, cents-off deals, displays, store demonstrators, premiums, and other incentives such as contests, trading stamps, and rebates. Sales promotion is an ongoing effort to maintain enthusiasm, so different strategies are used over time to keep the ideas fresh.

FROM THE PAGES OF...
Entrepreneur® MAGAZINE

Word-of-Mouth Promotions

Visual Dialogues makes durable maps for bikers and hikers. Company founder Rick McEwan is an artist/back-packer who discovered that regular maps could get ruined in the rain and other happenings along the hiking trail. He began making durable maps and even produces maps on T-shirts. His maps and T-shirts are sold via catalog and through 300 retail outlets. But ask McEwan what his promotion secret is, and he'll tell you, "Word of mouth is the secret behind the company's sales. Our biggest advertisement is our name and address on the maps. We get lots of orders from those."

Source: Robin Montgomery, "Top of the Charts," *Entrepreneur*, October 1994, p. 13.

One popular sales promotion tool is *sampling*. Often consumers won't buy a new product unless they've had a chance to try it. As a consequence, stores often have people standing in the aisles handing out samples of food and beverage products. Sampling is thus a quick effective way of demonstrating a product's superiority at the time when consumers are making a purchase decision.[12]

PUBLIC RELATIONS AND PUBLICITY

Public relations (PR) is defined by *Public Relations News* as the management function that evaluates public attitudes, identifies the policies and procedures of an individual or an organization with the public interest, and executes a program of action to earn public understanding and acceptance. In other words, a good public relations program has three steps:

1. Listen to the public. Public relations starts with good marketing research ("evaluates public attitudes").

2. Develop policies and procedures in the public interest. We don't earn understanding by bombarding the public with propaganda; we earn understanding by having programs and practices in the public interest.

public relations
The management function that evaluates public attitudes, develops policies and procedures consistent with the public interest, and takes steps to earn public understanding and acceptance.

Displays (store displays)	Rebates (refunds from producers)
Contests ("You may have won $1 million!")	Lotteries
Samples (toothpaste, soap)	Audiovisual aids
Coupons (25 cents off)	Catalogs
Premiums (free glass when you buy a meal)	Demonstrations
Shows (fashion shows)	Special events
Deals (price reductions)	Exhibits
Trade shows	Portfolios for salespeople
Bonuses (buy one, get one free)	Conventions
Incentives (the gift in a Cracker Jack box)	Sweepstakes

FIGURE 16.6

SALES PROMOTION TECHNIQUES
Spend some time with this list. Most students aren't familiar with all the activities involved in sales promotion. This is the time to learn them.

Making Ethical Decisions

Guilt by Association

Suppose you're CEO of an international public relations firm. You're approached by the dictator of a foreign country who has been linked to international drug trafficking. You feel these charges against him are well founded and have little doubt of his guilt. He offers $1 million for your firm's advice on how to change his image. He agrees to keep your relationship confidential and to pay you from an account unrelated to him. What are your alternatives? What are the consequences of each alternative? Which alternative is most ethical? Which do you choose?

3. Inform people of the fact that you're being responsive to their needs. It's not enough to simply have programs in the public interest. You have to tell the public about those programs so that they know you're being responsive.

••• GLOBAL PUBLIC RELATIONS •••

Pause for a moment and think of countries such Mexico, China, Japan, and India. What are your initial impressions? Why? A few moments' reflection will tell you that almost everything you know or believe about a country is based on what you've heard on the radio, seen on TV, or read about in a magazine or newspaper. If you have a favorable impression, that country has done a relatively good PR job. If you have a negative impression, it may be that the media created it or the country may have ignored its PR role.

OS&A Research and Strategy (a public opinion research firm) is working with the U.S. Department of Housing and Urban Development (HUD) to improve HUD's image. The company designed 19 surveys to sample the attitudes and observations of HUD's customers, ranging from individuals to mortgage lenders. This effort is just one of many being undertaken in the 1990s to improve government's image.[13]

A key industry for most countries is tourism. The best way to increase tourism is to get favorable publicity in other countries' media and through travel agents, tour clubs, and other major influentials. Can you see the value of PR people giving speeches, film presentations, and other promotional efforts to these groups?

We don't want to belabor the point that public relations is important for countries, cities, and communities as well as businesses. But we do want to expand your horizons a bit to see public relations and its main concern (public opinion) as a critical function for all organizations and individuals hoping to establish mutually satisfying relationships with others.

••• PUBLICITY •••

publicity
Any information about an individual, a product, or an organization that is distributed to the public through the media, that is not paid for, or controlled by, the sponsor.

Publicity is one of the major functions of the public relations department. Here's how it works. Suppose when we want to introduce our new Fiberrific cereal to consumers, we have very little money to promote it. We want to get some initial sales to generate funds. One effective way to reach the public is through publicity. **Publicity** is any information about an individual, product, or organization that's distributed to the public through the media and that's not

paid for, or controlled by, the sponsor. We might prepare a publicity release describing Fiberrific and the
research findings supporting its benefits and send it
to the various media. Much skill is involved in writing the story so that the media will want to publish it.
Release of the news about Fiberrific will reach many
potential buyers (and investors, distributors, and
dealers), and we may be on our way to becoming
wealthy marketers.

The best thing about publicity is that the various
media will publish publicity stories free-of-charge if the
material seems interesting or newsworthy. The idea,
then, is to write publicity that meets those criteria.

Besides being free, publicity has several further
advantages over other promotional tools, such as
advertising. For example, publicity may reach people
who wouldn't read an ad. Publicity may be placed on
the front page of a newspaper or in some other
prominent position. Perhaps the greatest advantage
of publicity is its believability. When a newspaper or
magazine publishes a story as news, the reader treats
that story as news—and news is more believable
than advertising.

There are several disadvantages to publicity as
well. For example, you have no control over how,
when, or if the media will use the story. The media
aren't obligated to use a publicity release and most
are thrown away. Furthermore, the story may be
altered so that it's not so positive. There's good publicity (IBM comes out with
a new supercomputer) and bad publicity (GM lays off 74,000 workers). Once a
story has run, it's not likely to be repeated. Advertising, on the other hand, can
be repeated as often as needed. One way to see that publicity is handled well by
the media is to establish a friendly relationship with media representatives,
cooperating with them when they seek information. Then when you want their
support, they're more likely to cooperate.

The Closest You Can Get To Heaven While Still On Earth

From the cloud-shrouded peaks of the Himalayas to the pink city of Jaipur, from thousands of ancient temples to the singular majesty of the Taj Mahal, India awakens the senses, quiets the mind and energizes the soul. So find out how the country Mark Twain called "paradise on earth" offers you the best of the ancient world and the twentieth century. Especially now: Air India's brand new fleet of Boeing 747-400s will whisk you to our world in the greatest of comfort and speed. For your free India Travel Guide call your local travel agent or the Government of India Tourist Office: New York (212) 586-4901, Los Angeles (213) 380-8855, Toronto (416) 962-3787. And discover the journey of perpetual wonder.

India
THE JEWEL OF ASIA

Call the number above or write to MSI, 25-15 50th Street, Dept. SAV395, Woodside, NY 11377.

This print ad for India is designed to create a favorable impression for the country and encourage tourism. An integrated marketing communication program would link such ads with a publicity campaign, a personal selling campaign, and a direct marketing campaign (direct mail) to create a unified campaign.

PREPARING THE PROMOTION MIX

Each target group calls for a separate promotion mix. For example, large,
homogeneous groups of consumers are usually most efficiently reached
through advertising. Large organizations are best reached through personal
selling. To motivate people to buy now rather than later, sales promotion
efforts such as coupons, discounts, special displays, premiums, and so on may
be used. Publicity adds support to the other efforts and can create a good
impression among all consumers. Word of mouth is often the most powerful
promotional tool and is generated effectively by listening, being responsive,
and creating an impression worth passing on to others.

••• PROMOTIONAL STRATEGIES •••

There are three ways to promote products' movement from producers to consumers. The first is called a *push strategy*. In a **push strategy**, the producer
uses advertising, personal selling, sales promotion, and all other promotional

push strategy
Use of promotional tools to convince wholesalers and retailers to stock and sell merchandise.

tools to convince wholesalers and retailers to stock and sell merchandise. If it works, consumers will then walk into the store, see the product, and buy it. The idea is to push the product down the distribution system to the stores. One example of a push strategy is to offer dealers one free case of soda for every dozen cases they purchase.

pull strategy
Use of promotional tools to motivate consumers to request products from stores.

A second strategy is called a *pull strategy*. In a **pull strategy**, heavy advertising and sales promotion efforts are directed toward consumers so that they'll request the products from retailers. If it works, consumers will go to the store and order the products. Seeing the demand for the products, the store owner will then order them from the wholesaler. The wholesaler, in turn, will order them from the producer. Products are thus pulled down through the distribution system. Dr Pepper has used TV advertising in a pull strategy to increase distribution. Tripledge wipers also reached retail stores through a pull strategy. Of course, a company could use both push and pull strategies at the same time in a major promotional effort.

The third way to move goods from producer to consumer is to make promotion part of a total systems approach to marketing. That is, promotion would be part of supply chain management ◀·· P.472 ··▶. In such cases, retailers would work with producers and distributors to make the supply chain as efficient as possible. Then a promotional plan would be developed for the whole system. The idea would be to develop a value package ◀·· P.435 ··▶ that would appeal to everyone: manufacturers, distributors, retailers, and consumers. The trend today is toward everyday low pricing because that results in the greatest profit for sellers and good bargains for consumers. The best deal for consumers is to use coupons and other deals, but that has proven less profitable for sellers and thus may be unsustainable for the long run.

••• OPENING COMMUNICATION •••
WITH ALL STAKEHOLDERS

It's not enough for a firm to have good relations with customers. They must also maintain good relations with stockholders, suppliers, financiers, the local community, and any other group or individual affected by the organization. That means that organizations must listen carefully to all stakeholders and respond accordingly. The best way to maintain such open communication is to establish an integrated marketing communication system. We'll discuss integrated marketing communication systems next.

CRITICAL THINKING

What kinds of problems can emerge if a firm doesn't communicate with environmentalists, the news media, and the local community? In your area have you seen examples of firms that aren't responsive to the community? What were the consequences?

PROGRESS CHECK

- What are the seven steps in the selling process?
- Promoters spend more money on sales promotion than on advertising. Figure 16.6 lists 21 different sales promotion techniques. Do you remember most of them?
- Could you describe how to implement a push strategy for Fiberrific cereal? A pull strategy?

INTEGRATED MARKETING COMMUNICATION (IMC) SYSTEMS

Interactive TV and other new technologies have forced marketers like Pepsico (see this chapter's opening profile) to take a new approach to promotion. The idea is to combine all promotional efforts into one unified package to heighten efficiency and effectiveness. That unified effort is called an integrated marketing communication system. An **integrated marketing communication (IMC) system** is a formal mechanism for uniting all the promotional efforts in an organization to make it more responsive to its customers and other stakeholders. In the past, advertising was created by ad agencies, public relations was created by PR firms, and so forth. There was little coordination between promotional efforts. Today, all that's changing in many companies.

integrated marketing communication (IMC) system
A formal mechanism for uniting all the promotional efforts in an organization to make it more responsive to its customers and other stakeholders.

... IMPLEMENTING AN INTEGRATED MARKETING ... COMMUNICATION SYSTEM

To implement an IMC system, you start with customers and stakeholders ◀--- P40 ---▶ and their information needs. Gathering such information and making that information accessible to everyone in the system is a key to future marketing success. All messages reaching customers, potential customers, and stakeholders must be consistent and coordinated. A communications specialist could be part of every cross-functional product development team to be sure that communication aspects of the product are given consideration from the very beginning.

World-class marketing communication demands a complete restructuring of the communication function.[14] Let's explore the three steps in developing an integrated marketing communication system:

1. *Listen constantly* to the groups affected by the organization (including customers, potential customers, and other stakeholders) and keep that information in a database. Make that information available to everyone in the organization. "Without specific customer information, the organization will continue to send out the wrong messages and information to the wrong people at the wrong time at an exorbitant cost."[15]

   An information database is critical to any successful program. Every organization that can afford it should keep information about its customers and other stakeholders in a database. There are companies that will assist you in establishing such a database. For example, Sprint Publishing and Advertising, a subsidiary of Sprint, has formed a unit called Integrated Marketing Services. This unit helps organizations with on-premise research services, database modeling, inbound and outbound telemarketing, and direct response services. In other words, Sprint Publishing is offering a unified communication effort that involves both listening and talking.

2. *Respond quickly* to customer and other stakeholder information by adjusting company policies and practices and by designing wanted products and services for target markets. A responsive firm adapts to changing wants and needs quickly and captures the market from other less responsive firms. That's why information is so vital to organizations today and why so much money is spent on computers to analyze data. One reason why small firms are capturing markets from large firms is that small firms tend to be better listeners, to have fewer layers of management in which information gets lost, and to be more responsive to changes in the market.

3. *Use integrated marketing communication* to let all customers and other stakeholders know that the firm is listening and responding to their needs.[16] All employees should be encouraged to join community organizations and volunteer for charitable causes. This makes the organization more visible and gives employees a chance to gather information from the public and to tell people about the firm's programs and products. When an organization is responsive to the public and lets that fact be known, it will more likely be profitable and grow, creating more jobs and more benefits for society. Ultimately, marketing is the way society meets its needs by exchanging goods and services. Integrated marketing communication systems create the information flows that make such exchanges mutually beneficial.

THE EFFECT ON TRADITIONAL MARKETING ORGANIZATIONS

Advertising agencies are the organizations most affected by the trend toward integrated marketing communication. Traditionally, agencies provided one service—the creation of advertising. Over time, they've added services such as direct marketing, sales promotion assistance, and database management so they could provide an integrated marketing communication package to advertisers. Leo Burnett Company was one of the first agencies to completely integrate. That was years ago. Today, many ad agencies are trying to integrate advertising, public relations, direct marketing, and other promotional tools into one integrated package.[17]

FROM INTEGRATED MARKETING COMMUNICATION TO INTEGRATED MARKETING

integrated marketing (IM)
The merging of all organizational efforts to please customers, employees, and other stakeholders.

Once firms have mastered the idea of integrated marketing communication, they can move on to adopt the concept of integrated marketing. **Integrated marketing (IM)** is the merging of all organizational efforts (not just promotion) to please customers, employees, and other stakeholders. In addition to integrating all *promotional* efforts, integrated marketing would combine those efforts with marketing research, product design, engineering, production, packaging, pricing, logistics, customer service, and all the other firm's functions.

IMPLEMENTING AN INTEGRATED MARKETING STRATEGY

Let's focus for a minute on an integrated marketing strategy for customers. Such a strategy begins by identifying very narrow customer groups that provide a clear marketing opportunity. You've learned how to do that using market segmentation. You then determine in detail what those customer groups want in a value package. Every effort should be made to determine what competition is already offering the customer. Then you develop a value package that's custom-designed for each customer or homogeneous customer group (*mass customization*).

A good way to ensure that the entire organization (and its suppliers and dealers) has a unified focus on this objective is to develop customer-oriented cross-functional teams that represent the various functions of the firm.

Included on the team may be customers, suppliers, and dealers. Each team's makeup may vary by customer group. The idea is to focus on customer needs. Organization structure must be flexible enough to respond to those needs.

The team would also conduct an audit to identify any other stakeholders whose needs must be met. The team would decide stakeholder priorities and develop appropriate marketing responses for each. Once that process was implemented, the company could truly say that it was customer-driven and had a world-class marketing and communications approach to all stakeholders.

PROGRESS CHECK

- What are the three steps in developing an integrated marketing communication system?
- How does integrated marketing differ from integrated marketing communication?

SUMMARY

1. Promotion is an attempt by marketers to persuade others to participate in exchanges with them.
   - *What are the six promotional tools that make up the promotion mix?*
   The six promotional tools are advertising, personal selling, word of mouth, sales promotion, public relations, and publicity.

1. List and describe the various elements of the promotion mix.

2. Many people mistake other promotional tools for advertising.
   - *How does advertising differ from the other promotional tools?*
   Advertising is limited to paid, nonpersonal communication through various media by organizations and individuals who are in some way identified in the advertising message.
   - *What are the advantages of using the various media?*
   You can review the advantages and disadvantages of the various advertising media in Figure 16.3.
   - *How's technology used in advertising?*
   Rather than passively *receive* programming (news, entertainment, and commercials), consumers using interactive TV can actively *control* what they receive and can conduct a dialogue with advertisers. They can eliminate commercials from shows or watch the commercials and respond electronically (including placing orders). Some on-line computer services will offer advertising—and nothing but advertising—on demand. There will be databases for "considered purchases," offering consumers in-depth information (via text, pictures, and sound) about cars, travel, consumer electronics, and other high-priced items.

2. Describe advantages and disadvantages of various advertising media and explain the latest advertising techniques.

3. Personal selling is the face-to-face presentation and promotion of products and services. It also involves the search for new prospects and follow-up service after the sale.
   - *What are the seven steps of the selling process?*
   The steps of the selling process are (1) prospect and qualify, (2) preapproach, (3) approach, (4) make presentation, (5) answer objections, (6) close sale, and (7) follow up.

3. Illustrate the seven steps of the selling process.

4. Word-of-mouth promotion encourages people to talk about an organization.
   - *What's the best way to generate positive word of mouth?*
   The best way to generate positive word of mouth is to have a good product, provide good services, and keep customers happy. Word-of-mouth promotion thus includes (1) focusing on customer satisfaction and quality, (2) delivering on promises, and (3) targeting opinion leaders.

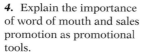

4. Explain the importance of word of mouth and sales promotion as promotional tools.

• *How are sales promotion activities used both within and outside the organization?*

Internal sales promotion efforts are directed at salespeople and other customer-contact people to keep them enthusiastic about the company. Internal sales promotion activities include sales training, sales aids, audiovisual displays, and trade shows. External sales promotion (promotion to consumers) involves using samples, coupons, cents-off deals, displays, store demonstrators, premiums, and other such incentives.

5. Describe the functions of the public relations department and the role of publicity in those functions.

5. Public relations is the management function that evaluates public attitudes, identifies the policies and procedures of an organization with the public interest, and executes a program of action to earn public understanding and acceptance.

• *What are the three major steps in a good public relations program?*

(1) Listen to the public. (Public relations starts with good marketing research.) (2) Develop policies and procedures in the public interest. (One doesn't earn understanding by bombarding the public with propaganda; one earns understanding by having programs and practices in the public interest.) (3) Inform people that you're being responsive to their needs.

• *What is publicity?*

Publicity is information distributed by the media that's not paid for, or controlled by, the sponsor. It's an effective way to reach the public. Publicity's greatest advantage is its believability.

6. Compare and contrast various promotional strategies such as push and pull strategies.

6. Marketers use various promotional strategies to move goods from producers to consumers.

• *What are the various promotional strategies?*

(1) In a push strategy, the producer uses advertising, personal selling, sales promotion, and all other promotional tools to convince wholesalers and retailers to stock and sell merchandise. (2) In a pull strategy, heavy advertising and sales promotion efforts are directed toward consumers so that they'll request the products from retailers. (3) A final way to move goods from producer to consumer is to make promotion part of a total systems approach to marketing. That is, promotion would be part of supply chain management, as discussed in Chapter 15. In such cases, retailers would work with producers and distributors to make the supply chain as efficient as possible.

7. Describe the three parts of an integrated marketing communication system and how such systems affect ad agencies.

7. An integrated marketing communication system is a formal mechanism for uniting all the promotional efforts in an organization to make it more responsive to its customers and other stakeholders.

• *How do you set up an integrated marketing communication system?*

It consists of three ongoing parts: (1) *Listen constantly* to all groups affected by the organization, keep that information in a database, and make that information available to everyone in the organization. (2) *Respond quickly* to customer and other stakeholder information by adjusting company policies and practices and by designing wanted products and services for target markets. (3) *Use integrated marketing communication* to let all customers and other stakeholders know that the firm is listening and responding to their needs.

• *How does IMC affect traditional marketing organizations?*

Ad agencies have been forced away from being narrow advertising specialists to becoming integrated marketing communication experts.

8. Integrated marketing is the merging of all organizational efforts (not just promotion) to please customers, employees, and other stakeholders.
   • **How can a company be sure that integrated marketing takes place?** A good way to ensure that the entire organization has a unified focus on this objective is to develop customer-oriented cross-functional teams that represent the various functions of the firm. Teams may include customers, suppliers, and dealers.

8. Discuss how integrated marketing evolves from integrated marketing communication.

KEY TERMS

advertising 493
direct marketing 492
infomercials 495
integrated
  marketing (IM) 510
integrated marketing
  communication
  (IMC) system 509

interactive
  television 497
mass
  customization 498
personal selling 500
promotion 492
promotion mix 493
prospecting 500

public relations
  (PR) 505
publicity 506
pull strategy 508
push strategy 507
sales promotion 504
word-of-mouth
  promotion 503

DEVELOPING WORKPLACE SKILLS

1. Review several newspapers and magazines for the purpose of evaluating the advertising. Choose several ads, contrasting those containing a lot of information with those that do not. Bring examples of each to class for discussion. Which are more effective in attracting consumer interest?

2. Scan your local newspaper for examples of publicity (stories about new products you see in the paper) and sales promotion (coupons, contests, sweepstakes). Share your examples and discuss the effectiveness of such promotional efforts with the class.

3. Select and bring to class a product that you think others would find interesting. Set up a role-playing situation in which you attempt to sell the product to your classmates in a five-minute sales presentation.

4. Interview at least three different salespeople in three different fields (e.g., insurance, automobiles, computers, real estate, and industrial products). Develop a chart comparing the attributes (e.g., compensation, levels of responsibility and authority, etc.) of each. Which appears to offer the best career potential? Why?

5. Make a list of 20 products (goods and services) that most students own or use and then debate which promotional techniques prompt you to buy these goods and services: advertising, personal selling, publicity, sales promotion, or word-of-mouth.

PRACTICING MANAGEMENT DECISIONS

〉〉 C A S E WAKING UP THE COFFEE INDUSTRY 〈〈

About 25 years ago, the number one drink in America was coffee. However, the trend for the coffee industry wasn't good. From the 1960s through the 1980s, coffee sales declined. By the end of the 1980s, soft drinks had replaced coffee as our favorite beverage.

The history of coffee sales is revealing. The original colonists were mostly tea drinkers, bringing the habit with them from England. There were some coffee drinkers in the Dutch colony called New Amsterdam (the future New

York). In 1773, the colonists dumped hundreds of chests of tea into Boston harbor in a protest over taxes, and thereafter America evolved into a coffee-drinking nation.

By 1962, coffee sales were up to $1 billion a year. Three fourths of the adult population drank an average of over three cups a day. The market looked so attractive at that time that Procter & Gamble bought the Folgers coffee company in 1963. But from 1963 on, coffee sales overall have declined.

What happened in the 1960s to change the market? A major factor was Pepsi and Coke's battle for the teenage drinker. Pepsi developed the theme of the Pepsi Generation. Coke responded with themes directed toward young people as well. Coffee ads, meanwhile, were directed toward the over-35 crowd. The spokespeople for coffee were middle-aged women, such as Mrs. Olsen, who promoted Folgers. Meanwhile, the Pepsi Generation grew up and took their preference for soft drinks with them.

More recently, coffee producers have been trying to woo back younger drinkers. Nescafe Silka, for example, is a "smooth, lighter coffee" aimed at 18- to 35-year-olds. Another campaign is aimed at the new generation of college students. The Coffee Development Group has 50 "coffee houses" on college campuses, providing a coffee grinder, a brewer, and a cappuccino machine, among other supplies. The idea is to get students back to drinking coffee. Recent studies have found that students are drinking soft drinks for breakfast. Coffee makers want to change that trend back to coffee for the morning meal.

Meanwhile, coffee shops such as Starbucks are leading a resurgence. They're cutting into the business of companies that have a much smaller selection such as Dunkin' Donuts. However, one factor may restrain the industry's comeback—specialty coffee prices have increased dramatically, due to the increased demand and an inadequate supply of beans. These price increases have cut into coffee shops' profits. Meanwhile, sales of canned coffee continue to decline. Now that consumers have had a taste of Starbucks and other "gourmet" brews, it's clear that's what they prefer, regardless of the cost.

Decision Questions

1. What would you recommend to coffee producers to win the college market back to coffee?

2. Would you develop different strategies for regular versus decaffeinated coffee? Why? Which would you emphasize for college students today, or would you try to balance your offerings of both?

3. What kind of marketing communication system might you establish to keep in touch with students and other young coffee drinkers?

4. You've talked with many college students and heard what they say about coffee versus soft drinks. What has your marketing intelligence system told you? What recommendation would you make to coffee producers based on that information? Would a focus group help to confirm those impressions?

Source: Kathleen Deveny, "For Coffee's Big Three, a Gourmet-Brew Boom Proves Embarrassing Bust," *The Wall Street Journal*, November 4, 1993, pp. B1 and B10; and Seth Lubove, "Coffee versus Gazebo Blend," *Forbes*, June 20, 1994, p. 112.

> VIDEO CASE   INTEGRATED MARKETING COMMUNICATION
>   AT SPRINT

Integrated marketing communication (IMC) means using multiple promotion tools (e.g., advertising, personal selling, publicity, sales promotion, and direct marketing) to reach a target audience with one, unified message. It is important when thinking about integrated communication to remember that everything about a product communicates, including its price, the brand name, where it is sold, and so forth. If there is one place to apply integrated marketing communication, it might well be the telecommunications industry. Few industries today are as competitive and AT&T, Sprint, and MCI are battling aggressively for this market. It's easy to understand why—each share point of the market is worth $1 billion!

In formulating its competitive strategy, Sprint decided to focus on the business customer, especially businesspeople who travel. Product research went into determining what this market wanted in a product and what the company's capabilities were. Integrated marketing communication thus leads to integrated marketing; that is, integrating product development with pricing, promotion, and research.

Sprint uses an account supervisor as the person to manage the integration of marketing and marketing communication. He or she sets up the links with other departments. Research was needed to learn more about the target market. It turns out that the market was largely male and between the ages of 25 and 54. Both qualitative and quantitative research was used to determine what these men wanted and how to reach them through the media.

The BIG IDEA was to sell the idea of voice recognition so that business travelers could simply say the name of a person and the phone number would be dialed automatically. This technology was so advanced that the image of Sprint as a whole was enhanced by its promotion. It even attracted college students when they were not the target market; they thought the idea was "cool."

The success of this new product, however, depended greatly on the use of integrated marketing communication. In addition to ads on TV and in business magazines, the company promoted the concept on the back of airline ticket jackets, in in-flight magazines, and at press conferences. Telemarketing was also used.

The program turned out to be a big hit. Much of its success was credited to leverage—the increased power of communication—created by an integrated campaign. That campaign, however, was part of a larger overall marketing strategy that called for segmentation, pricing, and numerous other marketing decisions.

Discussion Questions

1. How was the promotion industry organized before so that marketing communication was *not* integrated? What changes had to be made to allow such integration?

2. Many college students have signed up for MCI or Sprint service. After making a considerable effort to attract these new customers, some students believe these companies have not followed up with good customer relations. How could phone companies use relationship marketing to *keep* these customers?

3. How does the idea of voice recognition compare to the lure of MCI's Friends and Family program as a promotional BIG IDEA?

Part 5

FUNDAMENTALS OF MARKETING

Marketing is a challenging and dynamic area in which to choose a career. The field is so varied, it can attract people with a tremendous variety of talents, skills, and interest areas. For example, the "number crunching" person could choose marketing research; artistic individuals might be attracted to advertising or sales promotion; and entrepreneurial types might choose wholesaling or retailing. There are dozens of other combinations.

Marketing is based on the exchange of goods and services. Like every other area of business, it is dynamic and always changing, especially with the current emphasis on international markets. Anyone who wants to be involved in this exciting area must be flexible and able to change with the times as tastes for new products and services change and as new markets open and old ones close. Marketing is an area that remains wide open.

SKILLS

Although marketing draws on talents from a variety of personality types and skill areas, some realistic generalizations can be made about skills that most marketers have in common. Marketers need to be people oriented, even the number crunchers mentioned above. They also need to be tuned in to the culture of the country or region where they are marketing. They need to sense trends and changing habits of customers. Above all, they must be effective communicators, possessing an ability to be heard and noticed as well as to hear and notice the needs of others. The amount of education required varies widely from position to position, and even firm to firm.

CAREER PATHS

Many marketing careers start out as sales positions. Sales is a challenging area in which individuals can prove themselves, using that success as a means of moving up to sales manager or other positions of responsibility. Advertising is another avenue of interest, especially for those who are attracted to the tantalizing mixture of psychology, communications, and art that advertisers use. Retailing also offers a variety of opportunities, some more marketing-oriented that others.

Not all positions in marketing require a four-year degree, although one is usually a formally stated requisite. In many companies, your skill level is the important issue. Marketing skills can often be developed in two-year business programs and in real-world experience. On-campus clubs such as FBLA (Future Business Leaders of America) and DECA (Distributive Education Clubs of America) can help you learn to compete in the world of marketing while still in school.

SOME POSSIBLE CAREERS IN MARKETING

Job Title	Salary	Job Duties	Career Path	Prospects
Market researcher	$23,000–$34,000 (start) Market research director, as much as $140,000.	Design surveys, opinion polls, and questionnaires; collect data using various methods.	Bachelor's degree with marketing courses. Some positions require only talent and desire to learn.	Good prospects through 2005. Fewer than 30,000 now employed in the United States.
Sales representative	$20,500–$100,000+ (depends both on the company and initiative of the individual).	Call on customers; fulfill needs; provide follow-up; sometimes deal with credit issues; report regularly to home office.	Training programs usually provided by company. Successful representatives are usually promoted to sales manager.	Many new opportunities in the future, especially in high tech and international sales.
Purchasing agent (buyer)	$25,200–$36,000 (usually depends on company size).	Stay informed about buying opportunities; maintain good relations with company sales force. Maintain positive relations with suppliers.	Usually start out as buyer trainee, or assistant buyer. Can be promoted to purchasing manager or merchandising manager.	Growth through 2005 will be steady, but below average for other positions.
Advertising agent or manager	$23,000–$36,500, depending on job title and experience.	Trainee positions are usually in copywriting, layout, or other less responsible positions. Copywriters must have a command of written English. Layout people need a talent for proportion and for predicting reader reaction.	Entry-level positions are usually in specific areas of advertising. A copywriter can be promoted to senior copywriter. The highest promotion will usually be to creative director.	Slow but steady growth through 2005.
Public relations specialist	$22,000–$46,500, depending on experience and size of firm.	Build and maintain a good image for the company. Communicate the goals and purposes of the company to the public and stockholders, if any. Must be good writer and speaker and be comfortable in all areas of the mass media.	College degree with entry-level experience (as an unpaid student trainee, etc.). Many PR people started in some other career, such as journalism, but made this career move later. Can be promoted to management, often outside of public relations, sometimes into market research.	More small companies are now using PR specialists. Future prospects are good to 2005, especially in smaller firms.
Marketing consultant	Varies greatly, because a consultant is in business for himself or herself.	Begin like any service-based entrepreneur. Need especially to make contacts with firms needing your service.	Intensive training needed; essential to be correct in advice. Serve as intern in consulting firm or start on your own with aggressive approach.	Growth very good through 2005, especially in areas of international and high tech marketing.

LYNN KASTNER, INTERNATIONAL MARKETING CONSULTANT

In 1990, changes in Lynn Kastner's personal life steered her back to college. Although she had not held a full-time job for 10 years, she had been actively engaged in serving her community as a trustee on several boards. Building on her bachelor's degree in psychology, Lynn conducted a careful review of the labor market. Two exciting and fast-moving areas that attracted her were marketing and international business. Her first international business class was team-taught by five instructors, each specializing in a different functional area of business. "This class excited me," Lynn says, "I could see the possibilities."

At Bellevue Community College in the state of Washington, Lynn pursued a degree in marketing and management and took all available courses in international studies. She also studied specific countries including China, Russia, and Japan. Any coursework that would enhance her understanding of the international arena was enthusiastically undertaken. Additionally, Lynn is currently studying the Mandarin Chinese language.

After graduation, Lynn used this knowledge to start and manage her own international marketing consulting firm, Kastner & Associates, in the Puget Sound area of Washington. With the help of her mentor and former business instructor, Mag Mallory, she launched a business that is already attracting attention in her area. Her consulting firm emphasizes cultural marketing issues, both domestically and in the countries Lynn has focused on.

"To be a successful international marketing consultant, one needs some important skills," Lynn says:

1. The ability to develop cross-cultural literacy and guard against the dangers of ethnocentrism—the belief that one's own ethnic group or culture is superior. Doing business in a different culture requires adaptation to the value systems and norms of that culture.
2. A broad base of knowledge and the skills to apply it. Because of its broad global environment, a number of disciplines (geography, history, anthropology, business, economics, and law) are useful to help explain the conduct of international business.
3. The ability to convey your expertise to others. This means having written, oral, and interpersonal communication skills that enable one to relate effectively. Be willing to get out of your comfort zone and approach people you haven't met.
4. The desire to specialize in a particular region or country and the confidence that you are the best. If you don't believe it, how will you sell yourself to potential clients?
5. The drive to continually update your skills through reading current books and periodicals in your area of interest and by attending relevant conferences and seminars.

Lynn's other area of interest is marketing research. Already, projects in that area have come to her firm. "The reputation is what counts," Lynn says. "Once that's established, the initial marketing of your services is easier, and you can concentrate on consulting rather than just selling yourself."

Lynn is a member of the World Trade Club of Seattle and the American Marketing Association. These organizations are excellent resources for networking, current information, and professional development. Lynn believes that success in business depends on being focused and willing to share knowledge and information. She is able to achieve this through her affiliations and strong desire to succeed in the international arena. Finally, Lynn believes you must know what you want, who you are, and where you can take your clients.

Special thanks to Judy Woo and Jack Perry, Bellevue Community College, for recommending Ms. Kastner for this Career Portfolio.

PART

6

DECISION MAKING: MANAGING INFORMATION

CHAPTER 17
USING TECHNOLOGY
TO MANAGE
INFORMATION

CHAPTER 18
UNDERSTANDING
FINANCIAL
INFORMATION AND
ACCOUNTING

USING TECHNOLOGY TO MANAGE INFORMATION

LEARNING GOALS

After you have read and studied this chapter, you should be able to

1. Outline the changing role of business technology.

2. Summarize the services available along the information highway, specifically those of on-line computer services and the Internet.

3. List the steps in managing information and identify the characteristics of useful information.

4. Describe the hardware used to travel the information highway and outline the benefits of the move toward computer networks.

5. Describe the computer software most frequently used in business.

6. Discuss the effects of information technology on management.

7. Identify the careers that are gaining or losing workers due to the growth of information technology.

HARRIET DONNELLY OF AT&T

Harriet Donnelly, an AT&T consumer products manager, travels the world with her office in her flight bag. Her six-pound office includes a notebook computer with a built-in fax modem, a pager, and a cellular phone. Her two-pound portable printer is usually left at home. Donnelly's computer is loaded with a word processing program to write text, a graphics program to design presentations, and an organizer program to manage her schedule and address book.

Donnelly checks her voice mail for messages three or four times a day. She returns urgent messages immediately, but does most of her communicating at night in her hotel room, returning all remaining messages left by voice mail, e-mail, and pager. Communicating abroad can be problematic because each country in Europe has different phone jacks. If Donnelly doesn't have the right adapter with her, she gets more sleep that night, but she doesn't feel good about it.

Donnelly likes the flexibility of working wherever and whenever she pleases. She says it takes away the nine-to-five restrictions and makes her more productive.

PCs and other technological breakthroughs—such as supercomputers, fax machines, and telecommunications equipment using fiber optics—are revolutionizing the way we do business and are increasing productivity. This is the Information Age. Businesses small and large will succeed or fail based on their ability to manage information. Computers play a large part in that process. But so do other kinds of equipment that will enable managers to make better decisions and communicate with each other, with customers, and with other companies, including suppliers. The late 1990s will be one of the most exciting times in history due to rapid technological developments along the information highway. The question is, Will you be able to keep up?

> *The ability of small business management to use the new computer and communication technologies to access information will determine a company's future just as much as product design or marketing savvy has in the past.*
>
> Larry Wilke, President of International Computer Programs, Inc.

data processing (DP)
Technology that supported existing business (primarily used to improve the flow of financial information).

information systems (IS)
Technology that helps companies *do business* (includes such tools as ATMs and voice mail).

information technology (IT)
Technology that helps companies *change business* by its applications to new methods of doing business.

Remote shopping networks such as the Home Shopping Club pictured here have minimized the importance of time and location in meeting customers needs. Couch potatoes no longer have to roll over to buy their new slippers; they just pick up the phone and order what they want, when they want it. Okay, they still have to get off the couch to answer the door when the mail carrier delivers the package, but you can bet somewhere there's a techie working on that.

THE ROLE OF INFORMATION TECHNOLOGY

Throughout this text, we've emphasized the need for managing information flows between businesses and their employees, businesses and their customers, and so on. Those managers who try to rely on the old ways of doing things simply won't be able to compete with those who have the latest in technology and know how to use it.

Business technology is continuously changing names and changing roles. In the 1970s, business technology was known as **data processing (DP)**. (There's often confusion between the words *data* and *information*. Data are raw, unanalyzed, and unsummarized facts and figures. Information is the processed and summarized data that can be used for managerial decision making.) DP's primary role was to support the existing business. It was primarily used to improve the flow of financial information. DP was hidden in a back room and rarely came in contact with customers.

In the 1980s, business technology changed names to **information systems (IS)**. IS moved out of the back room and into the center of the business. Its role changed from supporting the business to *doing* business. Customers interacted with technology in such ways as using automatic teller machines (ATMs) and voice mail. As business made greater use of technology, it became more dependent on it.

Until the late 1980s, business technology was just an addition to the existing way of doing business. It was a matter of using new technology on *old* methods. But things started to change as the 1990s approached. Businesses shifted to using new technology on *new* methods. Technology's new name became **information technology (IT)** and its role became to *change* business.

••• HOW INFORMATION TECHNOLOGY CHANGES BUSINESS •••

Time and place have always been at the center of business. Customers had to go to the business during business hours to satisfy their needs. We went *to* the store to buy clothes. We went *to* the bank to arrange for a loan. The businesses decided *when* and *where* we did business with them. Today IT allows businesses to deliver products and services whenever and wherever it's convenient for the customer. Thus, you can order clothes from the Home Shopping Network and arrange a home mortgage loan by phone.

Consider how IT has changed the entertainment industry. If you wanted to see a movie 30 years ago, you had to go to a movie theater. Twenty years ago you could wait for it to be on TV. Ten years ago you could wait for it to be on cable TV. Today you can go to a video store and rent it. Now you can even order video on demand by satellite or cable.

Organization	Technology is breaking down corporate barriers, allowing functional departments or product groups (even factory workers) to share critical information instantly.
Operations	Technology shrinks cycle times, reduces defects, and cuts waste. Service companies use electronic data interchange to streamline ordering and communication with suppliers and customers.
Staffing	Technology eliminates layers of management and cuts the number of employees. Companies use computers and telecommunication equipment to create "virtual offices" with employees in various locations.
New products	Information technology cuts development cycles by feeding customer and marketing comments to product development teams quickly so that they can revive products and target specific customers.
Customer relations	Customer service representatives can solve customers' problems instantly by using companywide databases to complete tasks from changing addresses to adjusting bills. Information gathered from customer service interactions can further stronger customer relationships.

FIGURE 17.1

HOW INFORMATION TECHNOLOGY IS CHANGING BUSINESS

Here are a few ways that information technology is changing businesses, their employees, suppliers, and customers.

Source: John Verity, "The Information Revolution," *Business Week/The Information Revolution*, 1994, pp. 11-18; and John Verity, "The Gold Mine of Data in Customer Service," *Business Week*, March 21, 1994, pp. 113–14.

As IT breaks time and location barriers, it creates organizations and services that are independent of location. For example, NASDAQ and SOFFEX are electronic stock exchanges without trading floors. Buyers and sellers make trades by computer.

Being independent of location brings work to people instead of people to work. With IT, work can flow more than 8,000 miles in a second, allowing businesses to conduct work around the globe continuously. We're moving toward what's called **virtualization;** that is, where you don't have a physical place to go but where everything is accessible through technology. For example, Harriet Donnelly in this chapter's opening profile has a virtual office in her flight bag. The technology she carries with her allows her to access people and information as if she were in an actual office. Likewise, virtual communities are forming as people who wouldn't otherwise have met communicate with each other through the virtual post office created by computer networks.[1]

Doing business is drastically different when companies understand how to use technological capabilities. Figure 17.1 gives other examples of how information technology changes business.

virtualization
Accessibility through technology that allows business to be conducted independent of location.

MOVING FROM INFORMATION TECHNOLOGY TOWARD KNOWLEDGE TECHNOLOGY

In the mid-1990s, we started moving away from information technology toward **knowledge technology (KT)**. Knowledge is information charged with enough intelligence to make it relevant and useful. KT will add a layer of intelligence to filter appropriate information and deliver it when it's needed. For example, consider the number 70. Doesn't mean much, does it? Change it to 70 percent and it means a little more, but still doesn't tell us a lot. Make it 70 percent chance of rain and we have more meaning.

Now let's imagine you're the first one on your block with a wristwatch featuring KT. As you walk out the door, the watch signals you that it has a message: "70 percent chance of rain in your city today." KT just gave

knowledge technology (KT)
Technology that adds a layer of intelligence to filter appropriate information and deliver it when it is needed.

SPOTLIGHT ON SMALL BUSINESS

Field of Dreams

American farms are among the small businesses that are learning to adapt to the Information Age. Infielder is a new computerized record-keeping system developed by a team of companies led by Monsanto and Apple Computer. The system uses a hand-held computer to record information as farmers go about their day. Farmers enter weather conditions, seed varieties, chemical or fertilizer applications, elevator scale receipts, and other information. At the end of the day, they transfer the data by connecting the hand-held computer to a personal computer that automatically updates field-by-field records on crops.

The detailed records help the farmers get the most from their land by helping them customize crop practices and maximize profit from each field. Farmers use Infielder to produce reports, charts, tables, and maps for agencies, landlords, or lenders. They can also use the hand-held computer to keep track of appointments or meetings.

Source: Jerri Stroud, "Infielder Is Chance to Field Crop Data," *St. Louis Post-Dispatch,* July 22, 1994, p. 1C·

you relevant information just when you needed it. Now you can head for class with an umbrella under your arm, knowing that you made an informed decision.

KT will change the traditional flow of information from an individual going to the database to the data coming to the individual. KT will "think" about the facts based on an individual's needs, reducing the time spent finding and getting information. Then businesspeople can spend more time doing what's important: *deciding* how to react to problems and opportunities.[2]

CRITICAL THINKING

Knowledge technology allows the database to go to the individual rather than the individual searching through the database. Can you imagine how you could use such a system? If you could design it yourself, what would it look like and what would it do?

CRUISING THE INFORMATION HIGHWAY

Much has been written about the information highway in recent years, yet many people are still confused about what this highway is and where it goes. In fact, technology experts themselves disagree about what it is and when it will be ready to travel. Some say that it's years from existence, while others say we're using it already whenever we use a modem to communicate with another computer.

Andrew Grove, Intel's CEO, thinks that both groups are correct. Grove objects to the term *information highway* itself because it implies that the ability to send large amounts of digital data will somehow "arrive." He says the ability to send data has been with us for some time and that it will simply continue to grow as technology progresses toward digital technology. Digital technology carries voices and other data encoded by and for computers. Digital data can be compressed to make more room on transmission lines and to speed the transfer of monster-size data products such as video programs. Instead of thinking of a system awaiting construction, Grove prefers to think

BUSINESS	LEADING ROLE	PARTICIPANTS
Local telephone service	Complete the "last mile" by providing high-capacity gateways to businesses and individuals	The Baby Bells: Ameritech, Bell Atlantic, Bell South, Nynex, Pacific Telesis, Southwestern Bell, U S West
Cable television	Same as above	Cablevision, Comcast, Cox Enterprises, TCI, Time Warner Cable, Viacom, others
Cellular, wireless communication service	Develop mobile, personal gateways capable of digital communication	Ardis, GTE/Contel, McCaw, Motorola, Nextal RAM, others
Long-distance telephone service	Provide a backbone of high-capacity data networks connecting regions	AT&T, MCI, Sprint, WilTel
Computers and electronics	Develop and market nodes for sending and receiving digital information	Apple, Digital Equipment, Hewlett-Packard, IBM, Intel, Oracle, PictureTel, Silicon Graphics, Sun Microsystems, others
Entertainment and information	"Content providers" compiling repositories of marketable data to sell over the superhighway	Capital Cities/ABC, CUC, QVC, Sony, Time Warner, Viacom, Walt Disney, others

Source: Jeffrey Zygmont, "A Hitchhiker's Guide to the Information Superhighway," *CFO*, May 1994, pp. 63–64.

of the **information highway** as an evolving concept that expands the role of telecommunications.[3] Figure 17.2 describes the businesses involved in helping the information highway evolve.

The evolution of the information highway will mean that today's voice-only telephone system will be replaced by a high-capacity data network that combines components of cable TV, cellular phones, and other wireless systems. What will appear to be a single network will actually be many coordinated networks and facilities. You'll be able to plug in an information appliance (perhaps a combination TV, computer, and telephone) as easily as you plug a toaster into an electrical socket today.[4]

{{ **FIGURE 17.2** }}

BUILDING THE INFORMATION HIGHWAY
The evolution of the information highway depends on the cooperation of many industries. This chart identifies the key businesses and their role in making the information highway a reality.

information highway
Telecommunications technology that allows users to send and receive large amounts of digital data.

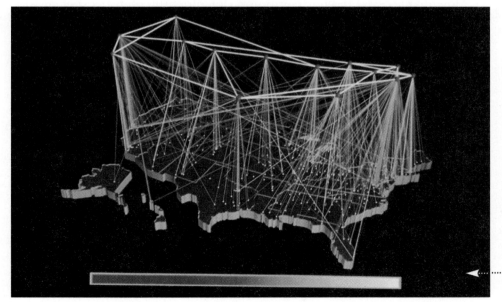

As 150,000 new users sign on the Internet each month, traffic on the information highway shows signs of congestion already. This photo from the National Science Foundation's networks shows the traffic pattern in 1994. The purple lines are all clear while the white lines indicate heavy backups.

On-line services such as CompuServe and America Online make navigating the information highway a bit less intimidating. A good service offers such valuable resources as tech support, small-business forums, on-line publications and databases, and up-to-the-minute market reports for investors. How do you select the right service for you? First determine what your needs are. Then read reviews of the services in journals such as *Home Office Computing* (the May 1995 issue compares six of the major services). Talk to friends and see what services they use and what features they find most helpful.

Internet
A connection of tens of thousands of interconnected computer networks that includes 1.7 million host computers.

··· DRIVERS ED FOR THE ··· INFORMATION HIGHWAY

The first thing you need to cruise the information highway is a computer with a modem (a device that connects your computer with other computers via phone lines) and basic communications software. That will get you as far as text-only on-line services such as Delphi, Genie, and the Well. Only words appear on your screen with these services so you may want to access (tap into) other services that offer pictures, drawings, video games, and other graphics such as Prodigy, America Online, and CompuServe. That will mean you'll need a little more sophisticated electronics in your computer, but if your computer was made during the 1990s, you should have what you need. Some on-line services require special software programs, but they'll usually send you those free.[5]

After you get the required software from the on-line service and install it according to their directions, you enter a password you make up and you're on the road. Each on-line service offers its own combination of services, but many have these features:[6]

Conversation: Most on-line services offer live discussions where you type in your comments and others respond immediately. Others only let you send messages and then have you check an electronic "bulletin board" to see if anyone responded. There can be open topics into which you just jump when you have a comment to make. Others are limited to specific topics.

Games: Some services offer games that you can play against either another person or the computer while you're on-line. (This can be expensive if the service charges for connect time.) Others allow you to download (copy) to your computer. Downloading requires special software and can take a few minutes. Some services also charge extra for downloading games.

News/reference/shopping: Some services offer news headlines, stock market information, access to encyclopedias and other databases such as Dow Jones, and shopping by computer. Prodigy reported that thousands of people logged on (called in) for information on the California earthquake on January 17, 1994.

Some services are easier to use than others. Prodigy and CompuServe offer easy-to-follow graphics to guide you on your quest. Others such as Delphi and Dow Jones News Retrieval require you to learn difficult commands to explore their databases. Perhaps the most difficult section of the information highway to navigate is the Internet. The **Internet** is a connection of tens of thousands of interconnected computer networks that includes 1.7 million host computers. Approximately 20 million people worldwide exchange electronic mail and search free computer databases.[7] Let's take a closer look at the Internet.

••• HOW TO DRIVE IN THE FAST LANE: THE INTERNET •••

The Internet is hardly new. The Pentagon built the network in 1969 when the world feared that a nuclear war would paralyze communications. The computer network was developed to reach far-flung terminals even if some connections were broken. The system took on a life of its own and grew as scientists and other academics used it to share data and electronic mail.[8] No one owns the Internet. There's no central computer; each message you send has an address code that lets any computer in the Internet forward it to its destination. There's no Internet manager. The closest thing to a governing body is the Internet Society in Reston, Virginia. This is a volunteer organization of 2,000 individuals and 84 corporate members who promote Internet use and oversee development of new communication software. Figure 17.3 describes how the Internet works.

Riders of the Internet use it for various activities:

Electronic Mail: The most popular corporate use of the Internet is e-mail. For example, researchers at GE's corporate R&D division send and receive 5,000 e-mail messages a day. A senior executive at Panasonics' U.S. operation uses e-mail to stay in touch with seven U.S. labs, many of his suppliers and customers, parent company Matsushita's Japanese lab, and his secretary, who's 20 feet away.

Collaboration: IBM engineers use the Internet when they do development work with other companies. Nick Trio of IBM insists, "To be technologically vital these days, you have to be on the Internet." Software developers in New York are collaborating with developers in New Jersey. The researchers use the Internet to share a workstation in New Jersey rather than commute back and forth to each others' labs.

Information gathering: Internet users can tap into such diverse institutions as the Federal Reserve and the Library of Congress. Thousands of news groups are filled with experts discussing their fields. There are groups on semiconductor manufacturing and education (as well as on pets, movies, cooking, and the Boy Scouts). The problem is that there's no unifying organization of the information. As one user says, "Imagine doing research at a vast archive with thousands of incomplete catalogues and no librarian."

Direct Marketing: InterCon Systems is a maker of Internet software. It has a reputation for providing excellent customer support via Internet. In addition to questions posed directly to them, InterCon developers read questions asked in other groups that discuss computer-related topics. They answer the ones they can whether or not the question (or the answer) has anything to do with InterCon products. InterCon's sales have more than doubled since it started in 1989.

The basic difficulty of the Internet is twofold: The traffic signs are written in UNIX and there's no defined structure for organizing information. UNIX is an operating system that was designed long before anyone thought of "user-friendly." Consider this example of a simple Internet address: bigk9(A)avm1.hq.umars.edu. Accuracy is critical here—one slip of the finger and your message goes nowhere or around the world instead of where you intended it. Even if you do master the intricacies of UNIX, you must then be patient enough to dig through the depths of millions of pages of electronic data to get to the information you need. Since the Internet doesn't require a prescribed structure for entering information, even experienced users have

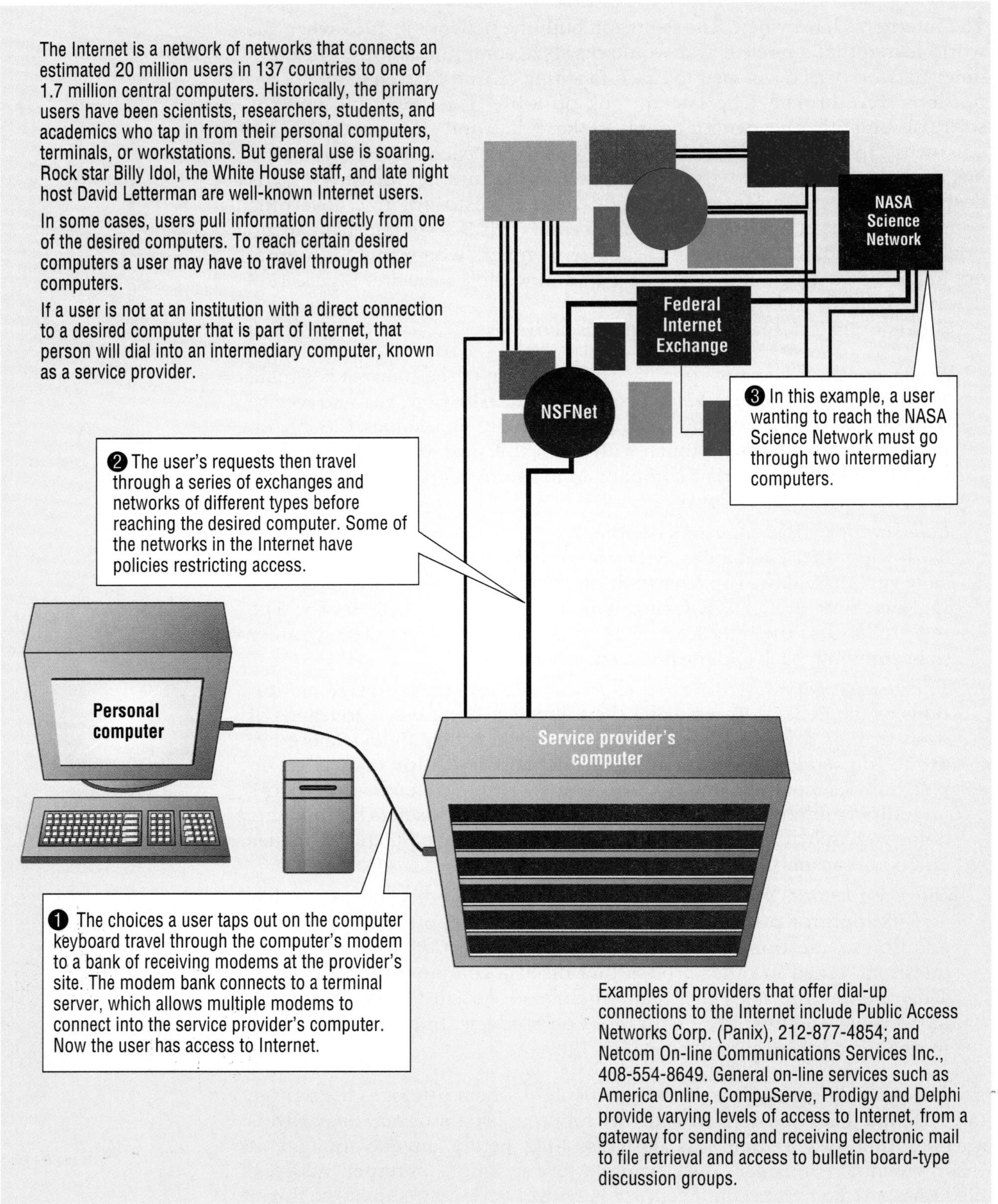

The Internet is a network of networks that connects an estimated 20 million users in 137 countries to one of 1.7 million central computers. Historically, the primary users have been scientists, researchers, students, and academics who tap in from their personal computers, terminals, or workstations. But general use is soaring. Rock star Billy Idol, the White House staff, and late night host David Letterman are well-known Internet users.

In some cases, users pull information directly from one of the desired computers. To reach certain desired computers a user may have to travel through other computers.

If a user is not at an institution with a direct connection to a desired computer that is part of Internet, that person will dial into an intermediary computer, known as a service provider.

NASA Science Network

Federal Internet Exchange

❸ In this example, a user wanting to reach the NASA Science Network must go through two intermediary computers.

NSFNet

❷ The user's requests then travel through a series of exchanges and networks of different types before reaching the desired computer. Some of the networks in the Internet have policies restricting access.

Personal computer

Service provider's computer

❶ The choices a user taps out on the computer keyboard travel through the computer's modem to a bank of receiving modems at the provider's site. The modem bank connects to a terminal server, which allows multiple modems to connect into the service provider's computer. Now the user has access to Internet.

Examples of providers that offer dial-up connections to the Internet include Public Access Networks Corp. (Panix), 212-877-4854; and Netcom On-line Communications Services Inc., 408-554-8649. General on-line services such as America Online, CompuServe, Prodigy and Delphi provide varying levels of access to Internet, from a gateway for sending and receiving electronic mail to file retrieval and access to bulletin board-type discussion groups.

Source: Peter Lewis, "Taking Care of Business," *St. Louis Post-Dispatch*, December 15, 1993, p. 11D. Reprinted with permission of the *St. Louis Post-Dispatch,* copyright 1993.

FIGURE 17.3

HOW THE INTERNET WORKS

difficulty retrieving information. New software is becoming available to make the Internet easier to use.[9] Mosaic is one of the most popular Internet graphic interfaces. Mosaic users navigate the Internet by simply pointing and clicking.[10]

*The Internet
Helps Small
Businesses Reach
Beyond Their
Borders*

Trade Point is a new service on the Internet that helps entrepreneurs market their products in countries around the world. Introduced in the United States in early 1995, the service boasts 50 cities (from London to Lusaka, Zambia) as "trade points" for fostering relationships between foreign partners in the hope of sparking profit-making alliances worldwide.

Using the service, you can obtain such information as the Commerce Department's index of companies that import and export to and from the United States. You can use reference materials for start-ups including listings of freight-forwarding companies and regulatory requirements, a database of lending institutions willing to fund overseas ventures, and credit reports from Graydon America.

You can also advertise your products or services in a multimedia catalog that includes full-color pages and audio and video clips. "If someone in Europe wants to find a women's shoe manufacturer interested in exporting, for example, he could easily call on-line to Trade Point USA and find all the firms that fit their profile," says Mark DeVoe, consulting manager for Digital Equipment Corporation, the company that backed the project along with IBM. Some people expect Trade Point to be a standard part of international business by 1997.

Source: Anne R. Field, "New Internet Service Helped You Venture Abroad," *Home Office Computing*, January 1995, p. 14.

For all of its negatives, the Internet is gaining fans at an amazing rate. Some 150,000 new users sign on each month.[11] You can access the Internet by contacting one of the many companies known as Internet providers. For names of providers, call NIC Information Services at 1–800–444–4345.

**PROGRESS
CHECK**

- How has the role of information technology changed since the days when it was known as data processing?
- In what way is knowledge technology different from information technology?
- List the features offered by on-line computer services.
- What is the Internet? Name its four major uses.

MANAGING INFORMATION

Even before computers, managers had to sift through mountains of information to find what they needed to help them make their decisions. Consider that since 1987 we've added over 130 million information receptacles (e-mail addresses, cellular phones, pagers, fax machines, voice mailboxes, and answering machines). That's a 365 percent increase from 1987.[12] Too much information can confuse issues rather than clarify them. How can managers keep from getting buried in the information overload? Stepping back and gaining perspective is the key to managing the sea of information you face.

The first step toward gaining perspective is to identify the four or five key goals you wish to reach. Eliminating information that's not related to those top priorities can get rid of half the information flowing into your office. For example, as we were assembling information to include in this chapter, we collected over 300 journal articles. Feeling the pressure of information overload, we identified the goals we wanted the chapter to accomplish and eliminated all the articles that didn't address those goals. As we further refined our goals, the stack of paper gradually dropped to a manageable size.

Obviously, not all of the information that ends up on your desk will be useful. Management information's usefulness depends on four characteristics of that information:

1. *Quality*. Quality means that the information is accurate and reliable. When the clerk at a fast-food restaurant enters your order into the cash register, it may be automatically fed to a computer, and the day's sales and profits can be calculated as soon as the store closes. The sales and expense data must be accurate, or the rest of the calculations will be wrong.

2. *Completeness*. There must be enough data to make a decision, but not too much to confuse the issue. As we've noted, today's problem is often too much data rather than too little.

3. *Timeliness*. Information must reach managers quickly. If a customer has a complaint, that complaint should be handled within a day. In the past, a salesperson might make a report to his or her manager; that report would go to a higher-level manager, and the problem may not be resolved for months. Electronic mail and other developments make it possible for marketing, engineering, and production to hear about a problem with a product the same day that the salesperson hears about it. Product changes can be made instantly using computer-integrated manufacturing as discussed in Chapter 9.

4. *Relevance*. Different managers have different information needs. Again, the problem today is that information systems often have too much data available. Managers must learn the questions to ask to get the answers they need.

Sorting out the useful information and getting it to the right people is the goal in solving information overload. There are software programs to do just that by filtering information so that users can get the customized information they need. For example, Individual Inc. of Cambridge, Massachusetts, will deliver customized news to you every morning by e-mail or fax. The software sorts through more than 3,000 news sources to find information that suits your identified needs.

Some people are concerned that only getting the information the computer thinks you need will eliminate a lot of other useful information you may find by luck. Software developers envision a program with a fortune dial that will allow you to regulate the amount of random information you receive with your customized news.

The important thing to remember when facing information overload is to relax. You can never read everything that's available. Set goals for yourself and do the best that you can. Remember, just because there's a public library doesn't mean you should feel guilty about not reading every book in it. And so it is with the information highway: You can't make every stop along the route, so plan your trip wisely and bon voyage!

THE ENABLING TECHNOLOGY: HARDWARE

We hesitate to discuss advances in computer hardware because what's powerful as we write may be obsolete by the time you read this. Thirty years ago the chairman of Intel Corp., Gordon E. Moore, made an observation that has

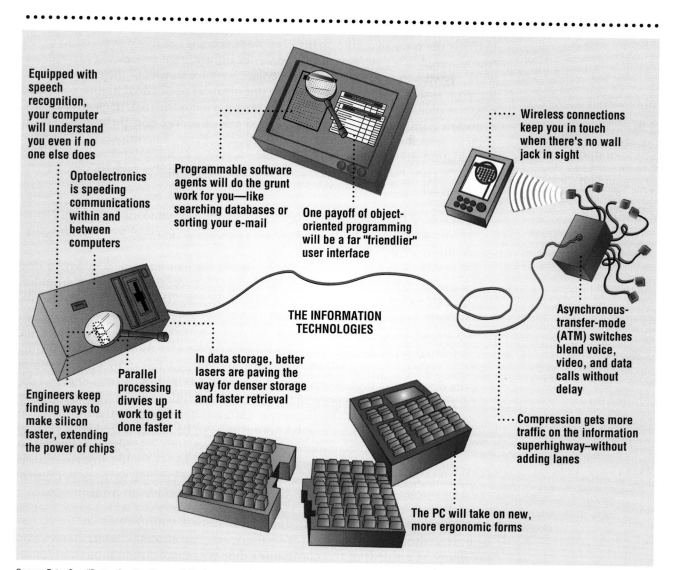

Equipped with speech recognition, your computer will understand you even if no one else does

Optoelectronics is speeding communications within and between computers

Programmable software agents will do the grunt work for you—like searching databases or sorting your e-mail

One payoff of object-oriented programming will be a far "friendlier" user interface

Wireless connections keep you in touch when there's no wall jack in sight

THE INFORMATION TECHNOLOGIES

Engineers keep finding ways to make silicon faster, extending the power of chips

Parallel processing divvies up work to get it done faster

In data storage, better lasers are paving the way for denser storage and faster retrieval

Asynchronous-transfer-mode (ATM) switches blend voice, video, and data calls without delay

Compression gets more traffic on the information superhighway—without adding lanes

The PC will take on new, more ergonomic forms

Source: Peter Coy, "Faster, Smaller, Cheaper," *Business Week/The Information Revolution*, 1994, pp. 54–57. Reprinted from a special issue of *Business Week* by special permission, copyright © 1994 by McGraw-Hill, Inc.

⟨⟨ **FIGURE 17.4** ⟩⟩

THE INFORMATION TECHNOLOGIES

since been called Moore's Law. Moore remarked that the computer chips' capacity doubles every year or so.[13] The million-dollar vacuum-tube computers that awed people in the 1950s couldn't keep up with a 1990s pocket calculator. In fact, a birthday card that plays "Happy Birthday" contains more computing power than existed before 1950.[14]

The speed of evolution in the computer industry has slowed little since Moore's remark. So rather than add potentially outdated facts to your information overload, we offer you a simple overview of the kind of computer technology available now or by the end of the 1990s.

Hardware includes computers, pagers, cellular phones, printers, and fax machines. The mobile worker will find travel-size versions of computers, printers, and fax machines that are almost as powerful and feature-laden as their big brothers. Figure 17.4 describes the information technologies that will carry you on your journey down the information highway.

Telecommunications hardware is no longer earthbound. Until 1994, airplane phones couldn't receive calls. Now you can pass a credit card through a swipe reader when you board the plane and any incoming calls are directed to your seat. Some planes boast fax machines that allow you to type a message on a seat-back display terminal and fax it to the ground.[15]

••• COMPUTER NETWORKS •••

network computing system (client/server computers)
Computer systems that allow personal computers (clients) to obtain needed information from huge databases in a central computer (server).

Perhaps the most dynamic change in recent years is the move away from mainframe computers that serve as the center of information processing toward network systems that allow many users to access information at the same time. In an older system, a central computer (mainframe) performed all the tasks and sent the results to a terminal that couldn't perform the task itself. In the new **network computing system** (also called **client/server computing**), the tasks such as searching sales records are handled by personal computers ("clients"). Information needed to complete the tasks is stored in huge databases controlled by the "server."[16] Networks connect people to people and people to data.

Networks have three major benefits:

They save time and money. SynOptics Communications found that electronic delivery of mail and files increased the speed of product-development by 25 percent.

Networks provide easy links across functional boundaries. It's easy to find someone who can offer insight to a problem's solution. The most common questions on computer bulletin boards begin, "Does anyone know . . .?" Usually someone does.

Companies can see their products more clearly. In traditional organizations, information is summarized so many times that it often loses its meaning. For example, a sales rep's two-page summary may be cut to a paragraph in the district manager's report and then to a few numbers on a chart in the regional manager's report. Networks catch raw information. Here's how networks helped Lotus Development: Instead of waiting for the information gained from 4 million annual phone calls to be summarized by technical support people, information now goes straight into a database, available on demand. Rather than accept someone else's idea of what information is needed, anyone can access the data and search according to his or her needs. As a result, many more employees watch the market from front-row seats.[17]

The move toward networks doesn't mean that mainframes are dead. Far from it. Using networks requires so many organizational changes that some (as many as a third) of the companies that try networking go back to mainframes. For the next decade or so, while organizations learn to let go of hierarchical management styles and feel more comfortable entrusting and empowering employees with the utility of information, the computing world will be a hybrid. PCs will take on more jobs with their speed, flexibility, and utility, while mainframes will handle large corporations' big jobs of storing, transferring, and processing large amounts of data.[18]

CRITICAL THINKING

How can the ability to communicate instantly with businesses and government organizations throughout the world affect world peace and world trade? Could the cooperation needed among telecommunications firms worldwide lead to more cooperation on other issues such as the environment, world health care, and worldwide exchanges of technical information?

SOFTWARE

As you know, computer software (programs) provide the instructions that enable you to tell the computer what to do. It's important to find the right software *before* finding the right hardware (equipment). Software is like a record. If you want to hear a certain singer or orchestra, you buy that

Legal Briefcase

Needed: A Balance of Free Trade and Public Policy

Most people in the communications industry think current U.S. telecom regulations are dangerously out of date as we speed along the information highway. Debates rage about how to develop new regulations that protect consumers without prohibiting the competition of free trade. The most challenging issues for government policy include

- *Cultivating new technology.* Government and industry must establish common standards for information to flow smoothly. However, if the standards are too rigid, the technology will quickly become obsolete.

- *Deregulation.* The speedy evolution of the information highway depends on increased competition among cable, phone, and computer companies. However, one segment may gain an unfair advantage if there's too much deregulation.

- *Universal access.* Congress wants to ensure that the telephone era policy of universal service (everyone has access) survives. Who should pick up the tab for wiring low-profit rural and poor customers' homes?

- *Balance between privacy and law enforcement.* How can the government keep data safe from criminals, while allowing law enforcers to tap in when necessary?

Source: John Carey, "From Internet to Infobahn," *Business Week/The Information Revolution*, 1994, pp. 32–36; and John Carey and Mark Lewyn, "Yield Signs on the Info Interstate," *Business Week*, January 24, 1994, pp. 88–90.

---

particular record. The record may be an old 78 or a new CD. The type of records you buy dictates what equipment you need.

Some software programs are easier to use than others. Some are more sophisticated and can perform more functions. You must decide what functions you want performed by a computer and then choose the appropriate software. That choice will help decide what make and power computer to buy.

Most software is distributed commercially through suppliers like retail stores and mail-order houses. Some software, called **shareware**, is copyrighted but distributed to potential customers free of charge. Users are asked to send a specified fee to the developer if the program meets their needs and they decide to use it. The shareware concept has become very popular and has dramatically reduced the price of software. Public domain software is software that's free for the taking.

Businesspeople most frequently use software for five major purposes: (1) writing (word processors), (2) manipulating numbers (spreadsheets), (3) filing and retrieving data (databases), (4) presenting information visually (graphics), and (5) communicating. Today's software can perform all five functions in one kind of program known as *integrated software* or *suites*. A new class of software program called *groupware* is emerging for use on networks.

shareware
Computer software that is copyrighted but distributed to potential customers free of charge. It is expected that users will send a fee to the developer if the software is found useful.

• • • WORD PROCESSING PROGRAMS • • •

Many users spend most of their time using a word processor. The most popular word processing programs can handle everything from a letter to a multi-chapter book. They can also produce designs that used to be done by powerful page-layout design programs.

Businesses use word processors to increase office productivity «∙∙ P.74 ∙∙». Standardized letters can be personalized quickly, documents can be updated by changing only the outdated text and leaving the rest intact, and contract forms can be revised to meet the stipulations of specific customers.

	A	B	C	D
	Fixed cost	Price	Unit variable cost	Break-even point
1				
2				
3				
4	2000	2.00	1	2000
5	2000	**2.50**	1	**1333**

Desktop publishing software combines word processing with graphics capabilities. A keystroke or a click of a mouse can change the style of type, the placement of a chart, or the size of the columns. Businesses can now publish their own professional-looking newsletters and presentations.

Of the many word processing software packages on the market, the three most popular are WordPerfect, Microsoft Word, and Ami Pro.[19]

••• SPREADSHEET PROGRAMS •••

spreadsheet program
A table made up of rows and columns which enables a manager to organize information.

A **spreadsheet program** is simply the electronic equivalent of an accountant's worksheet. A spreadsheet is a table made up of rows and columns that enables a manager to organize information. Using the computer's speedy calculations, managers have their questions answered almost as fast as they can ask them. For example, suppose we use a spreadsheet to figure the break-even point (Chapter 14) for our Fiberrific cereal. The spreadsheet contains the appropriate formula for calculating the break-even point. Our calculations show that at a price of $2 a box, we must sell 2,000 boxes to break even. We now think we can raise our price because of increased demand caused by a government study that links eating oat bran with lowering cholesterol levels. We can ask, "What if we raise the price of Fiberrific to $2.50?" Once we simply insert $2.50 in the price cell (the point where columns and rows intersect), the computer will tell us instantly that we must sell only 1,333 boxes to break even. (See Figure 17.5.)

Of course, this is a simple example. Businesses often develop very complex spreadsheets using hundreds of columns and rows. Popular programs include Lotus 1-2-3, Quattro Pro, and Excel.

••• DATABASE PROGRAMS •••

database program
Computer software that allows users to store and manipulate information that is normally kept in lists (names and addresses, inventories, etc.).

Database programs allow you to work with information you normally keep in lists: names and addresses, schedules, inventories, and so forth. Simple commands allow you to add new information, change incorrect information, and delete out-of-date or unnecessary information. Most programs have features that let you print only certain information, arrange records in the order you want them, and change the way information is displayed. Using database programs, you can create reports with exactly the information you want and the way you want the information to appear. Leading database programs include Q & A, Access, Approach, Paradox, PFS: Professional File, PC-File, dBase IV, R base, and HyperCard for Apple computers.

• • • GRAPHICS PROGRAMS • • •

A picture speaks a thousand words. Why should we study a thousand-line report to identify the leading Fiberrific salesperson when a glance at a computer-generated bar graph can show us in an instant? Computer graphics programs can use data from spreadsheets to visually summarize information by drawing bar graphs, pie charts, and line charts. Do you need to change a figure or label? No need to search for the eraser, ruler, and compass. Simply insert the new data and, presto, the computer changes the lines or curves and your new chart is ready for presentation. Would you rather have a pie chart than the bar graph? No problem for a computer with a good graphics program. Some popular graphics programs include MacDraw for Macintosh computers, Harvard Graphics, Freelance Plus, Windows Draw, and Applause II.

• • • COMMUNICATIONS PROGRAMS • • •

Communications software makes it possible for different brands of computers to transfer data to each other. The software translates the data into ASCII (American Standard Code for Information Interchange), the common standard all computer manufacturers have agreed to adopt. These programs enable a computer to exchange files with other computers, retrieve information from databases, and send and receive electronic mail. Such programs include Microsoft Mail, Crosstalk Mk., Smartcom, ProComm, and Telik.

communications software
Computer software that makes it possible for different brands of computers to transfer data to each other.

• • • INTEGRATED PROGRAMS • • •

It may occur to you that having all these different software packages might become cumbersome. It may be hard to cut and paste information generated in one program (such as a spreadsheet) into another (perhaps a word processing document). One solution is an **integrated software package** (also called a **suite**) that offers two or more applications in one package. With these programs, you can share information across applications easily. Most such packages include word processing, database management, spreadsheet, graphics, and communications. Suites include Microsoft Office, Lotus SmartSuite, and Borland Office.

integrated software package (suite)
Computer software that offers two or more applications in one package.

• • • GROUPWARE • • •

As businesses move toward networking, a new class of software called *groupware* is emerging. **Groupware** is software that allows people to work collaboratively and share ideas. The programs we just discussed (word processing, databases, etc.) were designed for people working alone at individual computers. Groupware runs on a network and allows people to work on the same project at the same time. Groupware also makes it possible for work teams to communicate together over time. Team members can swap leads, share client information, keep tabs on news events, and make suggestions to one another. The computer becomes a kind of team memory where every memo and idea is stored for quick retrieval any time.[20] The most popular groupware today is Lotus Notes, but other programs are under development.

groupware
Computer software that allows people to work collaboratively and share ideas.

Making Ethical Decisions

Superhighway Robbery

Computer software, particularly the applications programs described in this text, take hundreds of hours to create. Anyone who has taken a basic programming course knows that developing such programs takes tremendous planning, effort, and tenacity. And anyone who has bought a software package knows it often takes a lot of money to buy one.

Suppose a friend of yours owns a program that you've been wanting to use for writing term papers. Your friend offers to make a "pirate" (illegal) copy for you. What are your alternatives? What will you do? What will be the consequences of your decision?

PROGRESS CHECK

- What four characteristics of information make it useful?
- How do computer networks change the way employees gather information?
- What are the seven major types of computer software used in business?

EFFECTS OF INFORMATION TECHNOLOGY ON MANAGEMENT

The increase of networked computers will affect management. Many bureaucratic functions can be replaced by technology. In Chapter 8 we talked about tall versus flat organization structures. Computers will eliminate middle management functions and thus flatten organization structures.[21] Hartford Insurance Company is now able to process the same number of claims with 30 percent fewer employees since it started using desktop computers.[22]

Perhaps the most revolutionary effect of computers may be the ability to allow employees to stay home and do their work from there (telecommuting). For example, Mrs. Donna Puccini works for Continental Illinois Bank. She and three other people work at home using word processors to generate letters, memos, and statistical tables. Her computer in a bedroom is linked to Continental's downtown office. Donna's work is transmitted to the office and back as easily as she could walk into the boss's office.

Naturally, such work involves less travel time and costs, and often increases productivity. Telecommuting helps companies save money by retaining valuable employees during long pregnancy leaves and by tempting experienced employees out of retirement. Telecommuting enables men and women to stay home with small children and is a tremendous boon for disabled workers. Employees who can work extra hours on their home computers rather than work late at the office report less stress and improved morale. Studies show that home offices increase both the amount and quality of work. However, these studies also show that telecommuting is only successful among self-starters, people who don't have home distractions, and those whose work doesn't require face-to-face interaction with co-workers.

Not all of computers' effects have been positive. One problem with computers today and in the future will be hackers, people who break into computer systems for illegal purposes such as transferring funds from someone's bank account to their own without authorization. In 1994, the Pentagon was unable to find the hackers who broke into its computers through the Internet

FROM THE PAGES OF...
Entrepreneur
MAGAZINE

Home-Based Business

Home-based businesses immediately run into zoning restrictions and other hassles when they try to hire other people. Simply finding parking space can be a problem. The solution? Home-based businesses are forming their own version of the virtual corporation. That is, entrepreneurs like John Seeley are setting up computer networks that allow their employees to stay home. Seeley's firm, Evaluation Research Associates, moved from downtown Ann Arbor, Michigan, to his home. All 10 of his employees decided to set up home-based offices with the firm. They communicate using e-mail, phones, and some face-to-face meetings.

Seeley hired an information technology specialist to design the system. To maintain some human contact, the staff meets every couple of weeks. Seeley passed on the savings from not having office space to his clients—nonprofit organizations. The savings came to some $200 per day per client. Work is now relaxed since employees can stay home, play the piano for stress relief, and still stay in close contact.

Source: Janean Huber, "Out of Site," *Entrepreneur*, April 1994, pp. 72–74.

and stole, altered, and erased records. Ironically, one of the Pentagon systems the hackers gained access to was computer security research.

There's also a problem with privacy as more and more personal information is stored in computers and people can access that data illegally.[23] Computer security is more complicated today than in the past. When information was processed in a mainframe environment, the single data center was easier to control since there was limited access. Today, however, computers are not only accessible in all areas within the company, but also with other companies with which the firm does business. The person who develops a foolproof lock for computer data certainly will make a fortune. The Pentagon alone budgets hundreds of millions of dollars for development and maintenance of its computer security system.[24]

Constant use of computers can create physical problems for workers. Repetitive hand movements are blamed for ligament damage known as *carpal tunnel syndrome.*

Another danger of automating offices is that the firm may become too impersonal, too mechanical. People are often hidden in cubicles behind a computer terminal, and human contact is minimized. Such isolation can be

Videoconferencing makes it possible to have business meetings in which all the people involved can see and interact with one another without flying from city to city. The savings are quite dramatic. What disadvantages, if any, do you see with this use of technology?

Managers Must	Workers Must
• Instill commitment in subordinates, rather than rule by command and control	• Become initiators, able to act without management direction
• Become coaches, training workers in necessary job skills, making sure they have resources to accomplish goals, and explaining links between a job and what happens elsewhere in the company	• Become financially literate so they can understand the business implications of what they do and changes they suggest
• Give greater authority to workers over scheduling, priority setting, and even compensation	• Learn group interaction skills, including how to resolve disputes within their work group and how to work with other functions across the company
• Use new information technologies to measure workers' performance, possibly based on customer satisfaction or the accomplishment of specific goals	• Develop new math, technical, and analytical skills to use newly available information on their jobs

Source: James B. Treece, "Breaking the Chains of Command," *Business Week/The Information Revolution*, 1994, pp. 112-14.

〘 FIGURE 17.6 〙

WHEN INFORMATION
TECHNOLOGY ALTERS THE
WORKPLACE

stressful and demoralizing. Managers of such workers need to practice more management by walking around, have more social functions, and provide more opportunities for interpersonal contact during breaks, at lunch, and after work.

Electronic communication can never replace human communication for creating enthusiasm and esprit de corps. Efficiency and productivity can become so important to a firm that people are treated like robots. In the long run, that may lower efficiency and productivity. Computers are a tool, not a total replacement for managers or workers. Creativity is still a human trait. Computers should aid creativity by giving people more freedom and time.[25] Figure 17.6 shows how information technology changes the way managers and workers interact.

Cyberspace communication adds another potential problem for managers: unedited postings to on-line services have led to libel accusations. For example, Stratton Oakmont Inc. is suing Prodigy and an anonymous writer who posted a note that accused Stratton of fraud in late 1994. Prodigy removed the remarks from its network a couple of weeks after it was posted, but Stratton says the damage has been done. It claims that Prodigy is responsible for what it publishes. Prodigy says there is no way it can read, much less edit, all the 75,000 notes sent on its network daily.[26]

Existing laws do not address the problems of today's direct, real-time communication. As more people merge onto the information highway, more legal issues will arise. Already copyright and pornography laws are crashing into the virtual world. Other legal questions, including intellectual property and contract disputes, on-line sexual and racial harassment, and the use of electronic communication to hawk crooked sales schemes, are being raised as 5.2 million people log on to commercial networks.[27]

TECHNOLOGY AND YOU

If you're beginning to think that being computer illiterate may be occupational suicide, you're getting the point. Workers in every industry come in contact with computers to some degree. Even burger flippers in fast-food chains read orders on computer screens. Economists estimate that workers who use computers earn 10 to 15 percent more than workers doing similar work without computers.[28] Figure 17.7 shows information technology's effects on careers.

Technological change and office automation will shrink these jobs . . .

PERCENT EMPLOYMENT CHANGE, 1992–2005	
Computer operators	−39%
Billing, posting, and calculating machine operators	−29%
Telephone operators	−28%
Typists and word processors	−16%
Bank tellers	−4%

Data: Bureau of Labor Statistics

. . . but technology also generates new openings in the info-tech world.

FIVE FASTEST-GROWING OCCUPATIONS REQUIRING A COLLEGE DEGREE, 1992–2005	
Computer engineers and scientists	112%
Systems analysts	110%
Physical therapists	88%
Special education teachers	74%
Operations research analysts	61%

Data: Bureau of Labor Statistics

Companies are doing more with less. Classic white-collar workers are being replaced with high-tech machines.

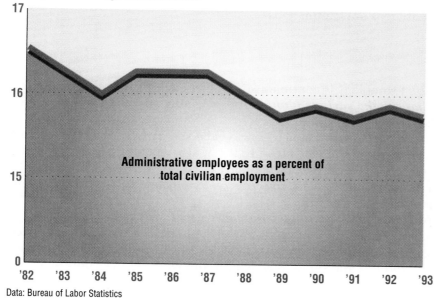

Administrative employees as a percent of total civilian employment

'82 '83 '84 '85 '86 '87 '88 '89 '90 '91 '92 '93

Data: Bureau of Labor Statistics

{{ FIGURE 17.7 }}

WINNERS AND LOSERS IN THE RACE DOWN THE INFORMATION HIGHWAY

As the information highway accelerates its evolution, many workers are forced from their obsolete jobs while others find higher-paying jobs.

Be your own boss. Computers linked to the information highway could open up new opportunities for entrepreneurs.

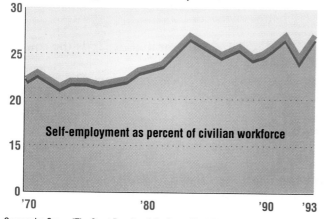

Self-employment as percent of civilian workforce

'70 '80 '90 '93

Source: Ira Sager, "The Great Equalizer," *Business Week/The Information Revolution,* 1994, pp. 100–107. Reprinted from the May 18, 1994, issue of *Business Week* by special permission, copyright © 1994 by McGraw-Hill, Inc.
Data: Bureau of Labor Statistics

But the impact of the information highway on jobs depends on government policy. Look at the effect of permitting the Baby Bells into new businesses.

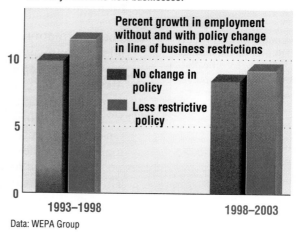

Percent growth in employment without and with policy change in line of business restrictions

- No change in policy
- Less restrictive policy

1993–1998   1998–2003

Data: WEPA Group

Don't feel alone if you're still computer illiterate. You have more than a few high-ranking executives in your ranks. For too long many executives have relied on secretaries to send their e-mail and information officers to generate financial information. Now they feel like they live in information igloos with no idea of what technology can do for them. They're at the mercy of technologists who want the latest and most powerful stuff out there whether the existing system is satisfactory or not. Embarrassed by their lack of computer skills, some execs are heading for the CEO Boot Camp, a retreat on Nantucket Island, where they learn that backspace is the little arrow on the right.[29]

As information technology eliminates old jobs while creating new ones, it's up to you to learn the skills you need to be certain you aren't left behind.

PROGRESS CHECK

- How has information technology changed the way people work?
- What are the disadvantages of information technology?
- What areas are losing jobs as information technology expands?
- What areas are gaining jobs?

SUMMARY

1. Outline the changing role of business technology.

1. Business technology is continuously changing names and changing roles.
   - *What are the various names and roles of business technology since 1970?*
   In the 1970s, business technology was called *data processing (DP)*; its role was to *support* existing business. In the 1980s, its name became *information systems (IS)* and its role changed to *doing* business. By the 1990s, business technology became *information technology (IT)*; its role is now to *change* business.
   - *How does information technology change business?*
   Information technology has minimized the importance of time and place to business. Businesses that are independent of time and location can deliver products and services whenever and wherever it's convenient for the customer. Figure 17.1 gives examples of how information technology changes business.
   - *What is knowledge technology?*
   Knowledge technology adds a layer of intelligence to filter appropriate information and deliver it when it's needed.

2. Summarize the services available along the information highway, specifically those of on-line computer services and the Internet.

2. The information highway is an evolving concept that expands the role of telecommunications.
   - *What do you need to drive on the information highway?*
   All you need is (1) to get a computer and a modem and (2) to sign up with an on-line computing service.
   - *What features do on-line computing services offer?*
   On-line computing services offer conversation (bulletin boards and e-mail), games, news, reference, and shopping.
   - *What is the Internet and what does it offer businesses?*
   The Internet is an independent computer network that includes 1.7 million host computers and 20 million users worldwide. It offers (1) e-mail, (2) ability to collaborate with others, (3) information gathering, and (4) direct marketing capabilities.

● *What are the Internet's drawbacks?*
The two basic difficulties with the Internet are (1) searching the databases requires knowledge of a complex operating system (UNIX) and (2) there's not a defined structure for organizing information.

3. Information technology multiplies the mountains of information available to businesspeople.

   ● *How can one deal with information overload?*
The most important step in dealing with information overload is to identify your four or five key goals. Eliminate information that won't help you meet those goals.

   ● *What makes information useful?*
The usefulness of management information depends on four characteristics: quality, completeness, timeliness, and relevance.

3. List the steps in managing information and identify the characteristics of useful information.

4. Computer hardware changes rapidly.

   ● *What has been the most dynamic change in computer hardware thus far in the 1990s?*
Perhaps the most dynamic change has been the move away from mainframe computers that serve as the center of information processing toward network systems that allow many users to access information at the same time.

   ● *What are the major benefits of networks?*
Networks' major benefits are (1) saving time and money, (2) providing easy links across functional boundaries, and (3) allowing employees to see their products more clearly.

4. Describe the hardware used to travel the information highway and outline the benefits of the move toward computer networks.

5. Computer software provides the instructions that enable you to tell the computer what to do.

   ● *What types of software programs are used by managers most frequently?*
Managers most often use word processing, electronic spreadsheet, database, graphic, and communication programs. A new class of software program called *groupware* allows people to work collaboratively and share ideas.

5. Describe the computer software most frequently used in business.

6. Information technology has a tremendous effect on how we do business.

   ● *What effect has information technology had on business management?*
Computers eliminate some middle management functions and thus flatten organization structures. Computers also allow workers to work from their own homes. On the negative side, computers sometimes allow information to fall into the wrong hands. Managers must find ways to prevent stealing by hackers. Computers also present the danger of making an organization too impersonal. Managers combat this by stressing social functions and providing opportunities for interpersonal contact.

6. Discuss the effects of information technology on management.

7. Information technology eliminates old jobs while creating new ones.

   ● *Which careers are gaining and losing workers because of the growth of information technology?*
Computer operators and word processors are among the shrinking jobs. As more employees can and do access information themselves, they no longer need others to do it for them. Computer engineers and systems analysts are in demand. Figure 17.7 shows other employment changes caused by the growth of information technology.

7. Identify the careers that are gaining or losing workers due to the growth of information technology.

KEY TERMS

communications software 537
data processing (DP) 524
database program 537
groupware 537
information highway 527
information system (IS) 524
information technology (IT) 524
integrated software package (suite) 537
Internet 528
knowledge technology (KT) 525
network computing system (client/server computing) 534
shareware 535
spreadsheet program 536
virtualization 525

DEVELOPING WORKPLACE SKILLS

1. Imagine that a rich relative has given you $3,000 to buy a computer system for use in school. Research the latest in hardware and software in computer magazines and then go to a computer store to try out alternatives. Make a list of what you intend to buy and then write a summary explaining the reasons for your choices.
2. Interview someone who bought a computer system to use in his or her business. Ask them about any problems they had in deciding what to buy or in installing and using the system. What training was necessary and available? What would they do differently next time? What software do they find especially useful?
3. Imagine that you are a purchasing manager for a large computer store near your campus. Design a two-page research survey to determine what software and hardware features students at the school need. Discuss your research questions and survey implementation strategy with the class.
4. Find someone who knows how to access the Internet. Choose a topic that interests you and then ask your friend to help you find and retrieve information pertaining to that topic. Select another topic and conduct the research on your own.
5. Computers abound on most college campuses. Where are they and what are they used for on your campus? Use a computer graphics program to create a chart that illustrates the types of software application programs used for various activities. For example, the library may record book checkouts and circulation using a database program. In addition to the library, consider computer usage in the student records office, food services, athletic department, business school, alumni office, and business office.

PRACTICING MANAGEMENT DECISIONS

CASE ELECTRONIC SHOPPING—WHAT NEXT?

Picture this: You walk into one of the new, large shopping malls. Maybe it's as big as the mile-long mall in Canada with 57 entrances. You dread the idea of going from store to store on a busy Saturday shopping for holiday gifts. Suddenly you notice something new in the center—a kiosk with a video screen inside. It looks like a giant video game. It's called an Electronistore.

Curious, you step inside and sit down. On the screen appears a hostess who welcomes you and asks whether you've used the service before. You say no by pressing a button, and step-by-step instructions appear.

You decide to explore the household appliances listing to see what's available. A subcategory of microwave ovens appears in the list. You ask for that file and see prices and product descriptions. If you want more details, you push the details button and get answers to questions such as whether the oven has a browning element.

Fascinated by the possibilities, you push buttons for other categories, such as stereo equipment and shoes. If you see what you want for yourself and for gifts, you can insert your credit card and place an order. There's no salesperson and no standing in line.

The Electronistore has several advantages:

- It allows for quick, easy comparison shopping.
- It provides in-depth product information.
- Merchandise can be demonstrated.
- Shoppers enjoy using the service.

Electronistores are just the beginning of interactive electronic shopping. Now you can call up all the information desired on your own computer screen using an on-line information service like CompuServe. You might want to do most of your shopping at home. (Prodigy dropped its grocery shopping service in 1991, however, because people didn't seem to enjoy buying food without touching and smelling it.) Your computer can be the equivalent of a giant catalog capable of demonstrating products and taking your order. That's the reality of the 1990s. What's next? Now that consumers can interact with producers electronically, what information needs to be exchanged, with what result?

Decision Questions

1. Which system seems to have the greater potential for success: electronic kiosks in stores or interactive TV in the home?

2. What kinds of services (not goods) could be sold over interactive TV systems?

3. Many people (especially those over 45) say there's no need for a home computer. "What do you use them for anyhow?" they say. Discuss the future of interactive TV and its uses for obtaining the latest in news, banking, shopping, and more. Brainstorm all the possibilities to get a view of the future.

4. How will electronic kiosks and interactive TV affect a person planning a career in personal selling?

• •

〰 VIDEO CASE   CRUISING THE INTERNET 〰

This era that we live in is called the "Information Age" and with good reason. Never before has so much information been available so quickly to so many people. Information will be even easier to obtain as businesses and other organizations, as well as individuals, put more information on the Internet.

The Internet is a system of linked computers which enables computer users to both communicate and exchange information. The information highway or I-way is the path taken to electronically find information and bring it home to your computer. Traveling the information highway is called "cruising the Internet" because you can elect to simply go for a ride to see what is available or pick a specific destination and go directly to that source.

Getting on the Internet is becoming easier and cheaper over time as new software programs are being developed to make cruising easier. Spry Inc., for example, sells a program called Internet-in-a-Box. Netscape Communications

Corporation has been giving away its Netscape Navigator Web. On-line services such as Prodigy, CompuServe, and America Online all have or are developing similar products.

Getting on the Internet is easy if you have a computer with a modem, a phone line, and the appropriate software. Once on the Internet, you will find numerous services designed to help you find what you want. Some of these are "librarians" that have names like Gopher and Veronica, but their names are less important than knowing what they can do for you in locating necessary information.

Learning to cruise the Internet is like learning to drive on any highway. You start off slowly learning the basics and before long you can send messages to friends on e-mail, chat with computer users all over the world, and, most importantly, tap into computer databases that contain works of art, music, books, magazines, newspapers, research reports, and almost anything else you need to know. The Internet will one day become your personal library, dictionary, communication system, and research assistant.

Discussion Questions

1. What is the easiest way for you to access the Internet? If you don't know, ask your instructor or local computer store personnel.

2. Soon you will be able to contact businesses directly on the Internet and ask them to demonstrate their products to you. How will this change the relationship between buyers and sellers? How will it affect the marketing function?

3. What are some of the uses that students can now make of the Internet? Ask your classmates to share some of their experiences in using the Net.

CHAPTER 18

UNDERSTANDING FINANCIAL INFORMATION AND ACCOUNTING

LEARNING GOALS

After you have read and studied this chapter, you should be able to

1. Understand the importance of financial information and accounting and its different uses in business.

2. Define and explain the different areas of the accounting profession.

3. Distinguish between accounting and bookkeeping and list the steps in the accounting cycle.

4. Explain the difference between the major financial statements.

5. Describe the roles of depreciation, LIFO, and FIFO in reporting financial information.

6. Explain the importance of ratio analysis in reporting financial information.

CONNIE CONNORS OF CVC COMMUNICATIONS

Connie Connors went to New York from California to pursue a career as a dancer. She became disillusioned with her career choice when the only compensation offered to dance in an MTV video was lunch. Connors ultimately decided that there was more promise in a business career and she started a public relations agency—CVC Communications—specializing in technology, education, and publishing.

It didn't take Connors long to learn the value of financial information and accounting. She estimated that within three years her agency would be doing at least $1.5 million in business. She borrowed $5,000 from a bank and another $5,000 from her parents to cover her estimated $10,000 cost of moving into her first office. Her accountant argued against the move. The total cost of the move actually exceeded $30,000. The magnitude of her miscalculation taught Connie the value of sound financial advice.

When revenues from the business reached $100,000 in the fourth quarter of 1989, Connie felt elated. However, her mood changed considerably when she learned that the $100,000 of revenue resulted in a $500 loss for the company after costs and expenses were deducted. To reduce expenses, Connie had to fire one of her employees. She knew it was time for more financial advice so she asked a friend (a consultant for a major accounting firm) for help to save the business. Her friend offered to coach her in accounting principles and sound financial management.

One of the first areas to focus on was expense control. Expenses at CVC had truly gotten out of hand. Salaries, rent, freelancers' fees, legal costs, phones, insurance, and office supplies rose in one year from $7,000 a month to $20,000 a month. Acting on the sound accounting advice she received, CVC's monthly expenses were cut and its profit margin increased.

Connie's accountant also taught her the importance of cash flow. The idea is to keep enough cash on hand to pay bills when they are due. You create a positive cash flow by increasing the amount of incoming cash and minimizing expense outflows. Any excess cash can be invested. Connie has also learned the value of financial ratios for measuring her firm's performance.

Controlling costs and managing cash flows are two keys to survival in business today. This chapter will teach you the importance of financial information and accounting fundamentals that Connie learned were so essential to business success. The chapter will also explore financial ratios that are critical for measuring and judging a company's performance.

⟨⟨ *Accounting is the language of business.*

anonymous ⟩⟩

THE IMPORTANCE OF FINANCIAL INFORMATION

Connie Connors's experience recurs hundreds of times every day throughout the country. Small businesses and sometimes even larger ones fail because they don't follow good financial procedures. Financial information is the heart that keeps competitive businesses beating. Accounting keeps the heartbeat stable.

Accounting is different from marketing, management, and human resource management in that we know almost nothing about accounting from experience. As consumers, we have all had some experience with marketing. As workers or students, we have observed and understand most management concepts. But accounting? What is it? Is it hard to learn? What do accountants do? Is it interesting? Is this a career path you may wish to pursue?

The fact is that you have to know something about accounting if you want to understand business. Furthermore, accounting isn't that hard. You'll have to learn a few terms; that's mandatory. You also have to understand the relationship of bookkeeping to accounting and how accounts are kept. That's not too difficult either. By making this effort you can avoid the problems Connie Connors and others have had when they plunged into the world of business. It's almost impossible to run a business effectively without being able to read, understand, and analyze accounting reports and financial statements.

Accounting reports and financial statements reveal as much about a business's health as pulse rate and blood pressure reports tell us about a person's health. Often a business seems to be doing quite well. Sales go up. Cash is generated to pay monthly expenses. Profits are high. But financial problems gradually start to plague the business. Costs accelerate. Expenses go unchecked. Cash flow becomes poor (meaning the business simply doesn't have funds available to pay its bills). The net result is business failure—thousands fail every year, many of them due to financial mismanagement.

This chapter will introduce you to the importance of obtaining financial information using basic accounting principles. After reading it, you should have a good idea of what accounting is, how it works, and why it's vital. Spend some time learning accounting terms and understanding accounting statements. It's important to understand how such statements are constructed, but it's more important to learn what they mean to the business. A few hours invested in learning this material will pay off repeatedly as you become more involved in business or investing, or simply in understanding what's going on in the world of business and finance. Also, accounting and finance professionals are in demand, so salaries are high.[1]

WHAT IS ACCOUNTING?

accounting
The recording, classifying, summarizing, and interpreting of financial events and transactions to provide management and other interested parties the information they need to make better decisions.

Financial information is primarily based on information generated from accounting. **Accounting** is the recording, classifying, summarizing, and interpreting of financial events and transactions to provide management and other interested parties the information they need to make better decisions. Financial transactions include buying and selling goods and services, acquiring

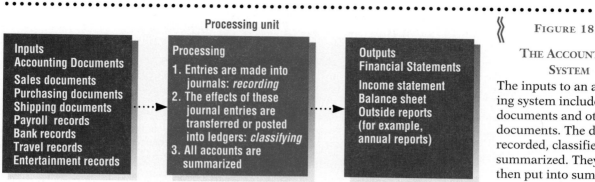

FIGURE 18.1

THE ACCOUNTING SYSTEM
The inputs to an accounting system include sales documents and other documents. The data are recorded, classified, and summarized. They're then put into summary financial statements such as the income statement and balance sheet.

insurance, and using supplies. These transactions may be recorded by hand, or they may be recorded in a computer system. Of course, the trend today is to use computers since the process is often repetitive and complex, and computers greatly simplify the task.

After the transactions have been recorded, they're usually classified into groups with common characteristics. For example, all purchases are grouped together, as are all sales transactions. A businessperson can thus obtain needed information about purchases, sales, and other transactions over a given period of time. The methods used to record and summarize accounting data into reports are called an **accounting system.** (See Figure 18.1.) Systems that use computers enable an organization to get financial reports daily if they wish. One purpose of accounting is to help managers evaluate the firm's financial condition and operating performance so they may make better decisions. Another is to report financial information to people outside the firm such as owners, creditors, suppliers, employees, and the government (for tax purposes).

In very basic terms, accounting is the measurement and reporting to various users (inside and outside the organization) of financial information about the firm's economic activities. (See Figure 18.2.) Accounting has been called the language of business, which may make you think accounting is only necessary for profit-seeking firms. But it's also the language used to report financial information about nonprofit organizations such as churches, schools, hospitals, fraternities, and units of government. Accounting work is divided into several major areas. Accountants can be called on to work in one or more of these areas. Let's review those areas next.

accounting system
The methods used to record and summarize accounting data into reports.

AREAS OF ACCOUNTING

Students sometimes believe that opportunities in accounting are limited because accounting is rather narrow in scope. Actually, nothing could be further from the truth. The accounting profession is divided into four key areas: managerial accounting, financial accounting, auditing, and tax accounting. All four areas present career opportunities for students who are willing to put forth the effort. Let's look at the different areas of accounting next.

••• MANAGERIAL ACCOUNTING •••

Managerial accounting is used to provide information and analyses to managers within the organization to assist them in decision making. Managerial accounting is concerned with measuring and reporting costs of production, marketing, and other functions (cost accounting); preparing budgets

managerial accounting
The provision of information and analyses to managers within the organization to assist them in decision making.

USERS	TYPE OF REPORT
Government taxing authorities (e.g., the Internal Revenue Service)	Tax returns
Government regulatory agencies	Required reports
People interested in the organization's income and financial position (e.g., owners, creditors, financial analysts, suppliers)	Financial statements found in annual reports (e.g., income statement, balance sheet, statement of cash flows)
Managers of the firm	Financial statements and various internally distributed financial reports

(planning); checking whether units are staying within their budgets (controlling); and designing strategies to minimize taxes (tax accounting). Simple analyses of corporate figures can disclose important information. For example, a slight month-to-month increase in payroll costs may not appear significant. But multiply that increase by 12 months, and the increase in costs can be disastrous. Monitoring figures such as profit margins, unit sales, travel expenses, cash flow, inventory, and other such data is critical to a firm's success.

If you're a business major, it's almost certain you'll be required to take a course in managerial accounting. You may even elect to pursue a career as a certified management accountant (CMA). A **certified management accountant** is a professional accountant who has met certain educational and experience requirements and been certified by the Institute of Certified Management Accountants. CMAs generally work within the organization as accountants with management responsibilities. Today, the majority of Fortune 500 firms prefer accountants who earn a CMA over accountants with a CPA. (See the next section.) With growing emphasis on global competition, company downsizing, and organizational cost cutting, managerial accounting may be one of the most important courses in your college career.

certified management accountant
A professional accountant who has met certain educational and experience requirements and been certified by the Institute of Certified Management Accountants.

••• FINANCIAL ACCOUNTING •••

Financial accounting differs from managerial accounting in that the information and analyses it develops are for use by people outside the organization. This information goes to owners and prospective owners, creditors and lenders, employee unions, customers, suppliers, government units, and the general public. These external users are interested in the organization's profits, its ability to pay its bills, and other financial information. Much of the information is contained in the company's **annual report,** a yearly statement of the financial condition and progress of an organization covering a one-year period.

It's critical for firms to keep accurate financial information. Because of this, many organizations employ **private accountants** who work for a single firm, government agency, or nonprofit organization. However, not all firms or nonprofit organizations want or need a full-time accountant. Therefore, thousands of accounting firms in the United States provide the accounting services an organization needs. A person who provides accounting services to individuals or businesses on a fee basis is called a **public accountant.** Such accountants can provide business assistance in many ways. They may design an accounting system for a firm, help select the correct computer and software to run the system, and analyze the financial strength of an organization right from the start. Many big accounting firms earn a sizable percentage of revenues from consulting and other services. Arthur Andersen & Co. (a major accounting firm) has watched its Andersen Consulting unit generate revenues of over $3 billion per year.[2]

financial accounting
The preparation of financial statements for people outside of the firm (for example, investors).

annual report
A yearly statement of the financial condition and progress of an organization covering a one-year period.

private accountant
Accountant who works for a single company.

public accountant
Accountant who provides accounting services to individuals or businesses on a fee basis.

Details, Details

Entrepreneurs often start their own businesses because it's an exciting way to make a living. Later they find that some parts of business ownership aren't exciting at all—to them. In fact, Alan Caruba of The Boring Institute asked entrepreneurs what activities they didn't enjoy. Top on the list was doing payroll. Also in the top 10 were collections and bills. (Of course, government paperwork was high on the list.)

How do entrepreneurs avoid such work? They hire someone else to do it for them. Usually that someone else is an accountant or someone good at accounting. Accounting can be an interesting occupation because it pays well and others are often willing to let you do it for them. Accountants are now increasingly involved in complex financial planning and that makes the job even more interesting and challenging.

Source: "Ho-Hum," *Entrepreneur*, May 1994, p. 14; and David R. Evanson, "Super CPAs," *Entrepreneur*, January 1995, pp. 43–45.

The accounting profession tries to ensure that financial reports of organizations are accurate. The independent Financial Accounting Standards Board (FASB) defines what are *generally accepted accounting principles (GAAP)* that accountants must follow. If financial reports are prepared "in accordance with GAAP," users know the information is reported according to standards agreed on by accounting professionals. The accounting profession also wants to ensure that the people firms hire as accountants are as professional as doctors and lawyers. Accountants who pass a series of examinations established by the American Institute of Certified Public Accountants (AICPA) and meet the state's requirement for education and experience are recognized as **certified public accountants (CPAs)**. CPAs have much prestige among their peers and the business community as a whole. Many small businesses are now turning to them for financial advice.[3] Why not check and see what it takes to become a CPA in your state. Ask an accounting instructor at your school or contact the American Institute of Certified Public Accountants.

certified public accountant (CPA)
Accountant who passes a series of examinations established by the American Institute of Certified Public Accountants (AICPA) and meets the state's requirements for education and experience.

auditing
The task of reviewing and evaluating the records used to prepare the company's financial statements.

independent audit
An evaluation and unbiased opinion about the accuracy of company financial statements.

••• AUDITING •••

The job of reviewing and evaluating the records used to prepare the company's financial statements is referred to as **auditing.** Accountants within the organization often perform internal audits to ensure that proper accounting procedures and financial reporting are being carried on within the company. Public accountants also conduct independent audits of accounting and related records. An **independent audit** is an evaluation and unbiased opinion about the accuracy of a company's financial statements. After an audit of a firm, accountants will provide an *auditor's opinion* that states if the company's financial reports have been prepared according to accepted

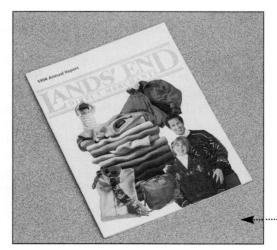

Financial analysts and other stakeholders of a firm are particularly interested in the information disclosed in the company's annual report. Annual reports such as this one for Lands' End highlight a company's financial condition, as well as its plans for the future. Generally, a company's annual report is provided free to anyone requesting a copy.

accounting principles. A firm's annual report often includes a written opinion from an auditor. An accountant who has a bachelor's degree, has two years of internal auditing experience, and has successfully passed an exam administered by the Institute of Internal Auditors can earn standing as a **certified internal auditor.**

certified internal auditor
An accountant who has a bachelor's degree, has two years of internal auditing experience, and has successfully passed an exam administered by the Institute of Internal Auditors.

••• TAX ACCOUNTING •••

Taxes are the price we pay for roads, parks, schools, police protection, and other functions provided by government. Federal, state, and local governments require submission of tax returns that must be filed at specific times and in a precise format. **Tax accountants** are trained in tax law and are responsible for preparing tax returns and developing tax strategies. Since governments often change tax policies according to needs or specific objectives, the tax accountant's job is certainly challenging. Also, as the burden of taxes grows in the economy, the tax accountant becomes increasingly important to the organization.

tax accountant
Accountant who is trained in tax law and is responsible for preparing tax returns and developing tax strategies.

Managerial and financial accounting, auditing, and tax accounting are the four key areas of accounting. Still, some people get confused about the difference between an accountant and a bookkeeper. We'll clarify that difference next, right after the Progress Check.

PROGRESS CHECK

- Can you explain the difference between managerial and financial accounting?
- Could you define accounting to a friend so that he or she would clearly understand what's involved?
- What's the difference between a private accountant and a public accountant?
- What are certified accountants in each area of accounting called?

ACCOUNTING VERSUS BOOKKEEPING

bookkeeping
The recording of business transactions.

Bookkeeping involves the recording of business transactions. Bookkeeping is an important part of accounting, but accounting goes far beyond the mere recording of data. Accountants classify and summarize the data provided by bookkeepers. They interpret the data and report them to management. They also suggest strategies for improving the firm's financial condition and progress. Accountants are especially valuable for income tax preparation and financial analysis.

If you were a bookkeeper, your first task would be to divide all the firm's paperwork into meaningful categories such as sales documents, purchasing receipts, and shipping documents. If you collected all this information, you'd have several piles of papers, much like the piles generated in the preparation of income tax forms. If this information wasn't compressed somehow, it would become unmanageable. Therefore, the bookkeeper must begin to record the data from the original transaction documents (the sales slips and so forth) into record books called *journals*. **Journals** are the books where accounting data are first entered. The term *journal* comes from the French word *jour*, which means day. A journal, therefore, is where the day's transactions are kept.

journal
Recording device used for the first recording of all transactions.

••• DOUBLE-ENTRY BOOKKEEPING •••

It's quite possible when recording financial transactions that you could make a mistake. For example, you could easily write $10.98 as $10.89. For that reason, bookkeepers record all their transactions in two places. They can then check one list against the other to make sure that they add up to the same amount. If they don't equal the same amount, the bookkeeper knows that he or she made a mistake.

The concept of writing every transaction in two places is called **double-entry bookkeeping.** For example, if the owner of a business put $15,000 of his or her own money into the company, the bookkeeper would debit (make an entry into) the cash account. (See Figure 18.3.) To keep the transaction in balance, a corresponding credit entry would be recorded in the capital (owners' equity) account. Debits and credits are thus always in balance. (*Debit* means a bookkeeping entry on the left side of the account; *credit* means an entry recorded on the right side of the account.) The details of double-entry bookkeeping can be easily learned in a class or on the job. For now, you should remember that a journal is the first place transactions are recorded, and they're recorded twice (in two different accounts).

Now, let's suppose a businessperson wanted to determine how much was paid for office supplies in the first quarter of the year. That would be difficult even with accounting journals. The businessperson would have to go through every transaction, seeking out those involving supplies and adding them up. Clearly, what a businessperson needs is another set of books that has pages labeled Office Supplies, Cash, and so on. Then entries in the journal could be transferred (posted) to these pages, and information about various accounts could be found quickly and easily. A **ledger** is a specialized accounting book in which information from accounting journals is accumulated into specific categories and posted so managers can find all the information about one account in the same place. All the journals are totaled and posted (recorded) into ledgers on a weekly, monthly, or quarterly basis. Computerized accounting programs often post into ledgers daily or instantaneously with journal entries. (See Figure 18.3.) This way the financial information is readily available whenever the organization needs it.

> **double-entry bookkeeping**
> A system of bookkeeping in which two entries in the journal are required for each company transaction.

> **ledger**
> Recording device in which information from accounting journals is categorized into homogeneous groups and posted so that managers can find all the information about one account in the same place.

Those of you who don't file the 1040EZ Form know how much paperwork can be involved in doing your own income taxes. There could be dozens of documents to sort through, add up, and so forth. Imagine having many times that paperwork every day and you'll appreciate a bookkeeper's value. Can you imagine how many different transactions a typical McDonald's restaurant has in a single day? You can see why most businesses prefer to hire someone to do the bookkeeping. Would it be worth the owner's time to do all the paperwork? Can you understand why many businesses find it easier to do this work on a computer?

CRITICAL THINKING

••• THE SIX-STEP ACCOUNTING CYCLE •••

The **accounting cycle** is a six-step procedure that results in the preparation and analysis of the two major financial statements: the balance sheet and the income statement. (See Figure 18.4.) The accounting cycle generally involves the work of both the bookkeeper and the accountant. The first three steps are continuous: (1) analyzing and categorizing documents, (2) putting the information into journals, and (3) posting that information into ledgers. The fourth step

> **accounting cycle**
> A six-step procedure that results in the preparation and analysis of the two major financial statements: the balance sheet and the income statement.

FIGURE 18.3

JOURNAL ENTRIES

This figure shows how the information from the journal is posted to various ledgers. The idea is to have all similar transactions in one place. That is, all cash transactions are recorded in one ledger account, all credit transactions in another.

General Journal					Page 1
Date	Account Titles and Explanation	Post Ref	Debit		Credit
1996 Feb 1	Cash	101	15000		
	Hugh Ownit, Capital	301			15000
	The owner invested				
	$15,000 cash in business				
4	Cash	101	5000		
	Accounts Receivable-Super Stores, Inc.	102			5000
	Collection on account				

General Ledger					
Cash					Account No. 101
Date	Explanation	Post Ref	Debit	Credit	Balance
1996 Feb 1					15000
1	Owner investment	G1	15000		30000
4	Super Stores, Inc.	G1	5000		35000

General Ledger					
Hugh Ownit, Capital					Account No. 301
Date	Explanation	Post Ref	Debit	Credit	Balance
1996 Feb 1					35000
1	Owner investment	G1		15000	50000

General Ledger					
Accounts Receivable, Super Stores, Inc.					Account No. 102
Date	Explanation	Post Ref	Debit	Credit	Balance
1996 Feb 1					7500
4	Payment on account	G1		5000	2500

trial balance

Totaling all of the debit balances and all of the credit balances in the ledgers to be sure debits equal credits.

involves preparing a trial balance. **A trial balance** involves summarizing all the data in the account ledgers to see whether the figures are correct and balanced. If they aren't correct, they must be corrected before the income statement and balance sheet are prepared. The fifth step, then, is to prepare an income statement and balance sheet. The sixth step is for the accountant to analyze the financial statements and evaluate the financial condition of the firm.

After the progress check, we'll look into the key financial statements and the important financial information each statement provides.

PROGRESS CHECK

- What's the difference between accounting and bookkeeping?
- What's the difference between an accounting journal and a ledger?

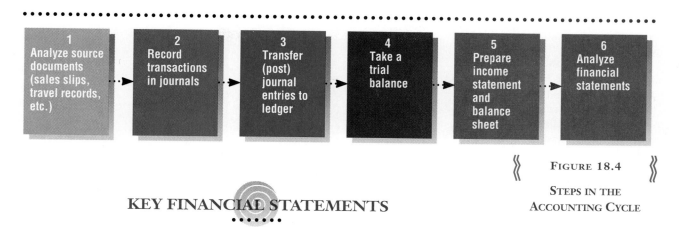

FIGURE 18.4

STEPS IN THE
ACCOUNTING CYCLE

KEY FINANCIAL STATEMENTS

A **financial statement** is the summary of all transactions that have occurred over a particular period. Financial statements indicate a firm's financial health. That's why they're of interest to stockholders (the owners of the firm); banks and bondholders (people who've loaned money to the firm); investors (people who may want to own part of the firm); unions; employees; and, of course, the Internal Revenue Service, which wants its share of the profits.

Two key financial statements, as you've learned, are

1. The *balance sheet,* which reports the firm's financial condition on a specific date.
2. The *income statement,* which reports revenues, costs, expenses, and profits (or losses) for a specific period of time, showing the results of operations during that period.

After taking an intensive accounting course, one reporter summarized the difference this way: "The balance sheet is a snapshot, while the income statement is a motion picture. The former tells what the company owns and owes on a certain day; the latter, what it sells its products for and what its selling costs are over a period of time."

To understand important financial information, you must be able to read and understand both the balance sheet and the income statement. Next we'll explore each statement in more detail.

••• THE BALANCE SHEET •••

A **balance sheet** is the financial statement that reports a firm's financial condition at a specific time. It's composed of three major accounts: assets, liabilities, and owners' equity. The term *balance sheet* implies that the report shows a balance, an equality between two figures. That is, the balance sheet shows a balance between assets on the one hand, and liabilities plus owners' equity on the other. The following analogy will help explain the idea of the balance sheet.

Let's say that you want to know what your financial condition is at a given point in time. Maybe you want to buy a new house or car and need to calculate the resources you have available to buy these things. First, you would add up everything you own: cash, property, money people owe you, and so forth. Subtract from that the money you owe others (for example, credit card debt, IOUs) and you have a figure that tells you that, as of today, you're worth so much. This is fundamentally what companies do in preparing a balance sheet.[4]

financial statement
The summary of all transactions that have occurred over a particular period.

balance sheet
Financial statement which reports the financial position of a firm on a specific date. A balance sheet is composed of assets, liabilities, and owners' equity.

CLASSIFICATIONS OF ASSETS

Assets are classified by how quickly they can be turned into cash (liquidity). The most liquid are called *current assets*. Those that are hard to sell quickly are called *fixed assets* or *property, plant, and equipment*. *Intangible assets* include patents and copyrights.

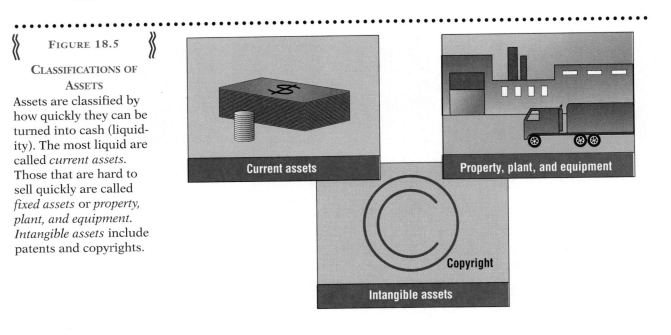

Current assets

Property, plant, and equipment

Copyright

Intangible assets

••• THE ACCOUNTS OF THE BALANCE SHEET •••

assets
The economic resources owned by the firm.

Assets are economic resources owned by the firm. Assets include productive items (such as equipment, buildings, land, furniture, fixtures, and motor vehicles) that help to generate income, as well as intangibles of value such as patents or copyrights. (See Figure 18.5.) Assets are listed according to their liquidity. **Liquidity** refers to how fast an asset can be converted into cash. For example, land is considered highly illiquid because it takes much time and paperwork to sell land. On the other hand, stock is considered highly liquid because it can be sold within minutes. Therefore, assets are divided into three categories according to how quickly they can be turned into cash:

liquidity
The ease with which an asset can be converted to cash.

1. **Current assets** are items that can be converted to cash within one year.
2. **Fixed assets** are items such as land, buildings, and equipment that are relatively permanent. (These assets are also referred to as *property, plant, and equipment*.)
3. **Intangible assets** include items of value such as patents and copyrights that do not have a physical form.

current assets
Resources, including cash or noncash items, that can be converted to cash within one year.

fixed assets
Resources of a permanent nature, such as land, buildings, furniture, and fixtures.

You can see why a key word in accounting is *assets*. Take a few minutes to go through the list of Classic Cereal Company's assets in Figure 18.6. Can you think of particular assets that you own? Do you have a car, life insurance, computer, sound equipment, and so on? Information concerning your assets is often required when seeking a small business loan.[5]

intangible assets
Items that are not included in the current and fixed assets categories. This catch-all category includes items such as patents and copyrights.

••• LIABILITIES AND OWNERS' EQUITY ACCOUNTS •••

liabilities
Amounts owed by the organization to others. Current liabilities are due in one year or less; long-term liabilities are not due within one year.

Another important term in accounting is *liabilities*. **Liabilities** are what the business owes to others. *Current liabilities* are payments due in one year or less; *long-term liabilities* are payments not due for one year or longer. As Figure 18.6 shows, common liability accounts recorded on a balance sheet include

1. *Accounts payable*—money owed to others for merchandise and services purchased on credit but not yet paid. If you have a bill you haven't paid, you have an account payable.

FIGURE 18.6

SAMPLE BALANCE SHEET

CLASSIC CEREALS, INC.
Balance Sheet
March 31, 1996

Assets

    Current assets

Cash	$ 15,000	
Accounts receivable	200,000	
Notes receivable	50,000	
Inventory	335,000	
Total current assets		$600,000

    Property, plant, and equipment

Land		$ 40,000	
Building and improvements	$200,000		
Less: Accumulated depreciation	– 90,000		
		110,000	
Equipment and vehicles	$120,000		
Less: Accumulated depreciation	– 80,000		
		40,000	
Furniture and fixtures	$ 26,000		
Less: Accumulated depreciation	– 10,000		
		16,000	
Total property, plant, and equipment			206,000

    Intangible assets

Goodwill	$ 20,000	
Research and development	80,000	
Total intangible assets		100,000
Total assets		$906,000

Liabilities and Stockholder's Equity

    Liabilities

      Current liabilities

Accounts payable	$ 40,000	
Notes payable (due Dec. 1996)	8,000	
Accrued taxes	150,000	
Accrued salaries	90,000	
Total current liabilities		$288,000

      Long-term liabilities

Notes payable (due Mar. 2004)	$ 35,000	
Bonds payable (due Dec. 2014)	290,000	
Total long-term liabilities		325,000
Total liabilities		$613,000

    Stockholder's equity

Common stock (1,000,000 shares)	$100,000	
Retained earnings	193,000	
Total stockholder's equity		293,000
Total liabilities & stockholder's equity		$906,000

2. *Notes payable*—short-term or long-term loans (e.g., from banks) that have a promise for future payment.

3. *Bonds payable*—money loaned to the firm that it must pay back. If a firm sells someone a bond, it agrees to pay that person back the money he or she lent you plus interest. (We'll discuss bonds in depth in Chapters 19 and 20.)

The value of things you own (assets) minus the amount of money you owe others (liabilities) is called *equity*. The value of what stockholders own in a firm (minus liabilities) is called *stockholders' equity* (or *shareholders' equity*). Because stockholders are the owners of a firm, stockholders' equity is also called *owners' equity* or *partnership equity*.

owners' equity
Assets minus liabilities.

The formula for **owners' equity,** then, is assets minus liabilities. Differences will exist in the owners' equity account according to the type of organization. Businesses that aren't incorporated identify the investment of the sole proprietor or partner through a *capital account*. For sole proprietors and partners, owners' equity means the value of everything owned by the business minus any liabilities of the owner(s) (for example, outstanding loans). For corporations, the owners' equity account records the owners' claims to funds they've invested in the firm (such as capital stock) plus earnings kept in the business and not paid out in dividends (**retained earnings**).

retained earnings
The amount left after a company distributes some of its net income to stockholders in the form of dividends.

••• THE FUNDAMENTAL ACCOUNTING EQUATION •••

Imagine that you don't owe anybody any money. That is, you don't have any liabilities. Then the assets you have (cash and so forth) are equal to what you own (equity). But if you borrow some money from a friend, you've incurred a liability. The assets that you hold are now equal to what you owe plus what you own. Translated into business terms,

$$\text{Assets} = \text{Liabilities} + \text{Owners' equity}$$

fundamental accounting equation
Assets =Liability + Owners' equity; it is the basis for the balance sheet.

This formula is called the **fundamental accounting equation.** It's the basis for the balance sheet. As Figure 18.6 highlights, on the balance sheet you list assets in a separate column from liabilities and owners' equity. The assets are equal to or are balanced with the liabilities and owners' equity. It's that simple. The complicated part is determining what's included in the asset account and what's included in the liabilities and owners' equity accounts. Businesspeople must understand the important financial information the balance sheet provides. Take a few moments and see what facts you can determine about Classic Cereal from this financial statement. Can you do a personal balance sheet for yourself?

PROGRESS CHECK

- What does it mean to list various assets by degree of liquidity?
- What goes into the account called *liabilities?*
- What's the formula for owners' equity?

••• THE INCOME STATEMENT •••

income statement
Financial statement which reports revenues and expenses over a specific period of time, showing the results of operations during that period. It summarizes all the resources that came into the firm (revenues), and all the resources that left the firm and the resulting net income or loss.

The financial statement that shows the "bottom line"—that is, profit after costs, expenses, and taxes—is the income statement. The **income statement** summarizes all the resources (called *revenue*) that came into the firm from operating activities, money resources that were used up, expenses incurred in doing business, and what resources were left after all costs and expenses, including taxes, were paid. **Net income or net loss** is the resources leftover, if any. (See Figure 18.7.) The income statement reports the results of operations over a particular period of time. The formulas for the income statement are

net income/net loss
Revenue minus expenses.

$$\text{Revenue} - \text{Cost of goods sold} = \text{Gross margin (gross profit)}$$

$$\text{Gross margin (gross profit)} - \text{Operating expenses} = \text{Net income or loss before taxes}$$

$$\text{Net income before taxes} - \text{Taxes} = \text{Net income (or net loss)}$$

FIGURE 18.7

SAMPLE INCOME
STATEMENT

CLASSIC CEREALS, INC.
Income Statement
For the Year Ended December 31, 1995

Revenues		
Gross sales		$ 720,000
Less: Sales returns and allowances	$ 12,000	
Sales discounts	8,000	– 20,000
Net sales		$700,000
Cost of goods sold		
Beginning inventory, Jan. 1		$ 200,000
Merchandise purchases	$400,000	
Freight	40,000	
Net purchases		440,000
Cost of goods available for sale		$ 640,000
Less ending inventory, Dec. 31		– 230,000
Cost of goods sold		– 410,000
Gross profit		$ 290,000
Operating expenses		
Selling expenses		
Salaries for salespeople	$ 90,000	
Advertising	18,000	
Supplies	2,000	
Total selling expenses		$ 110,000
General expenses		
Office salaries	$ 67,000	
Depreciation	1,500	
Insurance	1,500	
Rent	28,000	
Light, heat, and power	12,000	
Miscellaneous	2,000	
	112,000	
Total operating expenses		222,000
Net income before taxes		$ 68,000
Less: Income tax expense		19,000
Net income after taxes		$ 49,000

Let's review some of the terms used in the income statement and their significance. Naturally, stockholders and other interested parties (such as lenders) want to know how the company is performing financially. This is valuable financial information. Let's take a moment to walk through the income statement and learn what each step means.

••• REVENUE •••

Revenue is the value of what's received from goods sold, services rendered, and other financial sources. Note the terms *revenue* and *sales*. Most revenue (money coming in to the firm) comes from sales, but there could be other sources of revenue such as rents received, money paid to the firm for use of its patents, or interest earned. Be careful not to confuse the terms *revenue* and *income*. Some people use them as if they were synonymous. But a

revenue
The value of what is received for goods sold, services rendered, and other sources.

glance at the income statement shows that revenue is at the top of the statement and income is at the bottom. Net income is revenue minus sales returns, costs, expenses, and taxes.

COST OF GOODS SOLD
··· (COST OF GOODS MANUFACTURED) ···

cost of goods sold (cost of goods manufactured)
A particular type of expense measured by the total cost of merchandise sold or cost of raw materials or parts and supplies used for producing items for resale.

Cost of goods sold (or **cost of goods manufactured**) measures the cost of merchandise sold or cost of raw materials or parts and supplies used for producing items for resale. To calculate how much a business earned by selling merchandise over the year, you subtract how much it spent to buy the merchandise from the revenue. That cost includes the purchase price plus any freight charges paid to bring in the goods plus the costs associated with storing the goods less the cost of any goods returned. In other words, all costs of buying and keeping merchandise for sale, including packaging, are included in the cost of goods sold.

gross margin
How much the firm earned by buying and selling or making and selling merchandise.

When you subtract the cost of goods sold from net sales, you get what's called *gross margin* or *gross profit*. **Gross margin** then, is how much the firm earned by buying (or making) and selling merchandise. In a service firm, there may be no cost of goods sold; therefore, net sales could equal gross margin. In a manufacturing firm, we'd estimate the cost of goods manufactured. In either case (selling goods or services), the gross margin doesn't tell you everything. You're also interested in net profit or net income. To get that, you must subtract expenses.

··· OPERATING EXPENSES ···

expenses
Costs incurred in operating a business, such as rent, utilities, and salaries.

To sell goods or services, a business has certain **expenses.** Obvious ones include rent, salaries, supplies, utilities, insurance, and depreciation of equipment. Accountants are trained to help you find other expenses you may need to deduct.

After all expenses are deducted, the firm's net income before taxes is determined. (See Figure 18.7.) After the allocation for taxes, we get to what people call the bottom line, which is the net income (or perhaps net loss) the firm incurred from operations. It answers the question, How much did the business earn?

You may not be familiar with these terms, but you use the concepts behind them all the time. For example, you can see the importance of keeping track of costs and expenses when you prepare your own budget. If your expenses (e.g., rent and utilities) exceed your revenues (how much you earn), you're in deep trouble. If you need more money (revenue), you could sell some of the things you own. The same is true of businesses.

So you see, businesses are much like you. They need to keep track of how much money they earn, how much they spend, how much cash they have on hand, and so on. The difference is that businesses tend to have more complex problems and more to record. (See Figure 18.8.) Cash flow is often a problem both businesses and individuals suffer. Keep this in mind as we explore accounting information in more depth.

PROGRESS CHECK

- What are the three formulas that make up the income statement?
- What's the difference between revenue and income on the income statement?

Legal Briefcase

Who's Accountable?

Accurate financial information is vital to understanding a firm's financial condition. But sometimes organizations decide to get a bit "creative" (some would say "deceptive") in reporting financial information. Actions or omissions can range from minor deceptions to actual serious misapplications of accounting principles. In reading a financial report, it's important to be alert to the seven most common uses of "slick accounting":

1. Recording revenue too soon.
2. Recording bogus revenue that doesn't exist.
3. Boosting income with one-time gains.
4. Shifting current expenses to a later period.
5. Failing to record or disclose all liabilities.
6. Shifting current income to a later period.
7. Shifting future expenses to the current period.

Any of these actions can affect the accurate financial picture of the firm. Can you see why it's important to have a basic understanding of financial statements and how they should be properly structured?

Source: Howard M. Schilit, "Is It Fraud, or Just Slick Accounting," *CFO*, August 1993, pp. 8-9; and Howard M. Schilit, *Financial Shenanigans* (New York: McGraw-Hill, 1993).

••• THE IMPORTANCE OF CASH FLOW ANALYSIS •••

Understanding cash flow problems is really rather simple. Let's say you borrow $10 from a friend to buy a used bike and agree to pay him back at the end of the week. You sell the used bike to someone else for $15. He agrees to pay you in a week also. It turns out that the person who bought the bike from you doesn't have the money in a week and tells you he'll pay you next month sometime. Meanwhile, your friend wants his $10 now! Eventually, you could make a $5 profit, but right now you have a cash flow problem. You owe $10

⟨⟨ **FIGURE 18.8** ⟩⟩

SAMPLE OF SPECIFIC ACCOUNT TITLES IN GENERAL ACCOUNT CLASSIFICATIONS

FOR THE BALANCE SHEET			FOR THE INCOME STATEMENT			
Assets	Liabilities	Stockholders' or Owners' Equity	Revenues	Cost of Goods Sold	Expenses	
Cash	Accounts payable	Capital stock	Sales revenue	Cost of buying goods	Wages	Interest
Accounts receivable	Notes payable	Retained earnings	Rental revenue	Cost of storing goods	Rent	Donations
Inventory	Bonds payable	Common stock	Commissions revenue		Repairs	Licenses
Investments	Taxes payable	Treasury stock	Royalty revenue		Travel	Fees
Equipment					Insurance	Supplies
Land					Utilities	Advertising
Buildings					Entertainment	Taxes
Motor vehicles					Storage	
Goodwill						

Reaching Beyond Our Borders

The Oil's Flowing but the Cash Isn't

In May 1994, after 16 months of intense negotiations, AT&T was awarded the largest telecommunications contract ever received outside the United States. The Kingdom of Saudi Arabia signed a $4 billion agreement with AT&T to modernize the country's phone system. The contract was a real coup since the competition included such global giants as Germany's Siemens, Alcatel Alsthom of France, NEC of Japan, and Northern Telecom of Canada.

When you think of Saudi Arabia, one thing comes to mind: oil. The Saudis pump 8 million barrels a day and supply almost 20 percent of the oil imports to the United States. With numbers like this, you may assume the Saudis could pay AT&T from petty cash funds. Well, surprise. The Saudis had to borrow the money from the U.S. government's Export–Import Bank to seal the deal.

As impossible as it may seem, Saudi Arabia, the world's number one oil producer, is having major cash flow problems. After years of deficit spending and falling oil prices, the Saudis are running out of cash. The prob-

lems have become so acute that King Faud was forced to announce across-the-board spending cuts of 19 percent. The Saudi government was unable to continue paying its bills. Unfortunately, the problems didn't stop there. The Saudi stock exchange fell 30 percent and some of the kingdom's largest business groups were also having trouble meeting financial obligations. For the first time in recent history, the Saudis found it hard to raise fresh cash. Several large New York–based banks refused loans to the government to pay a $1.85 billion installment due to the McDonnell Douglas Company. The risk was considered too high.

If oil prices rebound, the Saudi economy may find some relief since the economy is 85 percent dependent on oil revenues. But answers to cash flow problems are never easy. Only time will tell if Saudi Arabia can bite the bullet and overcome its cash crisis.

Source: John Rossant and Stanley Reed, "The Saudis Are Buying—but with Whose Money?" *Business Week*, May 23, 1994, pp. 28–29.

and have no cash. What would you do if your friend insisted on being paid? If you were a business, you might go bankrupt even though you have the potential for profits.

A business can often increase both sales and profit, but still suffer deeply from cash flow problems. That happened to Connie Connors in this chapter's opening profile. **Cash flow** is simply the difference between cash flowing in and cash flowing out of a business. Poor cash flow is a key operating problem of many businesses.[6] Here's how cash flow problems occur in a growing business: A company's growing rapidly. Everyone's excited! To meet customers' demands, more and more goods are bought on credit. (No cash is involved.) Similarly, more and more goods are sold on credit. (No cash is involved.) This goes on for quite a while until the firm uses up all its credit with banks and others that lend it money. The firm then requests more money from the bank to pay a crucial bill. The bank refuses the loan because the credit limit has been reached. All other credit sources refuse a loan as well. The company desperately needs funds to pay its bills, or else its creditors could force it into bankruptcy. The company could survive if its customers would pay their bills, but they're too slow in paying to solve the problem. All too often, the company does go into bankruptcy, all because there was no cash available when it was most needed.

Clearly, one of the critical relationships a businessperson makes is with his or her banker. Obviously, one solution to cash flow problems is to develop a great relationship with your bank. You can also see one of the vital services accounting provides to the firm. Accountants tell the firm if it needs cash and

cash flow
The difference between cash receipts and cash disbursements.

FIGURE 18.9

STATEMENT OF CASH
FLOWS

CLASSIC CEREALS, INC.
Statement of Cash Flows
For the Year Ended December 31, 1996

Cash flows from operating activities		
Cash received from customers	$150,000	
Cash paid to suppliers and employees	(90,000)	
Interest paid	(5,000)	
Income tax paid	(4,500)	
Interest and dividends received	1,500	
Net cash provided by operating activities		$52,000
Cash flows from investing activities		
Proceeds from sale of plant assets	$ 4,000	
Payments for purchase of equipment	(10,000)	
Net cash provided by investing activities		(6,000)
Cash flows from financing activities		
Proceeds from issuance of short-term debt	$ 3,000	
Payment of long-term debt	(7,000)	
Payment of dividends	(15,000)	
Net cash inflow from financing activities		(19,000)
Net change in cash and equivalents		$27,000
Cash balance, December 31, 1995		(2,000)
Cash balance, December 31, 1996		$25,000

how much. It's up to the finance managers to decide how and where to get the money needed. The statement of cash flows is a good barometer of the cash position within a firm.

••• THE STATEMENT OF CASH FLOWS •••

In 1988, the Financial Accounting Standards Board required the statement of cash flows to replace the statement of changes in financial position. The **statement of cash flows** reports cash receipts and disbursements, related to the firm's major activities:

Operations.

Investments.

Financing.

Figure 18.9 shows a statement of cash flows. This statement answers such questions as, How much cash came into the business from current operations? That is, how much cash came into the firm from buying and selling goods and services? Was cash used to buy stocks, bonds, or other investments? Were some investments sold that brought in cash? How much money came in from issuing stock, and how much went out for paying dividends? Other financial transactions are analyzed to see their effect on the firm's cash position.

The firm analyzes all of the cash changes due to operating, investing, and financing to learn the net cash position. The cash flow statement also gives the firm some insight into how to better handle cash so that no cash flow problems occur in the future.

statement of cash flows
Report of cash receipts and disbursements related to the firm's major activities: operations, investments, and financing.

Making Ethical Decisions

Oh, My Aching Bank!

You're a small manufacturing firm's only accountant. You have full charge of the books of the company, which isn't in good shape because of an economic downturn.

You know that your employer is going to ask the bank for an additional loan so that the company can continue to pay its bills. Unfortunately, the financial statements for the year won't show good results, and you know that the bank won't approve a loan increase based on those figures.

Your boss approaches you in early January before you've closed the books for the year. He suggests that perhaps the statements can be improved by treating sales made at the beginning of January as if they were made in December. He also asks you to do a number of other things to cover up the trail so the auditors won't discover the "padding" of the years' sales.

You know that it's against the professional rules of your accounting organization, and you argue with your boss. Your boss tells you that if the company doesn't get the additional bank loan, it will likely close and you'll be out of a job. You believe that your boss is probably right and you know that it's a bad time to be looking for work.

What are your alternatives? What are the likely consequences of each alternative. What will you do?

APPLYING ACCOUNTING KNOWLEDGE

If accounting were nothing more than the repetitive function of gathering and recording transactions and preparing financial statements, the major functions could be assigned to computers. In fact, most medium-size and large firms have done just that. The truth is that *how* you record and report data are critical.

Take depreciation, for example. **Depreciation** is the systematic write-off of the value of a tangible asset over its estimated useful life. Companies are permitted to use depreciation as an expense of business operations. Subject to certain technical rules, which are beyond the scope of this chapter, a firm may use one of several different techniques for calculating depreciation. Each technique results in a different bottom line, in other words, a different net income. Accountants can offer financial advice and recommend ways of handling depreciation—as well as insurance, investments, and other accounts—that also will affect the firm's bottom line.

One of the more complex issues in accounting is how to handle inventory. Inventories are a critical part of a company's financial statements. This shows up in the cost of goods sold (or cost of goods manufactured) section of the income statement. When a firm takes merchandise from inventory and sells it, it has several different ways of calculating that item's cost. One way is to take the oldest merchandise first, as is done in supermarkets. Clerks stack the old merchandise in front of the new merchandise so that the old merchandise sells first. This is called **FIFO (first in, first out).** In accounting, what counts isn't whether the item was really first in; what counts is how much the accountants say that item cost. Let's say, for example, that a college bookstore has been buying textbooks for resale. It buys a textbook in 1995 for $50. Because of inflation, it buys another copy of the same textbook in 1996 for $60. Now it has two textbooks to sell. If the accountant used the FIFO technique, the cost of goods sold would be $50, because the textbook that was bought first (in 1995) cost $50.

depreciation
The systematic write-off of the value of an asset over its estimated useful life.

FIFO
(first in, first out)
Accounting technique for calculating cost of inventory based on first in, first out.

	FIFO	LIFO
Revenue	$65	$65
Cost of goods sold	$50	$60
Income before taxes	$15	$ 5
Taxes of 40%	$ 6	$ 2
Net income	$ 9	$ 3

FIGURE 18.10
ACCOUNTING USING
LIFO VERSUS FIFO
INVENTORY VALUATION

A second approach would be to use a technique called **LIFO (last in, first out).** Using that strategy, the bookstore's cost of goods sold for the textbook would be $60. Can you see the difference in the two accounting approaches on the bottom line? The books are the same and contain the same information. However, if the book is sold for $65, FIFO would report $10 more of net income before taxes than LIFO. (See Figure 18.10.) If a firm switched from a LIFO to a FIFO system, you can see that such a change would make it appear that the firm made more money when, in fact, nothing changed but the accounting system. That's why the American Institute of Certified Public Accountants (AICPA) is adamant that readers of financial statements are given complete information concerning the firm's financial operations. Companies have to include a notation of any change in inventory valuation in their annual reports.

**LIFO
(last in, first out)**
Accounting technique for calculating cost of inventory based on last in, first out.

- What is cash flow, and how can a small business protect itself against cash flow problems before they occur?
- Why are cash flows statements relevant?
- What's the difference between LIFO and FIFO inventory valuation?
- How could the use of these methods change financial information?

**PROGRESS
CHECK**

USING FINANCIAL RATIOS

Every person in an organization should know the importance of accurate financial information. What's especially helpful in financial analysis is the use of ratios to measure a company's health. Most of you are familiar with ratios— we use them all the time. For example, in basketball, the percentage of shots made from the foul line versus attempts is measured by a ratio. A player who shoots 85 percent from the foul line is considered an outstanding foul shooter, so it's wise not to foul this person. Ratios are easy to compute, and yet they provide valuable information about an athlete's or firm's performance. Understanding business ratios is key to sound financial analysis. Let's look at some ratios businesspeople use in four key categories: liquidity ratios, leverage (debt) ratios, profitability (performance) ratios, and activity ratios.

••• LIQUIDITY RATIOS •••

Liquidity ratios measure the company's ability to pay its short-term debts. These ratios are of particular importance to the firm's creditors who expect to be paid on time. The two primary indicators of a company's liquidity are the current ratio and the acid-test ratio. The current ratio is the ratio of a firm's current assets to its current liabilities. This information can be found on the firm's balance sheet. Let's say that Miller's Auto Repair has $25,000 of current assets and $10,000 of current liabilities. Its current ratio is thus 2.5. This means the company has $2.50 of current assets for every $1 of current liabilities.

$$\text{Current ratio} = \frac{\text{Current liabilities}}{\text{Current assets}} = \frac{\$25,000}{\$10,000} = 2.5$$

The purpose of the current ratio is to evaluate the firm's ability to pay its bills in the short run. (In other words, can it pay its short-term bills with its short-term assets?) At first glance, this may sound like the firm is well positioned financially for the short term. Nonetheless, the ratio should be compared to competing firms within the industry to measure how the company sizes up to its main competitors. The firm also needs to evaluate the ratio from the previous year to note any significant changes. Usually, a 2 to 1 ratio of current assets to current liabilities is considered sound.

The second key liquidity ratio is called the *acid-test ratio* (also called the *quick ratio*). The acid-test ratio measures the cash, marketable securities, and receivables of the firm in relation to its current liabilities. This ratio is considered critical to firms that have difficulty converting inventory into quick cash. It helps answer the question, If sales drop off and we can't sell our inventory, can we still pay our short-term debt?

Though it varies by industry, in general, an acid-test ratio of at least 1.0 is considered sound. If an organization can't meet its short-term debt, it often has to go to a high-cost lender for financial assistance.

$$\text{Acid-test ratio} = \text{Cash} + \text{Marketable securities} + \frac{\text{Receivables}}{\text{Current liabilities}} = \frac{\$15,000}{\$10,000} = 1.5$$

••• LEVERAGE (DEBT) RATIOS •••

Leverage (debt) ratios refer to the degree to which a firm relies on borrowed funds in its operations. A firm that takes on too much debt could have problems repaying its lenders or meeting promises to stockholders. These two groups are generally very interested in a firm's debt ratios. The debt to owners' equity ratio measures the degree to which the company is financed by borrowed funds that must be repaid:

$$\text{Debt to owners' equity ratio} = \frac{\text{Total liabilities}}{\text{Owners' equity}} = \frac{\$150,000}{\$275,000} = 54.5\%$$

A ratio above 1 (or 100 percent) shows that a firm actually has more debt than equity. It's a good bet this firm could be quite risky to both lenders and investors. But remember, it's always important to compare ratios to other firms in the same industry because debt financing is more acceptable in some industries than others. Comparisons with past years' ratios can also identify trends within the firm or industry.

••• PROFITABILITY (PERFORMANCE) RATIOS •••

A firm's financial performance is measured by using profitability ratios (also called *performance ratios*). Profitability ratios measure how effectively the firm is using its various resources to achieve profits. Management's performance is often carefully measured by using profitability ratios. Three of the more important ratios used are earnings per share, return on sales, and return on equity.

Earnings per share measures the profit a company earns for each share of common stock it has outstanding. As you probably guessed, this is a crucial ratio for corporations since earnings stimulate growth in the company and pay for stockholders' dividends. Earnings per share is calculated as follows:

$$\text{Earnings per share} = \frac{\text{Net income}}{\text{Number of common shares outstanding}} = \frac{\$120,000}{100,000} = \$0.12 \text{ earnings per share}$$

Earnings per share is an excellent indicator of a firm's current performance and growth on a year-by-year basis. Continued earnings growth is well received by both investors and lenders.

Another reliable measure of performance is obtained by using a ratio based on the return on sales. Firms use this ratio to see if they're doing as well as their competition in generating income from their sales. Return on sales is calculated by comparing a company's net income with its total sales.

$$\text{Return on sales} = \frac{\text{Net income}}{\text{Net sales}} = \frac{\$50,000}{\$500,000} = 10\% \text{ return on sales}$$

Return on equity measures how much was earned for each dollar invested by owners. It's calculated by comparing a company's net income with its total owners' equity:

$$\text{Return on equity} = \frac{\text{Net income}}{\text{Total owners' equity}} = \frac{\$50,000}{\$150,000} = 33\% \text{ return on equity}$$

The level of risk involved in the industry and competing firms' return on equity are important in assessing a firm's performance. The higher the risk involved, normally the higher the return on equity expected by investors.

It's important to remember that profits help companies grow.[7] Therefore, these and other profitability ratios are considered vital measurements of company growth and management performance.

••• ACTIVITY RATIOS •••

Converting the firm's resources to profits is a key function of management. Activity ratios measure the effectiveness of the firm's management in using its available assets.

The inventory turnover ratio measures the speed of inventory moving through the firm and its conversion into sales. Inventory sitting idly in a business costs money. The more efficiently the firm manages its inventory, the higher the return. We measure the inventory turnover ratio as

$$\text{Inventory turnover ratio} = \frac{\text{Cost of goods sold}}{\text{Average inventory}} = \frac{\$320,000}{\$116,000} = 2.75 \text{ times}$$

A lower than average inventory turnover ratio often indicates obsolete merchandise or poor buying practices. A higher than average ratio may note an understocked condition where sales can be lost because of inadequate stock. An acceptable turnover ratio is often determined on an industry-by-industry

SPOTLIGHT ON
SMALL BUSINESS

*Keeping a Smile
on Your
Banker's Face*

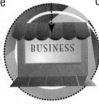

As you've learned, positive or negative relations with your banker can often predict success or failure for a business, especially a small business. Entrepreneurs learn fast that keeping their banker happy can pay off, particularly if the company finds itself in a financial crunch. How do you keep your banker happy? One answer is to use accounting information. Few entrepreneurs realize that financial ratios are important to bankers and are often the basis of their decisions concerning financing requests.

Financial ratios not only can help the entrepreneur manage his or her business more efficiently, but they also can make your banker a more reliable business partner. Bankers see ratios as useful measurements to use when comparing a company's financial position to that of competing companies. Also, they see ratios as an effective guide in evaluating the firm's performance to industry standards or trends in the market. What are some important ratios at which bankers look closely?

Banks feel a firm's ability to repay bank loans and make timely interest payments is crucial in measuring financing requests. Therefore, liquidity ratios such as the current ratio are important in determining the firm's short-term financial strength. Is it best for a firm to always maintain a high current ratio? Not necessarily! If a company has too high a current ratio, bankers may feel it's

making poor use of resources. If your current ratio is falling, you must be prepared to make a case to explain why this is happening. Keeping track of inventory and the firm's debt position will also impress your banker. Low inventory turnover could suggest to bankers that trouble is ahead. Excess inventory can boost interest rates and possibly lower profits. Ratios such as inventory turnover can offer valuable insights into preventing these problems and keeping the bank on your side. Debt is a potential source of worry for both the businessperson and the bank. Therefore, debt to equity and total debt to total assets are ratios of major concern to the business and the bank.

How can small-business managers build a working relationship with their bankers? They should regularly prepare and update a report binder that contains key financial ratios as well as cash flow forecasts and projections. Entrepreneurs must then discuss with the banker what ratios are perhaps most relevant to their businesses and then keep track of them on a regular basis. With such diligence, you not only build a good working relationship with your banker, but you also build a partnership with an informed partner.

Source: Richard J. Maturi, "The Numbers Game," *Inc.*, October 1991, pp. 42–45.

basis. Managers need to be aware of proper inventory control to ensure proper performance. Have you ever worked as a food server in a restaurant? How many times did your employer expect you to "turn over" a table in an evening? The more times a table turns, the higher the possible return to the owner.

Accountants and finance professionals use several other specific ratios besides the ones we've discussed to learn more about a firm's financial condition. The key purpose here is to acquaint you with the idea of what ratios are and how they're used. It's also important for you to note that financial analysis begins where accounting statements end.

THE IMPACT OF COMPUTER TECHNOLOGY IN ACCOUNTING

After reading the previous sections that specify the number of accounts a firm must keep, the reports that need to be generated, and the importance of ratio analysis, you no doubt recognize the value of computers in the accounting process. Even owners of relatively small businesses are learning that data

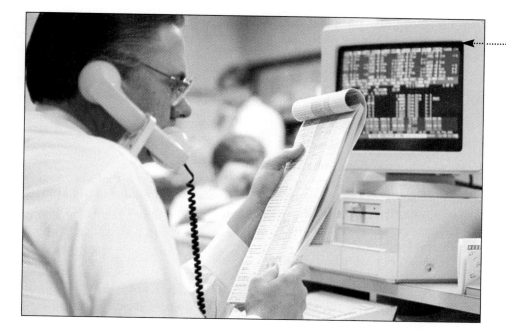

Computers have made the accounting process much faster and easier. Businesses of all sizes can enjoy the benefits of computerized accounting systems. As the cost of hardware and software decreases, and applications continue to grow, many home-based businesses will benefit from computerized accounting information.

processing (like keeping and analyzing accounting records) is usually best done by a computer. Computers can record and analyze data and print out financial reports providing continuous financial information for the business.

It's now possible to have continuous auditing (that is, testing the accuracy and reliability of financial statements) because of computers. One large auditing firm, Coopers & Lybrand, hopes to link its computers to clients' computers using Coopers' software to continuously analyze and to test the correct functioning of its clients' systems. Such continuous auditing could help prevent bank failures and other business bankruptcies by spotting trouble at its early stages.

There are now software programs that allow even novices to do sophisticated financial analyses within days. But no computer yet has been programmed to make good financial decisions by itself. A computer is a wonderful tool, however, in the hands of trained accountants who understand the data. They know which strategy produces the best accounting results. Business owners should understand exactly what computer system is best suited for their particular needs. Once criteria are determined, a small business must develop its accounting system so that it works on these predesigned systems. That's one reason why we recommend that all prospective small-business owners hire or consult with an accountant before they get started in business.

Trained accountants can assist the firm in reaching its financial reporting objectives by using legal, established accounting procedures. You see from this chapter that there's more to accounting than meets the eye. It can be fascinating. Minority students will find opportunities in all accounting firms. One of the faster-growing firms is Mitchell, Titus & Company, the largest minority-owned CPA firm in the country.[8] What can be especially fascinating and challenging for all students is to understand how finance specialists use accounting and financial information to keep a business sound financially. We'll explore this process in Chapter 19.

- Look back at the financial statements of Classic Cereal in Figures 18.6 and 18.7. Can you calculate the company's current ratio, acid-test ratio, debt to equity ratio, and return on sales? Check with your instructor concerning your accuracy.

- What's the most important thing for a company to remember in deciding on a particular accounting strategy using available software?

PROGRESS CHECK

SUMMARY

1. Understand the importance of financial information and accounting and its different uses in business.

2. Define and explain the different areas of the accounting profession.

3. Distinguish between accounting and bookkeeping and list the steps in the accounting cycle.

4. Explain the difference between the major financial statements.

1. Financial information is critical to an organization's growth and development. Accounting provides the information necessary to measure a firm's financial condition.
   - ***What is accounting?***
   Accounting is the recording, classifying, summarizing, and interpreting of financial events and transactions that affect an organization. The methods used to record and summarize accounting data into reports are called an *accounting system.*

2. The accounting profession covers four major areas.
   - ***How does managerial accounting differ from financial accounting?***
   Managerial accounting provides information and analyses to managers within the firm to assist them in decision making. Financial accounting provides information and analyses to *external* users of data such as creditors and lenders.
   - ***What's the job of an auditor?***
   Auditors review and evaluate the standards used to prepare a company's financial statements. An independent audit is conducted by a public accountant; it's an evaluation and unbiased opinion about the accuracy of a company's financial statements.
   - ***What's the difference between private and public accountants?***
   A public accountant provides services for a fee to a variety of companies, whereas a private accountant works for a single company. Private and public accountants do essentially the same things with the exception of independent audits. Private accountants do perform internal audits, but only public accountants supply independent audits.

3. Many people confuse bookkeeping and accounting.
   - ***What's the difference between bookkeeping and accounting?***
   Bookkeeping is part of accounting, but only the mechanical part of recording data. Accounting also includes classifying, summarizing, interpreting, and reporting data to management.
   - ***What are journals and ledgers?***
   Journals are original-entry accounting documents. That means they're the first place transactions are recorded. Summaries of journal entries are recorded (posted) into ledgers. Ledgers are specialized accounting books that arrange the transactions by homogeneous groups (accounts).
   - ***What are the six steps of the accounting cycle?***
   The six steps of the accounting cycle are (1) analyzing documents, (2) recording the information into journals, (3) posting that information into ledgers, (4) preparing a trial balance, (5) preparing the income statement and balance sheet, and (6) analyzing financial statements.

4. Financial statements are a critical part of the firm's financial position.
   - ***What's a balance sheet?***
   A balance sheet reports a firm's financial position on a particular day. The fundamental accounting equation used to prepare the balance sheet is

$$\text{Assets} = \text{Liabilities} + \text{Owners' equity}$$

   - ***What are the major accounts of the balance sheet?***
   Assets are economic resources owned by the firm, such as buildings and machinery. Liabilities are amounts the firm owes to others (for example, creditors, bondholders). Owners' equity is the value of the things the firm owns (assets) minus any liabilities; thus, owners' equity equals assets minus liabilities.

• **What's an income statement?**

An income statement reports revenues, costs, and expenses for a specific period of time (e.g., for the year ended December 31, 1996). The formula is

Revenue – Sales returns – Cost of goods sold =
Gross margin – Operating expenses =
Income before taxes – Taxes = Net income or net profit

(Note that income and profit mean the same thing.)

• **What's a statement of cash flows?**

Cash flow is the difference between cash receipts and cash disbursements. The statement of cash flows reports cash receipts and disbursements related to the firm's major activities: operations, investments, and financing.

5. Applying accounting knowledge makes the reporting and analysis of data a challenging occupation. Depreciation is a key account that accountants evaluate. Two accounting techniques for valuing inventory are LIFO and FIFO.

• **What's depreciation?**

Depreciation is the systematic write-off of a tangible asset's value over its estimated life. Depreciation must be noted on both the balance sheet and the income statement.

• **What are LIFO and FIFO?**

LIFO (last in, first out), and FIFO (first in, first out) are methods of valuing inventory. Which method you use affects net income.

5. Describe the roles of depreciation, LIFO and FIFO in reporting financial information.

6. Financial ratios are a key part of analyzing financial information.

• **What are the four key categories of ratios?**

The four key categories of ratios are liquidity ratios, leverage (debt) ratios, profitability (performance) ratios, and activity ratios.

• **What's the major value of ratio analysis to the firm?**

Ratio analysis provides the firm with financial information about its financial position in key areas compared to (1) comparable firms in its industry and (2) its past performance.

• **How can computers help accountants?**

Computers can record and analyze data and provide financial reports. Software can continuously analyze and test accounting systems to be sure they're functioning correctly. Computers can help decision making by providing appropriate information, but they can't make good financial decisions independently. Accounting creativity is still a human trait.

6. Explain the importance of ratio analysis in reporting financial information.

accounting 550
accounting cycle 555
accounting system 551
annual report 552
assets 558
auditing 553
balance sheet 557
bookkeeping 554
cash flow 564
certified internal auditor 554
certified management accountant 552

certified public accountant (CPA) 553
cost of goods sold (cost of goods manufactured) 562
current assets 558
depreciation 566
double-entry bookkeeping 555
expenses 562
FIFO (first in, first out) 566
financial accounting 552

financial statement 557
fixed assets 558
fundamental accounting equation 560
gross margin 562
income statement 560
independent audit 553
intangible assets 558
journal 554
ledger 555
liabilities 558

KEY TERMS

LIFO (last in, first out) 567

liquidity 558

managerial accounting 551

net income/net loss 560

owners' equity 560

private accountant 552

public accountant 552

retained earnings 560

revenue 561

statement of cash flows 565

tax accountant 554

trial balance 556

DEVELOPING WORKPLACE SKILLS

1. Take a sheet of paper and on every fourth line, write one of the following headings: assets, liabilities, owners' equity, expenses, cost of goods sold (or cost of goods manufactured), and revenues. Then list as many items as you can under each heading. When you are finished, look up the lists provided in the text and add to your own. Keep the lists for your notes. As you complete the lists, create a mental picture of each account so that you can understand the concepts behind accounts and accounting.

2. Prepare your own income statement. See how far you can get without looking back to Figure 18.7. Then look in the text to see what you have forgotten, if anything.

3. Use a computer and spreadsheet software to prepare your own balance sheet. Remember the simple formula: Assets = Liabilities + Owners' equity. Check your balance sheet against the one in Figure 18.6.

4. Place yourself in the role of small business consultant. One of your clients, Pennsylvania Place Antiques, has been very successful and would like to open two more stores, but from time to time they've experienced cash flow problems. Draft an advisory memo proposing a more conservative expansion strategy identifying the potential problems with rapid growth.

5. The text describes two ways of determining the cost of goods sold: FIFO (first in, first out) and LIFO (last in, first out). Compute the net income using FIFO and LIFO with the information listed below. Which strategy is best?

Beginning inventory:	25,000 units @ $20.00
Purchases (new inventory):	25,000 units @ 25.00
Sales:	25,000 units @ 55.00
Tax rate:	33%

. . . .

PRACTICING MANAGEMENT DECISIONS

〈〈 C A S E APPLYING FINANCIAL INFORMATION 〉〉

DaVinci Paint and Decorating was started by Keith Allen when he was a senior in high school. As the business grew, Keith hired several friends and over time the company began to prosper. At first he didn't consider keeping records that important. But now he's in a position to begin keeping better records. Keith has written down some of his figures, yet he isn't quite sure how to interpret them. He plans to request another loan from a local bank and has been told to prepare a balance sheet to calculate his financial position. These are his figures:

Cash on hand	$5,100
Equipment loan	1,200
Supplies	500

Bank loan	7,500
Truck	13,750
Equipment	4,520
Money owed supplier	900
Office furniture	945
Accounts receivable	2,400
Notes payable	1,900

Keith collected some other figures he felt might be important in determining his firm's performance. These were put together fast and in no apparent order:

Income from work	$74,000
Salaries to employees	38,000
Advertising expense	1,720
Insurance	2,000
Office costs (rent, heat, etc.)	8,040
Depreciation on truck	4,000

Keith also recently purchased some wallpapering materials for $1,800 for a job he expects to start in a week.

Decision Questions

1. What additional information, if any, would you need to construct a balance sheet? If his company is a sole proprietorship, can you prepare a balance sheet for Keith from the information provided? Is Keith in a strong or poor financial condition? How can you determine this?

2. Prepare an income statement you could use to show Keith how such a financial statement looks. How much did Keith earn before taxes?

3. Is the bank being unreasonable by asking Keith to put together a balance sheet? What else might the bank be interested in if Keith wants a loan?

• •

〉〉 VIDEO CASE LEARNING THE LANGUAGE OF BUSINESS 〈〈

Games and sports are more fun to play when you know the rules and regulations. Once you begin playing, it's a challenge to see how well you can do relative to other players. Each game has its own rules and measures of success. In baseball, you can strike out 2 out of 3 times at bat yet still be considered a good player. In basketball, on the other hand, if you miss 2 out of 3 foul shots you wouldn't seem so good.

Businesses also follow rules and regulations. As in sports, there are various ways of "scoring" and measuring the effectiveness of one business against others in the same field. For example, you can compare supermarkets to other supermarkets in efficiency, return on investment, turnover of goods, and so forth.

The people who keep such records are called accountants. Their function is to act as the score and record keepers of business. Accounting is thus called "the language of business" because accounting terms such as assets, liabilities, revenues, expenses, and owners' equity are as important to business as "balls," "strikes," and "outs" are to baseball.

The score sheets in accounting, as you have read in this chapter, include the income statement, the balance sheet, and the statement of cash flows. Such statements tell a business how it is doing *internally*. But how does the success of the business *compare to its competitors?* Lots of people would like to know that answer: potential stockholders, union negotiators, potential employees, bankers, and other lenders. Accountants calculate and prepare such comparison measures as return on investment, inventory turnover, debt ratios, price/earnings ratios, and more. In order to be considered a pro in business, you have to know the language and the importance and meaning of key ratios. Just as a professional baseball player can tell you his or her batting average, a professional businessperson can tell you his or her company's return on investment and explain its significance.

Decision Questions

1. Which accounting terms and concepts do you need to know to prepare a balance sheet? What is the formula?

2. Which terms and concepts do you need to know to prepare an income statement?

3. Why should accountants compare the success of one business against others?

4. Can you prove that you are ready for at least the amateur ranks of business by explaining what is meant by ROI, cash flow, and the PE ratio?

Part 6
MANAGING INFORMATION (INFORMATION SYSTEMS)

Information management is a major growth industry of the future. To understand either the past or the present conditions of a company, we must have information. The process of getting the right information and processing it efficiently is an important part of staying competitive in today's business world. In a world constantly reshaped by new technology, the field of information management plays a key role.

Changing technologies have created a large number of different job titles in this exciting area. Careers are available in: information systems management, computer programming, cost estimating, and troubleshooting, just to name a few. All future forecasts predict that career opportunities in computer-related businesses and industries will continue to grow more rapidly than the average for other occupations.

SKILLS

Anyone who chooses to work with information technology should be comfortable with change and have a willingness to keep abreast of changes. Such a person also needs to have an interest in and aptitude for data and information and have an ability to see trends and relationships. People in this area are usually involved in some way with problem solving. An aptitude for seeing possible solutions to problems is important.

CAREER PATHS

In this ever-changing field, up-to-date knowledge is the key. A formal education in computer science, for example, would be almost useless if it was obtained 10 years ago and not updated. Most employers prefer hiring people who have had recent college coursework in software applications, programming, and general business. Business knowledge is important for the employee to place his or her work in context.

Computer skills are taught at public and private vocational schools, community colleges, and universities. Many programmers and systems analysts are college graduates, and a degree is helpful in getting hired. However, vocational schools can often provide the knowledge and skill necessary to excel.

SOME POSSIBLE CAREERS IN INFORMATION SYSTEMS

Job Title	Salary	Job Duties	Career Path	Prospects
Systems analyst	$26,500–$47,000 Median: $42,000.	Advise computer programmers on problem solutions. Implement management decision on data processing issues.	Can start as a trainee, then be promoted into management.	One of the fastest-growing occupations through 2005.
Computer programmer	$21,000–$39,500.	Work for systems analyst to write programs needed by management.	Entry-level positions often involve inputting and other less technical tasks. Promotions often mean greater task complexity. Sometimes start out as programmer.	Growth will be faster than average through 2005. Driven by growth of construction industries.
Cost estimator	$17,000–$75,000.	Prepare specifications using precedent, math, and computer data to predict cost requirements.	Career path varies greatly from company to company and from industry to industry.	Prospects are fair through 2005.
Operations research analyst	$30,000–$50,000, Top salaries: $90,000+.	Solve problems by the use of computerized data. Nature of problems varies.	Master's degree very desirable. High level of computer skills is mandatory. Promotion into management quite possible. Bachelor's degree graduates start as research assistants.	Growth slow but definite through 2005.

DAVID GOODMAN, COMPUTERIZED TROUBLESHOOTER

As a student at Lansing Community College in Michigan, David Goodman knew only that he wanted a career in business. Like many students, he had to do some career exploration before he finally found his niche. In David's case, that niche was in the data processing area. As a student, he worked in computer systems, while he held another job at a local McDonald's. In 1990, he graduated with an associate's degree in marketing. Both marketing and data processing were in his future.

While he was still a student, a hypermarket called Meijer, Inc., hired him. In that company, David was able to learn various aspects of marketing and data processing. His favorite job during his student days was his position as advertising manager for *The Lookout,* the student newspaper at Lansing Community College, where he worked while still employed by Meijer. This position allowed him to see advertising from a unique perspective and to travel all over the country to journalism competitions among community colleges. For over two years he also worked for the *Greater Lansing Business Monthly.* There he was able to use both his computer skills and his marketing talent. In 1992, David was awarded a Certificate of Recognition from the Lansing Chamber of Commerce for his accomplishments in both college and the community.

Today he works for EDS at its Pontiac headquarters in the roadside assistance program. When motorists have problems, they contact Dave's office, and he uses his data processing resources to solve them. The computer system that he runs is the source of the data he needs in emergency situations. Besides computer skills, this job requires the ability to empathize with others, to communicate with them, and to choose the right solution for their problem.

To be successful at a job like this, David says, requires oral communications as the number one skill. "That includes listening skills as well as speaking skills," he reflects. David reports that learning how to listen can be the telling difference between failure and success in this job. "People who are in trouble don't always say what they really mean. It takes a good listener to hear through the emotions and frustrations to the real needs."

Also, it's a job where you never stop learning. David is not planning for this job to be the final stop on his career ladder. He has his eyes on research and development. "R & D is customer-feedback oriented," he says. "I want to be a part of that, because it involves both the computer skills and the people abilities that I am developing now." Research and development will also allow David a chance to use the creativity he's using now, but in a new and different context.

His advice to those still in college is to learn as much as possible from everything you do, both inside the classroom and out. Always maintain a learning attitude, and knowledge will come to you in ways you wouldn't expect. "Have a general plan and follow it through, even if it contains a few detours along the way, and don't ever be afraid to do some career exploration."

Special thanks to Bill Motz, Lansing Community College, for recommending David Goodman for this career portfolio.

PART 7

MANAGING FINANCIAL RESOURCES

CHAPTER 19
USING FINANCIAL
RESOURCES

CHAPTER 20
FINANCING AND
INVESTING THROUGH
SECURITIES MARKETS

CHAPTER 21
UNDERSTANDING
MONEY AND FINANCIAL
INSTITUTIONS

CHAPTER 22
DEVELOPING AND
MANAGING YOUR
PERSONAL FINANCES

APPENDIX
MANAGING RISK

CHAPTER 19

USING FINANCIAL RESOURCES

LEARNING GOALS

After you have read and studied this chapter, you should be able to

1. Explain the role and importance of finance.

2. Describe the responsibilities of financial managers.

3. Outline the steps in financial planning by explaining the process of forecasting financial needs, developing budgets, and establishing financial controls.

4. Recognize the financial needs that must be met with available funds.

5. Distinguish between short-term and long-term financing and between debt capital and equity capital.

6. Identify and describe several sources of short-term financing.

7. Identify and describe several sources of long-term financing.

JUDY LEWENT, CFO OF MERCK & COMPANY

Judy Lewent has put her education to good use. A graduate of MIT's Sloan School of Management, she worked as division controller at Pfizer before joining pharmaceutical giant Merck in 1980. After serving three years as company treasurer, Lewent became CFO (chief financial officer) in 1990. Today, she sits on the 10-member management committee at Merck and is considered one of the most powerful women in corporate America.

Lewent's job at Merck is intense and challenging. Think about what she must face for just a moment. The pharmaceutical industry is extremely competitive. In addition, the business requires costly, time-consuming research that may not pay off for many years. Merck invests more than $1 billion per year in research, yet estimates are that it takes from 10 to 12 years and costs $359 million to develop a new drug. To further compound this problem, only 3 out of 10 drugs brought to market ever return the cost the company spent on their development. As you might suspect, the question, Do we continue to invest?, is asked often in the course of product development. Add other complexities—such as health care reform, the emerging generic drug market, and an unpredictable global market with fluctuating currencies—and it's easy to see why the words *risk/return* take on such importance in Judy Lewent's job.

Lewent believes the challenge of chief financial officers today is to help overcome the negative perception that U.S. companies pursue short-term financial gains at the expense of long-term growth. Merck, like many other successfully managed companies, allies the role of finance with research, marketing, and production to maximize value. Lewent and her 500-member finance team are charged with developing the financial plan to deal with the high-stakes nature of this changing industry.

The ideas of risk, complexity, and uncertainty clearly define the business environment of the 1990s. Add the challenges of instability in global markets, interest rate fluctuations, and enhanced expectations of investors and lenders and you see the challenge of sound financial management. Let's explore the role of finance in the organization and the tools financial managers use in seeking financial stability and future growth in the firm.

Imagine that a company is a car, and the role of financing becomes clear. In essence, it's fuel. In financing a company, then, the entrepreneur must answer two crucial questions: Where is the company now? and Where do you want to take it? From there it's simply a matter of deciding when to fill up, at which station, and at what cost.

Unfortunately, many young companies sputter to a halt under a sign that says a gas station is still 35 miles away. Sometimes the entrepreneur simply underestimates the need for fuel. Other times the problem is the distance to the destination. The simplest mistakes overlap, snowball, and lead to disaster.

Eileen Davis

THE ROLE OF FINANCE

Let's compare the roles of an accountant and a financial manager. An accountant is like a skilled lab technician who takes blood samples and other measures of a person's health and writes the findings on a health report (the equivalent of a set of financial statements). A financial manager for a business is the doctor who interprets the report and makes recommendations to the patient regarding changes that would improve health. Financial managers use the data prepared by the accountants and make recommendations to top management regarding strategies for improving the health (financial strength) of the firm.

A manager can't make sound financial decisions without understanding accounting information. That's why we examined accounting in Chapter 18. Similarly a good accountant needs to understand finance. Accounting and finance, finance and accounting—the two go together like peanut butter and jelly. In organizations, both the accounting and finance functions are generally under the control of a person such as Judy Lewent, who serves as a chief financial officer (CFO). Finance is a critical activity in any size organization.

As you may remember from Chapter 6, financing a small business is a difficult but essential function if a firm expects to survive those important first five years. The need for careful financial management is an ongoing challenge a business of any size must face throughout its entire life. Chrysler Corporation faced extinction in the late 1970s due to severe financial problems. Had it not been for a $1 billion government-backed loan, Chrysler might have joined the ranks of defunct auto companies such as Packard and Hudson. Three of the most common ways for any firm to fail financially are

1. Undercapitalization (not enough funds to start with).
2. Poor control over cash flow (cash in minus cash out).
3. Inadequate expense control.

••• THE IMPORTANCE OF UNDERSTANDING FINANCE •••

Consider the financial problems encountered by a small organization called Parsley Patch. This company was started on a shoestring budget by two women. It began when Elizabeth Bertani prepared salt-free seasonings for her husband, who was on a salt-free diet. Her friend Pat Sherwood thought the seasonings were good enough to sell. Mrs. Bertani agreed, and Parsley Patch, Inc., was born.

The business began with an investment of $5,000, which was eaten up for a logo and a label design. Mrs. Bertani and Ms. Sherwood quickly learned the importance of capital in getting the business going. Eventually, the two women personally invested more than $100,000 to keep the business from experiencing severe undercapitalization.

Everything was going well. Hundreds of gourmet shops adopted the product line, but sales were still below expectations. Finally, the women decided the health-food market offered more potential because salt-free seasonings were a natural for people with restricted diets. The choice was a good one. Sales took off and were approaching $30,000 a month. The problem was no profits. Elizabeth and Pat hadn't been trained in cash flow procedures or in controlling expenses. In fact, they were told not to worry about costs, and they hadn't. They eventually hired a CPA and an experienced financial manager who taught them how to compute the costs of various blends they produced and how to control their expenses. They also offered insight into how to control cash coming in and out of the company. Soon they earned a comfortable margin on operations that ran close to $1 million a year. Luckily, they were able to turn things around before they went broke.

If Elizabeth and Pat had understood finance before starting their business, they might have avoided many of their problems. The key word here is *understand*. You don't have to pursue finance as a career to understand finance. Financial understanding is important to anyone who wants to invest in stocks and bonds, start a small business, or plan a retirement fund. In short, finance and accounting are two areas everyone involved in business should study. Let's look at what finance is all about.

WHAT IS FINANCE?

Finance is the function in a business that acquires funds for the firm and manages funds within the firm (for example, preparing budgets, doing cash flow analysis, and planning for the expenditure of funds on such assets as plant, equipment, and machinery). Without a carefully calculated financial plan, a firm has little chance for survival regardless of its product or marketing effectiveness. **Financial management** is the job of managing a firm's resources so it can meet its goals and objectives. Most organizations have a manager in charge of financial operations. Generally, this person is the chief financial officer. But sometimes financial management is in the hands of a person known as the treasurer or vice president of finance. A comptroller is the chief accounting officer. Figure 19.1 shows what a finance person does. As you see, the fundamental charge is to obtain money and then plan, use, and control money effectively. That includes managing cash, accounts receivable, and inventory. Where a company's cash is invested may have a major impact on profits.

finance
The function in a business responsible for acquiring funds for the firm, managing funds within the firm, and planning for the expenditure of funds on various assets.

financial management
Management of the firm's resources so it can meet its goals and objectives.

• Planning	• Collecting funds (credit management)
• Budgeting	• Auditing
• Obtaining funds	• Managing taxes
• Controlling funds (funds management)	• Advising top management on financial matters

FIGURE 19.1

WHAT FINANCIAL MANAGERS DO
All these functions depend greatly on the information provided by the accounting statements discussed in Chapter 18.

You're probably familiar with several finance functions such as buying merchandise on credit and collecting payment from customers. Both credit and collections are important responsibilities of financial managers. Financial managers must also be sure that the company doesn't lose too much money to bad debts (people or firms that don't pay). Naturally, this means that the finance department is responsible for collecting overdue payments. These functions are critical to all types of businesses—especially small and medium-size businesses, which typically have smaller cash or credit cushions than large corporations.

As Chapter 18 said, tax payments represent an outflow of cash from the business. Therefore, they too fall under finance. As tax laws and tax liabilities have changed, finance people have taken on the increasingly important responsibility of tax management. Tax management is the analysis of tax implications of various managerial decisions in an attempt to minimize taxes paid by the business. (Remember Chapter 18's discussion of tax accounting and issues such as LIFO and FIFO?) Businesses of all sizes must concern themselves with managing taxes.

It's the internal auditor, usually a member of the firm's finance department, who checks on the journals, ledgers, and financial statements prepared by the accounting department to make sure that all transactions have been treated in accordance with established accounting rules and procedures. If there were no such audits, accounting statements would be less reliable. Therefore, internal auditors should be objective and critical of any improprieties or deficiencies they might note in their evaluation. Regular internal audits offer the firm assistance in the important role of financial planning, which we'll look at next.

CRITICAL THINKING

Can you see the link between accounting and finance? They're mutually supportive functions in a firm. A firm can't get along without accounting, but neither can it prosper without finance. The importance of finance is such that many successful finance executives go on to become presidents and chief executive officers. What would be the advantages and disadvantages of having a president with a finance background versus a marketing background? Do you think Judy Lewent might be in line to become CEO of Merck in the future? Why?

Expansion into global markets requires careful financial and technical analysis, as well as many risks. Southwestern Bell and Telmex entered a joint venture in 1990 to build one of the fastest growing telephone companies in the world.

FINANCIAL PLANNING

Planning has been a continuous theme of this book. We've stressed its importance as a managerial function and offered insights into planning your career. Financial planning involves analyzing short-term and long-term money flows to and from the firm. The overall objective of financial planning is to optimize profits and make the best use of money. Financial planning is one of the key responsibilities of the financial manager. It's probably safe to assume that we all could use better financial planning in our lives.

Financial planning involves three steps: (1) forecasting both short-term and long-term financial needs, (2) developing budgets to meet those needs, and (3) establishing financial control to see how well the company is following the financial plans. Let's look at each step's important role in the financial health of an organization.

••• FORECASTING FINANCIAL NEEDS •••

Forecasting is an important component of financial planning. (See Figure 19.2.) A **short-term forecast** is a prediction of revenues, costs, and expenses for a period of one year or less. This forecast is the foundation for most other financial plans so its accuracy is critical. Part of the short-term forecast may be in the form of a **cash flow forecast,** which projects the expected cash inflows and outflows in future periods, usually months or quarters. Naturally, the inflows and outflows recorded in the cash flow forecast are based on expected sales revenues and on various costs and expenses incurred and when they'll come due. A firm often uses past financial statements as a basis for expected sales and various costs and expenses.

A **long-term forecast** is a prediction of revenues, costs, and expenses for a period longer than 1 year, sometimes as far as 5 or 10 years into the future. This forecast plays a crucial part in the company's long-term strategic plan. Remember, the strategic plan asks questions such as these: What business are we in, and should we be in it five years from now? How much money should we invest in automation and new plant and equipment over the next decade? Will there be cash available to meet long-term obligations?

The long-term financial forecast gives top management as well as operations managers some sense of the income or profit potential possible with different strategic plans. Additionally, long-term projections assist financial managers with the preparation of company budgets.

short-term forecast
A prediction of revenues, costs, and expenses for a period of one year or less.

cash flow forecast
A prediction of cash inflows and outflows in future periods.

long-term forecast
A prediction of revenues, costs, and expenses for a period longer than 1 year, sometimes extending 5 or 10 years into the future.

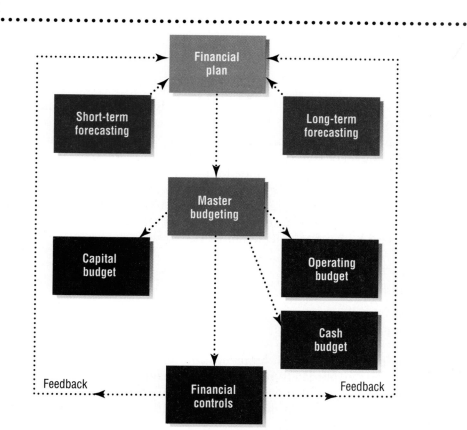

FIGURE 19.2

FINANCIAL PLANNING
Note the close link between financial planning and budgeting.

Reaching Beyond Our Borders

Dear Walt and Mickey, Welcome to Realityland

Imagine the impossible—Mickey Mouse roaming the streets of Paris looking for a small handout of cheese. Sound unlikely? Probably so, but things at the Paris Disney (formerly Euro Disney) complex have been nothing short of a financial disaster. It seems that Paris Disney is awash in a sea of debt that the company has suggested could close the park.

According to Rebecca Winnington-Ingram of Morgan Stanley International, "The park is making money. It's the underlying financial structure that is unbearable." Disney wants its banks to convert some of the debt to equity and cut interest on loans to help lighten the firm's estimated $290 million in annual debt service. Banks aren't receptive to the idea and suggest that Disney inject some new funds. Meanwhile, Paris Disney stock has plunged and bondholders are threatening to sue.

Things weren't always so dismal and may not remain so. When Disney first announced its plans to open the park in the Paris suburb, the French government was ecstatic. Financiers also took well to the Disney name and reputation. Sixty international banks waited in line to court the company with billions of francs. Analysts suggest that Disney's over-commitment in hotel development may be at the heart of the company's problem. Also, failure to accurately assess the influence of French culture caused some early problems. Nevertheless, help may be on the way.

Saudi Prince Al-Walid bin Talal has offered to invest up to $430 million in new equity to keep the park open. He would purchase shares that three French banks have expressed little interest in owning. With this new infusion of cash and a proposed restructuring of debt, the park should remain on stable financial footing for the next two years. The end of the recession in Europe and the opening of the London-to-Paris channel train (Eurostar) could also enhance attendance at the park. But Mickey's trip through financial realityland is by no means over.

Source: Peter Gumbel, "Marketing Changes Boost Euro Disney as Debt-Restructuring Talks Approach, *The Wall Street Journal*, January 12, 1994, pp. A1 and A12; Jolie Solomon, "Mickey's Trip to Trouble," *Newsweek*, February 14, 1994, pp. 34–39; Stewart Toy and Paula Dwyer, "Is Disney Headed for the Euro-Trash Heap?" *Business Week*, January 24, 1994, p. 52; and Stewart Toy, "EuroDisney's Prince Charming?" *Business Week*, June 13, 1994, p. 42.

••• DEVELOPING BUDGETS •••

budget
A financial plan that allocates resources based on projected revenues.

A budget is a financial plan. Specifically, a **budget** sets forth management's expectations for revenues and, based on those financial expectations, allocates the use of specific resources throughout the firm. You may live under a carefully constructed budget of your own. A business operates in the same way. A budget becomes the primary basis and guide for the firm's financial operations.

Most firms compile yearly budgets from short-term and long-term financial forecasts. Therefore, since budgeting is clearly tied to forecasting, financial managers must take forecasting responsibilities seriously. There are usually several budgets established in a firm:

An operating budget.

A capital budget.

A cash budget.

A master budget.

operating budget
The projection of dollar allocations to various costs and expenses needed to run or operate the business.

An **operating budget** is the projection of dollar allocations to various costs and expenses needed to run or operate the business, given projected revenues. How much the firm will spend on supplies, travel, rent, advertising, salaries, and so forth is determined in the operating budget.

FIGURE 19.3

A SAMPLE CASH BUDGET

Fiberrific, Inc.
Monthly Cash Budget

FIBERRIFIC, INC.

	January	February	March
Sales forecast	$50,000	$45,000	$40,000
Collections			
Cash sales (20%)		9,000	8,000
Credit sales (80% of past month)		40,000	36,000
Monthly cash collection		$49,000	$44,000
Payments schedule			
Supplies and material		$11,000	$10,000
Salaries		12,000	12,000
Direct labor		9,000	8,000
Taxes		3,000	3,000
Other expenses		7,000	6,000
Monthly cash payments		$42,000	$39,000
Cash budget			
Cash flow		$ 7,000	$ 5,000
Beginning cash		−1,000	6,000
Total cash		$ 6,000	$11,000
Less minimum cash balance		−6,000	−6,000
Excess cash to market securities		$ 0	$ 5,000
Loans needed for minimum balance		0	0

A **capital budget** highlights the firm's plans for purchasing major assets (such as property, buildings, and equipment) that often require large sums of money.

A **cash budget** estimates the projected cash balance at the end of a given period (for example, monthly, quarterly). Cash budgets can be important guidelines that assist managers in anticipating borrowing, debt repayment, cash disbursements, and short-term investment expectations. Cash budgets help the firm plan for cash shortages or surpluses. The cash budget is often the last budget prepared. Figure 19.3 shows a sample cash budget.

A **master budget** ties together all the above-mentioned budgets and summarizes the proposed financial activities of the firm.

Clearly, financial planning plays an important role in the firm's operations. This planning often determines what long-term investments to make, when specific funds will be needed, and how the funds will be generated. Once a company has projected its short-term and long-term financial needs and established budgets to show how funds will be allocated, the final step in financial planning is to establish financial controls.

capital budget
The firm's spending plans for major asset purchases that often require large sums of money.

cash budget
Projects the cash balance at the end of a given period.

master budget
The financial plan that summarizes the operating, capital, and cash budgets.

••• ESTABLISHING FINANCIAL CONTROLS •••

Financial control means that the actual revenues, costs, and expenses (including the cash flow projections) are periodically reviewed and compared with projections. Managers can identify deviations and take corrective action if necessary. Such controls provide feedback to help reveal which accounts,

financial control
A process that periodically compares the actual revenue, costs, and expenses with projections.

Making Ethical Decisions

How Much Is Enough?

You are a department manager for a major consumer products firm. Each year your supervisor asks that you prepare a short-term financial forecast and operating budget for the coming fiscal year. Your department's appropriations are determined; funds are allocated from the forecast and budget you present. Preliminary analysis indicates that your department could survive the next year's operations with exactly the same budget that was allocated to you last year. The problem is, you wonder that by not requesting additional funds for this year, the firm will expect you to keep your departmental costs down each and every year. You realize your supervisor would certainly approve a 10 percent increase in your budget appropriations just on his trust in you. You might even be able to get a 15 percent increase with little questioning of actual need. What will you do? What could result from your decision?

which departments, and which people are varying from the financial plans. Such deviations may or may not be justified. In either case, managers can make some financial adjustments to the plan. After the Progress Check we'll explore specific reasons why firms need to have funds readily available.

PROGRESS CHECK

- Name three finance functions that are important to the firm's overall operations and performance.
- What are the three primary financial problems that often cause firms to fail?
- How do short-term and long-term financial forecasts differ?
- What's the organization's purpose in preparing budgets? Can you identify at least three different types of budgets?

THE NEED FOR OPERATING FUNDS

Continuous sound financial management is essential to businesses because the need for operating funds never seems to cease. Also, like our personal financial needs, the capital needs of a business change over time. For example, as a small business grows, its financial requirements shift considerably. (Remember the example of Parsley Patch.) The same is true with large corporations such as AT&T and PepsiCo. As they venture into new product areas or markets, their capital needs increase. Different firms need funds available for different reasons. However, in virtually all organizations, funds must be available to finance certain operational needs. Let's look at the financial needs that affect both the smallest and the largest of businesses.

••• MANAGING DAILY BUSINESS OPERATIONS •••

If workers are scheduled to be paid on Friday, they don't want to have to wait until Monday for their paychecks. If tax payments are due on the 15th of the month, the government expects the money on time. If the interest payment on a business loan is due on the 30th, the lender doesn't mean the 1st of the next month. As you can see, funds have to be available to meet the daily operational costs of the business.

Ed Goldman was a gas station operator when his wife sent him out to buy some ice. He asked the owner of the ice machine to send his supplier to his gas station. Ed loved the idea of selling ice, and eventually sold his gas station to make ice full time. Now his company, Cubex, sells and leases ice machines to others.

Ed has some advice for entrepreneurs looking to finance their businesses: "Keep a careful eye on your

Advice from the Ice Man

working capital, borrow from someone you know rather than a bank, and keep personal spending in line with business growth. Put those things together and offer quality and service at a good price, and you can succeed."

Source: William Slattery, "Freeze Fame," *Entrepreneur*, January 1994, pp. 250–54.

The challenge of sound financial management is to see that funds are available to meet these daily cash needs without compromising the firm's investment potential. Money has what's called a *time value*. In other words, if someone offered to give you $200 today or $200 one year from today, you'd benefit by taking the $200 today. Why? A very simple reason. You could start collecting interest on the $200 you receive today, and over a year's time, your money would grow. In business, the interest gained on the firm's investments is important in maximizing the profit the company will gain. For this reason, financial managers often try to keep cash expenditures at a minimum, to free funds for investment in interest-bearing accounts. It's not unusual for finance managers to suggest the firm pay bills as late as possible (unless a cash discount is available) and collect what's owed to it as fast as possible. This way they maximize the investment potential of the firm's funds. Efficient cash management is particularly important to small firms in conducting their daily operations.

••• MANAGING ACCOUNTS RECEIVABLE •••

Financial managers know that making credit available helps to keep current customers happy and attracts new customers. In today's highly competitive business environment, many businesses couldn't survive without making credit available to customers.

The major problem with selling on credit is that as much as 25 percent or more of the business's assets could be tied up in accounts receivable. This means that the firm needs to use some of its available funds to pay for the goods or services already given customers who bought on credit. This outflow of funds means financial managers must develop efficient collection procedures. For example, businesses often provide cash or quantity discounts to buyers who pay their accounts by a certain time. Also, finance managers carefully scrutinize old and new credit customers to see if they have a favorable history of meeting their credit obligations on time. In essence, the firm's credit policy reflects its financial position and its desire to expand into new markets.

One way to decrease the time and, therefore, expense of collecting accounts receivable is to accept bank credit cards such as Mastercard or Visa. This is convenient for both the customer and the merchant. Banks have already established the customer's creditworthiness, which reduces the business's risk. On the other hand, businesses must pay a fee to offer credit cards, and that fee may seriously cut into profits. This is especially costly for small businesses.

••• OBTAINING NEEDED INVENTORY •••

As we noted earlier, the marketing concept implies a clear consumer orientation. This focus on the customer means that service and availability of goods are vital if a business expects to prosper in today's markets. Therefore, to satisfy customers, businesses must maintain inventories that involve a sizable expenditure of funds. Although it's true that the firm expects to recapture its investment in inventory through sales to customers, a carefully constructed inventory policy assists in managing the use of the firm's available funds and maximizing profitability. For example, an owner of a neighborhood ice cream parlor ties up more funds in inventory (ice cream) in the summer months than in winter. It's obvious why. Demand for ice cream goes up in the summer. As you learned in Chapter 9, innovations such as just-in-time inventory are reducing the amount of funds a firm must tie up in inventory.

••• MAJOR CAPITAL EXPENDITURES •••

capital expenditures
Major investments in long-term assets such as land, buildings, equipment, or research and development.

Capital expenditures are major investments in long-term assets such as land, buildings, equipment, or research and development. In many organizations, the purchase of major assets—such as land for future expansion, plants to increase production capabilities, research to develop new products, and equipment to maintain or exceed current levels of output—is essential. As you might imagine, these expenditures can require a huge portion of the organization's funds. Remember the situation confronting companies such as Merck? They often must spend large sums of money for research to develop products that may not be commercially successful. Therefore, it's critical that the company weigh all the possible options before it commits what may be a large portion of its available resources. For this reason, financial managers and analysts evaluate the appropriateness of such purchases or expenditures. Consider the situation in which a firm needs to expand its production capabilities due to rising demand. One option is to buy land and build a new plant from scratch. Another option would be to purchase an existing plant or consider renting. Can you think of financial and accounting considerations that would come into play in this decision?

The firm's need for available funds raises several questions: How does the firm obtain funds to finance operations and other business necessities? How long will specific funds be needed by the organization? Will funds have to be repaid at a later date? How much will the needed funds cost? Will these funds come from internal sources or external sources? These questions will be addressed in the next section, after the Progress Check.

PROGRESS CHECK

- Money is said to have a time value. What does this mean?
- Why are accounts receivable a financial concern to the firm?
- What's the major reason organizations spend a good deal of their available funds on inventory and major assets?

ALTERNATIVE SOURCES OF FUNDS

Earlier in the chapter, you learned that finance is the function in a business that's responsible for acquiring and managing funds for the firm. Determining the amount of money needed for various time periods and finding out the most appropriate sources from which to obtain these funds are fundamental steps in sound financial management. Next we'll look at methods of acquiring funds from a variety of sources. Before we begin this discussion, it's important to highlight some key distinctions involved in funding the firm's operations.

Organizations typically encounter short- and long-term financing needs. **Short-term financing** refers to needs for capital that will be repaid within one year. On the other hand, **long-term financing** refers to capital needs for major purchases that will be repaid over a specific time period longer than one year. We'll explore sources of both short- and long-term financing in the next sections. Businesses can use different methods of raising money. Large firms can seek to raise money through borrowing (debt), from selling ownership (equity), or from profits (retained earnings). **Debt capital** refers to funds raised through various forms of borrowing that must be repaid. Funds borrowed could be either short-term (due to be repaid within one year) or long-term (due over a period longer than one year). **Equity capital** is money raised from within the firm or through the sale of ownership in the firm.

short-term financing
Financing that will be repaid within one year.

long-term financing
Financing that will be repaid over a specific time period longer than one year.

debt capital
Funds raised by borrowing money through the sale of bonds or from banks and other lending institutions.

equity capital
Funds raised within the company or from selling ownership in the firm.

OBTAINING SHORT-TERM FINANCING

The bulk of a finance manager's job isn't involved with obtaining long-term funds. The firm's nitty-gritty, day-to-day operation calls for careful management of short-term financial needs. Firms need to borrow short-term funds for purchasing additional inventory or for meeting bills that come due unexpectedly. Much like your personal financial needs, a business sometimes needs to obtain short-term funds when other funds run out. This is particularly true of small businesses. It's rare that new small businesses even attempt to find funding for long-term needs. They're concerned more with just staying afloat until they can build capital and creditworthiness. Short-term financing can be obtained in several different ways. Also, suppliers of short-term financing can require that the funds provided be secured or unsecured. Let's look at the major forms of short-term financing.

••• TRADE CREDIT •••

The most widely used source of short-term funding, trade credit, is the least expensive and most convenient form of short-term financing. **Trade credit** means that a business is able to buy goods today and pay for them sometime in the future. When a firm buys merchandise, it receives an invoice (bill) much like the one you receive when you buy something on credit.

Often a business invoice contains terms such as "2/10, net 30." This means that the buyer can take a 2 percent discount for paying within 10 days. The total bill is due in 30 days if the purchaser doesn't take advantage of the discount. Finance managers should pay attention to such discounts. This creates an opportunity to reduce the cost of financing. Think about it for a moment—if the discount is 2/10, net 30, the purchaser will pay 2 percent more for waiting an extra 20 days to pay the invoice. Some uninformed businesspeople feel that 2 percent is insignificant and pay their bills after the discount period. However, by paying in 30 days instead of 10 days, the firm loses 2 percent for waiting. In the course of a year, two percent for 20 days is an annual rate of 36 percent interest (because there are 18 20-day periods in the year). If the firm can pay within 10 days, it needlessly increases its cost of financing by not doing so.

trade credit
The practice of buying goods now and paying for them later.

••• PROMISSORY NOTES •••

promissory note
A written contract with a promise to pay.

Some suppliers hesitate to give trade credit to organizations with a poor credit rating, no credit history, or a history of slow payment. In such cases, the supplier may insist that the customer sign a promissory note as a condition for obtaining credit. A **promissory note** is a written contract with a promise to pay. Promissory notes can be sold by the supplier to a bank at a discount (the amount of the note less a fee for the bank's services).

••• FAMILY AND FRIENDS •••

Another source of short-term funds for many small firms is money loaned to them by family and friends. Because short-term funds are needed for periods of less than a year, friends are sometimes willing to help. Such loans can be dangerous if the firm doesn't understand cash flow. As we discussed earlier, the firm may suddenly find several bills coming due at the same time and have no other sources of funds. It's better, therefore, not to borrow from friends; instead, go to a commercial bank that understands the risk and can help analyze future financial needs. If you do borrow from family or friends, it's best to be professional about the deal and (1) agree on terms at the beginning, (2) write an agreement, and (3) pay them back the same way you would a bank loan.

••• COMMERCIAL BANKS •••

Banks are often reluctant to loan money to small businesses. Nonetheless, the most promising and best-organized ventures can sometimes get bank loans. If they're able to get such a loan, small to medium-size businesses should have the person in charge of the finance function keep in close touch with the bank. It's wise to see a banker periodically (as often as once a month) and send the banker all financial statements so that the bank continues to supply funds when needed.

Try to imagine different kinds of businesspeople going to the bank for a loan, and you'll get a better feel for the role of the financial manager. Picture, for example, a farmer going to the bank to borrow funds for seed, fertilizer,

Farmers are an example of businesspeople that need to develop a solid working relationship with a bank. It's commonplace for farmers to need assistance from the bank to borrow funds for seed, fertilizer, and equipment that must be purchased in the spring. Farmers plan to pay back the loans when the crops are harvested in the fall.

A bank can help with financing such needs and offer other important financial management advice if they are given the right information.

equipment, and other needs. Such supplies may be bought in the spring and paid for when the fall harvest comes in. Now picture a local toy store buying merchandise for Christmas sales. The money for such purchases might be borrowed in June and July and paid back after Christmas. A restaurant may borrow funds at the beginning of the month and pay by the end of the month. Can you see that how much a business borrows and for how long depends on the kind of business it is and how quickly the merchandise purchased with a bank loan can be resold or used to generate funds?

Like you, a business sometimes finds itself in a position where many bills come due at once: utilities, insurance, payroll, new equipment, and more. Most times, such sudden cash needs can be met. But sometimes a business gets so far into debt, so far behind in its payments, that the bank refuses to lend it more. Suddenly the business can't pay its bills. More often than not, this results in bankruptcy or business failure, and you can chalk up another business failure to cash flow problems.

We hope you see now how important it is for the finance or accounting person to do a cash flow forecast. By anticipating times when many bills will come due, a business can begin early to seek funds or sell other assets to prepare for the crunch. Can you see also why it's important for a businessperson to keep friendly and close relations with his or her banker? The banker may spot cash flow problems early and point out the danger. Or the banker may be more willing to lend money in a crisis if the businessperson has established a strong, friendly relationship built on openness and trust. It's always important to remember that your banker wants you to succeed almost as much as you do. Bankers can be an invaluable support—especially to small, growing businesses.

DIFFERENT FORMS OF BANK LOANS   The most difficult kind of loan to get from a bank or other financial institution is an **unsecured loan** (a loan that's not backed by any specific assets as collateral). Normally, only highly regarded customers of the bank receive unsecured loans.

A **secured loan** is one backed by something valuable, such as property. If the borrower fails to pay the loan, the lender may take possession of the collateral. That takes some of the risk out of lending money. Accounts receivable are assets that can be quickly converted into cash. Therefore, they're often used as security. When accounts receivable or other assets are used as collateral for a loan, the process is called **pledging.** Some percentage of the value of accounts receivable pledged is advanced to the borrowing firm. Then as customers pay off their accounts, the funds received are forwarded to the firm's lender in repayment of the advance. **Inventory financing** means that inventory such as raw materials (for example, coal or steel) or other inventory is used as collateral or security for a loan. Other property can also be used as collateral, including buildings, machinery, and other things of value (for example, company-owned stocks and bonds).

If you develop a good relationship with a bank, often the bank will open a line of credit for you. A **line of credit** means the bank will lend your business a given amount of unsecured short-term funds, provided the bank has the funds readily available. In other words, a line of credit isn't guaranteed to a business. The primary purpose of a line of credit is to speed the borrowing process so that a firm doesn't have to go through the hassle of applying for a new loan every time it needs funds. The funds are generally available as long as the credit ceiling set by the bank isn't exceeded. As businesses mature and become more financially secure, the amount of credit often is increased. Some firms will apply for a **revolving credit agreement,** which is a line of credit that's guaranteed. However, the bank usually

unsecured loan
A loan that is not backed by any specific assets as collateral.

secured loan
A loan that is backed by something valuable.

pledging
Using accounts receivable or other assets as collateral for a loan.

inventory financing
Using inventory as collateral or security for a loan.

line of credit
The amount of unsecured short-term credit a bank will lend a borrower that is agreed to ahead of time.

revolving credit agreement
A line of credit that is guaranteed by the bank.

charges a fee for guaranteeing such an agreement. A line of credit and revolving credit agreements are particularly good ways of obtaining funds for unexpected cash needs.

A financial manager may also obtain short-term funds from **commercial finance companies.** These organizations make short-term loans to borrowers that offer tangible assets as collateral. Since commercial finance companies are willing to accept higher degrees of risk than commercial banks, the interest rates charged are usually higher than banks' rates. General Electric Capital Services is the largest commercial finance company in the United States.[1]

commercial finance companies
Organizations that make short-term loans to borrowers that offer tangible assets as collateral.

••• FACTORING •••

factoring
Selling accounts receivable for cash.

One relatively expensive source of short-term funds for a firm is **factoring** (the process of selling accounts receivable for cash). Here's how it works: A firm sells many of its products on credit to consumers and other businesses. Some of these buyers are slow in paying their bills. The company may thus have a large amount of money due in accounts receivable. A factor buys the accounts receivable from the firm at a discount for cash. The factor then collects and keeps the money that was owed the original firm. How much this costs the firm depends on the discount rate the factor requires. The discount rate for factoring depends on the age of the accounts receivable, the nature of the business, and the conditions of the economy.

Factoring is often an expensive way of raising cash, but it is very popular among small businesses.[2] Factoring can be less expensive when the company raising money agrees to reimburse the factor for slow-paying accounts. Factoring charges are much lower if the company assumes the risk of those people who don't pay at all. For example, MPG, Inc., is a rapidly growing commercial printing company. Its bank refused to increase its credit limit, so MPG went to Allstate Financial Corp., a factor. Each month, MPG sends Allstate $100,000 worth of accounts receivable. Allstate wires MPG's bank $75,000 within 24 hours. In other words, MPG turns $100,000 of accounts receivable into $75,000 cash almost immediately. Allstate charges a 2 percent fee for this service ($2,000) if customers pay within 15 days. If customers take 30 days to pay, the rate goes up to 4 percent. The rate goes up 2 percent for every 15-day period thereafter until 90 days have passed. As Allstate collects from MPG's customers, it sends the remaining money to MPG minus the fee. The cost of the factor, therefore, varies according to how long customers take to pay. It could go as high as 10 percent per month.

••• COMMERCIAL PAPER •••

commercial paper
A short-term corporate equivalent of an IOU that is sold in the marketplace by a firm; it matures in 270 days or less.

Sometimes a large corporation needs funds for a few months and wants to get lower rates than those charged by banks. One strategy is to sell commercial paper. **Commercial paper** consists of unsecured promissory notes, in amounts ranging from $25,000 and up, that mature in 270 days or less. The promissory note states a fixed amount of money the business agrees to repay to the lender on a specific date. The interest rate being charged is stated in the note. Commercial paper is unsecured and is sold at a public sale, so only the more financially stable firms can sell it. It's a way to get short-term funds for less than bank rates. Since most commercial paper comes due in 30 to 90 days, it's also an investment opportunity where buyers of commercial paper can put up cash for short periods to earn some interest.

SPOTLIGHT ON SMALL BUSINESS

Financing a Small Business

If you're starting or running a small business, you know that one of a small business owner's hardest jobs is to find money when it's really needed. The text has already discussed many sources of funds, but here are some other places you may want to search:

1. *State funds.* State funding programs like the Ben Franklin Partnership in Pennsylvania will provide outright grants as well as venture capital in return for ownership in the business. The SBA offers a booklet called "Capital Formation in the States," which lists funds operated by some states.

2. *Potential customers or suppliers.* Companies like Du Pont have funded young companies with which they already do business and with which they plan to develop and market a product. To find this type of investor, use the *Standard Industrial Classification Manual* or Dun's Marketing Services' *Million Dollar Directory* to locate large companies in your industry.

3. *Small business investment companies (SBICs).* The best way to find an SBIC is through the National Association of Small Business Investment Companies or the National Association of Investment Companies.

4. *Community development funds.* Communities sometimes invite companies that will provide jobs for their citizens by making loans and equity investments. Ask the National Congress for Community Economic Development or your state's department of economic development about community funds in your area.

5. *Accounting firms.* Most big accounting firms can help small businesses in two ways: by discounting their fees in hopes of increasing them as your company grows and by introducing you to potential investors. Call the small business divisions of big accounting firms to get the names of people who work with new businesses.

6. *Small business incubators.* Incubators provide new businesses with shared office services and can assist in raising money from outside sources. For information, contact the National Business Incubation Association in Carlisle, Pennsylvania. Large corporations and universities also operate incubators.

7. *Successful local entrepreneurs.* Experienced entrepreneurs may help when established sources don't. They may offer funds in exchange for equity. The only way to find such an investor is by networking (getting out and meeting people).

8. *Partners.* You may want to review Chapter 5 to see the advantages and disadvantages of taking on partners. You may also find investors on the Internet. Business Opportunities Online, Inc., is just one of many online services that help you find investors.

9. *Banks.* You've already learned how hard it is to get financing from a bank. Small-business loans are considered very risky. Nonetheless, a few such loans are made.

10. *Venture capital firms and venture lessors.* Talking to a venture capital firm will help you to discover other sources of funds. Venture lessors will rent equipment to brand new companies in return for a high rental rate and a share in the company's ownership.

Source: Ann Monroe, "The Search for Capital," *CFO*, May 1993, pp. 28–35; Marie-Jeanne Juilland, "Alternatives to a Rich Uncle," *Venture*, May 1988, pp. 62–68; Thomas Hierl, "Look at Every Option—and Beyond," *Nation's Business*, July 1991, p. 9; and David R. Evanson, "Found Money," *Entrepreneur*, April 1995, pp. 108–15.

- What do the terms 3/10, net 25 mean?
- What's the difference between trade credit and a line of credit at a bank?
- What's meant by factoring? What are some considerations set in establishing a discount rate in factoring?
- How does commercial paper work, and what's the main advantage of issuing commercial paper?

PROGRESS CHECK

OBTAINING LONG-TERM FINANCING

Financial planning and forecasting help the firm to develop a financial plan. This plan specifies the amount of funding that the firm will need over various time periods and the most appropriate sources of those funds. In setting long-term financing objectives, the firm generally asks itself three major questions:

1. What are the organization's long-term goals and objectives?
2. What are the financial requirements needed to achieve these long-term goals and objectives?
3. What sources of long-term capital are available, and which will best fit our needs?

In business, long term capital is used to buy fixed assets such as plant and equipment and to finance expansion of the organization. In major corporations, decisions involving long-term financing normally involve the board of directors and top management as well as finance and accounting managers. Judy Lewent in the chapter's profile sits on the 10-member management committee at Merck, which makes senior policy decisions involving factors such as long-term financing.[3] In some instances, an expert like an investment banker may be involved. In smaller businesses, the owners are always actively involved in analyzing financing opportunities.

Initial long-term financing usually comes from two major sources: debt capital or equity capital. Let's look at these sources of long-term funds next.

••• DEBT FINANCING •••

Long-term financing of a business can be achieved by securing debt capital. Funds that a firm gets from lending institutions or from the sale of bonds is called *debt capital*. With debt financing, the company has a *legal obligation* to repay the amount borrowed.

Once a firm is established and has developed rapport with a bank, insurance company, pension fund, commercial finance company, or other financial institution, it can often secure a long-term loan. Long-term loans are usually repaid within 3 to 7 years, but may extend to 15 or 20 years. For such loans, a business must sign a **term-loan agreement** (a promissory note that requires the borrower to repay the loan in specified installments—for example, monthly or yearly). A major advantage is that the interest paid on debt is tax-deductible.

Long-term loans are often more expensive than short-term loans because larger amounts of capital are borrowed. Also, since the repayment period could be as long as 20 years, recovering the capital is less secure. Therefore, most long-term loans require some form of collateral, including real estate, machinery, equipment, or stock. Lenders will also often require certain restrictions on a firm's operations to force it to act responsibly in its business practices. The interest rate for these loans is based on the adequacy of collateral, the firm's credit rating, and the general level of market interest rates. The greater risk a lender takes in making a loan, the higher rate of interest it requires. This is known as the **risk/return trade-off.**

If an organization can't attain its long-term financing needs from a lending institution, it may decide to issue bonds. To put it simply, a bond is like a company IOU with a promise to repay on a certain date. It's a binding contract through which an organization agrees to specific terms with investors in return for investors lending money to the company. The terms of the

term-loan agreement•
A promissory note that requires the borrower to repay the loan in specified installments.

risk/return trade-off
The principle that the greater risk a lender takes in making a loan, the higher the interest rate required.

agreement in a bond issue are referred to as the **indenture terms.** We'll discuss bonds in more depth in the next chapter. Now, let's see how bonds fit into a firm's long-term financing plans.

SECURED AND UNSECURED BONDS A bond is a long-term debt obligation of a corporation or government. (See Figure 19.4.) You are probably somewhat familiar with bonds. For example, you may own investments like U.S. Government Savings Bonds; or perhaps you volunteered your time to help a local school district pass a bond issue. Businesses compete with government for the sale of bonds. Investors measure the risk involved in purchasing a bond with the *return* (interest) the bond promises to pay.

Like other forms of long-term debt, bonds can be secured or unsecured. **Secured bonds** are issued with some form of collateral, such as real estate, equipment, or other pledged assets. If the bond's indenture terms are violated, the bondholder can issue a claim on the collateral offered. An **unsecured bond** is a bond that's backed only by the organization's reputation and bondholders' trust in the issuer. These bonds are generally referred to as *debenture bonds.* Bonds are a key form of long-term financing. If bonds interest you, stay tuned for Chapter 20, where we discuss them in detail.

1. Federal, state, and local governments
2. Federal government agencies
3. Corporations
4. Foreign governments and corporations

Source: The Wall Street Journal Guide to Money & Markets.

FIGURE 19.4

WHO CAN ISSUE BONDS?

indenture terms
The terms of agreement in a bond.

secured bonds
Bonds backed by some tangible asset that is pledged to the investor if the principal is not paid back.

unsecured bonds
Bonds which are not backed by any collateral.

••• EQUITY FINANCING •••

If a firm can't secure a long-term loan from a lender or issue bonds to investors, it often turns to the last alternative for long-term financing: equity capital. Equity financing comes from the owners of the firm. Therefore, equity financing is generated by (1) selling ownership in the firm in the form of stock or (2) using retained earnings the firm has reinvested in the business. (Figure 19.5 highlights the differences between debt and equity financing.) A business can also look to equity financing from venture capitalists. We'll discuss issuing stock at length in the next chapter. Here a basic understanding of stock as a source of equity financing is enough.

SELLING STOCK Regardless of whether a new firm can obtain debt financing, there usually comes a time when even more funds are required. One way to obtain needed funds is to sell ownership shares (called *stock*) in the firm to the public. The key word to remember here is *ownership.* An organization's

	TYPE OF FINANCING	
Conditions	Debt	Equity
Management influence	There's usually none unless special conditions have been agreed upon.	Common stockholders have voting rights.
Repayment	Debt has a maturity date. Principal must be repaid.	Stock has no maturity date. The company is never required to repay equity.
Yearly obligations	Payment of interest is a contractual obligation.	The firm isn't legally liable to pay dividends.
Tax benefits	Interest is tax-deductible.	Dividends are paid from after-tax income and aren't deductible.

FIGURE 19.5

DIFFERENCES BETWEEN DEBT AND EQUITY FINANCING

board of directors generally determines the exact number of shares of stock into which a firm will be divided. In seeking equity financing, the board can authorize to sell all the stock of the firm or part of it. Shares of stock the company decides not to offer for sale are referred to as *unissued stock*.

Issuing stock to the public as a means of equity financing is by no means automatic. Companies can only issue stock for sale to the public if they meet requirements set by the Securities and Exchange Commission (SEC).

••• RETAINED EARNINGS •••

A major source of long-term funds for a firm is income that it earns from its operations. This is especially true of small businesses since they have fewer financing alternatives available to them. However, large corporations also depend on profits to assist with long-term costs the firm expects to incur. You probably remember from Chapter 18 that the profits the company keeps and reinvests in the firm are called *retained earnings*.

Retained earnings are generally the most favored source of long-term capital in the firm. Using retained earnings saves the company interest payments, dividends, and any possible underwriting fees. Also, there's no dilution of ownership. Nevertheless, many organizations don't have on hand sufficient retained earnings to finance extensive capital improvements or expansion. Think about it for a moment. If you wanted to buy an expensive personal asset such as a new car, the ideal way to do it would be to go to your personal savings account and take out the necessary cash to pay for the car. No hassle! No interest! Unfortunately, few people can do this since people rarely have such large amounts of cash available. Most businesses are no different. Even though they'd like to finance long-term needs from operations, few have the resources on hand to accomplish this.

••• VENTURE CAPITAL •••

The hardest time for a firm to raise money is when it's just starting. The company typically has few assets so its chance of borrowing significant amounts of money from a bank is slim.

Venture capital firms are one of the sources of start-up capital for new companies.[4] Venture capital (money invested in new companies with great profit potential) helped such fast-growth companies as Intel, Apple Computer, Compaq, and Sun Microsystems get started.

The venture capital industry began about 50 years ago as an alternative investment vehicle for wealthy families such as the Rockefellers. They financed Sanford McDonnell, for example, when he was still operating out of a hangar. That small venture grew into McDonnell Douglas, the large aerospace and defense contractor. The venture capital industry grew significantly in the 1980s, when the new high-tech companies were being started. *Inc.* magazine surveyed 89 fast-growing companies to see how they financed their growth. The number one source of funds was venture capital—44 percent of the firms had used it.

A finance manager has to be careful when choosing a venture capital firm to help finance a new business. For one thing, the venture capital firm often will want a stake in owning the business. More important, the venture capital firm should be able to come up with more financing if the firm needs it. The search for venture capital begins with a good business plan. (See Chapter 6.) This document must convince investors that the firm will be a success. Part of the business plan may be a financing proposal that spells out how much is needed, how it's to be raised, and how it will be paid back.

Legal Briefcase

Derivatives Are Risky Business

Swaps, captions, underlying, look backs, rho, theta, floortion, vega, and spreadtion. Does that sound like the lineup of horses running in the Kentucky Derby? Well, it's not. However, some financial analysts suggest firms using these finance strategies might in fact be assuming more risk than wagering the company treasury on a horserace.

The preceding strategies are all part of the derivatives industry. Derivatives have grown with incredible speed to become an enormous, yet very controversial financial force in business. But relax—we won't force you to suffer any undue stress by trying to explain exactly how derivatives work. Quite frankly, most well-informed businesspeople have little understanding of what's involved in derivatives contracts. Nonetheless, the scope of this market, lack of financial reporting requirements, and potential risk involved have everyone from small investors to the Federal Reserve Board calling for scrutiny.

When Proctor & Gamble announced a $102 million loss on complex derivatives contracts, and Orange County, California, declared bankruptcy, the white flag was raised.

P&G officials actually admitted they didn't really understand what they'd gotten into. The problem was compounded by the fact that company financial statements made little mention of its involvement with derivatives. Unfortunately, this lack of financial disclosure is common in the United States. Information about a firm's activity in derivatives is virtually nonexistent in its annual report or financial disclosure documents.

The question of regulation is on the minds of many. The Securities and Exchange Commission, Financial Accounting Standards Board, and Congressional Banking Committee have all targeted the disclosure issue. Yet any reforms are expected to be slow in coming. With an estimated $16 trillion (that's right, *trillion*) in derivative contracts globally, let's hope a financial timebomb doesn't detonate.

Source: Kelley Holland, William Glasgall, Maria Mallory, Rick Melcher, and Greg Burns, "A Black Hole in the Balance Sheet," *Business Week*, May 16, 1994, pp. 80–82; and Thomas Burdick and Charlene Mitchell, "Betting on Derivatives Involves High Risks," *The Washington Times*, March 7, 1995, p. B7.

The dangers of having the wrong venture capital firm are illustrated in the experience of Jon Birck, who started Northwest Instrument Systems with money from a venture capital firm. He worked until 11 or 12 each night to build the company. One day he was asked to leave by the venture capital firm, which wanted a more experienced chief executive officer to protect its investment. Birck had dedicated three years to the company. He had left a secure job, put his marriage on the line, taken out a second mortgage on his house, and given himself a below-average salary; and then, just when the firm was ready for rapid growth, he was asked to resign.

As Jon Birck's story shows, financing a firm's long-term needs clearly involves a high degree of risk—especially when firms borrow needed funds. Therefore, you might be inclined to ask, Why do firms borrow funds instead of using equity funding? The reason involves the use of leverage. Let's look at this next.

••• USING LEVERAGE •••

Raising needed funds through borrowing to increase the firm's rate of return is referred to as **leverage.** While it's true that debt through borrowing increases the risk of the firm, it also enhances the firm's ability to increase profitability. A key job of the finance manager or CFO is to forecast and manage the borrowed funds. If the firm's earnings are larger than the interest payments on the funds

leverage
Raising needed funds through borrowing.

FIGURE 19.6

USING LEVERAGE VERSUS
EQUITY FINANCING:
FIBERRIFIC INC. NEEDS TO
RAISE $500,000

LEVERAGE—SELLING BONDS		EQUITY—SALE OF STOCK	
Common stock	$ 50,000	Common stock	$500,000
Bonds (at 10% interest)	450,000		
	$500,000		$500,000
Earnings	$125,000	Earnings	$125,000
Less bond interest	45,000		
	$ 80,000		$125,000
Return to stockholders	$80,000 / $50,000 = 160%	Return to stockholders	$125,000 / $500,000 = 25%

borrowed, stockholders earn a higher rate of return than if equity financing were used. (See Figure 19.6.) However, if the earnings are less than the interest on borrowed funds, shareholders will lose money on their investment.

Normally, it's up to each individual firm to determine exactly what's a proper balance between debt and equity financing. Viacom took on $8 billion of new debt in its takeover fight for control of Paramount.[5] On the other hand, firms such as Wrigley's, Hershey, and Blockbuster Entertainment (which became part of Viacom in 1994) have little long-term debt. According to Standard & Poor's and Moody's Investor Services, the average debt of a large industrial corporation ranges between 35 and 40 percent. As bank loan requirements get higher and investors grow more demanding, we predict that finance managers' jobs will be more difficult and challenging.[6]

The next chapter looks at stocks and bonds and other investment topics both as financing tools and as investment options. You'll learn about the stock exchanges, how to buy and sell stock, how to choose the right investment, how to read the stock and bond quotations in *The Wall Street Journal* and other newspapers, and more. Finance takes on a whole new dimension when you see how you can participate in financial markets yourself.

**PROGRESS
CHECK**

- What are the two major forms of debt financing available to the firm?
- How does debt financing differ from equity financing?
- What are the two major forms of equity financing available to the firm?
- What is leverage and why do firms use it?

SUMMARY
•••••••

1. Explain the role and importance of finance.
2. Describe the responsibilities of financial managers.

1. Sound financial management is critical to any business's well-being.
   - ***What are the most common reasons firms fail financially?***
   The most common financial problems are (1) undercapitalization, (2) poor control over cash flow, and (3) inadequate expense control.

2. Finance is that function in a business responsible for acquiring funds for the firm, managing funds within the firm (for example, preparing budgets and doing cash flow analysis), and planning for the expenditure of funds on various assets.
   - ***What do finance managers do?***
   They plan, budget, control funds, obtain funds, collect funds, audit, manage taxes, and advise top management on financial matters.

3. Financial planning involves short- and long-term forecasting, budgeting, and financial controls.
   - ***Define the four budgets of finance.***
   The operating budget is the projection of dollar allocations to various costs and expenses given various revenues. The capital budget is the spending plan for expensive assets such as property, plant, and equipment. The cash budget is the projected cash balance at the end of a given period. The master budget summarizes the other three budgets.

   3. Outline the steps in financial planning by explaining the process of forecasting financial needs, developing budgets, and establishing financial controls.

4. During the course of a business's life, its financial needs shift considerably.
   - ***What are the major needs for funds that firms experience?***
   Businesses have financial needs in four major areas: (1) managing daily business operations, (2) managing accounts receivable, (3) obtaining needed inventory, and (4) planning major capital expenditures.

   4. Recognize the financial needs that must be met with available funds.

5. Businesses often have needs for short-term and long-term financing and for debt capital and equity capital.
   - ***What's the difference between short-term and long-term financing?***
   Short-term financing refers to funds that will be repaid in less than one year, whereas long-term financing is money obtained from the owners of the firm and lenders who don't expect repayment within one year.
   - ***What's the difference between debt capital and equity capital?***
   Debt capital refers to funds raised by borrowing (going into debt), whereas equity capital is raised from within or by selling ownership (stock) in the company.

   5. Distinguish between short-term and long-term financing and between debt capital and equity capital.

6. There are many sources for short-term financing including trade credit, promissory notes, family and friends, commercial banks, factoring, and commercial paper.
   - ***Why should businesses use trade credit?***
   Trade credit is the least expensive form of short-term financing. It's also the most convenient. Businesses can buy goods today and pay for them sometime in the future.
   - ***What's a line of credit?***
   It's an agreement by a bank to loan a specified amount of money to the business at any time if the money is available. A revolving credit agreement is a line of credit that guarantees a loan will be available—for a fee.
   - ***What's the difference between a secured loan and an unsecured loan?***
   An unsecured loan has no collateral backing it. A secured loan is backed by an asset such as accounts receivable, inventory, or other property of value.
   - ***Is factoring a form of secured loan?***
   No, factoring means selling accounts receivable at a discount to a factor.
   - ***What's commercial paper?***
   It's a corporation's unsecured promissory note maturing in 270 days or less.

   6. Identify and describe several sources of short-term financing.

7. One of a finance manager's important functions is to obtain long-term capital.
   - ***What are the major sources of long-term financing?***
   The major sources are debt financing (selling bonds and obtaining long-term loans from banks and other financial institutions) and equity financing (obtaining funds through the sale of stock, venture capital firms, and retained earnings).
   - ***What are the two major forms of debt financing?***
   Debt capital comes from two sources: selling bonds and borrowing from individuals, banks, and other financial institutions. Bonds can be secured by some form of collateral or they can be unsecured. The same is true of loans.

   7. Identify and describe several sources of long-term financing.

- ***What are the major sources of equity financing?***

Equity capital comes from the sale of stock, venture capital firms, and retained earnings, profits from the firm retained rather than paid out in dividends.

- ***What's leverage and how do firms use it?***

Leverage is raising funds from borrowing. It involves the use of borrowed funds to invest in such undertakings as expansion and research and development. Firms measure the risk of borrowing against the potential for higher profits.

KEY TERMS

budget 588
capital budget 589
capital expenditures 592
cash budget 589
cash flow forecast 587
commercial finance companies 596
commercial paper 596
debt capital 593
equity capital 593
factoring 596
finance 585
financial control 589
financial management 585
indenture terms 599
inventory financing 595
leverage 601
line of credit 595
long-term financing 593
long-term forecast 587
master budget 589
operating budget 588
pledging 595
promissory note 594
revolving credit agreement 595
risk/return trade-off 598
secured bonds 599
secured loan 595
short-term financing 593
short-term forecast 587
term-loan agreement 598
trade credit 593
unsecured bond 599
unsecured loan 595

DEVELOPING WORKPLACE SKILLS

1. Obtain annual reports from at least three different corporations. Compare the balance sheets. Which assets are fixed and what is their value? How much has each company borrowed? Based on your analysis, which company is in the best financial health? Why?
2. Visit or call a lending officer in a local bank. Ask what the current interest rate is and what rate small businesses would pay for short-term and long-term loans. Ask for blank forms that borrowers use to apply for loans. Share these forms with your class and explain the types of information they ask for.
3. Use information from Standard & Poor's and Moody's Investor Service to evaluate three bonds. Ask the librarian what similar references are available. Report what you find to the class.
4. One small-business consultant said that the most difficult concept to get across to small-business owners was the need to take all trade credit (e.g., 2/10, net 30). He simply could not convince owners that they would save over 36 percent by doing that. Explain the concept to the class to show your own understanding.
5. The "banking crisis" of the early 1990s made banks even more reluctant to lend money to small businesses. Assume you are a small business consultant. Draft a memo to your clients advising them regarding the best sources for financing.

PRACTICING MANAGEMENT DECISIONS

CASE FINANCING NONPROFIT ORGANIZATIONS

Looking for a career that's challenging, with opportunities for advancement and large numbers of openings? Then welcome to the world of financial management in nonprofit organizations « P.32 ». Nonprofits are crying for the talents of skilled financial managers (who often overlook nonprofits in favor of profit-seeking firms).

The size and scope of the nonprofit sector often surprise even seasoned business professionals. Also, misconceptions abound about work in nonprofits. For starters, the nonprofit sector of the economy is valued at approximately $500 billion per year. This makes the nonprofit sector twice as large as the construction industry in the United States. Also, when the term *nonprofit* comes to mind, the first perception may be church-sponsored bingo games or bake sales. In reality, the nonprofit sector contains such notables as the National Football League and the National Audubon Society, neither of which sponsors bingo.

There are also problems at the top of many nonprofit organizations. According to David LaGreca, a manager with Volunteer Consulting Group (VCG), top management positions at nonprofits are often filled with highly trained people, such as social workers. These individuals frequently have specific skills but lack the training and business expertise of executives at profit-seeking firms. LaGreca also notes that it's often hard to recruit qualified individuals to serve on nonprofit boards. Many feel that the possibility of scandal in the operations of a nonprofit could damage their reputation or tarnish the image of other groups with which they're associated.

Decision Questions

1. Is the job of a financial manager in a nonprofit organization different from that of a financial manager with a profit-seeking firm?

2. Should financial managers in nonprofit organizations be compensated equally to their counterparts in profit-seeking firms? Why?

3. Do you see the nonprofit financial manager's job getting easier or harder in the future? Why?

Source: Ann Monroe, "A World of Difference," *CFO*, September 1993, pp. 34–44.

• •

〉〉 VIDEO CASE THE ROLE OF THE FINANCIAL MANAGER 〈〈

The role of the financial manager is one of the most complex roles in business. These managers are responsible for forecasting financial needs, budgeting, obtaining and controlling funds, auditing, managing accounts receivable, and advising management on financial affairs. In addition, financial managers handle tax questions, manage cash, and do internal audits. In short, financial managers are responsible for anything having to do with obtaining, spending, and managing money.

Financial management, then, can be defined simply as assuming responsibility for acquiring the necessary funds to start a business and then to manage the cash inflow and outflow once it is established. But such a definition doesn't capture the dynamics of financial management. It may be easier to picture part of finance as a four-step process: (1) forecasting financial needs, (2) preparing budgets, (3) establishing controls to ensure the company follows its financial plans, and (4) obtaining short-term and long-term financing.

Short-term financing involves the use of trade credit, issuing promissory notes, borrowing from friends and family, going to commercial banks, and collecting funds from those who owe the company. Financial mangers are responsible for minimizing the costs of borrowing and decreasing costs in general.

Long-term financing, on the other hand, is usually provided by retained earnings (profit not distributed in the form of dividends) or from the sale of stock or bonds. When a company sells stock, the ownership is spread among many people. A board of directors represents these owners, and the board selects the company's managers. When a company sells bonds, it obtains funds without losing any of its ownership. A bond is more like a corporate IOU. The rate a company must pay depends on the economy and competition from government bonds.

Clearly, financial managers are in touch with the company's life blood: money. In many ways, financial management is a form of risk management. Financial managers must weigh the risks of borrowing money against the potential earnings. They must also weigh the risks of investing the firm's profits in the stocks or bonds of other companies or in other types of investments. Additionally financial managers play key roles in deciding which of the firm's projects to finance and which to deny or cut off. Given such responsibility, it's easy to see why finance is both a rewarding and challenging career possibility.

Decision Questions

1. What are the financial conditions of the economy today and how do those conditions affect financial managers?

2. If you were a financial manager today at a major corporation, would you try to raise investment capital through the sale of stock or bonds or some other source? Why?

3. What is the relationship between accounting and finance? Could you be an outstanding financial manager without a good understanding of accounting?

4. Does finance seem like a good career for you? Why or why not?

CHAPTER 20

FINANCING AND INVESTING THROUGH SECURITIES MARKETS

LEARNING GOALS

After you have read and studied this chapter, you should be able to

1. Understand the functions of securities markets and how businesses and individuals can make use of their services.

2. Compare the advantages and disadvantages of selling bonds and identify the classes and features of bonds.

3. Compare the advantages and disadvantages of issuing stock and outline the differences between common and preferred stock.

4. Identify the various stock exchanges and describe how to invest in securities markets and choose among different investment strategies.

5. Describe the opportunities bonds offer as investments and explain what's meant by junk bonds.

6. Explain the opportunities that stock, mutual funds, and commodities offer and explain the advantage of diversifying investments.

7. Explain securities quotations listed in the financial section of a newspaper, tell how the Dow Jones Averages affect the market, and discuss investment bankers' and institutional investors' roles in securities trading.

JEROME DODSON, MUTUAL FUND MANAGER

You'll learn in this chapter that one way to decrease the risk of investing is to put your money in a mutual fund. In mutual funds, the fund manager uses money pooled from many individuals to invest in a variety of companies, thus spreading the risk. Jerome Dodson, founder and manager of Parnassus Fund, named his fund after the mountain where an oracle gave advice in Greek fables. Often the oracle's advice went against conventional wisdom. Dodson tends to go against conventional wisdom himself. He won't buy stocks in booming companies if they don't meet his standards for commitment to social responsibility.

Dodson has five screens for choosing companies in which to invest: (1) treatment of employees, (2) equal employment opportunity, (3) environmental protection, (4) community relations, and (5) ethical business practices. He doesn't invest in five industries: alcohol, tobacco, gambling, nuclear power, and weapons. How does Dodson's dealing exclusively in socially responsible companies pay off? In 1993, the $92 million fund was up 29.5 percent and its average return for the previous three years was 37.7 percent. Compare that to the Standard & Poor's 500's three-year average of 19.1 percent and you'll see that Dodson is ahead of the pack.

In this chapter, we'll explore securities markets and how they assist in securing long-term financing objectives of firms as well as provide investment opportunities for large and small investors. Read this chapter carefully, and, who knows, maybe you'll be running your own mutual fund some day.

}} *If you're so smart, why aren't you rich?*

anonymous }}

THE FUNCTION OF SECURITIES MARKETS

Securities markets such as the New York Stock Exchange serve two major functions: They help businesses find long-term funding and they give investors a place to buy and sell investments such as stocks and bonds. Businesses benefit from securities markets by obtaining the capital they need to finance beginning operations, expand, and buy needed goods and services. Investors benefit from the securities market by having a convenient place to buy and sell stocks, bonds, mutual funds, and other investments. In this chapter, we'll look at securities from the perspectives of both financing and investing.

Securities markets are divided into primary and secondary markets. *Primary markets* handle the sale of new securities. You should understand that corporations only make money on the sale of their securities once—when they're first bought on the primary market. After that, the *secondary market* handles the trading of securities between investors; proceeds of the sale go to the investor selling the stock, not the corporation. For example, if we, as the makers of Fiberrific, sell 20,000 shares of stock in our company at $15 a share, we raise $300,000. However, if shareholder Jones sells 100 shares of his Fiberrific stock to Investor Smith, we at Fiberrific collect nothing. Smith bought the stock from Jones, not Fiberrific.

The importance of long-term funding to businesses can't be overemphasized. A common mistake many new companies make is starting without sufficient capital. Businesses normally prefer to meet their long-term financial needs by using their retained earnings or by borrowing from a lending institution such as a commercial bank or insurance company. However, if they can't get sufficient funding from these sources, businesses can often obtain additional long-term funding through either debt or equity financing. As you remember from Chapter 19, debt financing often involves issuing bonds, and equity financing involves selling stock in the corporation. In this chapter, you'll learn more about these two major types of long-term financing. Let's begin by looking at debt financing.

DEBT FINANCING THROUGH SELLING BONDS

bond
A corporate certificate indicating that a person has loaned money to a firm.

Commercial banks, savings and loan associations, insurance companies, and other lending institutions lend money to businesses to facilitate long-term operations. However, as profit-seeking businesses themselves, these lenders often won't make loans they feel are too risky and may not be repaid. Also, as their capital needs change, they may not have the requested loan amounts available. For this reason, firms often issue corporate bonds to raise capital. To put it simply, a **bond** is a corporate certificate indicating that a person has loaned money to a firm. (See Figure 20.1.) With debt financing through bonds, the company has a legal obligation to pay regular interest payments to investors and repay the entire principal at a prescribed time called the *maturity date*. Let's explore the language of bonds a bit more carefully so you clearly understand what's involved.

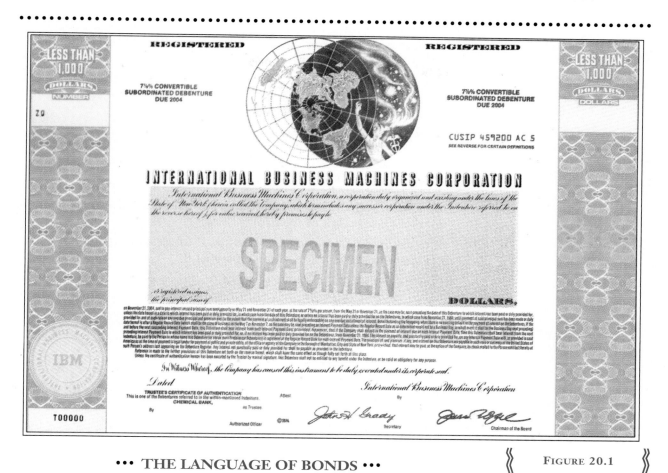

••• THE LANGUAGE OF BONDS •••

A bond is a contract of indebtedness issued by a corporation or government unit that promises payment of a principal amount at a specified future time plus interest. **Interest** is the bond issuer's payment to bondholders for use of the borrowed money. Interest rates paid on bonds are also called a bond's *coupon rate*. As you may suspect, the interest rate paid varies based on factors such as the state of the economy and the reputation of the company.[1] The interest rate paid by U.S. government bonds also affects the interest rate a firm must agree to pay. Since government bonds have the backing of the U.S. Treasury, they're considered safe investments. Generally, once an interest rate is set for specified bonds, it can't be changed. **Principal** refers to the face value of the bond. (Bonds are almost always issued in multiples of $1,000.)

The **maturity date** refers to the date on which the issuer of a bond must pay the principal to the bondholder. For example, if your company issues a $1,000 bond with an annual interest rate of 9 percent and a maturity date of 2016, your firm is agreeing to pay bondholders $90 in interest each year until a specified date in 2016, when you must repay them the full $1,000. There's no set time limits on bond issues. Borrowers issue bonds in many maturities. Some have a three-year maturity; others mature at a much later date. In fact, some firms have recently issued 50-year bonds that will mature in 2045.[2]

••• ADVANTAGES AND DISADVANTAGES OF SELLING BONDS •••

As a means of meeting long-term capital needs, bonds offer advantages to an organization. The decision to issue bonds is often based on careful evaluation of advantages such as:

FIGURE 20.1

A SAMPLE BOND CERTIFICATE FROM IBM
This is a convertible bond, meaning that it can be converted into shares of stock at a later date. It's also a debenture bond, meaning it's backed by corporate assets not otherwise pledged. The bond will pay you 7⅞ percent interest until the year 2004, when the principle ($1,000) will be repaid.

interest
The payment the issuer of a bond makes to bondholders for the use of borrowed money.

principal
The face value of a bond.

maturity date
The date on which the issuer of a bond must pay the principal of the bond to the bondholder.

- Bondholders have no vote on corporate affairs; thus, management maintains control over the firm's operations. Remember, bondholders are creditors of the firm, not owners as stockholders are.
- The interest paid on bonds is a deductible expense to the firm's operations. Remember from Chapter 18, expenses help limit a firm's tax responsibilities to the government.
- Bonds are a temporary source of funding for a firm. They're eventually repaid, at which point the debt obligation is eliminated.

But bonds also have their drawbacks:

- Bonds are an increase in debt (liabilities) and may adversely affect the market's perception of the firm.
- Interest on bonds is a legal obligation. If interest isn't paid, bondholders can take legal action to force payment.
- The face value of the bonds must be repaid on the maturity date. This could cause a possible cash shortage in the firm when repayment of the bonds comes due.

••• DIFFERENT CLASSES OF BONDS •••

debenture bond
A bond that is unsecured (i.e., not backed with any collateral such as equipment).

An organization can issue two classes of corporate bonds. The first class is unsecured bonds (bonds that aren't supported by any type of collateral). In other words, the only security the bondholder has is the reputation and credit rating of the company. Unsecured bonds are usually called **debenture bonds** and are issued only by well-respected firms with excellent credit ratings.

The second class of bonds is secured bonds. These are bonds backed by some tangible asset that's pledged to the bondholder if interest isn't paid or principal isn't paid back. There are several kinds of secured bonds:

- *Mortgage bonds* are ensured by the company's real assets such as land and buildings. They're the most common of secured bonds and among the most desirable.
- *Collateral trust bonds* are backed by the stock that the company owns and that's held in trust by a commercial bank (thus the word *trust* in their name).
- *Equipment trust bonds* are backed by the equipment the company owns. This may include trucks, aircraft, and other equipment that's widely used in industry. Such items make excellent collateral since they can be taken over easily and have good resale value.

As you can see, secured bonds are a relatively safe investment in that the risk to bondholders is reduced. Figure 20.2 describes several kinds of bonds. Bonds don't all include the same features. Let's look at special features they sometimes offer.

••• SPECIAL FEATURES OF BONDS •••

sinking fund
Provision of a bond which requires the issuer to retire (put in a trust fund), on a periodic basis, some part of the bond principal prior to maturity.

By now you should know that bonds are issued with an interest rate, are either unsecured or secured by collateral, and must be repaid at their maturity date. This repayment requirement often encourages firms to establish what's called a *sinking fund* to ensure that funds are available to repay bondholders on the maturity date. **Sinking fund** bond issuers regularly set aside

Bond	Description
Collateral trust	These bonds are secured by the general credit of the issuer as well as the specific property for which they're issued.
Convertible bond	These bonds can be exchanged for another security, usually common stock.
Debenture	These bonds are secured only by the general credit of the firm plus any unpledged assets.
Mortgage bond	These bonds are secured by real property (for example, buildings).
Municipal bond	These bonds are issued by the state or local government; interest payments are exempt from federal taxes.
Yankee bond	These bonds are issued by a foreign government and are payable in U.S. dollars.
Zero-coupon bond	These bonds pay no interest prior to maturity; the return comes from the difference between purchase price and the face (par) value.

As you can see, there are all kinds of bonds available with different risks, and bonds for every kind of investor. Zero-coupon bonds are growing in popularity. Watch for stories about them in the business press.

FIGURE 20.2

SAMPLE OF DIFFERENT BONDS AVAILABLE IN THE MARKET

funds in a reserve account (a sinking fund) so that enough will be accumulated by the maturity date to pay off the bond. Sinking funds can be attractive to firms and investors for several reasons:

- They provide for an orderly retirement of a bond issue.
- They reduce the risk of not being repaid and are therefore more attractive as an investment alternative.
- The bond's market price is supported because the risk of the firm's not being able to repay the principal on the maturity date is reduced.

Another special feature that could be included in a bond issue is a call provision. A **call provision** permits the bond issuer to pay off a bond prior to its maturity date. Call provisions must be included when a bond is originally issued; bondholders should be aware of this. Why would an organization want to repay a bond issue before its maturity date? Let's see why.

Call provisions give companies discretion in their long-term forecasting. Suppose a company issued $50 million in 20-year bonds in 1995 with an interest rate of 10 percent. The yearly interest expense would be $5 million. If in 1998 the same quality bonds are yielding only 7.5 percent interest, the firm would be paying $1.25 million in excess interest yearly. It's clear that it would benefit the firm to call in the bonds and perhaps reissue new bonds at the lower rate. However, one problem surfaces with call provisions: Investors aren't particularly fond of them. This often forces issuers of bonds to agree to *staggered calls*. For example, a 20-year bond issue may have staggered calls of five years. This means a bond issued in 1996 couldn't be called until 2001. Having the five years of expected bond interest helps keep investors happy.

A last feature that can be included in bonds is convertibility. A **convertible bond** is one that can be converted into shares of common stock in the issuing company. This can be an added incentive for an investor to buy a convertible bond because common stock has the potential to grow over time.[3] When we discuss common stock, this advantage will become evident to you.

call provision
Clause in a bond which gives the issuer of the bond the right to pay off the bond before its maturity.

convertible bond
A bond that can be converted into shares of common stock.

PROGRESS CHECK

- Why are bonds considered to be a form of debt financing?
- What's meant if a firm states it's issuing a 9 percent debenture bond due in 2008?
- Explain the difference between an unsecured bond and a secured bond.
- Why do issuing companies typically like to include call provisions in their bonds?

EQUITY FINANCING THROUGH SELLING STOCK

Equity financing is another form of long-term funding. Equity financing is the obtaining of funds by selling ownership in the corporation.

There are two classes of equity instruments: preferred stock and common stock. We'll discuss them separately after a brief look at the language of stock and the advantages and disadvantages of selling stock as a financing alternative.

••• THE LANGUAGE OF STOCK •••

stocks
Shares of ownership in a company.

stock certificate
Evidence of ownership that specifies the name of the company, the number of shares it represents, and the type of stock it is.

par value
A dollar amount assigned to shares of stock by the corporation's charter. The par value is printed on the front of a stock certificate and is used to compute the dividends of a preferred stock.

dividends
The part of the firm's profits that goes to stockholders.

Stocks are shares of ownership in a company. A **stock certificate** is evidence of ownership that specifies the name of the company, the number of shares it represents, and the type of stock it is. (See Figure 20.3.) Certificates sometimes indicate a **par value** (a dollar amount assigned to shares of stock by the corporation's charter). The par value of a share of stock may be nowhere near the stock's market value (the actual price at which the stock could be sold in the open market). The major use of par value today is in assigning the dollar value upon which dividends on preferred stock are paid. Par value means little to common stocks and many corporations issue "no par" common stock. (We explain this below.) **Dividends** are the part of a firm's profits that are distributed to shareholders. Dividends could be distributed in the form of cash or more shares of stock.[4]

FIGURE 20.3

STOCK CERTIFICATE FOR PET INC.
Examine this certificate for key information about this stock.

••• ADVANTAGES AND DISADVANTAGES OF ISSUING STOCK •••

Securities markets contain the names of almost every large company in the United States. Evidently, companies must feel that equity financing is a good way to raise long-term funds. Here are some advantages of issuing stock:

- Because stockholders are owners of the business, their investment never has to be repaid. Therefore, funds are available long-term for acquiring land, buildings, machinery, and other assets.
- There's no legal obligation to pay dividends to stockholders. Income instead can be ploughed back into the firm for future asset purchases, investments, or expansion. (You may recall, this is referred to as *retained earnings*.)
- Selling stock can actually improve the condition of the firm's balance sheet. How? No debt is incurred, and the company is stronger financially.

Nonetheless, as the saying goes, there's no such thing as a free lunch. There are disadvantages to selling equity in a firm as well:

- As owners of the firm, stockholders (usually only common stockholders) have the right to vote for the board of directors. You may remember from Chapter 5 that the corporation's board of directors decides who'll manage the firm and what the firm's policies will be. Hence, the firm's direction can be altered significantly through the sale of stock.
- Dividends are paid out of profit after taxes. Thus, paying dividends is more costly than paying interest, which is tax-deductible. Dividends, in other words, are taxed twice—once to the firm and once to the stockholder.
- Management decision making is often tempered by the need to keep the firm's stockholders happy.

As you just read, there are two classes of stock: preferred and common. (See Figure 20.4.) Let's look at these forms of equity financing and see how they differ.

Stock	Description
Classified common stock	This stock consists of two or more classes of common stock that have different voting rights or claims on dividends. For example, class A common stock may go to the general public and class B may go to the original owners. Class A stock may carry no voting rights, but its holders may receive larger dividends. The owners thus retain control of the firm.
Convertible preferred stock (no voting rights)	This stock can be exchanged for shares of common stock at a predetermined exchange rate.
Cumulative preferred stock (no voting rights)	This stock pays a dividend every year. If the dividend isn't paid, the amount owed accumulates and must be paid before common stockholders receive any dividends.

FIGURE 20.4

THREE TYPES OF STOCK AVAILABLE IN THE MARKET

Most investors deal only in common stock. Some prefer the special rights that come with preferred stock, however.

preferred stock
Stock that gives owners preference in the payment of dividends and an earlier claim on assets if the business is sold but that does not include voting rights.

Preferred stock gives its owners preference in the payment of dividends and an earlier claim on assets if the company is liquidated (forced out of business with its assets sold). However, it normally doesn't include voting rights in the firm. Preferred stock is frequently called a *hybrid investment* in that it has characteristics of both bonds and stocks. To illustrate what we mean, consider the treatment of preferred stock dividends.

Preferred stock dividends differ from common stock dividends in several ways. Preferred stock is generally issued with a par value. The par value becomes the basis for the dividend the firm is willing to pay. For example, if a par value of $100 is attached to a share of preferred stock and a dividend rate of 8 percent is attached to the same issue, the firm is committing to an $8 dividend for each share of preferred stock the investor owns. (Eight percent of $100 is $8.) The company would pay the owner of 100 shares of this preferred stock a yearly dividend of $800. Furthermore, this dividend is *fixed*, meaning it shouldn't change year by year.[5] Also, if the firm declares that dividends are to be paid, the dividends on preferred stock *must* be paid in full before any common stock dividends can be distributed. But preferred stockholders normally don't have voting rights in electing board directors for this preferred dividend treatment.

As you can see, a similarity exists between preferred stock and bonds in that both have a face (or par) value and both have a *fixed* rate of return. Why not just refer to preferred stock as a form of bond? Remember, bondholders *must* receive interest and *must* be repaid the face value of the bond on a maturity date. Preferred stock dividends are generally fixed but don't legally *have* to be paid, and the stock *never* has to be repurchased. Remember, too, the price of the stock can go up, resulting in a higher profit than a comparable bond. On the other hand, the stock price could also go down.

••• SPECIAL FEATURES OF PREFERRED STOCK •••

Because preferred stock is a hybrid investment, it can have special features that aren't available to common stock. For example, like bonds, preferred stock could be issued with a call provision. In other words, the firm could call in the shares of preferred stock for repurchase. As an investor, you'd be required to sell back your shares of preferred stock to the firm. As with bonds, the investor should be apprised of this call feature of the stock. Preferred stock could also be convertible, that is, convertible to shares of common stock. Again, the similarities between preferred stock and bonds are evident.

cumulative preferred stock
Preferred stock which accumulates unpaid dividends.

One important feature of preferred stock is that it can be cumulative. **Cumulative preferred stock** guarantees an investor that if one or more dividends aren't paid, the missed dividends will be accumulated. All the dividends, including back dividends, must be paid in full before *any* common stock dividends can be distributed. For example, as producers of Fiberrific we may decide not to pay our cumulative preferred stockholders the planned 3 percent dividend this period in order to retain funds for further research and development. The cumulative preferred stockholders must be paid 6 percent dividends the following period before we can pay any dividends to common stockholders. If preferred stock is *noncumulative*, any dividends missed are lost to the stockholder. Figure 20.5 illustrates how this process works.

If preferred stock doesn't meet the objectives of the firm or individual investor, the alternative of issuing or investing in common stock is available. Let's look at this interesting alternative.

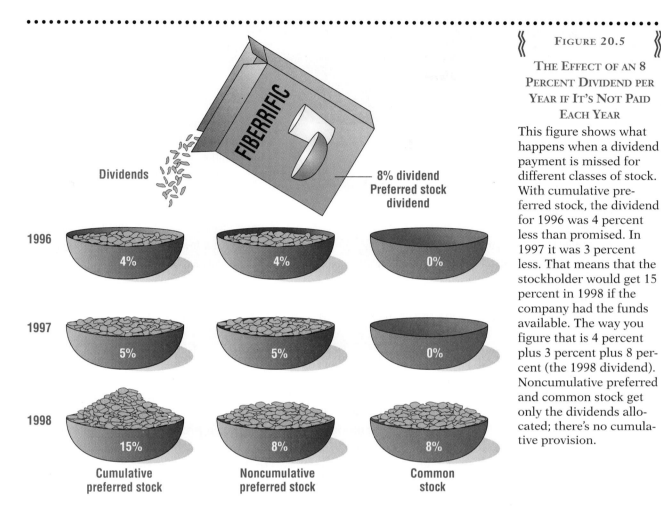

FIGURE 20.5

THE EFFECT OF AN 8
PERCENT DIVIDEND PER
YEAR IF IT'S NOT PAID
EACH YEAR

This figure shows what happens when a dividend payment is missed for different classes of stock. With cumulative preferred stock, the dividend for 1996 was 4 percent less than promised. In 1997 it was 3 percent less. That means that the stockholder would get 15 percent in 1998 if the company had the funds available. The way you figure that is 4 percent plus 3 percent plus 8 percent (the 1998 dividend). Noncumulative preferred and common stock get only the dividends allocated; there's no cumulative provision.

••• ISSUING COMMON STOCK •••

Common stock represents ownership privileges in a firm. These privileges include the rights (1) to vote for the board of directors and (2) to receive some of the firm's profits through dividends, when they're declared by the firm's board of directors. Also, by voting for the board of directors of a corporation, stockholders can influence corporate policy since the board selects the firm's top management and makes major policy decisions. In general, shareholders' voting rights are based on one vote for each share of stock held. Also, due to what's called a **preemptive right,** common stockholders have the first right to purchase any new shares of common stock the firm decides to issue; this helps common stockholders maintain a proportional share in the company.

Common stock is considered to be more risky and speculative than either bonds or preferred stock. Remember, common stockholders receive dividends only *after* both bondholders and preferred stockholders receive their interest and dividends. Also, if a company is forced to close, common stockholders share in the firm's assets only *after* bondholders and preferred stockholders recover their investments. Why would someone select common stock as an investment alternative? Because the risk is often accompanied by higher returns. We'll look at stocks and bonds from an investor's perspective after we discuss the role of stock exchanges.

common stock
The most basic form of ownership of firms; it includes voting rights and dividends, if dividends are offered by the firm.

preemptive right
Common stockholders' right to purchase any new shares of common stock the firm decides to issue.

FROM THE PAGES OF...
Entrepreneur®
MAGAZINE

Initial Public Offerings (IPOs)

For a small business to become a big business, a great deal of money is needed. Usually that money comes from stockholders. The process of finding stockholders is rather sophisticated. Nonetheless, some 707 companies raised over $41.5 billion in 1993 with IPOs (initial public offerings of stock).

People are unsure about where to invest their money these days. Should they invest in stock or bonds, or should they keep the money in the bank? Many people are interested in new ventures because they offer so much potential. Of course, they're also risky.

Surprisingly, it's somewhat easier to raise $8 to $15 million in investment capital than it is to raise $5 million.

This is because institutions are interested in investing, but they don't want to make too many small investments in companies they can't follow closely. They'd rather make a larger investment and keep track of the company.

Companies looking for smaller amounts are now going on the Internet and telling their story. Investors can read about companies and invest a few thousand dollars to help a small business grow into a large one.

Source: David R. Evanson, "Let's Make a Deal," *Entrepreneur,* April 1994, pp. 83–88.

PROGRESS CHECK

- Name at least two advantages and two disadvantages of issuing stock as a form of equity financing.
- What are the major differences between preferred stock and common stock?
- In what ways are preferred stock and bonds similar? How are they different?
- How does an investor benefit by owning cumulative preferred stock as opposed to noncumulative preferred?

STOCK EXCHANGES

stock exchange
An organization whose members can buy and sell securities to the public.

As its name implies, a **stock exchange** is an organization whose members can buy and sell (exchange) securities for the public. Brokerage firms purchase memberships or *seats* on the exchanges. Since the number of seats is limited, competition drives their price up. For example, the New York Stock Exchange (NYSE) has only 1,366 members.

There are stock exchanges all over the world in cities such as Paris, London, Madrid, Sydney, Buenos Aires, and Tokyo. It's exciting to see previously communist countries such as Hungary and Poland opening up stock exchanges. These nations are actively seeking American financial advisors to ease the transition and create modern exchanges.[6] (Be sure to read the box Reaching Beyond Our Borders.) These exchanges enable businesses and individuals to buy securities from companies almost anywhere in the world. If you hear of a foreign company that has great potential for growth, you can usually obtain shares of its stock with little difficulty from a U.S. broker who has access to the foreign stock exchanges. Daimler-Benz AG, the world's leading truck maker, became the first German company to list its securities on the New York Stock Exchange. Some brokers are predicting that foreign markets may deliver handsome rewards as the global economy becomes more of a reality.[7]

Stock exchanges buy and sell securities for the public. National exchanges, like the New York Stock Exchange (NYSE) pictured here, exchange securities of companies from all over the country through its 1,366 members. Membership on the exchange is limited and very expensive. However, seats on the exchange are coveted since the stock of most major companies in the United States are traded on the "Big Board," as the New York Stock Exchange is often called.

••• U.S. EXCHANGES •••

The largest stock exchange in the United States, the New York Stock Exchange, lists about 2,400 common stocks.[8] The second largest U.S. exchange, the American Stock Exchange (AMEX), is also located in New York. It lists about 1,000 common stocks, preferred stocks, and warrants. These two exchanges are called *national exchanges* because they handle stocks of companies from all over the United States. The AMEX is trying to increase its listings by lowering the listing requirements. The new rules will allow growing companies to be listed with much lower earnings and lower net worth.[9] That will enable the AMEX to increase its profits, because it charges companies for being listed.

In addition to the national exchanges, there are regional exchanges in cities such as Chicago (Midwest), San Francisco (Pacific Coast), Philadelphia, Boston, Cincinnati, Spokane, and Salt Lake City. These regional exchanges deal mostly with firms in their own areas.

••• THE OVER-THE-COUNTER (OTC) MARKET •••

The **over-the-counter (OTC) market** provides a means to trade stocks not listed on the national securities exchanges. The OTC market is made up of a network of several thousand brokers. These brokers maintain contact with each other and buy and sell securities for the public. A nationwide electronic system communicates trades to the brokers. The system is known as the **National Association of Securities Dealers Automated Quotation System (NASDAQ**—pronounced *nazz-dak*).

Originally, the over-the-counter market dealt mostly with small firms that couldn't qualify for listing on the national exchanges or didn't want to bother with the procedures. Today, however, well-known firms such as Apple, MCI,

over-the-counter (OTC) market
Exchange that provides a means to trade stocks not listed on the national exchanges.

National Association of Securities Dealers Automated Quotation System (NASDAQ)
A nationwide electronic system which communicates over-the-counter trades to brokers.

*Calling All
Brokers: How to
Build New
Exchanges*

In 1991, with much hoopla and enthusiasm, Poles transformed the former Communist Party Headquarters into the Warsaw Stock Exchange. However, after a short period of time, it was apparent these new "capitalists" knew little more than the basics of buying and selling securities. The exchange wasn't equipped to deal with such essentials as financial disclosure or insider trading. With the help of Robert Strahota, an official with the U.S. Securities and Exchange Commission, operations changed. Today the exchange is booming and volume has topped a respectable $100 million a week.

Strahota is just one of many U.S. securities regulators lending their expertise to emerging marketplaces that hope to become bustling international exchanges. From Costa Rica to Shanghai, the desire to implement American-based trading systems has exploded. Experts note that if U.S. expertise were a stock itself, trading would be halted by an order imbalance (a situation where demand far exceeds supply). According to Rudolf van der Bijl of the World Bank's International Finance Group, other nations look to the United States "because it's viewed as the safest and most important market." Even developed exchanges in the European Union are looking to put together a Europewide stock market for growth companies that mimics our NASDAQ exchange. It's no wonder that representatives from the National Association of Securities Dealers (NASD) have visited Europe as well as India, Malaysia, Pakistan, and Thailand in an attempt to export electronic market systems.

Perhaps the most critical challenge will come in the booming Asian exchange markets where emerging financial players such as Hong Kong's Peregrine Investments hope to become the Merrill Lynch of Asia. Peregrine recently surpassed $1 billion in capital and promises solid future growth. However, many concerned market watchers doubt that Asian markets will readily embrace Western standards of regulation and disclosure. Ancient traditions that fuel secret dealings and old-boy networks will be hard to break. Nonetheless, making financial markets work has become a priority in Asian markets. With the phenomenal growth of exchanges such as the Shanghai Securities Exchange, which trades $700 million a day although it was only founded in 1990, the stakes are too high to pass up.

Source: Richard Evans and Paula Dwyer, "NASDAQ with a European Accent?" *Business Week*, June 27, 1994, p. 73; Michael Schroeder, "Babysitting the World's Emerging Bourses," *Business Week*, November 1, 1993, pp. 112–14; and William Glasgall, Pete Engardio, and Joyce Barnathan, "A Millionaire a Minute," *Business Week*, November 29, 1993, pp. 110–11.

and Microsoft prefer to have their stock traded on the OTC market because the trades are done electronically. The NASDAQ exchange currently lists over 4,600 firms on its exchange—nearly twice the number on the NYSE.[10]

The OTC market also handles most corporate and U.S. government bonds as well as many city and state government bonds. Common stock of most insurance companies and banks as well as the stock of many smaller firms is traded on the OTC market. If you look in *The Wall Street Journal* under "NASDAQ Bid and Ask Quotations," you'll see that the price of over-the-counter stocks is determined by supply and demand, as reflected in "bid" and "ask" prices.

••• SECURITIES REGULATIONS •••

prospectus
A condensed version of economic and financial information prepared for the SEC that must be sent to purchasers.

The Securities Act of 1933 protects investors by requiring full disclosure of financial information by firms selling new stocks or bonds. A registration statement with detailed economic and financial information relevant to the firm must be filed with the Securities and Exchange Commission (SEC). A condensed version of that registration document—called a **prospectus**—must be sent to purchasers.

The Securities and Exchange Act of 1934 created the SEC. The **Securities and Exchange Commission** has responsibility at the federal level for regulating the various exchanges. Those companies trading on the national exchanges must register with the SEC and provide annual updates. The act established guidelines to prevent insiders from taking advantage of their privileged information. **Insider trading** involves the use of knowledge or information that individuals gain through their position that allows them to benefit unfairly from fluctuations in security prices. Originally, *insider* was narrowly defined as a company's directors, employees, and relatives. Today, the term has been broadened to include just about anyone who has information that's not available to the general public. Pressure is even being applied to mutual funds to avoid any hint of problems or scandals such as the 1980s experienced.[11]

The securities industry provides many opportunities for financing and investment. It's also a source of challenging, rewarding careers. If you like a fast-paced, tension-filled, action-driven, continuously changing work environment, this may be the place for you.

> **Securities and Exchange Commission (SEC)**
> Federal government agency which has responsibility for regulating the various exchanges.

> **insider trading**
> The use of knowledge or information that a person gains through his or her position that allows the person to benefit from fluctuations in stock prices.

HOW TO INVEST IN SECURITIES MARKETS

Investing in bonds, stocks, or other investments isn't hard at all. First, you have to decide what bond or stock you want to buy. That's perhaps the most difficult part of the procedure. Then you call a stockbroker. (They're listed in the phone book.) A **stockbroker** is a market intermediary who buys and sells securities for clients. The broker, who's a registered representative authorized to trade in stocks and bonds, calls a member of the stock exchange who represents the firm for which the broker works. That member goes to the place where the bond or stock you want is traded and negotiates a price. When the transaction is completed, the trade is reported back to your broker, who calls you. The brokerage firm's size often affects how fast an investor receives confirmation of a trade. For example, giant firms like Merrill Lynch have an automated order system that allows its brokers to enter your order the instant you ask for it; seconds later, the order can be confirmed.[12]

> **stockbroker**
> A market intermediary who buys and sells securities for clients.

The same procedure is followed if you wish to *sell* stocks or bonds. If you choose, the broker will keep the stock or bond certificate for you for safekeeping or so that you can sell it easily and quickly, with just a telephone call. The broker is also a valuable source of information about what stocks or bonds might best meet your financial objectives. It's important that you learn about and follow stocks and bonds on your own, though, because stock analysts don't always give the best advice to meet your specific expectations and needs. In fact, a Stockholm newspaper gave five Swedish stock analysts and a chimpanzee the equivalent of $1,250 each to make as much money as they could in the stock market. The chimp, who made his selection by throwing darts, won the competition.[13]

There are other ways to buy stocks if you're interested. In fact, only about 45 percent of stock is bought through brokers. The rest of the stock is bought through employee stock purchase plans (like the ones discussed in Chapter 12), mutual funds, dividend reinvestments, banks, and private sales.[14] Let's look at some alternatives you should consider before investing.

••• CHOOSING THE RIGHT INVESTMENT STRATEGY •••

Broadly speaking, *investing* means committing capital with the expectation of making a profit. The first step in an investment program is for the investor to analyze his or her specific situation. The analysis should consider income desired, cash requirements, level of risk, and so forth. As you might suspect, investment objectives change over the course of a person's life. A second step is to select general types of investments that best fit the specific needs of the investor. For example, investors should decide how much, if any, of their assets should be committed to real estate, bonds, stocks, or commodities (e.g., gold and silver). The third step is to select specific investments within the general areas. For example, should the investor choose the common or preferred stock of Procter & Gamble or Philip Morris? Would the investor's objectives be best served by a corporate-issued or government-issued bond? Generally, there are five criteria to use when selecting an investment option:

1. *Investment risk*—the chance that an investment and all its accumulated yields will be worth less at some future time than when the investment is made.
2. *Yield*—the increase in the value of an investment over time, usually a year.
3. *Duration*—the length of time assets are committed.
4. *Liquidity*—how quickly one can get back invested funds when they're desired.
5. *Tax consequences*—how the investment will affect the investor's tax situation.

Since new investors aren't generally well versed in the world of investing and choosing proper investment strategies, an investment planner can be useful. Let's look at the potential that bonds offer as an investment.

INVESTING IN BONDS

As an investment, bonds are rather safe. However, two questions often bother first-time investors concerning the purchase of a corporate bond. One question is, If I purchase a corporate bond, do I have to hold it to the maturity date? No! You don't have to hold a bond until maturity because bonds are bought and sold daily on major exchanges such as the New York Stock Exchange. However, if you sell your bond to another investor before its maturity date, you aren't guaranteed to get its face value (usually $1,000). For example, if your bond doesn't have features (interest rate, early maturity, etc.) that make it attractive to other investors, you may be forced to sell your bond at a *discount*. On the other hand, if your bond is highly valued by other investors, you may be able to sell your bond above the face value or at a *premium*. Bond prices fluctuate with interest rates. As interest rates go up, bond prices fall and vice versa. If interest rates double after you buy a bond at a certain rate, the price you can get for the bond could very well be cut in half. Thus, like all investments, bonds can be risky.[15]

The second question on investors' minds is, How do I know how risky a particular bond issue is as an investment? Fortunately, two companies—Standard & Poor's Investment Advisory Service and Moody's Investor Service—rate the level of riskiness of many corporate and government bonds. Naturally, the higher the risk associated with the bond issue, the higher the interest rate the organization must offer investors. (Remember the risk/return trade-off from the previous chapter.) Investors won't assume high levels of risk if they don't believe the potential return is worth it. The Chrysler Corporation found this out when Standard & Poor's lowered Chrysler's bonds' rating into the realm of speculative, high-risk investments (junk bonds). Consequently, Chrysler had to pay more to borrow money. What do we mean by junk bonds, and why are investors often leery of them? Let's take a look.

••• INVESTING IN •••
HIGH-RISK BONDS

High-risk, high-interest bonds are called **junk bonds**. Standard & Poor's Investment Advisory Service and Moody's Investor Service regard junk bonds as non–investment-grade bonds because of their high-risk and high–interest-rate features.

Why are junk bonds considered so risky, and why are firms forced to pay high interest rates to sell them? Remember, risk and return are closely related: The higher the risk, the higher the interest rate must be to attract buyers. Plus, most junk bonds' ability to pay depends on the company's asset valuation remaining high and its cash flow staying strong. If the company can't pay off the bond, the investor is left with a bond that isn't worth more than the paper it's written on—junk.[16]

High risk financing can be extremely risky even for the most experienced borrower. Donald Trump financed his Trump Taj Mahal in Atlantic City with junk bonds. When the junk bond market weakened in the early 1990s the Donald was forced to compromise with bondholders to keep the investment operating. Securities markets impose risks on all investors. Even very sophisticated investors like Mr. Trump can lose during unstable economic times.

junk bonds
High-risk, high-interest bonds.

• What's the primary purpose of a stock exchange? Can you name the largest stock exchange in the United States?

• What role do Standard & Poor's and Moody's Investor Service play in bond markets?

• What's a junk bond?

PROGRESS CHECK

INVESTING IN STOCKS AND OTHER INVESTMENTS
•••••••

Investing in stock is a chance for investors to share in the success of emerging or expanding companies. Investors can choose the stock investment that best fits their overall investment objectives.

It's important to remember that the market price of common stock is very dependent on the overall performance of the corporation in meeting its business objectives. Common stock is often referred to as *participating stock*. Stockholders participate in the firm's success or failure. Common stock offers great opportunities but is subject to a high degree of risk, as the stock market crash of 1987 showed. Later in this chapter, we'll look at that crash and see how investments in stock can be very speculative.

Two of the more frequently heard terms regarding stock investors are *bulls* and *bears*. Bulls are investors who believe that stock prices are going to rise. They buy stock in anticipation of the increase. When stock prices are rising, it's called a *bull market*. Bears are investors who expect stock prices to decline. They tend to sell their stocks before prices fall. When stock prices decline steadily, it's known as a *bear market*.

This announcement is neither an offer to sell nor a solicitation of an offer to buy these securities. The offer is made only by the Prospectus.

February 21, 1995

1,000,000 Shares

aSYST
TECHNOLOGIES

Common Stock

Price $32 Per Share

Copies of the Prospectus may be obtained in any State in which this announcement is circulated only from such of the undersigned as may legally offer these securities in such State.

Needham & Company, Inc.   **Adams, Harkness & Hill, Inc.**

Bear, Stearns & Co. Inc.   **Alex. Brown & Sons**   **Hambrecht & Quist**
                                        Incorporated   *Incorporated*
Lehman Brothers   **Montgomery Securities**   **PaineWebber Incorporated**

Robertson, Stephens & Company   **SoundView Financial Group, Inc.**

Investors often look to stock as a means of sharing in the growth of an emerging or expanding company. To inform the public about stock offerings, companies often make use of "Tombstone" announcements like the one pictured here. The "Tombstone" announcement provides basic information about the security (stock, bond, etc.) the company is offering for investment. Can you make out the key information provided in this "Tombstone" announcement?

growth stocks
Stocks of companies whose earnings are expected to grow faster than other stocks or the overall economy.

income stocks
Stocks that offer a high dividend.

blue chip stocks
Stocks of high-quality companies.

penny stock
A stock that sells for less than $5.

market order
Instructions to a broker to buy stock at the best price obtainable in the market now.

limit order
Instructions to a broker to purchase stock at a specific price, if and when that price becomes possible.

buying on margin
The purchase of stocks by borrowing some of the purchase cost from the brokerage firm.

Several investment opportunities in stock are available. For example, an investor may select a growth stock as a personal investment choice. **Growth stocks** are stocks of corporations whose earnings are expected to grow faster than other stocks or the overall economy. They are often relatively speculative and generally pay rather low or no dividends, but the potential for growth is strong. L.A. Gear, Inc., was such a growth stock. The footwear company went from an initial offering of $2.75 a share to $50 a share in less than a year. The company then dropped back to about $6 a share. **Income stocks** are stocks that offer investors a rather high dividend yield on their investment. Public utilities are often considered to be good income stocks, as are blue chip stocks. **Blue chip stock** is the stock of a firm that's considered to be of high quality and limited risk. Major corporations such as Boeing and Coca-Cola are considered to be blue chip stocks. Investors can even invest in a type of stock called a **penny stock** (one that sells for less than $5). Such stocks frequently represent ownership in firms such as mining companies and are often highly speculative. Since they're so speculative, they are very risky investments.

• • • BUYING STOCK: MARKET AND LIMIT ORDERS • • •

Buying and selling stock offers investors more options for placing an order than does buying and selling bonds. A **market order** tells the broker to buy or to sell a security immediately at the best price available. This type of order can be processed quickly, and the trade price can be given to the investor in minutes. A **limit order** tells the broker to buy or to sell stock at a specific price if and when that price becomes possible. Let's say, for example, that a stock is selling for $40 a share, and you feel it's likely to drop a little before it goes higher. You could place a limit order at $38. The broker would purchase the stock at that amount if the stock drops. If the stock never falls to $38, no order would be processed.

• • • BUYING STOCK ON MARGIN • • •

Buying on margin involves the purchase of stocks by borrowing some of the purchase cost from the brokerage firm. *Margin* refers to the amount of money an investor must invest in the stock. The Board of Governors of the Federal Reserve System sets margin rates in the market. You can read about this in detail in Chapter 21. Thus, if the margin is 50 percent, the investor may borrow up to 50 percent of the stock's purchase price from a broker. Obviously, the investor's idea is to buy shares of stock that he or she believes are going up in value. However, buying stocks on margin also has a downside. The credit extended by the broker must be repaid with interest by the investor. Additionally, if the stock's value goes down, the broker will issue a *margin call* requiring the investor to come up with more money to cover the losses the stock has suffered. If the investor is unable to make the margin call, the broker can legally sell off shares of stock to reduce the broker's chance of loss. Margin calls can force the investor to repay a significant portion of the loss within days or even hours.[17]

Investing in the stock of fast-growing companies is an investor's dream. Imagine buying shares at an early point in a firm's life cycle when profits and revenues are soaring. As the stock's price skyrockets, investors have little to think about except how and where to spend their earnings. Easy Street seems just around the corner. Unfortunately, investors often find Easy Street filled with potholes and dangerous curves. Investing in small growth companies is a risky business.

Here are some tips from the pros concerning investing in hot growth companies. They aren't foolproof but may help you hunt for that dream stock.

How to Make Money in Hot Growth Companies

- Watch revenue growth. Companies with steady, uninterrupted sales gains of at least 30 percent may have tapped a need or niche in the marketplace.

- Look for earnings that are growing rapidly and steadily, at least 30 percent a year. Solid growth companies should be able to finance their own expansion.

- Watch the price/earnings ratio. (Remember Chapter 18.) Don't let it grow too high.

- Look at long-term trends. Will the company have a viable stream of revenues over the long term?

  - Are new competitors on the horizon? Is its product or service extremely price-sensitive?

  - Who are the firm's accountants? An audit by a big-name accounting firm can be a real help but no guarantee that everything is fine financially.

- Look for momentum (what Wall Street calls "relative strength"). Look for firms that are outperforming at least 80 percent of the market.

- Evaluate the management team. Is a solid team in place or does the firm still depend on the wits of the entrepreneur? Managers with at least 10 years of industry experience are often invaluable.

Source: "A Guide to Investing in Hot Growth Companies," *Business Week*, May 23, 1994, p. 92.

Buying on margin is more appropriate for risk takers willing to speculate than for more conservative investors. This leveraging of one's investments can greatly exaggerate both the percentage of any profit made and the percentage of any losses incurred. The possibility of greater rate of return is, of course, accompanied by the greater risk of loss.

• • • STOCK SPLITS • • •

Companies and brokers prefer to have stock purchases conducted in **round lots** (purchases of 100 shares at a time). The problem is that many investors can't afford to buy 100 shares of a stock in companies that may be selling for $120 or so per share. Therefore, to make it easier for investors to buy in round lots, companies often announce **stock splits**; that is, they issue two or more shares for every share of stock outstanding. For example, if Fiberrific stock were selling for $120 a share, Fiberrific could declare a three-for-one split. Everyone who owned one share of Fiberrific would now own three shares— but each share would now be worth only $40. A round lot would now cost $4,000 instead of $12,000, as was the case at $120 per share. In stock splits, both companies and investors win. The advantage to the company is that it may be able to sell more shares at lower prices. The advantage to shareholders is that demand for the stock at $40 per share may be greater than demand

round lots

Purchases of 100 shares of stock at a time.

stock splits

Giving stockholders two or more shares of stock for each one they own.

Mutual funds are probably the best alternative small investors can select to begin an investment program. However, funds differ considerably in objectives. Jerome Dodson's Parnassus Fund (the opening profile) only invests in socially responsible companies. This is also the objective of Neuberger & Berman, a socially responsive fund that invests only in companies responsive to the environment, workplace diversity, and fair employment practices.

mutual fund

An organization that buys stocks and bonds and then sells shares in those securities to the public.

diversification

Buying several different investments to spread the risk.

at $120 per share. Thus, the stock price may go up. In fact, many investors buy in odd lots; that is, fewer than 100 shares. Your broker handles all the details of such purchases, but it's important to note that brokers charge a higher price for a transaction if the buyer purchases in odd lots.

••• INVESTING IN MUTUAL FUNDS •••

A **mutual fund** is an organization that buys stocks and bonds and then sells shares in those securities to the public. Mutual funds have the expertise to pick what they consider to be the best stocks and bonds available. The benefit to you is that you can buy shares of the mutual funds and thus share in the ownership of many different companies that you couldn't afford to invest in individually. In essence, the fund helps you to diversify and offers management of your investment, normally for a small fee. Jerome Dodson in the profile at the beginning of this chapter is a successful mutual fund money manager. Today, mutual funds control about $2 trillion of investors' funds. That's equal to approximately 86 percent of bank deposits.[18]

Mutual funds are probably the best way for smaller investors to begin. A variety of funds is available. There are conservative funds that invest only in government securities or bonds. Others specialize in high-tech firms, foreign companies, precious metals, and other high-risk investments. Jerome Dodson's fund only invests in socially responsible companies. A stockbroker or financial planner can help you find the mutual fund that best fits your investment objectives. Banks also offer mutual funds.[19] With a little research, you can buy some funds directly and save any sales fees.

The key point to remember is that the average small investor has a way to spread the risk of stock ownership by owning shares in many different companies through the purchase of shares in a mutual fund. Most investment advisors put mutual funds high on the list of recommended investments for beginning investors. But check the costs involved in a mutual fund—they can differ. A true *no-load fund* is one that charges no commission to either buy or sell its shares. A *load fund* charges a commission to either buy shares in the fund or to sell shares you hold in the fund. A careful investor also checks for other fees and charges imposed by the company managing a fund.

••• DIVERSIFYING INVESTMENTS •••

Diversification consists of buying several different investment alternatives to spread the risk of investing.[20] For example, an investor may put 20 percent of his or her money into high-risk growth stocks. Another 30 percent may be invested in conservative government bonds, 15 percent in commodities, and 20 percent in a mutual fund. The rest could be placed in the bank for emergencies and possible other investment opportunities. By diversifying investments, the investor diminishes the chance of losing everything. This investment strategy is often referred to as a *portfolio strategy*. Stockbrokers are trained in advising clients about the portfolio that would best fit their financial objectives. But be aware that some investments carry heavy risks. Let's look at one.

••• INVESTING IN COMMODITIES •••

Commodities are generally considered high-risk investments for most people. However, trading in commodities can also be a vehicle for protecting businesspeople, farmers, and others from wide fluctuations in commodity prices and thus can be a conservative investment strategy. Let's see how this works.

A **commodity exchange** specializes in buying and selling precious metals and minerals (e.g., silver, foreign currencies, gasoline) and agricultural goods (e.g., wheat, cattle, sugar). The Chicago Board of Trade (the largest commodity exchange) is involved with a wide range of commodities including corn, plywood, silver, gold, and U.S. Treasury bonds. The Chicago Mercantile Exchange (the second largest) deals in commodities such as cattle, hogs, pork bellies (bacon), potatoes, and various foreign currencies.

Commodity exchanges operate much like stock exchanges in that members of the exchange meet on the floor to exchange goods. Yet the commodities exchanges' appearance is quite different. All transactions for a specific commodity take place in specific trading areas (rings). Trades result from the meeting of a bid and offer in an open competition among exchange members. Bids and offers are made in a seemingly impossible-to-understand blend of voices, with all participants shouting at once.

Commodities trading demands much expertise and involves a high degree of risk. Unfortunately, most people who speculate in commodities lose money. But many companies use commodities markets to their advantage by dealing in the futures market. **Futures markets** involve the purchase and sale of goods for delivery sometime in the future. Buying or selling in the futures markets is known as **hedging**. Hedging is an important risk management tool for those who produce, process, market, and use commodities. Take, for example, a farmer who has oats growing in the field. He or she isn't sure what price the oats will sell for at harvest time. To be sure of a price, the farmer would sell the oats on the futures market. The price would then be fixed, and the farmer could plan accordingly. On the other hand, as producers of Fiberrific, we're worried about the possibility of oat prices rising. By hedging (buying the oats in the futures market), we know what we will have to pay for the oats and can plan accordingly.

Hedging, therefore, gives businesses a form of price insurance that enables them to focus on their primary function without worrying about fluctuations in commodity prices. Those who own a commodity can offset the risk of a price decline by selling futures contracts. Those who'll need a commodity in the future can offset a price rise by purchasing the commodity ahead of time. All this is possible because of commodity exchanges.

commodity exchange
Securities exchange which specializes in the buying and selling of precious metals and minerals (e.g., silver, foreign currencies, gasoline) and agricultural goods (e.g., wheat, cattle, sugar).

futures market
The purchase and sale of goods for delivery sometime in the future.

hedging
Buying or selling commodities in the futures market.

- What does buying on margin mean? How does it work?
- What's a stock split? What advantages are there to companies splitting shares of stock?
- What are mutual funds? How do they benefit small investors?
- Why would a restaurant owner be interested in the futures market?

PROGRESS CHECK

UNDERSTANDING SECURITIES MARKET INFORMATION

Investors can find a wealth of investment information in daily newspapers and various magazines. Such information is meaningless, though, until you understand what the data mean. Look through *The Wall Street Journal, Barron's*, and your local newspaper's business section. Listen carefully to the business reports on radio and TV, and watch a couple of business-oriented television shows. Listen for the terms and the different viewpoints. Investing is an inexact science, and few people are consistently right in predicting future stock and bond prices. Every time someone sells a stock (believing it will go up no further), someone else is buying it (believing it will go still higher). The following material will give you a good start toward understanding investment information.

••• BOND QUOTATIONS •••

Bonds are issued by both corporations and government units. Government issues are covered in *The Wall Street Journal* in a table called Treasury Issues. These issues are traded on the over-the-counter market. The price is quoted as a percentage of the face value. The interest rate is often followed by an "s" for easier pronunciation. For example, 9 percent bonds due in 1999 are called nines of ninety-nine.

Figure 20.6 gives a sample of bond quotes for corporations. As you look through the sample quotes, note the variation in interest rates and the maturity dates. There are so many variables to consider in buying specific issues of stocks and bonds that most people rely on experts to help them choose the best investments. Nonetheless, the more you know about these investments, the better prepared you are to talk intelligently with investment counselors and be sure their advice is consistent with your best interests. It bears repeating that the easiest way to buy bonds and diversify at the same time is to buy into a bond mutual fund.

FIGURE 20.6

UNDERSTANDING BOND QUOTATIONS IN NEWSPAPERS
Bonds are usually issued in $1,000 denominations so a price of 90 is really $900. Note that some bonds yield as high as 11.7 percent. How does that compare to a yield from a bank account?

CV means convertible bond.

These Lowen bonds are due in 1996 and originally paid $8^1/_8$%. The current yield is 9.4%.

$5000 worth of bonds were traded that day.

This bond sold for a high of $900 and the low for the day was $890. It ended the day at $900, up $70 from the previous day.

Bonds	Cur Yld	Vol	High	Low	Close		Net Chg
LaQuin 10s02	cv	4	102	102	102	–	$1^1/_4$
LearS 10s04	10.0	3	100	100	100	+	$1^5/_8$
LearS $11^1/_2$98	11.1	5	$103^1/_2$	$103^1/_2$	$103^1/_2$	–	$1^1/_2$
LearS $11^1/_4$98	10.8	2	$104^1/_4$	$104^1/_4$	$104^1/_4$	–	$^3/_4$
Leget $6^1/_2$06	cv	36	103	102	102		. . .
LipGp $8^5/_8$01	9.4	10	$92^1/_8$	$92^1/_8$	$92^1/_8$	–	$1^7/_8$
LincFl $8^1/_2$96	8.7	5	$97^1/_2$	$97^1/_2$	$97^1/_2$	–	$1^3/_8$
LomN 7s11	cv	4	104	104	104		. . .
LonSI $11^1/_4$90	11.7	5	$100^3/_8$	$100^3/_8$	$100^3/_8$	–	2
Loral $7^1/_4$10	cv	2	121	121	121	–	$^1/_2$
Lorilld $6^7/_8$93	7.6	62	$90^7/_8$	$90^3/_8$	$90^3/_8$		. . .
LouGs $9^1/_4$00	9.2	10	$101^1/_8$	101	101		. . .
Lowen $8^1/_8$96	9.4	18	90	89	90	+	7
viLykes $7^1/_2$94N f	. . .	35	$19^1/_2$	18	18	–	1
viLykes $7^1/_2$94f	. . .	79	$20^1/_2$	$19^7/_8$	$20^1/_2$	+	$^7/_8$
viLykes 11s00f	. . .	25	21	$20^1/_2$	$20^1/_2$	–	$^1/_2$
MACOM $9^1/_4$06	cv	30	101	$99^1/_4$	$99^1/_4$	–	$1^1/_4$

••• STOCK QUOTATIONS •••

If you look in the Money & Investing section of *The Wall Street Journal*, you'll see stock quotations from the New York Stock Exchange, the American Stock Exchange, and the NASDAQ over-the-counter markets. Notice the headings at the top of the columns. To understand the headings, look carefully at Figure 20.7. (This example highlights the information on the New York and American Stock Exchanges.) Stocks are quoted in eighths of a dollar, illustrated as fractional amounts. For example, a stock listed at \$65 7/8 is selling for \$65.875. Preferred stocks are identified by the letters *pf* following the abbreviated company name. Corporations can have several different preferred stock issues listed. With careful attention to detail, you can start to track selected stocks' performance by following this information daily in financial publications. Exactly what do these columns and headings tell you? Let's find out.

Moving carefully from left to right, these figures tell you the high price over the past 52 weeks; the low price; the abbreviated company name; the dividend paid (if any); the dividend yield (the return expected); the price/earnings ratio (the price of the stock divided by the per share earnings); the number of shares traded that day; the high, low, and closing prices

FIGURE 20.7

UNDERSTANDING STOCK QUOTATIONS IN NEWSPAPERS

Read across International Paper (Int Paper) and you'll see that the highest it sold for in the past 52 weeks was \$68.50 and that the lowest was \$44.25. The stock pays a dividend of \$2.40 and yields 3.6 percent. The price divided by earnings is 20 (the P/E ratio), and 567,900 shares were traded this day. The high for the day was \$65.875, and the low was \$64. The stock last sold for \$65.875 per share. The price went up \$1.875 from the previous day's close.

This stock yields 8.0%

52 Weeks				Yld	P-E	Sales				Net
High	Low	Stock	Div.	%	Ratio	100s	High	Low	Close	Chg
203	140	Inter pf	7.75	4.2	...	..1	186	186	186	+ 4 1/2
12	4 3/4	Intrtst	.10	1.7	...	1683	6 1/8	5 7/8	6	...
73 5/8	39 3/8	Intrtk	2.60	3.8	14	26	69 1/4	68 3/8	69 1/4	+ 3/4
15	6 3/8	Intmed	...	...	95	584	14	12 3/4	13 1/4	+ 1/2
24 3/4	16 1/2	IntAlu	.72	3.6	12	33	20	20	20	...
161 7/8	122 1/4	IBM	4.40	3.3	13	13237	135 1/4	133 3/4	134 1/4	+ 1/4
36 3/4	23 3/8	IntCtrl	.50	2.0	12	98	25 1/2	25 1/8	25 1/2	+ 1/4
48 7/8	28 3/8	IntFlav	1.16	2.5	21	291	45 7/8	45 5/8	45 3/4	- 1/8
42 1/4	27 1/8	IntMin	1.00	3.6	...	615	27 3/4	27 1/4	27 3/4	+ 1/8
50 3/8	46	IntM pfA	3.75	8.0	...	104	46 3/4	46 1/2	46 3/4	+ 1/4
31 5/8	21	InMult s	...	...	14	94	28 1/2	28	28 1/2	+ 1/2
68 1/2	44 1/4	IntPaper	2.40	3.6	20	5679	65 7/8	64	65 7/8	+ 1 7/8
12 3/8	6 3/8	IntRc s	...	...	...	157	7 1/8	6 3/4	6 7/8	- 1/2
44 3/4	21	IT Crp	...	...	34	149	42 3/8	42	42 3/8	+ 7/8
30 3/8	18	IntpbG s	.60	2.2	16	987	28	26 7/8	27 3/4	+ 1 1/8
34	18 3/8	IntBakr	...	...	10	34	31 1/4	30 3/4	31	+ 1/4
31 5/8	19	IntstPw	1.96	6.4	15	46	30 5/8	30 3/8	30 1/2	...
15 3/4	8 7/8	IntSec	.40	3.4	10	8	11 7/8	11 7/8	11 7/8	+ 1/8
46 3/4	29 7/8	IowlIG	2.90	6.5	11	694	45 1/4	44 3/8	44 3/8	- 3/8
27 1/2	20 1/2	Iowill pf	2.31	9.1	...	z100	25 1/2	25 1/2	25 1/2	- 7/8
26 1/4	15 1/2	IowaR s	1.60	6.1	13	151u	26 3/8	25 7/8	26 3/8	+ 1/4
57	32 3/4	Ipalco	3.04	5.4	15	253	56 7/8	56	56 7/8	+ 3/8
14 1/2	10	IpcoCo	.36	3.3	10	12	10 7/8	10 5/8	10 7/8	+ 1/8
59 1/4	32 1/2	IrvBnk	2.08	3.8	8	113	54 3/4	54 1/8	54 3/4	+ 1/4
54 3/4	49	IrvBk pf	3.87e	7.6	...	49	51	50 5/8	50 7/8	+ 3/8
17 7/8	9 3/4	Italy n	...	...	...	56	11	10 3/4	10 7/8	...

High and low price for last 52 weeks

IBM pays a dividend of \$4.40

Abbreviated name of company International Paper

Pf stands for preferred stock. The rest are common stock

The price of this stock is 14 times its earnings

International Paper's highest price for the day was \$65.875, the lowest was \$64.00, and at the close of trading was \$65.875. It was up \$1.875 from the previous day's close.

3400 shares of this stock traded that day

This stock went up \$.25 since the previous day's close.

for the day; and net change in price from the previous day. Look through the columns and find the stock that pays the highest yield. Spend a little time looking through the figures until they make sense to you.

... MUTUAL FUND QUOTATIONS ...

We noted that one way to get expert investment advice, to diversify your investments among various stocks and bonds, and to purchase such securities at a minimum cost is to buy into mutual funds. Look up *The Wall Street Journal*'s listing of mutual funds. Note that some funds have the letters NL after them (in the second to the last column). This indicates that (1) the fund is a *no-load fund* and (2) these shares can be bought without paying a commission to a salesperson or a fee to enter the fund. (See Figure 20.8.) But note that you may pay an annual fee for management advice. The other figure you'll notice when you look up mutual funds is *NAV (net asset value)*. NAV is the market value of a mutual fund portfolio divided by the number of shares it has outstanding.

Remember, it's easy to buy a no-load mutual fund directly and save the broker's commission. Often, ads for funds can be found in *The Wall Street Journal* and other business publications. Switching your money from a bond fund to a stock fund and back is generally no harder than making an 800-number phone call. Check it out; there are over 6,000 funds to choose from.

FIGURE 20.8

MUTUAL FUND QUOTATIONS

	Inv Obj	NAV	Offer Price	NAV Chg	YTD	Total Return 13 wks	Total Return 3 yrs
AIM Funds:							
AdIGV p	BST	9.63	9.73		+0.1	+0.2	NS ..
Agrsv p	SML	24.43	25.85	−0.09	−0.1	−1.2	+25.2 A
BalB t	S & B	15.30	15.30	−0.04	−4.2	+0.3	NS ..
Chart p	G & I	8.73	9.24	−0.03	−2.7	0.0	+7.0 D
Const p	CAP	16.57	17.53	−0.16	−5.3	−2.9	+16.8 A
BalA p	S & B	15.29	16.05	−0.05	−3.9	+0.5	+12.3 A
GoScA p	BND	9.38	9.85	+0.01	−2.8k	+0.8k	+6.2k E
GrthA p	GRO	10.29	10.89	−0.09	−9.1	−5.2	+2.1 E
GrthB t	GRO	10.22	10.22	−0.09	−9.6	−5.5	NS ..
HYIdA p	BHI	9.34	9.81	. . .	−2.0k	−0.7k	+15.4k B
HYIdB t	BHI	9.33	9.33	. . .	−2.4k	−1.0k	NS ..
IncoA p	BND	7.49	7.86	. . .	−7.6k	−0.7k	+8.8k B
IntlE p	ITL	13.02	13.78	−0.07	−0.2	+2.4	NS ..
LimM p	BST	9.96	10.06	+0.01	+0.5	+0.8	+5.5 C
MunIA p	GLM	8.16	8.57	+0.02	−2.2k	+2.2k	+8.4k A
Sumlt	GRO	9.14	NA	−0.08	−5.8	−2.2	+7.7 C
TeCt p	SSM	10.72	11.25	+0.03	−2.2k	+1.9k	+7.9k B
TF Int	IDM	10.65	10.76	+0.02	−1.0k	+1.6k	+7.1k B
UtlIA p	SEC	12.35	13.07	+0.01	−10.1k	−2.3k	+8.9k C
UtlIB t	SEC	12.35	12.35	+0.01	−10.4k	−2.5k	NS ..
ValuA p	GRO	20.83	22.04	−0.11	0.0	−0.5	+17.5 A
ValuB t	GRO	20.74	20.74	−0.12	−0.4	−0.8	NS ..
Weing p	GRO	16.65	17.62	−0.12	−2.9	−1.1	+4.9 E

Change in NAV from previous day

Price to buy one share

Return on investment year-to-date 13 weeks over 3 year periods

Investment objective of the fund. GRO means growth fund. (Other mutual fund objective categories can be found in *The Wall Street Journal*.)

NAV refers to net asset value of the fund.

Contact several different funds for information. They're generally happy to accommodate you. Remember, it's a great way to begin investing for your future financial needs.

••• THE DOW JONES AVERAGES •••

Whether you listen to the evening news on TV or stock reports on the radio, you'll hear announcers say things like "The Dow industrials are up five points today in active trading." A gentleman named Charles Dow is responsible for this. Dow began the practice of measuring stock averages in 1884 when he added the prices of 11 important stocks and divided the total by 11 to get an average. Today, the Dow remains a barometer used to measure the market's direction.

The **Dow Jones Industrial Average** was broadened in 1982 to include 30 stocks. New stocks are substituted when deemed appropriate. For example, the list was changed in 1991 to reflect the increase in the service sector. The 30 stocks in the Dow Jones Industrial Average include such notables as Du Pont, Eastman Kodak, GE, IBM, Sears, Philip Morris, and Coca-Cola. McDonald's Corporation became the first food retailing company to be included in the Dow Jones Industrial Average. (See Figure 20.9.) Again, the assumption is that the average indicates the market's direction over time. Some critics argue, however, that the 30-company sample is too small to get a good statistical representation.

Dow Jones Industrial Average
The average cost of 30 specific industrial stocks; used to give an indication of the direction of the market over time.

••• INVESTMENT BANKERS AND INSTITUTIONAL INVESTORS •••

Investment bankers are important players in securities markets. **Investment bankers** are specialists in assisting in the issue and selling of new securities. Companies such as Goldman Sachs, Morgan Stanley, and Salomon Brothers are important investment banking firms. Investment bankers provide valuable services to firms issuing new securities.

Investment bankers provide *underwriting* of a new issue of bonds or stocks. In other words, the investment banking firm purchases the entire bond or stock issue a firm wishes to sell at an agreed-upon discount. For example, if Fiberrific wanted to raise $100 million in new financing from a bond issue, an investment banking firm could offer to buy the entire issue for $98 million (a 2 percent discount). Fiberrific is spared the difficulties and risks associated with marketing and selling the issue to potential investors. The investment banker, being a market specialist, then sells the issue in the open market to private or institutional investors at the full $100 million price.

investment bankers
Specialists in assisting in the issue and selling of new securities.

Alcoa	Eastman Kodak	3M Corp.
Allied Signal	Exxon	Philip Morris
American Express	General Electric	Procter & Gamble
AT&T	General Motors	Sears Roebuck
Bethlehem Steel	Goodyear	Texaco
Boeing	IBM	Union Carbide
Caterpillar	International Paper	United Technologies
Chevron	J. P. Morgan	Walt Disney
Coca-Cola	McDonald's	Westinghouse
Du Pont	Merck	Woolworth

FIGURE 20.9

DOW JONES' 30 INDUSTRIAL STOCKS

Legal Briefcase

Institutional Investors Have Unfair Advantages in IPO Markets

It's often said that one good idea is all it takes to make a fortune. Investing in such an idea can also be a path to financial security. Therefore, it's not surprising that the IPO (initial public offering) market has been a hotbed of interest for individual investors looking to score big on new ideas and companies. In 1993, underwriters in this market raised a record $57.5 billion in equity capital for emerging companies such as Boston Chicken, Physician Corporation of America, and the Vermont Teddy Bear Company. Did hot IPOs such as these help individual investors realize that dream of scoring big? Not according to many experts who follow this market.

Professor Lynn Stout of the Georgetown University Law Center has been emphatic in criticizing individual investors' small chance of playing on a level field with the large institutions (mutual funds, pension funds, etc.) that control this market. Wall Street syndicate managers admit that institutions get to buy as much as 60 to 80 percent of the shares of certain "hot" deals. Additionally, critics argue that the portion of shares left for small investors is often distributed according to internal politics, favoritism, and rewards to good customers.

Getting a large slice of the best offerings isn't the only advantage afforded to large institutional investors. They also have a good deal more flexibility in trading their shares after the initial purchase. For example, brokerage firms often penalize small investors that "flip" IPOs (that is, turn a quick profit by selling a new issue) but allow large institutions to flip with no penalty. Institutional investors are also privy to more in-depth information than individual investors ever see. Some firms even provide elaborate "road shows" that promote the stock offering and disclose important information about the company and the deal. Small investors must rely on the information in the prospectus required by law.

If securities markets fail to deal with these shortcomings, the Securities and Exchange Commission may be forced to investigate. Many feel that the IPO market, even with all its strengths, is being distorted and not serving all investors. You be the judge.

Source: Philip Zweig and Leah Nathans Spiro, "Beware the IPO Market," *Business Week,* April 4, 1994, pp. 84–90; and Richard A. Melcher and Gail DeGeorge, "Does Scott Beck Have Another Winning Recipe?" *Business Week,* December 13, 1993, p. 100.

---

institutional investors
Large investors such as pension funds, mutual funds, insurance companies, and banks.

Institutional investors are large investors such as pension funds, mutual funds, insurance companies, and banks. Institutional investors are the most important financial force in securities markets. As you'll see in the next section, many experts consider program trading by institutional investors to be a major cause of the crash in 1987.

CRITICAL THINKING

What form of investment seems most appropriate to your needs now? Do you suspect your objectives and needs will change over time? Would investing other people's money be an interesting career to pursue? What problems might stockbrokers or mutual fund managers face on the job?

••• THE STOCK MARKET CRASH OF 1987 •••

On October 19, 1987, the stock market suffered the largest one day drop in its history. The Dow Jones Industrial Average fell 508 points. What does that mean? In just six and one-half hours of trading, a half-trillion dollars vanished before bewildered investors' eyes. How much is a half-trillion dollars? According to Paul Erdman, a noted economist, "A half-trillion dollars is more

Making Ethical Decisions

Inside Scoop

Imagine that you're a reporter for a local newspaper. You're writing an article on Mega Machinery, Inc., the area's largest industrial company. In the course of your research, a disgruntled Mega employee tells you of the company's plans to take over MiniMach, a competing firm. Buying MiniMach stock now before the takeover attempt becomes public knowledge will surely allow you to reap a huge profit when Mega offers top dollar for the MiniMach stock. What are the ethical considerations in this situation? What are your alternatives? What are the consequences of each alternative? What will you do?

than all the people of Central America plus most of the inhabitants of Eastern Europe earn in an entire year." Sam Walton lost over a billion dollars that day on his shares of Wal-Mart Stores, the discount store chain he founded. The crash prompted another billionaire, H. Ross Perot, to caution, "It was God tapping us on the shoulder and warning us to get our act together before we get the big shock."

What caused the crash of 1987? Ask a dozen financial analysts and you might get a dozen different responses. However, many analysts attest that "program trading" was a big cause of stock prices' falling to disastrous levels. In **program trading**, investors give their computers instructions to automatically sell if the price of their stock dips to a certain price to avoid potential losses. A threatening price automatically triggers a sell order. Assured that the computer is managing their portfolios, investors can then tend to other business. On Black Monday (as the crash is called), the computers became trigger-happy. Sell orders caused many stocks to fall to unbelievable depths.

Some investing lessons that can be learned from the crash of 1987: Be ready for volatility—it's the nature of the market; be careful of small, thinly traded stocks; look at the market globally and remember that all nations' economies and markets are tied together today; be diversified in your investments; don't gamble with borrowed money; and take a long-term perspective in dealing in securities markets. You may want to refer to this chapter again when you read about personal finance in Chapter 22.

program trading
Giving instructions to computers to automatically sell if the price of stock dips to a certain price to avoid potential losses.

PROGRESS CHECK

- What does the Dow Jones Industrial Average measure? Why is it so important?
- What services do investment banking firms provide in securities markets?
- Why are institutional investors important to securities markets?
- What do the letters SEC stand for? Exactly what does the SEC do?

SUMMARY

1. Securities markets provide opportunities for businesses and investors.
   - ***What opportunities are provided to businesses and individual investors by securities markets?***

   Businesses are able to raise capital to help finance major needs of the firm. Individual investors can share in emerging firms' success and growth by investing in the firm.

1. Understand the functions of securities markets and how businesses and individuals can make use of their services.

2. Compare the advantages and disadvantages of selling bonds and identify the classes and features of bonds.

2. Companies can raise capital by debt financing, which involves issuing bonds.
   - *What are the advantages and disadvantages of issuing bonds?*
   Advantages of issuing bonds include the following: (1) Management retains control since bondholders can't vote; (2) interest paid on bonds is tax-deductible; and (3) bonds are only a temporary source of finance. As for disadvantages: (1) Because bonds are an increased debt, they may affect the market's perception of the company adversely; (2) interest on bonds must be paid; and (3) the face value must be repaid on the maturity date.
   - *Are there different types of bonds?*
   Yes. There are unsecured (debenture) and secured bonds. Unsecured bonds aren't supported by collateral, whereas secured bonds are backed by tangible assets such as mortgages, stock, and equipment.

3. Compare the advantages and disadvantages of issuing stock and outline the differences between common and preferred stock.

3. Companies can also raise capital by equity financing, which involves selling stock.
   - *What are the advantages and disadvantages of selling stock?*
   Advantages of selling stock include the following: (1) The stock never has to be repaid since stockholders are owners in the company; (2) there's no legal obligation to pay dividends; and (3) no debt is incurred so the company is financially stronger. As for disadvantages: (1) Stockholders are owners of the firm and can affect its management through the selection of the board of directors; (2) it's more costly to pay dividends since they're paid after taxes; and (3) managers may be tempted to make stockholders happy in the short term rather than plan for long-term needs.
   - *What are the differences between common and preferred stock?*
   Common stockholders have voting rights in the company. Preferred stockholders have no voting rights. In exchange for voting privileges, preferred stocks offer a fixed dividend that must be paid in full before common stockholders receive a dividend.

4. Identify the various stock exchanges and describe how to invest in securities markets and choose among different investment strategies.

4. Stock exchanges give investors various options for investing in securities markets.
   - *What's a stock exchange?*
   An organization whose members can buy and sell securities.
   - *What are the different exchanges?*
   There are stock exchanges all over the world. The largest U.S. exchange is the New York Stock Exchange (NYSE). It and the American Stock Exchange (ASE) together are known as *national exchanges* because they handle stock of companies all over the country. In addition, several regional exchanges deal with companies in their own areas.
   - *What's the over-the-counter (OTC) market?*
   OTC is a system for exchanging stocks not listed on the national exchanges. It also handles bonds issued by city and state governments.
   - *How do investors normally make purchases in securities markets?*
   Investors generally purchase investments through market intermediaries called *stockbrokers*, who provide many different services to investors.
   - *What are the criteria for selecting investments?*
   They are (1) risk, (2) yield, (3) duration, (4) liquidity, and (5) tax consequences.

5. Describe the opportunities bonds offer as investments and explain what's meant by junk bonds.

5. Bonds present opportunities for investors.
   - *What's the difference between a bond selling at a discount and a bond selling at a premium?*
   A bond selling at a premium is a bond that can be sold in securities markets at a price above its face value. A bond selling at a discount is a bond that can be sold in securities markets but at a price below its face value.

- ● *What's a junk bond?*

Junk bonds are high-risk, high-interest bonds that speculative investors often find attractive investments.

6. Stock, mutual funds, and commodities present opportunities for investors to enhance their financial position.

   ● *What's a market order?*

   A market order tells a broker to buy or sell a security immediately at the best price available. A limit order tells the broker to buy or sell at a specific price if and when that price becomes possible.

   ● *What does buying on margin mean?*

   It means that the investor borrows up to 50 percent of the cost of the stock from the broker so he or she can get more shares.

   ● *What does it mean when a stock splits?*

   When a stock splits, stockholders receive two or more shares for each share they own. Each share is then worth half or less of the original share. Therefore, while the number of shares increases, the total value of the stockholders' holdings stays the same. The lower price per share may increase demand for the stock.

   ● *What's diversification?*

   Diversification means buying several different types of investments (e.g., government bonds, corporate bonds, preferred stock, common stock) with different degrees of risk. The purpose is to reduce the overall risk an investor would assume by just investing in one type of security.

   ● *How can mutual funds help individuals diversify their investments?*

   A mutual fund is an organization that buys stocks and bonds and then sells shares in those securities to the public. Individuals who buy shares in a mutual fund can invest in many different companies they couldn't afford to invest in otherwise.

   ● *What are commodity exchanges?*

   Commodity exchanges specialize in buying and selling precious metals and minerals (e.g., silver, oil) and agricultural goods (e.g., wheat, cattle, sugar).

   ● *What's hedging? How does it help buyers and sellers of commodities decrease their risks?*

   Hedging is buying or selling commodities in the futures market. Hedging decreases the risks of buying and selling commodities because it fixes the price for the commodities. For example, if you have wheat growing in the field, you can sell it now in the futures market and know exactly how much money to expect at harvest time.

7. The security quotations are listed in the daily papers.

   ● *What information do stock quotations give you?*

   Stock quotations give you all kinds of information: the highest price in the past 52 weeks; the lowest price; the dividend yield; the price/earnings ratio; the total shares traded that day; and the high, low, close, and net change in price from the previous day. Bond quotations give you similar information regarding bonds.

   ● *What's the Dow Jones Industrial Average?*

   The Dow Jones Industrial Average is the average price of 30 specific stocks traded on the New York Stock Exchange.

   ● *How are securities exchanges regulated?*

   Securities exchanges are regulated by the Securities and Exchange Commission (SEC).

   ● *What's insider trading?*

   Insider trading involves the use of information or knowledge that individuals gain through their position that allows them to benefit unfairly from fluctuations in security prices.

---

6. Explain the opportunities that stock, mutual funds, and commodities offer and explain the advantage of diversifying investments.

7. Explain securities quotations listed in the financial section of a newspaper, tell how the Dow Jones Averages affect the market, and discuss investment bankers' and institutional investors' roles in securities trading.

KEY TERMS

blue chip stocks 624
bond 610
buying on margin 624
call provision 613
commodity
  exchange 627
common stock 617
convertible bond 613
cumulative preferred
  stock 616
debenture bond 612
diversification 626
dividends 614
Dow Jones Industrial
  Average 631
futures market 627
growth stocks 624
hedging 627

income stock 624
insider trading 621
institutional
  investors 632
interest 611
investment banker 631
junk bonds 623
limit order 624
market order 624
maturity date 611
mutual fund 626
National Association
  of Securities Dealers
  Automated
  Quotation System
  (NASDAQ) 619
over-the-counter
  (OTC) market 619
par value 614

penny stock 624
preemptive right 617
preferred stock 616
principal 611
program trading 633
prospectus 620
round lot 625
Securities and
  Exchange
  Commission
  (SEC) 621
sinking fund 612
stock certificate 614
stock exchange 618
stock split 625
stockbroker 621
stocks 614

DEVELOPING WORKPLACE SKILLS

1. Write the Education Department, *The Wall Street Journal,* 200 Burnett Road, Chicopee, MA 01020, and have them send you the Student Edition. It explains all the columns and charts. Discuss this edition with your class.

2. Read *The Wall Street Journal* daily for several weeks. Choose and track several stocks in different industries. Use a computer to graphically display the trends of each. Does this exercise help you in your analysis of their performance?

3. See if anyone is interested in setting up an investment game in your class. Each student should choose one stock and one mutual fund. Record each student's selection and its price on a chart. In six weeks, look up and chart the prices again. The student with the largest percentage gain wins.

4. Businesses in the 1990s are trying to raise money by selling stock. During the 1980s, most businesses tried to raise money by selling bonds. Prepare an analysis explaining what happened to force businesses to switch. Compare your conclusions with those of your classmates.

5. Analyze the risks and opportunities of investing today in stocks, bonds, and mutual funds. Assume your Great Aunt Hildi just left you $10,000. Since you and your parents already saved enough money to cover your college bills, you decide to invest the money so that you can start your own business after you graduate. How will you invest your money? Why? Name specific investments.

PRACTICING MANAGEMENT DECISIONS

§ CASE   BONDS OR STOCK? THAT IS THE QUESTION. §

In 1973, Carlos Galendez had dreams but very little money. He spent more than 10 years working as a dishwasher and then cook for a major restaurant. His dream was to save enough money to start his own Mexican restaurant. In 1975, his dream finally came true. With a loan from the Small Business

Administration, he opened his first Casa de Carlos restaurant. His old family recipes and appealing decor helped the business gain immediate success. He repaid his small-business loan within 14 months and immediately opened a second and then a third location. By 1977, Casa de Carlos was the largest Mexican restaurant chain in the nation.

In 1978, the company decided to go public. Carlos believed that continued growth was beneficial to the company and that offering ownership was the way to bring in loyal investors. Nevertheless, he made certain his family maintained controlling interest in the firm's stock. Therefore, in its initial public offering, Casa de Carlos offered to sell only 40 percent of the available shares in the company to investors. The Galendez family kept control of the remaining 60 percent.

As the public's craving for Mexican food grew, so did the fortunes of Casa de Carlos, Inc. Heading into the 1980s, the company enjoyed the position of being light on debt and heavy on cash. But in 1985, the firm's debt position changed when it bought out Captain Al's Seafood Restaurants. Three years later, it expanded into full-service wholesale distribution of seafood products with the purchase of Mariner Wholesalers. The firm's debt increased, but the price of its stock was up and demand in all three operations was booming.

In 1990, Carlos Galendez died. His oldest child, Maria, was selected to take control as chief executive officer. Maria had learned the business from her father. He taught her to keep an eye out for opportunities that seemed fiscally responsible. Unfortunately, in 1993 the firm's fortunes began to shift. Two major competitors were taking market share from Casa de Carlos, and the seafood venture began to flounder (pun intended). The recession in the early 1990s didn't help either. Consumers spent less, causing severe cash problems. Maria Galendez had to decide how to get the funds the firm needed for improvements and other expenses. Banks wouldn't expand the firm's credit line so she was forced to consider a bond or stock offering to raise capital.

Decision Questions

1. What advantages and disadvantages should Maria consider before offering bonds to investors?

2. What would be the advantages and disadvantages of the company's offering new stock to investors?

3. Are any other options available to Maria Galendez?

4. What choice would you make? Why?

• •

❱❱ VIDEO CASE   WHY STOCK, WHY BONDS? ❱❱

The average small company never gets involved with stocks and bonds. It has to raise money through loans and from other means. Eventually, however, some small companies become bigger, and that's the time when they may want to sell stock or bonds to raise large amounts of money for growth and expansion.

A bond is like a corporate IOU. The bond certificate is the paper that spells out the terms of the agreement. It states when the bond will be paid, what the interest rate is, and the principal. Most bonds come in $1,000 denominations. One advantage for a company selling bonds rather than stocks is that bond holders do not get a vote in running the company. Furthermore, the interest paid to bondholders is tax deductible. If interest rates are not too high, therefore, bonds are a good way to raise money. However, bonds increase debt, and that doesn't look good on financial statements. Moreover, bonds are a legal obligation; that is, you have to pay the money back. As far as investors are concerned, they would prefer a secured bond, one that is backed by some collateral such as securities, real estate, or equipment. Unsecured bonds are called debentures and are usually issued by financially secure firms such as Xerox.

If you want maximum security in a bond, buy those sold by the U.S. government. Why? The federal government is unlikely to go bankrupt.

In determining when to buy, it's important to recognize that there are favorable and unfavorable times to purchase bonds. The best time to buy bonds is when interest rates are high and falling. Bond prices rise when interest rates fall. It is bad, therefore, to buy bonds when interest rates are low and rising. The bond price will fall in that case. Junk bonds promise high interest rates, but the risk assumed by the buyer is higher also.

Companies may prefer to raise money by selling stock. Stock doesn't pay interest; it pays dividends (some share of profits). The advantages of selling stock is that the money never has to be repaid. After all, the holders of the stock are the owners of the firm. They don't have to pay themselves anything. Furthermore, there is no legal demand that dividends be paid and many companies do not. Profits not paid to stockholders in the form of dividends are called retained earnings.

Common stock is, as it sounds, the most common form sold. Such stock provides its owners with voting rights with respect to certain issues affecting the company. Preferred stock carries no voting rights, but the owners have first rights to any dividends the company pays. Generally, owners of common stock make more money in the long run than people who buy bonds—a lot more.

If you are interested in buying stock, you may want to buy from a mutual fund. A mutual fund buys stock in a variety of companies and then sells shares of those holdings to the public. You get the advantage of a diversified group of stocks and the expertise of those who buy them.

The stock market was a great invention because it made it possible for people in the United States to invest in companies and it made it easier for companies to raise money. It was a mutually beneficial exchange relationship. As companies prosper and grow, they hire more people and pay more taxes to the government. They also create wealth for their owners. And since it is relatively easy to become an owner (stockholder), it should be relatively easy to become wealthy. You just have to pick the right stock in the right company. Maybe it's not so easy after all.

Decision Questions

1. As an investor, what do you see as the advantages of buying stock versus bonds? What is an easy way to diversify your risk?

2. There are mutual funds that buy both stocks and bonds. What would be the advantages and disadvantages of investing your money in such a fund?

3. Imagine that you are the owner of a small firm and you need to raise money to expand. Which would you prefer to offer first: bonds or stock? Why?

4. People often say that bonds are a safer investment than stock. Do you agree? Why?

CHAPTER 21

UNDERSTANDING MONEY AND FINANCIAL INSTITUTIONS

LEARNING GOALS

After you have read and studied this chapter, you should be able to

1. Explain what money is and the importance of the money supply to domestic and international exchange.

2. Describe how the Federal Reserve controls the money supply.

3. Trace the history of banking and the Federal Reserve System.

4. Describe the various institutions in the U.S. banking system.

5. Explain the importance of the Federal Deposit Insurance Corporation and other organizations that guarantee funds.

6. Discuss the future of the banking system.

7. Explain the role and importance of international banking.

ALAN GREENSPAN, CHAIRMAN OF THE FEDERAL RESERVE

Alan Greenspan was born in New York, the only son of Herbert (a broker) and Rose Greenspan. He went to George Washington High School, later studied music at Julliard, and played the clarinet for a year or so in a jazz band.

When music's attraction declined, Greenspan decided to go to New York University, where he majored in economics. He received his degree summa cum laude in 1948. He went on to get his M.A. in economics at NYU and started doctoral studies under Arthur Burns at Columbia. Arthur Burns later became chairman of the Federal Reserve Board.

Greenspan began work as an economist for the Conference Board, a nonprofit research group. Later he started his own consulting firm. He went on to teach economics at NYU for a couple of years; the school granted him a doctorate later. His firm, Townsend-Greenspan, provided research, forecasts, and other economic consulting services to major firms. He also devoted his energies to public service and began a distinguished career in government that included service for four presidents.

As one of President Nixon's top economic aides, Greenspan worked on several economic task forces and served as an informal adviser. As chairman of the Council of Economic Advisers under President Ford, he became an intense inflation fighter. He also argued that government spending must be cut. That's one reason why President Reagan chose him to be chairman of the Federal Reserve System (the Fed). In 1991, President George Bush reappointed Greenspan to another term, citing his success in fighting inflation and leading the economic recovery from the recession of 1990. President Clinton retained him for much the same reason.

Dr. Greenspan has occupied one of the most powerful positions in the country for the past several years. As chairman of the Federal Reserve, he has control over the nation's money supply. During 1994 Greenspan increased interest rates six times and he raised them once more in early 1995. *The Wall Street Journal* reported that "Greenspan's remarks [about raising rates] rattled stock and bond investors, sending prices lower." Clearly Alan Greenspan is a person to watch. It's also important to understand his role in the economy, especially banking.

> *Money makes money, and the money money makes, makes more money.*
>
> *Benjamin Franklin*

THE IMPORTANCE OF MONEY

The U.S. economy is heavily dependent on money: its availability, its value relative to other currencies, and its cost. Economic growth and the creation of jobs depend on money. Money is so important to the economy that many institutions have evolved to manage money and to make it available to you when you need it. Today you can easily get money from an automated teller machine (ATM) almost anywhere in the world. You don't have to have cash anymore to buy things. Most organizations will accept a check or credit card to pay for things you buy. Behind the scenes of this free flow of money is a complex system of banking that makes it possible for you to do all these things.

The banking system is becoming more complex all the time because the flow of money from country to country is as free as the flow from state to state. Therefore, what happens to any major country's economy has an effect on the U.S. economy and vice versa. For example, when Japan's stock market fell dramatically in the early 1990s, the flow of money from Japan to the United States slowed considerably. Also, Japanese cars became much more expensive for American consumers and American products became much less expensive for Japanese consumers.

Clearly, there's more to money and its role in the economies of the world than meets the eye. There's no way to understand the U.S. economy without understanding global money exchanges and the various institutions involved in the creation and management of money. We'll explore such institutions in this chapter. Let's start at the beginning by discussing exactly what people mean when they say "money" and how the supply of money affects the prices you pay for goods and services.

••• WHAT IS MONEY? •••

money
What people will generally accept as payment for goods and services.

Money is anything that people generally accept as payment for goods and services. In the past, objects as diverse as salt, feathers, stones, and rare shells have been used as money. *Barter* is the trading of goods and services for other goods and services directly. For example, you could give someone a pig and they could give you materials to build your home. Many people still barter goods and services without what you call money. The problem is that pigs and lumber are difficult to carry around. People need some object that's more portable, divisible, durable, and stable so that they can trade goods and services without carrying the actual goods around with them. One answer to that problem was to create coins made of silver or gold. Coins met all the standards for a more useful money:

> *Portability.* Coins were a lot easier to take to market than were pigs or other heavy products.
>
> *Divisibility.* Different-sized coins could be made to represent different values. For example, previous to 1963 a U.S. quarter had half as much silver content as a half dollar and a dollar had four times the silver of a quarter. Today's coins are no longer made of silver because it was too expensive to make them, but the values remain.

Stability. Everybody agreed on the value of coins so the value of money became relatively stable. In fact, U.S. money became so stable that much of the world uses U.S. dollars as *the* measure of value.

Durability. Coins last for thousands of years, even when they've sunk to the bottom of the ocean, as you've seen when divers find old Roman coins in sunken ships.

Coins and paper money thus become units of value and a means of making exchanges easier. Most countries have their own coins and paper that they use as money; they're all about equally portable, divisible, and durable. However, they're not always equally stable. For example, the value of money in Russia is so uncertain and so unstable that other countries won't accept Russian money in international trade. For Russia to become a global trader, it must develop money that's tradeable in world markets. When Poland made its money more stable in the early 1990s, global trade for that country grew tremendously.

• • • WHAT IS THE MONEY SUPPLY? • • •

This chapter's profile says that Alan Greenspan is in control of the money supply. Two questions emerge from that simple statement: (1) What is the money supply? and (2) Why does it need to be controlled? The value of money depends on the **money supply;** that is, how much money there is to buy available goods and services.

There are several definitions of the money supply. They're called *M-1*, *M-2*, and so on. The *M* stands for money, and the 1 and 2 stand for different definitions of the money supply. **M-1,** for example, includes **currency** (coins and paper bills), money that's available by writing checks, and money that's held in traveler's checks; that is, money that is quickly and easily raised. **M-2** includes everything in M-1 plus money in savings accounts (time deposits) and money in money market accounts, mutual funds, certificates of deposit, and the like; that is, money that may take a little more time to obtain than currency. M-2 is the most commonly used definition of money. You'll learn more about money and the money supply if you study finance and economics.

• • • WHY DOES THE MONEY SUPPLY NEED • • • TO BE CONTROLLED?

Imagine what would happen if governments were to distribute twice as much money as exists now. They could do that by making more coins and paper money. There would be twice as much money available, but there would be the same amount of goods and services. What would happen to prices in that case? Pause and think about the answer for a minute.

The answer is that prices would go up because more people would try to buy goods and services with their money and would bid up the price to get what they wanted. This is called *inflation.* Some people call it "Too much money chasing too few goods." You may want to review Chapter 2 to see how supply and demand affect prices.

On the other hand, what would happen if someone took some of the money out of the economy? What would happen to prices? Prices would go down because there would be an oversupply of goods and services compared to the money available to buy them. Take too much money out of the economy and a recession might occur. That is, people would lose jobs and the economy would stop growing.

money supply
The sum of all the funds that the public has immediately available for buying goods and services.

M-1
Money that is quickly and easily raised (currency, checks, travelers' checks, and the like).

currency
All coin and paper money issued by the Federal Reserve banks and all coins.

M-2
Money included in M-1 plus money that may take a little more time to raise (savings accounts, money market accounts, mutual funds, certificates of deposit, and the like).

Japanese cars and other products become much more expensive to U.S. buyers when the value of the dollar drops, as it did in the mid-1990s. On the other hand, U.S. goods during these periods are much less expensive to the Japanese, but due to trade restrictions imposed by Japan on numerous products U.S. companies historically haven't benefited. What would happen to Japanese auto sales in the United States if they allowed prices to rise according to the value of the yen?

Why does the money supply need to be controlled? The money supply needs to be controlled because the prices of goods and services can be somewhat managed by controlling the amount of money available in the economy. And those controls have an effect on employment and economic growth or decline. The same is true in international markets.

••• THE GLOBAL EXCHANGE OF MONEY •••

falling dollar
The value of the dollar changes such that the amount of goods and services you can buy with a dollar goes down.

rising dollar
The value of the dollar changes such that the amount of goods and services you can buy with a dollar goes up.

During the mid-1990s, the American dollar was falling relative to the Japanese yen. A **falling dollar** means that the amount of goods and services you can buy with a dollar goes down. A **rising dollar** means that the amount of goods and services you can buy with a dollar goes up. Thus, the price you pay for a Japanese car today is higher than a few years ago because of the falling dollar relative to the Japanese yen (their unit of currency).[1]

Although the dollar was weak relative to the Japanese yen, it was strong relative to other currencies. What makes the dollar weak or strong is the position of the U.S. economy relative to other economies. When the economy is strong, people want to buy dollars and the value of the dollar rises. When the economy is perceived as weakening, however, people no longer desire dollars and the value of the dollar falls. The value of the dollar depends on a strong economy, and a strong economy depends on a ready supply of money. Clearly, control over the money supply is important. In the following section, we'll discuss who controls the money supply and how it's done. Then we'll explore the U.S. banking system and how it loans money to businesses and individuals such as you and me.

CRITICAL THINKING

What will happen to the value of the dollar in Japan if U.S. customers stop buying Japanese cars and other products because of higher prices? What will happen to the value of the yen? Can you see that eventually Japanese car prices will fall?

CONTROL OF THE MONEY SUPPLY

You can see that money plays a huge role in the American economy and in the economies of the rest of the world. Therefore, it's important to have an organization that controls the money supply to try to keep the U.S. economy from growing too fast or too slowly. Theoretically, you can keep the economy growing without causing inflation with the proper monetary policy. (See Chapter 2 for a review of monetary policy.) The organization in charge of monetary policy is the Federal Reserve System (the Fed); the person in charge is Alan Greenspan, whom you read about in this chapter's profile. The head of the Federal Reserve is one of the most influential people in the world because he or she controls the money that much of the world depends on for trade.

The Fed's tools to regulate the money supply fall into three categories: reserve requirements, open-market operations, and the discount rate. Let's look at how the Fed uses these tools.

••• THE RESERVE REQUIREMENT •••

The **reserve requirement** is a percentage of commercial bank's checking and savings accounts that must be physically kept in the bank (for example, as cash in the vault) or in a non–interest-bearing deposit at the local Federal Reserve district bank. For instance, if Omaha Security Bank holds deposits of $100 million and the reserve requirement is, say, 10 percent, then the bank must keep $10 million to meet the reserve requirement. If the Fed were to increase the reserve requirement to 11 percent, then the bank would have to put an additional $1 million on reserve. This would reduce the funds available from the bank for loans. Consequently, the money supply would be reduced and prices would likely fall.

The reserve requirement is the Fed's most powerful tool. When the Fed increases the reserve requirement, banks have less money for loans and make fewer loans. Money becomes more scarce, which in the long run tends to reduce inflation. A *decrease* of the reserve requirement, on the other hand, increases the funds available to banks for loans, so banks make more loans and money becomes more readily available. Such an increase in the money supply stimulates the economy to achieve higher growth rates but can also create inflationary pressures. For example, Alan Greenspan cut the reserve requirement from 12 to 10 percent in 1992 to stimulate the economy. The economy began growing more rapidly. By 1994, the Fed reported that American factories were busier than they had been for five years.[2]

reserve requirement
A percentage of member-bank funds that must be deposited in the Federal Reserve System.

••• OPEN-MARKET OPERATIONS •••

Open-market operations are the Fed's most commonly used tool. They involve the buying and selling of U.S. government securities by the Fed with the goal of regulating the money supply.

The federal government issues U.S. government securities (bonds) and sells them to the public. These securities pay interest to owners and are guaranteed by the federal government. Consequently, they're considered to be a stable, relatively low-risk form of investment.

How does the Fed use U.S. government securities to control the money supply? When the Fed wants to decrease the money supply, it sells government securities. The money it gets as payment is taken out of circulation,

open-market operations
The buying and selling of U.S. government securities by the Fed with the goal of regulating the money supply.

decreasing the money supply. If the Fed wants to increase the money supply, it buys government securities from individuals, corporations, or organizations that are willing to sell. The money paid by the Fed in return for these securities enters circulation, resulting in an increase in the money supply.

••• THE DISCOUNT RATE •••

The Fed has often been called *the banker's bank*. One reason for this is that member banks can borrow money from the Fed and then pass it on to their customers as loans. The **discount rate** is the interest rate that the Fed charges for loans to member banks. An increase in the discount rate by the Fed discourages banks from borrowing and consequently reduces the number of available loans, resulting in a decrease in the money supply. On the other hand, lowering the discount rate encourages member bank borrowing and increases the funds available for loans, which increases the money supply. As you can see, the whole banking industry is affected by actions taken by the Federal Reserve System. In the following sections, we'll briefly discuss the history of banking to give you some background information for understanding why the Fed came into existence. Then we'll explore what's happening in banking today.

discount rate
The interest rate that the Fed charges for loans to member banks.

PROGRESS CHECK

- What's "money"?
- What are the characteristics of "useful" money?
- What's the "money supply" and why is it important?
- What are the various ways the Federal Reserve controls the money supply?

THE DEVELOPMENT OF THE FEDERAL RESERVE SYSTEM

This country's system of money and banking was slow to develop. There were no banks in the colonies at first. Strict laws limited the number of coins that could be brought to the colonies. Thus, colonists were forced to barter. Remember, that means to trade goods for goods (for example, cotton and tobacco for shoes and lumber).

The demand for money was so great that Massachusetts issued its own paper money in 1690; other colonies soon followed suit. Land banks were established to lend money to farmers. (Note that banks were used as a means to grow the economy.) Britain—which still ruled the colonies back then—ended both practices by 1741. In fact, in Pennsylvania during the American Revolution, a new bank was formed to finance the war against England. Yes, the government needs banks too.

In 1781, Alexander Hamilton persuaded Congress to form a central bank (a bank where banks could keep their funds and borrow funds if needed) over the objections of Thomas Jefferson and others. It was the first version of a federal bank. It closed in 1811, only to be replaced in 1816 because state-chartered banks couldn't support the War of 1812. The battle between the Second (Central) Bank of the United States and state banks got hot in the 1830s. Several banks in President Andrew Jackson's home state were hurt by pressure from the Central Bank. The fight ended when the bank was closed in 1836.

By the time of the Civil War, the banking system was a mess. Many different banks issued different kinds of currencies. During the war, coins were hoarded because they were worth more as gold and silver than as coins. The chaos continued, reaching something of a climax in 1907, when many banks failed. People got nervous about their money and went to the bank to withdraw their funds. Shortly thereafter, the cash ran out and some banks had to refuse money to depositors.

The cash shortage problems of 1907 led to the formation of an organization that could lend money to banks—the Federal Reserve System. It was a lender of last resort in such emergencies. Under the Federal Reserve Act of 1913, all federally chartered banks had to join the Federal Reserve. State banks could also join. The Federal Reserve became the banker's bank. If banks had excess funds, they could deposit them in the Fed; if extra money was needed, they could borrow it from the Fed. The Federal Reserve System has been intimately related to banking ever since.

••• THE GREAT DEPRESSION •••

The Federal Reserve System was designed to prevent a repeat of the 1907 panic. Nevertheless, the stock market crash of 1929 led to bank failures in the early 1930s. The stock market began tumbling, and people had to rush to the bank to get money to cover their positions in the stock market. In spite of the Federal Reserve System, the banks ran out of money. States were forced to close banks. President Franklin D. Roosevelt extended the period of the bank closings in 1933 to gain time to come up with some solution to the problem.

In 1933 and 1935, Congress passed legislation to strengthen the banking system. The most important move was to establish federal deposit insurance. You'll learn more about federal deposit insurance later in this chapter. At this point, it's important that you know that the government started an insurance program to further protect us from bank failures in the 1930s, during the Great Depression.

••• THE FEDERAL RESERVE AND ••• THE BANKING INDUSTRY

The Federal Reserve System, commercial banks, and savings and loan associations (S&Ls) have been in the news for over a decade. Some banks were in the news because of the loans they made to foreign countries—loans that may not be paid back. Many S&Ls were in the news because of failures throughout the country. Because of deflation and new tax laws in the 1980s, land values declined, and farmers and builders couldn't make their mortgage payments. This put great pressure on the S&Ls and banks that had loaned money to investors. S&Ls made other risky loans that turned out to be unprofitable, plunging the industry into debt. The bailout of the S&Ls is estimated to cost each American family up to $17,000 in tax dollars over the next three decades.

This newspaper from 1929 announced the stock market crash. The Great Depression lasted until the 1940s. Government, along with the securities and banking industries, has done a great deal since then to prevent a recurrence. For example, the FDIC now covers deposits in banks up to $100,000. That is, you and I guarantee those deposits. What are some of the events happening in the United States economy that threaten another banking crisis? What is being done to avert such a crisis?

Finally, the Federal Reserve has been in the news as it tries to keep the economy growing at an even pace. In the early 1990s, the Fed pumped up the money supply and lowered interest rates to get the economy moving. As inflation threatened in 1994, the Fed increased short-term interest rates. That caused bond prices to fall and threatened the stock market. Alan Greenspan became the center of attention as the whole financial community waited for the Fed's next move.

Some people felt that inflation was coming to the United States and applauded the Fed for hiking up interest rates. That would cut inflation and let the economy grow slowly but surely. Others felt that there was no inflation threat and that higher interest rates would slow the economy so much that a new recession would occur. In short, the whole world is watching the Federal Reserve System to see what direction the U.S. economy will take next. No group of people is more concerned than the nation's bankers. When the Fed raises the interest rates it charges banks (the *discount rate*), banks must raise their rates on mortgage loans, car loans, and the like. If rates get too high, people stop buying homes and cars, and the banks don't earn as much money making such loans.

stagflation
Period of both slow growth and inflation.

Businesses are also concerned because higher bank rates mean a higher cost of borrowing money. If businesses stop borrowing, then business growth slows, people are fired, and the whole economy stagnates. In fact, it's quite possible to have both slow growth and inflation. (That's called **stagflation**.) Thus, money and banking are critical to business leaders. You now know about money and the money supply. The following sections explore banking and its importance to businesspeople.

THE AMERICAN BANKING SYSTEM

The American banking system consists of commercial banks, savings and loan associations, credit unions, and mutual savings banks. In addition, various organizations perform several banking functions, although they aren't true banks. These nondeposit institutions (often called **nonbanks**) include pension funds, insurance companies, commercial finance companies, consumer finance companies, and brokerage houses. We'll discuss the activities and services provided by each of these institutions, starting with commercial banks.

nonbanks
Financial organizations that accept no deposits, but offer many of the services provided by regular banks (pension funds, insurance companies, commercial finance companies, consumer finance companies, and brokerage houses).

••• COMMERCIAL BANKS •••

commercial bank
A profit-making organization that receives deposits from individuals and corporations in the form of checking and savings accounts and uses some of these funds to make loans.

A **commercial bank** is a profit-making organization that receives deposits from individuals and corporations in the form of checking and savings accounts and then uses some of these funds to make loans. This is the institution entrepreneurs often turn to for loans. Commercial banks have two types of customers: depositors and borrowers (those who take out loans). A commercial bank is equally responsible to both types of customers. Commercial banks try to make a profit by efficiently using the funds given to them by depositors. In essence, a commercial bank uses customer deposits as inputs (on which it pays interest) and invests that money in interest-bearing loans to other customers (mostly businesses). Commercial banks make a profit if the revenue generated by loans exceeds the interest paid to depositors plus all other operating expenses.

SERVICES PROVIDED BY COMMERCIAL BANKS Individuals and corporations that deposit money in a checking account have the privilege of writing personal checks to pay for almost any purchase or transaction. The technical name for a checking account is a **demand deposit**, because the money is available on demand from the depositor. Typically, banks charge individual consumers a service charge for check-writing privileges or demand a minimum deposit. Banks might also charge a small handling fee for each check written. For corporate depositors, the amount of the service charge depends on the average daily balance in the checking account, the number of checks written, and the firm's credit rating and credit history.

In the past, checking accounts paid no interest to depositors, but interest-bearing checking accounts have experienced phenomenal growth in recent years. Most commercial banks offer NOW and Super NOW accounts to their depositors. A NOW (negotiable order of withdrawal) account typically pays an annual interest rate but requires depositors always to maintain a certain minimum balance in the account (for example, $500) and restricts the number of checks that depositors can write each month.

A Super NOW account pays higher interest to attract larger deposits. However, Super NOW accounts require a larger minimum balance. They typically offer free, unlimited check-writing privileges. Individual banks determine the specific terms for their NOW and Super NOW accounts.

In addition to these types of checking accounts, commercial banks offer a variety of savings account options. A savings account is technically called a **time deposit** because the bank can require a prior notice before withdrawal. One common form of savings account is called a *passbook savings account*. Here depositors have no checking privileges, but can withdraw money at any time.

A *certificate of deposit (CD)* is a time-deposit (savings) account that earns interest to be delivered at the end of the certificate's maturity date. The depositor agrees not to withdraw any of the funds in the account until the end of the specified period. CDs are now available for periods of three months up to five years; interest rates vary, depending on the period of the certificate. The interest rates also depend on economic conditions and the prime rate at the time of the deposit. In addition to the checking and savings accounts discussed above, commercial banks offer a variety of other services to their depositors including automated teller machines and credit cards.

Automated teller machines (ATMs) give customers the convenience of 24-hour banking at a variety of outlets such as supermarkets, department stores, and drugstores in addition to the bank's regular branches. Depositors can now get cash, transfer funds, and make deposits at their own discretion with the use of a computer-coded personalized plastic access card.

Commercial banks also offer credit cards to creditworthy customers, inexpensive brokerage services, financial counseling, automatic payment of telephone bills, safe deposit boxes, tax-deferred individual retirement accounts (IRAs) for qualified individuals and couples, traveler's checks, and overdraft

Bank on the environment of Vermont.

We'll put your money where your values are.

More people want to have a say in how banks use their deposits. Vermont National Bank has responded by allowing depositors to specify that their accounts be used for loans meeting certain social criteria. By using deposits for loans in the areas of affordable housing, agriculture, education, the environment, and dual–bottom-line businesses (businesses with a social and financial bottom line), the bank allows depositors to influence how their money is put to work for their community.

demand deposit
The technical name for a checking account; the money can be withdrawn on demand at any time by the owner.

time deposit
The technical name for a savings account for which the bank requires prior notice before withdrawal.

checking account privileges. (This means preferred customers can automatically get loans at reasonable rates when they've written checks exceeding their account balance.) Figure 21.1 lists key banking services.

SERVICES TO BORROWERS   Commercial banks offer a variety of services to individuals and corporations in need of a loan. Generally, loans are given based on the recipient's creditworthiness. Banks want to manage their funds effectively and are supposed to screen loan applicants carefully to ensure that the loan plus interest will be paid back on time.

To get a loan to buy a house or other expensive item in the future, you must develop a good credit history as early as possible. This is easier said than done, so carefully consider the following tips to develop a good credit history:

- Open a checking and savings account at a financial institution. Manage these accounts in a way that would avoid bad checks, overdrawn balances, and so forth. It's also important to keep some money in savings at all times. Prospective lenders could interpret this as a sign of efficient money management.
- Establish credit with a department store or oil company. It's usually easier to get credit from such sources than from a financial institution in the form of a credit card. Pay your bills on time to avoid having to pay finance charges. This should enhance your creditworthiness when you apply for a credit card.
- Pay all your rent, utility, and telephone bills promptly. This way you can get valuable references when you need them.
- Get a credit card from a financial institution. No matter how small the initial credit allowance might be, having a credit card is one of the best ways to develop a good credit history quickly. Remember that the more responsible you are in managing your credit card account, the more credit you can get in the future.

BUSINESS LOANS   Business loans are normally characterized as short-term or long-term, depending on whether they're to be repaid within one year or over a longer period of time. Short-term loans have to be paid within one year. Many businesses borrow on a short-term basis to get urgently needed cash for items such as seasonal inventory. Businesses find it useful to establish a line of credit before they actually need money. This involves getting approval for a specified loan amount beforehand, so the firm can immediately borrow the money whenever it's needed.

FIGURE 21.1

SERVICES AVAILABLE AT MOST COMMERCIAL BANKS
The number of services has expanded recently as banks seek to provide more and more assistance to consumers and businesses.

- Demand deposits (checking accounts)
- Time deposits (savings accounts)
- Loans
- Financial counseling
- Safe deposit boxes
- Certified checks
- Overdraft protection
- Insurance
- Traveler's checks
- Credit cards
- Certificates of deposit (CDs)
- NOW accounts
- Super NOW accounts
- Telebanking
- Automated teller machines (ATMs)
- Brokerage services

Long-term loans are those payable in a period that exceeds one year. Typically, long-term loans must be repaid within 2 to 5 years but could also be extended for longer periods (up to 20 years). Banks give long-term loans to individuals, corporations, and domestic and foreign governments. The interest charged for most long-term loans to large corporations and governments is negotiated between the two parties. Often, such loans require a long, exhausting round of bargaining before terms of the loan (interest charged, repayment period, types and amount of collateral required, default options, and so forth) are mutually agreed upon. Most loans by law require collateral.

• • • SAVINGS AND LOAN ASSOCIATIONS (S&Ls) • • •

A **savings and loan association** is a financial institution that accepts both savings and checking deposits and provides home mortgage loans. S&Ls are often known as *thrift institutions* since their original purpose was to promote consumer thrift and home ownership. To help them encourage home ownership, thrifts were permitted to offer slightly higher interest rates on savings deposits (than banks) to attract a larger pool of funds. These funds were then used to offer long-term fixed-rate mortgages at whatever the rate was at the time.

With the abrupt rise in interest rates in the late 1970s, S&Ls found themselves in deep financial trouble. The problem occurred because they were forced to pay depositors higher interest rates than before, while their revenues from the low-rate, long-term mortgage loans held constant. Thus, the S&Ls' costs kept going up while their income remained the same. Unable to pay a substantially higher interest rate than their competitors (commercial banks), S&Ls began to lose a large proportion of their depositors, with catastrophic results for many S&Ls.

Between 1979 and 1983, about 20 percent of the nation's S&Ls failed because of unbearable financial pressure. Faced with this situation in 1981, the federal government permitted S&Ls to offer NOW and Super NOW accounts, to allocate up to 10 percent of their funds to commercial loans, and to offer mortgage loans with adjustable interest rates based on market conditions. In addition, S&Ls were permitted to offer a variety of other banking services, such as financial counseling to small businesses and credit cards. As a result, S&Ls became much more similar to commercial banks—even though the rules governing them were different.

In the early 1990s, the S&L industry's problems caught the nation's attention. Newspapers and TV regularly reported the failure of one S&L after another. Deposits in these S&Ls were insured by the U.S. government, but the government agencies didn't have the money to pay for such losses. In the long run, taxpayers like you and me will be bailing out the failed S&Ls until the system is restructured.

Some S&L directors were sentenced to prison for defrauding investors and mismanaging funds. The investigation of Charles Keating of Lincoln Savings and Loan led to the halls of the U.S. Senate. Five U.S. senators were cited for ethical violations in trying to aid Mr. Keating. As this text is being written, President and Mrs. Clinton are being investigated for their involvement with a failed savings and loan. It too lost millions of dollars during this period.

Banks and S&Ls made many home mortgage loans in the early 1990s at relatively low interest rates. By 1994, interest rates were once more on the rise. Could more S&Ls fail in coming years? Possibly. In other words, the banking crisis may not be over yet. One alternative place to put your money, if you qualify, is a credit union.

savings and loan associations (S&Ls)
Financial institutions that accept both savings and checking deposits and provide home mortgage loans.

Dino Raimondi of Adult Basic Learning Environment in Redlands, California, was looking for a way to offer his employees good, varied benefits. His answer was to join San Bernardino County Credit Union. He found that a credit union gave employees access to payroll deduction plans, low-interest loans, and savings programs. This can increase employee morale.

Deposits are usually backed by the National Credit Union Share Insurance Fund (NCUSIF). It's generally considered to be much stronger than the fund that

Checking Out Credit Unions

backs S&Ls and banks. Check to make sure that your local credit union belongs; some are privately insured. Credit unions differ from banks in that they aren't for profit, their members are their owners, and their board of directors is made up of volunteers. Because they're not-for-profit organizations, they can offer better rates on savings accounts and can lend money for less than other financial institutions.

Source: Molly Klimas, "Extra Credit," *Entrepreneur*, April 1994, pp. 158–62.

••• CREDIT UNIONS •••

credit unions

Nonprofit, member-owned financial cooperatives that offer basic banking services such as accepting deposits and making loans; they may also offer life insurance and a limited number of home mortgages.

Credit unions are nonprofit, member-owned financial cooperatives that offer basic banking services such as accepting deposits and making loans to their members. Typically, credit unions offer their members interest-bearing checking accounts (called *share draft accounts*) at relatively high rates, short-term loans at relatively low rates, financial counseling, life insurance policies, and a limited number of home mortgage loans. Credit unions may be thought of as financial cooperatives organized by government agencies, corporations, unions, or professional associations. As not-for-profit institutions, credit unions enjoy an exemption from federal income taxes. Nationwide, more than 14,500 credit unions serve over 65 million members. By the end of the decade, they hope to have over 100 million members.[3] The Entrepreneur box discusses small-business owners' use of credit unions.

••• OTHER FINANCIAL INSTITUTIONS •••

Nonbanks are financial organizations that accept no deposits but offer many of the services provided by regular banks. Nonbanks include life insurance companies, pension funds, brokerage firms, commercial finance companies, and corporate financial services. As competition between these organizations and banks increases, the dividing line between banks and nonbanks is becoming less and less apparent. The diversity of financial services and investment alternatives offered by nonbanks has caused banks to expand the services they offer.

You know that life insurance companies provide financial protection for policyholders who periodically pay premiums. In addition, they invest the funds they receive from policyholders in corporate and government bonds. In recent years, more insurance companies have begun to provide long-term financing for real estate development projects.

pension funds

Amounts of money designated by corporations, nonprofit organizations, or unions to cover part of the financial needs of members when they retire.

Pension funds are amounts of money put aside by corporations, nonprofit organizations, or unions to cover part of the financial needs of members when they retire. Contributions to pension funds are made either by employees alone or by both the employer and employees. A member may begin to collect a monthly draw on this fund upon reaching a certain retirement age. To generate additional income, pension funds typically invest in low-return but safe corporate stocks or in other conservative investments such as government securities and corporate bonds.

Many large pension funds such as the California Public Employees Retirement System (CalPERS) are becoming a major force in U.S. financial markets. Formidable rivals such as Teachers Insurance & Annuity Association (TIAA) lend money directly to corporations.

Brokerage firms have traditionally offered services related to investments in the various stock exchanges in this country and abroad. However, brokerage houses have made serious inroads into regular banks' domain by offering high-yield combination savings and checking accounts. In addition, brokerage firms offer checking privileges on accounts (money market accounts). Also, investors can get loans from their broker, using their securities as collateral.

Brokerage firms have enjoyed significant growth as more investors learn of the options they offer. But brokerage houses are aware that stock market performance is a sensitive issue to investors. They recall how interest fell off somewhat in the late 1980s because the stock market fell. Nonetheless, brokerages likely will present an increasingly strong challenge for regular banks and S&Ls—especially if banks and S&Ls cannot shed the image of being unreliable.

Commercial and consumer finance companies offer short-term loans to businesses or individuals who either can't meet the credit requirements of regular banks or else have exceeded their credit limit and need more funds. These finance companies' interest rates are higher than regular banks'. The primary customers of these companies are new businesses and individuals with no credit history. In fact, college students often turn to consumer finance companies for loans to pay for their education.

Corporate financial systems established at major corporations such as General Electric, Sears Roebuck, General Motors, and American Express offer considerable financial services to customers.

To compete with such nonbank organizations, banks have had to offer something extra—guaranteed savings. Way back in the 1930s, Congress decided to guarantee bank savings so people would feel secure keeping their money in banks and S&Ls. Those guarantees came back to haunt Congress when banks and S&Ls made risky loans in the 1980s with the thought that such loans were guaranteed by the government. There was no way the bankers could lose if the loans fell through; after all, deposits were guaranteed. The temptation to make risky loans became too great. Banks and S&Ls made many loans that failed. That led to the banking crisis we're still experiencing to some extent. In the next section, we'll explore the history of bank protection.

> **commercial and consumer finance companies**
> Institutions that offer short-term loans to businesses or individuals who either can't meet the credit requirements of regular banks or else have exceeded their credit limit and need more funds.

Do you keep your savings in a bank, an S&L, a credit union, or some combination? Have you compared the benefits you could receive from each? Why do these institutions offer different interest rates?

CRITICAL THINKING

- Why did the United States need a Federal Reserve Bank?
- What's the "discount rate"?
- What's the difference between a bank, a savings and loan association, and a credit union?
- What's a "nonbank"?

PROGRESS CHECK

PROTECTING YOUR FUNDS

The American economic system learned a valuable lesson from the depression of the 1930s. To avoid the chance of investors being completely wiped out during an economic downturn, several organizations evolved to protect your money. The three major sources of financial protection are the Federal Deposit Insurance Corporation (FDIC), the Savings Association Insurance Fund (SAIF) (originally called the Federal Savings and Loan Insurance Corporation or FSLIC), and the National Credit Union Administration (NCUA). All three insure deposits in individual accounts up to $100,000. In the early 1990s, the FDIC and the FSLIC were tested to their limits by S&L and commercial bank failures. Let's explore these organizations and the challenges they face.

... THE FEDERAL DEPOSIT INSURANCE ... CORPORATION (FDIC)

Federal Deposit Insurance Corporation (FDIC)
An independent U.S. government agency that insures bank deposits.

The **Federal Deposit Insurance Corporation (FDIC)** is an independent agency of the U.S. government that insures bank deposits. If a bank were to fail, the FDIC would arrange to have its accounts transferred to another bank or pay off depositors up to a certain amount. (This amount has increased over the years and is now $100,000 per account.) The FDIC covers about 13,000 institutions, mostly commercial banks.

••• THE SAVINGS ASSOCIATION INSURANCE FUND (SAIF) •••

Savings Association Insurance Fund (SAIF)
Part of the FDIC that insures holders of accounts in savings and loan associations.

The **Savings Association Insurance Fund (SAIF)** insures holders of accounts in savings and loan associations. It's now part of the FDIC. As just noted, it was originally called the Federal Savings and Loan Insurance Corporation (FSLIC) and was an independent agency. A brief history will show why the association was created.

Both the FDIC and the FSLIC were started during the Great Depression. The FDIC was begun in 1933, and the FSLIC in 1934. Some 1,700 bank and thrift institutions failed during the previous few years, and people were losing confidence in them. The FDIC and FSLIC were designed to create more confidence in banking institutions.

For some 50 years, the FSLIC and the FDIC were successful in covering losses from thrift and bank institution failures. During the 1980s, however, the thrift institutions of America began to fail. Losses in the banking and S&L industry were predicted to be in the range of $500 billion.

Many banks and S&Ls went out of business and their assets (largely real estate property they owned) were turned over to the government. Remember, the government (read you and me) was responsible for making sure that depositors got their money back. In 1989, the government created the Resolution Trust Corporation (RTC) to sell the real estate. The money from these sales went to pay back the money the government lost from the S&L crisis. In fact, the federal deficit was lower in 1994 as a result of these paybacks.

To get more control over the banking system in general, the government placed the FSLIC under the Federal Deposit Insurance Corporation (FDIC) and gave it a new name: The Savings Association Insurance Fund.

Making Ethical Decisions

How High Can You Go?

Imagine you're one of the new financial officers sent in by the Resolution Trust Corp. to help bail out an S&L that's in danger of going under. One cause of the S&L's trouble was its unsafe and unsound real estate acquisition practices. One of your attempts to save the S&L was to shut down its real estate development operations. This seemed like a logical move since their real estate investments were unsound. However, these investments were an important source of revenue.

It didn't take long to see that another problem was created by cutting off these revenues when interest payments came due each day on depositors' CDs. Your fellow managers suggest attracting new deposits by promising extremely high rates on CDs. Rather than invest these new deposits, they suggest using them to pay the interest on earlier deposits and redemptions of CDs as they come due. Since the government insures accounts up to $100,000 regardless of the soundness of the institution, this strategy seems plausible. What would be the consequences of such a plan? What ethical problems does this plan create? Would you agree to such a plan?

THE FUTURE OF BANKING

What will be the future of banks and savings and loans in the 21st century? The answer lies in the decisions made by the Federal Reserve and the U.S. Congress and in the overall strength of the U.S. and world economies. One thing is certain—the U.S. financial community and the U.S. economy are in a relatively weak state. Federal debt and personal debt keep rising, and the banking industry isn't prepared to handle another major crisis.

Another certainty is that banks as we've traditionally known them will change. Banks are readying themselves to sell everything from insurance to mutual funds when the law allows. Many changes are needed to further strengthen the banking system. You should know what's happening in banking today because the weakness of the banking system can weaken the whole economic system. More important, from your individual perspective, you could find yourself short of cash if the bank or S&L you use suddenly goes bankrupt or closes for a few months to reorganize. Remember, you should shop for the right institution to serve your financial needs just as you shop for the right supermarket, hair stylist, or college.

It's impossible to predict the future of an economy. The economy has changed from the time this text was written. You can see for yourself what has happened over the past few years. One thing's certain—U.S. financial institutions have been going through troubled times. We can learn as much from this lesson as we learned from the lessons of the 1930s. Mistakes can become strengths if the right decisions are made and financial institutions are restructured for the future. In the next section, we'll discuss recent trends in banking that may strengthen America's financial base.

••• INTERSTATE BANKING •••

From earlier chapters of this text, you've learned that businesses are reorganizing to become more efficient and effective. Many businesses have done this through a whole series of mergers and acquisitions creating larger businesses

The Success of 1st Business Bank

*M*ergermania appears to be the key banking buzzword of the 1990s. Can small banks possibly survive such mammoth competition? Yes. However, small banks will probably follow the lead of institutions such as Los Angeles's 1st Business Bank. With assets of only $566 million, 1st Business Bank is hardly a rival to Citicorp (with assets of over $200 billion). Nonetheless, 1st Business Bank has some of the best results in the banking industry. How does it manage to produce these results?

1st Business Bank could be called a *niche bank*. It built its niche by serving companies with annual sales between $3 million and $100 million, almost all of them privately owned. Its founders felt these companies weren't likely to receive costly personal service and attention from major banks that concentrate on bigger companies. 1st Business Bank provides its midsize customers with service bordering on the extreme. For example, the bank sends couriers to pick up customers' deposits rather than make customers come to the bank. In addition, account officers and clients meet at least every six months to analyze each customer's cash flow, working capital, leverage and debt servicing capability, and other important financial information.

1st Business Bank's chairperson likes to say, "We are collectors of fine companies." 1st Business Bank feels its niche will make it a $1 billion bank. In the near future, however, small banks like 1st Business will come up against tougher competition from interstate banks that are often more efficient. To remain competitive, smaller banks will have to continue offering better service to niche markets.

Source: John Taylor, "Niche Player: A Bank Need Not Be All Things to All People: Los Angeles' 1st Business Bank Is Thriving when Most Banks Are Suffering," *Forbes*, April 1, 1991; and Greg Wilson, "Interstate Banking—Now," *The Wall Street Journal*, March 16, 1994, editorial page.

that are more entrepreneurial in nature. That is, although the businesses are large, they give their individual units more freedom to be responsive to the market.

This trend is also occurring in banking. There are indications that a massive wave of bank mergers and buyouts will be necessary if the banking industry is to remain competitive. A bill approved by the House–Senate conference committee will enable all banks to cross state lines beginning in 1997. Eventually, this will enable you to obtain funds from an automatic banking system anywhere in the United States, if not the world.[4]

••• EXPANDING WHAT BANKS DO •••

State banks have taken the lead in giving banks freedom to go into other businesses through acquisitions. For many years, banks in Minnesota and North Carolina, for example, have been allowed to sell insurance. In states such as Massachusetts and New Jersey, banks can engage in brokerage and underwriting, aspects of the "big three" nonbanking businesses: insurance, securities (stocks and bonds), and real estate. Today, banks may provide services in all three areas in certain states. Federal banks will likely receive the same rights if present trends continue. One area of explosive potential growth is bank-sponsored mutual funds.

••• THE ELECTRONIC FUNDS TRANSFER SYSTEM (EFTS) •••

Today, the whole banking system is on the brink of a major revolution in its day-to-day operations. The way things are done today—depositing money, writing checks, protecting against bad checks, and so on—is expensive.

Imagine the cost to the bank of approving a check, processing it through the banking system, and mailing it back to you. Something has to be done to make the system more efficient.

One step in the past was to issue credit cards. Credit cards cut down on the flow of checks, but they too have their costs: There's still paper to process, and there's a chance for credit card fraud.

This is leading to a society in which exchanges of money are done electronically with no paperwork involved; the system is called an **electronic funds transfer system (EFTS)**. Many firms now give you a card much like a credit card. Retailers put that card into a slot in a cash register (which they call a *point-of-sale terminal*). When the sale is recorded, an electronic signal is sent to the bank, transferring funds from your account to the store's account automatically. No paperwork is involved. In fact, it's possible that someday you'll no longer receive a paycheck either. Rather, your employer will send the money electronically to the bank, and the bank will transfer funds from your employer's account to your account. You can see why it's called an *electronic funds transfer system*. This system's already in place for social security recipients.

Naturally, such a system would be too complex if there were many banks dealing with many employers and individuals. To make the system work, it's better to have a few large banks that operate most efficiently. As we've already noted, this trend is already occurring. These banks won't necessarily be located in expensive urban areas. Because most transactions will be done electronically, the banks can locate in inexpensive rural areas. All in all, the system will be much more efficient and will have many benefits for both banks and individuals. On the other hand, some consumers dislike electronic banking. They worry that electronic accounts aren't very private. They also could miss having paper evidence of having paid bills.

On the positive side, banks will have less of a burden from processing checks and managing credit card fraud and bad checks. Bank-at-home services enable you to transfer funds among accounts, make payments of various kinds (for example, utility bills and mortgage payments), and receive all kinds of information about your account. You can also buy and sell stock, get stock quotations, and more.[5] More and more banks are now offering online banking services so you can use your computer to do your banking. **Virtual banking** is the term used to describe interactive home banking where all contact is made electronically.[6]

electronic funds transfer system (EFTS)
A computerized system which electronically performs financial transactions such as making purchases, paying bills, and receiving paychecks.

virtual banking
Interactive home banking where all contact is made electronically.

- What's the difference between the FDIC and the SAIF?
- What are two major trends in banking today?
- Describe an electronic funds transfer system (EFTS). What are its benefits?

PROGRESS CHECK

INTERNATIONAL BANKING AND BANKING SERVICES

Banks help businesses conduct business in other countries by providing three services: letters of credit, banker's acceptances, and currency exchange. If a U.S. company wants to buy a product from Germany, the company could pay a bank to issue a letter of credit. A **letter of credit** is a promise by the bank to pay the seller a given amount if certain conditions are met. For example, the German company may not be paid until the goods have arrived at the U.S.

letter of credit
A promise by a bank that a given amount will be paid if certain conditions are met.

banker's acceptance
A promise that the bank will pay some specified amount at a particular time.

currency exchange
Exchange of currency from one country with currency from another country.

company's warehouse. A **banker's acceptance** promises that the bank will pay some specified amount at a particular time. No conditions are specified. Finally, a company can go to a bank and exchange American dollars for German marks; that's called **currency exchange**.

Banks are making it easier for you and other tourists to buy goods and services overseas as well. Automatic teller machines now provide pounds, francs, lira, marks, and other foreign currencies through your personal Visa, MasterCard, Cirrus, Plus, or American Express card. You can usually get a better exchange rate with an ATM than you can from your hotel or corner money exchange facility.[7]

••• LEADERS IN INTERNATIONAL BANKING •••

This chapter focused on banking within the United States. In the future, though, it's likely that many crucial financial issues will be international in scope. In today's financial environment, it's foolish to discuss the American economy apart from the world economy. If the Federal Reserve decides to lower interest rates, foreign investors can withdraw their money from the United States in minutes and put it in countries with higher rates. Of course, the Fed's increasing interest rates can draw money to the United States equally quickly.

Today's money markets form a global market system. The United States is just a part, although a major part, of that system. International bankers tend not to be nationalistic in their dealings. That is, they send money to those countries where they can get a maximum return for their money at a reasonable risk. For example, in the 1980s, U.S. bankers loaned billions of dollars to newly industrialized Third World countries to help them finance development of oil and other industries. But when demand for oil dropped, these countries couldn't repay their debts and many major U.S. banks lost billions of dollars. The same is true of banks in the former West Germany and other countries that made similar loans. Such risky loans can weaken the financial system of the world. Thus, the success of American business is directly tied to the success of businesses throughout the world, including Mexico. That's a major reason why President Clinton helped Mexico with its debt problems in 1995.

Today's international finance markets involve holdings of almost $3 trillion. Just $1 trillion could buy every manufacturing corporation in the United States as well as all the livestock, crops, buildings, and machinery of America's farms! Every year, these banks and nonfinancial corporations lend more than $300 billion to governments and nonfinancial corporations, including U.S. firms. That is, every year, international banks lend enough to purchase every new factory, railroad, port, ship, power plant, and other productive facility built in America that year plus all the machinery in them.

Who supervises all of these transactions in foreign countries? Nobody. The Federal Reserve is virtually powerless in these international markets except for regulating the actions of U.S. banks. The net result of international banking and finance has been to link the economies of the world into one interrelated system with no regulatory control.

American firms must compete for funds with firms all over the world. An efficient firm in London or Tokyo is more likely to get international financing than a less efficient firm in Detroit or Chicago. Of the world's top 30 banks, only 1 (Citicorp) is in the United States. The top 8 are all Japanese banks. In fact, Japan has 17 of the top 30 banks. France has 5 in the top 30, Germany and Britain each has 2, and China and the Netherlands each has 1.[8] Clearly, the United States doesn't dominate world banking.

Reaching Beyond Our Borders

BCCI, the Bank of Crooks and Criminals, International

Many in the banking world felt that the Bank of Credit & Commerce, International (BCCI), was a textbook example of what's wrong in international banking. The bank was fined for laundering drug money in Florida and was involved in a foreign exchange scandal in Kenya. Its customers included former Panamanian strongman Manuel Noriega and Colombian drug lords. Yet for almost 20 years, BCCI stayed one step ahead of the law. This financial reign of terror came to a crashing end in the early 1990s when bank regulators from the United States, Britain, and five other countries shut down BCCI. The estimated losses from BCCI's operations amounted to almost $5 billion, making it one of the world's biggest banking failures. How did all this happen, and what can be done to prevent future BCCIs from developing?

Most experts agree that the absence of any type of global regulatory agency permitted BCCI to remain untouchable. For example, the bank's registered home base was Luxembourg, but its managers worked from London. Its shareholders were wealthy Persian Gulf oil sheiks, and its assets were tangled in a branch network that included 70 different countries. Many operations were channeled through the Cayman Islands. The complexity of the bank prevented any banking authority from performing regulatory audits. Fraud, corruption, and money laundering became the order of the day. *Time* magazine called the bank "the largest corporate criminal enterprise ever."

BCCI's actions have caused many industrialized nations to consider tighter controls on international banks. The bank was so bad that it earned the name "The Bank of Crooks and Criminals, International." The U.S. Senate and Federal Reserve support global actions to control international banking activity. International banks will undergo more intensive scrutiny in the future to attempt to prevent another BCCI-type scandal.

Meanwhile, U.S. authorities were able to convince authorities in Abu Dhabi to free all records of BCCI files in return for dropping all criminal charges against Abu Dhabi officials. Furthermore, the Abu Dhabi government allowed the United States to keep some $400 million being held in the United States. As a consequence of these recent actions, we may eventually learn how such a scandal could go on so long without being detected.

Source: Mark Maremont, Blanca Riemer, Gail DeGeorge, Suzanne Woolley, and Catherine Yang, "The Long and Winding Road to BCCI's Dead End," *Business Week*, July 22, 1991, pp. 54–55; Jonathan Beaty and S. C. Gwynne, "The Dirtiest Bank of All," *Time*, July 29, 1991, pp. 42–47 and Mark Maremont, "BCCI: Justice May Finally Prevail," *Business Week*, January 31, 1994, p. 59.

What all this means to you is that banking is no longer a domestic issue; it's an international issue. To understand the U.S. financial system, you must learn about the global financial system. To understand America's economic condition, you'll have to learn about the economic condition of countries throughout the world. What has evolved, basically, is a world economy financed by international banks. The United States is just one player in the game. To be a winning player, America must stay financially secure and its businesses must stay competitive in world markets. That will be the challenge of the 1990s and beyond. You should read all you can about international business and take courses in it if possible. You won't be living and working in a U.S. economy in the 21st century; you'll be living in a world economy.

- What are the major functions of the Federal Reserve? What other functions does it perform?
- How is the Federal Reserve organized?
- How does the Federal Reserve control the money supply?
- What's the significance of international banking?

PROGRESS CHECK

SUMMARY

1. Explain what money is and the importance of the money supply to domestic and international exchange.

1. Money is anything that people generally accept as payment for goods and services.
   - *How is the value of money determined?*
   The value of money depends on the money supply; that is, how much money is available to buy goods and services. Too much money in circulation causes inflation. Too little money causes recession and unemployment.

2. Describe how the Federal Reserve controls the money supply.

2. Because the value of money is so important to the domestic economy and international trade, an organization was formed to control the money supply.
   - *What's that organization and how does it work?*
   The Federal Reserve makes financial institutions keep funds in the Federal Reserve System (reserve requirement), buys and sells government securities (open-market operations), and loans money to banks (the discount rate). To increase the money supply, the Fed would cut the reserve requirement, buy government bonds, and lower the discount rate.

3. Trace the history of banking and the Federal Reserve System.

3. There were no banks and coins were limited in the American colonies at first. The colonists traded goods for goods instead of using money.
   - *How did banking evolve in the United States?*
   Massachusetts issued its own paper money in 1690; other colonies followed suit. British land banks lent money to farmers but ended such loans by 1741. After the revolution, there was much debate about the role of banking, and there were heated battles between the Central Bank of the United States and state banks. The banking system was a mess by the time of the Civil War, with many banks issuing different kinds of currency. Eventually, a federally chartered and state-chartered system was established, but chaos continued until many banks failed in 1907. The system was revived by the Federal Reserve only to fail again during the Great Depression. The Fed, banks, and S&Ls were in the news during the 1990s because many banks and S&Ls failed and the Federal Reserve kept raising interest rates. These events greatly impacted the economy.

4. Describe the various institutions in the U.S. banking system.

4. Savings and loans, commercial banks, and credit unions are all part of the banking system.
   - *How do they differ from one another?*
   Before deregulation in 1980, commercial banks were unique in that they handled both deposits and checking accounts. At that time, savings and loans couldn't offer checking services; their main function was to encourage thrift and home ownership by offering high interest rates on savings accounts and providing home mortgages. Deregulation closed the gaps between banks and S&Ls so that they now offer similar services.
   - *What kinds of services do they offer?*
   Banks and thrifts offer such services as passbook savings accounts, NOW accounts, CDs, loans, individual retirement accounts (IRAs), safe deposit boxes, and traveler's checks.
   - *What is a credit union?*
   A credit union is a member-owned cooperative that operates much like a bank in that it takes deposits, allows you to write checks, and makes loans. It also may sell life insurance and make home loans. Because credit unions are member-owned cooperatives rather than profit-seeking businesses like banks, credit union interest rates are sometimes higher than those from banks, and loan rates are often lower.

• *What are some of the other financial institutions that make loans and do other banklike things?*

These nonbanks include life insurance companies that loan out their funds, pension funds that invest in stocks and bonds and make loans, brokerage firms that offer investment services, and commercial finance companies.

5. The government has created organizations to protect depositors from losses such as those experienced during the Great Depression.

• *What agencies ensure that the money you put into a bank, S&L, or credit union is safe?*

Money deposited in banks is insured by an independent government agency, the Federal Deposit Insurance Corporation (FDIC). Money in S&Ls is insured by another agency connected to the FDIC, the Savings Association Insurance Fund (SAIF). These organizations protect your savings up to $100,000 per account.

5. Explain the importance of the Federal Deposit Insurance Corporation and other organizations that guarantee funds.

6. There will be many changes in the banking system in coming years.

• *What are some major changes?*

One important change will be the advent of interstate banking. Another change will be more services offered by banking including insurance, securities (stocks, bonds, and mutual funds), and real estate sales. Electronic funds transfer systems will make it possible to buy goods and services with no money. Automatic teller machines enable you to get foreign currency whenever you want it in a foreign country.

6. Discuss the future of the banking system.

7. Today's money markets aren't nationalistic; they're global markets.

• *What do we mean by global markets?*

Global markets mean that banks don't necessarily keep their money in their own countries. They send it where they get the maximum return. International finance markets hold almost $3 trillion.

• *What does this mean to you?*

Since finance is now an international rather than a domestic issue, you should understand the global financial system as well as the U.S. financial system. You should learn about the economies of countries throughout the world since we're living in a world economy.

7. Explain the role and importance of international banking.

banker's
  acceptance 658
commercial and
  consumer finance
  companies 653
commercial bank 648
credit unions 652
currency 643
currency
  exchange 658
demand deposit 649
discount rate 646
electronic funds
  transfer system
  (EFTS) 657

falling dollar 644
Federal Deposit
  Insurance
  Corporation
  (FDIC) 654
letter of credit 657
M-1 643
M-2 643
money 642
money supply 643
nonbanks 648
open-market
  operations 645
pension funds 652

reserve
  requirement 645
rising dollar 644
savings and loan
  associations
  (S&Ls) 651
Savings Association
  Insurance Fund
  (SAIF) 654
stagflation 648
time deposit 649
virtual banking 657

KEY TERMS

DEVELOPING WORKPLACE SKILLS

1. Paper money is issued by 12 Federal Reserve district banks. Collect $1 bills issued by as many of these Fed banks as possible. Which district bank is responsible for issuing most of the bills you have seen? Can you explain why?

2. Examine the business section of your daily newspaper and look at the exchange rates table that lists the equivalent price of foreign currency in U.S. dollars. Note which foreign currencies are priced less than the U.S. dollar and which cost more. Choose one and list the reasons for the difference.

3. Visit a local financial institution and ask for their high-yield interest rates (time deposits). Do you think they provide a satisfactory return on investment (ROI)? What are the pros and cons of such an investment?

4. Would you recommend that the government stop guaranteeing deposits in banks and savings and loan corporations? What are the advantages and disadvantages of such a proposal? Is there a compromise you can formulate?

5. Research the trends in M-1 and other money measures in *The Wall Street Journal*. What are the trends? See if you can find articles linking money supply with economic conditions. Report what those articles say to the class and make a prediction about future economic growth given the money supply changes in the last six months.

PRACTICING MANAGEMENT DECISIONS

⟨⟨ CASE   LEARNING ABOUT THE FEDERAL RESERVE SYSTEM ⟩⟩

Unlike other cases in this text, the facts and figures for this case must be gathered by you. Consult *The Wall Street Journal* or other business publications to see how the Federal Reserve System is strengthening the economy. This is an important exercise because so few people know much about the Federal Reserve.

The Coalition for Monetary Education conducted a random survey of 2,000 people to see what they knew about the Federal Reserve and monetary policy in general. Only about 1 percent (some 20 out of 2,000) understood the monetary basics.

Over 75 percent of the respondents knew that the Federal Reserve Board controlled the money supply. But only 9 percent of those polled were aware that the Federal Reserve's policies influenced the inflation rate, and only 13 percent were aware that the Fed's policies affected interest rates.

Only 31 percent of the people knew that U.S. currency isn't redeemable in gold or silver. Less than 30 percent knew that bank failures were widespread. Reacting to these findings, the coalition planned a campaign to educate the public about the effect of federal policies on banking.

Decision Questions

1. How do the Federal Reserve's policies affect interest rates and the inflation rate? Why is it important for people to know that?

2. What action, if any, has the Federal Reserve taken in the past year to control the money supply and inflation? What are the results? (The answer to this question can be found in past issues of *The Wall Street Journal*.)

3. Go back to Chapter 2 and read about fiscal and monetary policy. Which seems to be having the greater effect on the U.S. economy today: monetary or fiscal policy? Why?

....

〉〉 VIDEO CASE   THE FEDERAL RESERVE SYSTEM 〉〉

The Federal Reserve Bank of Dallas is just one of 12 regional Federal Reserve Banks and 25 branch offices. The Federal Reserve System was created in 1913 to strengthen the banking system. The fundamental idea was to establish a central bank that could lend money to member banks when needed. The Federal Reserve was also made responsible for the nation's monetary policy. It is important to understand that the Federal Reserve (or Fed) is not a government agency; it is independent of the government. The head of the Federal Reserve is appointed by the president and confirmed by the Senate, but the decisions the Federal Reserve Board makes are independent.

Basically the Fed controls the nation's money supply and credit, it supervises state member banks and inspects bank holding companies, and it operates as a bank for financial institutions and the federal government. It makes money by collecting interest on government securities that it owns, by making loans to financial institutions, and by collecting fees for processing checks.

The primary goals of the Fed include a high level of employment, the assurance of economic growth, and the creation of stable prices. To do that, the Fed uses several strategies: (1) Reserve requirements: each member bank is required to hold some percentage of their deposits in the Fed. If the reserve requirement is raised, less money will be available to lend. (2) Open market operations: the Fed buys and sells bonds to the public. When it sells bonds, money is taken out of the economy and slows growth. When it buys bonds, money is put into the economy and promotes growth. (3) Interest rates: the Fed loans money to banks at what is called the discount rate. When rates go up, money is more expensive and slows the economy. When rates go down, money is less expensive and the economy picks up momentum.

The Federal Reserve Banks also act as automated clearing houses. That is, they electronically pay checks for businesses and the government. Eventually, such payments may replace checks entirely. You can buy Treasury bills, notes, and bonds from the Fed. Treasury bills come in denominations of $10,000 and can be purchased for 13, 26, and 52 weeks. Notes and bonds have longer maturities. When the economy is unstable, as it was in the early 1990s, Treasury bonds are a secure place to put your money.

Discussion Questions

1. During 1994 and early in 1995, the Federal Reserve System increased interest rates several times with the hope of slowing the economy and preventing inflation. What is the situation with regard to growth and inflation now? Given current economic conditions, what should the Federal Reserve do next?

2. What interest rate is the Federal Reserve paying at present for Treasury bills, notes, and bonds? Are the rates competitive with your local bank? With those paid by money market funds?

3. Is there a Federal Reserve branch near you? If so, plan to visit it and research the process for buying Treasury bonds.

CHAPTER 22

DEVELOPING AND MANAGING YOUR PERSONAL FINANCES

LEARNING GOALS

After you have read and studied this chapter, you should be able to

1. Describe how best to manage your assets.

2. Explain the best way to accumulate capital and begin investing.

3. Compare and contrast various types of life and health insurance alternatives.

4. Outline a strategy for retiring with enough money to last a lifetime.

EILLEN DORSEY AND WALTER HILL, JR., OF ECS TECHNOLOGIES

Eillen Dorsey and Walter Hill, Jr., are successful entrepreneurs today because early in life they learned the importance of personal financial planning. The youngest of eight children, Eillen was reared in Harford County, Maryland. Her parents taught her that if she dreamed long and hard enough and was committed to her dream, she could turn it into reality. But that meant saving her money for college and then for investment.

Eillen attended Catonsville and Essex Community Colleges. Both inside and outside of school, Eillen began building a network of people who worked in corporate America and in local government agencies. She developed a particularly strong relationship with Walter Hill, Jr., who had attended Morgan State University and the University of Maryland. Walter also knew the value of savings.

Using the money they saved, Eillen and Walter wanted to start a minority firm in the Baltimore, Maryland, area. They noted that almost every corporation producing machinery had to buy some type of electrical components. They also knew that many of those companies were interested in doing business with a minority firm, so they saw an opportunity to become entrepreneurs.

Eillen had been a salesperson for Technico, an electrical component company, and was familiar with firms that wanted electrical components. Walter was working at Westinghouse and also knew people in industry. They quit their respective companies to form ECS Technologies.

Each partner contributed $5,000 to get the business started. They secured a $35,000 loan by using their homes as equity. Their homes thus became an important investment vehicle as well. The partners had already won a contract before they applied for the loan, making it easier for the lender to make the loan. Because the partners had invested their own money and assets, the banks were willing to give them a line of credit totaling $200,000.

Minority entrepreneurs who've saved their money and invested in small firms, like Eillen and Walter, have had great success all across the United States. In Connecticut, Wiley Mullins is annually selling almost $2 million worth of Wiley's Healthy Southern Classics. In North Carolina, Larry Harris is selling some $3.5 million worth of Harris Electronics' seatbelt chimes and related goods. In Kansas, Cleo and Mitchell Littleton (father and son) are grossing some $1 million a year in the environmental clean-up business. In Dallas, Joyce Foreman owns Foreman Office Products. There are over 23,000 businesses owned by African-Americans in the Los-Angeles/Long Beach area alone. There are over 15,000 in Chicago. Many of them can tell a success story much like that of Eillen and Walter. Such success stories usually begin with personal financial planning for start-up money.

> *The essential first rule of money management: Spend less than you earn.*
>
> *Andrew Tobias*

THE NEED FOR PERSONAL FINANCIAL PLANNING

If you talk to entrepreneurs like Eillen Dorsey and Walter Hill, you'll learn that one of the hardest parts of entrepreneurship is raising the money you need to start and keep your business going. As you ponder the job prospects today, you'll see that the chance for finding an excellent job and then moving up through management is much less today than it was in the past. Many middle management jobs have been eliminated so there are many people competing for fewer and fewer management jobs. Even if you're relatively successful, you may find, as Dorsey and Hill did, that owning your own firm is more interesting and financially rewarding.

But it's not easy to become an entrepreneur. You have to start thinking and acting like an entrepreneur long before you start your own business. All of us can do that rather easily, however, by learning to manage our own careers and finances. The planning, budgeting, controlling, and self-disciplining needed to save money will prove invaluable as you start your own firm. Whether or not you intend to become an entrepreneur, it's wise to learn personal financial planning. There are about 1.3 million people in the United States who have a net worth of at least $1 million.[1] You could be one of them if you are successful in your career and learn to save and invest your money properly. (See the Entrepreneur box.) That's what this chapter is about—personal finance.

••• SIX STEPS IN LEARNING TO CONTROL YOUR ASSETS •••

The only way to accumulate enough money to start your own business or to make any other prudent investment, using your own wages as a base, is to *make more than you spend*! I know you may find it hard to save today, but saving money today isn't only possible, it's imperative if you want to accumulate enough money to start a business, save for retirement, or take great vacations. Here are six steps you can take today to get control of your finances:

STEP 1. TAKE AN INVENTORY OF YOUR FINANCIAL ASSETS. This means that you need to develop a balance sheet for yourself. Remember, a balance sheet is based on the formula:

$$\text{Assets} - \text{Liabilities} = \text{Equity}$$

You can develop your own balance sheet by listing assets on one side and liabilities (e.g., mortgage, credit card debt, and auto loans) on the other. Assets include anything you own: TV, VCR, computer, bicycle, car, jewelry, clothes, and so on.

If your liabilities exceed your assets, you aren't on the path to financial security. You need some discipline in your life. Since we're talking about accounting, let's talk again about an income statement. At the top of the statement is revenue. You subtract costs and expenses to get net income or profit. Have you done that for your own enterprise, You Incorporated? The easiest

William Jeffrey Thompson of Ada, Oklahoma, was chosen as the Small Business Administration's special award winner in 1994. While a sophomore in high school, Jeffrey invested some $2,000 he had earned delivering papers to start a small business. Seven years later, his company, Peripheral Outlet, Inc.—a distributor and reseller of Macintosh computer memory products—had 18 employees and sales of $12.5 million a year. Thompson went on to major in finance at the University of Oklahoma.

From Paper Boy to Entrepreneur

Thompson's story is just one more example of an entrepreneur who used his or her savings to start a small business. The point of this chapter is to show you ways to save and invest your money so that you can maximize your options and act quickly when an opportunity presents itself.

Source: Erskine Bowles, "And the Winner Is," *Entrepreneur*, July 1994, p. 228.

place to begin is to list all your sources of revenue: your job, your investments, and so on. You'll then know how much revenue you have each month and what your net worth is—an excellent start.

STEP 2. KEEP TRACK OF *ALL* YOUR EXPENSES. This is a rather tedious but necessary chore if you want to learn discipline. In other words, you have to write down every single penny you spend each day. Most people like to have a category called *miscellaneous* where they put expenditures for things like cafe lattes, but you won't believe how much you fritter away on "miscellaneous" items unless you keep a detailed record for at least a couple of months.

Young married couples often find themselves running out of money. In such circumstances, each person tends to blame the other for excessive spending. The only way to trace where the money goes is to keep track of every cent you spend. Actually, it can turn out to be an enjoyable task because it gives you such a feeling of control. Here's how to proceed: Carry a notepad with you wherever you go and record what you spend as you go through the day. Those pieces of paper are your journals. At the end of the week, record your journal entries into a record book. (Accountants call it a *ledger*.)

Develop certain categories (accounts) to make the task easier and more informative. For example, you can have a category called Food for all food from the grocery store and miscellaneous food you bought during the week. You might want to have a separate account for meals eaten away from home because you can dramatically cut such costs if you make your lunches at home. Other accounts could include entertainment, donations to charity, and gifts. You can develop your accounts based on what's most important to you or where you spend the most money.

By keeping such records, you'll know for sure where your money is going. In California, Mike Yorkey and his wife kept such records. They found that they spent $2,534 more than they earned in one year. By going over their income statement, they learned where their money was going and cut back on unneeded expenditures. As a result, they came out $1,141 ahead the next year.[2] That money could then be saved for anything they wanted, including buying a business, investing for their children's education, or planning for retirement.

Budgeting and saving are such important activities to a family that everyone should be involved. By keeping track of every dollar spent over a period of time, you can learn exactly where your money is going and then plan to budget it carefully. Detailed, accurate records are especially helpful when it comes time to pay taxes.

STEP 3. PREPARE A BUDGET. Once you know your financial condition and the sources of revenue and expenses, you're prepared to make a personal budget. The budget should be based on your financial goals (e.g., money to start a business, money for retirement). It's important to include large purchases you're likely to make (such as a car or new roof for the house). For such expenditures, it's smart to save so much each month in a separate account. Then when it comes time to make that purchase, you have the cash so you won't have to pay any finance charges. The idea is to spend less than you take in. When you do that, you'll see why the government has so much trouble balancing the budget. It's hard to cut back on expenses; nonetheless, it's critical to financial health—for you and the government alike.

Other items that are important in a household budget include life insurance, car insurance, and medical care costs. You'll learn that running a household's finances is similar to running a small business's. It takes the same careful record keeping (if only for taxes), the same budgeting process and forecasting, the same control procedures, and often (sadly) the same need to periodically borrow funds. Suddenly, concepts such as credit and interest rates become only too real. This is where some knowledge of finance, investments, and budgeting pays off.

STEP 4. PAY OFF YOUR DEBTS. The first thing to do with any extra money you have is to pay off your debts. Start with the debts that carry the highest interest rates. Credit card debt, for example, may be costing you 16 percent or more a year. Merely paying off such debts will set you on a path toward financial freedom. It's better to pay off such debts at 16 percent plus than to put the money in a bank earning only 5 percent or so.[3]

STEP 5. START A SAVINGS PLAN. The best way to save money is to pay yourself first. That is, take your paycheck, take out money for savings, and then plan what to do with the rest. We do that at our homes, and we take out some money for charity as well. It's much easier to write checks to charities at the end of the year when the money is already in an account. You can arrange with your bank or mutual fund to deduct a certain amount every month.

STEP 6. IF YOU HAVE TO BORROW MONEY, ONLY BORROW IT TO BUY ASSETS THAT HAVE THE POTENTIAL TO INCREASE IN VALUE, SUCH AS A HOUSE. Don't borrow for expenses; you'll only get into more debt that way.

If you can manage enough discipline to carry out all six of these steps, you'll not only have money for investment and retirement, you'll have developed the financial techniques needed to run a small business. At first you may find it hard to live within a budget. Nonetheless, the payoff is well worth the pain. Most marriage difficulties center around money, so you'll be not only more secure financially, but potentially more secure in your relationship as well.

One asset you're already accumulating is a college education. As the world moves toward an information economy, education will become a more and more important investment. One of the next college requirements may be a course in personal finance.[4]

••• EDUCATION—THE BEST INVESTMENT •••

Throughout history an investment in education has paid off regardless of the state of the economy or political ups and downs. Everyone knows the benefits of getting a graduate degree in business, but those benefits are usually stated in terms of money or position. For example, a college graduate will earn, on the average, about $1,421,000 in his or her lifetime. A high school graduate will earn only $609,000.[5]

Investing in an education in areas such as art, literature, philosophy, psychology, music, and logic pays off as well. We can live a richer, fuller, more enjoyable life when we fully appreciate music, drama, and knowledge for its own sake.

When planning for your financial future, it's wise to think of what you'll do when you become financially secure. Life is more than working and making money. An investment in education may expose you to other countries, other languages, new ideas, and different ways of life. If you invest in yourself, you'll be making the best investment of all.

Many people use their education to find successful careers in business and to improve their earning potential, but at retirement they have little to show for their efforts. Making money is one thing; saving, investing, and spending it wisely are something else. Less than 10 percent of the U.S. population has accumulated enough money by retirement age to live comfortably.

BUILDING YOUR CAPITAL ACCOUNT

The path to success in a capitalist system is to have capital (money) to invest, yet the trend today for young graduates is not only to be capital-poor, but to be in debt. As you've read, accumulating capital takes discipline and careful planning.

The principle is simple: To accumulate capital, you have to earn more than you spend. For a young couple, that process may be easier than you might expect. Let's assume that a couple gets married soon after college. What to do next?*

The first step for both husband and wife is to find employment. Both people will want to work for several years before having children. During those years, the couple should try to live, as much as possible, on just *one* income. The other income can then be used to generate more capital. It may be invested in a mutual fund or some other relatively safe investment. Part of it could be invested in more risky investments for rapid capital accumulation, including your own business.

Living on one income is extremely difficult for the average young married couple. Most couples are eager to spend their money on a new car, furniture, stereo, clothes, and the like. They tend to look for a fancy apartment with all the amenities. A capital-generating strategy may require forgoing most (not all) of these purchases to accumulate investment money. The living style

---

*We aren't pushing you to get married. In fact, it's not true that two can live as cheaply as one. Staying single is one way to accumulate capital, especially if you live at home for a few years after college.

FIGURE 22.1

HOW MUCH HOUSE CAN
YOU AFFORD?
Monthly mortgage pay-
ments—including inter-
est, principal, real estate
taxes, and insurance—
generally shouldn't
amount to more than 28
percent of monthly
income. Assuming that
principal and interest
equal 25 percent of
household income, and
taxes and insurance equal
3 percent, here's how
much people in various
income categories can
afford to pay for a home
if they use a 30-year
mortgage and make a 10
percent down payment.

| | INTEREST RATE | | | |
Income	7%	8%	9%	10%
$ 25,000	$104,167	$ 94,516	$ 86,180	$ 79,015
50,000	208,333	189,033	172,360	158,030
75,000	312,500	283,549	258,540	237,044
100,000	416,667	378,065	344,720	316,059

Source: National Association of Home Builders.

required is close to the one adopted by most college students: a relatively inexpensive apartment furnished in hand-me-downs from parents, friends, and
Goodwill. For five or six years, the couple can manage with the old stereo,
used cars, and a few nice clothes. The living style desired is one of sacrifice,
not luxury. It's important not to feel burdened by this plan; instead, feel happy
knowing that your financial future will be more secure.

After six years of living on one income, the savings can grow to about
$96,000 (after taxes) for a pair of college graduates (saving $16,000 per year).
What to do with the money? The first investment might be a moderately
priced home. This investment should be made as early as possible. The purpose of this investment is to lock in payments for your shelter at a given
amount. This is possible with ownership, but not by renting. Through the
years, home ownership has been a wise investment. Figure 22.1 will help you
decide how much house you can afford.

••• APPLYING THE STRATEGY •••

Some people have used the seed money from this strategy to buy duplex homes
(two attached homes). They live in one and rent the other. The rent covers a
good part of the payments for both homes, so they can be housed very cheaply
while their investment in a home appreciates. They learn that it's quite possible
to live comfortably, yet inexpensively, for several years. In this way they accumulate capital. As they grow older, they see that such a strategy has put them
years ahead of their peers in terms of financial security. They can eventually
sell their duplex home and buy a single-family home with the profits. The
money saved can also be invested in everything from stocks and bonds to precious metals, insurance, additional real estate, and higher education.

This strategy may seem too restrictive for you, but you still can apply the
principles. The idea is to generate capital to invest. After all, this is basically a
capitalist society, and in such a society you're lost without capital. A couple is
wise to plan their financial future with the same excitement and dedication as
they plan their lives together. Even a modest saving of $6,000 a year will allow a
couple to buy a small home in a few years and begin an investment program.
Remember, money that earns 12 percent annually doubles in just six years! (See
the rule of 72.) An annual investment of $6,000 for six years can grow with com-
pounding to a total of over $50,000—a healthy start for any couple.

••• REAL ESTATE: A SECURE INVESTMENT •••

One of the better investments a person can make is in his or her own home.
Homes may grow in value each year. (They have historically.) Home prices in
some areas declined during the late 1980s and early 1990s, but in most

regions of the country prices are now on the rise again. Homes provide several investment benefits. First of all, a home is the one investment that you can live in. Once you buy a home, the payments are relatively fixed (though taxes and utilities go up, as you'll see if you do buy). As your income rises, the house payments get easier and easier to make, but renters often find that rents tend to go up at least as fast as income.

Paying for a home is a good way of forcing yourself to save. Every month you must make the payments. Those payments are an investment that will prove very rewarding over time for most people. As mentioned earlier, an investment in a duplex or small apartment building is also an excellent strategy. As capital accumulates and values rise, an investor can sell and buy an even larger apartment complex. Many fortunes have been made in real estate in just such a manner. The two entrepreneurs in this chapter's profile also learned that a home is a good asset to use when applying for a loan.

Here are some figures to give you a feel for the role of real estate in today's investment programs: For all people under age 45, one half of their assets are in real estate, and only $3,000 on average is invested in securities (stocks and bonds). For those over age 45, only 39 percent of assets are in real estate, with $13,000 in securities.

••• TAX DEDUCTION AND HOME OWNERSHIP •••

Buying a home is likely to be the largest and most important investment you'll make. It's nice to know that the federal government is willing to help you with that investment. Here's how: Interest on your home mortgage payments is tax-deductible. So are your real estate taxes. During the first few years, almost all the mortgage payments go for interest on the loan so almost all the early payments are tax-deductible—a tremendous benefit for homeowners. If, for example, your payments are $1,000 a month and your joint income is in the 28 percent tax bracket, then during the early years of your mortgage Uncle Sam will, in effect, give you credit for about $280 of your payment, lowering your real cost to $720. This makes home ownership much more competitive with renting than it may appear on the surface. Home ownership is one of the few tax shelters left in the new tax bills.

Real estate people will tell you that there are three keys to getting the optimum return on a home: location, location, and location. A home in the "best part of town," near schools, shopping, and work, is the best financial investment. Most young couples tend to go further away from town where homes are less expensive, but such homes are likely to appreciate in value much more slowly. It's better, from a financial viewpoint, to buy a smaller home in a great location.

- What are the six steps you can take today to control your finances?
- What's called "the best investment"?
- What steps should a couple follow to develop capital?
- Why is real estate a good investment?

PROGRESS CHECK

LEARNING TO MANAGE CREDIT AND INSURANCE
•••••••

Known as *plastic* to young buyers, credit cards are no doubt familiar to you. Names like Visa, MasterCard, American Express, Discover, Diners Club, and Carte Blanche are well known to most people. In a credit card purchase,

Which credit card you get may make a big difference in how much interest you pay. Wachovia, for example, has a Prime for Life card that charges only the prime rate—now around 9 percent. However, the fee for a year is $88. You can get other cards for no annual fee, but they typically charge a much higher interest rate. If you always pay on time, they would actually be a better deal.

finance charges after the first 25 or 30 days usually amount to about 15 to 20 percent annually. This means if you finance a car, home appliances, and other purchases by plastic, you may pay much more than if you pay with cash. A good personal financial manager, like a good businessperson, pays on time and takes advantage of savings made possible by paying early. Those couples who've established a capital fund can tap that fund to make large purchases and pay the fund back (with interest if so desired) rather than pay a bank.

Credit cards are an important element in a personal financial system even if they're rarely used. First of all, many merchants demand credit cards as a form of identification. It's often difficult or impossible to buy certain goods or even rent a car without owning a credit card because businesses use them for identification.

Secondly, credit cards are a way to keep track of purchases. A gasoline credit card, for example, gives you records of purchases over time for income tax and financial planning purposes. It's sometimes easier to write one check at the end of the month for several purchases than to carry cash around. Besides, cash may be stolen or lost.

Finally, a credit card is simply more convenient. If you come upon a special sale and need more money than you usually carry, a credit card is a quick, easy way to pay. You can carry less cash and don't have to worry about keeping your checkbook balanced as often.

If you do use a credit card, pay the balance in full during the grace period. Not having to pay 16 percent is as good as earning 16 percent tax-free. Also, choose a card that pays you back in cash, like the Discover card, or in frequent flier miles. The value of these givebacks can be as high as 5 percent. Rather than pay 16 percent, you earn 5 percent—quite a difference.[6]

The danger of a credit card is the flip side of its convenience. Too often, consumers buy goods and services that they wouldn't normally buy if they had to pay cash or write a check on funds in the bank. Consumers often pile up debts using credit cards to the point where they're unable to pay. If you aren't

---

College Students Need Credit Education

Ruth Susswein, executive director of Bancard Holders of America, feels that there should be mandatory personal finance classes in schools. It was reported that 64 percent of all college undergraduates have at least one credit card. The danger is that students may use those cards for purchases that will put them into too much debt. According to Susswein, some students have charged up to $10,000 in clothes and have used their cards for ski trips to Switzerland.

It's extremely important for college students to learn how to use credit cards and to manage their personal finances. After all, they're building up a credit history that either will support them when they seek to borrow funds in the future or will be a major hindrance.

Source: Vivian Marino, "Personal Finance 101 May Be the Next College Requirement," *The Philadelphia Inquirer*, August 20, 1994, pp. D1 and D2.

the type who can stick to a financial plan or household budget, it may be better not to have a credit card at all. Credit cards are a helpful tool to the financially careful buyer. They're a financial disaster to people with little financial restraint and tastes beyond their income.

• • • BUYING LIFE INSURANCE • • •

One of the last things a young couple thinks about when they get married is the idea that one of them may get sick or have an accident and die. It's not a pleasant thought. Even more unpleasant, though, is the reality of young people dying every day in accidents and other unexpected ways. You have only to know one of these families to see the emotional and financial havoc such a loss causes.

Today, with so many husbands and wives both working, the loss of a spouse means a sudden drop in income. To protect each other from such devastation, a couple should invest in life insurance for both husband and wife. Both should be covered under one policy because it's cheaper that way.

Today, the preferred form of life insurance is called **term insurance.** Term insurance is pure insurance protection for a given number of years. Every few years, you must renew the policy, whose fee usually gets higher and higher. (See Figure 22.2.)

term insurance
Pure insurance protection for a given number of years.

A popular alternative in the past has been **whole life insurance** (a combination insurance plan and savings plan). The problem was that the savings portion simply wasn't competitive with the rates available in mutual funds and other investment alternatives.

whole life insurance
A combination insurance plan and savings plan.

Today, life insurance companies are becoming more aggressive in winning investment dollars. One new plan, **variable life insurance,** is a whole life policy whose benefits vary (thus the term *variable life*) based on the insurance company's success in investing those funds. The money is placed in a portfolio that usually includes some stock, bonds, real estate, and other investments.[7] With such a policy, the benefits are guaranteed not to go below a certain amount. However, if the portfolio of stocks, bonds, and other investments does well, the benefits will increase. Buying such a policy is a way to get insurance and have a diversified investment account for your family. It's also one more way that people like you and me have a vested interest in U.S. business. How much we get from insurance is tied to the success of the economy.

variable life insurance
A whole life policy whose benefits vary based upon the investment performance of the insurance company.

Another relatively new type of policy, **universal life insurance,** is a combination of term insurance and an accumulation fund, usually based mostly on debt instruments (bonds). Policy owners can switch funds to buy more insurance or more bonds. The interest rates earned are close to those in the market after an initial fund of $1,000 is accumulated.

universal life insurance
A combination of term insurance and an accumulation fund, usually based on bonds.

INSURANCE NEEDS IN EARLY YEARS ARE HIGH.	INSURANCE NEEDS DECLINE AS YOU GROW OLDER.
1. Children are young and need money for education.	1. Children are grown.
2. Mortgage is high relative to income.	2. Mortgage is low or completely paid off.
3. Often there are auto payments and other bills to pay.	3. Debts are paid off.
4. Loss of income would be disastrous.	4. Insurance needs are few.
	5. Retirement income is needed.

FIGURE 22.2

WHY BUY TERM INSURANCE?

adjustable life insurance
Insurance policy that allows policyholder to switch back and forth from whole life to term as one's needs change.

Even more creative policies are now coming on the market. They may give the policyholder the freedom to switch from whole life to term and back as life's circumstances change. This is called **adjustable life insurance**. Other policies combine features of variable life, universal life, and adjustable life policies. Such policies may be considered as part of a total life savings and insurance plan. If people have the discipline to do it, though, the best option is straight term insurance with the idea that additional funds will be invested each year. That will result in the largest overall return as long as the plan is followed.

CRITICAL THINKING

There are many career openings available in life insurance companies. The new policies are far superior to the old policies, and they should be easier to sell. Now that so many women are working, there's a growing need to sell additional insurance to professional women. Talk to people who sell these new policies. Are they enthusiastic? Would you enjoy such work? By now, you've probably gotten the idea that everyone you talk to is a potential source of information about careers. Right. Keep looking, and you'll find hundreds of interesting, challenging careers.

••• BUYING HEALTH INSURANCE •••

You're likely to have health insurance coverage through your employer. If not, you can buy insurance from a health insurance provider (for example, Blue Cross/Blue Shield) or a local health maintenance organization (HMO). Most people don't realize the benefit of having company-paid health insurance until they have to pay for the insurance on their own. The cost is quite high.

One choice you may have to make is between Blue Cross/Blue Shield coverage or an HMO. For a young couple, an HMO is often an attractive alternative since HMOs stress preventive health care. Emphasis is on checkups and the prevention of illness, although hospital care is also provided. Different plans have different policies regarding your freedom to select doctors and so on. Such a decision shouldn't be taken lightly. Talk to people who have had both options. Learn the advantages and disadvantages. Assess your family's needs, and then choose.

It's dangerous financially not to have any health insurance. Hospital costs are simply too high to risk financial ruin by going uninsured. In fact, it's often a good idea to supplement health insurance policies with more disability insurance that pays part of the cost of a long-term sickness or an accident. Your chances of becoming disabled at an early age are much higher than your chances of dying from an accident. Therefore, it's important to have the proper amount of disability insurance. (See your agent.) The cost is relatively low to protect yourself from losing your livelihood for an extended period.

••• BUYING OTHER INSURANCE •••

You should buy insurance for your car. Get a large deductible of $500 to keep the premiums low and cover small damage on your own. You'll also need liability insurance to protect yourself against being sued by someone accidentally injured by you. Often you can get a discount by buying all your insurance with one company. GEICO, for example, gives discounts for safe driving, getting good grades, and more.

PLANNING YOUR RETIREMENT

It may seem too early to begin planning your retirement, but not to do so would be a big mistake. Successful financial planning means long-range planning, and retirement is a critical phase of life. What you do now could make a world of difference in your quality of life after age 65.

••• SOCIAL SECURITY •••

Social security is the term used to describe the Old-Age, Survivors, and Disability Insurance Program established by the Social Security Act of 1935. There's no question that by the time you retire, there will have been significant changes in the social security system. The problem is that the system can't afford to pay out more than it takes in. The number of people retiring and living longer is increasing dramatically, though the number of workers paying into social security per retiree is declining. The result is likely to be (1) a bankrupt program, (2) serious cuts in benefits, likely to include a much later retirement age and reduced cost-of-living adjustments (COLAs), or (3) much higher social security taxes.[8] Don't count on social security to provide you with ample funds for retirement. Rather, you should plan now to save funds for your nonworking years. (See Figure 22.3.) Recognizing social security's potential downfall, the government has established incentives for you to save money now for retirement. Here are the specifics.

social security
Retirement benefits provided by the Social Security Act of 1935.

〉〉 FIGURE 22.3 〈〈

THE FATE OF YOUR SOCIAL SECURITY INVESTMENT
This chart shows that, at present rates, social security funds will run out in the year 2048. That is about 50 years from now. Much sooner than that, the outgo will exceed revenues. It's a good idea to begin your own retirement account to supplement social security. You're likely to live a long time after retirement and will need the money.

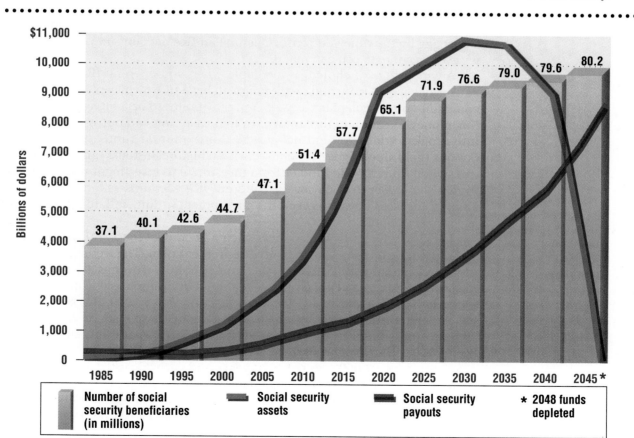

Source: Social Security Administration data.

DEDUCTIONS FOR PARTICIPANTS IN EMPLOYER-SPONSORED RETIREMENT PLANS This chart will tell you whether your initial contribution to an IRA is fully tax-deductible. It is if your adjusted gross income is under $40,000 and are married or under $25,000 and are unmarried. If your adjusted gross income is between $40,000 and $50,000 and you are married, you can still get a partial deduction. In all cases, however, the earnings are tax-deductible—and that's important to building a retirement account.

individual retirement account (IRA)
Tax-deferred retirement investment plan.

ADJUSTED GROSS INCOME	IRA TAX DEDUCTIBILITY
Under $40,000, married (under $25,000, unmarried)	Full tax deduction
$40,000–$50,000, married ($25,000–$35,000, unmarried)	Partial deduction, reduced proportionately
Over $50,000, married (over $35,000, unmarried)	Contributions not tax-deductible

••• INDIVIDUAL RETIREMENT ACCOUNTS (IRAS) •••

An **IRA (individual retirement account)** is a tax-deferred investment plan that enables you and your spouse to save part of your income for retirement. In effect, its a government-sponsored tax shelter. Neither the money you put into the fund nor its earnings are taxed until you take them out when you retire. At that time, your tax rate should be lower than it is during your work years.

IRA accounts are one of the most important tax breaks ever made for workers. Everyone who works is eligible, even part-time workers. This includes people who are already covered by company retirement plans. However, the initial contribution isn't tax free if you have a company retirement plan and make over $35,000 per year. (See Figure 22.4.)

The amount you can put into an IRA has increased through the years. Now the dollar amount is $2,000 per year. (Check the latest figures.) If you begin saving now, the money will compound over and over and become quite a nest egg by the time you retire. Opening an IRA account may be one of the wisest investments you can make.[9]

A wide range of choices is available when you open an IRA. Your local bank, savings and loan, and credit union all have IRA savings plans. Insurance companies offer such plans as well. You may prefer to be a bit aggressive with this money to earn a higher return. In that case, you can put your IRA funds into stocks, bonds, or mutual funds. Some mutual funds have multiple options (gold stocks, government securities, high-tech stocks, and more). You can switch from fund to fund or from investment to investment with your IRA funds. You can even open several different IRA accounts as long as the total amount invested doesn't exceed the government's limit. Talk to a broker and learn your options.

Let's see why an IRA account is such a good deal for a young investor if you don't have a company-sponsored retirement plan. The tremendous benefit is the fact that neither the invested money not the earnings are taxed. That means fast returns and good returns for you. For example, say you put $2,000 a year into an IRA. Normally, you'd pay taxes on that $2,000. But because you put the money into an IRA, you won't have to pay those taxes. If you're in the 28 percent tax bracket, that means you save $560 in taxes! Put another way, the $2,000 you save only costs you $1,440—a huge bargain.

If you save $2,000 a year for 20 years and earn 12 percent a year, you'll accumulate savings of over $160,000 in just 20 years and over $540,000 in 30 years. If you start when you are just out of school, you'll be a millionaire by the time you retire. All you have to do is save $2,000 a year and earn 12 percent. Can you see why investment advisors often say that an IRA account is the best way to invest in your retirement?

You can't take the money out until you are 59 years old without paying a 10 percent penalty and paying taxes on the income. That's really a benefit for you, because it's less tempting to tap the fund when an emergency comes up or you see the car of your dreams. On the other hand, the money is there if a real emergency arises.

When you make financial plans, be sure to explore an IRA. It's a sure path to being a millionaire some day and to having the funds available to further enjoy your retirement years. You might consider contributing to an IRA through payroll deductions to ensure the money's invested before you're tempted to spend it.

••• 401(k) PLANS •••

Many companies now offer **401(k) retirement plans** that have three benefits: (1) The money you put in reduces your present taxable income, (2) tax is deferred on the earnings, and (3) employers often match part of your deposit—50 cents or more for every dollar deposited. You should deposit at least as much as your employer matches, often up to 6 percent of your salary up to $9,240. You normally can't withdraw funds from this account until you're 59, but often you can borrow from the account. Check with your employer about the plan at your organization. The amount of assets in such plans has more than doubled to $475 billion since 1988, proving this savings technique's popularity.

You can usually select how the money in a 401(k) plan is invested: stocks, bonds, and, in some cases, real estate. Again, plans vary, so check with your employer. But financial advisors will tell you that 401(k) plans are a wonderful investment. If the policy is held until death, no income taxes will ever be due on the investment gains that have built up in the policy.

••• KEOGH PLANS •••

Millions of small-business people don't have the benefit of a corporate retirement system. Such people can contribute to an IRA account, but the amount they can invest is limited. The alternative for all those doctors, lawyers, real estate salespeople, artists, writers, small-business people, and other self-employed people is to establish their own **Keogh plan.** It's like an IRA for entrepreneurs. (Also check into IRA–SEP plans.)

The advantage of Keogh plans is that the maximum that can be invested is more than $30,000 per year. (The limit was $30,000 in 1984, and cost of living adjustments are added from 1986 on.) The original amount was much lower, but the government wanted to encourage self-employed people to build retirement funds. Both IRA and Keogh plans could be considered backup plans to protect people against the likely declines in the value of the social security system. Even without any cuts, social security simply won't provide enough for a comfortable retirement.

IRA savings accounts are free from taxes until you cash them in. A no-load equity fund means that you don't have to pay a salesperson's commission when you buy into one. You can pick up the phone, dial an 800 number, and choose from several different types of funds, bonds, CDs, and more. This ad for Fidelity is typical of those you will find in the various media for most types of investments.

401(k) retirement plan
Retirement plan that reduces your present taxable income, defers tax on your earnings, and allows employers to match part of your deposit.

Keogh plan
Retirement plan for self-employed people that allows the investment of more than $30,000 per year. Keogh funds and their returns are not taxed.

Like IRA accounts, Keogh funds aren't taxed, nor are the returns the funds earn. Thus, a person in the 28 percent tax bracket who invests $10,000 yearly in a Keogh saves $2,800 in taxes. That means, in essence, that the government is financing 28 percent of his or her retirement fund. As with an IRA, this is an excellent deal.

If a person were to put the full $30,000 a year into a Keogh plan that earns 10 percent a year, he or she would have over $5 million in the account after 30 years.

As with an IRA account, there's a 10 percent penalty for early withdrawal. Also like an IRA, funds may be withdrawn in a lump sum or spread out over the years. However, the key decision is the one you make now—to begin early to put funds into an IRA or Keogh plan (or both), so that the magic of compounding can turn that money into a sizable retirement fund.

Financial planning becomes more complex as you begin to create an investment strategy and portfolio. A certified financial planner (CFP) has the professional expertise you often need when making such decisions. This ad, sponsored by the Institute of Certified Financial Planners, emphasizes their professionalism and qualifications.

••• FINANCIAL PLANNERS •••

If the idea of developing a comprehensive financial plan for your family seems overwhelming, relax; help's available. The people who assist families in developing a comprehensive program that covers investments, taxes, insurance, and other financial matters are called *financial planners*. Be careful, though; everybody and his brother or sister are claiming to be financial planners today. Many are simply life insurance salespeople or mutual fund salespeople who call themselves financial planners.

In the past few years, there has been an explosion in the number of companies offering financial services. Such companies are sometimes called *one-stop financial centers* or *financial supermarkets* because they provide a variety of financial services ranging from banking service to mutual funds, insurance, tax assistance, stocks, bonds, and real estate. It pays to shop around for financial advice. You can go to an independent financial planner or a financial service company. In either case, ask around among your friends and family. Find someone who understands your situation and is willing to spend some time with you.

Most financial planners begin with life insurance. They feel that most people should have basic term insurance coverage. They also explore your health insurance plans. They look for both medical expense and disability coverage. They may also recommend major medical protection to cover catastrophic illnesses.

Financial planning covers all aspects of investing, all the way to retirement and death. (Planning for estate taxes is important early in life.) Financial planners can steer you into the proper mix of IRA investments, stocks, bonds, precious metals (for example, gold), real estate, and so on.

If all of this sounds interesting to you, maybe you'd enjoy a career as a financial planner. You could work independently and be a real asset to young people in need of counsel and advice. Find a financial planner in your area. Discuss what financial planners do and what recommendations they're now making for a person in your position. This fascinating field could be a rewarding career.

- What are three advantages of using a credit card?
- What are the advantages of term insurance over any other kind?
- What are the advantages of investing through an IRA account? A Keogh account? A 401(k) account?

PROGRESS CHECK

1. There are six steps you can take today to get control of your finances.
   - ***What are the six steps to managing personal assets?***
   (1) Take an inventory of your financial assets. That means that you need to develop a balance sheet for yourself: assets minus liabilities equals equity. (2) Keep track of *all* your expenses. (3) Prepare a budget. (4) Pay off your debts. (5) Start a savings plan. The best way to save money is to pay yourself first. That is, take your paycheck, take out money for savings, and then plan what to do with the rest. (6) If you have to borrow money, only borrow it to buy assets that have the potential to increase in value, such as a house.

SUMMARY

1. Describe how best to manage your assets.

2. To accumulate capital, you must earn more than you spend.
   - ***How can a person accumulate enough capital to become financially secure?***
   Let's use a young married couple as an example. The first step, after marriage, is to find jobs for both husband and wife. Both will want to work for several years before having children. During those years, they should try to live, as much as possible, on just one income. The other income can then be used to generate more capital. They can live frugally for five or six years, investing the money they save wisely; real estate is a great start.

2. Explain the best way to accumulate capital and begin investing.

3. Term insurance is pure insurance protection for a given number of years.
   - ***Why is term insurance preferred?***
   You can buy much more term insurance than whole life insurance for the same amount of money. If you want a savings plan, you can do much better on your own than most insurance plans.
   - ***Do I need other insurance?***
   It's important to have health insurance to protect against large losses. You also need car insurance (get a large deductible—$500 or so) and liability insurance in case you injure someone.

3. Compare and contrast various types of life and health insurance alternatives.

4. It may seem too early to begin planning your retirement, but not to do so would be a big mistake. Successful financial planning means long-range planning, and retirement is a critical phase of life.
   - ***What are some investment tips for staying financially secure for a lifetime?***
   Supplement social security with savings plans of your own. Everyone should have an IRA plan to begin with. Let the government pay for some of your retirement savings. All tax-free savings are good. That's why a Keogh plan or an IRA–SEP is wise. An IRA–SEP is a savings plan for entrepreneurs. If you work for someone else, check out the 401(k) plan.

4. Outline a strategy for retiring with enough money to last a lifetime.

adjustable life insurance 676
401(k) retirement plan 679
IRA (individual retirement account) 678

Keogh plan 679
social security 677
term insurance 675
universal life insurance 675

variable life insurance 675
whole life insurance 675

KEY TERMS

1. Few things are more surprising to a new college graduate than the cost of living, single or married, in an apartment. To prevent such surprises, research and calculate these costs now and share them with the class. Be sure to include rent, utilities, food, clothes, health care, insurance (life, auto, disability), auto expenses, vacation, charity, recreation, furniture, and depreciation (auto). Then discuss the concept of living on one income, given these figures.

2. Talk with your parents or others you know who have invested in a family home. What appreciation have they gained on the purchase price? What other benefits has the home brought? Compose a list of the benefits and drawbacks of owning a home and real estate in general as an investment.

3. For one month keep a record of every expenditure you make. Based on the results, share what you learn with your class. Use a computer spreadsheet or personal finance software to establish an annual budget.

4. Debate the following statement: "The best investment one can make is in education, including education in the arts, literature, music, and dance." Take the side you do not now believe to see how others think.

5. Are you familiar with all of the options available on various credit cards? If not, call several companies to find the best deal. Create a chart that compares the various options. Be sure to include annual fees and interest rates.

· ·

PRACTICING MANAGEMENT DECISIONS

〉〉 CASE   BECOMING FINANCIALLY SECURE 〉〉

Mike and Priscilla Thomas are a married couple with two incomes and no children. Their cars are both paid for. They've saved enough money to buy a new house without selling their old one. (Real estate is typically a sound investment.) They're renting out their town house for added income. They hope to buy more rental property to use as income producers so that they can both retire at age 50!

Priscilla runs a company called Cost Reduction Services and Associates. It advises small firms on ways to cut overhead expenses. The couple also owned a window-washing business when they were in college. She loves being in business for herself because "When you own your own business, you can work hard and you get paid for your hard work." Mike is a pharmaceutical salesperson.

How did the Thomases get the money to start their own businesses and buy a couple of homes? They committed themselves from the beginning of their marriage to live on Mike's income and to save her income. Furthermore, they decided to be frugal on spending. The goal of early retirement was their incentive. They "lived like college kids" for five years, cutting out coupons and saving every cent they could. They don't go out to eat much and they rent movies for their VCR. Their first investment was a town house. They followed the advice of "buy the most house you can afford." They used the tax deductions to help offset their income.

Mike puts 13 percent of his salary (the maximum) into his company's 401(k) plan. It's invested in a very aggressive growth fund: half U.S. stocks and half international stocks.

Now that the couple is financially secure, they're planning to have children.

Decision Questions

1. What steps would the average young couple have to follow to be like Mike and Priscilla and become financially secure all their lives?

2. What kind of goals could you establish to make it worthwhile to scrimp and save your money rather than spend it on today's pleasures?

3. How much money would one person have to earn to support two people living in an apartment in your area?

4. Can you see now why money management is one of the keys to both entrepreneurship and personal financial security?

Source: Jerry Knight, "Mike and Priscilla's DINK Adventure," *Washington Post*, July 24, 1994, p. H5.

••

VIDEO CASE   EMPLOYEE SAVINGS PLANS—WORKING WITH BROKERS

You may feel uncertain when it comes to planning your financial future, but you aren't alone. Even large firms like Mobil Oil need help when it comes to financial planning. At one time, Mobil ran its own savings plan for employees, but it recently outsourced the plan to Merrill Lynch. You too can turn to a brokerage firm to help you manage your investments. On the other hand, helping others plan their investments may look like an interesting career possibility.

By working with a broker like Merrill Lynch, the employees at Mobil found more investment flexibility, additional choices, automated transactions (24 hours a day, 7 days a week), and better investment information. They can make fund transfers and withdrawals, apply for loans, check savings rate changes, change the direction of their savings plans, and even customize their PIN numbers (private investment number). All of this is done with the utmost of privacy because the broker handling your account deals with numbers and doesn't have to know your name.

Merrill Lynch handles some $510 billion in investments for Mobil and other big corporate accounts as well as smaller accounts for individual investors. After observing what such account people do, you may be interested in being a broker yourself or working for a brokerage firm on corporate accounts.

Merrill Lynch, like most brokerage firms, has several funds where you can invest your money. There are a number of stock funds, including an international fund, that feature investments in different types of companies and industries (e.g., technology). They also manage a group of bond funds. Managing your money in such an account makes it possible to accumulate the funds required to invest in or purchase your own business, buy a home, plan your retirement, and make other financial plans.

Discussion Questions

1. How appealing does a career in a firm like Merrill Lynch seem to you? What do you find attractive or unattractive about such a career?

2. When you see employees at Mobil and other major firms carefully planning their financial futures, does it motivate you to begin such planning yourself? Why?

3. When you see how easy it is to deal with brokers—by simply picking up a phone and giving them the necessary information—does it encourage you to invest your money in such an account? Why?

4. When you are starting a career, the idea of saving for the future may seem less important. What are the primary benefits of consulting with a financial planning professional early in your career?

APPENDIX

MANAGING RISK

THE INCREASING CHALLENGE OF RISK MANAGEMENT

The management of risk is a major issue for businesses throughout the country. Every day you hear about an earthquake, flood, fire, airplane crash, riot, or truck accident that destroyed property or injured someone. Such reports are so much a part of the news that we tend to accept these events as part of everyday life (the 1992 Los Angeles riots alone cost insurers $775 million).

Such events mean much more to the businesspeople involved. They must pay to restore the property and compensate those who are injured. In addition to the newsmaking stories, thousands of other incidents might involve businesspeople in lawsuits. They include everything from job-related accidents to people being injured from using a business's products.

MANAGING RISK

The term **risk** refers to the chance of loss, the degree of probability of loss, and the amount of possible loss. There are two different kinds of risk:

- **Speculative risk** involves a chance of either profit or loss. It includes the chance a firm takes to make extra money by buying new machinery, acquiring more inventory, and making other decisions in which the probability of loss may be relatively low and the amount of loss is known. An entrepreneur takes speculative risk on the chance of making a profit. In business, building a new plant is a speculative risk because it may result in a loss or a profit.

- **Pure risk** is the threat of loss with no chance for profit. Pure risk involves the threat of fire, accident, or loss. If such events occur, a company loses money; but if the events do not occur, the company gains nothing.

The risk that is of most concern to businesspeople is pure risk. Pure risk threatens the very existence of some firms. Once such risks are identified, firms have several options:

1. Reduce the risk.
2. Avoid the risk.
3. Self-insure against the risk.
4. Buy insurance against the risk.

risk
The chance of loss, the degree of probability of loss, and the amount of possible loss.

speculative risk
A type of risk that involves a chance of either profit or loss.

pure risk
The threat of loss with no chance for profit.

We will discuss the option of buying insurance in detail later in this appendix. In the next sections, we will discuss each of the alternatives for managing risk. These are the steps that should be taken first in order to lower the need for outside insurance.

••• REDUCING RISK •••

A firm can reduce risk by establishing loss-prevention programs such as fire drills, health education, safety inspections, equipment maintenance, accident prevention programs, and so on. Many retail stores, for example, have mirrors, video cameras, and other devices to spot and prevent shoplifting. Water sprinklers and smoke detectors are used to minimize fire loss. In industry, most machines have safety devices to protect workers' fingers, eyes, and so on. Employees, as well as managers, can reduce risk. For example, truck drivers can wear seat belts to minimize injuries from accidents, and operators of loud machinery can wear earplugs to reduce the chance of hearing loss.

The key, therefore, to an effective risk management strategy is a good loss-prevention program. However, high insurance rates have forced some people to go beyond merely preventing risks to the point of avoiding risks—and in extreme cases by going out of business.

••• AVOIDING RISK •••

Many risks cannot be avoided. There is always the chance of fire, theft, accident, or injury. On the other hand, some companies are avoiding risk by not accepting hazardous jobs and by outsourcing shipping and other functions. The threat of lawsuits has driven away some drug companies from manufacturing vaccines, and some consulting engineers refuse to work on hazardous sites. Some companies are losing outside members of their boards of directors for lack of liability coverage protecting them from legal action against the firms they represent.

••• SELF-INSURING •••

self-insurance
Putting funds away to cover routine claims rather than buying insurance to cover them.

Many companies and municipalities have turned to **self-insurance** because they either can't find or can't afford conventional property/casualty policies. Such firms set aside money to cover routine claims and buy only "catastrophe" policies to cover big losses. In other words, they lower the cost of insurance by paying for smaller losses and then taking out insurance for larger losses.

Self-insurance is most appropriate when a firm has several widely distributed facilities. The risk from fire, theft, or other catastrophe is then more manageable. Firms with huge facilities, in which a major fire or earthquake could destroy the entire operation, usually turn to insurance companies to cover the risk.

One of the more risky strategies for self-insurance is for a company to "go bare," paying claims straight out of its budget. The risk here is that the whole firm could go bankrupt over one claim, if the damages are high enough. A less risky alternative is the forming of "risk retention groups"—insurance pools that share similar risks. It is estimated that about one third of the insurance market is using such alternatives.

••• BUYING INSURANCE TO COVER RISK •••

Although well-designed, consistently enforced risk-prevention programs reduce the probability of claims, accidents do happen. Insurance is the armor individuals, businesses, and nonprofit organizations use to protect themselves from various financial risks. For this protection such organizations spend about 10 percent of GDP on insurance premiums. We will continue our discussion of insurance by identifying the types of risks that are uninsurable, followed by those that are.

WHAT RISKS ARE UNINSURABLE?   One thing all organizations learned from the insurance crisis is that not all risks are insurable, even risks that once were covered by insurance. An **uninsurable risk** is one that no insurance company will cover. Examples of things that you cannot insure include *market risks* (e.g., losses that occur because of price changes, style changes, or new products that make your product obsolete); *political risks* (e.g., losses from war or government restrictions on trade); some *personal risks* (such as loss of a job); and some *risks of operation* (e.g., strikes or inefficient machinery).

WHAT RISKS ARE INSURABLE?   An **insurable risk** is one that the typical insurance company will cover. Generally, insurance companies use the following guidelines when evaluating whether or not a risk is insurable:

1. The policyholder must have an **insurable interest**. You cannot, for example, buy fire insurance on your neighbor's house and collect if it burns down.
2. The loss should be measurable.
3. The chance of loss should be measurable.
4. The loss should be accidental.
5. The risk should be dispersed; that is, spread among different geographical areas so that a flood or other natural disaster in one area would not bankrupt the company.
6. The insurance company can set standards for accepting risks.

THE LAW OF LARGE NUMBERS

An **insurance policy** is a written contract between the insured (an individual or organization) and an insurance company that promises to pay for all or part of a loss. A **premium** is the cost of the policy coverage to the insured or the fee charged by the insurance company.

As in all private businesses, the objective of an insurance company is to make a profit. To assure that it makes a profit, an insurance company gathers data to determine the extent of the risk. What makes the acceptance of risk possible for insurance companies is the law of large numbers.

There is much difference among insurance companies, but the policies are so complex that one has difficulty choosing the best plan. A good insurance agent can help you find the best policy for your needs. Ads like this one also help you narrow your choices.

uninsurable risk
Risk that a typical insurance company will not cover.

insurable risk
Risk that a typical insurance company will cover.

insurable interest
Possibility of policyholder to suffer a loss.

insurance policy
A written contract between the insured and an insurance company that promises to pay for all or part of a loss.

premium
The fee charged by an insurance company for an insurance policy.

law of large numbers
Principle which states that if a large number of people or organizations are exposed to the same risk, a predictable number of losses will occur.

The **law of large numbers** states that if a large number of people or organizations are exposed to the same risk, a predictable number of losses will occur during a given period of time. Once the insurance company calculates these figures, it can determine the appropriate premiums. The premium is supposed to be high enough to cover expected losses and yet earn a profit for the firm and its stockholders. Today, many insurance companies are charging high premiums, not for past risks, but for the anticipated costs associated with more court cases and higher damage awards.

RULE OF INDEMNITY

rule of indemnity
Insurance restriction which states that an insured person or organization cannot collect more than the actual loss from an insurable risk.

The **rule of indemnity** says that an insured person or organization cannot collect more than the actual loss from an insurable risk. One cannot gain from risk management; one can only minimize losses. One cannot, for example, buy two insurance policies and collect from both for the same loss. If a company or person carried two policies, the two insurance companies would calculate any loss and divide the reimbursement.

SOURCES OF INSURANCE

stock insurance company
Insurance company owned by stockholders, just like any other investor-owned company.

mutual insurance company
Insurance firm owned by its policyholders.

There are two major types of insurance companies. A **stock insurance company** is owned by stockholders, just like any other investor-owned company. A **mutual insurance company** is owned by its policyholders. The largest life insurance company, Prudential, is a mutual insurance company. A mutual insurance company, unlike a stock company, does not earn profits for its owners. It is a not-for-profit organization, and any excess funds (over losses, expenses, and growth costs) go to the policyholder/investor in the form of dividends or premium reductions.

TYPES OF INSURANCE

property losses
Losses resulting from fires, accidents, theft, or other perils.

liability losses
Losses resulting from property damage or injuries suffered by others for which the policyholder is held responsible.

As we have discussed, risk management consists of reducing risk, avoiding risk, self-insuring, and buying insurance. There are many types of insurance that cover various losses: property and liability insurance, health insurance, and life insurance. **Property losses** result from fires, accidents, theft, or other perils. **Liability losses** result from property damage or injuries suffered by others for which the policyholder is held responsible. Insurance coverage is available from public sources (state or federal government agencies) or private companies (stock companies or mutual companies). Figure A.1 outlines the various types of public insurance and what each normally covers.

HEALTH INSURANCE

Business and nonprofit organizations may offer their employees an array of health care benefits to choose from. Everything from hospitalization to physician fees, eye exams, dental exams, and prescriptions can be covered. Often,

Type of Insurance	What It Does
Workers' Compensation	Provides compensation for workers injured on the job. Includes payment of wages, medical care, job placement, and vocational rehabilitation.
Unemployment Compensation	Provides financial benefits, job counseling, and placement services for unemployed workers.
Social Security	Provides retirement benefits, life insurance, health insurance, and disability income insurance.
Federal Housing Administration (FHA)	Provides mortgage insurance to lenders to protect against default by home buyers.
National Flood Insurance Association	Provides compensation for damage caused by flooding and mud slides to properties located in flood-prone areas.
Federal Crime Insurance	Provides insurance to property owners in high crime areas.
Federal Crop Insurance	Provides compensation for damaged crops.
Pension Benefit Guaranty Corporation	Insures pension plans to prevent loss to employees if the company declares bankruptcy or goes out of business.

employees may choose between options from health care providers (for example, Blue Cross/Blue Shield); **health maintenance organizations (HMOs),** which require employees to choose from a restricted list of doctors and hospitals; or **preferred provider organizations (PPOs),** which are like HMOs but allow employees to choose their own physicians. Figure A.2 includes the various types of health insurance.

••• THE HEALTH INSURANCE CRISIS •••

The crisis in health insurance is that some 37 million Americans do not have any health insurance. The cost of the U.S. health care system is extremely high by world standards and is rising dramatically. Proposed solutions include mandatory care programs, a single comprehensive plan, and government assistance in buying individual insurance.

Under a mandatory care program, all companies would have to insure their employees or contribute to a federal fund that would cover the uninsured. People have called this a "play or pay" system. Small businesses object to this solution because the cost to them would be too high. Such a system could eventually lead to national health insurance. That is what some lawmakers proposed, but failed to pass through Congress in 1994.

The second proposal is to replace the current patchwork system with a single comprehensive plan, financed by the taxpayers. A national health insurance plan modeled after Canada's plan may save the United States some $75 billion. Much of the savings would come from reducing the paperwork from 1,500 insurance companies using a variety of forms. However, Canada's health insurance program has its problems; for example, people often have to wait long periods for elective as well as some other forms of nonemergency surgery.

The third proposal would be for consumers to buy their own insurance, with the government assisting those who cannot afford it. Whichever plan is ultimately adopted, it will doubtlessly alienate one or more influential interest groups, such as insurance companies, doctors, patients, or drug companies.

⦃ FIGURE A.1 ⦄

PUBLIC INSURANCE
State or federal government agencies that provide insurance protection.

health maintenance organizations (HMOs)
Health care organizations that require policyholders to choose from a restricted list of doctors and hospitals.

preferred provider organizations (PPOs)
Health care organizations similar to HMOs, but that allow policyholders to choose their own physicians.

Types of Insurance	What It Does
Property and Liability	
Fire	Covers losses to buildings and their contents from fire.
Automobile	Covers property damage, bodily injury, collision, fire, theft, vandalism, and other related vehicle losses.
Homeowners'	Covers the home, other structures on the premises, home contents, expenses if forced from the home because of an insured peril, third-party liability, and medical payments to others.
Computer Coverage	Covers loss of equipment from fire, theft, and sometimes spills, power surges, and accidents.
Professional Liability	Protects from suits stemming from mistakes made or bad advice given in a professional context.
Business Interruption	Provides compensation for loss due to fire, theft, or similar disasters that close a business. Covers lost income, continuing expenses, and utility expenses.
Nonperformance Loss Protection	Protects from failure of a contractor, supplier, or other person to fulfill an obligation.
Criminal Loss Protection	Protects from loss due to theft, burglary, or robbery.
Commercial Credit Insurance	Protects manufacturers and wholesalers from credit losses due to insolvency or default.
Public Liability Insurance	Provides protection for businesses and individuals against losses resulting from personal injuries or damage to the property of others for which the insured is responsible.
Extended Product Liability Insurance	Covers potentially toxic substances in products; environmental liability; and, for corporations, directors and officer liability.
Fidelity Bond	Protects employers from employee dishonesty.
Surety Bond	Covers losses resulting from a second party's failure to fulfill a contract.
Title Insurance	Protects buyers from losses resulting from a defect in title to property.
Health Insurance	
Basic Health Insurance	Covers losses due to sickness or accidents.
Major Medical Insurance	Protects against catastrophic losses by covering expenses beyond the limits of basic policies.
Hospitalization Insurance	Pays for most hospital expenses.
Surgical and Medical Insurance	Pays costs of surgery and doctor's care while recuperating in a hospital.
Dental Insurance	Pays a percentage of dental expenses.
Disability Income Insurance	Pays income while the insured is disabled as a result of accident or illness.
Life Insurance	
Group Life Insurance	Covers all the employees of a firm or members of a group.
Owner or Key Executive Insurance	Enables businesses of sole proprietors or partnerships to pay bills and continue operating, saving jobs for the employees. Enables corporations to hire and train or relocate another manager with no loss to the firm.
Retirement and Pension Plans	Provides employees with supplemental retirement and pension plans.
Credit Life Insurance	Pays the amount due on a loan if the debtor dies.

FIGURE A.2

PRIVATE INSURANCE
Insurance companies not government-owned (stock companies or mutual companies).

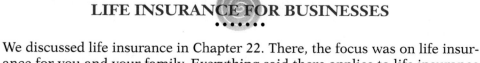

LIFE INSURANCE FOR BUSINESSES

We discussed life insurance in Chapter 22. There, the focus was on life insurance for you and your family. Everything said there applies to life insurance for business executives as well. The best coverage for most individuals is term insurance, but dozens of new policies with interesting features have been emerging recently. Figure A.2 lists various types of life insurance.

THE RISK OF DAMAGING THE ENVIRONMENT

Several incidents over the last few years have focused attention on a major risk that businesses face—pollution liability. One of the most publicized cases was the Manville Corporation's problems with asbestos. When the health hazards of asbestos were discovered, Manville was hit with 16,500 lawsuits, and the prospects were for 32,000 more lawsuits. To minimize the cost of such lawsuits, Manville asked for court protection under Chapter 11 of the Federal Bankruptcy Code.

The risk of environmental harm reaches international proportions in issues such as acid rain. One international incident that had dramatic consequences for businesses was the disaster in Bhopal, India, late in the 1980s. A chemical gas leak from a Union Carbide plant killed over 2,000 people and seriously injured thousands more. Public concern was raised over a similar Union Carbide plant in Institute, West Virginia.

The explosion of the Chernobyl nuclear plant in the former USSR caused much concern throughout the world. Due to violations of various safety standards several U.S. nuclear power plants have been shut down. Yet since coal-fired power plants are said to cause acid rain and other inexpensive fuel sources haven't been developed, there may be more research into nuclear plants in order to make them safer. Clearly, this will be an issue well into the next century.

Many feel there is a need for a more careful evaluation of environmental risks. For example, the government is spending $6.1 billion on hazardous waste dumps, which may cause 500 cancer deaths per year, and only $100 million on radon, which could cause 20,000 lung cancer deaths per year. We need a better way of assessing and managing those risks. While Americans tend to worry about oil spills, acid rain, pesticides, nuclear power plants, and hazardous wastes, some experts see greater risks in radon, lead, indoor air pollution, and fumes from chemicals. How much risk is there in global warming and depletion of the ozone layer? We don't yet know, but the risks may be substantial.

Clearly, risk management now goes far beyond the protection of individuals, businesses, and nonprofit organizations from known risks. It means the evaluation of global risks such as acid rain, global warming, and the depletion of the ozone layer. It also means prioritizing these risks so that international funds can be spent where they can do the most good. No insurance company can protect humanity from such risks. These risks are the concern of international governments throughout the world with the assistance of the international scientific community. They should also be your concern as you study risk management in all its dimensions.

health maintenance organizations (HMOs) 689
insurable interest 687
insurable risk 687
insurance policy 687
law of large numbers 688
liability losses 688
mutual insurance company 688
preferred provider organizations (PPOs) 689
premium 687
property losses 688
pure risk 685
risk 685
rule of indemnity 688
self-insurance 686
speculative risk 685
stock insurance company 688
uninsurable risk 687

 KEY TERMS

Part 7

FINANCIAL MANAGEMENT (FINANCE AND ACCOUNTING)

Accounting and finance are career areas that have existed for many centuries. Records discovered in the ruins of ancient Babylon dating back to 300 BC show that financial records were kept by the ancients. European monarchs, particularly in the 18th and 19th centuries, relied on bankers and other professional financiers to recover from wars and to build the new industrial revolution.

Today, accountants and financial managers are as much in demand as ever. Computerization has enriched both career areas immensely. Because of changing laws and regulations, companies and their personnel in these positions must place a greater emphasis than ever on accurate reporting of financial data. This field, like so many others, is dynamic and changing.

Nearly two million people work in some area of finance or accounting, most as accountants, financial managers, banking personnel, or financial consultants. Nearly every company—whether in manufacturing, transportation, retailing, or a variety of services—employs one or more financial managers. Accountants and bookkeepers are equally in demand.

SKILLS

Anyone who enters these areas must have a mathematical aptitude, an interest in numbers, and a considerable amount of patience. As with nearly every other area, speaking and writing skills are a must, because the financial information must be communicated to people. Good ethical judgment is also essential, because areas of finance and accounting both contain more "gray areas" than many of us imagine.

CAREER PATHS

A bachelor's degree in accounting or finance is usually a prerequisite, although accountants with two-year degrees and outstanding abilities have been hired as bookkeepers and accounting assistants. In some states, tax preparers do not need formal degrees, only mastery of current tax law. In all cases, though, continuing education is becoming increasingly important because of the growing complexity of global commerce, changing federal and state laws, and the constant introduction of new, complex financial instruments.

A well-trained, experienced financial manager is a prime candidate for promotion into top management. Junior public accountants usually advance to semisenior positions within two to five years and to senior positions within six to eight years. Although advancement can be rapid for well-prepared accountants, especially in public accounting, employees without adequate college preparation are often dead-ended in routine jobs. Also, even CPAs must constantly be reeducated in today's changing environment.

SOME POSSIBLE CAREERS IN ACCOUNTING AND FINANCE

Job Title	Salary	Job Duties	Career Path	Prospects
Accountant	Entry level: $28,000 (bachelor's degree) Experienced: $36,500–$50,400+.	Depends on size and nature of firm as well as specific job title. Public accountants work independently on a fee basis. Private accountants handle financial records in the company where they are salaried employees. The general accountant supervises, installs, and devises systems. The cost accountant determines unit costs of products and services. The auditor examines and vouches for the accuracy of records.	Start with either an accounting degree or many courses in accounting. Certified Public Accountant must take comprehensive exam, then intern as auditor for two years. Able accountants, especially CPAs, can be promoted rapidly. By specializing in certain accounting areas, an accountant can often be promoted.	Openings in all accounting areas are expected to grow faster than the average for other business specialists through 2005.
Financial manager	$20,200–$77,800 Median: $39,700.	As with accountants, duties depend on size and nature of firm as well as specific job title. Titles include treasurer, controller, credit manager, cash manager. Controllers direct preparation of financial reports; cash and credit managers monitor and control the flow of receipts and disbursements; risk and insurance managers work to minimize risk and cut risk costs.	Most start with a degree in finance or accounting. A Master of Business Administration degree (MBA) is becoming increasingly required by some companies. Often promoted into top management.	Number of applicants continues to grow and may exceed the number of openings in the next 10 years.
Securities sales workers	Trainees and beginners start $17,500–$23,000. Once established, changes to commission only. Experience workers earn from $65,000 upward.	Open accounts for new customers, execute buy and sell orders based on information from the securities exchange. Get information on company's progress from the research dept. Must be able to anticipate buying and selling trends in the markets.	Many brokerage concerns hire trainees, then place them on a probationary track of around six months. Depending on ability and ambition, promotion can be rapid.	For the talented and ambitious person, the opportunities will remain numerous through 2005.

LORI GEISLER, CERTIFIED PUBLIC ACCOUNTANT INTERN

When Lori Villagomez Geisler graduated with a degree in economics from The University of California at San Diego, she was hired almost at once by a large equipment leasing company. Her first job involved calling on mid-sized businesses, financing computer acquisitions and upgrades. After a year of this life, Lori found herself in real estate finance, working as a loan officer. Still not totally happy with her career moves, she began taking business classes at Palomar College in nearby San Marcos and at the Irvine campus of the University of California. With some important accounting courses under her belt, she applied for a position as an accountant with a computer manufacturing company, a company that specialized in memory upgrades. She reported directly to the controller.

Soon, the accounting world showed her that a Certified Public Accounting credential was going to be necessary if Lori was to achieve the goals she had set. First, she had to complete the required courses for the California CPA exam. Then she studied diligently for the exam itself, an exam that Lori describes as "the most grueling and difficult exam I have ever faced." In nearly every section of the exam, she found herself saying, "I should have studied more in this area." Despite her misgivings, she passed the entire exam the first time.

But passing the exam was still not the end. As is the case in every state, the young accountant now had to go through two years of an auditing internship before becoming a full-fledged CPA. Now, in her internship, she is dealing with a great variety of clients, and, as she puts it, is "learning, learning, learning as she goes." Her biggest hurdles are behind her.

Lori Geisler says that despite the importance of quantitative tools and a solid background in accounting courses, the most important skill for an accountant to master is communication—both oral and written. Why writing? She says that one's success as an accountant serving the public depends on credibility. "That credibility is usually established by writing narratives that explain the procedures that I used and how I arrived at my conclusions." As for the oral component, she says that an accountant spends much of her day interviewing staff and management. Not only do you need credibility, you need to understand all of the aspects of the department or company that will have impact on the accounting function. "And you have to be a team player," she concludes. When you're a CPA, you're only going to stay at a work site for a few weeks. You need to be considerate of others you are working with temporarily. You can't leave early or in any other way act like you're special.

The future looks positive for Lori Geisler. The market for Certified Public Accountants continues to be very good, and she will likely be able have a large hand in building her own clientele once she has completed her internship. "Accounting is an extremely rewarding field," Lori says. "You see projects from beginning to end. And you can be a real help to companies and the people who run them. It's a very fulfilling career."

Special thanks to Tom Humphrey, Palomar College, San Marcos, California, for recommending Ms. Geisler for this career portfolio.

CHAPTER NOTES

Prologue

Profile source: Ingrid Abramovitch, "Myth of the Gunslinger," *Success*, March 1994, pp. 34–40; Jane Seaberry, "Some Teens Learn Business from the Boss's Perspective," *The Washington Post*, May 19, 1992, pp. D1 & D4; and "2 Find a High Demand to KART Kids," *Chicago Tribune*, March 13, 1995, Sec. 4, p. 6.

1. "The Diploma Dividend," *Washington Post*, July 22, 1994, p. D1.

2. "The Power of Computers," *Fortune*, May 17, 1993, p. 24.

Chapter 1

Profile source: Jeanne Saddler, "Young Risk-Takers Push the Business Envelope," and Brett Pulley, "Me and My Homey's Era Spans Ventures," in *The Wall Street Journal*, May 15, 1994, pp. B1 and B2; "CBS This Morning," September 7, 1994 (an interview with La-Van Hawkins); and Marc Rice, "Payback: Burger Mogul Provides an Economic Lifeline," *St. Louis Post-Dispatch*, September 1, 1994, p. 8C.

1. Lois Jackman, "How We Cater to Individuals," *Nation's Business*, October 1994, p. 9.

2. "Opening Doors," *Entrepreneur*, October 1994, p. 14.

3. Patricia Shiff Estess, "Made in America," *Entrepreneur*, September 1994, p. 88.

4. "Entrepreneurs and Ethnicity," *Fortune*, October 3, 1994, p. 29.

5. Evan Ramstad, "Flair for Software," *The Washington Times*, September 20, 1994, pp. B7 and B12.

6. Howard Gleckman, Susan B. Garland, Richard A. Melcher, and Joseph Weber, "Downsizing Government," *Business Week*, January 23, 1995, pp. 34–39.

7. Debra Phillips, "The New Service Boom," *Entrepreneur*, August 1994, pp. 134–40.

8. "Index of Foreign Billionaires," *Forbes*, July 18, 1994, pp. 152–54.

9. "Business Startups: On the Rise Again," *Forbes*, June 6, 1994, p. 37.

10. "Performance," *Fortune*, May 30, 1994, p. 232.

11. "It's a Job," *Business Ethics*, April 1994, p. 10.

12. "Performance," *Fortune*, May 30, 1994, p. 232.

13. "Plenty of Bang for the Buck," *Business Week*, January 1995, p. 24.

14. Michael R. Sesit, "Americans Pour Money into Foreign Markets," *The Wall Street Journal*, April 15, 1994, pp. C1 and C13.

15. Udayan Gupta, "Investors Find Think-Small Strategy Works in Poland," *The Wall Street Journal*, August 4, 1994, p. B2; and Simon Johnson and Gary Loveman,

"Starting Over: Poland after Communism," *Harvard Business Review*, March–April 1995, pp. 44–57.

16. "Why Europe Has a Job Problem," *Fortune*, March 20, 1995, p. 42.

17. William J. Bennett, "The Best Welfare Reform: End It," *The Washington Post*, March 30, 1994, p. A19.

18. Janet Novack, "Twisting the Numbers," *Forbes*, March 13, 1995, p. 68.

19. Benjamin Forgey, "Barn Raising: A Bittersweet Exhibit," *The Washington Post*, March 19, 1994, pp. D1 and D4.

20. "Travel and Tourism: A Powerful Force for America's Future," Supplement to *The Washington Post*, April 20, 1994, pp. 1–15.

Chapter 2

Profile source: Joel Simon, "Eye of the Storm," *Success*, March 1994, pp. 42–43.

1. "Silly Summit," *Forbes*, April 25, 1994, p. 24.

2. Donald Lambro, "Where the Jobs Are . . . Where They Aren't," *The Washington Times*, March 18, 1994, p. A23.

3. "Slaying the Mandate Monster," *The Wall Street Journal*, January 9, 1995, p. A14.

4. "The Balanced Budget Amendment: A Contract with Evasion," *The Wall Street Journal*, January 12, 1995, p. A15.

5. Howard Gleckman, Susan B. Garland, Richard A. Melcher, and Joseph Weber, "Downsizing Government," *Business Week*, January 23, 1995, pp. 34–39.

6. Peter Brimelow, "The Grab Goes On," *Forbes*, March 28, 1994, pp. 58–60.

7. Benjamin Forgey, "Barn Raising: A Bittersweet Exhibit," *The Washington Post*, March 19, 1994, pp. D1 and D4.

8. Donald Lambro, "How High Taxes Undermine Families," *The Washington Times*, March 13, 1995, p. A19.

9. Christopher Farrell, "The Dollar Doesn't Deserve this Dumping," *Business Week*, March 20, 1995, p. 51.

10. Patrick Buchanan, "Where the Deficit Is Headed and Why," *The Washington Times*, January 16, 1995, p. A18.

11. "The Job Congress Was Elected to Do," *The Washington Times*, February 28, 1995, p. A20.

Chapter 3

Profile source: Carson Reed, "Colorado Businesswomen's China Mission," *Colorado Business*, November 1, 1990; Dave Savona, "Pacific Rim Networking," *International Business*, February 1992, pp. 44–47; Niklas von Daehne, "Total Dedication," *Success*, July/August 1994, p. 16; and Robert Lenzer, "Buy China—Carefully," *Forbes*, March 13, 1995, pp. 58–60.

1. Bill Saporito, "Where the Global Action Is," *Fortune*, Autumn/Winter 1993, pp. 63–65.

2. Douglas Harbrecht and Neil Gross, "The Secret Weapon That Won't Start a Trade War," *Business Week*, March 7, 1994, p. 45.

3. Anne R. Field, "New Interest Service Lets You Venture Abroad," *Home Office Computing*, January 1995, p. 14.

4. Richard A. Melcher, Julie Flynn, and Robert Neff, "Anheuser-Busch Says Skoal, Salud, Prosit," *Business Week*, September 20, 1993, pp. 76–77.

5. Louis S. Richman, "What's Next after GATT's Victory?" *Fortune*, January 10, 1994, pp. 66–71.

6. Robert Neff, "Tough Talk: Are the U.S. and Japan Headed for a Trade War?" *Business Week*, February 28, 1994, pp. 26–31.

7. Michael J. Mandel, Gary Williams, and Stephen Baker, "America's Trade Gap: The Good News in the Bad News," *Business Week*, February 6, 1995.

8. Sue Bae Kim, "Foreign Direct Investment: Gift Horse or Trojan Horse?" *Weekly Letter (Federal Reserve Bank of San Francisco)*, March 20, 1993, pp. 1–3.

9. Paul Krugman, "Competitiveness: Does It Matter?" *Fortune*, March 7, 1994, pp. 109–15.

10. Amy Barrett and Zachary Schiller, "Nestlé: A Giant in a Hurry," *Business Week*, March 22, 1993, pp. 50–54.

11. Valarie Reitman, "India Anticipates the Arrival of the Beefless Big Mac," *The Wall Street Journal*, January 3, 1994, p. B1.

12. Joel Bleeke and David Ernst, "Is Your Strategic Alliance Really a Sale?" *Harvard Business Review*, January–February 1995, pp. 97–105.

13. Moreton Binn, "Trade Master," *Success*, April 1992, p. 10.

14. Bradley Johnson, "Apple Wants Unified Worldwide Image," *Advertising Age*, April 12, 1993, p. 2.

15. Douglas Zehr, "In Puerto Rico, Kids 'R' Not Us," *Business Week*, February 24, 1994, p. 8.

16. Owen Ullmann, Pete Engardio, and Bill Hinchberger, "The Global Greenback," *Business Week*, August 9, 1993, pp. 43–44.

17. James S. Altschul, "Hands across the Water," *CFO*, February 1994, pp. 53–54.

18. Paul Blustein, "Tariffs Not the Key to Japanese Market," *Washington Post*, January 4, 1992, pp. B1 and B6.

19. Merrill Goozner, "Powerful Yen Makes It Even Costlier for Foreign Firms to Set Up in Japan," *Chicago Tribune*, March 12, 1995, Sec. 7, p. 1.

20. Robert West, "The Big New Import/Export Opportunities," *Boardroom Reports*, February 15, 1995, pp. 11–12.

21. Charlotte Grimes, "GATT Pact Sails through Senate," *St. Louis Post-Dispatch*, December 2, 1994, p. 1A.

22. Richman, "What's Next after GATT's Victory?", pp. 66–71.

23. Christopher Power, Rose Brady, Joyce Baranthan, and Karen Lewry Miller, "Second Thoughts on Going Global," *Business Week*, March 13, 1995, pp. 48–49.

24. Martin Sieff, "With NAFTA Here, Is TRAFTA on Way?" *The Washington Times*, April 16, 1995, pp. A1 and A13.

25. Geri Smith, Elisabeth Malkin, David Woodruff, Stanley Reed, and William Glasgall, "Mexico: Can It Cope?" *Business Week*, January 16, 1995, pp. 42–55.

26. "China Is It: Coke Invests $150 Million in Huge Market," *St. Louis Post-Dispatch*, November 7, 1993, p. 8E.

27. John J. Curran, "China's Investment Boom," *Fortune*, March 7, 1994, pp. 116–24.

28. Ibid.

29. David Savona, "The Deep China Deficit," *International Business*, March 1995, p. 82.

30. "U.S., China Sign Pact on Trade," *St. Louis-Post Dispatch*, February 27, 1995, pp. A1 and A5.

31. Paul Hofheinz, "Rising in Russia," *Fortune*, January 24, 1994, pp. 92–97.

32. "Western Decadence: MTV Hits Russia," *St. Louis Post-Dispatch*, July 10, 1993, p. 4A.

33. Neela Banerjee, "Russia Is Snickering after Mars Invades and Captures Market," *The Wall Street Journal*, July 13, 1993, p. B1.

Chapter 4

Profile source: Larry Armstrong, "From Riot and Ruin, a Surprising Harvest," *Business Week*, May 9, 1994, p. 38; and "Good Guys Finish First," *Business Ethics*, March/April 1995, p. 13.

1. Lynn Sharp Paine, "Managing for Organizational Integrity," *Harvard Business Review*, March–April 1994, pp. 106–17.

2. Mary Scott, "Ben and Jerry's CEO: Expand Internationally," *Business Ethics*, March/April 1995, p. 9.

3. Suzanne Wooley, "Smile, Cheater, You're on Candid Camera," *Business Week*, October 4, 1993, pp. 100–2.

4. Kenneth Blanchard and Norman Vincent Peale, *The Power of Ethical Management* (New York: William Morrow, 1988); and Diane Cole, "Companies Crack Down," *Managing Your Career*, a publication of *The Wall Street Journal*, Spring 1991, pp. 8–10.

5. Michael Lane, "Improving American Business Ethics in Three Steps," *The CPA Journal*, February 1, 1991; and Susan Sonnesyn, "A Question of Ethics," *Training and Development Journal*, March 1, 1991.

6. Kenneth E. Goodpaster and Gary Atkinson, "Stakeholder, Individual Rights, and the Common Good," *Phi Kappa Phi Journal*, Winter 1992, pp. 14–17.

7. Dan Callahan, "And on Page Six, We Review the Fun Index," *Business Ethics*, March/April 1995, p. 41.

8. Christopher Lasch, "A Skewed View of What Ails America," *Business Week*, February 6, 1995.

Chapter 5

Profile source: Louis S. Richman, "Rekindling the Entrepreneurial Fire," *Fortune*, February 21, 1994, p. 112; and Jerry A. Tennenbaum, "Food Franchisers Expand by Pursuing Customers into Every Nook and Cranny," *The Wall Street Journal*, October 26, 1994, p. B1.

1. "Anatomy of a Start-Up: The Hard Part," *Inc.*, April 1991, p. 55.

2. Don Wallace, "Power in Numbers," *Home Office Computing*, February 1994, pp. 56–61.

3. John Dorfman, "Master Limited Partnerships Regain Fans Thanks to Special Treatment of Payouts," *The Wall Street Journal*, August 19, 1993, p. C1.

4. George Rohe, "Important Tax Cutting Strategies," *Boardroom Reports*, April 16, 1995, pp. 11–12.

5. Daniel R. Zajac, "Esprit De Corporation," *Entrepreneur*, January 1995, pp. 284–89.

6. Robert F. Hartley, *Marketing Mistakes* (New York: John Wiley & Sons, 1995), p. 63.

7. Peter Weaver, "Heightened Scrutiny for S Corporations," *Nation's Business*, February 1995, p. 37.

8. David R. Evanson, "S Is More," *Entrepreneur*, February 1995, pp. 40–43.

9. Michael Seltz, "Fast-Growing Firms Mull Tax-Saving Structure Change," *The Wall Street Journal*, November 3, 1994, p. B2.

10. Ripley Hotch, "The Latest on LLCs: Uniform Law Advances," *Nation's Business*, November 1994, p. 8.

11. "Merger Mania," *Fortune*, October 3, 1994, p. 20.

12. Randall Smith, "Merger Activity Shifts into High Gear as the Information Superhighway Opens," *The Wall Street Journal*, January 3, 1994, p. R8; and Randall Smith and Greg Steinmetz, "Mergers Surge as Firms Find a Rising Economy and Cheap Financing," *The Wall Street Journal*, March 6, 1994, pp. A1 and A5.

13. Gary Strauss, "Foreigners Digesting U.S. Food Firms," *USA Today*, September 10, 1993, p. B1.

14. Jeffrey A. Tannenbaum, "FTC Says Franchisers Fed Clients a Line and Failed to Deliver," *The Wall Street Journal*, May 16, 1994, pp. A1 and A10.

15. Greg Matusky and John P. Hayes, "Franchising's Great Transformations," *Inc.*, April 1990, pp. 87–99.

16. Carol Steinberg, "What's Behind the Global Franchise Boom," *World Trade*, April 1993, p. 148.

17. Jeffrey A. Tannenbaum, "Retail Franchises Appear Riskier than Other Start-Ups," *The Wall Street Journal*, February 28, 1995, p. B2.

18. Andrew E. Serwer, "Trouble in Franchise Nation," *Fortune*, March 6, 1995, pp. 115–29.

19. Jeffrey A. Tannenbaum, "Franchisees Take Complaints against Pearle to FTC," *The Wall Street Journal*, February 16, 1994, p. B2.

20. Udayan Gupta, "Inroads into Franchises by Minorities Are Uneven," *The Wall Street Journal*, October 8, 1990, p. B1.

21. Gregory Matusky, "The Best Home-Based Franchises," *Home Office Computing*, December 1993, pp. 79–83.

22. Janet Lee, "Food Co-Ops: What Hippies Did Right," *Business Week*, November 29, 1993, p. 146.

23. Norm Alster, "Getting the Middleman's Share," *Forbes*, July 4, 1994, pp. 108–9.

Chapter 6

Profile source: "Topsy Tale," *St. Louis Post-Dispatch*, February 13, 1994, p. 3E.

1. Brent Bowers and Udayan Gupta, "Golden Touch," *The Wall Street Journal*, October 19, 1994, pp. A1 and A13.

2. Jim Schutze, "Corporate Dropouts," *Home Office Computing*, February 1993, pp. 47–53.

3. Bowers and Gupta, "Golden Touch."

4. Brian Dumaine, "America's Smart Young Entrepreneurs," *Fortune*, March 21, 1994, pp. 34–48.

5. This section is based on John Naisbitt and Patricia Aburdene, *Re-inventing the Corporation* (New York: Warner Books, 1985).

6. Gary McWilliams, "At Compaq, a Desktop Crystal Ball," *Business Week*, March 20, 1995, pp. 96–97.

7. Wilma Randle, "3M Trying to Innovate, Preserve," *Chicago Tribune*, March 7, 1994, pp. 1 and 8.

8. Eric Schine, "Out at the Skunk Works, the Sweet Smell of Success," *Business Week*, April 26, 1993, p. 101.

9. Cynthia E. Griffin, "Going Home," *Entrepreneur*, March 1995, pp. 120–25.

10. Wilma Randle, "Sowing Seeds," *Chicago Tribune*, October 27, 1993, Section 7, pp. 3 and 14; and Cynthia Todd, "Black Businesswomen Make Their Own Success," *St. Louis Post-Dispatch*, April 4, 1994, pp. 1A and 6A.

11. Gene Koretz, "Small Business Is Putting Some Snap in the Job Market," *Business Week*, April 25, 1994, p. 26.

12. "Where the New Jobs Are," *Business Week*, March 20, 1995, p. 24.

13. Koretz, "Small Business."

14. Nick Sullivan, "Tom Peters: Small Is Beautiful," *Home Office Computing*, January 1993, pp. 56–57.

15. Gene Koretz, "A Surprising Finding on New-Business Mortality Rates," *Business Week*, June 14, 1993, p. 22; and James Aley, "Debunking the Failure Fallacy," *Fortune*, September 6, 1993, p. 21.

16. Charles Burck, "Learning from a Master," *Fortune*, December 27, 1993, p. 144.

17. Brian O'Reilly, "The New Face of Small Business," *Fortune*, May 2, 1994, pp. 82–88.

18. Maury Klein, "The First Tycoon," *Forbes*, October 22, 1990, pp. 44–52.

19. Imran Husain, "After Hours," *Entrepreneur*, March 1995, pp. 230–33.

20. Jerri Stroud, "Tilling Their Fields of Dreams," *St. Louis Post-Dispatch*, February 26, 1995, pp. E1 and E8.

21. Daniel Grebler, "Even if You're Just Starting, Make Sure to Plan for End," *St. Louis Post-Dispatch*, March 13, 1995, p. 19BP.

22. Cynthia E. Griffin, "Growing Places," *Entrepreneur*, February 1995, pp. 108–13.

23. Nancy Nisselbaum, "Where Women Find Financing," *Home Office Computing*, April 1994, p. 18.

24. Paul Edwards and Sarah Edwards, "Little Loans, Big Benefits," *Home Office Computing*, July 1993, pp. 54–60.

25. Jeanne Saddler, "Small SBA Loans Planned to Put the Poor in Business," *The Wall Street Journal*, December 14, 1990, p. B2.

26. "Survival Guide for SBA Loans," *Home Office Computing*, March 1993, p. 14.

27. Amy Barrett, "Giant Steps for Small Business," *Business Week*, May 9, 1994.

28. "In Living Color," *Entrepreneur*, March 1995, p. 32.

29. Crystal Waters, "Not Just Another Pretty Face," *Home Office Computing*, June 1993, pp. 44–47.

30. Anne B. Fisher, "Profiting from Crisis," *Fortune*, February 7, 1994, p. 166.

31. Judith Broadhurst, "Shop Smart for an Accountant," *Home Office Computing*, April 1994, pp. 32–34.

32. "Technology's Hot," *Inc.*, January 1995, p. 102.

33. Deborah Jacobs, "Prepaid Legal Plans: Get Basic Legal Advice Year-Round for a Set Fee," *Home Office Computing*, February 1993, p. 56.

34. Jennifer Zaino, "What a Deal!" *Home Office Computing*, March 1994, pp. 39–43.

35. Rosalind Resnick, "The Electronic Schmooze," *Home Office Computing*, January 1994, pp. 86–88.

36. Amy Barrett, "It's a Small (Business) World," *Business Week*, April 17, 1995, pp. 96–101.

Chapter 7

Profile source: Dana Wechsler Linden, "The Mother of Them All," *Forbes*, January 16, 1995, pp. 75–76; and Noel Tichy and Ram Charon, "The CEO as Coach," Harvard Business Review, March-April 1995, pp. 69–78.

1. Mark Hendricks, "Who's the Boss?" *Entrepreneur*, January 1995, pp. 54–55; and Noel Tichy and Lawrence A. Bossidy, "The CEO as Coach," *Harvard Business Review*, March–April 1995, pp. 69–78.

2. Michael H. Jordan, "The Role of Top Management," *Harvard Business Review*, January–February 1995, pp. 142–144.

3. Rahul Jacob, "How to Retread Customers," *Fortune*, Autumn/Winter 1993, pp. 23–24.

4. John A. Byrne, "Borderless Management," *Business Week*, May 23, 1994, pp. 24–26.

5. Nick Sullivan, "Tom Peters: Small Is Beautiful," *Home Office Computing*, January 1993, pp. 56–57.

6. Jeffrey A. Tannenbaum, "Entrepreneurs Thrive by Helping Big Firms Slash Costs," *The Wall Street Journal*, November 10, 1993, p. B2.

7. Andrew Campbell, Michael Goold, and Marcus Alexander, "Corporate Strategy: The Quest for Parenting Advantage," *Harvard Business Review*, March–April 1995, pp. 120–32.

8. Dori Jones Yang, "When the Going Gets Tough, Boeing Gets Touchy-Feely," *Business Week*, January 17, 1994, pp. 65–67.

9. Chad Rubel, "Empower Employees So You Can Satisfy Customers," *Marketing News*, March 27, 1995, p. 14.

10. Joy Riggs, "Empowering Workers by Setting Goals," *Nation's Business*, January 1995, p. 6.

11. Michael Elliott, "Take Me to Your Leader," *Newsweek*, April 25, 1994, p. 67.

12. Walter Kiechell III, "A Manager's Career in the New Economy," *Fortune*, April 4, 1994, pp. 68–72.

13. Michael Barrier, "The Changing Face of Leadership," *Nation's Business*, January 1995, pp. 41–42.

14. B. G. Yovovich, "Convergence Creates New Executive Breed," *Business Marketing*, January 1995, p. 5.

15. Sunita Wadekar Bhargava and Fred F. Jespersen, "Portrait of a CEO," *Business Week*, October 11, 1993, pp. 64–65.

Chapter 8

Profile source: Louis S. Richman, "Reengineering under Fire," *Fortune*, April 18, 1994, p. 186; John Hillkirk, "Challenging Status Quo Now in Vogue," *USA Today*, November 9, 1994, pp. B1 and B3; and Ronald E. Yates, "The New Fix for Corporate America's Organizational Ills? Reengineering," *Chicago Tribune*, October 17, 1993, Sec. 7, pp. 1 and 6.

1. Earl Naumann, *Creating Customer Value* (Cincinnati: Thompson Executive Press, 1995), pp. 212–213.

2. Elios Pascual, "Mack Learns the Error of False Pride," *The Wall Street Journal*, July 11, 1994, p. A12.

3. Glenn M. Parker, *Cross-Functional Teams* (San Francisco: Jossey-Boss, 1994).

4. Robert H. Waterman, *What America Does Right* (New York: W.W. Norton, 1994).

5. Brian Dumaine, "The Trouble with Teams," *Fortune*, September 5, 1994, pp. 86–92.

6. Rahul Jacob, "The Struggle to Create an Organization for the 21st Century," *Fortune*, April 3, 1995, pp. 90–99.

7. Lori Ioannou, "The Journey Toward Empowerment," *International Business*, January 1995, p. 74.

8. Jessica Lipnack and Jeffrey Stamps, *The TeamNet Factor* (Essex Junction, Vt.: Oliver Wight Publications, 1993).

9. Ibid.

10. John Rossant, "Strategies," *Business Week*, January 23, 1995, pp. 82–83.

11. Michael Hammer and James Champy, *Reengineering the Corporation* (New York: HarperCollins, 1993).

12. John P. Kotter, "Leading Change: Why Transformation Efforts Fail," *Harvard Business Review*, March–April 1995, pp. 59–67.

13. Thomas J. Kiely, "Managing Change: Why Reengineering Projects Fail," *Harvard Business Review*, March–April 1995, p. 15.

14. *Better Change* (Burr Ridge, Ill.: Richard D. Irwin, 1995).

15. Michael Rothchild, "Coming Soon: Internal Markets," *Forbes ASAP*, June 7, 1993, pp. 19–21.

16. John P. Kotter, "Leading Change: Why Transformation Efforts Fail," *Harvard Business Review*, March–April 1995, pp. 59–67.

17. Michael Meyer and Nancy Hass, "Simon Says, 'Out!'" *Newsweek*, June 27, 1994, pp. 42–44.

Chapter 9

Profile source: Erie Norton, "Future Factories," *The Wall Street Journal*, January 13, 1993, p. A8.

1. James Brian Quinn, *Intelligent Enterprise* (New York: Free Press, 1992).

2. Dave Savona, "Talking Real Estate," *International Business*, February 1995, p. 81.

3. "International Site Selection," *International Business*, June 1993, an ad for Arthur Andersen between pages 26 and 27.

4. Jon Margolis, "The Computer Cowboys," *Chicago Tribune*, November 18, 1993, Sec. 5, p. 2.

5. Jennifer A. Cinguina, "To Rent or Buy Abroad," *International Business*, September 1994, p. 111.

6. "Luring Factories to Landfills," *Business Week*, March 6, 1995, p. 58.

7. Andrew S. Grove, *High Output Management* (New York: Random House, 1983).

8. "New Software = Faster Factories," *ASAP*, October 10, 1994, pp. 36–41.

9. Fred R. Bleakley, "Strange Bedfellows," *The Wall Street Journal*, January 3, 1995, pp. A1 and A6.

10. William H. Davidow and Michael S. Malone, *The Virtual Corporation* (New York: HarperCollins, 1992).

11. James B. Treece, "Motown's Struggle to Shift on the Fly," *Business Week*, July 11, 1994, pp. 111–12.

12. Jerry Bowles and Joshua Hammond, *Beyond Quality* (New York: Berkley Books, 1992).

13. Davidow and Malone, *Virtual Corporation*.

14. Peter M. Senge, *The Fifth Discipline* (New York: Doubleday, 1990).

15. Alison L. Sprout, "Talking to Robots Made Easy," *Fortune*, October 31, 1994, p. 240.

16. "Custom Made," *Success*, October 1994, p. 28.

17. Walter S. Mossberg, "Personal Technology," *The Wall Street Journal*, October 27, 1994, p. B1.

18. Tom Hout and George Stalk, Jr., *Competing Against Time* (New York: Free Press, 1990).

19. Damon Darlin, "Automating the Automators," *Forbes*, February 14, 1994, pp. 156–60.

20. Louis S. Richman, "Why the Economic Data Mislead Us," *Fortune*, March 8, 1993, pp. 108–13.

21. "The Big Payoff from Computers," *Fortune*, March 7, 1994, p. 28.

22. "Technology Is Fueling Retail Productivity, But Slowing Job Gains," *Business Week*, May 10, 1993, p. 16.

Chapter 10

Profile source: Kenneth Labich, "Is Herb Kelleher America's Best CEO?" *Fortune*, May 2, 1994, pp. 44–52; Wendy Zellner, "Southwest," *Business Week*, February 13, 1995; and Howard Banks, "Recovery," *Forbes*, March 27, 1995, pp. 79–80.

1. Robert Frank, "Driving Harder: As UPS Tries to Deliver More to Its Customers, Labor Problems Grow," *The Wall Street Journal*, May 24, 1994, pp. A1 and A5.

2. Abraham H. Maslow, *Motivation and Personality* (New York: Harper, 1954).

3. Robert D. Hof, "The Education of Andrew Grove," *Business Week*, January 16, 1995.

4. For more on Theory Y, see Douglas McGregor, *The Human Side of Enterprise* (New York: McGraw-Hill, 1970).

5. William G. Ouchi, *Theory Z: How American Business Can Meet the Japanese Challenge* (Menlo Park, Calif.: Addison-Wesley, 1981).

6. Frederick Herzberg, *Work and the Nature of Man* (World Publishers, 1966).

7. Virginia Baldwin Hick, "What Works at Work: Kind Word from Boss," *St. Louis Post-Dispatch*, January 3, 1994, p. 1C.

8. "Loyalty Surprise," *Boardroom Reports*, March 15, 1994, p. 10; and "Brainstorming," *Boardroom Reports*, April 15, 1994, p. 15.

9. Jim Barlow, "Company Loyalty: The Feeling Is Mutual," *The Washington Times*, April 18, 1994, p. E13.

10. Brian Dumaine, "The Bureaucracy Busters," *Fortune*, June 17, 1991, pp. 111–20.

11. Mark Maremont, "Kodak's New Focus," *Business Week*, January 30, 1995.

12. Barrie McKenna, "Reborn in Rimouski," *Globe and Mail*, July 20, 1993, p. B20.

13. Glenn M. Parker, *Cross-Functional Teams* (San Francisco: Jossey-Bass, 1994).

14. Joseph B. White and Oscar Suris, "New Pony: How a 'Skunk Works' Kept the Mustang Alive—on a Tight Budget," *The Wall Street Journal*, September 21, 1993.

15. Thomas A. Stewart, "The Leading Edge," *Fortune*, May 15, 1995, pp. 123–24.

16. Alan Farnham, "Mary Kay's Lessons in Leadership," *Fortune*, September 20, 1993, pp. 68–77.

17. Sherwood Ross, "A Little Thanks Can Save Employers a Lot of Money," *St. Louis Post-Dispatch*, January 30, 1995, p. 18BP.

Chapter 11

Profile source: Jaclyn Fierman, "The Contingency Work Force," *Fortune*, January 24, 1994, pp. 30–36; "Boss Is a Temp," *St. Louis Post-Dispatch*, April 24, 1994, p. 8E; and Virginia Baldwin Hick, "Full-Time Jobs Decline for Nation's Work Force," *St. Louis Post-Dispatch*, September 1993, pp. 1 and 6.

1. Alan Deutschman, "How H-P Continues to Grow and Grow," *Fortune*, May 2, 1994, pp. 90–100.

2. Kevin Kelly, "Motorola: Training for the Millennium," *Business Week*, March 28, 1994, pp. 158–63; Ronald Henkoff, "Companies That Train Best," *Fortune*, March 22, 1993, pp. 62–75; and Dale Dauten, "Motorola Creates Personal Victories, Corporate Success," *St. Louis Post-Dispatch*, March 14, 1994, p. 5BP.

3. Lara Viani, "Steelwire Wins Contract for Retraining Program," *American Metal Market*, June 4, 1991.

4. Deborah Teschke, "Nursing Home Fights Fiscal Strain with Staff Retraining Program," *Healthcare Financial Management*, May 1, 1991.

5. Stratford Sherman, "How Will We Live with the Tumult?" *Fortune*, December 18, 1993, pp. 123–25.

6. "Stop That Chitchat," *The Washington Times*, March 30, 1993, p. F2.

7. "Drug Testing Rises," *St. Louis Post-Dispatch*, April 7, 1994, p. 8C; and "Testing . . . Testing," *Business Week*, May 2, 1994, p. 6.

8. Rita Bailey, "Southwest," *Business Week*, February 13, 1995.

9. Harvey Robbins and Michael Finley, *Why Teams Don't Work* (Princeton, N.J.: Peterson's Pacemaker Books, 1995).

10. Stewart Toy, "Mickey Goes to Charm School," *Business Week*, February 13, 1995.

11. "Corporate America's New Lesson Plan," *Business Week*, October 25, 1993, pp. 102–5.

12. Elizabeth Lesly, "Inside the Black Business Network," *Business Week*, November 29, 1993, pp. 70–81.

13. Amanda Bennett, "Bu Xinsheng: China's Model Manager," *The Wall Street Journal*, May 30, 1984, p. 36.

14. Ronald E. Yates, "Molding a New Future," *Chicago Tribune*, January 2, 1994, pp. 1 and 6.

15. Shawn Tully, "Your Paycheck Gets Exciting," *Fortune*, November 1, 1993, pp. 83–98.

16. Neela Banerjee, "Rebounding Earnings Stir Old Debate on Productivity's Tie to Profit-Sharing," *The Wall Street Journal*, April 12, 1994, pp. A2 and A14.

17. Jaclyn Fierman, "The Perilous New World of Fair Pay," *Fortune*, June 13, 1994, pp. 57–64.

18. John O. Whitney, *The Trust Factor* (New York: McGraw-Hill, 1994).

19. Roger Thompson, "Benefit Costs Surge Again," *Nation's Business*, February 1993, pp. 38–39.

20. Ibid.

21. Tim Smart, "IBM Has a New Product: Employee Benefits," *Business Week*, May 10, 1993, p. 58.

22. Bill Graham, "It's Not the Savings," *CFO*, October 1993, p. 14.

23. Jaclyn Fierman, "Are Companies Less Family-Friendly?" *Fortune*, March 21, 1994, pp. 64–67.

24. Julia Lawlor, "Flexible Work Policies a Myth for Most," *USA Today*, August 20, 1993; and Lisa Genasci, "Flexible Working Arrangements Still Resisted Despite Productivity Gains," *The Washington Times*, September 25, 1993, pp. D5 and D8.

25. Sue Shellenbarger, "More Companies Experiment with Workers' Schedules," *The Wall Street Journal*, January 13, 1994, pp. B1 and B6.

26. Roberta Maynard, "The Growing Appeal of Telecommuting," *Nation's Business*, August 1994, pp. 61–62.

27. Virginia Baldwin Hick, "'Virtual Office' Means More Home Work," *St. Louis Post-Dispatch*, March 21, 1994, pp. B1 and B2.

28. Bob Weinstein, "New Frontiers," *Entrepreneur*, May 1995, pp. 158–65.

29. Tim Smart, "Let the Good Times Roll—and a Few More Heads," *Business Week*, January 31, 1994, pp. 28–29; and William Flannery, "The Big Picture: Author Shares His View of Future," *St. Louis Post-Dispatch*, January 30, 1995, p. 6BP.

30. "Bye-Bye, Boot-Out Benefits," *Business Week*, January 31, 1994, p. 8; Peter M. Panken, "How to Keep Firing from Backfiring," *Boardroom Reports*, July 1, 1993, pp. 3–4; and Rebecca Mann, "How to Prevent Employee Lawsuits," *St. Louis Post-Dispatch*, March 3, 1995, p. 7B.

31. Carol Kleiman, "Early Bird Catches the Best Retirement Offer," *Chicago Tribune*, August 21, 1993, p. D5.

32. Catherine Yang, "Affirmative Action a 'Race-Neutral' Helping Hand?" *Business Week*, February 27, 1995.

33. Tim Poor, " 'Glass Ceiling' Won't Vanish Overnight," *St. Louis Post-Dispatch*, March 21, 1995, p. 11B; and "An Unbreakable Glass Ceiling?" *Business Week*, March 20, 1995, p. 42.

34. Catherine Yang, "Business Has to Find a New Meaning for 'Fairness,'" *Business Week*, April 12, 1993.

35. Robert J. Samuelson, "R.I.P. the Good Corporation," *Newsweek*, July 5, 1993, p. 41.

36. Marcia Bradford, "Basic Training," *Entrepreneur*, December 1993, pp. 154–56; and Aaron Bernstein, "How Much Good Will Training Do?" *Business Week*, February 22, 1993, pp. 76–77.

Chapter 12

Profile source: Bill Saporito, "The Owners' New Game Is Managing," *Fortune*, July 1, 1991, pp. 86– 91; David Greising, "The Toughest ;ns&?!%;ns in Sports," *Business Week*, June 15, 1992, pp. 100–04; E. Compte and S. N. Chakravarty, "How High Can David Stern Jump," *Forbes*, June 7, 1993, pp. 42–44; and Carl Desens and Eileen Drage O'Reilly, "The NBA's Fast Break Overseas," *Business Week*, December 4, 1994, p. 94.

1. Ellen Joan Pollock, "Arbitrator Finds Role Dwindling as Rivals Grow," *The Wall Street Journal*, April 28, 1993, p. B1.

2. Rochelle Sharpe, "Striking Out," *The Wall Street Journal*, February 8, 1994, p. A1.

3. Kevin Kelly, "Picket Lines? Just Call 1-800-Strikebreaker," *Business Week*, March 27, 1995, p. 42.

4. Christopher Conte, "Labor's Glass Ceiling: Despite a Growing Role, Women Lack Clout in Unions," *The Wall Street Journal*, February 9, 1993, p. 1A.

5. Marcus Mabry, "New Hopes for Old Unions," *Newsweek*, February 24, 1992, p. 39.

6. Daniel Seligman, "Big Labor's Last Stand," *Fortune*, October 18, 1993, pp. 170–71.

7. Peter Nulty, "Look What the Unions Want Now," *Fortune*, February 8, 1993, pp. 128–33.

8. Bruce Bartlett, "Downward Trend for Unions," *The Washington Times*, March 6, 1995, p. A17.

9. Frank Swoboda, "As Economy Remakes Itself, Fewer Wear the Union Label," *Washington Post*, October 6, 1993, pp. F1–F3.

10. Ibid.

11. Perkins, "Unions."

12. Nulty, "Look What Unions Want."

13. "Executive Pay," *The Wall Street Journal*, April 12, 1995, p. R15.

14. John A. Byrne, Lori Bongiorno, and Ronald Grover, "That Eye-Popping Executive Pay," *Business Week*, April 25, 1994, pp. 52–58.

15. Joann S. Lublin, "Firms Forfeit Tax Break to Pay Top Brass $1 Million-Plus," *The Wall Street Journal*, April 21, 1994, pp. B1–B4.

16. John A. Byrne, "That's Some Pay Cap, Bill," *Business Week*, April 25, 1994, p. 57.

17. Ibid.

18. Janice Castro, "How's Your Pay? CEO's: No Pain, Just Gain," *Time*, April 15, 1991.

19. John A. Byrne, "Their Cup Runneth Over Again," *Business Week*, March 28, 1994, pp. 26–28.

20. Julie Amparano Lopez, "A Better Way? Setting Your Own Pay—and Other Unusual Compensation Plans," *The Wall Street Journal*, April 13, 1994, p. R6.

21. Byrne, Bongiorno, and Grover, "That Eye-Popping Executive Pay."

22. Greg Burns, "Is Kemper Trying to Give Away the Store," *Business Week*, January 23, 1995.

23. Sue Shellenbarger, "So Much Talk, So Little Action," *The Wall Street Journal*, June 21, 1993, pp. R1–R4.

24. Ibid.

25. Valerie Reitman, "It's All Relative," *The Wall Street Journal*, April 13, 1994, pp. R7–R12.

26. Sharon Walsh, "Hushing Up Harassment?" *The Washington Post*, April 9, 1995, pp. H1 and H7.

27. Sharon Nelton, "Sexual Harassment: Reducing the Risk," *Nation's Business*, March 1995, pp. 24–26.

28. Shellenbarger, "So Much Talk."

29. Carol Kleiman, "GE Finds Its Family Policies Bring Good Things to Employees' Lives," *Washington Post*, September 29, 1992, p. 3B.

30. Dyan Machan, "The Mommy and Daddy Track," *Forbes*, April 16, 1990, pp. 162–63.

31. Michelle Galen and Mike McNamee, "We're Cheating the Kids," *Business Week*, February 20, 1995.

32. Sue Shellenbarger, "The Aging of America Is Making Elder Care a Big Workplace Issue," *The Wall Street Journal*, February 16, 1994, pp. A1–A6.

33. Sue Shellenbarger, "Firms Try Harder, but Often Fail to Help Workers Cope with Elder-Care Problems," *The Wall Street Journal*, June 23, 1993, pp. B1–B4.

34. Meg Cox, "New Magazines Cater to People with HIV," *The Wall Street Journal*, March 1, 1994, p. B1.

35. "Workplace; Odd Jobs," *The Washington Post*, April 4, 1993, p. 12.

36. Jolie Solomon, Patricia King, Carolyn Friday, Peter Annin, D. Richard Silva, Seema Nayyar, and Roger O. Crockett, "Waging War in the Workplace," *Newsweek*, July 19, 1993, pp. 30–34.

37. Mark Krantz, "The Economic Evangelist Who Came Up with the ESOP," *Investor's Business Daily*, February 24, 1995, p. A1.

38. Robert Rose and Erle Norton, "ESOPs Fables," *The Wall Street Journal*, December 23, 1993, pp. A1–A6.

39. Dan Lavin, "Millionaires at Work," *Fortune*, April 3, 1995, pp. 20–21.

40. Rose and Norton, "ESOPs Fables."

41. Steven Baker and Keith L. Alexander, "The Owners vs. the Boss at Weirton Steel," *Business Week*, November 15, 1993, p. 38.

42. Frank Swoboda, "This ESOP Fabel Pits Union against Management," *The Washington Post*, January 22, 1995, p. H6.

Chapter 13

Profile source: Bradford McKee, "If the Shoe Fits, They'll Be Back," *Nation's Business*, July 1992, p. 8; and Joan Koob Cannie, "We Are the Champions," *Small Business Reports*, January 1993, pp. 31–41.

1. Paul Kahn, "Service Quality as Strategy," in Eberhard E. Scheuing and William F. Christopher (eds.), *The Service Quality Handbook* (New York: American Management Association, 1993).

2. Rance Crain, "Success Will Depend on Team Approach," *Marketing News*, March 1994, p. 9.

3. Michael Selz, "Testing Self-Managed Teams, Entrepreneur Hopes to Lose Job," *The Wall Street Journal*, January 11, 1994, p. B1.

4. Jill Griffin, "Customer Loyalty," *Boardroom Reports*, April 1, 1995, pp. 1–2.

5. This quote is from one of the first and best books on relationship marketing: Regis McKenna, *Relationship Marketing* (Reading, Mass.: Addison-Wesley, 1991).

6. John A. Baugh and Christopher W. Rusbuldt, "What the Analysts Say," *Washington Business*, January 31, 1994, p. 31.

7. William H. Davidow and Michael S. Malone, *The Virtual Corporation* (New York: HarperBusiness, 1992), p. 153.

8. "1995: Year of the Customer," *Business Marketing*, January 1995, p. 8.

9. James C. Lawson, "Chipmaker Carves Out a Niche," *Business Marketing*, January 1995, p. 4.

Chapter 14

Profile source: Alan Farnham, "America's Most Admired Company," *Fortune*, February 7, 1994, pp. 50–54; Marshall Loeb, "How to Grow a New Product Every Day," *Fortune*, November 14, 1994, pp. 269–70; and Raul Jacob, "Corporate Reputations," *Fortune*, March 6, 1995, pp. 54–64.

1. Anne H. Soukhanov, "Constant Whitewater," *Atlantic Monthly*, February 1995, p. 116.

2. Michael Selz, "Start-Up Tries to Break the Club's Lock on Car Security," *The Wall Street Journal*, October 24, 1994, pp. B1 and B2.

3. Les Burch, "Moving Away from 'Me Too,'" *Nation's Business*, August 1994, p. 6.

4. Eben Shapiro, "Portions and Packages Grow Bigger and BIGGER," *The Wall Street Journal*, October 12, 1993, pp. B1 and B6.

5. Jack Edmonston, "Taxing Ad Spending to Reflect Equity," *Business Marketing*, January 1995, p. 20.

6. Phyllis Berman, "We Don't Do an Exact Copy," *Forbes*, October 10, 1994, pp. 78–79.

7. *Marketing Tools*, November–December 1994, p. 20.

8. Bill Wagner, "What's the Big Idea?" *Business Ethics*, January/February 1995, p. 18.

9. "'Economy Puts Focus on 'Value' Heinz Chairman O'Reilly Says, and That's Bad for Food Brands," *Advertising Age*, July 19, 1993, pp. 1 and 4.

10. "Wal-Mart's Price War: David versus Goliath," *U.S. News & World Report*, October 25, 1993, p. 14.

11. Peter F. Drucker, "The Five Deadly Business Sins," *The Wall Street Journal*, October 21, 1993, p. A18.

12. Bridget O'Brian, "Continental's CALite Hits Some Turbulence in Battling Southwest," *The Wall Street Journal*, January 10, 1995, pp. A1 and A5.

13. Jennifer Lawerence, "Major Airlines Look for Lift from Low Pricing," *Advertising Age*, February 14, 1994, p. 8; and Kenneth Labich, "Is Herb Kelleher America's Best CEO?" *Fortune*, May 2, 1994, p. 45.

14. Bob Weinstein, "Price Pointers," *Entrepreneur*, February 1995, pp. 48–53.

15. Ibid.

Chapter 15

Profile source: Joan M. Feldman, "Now, More than Ever, Time Is Money," *Air Transport World*, March 1993, pp. 46–52; Gregory L. Miles, "Exporters' New Bully Stick," *International Business*, December 1993, pp. 46–49; and Gregory Miles, "New Age Logistics Units Woo Customers Via Information Technology," *International Business*, January 1995, pp. 32–36.

1. Joan M. Feldman, "Now, More than Ever, Time Is Money," *Air Transport World*, March 1993, pp. 46–52.

2. Robert C. Borsch, "Supply Chain Management," *Boardroom Reports*, July 15, 1994, pp. 9–10.

3. Ronald Henkoff, "Delivering the Goods," *Fortune*, November 28, 1994, pp. 64–78.

4. Ivan T. Hofman, "Current Trends in Small-Package Shipping," *International Business*, March 1994, p. 33.

5. "Unlocking the Secrets of ECR," *Progressive Grocer*, January 1994, p. 3.

6. Marita van Oldenborgh, "Power Logistics," *International Business*, October 1994, pp. 32–34.

7. Gregory L. Miles, "Marriages of Convenience," *International Business*, January 1995, pp. 32–36.

8. "The Air Freight Industry Focuses on Global Customers," *International Business*, October 1994, p. 47.

9. Richard C. Morris, "They Ship Horses, Don't They?" *Forbes*, November 7, 1994, pp. 445–46.

10. "The Future of Truck Transportation," an ad in *Fortune*, April 3, 1995, pp. 107–20.

11. Zina Moukheiber, "Retailing," *Forbes*, January 2, 1995, pp. 190–93.

12. "Dayton's Is Top Retailer in Customer Satisfaction Survey," *Marketing News*, June 6, 1994, p. 8.

13. Christie Brown, "Pooper Scooper Dooper," *Forbes*, February 13, 1995, pp. 78–82.

14. Robert Kahn, "Lessons from Wal-Mart," *Bottom Line Personal*, June 1, 1994, pp. 11–12.

15. Ellen Neuborne, "Small Stores Doing Big Business," *USA Today*, June 22, 1994, p. B1.

Chapter 16

Profile source: Gary Levin, "Pepsi-Cola Taps Rapp for Push in Direct Marketing," *Advertising Age*, December 13, 1993, pp. 3 and 45; Jonathan Berry, "A Potent New Tool for Selling: Database Marketing," *Business Week*, September 5, 1994, pp 56–62; and Niklas Von Daehne, "Court Your Customers with Database Marketing," *Success*, January/February 1995, p. 50.

1. Yvonne Nava, "Apple's First Infomercial," *Business Marketing*, February 1995, p. A7.

2. A letter to the editor of the *Harvard Business Review*, March–April 1994, p. 180.

3. David M. Johnson, "The Internet Frontier," *Business Marketing*, February 1995, p. A4.

4. Debra Aho, "The Ads Stand Alone," *Advertising Age*, May 16, 1994, p. 23.

5. Debra Aho, "Ad Agency Just a Click Away," *Business Marketing*, March 1994, p. 14.

6. Gary Levin, "Global PR Efforts on the Wane," *Advertising Age*, May 16, 1994, p. 28.

7. Joseph Pine II, Don Peppers, and Martha Rogers, "Do You Want to Keep Your Customers Forever?" *Harvard Business Review*, March–April 1995, pp. 103–14.

8. For more on this, see Patricia Sellers, "The Best Way to Reach Your Buyers," *Fortune*, Autumn–Winter 1993, pp. 13–17.

9. Joe Mullich, "Copying Xerox's Style," *Business Marketing*, November 1994, pp. 1 and 48.

10. "Send Testimonials to Current Customers," *Boardroom Reports*, December 1, 1994, p. 6.

11. Kathleen Deveny and Richard Gibson, "Awash in Coupons? Some Firms Try to Stem the Tide," *The Wall Street Journal*, May 10, 1994, pp. B1 and B10.

12. Gabriella Stern, "With Sampling, There Is Too a Free Lunch," *The Wall Street Journal*, March 11, 1994, pp. B1 and B6.

13. Patrice Hill, "PR Researchers Help 'Reinvent' Government," *The Washington Times*, October 24, 1994, p. A17.

14. Don E. Schultz, "Making Mid-Decade Course Corrections," *Marketing News*, February 13, 1995, p. 10.

15. Don E. Schultz, "Maybe We Should Start All Over with an IMC Organization," *Marketing News*, October 25, 1993, p. 8.

16. Kim Cleland, "Few Wed Marketing, Communications," *Advertising Age*, February 27, 1995, p. 10.

17. Rick Fizdale, "Fully Integrating Marketing Equation," *Advertising Age*, September 12, 1994, p. S-2.

Chapter 17

Profile source: Alison L. Sprout, "Saving Time around the Clock," *Fortune*, December 13, 1993, p. 157.

1. John W. Verity, "The Information Revolution," *Business Week/The Information Revolution*, 1994, pp. 10–18.

2. This section is based on Rudy Puryear, "The Moment of Value," *Outlook*, vol. 4, 1994.

3. Geoff Lewis and Robert D. Hof, "The World According to Andy Grove," *Business Week/The Information Revolution*, 1994, pp. 76–78.

4. Catherine Arnst, "The Information Appliance," *Business Week*, November 22, 1993, pp. 98–110.

5. Jeffery Zygmont, "A Hitchhiker's Guide to the Information Superhighway," *CFO*, May 1994, pp. 63–64.

6. This section is based on Eliot Kleinberg, "How to Drive on the Information Highway," *The Washington Times*, April 18, 1994, p. E5.

7. Edward Baig, "Ready to Cruise the Internet," *Business Week*, March 28, 1994, p. 180–81.

8. John Carey, "From Internet to Infobahn," *Business Week/The Information Revolution*, 1994, pp. 32–36.

9. Clifford Stoll, "The Internet? Bah!" *Newsweek*, February 27, 1995, p. 41.

10. This section is based on Rick Tetzeli, "The Internet and Your Business," *Fortune*, March 7, 1994, pp. 86–96; and Tom Goodrich, "Mining the Internet: Tools for Access and Navigation," *Syllabus*, November/December 1994, pp. 16–22.

11. John Krick, "What Every Business Should Know about the Internet," *Boardroom Reports*, July 1, 1994, pp. 3–4; and Jennifer Tanaka and Adam Rogers, "Navigating the Internet," *Newsweek*, January 30, 1995, p. 66.

12. Rick Tetzeli, "Surviving Information Overload," *Fortune*, July 11, 1994, pp. 60–65.

13. Peter Coy, "Faster, Smaller, Cheaper," *Business Week/The Information Revolution*, 1994, pp. 54–57.

14. John Huey, "Waking Up to the New Economy," *Fortune*, June 27, 1994, pp. 36–46.

15. Mark Lewyn, "Going Places," *Business Week/The Information Revolution*, 1994, pp. 176–78.

16. Bill Laberis, "Pull the Plug on Computer Hype," *The Wall Street Journal*, April 25, 1994, p. A12.

17. Thomas A. Stewart, "Managing in a Wired Company," *Fortune*, July 11, 1994, pp. 44–56.

18. Michael Meyer, "Rethinking Your Mainframe," *Newsweek*, June 6, 1994, p. 49.

19. Stephen H. Wildstrom, "Suite Simplicity," *Business Week/The Information Revolution*, 1994, p. 158.

20. Alicia Hills Moore, "You Desktop in the Year 1996," *Fortune*, July 11, 1994, pp. 86–98.

21. James B. Treece, "Breaking the Chains of Command," *Business Week/The Information Revolution*, 1994, pp. 113–14.

22. Peter McGrath, "Info 'Snooper-Highway,'" *Newsweek*, February 27, 1995, pp. 60–61.

23. Michael Meyer, "Considering the PC Paradox," *Newsweek*, February 27, 1995, pp. 48–49.

24. "Hackers Tap Computers in Pentagon," *St. Louis Post-Dispatch*, July 22, 1994, pp. 1A and 7A.

25. David Kirkpatrick, "Making It All Worker-Friendly," *Fortune*, Autumn 1993, pp. 44–53.

26. Catherine Yang, "Flamed with a Lawsuit," *Business Week*, February 6, 1995.

27. Michael Himowitz, "Know What Your Kid's Doing on the Internet," *St. Louis Post-Dispatch*, March 15, 1995, p. 5C.

28. Michael J. Mandel, "The Digital Juggernaut," *Business Week/The Information Revolution*, 1994, pp. 22–30.

29. Michael Meyer, "The Fear of Flaming," *Newsweek*, June 20, 1994, p. 54.

Chapter 18

Profile source: Connie Connors, "The Rise and Fall and Rebirth of a Business," *Home-Office Computing*, March 1991, pp. 39–45; and Joan C. Szabo, "Outside Help with Cash Flow," *Nation's Business*, March 1995, pp. 38–39.

1. Sheryl Silver, "Accounting & Finance: Hiring Heats Up," *Washington Post*, September 25, 1994, p. K7.

2. Ronald Henkoff, "Inside Andersen's Army of Advice," *Fortune*, October 4, 1993, pp. 78–86.

3. David R. Evanson, "Super CPAs," *Entrepreneur*, January 1995, pp. 43–45.

4. Bob Weinstein, "Balancing Act," *Entrepreneur*, March 1995, pp. 56–61.

5. John T. Hiatt, "Corporate Buried Treasure," *International Business*, February 1994, pp. 32–36.

6. Szabo, "Outside Help."

7. "Getting Ahead of the Profitability Learning Curve," *Industrial Launderer*, April 1994, pp. 39–42.

8. Matthew S. Scott, "2 Decades in the Black," *Black Enterprise*, October 1994, pp. 150–56.

Chapter 19

Profile source: Nancy A. Nichols, "Scientific Management at Merck: An Interview with CFO Judy Lewent," *Harvard Business Review*, January/February 1994, pp. 89–99; Judy Lewent, "A Long-Term Vision for Finance," *CFO*, July 1993, p. 6; Phillip L. Zweig, "The High Art of Hedging at Merck," *Business Week*, October 31, 1994, p. 88; and "The Best of 1994," *Business Week*, January 9, 1995, pp. 101–19.

1. Terence P. Paré, "GE Monkeys with Its Money Machine," *Fortune*, February 21, 1994, pp. 81–87.

2. Leonard Machlis, "Factoring: Affordable, Effective Financing," *Bottom Line/Business*, June 1, 1995, pp. 3–4.

3. Nancy A. Nichols, "Scientific Management at Merck: An Interview with CFO Judy Lewent," *Harvard Business Review*, January/February 1994, pp. 89–99.

4. Jenny C. McCune, "Job One: Find Money," *Success*, December 1994, pp. 23–33.

5. Laura Landro and Johnnie L. Roberts, "Viacom Is Set to Grow into Media Colossus—or Burdened Giant," *The Wall Street Journal*, February 16, 1994, pp. A1–A6.

6. David R. Evanson, "10 Creative Ways to Get the Cash You Need," *Entrepreneur*, April 1995, pp. 108–15.

Chapter 20

Profile source: John Yatt, "A Fund That Does Well by Doing Good," *Fortune*, December 13, 1993, p. 40; and Laura Zinn and Michael O'Neal, "Will Politically Correct Sell Sweaters?" *Newsweek*, March 16, 1992, pp. 60–61.

1. Philip L. Zweig, "Sweet Yields Are Starting to Make Bonds Look Very Tempting," *Business Week*, December 26, 1994, pp. 138–39.

2. Larry Light, Tim Smart, Chuck Hawkins, and Dori Jones Young, "As Long Bonds Get Longer, Do They Get Riskier?" *Business Week*, June 28, 1993, pp. 92–93.

3. Pam Black, "A Safer Way to Drive Down Wall Street," *Business Week*, May 15, 1995, p. 148.

4. James S. Altschul, "Cheap Tricks with Stock Dividends," *CFO*, May 1993, pp. 65–68.

5. Ibid.

6. Michael Schroeder, "Babysitting the World's Emerging Bourses," *Business Week*, November 1, 1993, pp. 112–15.

7. Michael R. Sesit, "Direct Access to World Markets Is Said to Be Easier and Cheaper," *The Wall Street Journal*, October 19, 1994, pp. C1 and C12.

8. Kevin McManus, "NASDAQ Battles for Bigger Share of Stock Market," *Washington Post*, March 7, 1994, p. 5.

9. Bill Graham, "Should the AMEX Get More Respect?" *CFO*, January 1994, pp. 53–54.

10. McManus, "NASDAQ Battles."

11. Geoffrey Smith, "Mutual Funds: The Rules on Insider Trading, Please," *Business Week*, January 31, 1994, p. 60.

12. Jolie Solomon and Daniel McGinn, "What Makes Them Tick," *Newsweek*, March 14, 1994, p. 40–42.

13. "Chimpanzee Beats 5 Swedish Analysts at Picking Stocks," *St. Louis Post-Dispatch*, September 8, 1993, p. C1.

14. "How Stock Is Purchased," *Los Angeles Times*, May 22, 1991, p. D3.

15. Pam Black, "Taking the Bafflement Out of Bonds," *Business Week*, March 29, 1993, pp. 98–99.

16. *The Turnaround Letter*, September 1994, pp. 1–8.

17. Georgette Jasen, "Pros and Cons of Borrowing from Your Broker," *The Wall Street Journal*, April 21, 1993, pp. C1–C4.

18. Brett D. Fromson, "If the Boom Goes Bust . . . ," *Washington Post*, March 19, 1994, pp. C1 and C8.

19. Jane Bryant Quinn, "Banks and the Shoeshine Market," *St. Louis Post-Dispatch*, March 7, 1994, p. 49.

20. Chet Currier, "You Won't Go Wrong if You Diversify," *The Washington Times*, April 17, 1995, p. B8.

Chapter 21

Profile source: Barbara Rudolph and Frederick Angeheuer, "A Conservative Who Can Compromise," *Time*, June 15, 1987, pp. 50–51; Patrice Hill, "Greenspan Warns of Falling Dollar," *The Washington Times*, July 21, 1994, pp. A1 and A9; H. Erich Heinemann, "Alan Greenspan Meets John Wayne," *The Washington Times*, December 17, 1994, p. D1, and Matthew Schifrin, "Financial Services," *Forbes*, January 2, 1995, pp. 164–67.

1. Christopher Farrell, "The Dollar Doesn't Deserve This Thumping," *Business Week*, March 20, 1995, p.51.

2. "Fed Squeezes Borrowers a Bit Tighter," *St. Louis Post-Dispatch*, August 17, 1994, pp. A1 and A8.

3. Jane Bryant Quinn, "Taking Aim at the People's Bank," *Newsweek*, August 8, 1994, p. 37.

4. Deborah Lohse, "Interstate Banking Promises Conveniences—and Costs," *The Wall Street Journal*, August 3, 1994, pp. C1 and C24.

5. Michelle Singletary, "Now, Home May Be Where the Bank Is," *Washington Business*, January 16, 1995, pp. 1 and 14–15.

6. B. G. Yovovich, "Banking on Home Interactivity," *Advertising Age*, January 16, 1995, pp. 21 and 23.

7. Peter Weaver, "ATMs Abroad Dispense Foreign Currency," *Nation's Business*, August 1994, p. 66.

8. "The 100 Largest Banking Companies," *Fortune*, August 22, 1994, p. 184.

Chapter 22

Profile source: Robert L. Wallace, *Black Wealth through Black Entrepreneurship* (Edgewood, Md.: Duncan & Duncan, 1993); "Entrepreneurs across America," *Entrepreneur*, June 1994, pp. 84–102; and Sharon Nelton, "The Family in Black Businesses," *Nation's Business*, January 1995, p. 54.

1. Marc Rice, "Road to Riches Traveled in Pickup, Not Ferrari," *The Washington Times*, May 14, 1994, p. D5.

2. Mike Yorkey, "Where Did All the Money Go?" *Focus on the Family*, April 1993, pp. 2–3.

3. Andrew Leckey, "Resolve to Cut Debt, Diversify Investments," *The Washington Times*, January 4, 1995, p. B7.

4. Vivian Marino, "Personal Finance 101 May Be the Next College Requirement," *The Philadelphia Inquirer*, August 20, 1994, p. D1.

5. U.S. Bureau of the Census, 1994.

6. Andrew Tobias, "You can Invest Shrewdly Now," *Parade Magazine*, March 20, 1994, pp. 18–19.

7. David Glick, "The 1995 Financial Services Report," an ad in *Forbes*, March 27, 1995.

8. "Baby Boomers Will Doom Social Security, Group Warns," *St. Louis Post-Dispatch*, August 18, 1994, p. 8A.

9. Vivian Marino, "Plant the Seed Early on, Watch the Money Grow," *The Washington Times*, March 17, 1995, p. B9.

10. Al Ehrbar, "How Washington Can Stop Its War on Savings," *Fortune*, March 6, 1995, pp. 133–50.

GLOSSARY

absolute advantage (p. 89) When a country has a monopoly on producing a product or is able to produce it at a cost below that of all other countries.

accounting (p. 550) The recording, classifying, summarizing, and interpreting of financial events and transactions to provide management and other interested parties the information they need to make better decisions.

accounting cycle (p. 555) A six-step procedure that results in the preparation and analysis of the two major financial statements: the balance sheet and the income statement.

accounting system (p. 551) The methods used to record and summarize accounting data into reports.

acquisition (p. 162) A company's purchase of the property and obligations of another company.

Active Corps of Executives (ACE) (p. 196) Volunteers from industry, trade associations, and education who counsel small business.

adjustable life insurance (p. 676) Insurance policy that allows policyholder to switch back and forth from whole life to term as one's needs change.

administered distribution system (p. 471) Distribution system in which all the marketing functions at the retail level are managed by producers.

administrative agencies (p. 131) Institutions created by Congress with delegated power to pass rules and regulations within their mandated area of authority.

adversarial marketing (p. 411) Buyers and sellers have different, often conflicting goals, so that what is good for one may not be good for the other.

advertising (p. 493) Paid, nonpersonal communication through various media by organizations and individuals who are in some way identified in the advertising message.

affirmative action (p. 361) Employment activities designed to "right past wrongs" endured by females and minorities.

agency shop agreement (p. 377) Clause in labor–management agreement that says employers may hire nonunion workers who are not required to join the union but must pay a union fee.

American Federation of Labor (AFL) (p. 374) An organization of craft unions that championed bread-and-butter labor issues.

analytic system (p. 281) Manufacturing systems that break down raw materials into components to extract other products.

annual report (p. 552) A yearly statement of the financial condition and progress of an organization covering a one-year period.

apprenticeship (p. 348) Training involving a new worker working alongside a master technician to learn the skills and procedures of a job.

arbitration (p. 379) The agreement to bring in an impartial third party (an arbitrator) to render a binding decision in a labor dispute.

assembly process (p. 281) Production process that puts together components.

assets (p. 558) The economic resources owned by the firm.

auditing (p. 553) The task of reviewing and evaluating the records used to prepare the company's financial statements.

autocratic leadership (p. 226) Leadership style that involves making decisions without consulting others and implies power over others.

balance of payments (p. 92) The difference between money coming into a country (from exports) and money leaving the country (for imports) plus money flows from other factors such as tourism, foreign aid, military expenditures, and foreign investment.

balance of trade (p. 92) The relationship of exports to imports.

balance sheet (p. 557) Financial statement which reports the financial position of a firm on a specific date. A balance sheet is composed of assets, liabilities, and owners' equity.

banker's acceptance (p. 658) A promise that the bank will pay some specified amount at a particular time.

bankruptcy (p. 140) The legal process by which a person or business, unable to meet financial obligations, is relieved of those debts by having the court divide any assets among creditors, freeing the debtor to begin anew.

bargaining zone (p. 379) Range of options between the initial and final offer that each party will consider before a union will strike or before management will close a plant.

bartering (p. 98) The exchange of goods or services for goods or services.

blue chip stocks (p. 624) Stocks of high-quality companies.

bond (p. 610)   A corporate certificate indicating that a person has loaned money to a firm.

bookkeeping (p. 554)   The recording of business transactions.

brand (p. 441)   A name, symbol, or design (or combination of these) that identifies the goods or services of one seller or group of sellers and distinguishes them from those of competitors.

brand association (p 444)   The linking of a brand to other, favorable images.

brand awareness (p. 443)   The first product recalled when a product category is mentioned.

brand equity (p. 443)   Combination of factors such as awareness, loyalty, perceived quality, the feeling and images, and any other emotion people associate with a brand name.

brand loyalty (p. 443)   The degree to which customers are satisfied, like the brand, and are committed to further purchases.

brand name (p. 407)   A word, letter, or group of words or letters that differentiates the goods and services of a seller from those of competitors.

breach of contract (p. 135)   Violation when one party fails to follow the terms of a contract.

break-even analysis (p. 454)   The process used to determine profitability at various levels of sales.

budget (p. 588)   A financial plan that allocates resources based on projected revenues.

bureaucracy (p. 244)   Organization with three layers of authority: (1) top managers who make decisions, (2) middle managers who develop procedures for implementing decisions, and (3) workers and supervisors who do the work.

business (p. 29)   Any activity that seeks profit by providing needed goods and services to others.

business law (p. 130)   Rules, statutes, codes, and regulations established to provide a legal framework within which business may be conducted and that are enforceable in court.

business plan (p. 189)   A detailed written statement that describes the nature of the business, the target market, the advantages the business will have over competitors, and the resources and qualifications of the owners.

buying on margin (p. 624)   The purchase of stocks by borrowing some of the purchase cost from the brokerage firm.

cafeteria-style fringe benefits (p. 356)   Fringe benefits plan which allows employees to choose the benefits they want up to a certain dollar amount.

call provision (p. 613)   Clause in a bond which gives the issuer of the bond the right to pay off the bond before its maturity.

capital budget (p. 589)   The firm's spending plans for major asset purchases that often require large sums of money.

capital expenditures (p. 592)   Major investments in long-term assets such as land, buildings, equipment, or research and development.

capitalism (p. 61)   An economic system in which all or most of the means of production and distribution are privately owned and operated for profit.

cash-and-carry wholesaler (p. 478)   A limited-function wholesaler that serves mostly smaller retailers with a limited assortment of products.

cash budget (p. 589)   Projects the cash balance at the end of a given period.

cash flow (p. 564)   The difference between cash receipts and cash disbursements.

cash flow forecast (p. 587)   A prediction of cash inflows and outflows in future periods.

centralized authority (p. 253)   Maintaining decision-making authority with the top level of management at its headquarters.

certification (p. 376)   Process of a union's becoming recognized by the NLRB as the bargaining agent for a group of employees.

certified internal auditor (p. 554)   An accountant who has a bachelor's degree, has two years of internal auditing experience, and has successfully passed an exam administered by the Institute of Internal Auditors.

certified management accountant (p. 552)   A professional accountant who has met certain educational and experience requirements and been certified by the Institute of Certified Management Accountants.

certified public accountant (CPA) (p. 553)   Accountant who passes a series of examinations established by the American Institute of Certified Public Accountants (AICPA) and meets the state's requirements for education and experience.

channel captain (p. 471)   The organization in the marketing channel that gets the other members to work together in a cooperative effort.

channel of distribution (p. 464)   Marketing middlemen such as wholesalers and retailers who join together to transport and store goods in their path (channel) from producers to consumers.

closed-shop agreement (p. 377)   Clause in labor–management agreement specified that workers had to be members of a union before being hired.

cognitive dissonance (p. 421)   Consumer doubts after the purchase about whether or not the purchase was the best product at the best price.

collective bargaining (p. 376)   The process whereby union and management representatives reach a negotiated labor-management agreement.

command economies (p. 63) Economic systems in which the government largely decides what goods and services will be produced, who will get them, and how the economy will grow.

commercial and consumer finance companies (p. 653) Institutions that offer short-term loans to businesses or individuals who either can't meet the credit requirements of regular banks or else have exceeded their credit limit and need more funds.

commercial bank (p. 648) A profit-making organization that receives deposits from individuals and corporations in the form of checking and savings accounts and uses some of these funds to make loans.

commercial finance companies (p. 596) Organizations that make short-term loans to borrowers that offer tangible assets as collateral.

commercial paper (p. 596) A short-term corporate equivalent of an IOU that is sold in the marketplace by a firm; it matures in 270 days or less.

commodity exchange (p. 627) Securities exchange which specializes in the buying and selling of precious metals and minerals (e.g., silver, foreign currencies, gasoline) and agricultural goods (e.g., wheat, cattle, sugar).

common law (p. 131) The body of law that comes from judges' decisions; also known as "unwritten law."

common market (p. 105) A regional group of countries that have no internal tariffs, a common external tariff, and a coordination of laws to facilitate exchange; an example is the European Union.

common stock (p. 617) The most basic form of ownership of firms; it includes voting rights and dividends, if dividends are offered by the firm.

communications software (p. 537) Computer software that makes it possible for different brands of computers to transfer data to each other.

comparable worth (p. 388) The demand for equal pay for jobs requiring similar levels of education, training, and skills.

comparative advantage theory (p. 89) Theory which asserts that a country should produce and sell to other countries those products that it produces most efficiently.

competitive benchmarking (p. 262) Rating an organization's practices, processes, and products against the world's best.

compliance-based ethics codes (p. 119) Ethical standards that emphasize preventing unlawful behavior by increasing control and by penalizing wrongdoers.

compressed workweek (p. 358) Work schedule that involves same number of hours per week in fewer days.

computer-aided design (CAD) (p. 187) The use of computers in the design of products.

computer-aided manufacturing (CAM) (p. 287) The use of computers in the manufacturing of products.

conceptual skills (p. 230) Ability to picture the organization as a whole and the relationship between the various parts.

conglomerate merger (p. 162) The joining of firms in completely unrelated industries.

Congress of Industrial Organizations (CIO) (p. 375) Union organization of unskilled workers which broke away from the AFL in 1935 and rejoined it in 1955.

consideration (p. 135) Something of value; it's one of the requirements of a legal contract.

Constant whitewater (p. 434) The unremitting turmoil in today's corporate life.

consumer market (p. 421) All individuals or households who want goods and services for personal consumption or use.

consumer price index (CPI) (p. 73) Monthly statistics that measure changes in the prices of about 400 goods and services that consumers buy.

consumerism (p. 138) A social movement that tries to increase the rights and powers of buyers in relation to sellers.

contingency planning (p. 216) Process of preparing alternative courses of action that may be used if the primary plans do not achieve the objectives of the organization.

continuous improvement (p. 259) Procedures designed to insure and inspire constant creative interaction and problem solving.

contract (p. 135) A legally enforceable agreement between two or more parties.

contract law (p. 135) Laws which specify what constitutes a legally enforceable agreement.

contract manufacturing (p. 96) Production of private-label goods by a company to which another company then attaches its brand name or trademark.

contractual distribution system (p. 470) Distribution system in which members are bound to cooperate through contractual agreements.

controlling (p. 214) Management function that involves checking to determine whether or not an organization is progressing toward its goals and objectives, and taking corrective action if it is not.

convenience goods and services (p. 437) Products that the consumer wants to purchase frequently and with a minimum of effort.

convertible bond (p. 613) A bond that can be converted into shares of common stock.

cooling-off period (p. 383) Period during which workers return to their jobs while the union and management continue negotiations.

cooperative (p. 163) An organization owned by members/customers who pay an annual membership fee and share in any profits (if it is a profit-making organization).

copyright (p. 133) Exclusive rights to materials such as books, articles, photos, and cartoons.

core competencies (p. 262) Functions that the organization can do as well as or better than anyone else in the world.

core time (p. 357) The period when all employees are present in a flextime system.

corporate distribution system (p. 470) Distribution system in which all the organizations in the channel are owned by one firm.

corporate philanthropy (p. 120) Dimension of social responsibility that includes charitable donations.

corporate policy (p. 120) Dimension of social responsibility that refers to the position a firm takes on social and political issues.

corporate responsibility (p. 120) Dimension of social responsibility that includes everything from minority hiring practices to the making of safe products.

corporation (p. 148) A legal entity with authority to act and have liability separate from its owners.

cost of goods sold (cost of goods manufactured) (p. 562) A particular type of expense measured by the total cost of merchandise sold or cost of raw materials or parts and supplies used for producing items for resale.

countertrading (p. 98) Bartering among several countries.

craft union (p. 373) Labor organization of skilled specialists in a particular craft or trade.

credit unions (p. 652) Nonprofit, member-owned financial cooperatives that offer basic banking services such as accepting deposits and making loans; they may also offer life insurance and a limited number of home mortgages.

critical path (p. 290) The sequence of tasks that takes the longest time to complete.

cross-functional teams (p. 256) Groups of employees from different departments who work together on a semi-permanent basis (as opposed to the temporary teams established in matrix-style organizations).

cumulative preferred stock (p. 616) Preferred stock which accumulates unpaid dividends.

currency (p. 643) All coin and paper money issued by the Federal Reserve banks and all coins.

currency exchange (p. 658) Exchange of currency from one country with currency from another country.

current assets (p. 558) Resources, including cash or noncash items, that can be converted to cash within one year.

damages (p. 135) The monetary settlement awarded to a person who is injured by a breach of contract.

data processing (DP) (p. 524) Technology that supported existing business (primarily used to improve the flow of financial information).

databank (p. 38) Electronic storage file for information.

database program (p. 537) Computer software that allows users to store and manipulate information that is normally kept in lists (names and addresses, inventories, etc.).

debenture bond (p. 612) A bond that is unsecured (i.e., not backed with any collateral such as equipment).

debt capital (p. 593) Funds raised by borrowing money through the sale of bonds or from banks and other lending institutions.

debtor nation (p. 94) Country that owes more money to other nations than they owe it.

decentralized authority (p. 253) Delegating decision-making authority to lower-level managers who are more familiar with local conditions.

decertification (p 376) Process by which workers take away a union's right to represent them.

decision making (p. 231) Choosing among two or more alternatives.

delegating (p. 230) Assigning authority and accountability to others while retaining responsibility for results.

demand (p. 69) The quantity of products that people are willing to buy at different prices at a specific time.

demand deposit (p. 649) The technical name for a checking account; the money can be withdrawn on demand at any time by the owner.

democratic (participative) leadership (p. 226) Leadership style that consists of managers and employees working together to make decisions.

demography (p. 42) The statistical study of human population to learn its size, density, and other characteristics.

departmentalization (p. 250) Dividing tasks into homogeneous departments such as manufacturing and marketing.

depreciation (p. 566) The systematic write-off of the value of an asset over its estimated useful life.

depression (p. 76) A severe recession.

deregulation (p. 142) Government withdrawal of certain laws and regulations that seem to hinder competition (for example, airline regulations).

devaluation (p. 101) Lowering the value of a nation's currency relative to other currencies.

direct marketing (p. 492) Marketing that allows consumers to buy products by interacting with various advertising media without meeting a salesperson face-to-face.

directing (p. 214) Management function that involves guiding and motivating others to achieve the goals and objectives of the organization.

discount rate (p. 646) The interest rate that the Fed charges for loans to member banks.

diversification (p. 626) Buying several different investments to spread the risk.

dividends (p. 614)   The part of the firm's profits that goes to stockholders.

double-entry bookkeeping (p. 555)   A system of bookkeeping in which two entries in the journal are required for each company transaction.

Dow Jones Industrial Average (p. 631)   The average cost of 30 specific industrial stocks; used to give an indication of the direction of the market over time.

downsizing (p. 28)   Making organizations more efficient by laying off workers.

drop shipper (p. 479)   A limited-function wholesaler that solicits orders from retailers and other wholesalers and has the merchandise shipped directly from a producer to a buyer.

dumping (p. 92)   Selling products for less in a foreign country than is charged in the producing country.

economics (p. 60)   The study of how society chooses to employ resources to produce various goods and services and distribute them for consumption among various competing groups and individuals.

efficient consumer response (ECR) (p. 472)   The electronic linking of firms to provide more efficient response to consumer needs.

electronic data interchange (EDI) (p. 472)   Software that enables the computers of producers, wholesalers, and retailers to talk with each other.

electronic funds transfer system (EFTS) (p. 657)   A computerized system which electronically performs financial transactions such as making purchases, paying bills, and receiving paychecks.

embargo (p. 103)   A complete ban on the import or export of certain products.

employee orientation (p. 348)   The activity that introduces new employees to the organization, to fellow employees, to their immediate supervisors, and to the policies, practices, and objectives of the firm.

employee stock ownership plan (ESOP) (p. 392)   A plan whereby employees can buy part or total ownership of the firm where they work.

empowerment (p. 220)   Giving employees the authority and responsibility to respond quickly to customer requests.

enterprise resource planning (ERP) (p. 282)   Computer-based production and operations system that links multiple firms into one, integrated production unit.

entrepreneur (p. 28)   A person who takes the risk of starting and managing a business.

entrepreneurial team (p. 181)   A group of experienced people from different areas of business who join together to form a managerial team with the skills needed to develop, make, and market new products.

entrepreneurship (p. 178)   The acceptance of the risk of starting and managing a new business.

equity capital (p. 593)   Funds raised within the company or from selling ownership in the firm.

esteem needs (p. 312)   The needs for self-confidence and status.

ethics (p. 117)   The study of standards of conduct and moral judgment.

ethnocentricity (p. 98)   The feeling that one's culture is superior to all others.

exchange rate (p. 101)   The value of one currency relative to the currencies of other countries.

exclusive distribution (p. 482)   The distribution strategy that uses only one retail outlet in a given geographic area.

expenses (p. 562)   Costs incurred in operating a business, such as rent, utilities, and salaries.

export trading companies (p. 95)   Companies that attempt to match buyers and sellers from different countries.

exporting (p. 88)   Selling products to another country.

express warranties (p. 134)   Specific representations by the seller regarding the goods.

extrinsic reward (p. 308)   Reinforcement from someone else as recognition for good work, including pay increases, praise, and promotions.

factoring (p. 596)   Selling accounts receivable for cash.

factors of production (p. 33)   The resources used to create wealth: land, labor, capital, entrepreneurship, and information.

falling dollar (p. 644)   The value of the dollar changes such that the amount of goods and services you can buy with a dollar goes down.

Federal Deposit Insurance Corporation(FDIC) (p. 654)   An independent U.S. government agency that insures bank deposits.

federal deficit (p. 79)   The difference between federal revenue and federal spending in any given year.

FIFO (first in, first out) (p. 566)   Accounting technique for calculating cost of inventory based on first in, first out.

finance (p. 585)   The function in a business responsible for acquiring funds for the firm, managing funds within the firm, and planning for the expenditure of funds on various assets.

financial accounting (p. 552)   The preparation of financial statements for people outside of the firm (for example, investors).

financial control (p. 589)   A process that periodically compares the actual revenue, costs, and expenses with projections.

financial management (p. 585)   Management of the firm's resources so it can meet its goals and objectives.

financial statement (p. 557)   The summary of all transactions that have occurred over a particular period.

fiscal policy (p. 77)   Government efforts to keep the economy stable by increasing or decreasing taxes or government spending.

fixed assets (p. 558)   Resources of a permanent nature, such as land, buildings, furniture, and fixtures.

flexible manufacturing (p. 284)   Totally automated production centers that can perform a variety of functions to produce different products.

flextime plans (p. 357)   Work schedule that gives employees some freedom to adjust when they work as long as they work the required number of hours.

floating exchange rate (p. 101)   Value of currencies fluctuate according to the supply and demand in the market for the currency.

focus group (p. 418)   A small group of people who meet under the direction of a discussion leader to communicate their feelings concerning an organization, its products, or other important issues.

Foreign Corrupt Practices Act of 1978 (p. 101)   Law that prohibits "questionable" or "dubious" payments to foreign officials to secure business contracts.

foreign direct investment (p. 94)   Buying of permanent property and businesses in foreign nations.

foreign subsidiary (p. 96)   A company owned by another company (parent company) in a foreign country.

form utility (p. 277)   The value added by the creation of finished goods and services using raw materials, components, and other inputs.

formal organization (p. 266)   The structure that details lines of responsibility, authority, and position. It is the structure that is shown on organizational charts.

401(k) retirement plan (p. 679)   Retirement plan that reduces your present taxable income, defers tax on your earnings, and allows employers to match part of your deposit.

franchise (p. 163)   The right to use a specific business's name and sell its products or services in a given territory.

franchise agreement (p. 163)   An arrangement whereby someone with a good idea for a business sells the rights to use the business name and sell its products or services to others in a given territory.

franchisee (p. 163)   A person who buys a franchise.

franchisor (p. 163)   A company that develops a product concept and sells others the rights to make and sell the products.

free market economies (p. 63)   Economic systems in which decisions about what to produce and in what quantities are decided by the market; that is, by buyers and sellers negotiating prices for goods and services.

free trade (p. 89)   The movement of goods and services among nations without political or economic obstruction.

free trade area (p. 106)   Market in which nations can trade freely without tariffs or other trade barriers.

fringe benefits (p. 355)   Benefits such as sick leave pay, vacation pay, pension plans, and health plans that represent additional compensation to employees.

full-service wholesaler (p. 478)   A merchant wholesaler that performs all distribution functions.

fundamental accounting equation (p. 560)   Assets = Liability + Owners' equity; it is the basis for the balance sheet.

futures market (p. 627)   The purchase and sale of goods for delivery sometime in the future.

Gantt chart (p. 291)   Bar graph showing production managers what projects are being worked on and what stage they are in on a daily basis.

General Agreement on Tariffs and Trade (GATT) (p. 104)   Agreement among 124 countries which provided a forum for negotiating mutual reductions in trade restrictions.

general partner (p. 151)   An owner (partner) who has unlimited liability and is active in managing the firm.

general partnership (p. 151)   A partnership in which all owners share in operating the business and in assuming liability for the business's debts.

generic goods (p. 443)   Nonbranded products that usually sell at a sizable discount from national or private brands, have very basic packaging, and are backed with little or no advertising.

generic name (p. 442)   The name of a product category.

givebacks (p. 384)   Concessions made by unions to help employers remain competitive and save jobs.

global marketing (p. 99)   Selling the same product in essentially the same way everywhere in the world.

goals (p. 215)   Broad, long-term accomplishments an organization wishes to attain.

goal-setting theory (p. 321)   Theory that setting specific, attainable goals can motivate workers and improve performance if the goals are accepted, are accompanied by feedback, and are facilitated by organizational conditions.

golden parachute (p. 387)   A sizable severance package for corporate managers whose jobs may be threatened by a takeover by another firm.

goods (p. 49)   Tangible products such as houses, food, and clothing.

green product (p. 411)   A product whose production, use, and disposal don't damage the environment.

grievance (p. 378)   A charge by employees that management is not abiding by the terms of the negotiated labor agreement.

gross domestic product (GDP) (p. 72)   The total value of goods and services produced in a country in a given year.

gross margin (p. 562)   How much the firm earned by buying and selling or making and selling merchandise.

groupware (p. 537)   Computer software that allows people to work collaboratively and share ideas.

growth stocks (p. 624)   Stocks of companies whose earnings are expected to grow faster than other stocks or the overall economy.

Hawthorne effect (p. 311)   The tendency for people to behave differently when they know they are being studied.

health maintenance organizations (HMOs) (p. 689)   Health care organizations that require policyholders to choose from a restricted list of doctors and hospitals.

hedging (p. 627)   Buying or selling commodities in the futures market.

hierarchy (p. 244)   Organization with several levels of managers.

horizontal merger (p. 162)   The joining of two firms in the same industry.

human relations skills (p. 230)   Ability to lead, communicate, motivate, coach, build morale, train, support, and delegate.

human resource management (p. 338)   The process of evaluating human resource needs, finding people to fill those needs, and getting the best work from each employee by providing the right incentives and job enrichment, all with the goal of meeting the objectives of the organization.

hygiene factors (p. 318)   Factors that cause dissatisfaction if they are missing, but do not motivate if they are increased.

implied warranties (p. 134)   Guarantees legally imposed on the seller.

import quota (p. 103)   Limiting the number of products in certain categories that can be imported.

importing (p. 88)   Buying products from another country.

income statement (p. 560)   Financial statement which reports revenues and expenses over a specific period of time, showing the results of operations during that period. It summarizes all the resources that came into the firm (revenues), and all the resources that left the firm and the resulting net income or loss.

income stock (p. 624)   Stocks that offer a high dividend.

incubators (p. 191)   Centers which provide "newborn" businesses (usually in technological industries) with low-cost offices and basic business services.

indenture terms (p. 599)   The terms of agreement in a bond.

independent audit (p. 553)   An evaluation and unbiased opinion about the accuracy of company financial statements.

individual retirement account (p. 678)   Tax-deferred retirement investment plan.

industrial goods (p. 438)   Products used in the production of other products.

industrial market (p. 422)   All individuals and organizations that want goods and services to produce other goods and services or to sell, rent, or supply the goods to others.

industrial marketing (p. 426)   The marketing of goods and services to manufacturers, institutions, commercial operations, and the government.

industrial unions (p. 374)   Labor organizations of unskilled workers in mass production–related industries such as automobiles and mining.

inflation (p. 75)   A general rise in the prices of goods and services over time.

infomercials (p. 495)   TV programs that are devoted exclusively to promoting goods and services.

informal organization (p. 266)   The system of relationships and lines of authority that develops spontaneously as employees meet and form power centers. It is the human side of the organization and does not show on any formal charts.

information highway (p. 527)   Telecommunications technology that allows users to send and receive large amounts of digital data.

information superhighway (I-way) (p. 37)   The network of computer and telecommunications equipment that links people throughout the world into one unified communications system.

information systems (IS) (p. 524)   Technology that helps companies do business (includes such tools as ATMs and voice mail).

information technology (IT) (p. 524)   Technology that helps companies change business by its applications to new methods of doing business.

information utility (p. 416)   Value added to products by opening two-way flows of information between marketing participants.

injunction (p. 382)   A court order directing someone to do something or refrain from doing something.

insider trading (p. 621)   The use of knowledge or information that a person gains through his or her position that allows the person to benefit from fluctuations in stock prices.

institutional investors (p. 632)   Large investors such as pension funds, mutual funds, insurance companies, and banks.

insurable interest (p. 687)   Possibility of policyholder to suffer a loss.

insurable risk (p. 687)   Risk that a typical insurance company will cover.

insurance policy (p. 687)   A written contract between the insured and an insurance company that promises to pay for all or part of a loss.

intangible assets (p. 558)   Items that are not included in the current and fixed assets categories. This catch-all category includes items such as patents and copyrights.

integrated marketing (IM) (p. 510)   The merging of all organizational efforts to please customers, employees, and other stakeholders.

integrated marketing communication (IMC) system (p. 509)   A formal mechanism for uniting all the promotional efforts in an organization to make it more responsive to its customers and other stakeholders.

integrated software package (suite) (p. 537)   Computer software that offers two or more applications in one package.

integrity (p. 117)   The honesty, sincerity, and morality of a person.

integrity-based ethics codes (p. 119)   Ethical standards that define the organization's guiding values, create an environment that supports ethically sound behavior, and stress a shared accountability among employees.

intensive distribution (p. 482)   The distribution strategy that puts products into as many retail outlets as possible, including vending machines.

interactive television (p. 497)   Technology that enables TV viewers to respond or get involved with TV programs and commercials electronically .

interest (p. 611)   The payment the issuer of a bond makes to bondholders for the use of borrowed money.

internal customers (p. 223)   Units within the firm that receive services from other units.

Internet (p. 528)   A connection of tens of thousands of interconnected computer networks that includes 1.7 million host computers.

intrapreneur (p.182)   A person with entrepreneurial skills who is employed in a corporation to launch new products; such people take hands-on responsibility for creating innovation of any kind in an organization.

intrinsic reward (p. 308)   The good feeling you have when you have done a job well.

inventory financing (p. 595)   Using inventory as collateral or security for a loan.

inverted organization (p. 266)   Organization that has contact people at the top and the chief executive officer at the bottom of the organization chart.

investment bankers (p. 631)   Specialists in assisting in the issue and selling of new securities.

invisible hand (p. 61)   The term coined by Adam Smith to describe the mechanism for creating wealth and jobs.

involuntary bankruptcy (p. 140)   Bankruptcy procedures filed by a debtor's creditors.

ISO 9000 (p. 48)   Quality management and assurance standards published by the International Organization for Standardization (ISO).

job analysis (p. 342)   A study of what is done by employees who fill various job titles.

job description (p. 342)   A summary of the objectives of a job, the type of work, the responsibilities of the job, the necessary skills, the working conditions, and the relationship of the job to other functions.

job enlargement (p. 321)   Job enrichment strategy involving combining a series of tasks into one assignment that is more challenging and interesting.

job enrichment (p. 319)   Efforts to make jobs more interesting, challenging, and rewarding.

job rotation (p. 321)   Job enrichment strategy involving moving employees from one job to another.

job sharing (p. 357)   An arrangement whereby two or more part-time employees share one full-time job.

job simplification (p. 321)   Process of producing task efficiency by breaking down the job into simple steps and assigning people to each of those steps.

job simulation (p. 349)   A training method that uses equipment that duplicates job conditions and tasks so that trainees can learn skills before attempting them on the job.

job specifications (p. 342)   Written summary of the qualifications required of workers to do a particular job.

joint venture (p. 97)   A partnership in which companies (often from two or more different countries) join to undertake a major project.

journal (p. 554)   Recording device used for the first recording of all transactions.

junk bonds (p. 623)   High-risk, high-interest bonds.

Keogh plan (p. 679)   Retirement plan for self-employed people that allows the investment of more than $30,000 per year. Keogh funds and their returns are not taxed.

Knights of Labor (p. 374) The first national labor union (1869).

knowledge technology (KT) (p. 525) Technology that adds a layer of intelligence to filter appropriate information and deliver it when it is needed.

laissez-faire (free-reign) leadership (p. 226) Leadership style that involves managers setting objectives and employees being relatively free to do whatever it takes to accomplish those objectives.

law of large numbers (p. 688) Principle which states that if a large number of people or organizations are exposed to the same risk, a predictable number of losses will occur.

leadership (p. 224) Creating a vision for others to follow, establishing corporate values and ethics, and transforming the way the organization does business so it is more effective and efficient.

lean manufacturing (p. 285) The production of goods using less of everything compared to mass production: half the human effort, half the manufacturing space, half the investment in tools, half the engineering time to develop a new product in half the time.

ledger (p. 555) Recording device in which information from accounting journals is categorized into homogeneous groups and posted so that managers can find all the information about one account in the same place.

letter of credit (p. 657) A promise by a bank that a given amount will be paid if certain conditions are met.

leverage (p. 601) Raising needed funds through borrowing.

leveraged buyout (LBO) (p. 162) An attempt by employees, management, or a group of investors to purchase an organization primarily through borrowing.

liabilities (p. 558) Amounts owed by the organization to others. Current liabilities are due in one year or less; long-term liabilities are not due within one year.

liability losses (p. 688) Losses resulting from property damage or injuries suffered by others for which the policyholder is held responsible.

licensing (p. 95) Agreement in which a producer allows a foreign company to produce its product in exchange for royalties.

LIFO (last in, first out) (p. 567) Accounting technique for calculating cost of inventory based on last in, first out.

limit order (p. 624) Instructions to a broker to purchase stock at a specific price, if and when that price becomes possible.

limited-function wholesaler (p. 478) A merchant wholesaler that performs only selected distribution functions.

limited liability (p. 151) The responsibility of a business's owners for losses only up to the amount they invest; limited partners and shareholders have limited liability.

limited-liability company (p. 160) A company similar to an S corporation but without the special eligibility requirements.

limited partner (p. 151) Owner who invests money in the business but does not have any management responsibility or liability for losses beyond the investment.

limited partnership (p. 151) A partnership with one or more general partners and one or more limited partners.

line of credit (p. 595) The amount of unsecured short-term credit a bank will lend a borrower that is agreed to ahead of time.

line personnel (p. 254) Employees who perform functions that contribute directly to the primary goals of the organization.

liquidity (p. 558) The ease with which an asset can be converted to cash.

lockout (p. 382) A management tool for putting pressure on unions by closing the business.

long-term financing (p. 593) Financing that will be repaid over a specific time period longer than one year.

long-term forecast (p. 587) A prediction of revenues, costs, and expenses for a period longer than 1 year, sometimes extending 5 or 10 years into the future.

loss (p. 29) When a business's costs and expenses are more than its revenues.

M-1 (p. 643) Money that is quickly and easily raised (currency, checks, travelers' checks, and the like).

M-2 (p. 643) Money included in M-1 plus money that may take a little more time to raise (savings accounts, money market accounts, mutual funds, certificates of deposit, and the like).

management (p. 213) The process used to accomplish organizational goals through planning, organizing, directing, and controlling people and other organizational resources.

management by objectives (MBO) (p. 322) A system of goal setting and implementation that involves a cycle of discussion, review, and evaluation of objectives among top and middle-level managers, supervisors, and employees.

management development (p. 350) The process of training and educating employees to become good managers and then developing managerial skills over time.

managerial accounting (p. 551) The provision of information and analyzes to managers within the organization to assist them in decision making.

managing diversity (p. 233) Building systems and a culture that unite different people in a common pursuit without undermining their diversity.

market (p. 193) People with unsatisfied wants and needs who have both the resources and willingness to buy.

market modification (p. 451) Technique used to extend the life cycle of mature products by finding new users and market segments.

market order (p. 624) Instructions to a broker to buy stock at the best price obtainable in the market now.

market segmentation (p. 422) The process of dividing the total market into several groups that have similar characteristics.

marketing (p. 406) The process of determining customer wants and needs and then providing customers with goods and services that meet or exceed their expectations.

marketing concept (p. 409) Refers to a three-part business philosophy: (1) a customer orientation, (2) training of all employees in customer service, and (3) a profit orientation.

marketing management (p. 413) The process of planning and executing the conception, pricing, promotion, and distribution [place] of ideas, goods, and services [products] to create mutually beneficial exchanges.

marketing middlemen (p. 464) Organizations that assist in the movement of goods and services from producer to industrial and consumer users.

marketing mix (p. 413) The ingredients that go into a marketing program: product, price, place, and promotion.

marketing research (p. 416) The process used both to determine what consumer and industrial clients want and need and to select the most effective way to satisfy those wants and needs.

mass customization (p. 285) Tailoring products to meet the needs of individual customers.

mass customization (p. 498) The design of custom-made products and promotions, including advertising.

mass marketing (p. 411) Developing products and promotions that are designed to please large groups of people.

master budget (p. 589) The financial plan that summarizes the operating, capital, and cash budgets.

master limited partnership (MLP) (p. 152) A partnership that looks much like a corporation in that it acts like a corporation, but is taxed like a partnership and thus avoids the corporate income tax.

materials handling (p. 477) The movement of goods within a warehouse, factory, or store.

matrix organization (p. 255) Organization in which specialists from different parts of the organization are brought together to work on specific projects but still remain part of a traditional line and staff structure.

maturity date (p. 611) The date on which the issuer of a bond must pay the principal of the bond to the bondholder.

mediation (p. 379) The use of a third party, called a mediator, to encourage both parties to continue negotiating.

mentor (p. 351) An experienced employee who supervises, coaches, and guides lower-level employees by introducing them to the right people and groups and generally being their organizational sponsors.

mercantilism (p. 103) The economic principle advocating the selling of more goods to other nations than a country buys.

merger (p. 162) The result of two firms forming one company.

middle management (p. 217) Level of management that includes plant managers and department heads who are responsible for tactical plans.

mixed economies (p. 64) Economic systems in which some allocation of resources is made by the market and some is made by the government.

monetary policy (p. 76) The management of the amount of money placed into the economy by the government and the management of interest rates.

money (p. 642) What people will generally accept as payment for goods and services.

money supply (p. 643) The sum of all the funds that the public has immediately available for buying goods and services.

monopolistic competition (p. 136) The market situation where there are a large number of sellers that produce similar products, but the products are perceived by buyers as different.

monopoly (p. 136) A market in which there is only one seller.

morality (p. 117) The attempt to live by certain values and standards of conduct accepted by society as right and wrong.

motion economy (p. 310) Theory that every job can be broken down into a series of elementary motions.

motivator (p. 318) Factors that provide satisfaction and motivate people to work.

multiculturalism (p. 43) Process of optimizing the contribution of people from different cultures.

multinational corporation (p. 107) An organization that does manufacturing and marketing in many different countries; it has multinational stock ownership and multinational management.

mutual fund (p. 626) An organization that buys stocks and bonds and then sells shares in those securities to the public.

mutual insurance company (p. 688) Insurance firm owned by its policyholders.

National Association of Securities Dealers Automated Quotation System (NASDAQ) (p. 619) A nationwide electronic system which communicates over-the-counter trades to brokers.

national debt (p. 79) The sum of all the federal deficits over time.

negotiable instruments (p. 134) Forms of commercial paper (such as checks) that are transferable among businesses and individuals.

negotiated labor-management agreement (p. 377) Settlement which sets the tone and clarifies the terms under which management and labor agree to function over a period of time.

net income/net loss (p. 560) Revenue minus expenses.

network computing system (client/server computing) (p. 534) Computer systems that allow personal computers (clients) to obtain needed information from huge databases in a central computer (server).

networking (p. 258) Linking organizations with communications technology in order for them to work together on common objectives.

networking (p. 351) The process of establishing and maintaining contacts with key managers in one's own organization and in other organizations and using those contacts to weave strong relationships that serve as informal development systems.

niche marketing (p. 425) The process of finding very small but profitable market segments and designing custom-made products for those people.

nonbanks (p. 648) Financial organizations that accept no deposits, but offer many of the services provided by regular banks (pension funds, insurance companies, commercial finance companies, consumer finance companies, and brokerage houses).

nonprofit organization (p. 32) An organization whose goals do not include making a personal profit for its owners.

North American Free Trade Agreement (NAFTA) (p. 105) An agreement through which the United States, Canada, and Mexico formed a free trade area.

objectives (p. 215) Specific, short-term statements detailing how to achieve an organization's goals.

off-the-job training (p. 349) Internal and external programs to develop a variety of skills and foster personal development away from the workplace.

oligopoly (p. 136) A form of competition where the market is dominated by just a few sellers.

on-the-job training (p. 348) Training program in which the employee immediately begins his or her tasks and learns by doing, or watches others for a while and then imitates them, all right at the workplace.

open-market operations (p. 645) The buying and selling of U.S. government securities by the Fed with the goal of regulating the money supply.

open-shop agreement (p. 378) Agreement in right-to-work states which gives workers the option to join or not join a union, if one exists in their workplace.

operating budget (p. 588) The projection of dollar allocations to various costs and expenses needed to run or operate the business.

organizational culture (p. 263) Widely shared values within an organization that provide coherence and cooperation to achieve common goals.

organizational design (p. 244) The establishment of manageable groups of people who have clear responsibilities and who know how to accomplish the objectives of the organization and the group.

organizing (p. 214) Management function that involves designing the organizational structure, attracting people to the organization (staffing), and creating conditions and systems that ensure that everyone and everything work together to achieve the objectives of the organization.

outsourcing (p. 262) Assigning various functions, such as accounting and legal work, to outside organizations.

over-the-counter (OTC) market (p. 619) Exchange that provides a means to trade stocks not listed on the national exchanges.

owners' equity (p. 560) Assets minus liabilities.

par value (p. 614) A dollar amount assigned to shares of stock by the corporation's charter. The par value is printed on the front of a stock certificate and is used to compute the dividends of a preferred stock.

partnership (p.148) A legal form of business with two or more owners.

patent (p. 132) Exclusive rights for inventors to their inventions for 17 years.

penetration strategy (p 455) Method of pricing by which a product is priced low to attract more customers and discourage competitors.

penny stock (p. 624) A stock that sells for less than $5.

pension funds (p. 652) Amounts of money designated by corporations, nonprofit organizations, or unions to cover part of the financial needs of members when they retire.

perfect competition (p. 136) The market situation where there are many sellers of nearly identical products and no seller is large enough to dictate the price of the product.

performance appraisal (p. 352) An evaluation of the performance level of employees against standards to make decisions about promotions, compensation, additional training, or firing.

personal selling (p. 500)   Face-to-face presentation and promotion of products and services plus searching out prospects and providing follow-up service.

physical distribution (logistics) (p. 464)   The movement of goods and services from producer to industrial and consumer users.

physiological needs (p. 312)   The needs for basic, life-giving elements such as food, water, and shelter.

place utility (p. 416)   Value added to products by having them where people want them.

planning (p. 214)   Management function that involves anticipating future trends and determining the best strategies and tactics to achieve organizational objectives.

pledging (p. 595)   Using accounts receivable or other assets as collateral for a loan.

possession utility (p. 416)   Value added to products by doing whatever is necessary to transfer ownership from one party to another.

preemptive right (p. 617)   Common stockholders' right to purchase any new shares of common stock the firm decides to issue.

preferred provider organizations (PPOs) (p. 689)   Health care organizations similar to HMOs, but that allow policyholders to choose their own physicians.

preferred stock (p. 616)   Stock that gives owners preference in the payment of dividends and an earlier claim on assets if the business is sold but that does not include voting rights.

premium (p. 687)   The fee charged by an insurance company for an insurance policy.

primary boycott (p. 381)   Union encouragement of members not to buy products of a firm involved in a labor dispute.

principal (p. 611)   The face value of a bond.

private accountant (p. 552)   Accountant who works for a single company.

private brands (p. 442)   Products that do not carry the manufacturer's name, and carry the name of a distributor or retailer instead.

process manufacturing (p. 281)   Production process which physically or chemically changes materials.

product (p. 407)   Any physical good, service, or idea that satisfies a want or need.

product differentiation (p.437)   The attempt to create product perceptions in the minds of consumers so that one product seems superior to others.

product liability (p. 131)   Laws that hold businesses liable for negligence in the production, design, sale, or use of products it markets.

product life cycle (p. 448)   The four-stage theoretical depiction of the process from birth to death of a product class: introduction, growth, maturity, and decline.

product line (p. 436)   A group of products that are physically similar or are intended for a similar market.

product manager (p. 444)   Coordinates all the marketing efforts for a particular product (or product line) or brand.

product mix (p. 436)   The combination of product lines offered by a manufacturer.

product modification (p. 451)   Technique used to extend the life cycle of mature products by changing the product quality, features, or style to attract new users or more usage from present users.

production (p. 277)   The creation of finished goods and services using the factors of production: land, labor, capital, entrepreneurship, and information.

production and operations management (p. 276)   Activities managers do to create goods and services.

productivity (pp. 46, 74)   The total output of goods and services in a given period of time divided by work hours (output per work hour).

profit (p. 29)   Earnings above and beyond what a business spends for salaries, expenses, and other costs.

program evaluation and review technique (PERT) (p. 290)   A method for analyzing the tasks involved in completing a given project, estimating the time needed to complete each task, and identifying the minimum time needed to complete the total project.

program trading (p. 633)   Giving instructions to computers to automatically sell if the price of stock dips to a certain price to avoid potential losses.

promissory note (p. 594)   A written contract with a promise to pay.

promotion (p. 492)   An attempt by marketers to inform people about products to persuade them to participate in an exchange.

promotion mix (p. 493)   The combination of tools marketers use to promote their products or services.

property losses (p. 688)   Losses resulting from fires, accidents, theft, or other perils.

prospecting (p. 500)   Researching potential buyers and choosing those most likely to buy.

prospectus (p. 620)   A condensed version of economic and financial information prepared for the SEC that must be sent to purchasers.

protective tariff (p. 103)   Import tax designed to raise the price of imported products so that domestic products are more competitive.

public accountant (p. 552)   Accountant who provides accounting services to individuals or businesses on a fee basis.

public relations (PR) (p. 505)   The management function that evaluates public attitudes, develops policies and procedures consistent with the public interest, and takes steps to earn public understanding and acceptance.

publicity(p. 506) Any information about an individual, a product, or an organization that is distributed to the public through the media, that is not paid for, or controlled by, the sponsor.

pull strategy (p. 508) Use of promotional tools to motivate consumers to request products from stores.

pure risk (p. 685) The threat of loss with no chance for profit.

push strategy (p. 507) Use of promotional tools to convince wholesalers and retailers to stock and sell merchandise.

quality (p. 48) Providing customers with high quality goods and services that go beyond the expected.

quality control (p. 291) The measurement of products and services against set standards.

quality of life (p. 31) The general well-being of a society.

rack jobber (p. 478) A full-service wholesaler that furnishes racks or shelves full of merchandise to retailers, displays products, and sells on consignment.

recession (p. 76) Two consecutive quarters of decline in the GDP.

recruitment (p. 343) The set of legal activities used to obtain a sufficient number of the right people at the right time to select those who best meet the needs of the organization.

reengineering (p. 260) The rethinking and radical redesign of organizational processes to achieve dramatic improvements in critical measures of performance.

relationship marketing (p. 411) Establishing and maintaining mutually beneficial exchange relationships with internal and external customers and all the other stakeholders of the organzation.

reserve requirement (p. 645) A percentage of member-bank funds that must be deposited in the Federal Reserve System.

restructuring (p. 245) Redesigning organizations to make them more productive.

retailer (p. 464) A marketing middleman that sells to consumers.

retained earnings (p. 560) The amount left after a company distributes some of its net income to stockholders in the form of dividends.

revenue (p. 561) The value of what is received for goods sold, services rendered, and other sources.

revenue tariff (p. 103) Import tax designed to raise money for the government.

reverse discrimination (p. 361) The feeling of unfairness unprotected groups may have when protected groups are given preference in hiring and promoting.

revolving credit agreement (p. 595) A line of credit that is guaranteed by the bank.

right-to-work laws (p. 378) Legislation which gives workers the right, under an open shop, to join or not join a union if it is present.

rising dollar (p. 644) The value of the dollar changes such that the amount of goods and services you can buy with a dollar goes up.

risk (p. 29, 685) The chance you take of losing time and money on a business that may not prove profitable.

risk/return trade-off (p. 598) The principle that the greater risk a lender takes in making a loan, the higher the interest rate required.

robot (p. 285) A computer-controlled machine capable of performing many tasks.

round lot (p. 625) Purchases of 100 shares of stock at a time.

rule of indemnity (p. 688) Insurance restriction which states that an insured person or organization cannot collect more than the actual loss from an insurable risk.

S corporation (p. 159) A unique government creation that looks like a corporation but is taxed like a sole proprietorship and partnership.

safety needs (p. 312) The needs for peace and security.

sales promotion (p. 504) The promotional tool that stimulates consumer purchasing and dealer interest by means of short-term activities (displays, shows and exhibitions, contests, etc.).

sample (p. 418) A representative group of a market population.

savings and loan associations (S&Ls) (p. 651) Financial institutions that accept both savings and checking deposits and provide home mortgage loans.

Savings Association Insurance Fund (SAIF) (p. 654) Part of the FDIC that insures holders of accounts in savings and loan associations.

scientific management (p. 309) The study of workers to find the most efficient way of doing things and then teaching people those techniques.

secondary boycott (p. 381) An attempt by labor to convince others to stop doing business with a firm that is the subject of a primary boycott.

secured bonds (p. 599) Bonds backed by some tangible asset that is pledged to the investor if the principal is not paid back.

secured loan (p. 595) A loan that is backed by something valuable.

Securities and Exchange Commission (SEC) (p. 621) Federal government agency which has responsibility for regulating the various exchanges.

selection (p. 344)   The process of gathering information to decide who should be hired, under legal guidelines, for the best interests of the individual and the organization.

selective distribution (p. 482)   Distribution strategy that uses only a preferred group of the available retailers in an area.

self-actualization needs (p. 312)   The needs to achieve and to be all you can be.

self-insurance (p. 686)   Putting funds away to cover routine claims rather than buying insurance to cover them.

Service Corps of Retired Executives (SCORE) (p. 196)   Part of SBA made up of experienced businesspeople who provide consulting services to small businesses for free (minus expenses).

services (p. 50)   Intangible products such as education, health care, and insurance.

sexual harassment (p. 389)   Unwelcome sexual advances, requests for sexual favors, and other conduct of sexual nature (verbal or physical).

shareware (p. 535)   Computer software that is copyrighted but distributed to potential customers free of charge. It is expected that users will send a fee to the developer if the software is found useful.

shop steward (p. 378)   A labor official who works permanently in an organization and represents employee interests on a daily basis.

shopping goods and services (p. 437)   Products that the consumer buys only after comparing quality and price from a variety of sellers.

short-term financing (p. 593)   Financing that will be repaid within one year.

short-term forecast (p. 587)   A prediction of revenues, costs, and expenses for a period of one year or less.

sinking fund (p. 612)   Provision of a bond which requires the issuer to retire (put in a trust fund), on a periodic basis, some part of the bond principal prior to maturity.

skimming price strategy (p. 455)   Method of pricing by which the product is priced high to make optimum profit while there is little competition.

small business (p. 183)   A business that is independently operated, is not dominant in its field, and meets certain size standards in terms of number of employees and annual receipts.

Small Business Investment Companies (SBICs) (p. 193)   Private investment companies which the Small Business Administration licenses to lend money to small businesses.

social audit (p. 124)   A systematic evaluation of an organization's progress toward implementing programs that are socially responsible and responsive.

social needs (p. 312)   The needs to feel loved, accepted, and part of the group.

social responsibility (p. 116)   A business's concern for the welfare of society as a whole.

social security (p. 677)   Retirement benefits provided by the Social Security Act of 1935.

socialism (p. 63)   An economic system based on the premise that businesses should be owned by the people (workers).

sole proprietorship (p. 148)   A business that is owned, and usually managed, by one person.

span of control (p. 249)   The optimum number of subordinates a manager should supervise.

specialty goods and services (p. 438)   Products that have a special attraction to consumers who are willing to go out of their way to obtain them.

speculative risk (p. 685)   A type of risk that involves a chance of either profit or loss.

spreadsheet program (p. 536)   A table made up of rows and columns which enables a manager to organize information.

staff personnel (p. 254)   Employees who perform functions that assist line personnel in achieving their goals.

stagflation (p. 648)   Period of both slow growth and inflation.

stakeholders (p. 40)   Those people who can affect or are affected by the achievement of an organization's objectives.

standard of living (p. 31)   The level of ability to buy goods and services.

statement of cash flows (p. 565)   Report of cash receipts and disbursements related to the firm's major activities: operations, investments, and financing.

statutory law (p. 131)   State and federal constitutions, legislative enactments, treaties, and ordinances (written laws).

stock certificate (p. 614)   Evidence of ownership that specifies the name of the company, the number of shares it represents, and the type of stock it is.

stock exchange (p. 618)   An organization whose members can buy and sell securities to the public.

stock insurance company (p. 688)   Insurance company owned by stockholders, just like any other investor-owned company.

stock split (p. 625)   Giving stockholders two or more shares of stock for each one they own.

stockbroker (p. 621)   A market intermediary who buys and sells securities for clients.

stocks (p. 614)   Shares of ownership in a company.

strategic (long-range) planning (p. 215)   Process of determining the major goals of the organization and the policies and strategies for obtaining and using resources to achieve those goals.

strike (p. 380) Union strategy of workers refusing to go to work in order to further their objectives after an impasse in collective bargaining.

strikebreaker (p. 382) Workers hired to do the jobs of striking workers until the labor dispute is resolved.

supervisory (first-line) management (p. 217) First level of management above workers; includes people directly responsible for assigning specific jobs to employees and evaluating their daily performance.

supply (p. 68) The quantity of products that manufacturers or owners are willing to sell at different prices at a specific time.

supply chain management (SCM) (p. 472) The overall process of minimizing inventory and moving goods through the channel faster by using computers to improve communications among the channel members.

synthetic systems (p. 281) Production processes which either change raw materials into other products or combine raw materials or parts into finished products.

tactical (short-range) planning (p. 215) Process of developing detailed, short-term strategies about what is to be done, who is to do it, and how it is to be done.

target marketing (p. 422) The process by which an organization decides which market segments to serve.

tax accountant (p. 554) Accountant who is trained in tax law and is responsible for preparing tax returns and developing tax strategies.

taxes (p. 138) Federal, state, and local governments' way of raising money.

technical skills (p. 230) Ability to perform tasks of a specific department (such as selling or bookkeeping).

telecommuting (p. 45) Working at home and keeping in touch with others in the work force using telecommunications.

telemarketing (p. 483) The sale of goods and services by telephone.

term insurance (p. 675) Pure insurance protection for a given number of years.

term-loan agreement (p. 598) A promissory note that requires the borrower to repay the loan in specified installments.

time deposit (p. 649) The technical name for a savings account for which the bank requires prior notice before withdrawal.

time utility (p. 416) Value added to products by making them available when they are needed.

time–motion studies (p. 310) Studies of the tasks performed to complete a job and the time needed to do each task.

top management (p. 217) Highest level of management, consisting of the president and other key company executives who develop strategic plans.

tort (p. 131) Wrongful conduct that causes injury to another person's body, property, or reputation.

total quality management (TQM) (p. 259) Satisfying customers by building in and ensuring quality from all departments in an organization.

trade credit (p. 593) The practice of buying goods now and paying for them later.

trade deficit (p. 92) Buying more goods from other nations than are sold to them.

trade protectionism (p. 102) The use of government regulations to limit the import of goods and services; based on the theory that domestic producers can survive and grow, producing more jobs.

trademark (p. 442) Brand that has been given exclusive legal protection for both the brand name and the pictorial design.

training and development (p. 348) All attempts to improve employee performance by increasing an employee's ability to perform through learning.

trial balance (p. 556) Totaling all of the debit balances and all of the credit balances in the ledgers to be sure debits equal credits.

truck jobber (p. 479) A small limited-function wholesaler that delivers goods by truck to retailers.

unemployment rate (p. 72) The number of civilians who are unemployed and tried to find a job within the prior four weeks.

Uniform Commercial Code (UCC) (p. 134) A comprehensive commercial law adopted by every state in the United States; it covers sales laws and other commercial law.

uninsurable risk (p. 687) Risk that a typical insurance company will not cover.

union (p. 372) Employee organizations that have the main goal of representing members in employee–management bargaining about job-related issues.

union security clause (p. 377) Provision in a negotiated labor-management agreement which stimulates that employees who benefit from a union must either join or pay dues to the union.

union shop agreement (p. 377) Clause in labor–management agreement which says workers do not have to be members of a union to be hired, but must agree to join the union within a prescribed period.

universal life insurance (p. 675) A combination of term insurance and an accumulation fund, usually based on bonds.

unlimited liability (p. 150) The responsibility of business owners for all of the debts of the business; making the personal assets of the owners vulnerable to claims against the business. Sole proprietors and general partners have unlimited liability.

unsecured bonds (p. 599) Bonds which are not backed by any collateral.

unsecured loan (p. 595) A loan that is not backed by any specific assets as collateral.

value package (p. 435) Everything that consumers evaluate when deciding whether or not to buy something.

value pricing (p. 453) Offering consumers brand name goods and services at fair prices.

variable life insurance (p. 675) A whole life policy whose benefits vary based upon the investment performance of the insurance company.

venture capitalist (p. 191) Individuals or organizations which invest in new businesses in exchange for partial ownership pf the company.

vertical merger (p. 162) The joining of two companies involved in different stages of related businesses.

vestibule training (p. 349) Training conducted out of the workplace where employees are given instructions on equipment similar to that used on the job.

virtual banking (p. 657) Interactive home banking where all contact is made electronically.

virtualization (p. 525) Accessibility through technology that allows business to be conducted independent of location.

vision (p. 214) A sense of why the organization exists and where it's heading.

voluntary bankruptcy (p. 140) Legal procedures initiated by a debtor.

welfare capitalism (p. 64) A mixed economy in which most of the wealth is generated by businesses, but the government plays a major part in allocating resources.

whole life insurance (p. 675) A combination insurance plan and savings plan.

wholesaler (p. 464) A marketing middleman that sells to organizations and individuals, but not final consumers.

word-of-mouth promotion (p. 503) Consumers talking about products they have liked or disliked.

yellow-dog contract (p. 382) A contract agreement whereby employees agreed not to join a union as a condition of employment (outlawed by the Norris-La Guardia Act).

CREDITS

Contents

p. v, Courtesy of UPS. p. v, Sally Wiener Grotta/The Stock Market. p. vii, Courtesy of Jones Worely Design, Inc. p. viii, Courtesy of the St. Louis Bread Company. p. xi, Courtesy of The Dial Corporation. p. ix, Courtesy of Ernst & Young. p. xiii, Courtesy of Peak Public Relations. p. xiv, Courtesy of Rail Europe.

Prologue

p. 3, Eugene Louie/San Jose Mercury News. p. 5, Courtesy of Triton College. p. 6, Courtesy of Texas Department of Commerce. p. 7, David Young-Wolff/PhotoEdit. p. 9, reprinted by permission of NEA, Inc. p. 10, John Thoeming. p. 11, John Thoeming.
Appendix: p. 17, John Thoeming. p. 20, John Thoeming.

Chapter 1

p. 27, Courtesy of Checkers, Inc. p. 28, Courtesy of Checkers, Inc. p. 31, Reprinted with permission of General Motors Corporation. p. 33, Courtesy of AFSCME. p. 38, Joe Sohm/Stock Boston. p. 39, Courtesy of Microsoft Corporation. p. 43, Mark Richards/PhotoEdit. p. 46, Bob Daemmrich/Sygma. p. 46, Bob Daemmrich/Sygma.

Chapter 2

p. 59, Thomas Long. p. 60, The Bettman Archive. p. 62, The Bettman Archive. p. 63, The Bettman Archive. p. 66, Perry Alan Werner/The Image Works. p. 67, Bill Truslow/Gamma-Liaison. p. 68, Swersey/Gamma-Liaison. p. 72, Lee Corkran/Sygma. p. 74, J. Pickerell/The Image Works. p. 75, Rob Crandall/The Image Works.

Chapter 3

p. 87, Peter Tenzer. p. 88, John Thoeming. p. 91, Courtesy of Tullycross Fine Irish Imports. p. 94, Courtesy of BMW. p. 96, Dave Brown/Nawrocki Stock. p. 97, John Thoeming. p. 99, Scott Wanner/Nawrocki Stock. p. 106, Jeffrey Markowitz/Sygma. p. 107, Courtesy of Canon, Inc.

Chapter 4

p. 115, Alan Levenson. p. 116, Sygma. p. 121, Courtesy of ITT Corporation. p. 121, W. Campbell/Sygma. p. 123, Tim O'Brien for Time. p. 125, John Thoeming.
Appendix: p. 133, Courtesy of Coca-Cola Company. p. 138, Peter Langone/Tony Stone Images.

Chapter 5

p. 147, Bill Lisenby/Courtesy of Blimpie International. p. 148, Courtesy of BellSouth Corporation. p. 150, Rob Crandall/The Image Works. p. 151, Giboux/Gamma-Liaison. p. 155, Courtesy of Nike, Inc. p. 158, Misha Erwitt/Sygma. p. 164, John Thoeming. p. 167, F. Hibon/Sygma.

Chapter 6

p. 177, Paula Nelson/Gamma-Liaison. p. 178, Delmas/Gamma-Liaison. p. 179, Courtesy of Ernst & Young. p. 182, Courtesy of 3M. p. 187, Andy Goodwin. p. 189, John Thoeming. p. 192, Courtesy of AT&T. p. 194, Courtesy of Go-Video, Inc. p. 197, Courtesy of the Southland Corporation.

Chapter 7

p. 211, Joan C. Tonn/Unwich Management Center. p. 213, Liane Enkelis/Stock Boston. p. 215, Frank Herholdt/Tony Stone Worldwide. p. 219, John Thoeming. p. 221, Courtesy of Boeing Company. p. 224, Courtesy of Saturn. p. 226, Focus on Sports. p. 233, Steve McAlister/The Image Bank.

Chapter 8

p. 243, Courtesy of Cavalier Gage & Electronic. p. 246, John Thoeming. p. 248, Reprinted with permission of General Motors Corporation. p. 255, Robert Brenner/PhotoEdit. p. 257, Paul Conklin/PhotoEdit. p. 261, Tony Freeman/PhotoEdit. p. 264, Sygma. p. 265, Courtesy of Unysis. p. 267, Bruce Ayers/Tony Stone Images.

Chapter 9

p. 275, Courtesy of Carlyle Compressor Company. p. 277, Ted Horowitz/The Stock Market. p. 279, Blake Discher/Sygma. p. 285, Seth Resnick/Stock Boston. p. 286, Courtesy of Converse, Inc. p. 287, Michael Melford/Sygma. p. 293, Tony Freeman/PhotoEdit.

Chapter 10

p. 307, Courtesy of Southwest Airlines. p. 308, Louis Psihoyos/Matrix. p. 311, Reproduced with permission of AT&T Corporate Archives. p. 314, N. Rowan/The Image Works. p. 316, Courtesy of Hewlett-Packard Company. p. 321, Courtesy of Harley-Davidson, Inc. p. 325, Used with permission of Ford Motor Company. p. 330, Courtesy of Radisson Hotels International, Inc.

Chapter 11

p. 337, Ed Kashi. p. 341, Courtesy of Rockwell International. p. 343, Bill Kniest/Courtesy College of Lake County Placement Office. p. 349, Lonnie Duka/Tony Stone Worldwide. p. 350, Courtesy of American Airlines. p. 353, Gordon Joffrion/Stock South. p. 356, John Thoeming. p. 359, Joe Cornish/Tony Stone Images.

Chapter 12

p. 371, Wide World Photos, Inc. p. 373, Wide World Photos, Inc. p. 383, Ron Maratea/International Stock. p. 386, Allan Tannenbaum/Sygma. p. 390, Courtesy of Marriott Corporation. p. 392, Allan Tannerbaum/Sygma. p. 394, Courtesy of United Airlines.

Chapter 13

p. 405, Carl Howard/Black Star. p. 406, Courtesy of GTE Sprint. p. 408, Rhonda Sidney/Stock Boston. p. 413, Courtesy of United Airlines. p. 415, Thelma Shumsky/The Image Works. p. 418, John Thoeming. p. 422, Steve Dunwell/The Image Bank. p. 427, John Thoeming. p. 427, John Thoeming.

Chapter 14

p. 439, Rocky Thies. p. 442, Courtesy of Blockbuster Entertainment. p. 442, Courtesy of Borden. p. 442, Courtesy of Amoco Corporation. p. 442, Courtesy of The Pepsi Cola Company. p. 443, Courtesy of Reebok. p. 446, John Thoeming. p. 448, Gamma-Liaison. p. 488, Gamma-Liaison. p. 454, Courtesy of Taco Bell. p. 456, Reprinted with permission of General Motors Corporation.

Chapter 15

p. 463, John Thoeming. p. 466, Courtesy of UPS. p. 469, John Thoeming. p. 472, Charles Gupton/Stock Boston. p. 475, John B. Corns/Courtesy of CSX Corporation. p. 477, John B. Corns/Courtesy of CSX Corporation. p. 481, John Thoeming. p. 484, Miro Vintoniv/Stock Boston.

Chapter 16

p. 491, John Thoeming. p. 493, Courtesy of Ben & Jerry's Homemade, Inc. p. 497, Courtesy of Club Med. p. 500, Courtesy of 3M. p. 502, John Zoiner/International Stock. p. 504, Used with permission of Ford Motor Company. p. 507, Courtesy of Government of India Tourist Office.

Chapter 17

p. 523, Andy Freeburg. p. 524, John McDermott/Tony Stone Images. p. 527, Courtesy of the NCSA. p. 528, Courtesy of CompuServe. p. 539, The Stock Market.

Chapter 18

p. 549, Copyright Donnelly Marks, 1991. p. 552, John Thoeming. p. 571, Stock Imagery.

Chapter 19

p. 583, Courtesy of Merck & Company. p. 586, Joe Baraban. p. 594, Ed Bock/The Stock Market.

Chapter 20

p. 609, Terry Parke. p. 619, Courtesy of New York Stock Exchange. p. 623, Darryl L. Heikes/Stock South. p. 626, Courtesy of Neuberger & Berman.

Chapter 21

p. 641, Courtesy of the Federal Reserve System. p. 644, J. L. Atlan/Sygma. p. 647, The Bettman Archive. p. 649, Courtesy of Vermont National Bank.

Chapter 22

p. 667, Courtesy of ECS Technologies. p. 670, B. Daemmrich/The Image Works. p. 674, Courtesy of Wachovia Bank of Georgia. p. 679, Courtesy of Fidelity Investments. p. 680, Courtesy of The Institute of Certified Financial Planners. p. 687, Courtesy of General Accident Insurance.

ᴀᴍᴇ Iɴᴅᴇx

A

Abramovitch, Ingrid, 3, CN1
Aburdene, Patricia, 326, CN3
Adams, Eric, 190
Aho, Debra, CN8
Akers, John, 122
Alexander, Keith L., CN7
Aley, James, CN3
Allen, Robert, 386
Alster, Norm, CN3
Altschul, James S., CN2, CN10
Amparano, Julie, CN7
Anderson, M.H., 148
Angeheuer, Frederick, CN10
Annin, Peter, CN7
Armstrong, Larry, 115, CN2
Arnst, Catherine, CN9
Ash, Mary Kay, 327-328
Ashley, Agibail, 188
Ashley, Andrew, 188
Atkinson, Gary, CN2
Autry, Robert, 435

B

Babbage, Charles, 309
Bahls, Jane Easter, 340, 380
Baig, Edward, CN9
Bailey, Jeff, 441
Bailey, Rita, CN5
Baker, Stephen, CN2
Baker, Steven, CN7
Bamathan, Joyce, 620, CN2
Band, Howard, CN5
Banerjee, Ashish, 499
Banerjee, Neela, CN2, CN6
Banks, Howard, 307
Barbalatt, Gerald A., CN3
Barlow, Jim, CN5
Barrett, Amy, CN2, CN4
Barrier, Michael, CN4
Barrill, G. Steven, 191
Bartlett, Sarah, CN9
Basham, Robert, 164
Baugh, John A., CN7
Beaty, Jonathan, 659
Bennett, Amanda, CN6
Bennett, William J., CN1
Berkowitz, Eric N., 16
Berman, Phyllis, CN7
Bernstein, Aaron, CN6
Bernstein, Norris, 115
Berry, Jonathan, CN8
Bertani, Elizabeth, 584-585
Berton, Lee, CN9
Bhargava, Sunita Wadekar, CN4
Biegeleisen, J.I., 13
Binn, Moreton, CN2

Biondi-Williams, Laura, 3
Birck, Jon, 601
Black, Pam, CN3, CN10
Blake, Pat, 319
Blanchard, Kenneth, CN2
Bleakley, Fred R., CN5
Blechman, Bruce, CN3
Blustein, Paul, CN2
Bohnengel, Andrew, 198
Bongiorno, Lori, CN6, CN7
Borsch, Robert C., CN8
Bossidy, Lawrence A., CN4
Bowers, Brent, CN3
Bowles, Erskine, 100, 669
Bowles, Jerry, CN5
Bradford, Marcia, CN6
Brennan, Jody, 375
Brimelow, Peter, CN1
Broadhurst, Judith, CN4
Brown, Christie, CN8
Brown, Paul B., 499
Browning, E. S., CN5
Bruno, Richard, 190
Buchanan, James, 60
Buchanan, Patrick, CN1
Buck, Pearl, 87
Bums, Greg, 601
Burch, Les, 436-437, CN7
Burck, Charles, CN3
Burns, Greg, CN7
Bu Xinsheng, 354
Byrne, John A., CN4, CN6, CN7

C

Campbell, Carroll, 94
Canion, Rod, 181
Cannie, Joan Koob, CN7
Carey, John, 535
Caruba, Alan, 553
Carvey, John, CN9
Castro, Janice, CN7
Chakravarty, S.N., 371, CN6
Champy, James, 244, CN4
Chase, Larry, 497
Christopher, William F., CN7
Cinguina, Jennifer A., CN5
Clark, Charlie, 437
Clark, Don, 169
Cleland, Kim, CN8
Climas, Molly, 652
Clinton, Bill (President), 93, 390
Coberly, Sally, 391
Compte, E., 371, CN6
Connors, Connie, 549, CN9
Conte, Christopher, CN6
Conza, Tony, 147
Cook, Scott, 179
Cook, Wirt, M., 480

Cooper, Helene, CN5
Cox, Meg, CN7
Coy, Peter, 533, CN9
Crain, Rance, CN7
Crockett, Roger 0., CN7
Crystal, Graef, 387
Curran, John J., CN2
Curry, Lynne, CN2

D

Daehne, Niklas, 87, CN1
Darlin, Damon, CN5
Dauten, Dale, CN5
Davidow, William H., CN5, CN7
Davis, Eileen, 584
DeGeorge, Gail, 632, 659
Dell, Michael, 179
Deming, W. Edwards, 294
Desens, Carl, 371, CN6
DeSimone, Livio "Desi," 182
Deutschman, Alan, CN5
Deveny, Kathleen, CN8
Disney, Walt, 180
Dodson, Jerome, 609
Donnelly, Harriet, 523
Dorfman, John, CN3
Dorsey, Eillen, 667
Drucker, Peter F., 34, 88, 213, 321, 387, CN8 du Pont, E.I., 32, 178
Dumaine, Brian, 259, CN3, CN4, CN5
Dunlap, R. Terren, 194
Dwyer, Paula, 620

E

Eastman, George, 178
Eckland, Coy G., 116
Edmark, Tomima, 177
Edmonston, Jack, CN7
Edwards, Alfred G., 13
Edwards, Paul, CN3
Edwards, Sarah, CN3
Eisner, Michael, 386, 387
Ellentuck, Albert B., CN3
Elliott, Michael, CN4
Engardio, Peter, 384, 620, CN2
Estess, Patricia Shiff, CN1
Evans, Richard, 620
Evanson, David R., 553, 597, 618, CN3, CN9

F

Farber, Henry, 384
Farnham, Alan, CN5, CN7
Farrell, Christopher, CN1, CN10
Faud, King, 564

Fayol, Henri, 245, 248
Feldman, Henry, 167-168
Feldman, Joan M., CN8
Feldman, Paul, 167
Field, Anne R., 531
Fierman, Jaclyn, 337, CN5, CN6, CN10
Firestone, Peter, 359
Fisher, Anne B., CN4, CN7
Fisher, Douglas, 464
Fisher, George, 325
Fizdale, Rick, CN8
Flannery, William, CN6
Flynn, Julie, CN2
Follett, Mary Parker, 211, 212
Forbes, Malcolm, 170
Ford, Henry, 178
Foreman, Joyce, 667
Forgey, Benjamin, CN1
Foster, Gerry, 423
Frank, Robert, 309, CN5
Friday, Carolyn, CN7
Fromson, Breet D., CN10
Fry, Art, 182

G

Galen, Michelle, CN7
Gamble, James, 178
Ganim, Barbara A., 13
Gannon, Tim, 164
Gantt, Henry L., 290
Garland, Susan B., CN1
Gasset, Jos Orgega y, 15
Gaston, Robert J., 191
Gates, William, 179
Geisler, Lori, 694
Genasci, Lisa, CN6
Geneen, Harold, 316
Gershman, Eric, 410
Gibson, Richard, CN8
Gilbreth, Frank, 310
Gilbreth, Lillian, 310
Glasgall, William, 601, 620, CN2
Gleckman, Howard, CN1
Goldman, Ed, 591
Goldman, Marshall, 169
Gompers, Samuel, 374, 376
Goodman, David, 579
Goodpaster, Kenneth E., CN2
Goodrich, Tom, CN9
Gordon, Lynn, 503
Gordon, Matt, 13
Grabill, Linda, 3
Graham, Bill, CN6, CN10
Grayson, Jaynell, 115
Grebler, Daniel, CN3
Greenspan, Alan, 641
Greenspan, Herbert, 641
Greenspan, Rose, 641
Greising, David, 371, CN6
Griffin, Cynthia E., CN3
Griffin, Jill, CN7
Grimes, Charlotte, CN2
Gross, Judith, 186
Gross, Nell, CN2
Grove, Andrew S., 313, 527, CN5
Grover, Ronald, CN6
Gumbel, Peter, 588

Gupta, Udayan, CN1, CN3, CN9
Gwynne, S.C., 659

H

Hamilton, Alexander, 646
Hammer, Michael, 244, CN4
Hammond, Joshua, CN5
Handler, James, CN9
Handler, Jeff, 100
Harbrecht, Douglas, 384, CN2
Harris, Jim, 181
Harris, Larry, 667
Hartley, Robert F., CN3
Hartley, Steven, 16
Hass, Nancy, CN4
Hawkins, Chuck, CN10
Hawkins, La-Van, 27, 28, 29, 30
Hayden, John, CN6
Hayes, John P., CN3
Heinemann, H. Erich, CN10
Hendricks, Mark, 250, CN4
Henkoff, Ronald, CN5, CN8, CN9
Herzberg, Frederick, CN5
Hewlett, William, 316
Hiatt, John T., CN9
Hick, Virginia Baldwin, 337, CN5, CN6
Hieri, Thomas, 597
Hill, Anita, 389
Hill, Patrice, CN8, CN10
Hill, Walter, Jr., 667
Hillkirk, John, 243, CN4
Himowitz, Michael, CN9
Hinchberger, Bill, CN2
Hof, Robert D., CN5, CN9
Hoffman, Ivan T., CN8
Hofheinz, Paul, CN2
Holland, Kelley, 601
Holt, Lirel, 250
Hotch, Ripley, CN3
Houghton, Jaime, 212
Hout, Tom, 286, CN5
Huber, Janean, 170, 539
Hudson, Hoyt, 187
Huey, John, CN9
Humphrey, Tom, 694
Hunter, Janet, 13
Husain, Imran, CN3

I

Ingrassia, Lawrence, 116
Ioannou, Lori, CN4

J

Jackman, Lois, 28, CN1
Jackson, Andrew, 646
Jackson, Victoria, 193
Jacob, Rahul, CN4
Jacob, Raul, CN7
Jacobs, Deborah, CN4
Jacobsen, Sally, 37
Jasen, Georgette, CN10
Jespersen, Fred F., CN4
Jobs, Steve, 179, 181
Johnson, Bradley, CN2
Johnson, David M., CN8

Johnson, Earvin (Magic), 391-392
Johnson, Simon, CN1
Jones, Bob, 466
Jones, Carl, 178
Jordan, Michael, 443
Jordan, Michael H., CN4
Juilland, Marie Jeanne, 597

K

Kahn, Paul, CN7
Kahn, Robert, CN8
Kamsky, Virginia, 87, 97, 102
Kantor, Mickey, 104
Kassouf, Thomas L., 275
Kastner, Lynn, 519-520
Kastre, Michael F., 13
Kastre, Nydia Rodriguez, 13
Keatley, Robert, CN2
Kelleher, Herb, 307
Kelly, Kevin, CN5, CN6
Kelso, Louis O., 386, 392
Kennedy, John F., 138
Kerin, Roger A., 16
Kiechell, Walter, III, CN4
Kiely, Thomas J., CN4
Kim, Sue Bae, CN2
King, Patricia, CN7
Kirchhoff, Bruce, 185
Kirkpatrick, David, CN9
Kleiman, Carol, CN6, CN7
Klein, Maury, CN3
Kleinberg, Eliot, CN9
Knight, Bobby, 226
Kocher, Bob, 405
Kocher, Candy, 405
Kohrs, Kenneth, 325
Koretz, Gene, CN3
Kotte, Erika, 123
Kotter, John P., CN4
Krantz, Mark, CN7
Krick, John, CN9
Krueger, Alan, 384
Krugman, Paul, CN2
Kuenheim, Eberhard, 94

L

Laberis, Bill, CN9
Labich, Kenneth, 108, 307, CN5, CN8
Lambro, Donald, CN1
Landro, Laura, CN9
Lane, Michael, CN2
Lans, Maxine S., 409
Lasch, Christopher, CN2
Lavin, Dan, CN7
Lawerence, Jennifer, CN8
Lawlor, Julia, CN6
Lawson, James C., CN7
Lee, Janet, CN3
Lenzer, Robert, CN1
Lesly, Elizabeth, CN6
Leung, Liza, 320
Levin, Gary, CN8
Levinson, Marc, 125
Levitt, Theodore, 498-499
Lewent, Judy, 583, CN9
Lewis, Geoff, CN9

Lewis, John L., 375
Lewis, Peter, 530
Lewyn, Mark, 535, CN9
Light, Larry, CN10
Linden, Dana Wechsler, 211
Lindorff, Dave, CN2
Lipnack, Jessica, 260, CN4
Littleton, Cleo, 667
Littleton, Mitchell, 667
Loeb, Marshall, CN7
Lohse, Deborah, CN10
Loomis, Carol, 601
Louganis, Greg, 392
Loveman, Gary, CN1
Lublin, Joann S., CN6
Lui, Philip, 28

M

Machan, Dyan, CN7
Malkin, Elisabeth, CN2
Mallory, Maria, 601
Malone, Michael S., CN5, CN7
Mancuso, Joseph R., 178, 180
Mandel, Michael J., CN2, CN9
Mann, Rebecca, CN6
Marbach, William D., CN5
Maremont, Mark, 659, CN5
Margolis, Jon, CN5
Marino, Vivian, 674
Marshall, Ray, 384
Marx, Karl, 62-63
Maslow, Abraham H., 312, CN5
Maturi, Richard J., 570
Matusky, Gregory, CN3
May, Robert, 463
Mayfield, Gloria Hilliard, 328
Mayo, Elton, 310-311
McCaw, Craig, 179
McCormick, John, 125
McCune, Jenny C., CN9
McEwen, Rick, 505
McGinn, Daniel, CN10
McGrath, Kathleen, 402
McGrath, Peter, CN9
McGregor, Douglas, 313, CN5
McKee, Bradford, CN7
McKenna, Barrie, CN5
McManus, Kevin, CN10
McNamee, Mike, CN7
McWilliams, Gary, CN3
Meany, George, 375
Melcher, Richard A., 601, 632,
    CN1, CN2
Meyer, Michael, CN4, CN9
Miles, Gregory L., CN8
Miller, Cyndee, 449
Mills, Helen, 62
Misner, Ivan R., 503
Mitchell, Russell, CN2
Miyares, Urban, 28
Monroe, Ann, 597, CN9
Montgomery, Robin, 505
Moore, Alicia Hills, CN9
Moore, Dan, 37
Moore, Gordon E., 532
Morin, Laura, 13
Morris, Richard C., CN8
Mossberg, Walter S., CN5

Motts, Bill, 579
Moukbeiber, Zina, CN8
Mueller, Al, 188
Mueller, Caroline, 188
Mullich, Joe, CN8
Mullins, Wiley, 667
Murto, Bill, 181

N

Nader, Ralph, 125
Naisbitt, John, 326, CN3
Nakarmi, Laxmi, 352
Naumann, Earl, CN4
Nava, Yvonne, CN8
Nayyar, Seema, CN7
Neff, Robert, 352, 384, CN2
Nelson, Kent, 309
Nelton, Sharon, 223
Neubome, Ellen, 116, 438, CN8
Newman, Paul, 125
Nicholas, Ted S., 159
Nichols, Nancy A., CN9
Nisselbaum, Nancy, CN3
Norback, Craig T., 191
North, Robert, 108
Norton, Erle, 275, CN4, CN7
Norton, Steve, 187
Novack, Janet, CN1
Nulty, Peter, CN6

O

O'Brian, Bridget, CN8
O'Neal, Michael, CN9
O'Neal, Raymond, 27, 28
O'Neal, Shaquille, 443
O'Reilly, Anthony J., 387
O'Reilly, Brian, 234, CN3
O'Reilly, Eileen Drage, 371, CN6
O'Rourke, Tracy, 288
Ono, Yumiko, CN2
Ouchi, William G., CN5
Ounjian, Marilyn, 167

P

Packard, David, 316
Packwood, Robert, 389
Paine, Lynn Sharp, 122, CN2
Panken, Peter M., CN6
Parcels, J. Roy, 499
Pare, Terence P., CN9
Parker, Glenn M., CN4, CN5
Parker, Sir Peter, 211
Pascual, Elios, CN4
Peale, Nornian Vincent, CN2
Pechter, Kerry, 449
Penney, J.C., 170
Peppers, Don, CN8
Perkins, Anne G., CN6
Perlberger, Jillian, 337
Perot, Ross, 105-106
Perry, Jack, 520
Peters, Tom, 219
Peterson, C.D., 154
Pfeiffer, Eckhard, 181
Phillips, Debra, 284, CN1

Pinchot, Elizabeth, 34, 212, 258
Pinchot, Gifford, 34, 212, 258
Pine, Joseph, II, CN8
Pitz, Mary Elizabeth, 13
Poe, Sheri, 320
Pollock, Ellen Joan, CN6
Poor, Tim, CN6
Powell, Bill, 292
Procter, William, 178
Puccini, Donna, 538
Pulley, Brett, 27, CN1
Puryear, Rudy, CN9

Q

Quinn, James Brian, CN4
Quinn, Jane Bryant, CN10

R

Raimondi, Dino, 652
Ramstad, Evan, CN1
Randle, Wilma, 182, CN3
Reagan, Ronald, 382
Reda, Ezzat, 28
Reda, Hussein, 28
Redstone, Sumner, 264
Reed, Carson, 87, CN1
Reed, Stanley, 564, CN2
Reichheld, Frederick F., 406
Reichheld, Robert, 412
Reimer, Blanca, 659
Reitman, Valerie, 92, CN2, CN7
Resnick, Rosalind, CN4
Rice, Fay, 441
Rice, Marc, 27, CN1
Richman, Louis S., 147, 243, CN2,
    CN4, CN5
Riggs, Joy, CN4
Ring, Trudy, 13
Roberts, Johnnie L., CN9
Roddick, Anita, 179, 320
Rogers, Adam, CN9
Rogers, Martha, CN8
Rogers, Mary, 30
Rolon, Carmen, 121
Rose, Robert, CN7
Rosenbluth, Hal, 338
Rosenthal, Jonathan, 123
Ross, Arnold S., 386
Ross, Sherwood, CN5
Rossant, John, 564, CN4
Rothchild, Michael, CN4
Rouleau, Marcel, 325
Rudelius, William, 16
Rudolph, Barbara, CN10
Rufkahr, Norma, 208
Rusbuldt, Christopher W., CN7

S

Saddler, Jeanne, 27, CN1, CN3
Sammons, Mary Beth, 198
Samuelson, Robert J., CN6
Sandler, Corey, 154
Saporito, Bill, 371, CN2, CN6
Savignac, Kris, 303
Savona, Dave, 87, CN1, CN4

Scharlach, Andrew, 391
Scheetz, P., 17
Scheuing, Eberhard E., CN7
Schifrin, Matthew, CN10
Schilit, Howard M., 563
Schiller, Zachary, CN2
Schine, Eric, CN3
Schmidt, Warren, 227
Schmitt, Wolfgang, 433, 434, 448
Schroeder, Michael, 620, CN10
Schultz, Don E., CN8
Schultz, Howard, 179
Schutze, Jim, CN3
Schwartzenegger, Arnold, 386
Scott, Matthew S., CN9
Seaberry, Jane, 3, CN1
Segal, Troy, CN7
Seligman, Daniel, CN6
Sellers, Patricia, CN8
Seltz, Michael, CN3
Selz, Michael, CN7
Senge, Peter M., CN5
Sensenbrenner, Joseph, 294
Serwer, Andrew E., CN3, CN10
Sesit, Michael R., CN1, CN10
Shapiro, Eben, 117, CN7
Sharpe, Rochelle, CN6
Shellenbarger, Sue, CN6, CN7
Sherman, Stratford, 292, CN5
Sherwood, Pat, 584-585
Silva, D. Richard, CN7
Silver, Sheryl, CN9
Silverman, Edward R., 438
Simon, Joel, 59, CN1
Simonds, Tom, 187
Simurda, Stephen J., 449
Singletary, Michelle, CN10
Singleton, J., 17
Slattery, William, 591
Smart, Tim, CN6, CN10
Smith, Adam, 60, 61, 71
Smith, Geoffrey, CN10
Smith, Geri, CN2
Smith, Randall, CN3
Smith, Wesley J., 195
Snyder, Richard, 264
Solomon, Alisa, CN7
Solomon, Jolie, 588, CN7, CN10
Soukhanov, Anne H., CN7
Spiro, Leah Nathans, 632
Spragins, Ellyn, 190
Sprout, Alison L., CN5, CN6, CN8
Stalk, George, Jr., CN5
Stamps, Jeffrey, 260, CN4
Steinberg, Carol, CN3
Steirunetz, Greg, CN3
Stem, Gabriella, CN8
Stephens, Uriah Smith, 374
Stern, David, 371
Stevens, Mark, 169

Stevenson, William J., 295
Stewart, Thomas A., CN9
Stodder, Gayle Sato, 412
Stoll, Clifford, CN9
Stollenwerk, John, 198
Stout, Lynn, 632
Strahota, Robert, 620
Stratico-Smith, Kelly, 3
Strauss, Gary, CN3
Strauss, Levi, 170
Stroud, Jerri, 526, CN3
Sullivan, Nick, CN3, CN4
Sundling, Gail, 405
Suris, Oscar, CN5
Surprise, Loyalty, CN5
Swoboda, Frank, CN6, CN7

T

Talbott, Mary, 408
Tanaka, Jennifer, CN9
Tannenbaum, Jeffrey A., CN3, CN4
Tannenbaum, Robert, 227
Taylor, Frederick, 211, 212, 309-310
Taylor, John, 656
Templeman, John, 384
Tennenbaum, Jerry A., 147, CN2
Tesak, Pablo, 59, 60, 71
Teschke, Deborah, CN5
Tetzeli, Rick, CN9
Thomas, Clarence, 389
Thompson, Roger, CN6
Thompson, Susan, 303
Thompson, William Jeffrey, 669
Thurlow, Heida, 194
Thwaits, James, 104
Tichy, Noel, CN4
Tierney, Robin, 108
Todd, Cynthia, CN3
Torry, Saundra, CN3
Touby, Laurel, CN4
Towles, Natalie, 150
Toy, Stewart, 588, CN6
Tran, David, 151
Tran, Robert, 151
Treece, James B., CN5, CN9
Trump, Donald, 303, 623
Tucker, Marc, 384
Tully, Shawn, CN6

U—V

Ullmann, Owen, CN2
Vanderbilt, Cornelius, 187
van Oldenborgh, Marita, CN8
Verity, John W., 525, CN8
Viani, Lara, CN5
Vijek, Mike, 402

Vittoria, Joseph, 394
Vizard, Mary McAleer, 195
Von Daehne, Niklas, CN8

W

Wagner, Betty, 243
Wagner, Bill, CN7
Walker, T.J., 178
Wallace, Don, 154, CN2
Wallach, Robert, 118
Walton, Sam, 29, 30, 34, 479
Wang, Charles, 38
Waterman, Robert H., CN4
Waters, Crystal, CN4
Weaver, Peter, CN10
Weber, Joseph, CN1
Weber, Max, 245, 247, 248
Weddle, Peter D., 13
Weinstein, Bob, CN8
Welch, Jack, 212, 276
Westinghouse, 276
Westmacott, Terence, 495
White, Joseph B., CN5
Whitney, John 0., CN6
Wildstrom, Stephen H., CN9
Wilke, Larry, 524
Wilkins, Robert, 279
Williams, Gary, CN2
Wilson, Greg, 656
Winfrey, Oprah, 386
Winter, Jerry, 491
Woo, Judy, 520
Woodruff, David, CN2
Wooley, Suzanne, 659, CN2
Woolley, Suzanne, CN4
Wu, Yee-Ping, 28

Y

Yang, Catherine, 659, CN6, CN9
Yang, Dori Jones, CN4
Yates, Ronald E., 243, 352, CN4, CN6
Yatt, John, CN2, CN9
Yorkey, Mike, 669
Young, Dori Jones, CN10
Youovich, B.G., CN10
Yovovich, B.G., CN4

Z

Zaino, Jennifer, CN4
Zehr, Douglas, CN2
Zellner, Wendy, 307, CN5
Zinn, Laura, CN9
Zweig, Philip L., CN10
Zweig, Phillip L., 632, CN9
Zygmont, Jeffery, CN9

COMPANY & PRODUCT INDEX

A

AAMCO, 470
Ace Hardware, 472
Adult Basic Learning
    Environment, 652
Allen-Bradley, 284
Allstate Financial Company, 596
American Express, 410
America Online, 496, 528
Amway, 484
Anheuser-Busch, 91
Apple Computer, 99, 179, 415, 600
Arco, 360
Associated Grocers, 471
AT&T, 221, 256, 386, 389, 390, 523,
    590
AT&T Universal Card Services,
    409, 482
Avis, 97, 198, 394
A&W Root Beer, 162

B

Bain & Company, 412
Bank of America, 180
Baskin-Robbins, 470
Baxter Healthcare Corporation, 410
Ben & Jerry's Homemade, 387
Bethlehem Steel, 276
Black & Decker, 472
Blimpie International Sandwich
    Shops, 147
Blockbuster Entertainment, 602
Blockbuster Video, 481
Blue Diamond, 170
Body Shop, 179
Boeing, 221
Border's Books, 481
The Boring Institute, 553
Bridgestone, 94
Bristol Myers, 108
Burger King, 293
Business Logistics Services, 463

C

Cadbury Schweppes, 161, 162
Caldor, 480
Campbell Soup, 97, 390, 422
Careers USA, 167
Carnegie-Mellon University, 295
Carrier Corporation, 275
Cavalier Gage and Electronic, 243,
    257
Chantal Cookware, 194
Chase Manhattan Bank, 87
Checkers (restaurant franchise),
    27, 29

Chrysler Corporation, 98, 410, 622
CIFRA SA, 97
Clark Equipment, 263
Cleveland Electric Illuminating
    Company, 474
Coastal, 32
Coca-Cola Company, 30, 96, 99,
    107, 108
Columbia Records, 94
Compaq Computer, 181, 600
CompuServe, 496, 528
Computer Associates
    International, 38
Continental Airlines, 454
Continental Illinois Bank, 538
Coors Ceramics, 282
Corning Glass, 385
Crown Zellerbach, 338
Cubex, 591
CVC Communications, 549

D

Daimler-Benz AG, 618
Dayton's, 481
Decorating Den, 166
Dell Computers, 179, 485
Delmar Bootery, 405
Delphi, 528
Department of Defense, 321
DFT Lighting, 402
Dillard's, 481
Dip 'N' Strip, 168
Direct Tire Sales, 219
Disney, 46, 99, 118, 387, 588
Domino's Pizza, 163, 218219
Dow Chemical, 125
Dr Pepper, 508
Dunkin' Donuts, 97
Du Pont Company, 32, 178, 221

E

Eastman Kodak, 132, 178, 386
Eaton Corporation, 275
ECS Technologies, 667
EDS, 579
Eli Lilly, 360
Ernst & Young, 288, 359
Exxon, 32, 155

F

Farmland Industries, Inc., 169
Federal Express (FedEx), 46, 155,
    463, 475, 482
Fields & Associates, 219
Firestone, 94

1st Business Bank, 656
Florida Power & Light, 410, 481
Flypaper, 27
Food from the 'Hood, 115
Ford Motor Company, 99, 178,
    284, 321, 325, 350, 410
Foreman Office Products, 667
French Meadow Bakery, 503
Furukawa Electric, 325

G

Gateway 2000, 485
General Electric, 155, 212, 221,
    257, 276
General Mills, 393
General Motors, 30, 39, 98, 125,
    155, 275, 284, 285, 410
Genie, 528
Genlyte Group, Inc., 402
GiftMaker, 285
Gillette, 108, 360, 386
GTE, 360

H

Haemonetic Corporation, 390
Hardee's Food System, 435
Harris Electronics,' 667
Hart, Schaffner, and Marx, 402
H.B. Fuller Company, 101102
Henkel, 9091
Hercules, 32
Herman Miller Inc., 387
Hershey, 602
Hertz, 198
Hewlett-Packard, 182, 316, 338
H.J. Heinz, 387
Holiday Inn, 163, 292
Honda, 94
Honeywell's Building Controls
    Division, 256
H&R Block, 480
Hull Industries, 435
Hyatt legal services, 480

I

IBM, 48, 99, 118, 121, 155, 257,
    260, 356, 386, 410, 415, 611
IGA food stores, 471
InForm Incorporated, 495
Inner City Foods, Incorporated, 27
Intel Corporation, 46, 219, 313,
    425, 527, 532, 600
InterCon Systems, 529
Intuit, 179
ITT, 316

J

Jazzercise, 166
J.C. Penney, 253, 393
Johnson & Johnson, 390

K

Kamsky Associates, 87
Kellogg, 386
Kentucky Fried Chicken, 97, 198, 470
Kids 'R' Us, 100
Kiwi International Airlines, 454
Kmart, 480
Kohl's Department Store, 402
Kraft General Foods, 162

L

Land O'Lakes, 170
Land's End, 485
Leo Burnett Company, 510
Levy Strauss & Co., 118
L.L. Bean, 485
Lockheed Corporation, 182
Lord & Taylor, 481

M

Mac's Place, 279
Marriott, 118, 390
Marshalls, 480
Mary Kay Cosmetics, 327328, 410, 484
Max Davis Accociates, 303
McCaw Cellular Communications, 179
McDonald's, 97, 118, 125, 163, 198, 253, 263, 293, 454, 470
McDonnell Douglas, 98, 600
MCI, 412
Mercedes Benz, 279, 280
Merck & Company, 583
Meridan Group, 91
Merry Maids, 168
Metropolitan Life Insurance Company, 481
Microsoft, 46, 179, 393
Midway Airlines, 454
Minnetonka, Inc., 90
Money Mailer, Inc., 167
Morton Salt Company, 439
Motel 6, 480
Motorola, 39, 46, 107, 221, 291, 338, 386
MPG, Inc., 596

N

Nabisco, 472
Nakano Vinegar Company, 97
National Basketball Association, 371
National Bicycle Industrial Company, 285
National Semiconductor, 463
Navistar, 276
Nestlé, 96

Nike, 30
Nordstrom, 481
North American Rayon, 395
Northwest Instrument Systems, 601

O

Ocean Spray, 170
Office Depot, 480
OS&A Research and Strategy, 506

P

Paramount, 602
Parker Jewish Geriatric Institute, 339
Parnassus Fund, 609
Parsley Patch, 584585, 590
Pepsico, 393, 491, 590
Peripheral Outlet, Inc., 669
Perrier, 441
Philip Morris, 108
Phillips Cables, Ltd., 325
Phillips-Fitel, 325
Phillips Van Heusen, 125
Phoenix Designs, 282
Pillsbury Company, 287, 440
Pizza Hut, 97
Polaroid, 132, 393
Price's Market, 405
Procter & Gamble, 178, 393, 436, 472
Prodigy Information Service, 485, 496, 528
ProductView Interactive, 496
Published Image, 410

R

Ramada Inn, 97
Rapp Collins Worldwide, 491
Red Devil, 282
Red Roof Inns, 480
Ritz-Carlton Hotel Company, 482
RJR Nabisco, 108
Robert Plan Corp., 118
Rubbermaid, 433, 448
Rug Doctor Pro, 168

S

Safeway, 30
Sam's Clubs, 479
Samuel Adams Boston Lager, 91
Sashco Sealants, Inc., 436
Saturn, 39
Scandinavian Airlines, 481
Schwab Mutual Funds, 481
Seabrook Marketing, 454
Sears, Roebuck & Company, 117, 125, 471
7-Eleven, 97, 163
Shell Oil, 32
Shenandoah Life, 257
Sherwin-Williams, 320
Simon & Schuster, 264
Southwest Airlines, 307, 454, 480

Southwire Company, 104
SpeeDee Oil Change & Tune-Up, 168
Squibb, 108
Stalk, George, Jr., 286
Staples, 480
Starbucks, 179
Stelco, Inc., 338
Stride Rite, 390
Sunkist, 170
Sun Microsystems, 600
Sunnen Products Co., 319

T

Taco Bell, 454
Target, 472, 480
Technico, 667
Tenneco, 32
Texas Instruments, 181, 410
3M Company, 104, 182, 472
Tokyo's Imperial Hotel, 481
Topsytail Co., 177
Towers Perrin, 389
Toyota, 39, 99, 284
Toys 'R' Us, 100, 481
Tupperware, 484

U

Unilever, 162
Unisys, 283
United Parcel Service, 310, 463
U.S. West, 391
USAir Group, 454
USX, 155, 276

V

Valu-Jet Airlines, 454
Varian Corporation, 288
Viacom, 264, 602
Victoria Jackson Cosmetics Company, 193

W

Wal-Mart, 29, 3031, 46, 97, 480, 482
Weirton Steel, 394
Welch's, 170
The Well, 528
Wells-Fargo Bank, 121
Western Auto, 471
Western Electric Company, 310
Westinghouse, 155, 410
Wiley's Healthy Southern Classics, 667
Wrigley's, 602

X

Xerox Corporation, 118, 120, 291, 410, 472, 503

Y

Yes I Can, 28

GENERAL INDEX

A

Absolute advantage, 89
Acceptance of offer, 135
Accountant
  ethics of, 566
  for small business, 194-195, 553
Accounting
  application of, 566-567
  assets, 558
  auditing, 553-554
  cash flow analysis, 563-565
  certified public accountant, 553
  compared with bookkeeping, 554
  computer technology impact on, 570-571
  creative, 563
  defined, 550-551
  FIFO (first in, first out), 566
  financial accounting, 552-553
  financial ratios, 567-570
  fundamental accounting equation, 560
  journals, 554, 556
  liabilities, 558-560
  LIFO (last in, first out), 567
  managerial accounting, 551-552
  reason for, 550
  scope of, 551
  six step accounting cycle, 555-556
  tax accounting, 554
Accounting cycle, defined, 555-556
Accounting system, defined, 551
Accounts payable, 558
Accounts receivable, 591
Acquisitions. See Mergers and acquisitions
Action-oriented, entrepreneurs, 180
Active Corps Executives (ACE), 196
Activity ratios, 569-570
Adaptive pricing, 455
Adjustable life insurance, defined, 676
Administered distribution systems, 471
Administration Industrielle et Generale (Fayol), 245-246
Administrative agencies, 131
  deregulation, 142-143
Advancement, 359-360
Adversarial marketing, 411
Advertising. See also Catalogs; Direct mail; Promotion
  categories of, 494

Advertising—*Cont.*
  customized, 498-499
  defined, 493
  global, 498-499
  importance of, 493-494
  infomercials, 495
  by marketing middlemen, 465
  technology in, 495-497
  value package and, 435
Advertising agencies, integrated marketing communication (IMC) systems effect on, 510
Advocacy advertising, 494
Affirmative action, defined, 361
African-American businesspeople, 27-28, 56, 115, 178, 667
Age discrimination, 362
Age Discrimination in Employment Act, 362
Agency shop agreement, 377
Aging of population, 44
Agricultural industry, evolution in United States, 49-50, 75
AIDS, 391-392
  ethics, 393
Air, goods shipped by, 475
Alcohol abuse, 392
Alcohol Labeling Legislation, 139
Alternative sources of funds, 592-593
American Federation of Labor (AFL), 374
American Free Trade Agreement (AFTA), 47
American Stock Exchange, 619
Americans with Disabilities Act, 362
Analytic systems, defined, 281
Annual report, defined, 552-553
Answering objections, in selling process, 502
Antitrust law
  Interstate Commerce Act of 1887, 137
  Sherman Antitrust Act, 137-138
Appearance, as quality cue, 443
Application form, for employment, 345, 346
Apprenticeship, 187-188
  defined, 348
Approach, in selling process, 501
Arbitration, 379
Arthur Young Guide to Raising Venture Capital (Barrill & Norbach), 191

Asian population of United States in future, 43
Assembly line workers, 276
Assembly process, defined, 281
Assets
  on balance sheet, 558
  fundamental accounting equation, 560
Associations, as nonprofit organizations, 32
Atmospherics, value package and, 435
Attorney, for small business, 196
Auditing, 553-554
  and computer technology, 571
  defined, 553
Auditor's opinion, 554
Autocratic leadership, 226
Automated teller machines (ATMs), 650
Automation, of offices, 538-540
Automobile Information Disclosure Act, 139
Automobile insurance, personal finances and, 676
Autonomy, as motivator, 320
Avoidance of risk, 686

B

Background investigations, for employment, 345
Balance of payments, defined, 92
Balance of trade
  defined, 92
  unfavorable, of United States, 93
Balance sheet, 557
  accounts of, 558
  account titles, 563
  assets, 558
  defined, 557
  fundamental accounting equation, 560
  liabilities, 558-560
  sample, 559
Baldrige Award, 48-49, 363
Banker's acceptance, 658
Banker's bank. See Federal Reserve
Banking
  electronic funds transfer system (EFTS), 656-657
  Federal Reserve, and, 647
  future of, 655

Banking—Cont.
importance in global markets,
102
international. See International
banking
interstate, 655-656
Bank loans
from commercial banks, 594-
596
forms of, 595-596
Bank of Credit and Commerce, 659
Bankruptcy
defined, 138
division of assets, 141
as labor-management conflict
tactic, 379
laws governing, 138-141
Banks
business loans, 650-651
cash flow, and, 564
entrepreneur relations with, 570
expansion of role, 656
services to borrowers, 650
small banks, 656
Bar codes
electronic data exchange and, 38
in information management, 38
Bargaining zone, defined, 379
Bartering. See also Countertrading
defined, 98
Basic Guide to Exporting, 91
Bear market, 623
Benchmarking, 262, 292
competitive benchmarking, 410
Benefit market segmentation, 423,
425
Benefits, 355-356
cafeteria benefits packages, 44,
356
child care, 390-391
elder care, 391
employee stock ownership plans
(ESOPs). See Employee stock
ownership plans (ESOPs)
flexible schedules, 356
fringe benefits, defined, 355
golden parachutes, 387-388
"price club," 59
proposed legislation, 362-363
sole proprietorship, 150
for two-income families, 44
Big business, versus small
business, 183
Blue chip stock, 624
Board of directors
compensation of, 387
conflict with, 158
Bond certificate, 611
Bond ratings, 622-623
Bonds
advantages of selling, 611-612
call provision, 613
classes of, 612

Bonds—Cont.
convertible, 613
debt financing, and, 610
defined, 610
disadvantages of selling, 611-612
features of, 612-613
high risk, 623
investing in, 622-623
quotation, 628
secured and unsecured, 599
sinking fund, 612-613
terminology of, 611
Bonds payable, 559
Bonus plans, 355
Bookkeeping
compared with accounting, 554
defined, 554
double-entry, 555
Borrowing
bank services to borrowers, 650
leverage, 601-602
for small business startup, 189
Boycott, 379, 380-381
Boy association, 443-444
Brand awareness, 443
Brand equity
building, 443
defined, 443
Brand loyalty, 443
Brand manager, 444
Brand name, 133
defined, 407
legal issues, 409
value package and, 435
Brands
brand categories, 442-443
brand equity, 441
defined, 441
product lines, 436
trademark, 442
Breach of contract, 135-136
Break-even analysis, 454-455
Bribery, 101, 124, 482
Broadcasting, 497
Brokerage firms, 652, 653
Brokerage services, service of
commercial bank, 650
Brokers, as marketing middlemen,
465
Budget
capital, 589
cash, 589
defined, 588
development of, 588-589
master, 589
operating, 588
Bull market, 623
Bull's eye marketing, 423
Bureaucracies, foreign, 101
Bureaucracy
bureaucratic organization
structure, 248

Bureaucracy—Cont.
defined, 244
fundamentals of, 244-245
productivity and quality in, 294
in small business, 250
Business. See also New businesses;
Nonprofit organizations;
Organization; Startup of
business; Termination of
business
customer-driven, 40
defined, 29
economics, relationship to, 60
fiscal policy effect on, 77-78
history of economics and, 62-66
information flows between
customers and, 38
ownership of, 36
relationship to government, 65-
66
Business culture, multiculturalism
providing enrichment of, 44
Business environment
effect on entrepreneurs, 35
monitored by information
technology, 38
Business failure, small business,
184-186
Business law
administrative agencies, 131
antitrust law. See Antitrust law
bankruptcy laws, 138-141
common law, 131
consumer protection law, 138
copyright, 133
defined, 130-131
deregulation, 142-143
need for laws, 130
patent law, 132-133
product liability, 131-132
statutory law, 131
tax laws, 138
tort law, 131
trademark, 133
Business plan, 188-190
venture capital, 600
Business purchase, small business,
188
Business-to-business marketing.
See Industrial marketing
Buying, in marketing, 414
Buying a business, small business,
188

C

Cable television, and information
highway, 527
CAD/CAM, 286-288
competition and, 276
computer-aided design (CAD),
defined, 287

CAD/CAM—*Cont.*
   computer-aided manufacturing (CAM), defined, 287
Cafeteria benefits packages, 44, 356
Call provision of bond, 613
Capital, factor of production, 34-35
Capital accumulation
   real estate investment, 672-673
   strategy for, 671-672
Capital budget, 589
Capital expenditures
   defined, 592
   operating funds, and, 592
Capitalism
   Adam Smith, and, 61
   basic rights of, 66-67
   defined, 61
   efficiency and, 71
   equality and, 71
   free-market capitalism, 62
   market choices, 65
   market control, 65
   social and economic goals, 65
   social freedoms, 65
   welfare capitalism, 64-66
   worker motivation, 65
Career development, as organizational strategy, 347
Career paths
   entrepreneurs, 207
   financial management, 692-694
   human resource management, 401
   information technology, 577-578
   management, 301-302
   marketing, 517-518
Careers, 5, 7, 12-13, 676, 680
   effect of information technology on, 541
   in logistics, 464
   in marketing, 518
   preparation for, 7-8
   variety of, 4-5
Carts and kiosks, 484
Cash-and-carry wholesaler, defined, 478
Cash budget, 589
Cash flow
   defined, 564
   in global business, 564
   statement of cash flows, 565
Cash flow analysis, 563-565
Cash flow forecast, 587
Catalogs, targeted through databases, 38
C corporation, 160
CD-ROM, for advertising, 495
Cellular communications, and information highway, 527
Centralization of authority, 251-253

Centralized authority, defined, 253
Certificates of deposit (CD), service of commercial bank, 650
Certification, defined, 376
Certified checks, service of commercial bank, 650
Certified internal auditor, 554
Certified management accountant, defined, 552
Certified public accountant (CPA), 553, 585
Chain of command, bureaucracy, 244
Challenge, for entrepreneurs, 179
Channel captain, 471
Channel of distribution
   for consumer goods, 465
   defined, 464
   for industrial goods, 465
Channel systems, 470
   administered distribution systems, 471
   channel captain, 471
   contractual distribution systems, 470-471
   corporate distribution systems, 470
Charities, as nonprofit organizations, 32
Charts, 290
Checking accounts. See Demand deposit
Chief executive officer (CEO), 217
   at bottom of organization chart, 261
   compensation of, 386-387
Chief financial officer (CFO), 584
Chief information officer (CIO), 37
Chief operating officer (COO), 217
Child care, 390-391
Child labor, 62
Child Protection Act, 139
Child Protection and Toy Safety Act, 139
Children, advertising targeted to, 421
Choice, freedom of, 67
Cigarette Labeling Act, 139
Civil Rights Act of 1964, 361
Civil Rights Act of 1991, 361, 389
Classified common stock, 615
Clayton Act, 137
Client/server computers, 534
Closed-shop agreement, 377
Close sale, in selling process, 502
Cognitive dissonance, defined, 421
Cold call, 500
Collaboration, using internet for, 529
Collateral, 598
Collateral trust bonds, 612, 613
Collective bargaining, 375-377
   defined, 376-377

Command economies, 63-64. See also Socialism
   moving toward welfare capitalism, 64-65
Commercial accounts, business-to-business selling, 502-503
Commercial banks, 649-651
   business loans, 650-651
   services available at, 649-651
   services to borrowers, 650
   short-term financing from, 594-596
Commercial finance companies, 596, 652, 653
Commercialization, new-product development, 444, 447
Commercial law. See Uniform Commercial Code
Commercial loan officer, for small business, 196
Commercial paper, 596
Commission plans, 355
Commodities, investing in, 627
Commodity exchange, 627
Common law, 131
Common markets, 104-105
Common stock, 617
Communication
   building teamwork through, 324-325
   among departments, in bureaucracy, 244
   management development, 350-351
   multilingual, 325
   performance evaluation, 352
   with stakeholders, 508
Communications software, 537
Communication technology. See Telecommunications
Communicator, manager as, 213
Communist Manifesto (Marx), 63
Communities, as stakeholders, 40
Comparable worth, defined, 388
Comparative advantage theory, 89
Comparison advertising, 494
Compensation, 353-354. See also Benefits; Executive compensation; Wages
   based on performance, 41
   employee stock ownership plans (ESOPs), 392-395
   executive compensation, 386-388
   golden parachutes, 387-388
   as motivator, 310-312
   pay equity, 388-389
   pay systems, 354-355
   profit, and, 29
   proposed legislation, 362-363
   restrictions on, 387
   of self-managed workers, 41
   strategic plan for, 342
   unions, and, 383

Competing Against Time (Hout & Stalk), 286
Competition. See also Antitrust law; Competitive environment; Free trade; International competition; Trade protectionism
CAD/CAM, 287
in exporting, 88-89
labor force, effect of, 339-340
meeting needs of community, and, 40
by meeting needs of employees, 41
meeting stakeholders' needs, 40
nonprice competition, 456-457
pleasing customers, and, 39-40
price determined by, 456
over product life cycle, 551
profit, and, 29
regaining competitive edge, 276
right to freedom of, 66-67
in time, 286
Competition-oriented pricing, 456
Competitive benchmarking, 410
defined, 262
Competitive environment, factors in, 39
Competitive pricing, 452
break-even analysis, 454-455
cost-based pricing, 453
pricing objectives, 452-453
pricing strategies, 455-456
value pricing, 453-454
Compliance-based ethics codes, 119
Compressed workweek, defined, 358
Computer-aided acquisition and logistics support (CALS), 288
Computer-aided design. See CAD/CAM
Computer-aided engineering, 288
Computer-aided manufacturing. See CAD/CAM
Computer chips, capacity of, 533
Computer crime, 538-539
Computer hardware, 532-533
Computer-integrated manufacturing (CIM), 287
Computer literacy, as necessary skill, 4, 540
Computer networks, 534
Computer programmer, 578
Computers. See also Information highway; Information technology
and accounting, 570-571
CAD/CAM, 286-288
computer-integrated manufacturing (CIM), 287
computerized factory, 288

Computers—*Cont.*
computer scheduling programs, 356
effects on management, 538-540
hand-held for placing orders, 495
hardware, 532-533
improving service sector productivity with, 293
and information highway, 527
mainframes, 534
networks, 534
on-line advertising, 494
physical problems caused by, 539
in small business, 480, 526
software. See Software
in traditionally nontechnological businesses, 37
troubleshooter, 579
Computer skills, 233
Computer software. See Software
Concentration, in industrial market, 426
Concept testing, 407, 445
Conceptual skills, 230
Conflict
corporation, 158
partnership, 152
Conglomerate merger, 161
Congress of Industrial Organizations (CIO), 375
Consideration, 135
Constant white water, defined, 434
Construction industry, employment increases in, 184
Consumer finance companies, 653
Consumer goods, channels of distribution for, 465
Consumerism, defined, 138
Consumer market, 422
convenience goods and services, 437
defined, 421
segmentation of, 422-425
shopping goods and services, 437
specialty goods and services, 438
Consumer needs, efficient consumer response (ECR), 472-473
Consumer price index (CPI), 72
inflation and, 75
Consumer products, 421
Consumer Product Safety Act, 139
Consumer protection laws, 138
list of, 139
Consumers
decision making process of, 420-421
marketing research as method of understanding, 419-420

Consumers—*Cont.*
purchases as signals to business, 67
responding to, 38
Containerization, 476
Contest, as sales promotion, 504
Contingency planning, 216
Contingent workers, 337. See also Outsourcing
Continuing education, 347
Continuous improvement, 410
defined, 259
Continuous process, 281
Contract
breach, 135-136
defined, 135
Contract employment, 184
Contract law
breach of contract, 135-136
defined, 135
description of, 134
effect on business, 36
Contract manufacturing. See Outsourcing
Contractual distribution systems, 470-471
Control function, 222
Controlling, 222-223
defined, 214
function of management, 213, 214
Control of money supply, 645
discount rate, 646
need for, 643-644
open-market operations, 645-646
reserve requirement, 645
Control procedures, competition and, 276
Control process, 222
Convenience goods and services, 437
Conversation, on information highway, 528
Convertible bonds, 613
Convertible preferred stock, 615
Cooling-off period, defined, 383
Cooperation
informal organization, and, 266-267
managers, and, 213
Cooperative
defined, 163
small business, 170
Coordinator, manager as, 213
Copyright, 133
Core competencies, defined, 262
Core time, defined, 357
Corporate code of conduct, 120
Corporate culture, effect on recruiting, 343
Corporate distribution systems, 470
Corporate ethical standards, 119-120

Corporate expansion. See Mergers and acquisitions
Corporate financial services, 652
Corporate philanthropy, 120
Corporate policy, 120
Corporate social responsibility, 120-124
Corporations
    advantages of, 155-156
    C corporation, 160
    changing atmosphere in, 326-327
    defined, 148
    disadvantages of, 156-158
    downsizing, 28
    of individual, 159
    S corporation, 159-160
    size of, 155
Corruption, effect on business, 36
Cost-based pricing, 453
Cost control
    employee compensation, 353-354
    site selection and, 276, 278-279
Cost estimator, 578
Cost of goods sold (manufactured), 562
Cost-oriented pricing, 455
Costs
    of advertising, 493-494
    of employee selection and training, 344-345
    for marketing middlemen, 466
    physical distribution systems, 476
Cottage industries, 358-359
Countertrading, 98
Coupons, 504
Cover letter, 20-22
Craft union, defined, 373
Creative accounting, 563
Credit
    in marketing, 414, 415
    personal finances, and, 673-675
Credit cards, 673-675
    service of commercial bank, 650
Credit unions, 652
Critical path, defined, 290
Cross-functional cooperation among departments, 256-259
Cross-functional teams, 182, 256-257, 270, 298, 410, 430
    cross-training programs, 347
    defined, 256
    global marketing with, 448
    implementing effectiveness of front-line people, 41
    limitations of, 257
    networking, and, 258
    self-managed. See Self-managed teams
Cross-training programs, 347
Cultural differences, effect on global trade, 98-100

Culture, defined, 421
Culture shock, 499
Cumulative preferred stock, 615, 616
Currency, 643
Currency exchange, 658
Currency shifts, effect on global trade, 101-102
Current assets, on balance sheet, 558
Customary pricing, 455
Custom-designed products, CAD/CAM, 287
Customer-driven business, 40
    bureaucracy, and, 244
Customer focus, and competition, 276
Customer needs/wants, 277
    in integrated marketing strategy, 511
Customer orientation, 409-410
Customer-oriented marketing, 405
Customer-oriented organization, 218-219, 265, 271, 350
Customer relations, changes made by information technology, 525
Customers. See also Consumers; Customer needs/wants
    contact with teams, 221
    delighting the customer, 409-410
    demands of, 39-40
    establishment of relationship with, 407
    in industrial market, 426
    information flows between businesses and, 38
    internal, 223, 262-263
    long-term relationships with, 411-412
    mass customization, 285-286
    meeting needs of, 193
    organizational structures changing to meet needs of, 41
    and profit, 411
    promotion of product to, 407
    as stakeholders, 40
Customer satisfaction, 193
    corporate management, and, 212
    success measurement by, 223-224
Customer service, 39, 64, 495
    physical distribution systems, 475-476
    small business, 184
Customization of product, 277
Customized advertising, 498-499
Cyclical unemployment, 72-73

D

Daily business operations, operating funds for, 590-591

Damages (monetary settlement), 135
Databank, defined, 38
Database software, 536-537
Data collection, in marketing research, 417-418
Data processing (DP), defined, 524
The Day America Told the Truth, 118
Daywork, 355
Dealers, as stakeholders, 40
Debenture, 613
Debenture bonds, 612
Debt. See Borrowing; National debt
Debt capital, 593
Debt financing, 598-599
    bonds, 610
Debtor nation, 94
Debt ratios, 568
Decentralization of authority, 251-253
Decentralized authority, defined, 253
Decertification, defined, 376
Decision making
    by consumers, 420-421
    defined, 231
    managerial accounting used in, 551-552
    participation by employees, 221
    process, 231
Deficit spending, 79
Delegation of authority, 194, 230-231
    delegating, defined, 230
    to lower-level managers and employees, 212
Delighting the customer, 39, 229, 409-410
Delivery, value package and, 435
Demand
    defined, 69
    equilibrium point, 69-70
    for industrial goods, 426
    relationship to price, 67
Demand curve, 69
Demand deposit, 650
Demand-oriented pricing, 456
Democratic leadership, 226
Demographic market segmentation, 422, 424
Demographic trends
    aging of population, 44
    multiculturalism, 43-44
    single-parent households, 45
    two-income families, 44-45
Demography, defined, 42
Departmentalization, 250-251
    defined, 250
    ways to departmentalize, 251-252

Depreciation, defined, 566
Depression, defined, 76
Derivatives disclosure, 601
Derived demand, 426
Design for manufacturability and
    assembly (DFMA), 288
Devaluation, defined, 101
Directing
    defined, 214
    function of management, 213,
    214
    in traditional organizations, 220
Direct mail, 493, 494. See also
    Catalogs
    advantages and disadvantages
    of, 495
    targeted through databases, 38
Direct marketing, 177
    defined, 492
    online, 485
    using internet for, 529
Direct sales, in industrial market,
    426
Disability discrimination,
    legislation, 362
Disabled businesspersons, 28, 362
Disagreement. See Conflict
Discharge. See Termination of
    employment
Discount rate, 646
Discrimination, 361-362
    pay equity, 388
    sexual harassment, 389
Distribution. See also Inventory
    efficient consumer response
    (ECR), 472-473
    electronic data interchange
    (EDI), 472
    global, 472
    international, 464, 476
    marketing middlemen. See
    Marketing middlemen
    retail middlemen, 479-480
    role in business, 464
    small businesses pooling efforts,
    220
    supply chain management
    (SCM), 471-472
    wholesale middlemen. See
    Wholesale middlemen
Distribution warehouse, 477
Distributor brands, 442
Diversification of portfolio, 626-
    627
Diversity, 43, 99 See also
    Multiculturalism
    in franchising, 166-167
    managing, through human
    relations skills, 233-234
    recruiting problems caused by,
    343-344
    small business, 340

Diversity—Cont.
    unions and, 384
Diversity of work force, and
    management, 212, 398-399
Dividends, 74
    defined, 614
    effect of, 617
Divisibility, of money, 642
Dollar, declining value of, 184
Double-entry bookkeeping, 555
Double stacks, 474
Dow Jones averages, 631
Dow Jones Industrial Average, 631
Downsizing, 212, 340
    corporations, 28
    defined, 28
    of government, 28
    through retirement, 360
    self-managed teams, and, 41
    termination of employees
    resulting from, 360
    unions and, 384
Drop shipper, 479
Drug testing, 392
Dumping
    defined, 92
    trade protectionism and, 102
Durability, of money, 643
Duration, as investment criteria,
    622

E

Early retirement, 360
Economic differences, effect on
    global trade, 100-101
Economic empowerment, and
    entrepreneurship, 27
Economic environment, effect on
    entrepreneurs, 35-37
Economics. See also Resource
    development
    defined, 60
    history of business and, 62-66
    importance of, 60
Economic system(s)
    business contribution to, 60
    capitalism. See Capitalism
    command economies, 63-64.
    See also Socialism
    comparisons of, 65
    free market economies, 63-64.
    See also Capitalism
    generation of wealth in, 31
    mixed economies, 63-64
    socialism. See Socialism
    welfare capitalism, 64-66
Economic system of United States,
    71-72, 72
    key economic indicators, 72-74
    move toward social programs, 71
Economy
    dependence on money, 642

Economy—Cont.
    importance of small business to,
    184
Education
    for career in international
    business, 89
    choice of college, 6-7
    continuing education, 347
    for entrepreneurs, 186-188
    of front-line personnel, 261
    for global markets, 47-48
    managerial skills, 233-235
    off-the-job training, 349
    technological change and
    requirements for, 212
    undereducation, 340
    value of, 4
Efficiency, goal of organizations,
    248
Efficient consumer response
    (ECR), 472-473
Elder care, 391
Electronic banking, 656-657
Electronic data interchange (EDI),
    38, 472
Electronic funds transfer system
    (EFTS), 656-657
Electronic mail. See E-mail
E-mail
    advertising through, 495
    communication by, 325
    on internet, 529
Embargo, defined, 103
Emerging economies,
    countertrading and, 98
Employee-management issues
    AIDS, 391-392
    child care, 390-391
    drug testing, 392
    elder care, 391
    employee stock ownership plans
    (ESOPs). See Employee stock
    ownership plans (ESOPs)
    equal pay for comparable jobs,
    388-389
    executive compensation, 386-388
    sexual harassment, 389
    violence in workplace, 392
Employee orientation, defined, 348
Employee relations, 194
Employees. See also Job creation;
    Lower-level employees
    compensation. See
    Compensation
    competing by meeting needs of,
    41
    delegation of authority to, 194,
    212
    disabled people as, 28
    education of, 212
    education requirements for self-
    management, 41

Employees—*Cont.*
internal customers, 410
investment by, 30
job satisfaction of, 194
labor unions. See Unions
management of, 194
number in public sector, 65
number in small business, 183
organizational structures
changing to meet needs of, 41
orientation, 348
partial ownership of business
by, 41
participation in decision
making, 221
participation in ownership. See
Employee stock ownership
plans (ESOPs)
in small business, 187, 194
as stakeholders, 40
temporary, 337
Employee stock ownership plans
(ESOPs), 385, 392-395
benefits of, 393-394
defined, 392
partial ownership of business by
employees, 41
problems with, 394-395
Employment at will, 360
Employment Retirement Income
Security Act (ERISA), 364
Employment tests, 345
Empowerment, 41, 211, 246, 495
defined, 220
employees meeting customer
needs, 41
with information technology,
495-496
inverted organization and, 261-
262
of teams, 220-221, 228
Ending of business. See
Termination of business
*End of Bureaucracy and the Rise of
the Intelligent Organization*
(Pinchot), 212
Enterprise resource planning, 282
Enterprise zones, 181
Entrepreneurial team, 181
Entrepreneur Readiness
Questionnaire, 204
Entrepreneurs. See also Small
business
advice for potential, 180
balance of risk and profit by, 29-
30
career paths for, 207
defined, 28
disabled people as, 28
education for, 186-188
effect of business environment
on, 35

Entrepreneurs—*Cont.*
effect of economic environment
on, 35-37
Entrepreneur Readiness
Questionnaire, 204
hours of work, 187
immigrants as, 28
job creating power of, 178-179
layoffs as opportunities for, 28
personality of, 180
reasons for becoming, 179
relations with bankers, 570
seed money, 191
skills needed by, 206-207
sources of capital for startup,
189
traits of, 179-180
unpleasant details of business,
553
using savings to start business,
669
women as, 28, 55, 177, 243
Entrepreneurship
defined, 178
economic empowerment, and, 27
encouragement of, 181
factor of production, 34-35
within firms, 182, 200-201
importance to wealth, 32
as primary source of wealth, 35
small business. See Small
business
Environment. See Natural
environment
Environmentalism, 42
Equal Employment Opportunity
Act, 361
Equal Employment Opportunity
Commission (EEOC), 361
Equality
capitalism and, 71
socialism and, 62-63
Equal Pay Act of 1963, 388
Equilibrium point, 69-70
Equipment. See Fixed assets
Equipment trust bonds, 612
Equity
defined, 559-560
owner's equity, 560
retained earnings, 560
Equity capital, 593
Equity financing, 599-600
through stock sale, 614-617
Esteem needs, defined, 312
Ethical alternatives in decision
making, 231
Ethical standards
corporate, 119-120
international, 124-126
legality, 116-117
Ethics. See also Social
responsibility
of accountant, 566

Ethics—*Cont.*
advertising to young people,
117, 421
AIDS, 393
appropriations requests, 590
bribery, 482
competition, and, 42
competition with former
employer, 182
controlling suppliers, 125
defined, 117
first-line managers, 220
global trade, 123
green packaging, 441
guilt by association, 506
inside information, 633
management, and, 117
in marketing decisions, 418-419
organizational culture, and, 265
organizational ethics, 118
outsourcing, 156
personal ethics, 118-119
recruitment from competition,
347
relocation of business, 280
restructuring, 263
software pirating, 538
tax fairness, 79
temporary employees, 327
Ethics codes, 119-120
Ethics management, 119
Ethnocentricity, 98
European Economic Community
(EEC). See European Union
(EU)
European Union (EU), 46-47, 104-
105
Event sponsorship, 443
Exchange efficiency, 465-466
Exchange rate, defined, 101
Exchange relationships, 465-466
Excise taxes, 140
Exclusive distribution, 482
Executive compensation, 386-388
golden parachutes, 387-388
Expenses. See also Costs
operating expenses, 562
Exporting, 90
defined, 88
goods and services, 91
by small business, 197-198
strategy for reaching global
markets, 95
tips for, 198
United States experience in, 93-
95
Exportise, 91
Exports, declining value of dollar,
and, 184
Export trading companies, 95
Express warranty, 134
External sales promotion, 504
Extrinsic reward, 308

F

Factoring, 596
Factors of production
defined, 33
listing of, 34-35-35
Failure of business, small business, 184-186
Fair Credit Reporting Act, 139
Fair Labor Standards Act, 374
Fair Packaging and Liability Act, 139
Fair trade agreements, 46-47
Falling dollar, 644
Family and Medical Leave Act, 390
Family businesses, 194
Farm, 169, 173, 191, 526, 594
Favorable balance of payments, 92
Federal deficit, 79
Federal Deposit Insurance Corporation (FDIC), 654
Federal Reserve
Alan Greenspan at, 641
banking industry, and, 647
open-market operations, 645-646
reserve requirement, 645
Federal Reserve System
Great Depression, and, 647
history of, 646-647
Federal Trade Commission Act, 137
Feedback, as motivator, 320
FIFO (first in, first out), 566
Finance
defined, 585-586
in marketing, 414, 415
reasons to understand, 584-585
role of, 584
Finance companies, 652, 653
Financial accounting, 552-553
defined, 553
Financial Accounting Standards Board (FASB), 553
Financial control, 589-590
Financial counseling, service of commercial bank, 650
Financial failure, reasons for, 584
Financial information, and accounting, 550
Financial institutions. See also Banks
commercial banks, 649-651
credit unions, 652
nonbanks, 652
savings and loan associations, 651
Financial management
alternative sources of funds, 592-593
careers in, 692-694

Financial Management—Cont.
defined, 585-586
leverage, 601-602
needed in nonprofit organizations, 33
operating funds, 590-592
Financial managers, functions of, 585
Financial planners, 680
Financial planning, 586-587
budget development, 588-589
financial control, 589-590
forecasting, 587
personal. See Personal financial planning
Financial ratios, 567
activity ratios, 569-570
debt ratios, 568
leverage ratios, 568
liquidity ratios, 567-568
performance ratios, 568-569
profitability ratios, 568-569
Financial reporting, and computer technology, 571
Financial resources
corporation, 155
partnership, 152
small business, 189
sole proprietorship, 150
venture capitalist, 191
Financial statements
balance sheet. See Balance sheet
defined, 557
income statement. See Income statement
statement of cash flows, 565
Finding Private Venture Capital for Your Firm (Gaston), 191
Finished goods, transportation modes, 473-475
Firing. See Termination of employment
First-line management, 217-218
directing by, 220
Fiscal policy, 76, 77
Fishyback, 474
Fixed assets, on balance sheet, 558
Flammable Fabrics Act, 139
Flat organization structures, 249
Flexible manufacturing, 284, 288
mass customization, 286
Flextime, defined, 357
Flextime plans, 357-358
Floating exchange rate, defined, 101
Flow of goods, electronic data exchange and, 38
Focus group, defined, 418
Focus on customer. See Customer focus
Follow up, in selling process, 502

Food, Drug, and Cosmetic Act, 139
Forecasting
financial needs, 587
human resource management, 341
Foreign Corrupt Practices Act of 1978, 101
Foreign direct investment
defined, 94
implications of, 94
in United States, 94-95
Foreign subsidiaries
defined, 96
strategy for reaching global markets, 96
Formal organization, defined, 266
Forms of business ownership, 148-150. See also Cooperative; Corporation; Franchise; Limited liability company; Partnership; S Corporation; Sole proprietorship
change in, 185
comparison of, 162
Form utility, 469
defined, 277
Fortune magazine, largest companies by state listing in, 32
401(k) retirement plans, 679
Franchise
advantages of, 164-165
disadvantages of, 165
diversity in franchising, 166-167
forms of, 163
home-based, 167-168
international, 164, 168
potential, 164
training for minorities in, 167
Franchise agreement, 163
Franchise corporation, 147
Franchisee, 163
Franchise operation, 147
Franchise systems, 470
Franchising, 30
strategy for reaching global markets, 97, 163-168
Franchisor, 163
Free-market capitalism, 62
Free market economies, 63-64. See also Capitalism
Free-market principles, 59
Free markets, 67
Free-market system, 67-70. See also Capitalism
global, 70
limitations of, 71
Free rein leadership, 226-227
Free trade. See also Trade protectionism
defined, 89
legal issues of, 535
between states, 46

Free trade agreements, 46-47
  effect on career opportunities, 47
Free trade area, 106
Frictional unemployment, 72
Fringe benefits. See Benefits
Front-line personnel
  empowerment of, 261
  reorganization of business to
    empower, 41
Full-service wholesaler, defined,
  478
Funding, alternative sources of
  funds, 592-593
Fur Products Labeling Act, 139
Futures market, 627

G

Gantt chart, 290-291
General Agreement on Tariffs and
  Trade (GATT), 104, 112
General and Industrial Management
  (Fayol), 245
Generally accepted accounting
  principles (GAAP), 553
General partner, 151
General partnership, 151
Generation of wealth, 31
Generic goods, 443
Generic name, 442
Geographic market segmentation,
  422, 423
Giveback, defined, 384
Glass ceiling, 55, 361-362
Global advertising, 498-499
Global business
  career in, 88
  cash flow, 564
  compensation in other
    countries, 387
  cross-functional teams, and,
    258-259
  culture shock, 499
  Euro Disney, 588
  funding for, 100
  German labor unions, 384
  internet, 531
  learning about management, 234
  loans to foreign countries, 647
  networking and, 258
  Paris Disney, 588
  Post-It notes, 182
  product design, 449
  self-managed teams, 258
  stock exchanges, 618
  strategic alliances, 169
Global competition, 33. See also
    Free trade
  corporate management, and,
    212
  free trade agreements, 46-47
  generating changes in
    production methods, 283

Global competition—*Cont.*
  innovation, and, 212
  international competition, 45-46
  marketing and, 434
  product development, 448
  unions, and, 383
Global distribution, 464
  air freight industry in, 475
  electronic data interchange
    (EDI) and, 472
Global environment, 45-48
Global exchange of money, 644
Global financing
  banking, importance in, 102
  sources of, 103
Global marketing
  cross-functional teams in, 448
  defined, 99
  language barriers in, 99
  measurement problems in, 99-
    100
Global markets
  advantages of multiculturalism
    when working in, 44
  banking, importance in, 102
  contract manufacturing and, 96
  cooperation among businesses
    in, 46
  countertrading and, 98
  cultural differences, and, 98-100
  currency shifts and, 101-102
  difficulties of trade, 98-102
  distribution in international
    markets, 476
  exporting and, 95
  foreign subsidiaries and, 96
  franchising and, 97
  free trade agreements, 46-47
  international joint ventures and,
    97-98
  legal and regulatory differences,
    and, 101
  licensing and, 95-96
  preparation for, 47-48
  small business in, 196, 197-198
  societal and economic
    differences, and, 100-101
  strategies for reaching, 95
  supply and demand, 70-71
  United States industries with
    highest potential in, 196
Global public relations, 506
Global Reach (Barnett & Muller),
  107
Global trade. See also Exporting;
    Importing; International trade
  constraints on, 103-104
  ethics in, 123
  future of, 107-108
  measuring, 92-93
  multinational corporations, 107
  small business in, 90
  United States experience, 93-95

Global trade—*Cont.*
  United States growth and, 87
Goals
  defined, 215
  performance monitoring, 223
Goal-setting theory, 321-323
Golden parachutes, 387-388
The Good Earth (Buck), 87
Goods
  defined, 49
  United States trade deficit in, 94
Government
  downsizing of, 28
  employment increases in, 184
  fostering of entrepreneurial
    growth by, 36-37
  relationship to business, 65-66
Government agencies
  as bureaucracy, 245
  as nonprofit organizations, 32
Government officials, as
    stakeholders, 40
Government ownership of
    business, 36
Government regulation
  administrative agencies, 131
  deregulation, 142-143
  effect on business, 36-37
  federal regulatory agencies, list
    of, 132
  as hidden tax, 78-79
Government securities, use in
    control of money supply, 645-
    646
Government spending
  federal deficit, 79
  national debt, 79-81
Grapevine, in informal
    organization, 266
Graphics software, 537
Great Depression, and Federal
    Reserve System, 647
Green packaging, 441
Green product, 411, 412
Grievance, defined, 378
Gross domestic product (GDP), 72
  distribution of, 74
  United States exports as
    percentage of, 93
Gross margin, 562
Gross profit, 562
Group cohesiveness, 267
Group norms, 266-267
Groupware, 537
Growth, small business, 186
Growth industries, geared to
    elderly, 44
Growth potential
  small business in international
    markets, 198
  sole proprietorship, 150
Growth stock, 624

Guarantee, value package and, 435
*Guide to Limited Liability
   Companies*, 160

H

Hardware. See Computer hardware
Hawthorne effect, 311
Hawthorne Studies (Mayo), 310-312
Health insurance, 688-689
   crisis in, 689
   personal finances and, 676
Health maintenance organizations
   (HMOs), 689
Hedging, 627
Hierarchy, defined, 244
High risk bonds, 623
Hiring, changes made by
   information technology, 525
Hispanic population of United
   States in future, 43
Home-based business, 539
   franchise, 167-168
   number in United States, 183
Home-based franchise, 167-168
Home-based work, 358-359, 375
Homebound workers, 359
Home ownership, as investment,
   672-673
Honesty, 118
Horizontal merger, 161
Hostile workplace, 389
Hourly wage, 355
House brands, 442
*How to Form Your Own
   Corporation without a Lawyer
   for Under $500* (Nicholas), 159
Human-integration manufacturing
   (HIM), 288
Human relations skills, 230, 233-234
Human resource management, 400
   career paths for, 401
   challenge of, 339-341
   changing role of, 339
   defined, 338
   effects of legislation on, 364
   employee sources, 344
   job analysis, 342
   legislation affecting, 361-362
   planning process for, 341-343
   promotion, 359-360
   reassignment, 359-360
   retirement, 360
   scheduling programs, 356-359
   skills, 400
   termination. See Termination of
      employment
Hygiene factors, defined, 318

I

Idea generation, new-product
   development, 444, 445

Immigrants, as entrepreneurs, 28
Immigration Act of 1990, 181
Implied warranty, 134
Importing
   defined, 88
   by students, 90-91
Import quota, defined, 103
Incentives, employee stock
   ownership plans (ESOPs), 393
Income statement, 557, 560-561
   account titles, 563
   cost of goods sold
      (manufactured), 562
   defined, 560
   operating expenses, 562
   revenue, 561-562
   sample, 561
Income stock, 624
Income taxes, 140
Incubators, 191
Independence, of entrepreneurs,
   179
Independent audit, 553
Indirect compensation. See Benefits
Individual retirement account
   (IRA), 678-679
Industrial accounts, business-to-
   business selling, 502-503
Industrial advertising, 494
Industrial goods, 438-439
   channels of distribution for, 465
   defined, 438
Industrial homeworkers, 375
Industrial market
   defined, 422
   industrial goods, 438-439
Industrial marketing, 426, 502-503
   defined, 426
Industrial park, as incentive for
   site selection, 280
Industrial Revolution, 373-374
Industrial unions, defined, 374-375
Inflation, 643
   consumer price index (CPI) and,
      75
   recession, and, 76
   rule of 72, and, 75-76
Influence peddling. See Bribery
Infomercials, 495
Informal organization, 266-267
   defined, 266
Information
   advertising, and, 493
   for decision making, 231
   defined, 524
   factor of production, 34-35
   as primary source of wealth, 35
Information Era, 34
Information highway, 526-527
   defined, 527
   evolution of, 527
   information superhighway
      (I -Way), defined, 37

Information highway—*Cont.*
   tutorial for using, 528
Information management, 577-
   579. See also Information
   technology
   issue in twenty-first century, 34
   needed in nonprofit
      organizations, 33
   perspective in, 531
Information superhighway
   (I-Way). See Information
   highway
Information systems (IS), 577-579
   defined, 524
Information technology, 37-38
   career paths for, 577-578
   changes in business attributable
      to, 524-525
   computer hardware, 532-533
   computer software. See
      Software
   defined, 524
   effect on careers, 541
   effect on management, 538-540
   getting help with, 195-196
   importance of, 37-38
   to knowledge technology, 525-
      526
   role of, 524
   site selection and, 280
   skills needed for, 577
   troubleshooter, 579
Information utility, 416, 470
Initial interview, 345
Initial public offering, 618
   institutional investors, and, 632
Injunction, defined, 382
Inner-city businesses, 27
Innovation, global competition,
   and, 212
Inputs, cost controls on, 278
Insider trading, 621, 633
Institutional advertising, 494
Institutional investors, defined,
   632
Insurable interest, 687
Insurable risk, 687
Insurance
   to cover risk, 687
   health, 688-689
   law of large numbers, 687-688
   life, for business, 690
   rule of indemnity, 688
   self-insurance, 686-687
   service of commercial bank, 650
   sources of, 688
   types of, 688
Insurance agent, for small
   business, 196
Insurance policy, 687
Intangible assets, on balance sheet,
   558
Integrated marketing, 510-511

Integrated marketing communication (IMC) systems, 509-510
defined, 509
Integrated marketing strategy implementation, 510-511
Integrated software package, 537
Integrity, defined, 117
Integrity-based ethics codes, 119
Intellectual property law, 132-133
Intensive distribution, 482
Interactive advertising, 494
Interactive television advertising, and, 495, 497
defined, 497
Interest, on bond, 611
Interfirm organization, 219-220
Intermittent process, 281
Intermodal marketing companies, 475
Intermodal shipping, 475
Internal auditor, 586
Internal customers, 223, 262-263, 410
Internal sales promotion, 504
International banking, 657-658
BCCI, 659
leaders in, 658-659
International business. See Global business
International competition, 45-46. See also Free trade; Global competition
free trade agreements, 46-47
International distribution, 464. See also Global distribution
International executives, 352
International franchise, 164
International joint ventures, strategy for reaching global markets, 97-98
International markets. See Global markets
International Organization for Standardization (ISO), 48-49
International quality standards, 48-49
International trade. See also Exporting; Global trade; Importing
defined, 89
joint ventures, 97-98
reasons for, 89
small business in, 197-198
world growth and, 87
Internet, 196, 544-546
defined, 528
difficulties with, 529-530
in global business, 531
history of, 529
how it works, 530
tutorial for, 529-531

Internet Society, 529
Interstate banking, 655-656
Interstate Commerce Act of 1887, 137
Interstate Commerce Commission, 137
Interviews, for employment, 345
Intrepreneurs, 34, 182
Intrinsic reward, 308
Inventory
in channel of distribution, 471-472
effect of databases on, 38
efficient consumer response (ECR), 472-473
electronic data exchange and, 38
human resource management, 341-342
operating funds, and, 592
Inventory control, with packaging, 440
Inventory financing, 595
Inverted organization, 261-262
Invest, defined, 29
Investigations, background, for employment, 345
Investment, 621
amount of return on, 30
bond quotation, 628
in bonds, 622-623
in commodities, 627
diversification, 626-627
by entrepreneurs, 181
in hot growth companies, 625
on margin, 624-625
mutual fund quotation, 630-631
in mutual funds, 626
in stock, 623-626
stock quotation, 629-630
stock splits, 625-626
strategy, 621-622
as use for money, 29
Investment bankers, 631-632
Investment risk, 622
"Investor visas," 181
"Invisible hand," 61
Involuntary bankruptcy, 140
IRA (individual retirement account), 678-679, 48-49
ISO 9000 standards, 48-49

J

JIT (Just-in-time inventory control), 283-284, 473
Job analysis, 342
Job creation, 31, 73
effect of free trade agreements, 47
by entrepreneurs, 178-179
"invisible hand," 61
by small business, 184

Job creation—*Cont.*
small business, 73
Job description, defined, 342
Job enlargement, defined, 321
Job enrichment, as motivator, 319-321
Job interview, preparation for, 22-24
Job rotation, 351
defined, 321
Job satisfaction, of employees, 194
Job search
cover letter, 20-22
research, 16-17
résumé, 18-20
strategy for, 15-16
Job security, unions and, 384
Job sharing, defined, 357
Job sharing plans, 357
Job simplification, defined, 321
Job simulation, 349-350
Job specifications, defined, 342
Joint ventures, 87, 97, 169
Journal, for accounting data, 554, 556
Just-in-time inventory control (JIT), 283-284, 473

K

Keogh plans, 679-680
Key economic indicators, 72
gross domestic product (GDP), 72, 74
price indexes, 72
unemployment rate, 72-73
Key personnel, front-line personnel, 261
Kiosks, 484
Knights of Labor, 374
Knockoff brands, 442
Knowledge technology (KT), 525-526
defined, 525

L

Labor
factor of production, 34-35
site selection and, 278
Labor legislation, 375-377
Labor-management agreement, 377
Labor-management conflicts
arbitration, 379
mediation, 379
resolution of, 378-379
tactics used in, 379
Labor-management relations. See Unions
Labor-Management Relations Act (Taft-Hartley Act), 374, 377

Labor-Management Reporting and
  Disclosure Act (Landrum-
  Griffin Act), 374
Laissez-faire leadership, 226-227
Land, factor of production, 34-35
Landrum-Griffin Act, 374
Language proficiency, advantages
  of, 87
Latino population of United States
  in future, 43
Law. See Business law
Law of large numbers, 687-688
Lawyer. See Attorney
Layers of management,
  bureaucracy, 244
Layoffs. See also Downsizing
  as opportunities for
    entrepreneurs, 28
Leaders
  managers differentiated from,
    224-225
  need for, 235
Leadership
  defined, 224
  needed in nonprofit
    organizations, 33
  rules of, 228
  small business, 220
  styles of, 225-228
  vision, and, 224
Lean manufacturing, 276, 285
  small business, 284
Learning, defined, 421
Leasing, possession utility and, 469
Ledger, defined, 555
Legal differences, effect on global
  trade, 101
Legal environment of business. See
  Business law
Legal issues
  brand name, 409
  creative accounting, 563
  derivatives disclosure, 601
  free trade, 535
  home-based business, 195
  institutional investors in initial
    public offerings, 632
  regulation, and growth, 37
  safety regulations, 295
  sentencing guidelines, 122
  tariffs, 105
Legality
  versus ethics, 116-117
  personal ethics and, 118
Legal restrictions
  on discharge, 344
  on recruiting, 343
Legislation. See also Legal
    restrictions
  affecting human resource
    management, 361-362
  affecting unions, 374, 375-377
  age discrimination, 362

Legislation—Cont.
  disability discrimination, 362
  effects on human resource
    management, 364
  sex discrimination, 361
  wages and benefits, proposed,
    362-363
Letter of credit, 657
Leverage, 601-602
Leveraged buyout (LBO), 161
Leverage ratios, 568
Liabilities
  on balance sheet, 558-560
  fundamental accounting
    equation, 560
Liability
  corporation, 155
  partnership, 152
  sole proprietorship, 150
Liability losses, 688
Licensing
  defined, 95
  strategy for reaching global
    markets, 95-96
Licensing agreements, 95-96
Life insurance
  for business, 690
  personal finances and, 675-676
Life insurance companies, 652
Life span
  corporation, 156
  partnership, 152
  sole proprietorship, 150
LIFO (last in, first out), 567
Limited-function wholesaler,
    defined, 478
Limited liability, 151, 155-156
  S corporation, 159
Limited liability company, 160
Limited partner, 151
Limited partnership, 151
Limit order, 624, 625
Line and staff organizations, 254
Line of credit, 595
Line organizations, 253-254
Line personnel, 254
Liquidity
  on balance sheet, 558
  as investment criteria, 622
Listening skills, 324-325
Loans
  from commercial banks, 594-596
  from family and friends, 594
  to foreign countries, 647
  service of commercial bank, 650
Location-independent business, 525
Location of business, 27. See also
    Site selection
  barriers broken by information
    technology, 524-525
  for exporting, 108
Lockouts, 379
  defined, 382

Logistics
  career opportunities in, 464
  defined, 464
Logistics systems, 473
Long-range planning, 215
Long-term financing, 593, 598
  bonds, 599, 610
  debt financing, 598-599
  equity financing, 599-600
  retained earnings, 600
  venture capital, 600-601
Long-term forecast, 587
Long-term loans, 651
Loose monetary policy, 77
Loss. See also Liability; Profit
  defined, 29
Lower-level employees, self-
    management by, 41
Loyalty, brand equity and, 443

M

M-1, 643
M-2, 643
Magazine advertising, 493, 494
  advantages and disadvantages
    of, 495
Magnuson-Moss Warranty—
    Federal Trade Commission
    Improvement Act, 139
Mainframe computers, 534
Management. See also
    Organization
  career paths for, 301-302
  changing approach to, 212
  control function, 222
  cooperation with unions, 385
  corporation, 156
  defined, 213
  delegation of authority, 194
  employee-management issues.
    See Employee-management
    issues
  ethics, and, 117
  first-line management, 217-218
  franchise, 164, 165
  hierarchy of managers, 217-218
  informal organization effect on,
    266
  information technology effects
    on, 538-540
  layers of, 244
  management development, 350-
    351
  middle management, 217
  organizational ethics, 118
  partnership, 152
  positions in, 302
  setting standards, 222-223
  skills at different levels of, 229-
    230
  small business, 187, 188

Management—*Cont.*
  sole proprietorship, 149, 150
  span of control, 249-250
  supervisory (first-line)
    management, 217-218
  tasks at different levels of, 229-
    230
  top management, 217
  unions, and. See Unions
Management by objectives (MBO),
  321-323
Management skills, learning, 147
Management studies
  early studies, 309
  Hawthorne Studies (Mayo),
    310-312
Managerial accounting, 551-552
Managerial decision making,
    employee stock ownership
    plans (ESOPs), 393
Managerial potential, 232
Managerial skills
  computer skills, 233
  human relations skills, 233
  learning, 232
  technical skills, 234-235
  time management skills, 234
  verbal skills, 232
  writing skills, 233
Managerial style
  changes in, 212
  and education of workers, 212
Managerial teams, entrepreneurial
    teams, 181
Managers
  changing role of, 212-213
  communication by and to, 324-
    325
  cooperation and, 213
  decision making by, 231
  delegation of authority to, 212
  empowerment of teams by, 220-
    221
  entrepreneurs turning company
    over to, 181
  ethics, 220
  hierarchy of managers, 217-218
  investment by, 30
  leaders differentiated from, 224-
    225
  management development, 350-
    351
  managerial accounting, 551-552
  motivation by. See Motivation
  need for, 235
  networking, importance of, 351
  responsibilities of, in future, 41
  role of, 220-221
  skills needed by, 301
  teamwork and, 213
Managing risk. See Risk
    management

Manufacturer, in exchange
    relationships, 465-466
Manufacturing. See also
    Production
  computer-integrated
    manufacturing (CIM), 287
  human-integration
    manufacturing (HIM), 288
  production management, 276-
    277
  relationship to service, 276-277
  small business, in global
    economy, 184
Manufacturing base, 276
Manufacturing industry
  employment increases in, 184
  evolution in United States, 50
Manufacturing resource planning,
  282
Margin, buying stock on, 624-625
Market(s)
  consumer market. See
    Consumer market
  defined, 193
  industrial market. See
    Industrial market
  responsiveness to, 212
  site selection and, 279
Market economy, 59
Marketer, form utility added by, 469
Marketing. See also Promotion
  adaptation to change, 407
  adversarial marketing, 411
  bull's eye marketing, 423
  business-to-business marketing.
    See Industrial marketing
  career paths for, 517-518
  career prospects in, 427
  customer-oriented marketing,
    405
  defined, 406
  different classes of consumer
    goods and services, 437-438
  direct selling, 484
  distribution, 407
  eight functions of, 414
  establishment of customer
    relationship, 407
  finding need, 406-407
  fundamentals of, 517-520
  global competition and, 434
  history of, 408-409
  industrial goods, 438-439
  integrated marketing, 510-511
  mass marketing, 411-412
  needed in nonprofit
    organizations, 33
  network marketing, 484-485
  new-product development, 444
  niche marketing, 425
  packaging, 439-441
  process of, 406-407

Marketing—*Cont.*
  product design to meet needs,
    407
  product life cycle, 448-451
  relationship marketing, 411,
    412
  skills required for, 517
  small businesses pooling efforts,
    220
  target marketing, 422
  telemarketing, 483
  utilities created by, 415-416
  value package. See Value
    package
Marketing communications
  communication with
    stakeholders, 508
  direct marketing. See Direct
    marketing
  importance of, 492
  integrated marketing
    communication (IMC)
    systems, 509-510
  promotion mix, 492-493
Marketing concept, 409
Marketing consultants, 503
  for small business, 196
Marketing environment, 413
Marketing management, 412-414
Marketing middlemen, 407
  defined, 464
  exchange efficiency and, 465-
    466
  information utility added by,
    470
  place utility added by, 469
  possession utility added by, 469-
    470
  role of, 464-465
  time utility added by, 469
  value created by, 466-468
Marketing mix, 413
Marketing research, 416
  defined, 416
  ethical decision making in, 418-
    419
  process of, 417-419
  topics of, 417
  understanding consumers
    through, 419-420
  uses for, 419-420
Marketing research study, for
    small business, 196
Market modification, 551
Market order, 624
Market price, 456
  equilibrium point, and, 70
Market segmentation, 422-425
  defined, 422
  in integrated marketing
    strategy, 510
Market surveys, 182

Maslow's hierarchy of needs, 312-313

Mass customization, 285-286, 510
defined, 498-499

Mass marketing, 411-412

Mass production, development of, 408

Master budget, 589

Master limited partnership, 152

Materials handling, 477

Materials requirement planning (MRP), 282

Matrix organizations, 254-256

Maturity date, of bond, 611

Measurement. See also Accounting of performance. See Performance measurement
productivity in service sector, 293
quality control, 291-292
of success. See Success measurement

Mediation, 379

Mediator, 379

Mentor, defined, 351

Mercantilism, defined, 103

Merchant wholesalers, 478-479

Mergers and acquisitions
acquisition, defined, 161
conglomerate merger, 161
golden parachutes, 387-388
horizontal merger, 161
leveraged buyout (LBO), 161
merger, defined, 161
small banks, 656
taking firm private, 161
types of mergers, 163
vertical merger, 161

Middle management, 217

Mining industry, employment increases in, 184

Minority-owned business, 27-28, 56, 183, 667

Mixed economy, 63-64
defined, 64
market choices, 65
market control, 65
social and economic goals, 65
social freedoms, 65
welfare capitalism, 64-66
worker motivation, 65

Monetary policy
defined, 76
role of Federal Reserve System in, 76-77
tight versus loose, 77

Money. See also Currency shifts
currency, 643
defined, 642-643
global exchange of, 644
importance of, 642
M-1, 643
M-2, 643

Money—Cont.
protection of, 654
uses for, 29

Money supply
control of. See Control of money supply
defined, 643
tightening or loosening of, 77

Monitoring, performance, 223

Monopolistic competition, 136

Monopoly, 136-137

Moore's Law, 533

Morale
employee stock ownership plans (ESOPs), 393
promotion from within company, 359

Morality, defined, 117

Mortgage bonds, 612, 613

Mortgages, 651

Most favored nation status, 107-108

Motion economy, 310

Motivation
comparison of Theories X, Y, and Z, 317
future of, 329-330
goal-setting theory, 321-323
Hawthorne Studies (Mayo), 310-312
Herzberg's motivating factors, 317-319
importance of, 308-309
job enrichment, 319-321
of lower-level employees, 41
management by objectives (MBO), 321-323
Maslow's hierarchy of needs, 312-313
promotion from within company, 359
sales promotion, 504
through self-managed teams, 325-326
small business, 320
Theory X (McGregor), 313-314, 315-316
Theory Y (McGregor), 313, 314-316
Theory Z (Ouchi), 316-317
through work content, 317-319

Motivators, defined, 318

Motor vehicle, goods shipped by, 474

Multicultural environment, 42-45

Multiculturalism, 178, 399
advantages for business, 43-44
defined, 43-44

Multilevel marketing, 484-485, 488

Multilingual communication, 325

Multinational corporations (MNC), 107

Municipal bond, 613

Mutual funds
investing in, 626

Mutual funds—Cont.
mutual fund quotation, 630-631
no-load fund, 630

Mutual insurance company, 688

N

Name recognition, franchise, 164

Narrowcasting, 497

National Association of Securities Dealers Quotation System (NASDAQ), 619

National brand names, 442

National Cooperative Business Association, 169

National Credit Union Administration, 654

National debt, 79-81

National Education Association, 375, 384

National Labor Relations Act (Wagner Act), 374, 376

National Labor Relations Board, 376

Natural environment
competition by concern for, 41-42
green product, 411
measure of success by contribution to, 223-224
risk of damage to, 691

Negotiable instruments
defined, 134
Uniform Commercial Code, 134

Negotiated labor-management agreement, 377

Net income, 560

Net loss, 560

Network computing system, defined, 534

Networking, 351
cross-functional teams, and, 258
defined, 258
small business, 260

Network marketing, 484-485

Networks, computer, 534

New businesses, number per year, 29

New products. See also Product development
changes made by information technology, 525

New-product success, 444

Newspaper advertising, 493, 494
advantages and disadvantages of, 495

New York Stock Exchange, 618, 619

Niche marketing
defined, 425
small business, 412, 656

No-load fund, 630

Nonprice competition, 456-457
Nonprofit organizations, 604-605
  business skills needed in, 33
  defined, 32-33
  productivity and quality in, 294
Nonstore retailing, 483
Nontariff barriers, 104
Norris-LaGuardia Act, 374, 379, 382
North American Free Trade
  Agreement (NAFTA), 46, 104,
  105-106, 377
*North American International
  Business* magazine, 109
Notes payable, 559
NOW accounts, service of
  commercial bank, 650
Nutrition Labeling and Education
  Act, 139

O

Objectives, defined, 215
Occupational Safety and Health
  Act (OSHA), 364
Odd pricing, 455
Off-brand products, 443
Offer, 135
Off-the-job training, 349
  for managers, 351
Old-boy network, 351
Oligopoly, 136
On-line advertising, 494
On-line services, 528
  for advertising, 496-497
On-the-job coaching, 350
On-the-job training, 348
Open-market operations, 645-646
Open-shop agreement, 378
Operating budget, 588
Operating expenses, 562
Operating funds, 590
  accounts receivable,
    management of, 591
  capital expenditures, 592
  daily business operations, 590-
    591
  inventory, 592
Operations, changes made by
  information technology, 525
Operations expert, 147
Operations management, in
  service sector, 293
Operations research analyst, 578
Opportunity, for entrepreneurs,
  179
Organization
  centralization of authority, 251-
    253
  changes made by information
    technology, 525
  decentralization of authority,
    251-253

Organization—*Cont.*
  departmentalization. See
    Departmentalization
  evolution of, 245-248
  formal organization, 266
  informal organization, 266-267
  inverted, 261-262
  outsourcing, 262-263
  pyramid shaped structure, 247
  responsive, designing, 248-249
  restructuring, 245
  span of control, 249-250
Organizational culture, 263-266
  communication and, 324
  defined, 263
  emphasis on service, 265
  service-oriented, 263-266
Organizational design, defined, 244
Organizational effectiveness,
  criteria for, 223-224
Organizational ethics, 118
Organizational hierarchy. See also
  Bureaucracy
  development of, 244
Organizational structure
  bureaucratic versus customer-
    focused, 264
  changing to meet needs of
    customers and employees, 41
  flat, 249
  inverted organization, 261-262
  outsourcing, 262-263
  tall, 249
Organization chart, 217
Organization models, 253
  line and staff organizations, 254
  line organizations, 253-254
  matrix organizations, 254-256
  organization types, 253-254
Organization theory
  background of, 245
  Fayol's principles of
    organization, 245-246
  Max Weber and, 247-248
Organized labor. See Unions
Organizer, manager as, 213
Organizing, 217-218
  customer-oriented organization,
    218-219
  defined, 214
  function of management, 213,
    214
  interfirm, 219-220
Orientation of employees, 348
Outdoor advertising, 494
  advantages and disadvantages
    of, 495
Output, 278
Outsourcing, 262, 284, 356
  contingent workers, 337
  contract manufacturing as
    strategy for reaching global
    markets, 96

Outsourcing—*Cont.*
  defined, 262
  downsizing as result of, 28
  ethics, 156
  internal customers, 262-263
  temporary employment, 337
Overdraft protection, service of
  commercial bank, 650
Over-the-counter market, defined,
  619
Owner's equity, 560
Ownership
  corporation, 156
  franchise, 164
  sole proprietorship, 149
Ownership change, corporation,
  156

P

Package, value package and, 435
Packaging, 439-441
  functions of, 440-441
  growing importance of, 440-441
Paperwork, corporation, 157
Partial ownership of business by
  employees, 41. See also
  Employee stock ownership
  plans (ESOPs)
Participative leadership, 226
Partnership, 147
  advantages of, 152
  defined, 148, 151
  disadvantages of, 152-153
  small business, 154
Part-time business, 187
Part-time employment, for two-
  income families, 44
Par value, defined, 614
Patent, 132-133
Patent law, 132-133
Pay. See Compensation; Salary;
  Wages
Pay equity, 388-389
Penetration strategy, 455
Penny stock, 624
Pension funds, 652-653
  defined, 652
Perceived quality, 443
Perfect competition, 136
Performance
  compensation based on, 41
  monitoring, 223
  training and development and,
    348
Performance appraisal
  defined, 352
  steps in, 352-353
Performance evaluation, 352
Performance measurement, and
  reengineering, 260
Performance ratios, 568-569

Performance standards, 352
Personal ethics, 118-119
Personal finances
    automobile insurance, 676
    capital account, 671-673
    credit, management of, 673-675
    financial planners, 680
    financial planning. See Personal
        financial planning
    health insurance, 676
    life insurance, 675-676
    retirement planning. See
        Retirement planning
Personal financial planning
    borrowing, 670-671
    budget preparation, 670
    controlling assets, 668
    debt reduction/elimination, 670
    education as investment, 671
    expense tracking, 669
    inventory of assets, 668-669
    need for, 668
    savings plan, 670
Personal selling, 500
    compared with direct
        marketing, 492
    defined, 500
    steps in process, 500-502
Personnel. See Human resource
    management
PERT chart, 290
Philanthropy, corporate, 120
Physical distribution (logistics),
    defined, 464
Physical distribution management,
    473
    transportation modes, 473-475
Physical distribution systems
    containerization, 476
    materials handling, 477
    selection criteria for, 475-476
    storage, 477
Physical exams, for employment,
    345-346
Physiological needs, defined, 312
Picketing/pickets, 379, 382
Piecework, 355
Piggyback shipments, 474
Pipeline, goods shipped by, 474-475
Place utility, 416, 469
Planner, manager as, 213
Planning. See also Financial
    planning; Personal financial
    planning
    creating vision, 214-216
    defined, 214
    examples of, 216
    forms of, 216
    function of management, 213,
        214
    in small business, 188-189
Plant. See Fixed assets
Pledging, 595

Pluralist approach to corporate
    responsibility, 122-123
Political economy, 103
Population
    aging of, 44
    Asian population of United
        States in future, 43
    changes in population of United
        States, 43
    demography, 42
    Hispanic population of United
        States in future, 43
    Latino population of United
        States in future, 43
    of United States, changes in, 43
    world growth, 88
Portability, of money, 642
Portfolio strategy, 626-627
Possession utility, 416
Post-Capitalist Society (Drucker), 34
Post-It notes, 182
Poverty, in single-parent
    households, 45
Preapproach, in selling process,
    500-501
Preemptive right, 617
Preferred provider organizations
    (PPOs), 689
Preferred stock, 615, 616
    features of, 616
    stock quotation, 629
Premium (insurance), 687
Presentation, in selling process, 502
Price
    competitive pricing. See
        Competitive pricing
    demand and, 69
    every day low pricing (EDLP), 460
    money supply and, 643-644
    nonprice competition, 456-457
    as quality cue, 443
    relationship to demand, 67
    supply and, 68-69
    value package and, 435
Price competition, by retailers, 480
Price indexes, 72
Price lining, 455
Prices of goods and services, and
    standard of living, 31
Price wars, avoidance of, 456-457
Pricing. See also Competitive
    pricing
    over product life cycle, 551
    value pricing, 453-454
Pricing strategy, 452-453, 455-456
Pricing tactics, 455
Primary boycott, 380
Primary data, 419
    in marketing research, 418
Principal, of bond, 611
Principles of Scientific Management
    (Taylor), 309
Private accountant, 552-553

Private brands, 442
Private insurance, 690
Private ownership of business, 36
Private property, right to, 66
Problem definition, in marketing
    research, 417
Process manufacturing, defined,
    281
Producer, form utility added by,
    469
Producer price index (PPI), 72
Product
    defined, 407
    life cycle of. See Product life
        cycle
Product advertising, 494
Product design
    global view of, 449
    to meet needs, 407
    for small business, 438
Product development, 434-435
    global competition, 448
    new-product ideas, 445
    process for, 444-445
Product differentiation, 437
    different classes of consumer
        goods and services, 437-438
Product failure, reasons for, 444
Production
    CAD/CAM, 286-288
    competing in time, 286
    computer-integrated
        manufacturing (CIM), 287
    defined, 277, 278
    determination of amount of, 67
    flexible manufacturing, 284
    fundamentals of, 277-278
    human-integration
        manufacturing (HIM), 288
    just-in-time inventory control,
        283-284
    lean manufacturing, 285
    mass customization, 285-286
    materials requirement planning,
        282
    modern techniques, 283
    process, 277
    quality control, 291-292
Production and operations
    management
    career potential in, 277
    computer-based, 282
    defined, 276
Production control
    Gantt chart, 290-291
    program evaluation and review
        technique (PERT), 290
Production goals, 281-282
Production management, 276-277
Production processes, 281-282
Productivity. See also Information
    technology; Motivation;
    Technology

Productivity—*Cont.*
  CAD/CAM, 287
  defined, 46, 74
  flextime, and, 357
  future of, 294-295
  goal-setting theory, 321-323
  improving, 292-293
  machinery and, 74
  in nonprofit organizations, 294
  output, and, 278
  in service economy, 74-75
  in service sector, 293
Product liability law, 131-132
Product life cycle, 448-551
  defined, 448
  extension of, 551
  importance of, 550-551
Product-line pricing, 455
Product lines, 436-437
  defined, 436
Product management, 444
  new-product development
    process, 444-445
  new-product success, 444
Product manager, 444
Product mix, 436-437
  defined, 436
Product modification, defined, 551
Profit. See also Loss
  average, 30
  break-even analysis, 454-455
  competition, effect on, 29
  and customers, 411
  defined, 29
  in definition of business, 29
  entrepreneurs, 179
  ethics and, 418
  executive compensation, and,
    386
  franchise, 165
  matching with risk, 29-30
  measure of success, 223-224
  merged with principles, 62
  partnership, 152
  over product life cycle, 551
  right to keep, after taxes, 66
  sole proprietorship, 149
  uses of, 29
  who earns, 30
Profitability ratios, 568-569
Profit orientation, 409, 410-411
Profit sharing, in small business,
  188
Profit-sharing plans, 355
Program evaluation and review
  technique (PERT), 290
Program trading, 633
Promissory note, 594
  commercial paper, 596
  term-loan agreement, 598
Promotion. See also Advertising;
  Public relations

Promotion—*Cont.*
  integrated marketing
    communication (IMC)
    systems, 509-510
  publicity, 506-507
  sales promotion, 504-505
  strategies, 507-508
  word-of-mouth, 503-505
Promotion (advancement), 359-360
Promotion (advertising), 407
  defined, 492
Promotion mix, 492-493
  defined, 493
  preparing, 507
Property. See Fixed assets
Property losses, 688
Property taxes, 140
Prospecting, 500
Prospectus, 620
Protective tariff, defined, 103
Prototype, 407
Psychographic market
  segmentation, 422, 424
Psychological pricing, 455
Public accountant, 553
Public insurance, 689
Publicity, 506-507
  defined, 506
Public relations, 505-506
  defined, 505
  global, 506
  publicity, 506-507
Public schools, as nonprofit
  organizations, 32
Public utilities, employment
  increases in, 184
Pull strategy, 508
Purchase of business, small
  business, 188
Purchasing cooperatives, 220
Purchasing power, and standard of
  living, 31
Pure Food and Drug Act, 139
Pure risk, 685
Push strategy, 507-508
  defined, 507

Q

Qualifying, in selling process, 500
Quality
  Baldrige Award, 48
  defined, 48
  effect on competition, 39
  global measures for, 48-49
  international competition, and,
    45-46
  in nonprofit organizations, 294
  perceived quality, 443
Quality control, 291-292. See also
  Total quality management
  (TQM)

Quality imperative, 48-49
Quality of life
  defined, 31-32
  site selection and, 279
Quickie options, 387
Quick response, 472

R

Rack jobber, defined, 478
Radio advertising, 493, 494
  advantages and disadvantages
    of, 495
Rail, goods shipped by, 473-474
Raw material inventory, 281
Raw materials, transportation
  modes, 473-475
Reassignment, 359-360
Recession
  defined, 76
  versus inflation, 76
Recordkeeping, small business,
  187, 194-195
Recruiting. See also Selection of
  employees
  from competition, 347
  defined, 343
  from diverse population, 343-
    344
  employee sources, 344
  employee stock ownership plans
    (ESOPs), 393
  outside influences on, 344
  strategic plan for, 342
Reengineering. See also
  Downsizing; Restructuring
  defined, 260
Reference group, defined, 421
Regulation. See Government
  regulation
Regulatory differences, effect on
  global trade, 101
Reinventing the Corporation
  (Naisbitt & Aburdene), 326
Relationship marketing, 411, 412,
  431, 437
Relocation, golden parachutes,
  387-388
Renting, possession utility and, 469
Reputation, as quality cue, 443
Research, in marketing, 414
Research and development,
  Skunkworks (Lockheed), 182
Reserve requirement, 645
Resolution Trust Corp., 655
Resource allocation by
  government, in welfare
  capitalism, 64
Resource development, defined, 60
Resource files, 7
Resources
  expansion by business, 60

Resources—*Cont.*
  site selection and, 278-279
Restructuring. See also
  Downsizing
  defined, 245
  reengineering, 260
  total quality management and,
    259-260
Résumé, 18-20
Retail advertising, 494
Retail cooperatives, 471
Retail distribution strategy, 482
Retailers
  defined, 464
  differentiated from wholesalers,
    478
  establishment of relations with,
    219
  in exchange relationships, 465-
    466
  time utility added by, 469
  top ten, 480
Retail industry, employment
  increases in, 184
Retailing
  direct marketing, 485
  direct selling, 484
  network marketing, 484-485
  nonstore retailing, 483
  telemarketing, 483
  vending machines, kiosks, and
    carts, 484
  wheel of retailing, 483
Retailing, nonstore, 483
Retailing, wheel of, 483
Retail middlemen, 479-480
Retail sale, defined, 478
Retained earnings, 560, 600
Retirement, 360
  Occupational Safety and Health
    Act (OSHA), 364
Retirement planning
  401(k) plans, 679
  individual retirement account
    (IRA), 678-679
  Keogh plans, 679-680
  social security, 677
Retraining, for new jobs, 338-339
Revenue
  defined, 29
  on income statement, 561-562
Revenue tariff, defined, 103
Reverse discrimination, defined,
  361
Revolving credit agreement, 595-
  596
Right-to-work laws, 378, 379
Rising dollar, 644
Risk, 55, 177
  defined, 29, 685
  economic environment and, 35-
    36
  entrepreneur, and, 28

Risk—*Cont.*
  of environmental damage, 691
  high risk bonds, 623
  insurance to cover, 687
  law of large numbers, 687-688
  in marketing, 414, 415
  matching with profit, 29-30
Risk management, 685-686
  risk avoidance, 686
  risk reduction, 686
  self-insuring, 686-687
Risk/return trade-off, 598
Risk taking, for entrepreneurs, 179
Robinson Patman Act, 137
Robot, 285
Rule of 72, 75-76
Rule of indemnity, 688

S

Safe deposit boxes, service of
  commercial bank, 650
Safety needs, defined, 312
Salary. See Compensation; Wages
Salary systems, 354-355
Sales. See also Personal selling
  business-to-business selling,
    502-503
  direct selling, 484
  by marketing middlemen, 465
  over product life cycle, 551
  telemarketing, 483
Sales forecast, 281
Sales law. See Uniform
  Commercial Code
Sales promotion, 504-505
  defined, 504
Sales taxes, 140
Sample, defined, 418
Sampling, sales promotion, 505
Savings accounts. See Time
  deposit
Savings and loan associations, 651
  failures of, 647
Savings and Loan Insurance
  Corporation (FSLIC), 654
Savings Association Insurance
  Fund (SAIF), 654
Scheduling, strategic plan for, 342
Scheduling programs, 356-357
  flextime plans, 357-358
  home-based work, 358-359
  job sharing plans, 357
Scientific management, 309-310
S corporation, 159-160
Screening and analysis, new-
  product development, 444,
  445-447
Secondary boycott, 381
Secondary sources of data, 419
Secured bonds, 599, 612
Secured loan, 595

Securities. See also Bonds; Stock
  initial public offering, 618
  prospectus, 620
Securities and Exchange Act of
  1934, 621
Securities and Exchange
  Commission (SEC), 621
  disclosure rules on executive
    compensation, 386
Securities markets. See also Stock
  exchanges
  commodities, 627
  function of, 610
  futures, 627
  institutional investors, 631-632
  investing in. See Investment
  investment bankers, 631-632
  investment information, 628-
    632
  over-the-counter market, 619-
    620
  stock market crash of 1987,
    632-633
Securities quotations
  bonds, 628
  Dow Jones averages, 631
  mutual funds, 630-631
  preferred stock, 629
  stock, 629-630
Securities regulation, 620-621
Seed money, 191
Segmentation of consumer market,
  422-425
Selection competition, by retailers,
  481
Selection of employees
  costs of, 344-345
  process, 345-347
  selection, defined, 344
  strategic plan for, 342
Selective distribution, 482
Self-actualization needs, defined,
  312
Self-direction, of entrepreneurs,
  180
Self-insurance, 686-687
Self-managed teams
  cross-functional, 221, 256-259
  downsizing and, 41
  global business, 258
  informal organization, and,
    266-267
  motivation through, 325-326
  movement toward, 221
  organizational culture, and, 265
  trend toward, 228-229
Self-management, teams, 41, 221
Self-nurturing, of entrepreneurs,
  180
Self-organization, teams, 221
Self-service outlets, importance of
  packaging in, 440
Selling, in marketing, 414

Senior citizens, 44
Service
  competition on, 456
  effect on competition, 39
  value package and, 435
Service competition, by retailers,
  480-481
Service Corps of Retired
  Executives (SCORE), 196
Service economy, productivity in,
  74-75
Service organizations, relationship
  to manufacturing
  organizations, 276-277
Services, defined, 50
Service sector
  employment increases in, 184
  evolution in United States, 50-51
  growth projections for, 50
  productivity in, 293
  unions in, 383
  value pricing in, 454
Sex discrimination
  legislation, 361
  pay equity, 388
  sexual harassment, 389
Sexual harassment, 389
Share draft account, 652
Shareholders, in S corporation,
  160
Shareware, defined, 535
Sherman Antitrust Act, 137-138
Shopping goods and services, 437
Shop steward, 378
Short-range planning, 215-216
Short-term financing, 593
  commercial banks, 594-596
  commercial paper, 596
  defined, 593
  factoring, 596
  family and friends, 594
  promissory notes, 594
  trade credit, 593
Short-term forecast, 587
Shrink wrapping, 476
Simulation exercises, as job
  training, 349-350
Single-parent households, 45
Sinking fund, 612-613
Site selection
  cost savings through, 276, 278-
  279
  in future, 279-280
  proximity to market, 279
  of small business, decision
  about, 187
Size, corporation, 156, 157
Skills
  categories of, 230
  at different levels of
  management, 229-230
  human resource management,
  400

Skills—Cont.
  learning management skills, 147
  needed by entrepreneurs, 206-
  207
  needed in nonprofit
  organizations, 33
  work force, changes in skill
  requirements, 212
Skill variety, as motivator, 320
Skimming price strategy, 455
Skunkworks (Lockheed), 182
Slavery, 62
Slow economy, downsizing as
  result of, 28
Small business. See also
  Entrepreneurs;
  Entrepreneurship
  accountant for, 194-195
  advanced training for, 185
  advantages of, 184, 185
  attorney for, 196
  versus big business, 183
  bull's eye marketing, 423
  bureaucracy in, 250
  causes for failure, 186
  classification of, 184
  commercial loan officer for, 196
  computer technology in, 480,
  526
  consulting advice for, 195-196
  cooperatives, 170
  creative product differentiation
  by, 437
  defined, 183
  diversity in, 340
  failure rate, 184-186
  financing, 189, 191, 591, 597
  flexibility in adapting to
  customer wants, 437
  getting experience in, 187
  in global market, 196, 197-198
  in global trade, 90
  growth, 186
  importance to economy, 184
  information sources for, 195-
  196
  insurance agent for, 196
  job creation, 73
  job creation by, 184
  leadership in, 220
  lean manufacturing, 284
  management, 187
  management of, 188
  managing employees, 194
  manufacturing, in global
  economy, 184
  manufacuturing automation,
  289
  marketing consultant, 196
  marketing research study for,
  196
  meeting needs of customers,
  193

Small business—Cont.
  motivation, 320
  networking, 260
  niches for, 184
  partnerships, 154
  part-time, 187
  percentage of United States
  business, 183
  planning for, 188-189
  pooling of efforts, 220
  product design for, 438
  profit sharing in, 188
  public offering, 618
  purchase of, 188
  recordkeeping, 194-195
  recordkeeping for, 187
  shopping from home, 498
  small banks, and mergers, 656
  starting, 183
  statistics about, 183
  unions, impact of, 372
  using savings to start, 669
  word-of-mouth promotion, 505
Small Business Administration
  (SBA), 183, 191-193
Small Business Investment
  Companies (SBICs), 193
Smart teams, 221
Smoot Hawley Act, 112
Social audit, 124
Social causes, as nonprofit
  organizations, 32
Social fairness. See Equality
Socialism
  consequences of, 63
  defined, 63
  market choices, 65
  market control, 65
  social and economic goals, 65
  social freedoms, 65
  worker motivation, 65
Social issues. See also Corporate
  social responsibility
  capitalism and, 64
  measure of success by
  contribution to, 223-224
Socialist approach to corporate
  responsibility, 122
Social needs, defined, 312
Social responsibility, 174
  business activities, 124
  corporate, 120-124
  defined, 116
  entrepreneurs, 62
  international, 124-126
  social auditing, 124
Social security, 677
Societal differences, effect on
  global trade, 100-101
Software, 534-535
  CAD/CAM, 287
  communications programs, 537
  database programs, 536-537

Software—Cont.
graphics programs, 537
groupware, 537
integrated programs, 537
pirating, 538
shareware, 535
spreadsheet programs, 536
word processors, 535-536
Sole proprietors, retirement of, 185
Sole proprietorship, 147
advantages of, 149-150
defined, 148
disadvantages of, 150-151
Span of control, 249-250
Specialty goods and services, 438
Specific performance, 135-136
Speculative risk, 685
Spending, fiscal policy, 77-78
Spreadsheet software, 536
Stability, of money, 643
Staffing, changes made by
information technology, 525
Staff personnel, 254
Stakeholders, 258, 334
communication with, 508
corporate responsibility to, 121-
123
defined, 40
pleasing, 410
satisfying needs of, 218
Standardization, in marketing,
414, 415
Standard of living, defined, 31
Standards, setting, 222-223
Startup of business
corporation, 157
franchise, 165
risk, and, 29
small business, 183
sole proprietorship, 149
venture capitalist, 191
Statement of cash flows, 565
Statistics, demography, 42
Statutory law, 131
Stock
advantages of issuing, 615
blue chip, 624
common, 617
defined, 614
disadvantages of issuing, 615
growth stock, 624
income stock, 624
investing in, 623-626
penny stock, 624
preferred, 615, 616
splits, 625-626
stock quotation, 629-630
terminology of, 614
types of, 615
Stockbroker, 621
Stock exchanges
defined, 618

Stock exchanges—Cont.
foreign, 620
over-the-counter market, 619-620
United States exchanges, 619
Stockholders
income of business going to, 74
as stakeholders, 40
Stock insurance company, 688
Stock market crash of 1987, 632-
633
Stock options, as executive
compensation, 387
Stock sales, as equity financing,
599-600
Stock splits, 625-626
Storage
in marketing, 414, 415
by marketing middlemen, 465
physical distribution systems,
477
Storage warehouse, 477
Strategic alliances
global business, 169
international joint ventures, 97
Strategic approach to corporate
responsibility, 121-122
Strategic (long-range) planning, 215
Strategy
investing, 621-622
portfolio strategy, 626-627
Strict liability, 132
Strikebreaker, defined, 382
Strikes, 379, 380-383
defined, 380
Structural unemployment, 72
Structure of business. See
Organization; Organizational
structure
Style changes, extending product
life cycle, 551
Subculture, defined, 421
Subsidiaries. See Foreign
subsidiaries
Success measurement, customer
satisfaction, 223-224
Suite (integrated software
package), 537
Super NOW accounts, service of
commercial bank, 650
Supervisor, manager as, 213
Supervisory (first-line)
management, 217-218
Supplier-producer relationships,
283
Suppliers
contact with teams, 221
establishment of relations with,
219
just-in-time inventory control,
283
as stakeholders, 40
Supply
defined, 68-69

Supply—Cont.
equilibrium point, 69-70
supply and demand, 67
Supply and demand
price determined by, 456
world markets, 70-71
Supply chain management (SCM),
471-472
Supply curve, 69
Synthetic systems, defined, 281
Systems analyst, 578

T

Tactical (short-range) planning,
215-216
Taft-Hartley Act, 374, 377
Taking firm private, 161
Tall organization structures, 249
Target market, 411
Target marketing, 422
Target pricing, 455
Tariffs, 105
Task identity, as motivator, 320
Task significance, as motivator,
320
Tax accountant, defined, 554
Tax accounting, 554
Taxation
corporation, 157
employee stock ownership plans
(ESOPs), 393
as investment criteria, 622
in S corporation, 160
site selection and, 280
sole proprietorship, 150
Tax codes, effect on economy, 66
Taxes
defined, 138
effect on business, 36-37
fiscal policy, 77-78
income of business going to, 74
paid by businesses, 31
paid by employees, 31
profit, and, 30
regulation as hidden tax, 78-79
tax fairness, 79
types of, list, 140
Tax laws, defined, 138
Team leaders, delegating by, 231
Teams. See also Cross-functional
teams; Self-managed teams
empowerment of, 220-221
entrepreneurial teams, 181
front-line personnel, 261
managers working in, 213
smart teams, 221
Triad Development Process
(Hewlett-Packard), 182
Teamwork
communication, and, 324-325
effect on recruiting, 343

Teamwork—*Cont.*
　managers, and, 213
Technical skills, 230, 234-235
Technological environment, effect
　on entrepreneurs, 37
Technology. See also Computers;
　　Information highway;
　　Information technology;
　　Telecommuting
　and accounting, 570-571
　in advertising, 495-497
　CAD/CAM, 286-288
　computer scheduling programs,
　　356
　corporate management, and, 212
　efficient consumer response
　　(ECR), 472-473
　electronic data interchange
　　(EDI), 472
　electronic funds transfer system
　　(EFTS), 656-657
　flexible manufacturing, 284
　job simulation, 350
　just-in-time inventory control,
　　283-284
　mass customization, 285-286
　on-line advertising, 494
　robot, 285
　shared, in international joint
　　ventures, 97
　shopping from home, 498
　telemarketing, 483
　training programs for change
　　in, 342
　unions, and, 383
　virtual office, 359
Telebanking, service of commercial
　　bank, 650
Telecommunications. See also
　　Information highway
　E-mail, 325
　interfirm organization and, 219
　online direct marketing, 485
　site selection and, 280
　in traditionally non-
　　technological businesses, 37
Telecommuting
　for two-income families, 44
　virtual office, 359
Telemarketing, 483
Telephone, impact of information
　　highway on, 527
Television advertising, 493-494
　advantages and disadvantages
　　of, 495
Temporary employment, 337. See
　　also Outsourcing
Termination of business
　corporation, 157
　sole proprietorship, 149
Termination of employment, 360.
　　See also Downsizing
　golden parachutes, 387-388

Termination of employment—*Cont.*
　layoffs, 28
　legal restrictions on discharge,
　　344
Term insurance, defined, 675
Term-loan agreement, 598
Testing
　employment tests, 345
　new-product development, 444,
　　446
Test marketing, 407
Textile Fiber Products
　　Identification Act, 139
*Theory of Social and Economic
　　Organizations* (Weber), 247
Theory X (McGregor), 313-314,
　　315-316
Theory Y (McGregor), 313, 314-316
Theory Z (Ouchi), 316-317
Thrift institutions, 651
Tight monetary policy, 77
Time
　barriers broken by information
　　technology, 524-525
　competing in, 286
Time commitment, sole
　　proprietorship, 150
Time deposit, 650. See also
　　Demand deposit
Time management skills, 234
Time-motion studies, 310
Time to market, 279
Time utility, 416, 469
Top management, 217
　directing by, 220
Tort law, 131
Total product offer, 426
Total quality competition, by
　　retailers, 481-482
Total quality management (TQM),
　　291, 334, 385, 481
　benchmarking, 262
　defined, 259
　delighting the customer, 409
　marketing concept and, 409
　restructuring, and, 259-260
Tradable currency, effect on
　　business, 36
Trade advertising, 494
Trade alliances
　European Union (EU), 46-47,
　　104-105
　General Agreement on Tariffs
　　and Trade (GATT), 104
　North American Free Trade
　　Agreement (NAFTA), 46, 104,
　　105-106
Trade credit, 593
Trade deficit
　defined, 92
　with Japan, 93
　of United States, 93-94

Trademark, 133, 442
Trade protectionism
　common markets, 104-105
　defined, 102-103
　General Agreement on Tariffs
　　and Trade (GATT), 104
Trade unions. See Unions
Training, in customer service, 409
Training and development
　apprentice programs, 348-349
　continuing education, 347
　costs of, 344-345
　cross-training programs, 347
　defined, 348
　empowerment of teams, and,
　　221
　job simulation, 349-350
　management development, 350-
　　351
　by managers, 41
　off-the-job training, 349
　on-the-job training, 348
　retraining, 338-339
　strategic plan for, 342
　vestibule training, 349
Training program development,
　　400
Transfers. See Human resource
　　management
Transition, from one type of
　　economy to another, 50-51
Transportation
　in marketing, 414, 415
　by marketing middlemen, 465
Transportation industry,
　　employment increases in, 184
Transportation modes, 473-475
Traveler's checks, service of
　　commercial bank, 650
Triad Development Process
　　(Hewlett-Packard), 182
Trial balance, 556
Trial periods of employment, 346-
　　347
Truck, goods shipped by, 474
Truck jobber, 479
Truthfulness, 118
Truth-in-Lending Act, 139
Two-income families, 44-45

U

Understudy positions, 350-351
Underwriting, 631
Unemployment rate, 72-73
Unfavorable balance of trade, of
　　United States, 93
Uniform Commercial Code (UCC).
　　See also Contract law
　negotiable instruments, 134
　purpose of, 134
　warranties, 134

Uniform Limited Liability Company Act, 160
Uniform pricing, 455
Uninsurable risk, 687
Unions
  apprenticeship required by, 349
  cooperation with management, 385
  defined, 372
  future of labor-management relations, 383-385
  goals of, 377-378
  history of, 373-375
  legislation affecting, 374, 375-377
  management tactics, in disputes, 382-383
  membership as percentage of workforce, 384, 385
  perspectives on, 372-373
  resolving disagreements. See Labor-management conflicts
  role change for, 385
  in service sector, 383
  site selection and, 278
  tactics of, in disputes, 380-382
  women in, 383
Union security clause, 377
Union shop agreement, 377
United Auto Workers, 381
United Food and Commercial Workers Union, 381
United Mine Workers Union, 375
United States economic system. See Economic system of United States
Universal life insurance, defined, 675
Universal Product Codes (UPC), 440
Universities, as bureaucracy, 245
Unlimited liability, 150
Unsecured bonds, 599, 612
Unsecured loan, 595
Urban business, 27
Utility, 468
  defined, 277
  form utility, 469
  information utility, 470
  place utility, 469
  possession utility, 469-470
  time utility, 469

V

Value package, 434-435
  defined, 435
  development of, 435
Value pricing, 453-454
  defined, 453
Values, vision and, 224-225
Vending machines, 484
Venture capital, 600-601
Venture capitalist, 191
Vertical merger, 161
Vestibule training, 349
Violence in workplace, 392
Virtual banking, 657
Virtualization, defined, 525
Virtual office, 359
Vision
  creation of, 214-216
  defined, 214-215
  values and, 224-225
Vocational Rehabilitation Act, 362
Volume market segmentation, 423, 425
Voluntary bankruptcy, 140

W

Wages, standard of living and, 31
Wagner Act, 374, 376
Warehouse, materials handling, 477
Warehouse clubs, 478-479
Warranties, 134
Water, goods shipped by, 474
Wealth
  age group of wealthiest citizens, 44
  business as opportunity to acquire, 29
  of countries, 34
  disparities in, 62
  importance of entrepreneurship to, 32
  primary source of, 34-35
Wealth creation
  Adam Smith, and, 61
  capitalism and, 61-62
  critical elements of, 34-35
  "invisible hand," 61
  socialism and, 64
Wealth of Nations (Smith), 61
Welfare capitalism, 64-66
Welfare society, 61
Wheeler-Lea Amendment of 1938, 137

Wheel of retailing, 483
Whole life insurance, defined, 675
Wholesale middlemen, 478
  merchant wholesalers, 478-479
Wholesaler
  defined, 464
  differentiated from retailer, 478
  in exchange relationships, 465-466
Wholesale sale, defined, 478
Wholesale-sponsored chains, 471
Wireless communications, and information highway, 527
Women
  as entrepreneurs, 28
  franchises owned by, 166-167
  owning small businesses, 183
  pay equity, 388
  sex discrimination. See Sex discrimination
  sexual harassment, 389
  in unions, 383
Word-of-mouth promotion, 503-505
Word processing software, 535-536
Work force, changes in skill requirements, 212
Workplace, alteration by information technology, 538-540
Work slowdowns, 379
World markets. See Global markets
World's Best Known Marketing Secret: Building Your Business with Word-of-Mouth Marketing (Misner), 503
World trade. See Exporting; Global trade; Importing; International trade
Writing skills, 233

Y

Yellow-dog contracts, 379
  defined, 382
Yellow pages advertising, 494
  advantages and disadvantages of, 495
Yield, as investment criteria, 622

Z

Zero-coupon bond, 613
Zero defects, 39